Statutory Instruments 1989

PART I

SECTION 2

Published by Authority

LONDON: HMSO

1992

I/2a

ISBN 0 11 840310 9

HMSO publications are available from:

HMSO Publications Centre
(Mail and telephone orders only)
PO Box 276, London, SW8 5DT
Telephone orders 071-873 9090
General enquiries 071-873 0011
(queuing system in operation for both numbers)

HMSO Bookshops
49 High Holborn, London, WC1V 6HB 071-873 0011 (Counter service only)
258 Broad Street, Birmingham, B1 2HE 021-643 3740
Southey House, 33 Wine Street, Bristol, BS1 2BQ (0272) 264306
9-21 Princess Street, Manchester, M60 8AS 061-834 7201
80 Chichester Street, Belfast, BT1 4JY (0232) 238451
71 Lothian Road, Edinburgh, EH3 9AZ 031-228 4181

HMSO's Accredited Agents
(see Yellow Pages)

and through good booksellers

Price for two sections £200 net

Printed in the United Kingdom for HMSO
Dd0717765 1/92 C7 G409 10170

Contents of the Edition

PART I

SECTION 1

SECTION 2

PART II

PART III

1989 No. 379

SOCIAL SECURITY

The Social Fund Maternity and Funeral Expenses (General) Amendment Regulations 1989

Made - - - -	*8th March 1989*
Laid before Parliament	*10th March 1989*
Coming into force	*1st April 1989*

The Secretary of State for Social Security, in exercise of the powers conferred by sections 32(2)(a) and 84(1) of the Social Security Act 1986(**a**) and of all other powers enabling him in that behalf, after agreement by the Social Security Advisory Committee that the proposals to make these Regulations should not be referred to it(**b**), hereby makes the following Regulations:–

Citation, commencement and interpretation

1.—(1) These Regulations may be cited as the Social Fund Maternity and Funeral Expenses (General) Amendment Regulations 1989 and shall come into force on 1st April 1989.

(2) In these Regulations "the General Regulations" means the Social Fund Maternity and Funeral Expenses (General) Regulations 1987(**c**).

Amendment of regulation 3 of the General Regulations

2. For paragraph (2) of regulation 3 of the General Regulations (interpretation) there shall be substituted the following paragraph –

> "(2) For the purposes of these Regulations, persons are to be treated as not being members of the same household in the circumstances set out in regulation 16(2) and (3) of the Income Support (General) Regulations 1987(**d**).".

Amendment of regulation 7 of the General Regulations

3. In regulation 7 of the General Regulations (entitlement to payments for funeral expenses)–

(a) in paragraph (1)(a) for the words "either income support, family credit or housing benefit" there shall be substituted the words "income support, family credit, housing benefit or community charge benefits(**e**)";

(**a**) 1986 c.50; section 32(2)(a) was amended by section 1 of the Social Fund (Maternity and Funeral Expenses) Act 1987 (c.7) and section 84(1) is cited only for the definitions of "prescribed" and "regulations".
(**b**) *See* section 10(2)(b) of the Social Security Act 1980 (c.30) and section 61(1)(b) of the Social Security Act 1986.
(**c**) S.I. 1987/481, amended by S.I. 1988/36.
(**d**) S.I. 1987/1967, amended by S.I. 1988/663.
(**e**) *See* section 20(1) of the Social Security Act 1986 (c.50); reference to community charge benefits was inserted by section 135 of, and Schedule 10 to, the Local Government Finance Act 1988 (c.41).

(b) after paragraph (2) there shall be inserted the following paragraph–

"(3) In this regulation, any reference to housing benefit includes a reference, in Scotland, to housing benefit in the form of a community charge rebate(**a**).".

Amendment of regulation 9 of the General Regulations

4. In regulation 9 of the General Regulations (effect of capital)–

(a) for paragraph (2) there shall be substituted the following paragraph –

"(2) For the purposes of paragraph (1) –

(a) any capital possessed by any person whose capital is, for the purposes of entitlement to income support, treated as that of the claimant by virtue of section 22(5) of the Social Security Act 1986 or the provisions of regulation 23(3) of the Income Support (General) Regulations 1987(**b**) (calculation of income and capital) shall be treated as that of the claimant; and

(b) subject to paragraph (3), the claimant's capital shall be calculated in the same manner as his capital is calculated under the Income Support (General) Regulations 1987 for the purposes of determining his entitlement to income support.";

(b) after paragraph (2) there shall be inserted the following paragraph –

"(3) For the purposes of paragraph (1) –

(a) any sum acquired by the claimant (whether as a loan or otherwise) on the express condition that it is to be used to meet the funeral expenses in respect of which the claim is made shall be disregarded;

(b) in the case of a claim for a maternity payment or a funeral payment which is made within 12 months of the death of the husband of the claimant, any lump sum payable to that claimant as a widow by virtue of section 24 of the Social Security Act 1975(**c**) shall be disregarded;

(c) the amount of any payment out of capital, other than capital disregarded under sub-paragraphs (a) and (b) above or under regulation 47 of, and Schedule 10 to, the Income Support (General) Regulations 1987 (capital disregards), which has already been made towards the funeral expenses (whether or not the expenses are within the scope of regulation 7(2)) shall be added back to that capital as if the payment had not been made.".

Revocation of regulation 10 of the General Regulations

5. Regulation 10 of the General Regulations (assessment of capital) shall be revoked.

Signed by authority of the Secretary of State for Social Security.

Peter Lloyd
Parliamentary Under-Secretary of State,
Department of Social Security

8th March 1989

(**a**) *See* section 28 of the Social Security Act 1986; reference to community charge rebate was inserted by S.I. 1988/1483.
(**b**) S.I. 1987/1967, amended by S.I. 1988/1228.
(**c**) 1975 c.14; section 24 was substituted by section 36(1) of the Social Security Act 1986.

EXPLANATORY NOTE

(This note is not part of the Regulations)

These Regulations further amend the Social Fund Maternity and Funeral Expenses (General) Regulations 1987 ("the General Regulations").

They make provision for persons in Scotland awarded community charge rebate in the year beginning 1st April 1989 and thereafter for persons in Great Britain awarded community charge benefits, to be eligible for a funeral payment (regulation 3).

They substitute a new paragraph for paragraph (2) of regulation 3 of the General Regulations to clarify the interpretation provisions in regard to treatment as members of a household (regulation 2); and amend the provisions dealing with capital to make it clear that, apart from those modifications which are specified, capital is to be calculated as for income support purposes (regulations 4 and 5).

STATUTORY INSTRUMENTS

1989 No. 380

AGRICULTURE

The Dairy Produce Quotas Regulations 1989

Made - - - -	*8th March 1989*
Laid before Parliament	*10th March 1989*
Coming into force -	*31st March 1989*

ARRANGEMENT OF REGULATIONS

REGULATION

The Minister of Agriculture, Fisheries and Food and the Secretary of State, being Ministers designated**(a)** for the purposes of section 2(2) of the European Communities Act 1972**(b)** in relation to the common agricultural policy of the European Economic Community, acting jointly in exercise of the powers conferred on them by that section and of all other powers enabling them in that behalf, hereby make the following Regulations:–

Title and commencement

1. These Regulations may be cited as the Dairy Produce Quotas Regulations 1989 and shall come into force on 31st March 1989.

Interpretation

2.—(1) In these Regulations, unless the context otherwise requires–

"Commission Regulation" means Commission Regulation (EEC)1546/88**(c)** laying down detailed rules for the application of the levy as amended by the Commission Regulations listed in Schedule 3;

(a) S.I. 1972/1811.
(b) 1972 c.68; section 2 is subject to Schedule 2 to that Act and is to be read, as regards England and Wales, with sections 37, 40 and 46 of the Criminal Justice Act 1982 (c.48) and S.I. 1984/447, as regards Scotland, with section 289GA of the Criminal Procedure (Scotland) Act 1975 (c.21) (as inserted by section 66(2) of the Criminal Justice (Scotland) Act 1987 (c.41)) and, as regards Northern Ireland, with S.I. 1984/703 (N.I.3) and S.R. (N.I.) 1984 No. 253.
(c) OJ No. L139, 4.6.88, p. 12.

"Community legislation" means Article 5c of Council Regulation 804/68, Council Regulation 857/84 and the Commission Regulation;

"consent or sole interest notice" means a notice, in relation to a holding or part of a holding, signed by the person required under these Regulations to provide the notice, that either–

(a) he is the occupier of that holding or part of a holding and no other person has an interest in that holding or part of the holding, or

(b) all persons having an interest in the holding or part of the holding the value of which interest might be reduced by the apportionment or prospective apportionment to which the notice relates agree to that apportionment or proposed prospective apportionment;

"Council Regulation 804/68" means Council Regulation (EEC) No. 804/68**(a)** on the common organisation of the market in milk and milk products as amended by the Council Regulations listed in Schedule 1;

"Council Regulation 857/84" means Council Regulation (EEC) No. 857/84**(b)** adopting general rules for the application of the levy in the milk and milk products sector, as amended by the Council Regulations listed in Schedule 2;

"cow" includes a heifer that has calved;

"dairy enterprise" means an area stated by the occupier of that area to be run as a self-contained dairy produce business;

"dairy produce" means the produce, expressed in kilograms or litres (one kilogram being 0.97116 litres) of milk, in respect of which levy is payable under the Community legislation;

"Dairy Produce Quota Tribunal" has the meaning assigned to it by regulation 32;

"dairy unit" means a set of buildings used for the production of dairy produce, the address of which is registered under these Regulations or, if not so registered, is registered for any purpose by a milk marketing board or under any enactment relating to conditions to be observed in the production of dairy produce;

"delivery" has the meaning assigned to it by Article 12(g) of Council Regulation 857/84 (which sets out definitions) and "deliver" shall be construed accordingly;

"development claim" means a claim based on Article 3(1) of Council Regulation 857/84 (which deals with milk production development plans and investments);

"direct sale" means a sale referred to in Article 12(h) of Council Regulation 857/84;

"direct sales quota" means quantity of dairy produce which may be sold by direct sale from a holding in a quota year without the direct seller in occupation of that holding being liable to pay levy;

"direct seller" means a producer selling dairy produce by direct sale;

"division" means a part of a holding in a region where the remainder of the holding is in another region;

"eligible heifer" means any heifer, which, at the date of service of the notice referred to in regulation 16(2)(b), was on land subject to the notice and which calves for the first time on a day when the notice has effect;

"farming press" means any newspaper, journal or similar publication considered by the Minister to be likely to be read by producers and purchasers;

"Formula B" has the meaning assigned to it by Article 5c(1) of Council Regulation 804/68 (which deals with implementation of the levy);

"Gazette" means, as respects anything in these Regulations relating to–

(a) England and Wales alone, the London Gazette,

(b) Scotland alone, the Edinburgh Gazette,

(c) Northern Ireland alone, the Belfast Gazette, and

(d) the United Kingdom, the London, Edinburgh and Belfast Gazettes;

"holding" has the meaning assigned to it by Article 12(d) of Council Regulation 857/84, but in relation to any region, it means the division of the holding in that region;

(a) OJ No. L148, 28.6.68, p. 13 (OJ/SE 1968(1) p. 176).
(b) OJ No. L90, 1.4.84, p. 13.

"identification" means a description of a holding specifying–

(a) the address of the producer farming the holding,

(b) where possible, the address of any dairy unit on that holding, and

(c) such other particulars, if any, as the Minister may require,

and "identify" and "identified" shall be construed accordingly;

"interest" includes the interest of a mortgagee or heritable creditor and a trustee, but does not include the interest of a beneficiary under a trust or settlement or, in Scotland, the estate of a superior;

"Intervention Board" means the Intervention Board for Agricultural Produce established under section 6(1) of the European Communities Act 1972;

"levy" means the levy, payable under the Community legislation to the competent authority referred to therein, described in Article 1 of Council Regulation 857/84 (which deals with the fixing of the levy);

"milk marketing board" means a milk marketing board constituted under the Agricultural Marketing Act 1958**(a)** or the Agricultural Marketing Act (Northern Ireland) 1964**(b)**;

"Minister", as respects anything in these Regulations relating to–

(a) England and Wales alone, means the Minister of Agriculture, Fisheries and Food and the Secretary of State for Wales acting jointly;

(b) Scotland alone, means the Secretary of State for Scotland,

(c) Northern Ireland alone, shall be construed in accordance with paragraph (3), and

(d) the United Kingdom, means the Ministers;

"Ministers" means all those to whom the definition of "the Minister" relates, acting jointly;

"national direct sales reserve" means the reserve constituted under regulation 7(1) of the 1984 Regulations for the purpose of Article 6(3) of Council Regulation 857/84 (which enables Member States to constitute a reserve from the national direct sales quota);

"national wholesale quota" means quota applied for the time being to the United Kingdom or any part thereof by or under Article 5c(3) and (4) of Council Regulation 804/68;

"new region" means a region the establishment of which is announced under regulation 7(1);

"occupier" includes, in relation to land in respect of which there is no occupier, the person entitled to grant occupation of that land to another person;

"old region" means a region the discontinuance of which is announced under regulation 7(1);

"producer" has the meaning assigned to it by Article 12(c) of Council Regulation 857/84;

"prospective apportionment" in relation to quota on a holding means apportionment of quota ascertained under regulation 11 which will take place if there is a change of occupation of a part of the holding to which the prospective apportionment relates within six months of that prospective apportionment;

"purchaser" has the meaning assigned to it by Article 12(e) of Council Regulation 857/84;

"purchaser details" means in relation to a producer, the name and address of any purchaser to whom that producer delivers, or intends to deliver, dairy produce by wholesale delivery and the proportions of that dairy produce which he delivers or intends to deliver to each;

"purchaser quota" means quantity of dairy produce which may be delivered by wholesale delivery to a purchaser, from holdings in a region, during a quota year without that purchaser being liable to pay levy;

"qualifying cow" means any eligible heifer which calves at a time when the number of eligible heifers exceeds the replacement number;

(a) 1958 c.47, to which there are amendments not relevant to these Regulations.
(b) 1964 c.13 (N.I.), to which there are amendments not relevant to these Regulations.

"qualifying day" means, in respect of any qualifying cow, the day it calves and each day or part of a day thereafter during which the notice referred to in regulation 16(2)(b) has effect;

"quota" means direct sales quota or wholesale quota, as the case may be;

"quota year" means a consecutive period described in the first subparagraph of Article 5c(1) of Council Regulation 804/68 (which deals with periods in respect of which levy is payable);

"regions" means regions into which the United Kingdom is divided for the purposes of Article 1(2) of Council Regulation 857/84 (which deals with regions);

"regional wholesale quota" has the meaning assigned to it by regulation 7(1);

"replacement number" means the nearest integer to 22 per cent of the total number of dairy cows on the land subject to the notice referred to in regulation 16(2)(b) as at the date of service of the notice;

"running regional wholesale reserve" means a reserve constituted under regulation 5(9) or 7(2)(b) of the 1984 Regulations, regulation 6(2) or 9 of the 1986 Regulations or regulation 7(2) or 13;

"secondary wholesale quota" means wholesale quota which was allocated under paragraph 12(5) of Schedule 2 to the 1984 Regulations in consequence of a claim based on Article 3(1) or (3) of Council Regulation 857/84 or Article 3 of the Commission Regulation;

"the 1984 Regulations" means the Dairy Produce Quotas Regulations 1984**(a)**;

"the 1986 Regulations" means the Dairy Produce Quotas Regulations 1986**(b)**;

"total direct sales quota" means the total quantity of dairy produce which may be sold by direct sale from a holding in a quota year without the direct seller in occupation of that holding being liable to pay levy;

"total wholesale quota" means the total quantity of dairy produce which may be delivered by wholesale delivery from a holding in a region in a quota year without the producer in occupation of that holding being liable to pay levy;

"transferee" means a person who replaces another person as occupier of a holding or part of a holding;

"transferor" means a person who is replaced by another person as occupier of a holding or part of a holding;

"wholesale delivery" means delivery from a producer to a purchaser;

"wholesale development award" means secondary wholesale quota consequent upon a development claim, and

"wholesale quota" means quantity of dairy produce which may be delivered by wholesale delivery to a purchaser (to the extent specified in relation to that purchaser under these Regulations), from a holding in a quota year without the producer in occupation of that holding being liable to pay levy;

(2) In these Regulations, unless the context otherwise requires–

(a) any reference to a numbered regulation or Schedule shall be construed as a reference to the regulation or Schedule so numbered in these Regulations,

(b) any reference in a regulation or Schedule to a numbered paragraph shall be construed as a reference to the paragraph so numbered in that regulation or Schedule, and

(c) any reference in a paragraph to a numbered or lettered subparagraph shall be construed as a reference to the subparagraph so numbered or lettered in that paragraph.

(3) In their application to Northern Ireland these Regulations shall have effect with the substitution, for references to the Minister, of references to the Department of Agriculture for Northern Ireland.

(a) S.I. 1984/1047; amended by S.I. 1984/1538, 1787 and S.I. 1985/509.
(b) S.I. 1986/470; amended by S.I. 1988/534 and S.I. 1989/16.

Establishment of quota

3. Total direct sales quota and total wholesale quota for any person and purchaser quota for any purchaser in respect of any quota year shall be established in accordance with these Regulations and the Community legislation.

Formula B

4. For the purposes of Article 5c(1) of Council Regulation 804/68 the levy system shall be implemented in accordance with Formula B.

Milk equivalence of cheese

5.—(1) For the purposes of Article 11 of the Commission Regulation (which deals with milk equivalence of cream, butter and cheese) the milk equivalence of cheese shall be calculated on the basis that each kilogram of cheese shall equal such quantity of milk referred to in paragraph (2) as is required to make that kilogram of cheese.

(2) The milk to which paragraph (1) relates is milk the fat content of which has not been altered since milking.

Fat content of milk

6. At the request of a producer to whom the second indented paragraph of the second paragraph of Article 12(1) of the Commission Regulation applies, the Minister shall decide, for the purposes of any levy, that the fat content which shall be considered as representative of the milk delivered to a purchaser by that producer shall be determined in accordance with that paragraph.

Regions

7.—(1) The Minister shall, in respect of each quota year, announce by advertisement published in the Gazette and farming press any change in the regions into which the United Kingdom is divided for the purposes of Article 1(2) of Council Regulation 857/84 (which deals with regions) and the allocation from the national wholesale quota of a regional wholesale quota for each region.

(2) Where, in respect of any quota year, the regional wholesale quota allocated for a region is increased in relation to the preceding quota year, the wholesale quota so added shall create, or be added to, the running regional wholesale reserve for that region.

(3) Where, in respect of any quota year, the regional wholesale quota allocated for a region is reduced in relation to the preceding quota year the wholesale quota so subtracted shall be satisfied from all persons with wholesale quota in proportion to the wholesale quota of each at the start of the quota year (the reduction of purchaser quota to be calculated in accordance with those reductions of wholesale quota).

(4) Where in respect of a quota year the direct sales quota allocated within a region is reduced in relation to the preceding quota year, the quota so subtracted shall be satisfied from all persons with direct sales quota in that region in proportion to the direct sales quota of each at the beginning of the quota year.

(5) Where, in respect of any quota year, there is a change of regions as described in paragraph (1), the following shall be deemed to have taken place, for the purposes of these Regulations, immediately before the end of the prior quota year–

(a) the adjustment of wholesale quota applicable to any holding affected by the change in accordance with the following calculations–

(i) where any holding in more than one old region is in one new region, by aggregating the total wholesale quota relating to that holding;

(ii) where any holding in one old region is in more than one new region, by allocating wholesale quota in accordance with paragraph (6) in relation to divisions in new regions;

(iii) where any holding in more than one old region is in more than one new region but in different divisions, by aggregating the total wholesale quota relating to that holding and allocating wholesale quota in accordance with paragraph (6) in relation to divisions in new regions;

(b) the calculation of the running regional wholesale reserve of each new region by aggregating the running regional wholesale reserves of each of the old regions and dividing the aggregate among the new regions proportionally in accordance with the total wholesale quota then allocated in each new region;

(c) the calculation of the regional wholesale quota of each new region by adding to its aggregate of wholesale quotas (taking account of subparagraph (a)) its running regional wholesale reserve calculated under subparagraph (b).

(6) An allocation is made in accordance with this paragraph by allocating to the division of a holding which contains the dairy unit (where that holding contains a single dairy unit) the total wholesale quota relating to that holding or (in respect of any other holding) allocating to each division of that holding a part of the total wholesale quota relating to that holding calculated proportionally in accordance with the area of that division.

(7) The Minister may at any time reallocate the national wholesale quota among the regions, and where such reallocation is unable to be achieved by the transfer of wholesale quota between running regional reserves, may reduce the regional wholesale quota allocated for a region, the reduction being satisfied from all persons in that region with wholesale quota in proportion to the wholesale quota of each person at the start of the quota year and may pay compensation to persons whose entitlement to quota is so reduced and shall announce these arrangements by advertisement published in the Gazette.

(8) For the purpose of any reallocation of national wholesale quota under paragraph (7) the Minister may remove wholesale quota from any running regional wholesale reserve and add it to any other running regional wholesale reserve.

Adjustment of purchaser quota

8.—(1) Where any wholesale quota is increased or reduced in accordance with the Community legislation or these Regulations, the purchaser quota of any purchaser to whom that quota is applicable shall be correspondingly increased or reduced.

(2) On any transaction to which Article 7(2) of Council Regulation 857/84 or Article 9(1)(d) of the Commission Regulation (which between them deal with replacements of purchasers and changes by producers from one purchaser to another) applies, any purchaser whose purchaser quota has been increased by virtue of that transaction shall, no later than a date 21 days after the date of the transaction, submit to the Minister–

(a) a statement of the transaction, that is to say a statement setting out (in accordance with Article 7(2) of Council Regulation 857/84 where applicable) the following particulars–

(i) the nature of the transaction;

(ii) the parties to the transaction;

(iii) the changes of purchaser quota of any purchaser to whom the transaction relates;

(iv) the changes in respect of matters referred to in the list, mentioned in regulation 25(2)(a)(iv) forming part of the wholesale register entry of each producer to whom the transaction relates; and

(b) a statement that all purchasers and all producers to whom the transaction relates either agree to, or (so far as the purchaser submitting the statement is aware) have no right to bring proceedings in respect of, the changes the particulars of which are set out in the statement of the transaction.

(3) Following a transaction referred to in paragraph (2) dairy produce previously delivered by wholesale delivery in the quota year of the transaction by any producer involved in that transaction to any purchaser involved in that transaction (and any levy paid or payable in respect of that dairy produce) shall be deemed, for the purpose of calculation of levy, to have been delivered (or paid or payable) proportionally in accordance with changes effected by that transaction.

(4) The Minister may provide such forms as he reasonably considers to be necessary for the purposes of this regulation.

Transfer of quota

9.—(1) For the purposes of Article 7 of Council Regulation 857/84 and Article 7 of the Commission Regulation (transfer of quota when any holding is sold, leased or transferred by inheritance) on a transfer of any holding or part of a holding, other than a transfer pursuant to an agreement to which paragraph 7 applies, the transferee shall submit to the Minister–

(a) within two months of the change of occupation of the holding or part of a holding, a duly completed form prescribed for this purpose from time to time by the Minister, and

(b) such other evidence relating to the transfer, and within such time, as the Minister may reasonably require.

(2) Notwithstanding paragraph (1) above, the Minister may decide, in respect of transfers of any holding or part of a holding in a quota year which have not been notified to him in writing by the transferee before a date to be determined by him in the following quota year, that for the purposes of any levy calculation–

(a) the unused quota transferred with such transfers shall not be treated as a part of the transferee's quota entitlement for the quota year in which the transfer took effect but shall nevertheless be treated as if it remained unused quota available for re-allocation by the Minister in the year in which the transfer took place, and

(b) a transferee shall not be entitled to demand that, by reason of such a transfer, an amendment be made to the amount of quota, if any, which has been reallocated to him under Schedule 8 for the quota year in which the transfer took effect.

(3) A decision by the Minister, together with the date determined by him under paragraph (2) above, shall be announced by advertisment published in the Gazette and the farming press at least two months before that date or, in the event that such publication is not possible for any reason, by such other means of publication as the Minister considers likely to come to the attention of producers.

(4) Where there is a transfer of the entirety of a holding it shall be presumed that the transferee intends to deliver dairy produce from the holding by wholesale delivery to the purchasers named, and in the proportions listed, in the transferor's entry in the wholesale register.

(5) Where there is a transfer of part of a holding–

(a) an apportionment of the quota relating to the holding shall be carried out in accordance with regulation 10, and

(b) dairy produce previously sold by direct sale or delivered by wholesale delivery from the holding in the quota year in which the change of occupation takes place shall be deemed, for the purposes of any levy, to have been sold or delivered from each part of the holding proportionally in accordance with that apportionment.

(6) A prospective apportionment of quota in respect of a part of a holding may be made in accordance with regulation 11.

(7) This Regulation shall not apply to the following–

(a) a licence to occupy land,

(b) the tenancy of any land under which a holding, or part of a holding, in England and Wales is occupied for a period of less than ten months,

(c) the lease of any land under which a holding, or part of a holding, in Scotland is occupied for a period of less than eight months,

(d) the tenancy of any land under which a holding, or part of a holding, in Northern Ireland is occupied for a period of less then twelve months,

(e) the lease of any land under which part of a holding in Scotland is occupied for a term of less than one year, where the area occupation of which changes is no larger than 5 hectares and is less than one quarter of the area of the remainder of the holding,

(f) the termination of a tenancy or lease to which sub-paragraph (b), (c), (d) or (e) applies.

Apportionment of quota

10. Subject to regulations 11(4) and 12, where there is a transfer of part of a holding the apportionment of the quota relating to that holding shall be carried out–

(a) where within two months of the change of occupation the transferee submits to the Minister–

(i) a duly completed form in accordance with regulation 9(1)(a),

(ii) a statement, signed by the transferor and the transferee, that they have agreed that the quota shall be apportioned according to areas used for milk production as specified in the statement, and

(iii) a consent or sole interest notice in respect of the entirety of the holding,

in accordance with that agreement,

(b) in all other cases–

(i) in England and Wales and Northern Ireland by arbitration in accordance with Schedules 4 and 6,

(ii) in Scotland in accordance with Schedule 5.

Prospective apportionment of quota

11.—(1) The occupier of the holding in respect of which the prospective apportionment of quota is to be applied shall submit to the Minister a statement–

(a) identifying the parts of the holding to which the prospective apportionment is to relate,

(b) containing such information relating to the holding as may reasonably be required by the Minister, and

(c) requesting either–

(i) that a prospective apportionment of quota relating to the holding be made according to areas used for milk production as at the date of the statement as specified in the statement, or

(ii) that a prospective apportionment of quota be ascertained by arbitration in accordance with Schedule 4 in England and Wales and Schedule 6 in Northern Ireland, and in Scotland in accordance with Schedule 5.

(2) The prospective apportionment of quota shall be made in accordance with Schedule 4, 5 or 6, as the case may be, unless a prospective apportionment has been specified in accordance with paragap 1(c)(i) and the occupier sends to the Minister a consent or sole interest notice in respect of the entirety of the holding, in the case of which, subject to regulation 12, the prospective apportionment shall be as so specified.

(3) A prospective apportionment of quota may be revoked by a notice in writing to the Minister, signed by the occupier of the holding to which the prospective apportionment relates and accompanied by a consent or sole interest notice in respect of that holding, that the occupier no longer wishes that prospective apportionment to have effect.

(4) Where there is a change of occupation of part of a holding and within the six months preceding that change of occupation–

(a) the occupier of that holding has submitted a statement referred to in paragraph 1 in respect of that part of that holding, or

(b) a prospective apportionment of quota relating to that part of that holding has been made by an arbitrator under Schedule 4 or 6, or under Schedule 5,

the apportionment of quota shall be carried out in accordance with–

(i) any prospective apportionment of quota relating to that part of that holding made under paragraph 2 and not revoked under paragraph 3,

(ii) if there is no such prospective apportionment, any prospective apportionment which is in the process of being made under paragraph 2 by virtue of a statement relating to that part of that holding under paragraph 1,

(iii) in any other case, regulation 9.

(5) The Minister shall maintain a record of each prospective apportionment made under this Regulation and Schedule 4, 5 or 6.

Notification by the Minister of apportionment of quota by arbitration

12. Where the Minister has reasonable grounds for believing that the areas used for milk production on a holding are not as specified in a statement made for the purpose of regulation 10(a)(ii) or 11(1)(c)(i) he shall give notice of this fact in writing to the person who made the statement and the apportionment or prospective apportionment of that quota shall then be made–

(a) in England and Wales and Northern Ireland by arbitration in accordance with Schedules 4 and 6,

(b) in Scotland in accordance with Schedule 5.

Reserves

13. There may be constituted for any region a running regional wholesale reserve and there may be added to the national direct sales reserve and to any appropriate running regional wholesale reserve such quota as is not for the time being allocated to any person.

Quota exchange

14. For the purposes of Article 5(5) and (6) of the Commission Regulation (which deals with changes from direct sales to wholesale delivery and vice versa) any person in a region may exchange direct sales quota for wholesale quota with any other person with a holding in the same region on such terms as those producers and the Minister may agree having regard to the provisions of the Community legislation.

Management of quota

15.—(1) For the purposes of Article 5c(1a) of Council Regulation 804/68 (temporary transfers of quotas) and subject to paragraph (2) a producer may make a temporary transfer within one region of part of the wholesale quota registered as his to another producer for a period of one quota year.

(2) Where there is an agreement to make a temporary transfer of quota pursuant to paragraph (1) the transferee shall before 31st July in the quota year in question give notification to the Minister of the agreement and of such particulars as the Minister may reasonably require.

Temporary reallocation of quota

16.—(1) For the purposes of Formula B, the Minister may, in any quota year, award to a producer referred to in paragraph (2) below a temporary reallocation of unused quota from the purchaser quota of the purchaser to whom that producer makes wholesale deliveries of dairy produce, in accordance with the provisions of this regulation.

(2) This regulation shall apply to–

(a) a producer to whom an award of quota has been made by the Dairy Produce Quota Tribunal, or one of the local panels constituted under regulation 6(2) of the 1984 Regulations, or to whom an allocation of quota has been made by the Minister under Schedule 12 to the 1986 Regulations, which award or amount of the allocation has been mistakenly entered in the registers prepared and maintained by the Minister under regulation 25 as an amount of quota being more than 100 litres in excess of the amount of the award or the allocation, and

(b) a producer who has quota registered as his in relation to a holding which is in whole or in part subject to a notice prohibiting or regulating the movement of dairy cows pursuant to an Order made under the Animal Health Act 1981**(a)** or the Diseases of Animals (Northern Ireland) Order 1981**(b)**.

(3) Subject to paragraph (4), a producer referred to in paragraph (2)(a) above may be awarded a temporary reallocation of unused quota for any quota year ending before 1 April 1992. The amount of any such award shall be calculated either–

(a) 1981 c.22.
(b) S.I. 1981/1115 (N.I. 22).

(a) as the amount by which the producer's production exceeds his quota entitlement in the quota year in question, or

(b) as the amount being the difference between the producer's quota entitlement in the quota year in question and the quota mistakenly having been registered as his, or

(c) as the amount referred to in paragraph (3)(b) above reduced by the amount, if any, by which the direct sales quota mistakenly having been registered as the producer's was less than the direct sales quota to which he is entitled in the quota year in question,

whichever amount is less.

(4) An award under paragraph (3) above shall be subject to the following conditions–

(a) a producer whose production in the quota year in question has not exceeded his quota entitlement shall not be entitled to receive an award for that year;

(b) a producer who transfers the whole of his quota under regulation 9, or exchanges the whole of his quota under regulation 14, shall not be entitled to receive an award for the quota year in which the transfer took effect or any future quota year;

(c) a producer who transfers a part of his quota under regulation 9, or exchanges a part of his quota under regulation 14, shall be entitled to receive an award for the quota year in which the transfer or exchange took effect reduced by the amount of quota transferred or exchanged;

(d) a producer who makes a temporary transfer of quota under regulation 15(1) shall not be entitled to receive an award in the same quota year;

(e) an award shall not be transferable to the transferee of any holding or part of a holding of a producer to whom an award has or may be made.

(5) Subject to paragraph (7), a producer referred to in paragraph (2)(b) above may be awarded a temporary reallocation of unused quota for any quota year in which the notice referred to in that paragraph has effect. The amount of any such award shall be calculated either–

(a) as the amount equal to 15 litres per qualifying cow per qualifying day in any quota year, or

(b) as the amount by which in the quota year in question the producer's production exceeds his quota entitlement,

whichever amount is less.

(6) Where the notice referred to in paragraph (2)(b) above continues beyond the quota year in respect of which a producer has received an award under paragraph (5) above, any award under that paragraph for the following quota year shall be calculated as if the number of the producer's qualifying cows were equal to that of his eligible heifers which calved during the period of the notice in that following quota year, notwithstanding that when any such heifers calved the number of eligible heifers did not exceed the replacement number.

(7) An award under paragraph (5) above shall be subject to the following conditions–

(a) the total amount of quota temporarily reallocated to producers from the purchaser quota of any purchaser shall not exceed 15 per cent of the total amount of unused quota available to that purchaser in any quota year and the Minister shall, to the extent that it is necessary so to do, abate in whole or in part each such temporary reallocation accordingly;

(b) a producer who transfers quota under regulation 9, or who makes a temporary transfer of quota under regulation 15(1), or purchases cows or in-calf heifers for dairy purposes, shall not be entitled to receive an award in the same quota year unless the Minister is satisfied that the agreement to transfer, temporarily transfer or purchase, was entered into before service of the notice to which paragraph (2)(b) above refers.

(8) In making any award of a temporary reallocation of unused quota for the purpose of this regulation the Minister shall afford priority to the producers referred to in paragraph (2)(a) above before making any award to the producers to whom paragraph (2)(b) above applies.

(9) In this regulation, "quota", except where otherwise described, means wholesale quota.

Special allocation of quota

17. Where, by reason of a mistake made by the Minister or any person acting on his behalf, a person has not been allocated any quota or has been allocated a smaller quantity of any such quota than he would have been allocated if the mistake had not been made, the Minister may allocate to that person such quota as will compensate, in whole or in part, for that mistake from the national direct sales reserve or from the appropriate running regional wholesale reserve, as the case may be.

Conversion of direct sales quota and wholesale quota

18. Schedule 7 shall apply in respect of the conversion of wholesale quota into direct sales quota and of direct sales quota into wholesale quota under Article 6a of Council Regulation 857/84.

Calculation of levy liability

19. Schedule 8 shall apply in respect of the reallocation of quota for the purposes of Article 4a of Council Regulation 857/84 and in respect of the calculation of levy liability for the purposes of Article 5c of Council Regulation 804/68.

Payment of levy

20.—(1) For the purposes of Article 16(3) of the Commission Regulation the time allowed for making the payment required to be made by Article 16(2) of that Regulation (time for payment of levy by direct sellers) shall be four months from the end of the quota year in respect of which the payment is made.

(2) Levy payable by virtue of Article 9(3) of Council Regulation 857/84 (payment of levy by direct sellers) or Article 15 of the Commission Regulation (payment of levy by purchasers) shall be recoverable by the Intervention Board.

Northern Ireland wholesale provision

21. The Minister may add to any exceptional hardship provision or small producers supplementary development provision from wholesale quota in any running regional wholesale reserve in Northern Ireland, in accordance with Schedule 9.

Functions of the Intervention Board for Agricultural Produce

22.—(1) The Intervention Board shall be–

(a) the agency appointed for the purposes of Article 9(3) of Council Regulation 857/84 (which deals with payment of levy by direct sellers), and

(b) the competent authority for the purposes of–

(i) Article 11 (which deals with equivalences),

(ii) Article 12(2) (which deals with increases in fat content),

(iii) Article 14(1) (which deals with records of wholesale deliveries),

(iv) Article 15 (which deals with payment of levy in respect of wholesale deliveries), and

(v) Article 16 (which deals with records of direct sales and payment of levy in respect thereof)–

of the Commission Regulation.

(2) The Intervention Board and any milk marketing board may enter into an agreement providing for the discharge by the milk marketing board, on behalf of the Intervention Board, of any functions of the Intervention Board under these Regulations or the Community legislation specified in the agreement, on such terms as may be specified in the agreement.

(3) In respect of any area which is not within the area of a milk marketing board, paragraph (2) shall have effect as if "person or milk marketing board" were substituted for "milk marketing board" wherever those words appear.

(4) The Intervention Board may, in respect of any person in whose name any direct sales quota is registered and who fails to submit to the Intervention Board within two months of the end of any quota year the statement required to be made by Article 16(1) of the Commission Regulation, make and recover a reasonable charge in respect of any visit to any premises reasonably required to be made by the Intervention Board to obtain that statement.

Functions under these Regulations

23.—(1) The Minister and any milk marketing board may enter into an agreement providing for the discharge by that milk marketing board, on behalf of the Minister, of any functions of the Minister under these Regulations or the Community legislation specified in the agreement, on such terms as may be specified in the agreement.

(2) In respect of any area which is not within the area of the milk marketing board, paragraph (1) shall have effect as if "person or milk marketing board" were substituted for "milk marketing board" wherever those words appear.

Disapplication of enactments

24. Nothing in section 47(2) of the Agricultural Marketing Act 1958**(a)** or section 23 of the Agricultural Marketing Act (Northern Ireland) 1964**(b)** (which restrict the disclosure of certain information obtained under those Acts) shall restrict or apply to the disclosure of any information if, and in so far as, the disclosure is required or authorised by these Regulations, the Community legislation or an agreement under regulation 22(2) or 23(1).

Registers to be prepared and maintained by the Minister

25.—(1) The Minister shall–

(a) prepare a direct sales register entry in respect of each direct seller setting out–

(i) his name,

(ii) his total direct sales quota, and

(iii) an identification of his holding.

and shall send each direct seller a copy of the entry relating to him, and

(b) maintain–

(i) a direct sales register (being a register of entries referred to in paragraph (1)(a)), and

(ii) a register of particulars of direct sales by each direct seller.

(2) For each region the Minister shall–

(a) prepare a wholesale register entry in respect of each producer in that region setting out–

(i) his name,

(ii) his total wholesale quota,

(iii) an identification of his holding in that region, and

(iv) a list–

—of the names and addresses of each purchaser in that region whose purchaser quota will be calculated to take into account that producer's total wholesale quota, and

—of the wholesale quota to be taken into account in those calculations for each such purchaser in respect of his purchaser quota set out in accordance with proportional divisions of wholesale quota based on purchaser details to be provided by the producer on request by the Minister

and shall send to each producer a copy of the entry relating to him and to each purchaser named on the list referred to in subparagraph (iv) a copy of the entry wherein he is so named,

(a) 1958 c.47, to which there are amendments not relevant to these Regulations.
(b) 1964 c.13 (N.I.), to which there are amendments not relevant to these Regulations.

(b) maintain–

(i) a wholesale register (being a register of entries referred to in paragraph (2)(a)) for each region, and

(ii) a register for each region of particulars of wholesale deliveries by each producer in that region.

(3) In respect of each purchaser the Minister shall–

(a) prepare a purchaser notice setting out–

(i) his name,

(ii) a description of his undertaking, and

(iii) his purchaser quota,

and shall send each purchaser a copy of the notice relating to him,

(b) maintain–

(i) a register of purchaser notices, and

(ii) a register of particulars of wholesale deliveries to each purchaser.

(4) For the purposes of paragraphs (1) and (2), where a holding comprises more than one dairy enterprise a direct seller or a producer may, on presenting to the Minister a consent or sole interest notice in respect of that holding, agree with the Minister the partition of that holding among separate direct sales register entries or wholesale register entries as specified in the agreement.

(5) The Minister shall amend the registers which he is required by this regulation to maintain to record any allocations or adjustments made under or by virtue of these Regulations, and shall inform any person to whom an amendment relates and any purchaser affected by an amendment of that amendment.

(6) In this regulation "direct seller" and "producer" include a person who has moved into occupation of land with quota, whether or not that person is engaged in the sale or delivery of dairy produce.

Inspection of entries in the Minister's registers

26. The Minister shall permit, during reasonable working hours, inspection of any entry relating to–

(a) a specific holding in the registers referred to in regulation 25(1)(b)(i) and 25(2)(b)(i) by any person who is the direct seller or producer in relation to, or gives the Minister a statement in writing that he has an interest in, that holding, and

(b) a specific purchaser in either register referred to in regulation 25(3)(b) by the purchaser,

and shall, on payment of a reasonable charge, forward a copy of that entry to any such person who requests it.

Registers to be maintained by purchasers

27.—(1) Each purchaser shall maintain, in respect of all producers whose register entries include that purchaser's name on the list referred to in regulation 25(2)(a)(iv)–

(a) a register as indicated in regulation 25(2)(b)(i) in respect of each of those producers, and

(b) a register of particulars of wholesale deliveries from each of those producers to that purchaser.

(2) Each purchaser shall amend his registers referred to in paragraph (1) on each occasion when, under these Regulations, the Minister's equivalent register is required to be amended in relation to producers registered in that purchaser's register.

Registers as evidence

28. Any entry in a register or notice required by these Regulations to be maintained by the Minister shall in any proceedings be evidence of matters stated therein.

Information

29.—(1) The Minister and the Intervention Board shall provide each other with such information and assistance as shall be required for the proper performance of their respective functions under these Regulations and the Community legislation.

(2) Each purchaser shall provide such information to the Minister as the Minister may reasonably require for the maintenance of his register of particulars of wholesale deliveries under regulation 25(2)(b)(ii) and regulation 25(3)(b)(ii).

(3) The Minister shall copy such records to each purchaser as that purchaser may reasonably require for the purposes of his registration obligations under these Regulations and Article 14(1) of the Commission Regulation.

Service of documents

30. Any document required by these Regulations to be served on any person may be served by post.

Penalties

31.—(1) Subject to paragraph (2), any person who–

(a) fails without reasonable excuse to comply with a requirement imposed on him by or under these Regulations or the Community legislation, or

(b) in connection with these Regulations or the Community legislation, makes a statement or uses a document which he knows to be false in a material particular or recklessly makes a statement or uses a document which is false in a material particular,

shall be guilty of an offence and liable, on summary conviction, to a fine not exceeding £2,000 and, on conviction on indictment, to a fine.

(2) Paragraph (1)(a) shall not apply to any failure by any person to comply with a requirement in an agreement referred to in regulation 22 or 23.

(3) The Minister may, following any conviction under paragraph (1)(b) against which there is no successful appeal, by notice served (within the period of 12 months following the date specified in paragraph (4)) on the person to whose quota that conviction relates reduce his quota to such extent as may reasonably be regarded by the Minister as being attributable to the falsehood on which the conviction was founded.

(4) The date referred to in paragraph (3) is–

(a) in the case of a conviction against which there is no appeal, the date on which the right to appeal against that conviction expires, and

(b) in the case of a conviction against which there is an unsuccessful appeal–

(i) if there is no right of appeal against the result of that unsuccessful appeal, the date of that result, and

(ii) if there is a right of appeal against that result but no appeal is made, the date on which that right of appeal expires.

Dairy Produce Quota Tribunals

32.—(1) The Dairy Produce Quota Tribunal for England and Wales, the Dairy Produce Quota Tribunal for Scotland, and the Dairy Produce Quota Tribunal for Northern Ireland constituted under regulation 6 of the 1984 Regulations shall continue in existence and, in respect of direct sales from a holding situated in more than one area of a Dairy Produce Quota Tribunal, the Dairy Produce Quota Tribunal the functions of which shall relate to those direct sales shall continue to be the Dairy Produce Quota Tribunal chosen for the purpose by the Ministers.

(2) Any reference in these Regulations to "The Tribunal" shall be treated as a reference to the appropriate Dairy Produce Quota Tribunal under paragraph (1).

(3) Schedule 10 shall apply in respect of the constitution, appointment of members, renumeration of members, staffing and procedure of Dairy Produce Quota Tribunals.

Revocation

33. The Regulations specified in Schedule 11 are hereby revoked.

In Witness whereof the Official Seal of the Minister of Agriculture, Fisheries and Food is hereunto affixed on 7th March 1989.

Trumpington
Parliamentary Secretary
Ministry of Agriculture, Fisheries and Food

8th March 1989

Sanderson of Bowden
Minister of State, Scottish Office

SCHEDULE 1

Regulation 2

RELEVANT AMENDMENTS TO COUNCIL REGULATION 804/68

Council Regulation	*Official Journal Reference*
856/84	L90, 1.4.84, p.10
1557/84	L150, 6.6.84, p.6
591/85	L68, 8.3.85, p.5
1298/85	L137, 27.5.85, p.5
2033/85	L192, 24.7.85, p.9
2893/85	L278, 18.10.85, p.9
3275/85	L314, 23.11.85, p.7
3571/85	L341, 19.12.85, p.11
1335/86	L119, 8.5.86, p.19
773/87	L78, 20.3.87, p.1
1105/87	L106, 22.4.87, p.33
2188/87	L203, 24.7.87, p.24
2998/87	L285, 8.10.87, p.1
487/88	L50, 24.2.88, p.12
744/88	L78, 23.3.88, p.1
1109/88	L110, 29.4.88, p.27

Regulation 2

SCHEDULE 2

AMENDMENTS TO COUNCIL REGULATION 857/84

Council Regulation	*Official Journal Reference*	*Article amended or added*
1557/84	L150, 6.6.84, p.6	Annex
590/85	L68, 8.3.85, p.1	4a
		6
		6a
		7
		12(e)
591/85	L68, 8.3.85, p.5	Annex
1305/85	L137, 27.5.85, p.12	1(1)
		3(3)
		4a(1)
		6(2)
		8
		9(1), 9(2), 9(4)
		10
		12(c)
2033/85	L192, 24.7.85, p.9	Annex
2893/85	L278, 18.10.85, p.9	Annex
3275/85	L314, 23.11.85, p.7	Annex
3571/85	L341, 19.12.85, p.11	Annex
1343/86	L119, 8.5.86, p.34	2(3)
		4(1)(a)
		4a(1)
		6(4)
		9(1), 9(4)
		Annex
1911/86	L165, 21.6.86, p.6	2
		6(1)
2316/86	L202, 25.7.86, p.3	2(1), 2(2)
		3
		6(1)
774/87	L78, 20.3.87, p.3	1(1)
		4a(1), 4a(3)
		9(4)
		10
1105/87	L106, 22.4.87, p.33	Annex
1899/87	L182, 3.7.87, p.39	4(1), 4(2)
2188/87	L203, 24.7.87, p.24	Annex
487/88	L50, 24.2.88, p.12	Annex
1110/88	L110, 29.4.88, p.28	4a(1)
		9(4)
		Annex

Regulation 2

SCHEDULE 3

AMENDMENTS TO COMMISSION REGULATION 1546/88

Council Regulation	*Official Journal Reference*	*Article amended or added*
2202/88	L195, 23.7.88, p.54	15(6)
		16(2), 16(3)
		19(3)
3086/88	L275, 7.10.88, p.14	12(1), 12(2)
		13(1)
		19(3)

Commission Regulation	*Official Journal Reference*	*Article amended or added*
215/89	L25, 28.1.89, p.72	1

SCHEDULE 4

Regulations 9, 10, 11 and 12

APPORTIONMENTS AND PROSPECTIVE APPORTIONMENTS BY ARBITRATION – ENGLAND AND WALES

Appointment and remuneration of arbitrator

1.—(1) In any case where an apportionment is to be carried out by arbitration an arbitrator shall be appointed by agreement between the transferor and transferee within the period of two months referred to in regulation 9(1)(a) (referred to in this paragraph as "the relevant period") and the transferee shall notify the Minister in writing of the appointment of the arbitrator within fourteen days from the date of the appointment.

(2) Notwithstanding subparagraph (1) above, the transferor or the transferee may at any time within the relevant period make an application to the President of the Royal Institution of Chartered Surveyors (referred to in this Schedule as "the President") for the appointment of an arbitrator from among the members of the panel referred to in paragraph 8 and the person who makes such an application to the President shall notify the Minister in writing of that fact within fourteen days from the date of the application.

(3) If at the expiry of the relevant period an arbitrator has not been appointed by agreement between the transferor or the transferee nor an application made to the President under subparagraph (2) above, the Minister shall make an application to the President for the appointment of an arbitrator.

(4) Where the Minister gives a notice in accordance with regulation 12 he shall make an application to the President for the appointment of an arbitrator and the Minister shall be a party to the arbitration.

2.—(1) In any case where a prospective apportionment is to be made by arbitration an arbitrator shall be appointed–

(a) where regulation 12 applies, by the President,

(b) in any other case, by agreement between the occupier and any other interested party, or, in default, by the President on an application by the occupier.

(2) Where subparagraph (1)(b) above applies, the occupier shall notify the Minister in writing of the appointment of the arbitrator pursuant to the agreement, or of the application to the President for the appointment of an arbitrator, within fourteen days from the date of the appointment of the arbitrator or the date of the application to the President, as appropriate.

3. An arbitrator appointed in accordance with paragraphs 1 and 2 above shall conduct the arbitration in accordance with this Schedule and shall base his award on findings made by him as to areas used for milk production in the five years preceding the change of occupation, or in the case of a prospective apportionment in the five years preceding the appointment of the arbitrator.

4.—(1) No application may be made to the President for an arbitrator to be appointed by him under this Schedule unless the application is accompanied by the prescribed fee for such an application; but once the fee has been paid in connection with any such application no further fee shall be payable in connection with any subsequent application for the President to exercise any function exercisable by him in relation to the arbitration by virtue of this Schedule (including an application for the appointment by him in an appropriate case of a new arbitrator).

(2) The prescribed fee for the purposes of this paragraph shall be that which from time to time is prescribed as the fee payable to the President under paragraph 1(2) of Schedule 11 to the Agricultural Holdings Act 1986**(a)**.

5. Where the Minister makes an application to the President under paragraphs 1(3) or (4) above, the fee payable to the President in respect of that application referred to in paragraph 4 above shall be recoverable by the Minister as a debt due from the other parties to the arbitration jointly or severally.

6. Any appointment of an arbitrator by the President shall be made by him as soon as possible after receiving the application.

7. A person appointed by the President as arbitrator shall, where the arbitration relates to a holding in Wales, and any party to the arbitration so requires, be a person who possesses a knowledge of the Welsh language.

(a) 1986 c.5.

8. For the purposes of paragraph 1(2) the panel of arbitrators shall be the panel appointed by the Lord Chancellor under paragraph 1(5) of Schedule 11 to the Agricultural Holdings Act 1986.

9. If the arbitrator dies, or is incapable of acting, or for seven days after notice from any party requiring him to act fails to act, a new arbitrator may be appointed as if no arbitrator had been appointed.

10. No party to the arbitration shall have power to revoke the appointment of the arbitrator without the consent of the other party; and his appointment shall not be revoked by the death of any party.

11. Every appointment, application, notice, revocation and consent under the foregoing paragraphs must be in writing.

12. The remuneration of the arbitrator shall be–

(a) where he is appointed by agreement between the parties, such amount as may be agreed upon by him and the parties or, in default of agreement, fixed by the registrar of the county court (subject to an appeal to the judge of the court) on an application made by the arbitrator or one of the parties,

(b) where he is appointed by the President, such amount as may be agreed upon by the arbitrator and the parties or, in default of agreement, fixed by the President,

and shall be recoverable by the arbitrator as a debt due from any one of the parties to the arbitration.

Conduct of proceedings and witnesses

13. The parties to the arbitration shall, within thirty-five days from the appointment of the arbitrator, or within such further period as the arbitrator may permit, deliver to him a statement of their respective cases with all necessary particulars and–

(a) no amendment or addition to the statement or particulars delivered shall be allowed after the expiry of the said thirty-five days except with the consent of the arbitrator,

(b) a party to the arbitration shall be confined at the hearing to the matters alleged in the statement and particulars delivered by him and any amendment or addition duly made.

14. The parties to the arbitration and all persons claiming through them respectively shall, subject to any legal objection, submit to be examined by the arbitrator, on oath or affirmation, in relation to the matters in dispute and shall, subject to any such objection, produce before the arbitrator all samples and documents within their possession or power respectively which may be required or called for, and do all other things which during the proceedings the arbitrator may require.

15. Any person having an interest in the holding to which the arbitration relates shall be entitled to make representations to the arbitrator.

16. Witnesses appearing at the arbitration shall, if the arbitrator thinks fit, be examined on oath or affirmation, and the arbitrator shall have power to administer oaths to, or to take the affirmation of, the parties and witnesses appearing.

17. The provisions of county court rules as to the issuing of witness summonses shall, subject to such modifications as may be prescribed by such rules, apply for the purposes of the arbitration as if it were an action or matter in the county court.

18.—(1) Subject to subparagraphs (2) and (3) below, any person who–

(a) having been summoned in pursuance of county court rules as a witness in the arbitration refuses or neglects, without sufficient cause, to appear or to produce any documents required by the summons to be produced, or

(b) having been so summoned or being present at the arbitration and being required to give evidence, refuses to be sworn or give evidence,

shall forfeit such fine as the judge of the county court may direct.

(2) A judge shall not have power under sub-paragraph (1) above to direct that a person shall forfeit a fine of an amount exceeding £10.

(3) No person summoned in pursuance of county court rules as a witness in the arbitration shall forfeit a fine under this paragraph unless there has been paid or tendered to him at the time of the service of the summons such sum in respect of his expenses (including, in such cases as may be

prescribed by county court rules, compensation for loss of time) as may be so prescribed for the purposes of section 55 of the County Courts Act 1984**(a)**.

(4) The judge of the county court may at his discretion direct that the whole or any part of any such fine, after deducting costs, shall be applicable towards indemnifying the party injured by the refusal or neglect.

19.—(1) Subject to subparagraph (2) below, the judge of the county court may, if he thinks fit, upon application on affidavit by any party to the arbitration, issue an order under his hand for bringing up before the arbitrator any person (in this paragraph referred to as a "prisoner") confined in any place under any sentence or under commital for trial or otherwise, to be examined as a witness in the arbitration.

(2) No such order shall be made with respect to a person confined under process in any civil action or matter.

(3) Subject to subparagraph (4) below, the prisoner mentioned in any such order shall be brought before the arbitrator under the same custody, and shall be dealt with in the same manner in all respects, as a prisoner required by a writ of habeas corpus to be brought before the High Court and examined there as a witness.

(4) The person having the custody of the prisoner shall not be bound to obey the order unless there is tendered to him a reasonable sum for the conveyance and maintenance of a proper officer or officers and of the prisoner in going to, remaining at, and returning from, the place where the arbitration is held.

20. The High Court may order that a writ of habeas corpus ad testificandum shall issue to bring up a prisoner for examination before the arbitrator, if the prisoner is confined in any prison under process in any civil action or matter.

Award

21.—(1) Subject to subparagraph (2) below, the arbitrator shall make and sign his award within fifty-six days of his appointment.

(2) The President may from time to time enlarge the time limited for making the award, whether that time has expired or not.

(3) The award shall fix a date not later than one month after the delivery of the award for the payment of any costs awarded under paragraph 25 below.

22. The award shall be final and binding on the parties and the persons claiming under them respectively.

23. The arbitrator shall have power to correct in the award any clerical mistake or error arising from any accidental slip or omission.

Reasons for award

24. If requested by any party to the arbitration, on or before the making of the award, to make a statement, either written or oral, of the reasons for the award the arbitrator shall furnish such a statement.

Costs

25. The costs of, and incidental to, the arbitration and award shall be in the discretion of the arbitrator who may direct to and by whom and in what manner the costs, or any part of the costs, are to be paid. The costs for the purposes of this paragraph shall include any fee paid to the President in respect of the appointment of an arbitrator and any sum paid to the Minister pursuant to paragraph 5.

26. On the application of any party, any such costs shall be taxable in the county court according to such of the scales prescribed by county court rules for proceedings in the county court as may be directed by the arbitrator under paragraph 25 above, or, in the absence of any such direction, by the county court.

27.—(1) The arbitrator shall, in awarding costs, take into consideration–

(a) the reasonableness or unreasonableness of the claim of any party, whether in respect of amount or otherwise,

(a) 1984 c.28.

(b) any unreasonable demand for particulars or refusal to supply particulars, and

(c) generally all the circumstances of the case.

(2) The arbitrator may disallow the costs of any witness whom he considers to have been called unnecessarily and any other costs which he considers to have been incurred unnecessarily.

Special case, setting aside award and remission

28. The arbitrator may, at any stage of the proceedings, and shall, upon a direction in that behalf given by the judge of the county court upon an application made by any party, state in the form of a special case for the opinion of the county court any question of law arising in the course of the arbitration and any question as to the jurisdiction of the arbitrator.

29.—(1) Where the arbitrator has misconducted himself, the county court may remove him.

(2) Where the arbitrator has misconducted himself, or an arbitration or award has been improperly procured, or there is an error of law on the face of the award, the county court may set the award aside.

30.—(1) The county court may from time to time remit the award, or any part of the award, to the reconsideration of the arbitrator.

(2) In any case where it appears to the county court that there is an error of law on the face of the award, the court may, instead of exercising its power of remission under subparagraph (1) above, vary the award by substituting for so much of it as is affected by the error such award as the court considers that it would have been proper for the arbitrator to make in the circumstances; and the award shall thereupon have effect as so varied.

(3) Where remission is ordered under that subparagraph, the arbitrator shall, unless the order otherwise directs, make and sign his award within thirty days after the date of the order.

(4) If the county court is satisfied that the time limited for making the said award is for any good reason insufficient, the court may extend or further extend that time for such period as it thinks proper.

Miscellaneous

31. Any amount paid, in respect of the remuneration of the arbitrator by any party to the arbitration, in excess of the amount, if any, directed by the award to be paid by him in respect of the costs of the award shall be recoverable from the other party or jointly from the other parties.

32. For the purposes of this Schedule, an arbitrator appointed by the President shall be taken to have been so appointed at the time when the President executed the instrument of appointment; and in the case of any such arbitrator the periods mentioned in paragraphs 13 and 21 above shall accordingly run from that time.

33. Any instrument of appointment or other document purporting to be made in the exercise of any function exercisable by the President under paragraphs 1, 2, 6, 7, 12 or 21 above and to be signed by or on behalf of the President shall be taken to be such an instrument or document unless the contrary is shown.

34. The Arbitration Act 1950**(a)** shall not apply to an arbitration determined in accordance with this Schedule.

Regulations 9, 10, 11 and 12

SCHEDULE 5

APPORTIONMENTS AND PROSPECTIVE APPORTIONMENTS BY ARBITRATION – SCOTLAND

PART I

GENERAL

1.—(1) Subject to subparagraphs (2) and (3) below, all apportionments and prospective apportionments in respect of holdings in Scotland shall be carried out by arbitration and the provisions of Part II of this Schedule shall apply.

(a) 1950 c.27, to which there are amendments not relevant to these Regulations.

(2) The Scottish Land Court shall carry out the apportionment or prospective apportionment where the holding or any part of the holding constitutes or, immediately prior to the transfer giving rise to the apportionment, constituted–

(a) a croft within the meaning of section 3(1) of the Crofters (Scotland) Act 1955**(a)**;

(b) a holding within the meaning of section 2 of the Small Landholders (Scotland) Act 1911**(b)**; or

(c) the holding of a statutory small tenant under section 32 of the Small Landholders (Scotland) Act 1911.

(3) Where subparagraph (2) above does not apply and the holding or any part of the holding constitutes or, immediately prior to the transfer giving rise to the apportionment, constituted an agricultural holding within the meaning of section 1 of the Agricultural Holdings (Scotland) Act 1949**(c)**, the Scottish Land Court shall carry out the apportionment or prospective apportionment if requested to do so by a joint application of all parties interested in the apportionment, made within the period of two months referred to in regulation 9(1)(a).

(4) Where the Scottish Land Court carries out any apportionment or prospective apportionment, Part III of this Schedule shall apply.

2. An arbiter or the Scottish Land Court, as the case may be, shall decide the apportionment on the basis of findings made as to areas used for milk production in the five years preceding the change of occupation or, in the case of a prospective apportionment, in the five years preceding the appointment of the arbiter or the application to the Scottish Land Court.

PART II

APPORTIONMENTS CARRIED OUT BY ARBITRATION

Appointment and remuneration of arbiter

3.—(1) In any case where the apportionment is to be carried out by arbitration, an arbiter shall be appointed by agreement between the transferor and transferee within the period of two months referred to in regulation 9(1)(a) (referred to in this paragraph as "the relevant period") and the transferee shall notify the Minister in writing of the appointment of the arbiter within fourteen days from the date of the appointment.

(2) Notwithstanding sub-paragraph (1) above, the transferor or the transferee may at any time within the relevant period make an application to the Minister for the appointment of an arbiter.

(3) If at the expiry of the relevant period an arbiter has not been appointed by agreement between the transferor and the transferee nor an application made to the Minister under subparagraph (2) above, the Minister shall at his own instance proceed to appoint an arbiter.

4.—(1) In any case where a prospective apportionment is to be made by arbitration, an arbiter shall be appointed by agreement between the occupier and any other interested party or, in default, by the Minister on an application by the occupier.

(2) Where an arbiter is appointed by agreement in terms of subparagraph (1) above, the occupier shall notify the Minister in writing of the appointment of the arbiter within fourteen days from the date of the appointment.

5.—(1) Where, in terms of a notice given by the Minister under regulation 12, an apportionment or prospective apportionment is to be carried out by arbitration, the Minister shall apply to the Scottish Land Court for the appointment of an arbiter.

(2) Any fee payable by the Minister on an application to the Scottish Land Court under subparagraph (1) above shall be recoverable by him as a debt due from the other parties to the arbitration jointly or severally.

(3) Where the Minister is to be a party to an arbitration (otherwise than in terms of a notice given under regulation 12), the arbiter shall, in lieu of being appointed by the Minister, be appointed by the Scottish Land Court.

(a) 1955 c.21; section 3(1) was amended by the Crofters (Scotland) Act 1961 (c.58), Schedule 1, Part II, paragraph 9.
(b) 1911 c.49.
(c) 1949 c.75.

6. If the person appointed arbiter dies, or is incapable of acting, or for seven days after notice from any party requiring him to act fails to act, a new arbiter may be appointed as if no arbiter had been appointed.

7. No party to the arbitration shall have power to revoke the appointment of the arbiter without the consent of all other parties.

8. Every appointment, application, notice, revocation and consent under the foregoing paragraphs must be in writing.

9. The remuneration of the arbiter shall be–

(a) where he is appointed by agreement between the parties, such amount as may be agreed upon by him and the parties, or, in default of agreement, fixed by the auditor of the sheriff court (subject to an appeal to the sheriff) on an application made by the arbiter or one of the parties;

(b) where he is appointed by the Minister, such amount as may be fixed by the Minister;

(c) where he is appointed by the Scottish Land Court, such amount as may be fixed by that Court;

and shall be recoverable by the arbiter as a debt due from any one of the parties to the arbitration.

Conduct of proceedings and witnesses

10. The parties to the arbitration shall within twenty-eight days from the appointment of the arbiter deliver to him a statement of their respective cases with all necessary particulars; and–

(a) no amendment or addition to the statement or particulars delivered shall be allowed after the expiry of the said twenty-eight days except with the consent of the arbiter;

(b) a party to the arbitration shall be confined at the hearing to the matters alleged in the statement and particulars delivered by him and any amendment or addition duly made.

11. The parties to the arbitration, and all persons claiming through them respectively, shall, subject to any legal objection, submit to be examined by the arbiter on oath or affirmation in relation to the matters in dispute and shall, subject as aforesaid, produce before the arbiter all samples, books, deeds, papers, accounts, writings and documents, within their possession or power respectively which may be required or called for, and do all other things which during the proceedings the arbiter may require.

12. Any person having an interest in the holding to which the arbitration relates shall be entitled to make representations to the arbiter. The Minister may make such representations where the arbitration follows on a notice given by him under regulation 12.

13. The arbiter shall have power to administer oaths, and to take the affirmation of parties and witnesses appearing, and witnesses shall, if the arbiter thinks fit, be examined on oath or affirmation.

Award

14.—(1) The arbiter shall make and sign his award within three months of his appointment or within such longer period as may, either before or after the expiry of the aforesaid period, be agreed to in writing by the parties or fixed by the Minister.

(2) The award shall fix a date not later than one month after the delivery of the award for the payment of any expenses awarded under paragraph 17 below.

15. The award to be made by the arbiter shall be final and binding on the parties and the persons claiming under them respectively.

16. The arbiter may correct in an award any clerical mistake or error arising from any accidental slip or omission.

Expenses

17. The expenses of and incidental to the arbitration and award shall be in the discretion of the arbiter, who may direct to and by whom and in what manner those expenses or any part thereof are to be paid, and the expenses shall be subject to taxation by the auditor of the sheriff court on the application of any party, but that taxation shall be subject to review by the sheriff.

18.—(1) The arbiter shall, in awarding expenses, take into consideration–

(a) the reasonableness or unreasonableness of the claim of any party, whether in respect of amount or otherwise;

(b) any unreasonable demand for particulars or refusal to supply particulars; and

(c) generally all the circumstances of the case.

(2) The arbiter may disallow the expenses of any witness whom he considers to have been called unnecessarily and any other expenses which he considers to have been incurred unnecessarily.

19. It shall not be lawful to include in the expenses of and incidental to the arbitration and award, or to charge against any of the parties, any sum payable in respect of remuneration or expenses to any person appointed by the arbiter to act as clerk or otherwise to assist him in the arbitration unless such appointment was made after submission of the claim and answers to the arbiter and with either the consent of the parties to the arbitration or the sanction of the sheriff.

Statement of case

20. The arbiter may at any stage of the proceedings, and shall, if so directed by the sheriff (which direction may be given on the application of any party), state a case for the opinion of the sheriff on any questions of law arising in the course of the arbitration. The opinion of the sheriff on any case shall be final.

Removal of arbiter and setting aside of award

21. Where an arbiter has misconducted himself the sheriff may remove him.

22. When an arbiter has misconducted himself, or an arbitration or award has been improperly procured, the sheriff may set the award aside.

Miscellaneous

23. Any amount paid in respect of the remuneration of the arbiter by any party to the arbitration in excess of the amount, if any, directed by the award to be paid by him in respect of the expenses of the award shall be recoverable from the other party or jointly from the other parties.

24. The Arbitration (Scotland) Act 1894**(a)** shall not apply to any arbitration carried out under this Schedule.

PART III

APPORTIONMENTS CARRIED OUT BY THE SCOTTISH LAND COURT

25. The provisions of the Small Landholders (Scotland) Acts 1886 to 1931 with regard to the Scottish Land Court shall, with any necessary modifications, apply for the purpose of the determination of any matter which they are required, in terms of paragraph 1 of this Schedule, to determine, in like manner as those provisions apply for the purpose of the determination by the Land Court of matters referred to them under those Acts.

26. Where an apportionment or prospective apportionment is to be dealt with by the Scottish Land Court, the party making application to that Court shall notify the Minister in writing of the application within fourteen days of its being lodged with the Court.

27. Where, in terms of a notice given by the Minister under regulation 12, an apportionment or prospective apportionment is to be carried out by the Scottish Land Court, any fee payable by the Minister to the Court shall be recoverable by him as a debt due from the other parties to the case jointly or severally.

28. Any person having an interest in the holding to which the apportionment or prospective apportionment relates shall be entitled to be a party to the proceedings before the Scottish Land Court. The Minister shall be entitled to be a party where the apportionment follows on a notice given by him under regulation 12.

(a) 1894 c.13 (57 and 58 Vict.).

Regulations 9, 10, 11 and 12

SCHEDULE 6

APPORTIONMENTS AND PROSPECTIVE APPORTIONMENTS BY ARBITRATION – NORTHERN IRELAND

1. Paragraphs 3 to 17 below shall apply to every arbitration in Northern Ireland.

2.—(1) The Arbitration Act (Northern Ireland) 1937**(a)** shall, except insofar as it is inconsistent with paragraphs 3 to 17 below, apply to every arbitration in Northern Ireland as if that arbitration were pursuant to an arbitration agreement and as if paragraphs 3 to 16 below were contained in an arbitration agreement.

(2) In this paragraph "arbitration agreement" has the same meaning as in section 30 of the Arbitration Act (Northern Ireland) 1937.

Appointment of arbitrator

3.—(1) In any case where an apportionment is to be carried out by arbitration an arbitrator shall be appointed by agreement between the transferor and transferee within the period of two months referred to in regulation 9(1)(a) (referred to in this paragraph as "the relevant period") and the transferee shall notify the Minister in writing of the appointment of the arbitrator within 14 days from the date of the appointment.

(2) Notwithstanding subparagraph (1) above, the transferor or the transferee may at any time within the relevant period make an application to the President of the Law Society of Northern Ireland (referred to in this Schedule as "the President") for the appointment of an arbitrator and the person who makes such an application to the President shall notify the Minister in writing of that fact within fourteen days from the date of the application.

(3) If at the expiry of the relevant period an arbitrator has not been appointed by agreement between the transferor and the transferee nor an application made to the President under subparagraph (2) above, the Minister shall make an application to the President for the appointment of an arbitrator.

(4) Where the Minister gives a notice in accordance with regulation 12 he shall make an application to the President for the appointment of an arbitrator and the Minister shall be a party to the arbitration.

4.—(1) In any case where a prospective apportionment is to be made by arbitration an arbitrator shall be appointed–

(a) where regulation 12 applies, by the President;

(b) in any other case, by agreement between the occupier and any other interested party, or, in default, by the President on an application by the occupier.

(2) Where subparagraph (1)(b) above applies, the occupier shall notify the Minister in writing of the appointment of the arbitrator pursuant to the agreement, or of the application to the President for the appointment of an arbitrator, within fourteen days from the date of the appointment of the arbitrator or the date of the application to the President, as appropriate.

5. An arbitrator appointed in accordance with paragraphs 1, 3, and 4 above shall conduct the arbitration in accordance with this Schedule and shall base his award on findings made by him as to areas used for milk production in the five years preceding the change of occupation, or in the case of a prospective apportionment in the five years preceding the arbitration.

6. No application may be made to the President for an arbitrator to be appointed by him under this Schedule unless the application is accompanied by the fee which shall be £50 for such an application; but once the fee has been paid in connection with any such application no further fee shall be payable in connection with any subsequent application for the President to exercise any function exercisable by him in relation to the arbitration by virtue of this Schedule (including an application for the appointment by him in an appropriate case of a new arbitrator).

7. Where the Minister makes an application to the President under paragraphs 3(3) or (4) above, the fee payable to the President in respect of that application referred to in paragraph 6 above shall be recoverable by the Minister as a debt due from the parties to the arbitration jointly or severally.

(a) 1937 c.8 (N.I.).

8. Any appointment of an arbitrator by the President shall be made by him within fourteen days after receiving the application.

9. If the arbitrator dies, or is incapable of acting, or for seven days after notice from any party requiring him to act fails to act, a new arbitrator may be appointed as if no arbitrator had been appointed.

10. A party to the arbitration shall have power to revoke the appointment of the arbitrator with the consent of all other parties.

11. Every appointment, application, notice, revocation and consent under the foregoing paragraphs shall be in writing.

Statement of case

12. The parties to the arbitration shall, within thirty-five days from the appointment of the arbitrator, deliver to him a statement of their respective cases with all necessary particulars and–

(a) no amendment or addition to the statement or particulars delivered shall be allowed after the expiry of the said thirty-five days except with the consent of the arbitrator;

(b) a party to the arbitration shall be confined at the hearing to the matters alleged in the statement and particulars delivered by him and any amendment or addition duly made.

Award

13. The arbitrator shall make and sign his award within fifty-six days of his appointment.

14. The arbitrator shall have power to correct in the award any clerical mistake or error arising from any accidental slip or omission.

Reasons for award

15. If requested by any party to the arbitration, on or before the making of the award, to make a statement, either written or oral, of the reasons for the award the arbitrator shall furnish such a statement.

16. For the purposes of this Schedule, an arbitrator appointed by the President shall be taken to have been so appointed at the time when the President executed the instrument of appointment; and in the case of any such arbitrator the periods mentioned in paragraphs 12 and 13 above shall run from that time.

17. Any person having an interest in the holding to which the arbitration relates shall be entitled to make representations to the arbitrator.

SCHEDULE 7

Regulation 18

CONVERSION OF DIRECT SALES QUOTA AND WHOLESALE QUOTA

1. An applicant for the conversion of direct sales quota into wholesale quota or wholesale quota into direct sales quota in respect of a quota year who has both wholesale quota and direct sales quota shall submit his application to the Minister no later than a date to be determined by the Minister in respect of each quota year and published in the Gazette.

2. An application referred to in paragraph 1 shall, in respect of the quota year concerned–

(a) state the amount of the applicant's direct sales quota and wholesale quota, his direct sales and wholesale deliveries of dairy produce, and

(b) provide such other information as may reasonably be required to be provided in order to enable the Minister to assess the factors referred to in Article 6a of Council Regulation 857/84.

3. The Minister shall calculate the amount of the applicant's direct sales quota or wholesale quota which has not been used in that quota year and which the applicant has available for conversion into wholesale quota or direct sales quota, as the case may be.

4. The Minister shall, within each purchaser area, convert into wholesale quota so much of applicants' unused direct sales quota as will not exceed the amount by which wholesale deliveries of dairy produce to that purchaser exceed the wholesale quota of that purchaser adjusted in accordance with Article 12(1) of the Commission Regulation.

5. The Minister shall convert into direct sales quota so much of applicants' unused wholesale quota as will not exceed the amount by which the aggregate direct sales of dairy produce of direct sellers exceed the aggregate direct sales quota, adjusted to take into account the conversion, if any, under paragraph 4, of direct sellers in that quota year.

6.—(1) The quantity of direct sales quota which is to be converted into wholesale quota by virtue of an application referred to in paragraph 1 shall be taken from the applicant's direct sales quota and added to the national direct sales reserve. An equivalent quantity shall be transferred from that reserve to the appropriate running regional wholesale reserve and allocated from that reserve to the applicant.

(2) The quantity of wholesale quota which is to be converted into direct sales quota by virtue of such an application shall be taken from the applicant's wholesale quota and added to the appropriate running regional wholesale reserve. An equivalent quantity shall be transferred from that reserve to the national direct sales reserve and allocated from that reserve to the applicant.

Regulation 19

SCHEDULE 8

CALCULATION OF LEVY LIABILITY

Wholesale quota

1. The Minister shall calculate–

(a) the amount, if any, by which the quantity of wholesale deliveries of dairy produce to each purchaser must be adjusted to take account of its fat content calculated in accordance with paragraph 12(1) of the Commission Regulation, and

(b) the amount, if any, by which the purchaser quota exceeds the quantity of wholesale deliveries of dairy produce to him, adjusted in accordance with subparagraph (a), and

(c) the amount, if any, by which the wholesale deliveries of dairy produce to each purchaser, adjusted in accordance with subparagraph (a), exceeds his purchaser quota, and

(d) the aggregate of the amounts referred to at subparagraph (b) by which the total purchaser quota of each purchaser which exceeds the quantity of wholesale deliveries of dairy produce to him, adjusted in accordance with subparagraph (a), do so in each region.

2. The aggregate, if any, referred to in paragraph 1(d) shall be reallocated among purchasers in that region in proportion to, and (so far as it is available) to the extent of, the amounts referred to at paragraph 1(c).

3. The Minister shall calculate for each purchaser the amount, if any, by which the amount in paragraph 1(c) exceeds the amount reallocated in paragraph 2.

4. The Minister shall direct each purchaser to convert into wholesale quota the direct sales quota of any applicant who has both direct sales and wholesale quota for conversion under Schedule 7 to the extent of the amount referred to in paragraph 3 or (so far as it is available) to the extent of the quantity of direct sales quota each applicant has available for conversion whichever is less.

5. The Minister shall calculate for each purchaser the amount, if any, by which the amount referred to in paragraph 3 exceeds the amount of direct sales quota which each purchaser has converted into wholesale quota under paragraph 4.

6. The Minister shall calculate in respect of each region–

(a) the amount, if any, by which the total purchaser quota of purchasers within that region taking into account the amount of quota converted in accordance with paragraph 4, exceeds or falls short of the quantity of wholesale deliveries of dairy produce to purchasers within that region, and

(b) the aggregate of the amounts by which all those amounts referred to in subparagraph (a) exceed the total regional wholesale deliveries of dairy produce.

7. The aggregate referred to in paragraph 6(b) shall be reallocated among purchasers in regions in which wholesale deliveries of dairy produce have exceeded the appropriate regional wholesale quota in proportion to, and (so far as it is available) to the extent of, the amount, if any,calculated for each purchaser under paragraph 5.

8. The Minister shall calculate for each purchaser the amount, if any, by which the amount referred to in paragraph 5 exceeds the amount, if any, reallocated to that purchaser under paragraph 7.

Direct sales quota

9. The Minister shall calculate, taking into account the conversion of direct sales quota at paragraph 4–

(a) the amount, if any, by which the quantity of dairy produce sold by direct sales from the holding of each direct seller exceeds the direct sales quota of that direct seller,

(b) the amount, if any, by which the quantity of dairy produce sold by direct sales from the holding of each direct seller located within a purchaser area falls short of, or exceeds, the direct sales quota of direct sellers in that area, and

(c) the aggregate of the amounts referred to in subparagraph (b) of this paragraph.

10. The Minister shall direct each purchaser to convert into direct sales quota the wholesale quota of any applicant who has both direct sales quota and wholesale quota for conversion under Schedule 7 to the extent of the aggregate referred to in paragraph 9(c) or (so far as it is available) to the extent of the quantity of wholesale quota each applicant has available for conversion in proportion to any excess attributable to the direct sellers under paragraph 9(b) whichever is less.

11. The Minister shall calculate–

(a) the amount, if any, by which the aggregate referred to in paragraph 9(c) exceeds the aggregate of the amounts converted under paragraph 10,

(b) the amount, if any, by which the amount referred to in paragraph 9(a) exceeds the amount of the direct seller's quota converted under paragraph 10, and

(c) the aggregate of the amounts referred to under subparagraph (b).

Amount of levy

12. The Minister shall calculate the rate of levy per litre, if any, to be paid by each direct seller on the amount at paragraph 11(b) by multiplying the amount referred to in paragraph 11(a) by the figure for levy calculated in accordance with Article 1 of Council Regulation 857/84 and dividing the resultant figure by the aggregate referred to in paragraph 11(c).

13. The Minister shall calculate the amount of levy to be paid by each purchaser by multiplying the amount, if any, referred to in paragraph 8 adjusted to take into account the conversion, if any, of wholesale quota under paragraph 10 by the figure for the levy calculated in accordance with Article 1 of Council Regulation 857/84.

14. Each purchaser shall pass on the burden to producers of the levy, if any, calculated in accordance with Article 5c (Formula B) of Council Regulation 804/68 taking into account the amounts of unused quota, if any, reallocated to that purchaser under paragraph 2 or paragraph 7 of this regulation and conversion of quota under paragraph 4 and paragraph 10.

15. For the purposes of this Schedule "purchaser area" means the geographical area from within which a purchaser purchases milk or other milk products or, in respect of any region from which no purchaser purchases milk or other milk products, means that region.

SCHEDULE 9

Regulation 21

NORTHERN IRELAND WHOLESALE PROVISION

PART I

EXCEPTIONAL HARDSHIP ALLOCATION

1. The Minister may at any time add to an exceptional hardship provision made under paragraph 17 of Schedule 2 to the 1984 Regulations. Where any such additional provision is made the Minister shall by advertisement published in the Gazette announce the amount of quota in that provision.

2. The Minister may allocate quota in any additional exceptional hardship provision to a producer who has previously made an exceptional hardship claim and who has been allocated an amount of quota, in furtherance of that claim, being less than the amount of quota determined by the Tribunal in respect of that claim.

3. For the purposes of paragraph 2 above, "exceptional hardship claim" means a claim which has been determined by the Tribunal in accordance with paragraph 17 of Schedule 2 to the 1984 Regulations.

PART II

SMALL PRODUCER SUPPLEMENTARY DEVELOPMENT ALLOCATION

4. The Minister may at any time add to a small producer supplementary development provision made under Schedule 13 to the 1986 Regulations. Where any such additional provision is made the Minister shall by advertisement published in the Gazette announce the amount of quota in that provision.

5. Any additional provision made under paragraph 4 above shall be allocated by the Minister to producers who had a wholesale development award and the aggregate of whose total direct sales quota and total wholesale quota, on the date determined by the Minister for the purposes of a provision under Schedule 13 to the 1986 Regulations, was less than 200,000 litres.

6. The amount of quota which may be allocated to a producer under paragraph 5 above shall be limited to–

(a) the amount determined in respect of that producer by the further examination body, or by the Tribunal, in accordance with paragraphs 9(3) and 10(1), respectively, of Schedule 2 to the 1984 Regulations, or

(b) 200,000 litres,

whichever amount is less.

7. Where a producer has transferred the occupation of all or part of his holding to another person, any allocation of quota in respect of that producer by virtue of paragraph 5 above shall be divided between that producer and the transferee in the proportion that the wholesale quota relating to the holding was apportioned.

Regulation 32

SCHEDULE 10

DAIRY PRODUCE QUOTA TRIBUNALS

PART I

DAIRY PRODUCE QUOTA TRIBUNALS (OTHER THAN FOR SCOTLAND)

1. Each Dairy Produce Quota Tribunal shall consist of up to ninety members appointed by the Minister, including a Chairman appointed by him.

2. The quorum for any determination by a Dairy Produce Quota Tribunal shall be three.

3. Any determination to be made by a Dairy Produce Quota Tribunal shall be made by a majority.

4. Each Dairy Produce Quota Tribunal may be serviced by a Secretary and such other staff as the Minister may appoint.

5. Any document purporting to be signed by the Chairman of or the Secretary to a Dairy Produce Quota Tribunal and purporting to state a determination (or guidance of) the Dairy Produce Quota Tribunal shall in any proceedings be evidence of such a determination (or such guidance).

6. The terms of appointment and the remuneration of the members, Secretary and other staff of a Dairy Produce Quota Tribunal shall be determined by the Minister.

7. Except as otherwise provided in these Regulations, the procedure of a Dairy Produce Quota Tribunal shall be such as their Chairman shall in his discretion determine.

PART II

THE DAIRY PRODUCE QUOTA TRIBUNAL FOR SCOTLAND

8. The Dairy Produce Quota Tribunal shall consist of up to twenty members appointed by the Minister.

9. The Dairy Produce Quota Tribunal shall sit in separate panels, and a determination of any such panel shall be treated as the determination of the Tribunal for the purpose of these Regulations.

10. Each panel constituted under paragraph 9 shall choose their own Chairman.

11. The quorum for any determination by the Dairy Produce Quota Tribunal shall be three.

12. Any determination to be made by the Dairy Produce Quota Tribunal shall be made by a majority.

13. Each panel constituted under paragraph 9 shall be serviced by a Secretary and such other staff as the Minister may appoint.

14. Any document purporting to be signed by the Chairman of or the Secretary to a panel constituted under paragraph 9 and puporting to state a determination of the Dairy Produce Quota Tribunal shall in any proceedings be evidence of such a determination.

15. The terms of appointment and the remuneration of–

(a) the members of the Dairy Produce Quota Tribunal, and

(b) the Secretary and other staff of a panel constituted under paragraph 9

shall be determined by the Minister.

16. Except as otherwise provided in these Regulations, the procedure of a panel constituted under paragraph 9 shall be such as their Chairman shall in his discretion determine.

17. A panel constituted under paragraph 9 may consult with any person whom the panel consider to be capable of assisting them in reaching their determination and, in the event of such consultation, the applicant whose special case claim is being examined by the panel shall be afforded the opportunity to comment, before the panel reach their determination, on any advice given by that person.

PART III

GENERAL

18. The Dairy Produce Quota Tribunals for England and Wales, Scotland and Northern Ireland shall, if so required by the Ministers, issue a joint written statement of general guidance in respect of the criteria to be used in reaching any determination in relation to direct sales quota, and each Dairy Produce Quota Tribunal shall make its determinations in accordance with those criteria.

SCHEDULE 11

Regulation 33

REVOCATION

Regulations revoked	*References*
The Dairy Produce Quotas Regulations 1986	S.I. 1986/470
The Dairy Produce Quotas (Amendment) Regulations 1988	S.I. 1988/534
The Dairy Produce Quotas (Amendment) Regulations 1989	S.I. 1989/16

EXPLANATORY NOTE

(This note is not part of the Regulations)

These Regulations consolidate with amendments the Dairy Produce Quotas Regulations 1986, the Dairy Produce Quotas (Amendment) Regulations 1988 and the Dairy Produce Quotas (Amendment) Regulations 1989. The Regulations apply throughout the United Kingdom, with the minor exception of regulation 21 which applies only to Northern Ireland, and come into force on 31 March 1989.

The main amendments are as follows–

1. Minor changes have been made to certain of the definitions in order to update them (regulation 2).

2. Article 12(1) of Commission Regulation (EEC) No. 1546/88 gives Member States a discretion to permit certain producers to choose an alternative base year in respect of which to calculate the fat content of their milk for levy purposes. The Regulations specifically enable the Minister to implement a producer's choice of an alternative base year (regulation 6).

3. Any change of occupation of a holding must be notified to the Minister within 2 months on a form which is to be prescribed for the purpose. Certain changes of occupation of small areas of land in England and Wales are no longer exempt from the application of the transfer rules. Also those transfer rules no longer apply where a person occupied land under such an agreement and lawfully continued in occupation until a date one month after the termination of his interest in the land (regulation 9).

   Transfers which take place immediately before the end of a quota year cause problems as regards the calculation of levy liability unless they are promptly notified to the Minister, as otherwise it is impossible to assess how much unused quota is available for re-allocation amongst over-quota producers. In order to minimise these problems the Minister may set a date after the end of the quota year in question by which the person to whom quota is transferred must notify him of the transfer. Anyone who fails to notify the Minister by that date may only make use of the transferred quota to offset his levy liability in the following quota year, not the year in which the transfer actually took place. Such quota is nevertheless to be treated as being available for re-allocation by the Minister in the year in which the transfer took place (regulation 9(2)(a)).

4. The provision which previously allowed a purchaser and producer to agree a change in the identification of that producer's holding for the purpose of management of wholesale quotas by purchasers has not been re-enacted.

5. The Minister has been given the power to make a temporary reallocation of quota, in certain circumstances, to producers to whom the Dairy Produce Quota Tribunal or one of its local panels has made an award of quota, or to whom the Minister has allocated quota under Schedule 12 to the 1986 Regulations, where that award or allocation of quota has been entered incorrectly in the quota register maintained by the Minister (regulation 16).

6. New arbitration procedures have been introduced which are similar to those which operate under the agricultural holdings legislation, and contain in particular new statutory time limits within which certain steps in the arbitration must be taken (Schedule 4, 5 and 6).

7. Supplementary levy liability is calculated at purchaser level for wholesale producers and nationally for direct sellers, which allows the unused quota of under quota producers to be used to offset over-production by over quota producers. The Minister is given a power to instruct purchasers of the optimum amount to convert to keep the United Kingdom's levy to a minimum (Schedule 7).

8. The provisions in relation to calculation of levy liability have been replaced to take into account the fact that deliveries of milk against a purchaser's quota must be adjusted having regard to any increase in the butterfat content before the process for calculating the liability for levy may commence (Schedule 8).

9. Certain provisions which previously applied throughout the United Kingdom, and which enabled the Minister to make allocations of quota to producers in a number of different circumstances, have been deleted because they are no longer relevant. In relation to Northern Ireland only, however, provisions have been retained to enable the Minister to make any additional allocation of quota in cases of exceptional hardship and to certain small producers (Schedule 9).

STATUTORY INSTRUMENTS

1989 No. 381 (L.5)

COUNTY COURTS

PROCEDURE

The County Court (Amendment No. 2) Rules 1989

Made - - - - *8th March 1989*

Coming into force *1st April 1989*

Citation and interpretation

1.—(1) These Rules may be cited as the County Court (Amendment No. 2) Rules 1989.

(2) In these Rules, unless the context otherwise requires, an Order referred to by number means the Order so numbered in the County Court Rules 1981 **(a)** and Appendix A, B or C means Appendix A, B or C to those Rules.

Costs

2. Order 38, rule 13(2) shall be amended by substituting, for the figures "£16.00" and "£22.50", the figures "£17.00" and "£24.00" respectively.

3. Order 38, rule 14(1) shall be amended by substituting, for the figures "£22.50", "£45.50" and "£89.50" wherever they appear in the Table, the figures "£24.00", "£48.00" and "£95.00" respectively.

4. Appendix A shall be amended by substituting, for the entries in the last 3 columns corresponding to the numbered items, the following–

" *Item No.*	*Scale 1* *£* *100–500*	*Scale 2* *£* *500–3,000*	*Scale 3* *£* *3,000+*
1.		FOR ALL SCALES 6.50–26.50	
2.		FOR ALL SCALES 6.50–25.50	
3.		FOR ALL SCALES 4.60 per page (or proportionately) 3.10 per page (or proportionately)	
4. (a)		FOR ALL SCALES 0.55 per page 0.93 per page 1.27 per page	

(a) S.I. 1981/1687; the relevant amending instruments are S.I. 1982/1140, 1983/1716, 1984/576, 1985/1269, 1986/636, 1987/493, 1397, 1988/278, 897 and 1989/236.

" *Item No.*	*Scale 1* £ *100–500*	*Scale 2* £ *500–3,000*	*Scale 3* £ *3,000+*
(b)		FOR ALL SCALES 0.19 per page 0.36 per page	
5.		FOR ALL SCALES 11–70	
6.	such sum as is fair and reasonable not exceeding 389	such sum as is fair and reasonable not exceeding 996	Discretionary
7.	6.50	6.50	11.00
8.		FOR ALL SCALES 11.00	
9.	not exceeding	not exceeding	not exceeding
(a)	29	80	99
(b)	6.50–14	6.50–21	6.50–27.50
10.		FOR ALL SCALES 3.50–10.50	
11.	not exceeding	not exceeding	not exceeding
(a)	49	118	171
(b)	6.50–16	6.50–58.50	6.50–85
12.(a)	28–100	34.50–231	Discretionary
(b)	14–51.50	17.50–116	Discretionary
(c)	10.50–41	13–57	15–79.50
(d)		FOR ALL SCALES 20	
(e) On conference in chambers or elsewhere: for each half hour or part thereof	6.50	10.50	15
and for leading counsel	7.50	18	28
(f)	6.50–11	11–29	13–41.50
(g)	4–12	12–34.50	14–70.50
(h)	7.50–20	20–57	23.50–116.50
13.(a)	7.65–20.50	7.65–57	7.65–73
(b)	7.65	7.65–20.50	7.65–29.50".

5. Appendix B, Part I, paragraph 4 shall be amended by substituting, for the Tables of Fixed Costs, the following Tables–

"TABLES OF FIXED COSTS

TABLE I

Where claim exceeds £25 but does not exceed £250

	Amount of charges £
(a) Where service is not by solicitor	21.00
(b) Where service is by solicitor	23.50

TABLE II

Where claim exceeds £250 but does not exceed £600

	Amount of charges £
(a) Where service is not by solicitor	28.00
(b) Where service is by solicitor	33.00

TABLE III

Where claim exceeds £600 but does not exceed £2,000

	Amount of charges £
(a) Where service is not by solicitor	47.00
(b) Where service is by solicitor	52.00

TABLE IV

Where claim exceeds £2,000

	Amount of charges £
(a) Where service is not by solicitor	51.00
(b) Where service is by solicitor	56.00".

6. Appendix B, Part II shall be amended by substituting, for the Table, the following Table–

" FIXED COSTS ON JUDGMENTS

Column 1	*Column 2 Sum of Money* A *Exceeding £25 but not exceeding £600*	B *Exceeding £600 but not exceeding £3,000*	C *Exceeding £3,000*
	£	£	£
(a) Where judgment is entered in a default action in default of defence	7.50	14.00	15.50
(b) Where judgment is entered on the defendant's admission and the plaintiff's acceptance of his proposal as to mode of payment	13.00	27.50	32.00
(c) Where judgment is entered on an admission delivered by the defendant and the court's decision is given as to the date of payment or instalments by which payment is to be made ..	17.50	35.00	41.50
(d) Where judgment is given in a fixed date action for– (i) delivery of goods, or (ii) possession of land suspended on payment of arrears of rent, whether claimed or not, in addition to current rent and the defendant has neither delivered a defence, admission or counter-claim nor otherwise denied liability	26.00	39.00	48.00

	Exceeding £500 but not exceeding £3,000	*Exceeding £3,000*
(e) Where summary judgment is given under Order 9, rule 14	60.50	69.00"

7. Appendix B, Part III shall be amended by substituting, for paragraphs (a) and (b) of item 7 and for the amounts to be allowed corresponding to the numbered items, the following–

"

	Amount to be allowed £
1.	8.50
2.	8.50
3.	1.50
4.	5.50
5.	17.00
6.	5.50
7. (a) where the money recovered is less than £60	one half of the amount recovered
(b) where the money recovered is not less than £60	31.50
8.	31.50
9.	5.25".

8. Appendix C, paragraph 2 shall be amended by substituting, for the Table, the following–

"

Column 1 *Scale*	*Column 2* *Amount of Charges*
Lower Scale	39.00–60.50
Scale 1	43.50–110.00
Scale 2	68.00–412.50
Scale 3	99.00–497.00"

Part II of the Family Law Reform Act 1987(a)

9. Order 47, rule 6 shall be amended as follows–

(1) In the heading, after the figures "1973", there shall be added the words "and Part II of the Family Law Reform Act 1987".

(2) For the word "minor", wherever occurring in paragraphs (1), (2), (3) and (4) otherwise than in the expression "the Guardianship of Minors Act 1971" or "the Guardianship of Minors Acts 1971 and 1973", there shall be substituted the word "child".

(3) In paragraph (1), after the words "under that Act", there shall be inserted the words "or under section 4 of the Family Law Reform Act 1987".

(a) 1987 c.42.

(4) In paragraph (2), after the figures "1973", there shall be inserted the words "or under section 4 of the Family Law Reform Act 1987".

(5) In paragraph (3), the words "(as applied by section 4(3D) of the Guardianship Act 1973 (**a**))" shall be omitted.

(6) After paragraph (3), there shall be inserted the following new paragraphs–

"(3A) Subject to the provisions of these rules, R.S.C. Order 90, rule 6A shall apply to applications made under sections 11B, 11C and 11D of the said Act of 1971.

(3B) A respondent to an application under the said sections 11B, 11C or 11D, who wishes to dispute paternity of the child with respect to whom the application is made,–

(a) shall file an answer; and

(b) shall not, unless the court otherwise directs, be required to file an affidavit under R.S.C. Order 90, rule 6A(4).

(3C) Without prejudice to Order 14, any party to an application under the said sections 11B, 11C or 11D may by letter require any other party–

(a) to give further information concerning any matter contained in any affidavit filed by or on behalf of that other party or any other relevant matter, or

(b) to furnish a list of relevant documents or to allow inspection of any such document,

and may, in default of compliance by the other party, apply to the registrar for directions.".

(7) In paragraph (5), after the words "Acts of 1971 and 1973", there shall be inserted the words "and under Part II of the Family Law Reform Act 1987".

(8) After paragraph (5), there shall be inserted the following new paragraph–

"(6) Applications under sections 9 and 10 of the said Act of 1971–

(a) which are unopposed; or

(b) for an order in terms agreed by the parties,

and applications under sections 11B, 11C and 11D of that Act may be made to the registrar and he may make such order as he thinks fit or may refer to the judge any matter which he thinks should properly be decided by the judge.".

We, the undersigned members of the Rule Committee appointed by the Lord Chancellor under section 75 of the County Courts Act 1984 (**b**), having by virtue of the powers vested in us in that behalf made the foregoing Rules, do hereby certify the same under our hands and submit them to the Lord Chancellor accordingly.

C. S. Stuart-White
R. Lockett
Nigel Fricker
R. Greenslade
Patrick Eccles
Gillian Stuart-Brown
Deirdre McKinney
R. E. Hammerton
K. H. P. Wilkinson
Timothy Stow
R. C. Newport

I allow these Rules, which shall come into force on 1st April 1989.

Mackay of Clashfern, C.

Dated 8th March 1989

(**a**) 1973 c.29; section 4(3D) was inserted by the Domestic Proceedings and Magistrates' Courts Act 1978 (c.22), section 44(2).
(**b**) 1984 c.28.

EXPLANATORY NOTE

(This Note is not part of the Rules)

These Rules amend the County Court Rules 1981 so as to–

(a) revise the provisions relating to costs (Rules 2 to 8); and

(b) give effect to Part II of the Family Law Reform Act 1987 (rights and duties of parents etc.) which makes provision for the financial support of children and persons over eighteen in full-time education (Rule 9).

STATUTORY INSTRUMENTS

1989 No. 382 (C.14)

FAMILY LAW

The Family Law Reform Act 1987 (Commencement No. 2) Order 1989

Made - - - - *8th March 1989*

The Lord Chancellor, in exercise of the powers conferred on him by sections 34(2) and 34(3) of the Family Law Reform Act 1987(**a**), hereby makes the following Order:

1. This Order may be cited as the Family Law Reform Act 1987 (Commencement No. 2) Order 1989.

2. The provisions of the Family Law Reform Act 1987 set out in the first column of Schedule 1 to this Order shall come into force on 1st April 1989.

3. The transitional provisions in Schedule 2 to this Order shall have effect.

Mackay of Clashfern, C.

Dated 8th March 1989

(**a**) 1987 c.42.

SCHEDULE 1

(1) *Provisions of the Act*	*(2)* *Subject matter of provisions*
Section 2	Construction of enactments relating to parental rights and duties
Section 3	Agreements as to exercise of parental rights and duties
Section 4	Parental rights and duties of father
Section 5	Exercise of parental rights and duties
Section 6	Appointment of guardians
Section 7	Rights with respect to adoption
Section 8	Rights where child in care etc
Section 10	Orders for custody on application of either parent
Section 11	Orders for custody in guardianship cases
Section 12	Orders for financial relief on application of either parent
Section 13	Orders for financial relief in guardianship cases
Section 14	Orders for financial relief for persons over eighteen
Section 15	Alteration of maintenance agreements during lives of parties
Section 16	Alteration after death of one party
Section 17	Abolition of affiliation proceedings
Section 24	Registration of father where parents not married
Section 25	Re-registration where parents not married
Section 30	Orders applying section 1 to other enactments
Section 33, insofar as it relates to amendments, transitional provisions and repeals which are not already in force, with the exception of the amendments to the Family Law Reform Act 1969(**a**) set out in paragraphs 21 to 25 of Schedule 2 to the Act.	Amendments, transitional provisions, savings and repeals

SCHEDULE 2

TRANSITIONAL PROVISIONS

1. The Act (including the repeals and amendments made by it) shall not have effect in relation to the variation, discharge, revival or enforcement of–

(a) orders made under the Guardianship of Minors Acts 1971 and 1973(**b**) before 1st April 1989; or

(b) orders made under the said Acts by virtue of paragraph 1 of Schedule 3 to the Act.

2. Paragraph 62 of Schedule 2 to the Act shall not have effect in relation to the revival of orders made under section 34(1)(b) of the Children Act 1975(**c**) before 1st April 1989.

3. Paragraph 69 of Schedule 2 to the Act, and the repeals made by Schedule 4 to the Act in section 20 of the Domestic Proceedings and Magistrates' Courts Act 1978(**d**), shall not have effect in relation to the revival of orders made under Part I of that Act before 1st April 1989.

(**a**) 1969 c.46.
(**b**) 1971 c.3; 1973 c.29.
(**c**) 1975 c.72.
(**d**) 1978 c.22.

EXPLANATORY NOTE

(This note is not part of the Order)

This Order brings into force on 1st April 1989 all those provisions of the Family Law Reform Act 1987 which are not already in force, with the exception of sections 9, 23 and 32, and paragraphs 21 to 25 of Schedule 2.

The effect of the provisions being brought into force is as follows:

(a) section 2 applies to the enactments listed in that section the principle laid down in section 1, namely that, unless the contrary intention appears, the relationship between two persons should be construed without regard to whether or not a person's parents were married to each other at any time;

(b) section 3 provides that an agreement may be made between the parents of a child, whether or not they have at any time been married to each other, as to the exercise by either of them of parental rights and duties during a period when they are not living together;

(c) section 4 enables a father who was not married to the mother at the time of their child's birth to apply to the court for an order that he is to share all the parental rights and duties with the mother;

(d) section 5 enables parents who were not married at the time of their child's birth, in certain circumstances to apply for the directions of the court upon matters affecting the child's welfare;

(e) sections 6, 7 and 8 make changes to the legal position of a father who was not married to the mother at the time of their child's birth, who has an order made under section 4 or a right to custody of the child, as regards guardianship, adoption, and with respect to his rights where the child is in care;

(f) sections 10 and 11 re-enact with amendments certain provisions of the Guardianship of Minors Act 1971 to deal with applications for custody and access upon the application of either parent and in guardianship cases;

(g) sections 12 to 17 abolish affiliation proceedings and provide for applications for financial provision for children to be made under the Guardianship of Minors Act 1971. Under these provisions, applications may be made to a magistrates' court, a county court or the High Court by either parent, whether or not they have been married to each other at any time;

(h) sections 24 and 25 make changes to the requirements for registration of the father where the parents of a child are not married, and for re-registration where no person has previously been registered as the child's father;

(i) section 30 enables the Lord Chancellor by statutory instrument to apply the rule of construction established by section 1 to such other enactments as may be specified;

(j) section 33 deals with amendments, transitional provisions, savings and repeals.

This Order also brings into force the transitional provisions specified in Schedule 2. The effect of paragraph 1 is that orders made before 1st April 1989 under the Guardianship of Minors Act 1971 and the Guardianship Act 1973 can be varied, enforced, discharged and revived as if the amendments and repeals in the 1987 Act had not been made. Similar provision is made in paragraphs 2 and 3 in respect of the power to revive orders for periodical payments in respect of children made before 1st April 1989 under the Children Act 1975 and Part I of the Domestic Proceedings and Magistrates Courts Act 1978.

NOTE AS TO EARLIER COMMENCEMENT ORDER

(This note is not part of the Order)

The following provisions of the Act were brought into force on the 4th April 1988 by the Family Law Reform Act 1987 (Commencement No. 1) Order 1988 (S.I. 1988/425):

Sections 1, 18, 19, 20, 21, 22, 26, 27, 28, 29, 31;

Section 33 (partially);

Section 34.

STATUTORY INSTRUMENTS

1989 No. 383 (L.6)

MAGISTRATES' COURTS

The Magistrates' Courts (Custodianship Orders) (Amendment) Rules 1989

Made - - - -	*8th March 1989*
Laid before Parliament	*10th March 1989*
Coming into force -	*1st April 1989*

The Lord Chancellor, in exercise of the powers conferred on him by section 144 of the Magistrates' Courts Act 1980**(a)**, after consultation with the Rule Committee appointed under that section, hereby makes the following Rules:–

1. These Rules may be cited as the Magistrates' Courts (Custodianship Orders) (Amendment) Rules 1989 and shall come into force on 1st April 1989.

2. In these Rules, the "1985 Rules" means the Magistrates' Courts (Custodianship Orders) Rules 1985**(b)**.

3. The 1985 Rules shall have effect subject to the following amendments:–

(a) in rule 4(3) for the words "In the case of an application" there shall be substituted the words "Where a complaint is made";

(b) in rule 6(1) for the words which follow the word "complaint;" in the second place where it occurs there shall be substituted the words "the court may direct that any of the persons (other than the applicant) specified in Rule 5(1) be made a defendant and the court shall cause notice of the proceedings to be served on any such defendant.".

4. In their application to any proceedings except proceedings in relation to which the Family Law Reform Act 1987**(c)** does not have effect, the 1985 Rules shall have effect subject to the following amendments:–

(a) in rule 5(17)(b) for the words "is illegitimate" there shall be substituted the words "was not married to the mother of the child at the time of his birth";

(b) in Form 1 in the Schedule, in the note on paragraph 3, for the words from the beginning to "he", there shall be substituted the words "If the child's father and mother were not married to each other at the time of his birth, give details of the putative father. If the putative father";

(c) in Form 4 in the Schedule, in the note on paragraph 4, the words "(excluding the father of an illegitimate child)" shall be omitted.

Dated 8th March 1989

Mackay of Clashfern, C.

(a) 1980 c.43; section 144 is extended by section 145 of that Act and by section 46(4) of the Children Act 1975 (c.72) as amended by the said Act of 1980, Schedule 7, paragraph 138.
(b) S.I. 1985/1695.
(c) 1987 c.42; section 33(2) and Schedule 3 provide that applications pending at the time when the provisions of the Family Law Reform Act 1987 come into force are not affected by those provisions.

EXPLANATORY NOTE

(This note is not part of the Rules)

These Rules amend the Magistrates' Courts (Custodianship Orders) Rules 1985. Paragraph (b) of rule 3 replaces, in relation to adoption, guardianship or custody applications treated as applications for custodianship orders, the requirement that the Court should make a defendant to an application so treated every person who would have been a defendant to a complaint for a custodianship order, by a discretion to make a defendant any such person as the court thinks appropriate. Paragraph (a) of rule 3 clarifies the wording of rule 4 of the 1985 Rules to make it clear that in the case of an application so treated it is not necessary for the person deemed to be an applicant to provide a medical report in relation to the child. Rule 4 deletes references in the 1985 rules to illegitimacy, thereby reflecting the general principle stated in section 1 of the Family Law Reform Act 1987 that references to any relationship between two persons shall be construed without regard to whether the father or mother of either of them have been married to each other at any time.

1989 No. 384 (L.7)

MAGISTRATES' COURTS

The Magistrates' Courts (Family Law Reform Act 1987) (Miscellaneous Amendments) Rules 1989

Made - - - -	*8th March 1989*
Laid before Parliament	*10th March 1989*
Coming into force	*1st April 1989*

The Lord Chancellor, in exercise of the power conferred on him by section 144 of the Magistrates' Courts Act 1980(**a**), after consultation with the Rule Committee appointed under the said section 144, hereby makes the following Rules:

1. These Rules may be cited as the Magistrates' Courts (Family Law Reform Act 1987) (Miscellaneous Amendments) Rules 1989 and shall come into force on 1st April 1989.

2. Subject to rule 3 of these Rules, the following Rules–

The Maintenance Orders (Facilities for Enforcement) Rules 1922(**b**)

The Magistrates' Courts (Maintenance Orders Act 1958) Rules 1959(**c**)

The Magistrates' Courts (Blood Tests) Rules 1971(**d**)

The Magistrates' Courts (Guardianship of Minors) Rules 1974(**e**)

The Magistrates' Courts (Forms) Rules 1981(**f**)

The Magistrates' Courts Rules 1981(**g**)

The Magistrates' Courts (Adoption) Rules 1984(**h**)

The Magistrates' Courts (Children and Young Persons) Rules 1988(**i**)

shall have effect subject to the amendments set out in the Schedule to these Rules.

(**a**) 1980 c. 43; section 144 is extended by section 145 of that Act and by section 16(5) of the Guardianship of Minors Act 1971 (c. 3) as amended by the Guardianship Act 1973 (c. 29), section 2 and Schedule 2, the Children Act 1975 (c. 72), Schedule 3, the Domestic Proceedings and Magistrates' Courts Act 1978 (c. 22), Schedule 2, and the Magistrates' Courts Act 1980, Schedule 7.

(**b**) S.I. 1922/1335, amended by S.I. 1970/762.

(**c**) S.I. 1959/3, amended by S.I. 1977/1890, 1980/1896, 1986/1962, and to which there are other amendments not relevant to these Rules.

(**d**) S.I. 1971/1991.

(**e**) S.I. 1974/706, amended by S.I. 1979/953, 1980/1585.

(**f**) S.I. 1981/533, to which there are amendments not relevant to these Rules.

(**g**) S.I. 1981/552, amended by S.I. 1983/523, 1985/1695, and to which there are other amendments not relevant to these Rules.

(**h**) S.I. 1984/611.

(**i**) S.I. 1988/913, to which there are amendments not relevant to these Rules.

3. These Rules shall not apply in relation to any application to a magistrates' court, any affiliation order or any order made under a provision of the Guardianship of Minors Acts 1971 and 1973(**a**) in relation to which the Family Law Reform Act 1987(**b**) does not have effect.

Dated 8th March 1989

Mackay of Clashfern, C.

(**a**) 1971 c. 3 and 1973 c. 29.

(**b**) 1987 c. 42; section 33(2) and Schedule 3 provide that applications pending and affiliation orders in force at the time when the provisions of the Family Law Reform Act came into force are not affected by those provisions. Under article 3 of and Schedule 2 to the Family Law Reform Act 1987 (Commencement No.2) Order 1989 (S.I. 1989/382) similar provision is made in respect of orders in force under the Guardianship of Minors Acts 1971 and 1973.

Rule 2

SCHEDULE

AMENDMENTS TO RULES

The Maintenance Orders (Facilities for Enforcement) Rules 1922

1. In rule 6 of the Maintenance Orders (Facilities for Enforcement) Rules 1922, for the words "an Affiliation Order" there shall be substituted the words "a magistrates' court maintenance order".

The Magistrates' Courts (Maintenance Orders Act 1958) Rules 1959

2. In rule 9 of the Magistrates' Courts (Maintenance Orders Act 1958) Rules 1959, and in Forms 18 and 19 in the Schedule to those Rules, for the words "affiliation Order" or "an affiliation order" in each place where they occur there shall be substituted the words "magistrates' court maintenance order" or "a magistrates' court maintenance order", as the case may be.

The Magistrates' Courts (Blood Tests) Rules 1971

3. In rule 3 of the Magistrates' Courts (Blood Tests) Rules 1971, the words "under the Affiliation Proceedings Act 1957 or any other complaint" shall be omitted.

The Magistrates' Courts (Guardianship of Minors) Rules 1974

4. In the Magistrates' Courts (Guardianship of Minors) Rules 1974, for the words "minor" and "minors" in every place where they occur (except in the title of those Rules or the citation of the Guardianship of Minors Act 1971) there shall be substituted the words "child" and "children" respectively.

5. In rule 2 of these Rules, in the definition of "court", after the words "magistrates' court" there shall be inserted the words ", except as provided by rule 9(9)".

6. In rule 7 of those Rules, for the word "maintenance" there shall be substituted the word "access".

7. In rule 8(2)(a) of those Rules, for the words from "legal custody" to the words "Act of 1971" there shall be substituted the words "actual custody of the child and, if different, the person who has legal custody of the child".

8. Rule 9(3) of those Rules shall be omitted.

9. For rule 9(4)(a) and (b) of those Rules there shall be substituted the following sub-paragraphs–

"(a) the person specified in sub-paragraphs (a), (b) and (d) of paragraph (2);

(b) the probation officer or local authority under whose supervision the child is; and

(c) if the application is for the variation of the order, any probation officer or local authority whom it is sought to substitute for the officer or local authority under whose supervision the child is.".

10. In rule 9(5)(a) of those Rules, for the words "sub-paragraph (a) of paragraph (3)" there shall be substituted the words "sub-paragraphs (a) and (d) of paragraph (2)".

11. Rule 9(6) of those Rules shall be omitted.

12. In rule 9(7) of those Rules, for the words "sub-paragraph (a) of paragraph (3)" there shall be substituted the words "sub-paragraphs (a) and (d) of paragraph (2)", and the proviso shall be omitted.

13. After rule 9(7) of those Rules there shall be inserted the following paragraphs–

"(8) For the purposes of paragraphs (4)(a), (5)(a) and (7)(a) above, a father who was not married to the mother of a child at the time of his birth shall not be treated as a parent of that child unless he has been adjudged by a court to be the father of that child or unless he was a party to the proceedings in which the order was made.

(9) in this rule, "court" means the High Court, a county court or a magistrates' court.".

The Magistrates' Courts (Forms) Rules 1981

14. In Form 114 in the Schedule to the Magistrates' Courts (Forms) Rules 1981, for the reference to sections 9, 10, 11 and 12C(5) of the Guardianship of Minors Act 1971 there shall be substituted a reference to sections 11B and 11C of that Act, and the reference to section 60 of the Magistrates' Courts Act 1980 shall be omitted.

The Magistrates' Courts Rules 1981

15. Rules 35 and 35A of the Magistrates' Courts Rules 1981 shall be omitted.

16. In paragraph (4)(b)(i) of rule 36 of those Rules, the reference to section 11 of the Guardianship of Minors Act 1971 shall be omitted.

17. In rules 41(1), 43, 44(1), 59(1), 61, 62, 63(1) and 69 of those Rules, for the words "affiliation order" in each place where they appear there shall be substituted the words "magistrates' court maintenance order".

18. In rule 51 of those Rules, after the words "the Children Act 1975" there shall be inserted the word "or" and the words "or section 6A(5) of the Affiliation Proceedings Act 1957" shall be deleted.

19. In rule 105 of those Rules, after the words "section 35 of the Matrimonial Causes Act 1973" there shall be inserted the words "or under section 15 of the Family Law Reform Act 1987" and at the end of the heading to that rule there shall be inserted the words "or under s. 15 of the Family Law Reform Act 1987".

20. In rule 106(1) of those Rules, for the words "section 60 of the Act of 1980 or section 9, 10, 11 or 12C(5)" there shall be substituted the words "sections 11B or 11C".

The Magistrates' Courts (Adoption) Rules 1984

21. In rule 5(4)(e) of the Magistrates' Courts (Adoption) Rules 1984, for the words "an illegitimate child" there shall be substituted the words "a child whose mother and father were not married at the time of his birth".

22. In Schedule 1 to those Rules, in Form 1–

(a) for paragraph 11 there shall be substituted the following paragraph:

"(11. The father and mother of the child were not married to each other at the time of his birth and .... of .... who is/claims to be the father–

(i) does/does not intend to apply for an order giving him all parental rights and duties with respect to the child;

(ii) does/does not intend to apply for the custody/care and control of the child.)";

(b) for the note on paragraph 3 in that Form there shall be substituted the following:

"Paragraph 3: If the child has previously been adopted, give the names of his adoptive parents and not those of his natural parents. If the father and mother of the child were not married to each other at the time of his birth, and a court has made an order giving the father all the parental rights and duties with respect to the child, or if the father has legal custody of the child by virtue of a court order, give details of the court order under paragraph 12."; and

(c) for the note on paragraphs 5 and 6 in that Form there shall be substituted the following:

"Paragraphs 5 and 6: Enter either in paragraph 5 or 6 the names of the persons mentioned in paragraphs 3 and 4, except that if the father and mother of the child were not married at the time of his birth the father of the child should be entered only if a court has made an order giving him all the parental rights and duties in respect of the child or if he has legal custody of the child by virtue of a court order. Where it is sought to dispense with parental agreement, enter in paragraph 6 one or more of the grounds set out in section 12(2) of the 1975 Act.".

23. In Form 6 in that Schedule–

(a) for the last sentence of the note on paragraph 9 there shall be substituted the following:

"If the father and mother of the child were not married to each other at the time of his birth, and a court has made an order giving the father all the parental rights and duties with respect to the child, or if the father has legal custody of the child by virtue of a court order, give details of the order under paragraph 19."; and

(b) for the first sentence of the note of paragraphs 11 and 12 in that form there shall be substituted the following:

"Paragraphs 11 and 12: Enter either in paragraph 11 or 12 the names of the persons mentioned in paragraphs 9 and 10, except that if the father and mother of the child were not married at the time of his birth the father of the child should be entered only if a court has made an order giving the father all the parental rights and duties in respect of the child or if he has legal custody of the child by virtue of a court order.".

24. In Form 7 in that Schedule, in the fifth paragraph of the Notes, for the words from the beginning of that paragraph to the words "court order;" there shall be substituted the following words:

"A father who was not married to the mother of a child at the time of his birth is not a parent for this purpose, but is a guardian if a court has made an order giving him all the parental rights and duties with respect to the child or if he has legal custody of the child by virtue of a court order;".

25. In Schedule 2 to those Rules, in paragraph 1–

(a) for sub-paragraph (b) there shall be substituted the following sub-paragraph:

"(b) whether the child's father and mother were married to each other at the time of his birth."; and

(b) in sub-paragraph (i) for the words "if the child is illegitimate" there shall be substituted the words "if the father and mother of the child were not married to each other at the time of his birth".

26. For the heading to paragraph 2 of the said Schedule, there shall be substituted the following:

"2. Each Natural Parent, including where appropriate the father who was not married to the child's mother at the time of his birth.".

27. In sub-paragraph (b) of paragraph 6 of the said Schedule, for the words "claiming to be the father of an illegitimate child" there shall be substituted the words "who was not married to the mother of the child at the time of his birth and who claims to be the father of the child".

The Magistrates' Courts (Children and Young Persons) Rules 1988

28. In the Magistrates' Courts (Children and Young Persons) Rules 1988, in rule 2(1), after the definition of the word "court", there shall be inserted the following definition:

"'parent', in the case of a child or young person whose father and mother were not married to each other at the time of his birth, has the same meaning as it has in section 70(1A) and (1B) of the Children and Young Persons Act 1969(**a**);".

29. In rule 14(3) of those Rules, after sub-paragraph (d), there shall be inserted the following sub-paragraph:

"(dd) where the father and mother of the relevant infant were not married to each other at the time of his birth, any person who is known to the applicant to have made an application for an order under section 4 of the Family Law Reform Act 1987 (parental rights and duties of father) which has not yet been determined;".

30. In rule 29(2) of those Rules–

(a) for the words "section 87(1)" in the second place where they occur there shall be substituted the words "section 87"; and

(b) after the word "applies" there shall be inserted the words "and a father of a child where an order is in force under section 4 of the Family Law Reform Act 1987 by virtue of which actual custody is shared between the mother and the father and section 8(3) of the Act of 1980(**b**) accordingly applies".

31. In rule 30(1) of those Rules–

(a) the word "and" which follows the words "voluntary organisation;" in the second place where they occur shall be omitted, and

(b) there shall be inserted at the end the following words–

"; and a local authority or voluntary organisation which is a party to any such proceedings and a parent who is the complainant in any such proceedings in a case where the mother and father of the child were not married to each other at the time of his birth shall send a notice specifying the time and place fixed for the hearing of the complaint to any person who is known to the local authority, voluntary organisation or parent, as the case may be, to have made an application for an order under section 4 of the Family Law Reform Act 1987 (parental rights and duties of father) which has not yet been determined.".

(**a**) 1969 c. 54; section 70(1A) and (1B) were inserted respectively by section 8(1) of and paragraph 26 of Schedule 2 to the Family Law Reform Act 1987 (c. 42).

(**b**) Section 8(3) was inserted by section 8(2) of the Family Law Reform Act 1987.

EXPLANATORY NOTE

(This note is not part of the Rules)

These Rules make amendments to the Maintenance Orders (Facilities for Enforcement) Rules 1922, the Magistrates' Courts (Maintenance Orders Act 1958) Rules 1959, the Magistrates' Courts (Blood Tests) Rules 1971, the Magistrates' Courts (Guardianship of Minors) Rules 1974, the Magistrates' Courts (Forms) Rules 1981, the Magistrates' Courts Rules 1981, the Magistrates' Courts (Adoption) Rules 1984 and the Magistrates' Courts (Children and Young Persons) Rules 1988. The amendments are all consequential upon the provisions of Parts I and II of the Family Law Reform Act 1987. Part I came into force on 4th April 1988 (the Family Law Reform Act 1987 (Commencement No.1) Order 1988 (S.I. 1988/425)). Part II, apart from section 9, comes into force on 1st April 1989 (the Family Law Reform Act 1987 (Commencement No.2) Order 1989 (S.I. 1989/382)).

Parts I and II of the 1987 Act establish the principle that references to any relationship between two persons shall be construed without regard to whether the father and mother of either of them have or had been married to each other at any time, and substitute in various existing enactments references to whether the mother and father of a child were married to one another at the time of his birth for references to illegitimacy. Under Part II of the 1987 Act affiliation proceedings under the Affiliation Proceedings Act 1957 (c.55) are abolished and amendments made to the Guardianship of Minors Acts 1971 and 1973 to enable financial provision for a child to be obtained, whatever the marital status of the parents, in proceedings under the Guardianship of Minors Act 1971. The amendments made by these Rules reflect those changes.

1989 No. 385 (L. 8)

MATRIMONIAL CAUSES
SUPREME COURT OF ENGLAND AND WALES
COUNTY COURTS

The Matrimonial Causes (Costs) (Amendment) Rules 1989

Made - - - -	*8th March 1989*
Laid before Parliament	*10th March 1989*
Coming into force	*1st April 1989*

We, the authority having power to make rules of court for the purposes mentioned in section 50 of the Matrimonial Causes Act 1973(**a**), in exercise of that power and the further power conferred on us by section 64 of the Family Law Act 1986(**b**), hereby make the following Rules:

1.—(1) These Rules may be cited as the Matrimonial Causes (Costs) (Amendment) Rules 1989 and shall come into force on 1st April 1989.

(2) In these Rules, unless the context otherwise requires, a rule or Schedule referrred to by number means the rule or Schedule so numbered in the Matrimonial Causes (Costs) Rules 1988(**c**).

2. For rule 11(1), there shall be substituted the following–

"(1) Subject to the following provisions of this rule, on any taxation of the costs of a litigant in person there may be allowed such costs as would have been allowed if the work and disbursements to which the costs relate had been done or made by a solicitor on the litigant's behalf together with any payments reasonably made by him for legal advice relating to the conduct of or the issues raised by the proceedings.".

3. In rule 11(3), for the sum "£6.50", there shall be substituted the sum "£7.00".

4. For Schedule 2, there shall be substituted the following Schedule–

(**a**) 1973 c.18; section 50 was amended by the Domicile and Matrimonial Proceedings Act 1973 (c.45), section 6(2); by the Inheritance (Provision for Family and Dependants) Act 1975 (c.63), section 26(2), Schedule; by the Children Act 1975 (c.72), section 108, Schedule 3, paragraph 79; by the Administration of Justice Act 1977 (c.38), Schedule 5 Part VI; by the Domestic Proceedings and Magistrates' Courts Act 1978 (c.22), section 89, Schedule 2, paragraph 40; by the Matrimonial Homes Act 1983 (c.19), Schedule 2; by the County Courts Act 1984 (c.28), section 148, Schedule 2 Part V, paragraph 44, and by the Family Law Act 1986 (c.55), section 68, Schedule 1, paragraph 15.
(**b**) 1986 c.55.
(**c**) S.I. 1988/1328.

"SCHEDULE 2

PART I

PREPARATION

Column 1	Column 2 High Court	Column 3 County Court
ITEM		
1. Writing routine letters	£3.50 per item	£3.00 per item
2. Receiving routine letters	£1.75 per item	£1.50 per item
3. Routine telephone calls	£3.50 per item	£3.00 per item
4. All other preparation work including any work which was reasonably done arising out of or incidental to the proceedings, interviews with client, witnesses, and other parties; obtaining evidence; preparation and consideration of, and dealing with, documents, negotiations and notices; dealing with letters written and received and telephone calls which are not routine	Where the proceedings were conducted in the divorce registry or in another court on the South-Eastern Circuit at the time when the relevant work was done: £38.50 per hour All other circuits: £36.00 per hour	 £34.00 per hour £32.00 per hour
5. In addition to items 1–4 above, to cover the general care and conduct of the proceedings	+50%	+50%
6. Travelling and waiting time in connection with the above matters	£26.50 per hour	£24.50 per hour

PART II

CONFERENCES WITH COUNSEL

7. Attending counsel in conference	£31.00 per hour	£27.00 per hour
8. Travelling and waiting	£26.50 per hour	£24.50 per hour

PART III

ATTENDANCES

9. Attending with counsel at the trial or hearing of any cause or the hearing of any summons or other application at court, or other appointment	£31.00 per hour	£27.00 per hour
10. Attending without counsel at the trial or hearing of any cause or the hearing of any summons or other application at court, or other appointment	£46.00 per hour	£43.00 per hour
11. Travelling and waiting	£26.50 per hour	£24.50 per hour

PART IV

FEES FOR JUNIOR COUNSEL

12. With a brief on an unopposed application for an injunction, or procedural issue	Standard £74.00 Maximum £122.00	£64.00 £106.00
13. With a brief on the trial of a cause or matter or on the hearing of an ancillary application or on a children appointment where the hearing lasts for		
(a) one hour	Standard £111.00 Maximum £223.00	£95.00 £191.00
(b) a half day	Standard £154.00 Maximum £254.00	£133.00 £223.00
(c) a full day	Standard £307.00 Maximum £488.00	£265.00 £424.00
(d) more than a full day	Discretionary	Discretionary
14. For each day or part of a day on which the trial of a cause or matter, or the hearing of an ancillary application, or a children appointment, is continued after the first day	Discretionary	Discretionary
15. Conference (including time reasonably spent in preparation and conference, but not otherwise remunerated)	Standard £17.00 per ½ hour	Standard £15.00 per ½ hour
16. (a) Complex items of written work (such as advices on evidence, opinions and affidavits of a substantial nature, requests for particulars or answers)	Standard £80.00 per item	Standard £69.00 per item
(b) All other written work	Standard £48.00 per item	Standard £42.00 per item
17. Except where the court is within 25 miles of Charing Cross or where there is no local Bar in the court town, or within 25 miles thereof, for travelling time	Standard £15.40 per hour + expenses	Standard £13.20 per hour + expenses

PART V

TAXATION AND REVIEW OF TAXATION

18. Preparing the bill (where allowable) and completing the taxation (excluding preparing for and attending the taxation).	£26.50–£74.00	£26.50–£42.50
19. Preparing for and attending the taxation (including travelling and waiting).	Discretionary	Discretionary
20. Review by registrar or judge (including preparation)	Discretionary	Discretionary".

Mackay of Clashfern, C.
Stephen Brown, P.
Mathew Thorpe, J.
Joyanne W. Bracewell
Roy Ward
C. F. Turner
Roger Bird
T. A. C. Coningsby
Eleanor F. Platt
Henry Hodge
M. J. W. Churchouse

Dated 8th March 1989

EXPLANATORY NOTE

(This Note is not part of the Rules)

These Rules amend the Matrimonial Causes (Costs) Rules 1988 so as to enable a litigant in person to claim as costs the cost of receiving legal advice (rule 2) and to revise the prescribed rates of costs (rules 3 and 4).

STATUTORY INSTRUMENTS

1989 No. 386(L.9)

SUPREME COURT OF ENGLAND AND WALES

The Rules of the Supreme Court (Amendment No.2) 1989

Made - - - - 8th March 1989

Laid before Parliament 10th March 1989

Coming into force in accordance with rule 1

We, the Supreme Court Rule Committee, having power under section 85 of the Supreme Court Act 1981(**a**) to make rules of court under section 84 of that Act for the purpose of regulating and prescribing the practice and procedure to be followed in the Supreme Court, hereby exercise that power as follows:

Citation and commencement

1.—(1) These Rules may be cited as the Rules of the Supreme Court (Amendment No.2) 1989 and shall come into force on 1st April 1989, except for rules 2 to 8, which shall come into force when Part VI of the Criminal Justice Act 1988(**b**) comes into force.

(2) In these Rules, an Order referred to by number means the Order so numbered in the Rules of the Supreme Court 1965(**c**).

Part VI of the Criminal Justice Act 1988

2. The Arrangement of Orders at the beginning of the Rules of the Supreme Court 1965 shall be amended by inserting, after the words "Drug Trafficking Offences Act 1986"(**d**), the words "and Part VI of the Criminal Justice Act 1988".

3. Order 11, rule 1(1) shall be amended by substituting a semi-colon for the full stop at the end of item (r) and by adding thereafter the following –

"(s) the claim is made under Part VI of the Criminal Justice Act 1988.".

4. For the title to Order 115 and for rule 1 of that Order, there shall be substituted the following –

(**a**) 1981 c.54. (**b**) 1988 c.33. (**c**) S.I. 1965/1776; the relevant amending instruments are S.I. 1969/1105, 1973/2046, 1985/846, 1986/632, 2289, 1987/1423, 1988/298, 1340. (**d**) 1986 c.32.

"DRUG TRAFFICKING OFFENCES ACT 1986 AND PART VI OF THE CRIMINAL JUSTICE ACT 1988
I. DRUG TRAFFICKING OFFENCES ACT

Interpretation

1.—(1) In this Part of this Order, "the Act" means the Drug Trafficking Offences Act 1986 and a section referred to by number means the section so numbered in the Act.

(2) Expressions used in this Part of this Order which are used in the Act have the same meanings in this Part of this Order as in the Act.".

5. In Order 115, rule 3(2)(b), for the words "that an information is to be laid that the defendant has or is suspected of having committed a drug trafficking offence", there shall be substituted the words "that, whether by the laying of an information or otherwise, a person is to be charged with such an offence".

6. In Order 115, for the references to section 26 in the heading to rule 12 and in rule 12, there shall be substituted references to section 26A.

7. In Order 115, for the references to section 26(3) in rule 13 and in the heading to rule 15, there shall be substituted references to section 26A(1).

8. After Order 115, rule 21, there shall be inserted the following new Part –

"II. PART VI OF THE CRIMINAL JUSTICE ACT 1988

Interpretation

22.—(1) In this Part of this Order, "the 1988 Act" means the Criminal Justice Act 1988 and a section referred to by number means the section so numbered in that Act.

(2) Expressions which are used in this Part of this Order which are used in the 1988 Act have the same meanings in this Part of this Order as in the 1988 Act.

Application of Part I of Order 115

23. Part I of Order 115 (except rule 11) shall apply for the purposes of proceedings under Part VI of the 1988 Act with the necessary modifications and, in particular, –

(a) references to drug trafficking offences and to drug trafficking shall be construed as references to offences to which Part VI of the 1988 Act applies and to committing such an offence;

(b) references to the Drug Trafficking Offences Act 1986 shall be construed as references to the 1988 Act and references to sections 4(2), 8, 9, 11, 12(1), 14(1), 19, 19(4), 26 and 26A of the 1986 Act shall be construed as references to sections 73(6), 77, 78, 80, 81(1), 83(1), 89, 89(5), 96 and 97 of the 1988 Act respectively;

(c) rule 3(2) shall have effect as if the following sub-paragraphs were substituted for sub-paragraphs (a) and (b) –

"(a) state, as the case may be, either that proceedings have been instituted against the defendant for an offence to which Part VI of the 1988 Act applies (giving particulars of the offence) and that they have not been concluded or that, whether by the laying of an information or otherwise, a person is to be charged with such an offence;

(b) state, as the case may be, either that a confiscation order has been made or the grounds for believing that such an order may be made;" and

(d) rule 7(3) shall have effect as if the words "certificate issued by a magistrates' court or the Crown Court" were substituted for the words "certificate issued by the Crown Court".".

Costs

9. For Order 62, rule 18(1), there shall be substituted the following –

"(1) Subject to the provisions of this rule, on any taxation of the costs of a litigant in person there may be allowed such costs as would have been allowed if the work and disbursements to which the costs relate had been done or made by a solicitor on the litigant's behalf together with any payments reasonably made by him for legal advice relating to the conduct of or the issues raised by the proceedings.".

10. Order 62, rule 18(3) shall be amended by substituting, for the sum "£6.50", the sum "£7.00".

Fixed costs

11. Appendix 3 to Order 62 shall be amended as follows –

(1) For Table A (Basic Costs) in Part I there shall be substituted the following Table –

"A. Basic Costs

	Amount to be allowed in cases under following sub-paragraphs of paragraph I of this Appendix		
	(a) £ p	*(b)* £ p	*(c)* £ p
If the amount recovered is –			
not less than £600			
but less than £2,000 –			
(i) where the writ was served by post	47.00	61.50	108.00
(ii) where the writ was served on the defendant personally	52.00	66.00	112.50
not less than £2,000			
but less than £3,000 –			
(i) where the writ was served by post	52.00	68.50	112.50
(ii) where the writ was served on the defendant personally	56.00	72.00	118.00
not less than £3,000	68.00	97.50	139.00"

(2) Table B (Additional costs) in Part I shall be amended by substituting, for the figures shown in columns (i) and (ii), the following figures –

	(i)	*(ii)*
(1)	7.25	9.50
(2)	17.00	36.00
(3)(a)	26.25	47.00
(b)	31.00	52.00
(4)	12.00	14.00
(5)	12.00	14.00
(6)	9.25	17.00

(3) Part III, paragraph 1 shall be amended by substituting, for the sum of "£6.25", the sum of "£6.50";

(4) Part III, paragraph 2 shall be amended by substituting, for the sum of "25.00", the sum of "26.50";

(5) Part III, paragraph 3 shall be amended as follows –

(a) for the sum of "£15.25" in sub-paragraph (a) there shall be substituted the sum of "£16.00";

(b) for the table "Basic Costs" in sub-paragraph (b) there shall be substituted the following table –

"(i) Basic Costs

If the amount recovered by the applicant from the garnishee is –

	£ p
less than £131	one half of the amount recovered
not less than £131	67.00";

(c) for the sum of "£11.50" in the table "Additional costs" in sub-paragraph (b) there shall be substituted the sum of "£12.00";

(6) Part III, paragraph 4 shall be amended by substituting, for the sums of "£71.00" and "£11.50", the sums of "£75.50" and "£12.00".

(7) Part III, paragraph 5 shall be amended by substituting, for the sums of "£27.00" and "£1.80", the sums of "£29.00" and "£1.90"

(8) Part III, paragraph 6 shall be amended by substituting, for the sum of "£33.25", the sum of "£35.50".

Part II of the Family Law Reform Act 1987(a)

12. In Order 18, rule 7A(2), for the word "was" (after the words "matrimonial proceedings or") there shall be substituted the words "has been found to be the father of a child in relevant proceedings before any court in England and Wales or has been".

13. Order 90 shall be amended as follows.

(1) In the heading to rule 5, there shall be inserted, after the figures "1973", the words "or under Part II of the Family Law Reform Act 1987".

(2) In rule 5(1), after the words "(in this Order referred to as the "Guardianship Acts")", there shall be inserted the words "or under section 4 of the Family Law Reform Act 1987".

(3) In rule 5(2), the words "(as applied by section 4(3D) of the said Act of 1973)" shall be omitted.

(4) In rules 5(3), 6(1) and 7, after the words "Guardianship Acts", there shall be inserted the words "or under Part II of the Family Law Reform Act 1987".

(5) In the heading to rule 6, for the words "guardianship summons", there shall be substituted the words "certain summonses relating to minors".

(6) After rule 6, there shall be inserted the following new rule –

"Additional provisions for applications for financial relief

6A.—(1) Except where the application is for a variation order, an application for an order under section 11B, 11C or 11D of the Act of 1971(**b**) shall be supported by an affidavit by the applicant containing full particulars of his property and income, and stating the facts relied on in support of the application; and where the application is for a property adjustment order the affidavit shall also contain full particulars, so far as they are known to the applicant, of the property in respect of which the application is made and of any property to which the person against whom the application is made is entitled either in possession or reversion.

(**a**) 1987 c.42. (**b**) 1971 c.3; section 11B, 11C and 11D were inserted by the Family Law Reform Act 1987 (c.42), sections 12, 13 and 14.

(2) Where an application for a property adjustment order relates to land, the application shall identify the land and –

(a) state whether the title to the land is registered or unregistered and, if registered, the Land Registry title number; and

(b) give particulars, so far as they are known to the applicant, of any mortgage of the land or any interest therein.

(3) A copy of the application shall be served on any mortgagee of whom particulars are given pursuant to paragraph (2)(b), and any person so served may apply to the court in writing, within 14 days after service, for a copy of the applicant's affidavit.

(4) Within 14 days after the service of an affidavit under paragraph (1) or (6), or within such other time as the court may fix, the person against whom the application is made shall file an affidavit in answer containing full particulars of his property and income.

(5) Any person who receives an affidavit following an application made in accordance with paragraph (3) may, within 14 days after receipt, file an affidavit in answer.

(6) Where an application is made for a variation order, the registrar may order the applicant to file an affidavit setting out full particulars of his property and income and the grounds on which the application is made.

(7) In this rule –

(a) "variation order" means an order varying, discharging, suspending or reviving an order previously made under section 11B, 11C, 11D or 12C(6) of the Act of 1971;

(b) "property adjustment order" means an order made under section 11B(2)(d) or (e) of the Act of 1971.".

(7) In the heading to rule 7, for the word "Guardianship", there shall be substituted the word "Certain".

Mackay of Clashfern, C.,
Lane, C.J.,
Donaldson of Lymington, M.R.,
Stephen Crown, P.,
N. Browne-Wilkinson, V-C.,
Dillon, L.J.,
Steyn, J.,
Millett, J.,
Hugh Bennett,
F.M. Ferris,
Michael S. Howells,
C.R. Berry.

Dated 8th March 1989

EXPLANATORY NOTE

(This note is not part of the Rules)

These Rules amend the Rules of the Supreme Court 1965 so as to –

(a) provide for applications to the High court under Part VI of the Criminal Justice Act 1988 (confiscation of the proceeds of an offence) and to amend the provisions relating to applications under the Drug Trafficking Offences Act 1986 to take account of the amendments made to that Act by the Criminal Justice Act 1988 (rules 2 to 8);

(b) enable a litigant in person to claim as costs the cost of receiving legal advice and to increase the costs allowed to a litigant in person (rules 9 and 10);

(c) increase the fixed costs recoverable under Appendix 3 to Order 62 (rule 11);

(d) give effect to Part II of the Family Law Reform Act 1987 (rights and duties of parents etc.) which makes provision for the financial support of children and persons over eighteen in full-time education (rules 12 and 13).

1989 No 387 (S.41)

NATIONAL HEALTH SERVICE, SCOTLAND

The National Health Service (General Ophthalmic Services) (Scotland) Amendment Regulations 1989

Made - - - -	*8th March 1989*
Laid before Parliament	*10th March 1989*
Coming into force	*1st April 1989*

The Secretary of State, in exercise of the powers conferred on him by sections 26, 105(7) and 108(1) of the National Health Service (Scotland) Act 1978(**a**) and of all other powers enabling him in that behalf, hereby makes the following Regulations:

Citation, commencement and interpretation

1.—(1) These Regulations may be cited as the National Health Service (General Ophthalmic Services) (Scotland) Amendment Regulations 1989 and shall come into force on 1st April 1989.

(2) In these Regulations, the "principal Regulations" means the National Health Service (General Ophthalmic Services) (Scotland) Regulations 1986(**b**).

Amendment of regulation 2 of the principal Regulations

2. In regulation 2(1) of the principal Regulations (interpretation)–

(a) after the definition of "Board" there shall be inserted the following definitions:–

""capital limit" means the amount prescribed for the purposes of section 22(6) of the Social Security Act 1986(**c**) as it applies to income support;

"complex appliance" means an optical appliance at least one lens of which–

(i) has a power in any one meridian of plus or minus 10 or more dioptres, or

(ii) is a lenticular lens;"

(b) after the definition of "doctor" there shall be inserted the following definition:–

""eligible person" means a person who in accordance with regulation 14, may have his sight tested under general ophthalmic services;"

(c) after the definition of "enactment" there shall be inserted the following definitions:–

""family credit" means family credit under Part II of the Social Security Act 1986;

"general ophthalmic services" means the services which a contractor must provide pursuant to paragraph 10 of the terms of service;

(**a**) 1978 c.29; section 26 was amended by the Health and Social Security Act 1984 (c.48) ("the 1984 Act"), section 1(5) and Schedule 1, Part II, paragraphs 1 to 4 and by the Health and Medicines Act 1988 (c.49) ("the 1988 Act"), section 13(4); section 105(7), which contains provisions relevant to the making of Regulations, was amended by the Health Service Act 1980 (c.53), Schedule 6, paragraph 5; section 108(1) contains definitions of "prescribed" and "regulations" relevant to the exercise of the statutory powers under which these Regulations are made.

(**b**) S.I. 1986/965, amended by S.I. 1988/543.

(**c**) 1986 c.50; regulation 45 of the Income Support (General) Regulations 1987 (S.I. 1987/1967) has prescribed the amount of £6,000 as the capital limit.

"income support" means income support under Part II of the Social Security Act 1986 and includes personal expenses addition, special transition addition and transitional addition as defined in regulation 2(1) of the Income Support (Transitional) Regulations 1987(**a**);

"notice of entitlement" means a notice issued under regulation 7 of the Remission Regulations for the purposes of remission of charges under the Act;"

(d) after the definition of "qualifications" there shall be inserted the following definition:–

"the Remission Regulations" means the National Health Service (Travelling Expenses and Remission of Charges) (Scotland) Regulations 1988(**b**) and a reference to those Regulations is to be construed as a reference to them as they have effect on the date of making of the National Health Service (General Ophthalmic Services) (Scotland) Amendment Regulations 1989 and as amended subsequently.";

(e) the definition of "sight test" shall be deleted.

Amendment of regulation 13 of the principal Regulations

3. Regulation 13 of the principal Regulations (payment for services) shall be renumbered paragraph (1) and there shall be inserted thereafter the following–

"(2) Where in accordance with regulation 14B(4) a Board has paid to a patient in respect of a testing of sight an amount which exceeds the fee payable to the contractor, in accordance with the Statement, for that testing, it shall deduct the excess from remuneration otherwise payable to the contractor."

Substitution of regulation 14 of the principal Regulations

4. For regulation 14 (sight tests) of the principal Regulations there shall be substituted the following–

"Sight Tests – eligibility

14.—(1) A person may have his sight tested under general ophthalmic services if, at the time of the testing of sight, he is–

(a) under the age of 16 years;

(b) under the age of 19 years and receiving qualifying full-time education within the meaning of section 26(1A) of the Act;

(c) a person whose resources are treated in accordance with paragraph (2) as being less than or equal to his requirements;

(d) a person who requires to wear a complex appliance;

(e) a person who has been certified as–

(i) so blind or

(ii) substantially and permanently handicapped by defective vision and likely to become so blind

as to be unable to perform any work for which eyesight is essential and in consequence is registered as such in a register maintained by or on behalf of a regional council or islands council;

(f) a person who is or has been diagnosed by a doctor as suffering from diabetes or glaucoma; or

(g) aged 40 or over and is the parent, brother or sister or child of a person who has been diagnosed by a doctor as suffering from glaucoma.

(2) A person's resources shall be treated as being less than or equal to his requirements if–

(a) he is in receipt of income support;

(b) he is a member of the same family as a person who is in receipt of income support;

(c) he is in receipt of family credit;

(d) he is a member of the same family as a person who is in receipt of family credit;

(**a**) S.I. 1987/1969 amended by S.I. 1988/521 and 670.
(**b**) S.I. 1988/546, amended by S.I. 1989/393.

(e) his income resources as calculated in accordance with regulation 6 of, and Schedule 1 to, the Remission Regulations for the purposes of remission of charges under the Act are less than or equal to his requirements as so calculated and his capital resources as so calculated do not exceed the capital limit; or

(f) he is a member of the same family as a person described in paragraph (e) of this paragraph.

(3) In paragraph 1(e) the expressions "regional council" and "islands council" have the meanings given to them respectively by the Local Government (Scotland) Act 1973(**a**).

(4) In paragraph (2)(b) and (f) "family" has the meaning assigned to it by section 20(11) of the Social Security Act 1986 as it applies to income support(**b**) and in paragraph 2(d) it has the meaning assigned to it by section 20(11) of that Act as it applies to family credit(**c**).

Sight tests – applications

14A.—(1) An eligible person who wishes to have his sight tested under general ophthalmic services may make an application to any contractor for his sight to be tested.

(2) The application shall be made on a form provided for that purpose to contractors by the Board and shall contain a written declaration signed by the applicant to the effect that he is an eligible person.

(3) In addition, a person who is an eligible person–

(a) but only by virtue of regulation 14(1)(c) and (2)(e) or (f) shall show to the contractor a current notice of entitlement;

(b) but only by virtue of regulation 14(1)(d), shall show to the contractor the prescription for a complex appliance given to him on the occasion when his sight was last tested;

(c) but only by virtue of regulation 14(1)(f), shall, on a form provided for that purpose to contractors by the Board, provide the contractor with the name and address of his doctor and give his consent to the Board seeking confirmation of his diabetes or glaucoma from his doctor.

(4) A contractor to whom an application for a testing of sight is made shall, before making any test of the person's sight–

(a) subject to paragraph (5), satisfy himself that the person is an eligible person and that the requirements of paragraph (2) and such of the requirements of paragraph (3) as are applicable are met;

(b) ensure that particulars of the patient and the approximate date of the last testing, if any, of his sight are inserted in a sight test form by the patient or on his behalf; and

(c) satisfy himself that the testing of sight is necessary.

(5) Where an eligible person to whom paragraph (3)(b) applies is unable to meet its requirements, the contractor may, instead of satisfying himself that those requirements are met, satisfy himself that the person is an eligible person by referring to his own records or by measuring the power of the lenses of the person's existing optical appliance by means of a focimeter or other suitable means.

Sight test treated as a test under general ophthalmic services

14B.—(1) A person whose sight is tested by a contractor but who was not an eligible person when the sight test began and–

(a) who is shown during the testing to fall within the description specified in sub-paragraph (d) of regulation 14(1); or

(b) who is shown, in accordance with paragraph (3), within 3 months after the testing to fall within either of the descriptions specified in sub-paragraph (e) or (f) of regulation 14(2),

shall be taken for the purposes of the testing to have so fallen immediately before his sight was tested.

(a) 1973 c.65.
(b) 1986 c.50; *see* S.I. 1987/1967 regulations 14 to 16, as amended by S.I. 1988/663 and 1445.
(c) *See* S.I. 1987/1973, regulations 6 to 9, as amended by S.I. 1988/660.

(2) Where paragraph (1) applies the testing shall be treated as a testing of sight under the Act for the purposes of regulation 8(1)(a) of the National Health Service (Optical Charges and Payments) (Scotland) Regulations 1989(**a**) as well as for the purposes specified in section 26(1E)(i) and (ii) of the Act.

(3) For the purposes of paragraph (1)(b) a person is shown to fall within the description specified in sub-paragraph (e) or (f) of regulation 14(2) if he presents to the Board a notice of entitlement which is effective for a period which includes the date of the testing of sight or for a period beginning no later than 14 days after the date of the testing of sight.

(4) Where a testing of a person's sight is treated by virtue of paragraphs (1)(b) and (3) as a testing of sight under the Act the Board shall, on being presented with a receipt for, or other evidence of, any fee paid for the testing, and on being satisfied as to its amount, pay to that person an amount equal to that fee.".

Amendment of regulation 15

5. For regulation 15(1)(b) there shall be substituted the following–

"(b) on behalf of any other person who is incapable of making such an application or giving such a signature by–

(i) an adult relative,

(ii) any other adult who has the care of that person, or

(iii) any other adult competent to make such an application or give such a signature in accordance with any rule of law."

Amendment of terms of service

6.—(1) Schedule 1 to the principal Regulations (terms of service) shall be amended according to the following provisions of this regulation.

(2) In paragraph 2, for sub-paragraph (c) there shall be substituted the following:–

"(c) regulation 9(2) to (6) of the National Health Service (Optical Charges and Payments) (Scotland) Regulations 1989;".

(3) In paragraph 5 (notices) for "the National Health Service (Payments for Optical Appliances (Scotland) Regulations 1986" there shall be substituted "the National Health Service (Optical Charges and Payments) (Scotland) Regulations 1989".

Michael B. Forsyth
Parliamentary Under Secretary of State,
Scottish Office

St. Andrew's House, Edinburgh
8th March 1989

(**a**) S.I. 1989/392.

EXPLANATORY NOTE

(This note is not part of the Regulations)

These Regulations amend the National Health Service (General Ophthalmic Services) (Scotland) Regulations 1986 which provide for the arrangements under which ophthalmic medical practitioners and ophthalmic opticians ("contractors") provide general ophthalmic services.

As a consequence of the Health and Medicines Act 1988, from 1st April 1989 only certain categories of persons will be entitled to sight tests under general ophthalmic services. Those persons are specified by regulation 4 as children (including those under 19 in full-time education), persons entitled to income support or to family credit or to full remission of certain National Health Service charges, persons needing complex optical appliances, the registered blind or partially sighted, diabetics, those suffering from glaucoma and certain relatives of those suffering from glaucoma.

Regulation 4 also provides for those shown as a result of the sight test to need a complex optical appliance or who establish entitlement to full remission of NHS charges after the test to be treated as having had their sight tested under general ophthalmic services, so that any fee paid may be recovered from the Health Board. The appropriate adjustment is made to the contractor's remuneration (regulation 3).

STATUTORY INSTRUMENTS

1989 No. 388 (S.42)

LEGAL AID AND ADVICE, SCOTLAND

The Criminal Legal Aid (Scotland) (Fees) Amendment Regulations 1989

Made - - - -	*9th March 1989*
Laid before Parliament	*10th March 1989*
Coming into force	*1st April 1989*

The Secretary of State, in exercise of the powers conferred upon him by section 33 of the Legal Aid (Scotland) Act 1986(**a**), and of all other powers enabling him in that behalf, hereby makes the following Regulations:

1.—(1) These Regulations may be cited as the Criminal Legal Aid (Scotland) (Fees) Amendment Regulations 1989 and shall come into force on 1st April 1989.

(2) In these Regulations "the principal Regulations" means the Criminal Legal Aid (Scotland) (Fees) Regulations 1987(**b**).

2. For the Table of Fees set out in Schedule 3 to the principal Regulations (Fees of Counsel) there shall be substituted the Table of Fees set out in the Schedule to these Regulations.

3. The amendments to the principal Regulations made by regulation 2 of these Regulations shall apply only to fees in relation to proceedings concluded on or after 1st April 1989.

St. Andrew's House, Edinburgh
9th March 1989

James Douglas-Hamilton
Parliamentary Under Secretary of State,
Scottish Office

(**a**) 1986 c.47.
(**b**) S.I. 1987/365; the relevant amending instruments are S.I. 1987/824 and 1988/421.

Regulation 2

SCHEDULE

TABLE OF FEES

CHAPTER 1 – JUNIOR COUNSEL

	Junior with Senior	*Junior alone*
1. *Trial per day*		
(a) In Edinburgh	£139.50	£196.50
(b) In Glasgow	£165.00	£241.50
(c) Elsewhere within 60 miles journey by road from Edinburgh	£171.00	£247.50
(d) In Aberdeen, Inverness or Dumfries	£235.00	£330.50
(e) Elsewhere beyond 60 miles journey by road from Edinburgh: Such fee as the auditor considers appropriate with regard to the journey involved and the level of fees prescribed in this paragraph.		
2. *Appeals, etc*		
(a) Drafting grounds of appeal against conviction, including any note of appeal	£36.00	£51.00
(b) Hearing in appeal against conviction – per day	£139.50	£196.50
(c) Note of adjustments to stated case	£36.00	£51.00
(d) Hearing on stated case or bill of suspension relating to conviction or conviction and sentence	£63.50	£82.50
(e) Any appeal against sentence including fee for drafting note of appeal	£25.50	£57.00
(f) Appeal relating to granting of bail	£19.00	£19.00
3. *Consultations*		
(a) In Edinburgh	£44.50	£63.50
Additional fee if held in prison	£7.00	£7.00
(b) Elsewhere within 60 miles journey by road from Edinburgh	£82.50	£108.00
(c) In Aberdeen, Inverness or Dumfries	£165.00	£196.50
(d) Elsewhere beyond 60 miles journey by road from Edinburgh: Such fee as the auditor considers appropriate with regard to the journey involved and the level of fees prescribed in this paragraph.		
4. Opinion on appeal, etc.		£38.00
5. Revisal of stated case		£38.00
6. Drafting bill of suspension		£38.00
7. Remits for sentence and pleas in mitigation		£38.00

CHAPTER 2 – SENIOR COUNSEL

1. *Trial – per day*	
(a) In Edinburgh	£254.50
(b) In Glasgow	£298.50
(c) Elsewhere within 60 miles journey by road from Edinburgh	£305.50
(d) In Aberdeen, Inverness or Dumfries	£413.00
(e) Elsewhere beyond 60 miles journey by road from Edinburgh: Such fee as the auditor considers appropriate with regard to the journey involved and the level of fees prescribed in this paragraph.	

2. *Appeals, etc*	
(a) Revising grounds of appeal against conviction, including any note of appeal	£70.00
(b) Hearing in appeal against conviction – per day	£254.50
(c) Note of adjustments to stated case	£70.00
(d) Hearing on stated case or bill of suspension relating to conviction or conviction and sentence	£126.50
(e) Any appeal against sentence including revisal of note of appeal	£82.50
(f) Appeal relating to granting of bail	£25.50
3. *Consultations*	
(a) In Edinburgh	£95.50
Additional fee if held in prison	£7.00
(b) Elsewhere within 60 miles journey by road from Edinburgh	£152.00
(c) In Aberdeen, Inverness or Dumfries	£292.50
(d) Elsewhere beyond 60 miles journey by road from Edinburgh: Such fee as the auditor considers appropriate with regard to the journey involved and the level of fees prescribed in this paragraph.	
4. Opinion on appeal	£57.00
5. Revisal of stated case	£57.00
6. Revisal of bill of suspension	£57.00
7. Remits for sentence and pleas in mitigation	£57.00

EXPLANATORY NOTE

(This note is not part of the Regulations)

These Regulations amend the Criminal Legal Aid (Scotland) (Fees) Regulations 1987 so as to increase the fees allowable to Counsel for criminal legal aid given under the Legal Aid (Scotland) Act 1986. The increased fees will apply to proceedings concluded on or after 1st April 1989. The overall increase is around 6%.

STATUTORY INSTRUMENTS

1989 No. 389 (S.43)

LEGAL AID AND ADVICE, SCOTLAND

The Legal Aid (Scotland) (Fees in Civil Proceedings) Amendment Regulations 1989

Made - - - -	*9th March 1989*
Laid before Parliament	*10th March 1989*
Coming into force	*1st April 1989*

The Secretary of State, in exercise of the powers conferred on him by sections 14A and 15 of the Legal Aid (Scotland) Act 1967(**a**) as read with section 45 of, and paragraph 3(1) of Schedule 4 to, the Legal Aid (Scotland) Act 1986(**b**), and of all other powers enabling him in that behalf, hereby makes the following Regulations:

1.—(1) These Regulations may be cited as the Legal Aid (Scotland) (Fees in Civil Proceedings) Amendment Regulations 1989 and shall come into force on 1st April 1989.

(2) In these Regulations "the principal Regulations" means the Legal Aid (Scotland) (Fees in Civil Proceedings) Regulations 1984(**c**).

2. For the Table of Fees in Schedule 3 to the principal Regulations there shall be substituted the Table of Fees set out in the Schedule to these Regulations.

3. The amendments to the principal Regulations made by regulation 2 of these Regulations shall apply only to fees in relation to work done on or after 1st April 1989.

James Douglas-Hamilton
Parliamentary Under Secretary of State,
Scottish Office

St Andrew's House, Edinburgh
9th March 1989

(**a**) 1967 c.43; section 14A was inserted by section 3 of the Divorce Jurisdiction, Court Fees and Legal Aid (Scotland) Act 1983 (c.12).
(**b**) 1986 c.47.
(**c**) S.I. 1984/519; the relevant amending instruments are S.I. 1985/557, 1986/681, 1987/825 and 1988/422.

Regulation 2

SCHEDULE

TABLE OF FEES

CHAPTER I – JUNIOR COUNSEL

PART I – UNDEFENDED ACTIONS OF DIVORCE OR SEPARATION-AFFIDAVIT PROCEDURE

1.	*Summons or other initiating writ*	
	(a) Subject to sub-paragraph (b) below the fees shall be–	
	(i) Where the facts set out in section 1(2)(b) (unreasonable behaviour) of the Divorce (Scotland) Act 1976(**a**) are relied on	£24.50
	(ii) Where the facts set out in section 1(2)(a) (adultery) or section 1(2)(c) (desertion) of the said Act are relied on and the action is not straightforward	£24.50
	(iii) Where the facts set out in the said section 1(2)(a) (adultery) or section 1(2)(c) (desertion) are relied on and the action is straightforward	£20.00
	(iv) Where the facts set out in section 1(2)(d) (2 years' non-cohabitation and consent) or 1(2)(e) (5 years' non-cohabitation) of the said Act are relied on	£20.00
	(b) Where common law interdict and/or any order under the Matrimonial Homes (Family Protection) (Scotland) Act 1981(**b**) or any other ancillary order is also sought, the fee shall be within the following range:–	
	From	£24.50
	To	£46.00
2.	*Minute*	
	(a) Minute involving arrangements for a child or children and/or financial provision	£18.00
	(b) Any other minute	£14.00
3.	*By Order Roll appearance*	£14.00
4.	*All other work*	
	The fees specified in Part IV shall apply.	

PART II – CONSISTORIAL ACTIONS OTHER THAN THOSE TO WHICH PART I APPLIES

1.	*Summons or other initiating writ*	
	The fees specified in Part I shall apply.	
2.	*Minute for pursuer relating to custody, aliment or access*	£20.50
3.	*Defences or answers*	
	(a) Defences or answers in purely skeleton form to preserve rights of parties	£11.50
	(b) Answers to minute	£18.00
	(c) The fee for defences or answers to which sub-paragraph (a) or (b) does not apply shall be within the following range:–	
	From	£20.00
	To	£41.00
4.	*Joint minute regulating custody, aliment or access*	
	Framing or adjusting the minute	£17.50
5.	*By Order Roll appearance*	£14.00

(**a**) 1976 c.39.
(**b**) 1981 c.59.

6. *All other work*

The fees specified in Part IV shall apply.

PART III – PETITIONS

1. *Petition (including any revisals thereto)*

(a) Petition for interdict	£52.00
(b) Other Outer House petitions	£34.50
(c) Inner House petition: such fee shall be allowed as appears to the auditor to provide reasonable remuneration for the work.	

2. *Answers (including any revisals thereto)*

(a) Petition for interdict	£52.00
(b) Other Outer House petitions	£32.00
(c) Inner House petitions: such fee shall be allowed as appears to the auditor to provide reasonable remuneration for the work.	

3. *All other work*

The fees specified in Part IV shall apply.

PART IV – ORDINARY ACTIONS

1. *Summons (including any revisals thereto)*

(a) Straightforward cases	£43.50
(b) Other cases	£57.00

2. *Defences (including any revisals thereto)*

(a) Where in purely skeleton form to preserve rights of parties	£11.50
(b) Otherwise the fee shall be within the following range, having regard to nature of summons:–	
From	£43.50
To	£57.00

3. *Adjustment of record*

(a) Adjustment fee (each occasion)	£18.00
(b) Additional adjustment fee, where skeleton defences require to be amplified, where additional parties are introduced, etc.	£43.50

4. *Specification of documents*

Standard calls only	£18.00

5. *Minutes, etc.*

(a) Formal amendments or answers	£16.50
(b) Amendments or answers other than formal	£29.00
(c) Revising and signing tender or acceptance	£7.50
(d) Note of exceptions	£18.00
(e) Abandonment, sist, restriction, etc.	£9.00
(f) Issue or counter issue	£9.00

6. *Notes*

(a) Note on quantum only	£46.00
(b) Note advising on tender or extra-judicial offer, where not merely confirming advice at consultation	£52.00
(c) Note on line of evidence	£52.00

(d) The fee for other types of note shall be within the following range:–

From £17.50

To £52.00

7. *Consultations*

(a) Before proof or trial, or otherwise involving a significant degree of preparation or lengthy discussion–

(i) Junior alone £63.50

(ii) Junior with Senior £34.50

(b) Other consultations–

(i) Junior alone £52.00

(ii) Junior with Senior £29.00

8. *Motions*

(a) Unopposed motions on By Order (Adjustment) Roll, etc. £9.00

(b) Opposed motions–

Attendance for up to half hour £18.00

Attendance for each subsequent half hour or part thereof £14.00

(c) Motions on By Order Roll (including advice) £16.50

9. *Procedure Roll, proof or jury trial* £189.00

(a) Junior alone – per day

(b) Junior with Senior – per day £143.50

10. *Inner House*

(a) Single Bills

(i) Unopposed £14.00

(ii) Opposed–

Attendance for each half hour or part thereof £20.50

(b) Reclaiming motion

(i) Junior opening or appearing alone – per day £201.00

(ii) Junior otherwise – per day £155.50

(c) Motion for new trial

(i) Junior alone – per day £201.00

(ii) Junior with Senior – per day £155.50

11. *Attendance at judgement* £16.50

(a) Outer House

(b) Inner House £20.50

CHAPTER II – SENIOR COUNSEL

CONSISTORIAL ACTIONS, PETITIONS AND ORDINARY ACTIONS

1. *Revisal of pleadings*

(a) Revisal of summons, defences, petition or answers £75.50

(b) Adjustment fee (open record) (each occasion) £29.00

2. *Minutes, etc. – revisal fees*

(a) Amendments (other than formal) or answers £32.00

(b) Admissions, tender or acceptance (in appropriate cases) £9.00

(c) Note of exceptions £9.00

3. *Notes*

(a) Note on quantum only £69.00

	(b) Advice on tender or extra-judicial offer where not merely confirming advice at consultation	£75.50
	(c) Note on line of evidence (revisal)	£75.50
	(d) The fee for other notes shall be within the following range:–	
	From	£23.50
	To	£75.50
4.	*Consultations*	
	(a) Before proof or trial, or otherwise involving a significant degree of preparation or lengthy discussion	£91.00
	(b) Other consultations	£75.50
5.	*Day in court*	
	(a) Inner House – per day	£270.00
	(b) Outer House – per day	£252.00

EXPLANATORY NOTE

(This note is not part of the Regulations)

These Regulations amend the Legal Aid (Scotland) (Fees in Civil Proceedings) Regulations 1984 so as to increase the fees allowable to counsel for legal aid in civil proceedings given under the Legal Aid (Scotland) Act 1967. The increased fees will apply to fees for work done on or after 1st April 1989.

The Legal Aid (Scotland) Act 1967 continues in effect, despite its general repeal by the Legal Aid (Scotland) Act 1986, in respect of legal aid applications which were granted before commencement of the 1986 Act on 1st April 1987. (See paragraph 3(1) of Schedule 4 to the 1986 Act.) It is thus only in respect of work done following upon such applications that these Regulations increase the fees.

The overall increase is around 6 per cent.

STATUTORY INSTRUMENTS

1989 No. 390 (S.44)

LEGAL AID AND ADVICE, SCOTLAND

The Legal Aid (Scotland) (Fees in Criminal Proceedings) Amendment Regulations 1989

Made - - - -	*9th March 1989*
Laid before Parliament	*10th March 1989*
Coming into force	*1st April 1989*

The Secretary of State, in exercise of the powers conferred on him by sections 14A and 15 of the Legal Aid (Scotland) Act 1967(**a**) as read with section 45 of, and paragraph 3(1) of Schedule 4 to, the Legal Aid (Scotland) Act 1986(**b**), and of all other powers enabling him in that behalf, hereby makes the following Regulations:

1.—(1) These Regulations may be cited as the Legal Aid (Scotland) (Fees in Criminal Proceedings) Amendment Regulations 1989 and shall come into force on 1st April 1989.

(2) In these Regulations "the principal Regulations" means the Legal Aid (Scotland) (Fees in Criminal Proceedings) Regulations 1984(**c**).

2. For the Table of Fees in Schedule 3 to the principal Regulations there shall be substituted the Table of Fees set out in the Schedule to these Regulations.

3. The amendments to the principal Regulations made by regulation 2 of these Regulations shall apply only to fees in relation to proceedings concluded on or after 1st April 1989.

James Douglas-Hamilton
Parliamentary Under Secretary of State,
Scottish Office

St Andrew's House, Edinburgh
9th March 1989

(**a**) 1967 c.43; section 14A was inserted by section 3 of the Divorce Jurisdiction, Court Fees and Legal Aid (Scotland) Act 1983 (c.12).
(**b**) 1986 c.47.
(**c**) S.I. 1984/520; the relevant amending instruments are S.I. 1985/554, 1986/674, 1987/826 and 1988/922.

Regulation 2

SCHEDULE

TABLE OF FEES

CHAPTER 1 – JUNIOR COUNSEL

	Junior with Senior	*Junior alone*
1. *Trial per day*		
(a) In Edinburgh	£139.50	£196.50
(b) In Glasgow	£165.00	£241.50
(c) Elsewhere within 60 miles journey by road from Edinburgh	£171.00	£247.50
(d) In Aberdeen, Inverness or Dumfries	£235.00	£330.50
(e) Elsewhere beyond 60 miles journey by road from Edinburgh: Such fee as the auditor considers appropriate with regard to the journey involved and the level of fees prescribed in this paragraph.		
2. *Appeals, etc.*		
(a) Drafting grounds of appeal against conviction, including any note of appeal	£36.00	£51.00
(b) Hearing in appeal against conviction – per day	£139.50	£196.50
(c) Note of adjustments to stated case	£36.00	£51.00
(d) Hearing on stated case or bill of suspension relating to conviction or conviction and sentence	£63.50	£82.50
(e) Any appeal against sentence including fee for drafting note of appeal	£25.50	£57.00
(f) Appeal relating to granting of bail	£19.00	£19.00
3. *Consultations*		
(a) In Edinburgh	£44.50	£63.50
Additional fee if held in prison	£7.00	£7.00
(b) Elsewhere within 60 miles journey by road from Edinburgh	£82.50	£108.00
(c) In Aberdeen, Inverness or Dumfries	£165.00	£196.50
(d) Elsewhere beyond 60 miles journey by road from Edinburgh: Such fee as the auditor considers appropriate with regard to the journey involved and the level of fees prescribed in this paragraph.		
4. Opinion on appeal, etc.		£38.00
5. Revisal of stated case		£38.00
6. Drafting bill of suspension		£38.00
7. Remits for sentence and please in mitigation		£38.00

CHAPTER 2 – SENIOR COUNSEL

1. *Trial – per day*	
(a) In Edinburgh	£254.50
(b) In Glasgow	£298.50
(c) Elsewhere within 60 miles journey by road from Edinburgh	£305.50
(d) In Aberdeen, Inverness or Dumfries	£413.00
(e) Elsewhere beyond 60 miles journey by road from Edinburgh: Such fee as the auditor considers appropriate with regard to the journey involved and the level of fees prescribed in this paragraph.	

2. *Appeals, etc.*

(a) Revising grounds of appeal against conviction, including any note of appeal	£70.00
(b) Hearing in appeal against conviction – per day	£254.50
(c) Note of adjustments to stated case	£70.00
(d) Hearing on stated case or bill of suspension relating to conviction or conviction and sentence	£126.50
(e) Any appeal against sentence including revisal of note of appeal	£82.50
(f) Appeal relating to granting of bail	£25.50

3. *Consultations*

(a) In Edinburgh	£95.50
Additional fee if held in prison	£7.00
(b) Elsewhere within 60 miles journey by road from Edinburgh	£152.00
(c) In Aberdeen, Inverness or Dumfries	£292.50
(d) Elsewhere beyond 60 miles journey by road from Edinburgh: Such fee as the auditor considers appropriate with regard to the journey involved and the level of fees prescribed in this paragraph.	

4. Opinion on appeal	£57.00
5. Revisal of stated case	£57.00
6. Revisal of bill of suspension	£57.00
7. Remits for sentence and pleas in mitigation	£57.00

EXPLANATORY NOTE

(This note if not part of the Regulations)

These Regulations amend the Legal Aid (Scotland) (Fees in Criminal Proceedings) Regulations 1984 so as to increase the fees allowable to counsel for legal aid in criminal proceedings given under the Legal Aid (Scotland) Act 1967. The increased fees will apply to proceedings concluded on or after 1st April 1989.

The Legal Aid (Scotland) Act 1967 continues in effect, despite its general repeal by the Legal Aid (Scotland) Act 1986, in respect of legal aid applications which were granted before commencement of the 1986 Act on 1st April 1987. (See paragraph 3(1) of Schedule 4 to the 1986 Act.) It is thus only in respect of proceedings following upon such applications that these Regulations increase the fees.

The overall increase is around 6 per cent.

STATUTORY INSTRUMENTS

1989 No. 391 (S.45)

LEGAL AID AND ADVICE, SCOTLAND

The Civil Legal Aid (Scotland) (Fees) Amendment Regulations 1989

Made - - - -	*9th March 1989*
Laid before Parliament	*10th March 1989*
Coming into force	*1st April 1989*

The Secretary of State, in exercise of the powers conferred upon him by section 33 of the Legal Aid (Scotland) Act 1986(**a**), and of all other powers enabling him in that behalf, hereby makes the following Regulations:

1.—(1) These Regulations may be cited as the Civil Legal Aid (Scotland) (Fees) Amendment Regulations 1989 and shall come into force on 1st April 1989.

(2) In these Regulations "the principal Regulations" means the Civil Legal Aid (Scotland) (Fees) Regulations 1987(**b**).

2. For the Table of Fees set out in Schedule 3 to the principal Regulations (Fees of Counsel for Proceedings in the Court of Session) there shall be substituted the Table of Fees set out in the Schedule to these Regulations.

3. The amendments to the principal Regulations made in regulation 2 of these Regulations shall apply only to fees for work done on or after 1st April 1989.

James Douglas-Hamilton
Parliamentary Under Secretary of State,
Scottish Office

St. Andrew's House, Edinburgh
9th March 1989

(**a**) 1986 c.47.
(**b**) S.I. 1987/366; the relevant amending instruments are S.I. 1987/823 and 1988/420.

SCHEDULE

Regulation 2

TABLE OF FEES

CHAPTER I – JUNIOR COUNSEL

PART I – UNDEFENDED ACTIONS OF DIVORCE OR SEPARATION-AFFIDAVIT PROCEDURE

1. *Summons or other initiating writ*

(a) Subject to sub-paragraph (b) below the fees shall be–

(i) Where the facts set out in section 1(2)(b) (unreasonable behaviour) of the Divorce (Scotland) Act 1976(**a**) are relied on — £24.50

(ii) Where the facts set out in section 1(2)(a) (adultery) or section 1(2)(c) (desertion) of the said Act are relied on and the action is not straightforward — £24.50

(iii) Where the facts set out in the said section 1(2)(a) (adultery) or section 1(2)(c) (desertion) are relied on and the action is straightforward — £20.00

(iv) Where the facts set out in section 1(2)(d) (2 years' non-cohabitation and consent) or 1(2)(e) (5 years' non-cohabitation) of the said Act are relied on — £20.00

(b) Where common law interdict and/or any order under the Matrimonial Homes (Family Protection) (Scotland) Act 1981(**b**) or any other ancillary order is also sought, the fee shall be within the following range:–

From — £24.50

To — £46.00

2. *Minute*

(a) Minute involving arrangements for a child or children and/or financial provision — £18.00

(b) Any other minute — £14.00

3. *By Order Roll appearance* — £14.00

4. *All other work*

The fees specified in Part IV shall apply.

PART II – CONSISTORIAL ACTIONS OTHER THAN THOSE TO WHICH PART I APPLIES

1. *Summons or other initiating writ*

The fees specified in Part I shall apply.

2. *Minute for pursuer relating to custody, aliment or access* — £20.50

3. *Defences or answers*

(a) Defences or answers in purely skeleton form to preserve rights of parties — £11.50

(b) Answers to minute — £18.00

(c) The fee for defences or answers to which sub-paragraph (a) or (b) does not apply shall be within the following range:–

From — £20.00

To — £41.00

4. *Joint minute regulating custody, aliment or access*

Framing or adjusting the minute — £17.50

5. *By Order Roll appearance* — £14.00

(**a**) 1976 c.39.
(**b**) 1981 c.59.

6. *All other work*

The fees specified in Part IV shall apply.

PART III – PETITIONS

1. *Petition (including any revisals thereto)*

(a) Petition for interdict	£52.00
(b) Other Outer House petitions	£34.50

(c) Inner House petition: such fee shall be allowed as appears to the auditor to provide reasonable remuneration for the work.

2. *Answers (including any revisals thereto)*

(a) Petition for interdict	£52.00
(b) Other Outer House petitions	£32.00

(c) Inner House petitions: such fee shall be allowed as appears to the auditor to provide reasonable remuneration for the work.

3. *All other work*

The fees specified in Part IV shall apply.

PART IV – ORDINARY ACTIONS

1. *Summons (including any revisals thereto)*

(a) Straightforward cases	£43.50
(b) Other cases	£57.00

2. *Defences (including any revisals thereto)*

(a) Where in purely skeleton form to preserve rights of parties	£11.50
(b) Otherwise the fee shall be within the following range, having regard to nature of summons:–	
From	£43.50
To	£57.00

3. *Adjustment of record*

(a) Adjustment fee (each occasion)	£18.00
(b) Additional adjustment fee, where skeleton defences require to be amplified, where additional parties are introduced, etc.	£43.50

4. *Specification of documents*

Standard calls only	£18.00

5. *Minutes, etc.*

(a) Formal amendments or answers	£16.50
(b) Amendments or answers other than formal	£29.00
(c) Revising and signing tender or acceptance	£7.50
(d) Note of exceptions	£18.00
(e) Abandonment, sist, restriction, etc.	£9.00
(f) Issue or counter issue	£9.00

6. *Notes*

(a) Note on quantum only	£46.00
(b) Note advising on tender or extra-judicial offer, where not merely confirming advice at consultation	£52.00
(c) Note on line of evidence	£52.00

	(d) The fee for other types of note shall be within the following range:–	
	From	£17.50
	To	£52.00
7.	*Consultations*	
	(a) Before proof or trial, or otherwise involving a significant degree of preparation or lengthy discussion–	
	(i) Junior alone	£63.50
	(ii) Junior with Senior	£34.50
	(b) Other consultations–	
	(i) Junior alone	£52.00
	(ii) Junior with Senior	£29.00
8.	*Motions*	
	(a) Unopposed motions on By Order (Adjustment) Roll, etc.	£9.00
	(b) Opposed motions– Attendance for up to half hour	£18.00
	Attendance for each subsequent half hour or part thereof	£14.00
	(c) Motions on By Order Roll (including advice)	£16.50
9.	*Procedure Roll, proof or jury trial*	
	(a) Junior alone – per day	£189.00
	(b) Junior with Senior – per day	£143.50
10.	*Inner House*	
	(a) Single Bills	
	(i) Unopposed	£14.00
	(ii) Opposed–	
	Attendance for each half hour or part thereof	£20.50
	(b) Reclaiming motion	
	(i) Junior opening or appearing alone – per day	£201.00
	(ii) Junior otherwise – per day	£155.50
	(c) Motion for new trial	
	(i) Junior alone – per day	£201.00
	(ii) Junior with Senior – per day	£155.50
11.	*Attendance at judgement*	
	(a) Outer House	£16.50
	(b) Inner House	£20.50

CHAPTER II – SENIOR COUNSEL

CONSISTORIAL ACTIONS, PETITIONS AND ORDINARY ACTIONS

1.	*Revisal of pleadings*	
	(a) Revisal of summons, defences, petition or answers	£75.50
	(b) Adjustment fee (open record) (each occasion)	£29.00
2.	*Minutes, etc. – revisal fees*	
	(a) Amendments (other than formal) or answers	£32.00
	(b) Admissions, tender or acceptance (in appropriate cases)	£9.00
	(c) Note of exceptions	£9.00

3.	*Notes*	
	(a) Note on quantum only	£69.00
	(b) Advice on tender or extra-judicial offer where not merely confirming advice at consultation	£75.50
	(c) Note on line of evidence (revisal)	£75.50
	(d) The fee for other notes shall be within the following range:–	
	From	£23.50
	To	£75.50
4.	*Consultations*	
	(a) Before proof or trial, or otherwise involving a significant degree of preparation or lengthy discussion	£91.00
	(b) Other consultations	£75.50
5.	*Day in court*	
	(a) Inner House – per day	£270.00
	(b) Outer House – per day	£252.00

EXPLANATORY NOTE

(This note is not part of the Regulations)

These Regulations amend the Civil Legal Aid (Scotland) (Fees) Regulations 1987 so as to increase the fees allowable to Counsel for civil legal aid (and for legal aid in certain proceedings relating to children) given under the Legal Aid (Scotland) Act 1986. The increase will apply to fees for work done on or after 1st April 1989. The overall increase is around 6%.

STATUTORY INSTRUMENTS

1989 No. 392 (S.46)

NATIONAL HEALTH SERVICE, SCOTLAND

The National Health Service (Optical Charges and Payments) (Scotland) Regulations 1989

Made - - - -	*9th March 1989*
Laid before Parliament	*10th March 1989*
Coming into force	*1st April 1989*

ARRANGEMENT OF REGULATIONS

The Secretary of State, in exercise of the powers conferred on him by sections 26, 70(1), 73(a), 74(a), 105 and 108(1) of, and paragraphs 2 and 2A of Schedule 11 to, the National Health Service (Scotland) Act 1978(**a**) and of all other powers enabling him in that behalf, hereby makes the following Regulations:

PART I

GENERAL

Citation, commencement and interpretation

1.—(1) These Regulations may be cited as the National Health Service (Optical Charges and Payments) (Scotland) Regulations 1989 and shall come into force on 1st April 1989.

(**a**) 1978 c.29; section 26 was amended by the Health and Social Security Act 1984 (c.48) ("the 1984 Act"), section 1(5) and Schedule 1, Part II paragraphs 1 to 4 and Schedule 8 and by the Health and Medicines Act 1988 (c.49) ("the 1988 Act"), section 13(4); section 70(1) was amended by the 1988 Act, Schedule 3; section 105, which contains provisions relevant to the making of regulations, amended by the Health Service Act 1980 (c.53), Schedule 6, paragraph 5; section 108(1) contains definitions of "prescribed" and "regulations" relevant to the exercise of the statutory powers under which these Regulations are made; Paragraph 2(1) of Schedule 11 was substituted by the 1988 Act, Schedule 2, paragraph 15(1); and paragraph 2A of Schedule 11 was inserted by the 1984 Act, Schedule 1, Part II, paragraph 7 and amended by the 1988 Act, section 13(2) and (5).

(2) In these Regulations, unless the context otherwise requires–

"the Act" means the National Health Service (Scotland) Act 1978;

"capital limit" means the amount prescribed for the purposes of section 22(6) of the Social Security Act 1986(**a**) as it applies to income support;

"child" means a person who is under the age of 16 years;

"complex appliance" means an optical appliance at least one lens of which–

(a) has a power in any one meridian of plus or minus 10 or more dioptres, or

(b) is a lenticular lens;

"eligible person" is to be construed–

(a) for the purposes of Part III, in accordance with regulation 3(2);

(b) for the purposes of Parts IV and V, in accordance with regulation 8(2) to (5);

"face value" means, in relation to a voucher on which is marked a letter code specified in column 2 of Schedule 1, the amount specified in relation to it in column 3 of that Schedule, plus the amount of any increase provided for by paragraph 1 of Schedule 3;

"family credit" means family credit under Part II of the Social Security Act 1986;

"income support" means income support under Part II of the Social Security Act 1986 and includes personal expenses addition, special transition addition and transitional addition as defined in regulation 2(1) of the Income Support (Transitional) Regulations 1987(**b**);

"Health Board" means a Health Board constituted under section 2 of the Act;

"minimum complex appliance payment" means, in relation to an optical appliance, the amount specified as such for the appliance in paragraph 2 of Schedule 3;

"NHS sight test fee" means, in relation to a sight test carried out either by ophthalmic medical practitioners or by opticians, the fee payable, in accordance with the Statement published under regulation 10 of the Ophthalmic Services Regulations, to an optician in respect of a sight test;

"notice of entitlement" means a notice issued under regulation 7 of the Remission Regulations for the purposes of remission of charges under the Act;

"ophthalmic list" means a list, prepared and published pursuant to regulations made under section 26(2) of the Act of medical practitioners and opticians who undertake to provide general ophthalmic services(**c**);

"Ophthalmic Services Regulations" means the National Health Service (General Ophthalmic Services) (Scotland) Regulations 1986(**d**);

"optician" means an ophthalmic optician;

"patient" means a person whose sight has been tested whether under the Act or otherwise;

"patient's contribution" means the amount specified under regulation 7(5) of the Remission Regulations as that for which there is no entitlement under those Regulations to remission of charges;

"redemption value" is to be construed–

(a) for the purposes of Part III, in accordance with regulation 7;

(b) for the purposes of Part IV, In accordance with regulation 15;

(c) for the purposes of Part V, in accordance with regulation 20;

"the Remission Regulations" means the National Health Service (Travelling Expenses and Remission of Charges) (Scotland) Regulations 1988(**e**) and a reference to those Regulations is to be construed as a reference to them as they have effect on the making of these Regulations and as amended subsequently;

"replacement" does not include the replacement of an optical appliance rendered unserviceable by fair wear and tear;

"responsible Board" means–

(**a**) 1986 c.50; regulation 45 of the Income Support (General) Regulations 1987 (S.I. 1987/1967) has prescribed the amount of £6,000 as the capital limit.

(**b**) S.I. 1987/1969, amended by S.I. 1988/521 and S.I. 1988/670.

(**c**) *See* S.I. 1986/965, regulation 6.

(**d**) S.I. 1986/965, amended by S.I. 1988/521 and S.I. 1989/387.

(**e**) S.I. 1988/546, amended by S.I. 1989/393.

(a) in relation to a voucher completed pursuant to regulation 4, the Health Board for the area in which the testing of sight to which it relates takes place;

(b) in relation to a voucher issued pursuant to regulation 9 or regulation 10 or completed pursuant to regulation 17, the Health Board for the area in which the supply, replacement or repair of the optical appliance to which it relates takes or is to take place;

(c) in relation to a voucher issued pursuant to regulation 11 or completed pursuant to regulation 17, the Health Board which issues or completes it;

"small glasses" means glasses the lens apertures of which have datum centres not more than 56 millimetres apart; and for this purpose "datum centre" is to be construed in accordance with Part I of British Standard 3521: 1962 (Glossary of Terms relating to Ophthalmic Lenses and Spectacles Frames) published by the British Standard Institution as effective on 9th March 1989;

"supplier" includes a person replacing or repairing an optical appliance;

"supply" includes the replacement of an optical appliance rendered unserviceable by fair wear and tear;

"voucher" means–

(a) in Part III, a sight test claim form supplied by the Secretary of State to those whose names are included in an ophthalmic list;

(b) in Part IV, a voucher form supplied–

(i) where a testing of sight is carried out otherwise than by a Health Board by the Secretary of State to the person who carries it out or to the Health Board;

(ii) where a testing of sight is carried out by a Health Board, by the Health Board;

(iii) for the purposes of regulation 10(4), by the Health Board to whom the application is made;

(c) in Part V, a voucher form supplied by the Secretary of State;

for the purposes of enabling a payment to be made under these Regulations.

(3) For the purposes of Schedule 1–

(a) where an optical appliance has lenses described in different paragraphs in column 1 of Schedule 1, the face value of a voucher for the appliance shall be determined according to whichever lens would provide the greater face value; and

(b) where an optical appliance has a bifocal lens, the power of the lens shall be determined according to the power of that segment of the lens designed to correct a defect in distant sight; and

(c) a monocle shall be treated as though it were glasses.

(4) In these Regulations, unless the context otherwise requires, a reference–

(a) to a numbered regulation, Part or Schedule is to the regulation in, Part of or Schedule to, these Regulations bearing that number;

(b) in a regulation to a numbered paragraph is to the paragraph in that regulation bearing that number;

(c) in Schedule 1 to a numbered paragraph is to the paragraph in column 1 in that Schedule bearing that number.

PART II

CHARGES

Charges for glasses and contact lenses

2.—(1) A charge of such sum as may be determined by or in accordance with directions given by the Secretary of State shall be made and recovered in accordance with paragraph (2) in respect of the supply of glasses and contact lenses under the Act.

(2) Where a charge is payable by virtue of paragraph (1) the Health Board, or other person on its behalf, that supplies or is to supply the glasses or contact lenses may–

(a) on arranging to supply the glasses or contact lenses, make the charge; and

(b) on supplying the glasses or contact lenses or having them available for supply, recover the charge from the patient (if it has not previously been paid).

PART III

PAYMENTS FOR COST OF SIGHT TESTS

Eligibility – sight tests

3.—(1) A payment shall be made as provided for by this Part of these Regulations to contribute to the cost of a testing of sight which the responsible Board accepts as having been incurred by an eligible person.

(2) An eligible person is a person whose income resources, as calculated in accordance with regulation 6 of, and Schedule 1 to, the Remission Regulations for the purposes of remission of charges under the Act, exceed his requirements as so calculated, but whose patient's contribution does not exceed the NHS sight test fee and whose capital resources as so calculated do not exceed the capital limit.

Completion and use of voucher – sight tests

4.—(1) A person who wishes a payment to be made by virtue of this regulation in his case shall–

(a) apply to the Secretary of State for a notice of entitlement;

(b) apply for his sight to be tested by an ophthalmic medical practitioner or optician whose name is included in an ophthalmic list;

(c) indicate to that practitioner or optician that he is an eligible person at the time of the application; and

(d) show to him a current notice of entitlement and permit him to copy such details as may be required for the purposes of regulation 5(2)(b)(ii).

(2) The ophthalmic medical practitioner or optician may then duly complete the relevant parts of the voucher with the name and address of the patient and the date of the testing of sight.

(3) The person whose sight is or is to be tested shall sign on the voucher a declaration in writing to the effect that he is an eligible person.

(4) The ophthalmic medical practitioner or optician may use the voucher as being in substitution for payment by the patient of an amount equal to its redemption value, being part of the cost incurred for the testing of sight.

Payments to sight testers

5.—(1) The responsible Board shall, if the conditions specified in paragraph (2) are fulfilled, make a payment of the voucher's redemption value to an ophthalmic medical practitioner or optician who has used a voucher in accordance with regulation 4(4).

(2) The conditions specified in paragraph (1) are that–

(a) the patient has signed the declaration referred to in regulation 4(3);

(b) the ophthalmic medical practitioner or optician has–

(i) made a claim for a payment on a duly completed voucher to the responsible Board within the period of three months beginning with the date of the testing of sight, and

(ii) informed the responsible Board of the amount of the patient's contribution.

Payments to patients in respect of sight tests

6.—(1) A payment may be made under this regulation by the responsible Board to an eligible person who incurs the cost of a testing of sight by an ophthalmic medical practitioner or optician whose name is included in an ophthalmic list, without a voucher being completed in accordance with regulation 4.

(2) A patient who wishes to receive a payment under this regulation shall–

(a) if he did not apply to the Secretary of State for a notice of entitlement before the date on which his sight was tested, apply to him for such a notice within the period of 14 days beginning with that date;

(b) apply to the responsible Board for a payment within the period of three months beginning with that date; and

(c) produce to the responsible Board within that period–

(i) a notice of entitlement effective for a period including the date on which his sight was tested or for a period beginning no later than 14 days after that date, and

(ii) the receipt for any fee paid for the testing of sight.

(3) On an application made in accordance with paragraph (2), the responsible Board shall, if satisfied as to the cost incurred for the testing of sight, make a payment to the patient of an amount equal to the redemption value of the voucher which could have been completed under regulation 4 if the patient had satisfied the requirements of regulation 4(1).

Redemption value – voucher for sight tests

7. For the purposes of this Part of these Regulations the redemption value of a voucher is the amount, if any, by which the patient's contribution falls short of the lesser of–

(a) the NHS sight test fee; or

(b) the full cost which would have been incurred by the patient for the sight test but for these Regulations.

PART IV

PAYMENTS FOR COST OF SUPPLY OF OPTICAL APPLIANCES

Eligibility – supply of optical appliances

8.—(1) A payment shall be made as provided for by this Part of these Regulations to meet, or to contribute towards, the cost incurred (whether by way of charge under the Act or otherwise) for the supply of an optical appliance for which a prescription has been given in consequence of a testing of sight of an eligible person–

(a) which took place under the Act; or

(b) which took place otherwise than under the Act and within the Health Board area in which the person whose sight was tested normally resides.

(2) An eligible person is a person who at the time of the supply of the optical appliance is any of the following:–

(a) a child;

(b) a person under the age of 19 years and receiving qualifying full-time education within the meaning of paragraph 7 of Schedule 12 to the Act(**a**);

(c) a person whose resources are treated, in accordance with paragraph (3), as being less than his requirements;

(d) a person whose income resources, as calculated in accordance with regulation 6 of, and Schedule 1 to, the Remission Regulations for the purposes of remission of charges under the Act, are equal to or exceed his requirements as so calculated but whose patient's contribution is nil or is less than the face value of a voucher issued to him under this Part of these Regulations and whose capital resources do not exceed the capital limit;

(e) a person to whom a prescription is issued for a complex appliance.

(**a**) Paragraph 7 was substituted by the Health Services Act 1980 (c.53), Schedule 5, Part II, paragraph 8.

(3) A person's resources shall be treated as being less than his requirements if–

(a) he is in receipt of income support;

(b) he is a member of the same family as a person who is in receipt of income support;

(c) he is in receipt of family credit;

(d) he is a member of the same family as a person who is in receipt of family credit;

(e) his income resources as calculated in accordance with regulation 6 of, and Schedule 1 to, the Remission Regulations for the purposes of remission of charges under the Act, are less than his requirements as so calculated and his capital resources as so calculated do not exceed the capital limit; or

(f) he is a member of the same family as a person described in paragraph (e) of this paragraph.

(4) In paragraph (3)(b) and (f) 'family' has the meaning assigned to it by section 20(11) of the Social Security Act 1986 as it applies to income support(**a**) and in paragraph 2(d) it has the meaning assigned to it by virtue of section 20(11) of that Act as it applies to family credit(**b**).

(5) For the purposes of regulation 11 and other provisions of this Part of these Regulations as they apply to payments where the testing of sight was by or on behalf of a Health Board, a person is also an eligible person if, because of the frequency with which the condition of his eyes changes, he is considered by the Health Board to be non-tolerant of his existing optical appliance.

Issue of vouchers by ophthalmic medical practitioners and opticians

9.—(1) A person making an application for a testing of sight pursuant to regulation 14 of the Ophthalmic Services Regulations who considers that he may be an eligible person and wishes a payment to be made under these Regulations in his case shall indicate to the ophthalmic medical practitioner or optician to whom the application is made that he may be an eligible person.

(2) An ophthalmic medical practitioner or optician who, following a testing of sight under the Opthalmic Services Regulations, issues a prescription for an optical appliance to a patient–

(a) who has indicated that he may be an eligible person; or

(b) who (whether or not he has so indicated) is issued with a prescription for a complex appliance,

shall, in the circumstances described in paragraph (4) but subject to paragraph (5), issue to the patient a voucher relating to the optical appliance prescribed on the same occasion as he issues the prescription in accordance with paragraph 10(3) of Schedule 1 to the Ophthalmic Services Regulations.

(3) The ophthalmic medical practitioner or optician issuing the voucher shall sign it and shall–

(a) mark on it the letter code specified in column 2 of Schedule 1 which relates to the type of optical appliance prescribed as set out in column 1 of that Schedule;

(b) duly complete the relevant parts of the voucher with the name and address of the patient, the patient's age if under 19, particulars of the prescription issued to the patient, the date on which the patient's sight was tested and the date of issue of the voucher.

(4) The circumstances referred to in paragraph (2) are where the ophthalmic medical practitioner or optician, having consulted any records which he has relating to the patient and made such enquiry of the patient as he considers relevant, is satisfied that–

(a) the patient requires an optical appliance for the first time or an optical appliance pursuant to a prescription the particulars of which differ from those relating to his existing appliance; or

(b) the patient requires an optical appliance because his existing optical appliance has been rendered unserviceable by fair wear and tear.

(**a**) 1986 c.50; see S.I. 1987/1967, regulations 14 to 16, as amended by S.I. 1988/663 and 1988/1445.
(**b**) S.I. 1987/1973, regulations 6 to 9, as amended by S.I. 1988/660.

(5) Where a patient requires an optical appliance pursuant to a prescription the particulars of which differ from those relating to his existing appliance only because the patient is non-tolerant of that appliance, and has been so since it was supplied to him, no voucher shall be issued unless the Health Board responsible for the arrangements for the sight test, being satisfied that the prescription for that existing appliance was clinically correct, has authorised the issue of a voucher.

(6) Unless regulation 10(4) applies, not more than one voucher shall be issued to a patient in respect of any one optical appliance prescribed.

(7) A person making an application to an ophthalmic medical practitioner or optician for a testing of sight otherwise than under general ophthalmic services who considers that he may be an eligible person by virtue of regulation 8(2)(d) and wishes a payment to be made under these Regulations in his case shall indicate to the ophthalmic medical practitioner or optician to whom the application is made that he may be an eligible person; and that practitioner or optician may, if he issues a prescription for an optical appliance, issue a voucher relating to it in accordance with paragraphs (2) to (6) as though the testing of sight were carried out and the prescription was issued under general ophthalmic services.

Issue of vouchers by Health Boards

10.—(1) Subject to paragraph (2), a patient whose sight has been tested by an ophthalmic medical practitioner or optician otherwise than under the Act who considers that he may be an eligible person by virtue of regulation 8(2)(d) and wishes a payment to be made under these Regulations in his case may apply in writing for a voucher to the Health Board for the area in which his sight was tested.

(2) An application made under paragraph (1) shall–

(a) state that the patient may be an eligible person by virtue of regulation 8(2)(d);

(b) be accompanied by the prescription issued to the patient or a copy of it; and

(c) be made within the period of one month beginning with the date of the testing of sight but before the patient arranges for the supply of his optical appliance.

(3) On an application made in accordance with paragraph (2) the responsible Board shall issue a voucher relating to the optical appliance prescribed and shall–

(a) mark on it the letter code specified in column 2 of Schedule 1 which relates to the type of optical appliance prescribed as set out in column 1 of that Schedule;

(b) duly complete the relevant parts of the voucher with the name and address of the patient, the patient's age if under 19, particulars of the prescription issued to the patient, the date on which the patient's sight was tested and the date of issue of the voucher; and

(c) return the patient any prescription that he may have submitted.

(4) Where, on an application by a patient within six months of a voucher having been issued to him under regulation 9(2) or (7), a Health Board is satisfied, having made such enquiries as it considers relevant, that the voucher has been lost or destroyed without having been presented to a supplier of optical appliances, it may issue to the patient a replacement voucher completed in accordance with regulation 9(3)(a) and (b), but with the date of issue of the voucher being that on which the replacement is issued.

Issue of vouchers by Health Boards in connection with the hospital eye service

11.—(1) A person whose sight is tested by or on behalf of a Health Board who considers that he may be an eligible person and wishes a payment to be made under these Regulations in his case shall indicate to that Health Board that he may be an eligible person.

(2) Where, following a testing of sight, a prescription for an optical appliance is issued to a patient–

(a) who has indicated that he may be an eligible person;

(b) who (whether or not he has so indicated) is issued with a prescription for a complex appliance; or

(c) who is an eligible person by virtue of regulation 8(5),

the Health Board by or on behalf of which the patient's sight was tested shall issue to the patient a voucher relating to the optical appliance prescribed.

(3) The Health Board issuing the voucher shall–

(a) mark on it the letter code specified in column 2 of Schedule 1 which relates to the type of optical appliance prescribed as set out in column 1 of that Schedule;

(b) duly complete the relevant parts of the voucher with the name and address of the patient, the patient's age if under 19, particulars of the prescription issued to the patient, the date on which the patient's sight was tested and the date of issue of the voucher.

Use of vouchers for the supply of optical appliances

12.—(1) Subject to paragraphs (4) and (5), a patient to whom a voucher, duly completed in accordance with regulation 9, 10 or 11, has been issued may present it to a supplier who supplies or is to supply him with an optical appliance, provided that the arrangements for supply are made within six months of the date on which the voucher was issued.

(2) A supplier may accept the voucher in substitution for payment by the patient of an amount equal to its redemption value, being the whole or part of the cost incurred for the supply of an optical appliance.

(3) A voucher relating to glasses may be accepted in connection with the supply of contact lenses.

(4) Before presenting the voucher to the supplier the patient shall sign on the voucher–

(a) a declaration in writing to the effect that he is an eligible person indicating the grounds of his eligibility;

(b) an undertaking in writing to the effect that, if he is unable to show that he is an eligible person, he will pay to the responsible Board an amount equal to the voucher's redemption value.

(5) A patient who is an eligible person only by virtue of regulation 8(2)(d) or by virtue of his resources being treated in accordance with regulation 8(3)(e) or (f) as being less than his requirements shall–

(a) before presenting the voucher to the supplier, apply to the Secretary of State for a notice of entitlement; and

(b) on the same occasion as he presents the supplier with a voucher in accordance with paragraph (1), show a current notice of entitlement to the supplier and permit him to copy such details as may be required for the purposes of regulation 13(2)(c)(iii).

Payments to suppliers

13.—(1) The Health Board shall, if the conditions specified in paragraph (2) are fulfilled, make a payment of a voucher's redemption value to a supplier who has accepted the voucher from a patient in accordance with regulation 12.

(2) The conditions referred to in paragraph (1) are that–

(a) the patient has signed the declaration and undertaking referred to in regulation 12(4) and acknowledged receipt on the voucher of the optical appliance supplied to him;

(b) the optical applicance is not sold or supplied in contravention of section 21(1) of the Opticians Act 1958(**a**);

(c) the supplier has–

(i) made and kept a written record of the supply and issued to the patient a receipt for any money received from the patient,

(ii) made a claim for a payment on a duly completed voucher to the responsible Board, within the period of 3 months beginning with the date of supply of the optical appliance,

(iii) where the patient has shown a notice of entitlement to him, informed the responsible Board of the amount of the patient's contribution, if any, and

(iv) where the claim relates to a voucher the value of which is increased in accordance with paragraph 1(1)(e) of Schedule 3, certified that the glasses supplied were small glasses.

(**a**) 1958 c.32; section 21 was amended by the 1984 Act, section 1(1) and by the 1988 Act, section 13(6) and (7).

Payments to patients in Health Board cases

14.—(1) A payment may be made under this regulation to a patient who–

(a) has been issued by a Health Board with a voucher only because he may be an eligible person by virtue of regulation 8(2)(d), or by virtue of his resources being treated in accordance with regulation 8(3)(e) or (f) as being less than his requirements; and

(b) incurs cost for the supply of an optical appliance without first having obtained a notice of entitlement and without presenting his voucher to a supplier.

(2) A patient who wishes a payment to be made to him under this regulation shall–

(a) apply to the Secretary of State for a notice of entitlement;

(b) sign the declaration and undertaking referred to in regulation 12(4);

(c) within the period of three months beginning with the date on which he was supplied with the optical appliance, apply to the responsible Board for a payment and send to that Board–

(i) the voucher issued to him,

(ii) a statement of the amount of his patient's contribution, if any, and

(iii) evidence of the cost incurred for the supply of the optical appliance.

(3) On an application made in accordance with paragraph (2), the responsible Board shall, if satisfied–

(a) that the patient was issued with a notice of entitlement;

(b) as to the amount of the patient's contribution; and

(c) as to the cost incurred for the supply of the optical appliance,

make a payment to the patient of the voucher's redemption value.

Redemption value of voucher – supply of optical appliances

15.—(1) Where an optical appliance was supplied otherwise than under the Act the redemption value of a voucher is, subject to paragraphs (3) to (5), the lesser of–

(a) the full cost which would have been payable by the patient for the supply but for these Regulations;

(b) the face value of the voucher.

(2) Where an optical applicance was supplied under the Act, the redemption value of a voucher is, subject to paragraphs (3) to (5), the lesser of–

(a) the amount of the charge under section 70(1) of the Act which would have been payable by the patient for the supply but for these Regulations;

(b) the face value of the voucher.

(3) In relation to payments to be made because of a person's eligibility by virtue of regulation 8(2)(d), the amounts taken for the purposes of paragraph (1)(a) and (b) or paragraph (2)(a) and (b) shall, subject to paragraph (4), be reduced–

(a) where no voucher was completed in accordance with Part III in respect of the testing of the patient's sight, by the amount of the patient's contribution;

(b) where such a voucher was completed and for the purposes of regulation 7 the patient's contribution exceeded the lesser of the amounts specified in regulation 7(a) and (b), by the amount of the excess.

(4) If a reduction made under paragraph (3) in the case of a patient to whom a prescription was issued for a complex appliance would render the redemption value of the voucher less than the minimum complex appliance payment, that value shall be the minimum complex appliance payment.

(5) Where the patient was an eligible person only because a prescription was issued to him for a complex appliance, the redemption value of a voucher shall be the minimum complex appliance payment, except that where–

(a) the appliance was supplied under the Act; and

(b) in accordance with directions given pursuant to regultion 2(1), the amount of a charge made for the supply under section 70(1) of the Act would, but for any maximum charge specified in the directions, have exceeded by any amount the charge actually made,

the redemption value shall be reduced by the amount of the excess.

PART V

PAYMENTS FOR COST OF REPLACEMENT OR REPAIR OF OPTICAL APPLIANCES

Eligibility – replacement or repair

16.—(1) A payment shall be made as provided for by this Part of these Regulations to meet, or contribute towards, any cost accepted by the responsible Board as having been incurred (whether by way of charge under the Act or otherwise) for the replacement or repair of an optical appliance for which a prescription is given in consequence of a testing of sight of–

(a) a child where the appliance needs replacement or repair in consequence of loss or damage;

(b) a person of any description specified in regulation 8(2)(c), (d) or (e) suffering from illness, where the appliance needs replacement or repair in consequence of its loss or damage and the responsible Board is satisfied, after making such enquiries as it considers relevant, that the loss or damage would not have occurred but for that illness.

(2) No payment shall be made by virtue or paragraph (1)(a) or (b) unless the responsible Board is satisfied, after making such enquiries as it considers relevant, that the full cost of replacement or repair cannot be met under the terms of any warranty, insurance or other arrangement made with the supplier or manufacturer of such an appliance.

Completion of vouchers

17.—(1) A patient who considers that a payment should be made under this Part of these Regulations in his case in respect of the replacement or repair of his optical appliance may indicate to the supplier that he wishes such a payment may be made.

(2) In the case of a replacement the supplier may–

(a) mark on a voucher the letter code specified in column 2 of Schedule 1 which relates to the type of optical appliance to be replaced as set out in column 1 of that Schedule;

(b) duly complete the relevant parts of the voucher with the name and address of the patient, the patient's age if under 16 and the date of issue of the voucher.

(3) In the case of a repair the supplier may–

(a) mark on a voucher the letter code specified in column 2 of Schedule 1 which relates to the type of optical appliance to be repaired as set out in column 1 of that Schedule;

(b) indicate on the voucher the nature of the repair of the applicance to be undertaken and, in particular, whether it comprises–

(i) the replacement or repair of one or more lenses, and, if so, of how many,

(ii) the repair of a frame and, if so, whether it is of the whole frame, the front of a frame or one or both sides of a frame;

(c) duly complete the relevant parts of the voucher with the name and address of the patient, the patient's age if under 16 and the date of issue of the voucher.

(4) The patient shall sign on the voucher–

(a) a declaration in writing to the effect that he is an eligible person, indicating the grounds of his eligibility;

(b) a declaration in writing to the effect that the optical appliance cannot be replaced or repaired free of charge under the terms of any warranty, insurance or other arrangement made with its supplier or manufacturer; and

(c) an undertaking in writing to the effect that, if he is unable to show that he is an eligible person, he will pay to the responsible Board an amount equal to the voucher's redemption value.

(5) A patient who is an eligible person only by virtue of regulation 8(2)(d) or only by virtue of his resources being treated in accordance with regulation 8(3)(e) or (f) as being less than his requirements shall show a current notice of entitlement to the supplier and permit him to copy such details as may be required for the purposes of regulation 19(2)(b)(iv).

(6) In a case to which regulation 16(1)(b) applies, a supplier intending to use the voucher under regulation 18 shall first submit it to the responsible Board so that it may be satisfied as to the circumstances in which the loss or damage occurred and give its approval to the use of the voucher.

Use of vouchers for replacement or repair

18. The supplier may use the voucher as being in substitution for payment by the patient of an amount equal to its redemption value, being the whole or part of the cost incurred for the replacement or repair.

Payments to suppliers - replacement or repair

19.—(1) The responsible Board shall, if the conditions specified in paragraph (2) are fulfilled, make a payment of a voucher's redemption value to a supplier who has used a voucher in accordance with regulation 18.

(2) The conditions referred to in paragraph (1) are that–

(a) the patient has signed the declarations and undertaking referred to in regulation 17(4) and acknowledged on the voucher that the optical appliance has been replaced or repaired; and

(b) the supplier has–

(i) made and kept a written record of the replacement or repair and issued to the patient a receipt for any money received from the patient;

(ii) obtained any prior approval required by regulation 17(6);

(iii) made a claim for payment on a duly completed voucher to the responsible Board within the period of three months beginning with the date of the replacement or repair of the optical appliance; and

(iv) where the person has shown a notice of entitlement to him informed the responsible Board of the amount of the patient's contribution, if any.

Redemption value of voucher – replacement or repair

20.—(1) Subject to paragraph (4), the redemption value of a voucher shall, in the case of a replacement, be the lesser of–

(a) the full cost which would have been payable by the patient for the replacement but for these Regulations;

(b) the face value of the voucher or, in the case of the replacement of one only of a pair of contact lenses, £26.50.

(2) Subject to paragraphs (3) and (4), the redemption value of a voucher shall, in the case of the repair of an appliance be the lesser of–

(a) the full cost which would have been payable by the patient for the repair but for these Regulations;

(b) the amount specified in column 2 of Schedule 2 which relates to the type of optical appliance repaired (identified in that column by reference to the relevant letter code as specified in Schedule 1) and to the nature of the repair specified in column 1 of Schedule 2, together with any increase provided for by Schedule 3.

(3) Where more than one repair is made to an appliance the amount taken for the purposes of paragraph (2)(b) as being specified in Schedule 2 shall be the aggregate of the relevant amounts ascertained in accordance with Schedule 2, except–

(i) that the element of the value of a voucher which relates to the repair of a frame shall not exceed £7.40; and

(ii) the maximum supplement payable under paragraph 1(1)(e) or (g) of Schedule 3 in respect of the repair of any one appliance shall not exceed £33.00.

(4) In the case of a person who was eligible for a payment to be made in his case only by virtue of regulation 8(2)(d), the amounts taken for the purpose of paragraphs (1)(a) and (b) and (2)(a) and (b) shall be reduced by the patient's contribution.

PART VI

MISCELLANEOUS

Amounts wrongly paid

21.—(1) Where a person who is not an eligible person declares on a voucher that he is an eligible person and in consequence the responsible Board makes a payment under these Regulations, the person who makes the declaration shall repay the amount of that payment to the responsible Board.

(2) Where a supplier makes a claim for payment to the responsible Board, representing that the conditions specified in regulation 5(2), 13(2) or 19(2) are fulfilled, but those conditions are not fulfilled and the Board makes a payment to the supplier under these Regulations, it may recover the amount of that payment from the supplier.

Signatures

22.—(1) A signature required by these Regulations may be given–

(a) on behalf of a child by either parent or, in the absence of both parents, the guardian or other adult person who has the care of the child;

(b) on behalf of any other person who is incapable of giving the signature, by–

(i) an adult relative,

(ii) any other adult who has the care of that person, or

(iii) any other adult competent so to sign in accordance with any rule of law;

(c) on behalf of any person under 18 years of age–

(i) in the care of a local authority under Part II of the Social Work (Scotland) Act 1968(**a**) or under the provisions of that Part as applied by section 44(5) of that Act(**b**), by a person duly authorised by that authority;

(ii) in the care of a voluntary organisation, by that organisation or a person duly authorised by them.

Revocations

23. The Regulations specified in column (1) of Schedule 4 are revoked.

Michael B. Forsyth
Parliamentary Under Secretary of State,
Scottish Office

St. Andrew's House, Edinburgh
9th March 1989

(**a**) 1968 c.49.
(**b**) Section 44(5) was amended by The Children Act 1975 (c.72), Schedule 3, paragraph 56 and by The Law Reform (Miscellaneous Provisions) (Scotland) Act 1985 (c.73), section 28.

SCHEDULE 1

Regulations 1(2), and (3), 9(3)(a), 10(3)(a), 11(3)(a), 17(2)(a) and (3)(a)

VOUCHER LETTER CODES AND FACE VALUES

Column 1 *Type of optical appliance*	Column 2 *Letter code*	Column 3 *Face value of voucher*
1. Glasses with single vision lenses of a power (plus or minus) not exceeding– (a) as respects any spherical power, 6 dioptres; (b) as respects any cylindrical power, 2 dioptres.	A	17.00
2. Glasses with single vision lenses not falling within paragraph 1 or 3.	B	28.00
3. Glasses with single vision lenses– (a) of a spherical power (plus or minus) exceeding 20 dioptres; (b) of a spherical power (plus or minus) exceeding 10 dioptres with any cylindrical power; (c) of a cylindrical power (plus or minus) exceeding 6 dioptres; or (d) in lenticular form.	C	46.00
4. Glasses with bifocal lenses of a power (plus or minus) not exceeding– (a) as respects any spherical power, 6 dioptres; (b) as respects any cylindrical power, 2 dioptres.	D	32.75
5. Glasses with bifocal lenses not falling within paragraph 4 or 6.	E	58.00
6. Glasses with prism segment bifocal lenses or glasses with bifocal lenses– (a) of a spherical power (plus or minus) exceeding 20 dioptres; (b) of a spherical power (plus or minus) exceeding 10 dioptres with any cylindrical power; (c) of a cylindrical power (plus or minus) exceeding 6 dioptres; and (d) in lenticular form.	F	98.00
7. Glasses not falling within any of paragraphs 1 to 6 for which a prescription is given in consequence of a testing of sight by a Health Board as part of the provision of ophthalmic services (other than general ophthalmic services).	G	98.00
8. Contact lenses for which a prescription is given in consequence of a testing of sight by a Health Board as part of the provision of ophthalmic services (other than general ophthalmic services).	H	26.50 per lens

Regulation 20(2) and (3)

SCHEDULE 2

VOUCHER VALUES – REPAIR

Column 1 *Nature of repair to appliance*	Column 2 *Letter codes – values*					
	A	B	C	D	E	F & G
	£	£	£	£	£	£
Repair or replacement of one lens	4.80	10.30	19.30	12.70	25.30	45.30
Repair or replacement of two lenses	9.60	20.60	38.60	25.35	50.60	90.60
Repair or replacement of–						
the front of a frame	6.60	6.60	6.60	6.60	6.60	6.60
a side of a frame	3.60	3.60	3.60	3.60	3.60	3.60
the whole frame	7.40	7.40	7.40	7.40	7.40	7.40
Maximum	17.00	28.00	46.00	32.75	58.00	98.00

SCHEDULE 3

Regulations 1(2), 13(2)(c)(iv) and 20(2) and (3)

PRISMS, TINTS, PHOTOCHROMIC LENSES, SMALL GLASSES AND SPECIAL FRAMES AND COMPLEX APPLIANCES

1.—(1) The amounts in column 3 of Schedule 1 and column 2 of Schedule 2 and in paragraph 2(a) and (b) of this Schedule shall be increased as follows:

(a) by £3.75 in respect of each single vision lens containing a necessary prism;

(b) by £4.75 in respect of each other lens containing a necessary prism;

(c) by £1.90 in respect of each necessary single vision tinted lens;

(d) by £2.40 in respect of each necessary other tinted lens;

(e) in respect of small glasses: by £33.00 in the case of supply or replacement of the glasses or repair of the whole frame; by £29.35 in the case of repair of the front of the frame; and by £15.85 in the case of repair of a side of a frame;

(f) where the voucher is issued by a Health Board (in connection with the hospital eye service) by £1.90 in respect of each necessary single vision photochromic lens and by £2.40 in respect of each necessary other photochromic lens;

(g) where the voucher is issued by a Health Board (in connection with the hospital eye service), in respect of glasses the frame of which is certified by the Health Board as being required to be specially manufactured on account of the patient's facial characteristics, by £33.00 in the case of supply or replacement of the glasses or repair of the whole frame, by £29.35 in the case of repair of the front of the frame and by £15.85 in the case of repair of a side of a frame.

(2) The increases provided for by sub-paragraph (1)(e), (f) and (g) of this paragraph do not apply in the case of a voucher relating to glasses if it is accepted in connection with the supply of contact lenses.

(3) In sub-paragraph (1) of this paragraph "necessary" in relation to a prism or a tinted or photochromic lens means that the prism, tint or photochromic quality has been prescribed on the basis of clinical need.

(4) Where the face value of a voucher is increased in accordance with sub-paragraph (1)(g) of this paragraph, it may not be further increased in accordance with sub-paragraph (1)(e) of this paragraph.

2. The minimum complex appliance payment is–

(a) for a complex appliance with single vision lenses only, £3.25;

(b) for any other complex appliance, £18.00;

plus, in each case, the amount of any increase provided for by paragraph 1 of this Schedule.

Regulation 23

SCHEDULE 4

REGULATIONS REVOKED

Column 1 *Regulations revoked*	Column 2 *References*
The National Health Service (Payments for Optical Appliances) (Scotland) Regulation 1986	S.I. 1986/966
The National Health Service (Payments for Optical Appliances) (Scotland) Amendment Regulations 1986	S.I. 1986/1192
The National Health Service (Payments for Optical Appliances) (Scotland) Amendment Regulations 1988	S.I. 1988/463
The National Health Service (Payments for Optical Appliances) (Scotland) Amendment (No. 2) Regulations 1988	S.I. 1988/545
The National Health Service (Payments for Optical Appliances) (Scotland) Amendment (No. 3) Regulations 1988	S.I. 1988/1425
The National Health Service (Payments for Optical Appliances) (Scotland) Amendment (No. 4) Regulations 1988	S.I. 1988/1950

EXPLANATORY NOTE

(This note is not part of the Regulations)

These Regulations introduce a scheme for a contribution to be made by Health Boards ("Boards") towards the cost incurred by certain people (specified in regulation 3) for a sight test (Part III) and a scheme for payments to be made by Boards in respect of the cost incurred by certain categories of persons (specified in regulation 16) for the replacement or repair of optical appliances (Part V). In addition the Regulations retain with modifications the scheme (introduced in 1986) for payments to be made by Boards in respect of the cost incurred by certain categories of persons (specified in regulation 8) for the supply of optical appliances (Part IV). Glasses and contact lenses will continue to be supplied by Boards as part of the hospital eye service and regulation 2 enables a charge to be made for those supplies (Part II).

Under Part III of these Regulations persons who are eligible for a contribution to be made towards the cost of their sight test are those who are entitled to partial remission of National Health Service (NHS) charges if the amount of the patient's contribution does not exceed the standard amount payable to opticians for sight tests under the NHS (sight test fee) and whose sight is tested by an ophthalmic medical practitioner or optician whose name is included in the ophthalmic list. The amount of the payment varies according to the patient's means but cannot exceed the sight test fee.

A person is eligible under Part IV of these Regulations if his sight is tested under the NHS or (in limited circumstances – regulation 8(1)(b)) if it is tested privately. A voucher is to be issued to a patient if he appears eligible for a payment under the Regulations. The voucher is required to bear a letter code which varies according to the type of appliance prescribed and indicates a monetary value (set out in Schedule 1). The patient may use the voucher towards the cost incurred by him for the supply of the optical appliance prescribed (regulation 12) and the supplier may, on submitting the voucher, claim a payment from the Health Board (regulation 13). The amount of that payment will vary according to whether or not the patient is required to make a contribution (which has the effect of reducing the voucher's value) and whether or not the optical appliance is a complex appliance (regulation 15). In some hospital eye service cases the payment may be made direct to the patient if he has been supplied with his optical appliance without using his voucher (regulation 14).

Voucher values for the supply of appliance are increased by between 4½ and 10 per cent and the voucher value for the supply of contact lenses is unchanged.

Part V of these Regulations makes provision for payments to be made for the cost of replacement and repair of optical appliances. Those eligible are children under 16 (where the appliance is lost or damaged) and others who are entitled to full or partial remission of NHS charges or need to wear complex appliances (where the appliance is lost or damaged as a result of illness) (regulation 16). In the case of a replacement, the voucher is completed in a similar way to a voucher for the supply of an optical appliance. In the case of repair the voucher must, as well as bearing a letter code, specify the nature of the repair to be carried out (the monetary value given to which is set out in Schedule 2 and is relevant to the amount of any payment made). In the case of replacements and repairs the amount of the payment varies according to the patient's means, so that if the patient is assessed as having to make a contribution the amount of any payment made is reduced (regulation 20).

Part VI deals with miscellaneous matters and contains provision for repayment of amounts wrongly paid (regulation 21) and for signatures by those under disability (regulation 22).

The instruments which these Regulations replace are revoked by regulation 23 and Schedule 4.

British Standard 3521:1962, referred to in regulation 1(2) of these Regulations, may be obtained from any of the sales outlets operated by the British Standards Institution or direct by post from the Institution at Linford Wood, Milton Keynes, MK14 6LE.

STATUTORY INSTRUMENTS

1989 No. 393 (S.47)

NATIONAL HEALTH SERVICE, SCOTLAND

The National Health Service (Travelling Expenses and Remission of Charges) (Scotland) Amendment Regulations 1989

Made - - - -	*9th March 1989*
Laid before Parliament	*10th March 1989*
Coming into force	
(a) for purposes of regulations 1 to 3	*1st April 1989*
(b) for all other purposes	*10th April 1989*

The Secretary of State for Scotland, in exercise of the powers conferred on him by sections 75A, 105 and 108(1) of the National Health Service (Scotland) Act 1978(**a**), and of all other powers enabling him in that behalf, hereby makes the following Regulations:

Citation, commencement and interpretation

1.—(1) These Regulations may be cited as the National Health Service (Travelling Expenses and Remission of Charges) (Scotland) Amendment Regulations 1989 and shall come into force, for the purposes of regulations 1 to 3, on 1st April 1989 and, for the purposes of regulation 4, on 10th April 1989.

(2) In these Regulations "the principal Regulations" means the National Health Service (Travelling Expenses and Remission of Charges) (Scotland) Regulations 1988(**b**).

Amendment of regulations 3 and 5 of the principal Regulations

2. In regulations 3(2)(b) and 5(2) of the principal Regulations for the words "section 70(1)" in each case, there shall be substituted the words "section 70(1A)".

Amendment of Table B in Part II of Schedule 1 to the principal Regulations

3. There shall be inserted in Table B of Part II of Schedule 1 to the principal Regulations–

(a) before the reference to regulation 17–

in column 1 the words "regulation 2", and in column 2 opposite those words, the following:–

"As if in paragraph (1)–

(a) there were inserted after the definition of "the Act", the following definition:

(**a**) 1978 c.29; section 75A was inserted by section 14(2) of the Social Security Act 1988 (c.7); section 105 which was amended by the Health Services Act 1980 (c.53), Schedule 6, paragraph 5(1) and Schedule 7 and by the Health and Social Services and Social Security Adjudications Act 1983 (c.41), Schedule 9, paragraph 24, contains provisions relevant to the making of regulations; section 108(1) contains definitions of "prescribed" and "regulations" relevant to the exercise of the statutory powers under which these Regulations are made.

(**b**) S.I. 1988/546.

"the 1987 Act" means the Abolition of Domestic Rates etc. (Scotland) Act 1987(**a**);

(b) there were inserted after the definition of "close relative" the following definitions:

""collective community charge contribution" means a payment to which section 11(11) of the 1987 Act refers;

"community charge" means a community charge imposed under section 7 of the 1987 Act and "personal community charge" shall be construed in accordance with that section and sections 8 and 10 of that Act;"

(b) in column 2 before the words "As if paragraphs 7, 8 and 10 were omitted", the following:–

"(m) (i) except where (ii) below applies, 80 per cent of liability in respect of a personal community charge or, as the case may be, 80 per cent of a collective community charge contribution, other than where payable by a registered student;

(ii) 80 per cent of liability in respect of the aggregate of the personal community charges or, as the case may be, of collective community charge contributions for which a couple or the members of a polygamous marriage are liable disregarding, where a member of the couple or that marriage is a registered student, the liability of such member for any such charges or contributions."

Substitution of Table B in Part II of Schedule 1 to the principal Regulations

4. In Part II of Schedule 1 to the principal Regulations Table B shall be deleted and there shall be substituted therefor, the following:–

"TABLE B

MODIFICATIONS OF PROVISIONS OF THE INCOME SUPPORT (GENERAL) REGULATIONS 1987 FOR THE PURPOSES OF PART II OF THIS SCHEDULE

Column 1 *Regulation or Schedule*	*Column 2* *Modification*
regulation 2	As if in paragraph (1)– (a) there were inserted after the definition of "the Act", the following definition: "the 1987 Act" means the Abolition of Domestic Rates etc. (Scotland) Act 1987(**a**); (b) there were inserted after the definition of "close relative" the following definitions: ""collective community charge contribution" means a payment to which section 11(11) of the 1987 Act refers; "community charge" means a community charge imposed under section 7 of the 1987 Act and "personal community charge" shall be construed in accordance with that section and sections 8 and 10 of that Act;"
regulation 17	As if for the words from "18 to 22" to "urgent cases)" there were substituted "18 to 21".
regulation 18	As if for the words from "19 to 22" to "urgent cases)" there were substituted "19 to 21".
regulations 19 to 21	As if in paragraph (1) in these Regulations the references to regulation 22 were omitted.

(**a**) 1987 c.47.

Column 1 *Regulation or Schedule*	*Column 2* *Modification*
Schedule 3	As if in paragraph 1– (a) sub-paragraph (aa) were deleted and there were inserted in substitution therefor– "(aa) all payments of interest and capital under an agreement for instalment purchase to buy the dwelling occupied as the home;" and (b) after sub-paragraph (h) there were added– "(i) mortgage capital payments; (j) payments in respect of an endowment policy in connection with the purchase of the dwelling occupied as the home; (k) payments by way of rent which do not otherwise fall within sub-paragraph (c) or (e) of this paragraph; (l) 80 per cent of the general rates payable in respect of any dwelling in England or Wales occupied as the home; (m)(i) except where (ii) below applies, 80 per cent of liability in respect of a personal charge or, as the case may be, 80 per cent of a collective community charge contribution, other than where payable by a registered student; (ii) 80 per cent of liability in respect of the aggregate of the personal community charges or, as the case may be, of collective community charge contributions for which a couple or the members of a polygamous marriage are liable disregarding, where a member of the couple or that marriage is a registered student, the liability of such member for any such charges or contributions. As if in paragraph 9(1) for the words "paragraph 1(c) to (h)" there were substituted the words "paragraph 1(c) to (h) and (k)". As if in paragraph 11, there were the following modifications:– (1) For sub-paragraph (1)(a) and (b) there were substituted:– "(1) Subject to the following provisions of this paragraph, the following deductions from the amount to be met under the preceding paragraphs of this Schedule in respect of housing costs shall be made– (a) in respect of a non-dependant aged 18 or more who is in remunerative work or is a person to whom regulation 3(3) applies (non-dependants)– (i) except where (ii) applies, the sum of £8.20; (ii) where the claimant or his partner is liable to pay general rates in respect of any dwelling in England and Wales occupied as the home or is a Crown tenant of a dwelling occupied in England and Wales as the home and paragraph 9(5)(a)(ii) or (b)(ii) applies, the sum of £11.20; (b) in respect of a non-dependant aged 18 or more to whom sub-paragraph (1)(a) does not apply– (i) except where (ii) or (iii) applies the sum of £3.45; (ii) where the claimant or his partner is liable to pay general rates in respect of any dwelling in England and Wales occupied as the home or is a Crown tenant of a dwelling occupied in England and Wales as the home and paragraph 9(5)(a)(ii) or (b)(ii) applies, the sum of £6.45; (iii) where (ii) applies but the non-dependant is aged under 25 and is in receipt of Income Support, the sum of £3.00". (2) In sub-paragraph (7)(d), there were added at the beginning the words: "except where paragraph (1)(b)(iii) applies," (3) paragraph 7(e) were omitted." As if paragraphs 5(a), 7, 8 and 10 were omitted.
Schedule 4	As if in paragraph 1(1)(a) the words from "but, except" to "paragraph 5" were omitted. As if paragraphs 4 to 12 were omitted.
Schedule 5	As if in paragraph 1(1)(a) the words from "but, except" to "paragraph 5" were omitted. As if paragraphs 4 to 10 were omitted.
Schedule 7	As if paragraphs 7 and 17 were omitted.

St. Andrew's House, Edinburgh
9th March 1989

Michael B. Forsyth
Parliamentary Under Secretary of State,
Scottish Office

EXPLANATORY NOTE

(This note is not part of the Regulations)

These Regulations amend the National Health Service (Travelling Expenses and Remission of Charges) (Scotland) Regulations 1988 ("the principal Regulations") to take into account the introduction into Scotland on 1st April 1989 of the community charge under the Abolition of Domestic Rates etc (Scotland) Act 1987, to make other amendments consequent upon changes in the method of calculating Income Support and Housing Benefit, and to make other minor amendments.

Regulation 2 amends a reference in the principal Regulations to section 70 of the National Health Service (Scotland) Act 1978 consequent upon an amendment made by the Health and Medicines Act 1988 which comes into force on 1st April 1989.

Regulation 3 brings into force on 1st April 1989 amendments to Table B in Part II of Schedule 1 to the principal Regulations to allow liability for personal community charge and collective community charge contributions to be taken into account in the assessment of the requirements of a claimant under the principal Regulations.

Regulation 4 amends Part II of Schedule 1 to the principal Regulations by substituting Table B in that Schedule. The new table contains the amendments relating to community charge and enables allowance to be made, in calculating a person's requirements to establish entitlement to remission of charges or payment of travelling expenses, for instalment payments made in buying a dwelling, and for reductions from housing costs made in respect of non-dependants of the person claiming remission or payment of travelling expenses under the principal Regulations. These changes come into force on 10th April 1989.

STATUTORY INSTRUMENTS

1989 No. 394

NATIONAL HEALTH SERVICE, ENGLAND AND WALES

The National Health Service (Dental Charges) Regulations 1989

Made - - - -	*8th March 1989*
Laid before Parliament	*10th March 1989*
Coming into force -	*1st April 1989*

ARRANGEMENT OF REGULATIONS

The Secretary of State for Health, in exercise of powers conferred by sections 35, 36, 37, 78(1A), 79(1), 79A, 81, 82(b), 83(a) and 83A of, and paragraphs 2(6) and 3(3) and (5) of Schedule 12 to, the National Health Service Act 1977**(a)** and of all other powers enabling him in that behalf, hereby makes the following Regulations:–

Citation, commencement and interpretation

1.—(1) These Regulations may be cited as the National Health Service (Dental Charges) Regulations 1989 and shall come into force on 1st April 1989.

(2) In these Regulations, unless the context otherwise requires–

(a) "the Act" means the National Health Service Act 1977;

"basic type" means, in relation to a dental appliance, a type no more expensive than that which is clinically necessary for such a reasonable standard of dental efficiency and oral health as is necessary to safeguard general health;

"the Board" means the Dental Practice Board constituted under section 37 of the Act**(b)**;

"bridge" means a fixed or a removable bridge which takes the place of any teeth;

"dental estimate form" has the same meaning as in the National Health Service (General Dental Services) Regulations 1973**(c)**;

"denture" does not include an obturator;

"patient" includes a person who pays or undertakes to pay a charge on behalf of a person to whom a dental appliance is supplied or to whom some other service is provided;

"Statement of Dental Remuneration" means the Statement published under regulation 23 of the National Health Service (General Dental Services) Regulations 1973;

"Statement remuneration" has the meaning assigned to it by regulation 4(2) and (3);

"supply", in relation to an appliance, includes its replacement;

(b) a reference to the Secretary of State includes a reference to a health authority exercising functions on his behalf**(d)**;

(c) a reference to a numbered regulation or Schedule is to the regulation in, or Schedule to, these Regulations bearing that number and a reference in a regulation or Schedule to a numbered paragraph is to the paragraph in that regulation or Schedule bearing that number.

Charges for supply of dental appliances

2.—(1) Subject to paragraph 2(3), (4) and (8) of Schedule 12 to the Act (which provides for circumstances in which no charge may be made) and to paragraph (2), a charge of the amount provided for by regulation 4 may be made and recovered under section 78(1A) of the Act in accordance with these Regulations in respect of the supply under the Act of dentures and bridges.

(2) No charge shall be made and recovered under section 78(1A) of the Act in respect of–

(a) a supply, otherwise than as part of general dental services, to a person who has undergone operative procedures affecting the mandible, the maxilla or the soft tissues of the mouth as part of treatment for invasive tumours; or

(b) a supply as part of general dental services for which a charge may be made under regulation 8(2).

(a) 1977 c.49; for the definitions of "prescribed" and "regulations" *see* section 128(1); section 37 was amended by section 12(2) and (3) of the Health and Medicines Act 1988 (c.49) ("the 1988 Act"); section 78(1A) and section 79A were inserted by, and section 79 was amended by, the 1988 Act, section 11; section 83A was inserted by the Social Security Act 1988 (c.7), section 14 and was amended by the 1988 Act, Schedule 2, paragraph 6; paragraph 2 of Schedule 12 was amended by the Health Services Act 1980 (c.53) ("the 1980 Act"), Schedule 5, paragraph 2, and by the 1988 Act, section 11(8) and Schedule 2, paragraph 8; paragraph 3 of Schedule 12 was amended by the 1980 Act, Schedule 5, paragraph 3.

(b) *See* section 12(1) of the 1988 Act.

(c) S.I. 1973/1468; the relevant amending instruments are S.I. 1980/986, 1985/1336, 1987/1965 and 1988/2265.

(d) *See* section 13 of the National Health Service Act 1977 and S.I. 1989/51.

Charges for other general dental services

3.—(1) Subject to section 79(1)(b) and (c) of, and paragraph 3(4) of Schedule 12 to, the Act (which provide for circumstances in which no charge may be made) and to paragraph (2), the amount of the charge which may be made and recovered under section 79(1) of the Act in respect of services provided as part of general dental services is that provided for by regulation 4.

(2) No charge shall be made and recovered under section 79(1) of the Act in respect of–

(a) the supply of a dental appliance described in regulation 2(1);

(b) a visit by a dental practitioner to a patient;

(c) the opening by a dental practitioner of his surgery outside his normal opening hours in order to provide emergency treatment; or

(d) the attendance at the surgery of a dental practitioner providing emergency treatment of a medical practitioner or of another dental practitioner, specifically with a view to the administration of a general anaesthetic in connection with emergency treatment.

Calculation of charges

4.—(1) Subject to paragraphs (4) and (5), the amount of the charge which may be made and recovered–

(a) under section 78(1A) of the Act for the supply of an appliance described in regulation 2(1);

(b) under section 79(1) of the Act for the provision of services other than those described in regulation 3(2),

is 75% of the Statement remuneration (rounded down, where necessary, to the nearest whole penny), being an amount not exceeding that which the Secretary of State considers to be the cost to the health service (within the meaning of section 79A(5) of the Act) of the supply or provision.

(2) In these Regulations "Statement remuneration" means–

(a) in relation to the supply (whether or not as part of general dental services) of an appliance described in regulation 2(1), the remuneration provided for by the Statement of Dental Remuneration as that payable to a dental practitioner for the supply of an appliance of that type;

(b) in relation to other services provided in pursuance of a contract or arrangement for the provision of general dental services, the total amount provided for by that Statement as that payable to the dental practitioner for the provision of those services under that contract or arrangement.

(3) For the purposes of paragraph (2), where the Statement remuneration for any service is a fee of such amount as the Board may in its discretion approve, whether or not subject to a maximum, the amount is–

(a) if the Board has approved a fee for the service, the amount of the fee so approved, notwithstanding any subsequent variation of that amount on appeal**(a)**;

(b) if the Board has refused to approve a fee for the service, the amount of any fee authorised for it on appeal.

(4) Where a dental practitioner–

(a) has, under a contract or arrangement for the provision of general dental services, begun to provide for a patient services which include the supply of an appliance described in regulation 2(1); and

(b) has referred that patient, for the supply of that appliance otherwise than as part of general dental services, to a health authority or to a person or body pursuant to arrangements made under section 23 of the Act,

the amount of the charge for that supply shall be calculated in accordance with Schedule 1, and the dental practitioner shall provide the health authority or other person or body

---

(a) *See* S.I. 1974/455, regulation 21; the relevant amending instrument is S.I. 1987/445.

with a written statement of the amounts mentioned in sub-paragraphs (a) and (b) of paragraph 1 of that Schedule.

(5) The amount of the charges payable under sections 78 and 79 of the Act in respect of all dental appliances supplied and other services provided in pursuance of any one contract or arrangement for the provision of general dental services shall not exceed £150 in the aggregate; and £150 is the sum prescribed for the purposes of paragraph 3(3) of Schedule 12 to the Act.

Conditions for exemption under the Act

5.—(1) It is a condition of the exemption under sub-paragraph (4) of paragraph 2 of Schedule 12 to the Act in respect of the supply of a dental appliance to a person otherwise than as part of general dental services–

(a) that a written declaration on a form provided for that purpose by the Secretary of State shall be made to the effect that that person is, at the time of the examination or first examination leading to the supply of the appliance, within one of the specified categories; and

(b) where the Secretary of State so requires, that the specified evidence shall be supplied by or on behalf of that person.

(2) It is a condition of the exemptions under sub-paragraph (4) of paragraph 2 and sub-paragraph (4) of paragraph 3 of Schedule 12 to the Act in respect of the supply of a dental appliance, or other services provided, to a person as part of general dental services–

(a) that a written declaration on a dental estimate form shall be made to the effect that that person is, on the date of the contract or arrangement for the services, within one of the specified categories; and

(b) where the Board so requires, that the specified evidence shall be supplied by or on behalf of that person.

(3) The declarations referred to in paragraphs (1)(a) and (2)(a) shall be made by the person to whom the services are to be provided, except that where the application for services is made by another person on his behalf**(a)** it shall be made instead by the person who applies for the services.

(4) Nothing in paragraph (1)(b) or (2)(b) prevents the Secretary of State or the Board from accepting evidence other than the specified evidence as establishing that a person is within one of the specified categories.

(5) In this regulation "the specified categories" means the categories of person specified in column (1) of Schedule 2 and "the specified evidence", in relation to any of those categories, means the evidence specified in relation to it in column (2) of that Schedule.

Making and recovery of charges

6.—(1) Where any charge is payable under section 78 of the Act in respect of the supply of a dental appliance under the Act otherwise than as part of general dental services, the Secretary of State or health authority may–

(a) on arranging to supply it, make the appropriate charge; and

(b) on supplying it or having it available for supply, recover the appropriate charge from the patient (if it has not previously been paid).

(2) In providing general dental services for which a charge may be made under section 78 or section 79 of the Act, a dental practitioner–

(a) may, on arranging to provide the service, make the appropriate charge;

(b) shall require the patient to acknowledge, on the appropriate part of the dental estimate form, and before that form is sent to the Board, his obligation to pay a charge which is made;

(c) may, on providing the service, recover the charge from the patient (if it has not previously been paid); and

(a) In the case of general dental services, *see* S.I. 1973/1468, regulation 17.

(d) shall, on receiving a sum in payment (in full or in part) of the charge, give a receipt for it on a form provided for that purpose by the Family Practitioner Committee or a form to the like effect.

(3) Where a declaration in support of a claim for exemption has been made under regulation 5(2)(a) but the claim is not substantiated, and in consequence of the claim a dental practitioner has not recovered a charge in respect of an appliance supplied or other services provided, the Family Practitioner Committee may recover the charge from the person who made the declaration (whether or not the obligation to pay has been acknowledged).

Remission and repayment

7.—(1) The charges which may be made and recovered by virtue of the preceding provisions of these Regulations are subject to the provisions of regulations made under section 83A of the Act providing for remission or repayment.

(2) In regulations 3(2)(b) and 5(2) of the National Health Service (Travelling Expenses and Remission of Charges) Regulations 1988**(a)** for "section 78(1)" there is substituted in each case "section 78(1A)".

Charges for more expensive supplies and repairs

8.—(1) Where the Secretary of State–

(a) supplies a dental appliance which is, at the request of the person supplied, of a type more expensive than the basic type; or

(b) repairs such a dental appliance at a cost exceeding that of repairing a dental appliance of the basic type,

he may make and recover from the patient a charge equal to the difference between the cost of supplying or repairing the appliance and the cost of supplying or repairing an appliance of the basic type, in addition to any charge authorised by section 78 of the Act.

(2) Where a dental practitioner providing general dental services, as part of those services and at the request of the person supplied,–

(a) supplies a denture which is of a type more expensive than the basic type;

(b) repairs such a denture at a cost exceeding that of repairing a denture of the basic type; or

(c) supplies a bridge which is of a type more expensive than a denture or a bridge of the basic type,

he may, subject to paragraph (4), make and recover from the patient in respect of the supply or repair of the appliance a charge of an amount calculated in accordance with Part I of Schedule 3.

(3) Part II of Schedule 3 shall have effect with respect to the procedure for determining the amount of the charge referred to in paragraph (2).

(4) In the case of an appliance supplied or repaired by a dental practitioner who is remunerated in accordance with Determination IV of the Statement of Dental Remuneration (salaried dentists), the Family Practitioner Committee, and not the dental practitioner, shall make and recover the charge.

Charges for replacement – general dental services

9.—(1) Where a dental practitioner providing general dental services replaces a dental appliance supplied as part of those services and it is determined in accordance with Schedule 4 that the replacement is necessitated by–

(a) an act or omission on the part of the person supplied; or

(b) if the act or omission occurred when the person supplied was under 16 years of age, an act or omission of the person supplied or of the person having charge of him when the act or omission occurred,

the dental practitioner may make and recover a charge from the relevant person.

(a) S.I. 1988/551.

(2) The amount of the charge to be made and recovered under paragraph (1) is, subject to paragraph (3), the Statement remuneration for the supply of the dental appliance.

(3) If the Family Practitioner Committee considers–

(a) that payment of the full amount of the charge under paragraph (1) would involve undue hardship to the relevant person; or

(b) that the replacement, though necessitated by the relevant person's act or omission, was not wholly necessitated by lack of reasonable care on his part,

it may determine that the charge shall not be payable, or that its amount shall be reduced.

(4) In this regulation, "relevant person" means–

(a) where paragraph (1)(b) applies, the person having charge of the person supplied when the act or omission occurred;

(b) in any other case, the person supplied.

Discontinuation of treatment – general dental services

10. A dental practitioner providing general dental services may decline–

(a) to begin treatment; or

(b) where treatment has begun, to continue with it,

until he or the Family Practitioner Committee has received payment of the amount of any charge payable to him or it in accordance with these Regulations.

Reduction of remuneration and accounting for charges – general dental services

11.—(1) Subject to paragraph (2), the remuneration which would otherwise be payable by a Family Practitioner Committee to a dental practitioner providing general dental services shall be reduced by the amount of the charges authorised by these Regulations in respect of those services.

(2) Paragraph (1) does not apply to remuneration under Determination IV of the Statement of Dental Remuneration (salaried dentists).

(3) A dental practitioner remunerated under Determination IV of the Statement of Dental Remuneration shall account for and pay to the Family Practitioner Committee, in such manner as it may require, the amount of any charges recovered from a patient under these Regulations.

Revocations, amendment, savings and application of Regulations

12.—(1) The regulations specified in column (1) of Schedule 5 are revoked to the extent specified in column (3) of that Schedule.

(2) In the National Health Service (General Dental Services) Regulations 1973–

(a) in regulation 26H, for "carried out pursuant to regulation 20" there is substituted "referred to in regulation 8(2) of the National Health Service (Dental Charges) Regulations 1989" and for "pursuant to regulation 21" there is substituted "in consequence of loss or damage".

(b) in Part I of Schedule 1 (terms of service), in paragraph 17(a), after sub-paragraph (ii), there is inserted the following sub-paragraph:–

"(iii) regulations 4(4), 6(2) and 8(2) to (4) of, and Schedule 3 to, the National Health Service (Dental Charges Regulations 1989;"

(3) These Regulations apply to the supply of a dental appliance otherwise than as part of general dental services only where the examination, or first examination, leading to the supply takes place on or after 1st April 1989; and where the examination or first examination leading to the supply takes place before 1st April 1989 the charge which may be made and recovered in respect of the supply shall be that authorised by the Act and regulations made under it as in force at the time of that examination or first examination.

(4) These Regulations apply to the provision of general dental services only where the contract or arrangement leading to the supply, as part of those services, of a dental appliance or to some other provision of general dental services is made on or after 1st April 1989; and where the contract or arrangement is made before that date, the charge

which may be made and recovered in respect of the supply or the other provision of general dental services shall be that authorised by the Act and regulations made under it as in force at the time when that contract or arrangement was made.

Signed by authority of the Secretary of State for Health

D. Mellor
Minister of State,
Department of Health

8th March 1989

Regulation 4(4)

SCHEDULE 1

CALCULATION OF CHARGE FOR SUPPLY OF APPLIANCE ON REFERRAL

1. There shall first be taken an amount ("£a") which is the greater of the following–

(a) the amount of the charges authorised by sections 78 and 79 of the Act which have been paid to the dental practitioner by the patient in respect of services provided under the contract or arrangement;

(b) the amount of the charges authorised by those sections, including any amount already paid, which would be payable to the dental practitioner by the patient in respect of those services if no charge fell to be made in respect of the supply of the appliance.

2. Then £a shall be compared with the full amount of the charges payable to the dental practitioner by the patient in respect of services provided under the contract or arrangement ("£b") and–

(a) if £a equals or exceeds £b, there is no charge for the supply of the appliance;

(b) if £a is less than £b, the charge for the supply of the appliance is–

(i) £b minus £a, or

(ii) 75% of the Statement remuneration for the supply of the appliance,

whichever is the lesser amount.

Regulation 5(5)

SCHEDULE 2

EXEMPTIONS – CATEGORIES AND EVIDENCE

(1) *Category*	(2) *Evidence*
1. Under 18 years of age.	**1.** The person's birth certificate.
2. 18 years of age and receiving qualifying full-time education (within the meaning of paragraph 7 of Schedule 12 to the Act).	**2.** The person's birth certificate and a document signed by the principal or other appropriate officer of the recognised educational establishment, or by or on behalf of the person providing instruction by other comparable means, to the effect that the person is receiving full-time instruction at the establishment or by other comparable means.
3. Expectant mother.	**3.** A certificate, signed by a registered medical practitioner, as to the pregnancy.
4. Having borne a child in the previous 12 months.	**4.** The child's birth certificate.

SCHEDULE 3

Regulation 8(2) and (3)

CHARGES FOR MORE EXPENSIVE SUPPLIES AND REPAIRS – GENERAL DENTAL SERVICES

PART I

AMOUNT OF CHARGE

1. The amount of the charge which may be made and recovered under regulation 8(2) is, subject to paragraph 2, £x plus £y where–

(a) £x is the amount of the charge which would be payable by the patient under section 78 of the Act in respect of the supply or repair of the appliance if it were an appliance of the basic type;

(b) £y is the difference between–

(i) the cost of supplying or repairing the more expensive appliance; and

(ii) the fees payable to the dental practitioner in accordance with Determination I of the Statement of Dental Remuneration in respect of the supply or repair of an appliance of the basic type, disregarding for this purpose any maximum fee in respect of combinations of dentures.

2. The aggregate of £x and the charges payable by the patient under section 78 and 79 of the Act in respect of services provided in pursuance of the contract or arrangement other than the supply or repair of the appliance ("the other charges") shall not exceed £150, so that–

(a) where the other charges are £150 or more, the amount of the charge referred to in paragraph 1 is £y only;

(b) where the other charges are of an amount less than £150, £x shall not exceed the difference between that amount and £150.

PART II

PROCEDURE

1. A dental practitioner who agrees to a request referred to in regulation 8(2) shall–

(a) complete, on a dental estimate form, an estimate for the treatment of the patient, including the supply or repair of an appliance of the basic type;

(b) complete a further estimate, on the supplementary estimate form set out in Determination VI of the Statement of Dental Remuneration or on a form to the like effect, of the cost of supplying or repairing the more expensive appliance;

(c) require the patient to sign both estimates;

(d) submit both estimates to the Board for approval of the treatment.

2. If the Board approves the estimates, it shall determine and indicate in the appropriate parts of the dental estimate form–

(a) the amount of the charge to be made and recovered under sections 78 and 79 of the Act for the treatment set out in the estimate referred to in paragraph 1(a), other than for the supply or repair of an appliance of the basic type;

(b) the amount of the charge which may be made and recovered under regulation 8(2) for the supply or repair of the more expensive appliance.

3. It is a condition of the approval by the Board of any estimate submitted under paragraph 1 that the dental practitioner shall comply, in respect of any such estimate, with the conditions with respect to materials set out in Determination III of the Statement of Dental Remuneration.

SCHEDULE 4

Regulation 9(1)

MANNER OF DETERMINING CHARGE FOR REPLACEMENT

1. Where the Board, on considering an estimate submitted for the approval of a free replacement of a dental appliance supplied as part of general dental services, considers that there are grounds for believing that the replacement is necessitated by such an act or omission as is referred to in regulation 9(1), it may refer the matter to the Family Practitioner Committee for investigation.

2. The Family Practitioner Committee shall make such inquiry into the matter referred as it thinks fit and if either–

(a) in its opinion the circumstances so require; or

(b) the person supplied or (if he is under 16 years of age) the person in charge of him so requires,

the inquiry shall take the form of an oral hearing by a sub-committee of the Family Practitioner Committee appointed for the purpose which shall report to the Family Practitioner Committee on the matter.

3. The Family Practitioner Committee, having considered any report made by its sub-committee under paragraph 2,–

(a) shall determine whether the replacement is necessitated by an act or omission on the part of the person supplied or (if the act or omission occurred when the person supplied was under 16 years of age) of the person supplied or of the person having charge of him when the act or omission occurred; and

(b) if it is so necessitated, shall determine, in accordance with regulation 9(2) and (3), the amount of the charge to be made and recovered.

4. The Family Practitioner Committee shall communicate its determination to–

(a) the relevant person (within the meaning of regulation 9(4));

(b) the dental practitioner replacing the appliance;

(c) the Board.

Regulation 12(1)

SCHEDULE 5

REVOCATIONS

(1) *Regulations revoked*	(2) *References*	(3) *Extent of revocation*
National Health Service (General Dental Services) Regulations 1973	1973/1468	Part V Schedule 1, paragraph 29
National Health Service (Charges for Appliances) Regulations 1974	1974/284	Regulations 4 and 8
National Health Service (General Dental Services) Amendment Regulations 1980	1980/986	Regulation 2(3)
National Health Service (Dental Charges) Regulations 1988	1988/473	The whole Regulations

EXPLANATORY NOTE

(This Note is not part of the Regulations)

These Regulations replace regulations providing for the making and recovery of charges for dental appliances supplied or repaired under the National Health Service (NHS) in England and Wales and for other dental treatment provided as part of NHS general dental services. Accordingly, these Regulations provide for charges for the following:–

the supply of dentures and bridges, whether or not as part of general dental services (regulations 2, 4 and 6 and Schedule 1);

the provision of other dental treatment as part of general dental services (regulations 3, 4 and 6);

the supply or repair, whether or not as part of general dental services, of dental appliances of a type more expensive than is clinically necessary (regulation 8 and Schedule 3);

the replacement, as part of general dental services, of dental appliances lost or damaged by an act or omission of the patient (regulation 9 and Schedule 4).

(Charges for replacement and repair under the NHS, otherwise than as part of general dental services, of dental appliances lost or damaged by an act or omission of the patient remain subject to the more general provisions as to appliances contained in the National Health Service (Charges for Appliances) Regulations 1974.)

The Regulations provide in addition for conditions for statutory exemptions (regulation 5 and Schedule 2), discontinuation of general dental services where charges are not paid (regulation 10), the reduction of a dental practitioner's remuneration by the amount of the charge which is recoverable under the Regulations (regulation 11) and the revocation of the superseded Regulations on dental charges (regulation 12 and Schedule 5).

There are three changes of substance made by these Regulations.

First, the basis of the charge for the supply of all dentures and bridges is altered from a specified amount to that which applies to other treatment, namely a formula of 75% of the fees which are or would be payable to a dentist providing general dental services for the supply of a denture or bridge of the relevant type. This increases charges for dentures by an average of about 10% and charges for bridges of the Maryland type by about 1.5%. Other charges are unaffected.

Secondly, a provision authorising additional charges for certain types of conservative treatment (gold inlays, pinlays or crowns) more expensive than clinically necessary is removed.

Thirdly, the scope of the condition that documentary evidence be produced when a claim is made to be exempt from charges for dental appliances or other treatment as part of general dental services is extended to cases where exemption is claimed on grounds of being under 18 or under 19 and in full-time education (regulation 5 and Schedule 2), and the nature of the evidence to be produced in all cases of exemption is specified in the Regulations.

STATUTORY INSTRUMENTS

1989 No. 395

NATIONAL HEALTH SERVICE, ENGLAND AND WALES

The National Health Service (General Ophthalmic Services) Amendment Regulations 1989

Made - - - -	*8th March 1989*
Laid before Parliament	*10th March 1989*
Coming into force	*1st April 1989*

The Secretary of State for Health, in exercise of powers conferred by sections 38(1), (3), (4), (5), (6) and (7), 39 and 126(4) of the National Health Service Act 1977(**a**) and of all other powers enabling him in that behalf, hereby makes the following Regulations:–

Citation, commencement and interpretation

1.—(1) These Regulations may be cited as the National Health Service (General Ophthalmic Services) Amendment Regulations 1989 and shall come into force on 1st April 1989.

(2) In these Regulations, the "principal Regulations" means the National Health Service (General Ophthalmic Services) Regulations 1986(**b**).

Amendment of regulation 2 of the principal Regulations

2. In regulation 2(1) of the principal Regulations (interpretation) –

(a) after the definition of "the 1984 Act" there is inserted the following definition:–

" "capital limit" means the amount prescribed for the purposes of section 22(6) of the Social Security Act 1986(**c**) as it applies to income support;";

(b) after the definition of "Committee" there is inserted the following definition:–

" "complex appliance" means an optical appliance at least one lens of which –

(i) has a power in any one meridian of plus or minus 10 or more dioptres, or

(ii) is a lenticular lens;";

(**a**) 1977 c.49; *see* section 128(1) for the definition of "prescribed" and "regulations". Section 38 was amended by section 1(3) of the Health and Social Security Act 1984 (c.48) ("the 1984 Act"), and by the Health and Medicines Act 1988 (c.49), section 13; section 39 was amended by section 1(4) of, and paragraph 1 of Schedule 1 to, the 1984 Act and by paragraph 52 of Schedule 1 to the Health Services Act 1980 (c.53). Sections 38 and 39 were each modified by S.I. 1985/39, Article 7. (**b**) S.I. 1986/975 amended by S.I. 1988/486. (**c**) 1986 c.50; regulation 45 of the Income Support (General) Regulations 1987 (S.I. 1987/1967) has prescribed the amount of £6,000 as the capital limit.

(c) after the definition of "doctor" there are inserted the following definitions:–

" "eligible person" means a person who, in accordance with regulation 13, may have his sight tested under general ophthalmic services;

"family credit" means family credit under Part II of the Social Security Act 1986;

"general ophthalmic services" means the services which a contractor must provide pursuant to paragraph 10 of the terms of service;

"income support" means income support under Part II of the Social Security Act 1986 and includes personal expenses addition, special transition addition and transitional addition as defined in regulation 2(1) of the Income Support (Transitional) Regulations 1987(**a**);";

(d) after the definition of "locality" there is inserted the following definition:–

" "notice of entitlement" means a notice issued under regulation 7 of the Remission Regulations for the purposes of remission of charges under the Act;";

(e) after the definition of "qualifications" there is inserted the following definition:–

" "the Remission Regulations" means the National Health Service (Travelling Expenses and Remission of Charges) Regulations 1988(**b**) and a reference to those Regulations is to be construed as a reference to them as they have effect on the making of the National Health Service (General Ophthalmic Services) Amendment Regulations 1989 and as amended subsequently;";

(f) the definition of "sight test" is omitted.

Amendment of regulation 12 of the principal Regulations

3. In regulation 12 of the principal Regulations (payment for services) after paragraph (1) there is inserted –

"(1A) Where in accordance with regulation 13B(4) a Committee has paid to a patient in respect of a testing of sight an amount which exceeds the fee payable to the contractor, in accordance with the Statement, for that testing, it shall deduct the excess from remuneration otherwise payable to the contractor."

Substitution of regulation 13 of the principal Regulations

4. For regulation 13 (sight tests) of the principal Regulations there are substituted the following regulations –

"Sight Tests – eligibility

13.—(1) A person may have his sight tested under general ophthalmic services if, at the time of the testing of sight, he is any of the following –

(a) a person who is under the age of 16 years;

(b) a person who is under the age of 19 years and receiving qualifying full-time education within the meaning of section 38(2) of the Act;

(c) a person whose resources are treated in accordance with paragraph (2) as being less than, or equal to, his requirements;

(d) a person who requires to wear a complex appliance;

(e) a person who is registered blind or partially sighted under section 29 of the National Assistance Act 1948(**c**);

(f) a person who has been diagnosed as suffering from diabetes or glaucoma;

(g) a person who is aged 40 or over and is the parent, brother, sister or child of a person who has been diagnosed as suffering from glaucoma.

(**a**) S.I. 1987/1969, amended by S.I. 1988/521 and 670. (**b**) S.I. 1988/551. (**c**) 1948 c.29; section 29(2) and (3) were repealed by the Local Government Act 1972 (c.70).

(2) A person's resources shall be treated as being less than or equal to his requirements if –

(a) he is in receipt of income support;

(b) he is a member of the same family as a person who is in receipt of income support;

(c) he is in receipt of family credit;

(d) he is a member of the same family as a person who is in receipt of family credit;

(e) his income resources as calculated in accordance with regulation 6 of, and Schedule 1 to, the Remission Regulations for the purposes of remission of charges under the Act are less than or equal to his requirements as so calculated and his capital resources as so calculated do not exceed the capital limit; or

(f) he is a member of the same family as a person described in paragraph (e) of this paragraph.

(3) In paragraph (2)(b) and (f) "family" has the meaning assigned to it by section 20(11) of the Social Security Act 1986 as it applies to income support(**a**) and in paragraph (2)(d) it has the meaning assigned to it by section 20(11) of that Act as it applies to family credit(**b**).

Sight tests – applications

13A.—(1) An eligible person who wishes to have his sight tested under general ophthalmic services may make an application to any contractor for his sight to be tested.

(2) The application shall be made on a form provided for that purpose to contractors by the Committee and shall contain a written declaration signed by the applicant to the effect that he is an eligible person.

(3) In addition, a person who is an eligible person –

(a) but only by virtue of regulation 13(1)(c) and (2)(e) or (f) shall show to the contractor a current notice of entitlement;

(b) but only by virtue of regulation 13(1)(d), shall show to the contractor the prescription for a complex appliance issued to him on the occasion when his sight was last tested;

(c) but only by virtue of regulation 13(1)(f), shall on a form provided for that purpose to contractors by the Committee provide the contractor with the name and address of his doctor and give his consent to the Committee seeking confirmation of his diabetes or glaucoma from his doctor.

(4) A contractor to whom an application for a testing of sight is made shall, before making any test of the person's sight –

(a) subject to paragraph (5), satisfy himself that the person is an eligible person and that the requirements of paragraph (2) and such of the requirements of paragraph (3) as are applicable are met;

(b) ensure that particulars of the patient and the approximate date of the last testing, if any, of his sight are inserted in a sight test form by the patient or on his behalf; and

(c) satisfy himself that the testing of sight is necessary.

(5) Where an eligible person to whom paragraph (3)(b) applies is unable to meet its requirements, the contractor may, instead of satisfying himself that those requirements are met, satisfy himself that the person is an eligible person by referring to his own records or by measuring the power of the lenses of the person's existing optical appliance by means of a focimeter or other suitable means.

(**a**) 1986 c.50; *see* S.I. 1987/1967 regulations 14 to 16 as amended by S.I. 1988/1445 and 663. (**b**) *See* S.I. 1987/1913, regulations 6 to 9 as amended by S.I. 1988/660.

Sight test treated as a test under general ophthalmic services

13B.—(1) A person whose sight is tested by a contractor but who was not an eligible person immediately before the testing and –

(a) who is shown during the testing to fall within the description specified in sub-paragraph (d) of regulation 13(1); or

(b) who is shown, in accordance with paragraph (3), within 3 months after the testing to fall within either of the descriptions specified in sub-paragraphs (e) or (f) of regulation 13(2),

shall be taken for the purposes of the testing to have so fallen immediately before his sight was tested.

(2) Where paragraph (1) applies the testing shall be treated as a testing of sight under the Act for the purposes of regulation 8(1)(a) of the National Health Service (Optical Charges and Payments) Regulations 1989(**a**) as well as for the purposes specified in section 38(6)(i) and (ii) of the Act.

(3) For the purposes of paragraph (1)(b) a person is shown to fall within a description specified in sub-paragraph (e) or (f) of regulation 13(2) if he presents to the Committee a notice of entitlement which is effective for a period which includes the date of the testing of sight or for a period beginning no later than 14 days after the date of the testing of sight.

(4) Where a testing of a person's sight is treated by virtue of paragraphs (1)(b) and (3) as a testing of sight under the Act the Committee shall, on being presented with a receipt for, or other evidence of, any fee paid for the testing, and on being satisfied as to its amount, pay to that person an amount equal to that fee.".

Amendment of terms of service

5.—(1) Schedule 1 to the principal Regulations (terms of service) is amended according to the following provisions of this regulation.

(2) In paragraph 2, for sub-paragraph (c) there is substituted the following:–

"(c) regulation 9(2) to (6) of the National Health Service (Optical Charges and Payments) Regulations 1989(**b**);".

(3) In paragraph 5 (notices) for "the National Health Service (Payments for Optical Appliances) Regulations 1986" there is substituted "the National Health Service (Optical Charges and Payments) Regulations 1989".

Signed by authority of the Secretary of State for Health

D. Mellor
Minister of State,
Department of Health

8th March 1989

(**a**) S.I. 1989/396. (**b**) S.I. 1989/396.

EXPLANATORY NOTE

(This note is not part of the Regulations)

These Regulations amend the National Health Service (General Ophthalmic Services) Regulations 1986 which provide for the arrangements under which ophthalmic medical practitioners and ophthalmic opticians ("contractors") provide general ophthalmic services.

As a consequence of the Health and Medicines Act 1988, from 1st April 1989 only certain categories of persons will be entitled to sight tests under the general ophthalmic services. Those persons are specified by regulation 4 as children (including those under 19 in full-time education), persons entitled to income support or to family credit or to full remission of certain National Health Service (NHS) charges, persons needing complex optical appliances, the registered blind or partially sighted, diabetics, those suffering from glaucoma and certain relatives of those suffering from glaucoma. Regulation 4 also provides for those shown as a result of the sight test to need a complex optical appliance or who establish entitlement to full remission of NHS charges after the test to be treated as having had their sight tested under general ophthalmic services, so that any fee paid may be recovered from the Family Practitioner Committee. The appropriate adjustment is made to the contractor's remuneration (regulation 3).

STATUTORY INSTRUMENTS

1989 No. 396

NATIONAL HEALTH SERVICE, ENGLAND AND WALES

The National Health Service (Optical Charges and Payments) Regulations 1989

Made - - - -	*8th March 1989*
Laid before Parliament	*10th March 1989*
Coming into force -	*1st April 1989*

ARRANGEMENT OF REGULATIONS

PART V

Payments for cost of replacement or repair of optical appliances

PART VI

Miscellaneous

The Secretary of State for Health, in exercise of powers conferred by sections 38(1), 39 and 78(1) of, and paragraphs 2 and 2A of Schedule 12 to, the National Health Service Act 1977**(a)** and of all other powers enabling him in that behalf, hereby makes the following Regulations:–

(a) 1977 c.49; *see* sections 128(1) for the definition of "prescribed" and "regulations". Section 38 was modified by S.I. 1985/39 and amended by section 1(3) of the Health and Social Security Act 1984 (c.48) ("the 1984 Act") and by the Health and Medicines Act 1988 (c.49) ("the 1988 Act"), section 13; section 39 was modified by S.I. 1985/39 and amended by section 1(4) of, and paragraph 1 of Part I of Schedule 1 to, the 1984 Act and paragraph 52 of Schedule 1 to the Health Services Act 1980 (c.53). Paragraph 2(1) of Schedule 12 was substituted by the 1988 Act, Schedule 2, paragraph 8(1); and paragraph 2A of Schedule 12 was inserted by the 1984 Act, Schedule 1, Part I, paragraph 3 and amended by section 13(2) and (3) of the 1988 Act.

PART I

GENERAL

Citation, commencement and interpretation

1.—(1) These Regulations may be cited as the National Health Service (Optical Charges and Payments) Regulations 1989 and shall come into force on 1st April 1989.

(2) In these Regulations, unless the context otherwise requires–

"the Act" means the National Health Service Act 1977;

"capital limit" means the amount prescribed for the purposes of section 22(6) of the Social Security Act 1986**(a)** as it applies to income support;

"child" means a person who is under the age of 16 years;

"complex appliance" means an optical appliance at least one lens of which–

(a) has a power in any one meridian of plus or minus 10 or more dioptres, or

(b) is a lenticular lens;

"eligible person" is to be construed–

(a) for the purposes of Part III, in accordance with regulation 3(2);

(b) for the purposes of Parts IV and V, in accordance with regulation 8(2) to (5);

"face value" means, in relation to a voucher on which is marked a letter code specified in column 2 of Schedule 1, the amount specified in relation to it in column 3 of that Schedule, plus the amount of any increase provided for by paragraph 1 of Schedule 2;

"family credit" means family credit under Part II of the Social Security Act 1986;

"income support" means income support under Part II of the Social Security Act 1986 and includes personal expenses addition, special transition addition and transitional addition as defined in regulation 2(1) of the Income Support (Transitional) Regulations 1987**(b)**;

"minimum complex appliance payment" means, in relation to an optical appliance, the amount specified as such for the appliance in paragraph 2 of Schedule 2;

"NHS sight test fee" means, in relation to a testing of sight carried out either by an ophthalmic medical practitioner or by an optician, the fee payable, in accordance with the Statement published under regulation 10 of the Ophthalmic Services Regulations, to an optician in respect of a testing of sight;

"notice of entitlement" means a notice issued under regulation 7 of the Remission Regulations for the purposes of remission of charges under the Act;

"opthalmic list" means a list, prepared and published pursuant to regulations made under section 39(a) of the Act of medical practitioners and opticians who undertake to provide general ophthalmic services**(c)**;

"Ophthalmic Services Regulations" means the National Health Service (General Opthalmic Services) Regulations 1986**(d)**;

"optician" means an ophthalmic optician;

"patient" means a person whose sight has been tested whether under the Act or otherwise;

"patient's contribution" means the amount specified under regulation 7(5) of the Remission Regulations as that for which there is no entitlement under those Regulations to remission of charges;

"redemption value" is to be construed–

(a) for the purposes of Part III, in accordance with regulation 7;

(b) for the purposes of Part IV, in accordance with reguation 15;

(c) for the purposes of Part V, in accordance with regulation 20;

(a) 1986 c.50; regulation 45 of S.I. 1987/1967 has prescribed the amount of £6,000 as the capital limit.
(b) S.I. 1987/1969 amended by S.I. 1988/521 and 670.
(c) *See* S.I. 1986/975, regulation 6.
(d) S.I. 1986/975 amended by S.I. 1988/486 and 1989/395.

"the Remission Regulations" means the National Health Service (Travelling Expenses and Remission of Charges) Regulations 1988**(a)** and a reference to those Regulations is to be construed as a reference to them as they have effect on the making of these Regulations and as amended subsequently;

"replacement" does not include the replacement of an optical appliance rendered unserviceable by fair wear and tear;

"responsible authority" means–

(a) in relation to a voucher completed pursuant to regulation 4, the Family Practitioner Committee for the locality in which the testing of sight to which it relates takes place;

(b) in relation to a voucher issued pursuant to regulation 9 or regulation 10 or completed pursuant to regulation 17 otherwise than by a health authority, the Family Practitioner Committee for the locality in which the supply, replacement or repair of the optical appliance to which it relates takes or is to take place;

(c) in relation to a voucher issued pursuant to regulation 11 or completed pursuant to regulation 17 by a health authority, the health authority which issues or completes it;

"small glasses" means glasses the lens apertures of which have datum centres not more than 56 millimetres apart; and for this purpose "datum centre" is to be construed in accordance with Part I of British Standard 3521: 1962 (Glossary of Terms relating to Ophthalmic Lenses and Spectacle Frames) published by the British Standard Institution as effective immediately before 8th March 1989;

"supplier" includes a person replacing or repairing an optical appliance;

"supply" includes the replacement of an optical appliance rendered unserviceable by fair wear and tear;

"voucher" means–

(a) in Part III, a voucher form supplied to those whose names are included in an ophthalmic list by the Secretary of State;

(b) in Part IV, a voucher form supplied–

(i) where a testing of sight is carried out otherwise than by a health authority by the Secretary of State to the person who carries it out or to the Family Practitioner Committee;

(ii) where a testing of sight is carried out by a health authority, by the health authority;

(c) in Part V, a voucher form supplied to a supplier, by the Secretary of State;

for the purposes of enabling a payment to be made under these Regulations.

(3) For the purposes of Schedule 1–

(a) where an optical appliance has lenses described in different paragraphs in column 1 of Schedule 1, the face value of a voucher for the appliance shall be determined according to whichever lens would provide the greater face value; and

(b) where an optical appliance has a bifocal lens, the power of the lens shall be determined according to the power of that segment of the lens designed to correct a defect in distant sight; and

(c) a monocle shall be treated as though it were glasses.

(4) In these Regulations, unless the context otherwise requires, a reference–

(a) to a numbered regulation, Part or Schedule is to the regulation in, Part of, or Schedule to, these Regulations bearing that number;

(b) in a regulation to a numbered paragraph is to the paragraph in that regulation bearing that number;

(c) in Schedule 1 to a numbered paragraph is to the paragraph in column 1 in that Schedule bearing that number.

(a) S.I. 1988/551.

PART II

CHARGES

Charges for glasses and contact lenses

2.—(1) A charge of such sum as may be determined by or in accordance with directions given by the Secretary of State shall be made and recovered in accordance with paragraph (2) in respect of the supply of glasses and contact lenses under the Act.

(2) Where a charge is payble by virtue of paragraph (1), the health authority, or other person on its behalf, that supplies or is to supply the glasses or contact lenses may–

(a) on arranging to supply the glasses or contact lenses, make the charge; and

(b) on supplying the glasses or contact lenses or having them available for supply, recover the charge from the patient (if it has not previously been paid).

PART III

PAYMENTS TOWARDS COST OF SIGHT TESTS

Eligibility—sight tests

3.—(1) A payment shall be made as provided for by this Part of these Regulations to contribute to the cost of a testing of sight which the responsible authority accepts as having been incurred by an eligible person.

(2) An eligible person is a person whose income resources, as calculated in accordance with regulation 6 of, and Schedule 1 to, the Remission Regulations for the purposes of remission of charges under the Act, exceed his requirements as so calculated, but whose patient's contribution does not exceed the NHS sight test fee and whose capital resources as so calculated do not exceed the capital limit.

Completion and use of voucher—sight tests

4.—(1) A person who wishes a payment to be made by virtue of this regulation in his case shall–

(a) apply to the Secretary of State for a notice of entitlement;

(b) apply for his sight to be tested by an ophthalmic medical practitioner or optician whose name is included in an ophtalmic list;

(c) indicate to that practitioner or optician that he is an eligible person at the time of the application;

(d) show to him a current notice of entitlement and permit him to copy such details as may be required for the purposes of regulation 5(2)(b)(ii).

(2) The ophthalmic medical practitioner or optician may then duly complete the relevant parts of the voucher with the name and address of the patient and the date of the testing of sight.

(3) The person whose sight is or is to be tested shall sign on the voucher a declaration in writing to the effect that he is an eligible person.

(4) The ophthalmic medical practitioner or optician may use the voucher as being in substitution for payment by the patient of an amount equal to its redemption value, being part of the cost incurred for the testing of sight.

Payments to sight testers

5.—(1) The responsible authority shall, if the conditions specified in paragraph (2) are fulfilled, make a payment of the voucher's redemption value to an ophthalmic medical practitioner or optician who has used a voucher in accordance with regulation 4(4).

(2) The conditions specified in paragraph (1) are that–

(a) the patient has signed the declaration referred to in regulation 4(3);

(b) the ophthalmic medical practitioner or optician has–
  (i) made a claim for a payment on a duly completed voucher to the responsible authority within the period of three months beginning with the date of the testing of sight, and
  (ii) informed the responsible authority of the amount of the patient's contribution.

Payments to patients in respect of sight tests

6.—(1) A payment may be made under this regulation by the responsible authority to an eligble person who incurs the cost of a testing of sight by an ophthalmic medical practitioner or optician whose name is included in an ophthalmic list, without a voucher being completed in accordance with regulation 4.

(2) A patient who wishes to receive a payment under this regulation shall–
(a) if he did not apply to the Secretary of State for a notice of entitlement before the date on which his sight was tested, apply to him for such a notice within the period of 14 days beginning with that date;
(b) apply to the responsible authority for a payment within the period of three months beginning with that date; and
(c) produce to the responsible authority within that period–
  (i) a notice of entitlement effective for a period including the date on which his sight was tested or for a period beginning no later than 14 days after that date, and
  (ii) the receipt for any fee paid for the testing of sight.

(3) On an application made in accordance with paragraph (2), the responsible authority shall, if satisfied as to the cost incurred for the testing of sight, make a payment to the patient of an amount equal to the redemption value of the voucher which could have been completed under regulation 4 if the patient had satisified the requirements of regulation 4(1).

Redemption value of voucher for sight test

7. For the purposes of this Part of these Regulations the redemption value of a voucher is the amount, if any, by which the patient's contribution falls short of the lesser of–
(a) the NHS sight test fee; or
(b) the full cost which would have been incurred by the patient for the sight test but for these Regulations.

PART IV

PAYMENTS FOR COST OF SUPPLY OF OPTICAL APPLIANCES

Eligibility—supply of optical appliances

8.—(1) A payment shall be made as provided for by this Part of these Regulations to meet, or to contribute towards, the cost incurred (whether by way of charge under the Act or otherwise) for the supply of an optical appliance for which a prescription has been given in consequence of a testing of sight of an eligible person–
(a) which took place under the Act; or
(b) which took place otherwise than under the Act and within the locality in which the person whose sight was tested normally resides or within a reasonable travelling distance of his home.

(2) An eligible person is a person who at the time of the supply of the optical appliance is any of the following:–
(a) a child;

(b) a person under the age of 19 years and receiving qualifying full-time education within the meaning of paragraph 7 of Schedule 12 to the Act**(a)**;

(c) a person whose resources are treated, in accordance with paragraph (3), as being less than his requirements;

(d) a person whose income resources, as calculated in accordance with regulation 6 of, and Schedule 1 to, the Remission Regulations for the purposes of remission of charges under the Act, are equal to or exceed his requirements as so calculated but whose patient's contribution is nil or is less than the face value of a voucher issued to him under this Part of these Regulations and whose capital resources do not exceed the capital limit;

(e) a person for whom a prescription is issued for a complex appliance.

(3) A person's resources shall be treated as being less than his requirements if–

(a) he is in receipt of income support;

(b) he is a member of the same family as a person who is in receipt of income support;

(c) he is in receipt of family credit;

(d) he is a member of the same family as a person who is in receipt of family credit;

(e) his income resources as calculated in accordance with regulation 6 of, and Schedule 1 to, the Remission Regulations for the purposes of remission of charges under the Act, are less than his requirements as so calculated and his capital resources as so calculated do not exceed the capital limit; or

(f) he is a member of the same family as a person described in paragraph (e) of this paragraph.

(4) In paragraph (3)(b) and (f) "family" has the meaning assigned to it by section 20(11) of the Social Security Act 1986 as it applies to income support**(b)** and in paragraph (2)(d) it has the meaning assigned to it by virtue of section 20(11) of that Act as it applies to family credit**(c)**.

(5) For the purposes of regulation 11 and other provisions of this Part of these Regulations as they apply to payments where the testing of sight was by a health authority, a person is also an eligible person if, because of the frequency with which the condition of his eyes changes, he is considered by the health authority to be non-tolerant of his existing optical appliance.

Issue of vouchers by ophthalmic medical practitioners or opticians

9.—(1) A person making an application for a testing of sight pursuant to regulation 13 of the Ophthalmic Services Regulations who considers that he may be an eligible person and wishes a payment to be made under these Regulations in his case shall indicate to the ophthalmic medical practitioner or optician to whom the application is made that he may be an eligible person.

(2) An ophthalmic medical practitioner or optician who, following a testing of sight under the Ophthalmic Services Regulations, issues a prescription for an optical appliance to a patient–

(a) who has indicated that he may be an eligible person; or

(b) who (whether or not he has so indicated) is issued with a prescription for a complex appliance,

shall, in the circumstances described in paragraph (4) but subject to paragraph (5), issue to the patient a voucher relating to the optical appliance prescribed on the same occasion as he issues the prescription in accordance with paragraph 10(1) of Schedule 1 of the Ophthalmic Services Regulations.

(3) The ophthalmic medical practitioner or optician issuing the voucher shall sign it and shall–

(a) mark on it the letter code specified in column 2 of Schedule 1 which relates to the type of optical appliance prescribed as set out in column 1 of that Schedule;

(a) Paragraph 7 was substituted by the Health Services Act 1980 (c.53), Schedule 5, paragraph 4.
(b) 1986 c.50; *see* S.I. 1987/1967 regulations 14 to 16 as amended by S.I. 1988/1445 and 663.
(c) S.I. 1987/1973 regulations 6 to 9 as amended by S.I. 1988/660.

(b) duly complete the relevant parts of the voucher with the name and address of the patient, the patient's age if under 19, particulars of the prescription issued to the patient, the date on which the patient's sight was tested and the date of issue of the voucher.

(4) The circumstances referred to in paragraph (2) are where the ophthalmic medical practitioner or optician, having consulted any records which he has relating to the patient and made such enquiry of the patient as he considers relevant, is satisfied that–

(a) the patient requires an optical appliance for the first time or an optical appliance to a prescription the particulars of which differ from those relating to his existing appliance; or

(b) the patient requires an optical appliance because his existing optical appliance has been rendered unserviceable by fair wear and tear.

(5) Where a patient requires an optical appliance to a prescription the particulars of which differ from those relating to his existing appliance only because the patient is non-tolerant of that appliance, and has been so since it was supplied to him, no voucher shall be issued unless the Family Practioner Committee responsible for the arrangements for the sight test, being satisfied that the prescription for that existing appliance was clinically correct, has authorised the issue of a voucher.

(6) Unless regulation 10(4) applies, not more than one voucher shall be issued to a patient in respect of any one optical appliance prescribed.

(7) A person making an application to an ophthalmic medical practitioner or optician for a testing of sight otherwise than under general ophthalmic services who considers that he may be an eligible person by virtue of regulation 8(2)(d) and wishes a payment to be made under these Regulations in his case shall indicate to the ophthalmic medical practitioner or optician to whom the application is made that he may be an eligible person; and that practitioner or optician may, if he issues a prescription for an optical appliance, issue a voucher relating to it in accordance with paragraphs (2) to (6) as though the testing of sight were carried out and the prescription were issued under general ophthalmic services.

Issue of vouchers by Family Practitioner Committees

10.—(1) Subject to paragraph (2), a patient whose sight has been tested by an ophthalmic medical practitioner or optician otherwise than under the Act who considers that he may be an eligible person by virtue of regulation 8(2)(d) and wishes a payment to be made under these Regulations in his case may, if he was not issued with a voucher under regulation 9(7), apply in writing for a voucher to the Family Practitioner Committee for the locality in which his sight was tested.

(2) An application made under paragraph (1) shall–

(a) state that the patient may be an eligible person by virtue of regulation 8(2)(d);

(b) be accompanied by the prescription issued to the patient or a copy of it; and

(c) be made within the period of one month beginning with the date of the testing of sight but before the patient arranges for the supply of his optical appliance.

(3) On an application made in accordance with paragraph (2) the responsible authority shall issue a voucher relating to the optical appliance prescribed and shall–

(a) mark on it the letter code specified in column 2 of Schedule 1 which relates to the type of optical appliance prescribed as set out in column 1 of that Schedule;

(b) duly complete the relevant parts of the voucher with the name and address of the patient, the patient's age if under 19, particulars of the prescription issued to the patient, the date on which the patient's sight was tested and the date of issue of the voucher; and

(c) return to the patient any prescription that he may have submitted.

(4) Where, on an application by a patient within 6 months of a voucher having been issued to him under regulation 9(2) or (7), a Family Practitioner Commmittee is satisfied, having made such enquiries as it considers relevant, that the voucher has been lost or destroyed without having been presented to a supplier of optical appliances, it may issue to the patient a replacement voucher completed in accordance with paragraph (3)(a) and (b), but with the date of issue of the voucher being that on which the replacement is issued.

Issue of vouchers by health authorities

11.—(1) A person whose sight is tested by a health authority who considers that he may be an eligible person and wishes a payment to be made under these Regulations in his case shall indicate to that health authority that he may be an eligible person.

(2) A health authority which, following a testing of sight, issues a prescription for an optical appliance to a patient–

(a) who has indicated that he may be an eligible person;

(b) who (whether or not he has so indicated) is issued with a prescription for a complex appliance; or

(c) who is an eligible person by virtue of regulation 8(5),

shall issue to the patient a voucher relating to the optical appliance prescribed.

(3) The health authority issuing the voucher shall–

(a) mark on it the letter code specified in column 2 of Schedule 1 which relates to the type of optical appliance prescribed as set out in column 1 of that Schedule;

(b) duly complete the relevant parts of the voucher with the name and address of the patient, the patient's age if under 19, particulars of the prescription issued to the patient, the date on which the patient's sight was tested and the date of issue of the voucher.

Use of vouchers for supply of optical appliances

12.—(1) Subject to paragraphs (4) and (5), a patient to whom a voucher, duly completed in accordance with regulation 9, 10 or 11, has been issued may present it to a supplier who supplies or is to supply him with an optical appliance, provided that the arrangements for supply are made within 6 months of the date on which the voucher was issued.

(2) A supplier may accept the voucher in substitution for payment by the patient of an amount equal to its redemption value, being the whole or part of the cost incurred for the supply of an optical appliance.

(3) A voucher relating to glasses may be accepted in connection with the supply of contact lenses.

(4) Before presenting the voucher to the supplier the patient shall sign on the voucher–

(a) a declaration in writing to the effect that he is an eligible person, indicating the grounds of his eligibility;

(b) an undertaking in writing to the effect that, if he is unable to show that he is an eligible person, he will pay to the responsible authority an amount equal to the voucher's redemption value.

(5) A patient who is an eligible person only by virtue of regulation 8(2)(d) or by virtue of his resources being treated in accordance with regulation 8(3)(e) or (f) as being less than his requirements shall–

(a) before presenting the voucher to the supplier, apply to the Secretary of State for a notice of entitlement; and

(b) on the same occasion as he presents the supplier with a voucher in accordance with paragraph (1), show a current notice of entitlement to the supplier and permit him to copy such details as may be required for the purposes of regulation 13(2)(c)(iii).

Payments to suppliers

13.—(1) Except where it was the supplier, the responsible authority shall, if the conditions specified in paragraph (2) are fulfilled, make a payment of a voucher's redemption value to a supplier who has accepted the voucher from a patient in accordance with regulation 12.

(2) The conditions referred to in paragraph (1) are that–

(a) the patient has signed the declaration and undertaking referred to in regulation 12(4) and acknowledged receipt on the voucher of the optical appliance supplied to him;

(b) the optical appliance is not sold or supplied in contravention of section 21(1) of the Opticians Act 1958**(a)**;

(c) the supplier has–

(i) made and kept a written record of the supply and issued to the patient a receipt for any money received from the patient,

(ii) made a claim for a payment on a duly completed voucher to the responsible authority, within the period of 3 months beginning with the date of supply of the optical appliance,

(iii) where the patient has shown a notice of entitlement to him, informed the responsible authority of the amount of the patient's contribution, if any, and

(iv) where the claim relates to a voucher the value of which is increased in accordance with paragraph 1(1)(e) of Schedule 2, certified that the glasses supplied were small glasses.

Payments to patients in health authority cases

14.—(1) A payment may be made under this regulation to a patient who–

(a) has been issued by a health authority with a voucher only because he may be an eligible person by virtue of regulation 8(2)(d), or by virtue of his resources being treated in accordance with regulation 8(3)(e) or (f), as being less than his requirements; and

(b) incurs cost for the supply of an optical appliance without first having obtained a notice of entitlement and without presenting his voucher to a supplier.

(2) A patient who wishes a payment to made to him under this regulation shall–

(a) apply to the Secretary of State for a notice of entitlement;

(b) sign the declaration and undertaking referred to in regulation 12(4);

(c) within the period of three months beginning with the date on which he was supplied with the optical appliance, apply to the responsible authority for a payment and provide that authority with–

(i) the voucher issued to him,

(ii) a statement of the amount of his patient's contribution, if any, and

(iii) evidence of the cost incurred for the supply of the optical appliance.

(3) On an application made in accordance with paragraph (2), the responsible authority shall, if satisfied–

(a) that the patient was issued with a notice of entitlement;

(b) as to the amount of the patient's contribution; and

(c) as to the cost incurred for the supply of the optical appliance,

make a payment to the patient of the voucher's redemption value.

Redemption value of voucher for supply of optical appliances

15.—(1) Where an optical appliance was supplied otherwise than under the Act the redemption value of a voucher is, subject to paragraphs (3) to (5), the lesser of–

(a) the full cost which would have been payable by the patient for the supply but for these Regulations;

(b) the face value of the voucher.

(2) Where an optical appliance was supplied under the Act, the redemption value of a voucher is, subject to paragraphs (3) to (5), the lesser of–

(a) the amount of the charge under section 78(1) of the Act which would have been payable by the patient for the supply but for these Regulations;

(b) the face value of the voucher.

(3) In relation to payments to be made because of a person's eligibility by virtue of

(a) 1958 c.32; section 21 was amended by the Health and Social Security Act 1984 (c.48), section 1(1) and by the Health and Medicines Act 1988 (c.49), section 13(6) and (7).

regulation 8(2)(d), the amounts taken for the purposes of paragraph (1)(a) and (b) or paragraph (2)(a) and (b) shall, subject to paragraph (4), be reduced–

(a) where no voucher was completed in accordance with Part III in respect of the testing of the patient's sight, by the amount of the patient's contribution;

(b) where such a voucher was completed and for the purposes of regulation 7 the patient's contribution exceeded the lesser of the amounts specified in regulation 7(a) and (b), by the amount of the excess.

(4) If a reduction made under paragraph (3) in the case of a patient for whom a prescription was issued for a complex appliance would render the redemption value of the voucher less than the minimum complex appliance payment, that value shall be the minimum complex appliance payment.

(5) Where the patient was an eligible person only because a prescription was issued for him for a complex appliance, the redemption value of a voucher shall be the minimum complex appliance payment, except that where–

(a) the appliance was supplied under the Act; and

(b) in accordance with directions given pursuant to regulation 2(1), the amount of a charge made for the supply under section 78(1) of the Act would, but for any maximum charge specified in the directions, have exceeded by any amount the charge actually made,

the redemption value shall be reduced by the amount of the excess.

PART V

PAYMENTS FOR COST OF REPLACEMENT OR REPAIR OF OPTICAL APPLIANCES

Eligibility – replacement or repair

16.—(1) A payment shall be made as provided for by this Part of these Regulations to meet, or contribute towards, any cost accepted by the responsible authority as having been incurred (whether by way of charge under the Act or otherwise) for the replacement or repair of an optical appliance for which a prescription is given in consequence of a testing of sight of–

(a) a child, where the appliance needs replacement or repair in consequence of loss or damage;

(b) a person of any description specified in regulation 8(2)(c), (d) or (e) suffering from illness, where the appliance needs replacement or repair in consequence of its loss or damage and the responsible authority is satisfied, after making such enquiries as it considers relevant, that the loss or damage would not have occurred but for that illness.

(2) No payment shall be made by virtue of paragraph (1)(a) or (b) unless the responsible authority is satisfied, after making such enquiries as it considers relevant, that the full cost of replacement or repair cannot be met under the terms of any warranty, insurance or other arrangement made with its supplier or manufacturer.

Completion of vouchers

17.—(1) A patient who considers that a payment may be made under this Part of these Regulations in his case in respect of the replacement or repair of his optical appliance may indicate to the supplier that he wishes such a payment may be made.

(2) In the case of a replacement, the supplier may–

(a) mark on a voucher the letter code specified in column 2 of Schedule 1 which relates to the type of optical appliance to be replaced as set out in column 1 of that Schedule;

(b) duly complete the relevant parts of the voucher with the name and address of the patient, the patient's age if under 16 and the date of issue of the voucher.

(3) In the case of a repair, the supplier may–

(a) mark on a voucher the letter code specified in column 2 of Schedule 1 which relates to the type of optical appliance to be repaired as set out in column 1 of that Schedule;

(b) indicate on the voucher the nature of the repair of the appliance to be undertaken and, in particular, whether it comprises–

(i) the replacement or repair of one or more lenses included in the appliance, and, if so of how many,

(ii) the repair of a frame and, if so, whether it is of the whole frame, the front of a frame or one or both sides of a frame;

(c) duly complete the relevant parts of the voucher with the name and address of the patient, the patient's age if under 16 and the date of issue of the voucher.

(4) The patient shall sign on the voucher–

(a) a declaration in writing to the effect that he is an eligible person, indicating the grounds of his eligibility;

(b) a declaration in writing to the effect that the optical appliance cannot be replaced or repaired free of charge under the terms of any warranty, insurance or other arrangement made with its supplier or manufacturer; and

(c) an undertaking in writing to the effect that, if he is unable to show that he is an eligible person, he will pay to the responsible authority an amount equal to the voucher's redemption value.

(5) A patient who is an eligible person only by virtue of regulation 8(2)(d) or only by virtue of his resources being treated in accordance with regulation 8(3)(e) or (f) as being less than his requirements shall show a current notice of entitlement to the supplier and permit him to copy such details as may be required for the purposes of regulation 19(2)(b)(iv).

(6) In a case to which regulation 16(1)(b) applies, a supplier intending to use the voucher under regulation 18 shall first submit it to the responsible authority so that it may be satisfied as to the circumstances in which the loss or damage occurred and give its approval to the use of the voucher.

Use of vouchers for replacement or repair

18. The supplier may use the voucher as being in substitution for payment by the patient of an amount equal to its redemption value, being the whole or part of the cost incurred for the replacement or repair.

Payments to suppliers for replacement or repair

19.—(1) Except where it was the supplier, the responsible authority shall, if the conditions specified in paragraph (2) are fulfilled, make a payment of a voucher's redemption value to a supplier who has used a voucher in accordance with regulation 18.

(2) The conditions referred to in paragraph (1) are that–

(a) the patient has signed the declarations and undertaking referred to in regulation 17(4) and acknowledged on the voucher that the optical appliance has been replaced or repaired; and

(b) the supplier has–

(i) made and kept a written record of the replacement or repair and issued to the patient a receipt for any money received from the patient;

(ii) obtained any prior approval required by regulation 17(6);

(iii) made a claim for payment on a duly completed voucher to the responsible authority within the period of 3 months beginning with the date of the replacement or repair of the optical appliance; and

(iv) where the person has shown a notice of entitlement to him, informed the responsible authority of the amount of the patient's contribution, if any.

Redemption value of voucher for replacement or repair

20.—(1) Subject to paragraph (4), the redemption value of a voucher shall, in the case of a replacement, be the lesser of–

(a) the full cost which would have been payable by the patient for the replacement but for these Regulations;

(b) the face value of the voucher or, in the case of the replacement of one only of a pair of contact lenses, £26.50.

(2) Subject to paragraph (4), the redemption value of a voucher shall, in the case of the repair of an appliance be the lesser of–

(a) the full cost which would have been payable by the patient for the repair but for these Regulations;

(b) the amount specified in column 2 of Schedule 3 which relates to the type of optical appliance repaired (identified in that column by reference to the relevant letter code as specified in Schedule 1) and to the nature of the repair specified in column 1 of Schedule 3, together with any increase provided for by Schedule 2.

(3) Where more than one repair is made to an appliance the amount taken for the purposes of paragraph (2)(b) as being specified in Schedule 3 shall be the aggregate of the relevant amounts ascertained in accordance with Schedule 3, except that the element of the value of a voucher which relates to the repair of a frame shall not exceed £7.40.

(4) In the case of a person who was eligible for a payment to be made in his case only by virtue of regulation 8(2)(d), the amounts taken for the purpose of paragraphs (1)(a) and (b) and (2)(a) and (b) shall be reduced by the patient's contribution.

PART VI
MISCELLANEOUS

Amounts wrongly paid

21.—(1) Where a person who is not an eligible person declares on a voucher that he is an eligible person and in consequence the responsible authority makes a payment under these Regulations, the person who makes the declaration shall repay the amount of that payment to the responsible authority.

(2) Where a supplier makes a claim for payment to the responsible authority, representing that the conditions specified in regulation 5(2), 13(2) or 19(2) are fulfilled, but those conditions are not fulfilled and the authority makes a payment to the supplier under these Regulations, it may recover the amount of that payment from the supplier.

Signatures

22.—(1) A signature required by these regulations may be given–

(a) on behalf of a child by either parent or, in the absence of both parents, the guardian or other adult person who has the care of the child;

(b) on behalf of any other person who is incapable of giving the signature, by a relative or any other adult who has the care of that person; or

(c) on behalf of any person under 18 years of age–

 (i) in the care of any authority to whose care he has been committed under the provisions of the Children and Young Persons Act 1969**(a)** or which has received him into care under the Child Care Act 1980**(b)**, by a person duly authorised by that authority;

 (ii) in the care of a voluntary organisation, by that organisation or a person duly authorised by them.

Revocations

23. The Regulations specified in column (1) of Schedule 3 are revoked.

Signed by authority of the Secretary of State for Health

D. Mellor
Minister of State,
Department of Health

8th March 1989.

(a) 1969 c.54.
(b) 1980 c.5.

Regulations 1(2), 9(3)(a), 10(3)(a), 11(3)(a), 17(2)(a) and (3)(a)

SCHEDULE 1

VOUCHER LETTER CODES AND FACE VALUES – SUPPLY AND REPLACEMENT

1 *Type of Optical Appliance*	2 *Letter Code*	3 *Face Value of Voucher*
1. Glasses with single vision lenses of a power (plus or minus) not exceeding– (a) as respects any spherical power, 6 dioptres; (b) as respects any cylindrical power, 2 dioptres.	A	£17.00
2. Glasses with single vision lenses not falling within paragraph 1 or 3.	B	£28.00
3. Glasses with single vision lenses– (a) of a spherical power (plus or minus) exceeding 20 dioptres; (b) of a spherical power (plus or minus) exceeding 10 dioptres with any cylindrical power; (c) of a cylindrical power (plus or minus) exceeding 6 dioptres; or (d) in lenticular form.	C	£46.00
4. Glasses with bifocal lenses of a power (plus or minus) not exceeding– (a) as respects any spherical power, 6 dioptres; (b) as respects any cylindrical power, 2 dioptres.	D	£32.75
5. Glasses with bifocal lenses not falling within paragraph 4 or 6.	E	£58.00
6. Glasses with prism segment bifocal lenses or glasses with bifocal lenses– (a) of a spherical power (plus or minus) exceeding 20 dioptres; (b) of a spherical power (plus or minus) exceeding 10 dioptres with any cylindrical power; (c) of a cylindrical power (plus or minus) exceeding 6 dioptres; and (d) in lenticular form.	F	£98.00
7. Glasses not falling within any of paragraphs 1 to 6 for which a prescription is given in consequence of a testing of sight by a health authority.	G	£98.00
8. Contact lenses for which a prescription is given in consequence of a testing of sight by a health authority.	H	£26.50 per lens

SCHEDULE 2

Regulations 1(2), 20(2)(b)

PRISMS, TINTS, PHOTOCHROMIC LENSES, SMALL AND SPECIAL GLASSES AND COMPLEX APPLIANCES

1.—(1) The amounts in column 3 of Schedule 1 and column 2 of Schedule 3 and in paragraph 2(a) and (b) of this Schedule shall be increased as follows:–

(a) by £3.75 in respect of each single vision lens containing a necessary prism;

(b) by £4.75 in respect of each other lens containing a necessary prism;

(c) by £1.90 in respect of each necessary single vision tinted lens;

(d) by £2.40 in respect of each necessary other tinted lens;

(e) by £33.00 in the case of supply or replacement of the glasses or repair of the whole frame, by £29.35 in the case of repair of the front of the frame and £15.85 in the case of repair of a side of a frame in respect of small glasses,

(f) where the voucher is issued or completed by a health authority, by £1.90 in respect of each necessary single vision photochromic lens and by £2.40 in respect of each necessary other photochromic lens;

(g) where the voucher is issued or completed by a health authority, by £33.00 in respect of glasses the frame of which is certified by the health authority as being required to be specially manufactured on account of the patient's facial characteristics.

(2) The increases provided for by sub-paragraph (1)(e), (f) and (g) of this paragraph do not apply in the case of a voucher relating to glasses if it is accepted in connection with the supply or replacement of contact lenses.

(3) In sub-paragraph (1) of this paragraph "necessary" in relation to a prism or a tinted or photochromic lens means that the prism, tint or photochromic quality has been prescribed on the basis of clinical need.

(4) Where the face value of a voucher is increased in accordance with sub-paragraph (1)(g) of this paragraph, it may not be further increased in accordance with sub-paragraph (1)(e) of this paragraph.

2. The minimum complex appliance payment is–

(a) for a complex appliance with single vision lenses only, £3.25;

(b) for any other complex appliance, £18.00;

plus, in each case, the amount of any increase provided for by paragraph 1 of this Schedule.

SCHEDULE 3

Regulation 20(2) and (3)

VOUCHER VALUES – REPAIR

1 *Nature of repair to appliance*	2 *Letter Codes – Values* A £	B £	C £	D £	E £	F and G £
Repair or replacement of one lens	4.80	10.30	19.30	12.70	25.30	45.30
Repair or replacement of two lenses	9.60	20.60	38.60	25.35	50.60	90.60
Repair or replacement of–						
the front of a frame	6.60	6.60	6.60	6.60	6.60	6.60
a side of a frame	3.60	3.60	3.60	3.60	3.60	3.60
the whole frame	7.40	7.40	7.40	7.40	7.40	7.40

Regulation 23

SCHEDULE 4

REGULATIONS REVOKED

1 *Regulations revoked*	2 *References*
The National Health Service (Payments for Optical Appliances) Regulations 1986	S.I. 1986/976
The National Health Service (Payments for Optical Appliances) Amendment Regulations 1986	S.I. 1986/1136
The National Health Service (Payments for Optical Appliances) Amendment Regulations 1988	S.I. 1988/428
The National Health Service (Payments for Optical Appliances) Amendment (No. 2) Regulations 1988	S.I. 1988/552
The National Health Service (Payments for Optical Appliances) Amendment (No. 3) Regulations 1988	S.I. 1988/1435
The National Health Service (Payments for Optical Appliances) Amendment (No. 4) Regulations 1988	S.I. 1988/1935

EXPLANATORY NOTE

(This note is not part of the Regulations)

These Regulations introduce a scheme for a contribution to be made by Family Practitioner Committees (FPCs) towards the cost incurred by certain people (specified in regulation 3) for a sight test (Part III) and a scheme for payments to be made by FPCs and Health Authorities (HAs) in respect of the cost incurred by certain categories of persons (specified in regulation 16) for the replacement or repair of optical appliances (Part V). In addition the Regulations retain with modifications the scheme (introduced in 1986) for payments to be made by FPCs and HAs in respect of the cost incurred by certain categories of persons (specified in regulation 8) for the supply of optical appliances (Part IV). Glasses and contact lenses will continue to be supplied by HAs as part of the hospital eye service and regulation 2 enables a charge to be made for those supplies (Part II).

Under Part III of these Regulations persons who are eligible for a contribution to be made towards the cost of their sight test are those who are entitled to partial remission of National Health Service (NHS) charges if the amount of the patient contribution does not exceed the standard amount payable to opticians for sight tests under the NHS (sight test fee) and whose sight is tested an ophthalmic medical practitioner or optician whose name is included in the opthalmic list. The amount of the payment varies according to the patient's means but cannot exceed the sight test fee.

A person is eligible under Part IV of these Regulations if his sight is tested under the NHS or (in limited circumstances – regulation 8(1)(b)) if it is tested privately. A voucher is to be issued to a patient if he appears eligible for a payment under the Regulations. The voucher is required to bear a letter code which varies according to the type of appliance prescribed and indicates a monetary value (set out in Schedule 1). The patient may use the voucher towards the cost incurred by him for the supply of the optical appliance prescribed (regulation 12) and the supplier may, on submitting the voucher, claim a payment from the FPC or HA (regulation 13). The amount of that payment will vary according to whether or not the patient is required to make a contribution (which has the effect of reducing the voucher's value) and whether or not the optical appliance is a complex appliance (regulation 15). In some hospital eye service cases the payment may be made direct to the patient if he has been supplied with his optical appliance without using his voucher (regulation 14). Voucher values for the purposes of supply are increased by between 4½ and 10%. The voucher value for contact lenses remains unchanged.

Part V of these Regulations makes provision for payments to be made for the cost of replacement and repair of optical appliances. Those eligible are children under 16 (where the appliance is lost or damaged) and others who are entitled to full or partial remission of NHS charges, or are persons who need to wear complex appliances (where the appliance is lost or damaged as a result of illness) (regulation 16). In the case of a replacement, the voucher is completed in a similar way to a voucher for the supply of an optical appliance. In the case of repair the voucher must as well as bearing a letter code, specify the nature of the repair to be carried out (the monetary value given to which is set out in Schedule 3 and is relevant to the amount of any payment made). In the case of replacements and repairs the amount of the payment varies according to the patient's means, so that if the patient is assessed as having to make a contribution the amount of any payment made is reduced (regulation 20).

Part VI deals with miscellaneous matters and contains provision for repayment of amounts wrongly paid (regulation 21) and for signatures by those under disability (regulation 22).

British Standard 3521: 1962, referred to in regulation 1(2) of these Regulations, may be obtained from any of the sales outlets operated by the British Standards Institution or direct by post from the Institution at Linford Wood, Milton Keynes, MK14 6LE.

STATUTORY INSTRUMENTS

1989 No. 397

INSOLVENCY

COMPANIES

INDIVIDUALS, ENGLAND AND WALES

The Insolvency (Amendment) Rules 1989

Made - - - -	*8th March 1989*
Laid before Parliament	*13th March 1989*
Coming into force	*3rd April 1989*

The Lord Chancellor, in the exercise of his powers under sections 411 and 412 of the Insolvency Act 1986(**a**), with the concurrence of the Secretary of State, and after consulting the committee existing for that purpose under section 413 of that Act, hereby makes the following Rules:–

Citation and commencement

1. These Rules may be cited as the Insolvency (Amendment) Rules 1989 and shall come into force on 3rd April 1989, and that day is referred to in these Rules as "the commencement date".

Interpretation

2.—(1) In these Rules references to the "the principal Rules" are to the Insolvency Rules 1986(**b**) and a Rule or Schedule referred to by number means the Rule or Schedule so numbered in the principal Rules.

(2) These Rules shall be read and construed as one with the principal Rules.

Application

3.—(1) Subject to paragraph (2), the principal Rules have effect in relation to insolvency proceedings to which the principal Rules apply by virtue of Rule 13.14 with the amendments set out in the Schedule to these Rules.

(2) The principal Rules as so amended apply to all such proceedings on and after the commencement date whenever those proceedings were commenced.

Mackay of Clashfern, C.

Dated 8th March 1989

I concur,

Francis Maude
Parliamentary Under-Secretary of State,
Department of Trade and Industry

Dated 8th March 1989

(**a**) 1986 c.45.
(**b**) S.I. 1986/1925, amended by S.I. 1987/1919.

SCHEDULE

Rule 3(1)

Amendment of Rule 6.223

1. At the end of Rule 6.223 there shall be added the words "or section 71 of the Criminal Justice Act 1988".

Amendment of Rule 12.3

2. In subparagraph (b) of paragraph (2) of Rule 12.3 there shall be added at the end the words "or section 71 of the Criminal Justice Act 1988".

Amendment of Schedule 3

3. For paragraphs 1–5 of Schedule 3 to the principal Rules there shall be substituted the following–

"**1.** For attendance	£56.43.
2. Per folio of written record	78.8p plus 4p per folio for all copies.
3. Travelling time	£5.93 per hour after first hour of each journey.

4. In addition to the items in paragraphs 1 to 3, the following London weighting allowances (see note below) are payable in relation to the location of the court or other place concerned–

Inner	*Intermediate*	*Outer*
£8.74 per day	£5.00 per day	£3.63 per day.

5. The amounts shown in paragraph 4 are subject to a maximum annual allowance of–

Inner	*Intermediate*	*Outer*
£1,750	£1,000	£725.".

EXPLANATORY NOTE

(This note is not part of the Rules)

These Rules make detailed amendments to the Insolvency Rules 1986 (as amended by the Insolvency (Amendment) Rules 1987), which set out detailed procedures for the conduct of all company and individual insolvency proceedings in England and Wales under the Insolvency Act 1986. These Rules apply to all insolvency proceedings to which the Insolvency Rules 1986 apply on and after 3rd April 1989, whether or not those proceedings were commenced before, on or after that date.

The amendments–

(a) are consequential on the coming into force on 3rd April 1989 of section 71 of the Criminal Justice Act 1988 (c.33); and

(b) provide for an increase in the remuneration payable to shorthand writers appointed in insolvency proceedings.

STATUTORY INSTRUMENTS

1989 No. 398

EDUCATION, ENGLAND AND WALES

The Education (School Hours and Policies) (Information) Regulations 1989

Made - - - -	*8th March 1989*
Laid before Parliament	*10th March 1989*
Coming into force	*1st April 1989*

In exercise of the powers conferred by section 8(5) and (7) of the Education Act 1980(**a**) and section 118(5) of the Education Reform Act 1988(**b**) the Secretary of State for Education and Science, as respects England, and the Secretary of State for Wales, as respects Wales, hereby make the following Regulations:

Citation, commencement and extent

1. These Regulations may be cited as the Education (School Hours and Policies) (Information) Regulations 1989 and shall come into force on 1st April 1989.

Interpretation

2.—(1) In these Regulations –

"the Act" means the Education Reform Act 1988;

"the 1981 Regulations" means the Education (School Information) Regulations 1981(**c**);

"education authority" means a local education authority;

"relevant education authority", in relation to a school, means the education authority by whom the school is maintained;

"maintained school" has the meaning assigned to it by section 25(1) of the Act;

"school prospectus" means a document of the kind referred to in paragraph (3) of Regulation 6 of the 1981 Regulations or (as the case may be) a document of a like nature which the governing body of a grant-maintained school are required by the school's articles of government to publish;

"governors' report" means a report of the kind referred to in section 30 of the Education (No.2) Act 1986(**d**) or section 58(5)(j) of the Act (as the case may be).

(2) In these Regulations, unless the context otherwise requires, any reference to a numbered regulation is a reference to the regulation bearing that number in these Regulations and any reference in a regulation to a numbered paragraph is to the paragraph of that regulation bearing that number.

(**a**) 1980 c.20. (**b**) 1988 c.40. (**c**) S.I. 1981/630; amended by S.I. 1983/41 and Regulation 6(3) is amended by Regulation 6 of these Regulations. (**d**) 1986 c.61.

Information to be made available by head teachers

3.—(1) The head teacher of every maintained school shall make available to parents of pupils at the school and other persons the information specified in paragraph (2) in the manner specified in paragraph (3).

(2) The information referred to in paragraph (1) is information consisting of –

(a) the times at which each school session begins and ends on a school day, and

(b) particulars of the charging and remissions policies determined by the governing body of the school under section 110 of the Act.

(3) Copies of the information shall be provided at the school for inspection by parents and other persons at all reasonable times on a school day and for distribution without charge to parents on request.

Information to be made available by education authorities

4.—(1) Every education authority shall make available information consisting of particulars of the charging and remissions policies determined by the authority under section 110 of the Act to the persons and in the manner specified in paragraph (2).

(2) Copies of the particulars shall be made available –

(a) for distribution without charge to parents on request, and for reference by parents and other persons –

(i) at the offices of the relevant education authority, and

(ii) at every school maintained by the relevant education authority, and

(b) for reference by parents and other persons at the public libraries in the area of that authority.

Changes in information to which Regulation 3(2)(b) applies

5.—(1) This Regulation applies to any significant change to the information to which Regulations 3(2)(b) applies which takes place after publication of the school prospectus in any school year but before completion of the preparation of the governors' report in that year.

(2) The governing body shall make available particulars of any such change at the same time, in the same manner, and to the same extent that they are required by the articles of government for the school to make copies of the governors' report available.

Amendment of the 1981 Regulations

6.—(1) The following paragraph shall be substituted for paragraph (3) of Regulation 6 of the 1981 Regulations –

"(3) In the case of any school –

(a) such information shall be published in a single document to be known as the school prospectus; and

(b) copies shall be made available at the school for distribution without charge to parents on request and for reference by parents and other persons."

(2) After paragraph 13 of Schedule 1 to the 1981 Regulations there shall be added the following paragraph –

"13A. The arrangements for parents and other persons to obtain copies of and to refer to particulars of the charging and remissions policies determined by the authority under section 110 of the Education Reform Act 1988(**a**)".

(3) After paragraph 13 of Schedule 2 to the 1981 Regulations there shall be added the following paragraph –

"13A.—(1) The times at which each school session begins and ends on a school day.

(**a**) 1988 c.40.

(2) A summary of the charging and remissions policies determined by the governing body of the school under section 110 of the Education Reform Act 1988."

Kenneth Baker
Secretary of State for Education and Science

3rd March 1989

Wyn Roberts
Minister of State, Welsh Office

8th March 1989

EXPLANATORY NOTE

(This note is not part of the Regulations)

These Regulations, which apply to schools maintained by local education authorities and to grant-maintained schools, impose obligations on head teachers, school governing bodies and local education authorities to make information available about school hours and charging and remissions policies.

The head teacher is required to make available to parents and others details of the times at which each school session begins and ends, and of the school governing body's charging and remissions policies determined under section 110 of the Education Reform Act 1988. This information is to be available for inspection at the school and parents are entitled to a free copy of it (regulation 3).

Local education authorities are required to make available details of their charging and remissions policies at specified locations (regulation 4).

If any change takes place in the governors' charging or remissions policies after the school prospectus has been published but before the governors' report has been completed, they are required to provide details of the change with their report (regulation 5).

The Education (School Information) Regulations 1981 are amended –

(a) so as to require the publication of information to which those and these regulations apply in a document to be known as a prospectus;

(b) by adding to the general information required by those regulations to be published by a local education authority details of the authority's arrangements for publicising their charging and remissions policies; and

(c) by adding to the specific information required to be published about individual schools information about school hours and the charging and remissions policies adopted by the governing body of each school.

STATUTORY INSTRUMENTS

1989 No. 404 (C.15)

HOUSING, ENGLAND AND WALES
HOUSING, SCOTLAND

The Housing Act 1988 (Commencement No. 4) Order 1989

Made - - - - 9th March 1989

The Secretary of State, in exercise of the powers conferred on him by section 141(2) and (4) of the Housing Act 1988**(a)**, and of all other powers enabling him in that behalf, hereby makes the following Order:

1.—(1) This Order may be cited as the Housing Act 1988 (Commencement No. 4) Order 1989.

(2) In this Order–

"the 1985 Act" means the Housing Associations Act 1985**(b)**, and

"the 1988 Act" means the Housing Act 1988.

2.—(1) Subject as hereinafter provided, the following provisions of the 1988 Act shall come into force on 1st April 1989–

Part II to the extent that it is not yet in force, except in so far as section 59 relates to paragraph 27 of Schedule 6,

section 129,

section 140(1) in so far as it relates to paragraph 66, 89, 97, 103 and 106–113 of Schedule 17, and

section 140(2) in so far as it relates to the repeals in–

(a) the 1985 Act, except for

(i) section 55, and

(ii) sections 56 and 57 in so far as they relate to hostel deficit grants,

(b) the Housing and Planning Act 1986**(c)** to the extent that such repeals are not yet in force,

(c) the Housing (Scotland) Act 1986**(d)**,

(d) the Landlord and Tenant Act 1987**(e)** to the extent that such repeals are not yet in force,

(e) the Local Government Act 1988**(f)**, and

(f) the Housing (Scotland Act 1988**(g)** to the extent that such repeals are not yet in force.

(a) 1988 c.50.
(b) 1985 c.69.
(c) 1986 c.63.
(d) 1986 c.65.
(e) 1987 c.31.
(f) 1988 c.9.
(g) 1988 c.43.

(2) The following provisions of the 1988 Act shall come into force on 5th April 1989–
Part IV to the extent that it is not yet in force,
section 127, and
section 140(1) in so far as it relates to paragraphs 17(1), 38 and 39 of Schedule 17.

3. The repeal and amendment of provisions of the 1985 Act shall be subject to the following provisions:

(a) the repeal of section 52 (circumstances in which grant may be reduced, suspended or reclaimed) and of section 16 of the Housing (Scotland) Act 1986 (which amends that section) shall not apply where section 52 would otherwise apply by virtue of events described in subsection (1) of that section occurring before 1st April 1989 (and in relation to sub-section (1)(b) the event in question is the land ceasing to be used, or to be available for use, as therein described);

(b) the repeal of section 53 (recoupment of surplus rental income) shall not apply in relation to any surpluses arising during a period which expires before 1st April 1989;

(c) there shall not apply in relation to revenue deficit grant payable to an association for a period which expires before 1st April 1989–

(i) the repeals of section 54 (revenue deficit grants), and sections 56 and 57 to the extent that they relate to revenue deficit grants,

(ii) the amendment to section 69A**(a)** (land subject to housing management agreement) by paragraph 29 of Schedule 6 to the 1988 Act, and

(iii) the substitution of the definition of "housing activities" in section 106(1) effected by paragraph 36 of Schedule 6 to the 1988 Act;

(d) the repeal of section 62 (grants for affording tax relief) and of paragraph 8(1) of Schedule 5 to the Housing and Planning Act 1986 (which amends that section) shall not apply in relation to a grant payable to an association in respect of a period which commences before 1st April 1989.

4. The amendment of section 69A of the 1985 Act (land subject to housing management agreement) by paragraph 29 of Schedule 6 to the 1988 Act does not apply for the purposes of hostel deficit grant payable under section 55 of the 1985 Act.

Nicholas Ridley
9th March 1989 One of Her Majesty's Principal Secretaries of State

---

EXPLANATORY NOTE

(This note is not part of the Order)

This Order brings into force on 1st April 1989 the following provisions of the Housing Act 1988–

(a) Part II (housing associations) to the extent that it is not in force, subject to provisions in articles 3(c) and 4;

(b) section 129, which provides for schemes to assist local housing authority tenants to obtain other accommodation;

(c) section 140 in relation to certain minor and consequential amendments in Schedule 17 and repeals in Schedule 18 (subject to the provisions of article 3).

(a) Section 69A was inserted by paragraph 42 of Schedule 5 to the Housing and Planning Act 1986.

It brings into force on 5th April 1989 those provisions of Part IV of the Housing Act 1988 (change of landlord) not yet in force (together with related minor amendments) and section 127) Preserved right to buy).

NOTE AS TO EARLIER COMMENCEMENT ORDERS

(This note is not part of the Order)

Provision	*Date of Commencement*	*S.I. No.*
Section 46(1) and (2) Section 47(2) Section 47(6) (partially) Sction 140(1) (partially)	1 December 1988	1988/2056
Section 140(1) (partially) Section 140(2) (partially)	2 January 1989	1988/2152
Section 49 Section 57 Section 59(1) Section 59(2) and (3) (partially) Section 94 Section 106 Sections 111 to 114 Section 119 Section 140(1) (partially) Section 140(2) (partially)	15 January 1989	1988/2152
Section 122 Section 124 Section 140(2) (partially)	10 March 1989	S.I. 1989/203

STATUTORY INSTRUMENTS

1989 No. 415

PENSIONS

The Personal Injuries (Civilians) Amendment Scheme 1989

Made - - - -	*9th March 1989*
Laid before Parliament	*10th March 1989*
Coming into force	
–for the purposes of articles 1, 2 and 4	*1st April 1989*
–for all other purposes	*10th April 1989*

The Secretary of State for Social Security, with the approval of the Treasury, in exercise of the powers conferred by sections 1 and 2 of the Personal Injuries (Emergency Provisions) Act 1939 (**a**) and now vested in him(**b**), and of all other powers enabling him in that behalf, hereby makes the following Scheme:

Citation, commencement and interpretation

1.—(1) This Scheme may be cited as the Personal Injuries (Civilians) Amendment Scheme 1989 and shall come into force for the purposes of this article and articles 2 and 4 on 1st April 1989 and for all other purposes on 10th April 1989.

(2) In this Scheme the expression "the principal Scheme" means the Personal Injuries (Civilians) Scheme 1983(**c**).

Amendment of article 2 of the principal Scheme

2. In paragraph (19) of article 2 of the principal Scheme (meaning of "public funds") after the words "any public, general or local Act", there shall be inserted the words "moneys provided under the Abolition of Domestic Rates Etc. (Scotland) Act 1987(**d**)".

Amendment of Article 18 of the principal Scheme

3. In Article 18 of the principal Scheme (unemployability allowances) in paragraph (2) for the amount "£1,404" there shall be substituted the amount "£1,482".

(**a**) 1939 c.82. (**b**) *See* Transfer of Functions (Ministry of Pensions) Order 1953 (S.I. 1953/1198), Article 2; Ministry of Social Security Act 1966 (c.20), section 2; Secretary of State for Social Services Order 1968 (S.I. 1968/1699), Article 2. (**c**) S.I. 1983/686, as amended by S.I. 1983/1164, 1540, 1984/1289, 1675, 1985/1313, 1986/628, 1987/191, 1988/367 and 2260. (**d**) 1987 c.47.

Amendment of article 28 of the principal Scheme

4. At the end of paragraph (1) of article 28 of the principal Scheme (Rent allowance for widows who have children) there shall be added the words "and to any community charge payable by her.".

Substitution of Schedules 3 and 4 to the Principal Scheme

5. For Schedules 3 and 4 to the principal Scheme (rates of pensions and allowances payable in respect of disablement and death) there shall respectively be substituted the Schedules set out in the Schedule hereto and numbered 3 and 4.

Signed by authority of the Secretary of State for Social Security.

Skelmersdale
Parliamentary Under-Secretary of State,
Department of Social Security

6th March 1989

We approve,

Alan Howarth
Stephen Dorrell
Two of the Lords Commissioners of Her Majesty's Treasury.

9th March 1989

Article 5

SCHEDULE

Schedules to be substituted in the principal Scheme

"SCHEDULE 3

Article 11

RATES OF PENSIONS AND ALLOWANCES PAYABLE IN RESPECT OF DISABLEMENT

Description of Pension or Allowance	*Rate*
1. Pension for 100 per cent. disablement under Article 11	£71.20 per week
2. Education allowance under Article 13	£120 per annum*
3. Constant attendance allowance –	
(a) under the proviso to Article 14	£57.00 per week*
(b) in any other case under that Article	£28.50 per week*
4. Exceptionally severe disablement allowance under Article 15	£28.50 per week
5. Severe disablement occupational allowance under Article 16	£14.25 per week
6. Allowance for wear and tear of clothing –	
(a) under Article 17(1)(a)	£61 per annum
(b) under Article 17(1)(b) and (2)	£97 per annum
7. Unemployability allowances –	
(a) personal allowance under Article 18(1)(i)	£46.30 per week
(b) additional allowances for dependants by way of –	
(i) increase of allowance in respect of a wife or a dependent husband under Article 18(5)(b)	£26.20 per week*
(ii) allowance in respect of an adult dependant under Article 18(5)(c)	£26.20 per week*
(iii) increase of allowance in respect of each child under Article 18(5)(d)	£ 8.95 per week

SCHEDULE 3 continued

Description of Pension or Allowance	*Rate*
8. Invalidity allowance payable under Article 19	
(a) if –	
(i) the relevant date fell before 5th July 1948; or	
(ii) on the relevant date the disabled person was under the age of 35; or	
(iii) on the relevant date the disabled person was under the age of 40 and had not attained the age of 65, in the case of the disabled person being a man, or 60, in the case of that person being a woman, before 6th April 1979 and the period in respect of which payment of the allowance is to relate begins on or after 6th April 1979	£ 9.20 per week
(b) if –	
(i) on the relevant date the disabled person was under the age of 45; or	
(ii) on the relevant date the disabled person was under the age of 50 and had not attained the age of 65, in the case of the disabled person being a man, or 60, in the case of that person being a woman, before 6th April 1979 and the period in respect of which payment of the allowance is to relate begins on or after 6th April 1979	£ 5.80 per week
(c) if heads (a) and (b) do not apply and on the relevant date the disabled person was a man under the age of 60 or a woman under the age of 55	£ 2.90 per week
9. Comforts allowance –	
(a) under Article 20(1)(a)	£12.30 per week
(b) under Article 20(1)(b) or 45(1)	£ 6.15 per week
10. Allowance for lowered standard of occupation under Article 21	£28.48 per week*
11. Age allowance under Article 22 where the degree of pensioned disablement is –	
(a) 40 or 50 per cent.	£ 5.00 per week
(b) 60 or 70 per cent.	£ 7.75 per week
(c) 80 or 90 per cent.	£11.10 per week
(d) 100 per cent.	£15.50 per week
12. Treatment allowances – increase of personal allowance under Article 23(2)	£15.50 per week*
13. Part-time treatment allowance under Article 25	£29.70 per day*
14. Mobility supplement under Article 25A	£27.10 per week

*Maximum.

SCHEDULE 4

Article 27

RATES OF PENSIONS AND ALLOWANCES PAYABLE IN RESPECT OF DEATH

Description of Pension or Allowance	*Rate*
1. Pension to widow –	
(a) under Article 27(1)	£56.65 per week
(b) under Article 27(2)	£13.08 per week
2. Rent allowance under Article 28	£21.55 per week*
3. Allowance under Article 29 or 50 to an elderly surviving spouse –	
(a) if age 65 but under age 70	£ 6.10 per week
(b) if age 70 but under age 80	£12.20 per week
(c) if age 80 or over	£15.30 per week
4. Pension under Article 30 to unmarried dependant who lived as spouse	£ 1.00 per week*
5. Pension to dependent widower under Article 32	£56.65 per week*
6. Allowances under Article 33 in respect of each child under the age of 15	£12.60 per week
7. Pension under Article 34(1) to a motherless or fatherless child under the age of 15	£13.80 per week
8. Pension or allowance under Article 35(3) to or in respect of a child over the age of 15 –	
(a) where the child has attained the age of 18 and is incapable of self-support by reason of an infirmity which arose before he attained the age of 15 –	£43.60 per week*
(b) any other case	£13.80 per week*
9. Education allowance under Article 36	£120 per annum*
10. Pensions to parents –	
(a) minimum rate under Article 38(4)	£ 0.25 per week
(b) maximum rate under Article 38(4) –	
(i) where there is only one eligible parent	£ 1.00 per week
(ii) where there is more than one eligible parent	£ 1.38 per week
(c) increase under the proviso to Article 38(4) –	
(i) where there is only one eligible parent	£ 0.38 per week*
(ii) where there is more than one eligible parent	£ 0.62 per week*
11. Pensions to other dependants –	
(a) for each juvenile dependant under Article 39(4)	£ 0.30 per week*
(b) aggregate rate under Article 39(4)	£ 1.00 per week*
(c) under Article 39(5)	£ 1.00 per week*

*Maximum".

EXPLANATORY NOTE

(This note is not part of the Scheme)

This Scheme further amends the Personal Injuries (Civilians) Scheme 1983 ("the principal Scheme") which makes provision for the payment of pensions and allowances to or in respect of civilians who were killed or injured in the 1939-45 War.

This Scheme raises the maximum amount of annual earnings which may be received by a disabled person while he is deemed to be unemployable for the purposes of unemployability allowances under Article 18 of the principal Scheme, and varies the rates of pensions and allowances in respect of disablement and death in the 1939–45 War (Articles 3 and 5, and the Schedule).

It also makes amendments (Articles 2 and 4) consequential upon the abolition in Scotland from 1st April 1989 of domestic rates and their replacement by community charge.

STATUTORY INSTRUMENTS

1989 No. 416

HOUSING, ENGLAND AND WALES
HOUSING, SCOTLAND
RATING AND VALUATION

The Housing Benefit (General) Amendment Regulations 1989

Made - - - -	*9th March 1989*
Laid before Parliament	*10th March 1989*
Coming into force	
for the purpose of regulations 1 to 6 and 9 to 11 to the extent that they relate to cases referred to in regulation 1(2)	*1st April 1989*
to the extent that they relate to any other case	*3rd April 1989*
for the purposes of regulations 7 and 8	*9th October 1989*

The Secretary of State for Social Security in exercise of powers conferred by sections 20(1)(c) and (8), 21(6)(b), 22(1), (8) and (9), 29 and 84(1) of the Social Security Act 1986(**a**) and section 166(1) to (3A) of the Social Security Act 1975(**b**) and of all other powers enabling him in that behalf, after consultation with organisations appearing to him to be representative of authorities concerned(**c**), and of all other powers enabling him in that behalf, by this instrument which is made before the end of a period of 12 months from the commencement of the enactments under which it is made, hereby makes the following Regulations:

Citation, commencement and interpretation

1.—(1) These Regulations may be cited as the Housing Benefit (General) Amendment Regulations 1989 and shall come into force as follows –

(a) regulations 1 to 6 and 9 to 11 in any case to which paragraph (2)(a) or (b) applies, on 1st April 1989 and in any other case, on 3rd April 1989;

(b) regulations 7 and 8, on 9th October 1989.

(2) This paragraph applies in any case where –

(a) rent is payable at intervals of one month or any other interval which is not a week or multiple thereof; or

(b) payments by way of rates are not made together with payments of rent at weekly intervals or multiples thereof.

(**a**) 1986 c.50; section 84(1) is an interpretation provision and is cited because of the meanings assigned to the words "prescribed" and "regulations". (**b**) 1975 c.14; section 166(3A) was inserted by section 62(1) of the Social Security Act 1986 and section 166(1) to (3A) was applied by section 83(1) of that Act. (**c**) *See* section 61(7) of the Social Security Act 1986.

(3) In these regulations "the General Regulations" means the Housing Benefit (General) Regulations 1987(**a**).

Amendment of regulation 3 of the General Regulations

2. In regulation 3 of the General Regulations (definition of non-dependant) –

(a) in paragraph (2)(e), for the words "liable to make payments" to the end there shall be substituted the words "liable to make payments on a commercial basis to the claimant or the claimant's partner or to whom or to whose partner the claimant or the claimant's partner is liable to make payments on a commercial basis, in respect of the occupation of the dwelling;";

(b) in paragraph (3), the words "a person who normally resides with a claimant and who is a boarder or" shall be omitted;

(c) at the end of paragraph (4) there shall be added the words "but not if each person is separately liable to make payments in respect of his occupation of the dwelling to the landlord.".

Amendment of regulation 24 of the General Regulations

3. In regulation 24 of the General Regulations (average weekly income other than earnings) the words "or regulation 27(4) (weekly amount of charitable or voluntary payment)" shall be omitted.

Amendment of regulation 61 of the General Regulations

4. In regulation 61 of the General Regulations (maximum housing benefit) after the words "non-dependants" there shall be inserted the words "or boarders".

Amendment of regulation 63 of the General Regulations

5. In regulation 63 of the General Regulations (non-dependant deductions) –

(a) in paragraph (1)(a) for the words "who is in remunerative work or who is a boarder" there shall be substituted the words "in remunerative work or a boarder aged 18 or over";

(b) in paragraph (2) after the words "remunerative work" there shall be inserted the words "and of a boarder aged 18 or over in remunerative work".

Amendment of Schedule 1 to the General Regulations

6. After sub-paragraph (4) of paragraph 1A of Schedule 1 to the General Regulations (amount ineligible for meals) there shall be added the following sub-paragraphs –

"(5) Where a charge for meals includes provision for meals for a person who is not a member of the claimant's family sub-paragraphs (2) to (4) shall apply as if that person were a member of the claimant's family.

(6) For the avoidance of doubt where the charge does not include provision for meals for a claimant or, as the case may be, a member of his family, sub-paragraphs (2) to (4) shall not apply in respect of that person.".

Amendment of Schedule 2 to the General Regulations

7. In Schedule 2 to the General Regulations (applicable amounts) –

(a) for paragraph 9 there shall be substituted the following paragraphs –

"Pensioner premium for persons under 75

9. The condition is that the claimant –

(a) is a single claimant or lone parent aged not less than 60 but less than 75; or

(b) has a partner and is, or his partner is, aged not less than 60 but less than 75.

(**a**) S.I. 1987/1971, relevant amending instruments are S.I. 1988/1444 and 661, 909, 1971.

Pensioner premium for persons 75 and over

9A. The condition is that the claimant –

(a) is a single claimant or lone parent aged not less than 75 but less than 80; or

(b) has a partner and is, or his partner is, aged not less than 75 but less than 80.";

(b) in paragraph 12(1)(a)(ii) for the words "solely on account of the maximum age for its payment being reached" there shall be substituted the words "either on account of the maximum age for this payment being reached or the payment of a retirement pension under the Social Security Act.";

(c) in paragraph 15 –

(i) for sub-paragraph (2) there shall be substituted the following sub-paragraphs –

"(2) Pensioner premium for persons aged under 75 –	2.
(a) where the claimant satisfies the condition in paragraph 9(a);	(a) £11.20;
(b) where the claimant satisfies the condition in paragraph 9(b).	(b) £17.05.
(2A) Pensioner premium for persons aged 75 and over –	2A.
(a) where the claimant satisfies the condition in paragraph 9A(a);	(a) £13.70;
(b) where the claimant satisfies the condition in paragraph 9A(b).	(b) £20.55.".

(ii) in sub-paragraph (3) for "£13.70" and "£19.50" there shall be substituted "£16.20" and "£23.00" respectively(**a**).

Amendment of Schedule 3 to the General Regulations

8. For paragraph 3 of Schedule 3 to the General Regulations (sums to be disregarded in the calculation of earnings) there shall be substituted the following paragraph –

"**3.**—(1) In a case to which this paragraph applies, £15; but notwithstanding regulation 19 (calculation of income and capital of members of a claimant's family and of a polygamous marriage) if this paragraph applies to a claimant it shall not apply to his partner except where, and to the extent that, the earnings of the claimant which are to be disregarded under this paragraph are less than £15.

(2) This paragraph applies where the claimant's applicable amount includes an amount by way of the disability premium or severe disability premium under Schedule 2 (applicable amounts).

(3) This paragraph applies where –

(a) the claimant is a member of a couple and his applicable amount would, but for the higher pensioner premium under Schedule 2 being applicable, include an amount by way of the disability premium under that Schedule; and

(b) he or his partner is under the age of 60 and at least one is engaged in employment.

(4) This paragraph applies where –

(a) the claimant's applicable amount includes an amount by way of the higher pensioner premium under Schedule 2; and

(**a**) Paragraph 15(3) of Schedule 2 was amended by article 18(9) of, and Schedule 10 to, the Social Security Benefits Up-rating Order 1989 (S.I. 1989/43).

(b) the claimant or, if he is a member of a couple, either he or his partner has attained the age of 60; and

(c) immediately before attaining that age he or, as the case may be, he or his partner was engaged in employment and the claimant was entitled by virtue of sub-paragraph (2) to a disregard of £15; and

(d) he or, if he is a member of a couple, he or his partner has continued in employment.

(5) This paragraph applies where –

(a) the claimant is a member of a couple and his applicable amount would include an amount by way of the disability premium under that Schedule, but for –

(i) the pensioner premium for persons aged 75 and over under Schedule 2 being applicable; or

(ii) the higher pensioner premium under that Schedule being applicable; and

(b) he or his partner has attained the age of 75 but is under the age of 80 and the other is under the age of 60 and at least one member of the couple is engaged in employment.

(6) This paragraph applies where –

(a) the claimant is a member of a couple and he or his partner has attained the age of 75 but is under the age of 80 and the other has attained the age of 60; and

(b) immediately before the younger member attained that age either member was engaged in employment and the claimant was entitled by virtue of sub-paragraph (5) to a disregard of £15; and

(c) either he or his partner has continued in employment.

(7) For the purposes of this paragraph, no account shall be taken of any period not exceeding eight consecutive weeks occurring on or after the date on which the claimant or, if he is a member of a couple, he or his partner attained the age of 60 during which either or both ceased to be engaged in employment or the claimant ceased to be entitled to income support.".

Amendment of Schedule 4 to the General Regulations

9. In paragraph 19 of Schedule 4 to the General Regulations (sums to be disregarded in the calculation of income other than earnings) at the end there shall be added the words "or a boarder".

Amendment of Schedule 5 to the General Regulations

10. In paragraph 24 of Schedule 5 to the General Regulations (capital to be disregarded) for the words "he left that dwelling" there shall be substituted the words "he ceased to occupy that dwelling or, where the dwelling is occupied as the home by the former partner who is a lone parent, for so long as it is so occupied".

Amendment of Schedule 6 to the General Regulations

11. In paragraph 9(c) of Schedule 6 to the General Regulations (matters to be included in notice of determination) after the reference "paragraph 5(2)" there shall be inserted the reference "or (2A)".

Signed by authority of the Secretary of State for Social Security

Peter Lloyd
Parliamentary Under-Secretary of State,
Department of Social Security

9th March 1989

EXPLANATORY NOTE

(This note is not part of the Regulations)

These Regulations further amend the Housing Benefit (General) Regulations 1987 in the following respects —

(a) they introduce an increased pension premium for persons aged 75 and over and uprate the amount of the higher pensioner premium with effect from 9th October 1989 (regulation 7); and provide for an earnings disregard of £15 where but for these changes a person would have been entitled to the disability premium (regulation 8);

(b) they provide for boarders not to be treated as non-dependants if they live in the household of another claimant and for a deduction to be made from the maximum housing benefit in respect of boarders aged 18 or over (regulations 2, 4 and 5);

(c) they make provision for property to be disregarded where it is occupied by a lone parent if he is the former partner of the claimant and for the disregard of payments made to the claimant by a boarder (regulations 9 and 10); and delete an obsolete reference (regulation 3);

(d) they provide, in assessing ineligible service charges, for a deduction in respect of meals to be made in respect of a person who is a member of the claimant's household but not a member of his family and make clear that such deductions are only to be made in respect of persons for whom the charge makes provision (regulation 6); and for the notice of award to specify the details of any fuel deduction made (regulation 11).

These Regulations are made before the expiry of 12 months from the commencement of the enactments under which they are made; they are accordingly exempt by section 61(5) of the Social Security Act 1986 from reference to the Social Security Advisory Committee and have not been so referred.

STATUTORY INSTRUMENTS

1989 No. 417

PENSIONS

The Pensions Increase (Local Authorities' etc. Pensions) (Amendment) Regulations 1989

Made - - - -	*9th March 1989*
Laid before Parliament	*10th March 1989*
Coming into force	*1st April 1989*

The Treasury, in exercise of the powers conferred upon the Minister for the Civil Service by section 5(2) of the Pensions (Increase) Act 1971(**a**), and now vested in them(**b**), and of all other powers enabling them in that behalf, hereby make the following Regulations:

1.—(1) These Regulations may be cited as the Pensions Increase (Local Authorities' etc. Pensions) (Amendment) Regulations 1989, and shall come into force on 1st April 1989.

(2) In these Regulations "the 1974 Regulations" means the Pensions Increase (Local Authorities' etc. Pensions) Regulations 1974(**c**).

2. In regulation 4(2) of the 1974 Regulations, for the words "paragraph 7", there shall be substituted the words "paragraph 7 or 8".

3. In regulation 5 of the 1974 Regulations there shall be added the following paragraph–

"(c) where the pension is a pension specified in paragraph 8 of that Schedule, in which case any such increase shall take effect from 1st April 1989.".

4. In the Schedule to the 1974 Regulations there shall be added the following paragraph–

"**8.** A pension payable by Scottish Homes out of a superannuation fund established and administered under the Local Government Superannuation (Scotland) Regulation 1987(**d**).".

Alan Howarth
Stephen Dorrell
Two of the Lords Commissioners of
Her Majesty's Treasury

9th March 1989

(**a**) 1971 c.56.
(**b**) S.I. 1981/1670.
(**c**) S.I. 1974/1740, amended by S.I. 1983/1315 and 1986/391.
(**d**) S.I. 1987/1850; amended by S.I. 1988/625.

EXPLANATORY NOTE

(This note is not part of the Regulations)

These Regulations amend the Pensions Increase (Local Authorities etc. Pensions) Regulations 1974 so as to provide for the payment of increases under the Pensions Increase Act 1971 on Scottish Homes pensions and so as to secure that the cost of such increases is to be borne by that body. Scottish Homes is a body established under section 1 of the Housing (Scotland) Act 1988 (c.43).

STATUTORY INSTRUMENTS

1989 No. 418

MEDICINES

The Medicines (Fees Relating to Medicinal Products for Human Use) Regulations 1989

Made - - - -	*9th March 1989*
Laid before Parliament	*10th March 1989*
Coming into force	*1st April 1989*

The Secretary of State concerned with health in England, the Secretaries of State respectively concerned with health and with agriculture in Wales and in Scotland, the Minister of Agriculture, Fisheries and Food, the Department of Health and Social Services for Northern Ireland and the Department of Agriculture for Northern Ireland, acting jointly, with the consent of the Treasury, in exercise of the powers conferred by section 1(1) and (2) of the Medicines Act 1971(**a**) and now vested in them(**b**) and of all other powers enabling them in that behalf, after consulting such organisations as appear to them to be representative of interests likely to be substantially affected by these Regulations(**c**), hereby make the following Regulations:–

PART I

GENERAL

Citation, commencement and scope

1.—(1) These Regulations may be cited as the Medicines (Fees Relating to Medicinal Products for Human Use) Regulations 1989 and shall come into force on 1st April 1989.

(2) Subject to paragraphs (3) and (4) below, these Regulations apply only to fees payable –

(a) in connection with applications for the grant, variation or renewal of licences or certificates under Part II of the Medicines Act 1968 relating wholly or partly to medicinal products for human use; or

(b) in respect of inspections made in connection with applications for the grant, renewal or variation of, or during the currency of any such licence or certificate.

(**a**) 1971 c.69, as amended by section 21 of the Health and Medicines Act 1988 (c.49); by virtue of section 1(3) of the 1971 Act expressions in that section have the same meaning as in the Medicines Act 1968 (c.67), as amended by the Transfer of Functions (Wales) Order 1969 (S.I. 1969/388). The expression "The Ministers" is defined in section 1(1) of the 1968 Act as so amended. (**b**) In the case of the Secretaries of State concerned with health in England and in Wales by virtue of Article 2(2) of, and Schedule 1 to, the Transfer of Functions (Wales) Order 1969; in the case of the Secretary of State concerned with agriculture in Wales by virtue of Article 2(3) of, and Schedule 1 to, the Transfer of Functions (Wales) (No. 1) Order 1978 (S.I. 1978/272); in the case of the Northern Ireland Departments by virtue of section 40 of, and Schedule 5 to, the Northern Ireland Constitution Act 1973 (c.36), and section 1(3) of, and paragraph 2(1)(b) of Schedule 1 to, the Northern Ireland Act 1974 (c.28). (**c**) *See* section 129(6) of the Medicines Act 1968 as extended to include regulations made under the Medicines Act 1971 by section 1(3)(b) of that latter Act.

(3) No fee shall be payable under these Regulations in connection with any application for the grant, variation or renewal of a licence or certificate under Part II of the Medicines Act 1968 by an authority constituted under the National Health Service Act 1977(**a**), the National Health Service (Scotland) Act 1978(**b**) or the Health and Personal Social Services (Northern Ireland) Order 1972(**c**) or in respect of any inspection made in connection with such an application or during the currency of a licence or certificate held by such an authority.

(4) No fee shall be payable under these Regulations in connection with any application for the grant, variation or renewal of a licence or certificate under Part II of the Medicines Act 1968 where that application is made at the specific written invitation of the licensing authority.

Interpretation

2.—(1) Except as provided in paragraph (2) below, expressions used in these Regulations have the same meaning as in the Medicines Act 1968.

(2) In these Regulations, "medicinal product" includes any substance or article specified in any order made under section 104 or 105(1)(a) of the Medicines Act 1968 which directs that Part II of that Act shall have effect in relation to such substance or article.

PART II

FEES FOR APPLICATIONS FOR LICENCES OR CERTIFICATES AND FOR INSPECTIONS IN CONNECTION THEREWITH

Applications for Licences

3. Subject to regulations 16 and 20 of these Regulations, in connection with an application for a product licence, a manufacturer's licence or a wholesale dealer's licence there shall be payable by the applicant –

(a) the fee prescribed in Part II of Schedule 1 to these Regulations in connection with that application; and

(b) in respect of any inspection of a description falling within paragraph 1 of Schedule 2 to these Regulations made in connection with that application the fee payable in accordance with paragraphs 2 to 5 of that Schedule.

Applications for Clinical Trial Certificates

4. Subject to regulation 20 of these Regulations, in connection with an application for a clinical trial certificate, there shall be payable by the applicant a fee of £8,000.

Applications for certificates for exports of medicinal products

5.—(1) In connection with an application for a certificate issued under section 50 of the Medicines Act 1968, there shall be payable by the applicant —

(a) if the applicant requests that the certificate be issued within 24 hours of receipt of the application, a fee of £100;

(b) in any other case, a fee of £50; and

(c) in either case —

(i) a fee of £10 for each certified copy of the original certificate requested by the applicant in excess of four, and

(ii) a fee of £50 for each set of certificates requested by the applicant in addition to one.

(**a**) 1977 c.49. (**b**) 1978 c.29. (**c**) S.I. 1972/1265 (N.I.14).

(2) In paragraph (1)(c)(ii) above, "set of certificates" means the original certificate plus up to four certified copies of that certificate.

PART III

FEES FOR APPLICATIONS FOR VARIATIONS OF LICENCES OR CERTIFICATES

Variations of Licences

6. Subject to regulations 9, 16 and 20 of these Regulations, in connection with an application under section 30 of the Medicines Act 1968 for the variation of a provision of a product licence, a manufacturer's licence or a wholesale dealer's licence, there shall be payable by the applicant –

(a) the fee prescribed in Part III of Schedule 1 of these Regulations; and

(b) in respect of any inspection of a description referred to in paragraph 1 of Schedule 2 to these Regulations made in connection with that application, the fee payable in accordance with paragraphs 2 to 5 of that Schedule.

Variations of Clinical Trial Certificates

7. Subject to regulations 8, 9 and 20 of these Regulations, in connection with an application under section 39(4) of the Medicines Act 1968 for variation of a provision of a clinical trial certificate, there shall be payable by the applicant a fee of £175.

Change of Name or Address in Clinical Trial Certificates

8. Where an application is made for a variation to a provision of the clinical trial certificate and the variation applied for consists of no more than a change of either or both the name and address of the holder of the certificate, there shall be payable by the applicant a fee of £50.

Applications for Multiple Variations

9. A separate fee shall be payable in respect of each variation of each provision of a licence or certificate applied for in any one application except that no separate fee shall be payable in respect of any variation which is related to or is consequential upon another variation of a provision of the same licence or certificate which is applied for in the same application.

PART IV

FEES FOR APPLICATIONS FOR RENEWALS OF LICENCES OR CERTIFICATES

Renewal of Licences

10. Subject to regulations 12, 16 and 20 of these Regulations, in connection with an application under section 24(2) of the Medicines Act 1968 for renewal of a product licence, a manufacturer's licence or a wholesale dealer's licence, there shall be payable by the applicant —

(a) the appropriate fee prescribed in Part IV of Schedule 1 to these Regulations; and

(b) in respect of any inspection of a description referred to in paragraph 1 of Schedule 2 to these Regulations made in connection with that application a fee payable in accordance with paragraphs 2 to 5 of that Schedule.

Renewal of Certificates

11. Subject to regulations 12 and 20 of these Regulations, in connection with an application under section 38(2) of the Medicines Act 1968 for renewal of a clinical trial certificate there shall be payable by the applicant a fee of £2,000.

Renewals in terms which are not identical to the existing licence or certificate

12. Where an applicant applies for renewal of a licence, or as the case may be, a clinical trial certificate so as to contain provisions which are not identical to that licence or certificate as in force at the date of that application, the fee payable under this Part of these Regulations shall be increased by an amount equal to the fee which would have been payable under Part III of these Regulations had he made a separate application for each variation of that licence or certificate.

PART V

FEES FOR INSPECTIONS MADE DURING THE CURRENCY OF A LICENCE

13.—(1) Subject to paragraph (4) below and to regulations 16 and 20 of these Regulations, a fee in accordance with paragraphs 2 to 5 of Schedule 2 to these Regulations shall be payable in respect of any inspection of a site made during the currency of a product licence, a manufacturer's licence or a wholesale dealer's licence (except for any inspection in respect of which a fee is otherwise payable under Parts III or IV of these Regulations).

(2) The fee payable under paragraph (1) above in respect of an inspection of a site made during the currency of a manufacturer's licence or a wholesale dealer's licence shall be payable by the holder of the manufacturer's or, as the case may be, the wholesale dealer's licence.

(3) Where a fee is payable under paragraph (1) above in respect of an inspection of a site located outside the United Kingdom, the fee shall be payable in equal proportions by each holder of a product licence in which that site is named as a possible site for manufacture of the medicinal product in respect of which the product licence is granted.

(4) No fee shall be payable in respect of any inspection of a site carried out within 6 months of a previous inspection in order to ascertain whether alterations or improvements to the premises concerned which were required in writing by the licensing authority as the result of that previous inspection have been implemented.

PART VI

ADMINISTRATION

Payment of fees to Ministers

14. Any sums which under the provisions of these Regulations become payable by way of, or on account of, fees shall be paid to one of the Ministers specified in section 1(1)(a) of the Medicines Act 1968.

Time for payment of fees in connection with applications or inspections and refunds of such fees

15.—(1) Subject to paragraphs (2) and (3) below, all sums payable by way of fees under these Regulations in connection with any application shall be payable at the time of the application.

(2) If, following either the determination of an application or an inspection, it becomes apparent that —

(a) a lesser fee was properly payable, the excess shall be refunded to the applicant or, as the case may be, the holder of the licence or certificate concerned; or

(b) a higher fee was properly payable, the balance due shall be payable within 14 days following written notice from the licensing authority to the applicant or, as the case may be, the holder of the licence or certificate concerned.

(3) All sums payable by way of fees in respect of inspections made either in connection with an application or during the currency of a licence or certificate shall become payable within 14 days following written notice from the licensing authority.

Waiver, Reduction or Refund of Fees

16. The licensing authority shall waive payment of, reduce any fee or part of a fee otherwise payable under these Regulations or refund the whole or part of any fee already so paid in any of the circumstances specified in Schedule 3 to these Regulations.

Suspension of Licences

17. Where any sum due by way of, or on account of, any fee or any part thereof payable under these Regulations remains unpaid by the holder of a licence or certificate, the licensing authority may serve a notice on him requiring payment of the sum unpaid and, if after a period of one month from the date of service of such notice, or such longer period as the licensing authority may allow, the said sum remains unpaid, the licensing authority may forthwith suspend the licence or certificate until such sum has been paid.

Civil proceedings to recover unpaid fees

18. All unpaid sums due by way of, or on account of, any fees payable under these Regulations shall be recoverable as debts due to the Crown.

PART VII

REVOCATION, SAVINGS AND TRANSITIONAL PROVISIONS

Revocation and Savings

19.—(1) Subject to paragraph (2) below, the Regulations specified in Schedule 4 to these Regulations are hereby revoked in so far as they apply in relation wholly or partly to medicinal products for human use.

(2) Paragraph (1) above shall not affect any notice given or any suspension made under the Regulations referred to in Schedule 4 to these Regulations and any such notice or suspension shall have effect as if given or made under these Regulations.

Transitional provisions

20.—(1) Subject to paragraphs (2) to (4) below, these Regulations shall not apply to any application made before 1st April 1989.

(2) A fee shall be payable in respect of any inspection made on or after 1st April 1989 in connection with any application made before that date as if these Regulations applied to that application.

(3) Where an application is made before 1st April 1989 to renew a licence or a certificate which is due to expire on or after 1st October 1989, a fee shall be payable in accordance with Part IV of these Regulations in connection with that application within 14 days following written notice from the licensing authority.

(4) In the case of an article or substance to which Part II of the Medicines Act 1968 applies by virtue of the Medicines (Surgical Materials) Order 1971(**a**), the fee payable under these Regulations in respect of an application for a product licence made on or before 31st March 1990 at the specific written invitation of the licensing authority shall be £250.

Signed by authority of the Secretary of State for Health

D. Mellor
Minister of State,
Department of Health

9th March 1989

Peter Walker
Secretary of State for Wales

8th March 1989

Malcolm Rifkind
Secretary of State for Scotland

8th March 1989

In Witness whereof the Official Seal of the Minister of Agriculture, Fisheries and Food is hereunto affixed on 8th March 1989.

John MacGregor
Minister of Agriculture, Fisheries and Food

Sealed with the Official Seal of the Department of Health and Social Services for Northern Ireland on 9th March 1989.

F.A. Elliott
Permanent Secretary

Sealed with the Official Seal of the Department of Agriculture for Northern Ireland on 9th March 1989.

W.J. Hodges
Permanent Secretary

We consent,

Stephen Dorrell
Kenneth Carlisle
Two of the Lords Commissioners
of Her Majesty's Treasury

7th March 1989

(**a**) S.I. 1971/1267.

SCHEDULE 1

Regulations 3(a), 6(a) and 10(a)

FEES FOR APPLICATIONS, VARIATIONS AND RENEWALS OF LICENCES

PART I

INTERPRETATION

1. In this Schedule —

"active ingredient" means the ingredient of a medicinal product in respect of which therapeutic efficacy is claimed;

"complex application" means an application, other than a major application, for a product licence or, as the case may be, for a variation to a product licence where the application —

(a) is subject to the procedure laid down in Article 9 of Council Directive 75/319/EEC(**a**);

(b) relates to a medicinal product which is intended to be used in accordance with an indication for use in respect of a new category of patients or as treatment for a new category of disease;

(c) relates to a medicinal product containing a new combination of active ingredients that have not previously been included in that combination in a medicinal product in respect of which a product licence (other than a product licence of right) has previously been granted in the United Kingdom;

(d) relates to a medicinal product containing a new excipient;

(e) relates to a medicinal product that is intended to be administered by a route of administration different from that used in the administration of any medicinal product which contains the same active ingredient as the product in question and in respect of which a product licence (other than a product licence of right) has previously been granted in the United Kingdom;

(f) relates to a medicinal product containing an active ingredient the manufacture of which involves a route of synthesis (or, in the case of a medicinal product not synthetically produced, a method of manufacture) different from that used in the manufacture of the active ingredient of any medicinal product which contains the same active ingredient as the product in question and in respect of which a product licence (other than a product licence of right) has previously been granted in the United Kingdom;

(g) relates to a medicinal product which is a controlled release preparation;

(h) relates to a sterile medicinal product the manufacture of which involves a method of sterilisation different from that used in the manufacture of any medicinal product which contains the same active ingredient as the product in question and in respect of which a product licence (other than a product licence of right) has previously been granted in the United Kingdom;

(i) relates to a sterile medicinal product the container of which is directly in contact with the medicinal product and is made from different material from the container of any medicinal product which contains the same active ingredient as the product in question and in respect of which a product licence (other than a product licence of right) has previously been granted in the United Kingdom;

(j) is an application to vary a product licence (parallel import) to include —

(i) importation of the same medicinal product bearing a marketing authorisation issued in a different Member State of the European Economic Community; or

(ii) importation of a medicinal product which is differently formulated from any other medicinal product in respect of which a product licence (parallel import) has previously been granted in the United Kingdom; or

(k) names as manufacturer of the active ingredient of the medicinal product in question a different manufacturer from the manufacturer of that active ingredient included in a medicinal product in respect of which a product licence (other than a product licence of right) has previously been granted in the United Kingdom;

"major application" means an application for a product licence in respect of a medicinal product containing a new active ingredient;

(**a**) O.J. No. L 147, 9.6.1975 p.13, as amended by Article 3 of Council Directive 83/570/EEC, O.J. No. L 332, 28.11.1983, p.1.

"new active ingredient" means an active ingredient that has not previously been included as an active ingredient in a medicinal product in respect of which a product licence (other than a product licence of right) has previously been granted in the United Kingdom;

"new excipient" means any ingredient of a medicinal product, other than an active ingredient, that has not previously been included in a medicinal product —

(a) which is intended to be administered by the same route of administration as the product in question; and

(b) in respect of which a product licence (other than a product licence of right) has previously been granted in the United Kingdom,

except that, in the case of a medicinal product intended to be administered orally, the expression does not include any ingredient specified in any enactment (including an enactment comprised in subordinate legislation) as an approved ingredient or additive in food or in a food product;

"product licence (parallel import)" means a product licence in respect of a medicinal product which is imported into the United Kingdom from another Member State of the European Economic Community; which has been granted a marketing authorisation in another Member State of the Community and which has no differences having therapeutic effect from a medicinal product in respect of which a product licence has previously been granted in the United Kingdom;

"simple application" means an application for a product licence to which Article 4.8(a)(i) of Council Directive 65/65/EEC(**a**) applies;

"standard application" means any application which is not a major, complex or simple application or an application for a product licence (parallel import).

PART II

FEES FOR APPLICATIONS FOR LICENCES

Product Licences

1. Subject to paragraphs 2 and 3 below, the fee payable under regulation 3(a) of these Regulations in connection with an application for a product licence of a kind described in Column 1 of the following Table shall be the fee specified in the corresponding entry in Column 2 of that Table:

Table

Column 1 *Kind of Application*		*Column 2* *Fee Payable*
1. Major application —		
(a) in respect of any such application —	1.(a)	£8,000
(i) to which paragraph 5 of Chapter III of Part 3 of the Annex to Council Directive 75/318/EEC(**b**) applies, or		
(ii) which relates to an article or substance in relation to which Part II of the Medicines Act 1968 has effect by virtue of an order made under section 104 or 105(1)(a) of that Act;		
(b) in any other case	1.(b)	£40,000
2. Complex application	2.	£6,000
3. Standard application	3.	£3,000
4. Simple application	4.	£1,500

(**a**) O.J. No. 22, 9.2.1965, p.369/65, as amended by Article 1.1 of Council Directive 87/21/EEC, O.J. No. L 15/36, 17.1.1987. (**b**) O.J. No. L 147, 9.6.1975, page 1.

Table (contd)

Column 1 *Kind of Application*	*Column 2* *Fee Payable*
5. Application for a product licence (parallel import) –	
(a) in a case where –	5.(a) £1,500
(i) no such licence has previously been granted in the United Kingdom which is in respect of the same product bearing a marketing authorisation issued in the same Member State of the European Economic Community as the product for which a licence is applied; or	
(ii) the application relates to a medicinal product which is differently formulated from any other medicinal product in respect of which a product licence (parallel import) has previously been granted in the United Kingdom;	
(b) in any other case.	5.(b) £1,000

2. Where a major application is made by a person who is already the holder of a clinical trial certificate in respect of a medicinal product containing the same active ingredient as the medicinal product in respect of which the product licence is applied for, the fee payable under regulation 3(a) of these Regulations in connection with that application shall be reduced by the amount of the fee paid in connection with the application for that certificate.

3.—(1) Subject to sub-paragraphs (2) and (3) below, where an application for a product licence is for more than one such licence each relating to a medicinal product containing the same active ingredient or combination of ingredients, the fee payable under regulation 3(a) of these Regulations shall be of an amount equal to the aggregate of the amounts payable under paragraph 1 above in respect of a separate application for each such licence.

(2) If the application is a major application, the amount payable shall be the amount payable in respect of a major application under paragraph 1 above plus —

(a) in respect of each additional product licence applied for which relates to a medicinal product of a different dosage form, the amount payable in respect of a complex application under paragraph 1 above; and

(b) in respect of each additional product licence applied for which relates to a medicinal product of the same dosage form but of a different strength of active ingredient or different combination of active ingredients, the amount payable in respect of a standard application under paragraph 1 above.

(3) If the application is a complex application, the amount payable shall be the amount payable in respect of a complex application under paragraph 1 above plus –

(a) in respect of each additional product licence applied for which relates to a medicinal product of a different dosage form, the amount payable in respect of a complex application under paragraph 1 above; and

(b) in respect of each additional product licence applied for which relates to a medicinal product of the same dosage form but of a different strength of active ingredient or different combination of active ingredients, the amount payable in respect of a standard application under paragraph 1 above.

Manufacturers' Licences

4.—(1) The fee payable under regulation 3(a) of these Regulations in connection with an application for a manufacturer's licence shall be —

(a) in a case to which sub-paragraph (2) below applies, £50;

(b) in any other case, £1,000; and

(c) in either case, if appropriate, a fee calculated in accordance with Schedule 2 to these Regulations in respect of any inspection made in connection with that application.

(2) This sub-paragraph applies to the case of an application for a manufacturer's licence which is limited solely to the manufacture or assembly of medicinal products, the sale or supply of which do not require a product licence and to which Article 2(2)(i)(e) of the Medicines (Exemption from Licences) (Special and Transitional Cases) Order 1971(**a**) applies.

Wholesale Dealers' Licences

5. The fee payable under regulation 3(a) of these Regulations in connection with an application for a wholesale dealer's licence shall be £650.

PART III

FEES FOR APPLICATIONS FOR VARIATIONS OF LICENCES

Product Licences

1. Subject to paragraph 4 below, the fee payable under regulation 6(a) of these Regulations in connection with an application for variation of a product licence shall be —

(a) in the case of a complex application, £1,250; and

(b) in any other case, £175.

Manufacturers' Licences

2. Subject to paragraph 4 below the fee payable under Regulation 6(a) of these Regulations in connection with an application for variation of a manufacturer's licence shall be —

(a) in the case of a manufacturer's licence referred to in paragraph 4(2) of Part II of this Schedule, £50; and

(b) in any other case, £175.

Wholesale Dealers' Licences

3. Subject to paragraph 4 below, the fee payable under regulation 6(a) of these Regulations in connection with an application for variation of a wholesale dealer's licence shall be £175.

Other Variations

4. The fee payable under regulation 6(a) of these Regulations in connection with an application for variation of a product licence, a manufacturer's licence or a wholesale dealer's licence shall be £50 where —

(a) the variation applied for consists of no more than a change of either or both the name and the address of the holder of the licence; and

(b) in the case of an application for variation of a manufacturer's licence or a wholesale dealer's licence only, any change of address does not involve a change of the site of manufacture or wholesale dealing.

PART IV

FEES FOR APPLICATIONS FOR RENEWALS OF LICENCES

Product Licences

1. The fee payable under Regulation 10(a) of these Regulations in connection with an application for renewal of a product licence shall be —

(a) in the case of a product licence of right £100;

(b) in the case of a product licence (parallel import), £500;

(c) except in a case to which sub-paragraphs (a) or (b) above applies, where the medicinal product to which the product licence relates falls within a description or class of medicinal product specified in an Order under section 58(1) of the Medicines Act 1968, £750; and

(d) in any other case, £500.

(**a**) S.I. 1971/1450; there are no relevant amending instruments.

Manufacturers' Licences

2. The fee payable under regulation 10(a) of these Regulations in connection with an application for renewal of a manufacturer's licence shall be —

(a) in the case of a manufacturer's licence referred to in paragraph 4(2) of Part II of this Schedule, £50;

(b) in any other case, £500.

Wholesale Dealers' Licences

3. The fee payable under regulation 10(a) of these Regulations in connection with an application for renewal of a wholesale dealer's licence shall be £325.

SCHEDULE 2

Regulations 3(b), 6(b), 10(b) and 13

FEES FOR INSPECTIONS

Interpretation

1.—(1) In this Schedule —

"major inspection" means an inspection at a site at which 60 or more relevant persons are employed;

"minor inspection" means an inspection at a site at which fewer than 10 relevant persons are employed;

"relevant person" means any person directly or indirectly engaged in, or assisting in, the manufacture or assembly of medicinal products and also includes any person connected with such production who is involved in management, quality control, site maintenance, packing, storage or distribution;

"standard inspection" means an inspection at a site at which 10 or more, but fewer than 60, relevant persons are employed.

(2) In calculating the number of relevant persons for the purposes of this Schedule, any person partly engaged in or assisting in the manufacture or assembly of medicinal products (whether as a part-time employee or by virtue of being only partly employed in such work) shall be included in the calculation but only as a fraction calculated by reference to the amount of time spent by that person engaged or assisting in the manufacture or assembly of medicinal products or, where such a calculation is inappropriate, by reference to the percentage of his job which relates to the manufacture or assembly of such products and, in either case, by comparison with the average working week of a relevant person engaged in full-time employment at the same site.

Fees

2. Subject to paragraphs 3 to 5 below, the fee payable in respect of an inspection under these Regulations shall be —

(a) except in the case of an inspection falling within sub-paragraphs (b) to (d) below —

(i) in respect of a minor inspection, £750;

(ii) in respect of a standard inspection, £1,500;

(iii) in respect of a major inspection, £3,000;

(b) where the site inspected is wholly or partly concerned with the manufacture of sterile products or the filling of the containers directly in contact with such products —

(i) in respect of a minor inspection, £1,250;

(ii) in respect of a standard inspection, £2,500;

(iii) in respect of a major inspection, £5,000;

(c) except in the case of an inspection falling within sub-paragraph (b) above or sub-paragraph (d) below, where the site inspected is concerned only with the assembly of medicinal products —

(i) in respect of a minor inspection, £500;

(ii) in respect of a standard inspection, £1,000;

(iii) in respect of a major inspection, £2,000;

(d) where the site inspected is limited solely to the manufacture or assembly of medicinal products, the sale or supply of which does not require a product licence and to which Article 2(2)(i)(e) of the Medicines (Exemption from Licences) (Special and Transitional Cases) Order 1971 applies, £50.

3.—(1) Subject to sub-paragraph (2) below, unless the applicant or, as the case may be, the holder of the licence establishes that an inspection is a minor inspection or a standard inspection, the fee payable shall be the appropriate fee specified in paragraph 2 above for a major inspection.

(2) If, following an inspection, it becomes apparent that the inspection fell into a different category from that established by the applicant or the holder of the licence, the fee payable under these Regulations in respect of that inspection shall be the fee payable in respect of an inspection falling within the category into which the inspection should have fallen.

4. In the case of an inspection in connection with the grant, variation or renewal of a wholesale dealer's licence or during the currency of such a licence, the fee payable under these Regulations shall be —

(a) except in a case falling within sub-paragraph (b) below, £650;

(b) where the site is that of a wholesale dealer whose licence is limited to dealing only in medicinal products falling within a description or class specified in an Order made under section 51(1) of the Medicines Act 1968, £250.

5. The fee payable in respect of an inspection at a site outside the United Kingdom shall be increased by an amount equal to the travelling and subsistence costs of the inspector relating to the inspection and any additional costs reasonably incurred by him in respect of that inspection as a result of its being at a site outside the United Kingdom (such as interpreter's fees).

Regulation 16

SCHEDULE 3

WAIVER, REDUCTION OR REFUND OF FEES

1. Where the manufacture, assembly, sale or supply of medicinal products of a particular class or description will be, or is likely to be, interrupted for a period and in consequence thereof the health of the community will be, or is likely to be, put at risk, any fees otherwise payable under these Regulations in connection with an application for the grant of a product licence or a manufacturer's licence relating to a medicinal product falling within that class or description shall be waived during that period or, if the period will, or is likely to, exceed 3 months, during the first 3 months of that period.

2.—(1) Subject to sub-paragraph (2) below, where an application for a product licence or a clinical trial certificate is withdrawn before determination by the licensing authority, the following percentage of the fee otherwise payable under regulation 3(a) or 4 of these Regulations in connection with that application shall be refunded or, if it has not yet been paid, shall be waived:—

(a) if the application has been received but no medical, scientific or pharmaceutical assessment thereof has begun, 90%;

(b) except in a case to which paragraph (c) below applies, if medical, scientific or pharmaceutical assessment has begun but not been completed, 50%;

(c) if a request for further information in connection with the application has been made by the licensing authority under section 44(1) of the Medicines Act 1968, 25%.

(2) If an application for a product licence or clinical trial certificate is withdrawn either after medical, scientific and pharmaceutical assessment has been completed or following consideration of that application by a committee established under section 4 of the Medicines Act 1968 or by the Medicines Commission, no refund or waiver of the fee payable under regulation 3(a) or 4 of these Regulations in connection with that application shall be made under this paragraph.

3. Where an application for a manufacturer's or a wholesale dealer's licence is withdrawn before determination by the licensing authority, the following percentage of the fee otherwise payable under regulation 3(a) of these Regulations in connection with that application shall be refunded or, if it has not yet been paid, shall be waived:–

(a) if the application is withdrawn before any inspection in connection with that application has been made, 90%;

(b) if such an inspection has been made, 50%.

4. Where the same site is inspected at the same time in connection with applications for the grant, variation or renewal of both a manufacturer's licence and a wholesale dealer's licence or during the currency of both such licences, the fee otherwise payable under these Regulations in respect of the inspection relating to the wholesale dealer's licence shall be waived.

SCHEDULE 4

Regulation 19(1)

REGULATIONS REVOKED IN SO FAR AS THEY APPLY IN RELATION WHOLLY OR PARTLY TO MEDICINAL PRODUCTS FOR HUMAN USE

The Medicines (Fees) Regulations 1978**(a)**

The Medicines (Fees) Amendment Regulations 1979**(b)**

The Medicines (Fees) Amendment Regulations 1980**(c)**

The Medicines (Fees) Amendment (No. 2) Regulations 1980**(d)**

The Medicines (Fees) Amendment Regulations 1982**(e)**

The Medicines (Fees) Amendment Regulations 1983**(f)**

The Medicines (Fees) Amendment Regulations 1985**(g)**

The Medicines (Fees) Amendment Regulations 1987**(h)**

(a) S.I. 1978/1121. **(b)** S.I. 1979/899. **(c)** S.I. 1980/16. **(d)** S.I. 1980/1126. **(e)** S.I. 1982/1121. **(f)** S.I. 1983/1731. **(g)** S.I. 1985/1231. **(h)** S.I. 1987/1439.

EXPLANATORY NOTE

(This note is not part of the Regulations)

These Regulations, which replace the Medicines (Fees) Regulations 1978 (as amended), prescribe fees in connection with applications and inspections relating to licences and certificates granted under the Medicines Act 1968 in so far as they apply to medicinal products for human use only.

These Regulations provide for fees to be payable for applications for the grant of product licences, manufacturers' licences, wholesale dealers' licences, clinical trial certificates and export certificates (Part II).

The Regulations also provide for fees to be payable for applications for variations of such licences or certificates (Part III) and for renewal thereof (Part IV). In addition the Regulations provide for fees to be payable in respect of inspections of sites carried out in connection with such applications for such licences or certificates and during the currency thereof (Part V).

Administrative provisions (Part VI) deal with time of payment and waiver or refund of fees in specified circumstances.

Part VII of the Regulations deals with revocations, savings and transitional provisions.

STATUTORY INSTRUMENTS

1989 No. 419

NATIONAL HEALTH SERVICE, ENGLAND AND WALES

The National Health Service (Charges for Drugs and Appliances) Regulations 1989

Made - - - -	*9th March 1989*
Laid before Parliament	*10th March 1989*
Coming into force -	*1st April 1989*

The Secretary of State for Health, in exercise of powers conferred by sections 41, 42, 77, 83 and 83A of, and paragraph 1 of Schedule 12 to, the National Health Service Act 1977**(a)** and of all other powers enabling him in that behalf, hereby makes the following Regulations:–

Citation and commencement

1. These Regulations may be cited as the National Health Service (Charges for Drugs and Appliances) Regulations 1989 and shall come into force on 1st April 1989.

Interpretation

2.—(1) In these Regulations, unless the context otherwise requires–

"the Act" means the National Health Service Act 1977;

"accepted disablement" means physical or mental injury or disease which is accepted by the Secretary of State as attributable to or aggravated by service in the armed forces of the Crown or such other service as he may determine;

"appliance" means a listed appliance within the meaning of section 41 of the Act but does not include a contraceptive appliance;

"chemist" includes any person, other than a doctor, providing pharmaceutical services;

"Committee" means Family Practitioner Committee;

"doctor" means a registered medical practitioner;

"drugs" includes medicines, but does not include contraceptive substances;

"elastic hosiery" means an above-knee, below-knee or thigh stocking;

"exemption" means any remission granted under these regulations from charges payable under these regulations;

"exemption certificate" has the meaning assigned to it by regulation 7(1);

"medical list" means the list of doctors prepared under regulation 4(1) of the Medical Services Regulations;

(a) 1977 c.49; *see* section 128 for the definitions of "prescribed" and "regulations"; section 41 was amended by the Health Services Act 1980 (c.53), section 20(1) and modified by S.I. 1985/39, Article 7(13); section 42 was substituted by the National Health Service (Amendment) Act 1986 (c.66), section 3(1) and amended by S.I. 1987/2202, Article 4; section 83A was inserted by the Society Security Act 1988 (c.7), section 14(1).

"the Medical Services Regulations" means the National Health Service (General Medical and Pharmaceutical Services) Regulations 1974**(a)**;

"oxygen concentrator" and "oxygen concentrator services" have the meanings assigned to them by regulation 26D of the Medical Services Regulations**(b)**;

"patient" means–

(a) any person for whose treatment a doctor is responsible under his terms of service;

(b) any person who applies to a chemist for the provision of pharmaceutical services including a person who applies on behalf of another person; or

(c) a person who pays or undertakes to pay on behalf of another person a charge for which these regulations provide;

"pre-payment certificate" has the meaning assigned to it by regulation 8(1);

"prescription form" means a form on which the provision of pharmaceutical services may be ordered by–

(a) a doctor in pursuance of a health authority's functions; or

(b) a doctor or dental practitioner under the provisions of their terms of service,

and which contains on its reverse side a form of declaration of entitlement to exemption;

"terms of service" in relation to doctors and chemists has the meaning assigned to it in regulation 2(1) of the Medical Services Regulations and in relation to dental practitioners the meaning assigned to it in regulation 2(1) of the National Health Service (General Dental Services) Regulations 1973**(c)**;

"the Travelling Expenses and Remission of Charges Regulations" means the National Health Service (Travelling Expenses and Remission of Charges) Regulations 1988**(d)**;

"treatment" includes examination and diagnosis.

(2) For the purposes of these Regulations the supply against an order on one prescription form–

(a) of quantities of the same drug in more than one container shall be treated as the supply of only one quantity of a drug;

(b) of more than one appliance of the same type, except in the case of elastic hosiery and tights, or of two or more component parts of the same appliance shall be treated as the supply of only one appliance.

(3) Unless the context otherwise requires, any reference in these Regulations to a numbered regulation or Schedule is a reference to the regulation in, or Schedule to, these Regulations which bears that number, and any reference in a regulation to a numbered paragraph is a reference to the paragraph bearing that number in that regulation.

Supply of drugs and appliances by chemists

3.—(1) A chemist who provides pharmaceutical services to a patient shall, subject to paragraph (2), make and recover from that patient–

(a) in respect of an item of elastic hosiery a charge of £2.80, that is to say a charge of £5.60, per pair;

(b) in respect of an oxygen concentrator, a charge of £2.80 for each month in which the chemist provides any oxygen concentrator services;

(c) in respect of the supply of each other appliance and of each quantity of a drug, a charge of £2.80.

(2) No charge shall be made and recovered under paragraph (1) where–

(a) there is exemption under regulation 6 and a declaration of entitlement to exemption on the prescription form is duly completed by or on behalf of the patient;

(a) S.I. 1974/160, relevant amending instruments are S.I. 1975/719, 1982/1283, 1985/39 and 1053.
(b) *See* S.I. 1985/955, regulation 2(5).
(c) S.I. 1973/1468, to which there are amendments not relevant to these Regulations.
(d) S.I. 1988/551.

(b) there is entitlement to remission of the charge under regulation 3 of the Travelling Expenses and Remission of Charges Regulations;

(c) the patient is resident in a school or institution the name of which is inserted on the prescription form by a doctor under his terms of service; or

(d) a chemist provides oxygen concentrator services to a patient in a month and a charge is already required to be made under these Regulations to that patient, whether by that or another chemist, in respect of another oxygen concentrator for that month or such charge would be required to be made but for any exemption.

(3) For the purposes of this regulation, where a drug ordered on a single prescription form is supplied by instalments, the charge of £2.80 payable for that drug shall be payable upon the supply of the first instalment.

(4) A chemist, notwithstanding the provisions of his terms of service, shall be under no obligation to provide pharmaceutical services in respect of an order on a prescription form unless he is first paid by the patient any charge required to be made and recovered by paragraph (1) in respect of that order.

(5) A chemist who makes and recovers a charge under paragraph (1) shall, if so required by the patient, give him a receipt for the amount received on a form provided for the purpose by the Committee which shall contain forms of declaration in support of an application for repayment and information as to whom an application for repayment shall be made.

(6) Any sum which would otherwise be payable by a Committee to a chemist in respect of the provision by him of pharmaceutical services shall be reduced by the amount of any charges which are required to be made and recovered by the preceding provisions of this regulation.

Supply of drugs and appliances by doctors

4.—(1) A doctor who provides pharmaceutical services to a patient shall, subject to paragraph (2), make and recover from that patient–

(a) in respect of the supply of an item of elastic hosiery a charge of £2.80, that is to say a charge of £5.60 per pair;

(b) in respect of the supply of each other appliance and of each quantity of a drug, a charge of £2.80.

(2) No charge shall be made and recovered under paragraph (1) where–

(a) there is exemption under regulation 6 and the patient or a person on his behalf declares, in writing if the doctor so requires, that he is entitled to exemption;

(b) there is entitlement to remission of the charge under regulation 3 of the Travelling Expenses and Remission of Charges Regulations; or

(c) the drugs or appliances are supplied in respect of two or more persons in a school or institution in which at least 20 persons are normally resident of whom at least 10 are his patients.

(3) For the purposes of this regulation, where a drug ordered on a single prescription form is supplied by instalments, the charge of £2.80 payable for that drug shall be payable upon the supply of the first instalment.

(4) A doctor shall, notwithstanding the provisions of his terms of service, be under no obligation to provide pharmaceutical services for which a charge is required to be made and recovered by paragraph (1) unless he is first paid the amount of that charge by the patient.

(5) A doctor who makes and recovers a charge under paragraph (1) shall, if so required by the patient, give him a receipt for the amount received on a form provided for the purpose by the Committee which shall contain forms of declaration in support of an application for repayment and information as to whom an application for repayment shall be made.

(6) A doctor shall as soon as practicable after the end of each month send a sum of money, equal to the total of the charges required to be made and recovered by him under

paragraph (1) during that month, to the Committee on whose medical list he is included, or, if he is included on more than one medical list, to the Committee which, under the provisions of the Statement published under regulation 24 of the Medical Services Regulations, pays him for the provision of general medical services on behalf of all the Committees concerned.

(7) Nothing in this regulation shall authorise the payment of a charge where the drug or appliance supplied either–

(a) is needed for immediate treatment and no order for the drug or appliance is made on a prescription form; or

(b) is administered or applied to the patient by the doctor personally.

Supply of drugs and appliances by health authorities

5.—(1) A health authority which supplies to a patient, for the purposes of his treatment, drugs otherwise than for administration at a hospital or appliances shall, subject to paragraph (2), make and recover from the patient–

(a) in respect of an item of elastic hosiery a charge of £2.80, that is to say a charge of £5.60 per pair;

(b) in respect of an appliance specified in column (1) of Schedule 1, the charge specified in relation to it in column (2) of that Schedule;

(c) in respect of tights, a charge of £5.60;

(d) in respect of the supply of each other appliance and of each quantity of a drug, a charge of £2.80.

(2) No charge shall be made and recovered under this regulation from a patient who is exempt–

(a) under paragraph 1(1)(a) to (d) of Schedule 12 to the Act;

(b) under regulation 6 and who provides such evidence of his exemption as the health authority may reasonably require; or

(c) by reason of being entitled to remission under regulation 3 of the Travelling Expenses and Remission of Charges Regulations.

(3) For the purposes of this regulation, where a drug ordered on a single prescription form is supplied by instalments, the charge of £2.80 payable for that drug shall be payable upon the supply of the first instalment.

(4) A health authority which makes and recovers a charge under this regulation shall, if so required by the patient, give him a receipt for the amount received on a form which shall contain forms of declaration in support of an application for repayment and information as to whom an application for repayment shall be made.

Exemptions

6.—(1) No charge shall be payable under regulation 3 or regulation 4 by–

(a) a person who is under 16 years of age;

(b) a person who is under 19 years of age and is receiving qualifying full-time education within the meaning of paragraph 7 of Schedule 12 to the Act**(a)**;

(c) a man who has attained the age of 65 years or a woman who has attained the age of 60 years;

(d) a woman with a valid exemption certificate issued by a Committee on the ground that she is an expectant mother or has within the last twelve months given birth to a live child or a child registrable as still-born under the Births and Deaths Registration Act 1953**(b)**;

(e) a person with a valid exemption certificate issued by a Committee on the ground that he is suffering from one or more of the following conditions–

(i) permanent fistula (including caecostomy, colostomy, laryngostomy or ileostomy) requiring continuous surgical dressing or an appliance;

(ii) the following disorders for which specific substitution therapy is essential–

(a) Paragraph 7 was substituted by the Health Services Act 1980 (c.53), Schedule 5, paragraph 4.
(b) 1953 c.20.

Addison's disease and other forms of hypoadrenalism,
diabetes insipidus and other forms of hypopituitarism,
diabetes mellitus,
hypoparathyroidism,
myasthenia gravis,
myxoedema;

(iii) epilepsy requiring continuous anti-convulsive therapy;

(iv) a continuing physical disability which prevents the patient from leaving his residence without the help of another person;

(f) a person with a valid exemption certificate issued by the Secretary of State in respect of the supply of drugs and appliances for the treatment of accepted disablement, but only in respect of those supplies to which the certificate relates;

(g) a person with a valid pre-payment certificate.

(2) No charge shall be payable under regulation 5–

(a) in respect of the supply of an appliance specified in column (1) of Schedule 1, by a person of a description specified in paragraph (1)(f);

(b) in respect of the supply of an appliance not so specified or of drugs, by a person of a description specified in any of sub-paragraphs (c) to (g) of paragraph (1).

(3) A charge referred to in column (1) of Schedule 1 shall, in the case of a person referred to in regulation 5 of the Travelling Expenses and Remission of Charges Regulations, be remitted to the extent specified in that regulation.

(4) An exemption by reference to age or the validity of an exemption certificate shall be determined by reference to the age or validity on the day on which–

(a) in the case of pharmaceutical services provided by a chemist, the order for drugs or appliances is presented for dispensing;

(b) in any other case, the drugs or appliances are supplied.

(5) Where a claim to exemption has been made but is not substantiated and in consequence of that claim a chemist, a doctor or a health authority has not recovered a charge in respect of the supply of any drugs or appliances, a Committee or that health authority shall recover such charge from the person concerned.

Certificates of exemption—application and issue

7.—(1) A person who wishes to claim exemption under the provisions of regulation 6(1)(d), (e) or (f) shall apply for a certificate conferring exemption (in these Regulations referred to as an "exemption certificate") to the Committee in the case of an exemption under sub-paragraph (d) or (e) on a form supplied for that purpose by the Committee and in the case of an exemption under sub-paragraph (f) to an office of the Department of Social Security on a form supplied for that purpose by the Secretary of State.

(2) A Committee, on being satisfied that an applicant is entitled to exemption under paragraph (1)(d), shall issue an exemption certificate which shall be valid–

(a) in the case of an expectant mother until the end of her pregnancy and, where she gives birth to a live child or a child registrable as still-born under the Births and Deaths Registration Act 1953, until the end of the period of twelve months beginning with the expected date of confinement;

(b) in the case of a mother who has given birth to a child, until the end of the period of twelve months beginning with the date of birth of that child.

(3) A Committee, on being satisfied that an applicant, not being a person entitled to exemption under the provisions of regulation 6(1)(a), (b) or (c), is entitled to exemption under regulation 6(1)(e) shall issue to the applicant an exemption certificate which shall be valid for such period as it may determine.

(4) The Secretary of State, on being satisfied that an applicant is entitled to exemption under regulation 6(1)(f), shall issue to the applicant an exemption certificate which shall be valid for such period as he may determine.

Pre-payment certificates

8.—(1) Subject to the following provisions of this regulation, a Committee on payment of the relevant sum prescribed by paragraph (5) shall as soon as reasonably practicable grant a certificate (in these regulations referred to as a "pre-payment certificate") to any person who duly completes and submits an application for it on a form provided for the purpose by the Committee.

(2) A pre-payment certificate shall be valid for a period of either four months or twelve months and an application for such a certificate shall indicate the period for which it is required to be valid.

(3) A pre-payment certificate which is granted confers on the person to whom it is granted exemption as provided by regulation 6 in respect of drugs and appliances supplied during the period for which it is valid.

(4) No pre-payment certificate shall be granted unless the application made for it is received less than one month before the date on which its period of validity is to begin.

(5) For the purposes of this regulation the prescribed sum shall be £14.50 for a pre-payment certificate valid for 4 months and £40.00 for a pre-payment certificate valid for 12 months.

(6) Where payment of a prescribed sum has been made under this regulation and, not more than one month after the date on which his certificate became valid, the person in respect of whom payment was made either becomes a person to whom any of the provisions of regulation 6(1)(b) to (f) applies, or dies, an application for repayment of that sum may be made, by or on behalf of that person or his estate, in accordance with paragraph (7).

(7) An application under paragraph (6) shall be made to the Committee which granted the certificate and shall be accompanied by the certificate (where granted) and a declaration in support of the claim, and the claim and any repayment shall be made in such manner and subject to such conditions as the Secretary of State may determine.

Repayment of charges

9.—(1) Where a charge has been paid under these Regulations by or on behalf of a person who was at the time of payment exempt from the requirement to pay that charge, an application for repayment of that charge may be made in accordance with paragraph (2) by or on behalf of that person.

(2) The application for repayment shall–

(a) be made to the person or body specified in the receipt which is given under regulation 3(5), 4(5) or 5(4) as being the person or body to whom application for repayment of charges is to be made;

(b) be made within such period of the supply of the drug or appliance, and in such form and manner, as the Secretary of State may determine for the applicant, any class of applicant or applicants generally;

(c) be accompanied by the receipt for the charge paid and a declaration as to the grounds of exemption.

(3) In the case of a charge under regulation 5 in respect of an appliance specified in column (1) of Schedule 1, the application shall be accompanied by the exemption certificate referred to in regulation 6(1)(f) and, if the patient was referred by a doctor to the health authority for treatment, either–

(a) a certificate from the doctor certifying that the treatment was for accepted disablement; or

(b) a statement that such a certificate was surrendered to the health authority on or before the supply of the appliance.

(4) The Secretary of State shall make arrangements for the repayment of any charge paid under these Regulations by a person who is entitled to exemption.

Application

10. These Regulations shall apply only where drugs and appliances are supplied on or after 1st April 1989.

Revocations

11. The Regulations specified in column (1) of Schedule 2 are hereby revoked to the extent specified in column (3) of that Schedule.

Signed by authority of the Secretary of State for Health

D. Mellor
Minister of State,
Department of Health

9th March 1989.

SCHEDULE 1

Regulation 5

CHARGES FOR FABRIC SUPPORTS AND WIGS

(1) *Specified Appliance*	(2) *Specified Charge*
Surgical Brassiere	£12.00
Abdominal or Spinal Support	£16.00
Stock Modacrylic Wig	£24.00
Partial Human Hair Wig	£62.00
Full Bespoke Human Hair Wig	£97.00

SCHEDULE 2

Regulation 12

REGULATIONS REVOKED

(1) *Regulations revoked*	(2) *Reference*	(3) *Extent of revocation*
The National Health Service (Charges for Drugs and Appliances) Regulations 1980	S.I. 1980/1503	The whole Regulations
The National Health Service (Charges for Drugs and Appliances) Amendment Regulations 1981	S.I. 1981/1714	The whole Regulations
The National Health Service (Charges for Drugs and Appliances) Amendment Regulations 1983	S.I. 1983/306	The whole Regulations
The National Health Service (Charges for Drugs and Appliances) Amendment (No. 2) Regulations 1983	S.I. 1983/1165	The whole Regulations
The National Health Service (Charges for Drugs and Appliances) Amendment Regulations 1984	S.I. 1984/298	The whole Regulations
The National Health Service (Charges for Drugs and Appliances) Amendment Regulations 1985	S.I. 1985/326	The whole Regulations
The National Health Service (Charges for Drugs and Appliances) Amendment (No. 2) Regulations 1985	S.I. 1985/1671	The whole Regulations
The National Health Service (Charges for Drugs and Appliances) Amendment Regulations 1987	S.I. 1987/368	The whole Regulations
The National Health Service (Charges for Drugs and Appliances) Amendment Regulations 1988	S.I. 1988/427	The whole Regulations
The National Health Service (General Medical and Pharmaceutical Services and Charges for Drugs) Amendment Regulations 1988	S.I. 1988/866	Regulation 3

EXPLANATORY NOTE

(This note is not part of the Regulations)

These Regulations replace with amendments the Regulations providing for the making and recovery of charges for drugs and appliances (other than dental and optical appliances) supplied under the National Health Service Act 1977.

Accordingly, these Regulations provide for charges for drugs and appliances supplied by doctors and chemists providing pharmaceutical services (regulations 3 and 4) and by health authorities to patients who are not resident in hospital (regulation 5).

The Regulations provide in addition for–

the reduction of a chemist's remuneration by the amount of the charge recoverable under the Regulations (regulation 3(6));

a doctor providing pharmaceutical services to send each month a sum equal to the total of the charges recovered under the Regulations to the Family Practitioner Committee which pays him for the provision of general medical services (regulation 4(6));

the remission of charges (regulations 3(2), 4(2), 5(2) and 6);

the application for and the issue of exemption certificates (regulation 2(1) and 7);

the payment for certificates granting exemption from charges otherwise exigible under these Regulations (regulation 8);

the repayment of charges (regulation 9); and

the revocation of the superceded Regulations on charges for drugs and appliances (regulation 11).

The amendments increase the charge for items on prescription or supplied to out-patients, and the monthly charge in respect of an oxygen concentrate supplied by a chemist, from £2.60 to £2.80. The charge for elastic stockings is increased from £2.60 to £2.80 each and for tights from £5.20 to £5.60. The charges for wigs are increased from £90.00 to £97. 00 (human hair wig), from £58.00 to £62.00 (partial human hair wig) and from £22.00 to £24.00 (modacrylic wig). The charge for fabric supports is increased from £15.00 to £16.00 and the charge for surgical brassieres is increased from £11.00 to £12.00. The sums prescribed for the grant of pre-payment certificates of exemption from charges are increased from £13.50 to £14.50 for a four month certificate and from £37.50 to £40.00 for a twelve month certificate.

The other amendments of substance are that there is no longer a provision enabling charges to be paid by means of postage stamps and there is no minimum period within which a claim for repayment of a charge wrongly paid has to be made.

STATUTORY INSTRUMENTS

1989 No. 420

INJURIES IN WAR COMPENSATION

The Injuries in War (Shore Employments) Compensation (Amendment) Scheme 1989

Made - - - - *1st March 1989*

The Defence Council, with the consent of the Treasury, in exercise of powers conferred by section 1 of the Injuries in War Compensation Act 1914 (Session 2)(**a**) and now vested in them(**b**), hereby make the following Scheme:–

1. The Injuries in War (Shore Employments) Compensation Scheme 1914(**c**) shall be amended as follows:–

In paragraph (3) thereof for the figures "£67.20", wherever they occur, there shall be substituted the figures "£71.20".

2. This Scheme shall have effect on and after 10 April 1989, so, however, that no payment shall be made thereunder in respect of any period before that date.

3. This Scheme may be cited as the Injuries in War (Shore Employments) Compensation (Amendment) Scheme 1989, and the Injuries in War (Shore Employments) Compensation Schemes 1914 to 1988 and this Scheme may be cited together as the Injuries in War (Shore Employments) Compensation Schemes 1914 to 1989.

Trefgarne
Michael Quinlan
Members of the Defence Council

Dated 1st March 1989

We consent,

Stephen Dorrel
David Lightbown
Two of the Lords Commissioners of Her Majesty's Treasury

(**a**) 1914 c.18 (5 & 6 Geo 5). (**b**) S.I. 1964/488. (**c**) Relevant amending instruments are S.I. 1949/2285 1961/1246 1971/1987, 1972/1280. 1973/1635, 1974/1104, 1975/265, 1696, 1976/1461, 1977/1836, 1978/1629, 1979/1506, 1980/1731, 1981/1475, 1983, 756, 1713, 1985/299, 1566, 1986/1095, 1987/529 and 1988/624.

EXPLANATORY NOTE

(This note is not part of the Order)

The Injuries in War (Shore Employments) Compensation Schemes 1914 to 1988 provide for the payment of weekly allowance to small numbers of ex-members of the Women's Auxiliary Forces who suffered disablement from their services overseas during the 1914–18 war. This amending Scheme provides that the maximum weekly allowance payable shall be increased from £67.20 to £71.20 and that other allowances shall be increased proportionately. The increase will take effect on and after 10 April 1989.

STATUTORY INSTRUMENTS

1989 No. 421

INCOME TAX

The Lloyd's Underwriters (Tax) Regulations 1989

Made - - - -	*10th March 1989*
Laid before the House of Commons	*10th March 1989*
Coming into force	*6th April 1989*

The Commissioners of Inland Revenue, in exercise of the powers conferred on them by paragraph 17(1) and (1A) of Schedule 16 to the Finance Act 1973(**a**) and paragraph 1(1) and (3) of Schedule 16A to that Act hereby make the following Regulations:

Citation, commencement and effect

1.—(1) These Regulations may be cited as the Lloyd's Underwriters (Tax) Regulations 1989 and shall come into force on 6th April 1989 but shall have effect for the year of assessment 1986–87 only.

(2) Except for regulations 2, 3, 7 and 21(1) to (3), the Lloyd's Underwriters (Tax) Regulations 1974(**b**) shall not have effect for the year of assessment 1986–87.

Interpretation

2.—(1) In these Regulations unless the context otherwise requires–

"Board" means the Commissioners of Inland Revenue;

"member" means an underwriting member of Lloyd's;

"Schedule 16" means Schedule 16 to the Finance Act 1973 and "Schedule 16A" means Schedule 16A to that Act;

"syndicate gains" means the chargeable gains accruing to a member on the disposal of assets forming part of a premiums trust fund;

"syndicate investment income" means the profits or gains arising to a member from assets forming part of a premiums trust fund;

"the Taxes Acts" means the Taxes Management Act 1970(**c**) and–

(a) the Tax Acts as defined in Schedule 1 to the Interpretation Act 1978(**d**), as originally enacted, and

(b) the Capital Gains Tax Act 1979(**e**) and all other enactments relating to capital gains tax.

(2) For the purposes of these Regulations an underwriting year corresponds to the year of assessment in which it ends.

Assessment and collection: general

3.—(1) Subject to paragraph (2) and regulations 4 to 9, the like provisions as are contained in the Taxes Acts relating to the assessment and collection of tax shall have effect in relation to tax charged in accordance with Schedule 16.

(**a**) 1973 c.51; paragraph 17(1) was amended by section 61(4)(a) of the Finance Act 1988 (c.39), and paragraph 17(1A) was inserted by section 61(4)(b) of that Act. Schedule 16A was inserted by the Finance Act 1988, section 58(4). (**b**) S.I. 1974/896, amended by S.I. 1974/1330. (**c**) 1970 c.9. (**d**) 1978 c.30. (**e**) 1979 c.14.

(2) The like provisions as are specified in the first column of the Schedule to these Regulations shall have effect in relation thereto as if the modifications specified in the second column had been made.

Date for payment

4.—(1) Subject to paragraph (2)–

(a) tax charged by an assessment on–

(i) the profits or gains arising to a member from his underwriting business, and

(ii) the profits or gains arising to him from assets forming part of a premiums trust fund,

shall be payable on or before 1st July 1990, and

(b) tax charged by an assessment on a member's syndicate gains shall be payable on or before 1st January 1990.

(2) Tax contained in an assessment made less than 30 days before, or after, the date specified in sub-paragraph (a) or (b) of paragraph (1) shall be payable at the expiration of a period of 30 days beginning with the date of the issue of the notice of assessment.

Set-off

5.—(1) Where any syndicate profit or loss returned by an agent under paragraph 2(1) of Schedule 16A includes any syndicate investment income which has suffered tax by way of deduction, the tax so deducted shall be set in the first place against the amount (if any) payable under paragraph 3(1)(a) of Schedule 16A.

(2) Where, under the provisions of section 87 of the Finance Act 1972**(a)**, the aggregate amount of any such income includes an amount of tax credit, the amount of that credit shall be set in the first place against the amount so payable.

(3) Where any such income includes interest or dividends to which the Income Tax (Building Societies) Regulations 1986(**b**) apply, the amount actually paid or credited shall be deemed to be a net amount corresponding to a gross amount from which income tax has been deducted at the basic rate for the year 1986–87.

Repayment

6. Where–

(a) any tax suffered by way of deduction on any syndicate investment income, or

(b) the amount of any tax credit included in the aggregate amount of any such income,

exceeds the amount (if any) payable by an agent under paragraph 3(1)(a) of Schedule 16A, the inspector shall pay the excess tax to the agent or, as the case may be, give credit to him for the balance of the tax credit.

Reasonable excuse

7. For the purposes of Schedule 16A, an agent shall be deemed not to have failed–

(a) to deliver a return of a syndicate profit or loss within the time specified in paragraph 2(2) of that Schedule, or

(b) to deliver a return apportioning a syndicate profit or loss within the period referred to in paragraph 7(3) of that Schedule,

if he delivered it within such further time, if any, as the inspector may have allowed; and where an agent had a reasonable excuse for not delivering such a return he shall be deemed not to have failed to deliver it unless the excuse had ceased and, after the excuse ceased, not to have failed to deliver it if he did so without unreasonable delay after the excuse had ceased.

(**a**) 1972 (c.41); subsection (2)(c) of section 87 was amended by the Finance Act 1980 (c.48), section 122(4) and Schedule 20, Part V, and subsection (6) was amended by the Finance Act 1978 (c.42), section 14 and Schedule 2, paragraph 15(6) and by the Finance Act 1984 (c.43), sections 17(2) and 128(6) and Schedule 7, paragraph 2(2)(b) and Schedule 23, Part VI. (**b**) S.I. 1986/482, amended by S.I. 1987/844, 1988/1011 and 1989/36.

Determinations and notices of determinations

8. The like provisions as are contained in sections 113(1B) and (3) and 114(2) of the Taxes Management Act 1970**(a)** shall apply to a determination or a notice of a determination under Schedule 16A as if the determination were an assessment and the notice of the determination were a notice of an assessment.

Error or mistake

9.—(1) If an agent alleges that a determination under paragraph 4 of Schedule 16A was excessive because of some error or mistake in a return made by him under paragraph 2 of that Schedule, he may by notice in writing at any time not later than six years after the end of the year of assessment 1988–89 make a claim to the Board for relief.

(2) On receiving the claim the Board shall inquire into the matter and having regard to all the relevant circumstances of the case, but subject to paragraph (3), give by way of repayment or otherwise such relief in respect of the error or mistake as is reasonable and just.

(3) No relief shall be given under this regulation in respect of an error or mistake as to the basis on which the syndicate profit or loss ought to have been computed where the return was in fact made on the basis or in accordance with the practice generally prevailing at the time when the return was made.

(4) An appeal may be brought against the decision of the Board on the claim, by giving written notice to the Board within 30 days of receipt of written notice of that decision and the Special Commissioners shall hear and determine the appeal in accordance with the principles to be followed by the Board in determining claims under this regulation; and either the appellant or the Board shall be entitled to require a case to be stated under the like provisions as are contained in section 56 of the Taxes Management Act 1970(**b**) but only on a point of law arising in connection with the computation of profits or losses.

(5) In this regulation "return" includes the documents referred to in paragraph 2(1)(b) and (c) of Schedule 16A.

Agents

10.—(1) For the purposes of Schedule 16A and of these Regulations, if the person who is acting as agent in respect of the underwriting year corresponding to the year of assessment 1986–87 is different from the person who was so acting at the end of that underwriting year (in this regulation referred to as "the original agent"), then "agent" has the meaning given to it by sub-paragraph (a) or, as the case may be, sub-paragraph (b) of paragraph (2).

(2) If the original agent ceases so to act–

(a) before the beginning of the year of assessment 1989–90, then "agent" means–

(i) the person who is so acting at the beginning of that year of assessment, or

(ii) if that person ceases so to act, such person as the Board may determine having regard to all the circumstances;

(b) after the end of the year of assessment 1988–89, then "agent" means such person as the Board may determine having regard to all the circumstances.

T J Painter
L J H Beighton
10th March 1989 Two of the Commissioners of Inland Revenue

(a) 1970 (c.9); subsection (1B) of section 113 was inserted by the Finance Act 1970 (c.24), Schedule 4, paragraph 10. **(b)** 1970 (c.9); subsection (3) of section 56 was amended by the Finance Act 1984 (c.43), section 127 and Schedule 22, paragraph 6, and subsection (9) was amended by the Finance (No. 2) Act 1975 (c.45), section 45(3).

Regulation 3(2)

SCHEDULE

Provisions	*Modifications*
Taxes Management Act 1970 (c.9)	
section 33(1)	For the words "(or, if the assessment is to corporation tax, the end of the accounting period) in which the assessment was made" substitute "1988–89".
section 34(1)	For the words "the chargeable period to which the assessment relates" substitute "the year of assessment 1988–89".
section 37(1)	For the words "that year" substitute "the year of assessment 1988–89".
section 40(1) and (2)	For the words from "the third year next following" to the end of each subsection substitute "the year of assessment 1991–92".
section 43(1)	For the words "the chargeable period to which it relates" substitute "the year of assessment 1988–89".
Income and Corporation Taxes Act 1970 (c.10)	
section 168(1)	For the words "two years" substitute "four years".
Finance Act 1971 (c.68)	
section 23(2) and (4)**(a)**	For the words "twelve months" substitute "three years".
Finance Act 1978 (c.42)	
section 30(1)	For the words "two years" substitute "four years".

(a) Subsections (2) and (4) of section 23 were amended by the Finance Act 1976 (c.40), section 36(10).

EXPLANATORY NOTE

(This note is not part of the Regulations)

These Regulations, which have effect for the year of assessment 1986–87 only, provide for the assessment and collection of tax charged on underwriting members of Lloyd's in accordance with Schedule 16 to the Finance Act 1973 ("Schedule 16") (so far as not provided for by Schedule 16A to that Act) ("Schedule 16A"). They also provide for the determination in certain circumstances of the person who is an agent in relation to a syndicate of underwriting members of Lloyd's for the purposes of Schedule 16A and these Regulations.

Regulation 1 provides for citation, commencement and effect, and regulation 2 contains definitions.

Regulation 3 applies provisions corresponding to provisions in the Taxes Acts to the assessment and collection of tax charged in accordance with Schedule 16, with certain modifications.

Regulation 4 provides dates on or before which tax charged by an assessment on underwriting profits and tax charged by an assessment on syndicate gains is payable.

Regulation 5(1) and (2), respectively, provide that any investment income which has suffered tax by way of deduction, and the amount of any tax credit included in the aggregate amount of any such income, shall be set against the amount payable under paragraph 3(1)(a) of Schedule 16, and regulation 5(3) makes provision in relation to building society interest and dividends to which the Income Tax (Building Societies) Regulations 1986 apply.

Regulation 6 provides for the repayment of tax to an agent and for the giving to him of tax credit.

Regulation 7 provides that in the circumstances there specified an agent shall be deemed not to have failed to comply with paragraph 2(2) or 7(3) of Schedule 16A.

Regulation 8 provides that section 113(1B) and (3) and 114(2) of the Taxes Management Act 1970 shall apply to a determination or notice of a determination under Schedule 16A.

Regulation 9 provides for the giving of relief if a determination is alleged to be excessive because of an error or mistake in a return.

Regulation 10 adds to the definition of "agent" contained in paragraph 1(1) of Schedule 16A.

Authority for the retrospective effect of these Regulations is given by paragraph 17(1A) of Schedule 16 and paragraph 1(3) of Schedule 16A.

STATUTORY INSTRUMENTS

1989 No. 422 (S.48)

HOUSING, SCOTLAND

The Housing (Scotland) (Superannuation Fund) Regulations 1989

Made - - - -	*9th March 1989*
Laid before Parliament	*10th March 1989*
Coming into force	*1st April 1989*

The Secretary of State, in exercise of the powers conferred on him by paragraph 10(4) of Schedule 1 to the Housing (Scotland) Act 1988(**a**), and of all other powers enabling him in that behalf, and with the consent of the Treasury, hereby makes the following Regulations:

Citation and commencement

1. These Regulations may be cited as the Housing (Scotland) (Superannuation Fund) Regulations 1989 and shall come into force on 1st April 1989.

Transfer of superannuation fund from the Scottish Special Housing Association to Scottish Homes

2.—(1) On 1st April 1989 the superannuation fund maintained immediately before that date by the Scottish Special Housing Association in terms of the provisions of the Local Government Superannuation (Scotland) Regulations 1987(**b**) shall by virtue of this regulation be transferred to Scottish Homes.

(2) On and after that date the function of administering that fund in accordance with those Regulations shall be exercised by Scottish Homes.

Consequential amendment of Local Government Superannuation (Scotland) Regulations 1987

3.—(1) For regulation A3 of the Local Government Superannuation (Scotland) Regulations 1987 there shall be substituted the following regulation:–

"Application of the Regulations to Scottish Homes, their employees, and former employees of the Scottish Special Housing Association

A3.—(1) Subject to paragraphs (2), (3) and (4), these Regulations shall apply to Scottish Homes and its employees as though Scottish Homes were a body described in Part I of Schedule 3 and an administering authority, and shall also apply to Scottish Homes and persons who were employed by the Scottish Special Housing Association but have not become employees of Scottish Homes as though Scottish Homes were an administering authority in respect of those persons.

(2) Where a person who was an eligible employee of the Scottish Special Housing Association has become an employee of Scottish Homes in consequence of an offer under paragraph 11 of Schedule 1 to the Housing (Scotland) Act 1988, these Regulations shall have effect as if his employments with the Scottish Special Housing Association and Scottish Homes were one continuous employment.

(**a**) 1988 c.43.
(**b**) S.I. 1987/1850, amended by S.I. 1988/625.

(3) Regulation P6 shall apply to Scottish Homes as if paragraph (2)(b) of that Regulation were deleted.

(4) For the purpose of Part D, "service" rendered to the Scottish Special Housing Association before 16th May 1945 shall not be construed as qualifying or reckonable service.".

(2) Schedule 2 to those Regulations shall be deleted.

James Douglas-Hamilton
Parliamentary Under Secretary of State,
Scottish Office

St. Andrew's House, Edinburgh
9th March 1989

We consent,

Alan Howarth
David Lightbown
Two of the Lords Commissioners of Her Majesty's Treasury

9th March 1989

EXPLANATORY NOTE

(This note is not part of the Regulations)

These Regulations transfer, at 1st April 1989, the superannuation fund maintained by the Scottish Special Housing Association and responsibility for administering the fund to Scottish Homes (regulation 2). They make consequential amendments to the Local Government Superannuation (Scotland) Regulations 1987 (regulation 3).

Scottish Homes is a statutory body established by section 1 of the Housing (Scotland) Act 1988. Section 3(1) of that Act dissolves the Scottish Special Housing Association at 1st April 1989 and transfers its assets to Scottish Homes.

STATUTORY INSTRUMENTS

1989 No. 423 (S.49)

HOUSING, SCOTLAND

The Right To Purchase From A Public Sector Landlord (Application Form) (Scotland) Regulations 1989

Made - - - -	*9th March 1989*
Laid before Parliament	*13th March 1989*
Coming into force	*3rd April 1989*

The Secretary of State, in exercise of the powers conferred on him by section 58(1) of the Housing (Scotland) Act 1988(**a**) and of all other powers enabling him in that behalf, hereby makes the following Regulations:

Citation and commencement

1. These Regulations may be cited as the Right To Purchase From A Public Sector Landlord (Application Form) (Scotland) Regulations 1989 and shall come into force on 3rd April 1989.

Interpretation

2. In these Regulations:

"the Act" means the Housing (Scotland) Act 1988;

"applicant" means a person who has been approved by Scottish Homes under section 57 of the Act or, as the case may be, Scottish Homes; and

"public sector landlord" has the same meaning as in section 56(3) of the Act.

Form of Notice

3. For the purposes of section 58(1) of the Act (which requires an applicant wishing to exercise the right conferred by Part III of the Act to acquire a house from a public sector landlord to serve a notice on that landlord), there is prescribed the notice in the form set out in the Schedule hereto or in a form substantially to the like effect.

James Douglas-Hamilton
Parliamentary Under Secretary of State,
Scottish Office

St. Andrew's House, Edinburgh
9th March 1989

(**a**) 1988 c.43.

SCHEDULE

Regulation 3

FORM OF NOTICE

HOUSING (SCOTLAND) ACT 1988

NOTICE OF APPLICATION TO PURCHASE UNDER SECTION 58

I, [insert name and address of applicant], hereby give notice that I seek to exercise the right conferred by Part III of the Housing (Scotland) Act 1988 ("the Act") to acquire the house specified in Part I of this Notice from you, [insert name and address of public sector landlord].

As required by section 58(1)(b) of the Act, this Notice is accompanied by the consent in writing of the qualifying tenant or tenants (including the persons mentioned in section 58(2) of the Act) to this approach being made to you. Information about the qualifying tenant(s) and those other persons is given in Part II of this Notice.

[Where the applicant is not Scottish Homes] I am approved by Scottish Homes under section 57 of the Act. I attach a copy of the document issued by Scottish Homes in terms of which I am approved.

Signed: ....

Date: ....

PART I

HOUSE TO BE ACQUIRED

Address of the house
to be acquired:

Any other heritable property which will reasonably serve a beneficial purpose in connection with the house which it is proposed to acquire:

PART II

INFORMATION ABOUT QUALIFYING TENANT(S) AND OTHER PERSONS

Name of tenant or,
in the case of joint tenants,
the name of each joint tenant:

Name of spouse of each tenant
(including any person living with
tenant as a spouse):

Date Tenancy Commenced:

EXPLANATORY NOTE

(This note is not part of the Regulations)

These Regulations prescribe the form of notice to be used by an applicant for the purpose of exercising the right conferred by Part III of the Housing (Scotland) Act 1988 to purchase a house belonging to a public sector landlord.

STATUTORY INSTRUMENTS

1989 No. 424

HARBOURS, DOCKS, PIERS AND FERRIES

The Harbour Works (Assessment of Environmental Effects) (No.2) Regulations 1989

Approved by both Houses of Parliament

Made - - - -	*9th March 1989*
Coming into force	*16th March 1989*

The Secretary of State for Transport and the Minister of Agriculture, Fisheries and Food as respects England, the Secretary of State for Wales as respects Wales and the Secretary of State for Scotland as respects Scotland, being Ministers designated(**a**) for the purposes of section 2(2) of the European Communities Act 1972(**b**) in relation to measures relating to the requirement for an assessment of the impact on the environment of projects likely to have significant effects on the environment, in exercise of the powers conferred by that section hereby make the following Regulations:–

Citation, Commencement and Extent

1.—(1) These Regulations may be cited as the Harbour Works (Assessment of Environmental Effects) (No.2) Regulations 1989.

(2) These Regulations shall come into force on the seventh day after the day on which they are made.

(3) These Regulations shall not extend to Northern Ireland.

Interpretation

2.—(1) In these Regulations, unless the context otherwise requires–

"the appropriate Minister" means

(a) in respect of harbour works not being works relating to fishery harbours or marine works, the Secretary of State for Transport;

(b) in respect of harbour works relating to fishery harbours in England, the Minister of Agriculture, Fisheries and Food;

(c) in respect of harbour works relating to fishery harbours in Wales, the Secretary of State for Wales;

(d) in respect of harbour works relating to marine works in Scotland, the Secretary of State for Scotland;

"developer" means any person who proposes to carry out or who carries out harbour works;

"the Directive" means Council Directive No. 85/337/EEC(**c**) on the assessment of the effect of certain public and private projects on the environment;

"environmental assessment" means an assessment in accordance with the Directive;

(**a**) S.I. 1988/785.
(**b**) 1972 c. 68.
(**c**) O.J. No. L175, 5.7.85, p. 40.

"fishery harbour" has the meaning assigned to it in section 21 of the Sea Fish Industry Act 1951(**a**);

"harbour" has the meaning assigned to it in section 57 of the Harbours Act 1964(**b**);

"harbour authority" means the harbour authority as defined in section 57 of the Harbours Act 1964 in relation to the harbour where the harbour works are proposed to be carried out;

"harbour works" means works involved in the construction of a harbour or in the making of modifications to an existing harbour;

"marine work" has the meaning assigned to it in section 57 of the Harbours Act 1964;

"operations" means the operations described in section 34(1) of the Coast Protection Act 1949(**c**);

"provisional order" has the meaning assigned to it in section 57 of the Harbours Act 1964.

(2) For the purposes of these Regulations a person carries out harbour works if he carries out the whole or any part of such works or any operation in connection with or for the purposes of such works.

(3) In these Regulations reference to a numbered regulation is a reference to the regulation bearing that number in these Regulations and any reference to a numbered paragraph or lettered sub-paragraph is a reference to the paragraph or sub-paragraph bearing that number or letter in these Regulations.

Scope

3. These Regulations apply to harbour works below the low water mark of medium tides, being works which are–

(a) not subject to planning control pursuant to the Town and Country Planning Act 1971(**d**) or the Town and Country Planning (Scotland) Act 1972(**e**) or pursuant to orders made in exercise of powers conferred by the said Acts; and

(b) not specifically described in or authorised to be carried out by a harbour revision order made pursuant to section 14 of the Harbours Act 1964, a harbour empowerment order made pursuant to section 16 of the Harbours Act 1964 or by a provisional order; and

(c) not specifically described in or authorised to be carried out by any enactment conferring powers to carry out works at a harbour.

Scrutiny of applications relating to harbour works

4.—(1) Where an application or notice of one of the following descriptions is made or given–

(a) an application for consent to the carrying out of operations pursuant to section 34 of the Coast Protection Act 1949;

(b) notice from a harbour authority pursuant to regulations made under section 37 of the Merchant Shipping Act 1988(**f**) that application has been made for a licence to carry out operations; or

(c) an application for the approval of any such work as is referred to in section 35(1)(g) of the Coast Protection Act 1949;

the appropriate Minister shall consider whether the application or notice relates in whole or in part to harbour works to which these Regulations apply and shall reach a decision thereon as soon as reasonably practicable.

(2) If the appropriate Minister decides that the application or notice relates to harbour works to which these Regulations apply, the proposed works shall not be commenced unless the appropriate Minister reaches a decision under regulation 4(5) or consents thereto under

(**a**) 1951 c. 30.
(**b**) 1964 c. 40.
(**c**) 1949 c. 74; section 34(1) was amended by section 36 of the Merchant Shipping Act 1988 (c. 12).
(**d**) 1971 c. 78.
(**e**) 1972 c. 52.
(**f**) 1988 c. 12.

regulation 8(3) or regulation 9(5) and he shall notify the developer of his decision and its effect forthwith.

(3) If the appropriate Minister decides that the application or notice relates in whole or in part to harbour works to which these Regulations apply, he shall consider whether–

(a) the proposed harbour works constitute a project which falls within Annex I of the Directive; or

(b) the proposed harbour works constitute a project which falls within Annex II of the Directive and, if so, whether their characteristics require that they should be made subject to an environmental assessment.

(4) The appropriate Minister may require the developer to provide him with such of the following information as he deems necessary to enable him to consider whether proposed harbour works being the subject of an application or notice referred to in paragraph (1) constitute a project falling within paragraph (3)–

(a) a brief description of the nature and purpose of the proposed harbour works;

(b) a plan sufficient to identify the location of the proposed harbour works;

(c) plans and sections showing the lines, situation and levels of the proposed harbour works; and

(d) such further information as he may specify in a particular case.

(5) If the appropriate Minister decides that proposed harbour works do not constitute a project falling within Annex I or Annex II to the Directive or that they constitute a project falling within Annex II the characteristics of which do not require that they should be made subject to an environmental assessment, he shall take no further action on the application or notice pursuant to these Regulations and he shall notify the developer and, in a case where a notice has been received under regulation 4(1)(b), the harbour authority, of his decision forthwith.

Harbour works subject to an environmental assessment

5.—(1) If the appropriate Minister decides that proposed harbour works constitute a project falling within Annex I of the Directive, or a project falling within Annex II and considers that their characteristics require that they should be made subject to an environmental assessment, he shall notify the developer and, in a case where a notice has been received under regulation 4(1)(b), the harbour authority, of his decision forthwith and direct the developer to supply him in such form as he may specify with the information referred to in Annex III to the Directive to the extent that he considers—

(a) that it is relevant to any stage of the procedure set out in these Regulations and to the specific characteristics of the proposed harbour works to which the application or notice relates and to the environmental features likely to be affected; and

(b) that (having regard in particular to current knowledge and methods of assessment) the developer may reasonably be required to compile that information.

(2) The information to be supplied to the appropriate Minister under paragraph (1) above shall include at least–

(a) a description of the proposed harbour works comprising information on the site, design and size of the proposed harbour works;

(b) a description of the measures envisaged in order to avoid, reduce and, if possible, remedy significant adverse effects;

(c) the data required to identify and assess the main effects which the proposed harbour works are likely to have on the environment;

(d) a non-technical summary of the information mentioned in sub-paragraphs (a) to (c) above.

Publication of notice by developer

6.—(1) Not less than 14 days before the developer provides the information to be supplied under regulation 5(1) to the appropriate Minister, he shall publish a notice in a local newspaper circulating in the locality of the harbour where the harbour works are proposed to be carried out stating—

(a) his name and the location and nature of the proposed harbour works;

(b) that he has applied for consent or approval to the carrying out of the proposed works and specifying the relevant provision pursuant to which consent or approval was applied for;

(c) that he has been directed to supply the information referred to in regulation 5(1);

(d) that a copy of any information supplied under regulation 4(4) together with the information to be supplied under regulation 5(1) may be inspected by members of the public at all reasonable hours;

(e) an address within the locality of the harbour where the harbour works are proposed to be carried out at which the documents open to inspection may be inspected, and the latest date on which they will be available (being a date not less than 42 days later than the date on which the notice is published);

(f) an address within the locality of the harbour where the harbour works are proposed to be carried out (whether or not the same as that named under sub-paragraph (e)) at which copies of the information to be supplied under regulation 5(1) may be obtained, for so long as stocks last, and, if a charge is to be made for a copy, the amount of the charge; and

(g) that any person who wishes to make representations concerning the proposed harbour works should do so in writing, within 7 days from the date specified in accordance with sub-paragraph (e), to the appropriate Minister.

(2) On the date of publication of the notice under paragraph (1) above the developer shall also post at a place to which members of the public have access at the offices of the harbour authority for the harbour in respect of which the harbour works are proposed to be carried out or if there is not such place, shall post outside the offices of the said harbour authority, a notice containing the information specified in paragraph (1).

(3) The developer shall ensure that the notice referred to in paragraph (2) is–

(a) left in position for a period of 42 days from the date of posting;

(b) posted by affixing it firmly to some object on the premises and is sited and displayed in such a way as to be easily visible to and legible by members of the public; and

(c) replaced if it is at any time removed, damaged or defaced.

(4) The information supplied to the appropriate Minister under regulation 5(1) shall be accompanied by–

(a) a copy of the notice referred to in paragraph (1) above certified by or on behalf of the developer as having been published in a named newspaper on a date specified in the certificate; and

(b) a certificate by or on behalf of the developer which states–

(i) that he has posted a notice at or outside the offices of the harbour authority for the harbour in which the harbour works are proposed to be carried out in accordance with paragraph (2) above, and when he did so; and

(ii) that he has complied with the requirements of paragraph (3)(b) and will comply with the requirements of paragraph 3(c) should this be necessary.

Consultation on and holding of inquiry into proposed harbour works

7.—(1) The appropriate Minister may direct the developer to supply such bodies as he may specify being bodies appearing to him to have environmental responsibilities, with copies of the information supplied to him under regulation 5(1).

(2) Where the developer is not the harbour authority, the appropriate Minister shall direct the developer to supply the harbour authority with copies of the information supplied to him under regulation 5(1).

(3) Where he has given a direction under paragraph (1) or (2) above the appropriate Minister shall consult the bodies specified therein or the harbour authority before reaching a decision on the merits of proposed harbour works.

(4) The appropriate Minister may if he thinks fit cause an inquiry to be held by a person appointed by him into a proposal to carry out harbour works and he shall afford to the developer, to any persons who have made representations to him and to the bodies specified or the harbour authority mentioned in any direction given under paragraph (1) or (2) above the opportunity to appear before the person appointed by him for the purpose.

Decisions on applications

8.—(1) Where the appropriate Minister is satisfied that the developer has complied with his direction under regulation 5(1), with regulation 6 and with any direction under regulation 7(1) or (2), and he has received the report of any inquiry held under regulation 7(4), he shall reach a decision on the merits of the proposed harbour works.

(2) In reaching his decision concerning proposed harbour works, the appropriate Minister shall consider the information supplied to him under regulation 5(1), any representations received pursuant to regulation 6(1) or 6(2), any consultations under regulation 7(3), and the report of any inquiry held under regulation 7(4), and he shall have regard in particular–

(a) to the effect of the proposed harbour works on the environment;

(b) to the desirability of the proposed works being carried out in the interests of securing the improvement, maintenance or management of the harbour in an efficient and economical manner or of facilitating the efficient and economic transport of goods or passengers by sea; and

(c) to any other benefits which may be derived from the proposed works.

(3) The appropriate Minister may–

(a) consent to the carrying out of the proposed harbour works either unconditionally or subject to such conditions as he sees fit; or

(b) refuse such consent.

(4) The appropriate Minister shall–

(a) notify his decision and the reasons and considerations upon which it was based to the developer and to all bodies and persons who were consulted on or made representations concerning the proposed harbour works; and

(b) publish his decision in such manner as he thinks fit.

(5) Any condition subject to which the appropriate Minister has consented to harbour works–

(a) shall (subject to paragraph (c) below) either remain in force for a specified period or remain in force without limit of time;

(b) shall (in addition to binding the developer to whom the consent is given) bind, so far as is appropriate, any other person who for the time being owns, occupies, or enjoys any use of the harbour works;

(c) may, if the appropriate Minister thinks fit, be revoked by him.

(6) A consent under paragraph (3) may be granted so as to continue in force, unless renewed, only if the harbour works for which the consent is granted are begun or completed within such period as may be specified in the consent, and any renewal of a consent may be limited in the same way.

Harbour works carried out without a decision

9.—(1) If a developer carries out harbour works to which it appears to the appropriate Minister that these Regulations apply and which have not been the subject of a decision under regulation 4(5), regulation 8 or this regulation, the appropriate Minister shall serve notice in writing on the developer requiring him, if appropriate, to cease the works forthwith and to supply the appropriate Minister with such of the information referred to in regulation 4(4) or, if applicable, in regulation 5(1) as he may specify within such period as he may specify.

(2) On receipt of the information required from the developer, the appropriate Minister shall consider the harbour works in accordance with these Regulations whether or not an application or notice has been received pursuant to regulation 4(1).

(3) If the developer no longer owns, occupies or enjoys any use of the harbour works when the appropriate Minister decides to serve a notice under paragraph (1) the notice may be served on any other person who for the time being owns, occupies or enjoys any use of the harbour works.

(4) If a developer fails to supply the appropriate Minister with such of the information referred to in regulation 4(4) as is specified in a notice served under paragraph (1) within the period specified therein, the appropriate Minister shall make such investigations as he considers necessary to enable him to decide whether the harbour works constitute a project the characteristics of which require that they should be made subject to an environmental

assessment and shall notify his decision to the developer under regulation 4(5) or regulation 5(1).

(5) If a developer fails to supply the appropriate Minister with such of the information referred to in regulation 5(1) as is specified in a notice served under paragraph (1) within the period specified therein, the appropriate Minister shall make such investigations, invite such representations and hold such consultations with bodies referred to in regulation 7 as he considers necessary to enable him to reach a decision on the merits of the harbour works.

(6) In reaching a decision under paragraph (5) the appropriate Minister shall have regard to the considerations specified in regulation 8(2).

(7) The provisions of regulation 8(3), (4), (5) and (6) shall apply in relation to a decision reached under paragraph (5) to the extent that they are appropriate.

Enforcement

10.—(1) If a developer carries out harbour works in respect of which consent has been refused under regulation 8 or regulation 9 or in contravention of a condition subject to which consent was granted, the appropriate Minister may serve notice in writing on the developer requiring him, within such period (not being less than thirty days) as may be specified in the notice, to remove the works and reinstate the site or to make such alterations thereto as may be so specified, or, if it appears to the appropriate Minister urgently necessary to do so, he may himself remove or alter the works and reinstate the site.

(2) If within the period specified in any notice under paragraph (1) the developer fails to comply with it, the appropriate Minister may himself remove or alter the works and reinstate the site as specified in the notice.

(3) Where the appropriate Minister removes or alters works and reinstates a site under paragraph (1) or (2), he shall be entitled to recover the expense, as certified by him, from the developer.

(4) If the developer no longer owns, occupies or enjoys any use of the harbour works when the appropriate Minister decides to serve a notice under paragraph (1), the notice may be served on any other person who for the time being owns, occupies or enjoys any use of the harbour works, and the references to the developer in paragraph (2), and in paragraph (3) in relation to any action taken by the appropriate Minister under paragraph (2), shall in that case have effect as a reference to the person on whom the notice is served.

Penalties

11.—(1) A person who issues a certificate purporting to comply with regulation 6(4) which contains a statement which he knows to be false or misleading in a material particular, or who recklessly issues a certificate purporting to comply with regulation 6(4) which contains a statement which is false or misleading in a material particular shall be guilty of an offence and liable on summary conviction to a fine not exceeding level 3 on the standard scale.

(2) A person who fails without reasonable excuse to comply with a notice served upon him under regulation 9(1) shall be guilty of an offence and liable on summary conviction to a fine not exceeding level 3 on the standard scale.

(3) Where a body corporate is guilty of an offence under paragraph (1) or (2) above and the offence is proved to have been committed with the consent or connivance of or to be attributable to any neglect on the part of any director, manager, secretary or other similar officer of the body corporate or any person who was purporting to act in any such capacity he, as well as the body corporate, shall be guilty of the offence and shall be liable to be proceeded against and punished accordingly.

(4) Where the affairs of a body corporate are managed by its members, paragraph (2) shall apply in relation to the acts and defaults of a member in connection with his functions of management as if he were a director of the body corporate.

20th February 1989	*Paul Channon* Secretary of State for Transport
1st March 1989	*John MacGregor* Minister of Agriculture, Fisheries and Food
8th March 1989	*Peter Walker* Secretary of State for Wales
9th March 1989	*James Douglas-Hamilton* Parliamentary Under Secretary of State for Scotland

EXPLANATORY NOTE

(This note is not part of the Regulations)

These Regulations implement for England and Wales and Scotland Council Directive 85/337/EEC of 27 June 1985 (O.J. No. L175 15.7.85, p. 40) on the assessment of the effects of certain public and private projects on the environment, in respect of certain harbour works, namely harbour works below medium low water mark for which consent under the Town and Country Planning Acts is not required and which are not authorised by or under any enactment.

Regulation 4 obliges the appropriate Minister to consider whether applications or notices received pursuant to the Coast Protection Act 1949 or other legislation relate to harbour works to which the Regulations apply. If he decides that they do, he must consider whether the proposed works fall within Annex I or Annex II to the Directive and, in the latter case, whether their characteristics require that they be made subject to an environmental assessment in accordance with the Directive. The works are not to be carried out unless the consent of the appropriate Minister is obtained or he has decided that an environmental assessment is not required.

Regulation 5 states that where the harbour works require the consent of the appropriate Minister, he shall direct the developer to supply him with such of the information specified in Annex III to the Directive as may be relevant and obtainable.

Regulation 6 provides that the developer must publish a notice in a local newspaper, and at or outside the premises of the harbour authority, indicating the nature of the proposed works, that he has been directed to supply the information specified in Annex III and stating where copies of the application and information may be inspected and obtained and how representations may be made. The developer is to furnish the appropriate Minister with a certificate to the effect that these steps have been carried out.

Regulation 7 provides for consultation with bodies having environmental responsibilities, and, in appropriate cases, with the harbour authority for the harbour at which the works are proposed to be carried out and the holding of inquiries into proposed works.

Regulation 8 requires the appropriate Minister to consider the information specified in Annex III to the Directive, any representations, consultations, and the report of any inquiry in reaching his decision and to have regard to the effect of the proposed works on the environment and on the development of the harbour. He is required to notify his decision and the reasons and considerations upon which it is based to the developer and to all bodies or persons who were consulted or made representations and to publish his decision.

Regulation 9 empowers the appropriate Minister to serve notice on a developer who carries out harbour works to which the Regulations apply and which may require to be subject to an environmental assessment, directing the developer to cease the works and to provide the appropriate Minister with specified information concerning the works to enable him to consider their status and merits. If the developer fails to provide the specified information, the appropriate Minister shall make such investigations as he considers necessary and shall proceed to reach a decision either on whether an assessment is required or, if appropriate, on the merits of the harbour works.

Regulation 10 deals with the enforcement of decisions pursuant to the Regulations by providing for the service of notice on the developer requiring him to remove the works and reinstate the site and empowering the appropriate Minister to take the necessary remedial action where a notice is not complied with.

If the developer no longer has any interest in the harbour works when a notice or application is sought to be served or made under regulation 9 or 10, the appropriate Minister may instead proceed against the person who is then interested in the harbour works.

Regulation 11 creates criminal offences in respect of non-compliance with the regulations. Where a certificate provided under regulation 6 is false or misleading the person who made it is guilty of an offence if he made it knowing it was false or misleading or recklessly. The offender is liable on a summary conviction to a fine not exceeding level 3 on the standard scale. Failure to comply with a notice served under regulation 9 is also an offence punishable on summary conviction by a fine not exceeding level 3 on the standard scale.

STATUTORY INSTRUMENTS

1989 No. 425

SEA FISHERIES

The Sea Fish Industry Authority (Levy) Regulations 1988 Confirmatory Order 1989

Made - - - -	*9th March 1989*
Laid before Parliament	*10th March 1989*
Coming into force -	*1st April 1989*

Whereas the Sea Fish Industry Authority (hereinafter referred to as "the Authority") have made the Sea Fish Industry Authority (Levy) Regulations 1988 (hereinafter referred to as "the Regulations");

And whereas the Authority have transmitted to the Minister of Agriculture, Fisheries and Food and the Secretaries of State respectively concerned with the sea fish industry in Scotland, Wales and Northern Ireland (hereinafter referred to as "the Ministers") the objections to the Regulations which have been duly made to the Authority and have not been withdrawn and the Ministers have considered such objections;

And whereas the Ministers have not considered it desirable to make any modifications in the Regulations;

Now, therefore, the Ministers, in exercise of the powers conferred on them by section 4(2) and (10) of the Fisheries Act 1981**(a)** and of all their other enabling powers, hereby make the following Order:–

Title and commencement

1. This Order may be cited as the Sea Fish Industry Authority (Levy) Regulations 1988 Confirmatory Order 1989 and shall come into force on 1st April 1989.

Confirmation

2. The Regulations are hereby confirmed and are set out in the Schedule to this Order.

Revocation

3. The Sea Fish Industry Authority (Levy) Regulations 1982 Confirmatory Order 1982**(b)** is hereby revoked.

In witness whereof the Official Seal of the Minister of Agriculture, Fisheries and Food is hereunto affixed on 2nd March 1989.

John MacGregor
Minister of Agriculture, Fisheries and Food

Sanderson of Bowden
2nd March 1989 Minister of State, Scottish Office

(a) 1981 c.29.
(b) S.I. 1982/168.

Peter Walker
9th March 1989 Secretary of State for Wales

Tom King
2nd March 1989 Secretary of State for Northern Ireland

SCHEDULE

Article 2

THE SEA FISH INDUSTRY AUTHORITY (LEVY) REGULATIONS 1988

Whereas it appears to the Sea Fish Industry Authority (hereinafter referred to as "the Authority") that it is desirable for the purpose of financing its activities to impose a levy on persons engaged in the sea fish industry in respect of sea fish and sea fish products, such levy to be payable on firsthand sales or trans-shipments within British fishery limits by way of firsthand sale;

Now therefore, the Authority in exercise of the powers conferred on it by sections 4 and 5 of the Fisheries Act 1981**(a)** hereby makes the following Regulations:–

Imposition of Levy

1.—(1) There shall be paid to the Authority subject to and in accordance with the provisions of these Regulations by every person who–

(a) purchases any sea fish or any sea fish product on a firsthand sale, or

(b) trans-ships within British fishery limits any sea fish or any sea fish product by way of firsthand sale,

a levy (hereinafter referred to as "the levy") at the rate per kilogram set out in the second column of the Schedule hereto in respect of any sea fish or sea fish product specified opposite thereto in the first column of the said Schedule so purchased or trans-shipped by him.

(2) The levy shall not be payable in respect of any live sea fish purchased for cultivation or in respect of canned or bottled sea fish or sea fish products.

(3) If any sea fish or any sea fish product is purchased on a firsthand sale through or from a wholesale merchant who sells on commission, the levy shall be paid to the Authority by the said wholesale merchant, who shall be entitled to recover as a civil debt from the purchaser of such sea fish product a sum equal to the amount of the levy so paid.

(4) Where the levy becomes payable by any person in respect of any sea fish or sea fish product trans-shipped within British fishery limits by way of firsthand sale by him, it shall not be payable by any person who subsequently purchases such fish or fish product.

(5) Where any sea fish or sea fish product is trans-shipped by way of sale within British fishery limits more than once, the levy shall be payable in respect of the first such trans-shipment only.

(6) Where the levy becomes payable in respect of any sea fish it shall not be payable in respect of the products of such sea fish.

Time Limits for Payment

2.—(1) Levy payable by a person who purchases any sea fish or sea fish product on a firsthand sale shall be paid to the Authority within seven days after the end of–

(a) the week during which there took place the firsthand sale of the fish or fish product in respect of which the levy is payable, or

(b) the week during which such fish or fish product was imported or brought into the country,

whichever is the later.

(2) Levy payable by a person who trans-ships any sea fish or sea fish product by way of firsthand sale shall be paid to the Authority within seven days after the end of the week during which there took place the trans-shipment of the fish or fish product in respect of which the levy is payable.

(a) 1981 c.29.

Keeping of Records

3.—(1) Every person engaged in the sea fish industry who sells sea fish or sea fish products otherwise than by retail shall keep or cause to be kept an accurate record of all his purchases and sales of sea fish and sea fish products (other than sales by retail), including in respect of each such purchase or sale–

(a) the date,

(b) the name and address of the seller or purchaser,

(c) the description of sea fish or sea fish product purchased or sold,

(d) the net weight of each description of sea fish or sea fish product purchased or sold,

(e) the price invoiced, and

(f) the place of landing or import, if known.

(2) Every person who carries on the business of selling sea fish or sea fish products by retail or the business of a fish fryer shall keep or cause to be kept an accurate record of all his purchases of sea fish and sea fish products, including in respect of each such purchase–

(a) the date,

(b) the name and address of the seller,

(c) the description of the sea fish or sea fish product,

(d) the net weight of each description of sea fish or sea fish product,

(e) the price invoiced, and

(f) the place of landing or import, if known.

(3) Every person engaged in the sea fish industry who trans-ships within British fishery limits by way of firsthand sale any sea fish or sea fish product shall keep an accurate record of all such trans-shipments including in respect of each one–

(a) the date,

(b) the names of the vessels from and to which the trans-shipment was made, together with their places of registration and registration numbers,

(c) the description of the sea fish or sea fish product,

(d) the net weight of each description of sea fish or sea fish product, and

(e) the price invoiced.

(4) In respect of every purchase, sale or trans-shipment of sea fish or sea fish product which it is customary or usual to sell, purchase or trans-ship by reference to a method of calculation of quantity other than a calculation by weight, the records which are required to be kept under paragraphs (1) to (3) of this regulation shall, in addition to and not in derogation of the requirements of those paragraphs, include particulars expressed by reference to the said method of calculation of quantity.

(5) The retention by any person of an accurate invoice or a copy thereof shall, as respects any of the matters mentioned in paragraphs (1) to (4) of this regulation of which sufficient particulars are contained therein, be deemed to be to that extent a compliance by that person with the provisions of the said paragraphs.

Making of Returns

4.—(1) Every person required to keep records in accordance with regulation 3 and who is liable to pay levy under regulation 1 hereof shall make returns in writing to the Authority in respect of each transaction so leviable. Such returns shall include the information in respect of which they are required to keep records in the said regulation 3.

(2) The returns required to be made in accordance with paragraph (1) above shall be made at the same time as levy is paid in accordance with regulation 1.

Interpretation

5. In these Regulations, unless the context otherwise requires, the following expressions have the meanings hereby respectively assigned to them–

"firsthand sale" means–

(a) in relation to any sea fish or sea fish product which has been first landed in the United Kingdom the first sale thereof (other than a sale by retail) whether prior to or after landing in the United Kingdom;

(b) in relation to any sea fish or sea fish product which has been first landed outside the United Kingdom and any sea fish product manufactured outside the United Kingdom from such sea fish or sea fish product which in either case is purchased by a person carrying on business in the sea fish industry and is imported or brought into the United Kingdom for the purposes of any such business, the first sale thereof (whether in the United Kingdom or elsewhere) to such a person as aforesaid;

(c) in relation to any sea fish or sea fish product which is trans-shipped within British fishery limits, the first sale thereof;

"pelagic fish" means herring, mackerel, pilchard, sprat, scad or whitebait;

"sale by retail" means a sale to a person buying otherwise than for the purpose of resale or processing or use as bait, and includes a sale to a person for the purposes of a catering business (other than a fish frying business); and "sell by retail" has a corresponding meaning;

"week" means a period of seven consecutive days ending at midnight on any Saturday;

"wholesale merchant" means a person selling or offering for sale sea fish or sea fish products otherwise than by retail.

Revocation

6. The Sea Fish Industry Authority (Levy) Regulations 1982**(a)** are hereby revoked.

Citation and commencement

7. These Regulations may be cited as the Sea Fish Industry Authority (Levy) Regulations 1988 and shall come into force on the day on which the confirmatory Order by Ministers comes into force.

The Common Seal of the
SEA FISH INDUSTRY AUTHORITY
was hereunto affixed
on the Twenty Fifth
day of November
Nineteen Hundred and Eighty Eight

in the presence of:–

Member: Ben Davies

Secretary: R Alaistair Davie

(a) Set out in the Schedule to S.I. 1982/168.

SCHEDULE

(1)	(2) *Rate per Kilogram*
Sea Fish	
Sea fish other than cockles or mussels or pelagic fish sold on a firsthand sale or pelagic fish trans-shipped within British fishery limits or sea fish sold for fishmeal production	0.7000 p
Cockles or mussels sold on a firsthand sale	0.3500 p
Pelagic fish sold on a firsthand sale or trans-shipped within British fishery limits	0.2000 p
Sea fish sold for fishmeal production	0.0350 p
Sea Fish Products	
Fresh, frozen or chilled sea fish	
Gutted	0.7000 p
Headless and gutted	0.9333 p
Fillets, skin on	1.4000 p
Fillets, skinless	1.7500 p
Fresh, frozen or chilled pelagic fish	
Gutted	0.2000 p
Headless and gutted	0.2667 p
Fillets, skin on	0.4000 p
Fillets, skinless	0.5000 p
Cockles or mussels without shell	0.7000 p
Smoked Sea Fish	
Headless and gutted	1.1667 p
Fillets, skin on	1.7500 p
Fillets, skinless	1.8667 p
Salted and Cured Sea Fish	
Wet	0.7000 p
Dried	1.0500 p
Sea fish products sold for fishmeal	0.0350 p
Sea fishmeal	0.1750 p
Any sea fish product not referred to above	1.4000 p

EXPLANATORY NOTE

(This note is not part of the Order)

This Order confirms Regulations made by the Sea Fish Industry Authority imposing for the purpose of financing its activities a levy in respect of sea fish and sea fish products landed in the United Kingdom or trans-shipped within British fishery limits.

The Order replaces and revokes the Sea Fish Industry Authority (Levy) Regulations 1982 Confirmatory Order 1982 (S.I. 1982/168) (article 3).

STATUTORY INSTRUMENTS

1989 No. 426

SEA FISHERIES

CONSERVATION OF SEA FISH

The Sea Fishing (Enforcement of Community Conservation Measures) (Amendment) Order 1989

Made - - - -	*9th March 1989*
Laid before Parliament	*10th March 1989*
Coming into force	*1st April 1989*

The Minister of Agriculture, Fisheries and Food and the Secretaries of State respectively concerned with sea fishing in Scotland, Wales and Northern Ireland, in exercise of the powers conferred on them by section 30(2) of the Fisheries Act 1981(**a**) and of all other powers enabling them in that behalf, hereby make the following Order:–

Title, commencement and interpretation

1. This Order may be cited as the Sea Fishing (Enforcement of Community Conservation Measures) (Amendment) Order 1989 and shall come into force on 1st April 1989.

(2) In this Order "the principal Order" means the Sea Fishing (Enforcement of Community Conservation Measures) Order 1986(**b**).

Amendment of the principal Order

2. The principal Order is hereby amended by substituting in article 2 thereof (interpretation) for the definition of the Council Regulation the following definition–

"the Council Regulation" means Council Regulation (EEC) No. 3094/86 laying down certain technical measures for the conservation of fishery resources(**c**), as amended by Council Regulation (EEC) No. 4026/86(**d**), Council Regulation (EEC) No. 2968/87(**e**), Council Regulation (EEC) No. 3953/87(**f**), Council Regulation (EEC) No. 1555/88(**g**), Council Regulation (EEC) No. 2024/88(**h**), Council Regulation (EEC) No. 3287/88(**i**), and Council Regulation (EEC) No. 4193/88(**j**);'.

Revocation

3. The Sea Fishing (Enforcement of Community Conservation Measures) (Amendment) (No. 2) Order 1988(**k**) is hereby revoked.

(**a**) 1981 c.29.
(**b**) S.I. 1986/2090, as amended by S.I. 1988/2300.
(**c**) OJ No L288, 11.10.86, p.l.
(**d**) OJ No L376, 31.12.86, p.l.
(**e**) OJ No L280, 3.10.87, p.l.
(**f**) OJ No L371, 30.12.87, p.9.
(**g**) OJ No L140, 7.6.88, p.l.
(**h**) OJ No L179, 9.7.88, p.l.
(**i**) OJ No L292, 26.10.88, p.5 as corrected in OJ No L8, 11.1.89, p.22.
(**j**) OJ No L369, 31.12.88, p.l.
(**k**) S.I. 1988/2300.

In witness whereof the Official Seal of the Minister of Agriculture, Fisheries and Food is hereunto affixed on 7th March 1989.

John MacGregor
Minister of Agriculture, Fisheries and Food

7th March 1989

Sanderson of Bowden
Minister of State, Scottish Office

9th March 1989

Peter Walker
Secretary of State for Wales

9th March 1989

Tom King
Secretary of State for Northern Ireland

EXPLANATORY NOTE

(This note is not part of the Order)

This Order further amends the Sea Fishing (Enforcement of Community Conservation Measures) Order 1986 ("the principal Order"), which makes provision for the enforcement of certain of the enforceable Community restrictions and obligations concerning technical measures for the conservation of fishery resources which are contained in Council Regulation (EEC) No. 3094/86 ("the Council Regulation").

In consequence of amendments made to the Council Regulation by Council Regulation (EEC) No. 4193/88, this Order further amends the definition of the Council Regulation in article 2 of the principal Order (interpretation) so as to provide for the inclusion of those amendments in that definition (article 2). It also incorporates corrections to Council Regulation (EEC) No. 3287/88 made by means of corrigenda in the Official Journal of the European Communities (OJ No. L8, 11.1.89, p.22).

The Order revokes the Sea Fishing (Enforcement of Community Conservation Measures) (Amendment) (No. 2) Order 1988 (S.I. 1988/2300) and incorporates its provisions in the new definition (article 3).

1989 No. 428

REPRESENTATION OF THE PEOPLE

The European Parliamentary Elections (Welsh Forms) Order 1989

Made - - - -	*9th March 1989*
Laid before Parliament	*20th March 1989*
Coming into force -	*21st April 1989*

In exercise of the powers conferred upon me by sections 2(1) and 3(4) of the Welsh Language Act 1967**(a)**, I hereby make the following Order:

1. This Order may be cited as the European Parliamentary Elections (Welsh Forms) Order 1989 and shall come into force on 21st April 1989.

2. The European Parliamentary Elections (Welsh Forms) Order 1979**(b)** is hereby revoked.

3. In this Order:

"the 1986 Regulations" means the European Parliamentary Elections Regulations 1986**(c)**; and

"the 1983 Act" means the Representation of the People Act 1983**(d)**.

4. Each of the forms set out in Schedule 1 to this Order is hereby prescribed as the version partly in Welsh and partly in English which shall be used at a European Parliamentary election in Wales, in place of:

(a) in the case of form 1, the notice required by rule 29(5) of the parliamentary elections rules in Schedule 1 to the 1983 Act (voting compartment notice)**(e)**, as applied by regulation 5 of, and Schedule 1 to, the 1986 Regulations;

(b) in the case of forms 2 and 3, forms E and F (official poll card for an elector and for a proxy), respectively, in Schedule 2 to the Representation of the People Regulations 1986**(f)**, as applied by regulation 5 of, and Schedule 2 to, the 1986 Regulations; and

(c) in the case of forms 4, 5 and 6, forms H, J and K (declarations of identity), respectively, in Schedule 2 to the Representation of the People Regulations 1986, as applied by regulation 5 of, and Schedule 2 to, the 1986 Regulations.

(a) 1967 c.66; section 2(1) was extended by paragraph 2(5) of Schedule 1 to the European Parliamentary Elections Act 1978 (c.10) (the citation of which Act has been amended by section 3(1)(b) and (2)(b) of the European Communities (Amendment) Act 1986 (c.58) on the coming into force of the Single European Act (Cmnd. 9758) on 1st July 1987).

(b) S.I. 1979/368; the citation of this instrument has been amended by section 3(1)(b) and (2)(b) of the European Communities (Amendment) Act 1986.

(c) S.I. 1986/2209; the citation of this instrument has been amended by section 3(1)(b) and (2)(b) of the European Communities (Amendment) Act 1986.

(d) 1983 c.2.

(e) Rule 29(5) was amended by paragraph 79 of Schedule 4 to the Representation of the People Act 1985 (c.50).

(f) S.I. 1986/1081.

5. Each of the forms set out in Schedule 2 to this Order is hereby prescribed as the Welsh version which may be used at a European Parliamentary election in Wales in place of the forms prescribed by the following provisions in the parliamentary elections rules in Schedule 1 to the 1983 Act, as applied by regulation 5 of, and Schedule 1 to, the 1986 Regulations, which provisions are:

(a) in the case of form 1, rule 35(1)(a),

(b) in the case of form 2, rule 35(1)(b),

(c) in the case of form 3, rule 35(2),

(d) in the case of forms 4, 5 and 6, the form of nomination paper, the form of directions for the guidance of the voters in voting**(a)** and the form of declaration to be made by the companion of a blind voter, respectively, set out in the Appendix to those rules.

6. The forms set out in Schedules 1 and 2 to this Order, except forms 1, 2 and 3 in Schedule 2, may be used with such modifications as circumstances require.

Home Office
9th March 1989

Douglas Hurd
One of Her Majesty's Principal Secretaries of State

(a) The form of directions for the guidance of the voters in voting was substituted by paragraph 86 of Schedule 4 to the Representation of the People Act 1985.

SCHEDULE 1

Article 4

Forms partly in Welsh and partly in English

Form 1

Vote for one candidate only. Put no other mark on the ballot paper or your vote may not be counted.

Pleidleisiwch i un ymgeisydd yn unig. Peidiwch â rhoi unrhyw farc arall ar y papur pleidleisio neu fe all na chaiff eich pleidlais ei chyfrif.

Form 2

Front of card
Wyneb y cerdyn

EUROPEAN PARLIAMENTARY ELECTIONS ACT 1978

DEDDF ETHOLIADAU SENEDD EWROP 1978

OFFICIAL POLL CARD
CERDYN PLEIDLEISIO SWYDDOGOL

Constituency Etholaeth	Number on Register Rhif ar y Gofrestr
Polling Day Dyddiad Pleidleisio	Name Enw...
Your polling station will be Eich gorsaf bleidleisio fydd .... Polling hours 7 am to 10 pm Oriau Pleidleisio 7 am i 10 pm	Address Cyfeiriad.. ....

Back of card
Cefn y cerdyn

EUROPEAN PARLIAMENTARY ELECTION

ETHOLIAD SENEDD EWROP

You need not take this card with you when you go to the polling station, but it will save time if you take it and show it to the clerk there.

Nid oes angen i chi fynd â'r cerdyn hwn gyda chi i'r orsaf bleidleisio, ond bydd yn arbed amser os ewch ag ef a'i ddangos i'r clerc yno.

When you go to the polling station, tell the clerk your name and address, as shown on the front of the card. The presiding officer will give you a ballot paper; see that he stamps the official mark on it before he gives it to you.

Pan ewch i'r orsaf bleidleisio, rhowch eich enw a'ch cyfeiriad i'r clerc fel yr ymddengys ar du blaen y cerdyn. Bydd y swyddog llywyddu yn rhoi i chi bapur pleidleisio; gwnewch yn siŵr ei fod yn stampio'r marc swyddogol arno cyn ei roi i chi.

Go to one of the compartments. Mark a cross (X) in the box on the right hand side of the ballot paper opposite the name of the candidate you are voting for.

Ewch i un o'r cabanau. Rhowch groes (X) yn y blwch ar ochr dde'r papur pleidleisio gyferbyn ag enw'r ymgeisydd yr ydych am bleidleisio drosto.

Fold the ballot paper in two. Show the official mark to the presiding officer, but do not let anyone see your vote. Put the ballot paper in the ballot box and leave the polling station.

Plygwch y papur yn ddau. Dangoswch y marc swyddogol i'r swyddog llywyddu, ond peidiwch â gadael i neb weld eich pleidlais. Rhowch y papur pleidleisio yn y blwch pleidleisiau ac ewch allan o'r orsaf bleidleisio.

Vote for one candidate only. Put no other mark on the ballot paper, or your vote may not be counted.

Pleidleisiwch i un ymgeisydd yn unig. Peidiwch â rhoi unrhyw farc arall ar y papur pleidleisio neu fe all na chaiff eich pleidlais ei chyfrif.

If by mistake you spoil a ballot paper, show it to the presiding officer and ask for another one.

Os bydd i chi ddifetha papur pleidleisio drwy gamgymeriad, dangsoswch y papur pleidleisio i'r swyddog llywyddu a gofynnwch am un arall.

If you have appointed a proxy to vote in person for you, you may nevertheless vote at this election if you do so before your proxy has voted on your behalf.

Os ydych wedi penodi dirprwy i bleidleisio'n bersonol ar eich rhan, fe allwch, er hynny, bleidleisio yn yr etholiad hwn yr un fath os gwnewch hynny cyn i'ch dirprwy bleidleisio ar eich rhan.

If you have been granted a postal vote, you will *not* be entitled to vote in person at this election, so please ignore this poll card.

Os rhoddwyd pleidlais drwy'r post i chi, *ni* fydd gennych hawl i bleidleisio'n bersonol yn yr etholiad hwn ac felly anwybyddwch y cerdyn pleidleisio hwn.

ISSUED BY THE RETURNING OFFICER
CYHOEDDWYD GAN Y SWYDDOG CANLYNIADAU

Form 3

Front of card
Wyneb y cerdyn

EUROPEAN PARLIAMENTARY ELECTIONS ACT 1978

DEDDF ETHOLIADAU SENEDD EWROP 1978

PROXY'S OFFICIAL POLL CARD
CERDYN PLEIDLEISIO SWYDDOGOL Y DIRPRWY

Proxy's name
Enw'r dirprwy ....
Proxy's address
Cyfeiriad y dirprwy ....

....

EUROPEAN PARLIAMENTARY ELECTION

ETHOLIAD SENEDD EWROP

Etholaeth ....Constituency

Polling day
Dyddiad pleidleisio ....
The poll will be open from 7 am to 10 pm
Oriau pleidleisio 7 am i 10 pm.

Back of card

Cefn y cerdyn

The elector named below whose proxy you are is entitled to vote at the polling station:–

Mae gan yr etholwr a enwir isod, yr ydych yn ddirprwy drosto, hawl i bleidleisio yn yr orsaf bleidleisio:–

....

....

To vote as proxy you must go to that polling station. Tell the clerk that you wish to vote as proxy; give the name and qualifying address of the elector as follows:–

I bleidleisio fel dirprwy, rhaid i chi fynd i'r orsaf bleidleisio honno. Dywedwch wrth y clerc eich bod am bleidleisio fel dirprwy: rhowch enw'r etholwr a'r cyfeiriad y cofrestrwyd ef o'i blegid, fel hyn:–

Number of Register
Rhif y Gofrestr ....

Name
Enw ....

Address
Cyfeiriad ....

....

The presiding officer will give you the elector's ballot paper. The method of voting as proxy is the same as for casting your own vote.

Fe rydd y swyddog llywyddu bapur pleidleisio'r etholwr i chi. Mae'r dull o bleidleisio fel dirprwy yr un fath â'r dull o roi eich pleidlais eich hun.

It is an offence to vote as proxy for some other person if you know that that person is subject to a legal incapacity to vote, e.g. if that person has been convicted and is detained in a penal institution in pursuance of his sentence. It is also an offence to vote at this election for more than two persons of whom you are not the husband, wife, parent, grandparent, brother, sister, child or grandchild.

Mae'n drosedd i chi bleidleisio fel dirprwy ar ran rhyw berson arall os gwyddoch fod y person hwnnw wedi'i anghymwyso yn ôl y gyfraith rhag pleidleisio, e.e. os cafwyd y person hwnnw'n euog a'i fod yn cael ei gadw mewn sefydliad cosbi yn unol â'r ddedfryd a gawsai. Trosedd hefyd yw pleidleisio yn yr etholiad hwn dros fwy na dau berson heb eich bod yn ŵr, gwraig, rhiant, tadcu, mamgu, brawd, chwaer, plentyn neu ŵyr neu wyres iddynt.

The person who appointed you as proxy may himself vote in person at this election if he is able, and wishes, to do so and if he votes before you vote on his behalf.

Gall y person a'ch penododd chi i weithredu fel dirprwy bleidleisio'n bersonol yn yr etholiad hwn os bydd yn gallu ac yn dymuno gwneud hynny a phleidleisio cyn i chi bleidleisio yn ei le.

ISSUED BY THE RETURNING OFFICER
CYHOEDDWYD GAN Y SWYDDOG CANLYNIADAU

Form 4

Front of form
Wyneb y ffurflen

EUROPEAN PARLIAMENTARY ELECTIONS ACT 1978
DEDDF ETHOLIADAU SENEDD EWROP 1978

Ballot Paper No ....
Rhif y Papur Pleidleisio ....

I hereby declare that I am the person to whom the ballot paper numbered as above was sent.

Yr wyf yn datgan drwy hyn mai fi yw'r person yr anfonwyd iddo/iddi'r papur pleidleisio â'r rhif uchod.

Voter's signature (or mark) ....

Llofnod y pleidleisiwr (neu farc) ....

The voter, who is personally known to me, has signed (or marked) this declaration in my presence.

Mae'r pleidleisiwr, a adnabyddir gennyf yn bersonol, wedi llofnodi (neu farcio) y datganiad hwn yn fy mhresenoldeb.

Witness's signature ....
Llofnod y tyst...

Name of witness ....
(CAPITAL LETTERS)

Enw'r tyst ....
(PRIFLYTHRENNAU)

Address of witness ....
(CAPITAL LETTERS)

Cyfeiriad y tyst ....
(PRIFLYTHRENNAU)
....

SEE INSTRUCTIONS ON THE BACK OF THIS FORM
GWELER Y CYFARWYDDIADAU AR GEFN Y FFURFLEN HON

Back of form

Cefn y ffurflen

INSTRUCTIONS TO THE VOTER

CYFARWYDDIADAU I'R PLEIDLEISIWR

1. You must sign (or mark) this declaration of identity in the presence of a person known to you. That person should then sign this declaration as a witness, adding his or her name and address. Without this the declaration will be invalid.

1. Rhaid i chi lofnodi (neu farcio) y datganiad hwn ynglŷn ag adnabyddiaeth ym mhresenoldeb person sy'n adnabyddus i chi. Dylai'r person hwnnw lofnodi'r datganiad hwn fel tyst, gan ychwanegu ei (h)enw a'i gyfeiriad/chyfeiriad. Heb hynny bydd y datganiad yn annilys.

2. Vote for one candidate only. Put no other mark on the ballot paper or your vote may not be counted.

2. Pleidleisiwch dros un ymgeisydd yn unig. Peidiwch â rhoi unrhyw farc arall ar y papur pleidleisio, neu efallai na chaiff eich pleidlais ei chyfrif.

3. Mark a cross (X) in the box on the right hand side of the ballot paper opposite the name of the candidate you are voting for. Do this secretly. If you cannot vote without assistance, the person assisting you must not disclose how you have voted.

3. Rhowch groes (X) yn y blwch ar ochr dde'r papur pleidleisio gyferbyn ag enw'r ymgeisydd y pleidleisiwch drosto. Gwnewch hyn yn gyfrinachol. Os na allwch bleidleisio heb gymorth, rhaid i'r person sy'n eich cynorthwyo beidio â datgelu sut y gwnaethoch bleidleisio.

4. Put the ballot paper in the small envelope marked "A" and seal it. Then put the envelope marked "A", together with the declaration of identity, in the larger envelope marked "B". Return it without delay. The ballot paper, in order to be counted, must be received by the returning officer not later than the close of the poll.

4. Rhowch y papur pleidleisio yn yr amlen fach a nodir ag "A" a seliwch hi. Yna rhowch yr amlen a nodir ag "A" ynghyd â'r datganiad ynglŷn ag adnabyddiaeth yn yr amlen fwy a nodir â "B". Dychwelwch hi ar unwaith. Er mwyn cael ei gyfrif, rhaid i'r papur pleidleisio gyrraedd y swyddog canlyniadau cyn i'r pleidleisio ddod i ben.

5. If you receive more than one ballot paper, remember that it is illegal to vote more than once (otherwise than as proxy) at the same election.

5. Os cewch fwy nag un papur pleidleisio cofiwch ei bod hi'n anghyfreithlon pleidleisio mwy nag unwaith (ac eithro fel dirprwy) yn yr un etholiad.

6. At this election you cannot vote in person at a polling station, even if you receive an official poll card.

6. Yn yr etholiad hwn, ni allwch bleidleisio'n bersonol mewn gorsaf bleidleisio, hyd yn oed os cewch gerdyn pleidleisio swyddogol.

7. If you inadvertently spoil your ballot paper, you can apply to the returning officer for another one. With your application you must return, in your own envelope, the spoilt ballot paper, the declaration of identity and the envelopes marked "A" and "B". Remember that there is little time available if a fresh postal ballot paper is to be issued and counted.

7. Os gwnewch ddistrywio'n ddamweiniol eich papur pleidleisio drwy'r post, gallwch wneud cais i'r swyddog canlyniadau am un arall. Gyda'ch cais rhaid i chi ddychwelyd, yn eich amlen eich hun, y papur pleidleisio a ddistrywiwyd, y datganiad ynglŷn ag adnabyddiaeth, ynghyd â'r amlenni a nodwyd "A" a "B". Cofiwch nad oes fawr o amser ar ôl os yw papur pleidleisio newydd i gael ei ddosbarthu a'i gyfrif.

Form 5

Front of form

Wyneb y ffurflen

EUROPEAN PARLIAMENTARY ELECTIONS ACT 1978

DEDDF ETHOLIADAU SENEDD EWROP 1978

Ballot Paper Nos ....

Rhifau'r Papurau Pleidleisio ....

I hereby declare that I am the person to whom the ballot papers numbered as above were sent.

Yr wyf yn datgan drwy hyn mai fi yw'r person yr anfonwyd iddo/iddi'r papurau pleidleisio â'r rhifau uchod.

Voter's signature (or mark) ....

Llofnod y pleidleisiwr (neu farc) ....

The voter, who is personally known to me, has signed (or marked) this declaration in my presence.

Mae'r pleidleisiwr, a adnabyddir gennyf yn bersonol, wedi llofnodi (neu farcio) y datganiad hwn yn fy mhresenoldeb.

Witness's signature..
Llofnod y tyst..

Name of witness ....
(CAPITAL LETTERS)

Enw'r tyst ....
(PRIFLYTHRENNAU)

Address of witness ....
(CAPITAL LETTERS)

Cyfeiriad y tyst ....
(PRIFLYTHRENNAU)

SEE INSTRUCTIONS ON THE BACK OF THIS FORM

GWELER Y CYFARWYDDIADAU AR GEFN Y FFURFLEN HON

Back of form

Cefn y ffurflen

INSTRUCTIONS TO THE VOTER

CYFARWYDDIADAU I'R PLEIDLEISIWR

1 You must sign (or mark) this declaration of identity in the presence of a person known to you. That person should then sign this declaration as a witness, adding his or her name and address. Without this the declaration will be invalid.

1. Rhaid i chi lofnodi (neu farcio) y datganiad hwn ynglŷn ag adnabyddiaeth ym mhresenoldeb person sy'n adnabyddus i chi. Dylai'r person hwnnw lofnodi'r datganiad hwn fel tyst, gan ychwanegu ei (h)enw a'i gyfeiriad/chyfeiriad. Heb hynny bydd y datganiad yn annilys.

2. At the European Parliamentary election, vote for one candidate only. *[At the election of .... vote for no more than .... candidates.] Put no other mark on the ballot paper or your vote may not be counted.

* *To be completed by the returning officer depending on the elections to which Regulation 78 applies.*

2. Yn yr etholiad Senedd Ewrop, pleidleisiwch dros un ymgeisydd yn unig. *[Yn etholiad .... peidiwch â phleidleisio dros fwy na .... ymgeisydd]. Peidiwch â rhoi unrhyw farc arall ar y papur pleidleisio, neu efallai na chaiff eich pleidlais ei chyfrif.

* *I'w lenwi ga y swyddog canlyniadau yn ôl yr etholiadau y mae Rheol 78 yn gymwys ar eu cyfer.*

3. Mark a cross (X) in the box on the right hand side of the ballot paper opposite the name[s] of the candidate[s] you are voting for. Do this secretly. If you cannot vote without assistance, the person assisting you must not disclose how you have voted.

3. Rhowch groes (X) yn y blwch ar ochr dde'r papur pleidleisio gyferbyn ag enw[au]'r ymgeisydd/ymgeiswyr y pleidleisiwch drosto/drostynt. Gwnewch hyn yn gyfrinachol. Os na allwch bleidleisio heb gymorth, rhaid i'r person sy'n eich cynorthwyo beidio â datgelu sut y gwnaethoch bleidleisio.

4. Put the ballot papers in the small envelope marked "A" and seal it. Then put the envelope marked "A", together with this declaration of identity, in the larger envelope marked "B". Return it without delay. The ballot papers, in order to be counted, must be received by the returning officer not later than the close of the poll.

4. Rhowch y papurau pleidleisio yn yr amlen fach a nodir ag "A" a seliwch hi. Yna rhowch yr amlen a nodir ag "A" ynghyd â'r datganiad hwn ynglŷn ag adnabyddiaeth yn yr amlen fwy a nodir â "B". Dychwelwch hi ar unwaith. Er mwyn cael eu cyfrif, rhaid i'r papurau pleidleisio gyrraedd y swyddog canlyniadau cyn i'r pleidleisio ddod i ben.

5. If you receive more than one ballot paper *relating to the same election*, remember that it is illegal to vote more than once (otherwise than as proxy) at that election.

5. Os cewch fwy nag un papur pleidleisio *sy'n gysylltiedig â'r un etholiad*, cofiwch ei bod hi'n anghyfreithlon pleidleisio mwy nag unwaith (ac eithrio fel dirprwy) yn yr etholiad hwnnw.

6. At these elections you cannot vote in person at a polling station, even if you receive an official poll card.

6. Yn yr etholiadau hyn, ni allwch bleidleisio'n bersonol mewn gorsaf bleidleisio, hyd yn oed os cewch gerdyn pleidleisio swyddogol.

7. If you inadvertently spoil any ballot paper, you can apply to the returning officer for a new one. If you do this you MUST RETURN ALL OF THE POSTAL BALLOT PAPERS YOU HAVE RECEIVED, together with the spoilt ballot paper. In addition, in your application for fresh postal ballot papers you MUST return, in your own envelope, the declaration of identity and the envelopes marked "A" and "B". Remember that there is little time available if fresh postal ballot papers are to be issued and counted.

7. Os gwnewch ddistrywio'n ddamweiniol unrhyw bapur pleidleisio drwy'r post, gallwch wneud cais i'r swyddog canlyniadau am un newydd. Os gwnewch hynny, RHAID I CHI DDYCHWELYD YR HOLL BAPURAU PLEIDLEISIO DRWY'R POST A GAWSOCH, ynghyd â'r papur pleidleisio a ddistrywiwyd. Hefyd, yn eich cais am bapurau pleidleisio newydd RHAID I CHI DDYCHWELYD, yn eich amlen eich hun, y datganiad ynglŷn ag adnabyddiaeth a'r amlenni a nodwyd "A" a "B". Cofiwch nad oes fawr o amser ar ôl os yw papur pleidleisio newydd i gael ei ddosbarthu a'i gyfrif.

Form 6

Front of form

Wyneb y ffurflen

EUROPEAN PARLIAMENTARY ELECTIONS ACT 1978
DEDDF ETHOLIADAU SENEDD EWROP 1978

To be returned with the [*insert colour of ballot paper*] coloured ballot paper.

I'w ddychwelyd gyda'r papur pleidleisio lliw [*nodwch liw'r papur pleidleisio*].

[*Insert colour of ballot paper*] coloured ballot paper No ....

Papur pleidleisio lliw [*Nodwch liw'r papur pleidleisio*] Rhif ....

I hereby declare that I am the person to whom the [*insert colour of ballot paper*] coloured ballot paper numbered above was sent.

Yr wyf yn datgan drwy hyn mai fi yw'r person yr anfonwyd iddo/iddi'r papur pleidleisio lliw [*nodwch liw'r papur pleidleisio*] â'r rhif uchod.

Voter's signature (or mark) ....

Llofnod y pleidleisiwr (neu farc) ....

The voter, who is personally known to me, has signed (or marked) this declaration in my presence.

Mae'r pleidleisiwr, a adnabyddir gennyf yn bersonol, wedi llofnodi (neu farcio) y datganiad hwn yn fy mhresenoldeb.

Witness's signature ....
Llofnod y tyst ....

Name of witness ....
(CAPITAL LETTERS)
Enw'r tyst ....
(PRIFLYTHRENNAU)

Address of witness ....
(CAPITAL LETTERS)
Cyfeiriad y tyst ....
(PRIFLYTHRENNAU)

SEE INSTRUCTIONS ON THE BACK OF THIS FORM

GWELER Y CYFARWYDDIADAU AR GEFN Y FFURFLEN HON

Back of form

Cefn y ffurflen

INSTRUCTIONS TO THE VOTER
CYFARWYDDIADAU I'R PLEIDLEISIWR

1. You must sign (or mark) this declaration of identity in the presence of a person known to you. *You are required to do this even if you have already signed (or marked) a similar declaration of identity in respect of another election to be held on the same day.* The person known to you should then sign this declaration as a witness, adding his or her name and address. Without this the declaration will be invalid.

1. Rhaid i chi lofnodi (neu farcio) y datganiad hwn ynglŷn ag adnabyddiaeth ym mhresenoldeb person sy'n adnabyddus i chi. *Mae'n ofynnol i chi wneud hynny hyd yn oed os ydych eisoes wedi llofnodi (neu farcio) datganiad tebyg ynglŷn ag adnabyddiaeth mewn perthynas ag etholiad arall a gynhelir ar yr un diwrnod.* Dylai'r person a adnabyddir gennych lofnodi'r datganiad hwn fel tyst, gan ychwanegu ei (h)enw a'i gyfeiriad/chyfeiriad. Heb hynny bydd y datganiad yn annilys.

2. Vote for one candidate only. Put no other mark on the ballot paper or your vote may not be counted.

2. Pleidleisiwch dros un ymgeisydd yn unig. Peidiwch â rhoi unrhyw farc arall ar y papur pleidleisio, neu efallai na chaiff eich pleidlais ei chyfrif.

3. Mark a cross (X) in the box on the right hand side of the ballot paper opposite the name of the candidate you are voting for. Do this secretly. If you cannot vote without assistance, the person assisting you must not disclose how you have voted.

3. Rhowch groes (X) yn y blwch ar ochr dde'r papur pleidleisio gyferbyn ag enw'r ymgeisydd y pleidleisiwch drosto. Gwnewch hyn yn gyfrinachol. Os na allwch bleidleisio heb gymorth, rhaid i'r person sy'n eich cynorthwyo beidio â datgelu sut y gwnaethoch bleidleisio.

4. Put the [*insert colour of ballot paper*] coloured ballot paper in the small envelope marked "A" and "Ballot paper envelope for the [*insert colour of ballot paper*] coloured ballot paper" and seal it. Then put the envelope marked "A" and "Ballot paper envelope for the [*insert colour of ballot paper*] coloured ballot paper", together with the declaration of identity, in the larger envelope marked "B" and "Covering envelope for the [*insert colour of ballot paper*] coloured ballot paper". TAKE CARE THAT YOU PLACE THE CORRECT BALLOT PAPER, BALLOT PAPER ENVELOPE AND DECLARATION OF IDENTITY IN THE CORRECT COVERING ENVELOPE AND RETURN IT WITHOUT DELAY, OTHERWISE YOUR VOTE MAY NOT BE COUNTED. The ballot paper, in order to be counted, must be received by the returning officer not later than the close of the poll.

4. Rhowch y papur pleidleisio lliw [*nodwch liw'r papur pleidleisio*] yn yr amlen fach a nodir ag "A" ac "Amlen papur pleidleisio ar gyfer y papur pleidleisio lliw [*nodwch liw'r papur pleidleisio*]" a seliwch hi. Yna rhowch yr amlen a nodir ag "A" ac "Amlen papur pleidleisio ar gyfer y papur pleidleisio lliw [*nodwch liw'r papur pleidleisio*]" ynghyd â'r datganiad ynglŷn ag adnabyddiaeth, yn yr amlen fwy a nodir â "B" a "Prif amlen ar gyfer y papur pleidleisio lliw [*nodwch liw'r papur pleidleisio*]". GOFALWCH EICH BOD YN RHOI'R PAPUR PLEIDLEISIO CYWIR A'R DATGANIAD YNGLŶN AG ADNABYDDIAETH YN Y BRIF AMLEN GYWIR A DYCHWELWCH HI AR UNWAITH, NEU EFALLAI NA CHAIFF EICH PLEIDLAIS EI CHYFRIF. Er mwyn cael ei gyfrif, rhaid i'r papur pleidleisio gyrraedd y swyddog canlyniadau cyn i'r pleidleisio ddod i ben.

5. If you receive more than one ballot paper, remember that it is illegal to vote more than once (otherwise than as proxy) at the *same election.* You are entitled to vote at different elections which are held on the same day.

5. Os cewch fwy nag un papur pleidleisio, cofiwch ei bod hi'n anghyfreithlon pleidleisio mwy nag unwaith (ac eithro fel dirprwy) yn *yr un etholiad.* Mae gennych hawl i bleidleisio mewn etholiadau gwahanol a gynhelir ar yr un diwrnod.

6. At this election you cannot vote in person at a polling station, even if you receive an official poll card.

6. Yn yr etholiad hwn, ni allwch bleidleisio'n bersonol mewn gorsaf bleidleisio, hyd yn oed os cewch gerdyn pleidleisio swyddogol.

7. If you inadvertently spoil your ballot paper, you can apply to the returning officer for another one. With your application you must return, in your own envelope, the spoilt ballot paper, the declaration of identity and the envelopes marked "A" and "B". Remember that there is little time available if a fresh postal ballot paper is to be issued and counted.

7. Os gwnewch ddistrywio'n ddamweiniol eich papur pleidleisio drwy'r post, gallwch wneud cais i'r swyddog canlyniadau am un arall. Gyda'ch cais rhaid i chi ddychwelyd, yn eich amlen eich hun, y papur pleidleisio a ddistrywiwyd, y datganiad ynglŷn ag adnabyddiaeth, ynghyd â'r amlenni a nodwyd "A" a "B". Cofiwch nad oes fawr o amser ar ôl os yw papur pleidleisio newydd i gael ei ddosbarthu a'i gyfrif.

Article 5

SCHEDULE 2

Forms in Welsh

Form 1

(i) "Ai chi yw'r person a gofrestrwyd yn y gofrestr etholwyr seneddol ar gyfer yr etholiad hwn fel hyn (*darllenwch y cofnod llawn yn y gofrestr*)?"

(ii) "A ydych eisoes wedi pleidleisio yma neu rywle arall, yn yr is-etholiad [etholiad cyffredinol] hwn, heblaw fel dirprwy ar ran rhyw berson arall?"

Form 2

(i) "Ai chi yw'r person y gwelir ei enw fel A.B. yn y rhestr ddirprwyon ar gyfer yr etholiad hwn, fel un sydd â hawl i bleidleisio fel dirprwy ar ran C.D.?"

(ii) "A ydych eisoes wedi pleidleisio yma neu rywle arall, yn yr is-etholiad [etholiad cyffredinol] hwn, fel dirpwy ar ran C.D.?"

Form 3

"Ai chi yw gŵr [gwraig], rhiant, tadcu [mamgu], brawd [chwaer], plentyn, neu ŵyr [wyres] C.D.?"

"A ydych eisoes wedi pleidleisio yn yr etholiad hwn ac yn yr etholaeth hon ar ran dau berson nad ydych yn ŵr [gwraig], rhiant, tadcu [mamgu], brawd [chwaer], plentyn, neu ŵyr [wyres] iddynt?"

Form 4

ETHOL CYNRYCHIOLYDD
I WASANAETHU YN SENEDD EWROP

Etholaeth ....

Yr ydym ni, sydd â'n henwau isod, ac sy'n etholwyr yn yr Etholaeth a enwyd, drwy hyn yn enwebu'r person a enwir isod i fod yn ymgeisydd yn yr etholiad a nodwyd.

Cyfenw'r ymgeisydd	Enwau eraill yn llawn	Disgrifiad	Cyfeiriad ei gartref yn llawn

Llofnodion	Rhif Etholiadol (gweler nodyn 3) Llythyren wahaniaethol	Rhif
Cynigydd	....	....
Eilydd	....	....
Yr ydym ni sydd â'n henwau isod, ac sy'n etholwyr yn yr Etholaeth a enwyd, yn cytuno drwy hyn â'r enwebiad hwn.		
1.	....	....
2.	....	....
3.	....	....
4.	....	....
5.	....	....
6.	....	....
7.	....	....
8.	....	....

9.	....	....
10.	....	....
11.	....	....
12.	....	....
13.	....	....
14.	....	....
15.	....	....
16.	....	....
17.	....	....
18.	....	....
19.	....	....
20.	....	....
21.	....	....
22.	....	....
23.	....	....
24.	....	....
25.	....	....
26.	....	....
27.	....	....
28.	....	....

NODIADAU

1. Tynnir sylw ymgeiswyr ac etholwyr at y rheolau ynglŷn â llenwi papurau enwebu, ac amodau eraill sy'n ymwneud ag enwebu a gynhwysir yn y rheolau etholiadau seneddol yn Atodiad 1, Deddf Cynrychiolaeth y Bobl 1983 fel y'u diwygiwyd ac fel y cawsant eu cymhwyso a'u newid ar gyfer ethol cynrychiolwyr y Deyrnas Gyfunol i'r Senedd gan Reolau Etholiadau Senedd Ewrop 1986.

2. Lle'r adnabyddir ymgeisydd yn arferol wrth ryw deitl gellir ei ddisgrifio wrth y teitl hwnnw fel pe bai'n gyfenw iddo.

3. Rhif etholiadol person yw ei rif yn y gofrestr a ddefnyddir yn yr etholiad (yn cynnwys llythyren wahaniaethol y dosbarth pleidleisio seneddol y mae wedi'i gofrestru ynddo) ac eithrio cyn i'r gofrestr gael ei chyhoeddi y gellir defnyddio yn lle hynny ei rif (os oes un) yn y rhestr etholwyr ar gyfer y gofrestr honno.

4. Ni chaiff etholwr roi enw wrth fwy nag un papur enwebu yn yr un etholiad.

5. Ni chaiff person sydd â' i enw ar y gofrestr neu'r rhestri etholwyr roi ei enw wrth bapur enwebu os yw'r cofnod yn rhoi fel dyddiad pryd y daw'n ddigon hen i bleidleisio ddyddiad ar ôl y diwrnod a benodir ar gyfer yr etholiad.

Form 5

CYFARWYDDYD I BLEIDLEISWYR WRTH BLEIDLEISIO

1. Pan roir i chi bapur pleidleisio gwnewch yn siŵr iddo gael ei stampio â'r marc swyddogol.

2. Ewch i un o'r cabanau pleidleisio. Rhowch groes (X) yn y blwch ar ochr dde'r papur pleidleisio gyferbyn ag enw yr ymgeisydd yr ydych am bleidleisio trosto.

3. Plygwch y papur yn ddau. Dangoswch y marc swyddogol i'r swyddog llywyddu, ond peidiwch â gadael i neb weld eich pleidlais. Rhowch y papur pleidleisio yn y blwch pleidleisiau a mynd allan o'r orsaf bleidleisio.

4. Pleidleisiwch i un ymgeisydd yn unig. Peidiwch â rhoi unrhyw farc arall ar y papur pleidleisio neu fe all na chaiff eich pleidlais ei chyfrif.

5. Os bydd i chi drwy gamgymeriad ddifetha eich papur pleidleisio, ewch a'i ddangos i'r swyddog llywyddu a gofyn am un arall.

Form 6

*Nodwch berthynas y cydymaith a'r pleidleisiwr

Gwnaed cais i mi, A.B. o .... gynorthwyo C.D. (*yn achos person dall sy'n pleidleisio fel dirprwy ychwaneger* pleidleisio fel dirprwy ar ran M.N.) sef rhif .... ar y gofrestr i gofnodi ei bleidlais yn yr etholiad a gynhelir yn awr yn yn yr etholaeth hon yn datgan drwy hyn [fod gennyf hawl i bleidleisio fel etholwr yn yr etholiad a enwyd] [fy mod yn* ..... i'r pleidleisiwr hwnnw ac wedi cyrraedd fy 18 mlwydd oed], ac na fu i mi o'r blaen gynorthwyo unrhyw bleidleisiwr dall [ac eithrio E.F., o, ...] i bleidleisio yn yr etholiad a enwyd.

(Llofnodwyd) A.B.

y .... dydd o fis 19

Yr wyf fi y gwelir fy llofnod isod sef swyddog llywyddu gorsaf bleidleisio .... ar gyfer Etholaeth .... yn tystio drwy hyn fod y datganiad uchod wedi ei ddarllen i ddechrau yng nghlyw'r datganwr a enwir uchod, a'i fod ef wedi ei lofnodi wedyn yn fy ngŵydd.

(Llofnodwyd) G.H.

y .... dydd of fis 19
am munud wedi ..... [a.m.] [p.m.]

NODYN:–Os bydd y person sy'n gwneud y datganiad uchod yn ystyriol ac yn fwriadol yn gwneud datganiad ffug ynglŷn ag unrhyw fater o bwys, bydd yn euog o drosedd.

EXPLANATORY NOTE

(This note is not part of the Order)

This Order replaces and revokes the European Parliamentary Elections (Welsh Forms) Order 1979 ("the 1979 Order"). The forms prescribed by Schedule 1 to this Order are versions partly in Welsh and partly in English which must be used at a European Parliamentary election in Wales for the purposes referred to in article 4 of this Order. The forms prescribed by Schedule 2 to this Order are Welsh versions of certain forms which may be used at a European Parliamentary election in Wales.

The differences between this Order and the 1979 Order are as follows. The bilingual versions of the official poll cards in Schedule 1 to this Order are based on the revised versions of those cards prescribed by the Representation of the People Regulations 1986, as applied by the European Parliamentary Elections Regulations 1986. In addition Schedule 1 now prescribes a bilingual version of the voting compartment notice and the declarations of identity prescribed by the Representation of the People Regulations 1986.

Schedule 2 to this Order omits the Welsh version of the declaration of secrecy consequent on the repeal of the requirement for such a declaration but includes the Welsh version of the directions for the guidance of the voters in voting.

NODYN ESBONIO

(Nid yw'r nodyn hwn yn rhan o'r Gorchymyn)

Mae'r Gorchymyn hwn yn disodli a diddymu'r European Parliamentary Elections (Welsh Forms) Order 1979 ("Gorchymyn 1979"). Mae'r ffurflenni a bennir gan Atodiad 1 y Gorchymyn hwn yn fersiynau rhannol Gymraeg a rhannol Saesneg y mae rhaid eu defnyddio mewn etholiad Senedd Ewrop yng Nghymru at y dibenion y cyfeirir atynt yn erthygl 4 y Gorchymyn hwn. Mae'r ffurflenni a bennir gan Atodiad 2 y Gorchymyn hwn yn fersiynau Cymraeg o rai ffurflenni y gellir eu defnyddio mewn etholiad Senedd Ewrop yng Nghymru.

Mae'r gwahaniaethau rhwng y Gorchymyn hwn a Gorchymyn 1979 fel a ganlyn. Seilir fersiynau dwyieithog y cardiau pleidleisio swyddogol yn Atodiad 1 y Gorchymyn hwn ar y fersiynau diwygiedig o'r cardiau hynny a bennwyd gan Reolau Cynrychiolaeth y Bobl 1986, fel y'u cymhwyswyd gan Reolau Etholiadau Senedd Ewrop 1986. Hefyd, mae Atodiad 1 bellach yn pennu fersiwn dwyieithog o'r rhybudd cabanau pleidleisio a'r datganiadau ynglŷn ag adnabyddiaeth a bennir gan Reolau Cynrychiolaeth y Bobl 1986.

Mae Atodiad 2 y Gorchymyn hwn yn hepgor fersiwn Cymraeg y datganiad cyfrinachedd o ganlyniad i ddiddymu'r gofyniad am ddatganiad o'r fath ond mae'n cynnwys fersiwn Cymraeg o'r cyfarwyddiadau i bleidleiswyr wrth bleidleisio.

STATUTORY INSTRUMENTS

1989 No. 429

REPRESENTATION OF THE PEOPLE

The Representation of the People (Welsh Forms) Order 1989

Made - - - -	*9th March 1989*
Laid before Parliament	*20th March 1989*
Coming into force	*21st April 1989*

In exercise of the powers conferred upon me by sections 2(1) and 3(4) of the Welsh Language Act 1967**(a)**, I hereby make the following Order:–

1. This Order may be cited as the Representation of the People (Welsh Forms) Order 1989 and shall come into force on 21st April 1989.

2. The Elections (Welsh Forms) Order 1970**(b)** is hereby revoked.

3. In this Order "the 1983 Act" means the Representation of the People Act 1983**(c)**.

4. Each of the forms set out in Schedule 1 to this Order is hereby prescribed as the version partly in Welsh and partly in English which shall be used:

(a) in the case of form 1, at a parliamentary election in Wales in place of the notice required by rule 29(5) of the parliamentary elections rules in Schedule 1 to the 1983 Act (voting compartment notice)**(d)**;

(b) in the case of form 2, as the proxy paper to be issued by the registration officer in Wales in place of form D (proxy paper) in Schedule 2 to the Representation of the People Regulations 1986**(e)**; and

(c) in the case of forms 3, 4 and 5, at a parliamentary election in Wales in place of forms H, J and K (declarations of identity), respectively, in Schedule 2 to the Representation of the People Regulations 1986.

5. Each of the forms set out in Schedule 2 to this Order is hereby prescribed as the Welsh version which may be used at a parliamentary election in Wales in place of the forms prescribed by the following provisions in the parliamentary elections rules in Schedule 1 to the 1983 Act, which provisions are:

(a) in the case of form 1, rule 35(1)(a),

(b) in the case of form 2, rule 35(1)(b),

(c) in the case of form 3, rule 35(2),

(a) 1967 c.66; section 2(1) was extended by section 22(1) of the Representation of the People Act 1985 (c.50).
(b) S.I. 1970/616.
(c) 1983 c.2.
(d) Rule 29(5) was amended by paragraph 79 of Schedule 4 to the Representation of the People Act 1985.
(e) S.I. 1986/1081; the form of proxy paper was amended by regulation 6 of, and paragraph 1 of Part I of Schedule 4 to, the European Parliamentary Elections Regulations 1986 (S.I. 1986/2209) (the citation of which has been amended by section 3(1)(b) and (2)(b) of the European Communities (Amendment) Act 1986 (c.58) on the coming into force of the Single European Act (Cmnd. 9758) on 1st July 1987).

(d) in the case of forms 4, 5 and 6, the form of nomination paper, the form of directions for the guidance of the voters in voting**(a)** and the form of declaration to be made by the companion of a blind voter, respectively, set out in the Appendix to those rules.

6. The forms set out in Schedules 1 and 2 to this Order, except forms 1, 2 and 3 in Schedule 2, may be used with such modifications as circumstances require.

Home Office
9th March 1989

Douglas Hurd
One of Her Majesty's Principal Secretaries of State

SCHEDULE 1

Article 4

Forms partly in Welsh and partly in English

Form 1

Vote for one candidate only. Put no other mark on the ballot paper or your vote may not be counted.

Pleidleisiwch i un ymgeisydd yn unig. Peidiwch â rhoi unrhyw farc arall ar y papur pleidleisio neu fe all na chaiff eich pleidlais ei chyfrif.

Form 2

Proxy paper
Papur dirprwy

REPRESENTATION OF THE PEOPLE ACTS
EUROPEAN PARLIAMENTARY ELECTIONS ACT 1978
DEDDFAU CYNRYCHIOLAETH Y BOBL
DEDDF ETHOLIADAU SENEDD EWROP 1978

Constituency
Etholaeth

Polling district
Dosbarth pleidleisio

Local government electoral area(s)
Rhanbarth(au) etholiadol llywodraeth leol

European Parliamentary constituency
Etholaeth Senedd Ewrop

Penodir

Name of proxy
Enw'r dirprwy ....

Address ....
Cyfeiriad ....

is hereby appointed as proxy for (Name of Elector)
drwy hyn yn ddirprwy dros (Enw'r Etholwr(aig)) ....

*[who is qualified to be registered for (Qualifying address)
sy'n gymwys i'w gofrestru/i'w chofrestru ar gyfer (Cyfeiriad cymhwyso)
....]

*[who qualifies as an overseas elector in respect of the above constituency
sy'n gymwys fel etholwr(aig) dramor mewn perthynas â'r etholaeth uchod]

(a) The form of directions for the guidance of the voters in voting was substituted by the Representation of the People Act 1985, Schedule 4, paragraph 86.

to vote for him/her at
i bleidleisio drosto/drosti yn

*[the *[parliamentary] [local government] [European Parliamentary] election for the above *[constituency] [electoral area] [European Parliamentary constituency]

[yr [etholiad seneddol] [llywodraeth leol] [Senedd Ewrop] ar gyfer yr *[etholaeth] [rhanbarth etholiadol] [etholaeth Senedd Ewrop] uchod.

on (date)
ar (dyddiad) ....]

*[any *[parliamentary or European Parliamentary election] [parliamentary, European Parliamentary or local government election] for the above *[parliamentary and European Parliamentary constituencies] [parliamentary and European Parliamentary constituencies and local government area(s).]

*[unrhyw *[etholiad seneddol neu etholiad Senedd Ewrop] [etholiad seneddol, etholiad Senedd Ewrop neu etholiad llywodraeth leol] ar gyfer yr *[etholaethau seneddol a Senedd Ewrop uchod] [etholaethau seneddol a Senedd Ewrop a rhanbarth (au) llywodraeth leol] uchod.]

*[This proxy appointment is not valid until
Nid yw penodiad y dirprwy hwn yn ddilys tan ....]

Signature
Llofnod ....

(Electoral Registration Officer)
(Swyddog Cofrestru Etholiadol)

Address...
Cyfeiriad ....

Date
Dyddiad ....

**Delete whichever is inappropriate*
Dileër yr hyn sy'n anghymwys

YOUR RIGHT TO VOTE AS PROXY
EICH HAWL I BLEIDLEISO FEL DIRPRWY

1. This proxy paper gives you the right to vote as proxy on behalf of the elector whose name is given overleaf.

1. Rhydd y papur dirprwy hwn hawl i chi bleidleisio fel dirprwy dros yr etholwr(aig) a enwir drosodd.

2. Your appointment as proxy may be for a particular election only, or it may be for an indefinite period. If it is for a particular election, you have the right to vote as proxy only at the election specified in the proxy paper. If it is for an indefinite period, you have in general the right to vote as proxy at any parliamentary, European Parliamentary or local election until the electoral registration officer informs you to the contrary. But if the person on whose behalf you have the right to vote as proxy qualifies as an overseas elector you may vote on his or her behalf only at parliamentary and European Parliamentary elections.

2. Gall eich penodiad fel dirprwy fod ar gyfer etholiad penodol yn unig, neu gall barhau am gyfnod amhenodol. Os yw ar gyfer etholiad penodol, mae gennych hawl i bleidleisio fel dirprwy yn unig yn yr etholiad a nodir yn y papur dirprwy. Os am gyfnod amhenodol y mae, mae gennych yr hawl fel rheol i bleidleisio fel dirprwy mewn unrhyw etholiad seneddol, etholiad Senedd Ewrop neu etholiad lleol nes i'r swyddog cofrestru etholiadol eich hysbysu i'r gwrthwyneb. Ond os yw'r person y mae gennych hawl i bleidleisio fel dirprwy drosto/drosti yn gymwys fel etholwr(aig) dramor cewch bleidleisio drosto/drosti yn unig mewn etholiadau seneddol ac etholiadau Senedd Ewrop.

3. When the elector applied for you to be appointed as proxy EITHER he or she was asked to state that he or she had consulted you and that you were capable of being and willing to be appointed as proxy OR you signed a statement stating that you were capable of being and willing to be appointed. You are capable of being appointed as proxy if you are at least 18 years old on polling day, a British or other Commonwealth citizen or a citizen of the Republic of Ireland and not for any reason disqualified from voting. If for some reason you are not capable of being, or willing to be, appointed as proxy, please write to the elector asking him to cancel the appointment.

3. Pan wnaeth yr etholwr(aig) gais i chi gael eich penodi yn ddirprwy, NAILL AI gofynnwyd iddo/iddi ddatgan iddo/iddi ymgynghori â chi a'ch bod yn gymwys i fod yn ddirprwy ac yn fodlon cael eich penodi NEU bu i chi lofnodi datganiad eich bod yn gymwys i fod yn ddirprwy ac yn fodlon cael eich penodi. Yr ydych yn gymwys i'ch penodi yn ddirprwy os ydych yn 18 oed o leiaf ar y dyddiad pleidleisio, yn ddinesydd Prydeinig neu'n ddinesydd un arall o wledydd y Gymanwlad neu yn ddinesydd Gweriniaeth Iwerddon a heb eich gwahardd rhag pleidleisio am unrhyw reswm. Os nad ydych, am unrhyw reswm, yn gallu bod yn ddirprwy neu yn fodlon cael eich penodi yn ddirprwy, byddwch cystal ag ysgrifennu at yr etholwr(aig) gan ofyn iddo/iddi ddileu'r pendodiad.

4. You may vote as proxy at the polling station allotted to the elector on whose behalf you are appointed. However, you may not vote as proxy at the same election for more than two electors of whom you are not the husband, wife, parent, grandparent, brother, sister, child or grandchild. Shortly before polling day you will be sent a proxy poll card telling you where the polling station is. You do not need to take either the poll card or this proxy paper to the polling station but you may find it helpful to do so. Remember that the elector may still vote in person. If he or she applies for a ballot paper at the polling station before you do you will not be able to vote as proxy on his or her behalf.

4. Cewch bleidleisio fel dirprwy yn yr orsaf bleidleisio a bennwyd i'r etholwr(aig) y penodwyd chi drosto/drosti. Er hynny, ni chewch bleidleisio fel dirprwy yn yr un etholiad dros fwy na dau o etholwyr nad ydych yn ŵr, gwraig, rhiant, tadcu neu famgu, brawd, chwaer, plentyn, ŵyr neu ŵyres iddynt. Ychydig cyn y dyddiad pleidleisio anfonir cerdyn pleidleisio dirprwy atoch yn dweud lle mae'r orsaf bleidleisio. Nid oes angen i chi fynd â'r cerdyn pleidleisio na'r papur dirprwy hwn gyda chi i'r orsaf bleidleisio, ond hwyrach y bydd o gymorth i chi wneud hynny. Cofiwch y caiff yr etholwr(aig) ddal i bleidleisio yn bersonol. Os bydd iddo/iddi wneud cais am bapur pleidleisio yn yr orsaf bleidleisio ni allwch bleidleisio fel dirprwy drosto/drosti.

5. If you cannot vote in person at the polling station the electoral registration officer may be able to allow you to vote as proxy by post. If your appointment is for an indefinite period, you may apply to vote by post throughout the period your appointment is in force if you live in a different electoral division from the elector's qualifying address—or if the addresses are in the same electoral division but in a different community in Wales. If you are registered for the same constituency or electoral area as the elector, you may apply if you are entitled to vote by post or proxy on your own behalf. In addition, you may vote by post at a particular election if the electoral registration officer is satisfied that you cannot reasonably be expected to vote in person at the elector's polling station. But the electoral registration officer cannot allow an application to vote by post at a particular election if he receives it after midday on the thirteenth working day before the poll.

5. Os na allwch bleidleisio yn bersonol yn yr orsaf bleidleisio, hwyrach y gall y swyddog cofrestru etholiadol ganiatáu i chi bleidleisio fel dirprwy trwy'r post. Os yw eich penodiad am gyfnod amhenodol, cewch wneud cais i bleidleisio trwy'r post trwy gydol y cyfnod y bydd eich penodiad mewn grym os ydych yn byw mewn adran etholiadol wahanol i gyfeiriad cymwys yr etholwr(aig)—neu os yw'r ddau gyfeiriad yn yr un adran etholiadol ond mewn cymdeithas wahanol yng Nghymru. Os cofrestrwyd chi yn yr un etholaeth neu ranbarth etholiadol â'r etholwr(aig), cewch wneud cais os oes gennych hawl i bleidleisio trwy'r post neu drwy ddirprwy ar eich rhan chi'ch hun. Hefyd, cewch bleidleisio trwy'r post mewn etholiad penodol os yw'r swyddog cofrestru etholiadol yn fodlon na ellir disgwyl yn rhesymol i chi bleidleisio yn bersonol yng ngorsaf bleidleisio'r etholwr(aig). Ond ni chaiff y swyddog cofrestru etholiadol ganiatáu cais i bleidleisio trwy'r post mewn etholiad penodol os daw i'w law ar ôl canol dydd ar y trydydd diwrnod gwaith ar ddeg cyn y bleidlais.

Form 3

Front of form
Wyneb y ffurflen

REPRESENTATION OF THE PEOPLE ACTS
DEDDFAU CYNRYCHIOLAETH Y BOBL

Ballot Paper No.
Rhif y Papur Pleidleisio ....

I hereby declare that I am the person to whom the ballot paper numbered as above was sent.

Yr wyf yn datgan drwy hyn mai fi yw'r person yr anfonwyd iddo/iddi'r papur pleidleisio â'r rhif uchod.

Voter's signature (or mark)
Llofnod y pleidleisiwr (neu farc) ....

The voter, who is personally known to me, has signed (or marked) this declaration in my presence.

Mae'r pleidleisiwr, a adnabyddir gennyf yn bersonol, wedi llofnodi (neu farcio) y datganiad hwn yn fy mhresenoldeb.

Witness's signature
Llofnod y tyst ....

Name of witness ....
(CAPITAL LETTERS)
Enw'r tyst ....
(PRIFLYTHRENNAU)

Address of witness ....
(CAPITAL LETTERS)
Cyfeiriad y tyst ....
(PRIFLYTHRENNAU)

SEE INSTRUCTIONS ON THE BACK OF THIS FORM
GWELER Y CYFARWYDDIADAU AR GEFN Y FFURFLEN HON

Back of form
Cefn y ffurflen

INSTRUCTIONS TO THE VOTER
CYFARWYDDIADAU I'R PLEIDLEISIWR

1. You must sign (or mark) this declaration of identity in the presence of a person known to you. That person should then sign this declaration as a witness, adding his or her name and address. Without this the declaration will be invalid.

1. Rhaid i chi lofnodi (neu farcio) y datganiad hwn ynglŷn ag adnabyddiaeth ym mhresenoldeb person sy'n adnabyddus i chi. Dylai'r person hwnnw lofnodi'r datganiad hwn fel tyst, gan ychwanegu ei (h)enw a'i gyfeiriad/chyfeiriad. Heb hynny bydd y datganiad yn annilys.

2. Vote for one candidate only. Put no other mark on the ballot paper or your vote may not be counted.

2. Pleidleisiwch dros un ymgeisydd yn unig. Peidiwch â rhoi unrhyw farc arall ar y papur pleidleisio, neu efallai na chaiff eich pleidlais ei chyfrif.

3. Mark a cross (X) in the box on the right hand side of the ballot paper opposite the name of the candidate you are voting for. Do this secretly. If you cannot vote without assistance, the person assisting you must not disclose how you have voted.

3. Rhowch groes (X) yn y blwch ar ochr dde'r papur pleidleisio gyferbyn ag enw'r ymgeisydd y pleidleisiwch drosto. Gwnewch hyn yn gyfrinachol. Os na allwch bleidleisio heb gymorth, rhaid i'r person sy'n eich cynorthwyo beidio â datgelu sut y gwnaethoch bleidleisio.

4. Put the ballot paper in the small envelope marked "A" and seal it. Then put the envelope marked "A", together with the declaration of identity, in the larger envelope marked "B". Return it without delay. The ballot paper, in order to be counted, must be received by the returning officer not later than the close of the poll.

4. Rhowch y papur pleidleisio yn yr amlen fach a nodir ag "A" a seliwch hi. Yna rhowch yr amlen a nodir ag "A" ynghyd â'r datganiad ynglŷn ag adnabyddiaeth yn yr amlen fwy a nodir â "B". Dychwelwch hi ar unwaith. Er mwyn cael ei gyfrif, rhaid i'r papur pleidleisio gyrraedd y swyddog canlyniadau cyn i'r pleidleisio ddod i ben.

5. If you receive more than one ballot paper, remember that it is illegal to vote more than once (otherwise than as proxy) at the same election.

5. Os cewch fwy nag un papur pleidleisio cofiwch ei bod hi'n anghyfreithlon pleidleisio mwy nag unwaith (ac eithro fel dirprwy) yn yr un etholiad.

6. At this election you cannot vote in person at a polling station, even if you receive an official poll card.

6. Yn yr etholiad hwn, ni allwch bleidleisio'n bersonol mewn gorsaf bleidleisio, hyd yn oed os cewch gerdyn pleidleisio swyddogol.

7. If you inadvertently spoil your ballot paper, you can apply to the returning officer for another one. With your application you must return, in your own envelope, the spoilt ballot paper, the declaration of identity and the envelopes marked "A" and "B". Remember that there is little time available if a fresh postal ballot paper is to be issued and counted.

7. Os gwnewch ddistrywio'n ddamweiniol eich papur pleidleisio drwy'r post, gallwch wneud cais i'r swyddog canlyniadau am un arall. Gyda'ch cais rhaid i chi ddychwelyd, yn eich amlen eich hun, y papur pleidleisio a ddistrywiwyd, y datganiad ynglŷn ag adnabyddiaeth, ynghyd â'r amlenni a nodwyd "A" a "B". Cofiwch nad oes fawr o amser ar ôl os yw papur pleidleisio newydd i gael ei ddosbarthu a'i gyfrif.

Form 4

Front of form
Wyneb y ffurflen

REPRESENTATION OF THE PEOPLE ACTS
DEDDFAU CYNRYCHIOLAETH Y BOBL

Ballot Paper Nos.
Rhifau'r Papurau Pleidleisio ....

I hereby declare that I am the person to whom the ballot papers numbered as above were sent.

Yr wyf yn datgan drwy hyn mai fi yw'r person yr anfonwyd iddo/iddi'r papurau pleidleisio â'r rhifau uchod.

Voter's signature (or mark)
Llofnod y pleidleisiwr (neu farc) ....

The voter, who is personally known to me has signed (or marked) this declaration in my presence.

Mae'r pleidleisiwr, a adnabyddir gennyf yn bersonol, wedi llofnodi (neu farcio) y datganiad hwn yn fy mhresenoldeb.

Witness's signature
Llofnod y tyst ....

Name of witness ....
(CAPITAL LETTERS)

Enw'r tyst ....
(PRIFLYTHRENNAU)

Address of witness ....
(CAPITAL LETTERS)

Cyfeiriad y tyst ....
(PRIFLYTHRENNAU)

SEE INSTRUCTIONS ON THE BACK OF THIS FORM
GWELER Y CYFARWYDDIADAU AR GEFN Y FFURFLEN HON

Back of form
Cefn y ffurflen

INSTRUCTIONS TO THE VOTER
CYFARWYDDIADAU I'R PLEIDLEISIWR

1. You must sign (or mark) this declaration of identity in the presence of a person known to you. That person should then sign this declaration as a witness, adding his or her name and address. Without this the declaration will be invalid.

1. Rhaid i chi lofnodi (neu farcio) y datganiad hwn ynglŷn ag adnabyddiaeth ym mhresenoldeb person sy'n adnabyddus i chi. Dylai'r person hwnnw lofnodi'r datganiad hwn fel tyst, gan ychwanegu ei (h)enw a'i gyfeiriad/chyfeiriad. Heb hynny bydd y datganiad yn annilys.

2. At the parliamentary election, vote for one candidate only. *[At the election of .... vote for no more than .... candidates.] Put no other mark on the ballot paper or your vote may not be counted.

**To be completed by the returning officer depending on the elections to which Regulation 78 applies.*

2. Yn yr etholiad seneddol, pleidleisiwch dros un ymgeisydd yn unig. *[Yn etholiad .... peidiwch â phleidleisio dros fwy na .... ymgeisydd]. Peidiwch â rhoi unrhyw farc arall ar y papur pleidleisio, neu efallai na chaiff eich pleidlais ei chyfrif.

**I'w lenwi gan y swyddog canlyniadau yn ôl yr etholiadau y mae Rheol 78 yn gymwys ar eu cyfer.*

3. Mark a cross (X) in the box on the right hand side of the ballot paper opposite the name of the candidate you are voting for. Do this secretly. If you cannot vote without assistance, the person assisting you must not disclose how you have voted.

3. Rhowch groes (X) yn y blwch ar ochr dde'r papur pleidleisio gyferbyn ag enw'r ymgeisydd y pleidleisiwch drosto. Gwnewch hyn yn gyfrinachol. Os na allwch bleidleisio heb gymorth, rhaid i'r person sy'n eich cynorthwyo beidio â datgelu sut y gwnaethoch bleidleisio.

4. Put the ballot papers in the small envelope marked "A" and seal it. Then put the envelope marked "A", together with this declaration of identity, in the larger envelope marked "B". Return it without delay. The ballot papers, in order to be counted, must be received by the returning officer not later than the close of the poll.

4. Rhowch y papurau pleidleisio yn yr amlen fach a nodir ag "A" a seliwch hi. Yna rhowch yr amlen a nodir ag "A" ynghyd â'r datganiad hwn ynglŷn ag adnabyddiaeth yn yr amlen fwy a nodir â "B". Dychwelwch hi ar unwaith. Er mwyn cael eu cyfrif, rhaid i'r papurau pleidleisio gyrraedd y swyddog canlyniadau cyn i'r pleidleisio ddod i ben.

5. If you receive more than one ballot paper *relating to the same election,* remember that it is illegal to vote more than once (otherwise than as proxy) at that election.

5. Os cewch fwy nag un papur pleidleisio *sy'n gysylltiedig â'r un etholiad,* cofiwch ei bod hi'n anghyfreithlon pleidleisio mwy nag unwaith (ac eithrio fel dirprwy) yn yr etholiad hwnnw.

6. At these elections you cannot vote in person at a polling station, even if you receive an official poll card.

6. Yn yr etholiadau hyn, ni allwch bleidleisio'n bersonol mewn gorsaf bleidleisio, hyd yn oed os cewch gerdyn pleidleisio swyddogol.

7. If you inadvertently spoil any ballot paper, you can apply to the returning officer for a new one. If you do this you MUST RETURN ALL OF THE POSTAL BALLOT PAPERS YOU HAVE RECEIVED, together with the spoilt ballot paper. In addition, in your application for fresh postal ballot papers you MUST RETURN in your own envelope, the declaration of identity and the envelopes marked "A" and "B". Remember that there is little time available if fresh postal ballot papers are to be issued and counted.

7. Os gwnewch ddistrywio'n ddamweiniol unrhyw bapur pleidleisio drwy'r post, gallwch wneud cais i'r swyddog canlyniadau am un newydd. Os gwnewch hynny, RHAID I CHI DDYCHWELYD YR HOLL BAPURAU PLEIDLEISIO DRWY'R POST A GAWSOCH, ynghyd â'r papur pleidleisio a ddistrywiwyd. Hefyd, yn eich cais am bapurau pleidleisio newydd RHAID I CHI DDYCHWELYD, yn eich amlen eich hun, y datganiad ynglŷn ag adnabyddiaeth a'r amlenni a nodwyd "A" a "B". Cofiwch nad oes fawr o amser ar ôl os yw papur pleidleisio newydd i gael ei ddosbarthu a'i gyfrif.

Form 5

Front of form
Wyneb y ffurflen

REPRESENTATION OF THE PEOPLE ACTS
DEDDFAU CYNRYCHIOLAETH Y BOBL

To be returned with the [*insert colour of ballot paper*] coloured ballot paper.
I'w ddychwelyd gyda'r papur pleidleisio lliw [*nodwch liw'r papur pleidleisio*].

[*Insert colour of ballot paper*] coloured ballot paper No.
Papur pleidleisio lliw [*Nodwch liw'r papur pleidleisio*] Rhif ....

I hereby declare that I am the person to whom the [*insert colour of ballot paper*] coloured ballot paper numbered above was sent.

Yr wyf yn datgan drwy hyn mai fi yw'r person yr anfonwyd iddo/iddi'r papur pleidleisio lliw [*nodwch liw'r papur pleidleisio*] â'r rhif uchod.

Voter's signature (or mark)
Llofnod y pleidleisiwr (neu farc) ....

The voter, who is personally known to me, has signed (or marked) this declaration in my presence.

Mae'r pleidleisiwr, a adnabyddir gennyf yn bersonol, wedi llofnodi (neu farcio) y datganiad hwn yn fy mhresenoldeb.

Witness's signature
Llofnod y tyst ....

Name of witness ....
(CAPITAL LETTERS)

Enw'r tyst ....
(PRIFLYTHRENNAU)

Address of witness ....
(CAPITAL LETTERS)

Cyfeiriad y tyst ....
(PRIFLYTHRENNAU)

SEE INSTRUCTIONS ON THE BACK OF THIS FORM
GWELER Y CYFARWYDDIADAU AR GEFN Y FFURFLEN HON

Back of form
Cefn y ffurflen

INSTRUCTIONS TO THE VOTER
CYFARWYDDIADAU I'R PLEIDLEISIWR

1. You must sign (or mark) this declaration of identity in the presence of a person known to you. *You are required to do this even if you have already signed (or marked) a similar declaration of identity in respect of another election to be held on the same day.* The person known to you should then sign this declaration as a witness, adding his or her name and address. Without this the declaration will be invalid.

1. Rhaid i chi lofnodi (neu farcio) y datganiad hwn ynglŷn ag adnabyddiaeth ym mhresenoldeb person sy'n adnabyddus i chi. *Mae'n ofynnol i chi wneud hynny hyd yn oed os ydych eisoes wedi llofnodi (neu farcio) datganiad tebyg ynglŷn ag adnabyddiaeth mewn perthynas ag etholiad arall a gynhelir ar yr un diwrnod.* Dylai'r person a adnabyddir gennych lofnodi'r datganiad hwn fel tyst, gan ychwanegu ei (h)enw a'i gyfeiriad/chyfeiriad. Heb hynny bydd y datganiad yn annilys.

2. Vote for one candidate only. Put no other mark on the ballot paper or your vote may not be counted.

2. Pleidleisiwch dros un ymgeisydd yn unig. Peidiwch â rhoi unrhyw farc arall ar y papur pleidleisio, neu efallai na chaiff eich pleidlais ei chyfrif.

3. Mark a cross (X) in the box on the right hand side of the ballot paper opposite the name of the candidate you are voting for. Do this secretly. If you cannot vote without assistance, the person assisting you must not disclose how you have voted.

3. Rhowch groes (X) yn y blwch ar ochr dde'r papur pleidleisio gyferbyn ag enw'r ymgeisydd y pleidleisiwch drosto. Gwnewch hyn yn gyfrinachol. Os na allwch bleidleisio heb gymorth, rhaid i'r person sy'n eich cynorthwyo beidio â datgelu sut y gwnaethoch bleidleisio.

4. Put the [*insert colour of ballot paper*] coloured ballot paper in the small envelope marked "A" and "Ballot paper envelope for the [*insert colour of ballot paper*] coloured ballot paper" and seal it. Then put the envelope marked "A" and "Ballot paper envelope for the [*insert colour of ballot paper*] coloured ballot paper", together with the declaration of identity, in the larger envelope marked "B" and "Covering envelope for the [*insert colour of ballot paper*] coloured ballot paper". TAKE CARE THAT YOU PLACE THE CORRECT BALLOT PAPER, BALLOT PAPER ENVELOPE AND DECLARATION OF IDENTITY IN THE CORRECT COVERING ENVELOPE AND RETURN IT WITHOUT DELAY, OTHERWISE YOUR VOTE MAY NOT BE COUNTED. The ballot paper, in order to be counted, must be received by the returning officer not later than the close of the poll.

4. Rhowch y papur pleidleisio lliw [*nodwch liw'r papur pleidleisio*] yn yr amlen fach a nodir ag "A" ac "Amlen papur pleidleisio ar gyfer y papur pleidleisio lliw [*nodwch liw'r papur pleidleisio*]" a seliwch hi. Yna rhowch yr amlen a nodir ag "A" ac "Amlen papur pleidleisio ar gyfer y papur pleidleisio lliw [*nodwch liw'r papur pleidleisio*]" ynghyd â'r datganiad ynglŷn ag adnabyddiaeth, yn yr amlen fwy a nodir â "B" a "Prif amlen ar gyfer y papur pleidleisio lliw [*nodwch liw'r papur pleidleisio*]". GOFALWCH EICH BOD YN RHOI'R PAPUR PLEIDLEISIO CYWIR A'R DATGANIAD YNGLŶN AG ADNABYDDIAETH YN Y BRIF AMLEN GYWIR A DYCHWELWCH HI AR UNWAITH, NEU EFALLAI NA CHAIFF EICH PLEIDLAIS EI CHYFRIF. Er mwyn cael ei gyfrif, rhaid i'r papur pleidleisio gyrraedd y swyddog pleidleisio cyn i'r pleidleisio ddod i ben.

5. If you receive more than one ballot paper, remember that it is illegal to vote more than once (otherwise than as proxy) at the *same election.* You are entitled to vote at different elections which are held on the same day.

5. Os cewch fwy nag un papur pleidleisio, cofiwch ei bod hi'n anghyfreithlon pleidleisio mwy nag unwaith (ac eithro fel dirprwy) yn *yr un etholiad.* Mae gennych hawl i bleidleisio mewn etholiadau gwahanol a gynhelir ar yr un diwrnod.

6. At this election you cannot vote in person at a polling station, even if you receive an official poll card.

6. Yn yr etholiad hwn, ni allwch bleidleisio'n bersonol mewn gorsaf bleidleisio, hyd yn oed os cewch gerdyn pleidleisio swyddogol.

7. If you inadvertently spoil your ballot paper, you can apply to the returning officer for another one. With your application you must return, in your own envelope, the spoilt ballot paper, the declaration of identity and the envelopes marked "A" and "B". Remember that there is little time available if a fresh postal ballot paper is to be issued and counted.

7. Os gwnewch ddistrywio'n ddamweiniol eich papur pleidleisio drwy'r post, gallwch wneud cais i'r swyddog canlyniadau am un arall. Gyda'ch cais rhaid i chi ddychwelyd, yn eich amlen eich hun, y papur pleidleisio a ddistrywiwyd, y datganiad ynglŷn ag adnabyddiaeth, ynghyd â'r amlenni a nodwyd "A" a "B". Cofiwch nad oes fawr o amser ar ôl os yw papur pleidleisio newydd i gael ei ddosbarthu a'i gyfrif.

Article 5

SCHEDULE 2

Forms in Welsh

Form 1

(i) "Ai chi yw'r person a gofrestrwyd yn y gofrestr etholwyr seneddol ar gyfer yr etholiad hwn fel hyn (*darllenwch y cofnod llawn yn y gofrestr*)?"

(ii) "A ydych eisoes wedi pleidleisio yma neu rywle arall, yn yr is-etholiad [etholiad cyffredinol] hwn, heblaw fel dirprwy ar ran rhyw berson arall?"

Form 2

(i) "Ai chi yw'r person y gwelir ei enw fel A.B. yn y rhestr ddirpwyon ar gyfer yr etholiad hwn, fel un sydd â hawl i bleidleisio fel dirprwy ar ran C.D.?"

(ii) "A ydych eisoes wedi pleidleisio yma neu rywle arall yn yr is-etholiad [etholiad cyffredinol] hwn fel dirprwy ar ran C.D.?"

Form 3

"Ai chi yw gŵr [gwraig], rhiant, tadcu [mamgu], brawd [chwaer], plentyn, neu ŵyr [wyres] C.D.?"

"A ydych eisoes wedi pleidleisio yn yr etholiad hwn ac yn yr etholaeth hon ar ran dau berson nad ydych yn ŵr [gwraig], rhiant, tadcu [mamgu], brawd [chwaer], plentyn, neu ŵyr [wyres] iddynt?"

Form 4

ETHOL AELOD
I WASANAETHU YN Y SENEDD DROS

Etholaeth ....

Yr ydym ni, sydd â'n henwau isod, ac sy'n etholwyr yn yr Etholaeth a enwyd, drwy hyn yn enwebu'r person a enwir isod i fod yn ymgeisydd yn yr etholiad a nodwyd.

Cyfenw'r ymgeisydd	Enwau eraill yn llawn	Disgrifiad	Cyfeiriad ei gartref yn llawn

Llofnodion	Rhif Etholiadol (gweler nodyn 3)	
	Llythyren wahaniaethol	Rhif
Cynigydd	....	....
Eilydd	....	....
Yr ydym ni sydd â'n henwau isod, ac sy'n etholwyr yn yr Etholaeth a enwyd, yn cytuno drwy hyn â'r enwebiad hwn.		
1.	....	....
2.	....	....
3.	....	....
4.	....	....
5.	....	....
6.	....	....
7.	....	....
8.	....	....

NODIADAU

1. Tynnir sylw ymgeiswyr ac etholwyr at y rheolau ynglŷn â llenwi papurau enwebu, ac amodau eraill sy'n ymwneud ag enwebu a gynhwysir yn rheolau etholiadau seneddol yn Atodiad 1, Deddf Cynrychiolaeth y Bobl 1983.

2. Lle'r adnabyddir ymgeisydd yn arferol wrth ryw deitl gellir ei ddisgrifio wrth y teitl hwnnw fel pe bai'n gyfenw iddo.

3. Rhif etholiadol person yw ei rif yn y gofrestr a ddefnyddir yn yr etholiad (yn cynnwys llythyren wahaniaethol y dosbarth pleidleisio seneddol y mae wedi'i gofrestru ynddo) ac eithrio cyn i'r gofrestr gael ei chyhoeddi y gellir defnyddio yn lle hynny ei rif (os oes un) yn y rhestr etholwyr ar gyfer y gofrestr honno.

4. Ni chaiff etholwr roi enw wrth fwy nag un papur enwebu yn yr un etholiad.

5. Ni chaiff person sydd â'i enw ar y gofrestr neu'r rhestri etholwyr roi ei enw wrth bapur enwebu os yw'r cofnod yn rhoi fel dyddiad pryd y daw'n ddigon hen i bleidleisio ddyddiad ar ôl y diwrnod a benodir ar gyfer yr etholiad.

Form 5

CYFARWYDDYD I BLEIDLEISWYR

1. Pan roir i chi bapur pleidleisio gwnewch yn siŵr iddo gael ei stampio â'r marc swyddogol.

2. Ewch i un o'r cabanau pleidleisio. Rhowch groes (X) yn y blwch ar ochr dde'r papur pleidleisio gyferbyn ag enw yr ymgeisydd yr ydych am bleidleisio trosto.

3. Plygwch y papur yn ddau. Dangoswch y marc swyddogol i'r swyddog llywyddu, ond peidiwch â gadael i neb weld eich pleidlais. Rhowch y papur pleidleisio yn y blwch pleidleisiau a mynd allan o'r orsaf bleidleisio.

4. Pleidleisiwch i un ymgeisydd yn unig. Peidiwch â rhoi unrhyw farc arall ar y papur pleidleisio neu fe all na chaiff eich pleidlais ei chyfrif.

5. Os bydd i chi drwy gamgymeriad ddifetha eich papur pleidleisio, ewch a'i ddangos i'r swyddog llywyddu a gofyn am un arall.

Form 6

Gwnaed cais i mi, A.B. o .... gynorthwyo C.D. (*yn achos person dall sy'n pleidleisio fel dirprwy ychwaneger* pleidleisio fel dirprwy ar ran M.N.) sef rhif .... ar y gofrestr i gofnodi ei bleidlais yn yr etholiad a gynhelir yn awr yn yr etholaeth hon yn datgan drwy hyn [bod gennyf hawl i bleidleisio fel etholwr yn yr etholiad a enwyd [fy mod yn* .... i'r pleidleisiwr hwnnw ac wedi cyrraedd fy 18 mlwydd oed], ac na fu i mi o'r blaen gynorthwyo unrhyw bleidleisiwr dall [ac eithrio E.F. o ....] i bleidleisio yn yr etholiad a enwyd.

*Nodwch berthynas y cydymaith a'r pleidleisiwr

(Llofnodwyd) A.B.

y .... dydd o fis .... 19 .

Yr wyf fi y gwelir fy llofnod isod sef swyddog llywyddu gorsaf bleidleisio .... ar gyfer Etholaeth yn tystio drwy hyn fod y datganiad uchod wedi ei ddarllen i ddechrau yng nghlyw'r datganwr a enwir uchod, a'i fod ef wedi ei lofnodi wedyn yn fy ngŵydd.

(Llofnodwyd) G.H.

y .... dydd o fis .... 19 .
am munud wedi .... [a.m.] [p.m.]

NODYN:– Os bydd y person sy'n gwneud y datganiad uchod yn ystyriol ac yn fwriadol yn gwneud datganiad ffug ynglŷn ag unrhyw fater o bwys, bydd yn euog o drosedd.

EXPLANATORY NOTE

(This note is not part of the Order)

This Order replaces and revokes the Elections (Welsh Forms) Order 1970 ("the 1970 Order"). The forms prescribed by Schedule 1 to this Order are versions partly in Welsh and partly in English which must be used in Wales for the purposes referred to in article 4 of this Order. The forms prescribed by Schedule 2 to this Order are Welsh versions of certain forms which may be used at a parliamentary election in Wales.

The differences between this Order and the 1970 Order are as follows. The bilingual versions of the forms in Schedule 1 to this Order are not prescribed by the 1970 Order. Schedule 2 to this Order omits the Welsh version of the declaration of secrecy consequent on the repeal of the requirement for such a declaration but includes the Welsh version of the directions for the guidance of the voters in voting.

NODYN ESBONIO

(Nid yw'r nodyn hwn yn rhan o'r Gorchymyn)

Mae'r Gorchymyn hwn yn disodli a diddymu'r Elections (Welsh Forms) Order 1970 ("Gorchymyn 1970"). Mae'r ffurflenni a bennir gan Atodiad 1 y Gorchymyn hwn yn fersiynau rhannol Gymraeg a rhannol Saesneg y mae rhaid eu defnyddio yng Nghymru at y dibenion y cyfeirir atynt yn erthygl 4 y Gorchymyn hwn. Mae'r ffurflenni a bennir yn Atodiad 2 y Gorchymyn hwn yn fersiynau Cymraeg o rai ffurflenni y gellir eu defnyddio mewn etholiad seneddol yng Nghymru.

Mae'r gwahaniaethau rhwng y Gorchymyn hwn a Gorchymyn 1970 fel a ganlyn. Ni phennwyd fersiynau dwyieithog y ffurflenni gan Atodiad 1 y Gorchymyn hwn gan Orchymyn 1970. Mae Atodiad 2 y Gorchymyn hwn yn hepgor fersiwn Cymraeg y datganiad cyfrinachedd o ganlyniad i ddiddymu'r gofyniad am ddatganiad o'r fath ond mae'n cynnwys fersiwn Cymraeg o'r cyfarwyddiadau i bleidleiswyr wrth bleidleisio.

STATUTORY INSTRUMENTS

1989 No. 430 (C.16)

HOUSING, ENGLAND AND WALES

The Housing and Planning Act 1986 (Commencement No. 13) Order 1989

Made - - - - 9th March 1989

The Secretary of State for the Environment, as respects England, and the Secretary of State for Wales, as respects Wales, in exercise of the powers conferred on them by section 57(2) of the Housing and Planning Act 1986**(a)** and of all other powers enabling them in that behalf, hereby make the following Order:

1. This Order may be cited as the Housing and Planning Act 1986 (Commencement No. 13) Order 1989.

2. Section 8 (preservation of right to buy on disposal to private sector landlord) of the Housing and Planning Act 1986 shall come into force on 5th April 1989.

Nicholas Ridley
9th March 1989 Secretary of State for the Environment

Peter Walker
9th March 1989 Secretary of State for Wales

EXPLANATORY NOTE

(This note is not part of the Order)

This Order brings section 8 of the Housing and Planning Act 1986 into force on 5th April 1989. Section 8 provides for the provisions of Part V of the Housing Act 1985 (c.68) (the right to buy) to continue to apply where a person ceases to be a secure tenant of a dwelling-house because the landlord has disposed of an interest in that dwelling-house in certain circumstances.

(a) 1986 c.63.

NOTE AS TO EARLIER COMMENCEMENT ORDERS

(This note is not part of the Order)

The following provisions of the Housing and Planning Act 1986 have been brought into force by commencement orders made before the date of this Order–

Provision	*Date of Commencement*	*S.I. No.*
sections 1 to 4 sections 10 to 14 sections 16 and 17 sections 19 and 20 sections 22 and 23 section 24 (partially) Part III (ss.27 to 29) Part VI (except for ss.40 to 43, 50 to 52 and parts of 49 and 53)	7th January 1987	1986/2262
section 49 (partially)	2nd March 1987	1987/304
section 40 section 49(2) (partially)	1st April 1987	1987/348
section 9	13th May 1987	1987/754
section 24(1) (partially)	22nd September 1987	1987/1554
sections 25, 50 and 51	1st October 1987	1987/1607
section 25 section 41 section 49(1) (partially) section 49(2) (partially)	2nd November 1987	1987/1759
section 18 (partially) section 24 (partially) Part V	11th December 1987	1987/1939
section 15 section 24(1) (partially)	17th February 1988	1987/2277
section 6	11th March 1988	1988/283
section 42 section 49(2) (partially)	17th November 1988	1988/1787

STATUTORY INSTRUMENTS

1989 No. 431

FINANCIAL SERVICES

The Financial Services Act 1986 (Miscellaneous Exemptions) Order 1989

Made - - - -	*13th March 1989*
Laid before Parliament	*13th March 1989*
Coming into force	*1st April 1989*

The Secretary of State, in exercise of his powers under section 46 of the Financial Services Act 1986(**a**) and of all other powers enabling him in that behalf, hereby makes the following Order:

1.—(1) This Order may be cited as the Financial Services Act 1986 (Miscellaneous Exemptions) Order 1989 and shall come into force on 1st April 1989.

(2) In this Order, "university" has the meaning given in section 43(6) of the Education (No. 2) Act 1986(**b**).

2. Each of the persons listed in the Schedule to this Order shall be an exempted person to the extent specified in that Schedule in relation to that person.

Francis Maude
Parliamentary Under Secretary of State,
Department of Trade and Industry

13th March 1989

(**a**) 1986 c.60; (power previously exercised in S.I. 1988/350 and 723).
(**b**) 1986 c.61.

SCHEDULE

Article 2

EXEMPTED PERSONS AND EXTENT OF EXEMPTION

1. The governing body of any university in receipt of funds administered by the Universities Funding Council or, in Northern Ireland, from the Department of Education for Northern Ireland on the advice of the Universities Funding Council when acting in the capacity of trustee or operator of any collective investment scheme established for objects connected with the relevant university.

2. The governing body of any institution within the PCFC funding sector within the meaning of section 120(8) of the Education Reform Act 1988(**a**) or of a designated assisted institution within the meaning of section 139(6) of that Act, when acting in the capacity of trustee or operator of a collective investment scheme for objects connected with the relevant institution.

3. Any person empowered by section 94 of the Mental Health Act 1983(**b**) to exercise the functions of a judge under Part VII of that Act when acting in the exercise of those functions.

4. Any person exercising the functions of the court under sections 5 or 8 of the Enduring Powers of Attorney Act 1985(**c**) when acting in the exercise of those functions.

EXPLANATORY NOTE

(This note is not part of the Order)

This Order provides for certain exemptions from the provisions of the Financial Services Act 1986 additional to those specified in Chapter IV of Part I of that Act and in the Financial Services Act 1986 (Miscellaneous Exemptions) Order 1988 and the Financial Services Act 1986 (Miscellaneous Exemptions) (No. 2) Order 1988. The persons specified in the Schedule to the Order are exempted from the requirement to obtain authorisation to the extent specified in the Schedule.

(**a**) 1988 c.40.
(**b**) 1983 c.20.
(**c**) 1985 c.29.

STATUTORY INSTRUMENTS

1989 No. 432 (S.50)

NATIONAL ASSISTANCE SERVICES

The National Assistance (Charges for Accommodation) (Scotland) Regulations 1989

Made - - - -	*7th March 1989*
Laid before Parliament	*20th March 1989*
Coming into force	*10th April 1989*

The Secretary of State, in exercise of the powers conferred on him by sections 22(3) and (4), 35(1) and 64(1) of the National Assistance Act 1948(**a**), and of all other powers enabling him in that behalf, hereby makes the following Regulations:

Citation, commencement and interpretation

1.—(1) These Regulations may be cited as the National Assistance (Charges for Accommodation) (Scotland) Regulations 1989 and shall come into force on 10th April 1989.

(2) These Regulations shall extend to Scotland only.

(3) In these Regulations–

"the Act" means the National Assistance Act 1948;

"Personal Injuries Scheme", "Service Pensions Instrument" and "1914-18 War Injuries Scheme" have the same meanings as in the Social Security (Overlapping Benefits) Regulations 1979(**b**);

a reference to a section of the Act is a reference to the section as applied by section 87(3) of the Social Work (Scotland) Act 1968(**c**) for the purposes of accommodation provided under that Act.

Revocation

2. The National Assistance (Charges for Accommodation) (Scotland) Regulations 1988(**d**) are hereby revoked.

Minimum charges

3.—(1) The liability of a person under section 22(3) of the Act (rate of liability to pay for accommodation provided under Part III of the Act) to pay for accommodation provided for him in premises managed by a local authority, or by an organisation with which arrangements have been made under section 26(1) of the Act, shall in no case be reduced below the sum of £34.90 per week.

(**a**) 1948 c.29; section 22(3) and (4) is applied by section 26(3) of that Act; section 22(3) and (4) and section 26(3) are applied by section 87(3) and (4) of the Social Work (Scotland) Act 1968 (c.49); section 64(1) contains a definition of "prescribed" relevant to the exercise of the statutory powers under which these Regulations are made.

(**b**) S.I. 1979/597; relevant amending instrument is S.I. 1980/1927.

(**c**) 1968 c.49; section 87(3) was amended by the Social Security Act 1980 (c.30), Schedule 4, paragraph 5(1), by the Health and Social Services and Social Security Adjudications Act 1983 (c.41), section 20(2), and by the Social Security Act 1986 (c.50), Schedule 10, paragraph 41(2).

(**d**) S.I. 1988/331.

(2) Where accommodation is provided for a child accompanied by a person over the age of 16, the liability of that person under section 22(3) and (7) of the Act to pay for the accommodation of that child shall in no case be reduced below whichever of the following sums is appropriate, that is to say–

(a) in respect of a child under the age of 11, the sum of £11.75 per week;

(b) in respect of a child aged 11 years or over but under the age of 16, the sum of £17.35 per week.

Sum needed for personal requirements

4. The sum which a local authority shall under section 22(4) of the Act assume that a person needs for his personal requirements shall be £8.70 per week except that, where that person is someone to whom there is payable attendance allowance under the provisions of section 35 of the Social Security Act 1975(**a**) or constant attendance allowance under any Personal Injuries Scheme, Service Pensions Instrument or any 1914-18 War Injuries Scheme, the said sum of £8.70 shall in respect of each week there is payable attendance allowance or constant attendance allowance be increased by the amount of such allowance.

Michael B. Forsyth
Parliamentary Under Secretary of State,
Scottish Office

St. Andrew's House, Edinburgh
7th March 1989

EXPLANATORY NOTE

(This note is not part of the Regulations)

These Regulations replace the National Assistance (Charges for Accommodation) (Scotland) Regulations 1988.

They increase from £32.90 to £34.90 the minimum weekly amount which a person is required to pay for accommodation provided for him under the Social Work (Scotland) Act 1968 (which by virtue of section 87(3) of that Act is to be regarded for purposes of charges as accommodation provided under Part III of the National Assistance Act 1948). They also increase the minimum weekly amount payable for that accommodation in respect of a child accompanying such a person, from £10.75 to £11.75 where the child is under the age of 11, and from £16.10 to £17.35 where he is between the ages of 11 and 16.

The Regulations also increase from £8.25 to £8.70 the weekly sum which, in assessing a person's liability to pay for such accommodation, a local authority is, in the absence of special circumstances, to assume will be needed for personal requirements.

(**a**) 1975 c.14; in section 35, subsections (2)(b), (3) and (4)(a) were amended, and subsections (2A) and (5A) inserted, by the Social Security Act 1979 (c.18), section 2; subsection (4A) was inserted by the Social Security Act 1980 (c.30), Schedule 1, paragraph 8; and subsection (6)(a) was amended by the National Health Service Act 1977 (c.49), Schedule 15, paragraph 63.

STATUTORY INSTRUMENTS

1989 No. 433 (S.51)

EDUCATION, SCOTLAND

The Grant-aided Colleges (Scotland) Grant Regulations 1989

Made - - - -	*9th March 1989*
Laid before Parliament	*20th March 1989*
Coming into force	*10th April 1989*

The Secretary of State, in exercise of the powers conferred on him by sections 73(c), 74(1) and 77 of the Education (Scotland) Act 1980(**a**), and of all other powers enabling him in that behalf, hereby makes the following Regulations:

Citation and commencement

1. These Regulations may be cited as the Grant-aided Colleges (Scotland) Grant Regulations 1989 and shall come into force on 10th April 1989.

Interpretation

2. In these Regulations, except where the context otherwise requires, the following expressions shall have the meanings hereby respectively assigned to them:–

"financial year" means the 12 month period ending on 31st March each year;

"governing body" means, in respect of a grant-aided college which is a college of education, the governing body of that college and, in respect of a grant-aided college which is a central institution (as defined in regulation 2(1) of the Central Institutions (Scotland) Regulations 1988(**b**), has the meaning given by that regulation;

"grant-aided college" has the meaning given by section 77(5) of the Education (Scotland) Act 1980.

Making of grants

3. Subject to the provisions of these Regulations, the Secretary of State may pay to the governing body of a grant-aided college–

(a) non-recurrent grants, being grants in aid of its expenditure on the acquisition of land, or rights therein, and buildings, on the erection, enlargement and improvement of buildings, on the supply of equipment and furnishings, on the provision and laying out of premises, including playing fields and other facilities for social activities and physical recreation, and generally on works of a permanent character; and

(b) recurrent grants, being grants in aid of its expenditure on administration, on the maintenance of the college, on the employment, education or training of staff, and for other purposes connected with such administration, maintenance, employment, education or training including works of a permanent but minor character.

(**a**) 1980 c.44.
(**b**) S.I. 1988/1715.

Determination and payment of grants

4.—(1) Grants under these Regulations shall be of such amount or at such rate and in respect of such period as the Secretary of State may determine.

(2) Grants under these Regulations may be paid as single payments or by instalments of such amounts and at such times as the Secretary of State may determine.

Conditions of all grants

5. The following conditions shall apply to the payment of all grants under these Regulations:–

(a) the governing body shall furnish such estimates of income and expenditure and shall give such other information to the Secretary of State as he may require;

(b) the governing body shall keep proper accounts;

(c) the accounts shall be prepared and audited to the satisfaction of the Secretary of State;

(d) the governing body shall submit audited accounts to the Secretary of State as soon as possible after the end of each financial year;

(e) the books and other documents relating to the governing body's accounts shall be open to inspection by the Secretary of State and by the Comptroller and Auditor General;

(f) the governing body shall not, without the prior written consent of the Secretary of State, borrow from any source or give any guarantee or indemnity; and

(g) the governing body shall comply with any requirements of regulations made under section 77 of the Education (Scotland) Act 1980 and any requirements imposed by these Regulations.

Additional condition of non-recurrent grants

6. It shall be an additional condition of the payment of non-recurrent grants that the governing body shall obtain the approval of the Secretary of State to–

(a) the purchase of any land, or rights therein, and buildings proposed to be acquired; or

(b) building or other works proposed to be undertaken;

with the aid of grant.

Additional conditions of recurrent grants

7. The following shall be additional conditions of the payment of recurrent grants:–

(a) the scales of tuition and other fees charged to students attending the grant-aided college shall be approved by the Secretary of State;

(b) the governing body shall comply with any direction given by the Secretary of State, after consultation with the governing body, as to the number of students of different categories to be admitted to the college in any period;

(c) the governing body shall, at such times and in such form as the Secretary of State may require, submit for his approval particulars of the courses to be provided in the grant-aided college, and shall comply with any direction given by him, after consultation with the governing body, as to the discontinuance of any such course;

(d) the total number of teaching staff employed in the grant-aided college shall be such as the Secretary of State may consider reasonable.

Requirements relating to grants

8.—(1) The following shall be requirements when any grant under these Regulations has been paid:–

(a) the governing body shall not dispose of any land or buildings provided, improved or maintained with the aid of grant without the prior approval of the Secretary of State;

(b) the governing body shall regularly review its holdings of land and buildings and (subject to paragraph (a) above and regulation 9(1)(b)) shall dispose of those which it considers are no longer needed;

(c) the governing body shall, at the request of the Secretary of State, repay to him so much of any grant as has not been used for the purposes for which it was given.

(2) It shall be an additional requirement when any grant under these Regulations has been paid to a college of education that the governing body shall (subject to regulation 9(1)(b)) dispose of any land or buildings which the Secretary of State, on being satisfied that they are no longer needed, directs it to dispose of.

Requirements relating to non-recurrent grants

9.—(1) The following shall be additional requirements when a governing body has received non-recurrent grant in respect of acquisition of, or expenditure on, any land or buildings:–

(a) no building works on the land or buildings (other than minor modifications or routine maintenance) shall be carried out without the prior approval of the Secretary of State;

(b) the governing body shall pay to the Secretary of State such portion of the proceeds of any disposal of the land or buildings (less any expenses incurred in the disposal) as he may determine after consultation with the governing body.

(2) The requirements specified in paragraph (1) above and in regulation 8(1)(a) of these Regulations shall apply when land or buildings have been provided with the aid of non-recurrent grant under the Further Education (Scotland) Regulations 1959**(a)** or the Colleges of Education (Scotland) Regulations 1987**(b)**, as the case may be, or under any earlier regulations enabling the payment of non-recurrent grant in respect of grant-aided colleges, as they apply when land or buildings have been provided with the aid of non-recurrent grant paid under these Regulations.

Power to withhold grants

10. The Secretary of State may reduce or withhold a grant if any condition imposed by these Regulations is not fulfilled.

Revocations

11. The following regulations are hereby revoked:–

(a) Part II of the Further Education (Scotland) Regulations 1959;

(b) regulation 4 of the Further Education (Scotland) Amendment Regulations 1979(**c**);

(c) in the Colleges of Education (Scotland) Regulations 1987–

(i) regulation 21(4); and

(ii) Part VIII.

Consequential amendments

12.—(1) In regulation 15 of the Central Institutions (Scotland) Amendment Regulations 1981(**d**) for the words "the Further Education (Scotland) Regulations" there shall be substituted the words "the Grant-aided Colleges (Scotland) Grant Regulations 1989".

(2) In regulation 13 of the Napier College of Commerce and Technology (No. 2) Regulations 1985(**e**) for the words "the Further Education (Scotland) Regulations 1959 to 1979" there shall be substituted the words "the Grant-aided Colleges (Scotland) Grant Regulations 1989".

(3) In regulation 13 of the Glasgow College of Technology (No. 2) Regulations 1985(**f**) for the words "the Further Education (Scotland) Regulations 1959 to 1979" there shall be substituted the words "the Grant-aided Colleges (Scotland) Grant Regulations 1989".

(**a**) S.I. 1959/477; the relevant amending instrument is S.I. 1979/1185.
(**b**) S.I. 1987/309.
(**c**) S.I. 1979/1185.
(**d**) S.I. 1981/1221.
(**e**) S.I. 1985/1163, as amended by S.I. 1988/1715.
(**f**) S.I. 1985/1164, as amended by S.I. 1988/1715.

St. Andrew's House, Edinburgh
9th March 1989

Michael B. Forsyth
Parliamentary Under Secretary of State,
Scottish Office

EXPLANATORY NOTE

(This note is not part of the Regulations)

These Regulations empower the Secretary of State to pay recurrent and non-recurrent grants to colleges of education and central institutions in Scotland (known collectively as "the grant-aided colleges"). They prescribe the conditions of, and requirements relating to, the payment of grants.

The regulations which previously empowered the Secretary of State to pay grants to the grant-aided colleges are revoked by these Regulations.

STATUTORY INSTRUMENTS

1989 No. 434 (S.52)

SHERIFF COURT, SCOTLAND

Act of Sederunt (Fees of Solicitors in the Sheriff Court) 1989

Made - - - -	*9th March 1989*
Laid before Parliament	*22nd March 1989*
Coming into force	*12th April 1989*

The Lords of Council and Session, under and by virtue of the powers conferred on them by section 40 of the Sheriff Courts (Scotland) Act 1907(**a**), and of all other powers enabling them in that behalf, do hereby enact and declare:

Citation and commencement

1.—(1) This Act of Sederunt may be cited as the Act of Sederunt (Fees of Solicitors in the Sheriff Court) 1989 and shall come into force on 12th April 1989.

(2) This Act of Sederunt shall be inserted in the Books of Sederunt.

Application

2.—(1) The Schedule to this Act of Sederunt applies to work done or expenses incurred on or after the date on which this Act of Sederunt comes into force.

(2) The Schedule to this Act of Sederunt shall not apply to fees for work done, expenses or outlays incurred or to the taxation of accounts for which the Secretary of State may make regulations under and by virtue of section 14A of the Legal Aid (Scotland) Act 1967(**b**) or section 33 of the Legal Aid (Scotland) Act 1986(**c**).

Revocation and saving

3.—(1) The Act of Sederunt (Fees of Solicitors in the Sheriff Court) 1988(**d**) is revoked.

(2) Notwithstanding the revocation in sub-paragraph (1) of this paragraph, the provisions of the Act of Sederunt (Fees of Solicitors in the Sheriff Court) 1988 shall continue to have effect in respect of work done expenses or outlays incurred, before the coming into force of this Act of Sederunt.

Edinburgh
9th March 1989

Emslie
Lord President, I.P.D.

(**a**) 1907 c.51; section 40 was amended by the Secretaries of State Act 1926 (c.18), section 1(3), the Administration of Justice (Scotland) Act 1933 (c.41), Schedule and the Divorce Jurisdiction, Court Fees and Legal Aid (Scotland) Act 1983 (c.12), Schedule 1, paragraph 7 and Schedule 2.
(**b**) 1967 c.43; section 14A was inserted by the Divorce Jurisdiction, Court Fees and Legal Aid (Scotland) Act 1983, section 3; the 1967 Act was repealed by the Legal Aid (Scotland) Act 1986 (c.47), Schedule 5, but continues to apply in respect of legal aid granted prior to the 1986 Act coming into force, by virtue of paragraph 3 of Schedule 4 to the 1986 Act.
(**c**) 1986 c.47; section 33 was amended by the Legal Aid Act 1988 (c.34), Schedule 4, paragraph 5.
(**d**) S.I. 1988/681.

SCHEDULE

Paragraph 2

GENERAL REGULATIONS

1. The Table of Fees in this Schedule shall regulate the taxation of accounts between (a) solicitor and client, client paying, (b) solicitor and client, third party paying and (c) party and party; and shall be subject to the aftermentioned powers of the sheriff to increase or modify such fees.

2. The pursuer's solicitor's account as between party and party shall be taxed by reference to the sum decerned for unless the sheriff otherwise directs.

3. Where an action has been raised under summary cause procedure, only expenses under Chapter IV of the Table of Fees shall be allowed unless the sheriff otherwise directs.

4. Fees for work done in terms of the Social Work (Scotland) Act 1968(**a**) shall be chargeable under Chapter III of the Table of Fees.

5. The sheriff shall have the following discretionary powers in relation to the Table of Fees:–

(a) In any case the sheriff may direct that expenses shall be subject to modification.

(b) In cases of importance or requiring special preparation, the sheriff may, upon a motion made not later than seven days after the date of any interlocutor disposing of expenses, pronounce a further interlocutor regarding these expenses allowing a percentage increase in a cause on the ordinary roll, not exceeding 50 per cent, and in a cause on the summary cause roll, not exceeding 100 per cent, of the fees authorised by this table to cover the responsibility undertaken by the solicitor in the conduct of the litigation. Where such an increase is allowed a similar increase may, if the sheriff so orders, be chargeable by each solicitor in the cause against his own client. In fixing the amount of the percentage increase the following factors shall be taken into account:–

(i) the complexity of the litigation and the number, difficulty or novelty of the questions involved;

(ii) the skill, specialised knowledge and responsibility required of and the time and labour expended by the solicitor;

(iii) the number and importance of the documents (however brief) prepared or perused;

(iv) the place and circumstances of the litigation or in which the solicitor's work of preparation for and conduct thereof has been carried out;

(v) the importance of the litigation or the subject-matter thereof to the client;

(vi) the amount or value of money or property involved;

(vii) any other fees and allowances payable to the solicitor in respect of other items in the same litigation and otherwise charged for in the account.

(c) Where a party or his solicitor on one side attends any diet of proof or debate or any meeting ordered by the sheriff and the other is absent or not prepared to proceed the sheriff shall have power to decern against the latter party for payment of such expenses as the sheriff may consider reasonable. If an appeal be abandoned, or any debate on preliminary pleas or otherwise ordered by the sheriff be departed from by any party and notice to that effect be given to the opposite party at least three lawful days before the date fixed for the hearing no debate fee shall be allowed; but failing such notice a debate fee shall be allowed to the respondent's or other party's solicitor of one-half of the amount which would have been allowed had the debate proceeded.

6. The expenses to be charged against an opposite party shall be limited to proper expenses of process without any allowance (beyond that specified in the Table of Fees) for preliminary investigations, subject to this proviso, that precognitions, plans, analyses, reports, and the like (so far as relevant and necessary for proof of the matters in the Record between the parties), although taken or made before the raising of an action or the preparation of defences, or before proof is allowed, and although the case may not proceed to trial or proof, may be allowed.

7. Save as otherwise provided in the Table of Fees it shall be in the option of the solicitor to charge an account either on the basis of the inclusive fees of Chapters I and II or on the basis of the detailed fees of Chapter III of the Table of Fees, but in accounts as between party and party it shall not be competent to make charges partly on the one basis and partly on the other. In accounts as between solicitor and client, however, it shall be competent to charge an account partly on the basis of the inclusive fees of Chapters I and II and partly on the basis of the detailed fees of Chapter III of the Table

(**a**) 1968 c.49.

of Fees, but if an inclusive fee is charged under Chapters I or II no work falling thereunder shall be charged again under Chapter III.

8. In order that the expenses of litigation may be kept within proper and reasonable limits only such expenses shall be allowed in the taxation of accounts between party and party as are necessary for conducting it in a proper manner. It shall be competent to the auditor to disallow all charges for papers, parts of papers or particular procedure or agency which he shall judge irregular or unnecessary.

9. Notwithstanding that a party shall be found entitled to expenses generally yet if on the taxation of the account it shall appear that there is any particular part of the litigation in which such party has proved unsuccessful or that any part of the expenses has been occasioned through his own fault he shall not be allowed the expense of such parts of the proceedings.

10. When a remit is made by the court regarding matters in the record between the parties to an accountant, engineer, or other reporter the solicitors shall not, without special agreement, be personally responsible to the reporter for his remuneration, the parties alone being liable therefor.

11. In all cases, the solicitor's outlays reasonably incurred in the furtherance of the litigation shall be allowed. These outlays shall include a charge in respect of posts and sundries of 12 per cent. of the taxed amount of fees.

12. In the taxation of accounts as between party and party where counsel is employed–

(a) counsel's fees and the fees for instruction of counsel in paragraph 19 of Chapter II or in a detailed account charged under Chapter III of the Table of Fees are to be allowed only where the sheriff has sanctioned the employment of counsel; and

(b) except on cause shown fees to counsel and solicitor for only one consultation in the course of the case are to be allowed except where counsel is employed both before the sheriff and the sheriff principal and there is a consultation prior to the debate on the appeal when fees for an additional consultation are to be allowed.

13. In the case of all solicitors' charges to which these Regulations relate, where those charges are taxable supplies in terms of the Finance Act 1972 and are supplied by a solicitor who is a taxable person within the meaning of that Act, an addition may be made to the charges of such amount as is equivalent to the rate of Value-Added Tax at the date of supply, and this additional sum shall be so described in the solicitor's account.

14. In Chapter IV of the Table of Fees–

(a) necessary outlays, including–

(i) in relation to Part II only, a charge in respect of post and sundries of 12 per cent. of the fees allowed;

(ii) fees for witnesses calculated as provided by Act of Sederunt;

are allowed in addition to the fees allowed under this Chapter;

(b) in Parts I and II, sheriff officers' fees and the costs of advertising are allowable as outlays;

(c) in Parts I and II, in respect of paragraph 3 (attendance at court), no fee is allowable for attendance at a continuation of the first calling, unless specially authorised by the court;

(d) in Part II, in respect of paragraph 7 (precognitions), in a case where a skilled witness prepares his own precognition or report, half of the drawing fee is allowable to the solicitor for revising and adjusting it;

(e) in Part II, in respect of paragraph 15, no fees shall be allowed in respect of accounts of expenses when the hearing on the claim for expenses takes place immediately on the sheriff or sheriff principal announcing his decision;

(f) all fees chargeable under this Chapter in respect of the actions mentioned in the left-hand column of the following table shall unless the sheriff, on a motion in that behalf, otherwise directs be reduced by the amount of the percentage specified opposite those actions in the right-hand column of the following table:–

TABLE

Actions	*Percentage reduction*
1. of a value* from £50 to £250	25%
2. of a value* of less than £50	50%
3. for recovery of possession of heritable property, if not defended	50%

* "value" in relation to any action in which a counterclaim has been lodged, is the total of the sums craved in the writ and the sum claimed, in the counterclaim.

(g) in Part I, in respect of paragraph 1 (instruction fees), in relation to actions for reparation there are allowable such additional fees for precognitions and reports as are necessary to permit the framing of the writ, together with necessary outlays in connection therewith; and

(h) in Part II, the fee allowable in respect of paragraph 14 (supplementary note of defence) is a fixed fee allowable only when a supplementary note of defence is ordained by the court.

TABLE OF FEES

CHAPTER I

PART I.—UNDEFENDED ACTIONS

(other than actions of divorce or of separation and aliment (affidavit procedure))

1. *Actions (other than those specified in paragraph 2 of this Chapter) in which decree is granted without proof–*

   (a) Inclusive fee to cover all work from taking instructions up to and including obtaining extract decree £55.00

   (b) In cases where settlement is effected after service of a writ but before the expiry of the *induciae* £47.50

   (c) If the pursuer's solicitor elects to charge this inclusive fee he shall endorse a minute to that effect on the initial writ before ordering extract of the decree. Outlays such as court dues for deliverance and posts shall be chargeable in addition and taxation shall be unnecessary.

2. *Actions of separation and aliment, adherence and aliment and custody and aliment where proof (other than by way of affidavit evidence) takes place–*

   (a) Inclusive fee to cover all work from taking instructions up to and including obtaining extract decree £260.00

   (b) If the pursuer's solicitor elects to charge this inclusive fee he shall endorse a minute to that effect on the initial writ after the close of the proof and before extract of the decree is ordered; and when the option is so exercised decree for expenses shall be granted against the defender for said sum together with the shorthand writer's fee actually charged as provided by Act of Sederunt and of other outlays up to £60 without the necessity for taxation. If outlays in excess of £60, excluding the shorthand writer's fee, are claimed, an account of such outlays shall be remitted to the auditor of court for taxation and the sum allowed for outlays shall be the amount of the account as taxed.

3. *Petition for appointment or discharge of a* curator bonis

   (a) Inclusive fee to cover all work enquiring into estate and taking instructions up to and including obtaining extract decree... ... ... £235.00

   (b) (i) If the solicitor elects to charge the inclusive fee and to recover only the normal outlays as set out in head (ii) of this sub-paragraph, he shall endorse on the petition before ordering extract of the decree a minute setting out the said fee and the outlays. Taxation of charges so specified shall not be necessary.

   (ii) The normal outlays referred to in head (i) of this sub-paragraph are:–
   reasonable fees for medical reports;
   court dues for deliverance;
   sheriff officers' fees for service;
   advertising costs incurred;
   posts and incidents; and
   Value Added Tax chargeable on solicitors' fees and posts.

PART II.—UNDEFENDED ACTIONS OF DIVORCE AND OF SEPARATION AND ALIMENT

(affidavit procedure)

1. In any undefended action of divorce or separation and aliment where–

(a) the facts set out in section 1(2)(b) (unreasonable behaviour) of the Divorce (Scotland) Act 1976 ("the 1976 Act") are relied upon;

(b) there is no crave relating to any ancillary matters; and

(c) the pursuer seeks to prove those facts by means of affidavits, the pursuer's solicitor may, in respect of the work specified in column 1 of Table A, charge the inclusive fee specified in respect of that work in column 2 of that Table.

TABLE A

Column 1 *Work done*	Column 2 *Inclusive fee* £
1. All work to and including the period of notice	182.50
2. All work from the period of notice to and including swearing affidavits	130.00
3. All work from swearing affidavits to and including sending extract decree	40.00
4. All work to and including sending extract decree	352.50
Add process fee	of 10%

2. In any undefended action of divorce or separation and aliment where–

(a) the facts set out in sections 1(2)(a) (adultery), 1(2)(c) (desertion), 1(2)(d) (two years' non-cohabitation and consent) and 1(2)(e) (five years' non-cohabitation) of the 1976 Act are relied on;

(b) there is no crave relating to any ancillary matters; and

(c) the pursuer seeks to prove those facts by means of affidavits,

the pursuer's solicitor may, in respect of work specified in column 1 of Table B, charge the inclusive fee specified in respect of that work in column 2 of that Table.

TABLE B

Column 1 *Work done*	Column 2 *Inclusive fee* £
1. All work to and including the period of notice	150.00
2. All work from the period of notice to and including swearing affidavits	72.00
3. All work from swearing affidavits to and including sending extract decree	40.00
4. All work to and including sending extract decree	262.00
Add process fee	of 10%

3. If–

(a) the pursuer's solicitor charges an inclusive fee under either paragraph 1 or paragraph 2 of this Part; and

(b) the action to which the charge relates includes a crave relating to an ancillary matter,

in addition to that fee he may charge, in respect of the work specified in column 1 of Table C, the inclusive fee specified in respect of that work in column 2 of that Table.

TABLE C

Column 1 *Work done*	Column 2 *Inclusive fee* £
1. All work to and including the period of notice	72.00
2. All work from the period of notice to and including swearing affidavits	42.00
3. All work under items 1 and 2	114.00
Add process fee	of 10%

4. If the pursuer's solicitor elects to charge an inclusive fee under this Part he shall endorse a minute to that effect on the initial writ before extract of the decree is ordered; and when the option is so exercised decree for expenses shall be granted against the defender for said sum together with outlays up to £85 inclusive of VAT without the necessity for taxation. If outlays in excess of £85 are claimed, an account of such outlays shall be remitted to the auditor of court for taxation and the sum allowed for outlays shall be the amount of the account as taxed.

CHAPTER II

DEFENDED ACTIONS

1.	*Instruction fee*—	
	(a) To cover all work (except as hereinafter otherwise specially provided for in this chapter) to the lodging of defences including copyings	£120.00
	(b) Where separate statement of facts and counterclaim and answers lodged, additional fee of	£42.00
2.	*Adjustment fee*—To cover all work (except as hereinafter otherwise specially provided for in this Chapter) in connection with the adjustment of the Record including (when appropriate) closing thereof, making up and lodging Closed Record and copyings–	
	(a) Agent for any party	£178.50
	(b) If action settled before Record is closed—each original party's agent ...	£120.00
	(c) If additional defender brought in before closing of Record—additional fee to each original party's agent	£21.00
	(d) If additional defender brought in after closing of Record—additional fee to each original party's agent	£30.00
3.	*Affidavit fee*—To framing affidavits, per sheet...	£7.50
4.	(a) *Debate fee*—To include preparation for and conduct of any hearing or debate other than on evidence, enquiring for cause at avizandum and noting interlocutor–	
	(i) When debate does not exceed 1 hour	£90.00
	(ii) For every quarter hour engaged after the first hour	£11.00
	(iii) Waiting time—per quarter hour	£10.00
	(b) *Interim Interdict Hearings*–	
	(i) Pursuer's solicitor—the same fees as for debate fee above, but to include both the appearance at lodging of writ and the hearing at second diet.	
	(ii) Defender's solicitor's fee where the debate does not exceed 1 hour	£52.50
	(iii) Waiting time—per quarter hour	£10.00
5.	*Precognitions*—Taking and drawing—per sheet	£18.00
	Note	
	Where a skilled witness prepares his own precognition or report, the solicitor shall be allowed half of above drawing fee for revising and adjusting it.	
6.	*Custody reports obtained under order of court*–	
	(a) Fee for all work incidental thereto	£40.00
	(b) Additional fee per sheet of report to include all copies required (maximum £25)	£5.50
7.	*Commissions to take evidence*–	
	(a) *On Interrogatories*–	
	(i) Fee to solicitor applying for commission to include drawing, intimating and lodging motion, drawing and lodging interrogatories, instructing commissioner and all incidental work (except as otherwise specially provided for in this chapter) but excluding attendance at execution of commission	£111.50
	(ii) Fee to opposing solicitor if cross-interrogatories prepared and lodged	£75.00
	(iii) If no cross-interrogatories lodged	£22.00
	(b) *Open Commissions*–	
	(i) Fee to solicitor applying for commission to include all work (except as otherwise specially provided for in this chapter) up to lodging report of commission but excluding attendance thereat	£67.00
	(ii) Fee to solicitor for opposing party	£37.00
	(iii) Fee for attendance at execution of commission—per quarter hour ...	£11.00
	(iv) Travelling time—per quarter hour	£10.00

8. *Specification of documents–*

(a) Fee to cover drawing, intimating and lodging specification and relative motion and attendance at court debating specification £46.00

(b) Inclusive fee to opposing solicitor £30.00

(c) Fee for citation of havers, preparation for and attendance before commissioner at execution of commission–

(i) Where attendance before commissioner does not exceed 1 hour £42.00

(ii) For each additional quarter hour after the first hour £11.00

(d) If commission not executed—fee for serving each party with copy of specification to include recovering and examining documents or productions referred to therein £10.00

9. *Amendment of Record–*

(a) Fee to cover drawing, intimating and lodging minute of amendment and relative motion and relative attendances at court–

(i) Where answers lodged £51.00

(ii) Where no answers lodged £33.50

(b) Inclusive fee to opposing solicitor–

(i) Where answers lodged £42.00

(ii) Where no answers lodged £28.00

(c) Fee for adjustment of minute and answers where applicable to be allowed in addition to each party £37.00

10. *Motions and minutes–*

(a) Fee to cover drawing, intimating and lodging any written motion or minute, including a reponing note, and relative attendances at court (except as otherwise provided for in this chapter)–

(i) Where opposed £52.50

(ii) Where unopposed (including for each party a joint minute other than under paragraph 15(b)) £37.00

(b) Fee to cover considering opponent's written motion, minute or reponing note, and relative attendances at court–

(i) Where motion, minute or reponing note opposed £30.00

(ii) Where motion, minute or reponing note unopposed £22.00

11. *Procedure preliminary to proof–*

(a) Fee to cover fixing diet of proof, citation of witnesses, and generally preparing for trial or proof and if necessary instructing shorthand writer–

(i) If action settled or abandoned not later than 14 days before the diet of proof £130.00

(ii) In any other case £216.00

(b) Fee to cover preparing for adjourned diet and all incidental work as in (a) if diet postponed for more than 6 days, for each additional diet £45.00

(c) Drawing and lodging an inventory of productions, lodging the productions specified therein, and considering opponent's productions (to be charged once only in each process) £22.00

(d) Where only one party lodges productions, opponent's charges for considering same £11.00

12. *Conduct of proof or trial–*

(a) Fee to cover conduct of proof or trial and debate on evidence if taken at close of proof—per quarter hour £11.00

(b) If counsel employed, fee to solicitor appearing with counsel—per quarter hour £10.00

(c) Waiting time—per quarter hour £10.00

13. *Debate on evidence–*

(a) Where debate on evidence not taken at conclusion of proof, preparing for debate £37.00

(b) Fee for conduct of debate—per quarter hour £11.00

(c) If counsel employed, fee to solicitor appearing with counsel—per quarter hour ... £10.00

(d) Waiting time—per quarter hour £10.00

14. *Appeals–*

(a) *To sheriff principal–*

(i) Fee to cover instructions, marking of appeal or noting that appeal marked, noting diet of hearing thereof and preparation for hearing £70.00

(ii) Fee to cover conduct of hearing—per quarter hour £11.00

(iii) If counsel employed, fee to solicitor appearing with counsel—per quarter hour £10.00

(iv) Waiting time—per quarter hour £10.00

(b) *To Court of Session–*

Fee to cover instructions, marking appeal or noting that appeal marked and instructing Edinburgh correspondents £35.00

15. *Settlements*

(a) *Judicial tender–*

(i) Fee for preparation and lodging or for consideration of minute of tender £42.00

(ii) Fee on acceptance of tender, to include preparation and lodging or consideration of minute of acceptance and attendance at court when decree granted in terms thereof £31.00

(b) *Extra-judicial settlement–*

Fee to cover negotiations resulting in settlement, framing or revising joint minute and attendance at court when authority interponed thereto £70.00

16. *Final procedure–*

(a) Fee to cover settling with witnesses, enquiring for cause at avizandum, noting final interlocutor £55.00

(b) Fee to cover drawing account of expenses, arranging, intimating and attending diet of taxation and obtaining approval of auditor's report and adjusting account with opponent where necessary, ordering, procuring and examining extract decree £45.00

(c) Fee to cover considering opponent's account of expenses and attending diet of taxation or adjusting account with opponent £16.00

17. *Copying fees–*

Copying all necessary papers by any means–

(a) First copy—per sheet £1.00

(b) Additional copies—per sheet £0.35

Note

A sheet shall be 250 words. When copied by photostatic or similar process, each page shall be charged as one sheet.

18. *Process fee–*

Fee to cover all consultations between solicitor and client during the progress of the cause and all communications, written or oral, passing between them—10 per cent. on total fees and copyings allowed on taxation.

19. *Fee for instruction of counsel–*

(a) Fee for instructing counsel to revise record £22.00

(b) Fee for instructing counsel to conduct debate, proof or trial... ... ... £46.00

(c) Fee for instructing counsel to conduct appeal to sheriff principal £46.00

Note

1. In each case to cover all consultations, revisal of papers and all incidental work.
2. Fee to counsel to be allowed as outlay.

CHAPTER III

CHARGES FOR TIME, DRAWING OF PAPERS, CORRESPONDENCE, ETC.

1. Attendance at court conducting trial proof or formal debate or hearing—per quarter hour £11.00

2. Time occupied in the performance of all other work including attendances with client and others and attendances at court in all circumstances, except as otherwise specifically provided–
   (a) Solicitor—per quarter hour £10.00
   (b) Allowance for time of clerk—one half of above.

   Note

   Time necessarily occupied in travelling to such to be chargeable at these rates.

3. Drawing all necessary papers (other than affidavits) (the sheet throughout this Chapter to consist of 250 words or numbers)—per sheet £5.00

4. Framing affidavits—per sheet £7.50

5. Revising papers where revisal ordered—for each five sheets £2.00

6. Copying all necessary papers by any means—
   (i) First copy—per sheet £1.00
   (ii) Additional copies—per sheet £0.35

   Note

   When copied by photostatic or similar process each page shall be charged as one sheet.

7. Certifying or signing a document £2.00

8. Perusing any document—per quarter hour £10.00

9. Lodging in process–
   Each necessary lodging in or uplifting from process; also for each necessary enquiry for documents due to be lodged £2.00

10. Borrowing process–
    Each necessary borrowing of process to include return of same £2.00

11. *Extracts–*
    Ordering, procuring and examining extracts, interim or otherwise £10.00

12. *Correspondence, intimations, etc.–*
    (a) Formal letters and intimations £1.00
    (b) Letters other than above—per page of 125 words £5.00
    (c) Telephone calls except under (d)... ... ... £2.00
    (d) Telephone calls (lengthy) to be treated as attendances or long letters.

13. *Citations–*
    Each citation of party or witness including execution thereof £5.00

14. *Instructions to officers–*
    (a) Instructing officer to serve, execute or intimate various kinds of writs or diligence including the examination of executions £2.00
    (b) For each party after the first on whom service or intimation is simultaneously made £2.00
    (c) Agency accepting service of any writ £5.00
    (d) Reporting diligence £5.00

15. *Personal diligence–*
    (a) Recording execution of charge £5.00
    (b) Procuring fiat £5.00

(c) Instructing apprehension £5.00

(d) Framing state of debt and attendance at settlement £6.00

16. *Sales–*

(a) Obtaining warrant to sell £5.00

(b) Instructing auctioneer or officer to conduct sale £5.00

(c) Perusing report of sale £5.00

(d) Reporting sale under poindings or sequestrations or any other judicial sales £5.00

(e) Noting approval of roup roll £5.00

(f) Obtaining warrant to pay £5.00

CHAPTER IV

SUMMARY CAUSES

PART I.—UNDEFENDED ACTIONS

1. To include—taking instructions, framing summons and statement of claim, obtaining warrant for service, serving, instructing service as necessary by sheriff officer (where appropriate), attendance endorsing minute for and obtaining decree in absence and extract decree and including posts and sundries £37.00

2. Service–

(a) citation by post wheresoever after the first citation for each party £4.00

(b) framing and instructing service by advertisement—for each party £12.00

3. Attendance at court £12.00

PART II.—DEFENDED ACTIONS

1. Instructions fee, to include taking instructions (including instructions for a counterclaim) framing summons and statement of claim, obtaining warrant for service, enquiring for notice of intention to defend, attendance at first calling, noting defence £51.00

2. Service–

(a) Citation by post within the United Kingdom, Isle of Man, Channel Islands, or the Republic of Ireland—for each party £4.00

Citation by post elsewhere—for each party £9.00

(b) Instructing service or reservice by sheriff officer including perusing execution of citation and settling sheriff officer's fee—for each party £4.00

(c) Framing and instructing service by advertisement—for each party £13.50

3. Attendance at court–

Attendance at any diet except as otherwise specifically provided £13.50

4. Preparing for proof, to include all work in connection with proof not otherwise provided for £46.00

5. Fee to cover preparing for adjourned diet and all incidental work if diet for more than six days—for each adjourned diet £22.00

6. (a) Drawing and lodging inventory of productions, lodging the productions specified therein and considering opponents' productions (to be charged only once in each process) £20.00

(b) Where only one party lodges productions, opponents' charges for considering same £9.00

7. Precognitions–

(a) Drawing precognitions, including instructions, attendances with witnesses and all relative meetings and correspondence—per witness £20.00

(b) Where precognitions exceed 2 sheets—for each additional sheet £9.00

8. Motions and minutes–	
Fee to cover drawing, intimating and lodging of any written motion or minute, excluding a minute or motion to recall decree, and relative attendance at court (except as otherwise provided in this chapter)–	
(a) Where opposed … … … … … … … … …	£28.00
(b) Where unopposed (including for each party a joint minute or joint motion)	£17.00
9. Fee to cover considering opponents' written motion or minute excluding minute or motion to recall decree and relative attendance at court–	
(a) Where motion or minute opposed … … … … … …	£22.00
(b) Where motion or minute unopposed … … … … … …	£13.50
10. Conduct of proof–	
(a) Fee to cover conduct of proof or trial and debate on evidence taken at close of proof—per half hour … … … … … … … …	£13.50
(b) Waiting time—per half hour … … … … … … …	£7.00
11. Settlements–	
(a) Judicial tender, fee for consideration of, preparing and lodging minute of tender	£28.00
(i) Fee for consideration and rejection of tenders … … … …	£20.00
(ii) Fee on acceptance of tender—to include preparing and lodging, or consideration of minute of acceptance and attendance at court when decree granted in terms thereof … … … … … … … … …	£20.00
(b) Extra judicial settlement—fee to cover negotiations resulting in settlement, framing or revising joint minute and attendance at court when authority interponed thereto… … … … … … … … … …	£46.00
12. Specification of documents–	
(a) Fee to cover drawing, intimating and lodging specification of documents and relative motion and attendance at court … … … … … …	£23.00
(b) Inclusive fee to opposing solicitor … … … … … …	£21.00
(c) Fee for citation of havers, preparation for and attendance before commissioner, to each party—for each half hour … … … … … … …	£13.50
(d) If alternative procedure adopted, a fee per person upon whom order served	£9.00
13. Commissions to take evidence—	
(a) Fee to cover drawing, lodging and intimating motion and attendance at court–	
(i) Where opposed … … … … … … … … …	£28.00
(ii) Where unopposed … … … … … … … … …	£17.00
(b) Fee to cover considering such motion and attendance at court–	
(i) Where opposed … … … … … … … … …	£22.00
(ii) Where unopposed … … … … … … … … …	£13.50
(c) Fee to cover instructing commissioner and citing witness … … …	£13.50
(d) Fee to cover drawing and lodging interrogatories and cross-interrogatories—per sheet … … … … … … … … … …	£9.00
(e) Attendance before commissioner—per hour … … … … …	£13.00
(f) Travelling time—per hour… … … … … … … …	£8.50
14. Supplementary note of defence (when ordained) … … … … …	£9.00
15. Appeals–	
(a) Fee to cover instructions, marking of appeal or noting that appeal marked, noting of diet of hearing thereof and preparation for hearing	£62.50
(b) Fee to cover conduct of hearing—per half hour … … … …	£13.50
16. Final procedure–	
(a) Fee to cover settling with witnesses, enquiring for cause at avizandum, noting final interlocutor … … … … … … … … …	£28.00

(b) Fee to cover drawing account of expenses, arranging intimating and attending hearing on expenses, and obtaining approval of sheriff clerk's report ... £28.00

(c) Fee to cover considering opponents' account of expenses and attendance at hearing on expenses £13.50

CHAPTER V

MERCANTILE SEQUESTRATION

Charge according to Chapter III.

CHAPTER VI

EXECUTRY BUSINESS–INTESTATE MOVEABLE SUCCESSION

1. Taking instructions to present petition for decree-dative, drawing petition and making necessary copies, lodging and directing publication, attendance at court, moving for decree-dative, extracting decree where necessary, and all matters incidental to petition—inclusive fee £54.00

2. Preliminary investigation and confirmation of executors–

   To be charged for according to general table of fees for conveyancing and general business in testate succession in force from time to time.

3. Bonds of caution–

   (a) Taking out bond of caution, getting it signed and lodged with clerk of court, and procuring attestation of cautioner's sufficiency £15.50

   (b) Where caution is found through the medium of a guarantee company for all the work in connection therewith £15.50

4. Restriction of caution–

   Taking instructions to prepare petition for restriction of caution, drawing petition and making necessary copies, lodging, instructing advertisement and all matters incidental to petition—inclusive fee £31.50

EXPLANATORY NOTE

(This note is not part of the Act of Sederunt)

This Act of Sederunt revokes the Act of Sederunt (Fees of Solicitors in the Sheriff Court) 1988, re-enacts that Act with a number of minor amendments and increases most of the fees in the Table of Fees in the Schedule to the Act by about 8 per cent.

1989 No. 435 (S.53)

COURT OF SESSION, SCOTLAND

Act of Sederunt (Rules of the Court of Session Amendment No.1) (Written Statements) 1989

Made - - - -	*7th March 1989*
Coming into force	*3rd April 1989*

The Lords of Council and Session, under and by virtue of the powers conferred on them by section 5 of the Court of Session Act 1988(**a**) and of all other powers enabling them in that behalf, do hereby enact and declare:

Citation and commencement

1.—(1) This Act of Sederunt may be cited as the Act of Sederunt (Rules of the Court of Session Amendment No.1) (Written Statements) 1989 and shall come into force on 3rd April 1989.

(2) This Act of Sederunt shall be inserted in the Books of Sederunt.

Conditions for receiving written statements in evidence without being spoken to by a witness

2. In the Rules of the Rules of the Court of Session(**b**), after rule 108, insert the following rule:–

"108A. Conditions for receiving written statements in evidence without being spoken to by a witness

(1) Any written statement (including an affidavit) or report, admissible under section 2(1)(b) of the Civil Evidence (Scotland) Act 1988(**c**) may be received in evidence in any category of civil proceedings without being spoken to by a witness subject to the provisions of this rule.

(2) The following provisions of this rule do not apply to any such written statement or report in respect of which express provision is made in these rules for its admissibility in evidence in relation to a particular category of civil proceedings.

(3) Application to the court to receive any such written statement or report in evidence without being spoken to by a witness shall be made by way of motion.

(4) Subject to paragraph (5), on enrolling any such motion, the applicant shall lodge–

(a) the written statement or report as a production;

(b) in any case where the other party or parties have not agreed to the written statement or report in question being received in evidence without being spoken to by a witness, an affidavit or affidavits in support of the motion stating–

(i) the name, designation, and qualifications (if any) of the author of the statement or report in question;

(ii) the circumstances in which it was written; and

(**a**) 1988 c.36, as amended by section 2(3) of the Civil Evidence (Scotland) Act 1988 (c.32).
(**b**) S.I. 1965/321; the relevant amending instrument is S.I. 1986/1955.
(**c**) 1988 c.32.

(iii) the reasons for the application.

(5) Paragraph (4) does not apply to an application made in respect of a written statement or report in the form of an affidavit which includes the information specified in sub-paragraph (b) of paragraph (4).

(6) Any such motion which is unopposed may be granted by the court without a hearing.

(7) On the hearing of any such motion, the court may grant the motion, with or without conditions, or may refuse it, or may continue the motion to enable such further information to be obtained as it may require for the purpose of determining the application.

(8) Expressions used in this rule and in the Civil Evidence (Scotland) Act 1988 shall have the meaning they have in that Act.".

Edinburgh
7th March 1989

Emslie
Lord President, I.P.D.

EXPLANATORY NOTE

(This note is not part of the Act of Sederunt)

This Act of Sederunt amends the Rules of the Court of Session to make provision for the procedure for receiving written hearsay evidence admissible under section 2 of the Civil Evidence (Scotland) Act 1988.

1989 No. 436 (S.54)

SHERIFF COURT, SCOTLAND

Act of Sederunt (Amendment of Ordinary Cause and Summary Cause Rules) (Written Statements) 1989

Made - - - -	*8th March 1989*
Coming into force	*3rd April 1989*

The Lords of Council and Session, under and by virtue of the powers conferred upon them by section 32 of the Sheriff Courts (Scotland) Act 1971(**a**) and of all other powers competent to them in that behalf, do hereby enact and declare:

Citation and commencement

1.—(1) This Act of Sederunt may be cited as the Act of Sederunt (Amendment of Ordinary Cause and Summary Cause Rules) (Written Statements) 1989 and shall come into force on 3rd April 1989.

(2) This Act of Sederunt shall be inserted in the Books of Sederunt.

Amendment of Ordinary Cause Rules

2. In the First Schedule to the Sheriff Courts (Scotland) Act 1907(**b**) (Ordinary Cause Rules), after rule 72, insert the following rule:–

"Conditions for receiving written statements in evidence without being spoken to by a witness

72A.—(1) Any written statement (including an affidavit) or report, admissible under section 2(1)(b) of the Civil Evidence (Scotland) Act 1988(**c**) may be received in evidence in any ordinary cause without being spoken to by a witness subject to the provisions of this rule.

(2) The following provisions of this rule do not apply to any such written statement or report in respect of which express provision is made in these rules for its admissibility in evidence in relation to a particular category of ordinary cause.

(3) Application to the sheriff to receive any such written statement or report in evidence without being spoken to by a witness shall be made by way of motion.

(4) Subject to paragraph (5), on enrolling any such motion, the applicant shall lodge–

(a) the written statement or report as a production;

(b) in any case where the other party or parties have not agreed to the written statement or report in question being received in evidence without being spoken to by a witness, an affidavit or affidavits in support of the motion stating–

(i) the name, designation, and qualifications (if any) of the author of the statement or report in question;

(ii) the circumstances in which it was written; and

(**a**) 1971 c.58; paragraph (e) of section 32(1) was substituted by section 2(4) of the Civil Evidence (Scotland) Act 1988 (c.32).

(**b**) 1907 c.51; First Schedule substituted by S.I. 1983/747.

(**c**) 1988 c.32.

(iii) the reasons for the application.

(5) Paragraph (4) does not apply to an application made in respect of a written statement or report in the form of an affidavit which includes the information specified in sub-paragraph (b) of paragraph (4).

(6) On the hearing of any such motion, the sheriff may grant the motion, with or without conditions, or may refuse it, or may continue the motion to enable such further information to be obtained as he may require for the purpose of determining the application.

(7) For the purpose of this rule—

(a) expressions used in this rule and in the Civil Evidence (Scotland) Act 1988 shall have the meaning they have in that Act;

(b) "affidavit" includes affirmation and statutory or other declaration;

(c) an affidavit shall be treated as admissible if it is duly emitted before a notary public or any other competent authority.".

Amendment of the Summary Cause Rules

3. In paragraph 3(2) of the Act of Sederunt (Summary Cause Rules, Sheriff Court) 1976(**a**) after "60" insert "72A".

Edinburgh
8th March 1989

Emslie
Lord President, IPD

EXPLANATORY NOTE

(This Note is not part of the Act of Sederunt)

This Act of Sederunt amends the Ordinary Cause and Summary Cause Rules of the Sheriff Court to make provision for the procedure for receiving written hearsay evidence admissible under section 2 of the Civil Evidence (Scotland) Act 1988.

(**a**) S.I. 1976/476; relevant amending instruments are S.I. 1983/747 and 1986/1966.

STATUTORY INSTRUMENTS

1989 No. 437

TRUSTEES

The Public Trustee (Fees) (Amendment) Order 1989

Made - - - - *9th March 1989*

Coming into force *1st April 1989*

The Treasury, in exercise of the powers conferred on them by section 9 of the Public Trustee Act 1906(**a**), and with the sanction of the Lord Chancellor, hereby make the following Order:

1. This Order may be cited as the Public Trustee (Fees) (Amendment) Order 1989 and shall come into force on 1st April 1989.

2. In article 20 of the Public Trustee (Fees) Order 1985 (**b**); the figure "1" shall be substituted for the figure "1 2/13" in paragraph (3).

Alan Howarth
Stephen Dorrell
Two of the Lords Commmissioners
of Her Majesty's Treasury

Dated 9th March 1989

I hereby signify my sanction

Dated 9th March 1989

Mackay of Clashfern, C.

EXPLANATORY NOTE

(This note is not part of the Order)

This Order amends the Public Trustee (Fees) Order 1985 by adjusting the withdrawal fee rate fixed by that Order.

(**a**) 1906 c.55, as amended by section 1 of the Public Trustee (Fees) Act 1957 (c.12) and section 2(1) of the Administration of Justice Act 1965 (c.2).
(**b**) S.I. 1985/373, as amended by S.I. 1988/571.

STATUTORY INSTRUMENTS

1989 No. 438

COMMUNITY CHARGES, ENGLAND AND WALES

The Community Charges (Administration and Enforcement) Regulations 1989

Made - - - -	*12th March 1989*
Laid before Parliament	*17th March 1989*
Coming into force	
except for regulations 4 and 5	*7th April 1989*
regulations 4 and 5	*22nd May 1989*

ARRANGEMENT OF REGULATIONS

PART I

General

PART II

Information and Inspection

PART III

Billing

PART IV

Enforcement

The Secretary of State for the Environment as respects England, and the Secretary of State for Wales as respects Wales, in exercise of the powers conferred on them by sections 5(3)(d), 10(6), 12(6), 14(7), 19, 23(3), 25, 31(10), 40(3), (4), (11) and (12), 143(1) and (2) and 146(6) of, and paragraph 10(1)(b) and (2) of Schedule 1, paragraphs 1 to 4, 6 to 8, 10 to 13 and 15 to 18 of Schedule 2, paragraph 6 of Schedule 3 and paragraphs 1 to 5, 7 to 24 and 26 to 28 of Schedule 4 to, the Local Government Finance Act 1988**(a)**, and of all other powers enabling them in that behalf, hereby make the following Regulations:

PART I

GENERAL

Citation, commencement and interpretation

1.—(1) These Regulations may be cited as the Community Charges (Administration and Enforcement) Regulations 1989 and except as mentioned in paragraph (2) shall come into force on 7th April 1989.

(2) Regulations 4 and 5 of these Regulations shall come into force on 22nd May 1989.

(3) In these Regulations "the Act" means the Local Government Finance Act 1988.

(a) 1988 c.41.

Service of notices

2. Where any notice which is required or authorised by these Regulations to be given to or served on any person falls to be given or served by or on behalf of the Common Council or by an officer of the Common Council, it may be given or served in any manner in which it might be given or served under section 233 of the Local Government Act 1972**(a)** if the Common Council were a local authority within the meaning of that section.

PART II

INFORMATION AND INSPECTION

Duty to supply information to registration officers

3.—(1) A person who has reason to believe he is or has been subject at any time on or after 1st December 1989 to a community charge of a charging authority shall inform the appropriate registration officer accordingly.

(2) A person who is shown in a charging authority's register as subject to a community charge of the authority and who has reason to believe that the item concerned contains an error or is not complete or up-to-date shall inform the appropriate registration officer accordingly.

(3) The information mentioned in paragraphs (1) and (2) is to be supplied within 21 days of the day on which the person first had reason to believe as mentioned in those paragraphs.

(4) In this regulation "the appropriate registration officer" means the registration officer of the charging authority with respect to whose community charge the person–

(a) has reason to believe he is or has been subject, or

(b) is shown as subject,

as the case may be.

Responsible individuals

4.—(1) The registration officer for a charging authority may, with the object of enabling him to form a view whether the responsible individual or any other person is, has been or is about to become subject to a community charge of the authority by virtue of any relevant property, request (by notice given in writing) a responsible individual as regards that property to supply to him such information as is specified in the notice.

(2) Each of the following is a responsible individual as regards any relevant property for the purposes of this regulation (so that one or more individuals may be responsible individuals with respect to the same property)–

(a) every individual aged 18 or over who is in occupation of the property,

(b) every individual aged 18 or over who holds a lease or underlease of the property, or who owns the property, and

(c) such other individual aged 18 or over whom the registration officer considers it appropriate to designate from time to time as a responsible individual with respect to the property.

(3) Information requested under paragraph (1) shall be supplied by the person requested to supply it if it is in his possession or control, and shall be so supplied within 21 days of the day on which the request is made.

(4) Without prejudice to section 233 of the Local Government Act 1972, a notice given under paragraph (1) in respect of persons falling within paragraph (2)(a) may be served by addressing it by the description of "occupier" of the relevant property (naming

(a) 1972 c.70; subsection (6) was repealed by the Local Government (Miscellaneous Provisions) Act 1976 (c.57), Schedule 2.

the relevant property) and by leaving it at, or (if the property has a postal address) by sending it by post to, the relevant property.

(5) If more than one person falls within the description in paragraph (2)(a) in respect of any relevant property and a notice given under paragraph (1) is served in the manner described in paragraph (4), their duty to supply the information is satisfied if one of the occupiers supplies it on behalf of all of them.

(6) A registration officer may revoke a designation under paragraph (2)(c).

(7) If any relevant property is a building or part of a building, an individual owns it for the purposes of paragraph (2)(b) only if he owns a freehold estate in it.

(8) In this regulation "relevant property" means a building, a part of a building, a caravan or a houseboat.

Other information from individuals

5.—(1) The registration officer for a charging authority may, for the purpose of carrying out his functions under Part I of the Act, request (by notice given in writing) any person falling within paragraph (2) to supply to him such information as is specified in the notice.

(2) A person falls within this paragraph if he is a person the officer making the request reasonably believes is, has been or is about to become subject to a community charge of the authority for which the officer is the registration officer.

(3) Information requested under paragraph (1) shall be supplied by the person requested to supply it if it is in his possession or control, and shall be so supplied within 21 days of the day on which the request is made.

Information from public bodies

6.—(1) The registration officer for a charging authority may, for the purpose of carrying out his functions under Part I of the Act, request (by notice given in writing) a person mentioned in paragraph (3) to supply to the officer such information as is specified in the notice and does not fall within paragraph (2).

(2) Information falls within this paragraph if–

(a) the information was obtained by the person concerned, or by a committee of such a person, in its capacity as police authority, or as a constituent council of such an authority,

(b) the information was obtained by the person concerned in its capacity as an employer, or

(c) the information consists of other than the name, address and any past or present place of residence of any person and the dates during which he is known or thought to have resided at that place.

(3) The persons referred to in paragraph (1) are–

(a) the registration officer for any other charging authority,

(b) the charging authority for which the officer making the request is the registration officer,

(c) any other charging authority,

(d) any precepting authority, and

(e) the electoral registration officer for any area in England and Wales.

(4) Information requested under paragraph (1) shall be supplied by the person requested to supply it if it is in his possession or control, and it shall be so supplied within 21 days of the day on which the request is made.

(5) A registration officer for a charging authority may (so far as he does not have the power to do so apart from this Part) supply relevant information to a registration officer for another charging authority even if he is not requested to supply the information.

(6) Information is relevant information for the purposes of paragraph (5) if–

(a) it was obtained by the first-mentioned officer in exercising his functions under Part I of the Act, and

(b) he believes it would be useful to the other officer in exercising his functions under that Part.

Supply of information to Secretary of State

7.—(1) The Secretary of State may, for the purpose of carrying out his functions under Part I of the Act, request (by notice given in writing) a registration officer for a charging authority to supply to him information which is specified in the notice and which was obtained by the officer for the purpose of carrying out his functions under that Part.

(2) Information requested under paragraph (1) shall be supplied by the officer if it is in his possession or control, and shall be so supplied within 21 days of the day on which the request is made.

Use of information by charging authority

8. In carrying out its functions under Part I of the Act, a charging authority may use information obtained under any other enactment provided it was not obtained by the authority, or by a committee of the authority, in its capacity as police authority, or as a constituent council of a police authority.

Notification of chargeable persons

9.—(1) Where a person becomes or ceases to be subject to a charging authority's community charge, and a registration officer makes an entry in the register accordingly, as soon as is reasonably practicable after doing so he shall send the person a copy of the item contained in the register in relation to the charge.

(2) Where a registration officer amends an item contained in the register in order to correct an error or render the item more complete or up-to-date, as soon as is reasonably practicable after doing so he shall send the person shown in the register as subject to the charge concerned a copy of the amended item.

Inspection of the register by chargeable persons

10.—(1) A person shown in a charging authority's register as subject at any time to a community charge of the authority may, at a reasonable place and time stated by the registration officer, inspect the item contained in the register in relation to the charge.

(2) If such a person requests the registration officer to supply a copy of such an item, the officer shall supply the copy to the person; but the authority may require a reasonable charge in respect of the supply of the copy, and if it does so the duty to supply it shall not arise unless the person pays the charge.

(3) If the register is not kept in documentary form, the duty to make an item available for inspection or to supply a copy of an item is satisfied if a print-out, photographic image or other reproduction of the item which has been obtained from the storage medium adopted in relation to the register is made available for inspection or is supplied (as the case may be).

Extracts of the register for public inspection

11.—(1) Every registration officer is to compile and then maintain–

(a) an extract taken from the information for the time being contained in the charging authority's register containing the information described in paragraph (2), and

(b) a list of the addresses of buildings and parts of buildings for the time being designated by the registration officer for the purposes of the charging authority's collective community charges.

(2) Subject to paragraph (3), the information to be contained in an extract compiled and maintained under paragraph (1)(a) is the address of every residence, property or dwelling (as the case may be) by virtue of which a person is subject to a community charge of the authority, together with the surname or family name of the person and the initial letters of any other names of his, without indication of sex.

(3) The information mentioned in paragraph (2) with respect to a person shall not be

included in the extract if, in the view of the registration officer, there is cause to believe that such inclusion might result in that or any other person being subject (whether in consequence of matrimonial dispute or otherwise) to threat of violence.

(4) The duty to compile and maintain an extract under paragraph (1)(a) is satisfied if the information required to be contained in it is entered in it not more than 6 months after the day the relevant information is entered in the register.

(5) An extract compiled and maintained under paragraph (1)(a)–

(a) shall be so organised that any address required to be contained in it immediately precedes the name of the person subject to the charge in relation to the address,

(b) shall not list the information required to be contained in it according to an order established by reference to the person's surname or family name, and

(c) shall not identify whether the community charge which arises by virtue of any residence, property or dwelling is a personal, standard or collective community charge.

(6) Any person may, at a reasonable time and place stated by the registration officer, inspect an extract and list maintained as mentioned in paragraph (1).

(7) Except so far as is necessary for the inspection of the extract or list in a case where paragraph (8) applies, the registration officer may not supply a copy of the extract and list to any person.

(8) If the extract or list are not maintained in documentary form, the duty to make them available for inspection is satisfied if a print-out, photographic image or other reproduction of them which has been obtained from the storage medium adopted in relation to them is made available for inspection.

Inspection of records supplied

12. An authority which, or an officer who, has received a copy of records under paragraph 1(4) of Schedule 2 shall allow a copy to be inspected by any individual liable to pay an amount to the chargeable person concerned under section 9 of the Act by way of contribution to the amount the chargeable person is liable to pay in respect of the charge to which the records relate.

PART III

BILLING

Interpretation and application of Part III

13.—(1) In this Part–

"demand notice" means the notice required to be served by regulation 14; and

"the relevant year" in relation to a notice means the chargeable financial year to which the notice relates.

(2) In this Part, "chargeable person" in relation to a chargeable financial year and a charging authority means a person entered on the authority's community charges register as subject in the year to a community charge of the authority; and in relation to a demand notice which falls to be issued before the chargeable financial year to which it relates, it includes a person who is shown in the authority's community charges register as subject to the charge concerned before the year begins and who is not shown at the time as ceasing to be subject to the charge on or before 1st April in the year.

(3) But a person is not to be treated for the purposes of this Part as shown as subject to a standard community charge on any day on which the property by virtue of which he is subject to it is shown in the register as falling for the day into a class for which the standard community charge multiplier is 0; and references in this Part to a person being or becoming subject to a charge, ceasing to be subject to a charge, or becoming subject

again to the same charge, and to the day on which he is so shown, shall be construed accordingly.

(4) Where references are made in this Part to the day on or time at which a notice is issued, they shall be taken to be references–

(a) if the notice is served in the manner described in section 233(2) of the Local Government Act 1972 by being left at, or sent by post to, a person's proper address, to the day on or time at which it is so left or posted, or

(b) in any other case, to the day on or time at which the notice is served.

(5) References in this Part to a person shown (or not shown) in a community charges register as subject on a day to a community charge, or to the day on which a person is shown in a community charges register as becoming subject or ceasing to be subject to a community charge, shall (subject to paragraph (3)) be construed in accordance with section 8 of the Act.

(6) This Part applies (amongst other matters) for the making of payments in relation to amounts that a person is liable to pay in respect of community charges as they have effect for a chargeable financial year; but its application in relation to a charge in respect of which a person has a joint and several liability under Part I of the Act is subject to the provisions of regulations 22 and 23 (joint and several liability).

(7) The provisions of this Part which provide for the repayment or crediting of any amount or the adjustment of payments due under a notice (including in particular paragraph 7 of Schedule 1) shall have effect subject to section 36(2) of the Act.

(8) References in this Part to a community charge do not include references to a charge to which persons are jointly subject under regulation 59 (co-owners), and references to a chargeable person shall be construed accordingly

The requirement for demand notices

14.—(1) For each chargeable financial year a charging authority shall serve a notice in writing on every chargeable person of the authority in accordance with regulations 15 to 18.

(2) Different notices shall be served for different chargeable financial years; and if a chargeable person is subject in any chargeable financial year to different community charges (whether by virtue of section 7(1) to (4) of the Act or otherwise), different notices shall be served in respect of each charge.

Service of demand notices

15.—(1) In the case of a personal community charge, the demand notice is to be served on or as soon as practicable after–

(a) except in a case falling within sub-paragraph (b), the day the charging authority has set the amount of its personal community charge for the relevant year for that part of its area which contains the residence by virtue of which the person is shown in the charging authority's register as subject to the charge, or

(b) if the person is not shown as subject to the charge on that day nor (in the event of a failure to meet the duty under section 32(2) of the Act) on any day in the relevant year preceding that day, the day on which the person is shown in the authority's register as becoming subject to it.

(2) In the case of a standard community charge, the demand notice is to be served on or as soon as practicable after–

(a) except in a case falling within sub-paragraph (b), the day the charging authority has set the amount of its personal community charge for the relevant year for that part of its area which contains the property by virtue of which the person is shown in the charging authority's register as subject to the charge, or

(b) if the person is not shown as subject to the charge on that day nor (in the event of a failure to meet the duty under section 32(2) of the Act) on any day in the relevant year preceding that day, the day on which the person is shown in the authority's register as becoming subject to it.

(3) In the case of a collective community charge, the demand notice is to be served on or as soon as practicable after–

(a) except in a case falling within sub-paragraph (b), the day the charging authority has set the amount of its personal community charge for the relevant year for that part of its area which contains the building constituting or containing the designated dwelling by virtue of which the person is shown in the charging authority's register as subject to the charge, or

(b) if the person is not shown as subject to the charge on that day nor (in the event of a failure to meet the duty under section 32(2) of the Act) on any day in the relevant year preceding that day, the day on which the person is shown in the authority's register as becoming subject to it.

(4) The part of a charging authority's area in which a residence, property or building is situated shall be determined for the purposes of this regulation in accordance with any rules for the time being in force under section 10(6), 12(6) or 14(7) of the Act (as the case may be).

Demand notices: personal and standard community charges

16.—(1) This regulation applies to demand notices served with respect to a personal or standard community charge.

(2) If the demand notice is issued before or during the relevant year and the chargeable person is shown in the charging authority's community charges register as subject to the charge on the day on which the notice is issued, the notice shall require payment of the amount specified in paragraph (3).

(3) The amount is the charging authority's estimate of the amount that the person will be liable to pay in respect of the charge as it has effect for the relevant year, made as respects periods in the year after the issue of the notice on the following assumptions–

(a) that the person will be subject to the community charge to which the notice relates on every day after the issue of the notice;

(b) if he is shown in the register as undertaking a full-time course of education on the day the notice is issued, that he will undertake such a course on every day after the issue of the notice;

(c) if the notice is issued with respect to a standard community charge, that the property by virtue of which he is shown in the register as subject to the charge will on every day after the issue of the notice be in the class specified in regulation 62 in which it is shown in the register as falling on the day the notice is issued; and

(d) if on the day the notice is issued a notification as to a community charge benefit to which he is entitled is in force under regulations made under section 31C(1) of the Social Security Act 1986**(a)**, and by virtue of regulations made under section 31A(1) of that Act the benefit allowed under that notification takes the form of a reduction in the amount the person is liable to pay in respect of the charge as it has effect with respect to that day, that on every day after that day he will be allowed the same reduction in that amount.

(4) If the demand notice is issued during the relevant year and if the chargeable person is not shown in the authority's register as subject to the charge on the day on which the notice is issued, the demand notice is to require payment of an amount equal to the person's liability in respect of the charge as it has effect for the period in the year up to the day on which he is last shown as ceasing to be subject to the charge.

(5) If a notice is served to which paragraph (4) applies, and after the person has been shown as ceasing to be subject to the charge he is subsequently shown as becoming subject again to the same charge in the year, a further notice shall be served on the chargeable person requiring payments in respect of the charge as it has effect for the period in the year after he is shown as becoming so subject; and regulations 15 to 17, 19

(a) 1986 c.50; sections 31A and 31C were inserted by, and other relevant amendments were made by, the Local Government Finance Act 1988 (c.41), Schedule 10.

and 20 (and, so far as applicable, Schedule 1) shall apply to the further notice with respect to that period, and the sum payable by the chargeable person with respect to that period, as if it were a demand notice given in relation to a different charge.

(6) If the demand notice is issued after the end of the relevant year, it shall require payment of the amount for which the chargeable person is liable in respect of the charge as it has effect for the year.

(7) If, after a demand notice to which paragraph (2) applies has been issued with respect to a standard community charge, an authority varies under section 40(6) of the Act a standard community charge multiplier as it applies to the property in relation to which the charge arises so that the estimate mentioned in paragraph (3) turns out to be wrong, the notice shall have no effect; and if the multiplier for the year is varied to other than 0 the charging authority shall as soon as practicable issue a fresh demand notice with respect to the charge.

Personal and standard community charges: payments

17.—(1) Unless an agreement under paragraph (3) in relation to the relevant year has been reached between the charging authority and the chargeable person before the demand notice is issued, a notice to which regulation 16(2) applies shall require the amount mentioned in regulation 16(3) to be paid by instalments in accordance with Part I of Schedule 1; and where such instalments are required Part II of the Schedule applies for their cessation or adjustment in the circumstances described in that Part.

(2) If an agreement under paragraph (3) in relation to the relevant year has been reached between the charging authority and the chargeable person before the demand notice is issued, a notice to which regulation 16(2) applies shall require the amount mentioned in regulation 16(3) to be paid in accordance with that agreement.

(3) A charging authority and a chargeable person may agree that the amount mentioned in regulation 16(3) which is required to be paid under a notice to which regulation 16(2) applies should be paid in such manner as is provided by the agreement, rather than in accordance with Schedule 1.

(4) Notwithstanding anything in the foregoing provisions of this regulation, such an agreement may be entered into either before or after the demand notice concerned is issued, and may make provision for the cessation or adjustment of payments, and for the making of fresh estimates, in the event of the estimate mentioned in regulation 16(3) turning out to be wrong; and if it is entered in into after the demand notice has been issued, it may make provision dealing with the treatment for the purposes of the agreement of any sums paid in accordance with Schedule 1 before it was entered into.

(5) A notice to which regulation 16(4) or (6) applies shall require payment of the amount concerned on the expiry of such period (being not less than 14 days) after the day of issue of the notice as is specified in it.

Collective community charges

18.—(1) A demand notice served with respect to a collective community charge shall require payments in respect of the charge as it has effect for the relevant year in accordance with paragraph 3 of Part I of Schedule 2.

(2) Part I of that Schedule shall also have effect for the compiling, retention, inspection and copying of records, the submission of returns and the adjustment of instalments in relation to such a charge.

(3) A person's liability to pay an amount under section 9 of the Act by way of contribution in relation to a collective community charge shall be discharged by the making of payments in accordance with Part II of Schedule 2; and information and receipts shall be supplied in accordance with that Part.

Notices: further provision

19.—(1) The calculation of such an amount as is mentioned in regulations 16(4) or (6) or paragraph 6(3) of Schedule 1 shall be made (so far as is relevant) by reference to the contents of the charging authority's community charges register at the time that the relevant notice given with respect to the amount is issued.

(2) No payment in respect of the amount that a chargeable person is liable to pay by way of community charge as it has effect for a chargeable financial year (whether interim, final or sole) need be made unless a notice served under this Part requires it.

(3) Where–

(a) a person is entered in the registers of two or more charging authorities as subject on the same day or days in a chargeable financial year to personal community charges of the authorities,

(b) he is liable to pay an amount under the Act to each authority in respect of its charge as it has effect for the year, and

(c) one or more of the entries is subject to an appeal or arbitration,

while any such appeal or arbitration is outstanding no amount shall be payable by virtue of any of the entries other than the entry which was made first.

(4) A person is liable to pay an amount for the purposes of paragraph (3)(b) notwithstanding that a notice remains to be given under this Part for a payment in respect of it to become due.

(5) An entry is to be treated as subject to an appeal or arbitration for the purposes of paragraph (3) upon the service of a notice in respect of it by the person in accordance with section 24 of the Act, and is to be treated as outstanding until any appeal under section 23 of the Act or arbitration under regulations made under paragraph 4 of Schedule 11 to the Act in relation to the matter by which he stated he was aggrieved in the notice is finally disposed of or abandoned or fails for non-prosecution; and the circumstances in which an appeal is to be treated as failing for non-prosecution include the expiry of any time prescribed under paragraph 8(2)(a) of that Schedule in consequence of which any such appeal would be required to be dismissed by a valuation and community charge tribunal.

(6) If on the first day on which any of the entries referred to in sub-paragraph (a) of paragraph (3) is made, two or more such entries are made, for the purposes of that paragraph–

(a) such one of the entries made on the first day as may be specified by the chargeable person within 14 days of the day on which, under regulation 9, he has received copies of the items required to be sent to him in relation to those entries, or

(b) in the absence of such a specification, such one of the entries made on the first day as may be agreed by the authorities concerned or, in the absence of such agreement, as may be determined by lot,

shall be treated as being the first entry.

(7) Any demand notice which relates to an entry with respect to which no amount is payable in consequence of paragraph (3) and which is given before the appeal or arbitration concerned is finally disposed of, abandoned or fails for non-prosecution shall be of no effect.

Failure to pay instalments: personal and standard community charges

20.—(1) Where–

(a) a demand notice has been served by a charging authority on a chargeable person,

(b) instalments are payable in respect of the charge to which the notice relates in accordance with Schedule 1,

(c) any such instalment is not paid in accordance with that Schedule,

the charging authority shall (unless all the instalments have fallen due) serve a further notice on the chargeable person stating the instalments required to be paid.

(2) If the chargeable person fails, within the period of 7 days beginning with the day of service of the further notice, to pay any instalments which are or will become due before the expiry of that period, the unpaid balance of the estimated amount shall become payable by him at the expiry of a further period of 7 days beginning with the day of the failure.

(3) If the chargeable amount proves to be greater than the estimated amount an additional sum equal to the difference between the two shall, on the service by the charging authority on the chargeable person of a notice stating the chargeable amount, be due from the person to the authority on the expiry of such period (being not less than 14 days) after the day of issue of the notice as is specified in it.

(4) If the chargeable amount proves to be less than the estimated amount the charging authority shall notify the chargeable person in writing of the chargeable amount; and any overpayment of the chargeable amount–

(a) subject to paragraph (8), shall be repaid if the chargeable person so requires, or

(b) in any other case shall (as the charging authority determines) either be repaid or be credited against any subsequent liability of the person to make a payment in respect of any community charge of the authority.

(5) If any factor or assumption by reference to which the estimated amount was calculated is shown to be false before the chargeable amount is capable of final determination for the purposes of paragraphs (3) and (4), the charging authority may, and if so required by the chargeable person shall, make a calculation of the appropriate amount with a view to adjusting the chargeable person's liability in respect of the estimated amount and (as appropriate) to–

(a) requiring an interim payment from the chargeable person if the appropriate amount is greater than the estimated amount, or

(b) subject to paragraph (8), making an interim repayment to the chargeable person if the appropriate amount is less than the amount of the estimated amount paid.

(6) The appropriate amount for the purposes of paragraph (5) is the amount which would be required to be paid under a demand notice if such a notice were issued with respect to the relevant year on the day that the notice under paragraph (7) is issued; and more than one calculation of the appropriate amount and interim adjustment may be made under paragraph (5) according to the circumstances.

(7) On calculating the appropriate amount the charging authority shall notify the chargeable person in writing of it; and a payment required under paragraph (5)(a) shall be due from the chargeable person to the charging authority on the expiry of such period (being not less than 14 days) after the day of issue of the notice as is specified in it.

(8) If the chargeable amount or the appropriate amount is less than the estimated amount in consequence of the chargeable person being shown in the community charges register as ceasing during the relevant year to be subject to the community charge to which the estimated amount relates, and the chargeable person is shown as becoming subject to a different community charge of the same charging authority on the same day as that on which he is shown as so ceasing, the charging authority may require that the amount of any overpayment mentioned in paragraph (4) or difference mentioned in paragraph (5)(b) should, instead of being repaid, be credited against the subsequent liability of the chargeable person in respect of the different charge.

(9) In this regulation–

"the appropriate amount" has the meaning given in paragraph (6);

"the chargeable amount" means the amount that the chargeable person is liable to pay in respect of the community charge to which the demand notice mentioned in paragraph (1)(a) relates as it has effect for the relevant year; and

"the estimated amount" means the amount last estimated under regulation 16(3) for the purposes of that notice or any subsequent notice given under paragraph 7(2) of Schedule 1 prior to the failure mentioned in paragraph (2) above, save that if in any case an interim adjustment has been made under paragraph (5), it means in relation to the next payment, repayment or interim adjustment in that case under this regulation (if any) the appropriate amount by reference to which the previous interim adjustment was so made.

Failure to submit returns or pay instalments: collective community charges

21.—(1) Where–

(a) a demand notice has been served by a charging authority on a chargeable person in respect of a collective community charge, and

(b) the chargeable person fails to submit a return or to pay an instalment in accordance with paragraphs 2, 3(1) to (3) and 4 of Schedule 2 on or before the day on which the return or the payment is due,

the unpaid balance of the estimated amount mentioned in paragraph (2) shall, subject to paragraphs (3) and (4), become payable by him on the day after the end of the period of 14 days beginning with the day of the failure.

(2) The estimated amount is the charging authority's estimate of the amount that the chargeable person will be liable to pay in respect of the charge as it has effect for the relevant year, made (so far as relevant) on the assumptions mentioned in paragraph (5).

(3) Paragraph (1) does not apply where returns have been submitted for all the periods in the relevant year during which the chargeable person is shown as subject to the charge, so that the amounts for which he is liable in respect of those periods are accordingly ascertained (and payable) under paragraph 3 of Schedule 2.

(4) Notwithstanding anything in paragraph (1) the unpaid balance shall not become payable unless at least 7 days have elapsed after the day of the service on the chargeable person by the charging authority of a notice requiring its payment and stating the estimated amount.

(5) The assumptions are–

(a) if the chargeable person is shown in the charging authority's community charges register as subject to the charge on the day on which the notice given under paragraph (4) is issued, that he will remain so subject for the remainder of the relevant year,

(b) if the chargeable person is not shown as subject to the charge on the day on which the notice is issued, that he will remain not subject to it for the remainder of the relevant year.

(6) If the chargeable amount proves to be greater than the estimated amount, an additional sum equal to the difference between the two shall, on the service by the charging authority on the chargeable person of a notice stating the chargeable amount, be due from the person to the authority on the expiry of such period (being not less than 14 days) after the day of issue of the notice as is specified in it.

(7) If the chargeable amount proves to be less than the estimated amount, the charging authority shall notify the chargeable person in writing of the chargeable amount; and any overpayment of the chargeable amount–

(a) shall be repaid if the chargeable person so requires, or

(b) in any other case shall (as the charging authority determines) either be repaid or be credited against any subsequent liability of the person to make a payment in respect of any community charge of the authority.

(8) If, after calculating the estimated amount, the charging authority is of the opinion that that amount is or may no longer be an accurate estimate of the amount that the chargeable person will be liable to pay in respect of the charge as it has effect for the relevant year (whether in consequence of the assumptions mentioned in paragraph (5) being shown to be false or otherwise), it may recalculate the estimated amount with a view to adjusting the chargeable person's liability in respect of the amount and (as appropriate) to–

(a) requiring an interim payment from the chargeable person if the recalculated amount is greater than the estimated amount, or

(b) making an interim repayment to the chargeable person if the recalculated amount is less than the amount of the estimated amount paid.

(9) A chargeable person may, if he has submitted returns under paragraph 2 of Schedule 2 for all return periods expiring before he makes the requirement, require a charging authority to recalculate the estimated amount under paragraph (8) having regard to the returns.

(10) The estimated amount is to be recalculated under paragraph (8) on the assumptions mentioned in paragraph (5) as if the notice referred to in the latter paragraph were the notice given under paragraph (11); and more than one recalculation and interim adjustment may be made under paragraphs (8) and (9) according to the circumstances.

(11) On recalculating the estimated amount under paragraph (8) the charging authority shall notify the chargeable person in writing of the recalculated amount; and a payment under paragraph (8)(a) shall be due from the chargeable person to the charging authority on the expiry of such period (being not less than 14 days) after the day of issue of the notice as is specified in it.

(12) The charging authority may, for the purposes of enabling it to make an estimate under paragraph (2) or (8), request (by notice in writing) the chargeable person to supply it with such information as is specified in the notice; and the information shall be supplied by the chargeable person if it is in his possession or control within 21 days of the day on which the request is made.

(13) In this regulation–

"the chargeable amount" means the amount that the chargeable person is liable to pay in respect of the charge to which the demand notice mentioned in paragraph (1)(a) relates as it has effect for the relevant year; and

"the estimated amount" means the amount estimated under paragraph (2), save that if in any case an interim adjustment has been made under paragraph (8), it means in relation to the next payment, repayment or interim adjustment in that case under this regulation (if any) the amount recalculated under that paragraph by reference to which the previous interim adjustment was so made.

Joint and several liability

22.—(1) Subject to regulation 23(1), both the chargeable person and a spouse of that person shall, with respect to a personal or standard community charge, if on any day in the chargeable period concerned the joint and several liability conditions are met and to the extent that it is unpaid, be jointly and severally liable to pay such fraction of–

(a) where the day by which all instalments payable under a demand notice in accordance with Schedule 1 are payable has passed, the aggregate amount of those instalments (together with the amount of any excess payable by the chargeable person in accordance with paragraph 7(5) of the Schedule),

(b) where regulation 20(2) applies, the estimated amount mentioned in that provision,

(c) the chargeable amount or appropriate amount stated in a notice given under regulation 20(3) or (7),

(d) the amount stated in a notice given under paragraph 6(3) of Schedule 1,

(e) the amount required to be paid by a demand notice to which regulation 16(4) or (6) applies, or

(f) the amount stated in a notice given to the chargeable person under regulation 26(2),

as is represented by $\frac{A}{B}$ where–

A is the number of days in the chargeable period on which the joint and several liability conditions are fulfilled with respect to the spouse, and

B is the number of days in the chargeable period.

(2) Subject to paragraph (5) and regulation 23(1), with respect to a standard community charge or collective community charge, both the chargeable person and a manager of that person shall, if on any day in the chargeable period concerned the joint and several liability conditions are fulfilled and to the extent that it is unpaid, be jointly and severally liable to pay such fraction of–

(a) any such amount as is mentioned in paragraph (1)(a) to (f),

(b) where regulation 21(3) applies, the amount for which the chargeable person is liable in respect of the charge as it has effect for the relevant year, or

(c) the estimated amount or chargeable amount stated in a notice given under regulation 21(4), (6) or (11),

as is represented by $\frac{A}{B}$ where–

A is the number of days in the chargeable period on which the joint and several liability conditions are fulfilled with respect to the manager, and

B is the number of days in the chargeable period.

(3) Where the fraction $\frac{A}{B}$ mentioned in paragraphs (1) and (2) gives a result of less than 1 and a person is accordingly solely liable with respect to a part of such an amount as is mentioned in those paragraphs and jointly and severally liable in respect of another part, any payment made by the person in respect of it (whether before or after the giving of a notice under regulation 23(1)) shall be treated as being made towards satisfaction of the part for which he is solely liable unless and until his liability in respect of that part is discharged.

(4) The joint and several liability conditions mentioned in paragraphs (1) and (2) are fulfilled on any day if on that day–

(a) as regards the spouse of a chargeable person, the chargeable person and the spouse are married to each other and the spouse is aged 18 or over, or

(b) as regards the manager of a chargeable person, the management arrangement concerned subsists and the manager is neither the chargeable person's employee nor (if an individual) aged under 18.

(5) A joint and several liability under paragraph (2) with respect to a standard community charge does not arise in relation to a manager unless the chargeable person is a company.

(6) The service on a manager of a document authorised or required to be served under this Part on the chargeable person with respect to whom he is the manager whilst the management arrangement concerned has effect shall be treated as service on the chargeable person.

(7) References in paragraph (1) to provisions of this Part, and to notices given under such provisions, includes references to those provisions (and notices given under those provisions) as applied by regulation 16(5) and paragraph 6(6) of Schedule 1.

(8) In this regulation and regulation 23–

"the chargeable period" has the meaning given in sections 16(2) and 17(2) of the Act (and accordingly regulation 13(3) does not apply to the determination of the period);

"management arrangement" has the meaning given in section 17(3) of the Act;

"manager" means a person with whom, on any day in the chargeable period, the chargeable person has a management arrangement, and who on the day is neither the chargeable person's employee nor (if an individual) aged under 18; and

"spouse" means a person to whom, on any day in the chargeable period, the chargeable person is married and who is aged 18 or over on the day.

(9) In determining for the purposes of this regulation and regulation 23–

(a) whether two people are married on any day, section 16(9) and (10) of the Act shall apply, and

(b) whether a management arrangement subsists on any day, section 17(9) of the Act shall apply.

Joint and several liability: further provision

23.—(1) An amount shall not be payable by a spouse or manager pursuant to regulation 22(1) or (2) unless a notice has been served on him by the charging authority stating the amount; and it shall be due from him to the authority at the expiry of such period (being not less than 14 days) after the day of issue of the notice as is specified in it.

(2) A notice under paragraph (1) may be served before the expiry of the chargeable period; and if on the day such a notice is issued the relevant year has not expired, it shall be assumed that the circumstances concerning any factor which might affect the

ratio $\frac{A}{B}$ in regulation 22(1) or (2) will remain as they stand at the time of issue of the notice; and without prejudice to the generality of the foregoing, the factors include–

(a) the question whether on any day the joint and several liability conditions will be fulfilled,

(b) the question whether the chargeable person will remain subject to the charge concerned.

(3) If a notice is served under paragraph (1) on such an assumption as is mentioned in paragraph (2), and the assumption is shown to be false, the charging authority shall serve a further notice on the spouse or manager (as the case may be) stating the revised sum for which he is jointly and severally liable under this regulation, calculated on the assumptions mentioned in paragraph (2) and as if the notice mentioned in that paragraph were the further notice served under this paragraph.

(4) If after a notice is served under paragraph (1) a notice is served on the chargeable person which adjusts an amount mentioned in regulation 22(1) or (2), or which otherwise notifies a change of the amounts with respect to which the spouse or manager has a joint and several liability under that regulation, a further notice shall also be served on the spouse or manager (as the case may be) stating the revised sum for which he is jointly and severally liable under the regulation.

(5) If the sum stated in the further notice served under paragraphs (3) or (4) is greater than the sum stated in the notice served under paragraph (1), the amount of the difference shall be due from the spouse or manager to the charging authority on the expiry of such period (being not less than 14 days) after the day of the further notice as is specified in it.

(6) If the sum stated in the further notice served under paragraph (3) or (4) is less than the sum stated in the notice served under paragraph (1) and there has been an overpayment by the spouse or manager, the amount overpaid–

(a) shall be repaid if the spouse or manager (as the case may be) so requires, or

(b) in any other case shall (as the charging authority determines) either be repaid or be credited against any subsequent liability of the person to make a payment in respect of any community charge of the authority.

(7) Regulations 20(5)(b) and 21(8)(b) apply as if the reference to the chargeable person includes, insofar as concerns the difference between the joint and several liability under regulation 22(1) or (2) of the spouse or manager in respect of the appropriate amount or recalculated amount referred to in those provisions and the amount he has paid in respect of the estimated amount so referred to, a reference to the spouse or manager, and as if the reference to regulation 20(8) were a reference to that provision as applied by paragraph (9) below; and accordingly any requirement which may be made by the chargeable person under regulation 20(5) or 21(9) for a calculation of the appropriate amount or for a recalculation of the estimated amount (as the case may be) may also be made by the spouse or manager.

(8) In a case where–

(a) payments have been made by the spouse or manager under regulation 22 or this regulation, and by the chargeable person, in respect of any amount for which the chargeable person is liable under this Part, and

(b) a sum would fall to be repaid to the chargeable person or credited against a liability of his if all those payments had been made by him,

the sum shall, to the extent that it does not exceed the payments made by the spouse or manager and the spouse or manager has not made recovery in respect of it under section 16(7) or 17(8) of the Act, be repaid to or credited in favour of the spouse or manager.

(9) If the circumstances described in regulation 20(8) have arisen, the charging authority may require that any amount of the overpayment or difference mentioned in that provision which might otherwise fall to be repaid to the spouse or manager should, instead of being repaid, be credited against any prospective liability of the spouse or manager under regulation 22 in respect of the different charge.

(10) An amount shall not be treated as overpaid for the purposes of paragraph (6) or paid for the purposes of paragraph (7) if recovery has been made in respect of it under section 16(7) or 17(8) of the Act.

Collection of penalties

24.—(1) Subject to paragraphs (2) to (4), where a penalty is payable by a person to a charging authority under paragraph 1 or 2 of Schedule 3 to the Act it may be collected, as the authority to which it is payable determines, either–

(a) by treating the penalty for the purposes of regulations 16 and 17 and Schedule 1 as it it were part of the amount that the person will be liable to pay in respect of a community charge as it has effect for a chargeable financial year as regards any demand notice issued pursuant to regulation 16(2) after the penalty is imposed, or

(b) by the service by the authority on the person of a notice requiring payment of the penalty on the expiry of such period (being not less than 14 days) after the issue of the notice as is specified in it.

(2) Where the imposition of a penalty is subject to an appeal or arbitration, no amount shall be payable in respect of the penalty while the appeal or arbitration is outstanding.

(3) The imposition of a penalty is to be treated as subject to an appeal or arbitration for the purposes of this regulation upon the service of a notice in respect of it by the person in accordance with section 24 of the Act, and is to be treated as outstanding until any appeal under section 23 of the Act or arbitration under regulations made under paragraph 4 of Schedule 11 to the Act in relation to the matter by which he stated he was aggrieved in the notice is finally disposed of or abandoned or fails for non-prosecution; and the circumstances in which an appeal is to be treated as failing for non-prosecution include the expiry of any time prescribed under paragraph 8(2)(a) of that Schedule in consequence of which any such appeal would be required to be dismissed by a valuation and community charge tribunal.

(4) A demand notice making provision for the recovery of a penalty which is subject to appeal or arbitration may not be issued under paragraph (1)(a) during the period that the appeal or arbitration concerned is outstanding; and where a penalty becomes subject to appeal or arbitration after the issue of a demand notice which makes such provision, such proportion of the instalments due under it as are attributable to the penalty shall not fall due until the appeal or arbitration is finally disposed of, abandoned or fails for non-prosecution.

(5) Where an amount has been paid by a person in respect of a penalty which is quashed under paragraph 1(8) or 2(12) of Schedule 3 to the Act, the charging authority which, or whose registration officer, imposed the penalty may allow the amount to him by way of deduction against any other sum which has become due from him under this Part (whether in respect of another penalty or otherwise); and any balance shall be repaid to him.

(6) Paragraphs (1) to (5) apply to penalties incurred under paragraph 2(8) to (11) of Schedule 3 to the Act before 1st April 1990 notwithstanding that no liability to pay amounts in respect of community charges arises before that date.

Appeals in relation to estimates

25. Section 23(2)(e) of the Act shall not apply where the ground on which the person concerned is aggrieved is that any assumption as to the future that is required by this Part to be made in the calculation of an amount may prove to be inaccurate.

Demand notices: final adjustment

26.—(1) This regulation applies where–

(a) a notice has been issued by a charging authority under this Part requiring a payment or payments to be made by a person in respect of his liability to pay a community charge as it has effect for a chargeable financial year or part of a chargeable financial year,

(b) the payment or payments required to be paid are found to be in excess of or less than his liability in respect of the charge as it has effect for the year or the part, and

(c) provision for adjusting the amounts required under the notice and (as appropriate) for the making of additional payments or the repaying or crediting of any amount overpaid is not made by any other provision of this Part, of the Act or of any agreement entered into under regulation 17(3) or paragraph 3(4) of Schedule 2.

(2) The charging authority shall as soon as practicable after the expiry of the year or the part of a year serve a further notice on the person stating the amount of his liability in respect of the charge as it has effect for the year or the part, and adjusting (by reference to that amount) the amounts required to be paid under the notice referred to in paragraph (1)(a).

(3) If the amount stated in the further notice is greater than the amount required to be paid under the notice referred to in paragraph (1)(a), the amount of the difference for which such other provision as is mentioned in paragraph (1)(c) is not made shall be due from the person to the charging authority on the expiry of such period (being not less than 14 days) after the day of issue of the notice as is specified in it.

(4) If there has been an overpayment, the amount overpaid for which such other provision as is mentioned in paragraph (1)(c) is not made–

(a) shall be repaid if the person so requires, or

(b) in any other case shall (as the charging authority determines) either be repaid or be credited against any subsequent liability of the person to make a payment in respect of any community charge of the authority.

PART IV

ENFORCEMENT

Interpretation and application of Part IV

27.—(1) In this Part–

"attachment of earnings order" means an order under regulation 32;

"charging order" means an order under regulation 44;

"debtor" means a person against whom a liability order has been made;

"earnings" has the meaning given in section 24 of the Attachment of Earnings Act 1971(**a**), and sections 6(2) and 25(4) of that Act shall apply for the purposes of this Part accordingly;

(**a**) 1971 c.32; section 24 was amended by the Social Security Pensions Act 1975 (c.60), Schedule 4, paragraph 15, the Merchant Shipping Act 1979 (c.39), section 39(1) the Social Security Act 1985 (c.53), Schedule 4, paragraph 1, and the Social Security Act 1986 (c.50), Schedule 10, paragraph 102.

"liability order" means an order under regulation 29; and

"net earnings" in relation to an employment means the residue of earnings payable under the employment after deduction by the employer of–

(a) income tax; and

(b) primary class 1 contributions under Part I of the Social Security Act 1975**(a)**.

(2) Regulations 28 to 47 apply for the recovery of a sum which has become payable to a charging authority under Part III and which has not been paid; but their application in relation to a sum for which persons are jointly and severally liable under that Part is subject to the provisions of regulation 48 (joint and several liability).

(3) References in this Part to a sum which has become payable and which has not been paid include references to a sum forming part of a larger sum which has become payable and the other part of which has been paid.

Liability orders: preliminary steps

28.—(1) Subject to paragraph (3), before a charging authority applies for a liability order it shall serve on the person against whom the application is to be made a notice ("reminder notice"), which is to be in addition to any notice required to be served under Part III, and which is to state every amount in respect of which the authority is to make the application.

(2) A reminder notice may be served in respect of an amount at any time after it has become due.

(3) A reminder notice need not be served on a person who has been served under regulation 20(1) or 21(4) with a notice in respect of the amount concerned; and in determining whether a person has been served for this purpose regulation 22(6) shall not have the effect of deeming him to have been served in a case where he has not in fact been so.

Application for liability order

29.—(1) If an amount which has fallen due under regulation 20(2) or 21(1) and (4) is wholly or partly unpaid, or (in a case where a reminder notice is required under regulation 28) the amount stated in the reminder notice is wholly or partly unpaid at the expiry of the period of 7 days beginning with the day on which the notice was served, the charging authority may, in accordance with paragraph (2), apply to a magistrates' court for an order against the person by whom it is payable.

(2) The application is to be instituted by making complaint to a justice of the peace, and requesting the issue of a summons directed to that person to appear before the court to show why he has not paid the sum which is outstanding.

(3) Section 127(1) of the Magistrates' Courts Act 1980**(b)** does not apply to such an application; but no application may be instituted in respect of a sum after the period of two years beginning with the day on which it became due under Part III.

(4) A warrant shall not be issued under section 55(2) of the Magistrates' Courts Act 1980 in any proceedings under this regulation.

(5) The court shall make the order if it is satisfied that the sum has become payable by the defendant and has not been paid.

(6) The order shall be made in respect of an amount equal to the aggregate of–

(a) the sum payable, and

(b) a sum of an amount equal to the costs reasonably incurred by the applicant in obtaining the order.

(a) 1975 c.14; *see* sections 1(2) and 4. Relevant amendments were made by the Social Security Pensions Act 1975 (c.60), Schedule 4, paragraph 36 and Schedule 5, the Education (School-leaving Dates) Act 1976 (c.5), section 2(4), the Social Security Act 1979 (c.18), section 14(1) and Schedule 3, paragraph 4, the Social Security and Housing Benefits Act 1982 (c.24), Schedule 5, the Social Security Act 1985 (c.53), sections 7(1) and (2) and 8(1), the Social Security Act 1986 (c.50), section 74 and Schedule 10, paragraph 104, and S.I. 1988/675.

(b) 1980 c.43.

Liability orders: further provision

30.—(1) A single liability order may deal with one person and one such amount as is mentioned in regulation 29(6) (in which case the order shall be in the form specified as form A in Schedule 3, or a form to the like effect), or, if the court thinks fit, may deal with more than one person and more than one such amount (in which case the order shall be in the form specified as form B in that Schedule, or a form to the like effect).

(2) A summons issued under regulation 29(2) may be served on a person–

(a) by delivering it to him,

(b) by leaving it at his usual or last known place of abode, or in the case of a company, at its registered office, or

(c) by sending it by post to him at his usual or last known place of abode, or in the case of a company, to its registered office.

(3) The amount in respect of which a liability order is made is enforceable in accordance with this Part; and accordingly for the purposes of any of the provisions of Part III of the Magistrates' Courts Act 1980 (satisfaction and enforcement) it is not to be treated as a sum adjudged to be paid by order of the court.

Duties of debtors subject to liability order

31.—(1) Where a liability order has been made, the debtor against whom it was made shall, during such time as the amount in respect of which the order was made remains wholly or partly unpaid, be under a duty to supply relevant information to the charging authority on whose application it was made.

(2) For the purposes of paragraph (1), relevant information is such information as fulfils the following conditions–

(a) it is in the debtor's possession or control,

(b) the charging authority requests him by notice given in writing to supply it; and

(c) it falls within paragraph (3).

(3) Information falls within this paragraph if it is specified in the notice mentioned in paragraph (2)(b) and it falls within one or more of the following descriptions–

(a) information as to the name and address of an employer of the debtor;

(b) information as to earnings or expected earnings of the debtor;

(c) information as to deductions or expected deductions from such earnings in respect of income tax, primary class 1 contributions under Part I of the Social Security Act 1975 or attachment of earnings orders made under this Part or under the Attachment of Earnings Act 1971;

(d) information as to the debtor's work or identity number in an employment, or such other information as will enable an employer of the debtor to identify him; or

(e) information as to sources of income of the debtor other than an employer of his.

(4) Information is to be supplied within 14 days of the day on which the request is made.

Making of attachment of earnings order

32.—(1) Where a liability order has been made and the debtor against whom it was made is an individual, the authority which applied for the order may make an order under this regulation to secure the payment of any outstanding sum which is or forms part of the amount in respect of which the liability order was made.

(2) Such an order–

(a) shall be expressed to be directed to a person who has the debtor in his employment, and shall operate as an instruction to such a person to make deductions from the debtor's earnings, and to pay the amounts so deducted to the authority;

(b) shall specify the sum to which the order relates, the rate at which the debtor's earnings are to be applied to meet the sum by way of deductions from his net earnings in accordance with regulation 33, and the period within which an amount deducted is to be paid to the authority; and

(c) shall remain in force until discharged under regulation 36(2) or the whole amount to which it relates has been paid (whether by attachment of earnings or otherwise).

(3) The authority may serve a copy of the order on a person who appears to the authority to have the debtor in his employment; and a person on whom it is so served who has the debtor in his employment shall comply with it.

Deductions under attachment of earnings order

33.—(1) The sum to be deducted by an employer under an attachment of earnings order on any pay day shall be–

(a) where the debtor's earnings from the employer are payable weekly, the sum specified in column 2 of Table A in Schedule 4 opposite the band in column 1 of that Table within which the net earnings payable by the employer on the pay-day fall;

(b) where his earnings from the employer are payable monthly, the sum specified in column 2 of Table B in that Schedule opposite the band in column 1 of that Table within which the net earnings payable by the employer on the pay-day fall;

(c) where his earnings from the employer are payable at regular intervals of a whole number of weeks or months, the sum arrived at by–

(i) calculating what would be his weekly or monthly net earnings by dividing the net earnings payable to him by the employer on the pay-day by that whole number (of weeks or months, as the case may be),

(ii) ascertaining the sum specified in column 2 of Table A (if the whole number is of weeks) or of Table B (if the whole number is of months) in Schedule 4 opposite the band in column 1 of that Table within which the notional net earnings calculated under paragraph (i) fall, and

(iii) multiplying that sum by the whole number (of weeks or months, as the case may be).

(2) Where the debtor's earnings from the employer are payable at regular intervals other than at intervals to which paragraph (1) applies, the sum to be deducted on any pay-day shall be arrived at by–

(a) calculating what would be his daily net earnings by dividing the net earnings payable to him by the employer on the pay-day by the number of days in the interval,

(b) ascertaining the sum specified in column 2 of Table C in Schedule 4 opposite the band in column 1 of that Table within which the notional net earnings calculated under sub-paragraph (a) fall, and

(c) multiplying that sum by the number of days in the interval.

(3) Where earnings are payable to a debtor by the employer by 2 or more series of payments at regular intervals–

(a) if some or all of the intervals are of different lengths–

(i) for the purpose of arriving at the sum to be deducted, whichever of paragraphs (1) and (2) is appropriate shall apply to the series with the shortest interval (or, if there is more than one series with the shortest interval, such one of those series as the employer may choose), and

(ii) in relation to the earnings payable in every other series, the sum to be deducted shall be 20 per cent. of the net earnings;

(b) if all of the intervals are of the same length, whichever of paragraphs (1) or (2) is appropriate shall apply to such series as the employer may choose and sub-paragraph (a)(ii) shall apply to every other series.

(4) Subject to paragraphs (5) and (6), where the debtor's earnings from the employer are payable at irregular intervals, the sums to be deducted on any pay-day shall be arrived at by–

(a) calculating what would be his daily net earnings by dividing the net earnings payable to him by the employer on the pay-day–

(i) by the number of days since earnings were last payable by it to him, or

(ii) if the earnings are the first earnings to be payable by it to him with respect to the employment in question, by the number of days since he began the employment;

(b) taking the sum specified in column 2 of Table C of Schedule 4 opposite the band in column 1 of that Table within which the notional net earnings calculated under sub-paragraph (a) fall; and

(c) multiplying that sum by the number of days mentioned in sub-paragraph (a).

(5) Where on the same pay-day there are payable to the debtor by the employer both earnings payable at regular intervals and earnings which are payable at irregular intervals, for the purpose of arriving at the sum to be deducted on the pay-day under the foregoing provisions of this regulation all the earnings shall be aggregated and treated as earnings payable at the regular interval.

(6) Where there are earnings payable to the debtor by the employer at regular intervals on one pay-day, and earnings are payable by the employer to him at irregular intervals on a different pay-day, the sum to be deducted on each of the pay-days on which the earnings which are payable at irregular intervals are so payable shall be 20 per cent. of the net earnings payable to him on the day.

Attachment of earnings orders: ancillary powers and duties of employers and others served

34.—(1) An employer who deducts and pays amounts under an attachment of earnings order may, on each occasion that he makes such a deduction, also deduct from the debtor's earnings the sum of one pound towards his administrative costs.

(2) An employer who deducts and pays amounts under an attachment of earnings order shall, in accordance with paragraph (3), notify the debtor in writing of the total amount of the sums so deducted under it (including sums deducted under paragraph (1)) up to the time of the notification.

(3) A notification under paragraph (2) must be given at the time that the pay statement given by the employer to the debtor next after a deduction has been made is so given, or if no such statements are usually issued by the employer, as soon as practicable after a deduction has been made.

(4) A person on whom a copy of an attachment of earnings order has been served shall, in accordance with paragraph (5), notify in writing the authority which made the order if he does not have the debtor against whom it was made in his employment or the debtor subsequently ceases to be in his employment.

(5) A notification under paragraph (4) must be given within 14 days of the day on which the copy of the order was served on him or the debtor ceased to be in his employment (as the case may be).

(6) While an attachment of earnings order is in force, any person who becomes the debtor's employer and knows that the order is in force and by what authority it was made shall notify that authority in writing that he is the debtor's employer.

(7) A notification under paragraph (6) must be given within 14 days of the day on which the debtor became the person's employee or of the day on which the person first knew that the order is in force and the identity of the authority by which it was made, whichever is the later.

Attachment of earnings orders: duties of debtor

35.—(1) While an attachment of earnings order is in force, the debtor in respect of whom the order has been made shall from time to time notify in writing the authority which made it of each occasion when he leaves an employment or becomes employed or re-employed, and (in a case where he becomes so employed or re-employed) shall include in the notification a statement of–

(a) his earnings and (so far as he is able) expected earnings from the employment concerned,

(b) the deductions and (so far as he is able) expected deductions from such earnings in respect of income tax and primary class 1 contributions under Part I of the Social Security Act 1975,

(c) the name and address of the employer, and

(d) his work or identity number in the employment (if any).

(2) A notification under paragraph (1) must be given within 14 days of the day on which the debtor leaves or commences (or recommences) the employment (as the case may be), or (if later) the day on which he is informed by the authority that the order has been made.

Attachment of earnings orders: ancillary powers and duties of authority

36.—(1) Where the whole amount to which an attachment of earnings order relates has been paid (whether by attachment of earnings or otherwise), the authority by which it was made shall give notice of that fact to any person who appears to it to have the debtor in his employment and who has been served with a copy of the order.

(2) The authority by which an attachment of earnings order was made may, on its own account or on the application of the debtor or an employer of the debtor, make an order discharging the attachment of earnings order; and if it does so it shall give notice of that fact to any person who appears to it to have the debtor in his employment and who has been served with a copy of the order.

(3) If an authority serves a copy of an attachment of earnings order in accordance with regulation 32(3), it shall (unless it has previously done so) also serve a copy of the order on the debtor.

Priority between attachment of earnings orders

37.—(1) Where an employer would, but for this paragraph, be obliged under regulation 32(3) to make deductions on any pay-day under two or more attachment of earnings orders made under this Part, he shall make deductions only with respect to the one which was made first until it ceases to be in force, and shall then deal with the other order or orders in like manner in the order in which they were made.

(2) Where an employer is or would, but for this paragraph, be obliged to comply at any time with an attachment of earnings order made under this Part and an order made under the Attachment of Earnings Act 1971 ("the 1971 Act")–

(a) if the order made under the 1971 Act was made first, whilst it is in force he shall comply only with the order made under the 1971 Act, or

(b) if the attachment of earnings order made under this Part was made first, whilst it is in force the attachable earnings for the purposes of Schedule 3 to the 1971 Act are to be treated as such of the attachable earnings mentioned in paragraph 3 of that Schedule**(a)** as remain after deduction of the amount to be deducted under the order made under this Part.

Attachment of earnings orders: persons employed under the Crown

38.—(1) Where a debtor is in the employment of the Crown and an attachment of earnings order is made in respect of him, for the purposes of this Part–

(a) the chief officer for the time being of the department, office or other body in which the debtor is employed shall be treated as having the debtor in his employment (any transfer of the debtor from one department, office or body to another being treated as a change of employment); and

(b) any earnings paid by the Crown or a Minister of the Crown, or out of the public revenue of the United Kingdom, shall be treated as paid by that chief officer.

(a) Paragraph 3 of Schedule 3 was amended by the Social Security (Consequential Provisions) Act 1975 (c.18), Schedule 2, paragraph 43, the Social Security Pensions Act 1975 (c.60), Schedule 5 and the Wages Act 1986 (c.48), Schedule 4, paragraph 4.

(2) If any question arises as to what department, office or other body is concerned for the purposes of this regulation, or as to who for those purposes is its chief officer, the question shall be referred to and determined by the Minister for the Civil Service.

(3) A document purporting to set out a determination of the Minister under paragraph (2) and to be signed by an official of the Office of that Minister shall, in any proceedings arising in relation to an attachment of earnings order, be admissible in evidence and be deemed to contain an accurate statement of such a determination unless the contrary is shown.

(4) This Part shall have effect in relation to attachment of earnings orders notwithstanding any enactment passed before 29th May 1970 and preventing or avoiding the attachment or diversion of sums due to a person in respect of services under the Crown, whether by way of remuneration, pension or otherwise.

Distress

39.—(1) Where a liability order has been made, the authority which applied for the order may levy the appropriate amount by distress and sale of the goods of the debtor against whom the order was made.

(2) The appropriate amount for the purposes of paragraph (1) is the aggregate of–

(a) an amount equal to any outstanding sum which is or forms part of the amount in respect of which the liability order was made, and

(b) a sum determined in accordance with Schedule 5 in respect of charges connected with the distress.

(3) If, before any goods are seized, the appropriate amount (including charges arising up to the time of the payment or tender) is paid or tendered to the authority, the authority shall accept the amount and the levy shall not be proceeded with.

(4) Where an authority has seized goods of the debtor in pursuance of the distress, but before sale of those goods the appropriate amount (including charges arising up to the time of the payment or tender) is paid or tendered to the authority, the authority shall accept the amount, the sale shall not be proceeded with and the goods shall be made available for collection by the debtor.

(5) The person levying distress on behalf of an authority shall carry with him the written authorisation of the authority, which he shall show to the debtor if so requested; and he shall hand to the debtor or leave at the premises where the distress is levied a copy of this regulation and Schedule 5 and a memorandum setting out the appropriate amount, and shall hand to the debtor a copy of any close or walking possession agreement entered into.

(6) A distress may be made anywhere in England and Wales.

(7) A distress shall not be deemed unlawful on account of any defect or want of form in the liability order, and no person making a distress shall be deemed a trespasser on that account; and no person making a distress shall be deemed a trespasser from the beginning on account of any subsequent irregularity in making the distress, but a person sustaining special damage by reason of the subsequent irregularity may recover full satisfaction for the special damage (and no more) by proceedings in trespass or otherwise.

(8) The provisions of this regulation shall not affect the operation of any enactment which protects goods of any class from distress.

(9) Nothing in the Distress (Costs) Act 1817**(a)**, as extended by the Distress (Costs) Act 1827**(b)**, (which makes provision as to the costs and expenses of the levying of certain distresses) shall apply to a distress under this regulation.

(a) 1817 c.93.
(b) 1827 c.17.

Appeals in connection with distress

40.—(1) A person aggrieved by the levy of, or an attempt to levy, a distress may appeal to a magistrates' court.

(2) The appeal shall be instituted by making complaint to a justice of the peace, and requesting the issue of a summons directed to the authority which levied or attempted to levy the distress to appear before the court to answer to the matter by which he is aggrieved.

(3) If the court is satisfied that a levy was irregular, it may order the goods distrained to be discharged if they are in the possession of the authority; and it may by order award compensation in respect of any goods distrained and sold of an amount equal to the amount which, in the opinion of the court, would be awarded by way of special damages in respect of the goods if proceedings were brought in trespass or otherwise in connection with the irregularity under regulation 39(7).

(4) If the court is satisfied that an attempted levy was irregular, it may by order require the authority to desist from levying in the manner giving rise to the irregularity.

Commitment to prison

41.—(1) Where a charging authority has sought to levy an amount by distress under regulation 39, the debtor is an individual, and it appears to the authority that no (or insufficient) goods of the debtor can be found on which to levy the amount, the authority may apply to a magistrates' court for the issue of a warrant committing the debtor to prison.

(2) On such application being made the court shall (in the debtor's presence) inquire as to his means and inquire whether the failure to pay which led to the liability order concerned being made against him was due to his wilful refusal or culpable neglect.

(3) If (and only if) the court is of the opinion that his failure was due to his wilful refusal or culpable neglect it may if it thinks fit–

(a) issue a warrant of commitment against the debtor, or

(b) fix a term of imprisonment and postpone the issue of the warrant until such time and on such conditions (if any) as the court thinks just.

(4) The warrant shall be made in respect of the relevant amount; and the relevant amount for this purpose is the aggregate of–

(a) the appropriate amount mentioned in regulation 39(2), or (as the case may be) so much of it as remains outstanding, and

(b) a sum of an amount equal to the costs reasonably incurred by the applicant in respect of the application.

(5) The warrant–

(a) shall state the relevant amount mentioned in paragraph (4),

(b) may be directed to the authority making the application and to such other persons (if any) as the court issuing it thinks fit, and

(c) may be executed anywhere in England and Wales by any person to whom it is directed.

(6) If–

(a) before the issue of a warrant the appropriate amount mentioned in regulation 39(2) (or so much of it as remains outstanding) is paid or tendered to the authority, or

(b) after the issue of the warrant, the amount stated in it is paid or tendered to the authority,

the authority shall accept the amount concerned, no further steps shall be taken as regards its recovery, and the debtor if committed to prison shall be released.

(7) The order in the warrant shall be that the debtor be imprisoned for a time specified in the warrant which shall not exceed 3 months, unless the amount stated in the warrant is sooner paid; but–

(a) where a warrant is issued after a postponement under paragraph (3)(b) and, since the term of imprisonment was fixed but before the issue of the warrant, the amount mentioned in paragraph (4)(a) with respect to which the warrant would (but for the postponement) have been made has been reduced by a part payment, the period of imprisonment ordered under the warrant shall be the term fixed under paragraph (3) reduced by such number of days as bears to the total number of days in that term less one day the same proportion as the part paid bears to that amount, and

(b) where, after the issue of a warrant, a part payment of the amount stated in it is made,the period of imprisonment shall be reduced by such number of days as bears to the total number of days in the term of imprisonment specified in the warrant less one day the same proportion as the part paid bears to the amount so stated.

(8) In calculating a reduction required under paragraph (7) any fraction of a day shall be left out of account; and rule 55(1), (2) and (3) of the Magistrates' Courts Rules 1981**(a)** applies (so far as is relevant) to a part payment as if the imprisonment concerned were imposed for want of sufficient distress to satisfy a sum adjudged to be paid by a magistrates' court.

Commitment to prison: further provision

42.—(1) A single warrant may not be issued under regulation 41 against more than one person, and shall be in the form specified as form C in Schedule 3, or in a form to the like effect.

(2) Where an application under regulation 41 has been made, and after the making of the inquiries mentioned in paragraph (2) of that regulation no warrant is issued or term of imprisonment fixed, the court may remit all or part of the appropriate amount mentioned in regulation 39(2) with respect to which the application related.

(3) Where an application under regulation 41 has been made but no warrant is issued or term of imprisonment fixed, the application may be renewed (except so far as regards any sum remitted under paragraph (2)) on the ground that the circumstances of the debtor have changed.

(4) A statement in writing to the effect that wages of any amount have been paid to the debtor during any period, purporting to be signed by or on behalf of his employer, shall in any proceedings under regulation 41 be evidence of the facts there stated.

(5) For the purpose of enabling enquiry to be made as to the debtor's conduct and means under regulation 41, a justice of the peace may–

(a) issue a summons to him to appear before a magistrates' court and (if he does not obey the summons) issue a warrant for his arrest, or

(b) issue a warrant for the debtor's arrest without issuing a summons.

(6) A warrant issued under paragraph (5) may be executed anywhere in England and Wales by any person to whom it is directed or by any constable acting within his police area; and section 125(3) of the Magistrates' Courts Act 1980 applies to such a warrant.

(7) Regulation 41 and this regulation have effect subject to Part I of the Criminal Justice Act 1982**(b)** (treatment of young offenders).

Insolvency

43.—(1) Where a liability order has been made and the debtor against whom it was made is an individual, the amount due shall be deemed to be a debt for the purposes of section 267 of the Insolvency Act 1986**(c)** (grounds of creditor's petition).

(2) Where a liability order has been made and the debtor against whom it was made is a company, the amount due shall be deemed to be a debt for the purposes of section 122(1)(f) of that Act (winding up of companies by the court).

(3) The amount due for the purposes of this regulation is an amount equal to any

(a) S.I. 1981/552.
(b) 1982 c.48.
(c) 1986 c.45.

outstanding sum which is or forms part of the amount in respect of which the liability order was made.

Charging orders

44.—(1) An application to the appropriate court may be made under this regulation where–

(a) a magistrates' court has made a liability order,

(b) the amount mentioned in regulation 29(6)(a) in respect of which the liability order was made is an amount the debtor is liable to pay under Part III in relation to a collective community charge, and

(c) at the time that the application under this regulation is made at least £1000 of the amount in respect of which the liability order was made remains outstanding.

(2) The application which may be made to the appropriate court under this regulation is an application by the authority concerned for an order imposing, on any interest held by the debtor beneficially in the relevant designated dwelling, a charge for securing the due amount; and the court may make such an order on such application.

(3) For the purposes of paragraph (2)–

(a) the authority concerned is the authority which applied for the liability order referred to in paragraph (1)(a),

(b) the relevant designated dwelling is the designated dwelling to which the community charge mentioned in paragraph (1)(b) relates,

(c) the due amount is the aggregate of–

(i) an amount equal to any outstanding sum which is or forms part of the amount in respect of which the liability order was made, and

(ii) a sum of an amount equal to the costs reasonably incurred by the applicant in obtaining the charging order,

(d) the appropriate court is the county court for the area in which the relevant designated dwelling is situated.

Charging orders: further provision

45.—(1) In deciding whether to make a charging order, the court shall consider all the circumstances of the case, and in particular any evidence before it as to–

(a) the personal circumstances of the debtor, and

(b) whether any other person would be likely to be unduly prejudiced by the making of the order.

(2) A charging order–

(a) shall specify the designated dwelling concerned and the interest held by the debtor beneficially in it, and

(b) may, as the court thinks fit, be made absolutely or subject to conditions as to the time when the charge is to become enforceable or as to other matters.

(3) A charge imposed by a charging order shall have the like effect and shall be enforceable in the same courts and in the same manner as an equitable charge created by the debtor by writing under his hand.

(4) The court by which a charging order was made may at any time, on the application of the debtor, the authority on whose application the order was made or any person interested in the designated dwelling, make an order discharging or varying the charging order.

(5) The Land Charges Act 1972**(a)** and Land Registration Act 1925**(b)** shall apply in

(a) 1972 c.61; section 6 of the Act was amended by the Supreme Court Act 1981 (c.54), Schedule 5, and the County Courts Act 1984 (c.28), Schedule 2, paragraph 18.

(b) 1925 c.21; section 49(1)(g) was inserted by the Charging Orders Act 1979 (c.53), section 3(3), and amended by the Drug Trafficking Offences Act 1986 (c.32), section 39(2) and the Criminal Justice Act 1988 (c.33), Schedule 15, paragraph 6.

relation to charging orders as they apply in relation to orders or writs issued or made for the purposes of enforcing judgments; and in section 49(1)(g) of the Land Registration Act 1925, after the words "Criminal Justice Act 1988" there are inserted the words ", or regulations under paragraph 11 of Schedule 4 to the Local Government Finance Act 1988".

(6) Where a charging order has been protected by an entry registered under the Land Charges Act 1972 or the Land Registration Act 1925, an order under paragraph (4) discharging the charging order may direct that the entry be cancelled.

Relationship between remedies

46.—(1) Where a warrant of commitment is issued against (or a term of imprisonment is fixed in the case of) a person under regulation 41(3), no steps, or no further steps, may be taken under this Part by way of attachment of earnings, distress, bankruptcy or charging of a designated dwelling in relation to the relevant amount mentioned in regulation 41(4).

(2) Steps under this Part by way of attachment of earnings, distress, commitment, bankruptcy, winding up or charging of a designated dwelling may not be taken while steps by way of another of those methods are being taken.

(3) Subject to paragraphs (1) and (2)–

(a) attachment of earnings or distress may be resorted to more than once, and

(b) attachment of earnings or distress may be resorted to in any order or alternately (or both).

(4) Where a step is taken for the recovery of an outstanding sum which is or forms part of an amount in respect of which a liability order has been made and under which additional costs or charges with respect to the step are also recoverable in accordance with this Part, any sum recovered thereby which is less than the aggregate of the amount outstanding and such additional costs and charges shall be treated as discharging first the costs and charges, the balance (if any) being applied towards the discharge of the outstanding sum.

Magistrates' courts

47.—(1) Justices of the peace for a commission area within which is situated the area of a charging authority shall have jurisdiction to act under the provisions of this Part as respects that authority.

(2) Subject to any other enactment authorising a stipendiary magistrate or other person to act by himself, a magistrates' court shall not under this Part hear a summons, entertain an application for a warrant or hold an inquiry as to means on such an application except when composed of at least two justices.

(3) References to a justice of the peace in regulations 29(2) and 40(2) shall be construed subject to rule 3 of the Justices' Clerks Rules 1970**(a)** (which authorises certain matters authorised to be done by a justice of the peace to be done by a justices' clerk).

Joint and several liability

48.—(1) This regulation has effect with respect to the application of regulations 28 to 47 to a sum for which persons are jointly and severally liable under Part III.

(2) A reminder notice shall be served in accordance with regulation 28(1) and (2) on every person against whom the application for a liability order is to be made except a chargeable person who has been served under regulation 20(1) or 21(4) with a notice in respect of the amount concerned; and in determining whether a person has been served for this purpose, regulation 22(6) shall not have the effect of deeming him to have been served in a case where he has not in fact been so.

(3) A liability order may be made against the chargeable person alone, or against that

(a) S.I. 1970/231, to which there are amendments not relevant to these Regulations.

person and the spouse or manager (as the case may be), but may not be made against the spouse or manager alone.

(4) Where a liability order has been made against both the chargeable person and the spouse or manager, subject to paragraph (9)–

(a) an attachment of earnings order may be made against one of them, or different such orders may be made against each;

(b) distress may be made against one of them or against each; and

(c) a charging order may be made against one of them or different such orders may be made against each.

(5) Where distress has been made against both the chargeable person and the spouse or manager, a warrant of commitment may be applied for against one of them or different warrants may be applied for against each.

(6) Where distress has been made against the chargeable person only, a warrant of commitment may be applied for against that person.

(7) Where a liability order has been made against a chargeable person and a spouse or manager, a warrant of commitment may not be applied for against the spouse or manager unless distress has been made against the chargeable person (as well as against the spouse or manager) and it appears to the authority concerned that no (or insufficient) goods of those persons can be found.

(8) Where a liability order has been made against a chargeable person and a spouse or manager, and a warrant for commitment is issued against (or a term of imprisonment is fixed in the case of) one of them under regulation 41(3), no steps, or further steps, may be taken under this Part against that one by way of attachment of earnings, distress or charging of a designated dwelling in relation to the amount mentioned in regulation 41(4).

(9) Where a liability order has been made against a chargeable person and a spouse or manager–

(a) steps by way of attachment of earnings, distress, commitment, bankruptcy, winding up or charging of a designated dwelling may not be taken against a person while steps by way of another of those methods are being taken against him, and

(b) subject to paragraph (10), steps by way of attachment of earnings, distress, or charging of a designated dwelling may not be taken against a person while steps by way of the same method or another of those methods are being taken against the other.

(10) Where a liability order has been made in respect of an amount against a chargeable person and a spouse of his and in making distress against one of them goods jointly owned by both are found, paragraph (9)(b) does not preclude distress being levied against those goods with respect to that amount; but in any subsequent proceedings under regulation 41 (commitment), charges arising under Schedule 5 from such distress shall be treated as charges relating to the person against whose goods the levy was intended to be made when the jointly owned goods were found, and not as charges relating to the other.

(11) Where a liability order has been made against a chargeable person and a spouse or manager in respect of an amount, paragraph 2(2) of Schedule 5 shall have effect so that if a charge has arisen against one of them under head B of the Table to paragraph 1 of the Schedule as regards a levy in respect of it, no further charge may be aggregated for the purposes of regulation 39(2) under heads A or B in consequence of any subsequent levy or attempted levy against either in respect of the amount; and if a charge has arisen under head A against one of them, it shall be treated as a charge under that head with respect to the other as well as that one for the purposes of the calculation of any subsequent charge under heads A or B against either.

(12) Where a liability order is made against a chargeable person in respect of an amount, and also against a spouse or manager of his (whether at the same time as the order against the chargeable person or subsequently and whether in respect of all or part of that amount), the order made as respects the spouse or manager shall not include

under regulation 29(6)(b) any additional sum in respect of the costs of obtaining the order against the spouse or manager, but the spouse or manager shall be treated as jointly and severally liable for the amount included in the order against the chargeable person in respect of costs, and the order against the spouse or manager shall (as regards regulation 29(6)(b)) be made in respect of the sum outstanding in relation to it.

(13) In this regulation "chargeable person", "spouse" and "manager" shall be construed in accordance with regulation 22.

Collective community charge contributions

49. A sum which has become payable to a chargeable person under regulation 18(3) but which has not been paid shall be recoverable in a court of competent jurisdiction.

Repayments

50. A sum which has become payable (by way of repayment) under Part III to a person other than a charging authority but which has not been paid shall be recoverable in a court of competent jurisdiction.

Offences

51.—(1) A person shall be guilty of an offence if, following a request under paragraph (2)(b) of regulation 31, he is under a duty to supply information and–

(a) he fails without reasonable excuse to supply the information in accordance with that regulation, or

(b) in supplying information in purported compliance with that regulation he makes a statement which is false in a material particular.

(2) Subject to paragraph (3), a person shall be guilty of an offence if, following the service of an attachment of earnings order on him under regulation 32(3), he is under a duty to comply with the order by virtue of that provision and he fails to do so.

(3) It shall be a defence for a person charged with an offence under paragraph (2) to prove that he took all reasonable steps to comply with the order.

(4) A person shall be guilty of an offence if he is under a duty to notify another person under regulation 34(2) and (3), 34(4) and (5), 34(6) and (7) or 35 and–

(a) he fails without reasonable excuse to notify the other person in accordance with the provision concerned, or

(b) in notifying the other person in purported compliance with the provision concerned he makes a statement which he knows to be false in a material particular or recklessly makes a statement which is false in a material particular.

(5) A person guilty of an offence under paragraph (1)(a) or (4)(a) shall be liable on summary conviction to a fine not exceeding level 2 on the standard scale.

(6) A person guilty of an offence under paragraph (1)(b), (2) or (4)(b) shall be liable on summary conviction to a fine not exceeding level 3 on the standard scale.

Miscellaneous provisions

52.—(1) Any matter which could be the subject of an appeal under section 23 of the Act may not be raised in proceedings under this Part.

(2) The contents of an item entered in a community charges register of a charging authority may be proved in proceedings under this Part either by–

(a) production of a copy of the relevant part of the register purporting to be certified by the registration officer maintaining the register to be a true copy, or

(b) evidence given in those proceedings as to the item by an officer of the charging authority authorised by it in that behalf who has inspected the register.

(3) If a liability order has been made and by virtue of–

(a) a notification which is given by the charging authority under regulation 20(4) or (7), 21(7) or (11), 23(4) or 26(2), or paragraph 6(3) or 7(2)(a) of Schedule 1, or

(b) section 36(2) of the Act applying in any case,

any part of the amount mentioned in regulation 29(6)(a) in respect of which the order was made would (if paid) fall to be repaid or credited against any subsequent liability, that part shall be treated for the purposes of this Part as paid on the day the notification is given or the amount in substitution is set under section 34 or 35 of the Act (as the case may be) and accordingly as no longer outstanding.

(4) If, after a warrant is issued or term of imprisonment is fixed under regulation 41(3), and before the term of imprisonment has begun or been fully served, a charging authority gives such a notification as is mentioned in paragraph (3)(a) in the case in question, or sets an amount in substitution so that section 36(2) of the Act applies in the case in question, it shall forthwith notify accordingly the clerk of the court which issued the warrant and (if the debtor is detained) the governor or keeper of the prison or place where he is detained or such other person as has lawful custody of him.

(5) If the debtor is treated as having paid an amount under paragraph (3) on any day, and–

(a) that day falls after the completion of the service of a term of imprisonment imposed under regulation 41 in respect of the amount he is treated as having paid, or

(b) the debtor is serving a term of imprisonment imposed under regulation 41 on that day and the amount he is treated as having paid exceeds the amount of any part payment which, if made, would cause the expiry of the term of imprisonment pursuant to paragraph (7)(b) of that regulation on that day,

the amount mentioned in sub-paragraph (a) or excess mentioned in sub-paragraph (b) shall be paid to the debtor or credited against any subsequent liability of his, as the debtor requires.

PART V

AREAS

Interpretation of Part V

53.—(1) References in this Part to the superficial extent of a building or a structure (where that structure is not a caravan or a houseboat) are to be treated as references–

(a) if the lowest floor of the building or structure is above ground level, to the floor area of the lowest floor measured externally,

(b) if all the building or structure is below ground level, to the floor area of its lowest floor measured internally, or

(c) in any other case, to the area of the building or structure measured externally on a horizontal plane at ground level.

(2) References in this Part to the superficial extent of a caravan, or of a structure where that structure consists of a caravan, are to be treated as references to its floor area measured externally.

(3) References in this Part to the superficial extent of a structure are, where that structure consists of a houseboat, to be treated as references to its enclosed volume.

(4) "Ground level" in paragraph (1) means the highest level of ground contiguous with–

(a) in the case of a building, the building,

(b) in the case of a structure where sub-paragraph (c) does not apply, the structure, or

(c) in the case of a structure which forms part of a larger building or structure, the larger building or structure.

Measurement of premises, etc.

54.—(1) For the purposes of section 2(4) of the Act, the greater or greatest part of premises is to be ascertained by reference to the superficial extent of the structure of which the premises consist or which forms part of the premises.

(2) In paragraph (1), "structure" does not include any structure not contiguous with the principal structure on the premises.

(3) For the purposes of sections 4(11) and 5(8) of the Act, the greater or greatest part of a building is to be ascertained by reference to its superficial extent.

(4) For the purposes of section 4(11) of the Act, the greater or greatest part of a caravan is to be ascertained by reference to its superficial extent.

(5) Where under the preceding paragraphs of this regulation no part of the superficial extent of any structure, building or caravan (as the case may be) can reasonably be ascertained to be greater than any other, the part of the premises, building or caravan concerned to be treated as the greater or greatest for the purposes of section 2(4), 4(11) or 5(8) of the Act shall be determined by agreement between the authorities within whose areas the several parts of that superficial extent are situated or, failing such agreement, by lot between those authorities.

Parts of charging authority's area: collective community charge

55.—(1) This regulation contains rules for the purposes mentioned in section 10(6) of the Act.

(2) A building shall be treated as contained in an authority's area if its greater or greatest part is treated by virtue of regulation 54(3) or (5) as situated in its area.

(3) In the following provisions of this regulation the relevant authority is the charging authority in whose area a building is, or is treated as, contained.

(4) Where a building (so far as it is in fact contained within the relevant authority's area) is contained wholly within a single part of the authority's area for which it has set an amount for its personal community charge for a chargeable financial year, the building shall be treated as contained within that part.

(5) Where a building is situated within more than one part of the area of the relevant authority for which it has set amounts for its personal community charge for the year, the building shall be treated as contained in whichever of those parts contains the greater or greatest part of the building, ascertained by reference to its superficial extent.

(6) Where it appears to the relevant authority that no such part of a building can reasonably be ascertained to be greater than any other for the purposes of paragraph (5), the building shall be treated as falling in such part of its area (being a part within which some of the building falls) as is determined by the authority.

Parts of charging authority's area: personal community charge

56.—(1) This regulation contains rules for the purposes mentioned in section 12(6) of the Act.

(2) A residence which consists of premises shall be treated as contained in an authority's area if the greater or greatest part of the premises is treated by virtue of regulation 54(1) or (5) as situated in its area.

(3) In the following provisions of this regulation–

(a) the relevant authority is the charging authority in whose area a residence consisting of premises is, or is treated as, contained; and

(b) the relevant structure is the structure of which such premises consist or which forms part of such premises.

(4) Where the relevant structure (so far as it is in fact contained within the relevant authority's area) is contained wholly within a single part of the authority's area for which it has set an amount for its personal community charge for a chargeable financial year, the residence concerned shall be treated as contained within that part.

(5) Where the relevant structure is situated within more than one part of the area of the relevant authority for which it has set amounts for its personal community charge for the year, the residence concerned shall be treated as contained in whichever of those parts contains the greater or greatest part of the structure, ascertained by reference to its superficial extent.

(6) Where it appears to the relevant authority that no such part of a structure can reasonably be ascertained to be greater than any other for the purposes of paragraph (5), the residence concerned shall be treated as falling in such part of its area (being a part within which some of the structure falls) as is determined by the authority.

(7) In paragraph (3)(b), "structure" does not include any structure not contiguous with the principal structure on the premises.

Parts of charging authority's area: standard community charge

57.—(1) This regulation contains rules for the purposes mentioned in section 14(7) of the Act.

(2) A property consisting of a building or self-contained part of a building shall be treated as contained in an authority's area if the greater or greatest part of the building of which it consists, or (in the case of property which is a self-contained part of a building) of the building of which it is part, is treated by virtue of regulation 54(3) or (5) as situated in its area.

(3) A property consisting of a caravan shall be treated as contained in an authority's area if the greater or greatest part of the caravan is treated by virtue of regulation 54(4) or (5) as situated in its area.

(4) In the following provisions of this regulation–

(a) the relevant authority is the charging authority in whose area a property is, or is treated as, contained; and

(b) the relevant building is the building of which a property consists or of which a property is a self-contained part; and

(c) the relevant caravan is the caravan of which a property consists.

(5) Where the relevant building or relevant caravan (so far as it is in fact contained within the relevant authority's area) is contained wholly within a single part of the authority's area for which it has set an amount for its personal community charge for a chargeable financial year, the property concerned shall be treated as contained within that part.

(6) Where the relevant building or relevant caravan is situated within more than one part of the area of the relevant authority for which it has set amounts for its personal community charge for the year, the property concerned shall be treated as contained in whichever of those parts contains the greater or greatest part of the building or caravan, ascertained by reference to its superficial extent.

(7) Where it appears to the relevant authority that no such part of a building or caravan can reasonably be ascertained to be greater than any other for the purposes of paragraph (6), the property concerned shall be treated as falling in such part of its area (being a part within which some of the building or caravan falls) as is determined by the authority.

PART VI

MISCELLANEOUS

Designated dwellings

58.—(1) A building falls into a prescribed description for the purposes of section 5(3)(d) of the Act if it falls within the description appearing in paragraph (2).

(2) The description is a building–

(a) which is a hostel, night shelter or other building for the time being providing residential accommodation, and

(b) which does so predominantly–

(i) in other than separate and self-contained sets of premises,

(ii) for people who have no fixed abode and no settled way of life, and

(iii) under licences to occupy the accommodation in favour of the residents which do not constitute tenancies.

Co-owners

59.—(1) This regulation applies in any case where (apart from this regulation) co-owners would be subject under the Act to different standard or collective community charges by virtue of the same property.

(2) Where this regulation applies–

(a) as regards the period for which the co-ownership subsists there shall be one charge only to which the co-owners are jointly subject, and with respect to which the registration officer for the charging authority concerned shall enter an item in the register compiled and maintained by him accordingly;

(b) the amount for which the co-owners are liable in respect of any such charge which is a standard community charge as it has effect for a chargeable financial year is to be calculated in accordance with section 14 of the Act (including any regulations made under section 14(7));

(c) the amount for which the co-owners are liable in respect of any such charge which is a collective community charge as it has effect for a chargeable year is to be calculated in accordance with section 15 of the Act;

(d) the co-owners shall be jointly and severally liable for the amount calculated in accordance with sub-paragraph (b) or (c); and

(e) section 16 or 17 of the Act shall have effect to make a spouse or manager of any of the co-owners jointly and severally liable also.

(3) There shall be different charges as regards each of the following–

(a) the period for which the co-ownership subsists (that is, for which the co-owners concerned are co-owners);

(b) any period for which one only of the co-owners has an interest in the building, part of a building or dwelling concerned, or is the owner of the caravan concerned; and

(c) any period for which there is a co-ownership as regards the property concerned but the participants of it do not correspond with those of the co-ownership mentioned in sub-paragraph (a) (whether because the number of members differs or because any of the personnel differs).

(4) Section 11(4) of the Act shall apply where different charges arise because of the operation of paragraph (3).

(5) If the other requirements mentioned in Class D or I (as the case may be) in regulation 62 are met, property shall be treated as falling in the class in question if the last of the co-owners subject to the charge concerned to have occupied the property on or before the day on which it was last occupied (construing those expressions in accordance with regulation 62(4) and (5)) satisfies the conditions described in sub-paragraphs (a) and (b) of the specification of class D.

(6) References to co-owners in this regulation include references to persons who together have an interest under a lease or underlease, and references to co-ownership shall be construed accordingly.

Co-owners: administration and enforcement

60.—(1) After paragraph 20 of Schedule 2 to the Act there is inserted–

"**21.** Where regulations dealing with co-owners are made under section 19 above, regulations under this Schedule may–

(a) include provision in relation to co-ownerships which is equivalent to that included under paragraphs 2 to 5 above in relation to other cases, with such modifications as the Secretary of State thinks fit, and

(b) modify, as the Secretary of State thinks fit, the application of regulations included under paragraphs 6 to 18 above as they have effect in relation to co-ownerships.".

(2) After paragraph 1(1)(e) of Schedule 4 to the Act there is inserted–

"(ee) any sum which has become payable under any provision included in regulations under paragraph 21(a) of that Schedule and has not been paid;".

(3) After Part VI of Schedule 4 to the Act there is inserted–

"PART VIA

CO-OWNERS

21A. This Part of this Schedule applies as regards the recovery of any sum falling within paragraph 1(1)(ee) above.

21B. Regulations under this Schedule may make, as regards the recovery of such a sum, provision equivalent to that included under Parts II to VI of this Schedule, subject to any modifications the Secretary of State thinks fit.".

Outstanding liabilities on death

61.—(1) This regulation applies where a person dies and at any time before his death–

(a) he was (or is alleged to have been) subject to a charging authority's community charge,

(b) he was (or is alleged to have been) liable to pay an amount under section 9 of the Act,

(c) he was (or is alleged to have been) liable, as spouse or manager, under section 16 or 17 of the Act, or

(d) a penalty was imposed on him under Schedule 3 to the Act.

(2) Where–

(a) before the deceased's death a sum has become payable by him under Part III or by way of relevant costs in respect of one of the matters mentioned in paragraph (1) but has not been paid, or

(b) after the deceased's death a sum would, but for his death (and whether or not on the service of a notice), become payable by him under Part III in respect of one of those matters,

his executor or administrator shall, subject to paragraph (3) and to the extent that it is not in excess of the deceased's liability under the Act (including relevant costs payable by him) in respect of the matter, be liable to pay the sum and may deduct out of the assets and effects of the deceased any payments made (or to be made).

(3) Where paragraph (2)(b) applies, the liability of the executor or administrator does not arise until the service on him of a notice requiring payment of the sum.

(4) Where before the deceased's death a sum in excess of his liability under the Act (including relevant costs payable by him) in respect of one of the matters mentioned in paragraph (1) has been paid (whether the excess arises because of his death or otherwise) and has not been repaid or credited under Part III, his executor or administrator shall be entitled to the sum.

(5) Costs are relevant costs for the purposes of paragraphs (2) and (4) if–

(a) an order or warrant (as the case may be) was made by the court in respect of them before the deceased's death under regulation 29(6)(b), 41(4)(b) or 44(3)(c)(ii), or in proceedings under regulation 49, or

(b) they are charges connected with distress which may be recovered pursuant to regulation 39(2)(b).

(6) A sum payable under paragraph (2) shall be enforceable in the administration of the deceased's estate as a debt of the deceased and accordingly–

(a) no liability order need be applied for in respect of it after the deceased's death under regulation 29, and

(b) the liability of the executor or administrator is a liability in his capacity as such.

(7) Regulation 52(1) and (2) applies to proceedings to enforce a liability arising under this regulation as it applies to proceedings under Part IV.

(8) The executor or administrator shall, until the completion of the administration of the deceased's estate, as regards any of the matters mentioned in paragraph (1) be treated as the deceased as respects the following provisions–

(a) regulation 3(2),

(b) regulation 5,

(c) regulation 9,

(d) regulation 10, and

(e) regulation 12;

and Schedule 3 to the Act (penalties) shall so far as relevant apply accordingly.

(9) But a notice given to the deceased under regulation 5(1) shall not have effect as a request which is made for the purposes of paragraph (8)(b) above until the executor or administrator is served with a copy of it.

(10) Insofar as is relevant to his liability under this regulation in the administration of the deceased's estate, the executor or administrator may institute, continue or withdraw proceedings (whether by way of appeal under section 23 of the Act or otherwise).

Standard community charge multipliers

62.—(1) The following are classes of property specified for the purposes of section

40(2) and (3) of the Act for which the standard community charge multiplier may not exceed 0–

Class A: unoccupied property which requires structural repair works to render it habitable, including unoccupied property with respect to which less than 6 months have elapsed since the day on which such repair works were substantially completed;

Class B: unoccupied property whose erection is not substantially completed, or which is in the course of structural alteration which has not been substantially completed, including unoccupied property with respect to which less than 6 months have elapsed since the day on which its erection or structural alteration was substantially completed;

Class C: unoccupied property with respect to which less than 3 months have elapsed since the relevant day;

Class D: unoccupied property with respect to which less than 12 months have elapsed since the day on which it was last occupied where–

(a) the person subject to the standard community charge arising by virtue of it is exempt from the personal community charge in consequence of the provisions of paragraph 8 or 9 of Schedule 1 to the Act; and

(b) he had his sole or main residence in the property immediately before he acquired his sole or main residence in the hospital, residential care home, nursing home, mental nursing home or hostel mentioned in paragraphs 8(1)(a) or 9(1)(a) of that Schedule, or he was detained as mentioned in paragraphs 8(1)(b) or (c) or 9(1)(b) of that Schedule (as the case may be);

Class E: unoccupied property where the person subject to the standard community charge arising by virtue of it is subject to the charge in his capacity as personal representative, and with respect to which either no grant of probate or of letters of administration has been made, or less than 3 months have elapsed since the day on which a grant of probate or of letters of administration was made;

Class F: property whose occupation is prohibited by law, or which is kept unoccupied by reason of action taken by or on behalf of the Crown or any local or public authority with a view to prohibiting its occupation or to acquiring it.

(2) The following are classes of property specified for the purposes of section 40(2) and (3) of the Act for which the standard community charge multiplier may not exceed 1–

Class G: caravans which do not fall into any of the foregoing classes;

Class H: property which does not fall into any of the foregoing classes and which, in consequence of conditions imposed on the grant of a planning permission under the Town and Country Planning Act 1971**(a)**, may not be occupied throughout the year.

(3) The following are classes of property specified for the purposes of section 40(2) and (3) of the Act (but for which no maximum standard community charge multiplier is specified under these Regulations)–

Class I: unoccupied property which does not fall into any of the foregoing classes and with respect to which 12 months or more have elapsed since the day on which it was last occupied, where the conditions described in sub-paragraphs (a) and (b) of the specification of class D are satisfied;

Class J: unoccupied property which does not fall into any of the foregoing classes, where the person subject to the standard community charge arising by virtue of it is subject to the charge in his capacity as personal representative, and with respect to which 3 months or more but less than 6 months have elapsed since the day on which a grant of probate or of letters of adminstration was made;

(a) 1971 c.78; section 29(1) was amended by the Housing and Planning Act 1986 (c.63), Schedule 11, paragraph 16.

Class K: unoccupied property which does not fall into any of the foregoing classes, where the person subject to the standard community charge arising by virtue of it is subject to the charge in his capacity as personal representative, and with respect to which 6 months or more but less than 12 months have elapsed since the day on which a grant of probate or of letters of administration was made;

Class L: unoccupied property which does not fall into any of the foregoing classes, where the person subject to the standard community charge arising by virtue of it is subject to the charge in his capacity as personal representative, and with respect to which 12 months or more have elapsed since the day on which a grant of probate or of letters of administration was made;

Class M: unoccupied property which does not fall into any of the foregoing classes, and with respect to which 3 months or more but less than 6 months have elapsed since the relevant day;

Class N: unoccupied property which does not fall into any of the foregoing classes, and with respect to which 6 months or more but less than 12 months have elapsed since the relevant day;

Class O: unoccupied property which does not fall into any of the foregoing classes, and with respect to which 12 months or more have elapsed since the relevant day;

Class P: property which does not fall into any of the foregoing classes.

(4) References in this regulation to property are references to the building, self-contained part of a building or caravan in respect of which the standard community charge concerned arises.

(5) Property is unoccupied at any time–

(a) for the purposes of classes D to F and I to L, if at the time no-one lives there; and

(b) for the purposes of classes A to C and M to O, if at the time no-one lives there and the property is substantially unfurnished.

(6) In this regulation "the relevant day" with respect to unoccupied property means the day on which the property concerned was last occupied (which is to be determined in accordance with paragraph (5)(b)), save that where property which was unoccupied becomes occupied on any day and becomes unoccupied again at the expiry of a period of less than 6 weeks beginning with that day, for the purposes of determining the relevant day (and only for that purpose) the property shall be treated as having remained unoccupied during that period; and the question whether a property was unoccupied, becomes occupied and becomes unoccupied again shall likewise be determined for that purpose in accordance with paragraph (5)(b).

Conditions for exemption of care workers

63.—(1) The conditions set out in paragraph (2) below are prescribed for the purposes of paragraph 10(1)(b) of Schedule 1 to the Act.

(2) The conditions are that–

(a) the person's employer with respect to the employment referred to in paragraph 10(1)(a) of that Schedule–

(i) is a public authority,

(ii) is a body established for charitable purposes only, or

(iii) is the other person, or one or more of the other persons, to whom care or support is provided under the employment, and was introduced to the person by a body established for charitable purposes only;

(b) the person is required to work under his contract of employment with that employer for at least 24 hours in each week providing the care or support;

(c) the person's salary or wages with respect to the hours he is so required to work do not exceed £25 a week; and

(d) the day falls within a period during which the person is resident in premises which are provided by or on behalf of that employer for the better performance of the person's duties under the employment.

(3) In paragraph (2)(a)(i) "public authority" means a local authority within the meaning of the Local Government Act 1972**(a)**, the Common Council of the City of London, the Council of the Isles of Scilly and the Crown.

9th March 1989

Nicholas Ridley
Secretary of State for the Environment

12th march 1989

Peter Walker
Secretary of State for Wales

SCHEDULE 1

Regulation 17(1)

PERSONAL AND STANDARD COMMUNITY CHARGE INSTALMENT SCHEME

PART I

PAYMENT OF THE AGGREGATE AMOUNT

1.—(1) This paragraph applies where the demand notice is issued on or before 31st December in the relevant year, but has effect subject to paragraph 3.

(2) The aggregate amount is to be payable in monthly instalments, the number of such instalments being 10 or, if less, the number of whole months remaining in the relevant year after the issue of the notice less one.

(3) The months in which the instalments are payable must be uninterrupted, but subject to that (and to paragraph 4) are to be such months in the relevant year as are specified in the notice; and the instalments are to be payable on such day in each month as is so specified.

(4) If the aggregate amount divided by the number of instalments gives an amount which is a multiple of 10 pence, the instalments shall be of that amount.

(5) If the aggregate amount so divided would not give such an amount, all but the first instalment shall be of an amount equal to A and the first instalment shall be of an amount equal to B, where–

$A=\frac{C}{D}$, rounded up or down (as the case may be) to the nearest multiple of 10 pence,

$B=C-((D-1)\times A)$,

C is equal to the aggregate amount, and

D is equal to the number of instalments to be paid.

2. Where the demand notice is issued between 1st January and 31st March in the relevant year, the aggregate amount is to be payable in a single instalment on such day as is specified in the notice.

3.—(1) If amounts calculated in accordance with paragraph 1 would produce an amount for an instalment of less than £5, the demand notice may require the aggregate amount to be paid–

(a) where the aggregate amount is less than £10, in a single instalment payable on such day as is specified in the notice, or

(b) where the aggregate amount is equal to or greater than £10, by a number of monthly instalments equal to the greatest whole number by which £5 can be multiplied to give a product which is less than or equal to the aggregate amount.

(2) The months in which the instalments under sub-paragraph (1)(b) are payable must be uninterrupted, but subject to that are to be such of the months in which, but for this paragraph, the instalments would have been payable under paragraph 1 as are specified in the demand notice; and the instalments are to be payable on such day in each month as is so specified.

(a) 1972 c.70; *see* section 270(1).

(3) Paragraph 1(4) and (5) applies to instalments under sub-paragraph (1)(b) as it applies to instalments under paragraph 1(2).

4. The demand notice shall be issued at least 14 days before the day on which the first instalment is due under it.

5. In this Part "the aggregate amount" means the amount referred to in regulation 16(3).

PART II

CESSATION AND ADJUSTMENT OF INSTALMENTS

6.—(1) This paragraph applies where the demand notice has been served on a chargeable person by a charging authority and after its issue the person is shown in the charging authority's community charges register as ceasing to be subject in the period to which the notice relates to the community charge concerned.

(2) Subject to sub-paragraphs (5) and (6), no payments of instalments falling due after the relevant day are payable under the notice.

(3) The charging authority shall on the relevant day or as soon as practicable after that day serve a notice on the chargeable person stating the amount of his liability in respect of the charge to which the demand notice relates as it has effect for the period in the relevant year up to the day on which he is shown as ceasing to be subject to the charge.

(4) If the amount stated under sub-paragraph (3) is less than the aggregate amount of any instalments which have fallen due on or before the relevant day, the difference shall go in the first instance to discharge any liability to pay the instalments (to the extent that they remain unpaid); and any residual overpayment–

(a) shall be repaid if the chargeable person so requires, or

(b) in any other case shall (as the charging authority determines) either be repaid or credited against any subsequent liability of the person to make a payment in respect of any community charge of the authority.

(5) If the amount stated under sub-paragraph (3) is greater than the aggregate amount of any instalments which have fallen due on or before the relevant day, the difference between the two shall be due from the chargeable person to the charging authority on the expiry of such period (being not less than 14 days) after the day of issue of the notice served under that sub-paragraph as is specified in it.

(6) If this paragraph applies in relation to a demand notice, and after the person has been shown in the register as ceasing to be subject to the charge he is shown as becoming subject again to the same charge in the relevant year, a further notice shall be served on the chargeable person requiring payments in respect of the charge as it has effect for the period in the year after he is shown as becoming so subject; and regulations 15 to 17, 19 and 20 (and, so far as applicable, this Schedule) shall apply to the further notice with respect to that period, and the sums payable by the chargeable person with respect to that period, as if it were a demand notice given in relation to a different charge.

(7) In this paragraph "the relevant day" means the day on which the person ceases to be subject to the charge or, if later, the day on which the entry on the register relating to the cessation is made.

7.—(1) This paragraph applies where the demand notice has been served on a chargeable person by a charging authority, the event mentioned in paragraph 6(1) has not occurred in relation to the notice, and

(a) the notice was so served on the understanding or assumption that on any day in the period to which the notice relates the person is not or will not be undertaking a full-time course of education, and after the issue of the notice the community charges register shows that person as undertaking such a course on that day;

(b) the notice was so served on the understanding or assumption that on any day in the period to which the notice relates the person is or will be undertaking a full-time course of education, and after the issue of the notice the community charges register shows that person as not undertaking such a course on that day;

(c) the notice was so served by reference to an amount set by the charging authority for its personal community charge for the relevant year and after the issue of the notice the authority sets a different amount for the charge in substitution for that amount under section 34 or 35 of the Act;

(d) the notice was so served in relation to a standard community charge, and the property by virtue of which the person is shown as subject or becoming subject to the charge is shown in the register as falling on any day in the period to which the notice relates into a class specified under regulation 62 for which the standard community charge multiplier is greater or less than that by reference to which the notice was issued;

(e) the notice was so served on the understanding or assumption that, on any day in the period to which the notice relates, the person is or will be entitled to a reduction in the amount he is liable to pay in respect of the community charge concerned under regulations made under section 31A(1) of the Social Security Act 1986, and he is allowed a larger or smaller reduction than had been so assumed;

(f) the notice was so served on the understanding or assumption that, on any day in the period to which the notice relates, the person is not or will not be entitled to a reduction in the amount he is liable to pay in respect of the community charge concerned under regulations made under section 31A(1) of that Act, and he is allowed such a reduction; or

(g) by virtue of regulations made under section 31D(1) to (3) of that Act a liability falls to be met by the person in respect of the community charge concerned in the manner mentioned in subsection (3)(b) of that section for which provision was not made in making the calculation under regulation 16(3) with respect to the notice.

(2) The charging authority shall on or as soon as practicable after the relevant day–

(a) serve a notice on the chargeable person which is to state the amount of the revised estimate mentioned in sub-paragraph (3), and

(b) adjust the instalments (if any) payable on or after the adjustment day ("the remaining instalments") so that they accord with the amounts mentioned in sub-paragraph (4).

(3) The revised estimate is the revised estimate of the charging authority of the amount that the person is liable to pay in respect of the charge as it has effect for the relevant year, made on the assumptions mentioned in regulation 16(3) and as if the notice mentioned in that provision were the notice referred to in sub-paragraph (2) above.

(4) The aggregate amount of the remaining instalments payable shall be equal to the amount by which the revised estimate mentioned in sub-paragraph (3) exceeds the aggregate amount of the instalments payable under the demand notice before the adjustment day; and the amount of each remaining instalment (if there are more than one) shall be calculated in accordance with paragraph 1(4) and (5) as if references in those provisions to the aggregate amount and to instalments were references to the aggregate amount of the remaining instalments and to the remaining instalments respectively.

(5) If the revised estimate mentioned in sub-paragraph (3) exceeds the aggregate amount of the instalments payable under the demand notice before the adjustment day, but no instalments are payable under it on or after that day, the amount of the excess shall be due from the chargeable person to the charging authority in a single instalment on the expiry of such period (being not less than 14 days) after the day of issue of the notice served under sub-paragraph (2) as is specified in it; and if in any case the revised estimate is less than the aggregate amount of the instalments payable before the adjustment day, any overpayment–

(a) shall be repaid if the chargeable person so requires, or

(b) in any other case shall (as the charging authority determines) either be repaid or credited against any subsequent liability of the person to make a payment in respect of any community charge of the authority.

(6) Where a notice has been given under sub-paragraph (2), in the operation of this paragraph as respects any further notice that may fall to be given under it, references in this paragraph to the demand notice and to amounts in respect of instalments payable under it shall be construed (so far as the context permits) as references to the demand notice, and amounts in respect of instalments payable under the notice, as from time to time previously adjusted under this paragraph; and in calculating the aggregate amount of instalments payable under a demand notice before the adjustment day for the purposes of sub-paragraphs (4) and (5) in consequence of the making of a revised estimate under sub-paragraph (3), there shall not count as so payable any amount in respect of such instalments which has fallen to be repaid (or credited) under section 36(2) of the Act or (on the occasion of the making of a previous revised estimate under sub-paragraph (3)) under sub-paragraph (5) above.

(7) In this paragraph–

"the adjustment day" means the day 14 days after the day the notice served under sub-paragraph (2) is issued; and

"the relevant day" means the day with respect to which the understanding or assumption mentioned in sub-paragraph (1)(a), (b), (e) or (f) is wrong, the day the amount set in substitution mentioned in sub-paragraph (1)(c) is so set, the day the property falls into the class mentioned in sub-paragraph (1)(d), or the day on which the liability to be met in the manner mentioned in sub-paragraph (1)(g) first so falls to be met (as the case may be).

8. More than one adjustment of amounts paid or payable under a demand notice may be made under this Part as the circumstances require.

Regulation 18

SCHEDULE 2

COLLECTIVE COMMUNITY CHARGES

PART I

RECORDS, RETURNS AND PAYMENTS

1.—(1) With respect to the collective community charge of a charging authority, the chargeable person shown in the community charges register of the authority as subject to it shall compile records containing the following information–

(a) the names of all individuals resident in the designated dwelling by virtue of which the charge arises who are qualifying individuals for the purposes of section 9 of the Act,

(b) the periods during which they are so resident, and

(c) the amounts payable by way of contribution for each day by the individuals.

(2) A record shall be retained until the expiry of the period of one year after the end of the contribution period to which it relates.

(3) The chargeable person shall allow the charging authority concerned or its registration officer to inspect the records within 5 days of the day on which he is requested by it or him (as the case may be) by notice in writing to do so.

(4) The chargeable person shall send a copy of the records retained by him to the charging authority concerned or to its registration officer within 21 days of the day on which he is requested by it or him (as the case may be) by notice in writing to do so.

2.—(1) A chargeable person shall submit a return for every return period in accordance with this paragraph for any chargeable financial year in relation to which he has been served with a demand notice issued with respect to a collective community charge.

(2) Each return is to state every amount that is or is to become payable by way of contribution under section 9 of the Act for each day falling within the return period, and is to be submitted to the charging authority which issued the demand notice.

(3) For a demand notice which is issued before or in April in the relevant year, each month in the year is a return period.

(4) For a demand notice which is issued after April in the relevant year but during that year–

(a) the first return period is to be the period up to the end of the month preceding that in which the notice was issued, and

(b) every month in the year after the first return period is itself to be a return period.

(5) For a demand notice which is issued after the relevant year, the return period is to be the relevant year.

(6) Returns relating to a return period for a chargeable financial year are to be submitted within 14 days of the day of service of the demand notice or of the expiry of the return period, whichever is the later.

3.—(1) Unless the charging authority and chargeable person have agreed otherwise under sub-paragraphs (4) and (5), at the same time that a return is submitted under paragraph 2 the chargeable person shall pay an instalment to the charging authority to which the return is submitted of an amount equal to the amount found by deducting amount B from amount A.

(2) Amount A is the total of all amounts which are or are to become payable to the chargeable person by way of contribution under section 9 of the Act for each day which falls within the return period to which the return which has been submitted relates.

(3) Amount B is an amount equal to the relevant proportion of amount A; and "the relevant proportion" for this purpose is the proportion specified in or (as the case may be) from time to time prescribed under section 15(4) of the Act in relation to the return period.

(4) A charging authority and a chargeable person may agree that the amount the person is liable to pay to the authority in respect of a collective community charge should be paid in such manner as is provided in the agreement, rather than in accordance with sub-paragraph (1).

(5) Such an agreement may be entered into either before or after the demand notice relating to the relevant year is issued; and if it is entered into after the demand notice has been issued, it may make provision dealing with the treatment for the purposes of the agreement of any sums paid in accordance with sub-paragraph (1) before it was entered into.

4.—(1) This paragraph applies where, after the service of a demand notice issued with respect to a collective community charge, a charging authority sets an amount for its personal community charge for the relevant year ("the new amount") in substitution for another amount ("the old amount") under section 34 or 35 of the Act which differs from the old amount.

(2) The charging authority shall as soon as practicable serve a notice on the chargeable person stating the new amount.

(3) If the new amount is greater than the old amount, any difference between the amount of an instalment paid under paragraph 3 before the service of the notice under sub-paragraph (2) and which was calculated by reference to the old amount, and the amount which, in consequence of the setting of the new amount, is in fact payable under that paragraph in respect of the instalment shall (subject to the terms of any agreement under paragraph 3(4) and (5)) be due from the chargeable person to the charging authority in a single instalment on the expiry of such period (being not less than 14 days) after the day of issue of the notice served under sub-paragraph (2) as is specified in it.

PART II

CONTRIBUTIONS

5.—(1) As soon as practicable after a dwelling has been designated as a designated dwelling and the chargeable person has been served with a demand notice in respect of his collective community charge specifying the amount of the charging authority's personal community charge, the chargeable person shall inform the contributors then resident in it that it has been designated, and supply them with information as to the days on which payments are due under paragraph 6, together with the amounts which are (or will be) so payable.

(2) Before or as soon as practicable after the contributor has become resident in a dwelling which has been designated as a designated dwelling, the chargeable person shall inform him that it is a designated dwelling, and supply him with information as to the days on which payments are due under paragraph 6, together with the amounts which are (or will be) so payable.

(3) As soon as practicable after the chargeable person has been served with a demand notice in respect of his collective community charge indicating that a charging authority has set a personal community charge for a chargeable financial year which differs from that for the previous year, he shall supply the contributors who have been supplied with information under sub-paragraph (1) or (2) with information as to the new amounts which are (or will be) payable under paragraph 6.

6.—(1) If the contributor is liable to make periodical payments of rent or other consideration in respect of his residence in the designated dwelling at intervals of a month or less, a payment on account of his liability under section 9 of the Act shall become due from him to the chargeable person on each day on which the rent or other consideration falls due during the contribution period ("a rent day"); and the payment due on a rent day shall relate to the contributions for such period of days falling after the rent day (but before the next rent day) or on or before the rent day as is determined by the chargeable person.

(2) If the contributor is not liable to make such periodical payments of rent or other consideration at the intervals mentioned in sub-paragraph (1), a periodical payment on account of his liability under section 9 of the Act shall become due from him to the chargeable person on such days during the contribution period, with such interval (not being greater than a month) between those days, as is determined by the chargeable person ("payment days"); and the payment due on a payment day shall relate to the contributions for such period of days falling after the payment day (but ending before the next payment day) or on or before the payment day as is determined by the chargeable person.

(3) The amount due in respect of a period determined under sub-paragraph (1) or (2) ("a payment period")–

(a) as regards any days in the period before the rent day or payment day to which the payment period relates, is the aggregate of the contributions payable by the contributor under section 9 of the Act for those days; and

(b) as regards any days in the period on or after the rent day or payment day to which the payment period relates, is the estimate of the chargeable person of the aggregate of the contributions payable by the contributor under section 9 of the Act for those days, made (subject to paragraph 7(2)) on the assumptions that on those days the chargeable person will remain subject to the charge and the conditions mentioned in subsection (1) of that section will be fulfilled.

7.—(1) When the contribution period ends, the chargeable person shall as soon as practicable calculate the liability of the contributor under section 9 of the Act in relation to that period and supply him with information as to the amount of the liability; and any amount paid by the contributor under this Part with respect to the period in excess of his liability under that section shall be repaid to him, and any amount paid by him which is less than his liability under that section shall be recoverable by the chargeable person from him.

(2) If it appears to the chargeable person (whether from information supplied by the contributor or otherwise) that in any payment period the contribution period will end, the amount payable under paragraph 6 in relation to the payment period shall, if the contributor so requires, be calculated (so far as applicable) on the assumption that it will so end, and not on the assumptions mentioned in paragraph 6(3)(b).

(3) If, by the time that an estimate or calculation under paragraph 6(3) falls to be made, the chargeable person has not been served with a demand notice indicating (nor otherwise notified by the charging authority as to) the amount of the authority's personal community charge for a chargeable financial year by reference to which the estimate or calculation so falls to be made, but he was served with a demand notice with respect to the previous chargeable financial year–

(a) until the notice is served or he is otherwise notified of the amount of the charge, payments under paragraph 6 shall be calculated by reference to the previous year's personal community charge; and

(b) as soon as the notice is served or he is otherwise so notified, such adjustments by way of repayments by the chargeable person or further payments by the contributor (as the case may be) with respect to past payments so calculated shall be made as will secure that the amounts paid represent the contributions due for the days to which those payments relate.

(4) If the charging authority sets an amount for its personal community charge under section 34 or 35 of the Act in substitution for an amount previously set by it, the chargeable person shall, on being notified of that, revise the information supplied to the contributors under paragraph 5 accordingly; and, such adjustments by way of repayments by the chargeable person or further payments by the contributor (as the case may be) with respect to past payments calculated by reference to the amount previously set but which relate to contributions which fall to be calculated by reference to the amount set in substitution shall be made as will secure that the amounts paid represent the contributions due for the days to which those payments relate.

8. The chargeable person shall, as soon as practicable after any payment by way of contribution is made by the contributor pursuant to this Part, supply him with a receipt for the payment.

9. In this Part "the chargeable person", "the contribution period" and "the contributor" have (subject to regulation 13(8)) the same meaning as in paragraph 4 of Schedule 2 to the Act.

SCHEDULE 3

Regulations 30(1) and 42(1)

ENFORCEMENT: PRESCRIBED FORMS

FORM A

LIABILITY ORDER IN RESPECT OF A COMMUNITY CHARGE

Regulation 29 of the Community Charges (Administration and Enforcement) Regulations 1989

.... Magistrates' Court

Date:

Defendant:

Address:

On the complaint of [ ] that the sum of [ ] is due from the defendant to the complainant under Part III of the Community Charges (Administration and Enforcement) Regulations 1989 and is outstanding, it is adjudged that the defendant is liable to pay the aggregate amount specified below, and it is ordered that that amount may be enforced in the manner mentioned in Part IV of those Regulations accordingly.

Sum payable and outstanding:

Costs of complainant:

Aggregate amount in respect of which the liability order is made:

Justice of the Peace

[*or* by order of the Court Clerk of the Court]

FORM B

LIABILITY ORDER IN RESPECT OF A COMMUNITY CHARGE

Regulation 29 of the Community Charges (Administration and Enforcement) Regulations 1989

.... Magistrates' Court

Date:

On the complaint of [ ] that the sums specified in the Table below are due under Part III of the Community Charges (Administration and Enforcement) Regulations 1989 from the defendants so specified to the complainant and are outstanding, it is adjudged that the defendants are liable to pay the aggregate amounts specified in respect of them in the Table, and it is ordered that those amounts may be enforced in the manner mentioned in Part IV of those Regulations accordingly.

TABLE

Name and address of defendant	*Sum payable and outstanding*	*Costs of complainant*	*Aggregate amount in respect of which the liability order is made with respect to the defendant.*

Justice of the Peace

[*or* by order of the Court Clerk of the Court]

FORM C

WARRANT OF COMMITMENT

Regulation 41 of the Community Charges (Administration and Enforcement) Regulations 1989

.... Magistrates' Court

Date:

Debtor:

Address:

A liability order ("the order") was made in respect of the debtor by the [ ] Magistrates' Court on [ ] under regulation 29 of the Community Charges (Administration and Enforcement) Regulations 1989 ("the Regulations").

The court is satisfied–

(i) that the [(*name of charging authority*)] ("the authority") sought under regulation 39 of the Regulations to levy by distress the amount then outstanding in respect of which the order was made of [ ], together with charges determined in accordance with Schedule 5 to the Regulations of [ ];

(ii) that no (or insufficient) goods of the debtor can be found by the authority on which to levy that amount; and

(iii) having inquired in the debtor's presence as to his means and as to whether the failure to pay which led to the order being made against him was due to his wilful refusal or culpable neglect, that it was due to such wilful refusal or culpable neglect.

The decision of the court is that the debtor be [committed to prison] [detained] for [ ] unless the aggregate amount mentioned below in respect of which this warrant is made is sooner paid.*

This warrant is made in respect of–

Amount outstanding (including charges) in respect of which distress was sought:

Costs of commitment of the authority:

Aggregate amount:

And you [(*name of person or persons to whom warrant is directed*)] are hereby required to take the debtor and convey him to [(*name of prison or place of detention*)] and there deliver the debtor to the [governor] [officer in charge] thereof; and you, the [governor] [officer in charge], to receive the debtor into your custody and keep the debtor for [(*period of imprisonment*)] from the debtor's arrest under this warrant or until the debtor be sooner discharged in due course of law.

Justice of the Peace

[*or* by order of the Court Clerk of the Court].

**Note:* The period of imprisonment will be reduced as provided by regulation 41(7)(b) of the Regulations if part payment is made of the aggregate amount.

SCHEDULE 4

Regulation 33

DEDUCTIONS TO BE MADE UNDER ATTACHMENT OF EARNINGS ORDER

TABLE A

DEDUCTIONS FROM WEEKLY EARNINGS

(1) *Net earnings*	(2) *Deduction*
Not exceeding £35	Nil
Exceeding £35 but not exceeding £55	£1
Exceeding £55 but not exceeding £65	£2
Exceeding £65 but not exceeding £75	£3
Exceeding £75 but not exceeding £80	£4
Exceeding £80 but not exceeding £85	£5
Exceeding £85 but not exceeding £90	£6
Exceeding £90 but not exceeding £95	£7
Exceeding £95 but not exceeding £100	£8
Exceeding £100 but not exceeding £110	£9
Exceeding £110 but not exceeding £120	£11
Exceeding £120 but not exceeding £130	£12
Exceeding £130 but not exceeding £140	£14
Exceeding £140 but not exceeding £150	£15
Exceeding £150 but not exceeding £160	£18
Exceeding £160 but not exceeding £170	£20
Exceeding £170 but not exceeding £180	£23
Exceeding £180 but not exceeding £190	£25
Exceeding £190 but not exceeding £200	£28
Exceeding £200 but not exceeding £220	£35
Exceeding £220 but not exceeding £240	£42
Exceeding £240 but not exceeding £260	£50
Exceeding £260 but not exceeding £280	£59
Exceeding £280 but not exceeding £300	£68
Exceeding £300	£68 in respect of the first £300 plus 50 per cent of the remainder.

TABLE B

DEDUCTIONS FROM MONTHLY EARNINGS

(1) *Net earnings*	(2) *Deduction*
Not exceeding £152	Nil
Exceeding £152 but not exceeding £220	£5
Exceeding £220 but not exceeding £260	£8
Exceeding £260 but not exceeding £280	£11
Exceeding £280 but not exceeding £300	£14
Exceeding £300 but not exceeding £320	£18
Exceeding £320 but not exceeding £340	£21
Exceeding £340 but not exceeding £360	£24
Exceeding £360 but not exceeding £380	£27
Exceeding £380 but not exceeding £400	£30
Exceeding £400 but not exceeding £440	£36
Exceeding £440 but not exceeding £480	£42
Exceeding £480 but not exceeding £520	£48
Exceeding £520 but not exceeding £560	£54
Exceeding £560 but not exceeding £600	£60
Exceeding £600 but not exceeding £640	£66
Exceeding £640 but not exceeding £680	£75
Exceeding £680 but not exceeding £720	£85
Exceeding £720 but not exceeding £760	£95
Exceeding £760 but not exceeding £800	£105
Exceeding £800 but not exceeding £900	£135
Exceeding £900 but not exceeding £1000	£170
Exceeding £1000 but not exceeding £1100	£207
Exceeding £1100 but not exceeding £1200	£252
Exceeding £1200 but not exceeding £1300	£297
Exceeding £1300	£297 in respect of the first £1300 plus 50 per cent of the remainder.

TABLE C

DEDUCTIONS BASED ON DAILY EARNINGS

(1) *Net earnings*	(2) *Deduction*
Not exceeding £5	Nil
Exceeding £5 but not exceeding £9	£0.20
Exceeding £9 but not exceeding £11	£0.50
Exceeding £11 but not exceeding £13	£1.00
Exceeding £13 but not exceeding £15	£1.20
Exceeding £15 but not exceeding £17	£1.40
Exceeding £17 but not exceeding £19	£1.70
Exceeding £19 but not exceeding £21	£2.10
Exceeding £21 but not exceeding £23	£2.50
Exceeding £23 but not exceeding £25	£3.00
Exceeding £25 but not exceeding £27	£3.60
Exceeding £27 but not exceeding £30	£4.50
Exceeding £30 but not exceeding £33	£5.30
Exceeding £33 but not exceeding £36	£6.70
Exceeding £36 but not exceeding £39	£8.00
Exceeding £39 but not exceeding £42	£9.40
Exceeding £42	£9.40 in respect of the first £42 plus 50 per cent of the remainder.

Regulation 39(2)(b)

SCHEDULE 5

CHARGES CONNECTED WITH DISTRESS

1. The sum in respect of charges connected with the distress which may be aggregated under regulation 39(2) shall be as set out in the following Table–

	(1) *Matter connected with distress*	(2) *Charge*
A	For making a visit to premises with a view to levying distress (whether the levy is made or not):	Reasonable costs and fees incurred, but not exceeding an amount which, when aggregated with charges under this head for any previous visits made with a view to levying distress in relation to an amount in respect of which the liability order concerned was made, is not greater than the relevant amount calculated under paragraph 2(1) with respect to the visit.
B	For levying distress:	An amount (if any) which, when aggregated with charges under head A for any visits made with a view to levying distress in relation to an amount in respect of which the liability order concerned was made, is equal to the relevant amount calculated under paragraph 2(1) with respect to the levy.
C	For the removal and storage of goods for the purposes of sale:	Reasonable costs and fees incurred.
D	For the possession of goods as described in paragraph 2(3)–	
	(i) for close possession (the man in possession to provide his own board):	£4.50 per day.
	(ii) for walking possession:	45p per day.
E	For appraisement of an item distrained, at the request in writing of the debtor:	Reasonable fees and expenses of the broker appraising.
F	For other expenses of, and commission on, a sale by auction–	
	(i) where the sale is held on the auctioneer's premises:	The auctioneer's commission fee and out-of-pocket expenses (but not exceeding in aggregate 15 per cent. of the sum realised), together with reasonable costs and fees incurred in respect of advertising.
	(ii) where the sale is held on the debtor's premises:	The auctioneer's commission fee (but not exceeding 7½ per cent. of the sum realised), together with the auctioneer's out-of-pocket expenses and reasonable costs and fees incurred in respect of advertising.
G	For other expenses incurred in connection with a proposed sale where there is no buyer in relation to it:	Reasonable costs and fees incurred.

2.—(1) In heads A and B of the Table to paragraph 1, "the relevant amount" with respect to a visit or a levy means–

(a) where the sum due at the time of the visit or of the levy (as the case may be) does not exceed £100, £12.50,

(b) where the sum due at the time of the visit or of the levy (as the case may be) exceeds that amount, 12½ per cent. on the first £100 of the sum due, 4 per cent. on the next £400, 2½ per cent. on the next £1,500, 1 per cent. on the next £8,000 and ¼ per cent. on any additional sum;

and the sum due at any time for these purposes means so much of the amount in respect of which the liability order concerned was made as is outstanding at the time.

(2) Where a charge has arisen under head B with respect to an amount, no further charge may be aggregated under heads A or B in respect of that amount.

(3) An authority takes close or walking possession of goods for the purposes of head D of the Table to paragraph 1 if it takes such possession in pursuance of an agreement which is made at the time that the distress is levied and which (without prejudice to such other terms as may be agreed) is expressed to the effect that, in consideration of the authority not immediately removing the goods distrained upon from the premises occupied by the debtor and delaying its sale of the goods, the authority may remove and sell the goods after a later specified date if the debtor has not by then paid the amount distrained for (including charges under this Schedule); and an authority is in close possession of goods on any day for these purposes if during the greater part of the day a person is left on the premises in physical possession of the goods on behalf of the authority under such an agreement.

3.—(1) Where the calculation under this Schedule of a percentage of a sum results in an amount containing a fraction of a pound, that fraction shall be reckoned as a whole pound.

(2) In the case of dispute as to any charge under this Schedule, the amount of the charge shall be taxed.

(3) Such a taxation shall be carried out by the registrar of the county court for the district in which the distress is or is intended to be levied, and he may give such directions as to the costs of the taxation as he thinks fit; and any such costs directed to be paid by the debtor to the charging authority shall be added to the sum which may be aggregated under regulation 39(2).

(4) References in the Table to paragraph 1 to costs, fees and expenses include references to amounts payable by way of value added tax with respect to the supply of goods or services to which the costs, fees and expenses relate.

EXPLANATORY NOTE

(This note is not part of the Regulations)

These Regulations, which are made under Parts I and II of the Local Government Finance Act 1988, make provision for the administration and enforcement of community charges arising under that Act and related matters.

Regulation 2, in Part I, applies section 233 of the Local Government Act 1972 to the service of notices by the Common Council of the City of London or its officers under the Regulations.

Regulations 3 to 6, in Part II, are concerned with the giving and obtaining of information for the purposes of the compilation and maintenance of community charges registers. They place a duty on individuals to inform the appropriate registration officer accordingly if they have reason to believe that they are or have been subject to a community charge, or that an item in the register concerning them contains an error, is incomplete or not up-to-date (regulation 3); and registration officers are empowered to request information from responsible individuals and certain other individuals (regulations 4 and 5), and from certain public bodies (regulation 6). Regulation 7 enables the Secretary of State to request information from registration officers, and regulation 8 permits charging authorities to use information (not being information obtained in their capacity as police authority) in the exercise of their functions under Part I of the Act. Regulation 9 requires a charging authority to send a copy of any entry or amended entry made in the register to the chargeable person, and regulation 10 permits a chargeable person to inspect an entry in the register relating to the charge to which he is subject.

Regulation 11 requires a charging authority to compile and maintain for public inspection an extract of the register and a list of buildings designated for the purposes of the collective community charge. Regulation 12 allows a person liable to contribute to the collective community charge payable by a chargeable person to inspect records received by the charging authority from the chargeable person.

Part III (regulations 13 to 26) is principally concerned with the billing of persons subject to community charges. It requires, amongst other matters, charging authorities to serve demand notices each year on chargeable persons (regulations 14 to 19) identifying the payments to be made in respect of community charges, and provides for certain of such payments to be payable by instalments during the year (Schedules 1 and 2). Schedule 2 (dealing with the collective community charge) also makes provision for the keeping of records, the making of returns, the payment of contributions, and the supply of information and receipts to contributors. Where a person fails to pay an instalment or submit a return in accordance with Schedule 1 or 2, in certain cases the unpaid balance of the charging authority's estimate of the chargeable amount for the year concerned will become payable immediately (regulations 20 and 21).

Regulations 22 and 23 provide for the billing of spouses or managers who are jointly and severally liable for any amount payable by a chargeable person and which has not been paid, and regulations 24 to 26 make provision for the collection of penalties imposed under Schedule 3 of the Act, restrict the grounds of appeal to valuation and community charge tribunals with respect to estimates, and require the final adjustment of amounts payable under notices given under the Regulations.

Part IV (regulations 27 to 52) is concerned with the enforcement of sums due under Part III. Amounts payable to a charging authority which are unpaid are recoverable under a liability order made by the magistrates' court (regulations 28 to 30), following the making of which the charging authority may request certain information of the debtor as to his employment or income (regulation 31), make an attachment of earnings order (regulations 32 to 38 and Schedule 4), levy distress (regulation 39 and Schedule 5), apply for the commitment of the debtor to prison if there are insufficient goods on which to make a levy (regulations 41 and 42), prove the debt in insolvency (regulation 43), or (in the case of a collective community charge) apply for a charging order (regulations 44 and 45). Regulation 48 applies the relevant provisions with modifications to cases of joint and several liability. Amounts payable by way of collective community charge contribution or of repayment are recoverable in a court of competent jurisdiction (regulations 49 and 50).

Regulation 51 makes provision for offences in the event of a failure of the debtor to supply information, or of an employer of his to comply with an attachment of earnings order or to provide certain information relevant to the order (or to deductions under it) in accordance with the Regulations. Regulation 52 precludes matters which can be raised by way of appeal to a valuation and community charge tribunal being raised in proceedings for recovery under Part IV, and provides for the case where the amounts required under a notice given under Part III are adjusted after a liability order has been made.

Regulation 54 contains rules for ascertaining what is to be treated as the greater or greatest part of premises, a building or a caravan for the purposes of establishing in which authority's area they are to be treated as situated where they are situated in more than one such area. Regulations 55 to 57 determine in which part of a charging authority's area a building, a residence consisting of premises, or a caravan is to be treated as situated where a charging authority has set different personal community charges for different parts of its area.

Part VI (regulations 58 to 63) is concerned with miscellaneous matters. It prescribes a description of dwelling for the purposes of section 5(3)(d) of the Act (regulation 58), and provides for cases where co-owners would otherwise be subject to different standard or collective community charges, so that amongst other matters, they are made jointly subject to a single charge (regulations 59 and 60). It makes provision for the enforcement of outstanding liabilities and other aspects of administration with respect to community charges, collective community charge contributions or penalties which remain outstanding on death (regulation 61), and regulation 62 specifies classes of property in relation to the setting of standard community charge multipliers under section 40 of the Act and maximum levels of multiplier with respect to certain of those classes.

Regulation 63 prescribes conditions which are to be fulfilled in order that a care worker may be exempt from the personal community charge.

STATUTORY INSTRUMENTS

1989 No. 439

COMMUNITY CHARGES, ENGLAND AND WALES

The Valuation and Community Charge Tribunals Regulations 1989

Made - - - -	*12th March 1989*
Laid before Parliament	*17th March 1989*
Coming into force	
for the purposes of regulations 4 to 8 and 11	*7th April 1989*
for all other purposes	*1st May 1989*

ARRANGEMENT OF REGULATIONS

PART I: GENERAL

PART II: ESTABLISHMENT OF TRIBUNALS

PART III: ADMINISTRATION

PART IV: COMMUNITY CHARGE APPEALS

The Secretary of State for the Environment as respects England and the Secretary of State for Wales as respects Wales, in exercise of the powers conferred on them by sections 143(2) and 146(6) of and paragraphs 1, 4 to 8, 11, 12 and 14 to 16 of Schedule 11 to the Local Government Finance Act 1988(**a**), and of all other powers enabling them in that behalf, and after consultation with the Council on Tribunals as required by section 10 of the Tribunals and Inquiries Act 1971(**b**) hereby make the following Regulations:

PART I
GENERAL

Citation and commencement

1. These Regulations may be cited as the Valuation and Community Charge Tribunals Regulations 1989 and shall come into force for the purposes of regulations 4 to 8 and 11 on 7th April 1989, and for all other purposes on 1st May 1989.

Interpretation

2.—(1) In these Regulations–

"the Act" means the Local Government Finance Act 1988;

"appointing body", in relation to any member, or any vacancy for a member, means the body which in accordance with regulation 4 had the power to appoint that

(**a**) 1988 c.41.
(**b**) 1971 c.62. Valuation and community charge tribunals were added to Schedule 1 to the 1971 Act by paragraph 41 of Schedule 12 to the 1988 Act.

member or has the power to fill that vacancy;

"area", in relation to a tribunal, unless the context otherwise requires, means the area for which it is established by regulation 3;

"chairman", in relation to a tribunal, means a person appointed to the position of chairman under regulation 8;

"clerk" means the clerk of the tribunal appointed in pursuance of regulation 11;

"establishment date", in accordance with regulation 3, means 1st May 1989;

"local valuation panel" means a local valuation panel established for the purposes of section 88 of the General Rate Act 1967(**a**);

"member" means a member of a tribunal;

"operative date" means 7th April 1989;

"president", in relation to a tribunal, means the president of that tribunal appointed under regulation 7; and

"tribunal", subject to regulation 15, means a tribunal established by regulation 3.

(2) In these Regulations a reference to a numbered section, unless the context otherwise requires, is a reference to the section so numbered in the Act.

(3) Any notice which is by virtue of any provision of these Regulations to be served on any person may be served by post.

PART II
ESTABLISHMENT OF TRIBUNALS

Establishment of tribunals

3. On 1st May 1989 there shall be established a valuation and community charge tribunal for each of the areas ascertained in accordance with column 1 of Schedule 1; and each tribunal shall be known by the name ascertained in accordance with column 2 with the addition of the words "Valuation and Community Charge Tribunal".

Membership

4.—(1) The Secretary of State shall determine the number of members of each tribunal, which where there is more than one appointing body provided in relation to that tribunal under paragraph (2) shall be a multiple of the number of those bodies.

(2) The members of each tribunal named in column 2 of Schedule 1 shall, subject to paragraphs (3) and (4), be appointed by the body or bodies specified in relation to that tribunal in column 3.

(3) Where there is more than one body specified as mentioned in paragraph (2)–

(a) the appointments shall be made by each body in equal proportions, and

(b) where the effect of a determination under paragraph (1) is to reduce the numbers of members of a tribunal, the number of members to be appointed by each body shall be reduced equally.

(4) Each person who immediately before the establishment date is a member of a local valuation panel and who has held office as such for more than one month shall on that date become a member of the tribunal established for the area for which that panel was constituted, and shall hold office subject to regulation 6 as if the period of his membership of the panel had been specified under paragraph (1) of that regulation.

(5) A person who becomes a member as provided by paragraph (4) shall be treated for the purposes of these Regulations as having been appointed by the body which appointed him a member of the local valuation panel.

Appointment of members

5.—(1) Where at the expiry of one week from the operative date or three months from a vacancy occurring, as the case may be, an appointing body has failed to make an appointment in accordance with regulation 4, that appointment may be made by the

(**a**) 1967 c.9.

Secretary of State after consultation with the president or, before the first appointment of a president, with the chairman of the local valuation panel for the area of the tribunal.

(2) No appointment under regulation 4(2) shall be valid if its effect would be that the number of members of the tribunal appointed by that body who are members of a charging authority exceeded the number equal to one third of the total of the number of members to be appointed by that body.

(3) Paragraph (2) shall not apply in relation to the appointment of any person who immediately before the operative date was a member of a local valuation panel; and shall not be construed as affecting the validity of the appointment of a member who becomes a member of a charging authority after his appointment takes effect.

Duration of membership

6.—(1) Each appointment of a member shall have effect for such period not exceeding six years as the body or person making the appointment may specify after consultation with the president or, before the first appointment of a president, with the chairman of the local valuation panel for the area of the tribunal.

(2) Each member shall hold office until whichever of the following first occurs–

(a) the period specified under paragraph (1) expires;

(b) notice of his removal under paragraph (3) takes effect;

(c) he becomes disqualified from membership as provided in regulation 9;

(d) he attains the age of 72 years;

(e) he resigns the office by notice in writing to the president;

(f) he retires in accordance with a determination under paragraph (4).

(3) The appointing body by which any member was, or fell to be, appointed shall, if so directed by the Secretary of State after consultation with that body and with the president, by notice in writing give that member such period of notice of termination of office under this paragraph as may be so directed.

(4) Where a determination under regulation 4(1) reduces the number of members of a tribunal, the member or members whose retirement is to effect the reduction shall, subject to paragraph (3), be determined by the appointing body or bodies.

The president

7.—(1) Within the prescribed period, the members of each tribunal shall in accordance with the following provisions of this regulation appoint a person to be president of the tribunal.

(2) The person to be appointed shall be a member of the tribunal and shall be determined by election by a simple majority of votes cast, each member having one vote.

(3) Where an election under paragraph (2) results in a tie, the person to be appointed from among the candidates with equal votes shall be determined by lot.

(4) The first election held in pursuance of this regulation shall not be held before the expiry of one week beginning on the day on which notice of the election is issued in accordance with paragraph (6) by the clerk of the local valuation panel for the area of the tribunal.

(5) No other election in pursuance of this regulation shall be held before the expiry of two weeks beginning on the day on which notice of the election is issued in accordance with paragraph (6) by the clerk of the tribunal.

(6) The notices required by paragraphs (4) and (5) shall be served on all persons who are members of the tribunal on the date on which the notice in question is issued.

(7) Where at the expiry of the prescribed period no election has taken place in accordance with the foregoing provisions of this regulation, the Secretary of State shall, after consultation with such of the members of the tribunal as he sees fit, appoint one of their number to be president.

(8) The president shall hold office until whichever of the following first occurs–

(a) the period of his membership for the time being specified under regulation 6(1) expires;

(b) he ceases to be a member of the tribunal;

(c) notice of his resignation under paragraph (9) takes effect;

(d) notice of termination under paragraph (10) takes effect.

(9) A president may resign his office as such by giving not less than one month's notice in writing to the Secretary of State.

(10) The Secretary of State may, after consultation with such of the members of a tribunal as he sees fit, by giving notice in writing to the president terminate his office as such.

(11) In this regulation, "the prescribed period" means three weeks beginning with the operative date, or three months beginning with a vacancy occurring in the office of president, as the case may be; and the validity of any election shall not be affected by there being a vacancy among the members of a tribunal.

Chairmen

8.—(1) The number of members of a tribunal to be appointed to the position of chairman shall be stated by the Secretary of State.

(2) Within the prescribed period, the members of a tribunal shall in accordance with this regulation appoint the appropriate number of chairmen by election from among their number; and the president may be appointed under this paragraph.

(3) The first election in pursuance of this regulation shall not be held before the expiry of one week beginning on the day on which notice of the election is issued in accordance with paragraph (5) by the clerk of the local valuation panel for the area of the tribunal.

(4) No other election in pursuance of this regulation shall be held before the expiry of two weeks beginning on the day on which notice of the election is issued in accordance with paragraph (5) by the clerk of the tribunal.

(5) The notices required by paragraphs (3) and (4) shall be served on all persons who are members of the tribunal at the date on which the notice in question is issued.

(6) The members elected as chairmen shall be the appropriate number of members who have the highest number of votes cast.

(7) For the purposes of paragraph (6) each member shall have a number of votes equal to the appropriate number, and may cast no more than one vote for each candidate; and where in relation to any vacancy the election results in a tie, the person or persons to be appointed from among the candidates with equal votes shall be determined by lot.

(8) Where at the expiry of the prescribed period no election has taken place in accordance with this regulation, the Secretary of State shall, after consultation with the president, appoint the appropriate number of members to be chairmen.

(9) A chairman shall hold office until whichever of the following first occurs–

(a) the period of his membership for the time being specified under regulation 6(1) expires;

(b) he ceases to be a member of the tribunal;

(c) he resigns by giving notice in writing to the president;

(d) notice of termination under paragraph (10) takes effect.

(10) The president–

(a) may after consultation with each of the tribunal's other chairmen by giving notice in writing to a chairman terminate his office; and

(b) shall if so directed by the Secretary of State give a chairman notice in writing terminating his office, which notice shall take effect on the expiry of such period as may be so directed.

(11) Before giving a direction under paragraph (10)(b) the Secretary of State shall consult the president.

(12) In this regulation–

"the appropriate number" means the stated number less the number of persons for the time being holding office as chairman;

"the prescribed period" means three weeks beginning with the operative date, or three months beginning with a vacancy occurring among the stated number, as the case may be; and

"the stated number" means the number stated by the Secretary of State in pursuance of paragraph (1).

Disqualification from membership

9.—(1) A person shall be disqualified from being appointed or continuing to be a member of a tribunal if he–

(a) has been adjudged bankrupt; or

(b) has made an arrangement with his creditors; or

(c) has, within the five years immediately preceding his appointment, or since his appointment, been convicted in the United Kingdom, the Channel Islands or the Isle of Man of any offence, and ordered to be imprisoned for a period of three months or more without the option of a fine, whether or not that sentence has been suspended; or

(d) is for the time being disqualified for being a member of a local authority in pursuance of section 19 or 20 of the Local Government Finance Act 1982 (**a**); or

(e) is aged 72 years or more.

(2) A disqualification attaching to a person by reason of paragraph (1)(a) shall cease–

(a) unless the bankruptcy order made against that person is previously annulled, on his discharge from bankruptcy; and

(b) if the bankruptcy is so annulled, on the date of the annulment.

(3) A disqualification attaching to a person by reason of paragraph (1)(b) shall cease–

(a) if he pays his debts in full, on the date on which the payment is completed; or

(b) in any other case, on the expiry of five years from the date on which the terms of the deed of composition or arrangement are fulfilled.

(4) For the purposes of paragraph (1)(c), the ordinary date on which the period allowed for making appeal from a conviction expires, or, if such an appeal is made, the date on which it is finally disposed of or abandoned or fails by reason of non-prosecution, shall be deemed to be the date of the conviction.

Allowances

10. Allowances to members in respect of travelling, subsistence and financial loss shall be payable to members as provided in Schedule 2.

PART III
ADMINISTRATION

Staff

11.—(1) Each tribunal shall appoint a clerk of the tribunal, and may appoint other employees.

(2) No appointment under paragraph (1) shall be valid unless it is made with the approval of the Secretary of State.

(3) The terms and conditions on which the clerk and the other employees are appointed shall be such as the tribunal may determine.

(4) The tribunal shall pay to its employees such remuneration and allowances as it may determine.

(5) No determination under paragraph (4) shall be valid unless made with the approval of the Secretary of State given with the Treasury's consent.

(**a**) 1982 c.32.

Administration

12.—(1) The functions of the tribunal under regulation 11 may be performed on its behalf by two or more of its members, who shall, subject to paragraph (2), include the president.

(2) Where it is impracticable for the president to perform any of his functions under paragraph (1), that function shall be performed by one of the tribunal's chairmen nominated by him for the purpose.

(3) The administration of members' allowances and of the remuneration and allowances of the tribunal's employees shall be the responsibility of the clerk.

(4) In respect of any payment under Schedule 2, each tribunal shall keep a record of the name of the recipient and the amount and reason for the payment, and shall permit any person authorised by the Secretary of State to inspect and make copies of such records.

Accommodation and equipment

13. The tribunal shall maintain a permanent office; and the clerk of the tribunal shall have the function on behalf of the tribunal of making such arrangements as shall secure that it has such other accommodation, and such secretarial and other equipment, as is sufficient for the performance of its functions.

Use of public rooms

14.—(1) The president or clerk of a tribunal may request the permission of a relevant council the whole or any part of whose area is within the area of the tribunal for the use of any premises belonging to that council by the tribunal or its members, clerk or employees, on such days as may be specified in the request.

(2) A council requested as provided in paragraph (1) shall not unreasonably withhold the permission requested, and shall be entitled to make reasonable charges in respect of such use.

(3) In this regulation "relevant council" means the council of any county, district or London borough and the Council of the Isles of Scilly.

PART IV
COMMUNITY CHARGE APPEALS

Interpretation

15. In this Part–

"appeal" means an appeal under section 23;

"notice of appeal" means a notice under regulation 18(1);

"registration officer" means a community charges registration officer appointed under section 26;

"tribunal", unless the context otherwise requires, means the members of a tribunal convened in accordance with this Part for the purposes of disposing of an appeal;

and any reference to a party to an appeal includes the appellant and any person entitled in pursuance of these Regulations to be served with a copy of the appellant's notice of appeal.

Jurisdiction

16.—(1) Subject to the provisions of this regulation, an appeal shall be dealt with by the tribunal established for the area of the charging authority or registration officer whose decision is the subject matter of the appeal.

(2) Where–

(a) a person is shown in more than one community charges register as subject to a personal community charge, and

(b) he appeals under section 23(2)(a) or (b) against both or all the entries, and

(c) in pursuance of paragraph (1) the appeals would fall to be dealt with by different tribunals, the appeals shall be dealt with by such one of those tribunals as he may choose.

(3) Where the appellant is a member of the tribunal by which, in pursuance of any provision of this regulation, his appeal would fall to be dealt with, it shall not be dealt with by that tribunal but by such other tribunal as may be appointed for the purpose by the Secretary of State.

Time limits

17.—(1) An appeal by a person who is aggrieved as mentioned in section 24(4)(a) or (b) shall be dismissed unless it is initiated in accordance with these Regulations not later than the expiry of two months beginning with the day on which the authority or, as the case may be, the registration officer notified him in accordance with that subsection that his grievance was believed not to be well founded, or that steps had been taken to deal with the grievance, as the case may be.

(2) Where as mentioned in section 24(4)(c) a person has not been notified as provided in section 24(4)(a) or (b), an appeal by that person shall be dismissed unless it is initiated within four months of the date of service of the aggrieved person's notice under section 24.

(3) Notwithstanding paragraphs (1) and (2), the president may authorise an appeal to be entertained where he is satisfied that the failure of the person aggrieved to initiate the appeal as provided by this regulation has arisen by reason of circumstances beyond that person's control.

Initiating an appeal

18.—(1) An appeal shall be initiated by serving on the clerk of the tribunal having jurisdiction in relation to the appeal a notice in writing (a "notice of appeal") containing the following information–

(a) the grounds on which the appeal is made;

(b) the date on which the aggrieved person's notice under section 24 was served on the charging authority or registration officer, as the case may be;

(c) the date, if any, on which he was notified by the authority or officer as mentioned in section 24(4)(a) or (b).

(2) The clerk shall notify the appellant that he has received the notice of appeal, and serve a copy of that notice on the charging authority or registration officer whose decision or action is the subject of the appeal, and any other charging authority or registration officer appearing to him to be concerned.

Arrangement for appeals

19. Subject to the provisions of this Part, it shall be the duty of the president to secure that arrangements are made for appeals initiated in pursuance of regulation 18 to be determined in accordance with the following provisions of these Regulations.

Withdrawal

20. Where notice in writing to that effect is given to the clerk before the commencement of a hearing or of consideration of written representations, an appeal may be withdrawn.

Disposal by written representations

21.—(1) An appeal may be disposed of on the basis of written representations if the following conditions are satisfied–

(a) all the parties have given their agreement in writing; and

(b) the respondent (or, if there is more than one, each of them) has, within 28 days of being notified by the clerk that the appellant has agreed to the appeal being disposed of by written representations, served on the clerk either a notice containing the reasons or further reasons for believing the appellant's grievance not to be well founded, or a notice stating that he or it does not intend to make further representations.

(2) The clerk shall within 14 days of receipt of a notice under paragraph (1)(b) serve on the appellant a copy of that notice and a statement of the effect of paragraph (3).

(3) After the expiry of 21 days from the issue of the notice to the appellant as mentioned in paragraph (2), the clerk shall submit copies of the notice of appeal, of any respondent's notice and any response to such a notice made by the appellant within 14 days of its service on him, to a tribunal constituted as mentioned in regulation 25(1).

(4) The tribunal may if it thinks fit require any party to furnish in writing further particulars of the grounds relied on and of any relevant facts or contentions.

Notice of hearing

22.—(1) Where the appeal is to be disposed of on the basis of a hearing, the clerk shall, not less than 21 days before the date in question, serve on the parties notice of the date, time and place appointed for the hearing.

(2) The clerk shall advertise the date, time and place appointed for any hearing by causing a notice giving such information to be affixed to the tribunal's office, to an office of the charging authority appointed by the authority for that purpose or to another conspicuous place within that authority's area.

(3) The notice required by paragraph (2) shall name a place where a list of the appeals to be heard (other than appeals in relation to an excepted register entry) may be inspected.

(4) In this regulation "excepted register entry" means any entry on the community charges register in relation to which, in pursuance of regulations under paragraph 17 of Schedule 2 to the Act, the registration officer is under no duty to include the name of the person who is the subject of the entry in the extract which is to be compiled from the information in the register.

Disqualification from participating

23.—(1) A person shall be disqualified from participating in the hearing or determination of, or acting as clerk or officer of a tribunal in relation to, an appeal if he is a member of a charging authority–

(a) whose decision is being appealed against or;

(b) whose registration officer took the decision which is being appealed against.

(2) A person shall be disqualified from participating in the hearing or determination of, or acting as clerk or officer of a tribunal in relation to an appeal, if the appellant is his spouse or he supports the appellant financially or is liable to do so.

(3) A person shall not otherwise be disqualified from acting in any capacity in relation to an appeal by reason only of the fact that he is a member of an authority which derives revenue directly or indirectly from charges which may be affected by the exercise of his functions.

Representation at the hearing

24. Any party to an appeal which is to be decided at a hearing may appear in person (with assistance from any person if he wishes), by counsel or solicitor, or any other representative (other than a person who is a member or an employee of the tribunal).

Conduct of the hearing

25.—(1) Subject to paragraph (2), a tribunal's function of hearing or determining an appeal shall be discharged by three members of the tribunal who shall include at least one chairman; and a chairman shall preside.

(2) Where all parties to an appeal who appear so agree, the appeal may be decided by two members of a tribunal, and notwithstanding the absence of a chairman.

(3) The hearing shall take place in public, unless the tribunal otherwise orders on the application of a party and on being satisfied that the interests of that party would be prejudicially affected.

(4) If at a hearing the appellant fails to appear, the tribunal may dismiss the appeal, and if any other party does not appear the tribunal may hear and determine the appeal in his absence.

(5) The tribunal hearing an appeal may require any witness to give evidence by oath or affirmation, and shall have power for that purpose to administer an oath or affirmation in due form.

(6) Parties at the hearing may be heard in such order as the tribunal may determine, and may examine any witness before the tribunal and call witnesses; and a hearing may be postponed or adjourned for such time, to such place and on such terms (if any) as the tribunal thinks fit.

(7) Subject to any provision of this Part, the tribunal shall conduct the hearing in such manner as it considers most suitable to the clarification of the issues before it and generally to the just handling of the proceedings; it shall so far as appears to it appropriate seek to avoid formality in its proceedings and it shall not be bound by any enactment or rule of law relating to the admissibility of evidence in proceedings before courts of law.

Evidence: general

26.—(1) This regulation applies to information supplied in pursuance of regulations under any of paragraphs 6 to 10 and 13 to 15 of Schedule 2 to the Act.

(2) Subject to the provisions of this regulation, information to which this regulation applies shall in any relevant proceedings be admissible as evidence of any fact included in such information; and any document purporting to contain such information shall, unless the contrary is shown, be presumed–

(a) to have been supplied by the person by whom it purports to have been supplied;

(b) to have been supplied by that person in any capacity in which it purports to have been supplied.

(3) Information to which this regulation applies shall not be used in any relevant proceedings by a charging authority or registration officer unless–

(a) not less than 14 days' notice, specifying the information to be so used and the residence and person to which it relates has previously been given to every other party to the proceedings; and

(b) any person who has given not less than 24 hours' notice of his intention to do so has been permitted by that authority or officer, at any reasonable time, to inspect and take extracts from the documents or other media in or on which such information is held.

(4) In this regulation "relevant proceedings" means any proceedings on or in consequence of an appeal, and any proceedings on or in consequence of a reference to arbitration under regulation 33.

Evidence of registers

27. An extract from a community charges register may be proved by the production of a copy of the relevant part of it purporting to be certified to be a true copy by the community charges registration officer.

Decisions on appeals

28.—(1) An appeal shall be decided by a majority of members participating; and where it falls to be disposed of by two members and they are unable to agree as to a decision, it shall be remitted by the clerk to be decided by a tribunal consisting of different members.

(2) The decision of the tribunal may be given orally or in writing; but the decision in a case which falls to be disposed of by written representations shall be given in writing.

(3) Where the decision is given in writing the decision and the reasons for the decision shall as soon as is reasonably practicable be notified in writing to the parties.

Orders

29.—(1) On or after deciding an appeal the tribunal may in consequence of the decision by order require–

(a) the alteration of any community charges register (prospectively or retrospectively);

(b) the alteration of any estimate made under regulations made under Schedule 2 to the Act;

(c) the revocation of any designation of an individual as a responsible individual in pursuance of regulations under Schedule 2 to the Act;

(d) the quashing of a penalty imposed under Schedule 3 to the Act;

(e) the revocation of a designation under section 5.

(2) An order may require any matter ancillary to its subject-matter to be attended to.

Records of decisions etc.

30.—(1) It shall be the duty of the clerk to make arrangements for each decision and each order made in pursuance of regulation 29 to be recorded, and the record shall include the particulars specified in Schedule 3.

(2) The record may be kept in any form, whether documentary or otherwise; and a copy of each entry shall be transmitted to each party to the appeal to which the entry relates.

(3) Any party to an appeal or the representative of such a party may, at a reasonable time stated by or on behalf of the tribunal concerned and without making payment, inspect records ("relevant records") which relate to decisions and orders of the tribunal which are required to be made by paragraph (1).

(4) If without reasonable excuse a person having custody of relevant records intentionally obstructs a person in exercising the right conferred by paragraph (3) he shall be liable on summary conviction to a fine not exceeding level 1 on the standard scale.

(5) No offence shall be committed under paragraph (4) by any person who refuses to permit the exercise of the right in the reasonable belief that to do so would be to incur the risk of violence to a person named in an entry.

(6) The member who presided at the hearing or determination of an appeal may authorise the correction of any clerical error in the decision or record, and a copy of the relevant entry as so amended shall be transmitted as required by paragraph (2).

(7) The production in any proceedings in any court of law of a document purporting to be certified by the clerk of a tribunal to be a true copy of a record or decision of that tribunal shall, unless the contrary is proved, be sufficient evidence of the document and of the facts it records.

Review of decisions

31.—(1) A tribunal constituted as provided in paragraph (2) shall have power on written application by a party to review and to revoke, vary or set aside by certificate under the hand of the presiding member any decision on the grounds that–

(a) the decision was wrongly made as a result of a clerical error;

(b) a party did not receive notice of the hearing leading to the decision and did not appear;

(c) new evidence, the existence of which could not have been ascertained by reasonably diligent inquiry or could not have been foreseen, has become available since the conclusion of the proceedings to which the decision relates; or

(d) the interests of justice otherwise require such a review.

(2) As far as is reasonably practicable, the tribunal appointed to consider an application for a review shall consist of the same members as constituted the tribunal which took the decision subject to review.

(3) If a tribunal in pursuance of this regulation revokes a decision, it shall set aside any order made in pursuance of that decision and shall order a re-hearing or redetermination before either the same or a different tribunal.

Appeals

32.—(1) An appeal shall lie to the High Court on a question of law arising out of a decision or order which is given or made by a tribunal on an appeal, and may be made by the appellant, the authority or registration officer whose decision he appealed against, or any other officer who was party to the appeal.

(2) An appeal under paragraph (1) may be dismissed if it is not made within 28 days of the date of the decision or order that is the subject of the appeal.

(3) The High Court may confirm, vary, set aside, revoke or remit the decision of the tribunal, and may make any order the tribunal could have made.

(4) Charging authorities and registration officers shall act in accordance with any order made by the High Court; and paragraph 9 or 10 (as the case may be) of Schedule 11 to the Act shall have effect subject to this requirement.

Arbitration

33.—(1) Where it is so agreed in writing between the persons who, if a question were to be the subject of an appeal to a tribunal, would be the parties to the appeal, the question shall be referred to arbitration.

(2) Section 31 of the Arbitration Act 1950 (**a**) shall have effect for the purposes of the referral of a question in pursuance of this regulation as if such referral were to arbitration under another Act within the meaning of that section.

(3) In any arbitration in pursuance of this regulation the award may include any order which could have been made by a tribunal in relation to the question; and paragraphs 9 and 10 of Schedule 11 to the Act shall apply to such an order as they apply to orders recorded in pursuance of these Regulations.

Nicholas Ridley
9th March 1989 Secretary of State for the Environment

Peter Walker
12th March 1989 Secretary of State for Wales

(**a**) 1950 c.27.

SCHEDULE 1

Regulations 3, 4

ESTABLISHMENT OF TRIBUNALS

1 *Area of jurisdiction*	2 *Name*	3 *Appointing body or bodies*
The area of each non-metropolitan county, other than Essex and Hampshire	The name of the county	The council of the county
Each of the following metropolitan counties: Merseyside, South Yorkshire, Tyne and Wear, West Yorkshire	The name of the county	The councils of the districts in the county
Essex		
The districts of Braintree, Maldon, Tendring and Uttlesford and the boroughs of Chelmsford and Colchester	Essex North	Essex County Council
The districts of Basildon, Brentwood, Castle Point, Epping Forest, Harlow and Rochford and the boroughs of Southend-on-Sea and Thurrock	Essex South	Essex County Council
Hampshire		
The districts of East Hampshire and Hart, the boroughs of Basingstoke and Deane, Rushmoor and Test Valley and the City of Winchester	Hampshire North	Hampshire County Council
The district of New Forest, the boroughs of Eastleigh, Fareham, Gosport and Havant and the cities of Portsmouth and Southampton	Hampshire South	Hampshire County Council
Greater London		
The London boroughs of Camden, Islington, Westminster; the Royal Borough of Kensington and Chelsea; the City of London; the Inner Temple; the Middle Temple	Central London	The councils of the boroughs comprised in the area and the Common Council
The London boroughs of Barking and Dagenham, Hackney, Havering, Newham, Redbridge, Tower Hamlets and Waltham Forest	London North East	The councils of the boroughs comprised in the area
The London boroughs of Barnet, Brent, Ealing, Enfield, Haringey, Harrow and Hillingdon	London North West	The councils of the boroughs comprised in the area
The London boroughs of Bexley, Bromley, Croydon, Greenwich, Lewisham and Southwark	London South East	The councils of the boroughs comprised in the area
The London boroughs of Hammersmith and Fulham, Hounslow, Kingston upon Thames, Lambeth, Merton, Richmond, Sutton, Wandsworth	London South West	The councils of the boroughs comprised in the area
Greater Manchester		
The boroughs of Bolton, Bury, Oldham, Tameside, Rochdale and Wigan	Manchester North	The councils of the districts comprised in the area
The boroughs of Stockport and Trafford and the cities of Manchester and Salford	Manchester South	The councils of the districts comprised in the area
West Midlands		
The City of Birmingham	Birmingham	Birmingham City Council

1 *Area of jurisdiction*	2 *Name*	3 *Appointing body or bodies*
The boroughs of Coventry and Solihull	Coventry and Solihull	Coventry City Council and Solihull Borough Council
The boroughs of Dudley, Sandwell, Walsall and Wolverhampton	West Midlands West	The councils of the districts comprised in the area
Isles of Scilly		
The Isles of Scilly	Isles of Scilly	The Council of the Isles of Scilly

Regulation 10

SCHEDULE 2

MEMBERS' ALLOWANCES

Financial loss allowance

1. In respect of his performance of any approved duty, a member shall be entitled to an allowance, not exceeding the appropriate amount specified in Table A, in respect of loss of earnings necessarily suffered, or individual expenses (other than expenses on account of travelling or subsistence) necessarily incurred by him for the purpose of enabling him to perform that duty.

TABLE A

For any approved duty whose duration does not exceed 4 hours................................£16.15
For any such duty whose duration exceeds 4 hours but not 24 hours £32.35
For any such duty whose duration exceeds 24 hours, £32.35 for each period of 24 hours plus the amount ascertained from this Table appropriate to the remainder of the period

Subsistence allowances

2.—(1) In respect of his performance of any approved duty, a member shall be entitled to an allowance not exceeding the appropriate amount specified in Table B and calculated in accordance with this paragraph.

TABLE B

For any approved duty whose duration–
exceeds 4 hours but not 8 hours £4.00
exceeds 8 hours but not 12 hours £7.00
exceeds 12 hours but not 16 hours £10.00
exceeds 16 hours £12.00

(2) For the purposes of this paragraph–

(a) where the member travels directly from, or to, his usual place of residence or business to, or from, the place at which the duty is to be performed, the duty shall be treated as beginning or, as the case may be, ending at the time at which he left or returned to that place of residence or business; and where he does not so travel, it shall be treated as beginning or, as the case may be, ending at the time at which he would ordinarily have left from, or returned to, that place;

(b) different periods of duty on any one day shall be added together;

(c) no more than one hour of any meal break may be treated as included in the performance of the duty.

3.—(1) In respect of his performance of any approved duty whose duration exceeds 4 hours, a member shall be entitled to an allowance of £4.00.

(2) Paragraphs (b) and (c) of paragraph 2(2) shall apply for the purposes of this paragraph.

4. Where by reason of the time at which an approved duty begins or ends a member necessarily spends a period of 24 hours or longer away from his usual place of residence, he shall be entitled to an allowance–

(a) not exceeding £60.40 per night spent away from that place of residence, in respect of a duty to be performed in inner London, or of attendance at the annual conference of the Rating and Valuation Association, or

(b) not exceeding £52.95 per night so spent in any other case,

but shall not be so entitled in relation to any such night in respect of which the member's overnight accommodation is provided at the expense of the Secretary of State.

Travelling allowances

5.—(1) In respect of his performance of any approved duty, a member shall be entitled to an allowance not exceeding the appropriate amount specified in this paragraph in respect of travel necessarily undertaken for the purpose of enabling him to perform the duty.

(2) Where the travel is by public transport, the appropriate amount is, subject to sub-paragraph (3), the amount of the fare paid by the member, not exceeding the ordinary fare or any available cheap fare or, where more than one class of travel is available, the first class fare.

(3) Where by reason of the time at which an approved duty begins or ends a member necessarily incurs expenses in connection with the provision of overnight sleeping accommodation on public transport, he shall be entitled to an allowance equivalent to the cost of such accommodation less one third of any allowance to which he is entitled under paragraph 4.

(4) Where the travel is by means of his own private motor vehicle, or such a vehicle provided for his use, the appropriate amount is 27.3p multiplied by the number of miles travelled, plus any expenditure in respect of parking fees, tolls, or the transport of the vehicle by ferry.

(5) Where the travel is by means of a taxi-cab or hired motor vehicle, the appropriate amount, subject to sub-paragraph (6), is 27.3p per mile multiplied by the number of miles travelled.

(6) Where the travel is by means of a taxi-cab solely by reason of urgency, the appropriate amount is the fare paid.

Interpretation

6. In this Schedule–

"approved duty" means attendance at any meeting of the tribunal or the doing of any thing for or in connection with the discharge of its functions; and

"inner London" means the City of London, the Inner Temple, the Middle Temple and the London boroughs of Camden, Greenwich, Hackney, Hammersmith and Fulham, Islington, Kensington and Chelsea, Lambeth, Lewisham, Southwark, Tower Hamlets, Wandsworth and Westminster.

SCHEDULE 3

Regulation 30

CONTENTS OF RECORDS

The appellant's name and address
The date of the appeal
The matter appealed against
The name of the charging authority or the title of any registration officer whose decision was appealed against
The date of the hearing or determination
The names of the parties who appeared, if any
The decision of the tribunal, and its date
The reasons for the decision
Any order made in consequence of the decision
The date of any such order

EXPLANATORY NOTE

(This note is not part of the Regulations)

These Regulations establish valuation and community charge tribunals and provide for the determination of appeals under section 23 of the Local Government Finance Act 1988 in connection with the system of community charges payable from 1st April 1990.

Parts II and III make provision for the establishment of the tribunals on 1st May 1989. Regulation 3 establishes tribunals for each of the areas set out in Schedule 1. Regulation 4 provides for the determination of the number of members of each tribunal and their appointment.

Regulations 5 and 6 regulate the appointment of members and the duration of their appointments. Regulations 7 and 8 deal with the appointment of the tribunal's president and its chairmen. Regulation 9 provides for the circumstances in which a person is to be disqualified from membership of a tribunal. Regulation 10 introduces Schedule 2, which sets out the allowances payable to members.

Matters relating to the staff, administration and accommodation and equipment for tribunals are dealt with in regulations 11 to 14.

Part IV provides for the procedure for dealing with appeals in relation to community charges. Regulation 16 makes provision for the areas in respect of which tribunals are to have jurisdiction under section 23 of the 1988 Act. Procedure prior to the hearing of an appeal is dealt with in regulations 17 to 20. Regulation 21 sets out the circumstances in which an appeal may be disposed of by written representations. Regulation 22 deals with notice of a hearing, regulation 23 with disqualification from participating in the determination of an appeal, and regulations 24 to 27 with procedure and evidence.

Regulations 28 to 30 deal with decisions and orders made by the tribunal and their recording. Regulation 31 enables a tribunal to review a decision, regulation 32 deals with appeals to the High Court on a question of law, and regulation 33 with the disposal of appeals by reference to arbitration.

STATUTORY INSTRUMENTS

1989 No. 440

RATING AND VALUATION

The Valuation and Community Charge Tribunals (Transfer of Jurisdiction) Regulations 1989

Made - - - -	*12th March 1989*
Laid before Parliament	*17th March 1989*
Coming into force	*1st May 1989*

The Secretary of State for the Environment as respects England and the Secretary of State for Wales as respects Wales, in exercise of the powers conferred on them by sections 117(8) and 143(1) and (2) of and paragraphs 3, 14 and 16 of Schedule 11 to the Local Government Finance Act 1988**(a)**, and section 48(6) of the General Rate Act 1967**(b)**, and of all other powers enabling them in that behalf, and after consultation with the Council on Tribunals as required by section 10 of the Tribunals and Inquiries Act 1971**(c)** hereby make the following Regulations:–

Citation and commencement

1. These Regulations may be cited as the Valuation and Community Charge Tribunals (Transfer of Jurisdiction) Regulations 1989 and shall come into force on 1st May 1989.

Interpretation

2. In these Regulations–

"the Act" means the Local Government Finance Act 1988;

"the 1967 Act" means the General Rate Act 1967;

"the transfer date" means 1st May 1989;

"tribunal" means a valuation and community charge tribunal established by regulations under Schedule 11 to the Act.

Transfer of jurisdiction

3.—(1) On and after the transfer date, tribunals shall (in addition to the jurisdiction conferred on them by section 23 of the Act) exercise the jurisdiction conferred on local valuation courts by–

(a) sections 73(2)(b), 74(3), 75 and 83(6) of the 1967 Act**(d)**;

(b) section 2(5B) and paragraph 11(2) of Schedule 1 to the Rating (Disabled Persons) Act 1978**(e)**;

(c) regulation 6 of the Mixed Hereditaments (Certificate) Regulations 1967**(f)**;

(a) 1988 c.41.
(b) 1967 c.9. The powers cited were conferred on the Minister of Housing and Local Government (by virtue of the definition of "Minister" in section 115(1)), and vested in the Secretary of State by S.I. 1970/1681.
(c) 1971 c.62. Valuation and community charge tribunals were added to Schedule 1 to the 1971 Act by paragraph 41 of Schedule 12 to the 1988 Act.
(d) Sections 73 and 74 were amended by the Rates Act 1984 (c.33), Schedule 1.
(e) 1978 c.40. Section 2(5B) was inserted by paragraph 22 of Schedule 1 to the Rates Act 1984.
(f) S.I. 1967/637.

(d) section 78 of the Land Drainage Act 1976**(a)**;

and on that date the local valuation courts shall be wound up.

(2) The jurisdiction transferred by paragraph (1) shall be exercised as regards appeals or applications instituted or made before, as well as those instituted or made on or after, the transfer date.

Transitional provisions

4.—(1) This regulation applies to any appeal or application instituted or made under any of the provisions mentioned in regulation 3(1).

(2) Any appeal or application which was instituted before the transfer date shall be continued as an appeal to the valuation and community charge tribunal established for the area for which was constituted the local valuation panel from among whose members the local valuation court to hear and determine the appeal fell to be convened.

(3) In relation to any appeal or, as the case may be, application made under a provision mentioned in paragraph (1)(a) to (c) of regulation 3 which is instituted on or after the transfer date, subject to the provisions mentioned in paragraph (4) the tribunal which is to hear and determine the appeal or application shall be the tribunal established for the area in which the hereditament is situated.

(4) The provisions referred to in paragraph (3) (which are saved by regulation 6(4)) are–

(a) regulation 3 (which deals with extensive undertakings) of the Rating Appeals (Local Valuation Courts) Regulations 1956**(b)**; and

(b) regulation 3 (which deals with contiguous and neighbouring hereditaments) of the Local Valuation Panels (Jurisdiction) Regulations 1967**(c)**.

(5) In relation to any appeal under section 78 of the Land Drainage Act 1976 which is instituted on or after the transfer date, the tribunal which is to hear and determine the appeal shall be determined in accordance with section 78 of the Land Drainage Act 1976 and the Drainage Rates (Appeals) Regulations 1970**(d)** (which are saved by regulation 6(4)), in each case as amended as provided by regulation 6.

5. Schedule 1 shall have effect to provide for continuity of employment in respect of the employees of local valuation panels.

Consequential and supplementary amendments, savings and repeals

6.—(1) The enactments and instruments mentioned in Schedule 2 shall on the transfer date be amended as provided in that Schedule.

(2) Notwithstanding section 117(1) of and Part I of Schedule 13 to the Act, the 1967 Act shall continue to have effect on and after 1st April 1990 in respect of appeals and applications under the enactments referred to in regulation 3(1) instituted before that date.

(3) But sections 88(1) to (4), sections 89 to 92 and 94 of the 1967 Act, section 79(8) of the Land Drainage Act 1976 and regulation 4(3) of the Rating Appeals (Local Valuation Courts) Regulations 1956 shall not have effect on and after the transfer date.

(4) Nothing in section 117(1) of the Act or in this regulation shall affect the Rating Appeals (Local Valuation Courts) Regulations 1956, the Local Valuation Panels (Jurisdiction) Regulations 1967 and the Drainage Rates (Appeals) Regulations 1970 (in each case as amended by Schedule 2) as they apply in respect of appeals and applications to which regulation 4 applies.

Nicholas Ridley
9th March 1989 Secretary of State for the Environment

Peter Walker
12th March 1989 Secretary of State for Wales

(a) 1976 c.70.
(b) S.I. 1956/632.
(c) S.I. 1967/636.
(d) S.I. 1970/1152.

SCHEDULE 1

Regulation 5

CONTINUITY OF EMPLOYMENT

1. This Schedule applies to any person (an "employee") who immediately before the transfer date is employed under a contract of employment with a local valuation panel.

2. The contract of employment between an employee and the local valuation panel shall not be terminated by that panel ceasing to exist, but shall have effect from the transfer date as if originally made between the employee and the tribunal ("the appropriate tribunal") established by regulation 3 of the Valuation and Community Charge Tribunals Regulations 1989**(a)** for the area for which that panel was established.

3. Without prejudice to paragraph 2–

(a) all the rights, powers, duties and liabilities of the panel under or in connection with a contract to which this Schedule applies shall on the transfer date by virtue of this paragraph be transferred to the appropriate tribunal; and

(b) anything done before the transfer date by or in relation to the panel in respect of that contract or the employee shall be deemed from that date to have been done by or in relation to the tribunal.

4. Paragraphs 2 and 3 are without prejudice to any right of an employee to terminate his contract of employment if a substantial change is made to his detriment in his working conditions; but no such right shall arise by reason only of the change of employer effected by this Schedule.

SCHEDULE 2

Regulation 6

AMENDMENTS TO RATING AND LAND DRAINAGE LEGISLATION

PART I

RATING APPEALS

1. The enactments and instruments mentioned in Table 1 shall be amended as indicated in that Table.

TABLE 1

*GENERAL RATE ACT 1967***(b)**

(1) *Provision*	(2) *Words to be replaced*	(3) *Words substituted*
section 70(5)	"the clerk to the local valuation panel"	"the clerk of the valuation and community charge tribunal"
section 72(1)	"any appeal to a local valuation court"	"any appeal to a valuation and community charge tribunal"
section 73(1) section 74(2)	from "the clerk" to "constituted" where second occurring	"the clerk of the valuation and community charge tribunal having jurisdiction in relation to the hereditament in question in accordance with regulations under Schedule 11 to the Local Government Finance Act 1988"
section 73(2)(b) section 74(3) section 83(9)	"appeal to a local valuation court"	"appeal to a valuation and community charge tribunal"

(a) S.I. 1989/439.
(b) c.9. Sections 70 to 76 were amended by the Rates Act 1984 (c.33), Schedule 1 paragraphs 12 to 18, with effect as provided in paragraph 19.

(1) *Provision*	(2) *Words to be replaced*	(3) *Words substituted*
section 74(3)	"the clerk to a local valuation panel"	"the clerk of a valuation and community charge tribunal"
section 75(b)	"the clerk of a local valuation panel"	"the clerk of a valuation and community charge tribunal"
section 76(1)	The whole subsection	"Where a copy of a proposal is transmitted to the clerk of a valuation and community charge tribunal and by virtue of section 73(2), 74(3) or 75 of this Act that transmission has effect as an appeal to the tribunal against an objection to the proposal, it shall be the duty of the president of that tribunal to make arrangements for the appeal to be determined."
section 76(2)	The whole subsection	"(2) The procedure of a valuation and community charge tribunal shall, subject to the Rating Appeals (Local Valuation Courts) Regulations 1956 and to this section, be such as the tribunal may determine; and unless subsection (2A) of this subsection applies, the tribunal (a) shall sit in public, unless the tribunal otherwise orders on the application of any party to the appeal and upon being satisfied that the interests of that party would be prejudically affected and (b) may take evidence on oath and shall have power to administer oaths. (2A) This subsection applies where all the parties who would be entitled to appear as provided in subsection (4) of this section have agreed that the appeal shall be determined on the basis of written representations. (2B) Where subsection (2A) applies, subsection (4) shall not apply, and the appeal shall be determined by a valuation and community charge tribunal constituted as provided in section 88(5) of this Act on the basis of any representations submitted in writing by the parties."
section 76(3)	From the beginning to "may hear and determine"	"Where, by virtue of section 75 of this Act, the transmission of a copy of a proposal relating to any hereditament has effect as an appeal to a valuation and community charge tribunal, the tribunal may determine"
	"the court shall not hear the first-mentioned appeal"	"the tribunal shall not determine the first-mentioned appeal"
section 76(4)	"an appeal to a local valuation court"	"an appeal to a valuation and community charge tribunal"
	"any witness before the court"	"any witness before the tribunal"

(1) *Provision*	(2) *Words to be replaced*	(3) *Words substituted*
section 76(5)	from "after hearing" to "shall give such directions"	"after considering the written representations of the parties mentioned in subsection (4) of this section, or such of them wish to make representations, or, as the case may be, hearing them or such of them as desire to be heard, the tribunal shall give such directions"
	"that contention appears to the court"	"that contention appears to the tribunal"
section 77	From the beginning to "the decision of the court"	"Any person who in pursuance of section 76 of this Act appears before a valuation and community charge tribunal on the hearing of an appeal, or any person who made representations in an appeal determined on the basis of written representations, who is aggrieved by the decision of the tribunal"
	"such of the persons as appeared"	"such of the persons as appeared or made representations"
	"any directions which the local valuation court might have given"	"any directions which the tribunal might have given"
section 78(1)	"before a local valuation court"	"before a valuation and community charge tribunal"
	"heard or determined by such a court"	"heard or determined by such a tribunal"
section 78(3)	"given by the local valuation court"	"given by the tribunal"
section 83(5)(b)	"to produce to him at the hearing"	"to produce to him at any hearing"
section 83(6)	"the court or tribunal"	"the tribunal"
section 83(7)	"proceedings before a court"	"proceedings before a tribunal"
section 83(8) section 83(9)	"a local valuation court"	"a valuation and community charge tribunal"
section 88	The whole section	"(5) Subject to subsection (6) of this section, the tribunal as constituted to hear or determine an appeal shall consist of– (a) a chairman appointed as provided by regulations for the time being in force under Schedule 11 to the Local Government Finance Act 1988, and (b) two other members of the tribunal. (6) With the consent of all the persons appearing before a tribunal on the hearing of an appeal, the appeal may be heard and determined by any two of the persons mentioned in subsection (5) of this section; but if the members of a tribunal so constituted are unable to agree on a decision, the appeal shall be reheard by a differently constituted tribunal."

(1) Provision	(2) Words to be replaced	(3) Words substituted
section 93(1)	"a local valuation panel or local valuation court"	"a valuation and community charge tribunal"
section 108(1)(c)	"any local valuation court"	"any local valuation court or valuation and community charge tribunal"
LOCAL GOVERNMENT ACT 1974(a)		
section 21(3)	"the court or arbitrator"	"the tribunal or arbitrator"
RATING (DISABLED PERSONS) ACT 1978(b)		
section 2(5B) Schedule 1 paragraph 11(2)	from "may appeal" to "the court may"	"may appeal to the valuation and community charge tribunal by sending a notice in writing to the clerk of the tribunal having jurisdiction in relation to the hereditament in question in accordance with regulations under Schedule 11 to the Local Government Finance Act 1988; and the tribunal may"
section 2(5C)	The whole subsection	"Section 76(2) to (2B) and (4) and section 77 of the said Act of 1967 (procedure of valuation and community charge tribunal and right of appeal to Lands Tribunal) shall, with the necessary modifications, apply to the proceedings and jurisdiction of a valuation and community charge tribunal under this section."
Schedule 1 paragraph 11(3)	The whole sub-paragraph	"Section 76(2) to (2B) and (4) and section 77 of the said Act of 1967 (procedure of valuation and community charge tribunal and right of appeal to Lands Tribunal) shall, with the necessary modifications, apply to the proceedings and jurisdiction of a valuation and community charge tribunal under this paragraph."
RATING APPEALS (LOCAL VALUATION COURTS) REGULATIONS 1956(c)		
regulation 2	the definition of "court"	" 'tribunal', unless the context otherwise requires, means the members of a valuation and community charge tribunal appointed in pursuance of regulations under Schedule 11 to the Local Government Finance Act 1988 to determine an appeal"
	the definition of "chairman"	" 'chairman' means the person presiding at a sitting of a tribunal"
	the definition of "the clerk"	" 'the clerk' means the clerk of the valuation and community charge tribunal from which the tribunal to determine the appeal is constituted"
	the definition of "party"	" 'party' means a person who appears or is entitled to appear at the hearing of the appeal, or who would have been so entitled had he not agreed that the appeal should be determined by written representations."

(a) 1974 c.7.
(b) 1978 c.40, as amended by paragraph 22 of Schedule 1 to the Rates Act 1984 (c.33).
(c) S.I. 1956/632.

(1) Provision	(2) Words to be replaced	(3) Words substituted
regulation 3	"The court to hear and determine"	"The tribunal to determine"
	"or to hear and determine"	"or to determine"
	"that local valuation panel"	"that valuation and community charge tribunal"
	"the area of any other local valuation panel"	"the area of any other such tribunal"
	"the appeal shall be heard and determined by a court consisting of members of such one of the panels"	"the appeal shall be determined by such one of the tribunals"
regulation 4	"fixed for the hearing of an appeal"	"fixed for any hearing of an appeal"
	"a court will sit"	"a tribunal will sit"
	"the offices of the local valuation panel"	"the office of the valuation and community charge tribunal"
regulation 5	"no member of the local valuation panel from which the court is constituted"	"no member of the valuation and community charge tribunal hearing the appeal"
regulations 6 to 9 regulation 10(2) and (3) regulation 11 regulation 12	"the court"	"the tribunal"
regulation 10(1)	from "the decision of the majority" to the end of the paragraph	"the decision of the majority of the members of the tribunal determining the appeal shall be the decision of the tribunal."

MIXED HEREDITAMENT (CERTIFICATE) REGULATIONS 1967(a)

regulation 6(1)	from "to the clerk" to "fall to be constituted"	"to the clerk of the valuation and community charge tribunal which would in accordance with regulations under Schedule 11 to the Local Government Finance Act 1988 have jurisdiction"
regulation 6(2) regulation 6(3)	"the clerk to the local valuation panel"	"the clerk of a valuation and community charge tribunal"
regulation 6(3)	"an appeal to the local valuation court"	"an appeal to the valuation and community charge tribunal"

(a) S.I. 1967/637.

(1) *Provision*	(2) *Words to be replaced*	(3) *Words substituted*
regulation 7(1)	The whole paragraph	"(1) Where by virtue of the foregoing regulation the sending of a certificate has effect as an appeal to a valuation and community charge tribunal, it shall be the duty of the president of that tribunal to make arrangements for an appeal under these regulations to be heard and determined. (1A) The procedure of a valuation and community charge tribunal shall, subject to the Rating Appeals (Local Valuation Courts) Regulations 1956 as applied and adapted by the Valuation and Community Charge Tribunals (Transfer of Jurisdiction) Regulations 1989 and to this regulation, be such as the tribunal may determine; and the tribunal– (a) shall sit in public, unless the tribunal otherwise order on the application of any party to the appeal and upon being satisfied that the interests of that party would be prejudicially affected; and (b) may take evidence on oath and shall have power to administer oaths."
regulation 7(2)	"an appeal to a local valuation court" "any witness before the court"	"an appeal to a valuation and community charge tribunal" "any witness before the tribunal"
regulation 7(3)	"the local valuation court may confirm"	"the tribunal may confirm"
regulation 8(1)	from "who in pursuance of" to "the decision of the court thereon"	"who in pursuance of regulation 7 of these regulations appears before a valuation and community charge tribunal on the hearing of an appeal and is aggrieved by the decision of the tribunal"
regulation 8(2)	"or the local valuation court"	"or the valuation and community charge tribunal"

2. The Local Valuation Panels (Jurisdiction) Regulations 1967**(a)** shall be amended by the substitution for references to a local valuation panel or a local valuation court of references to a valuation and community charge tribunal.

3.—(1) In the Lands Tribunal Rules 1975**(b)**–

(a) in rule 2–

(i) in the definitions of "drainage rates appeal" and "rating appeal", after "local valuation court" there shall be added "or valuation and community charge tribunal";

(ii) for the definition of "valuation proceedings" there shall be substituted–

" 'valuation proceedings' means proceedings before a local valuation court or a valuation and community charge tribunal, or proceedings begun before a local valuation court and continued before a valuation and community charge tribunal;"

(b) for the references to a local valuation court in rules 9(1), 37, 42(1) and 54(2), in Form 2 in Schedule 1 and item 6 of Schedule 2 there shall be substituted a reference to a valuation and community charge tribunal.

(2) The amendments made by paragraph (1)(b) shall not have effect in relation to decisions of a local valuation court made before the transfer date.

(a) S.I. 1967/636.
(b) S.I. 1975/299.

PART II

LAND DRAINAGE APPEALS

4. The Land Drainage Act 1976**(a)** shall be amended as indicated in Table 2.

TABLE 2

(1) *Provision*	(2) *Words to be replaced*	(3) *Words substituted*
section 78(5)	paragraphs (a) and (b)	" (a) the clerk of the valuation and community charge tribunal established in accordance with regulations under Schedule 11 to the Local Government Finance Act 1988 for the area in which the land to which the determination relates is situated, or (b) where different parts of that land are situated in different areas for which such tribunals are established, the clerk of such one of those tribunals as may be determined by or under the Drainage Rates (Appeals) Regulations 1970."
section 78(6)	"a local valuation court"	"a valuation and community charge tribunal"
section 79(1)	subsections (1) and (2)	"(1) It shall be the duty of the president of the valuation and community charge tribunal to whose clerk a notice of objection is transmitted in pursuance of section 78 above to arrange for the appeal to which the notice relates to be heard and determined; and subsections (5) and (6) of section 88 of the General Rate Act 1967 shall apply to the constitution the tribunal to hear and determine the appeal and to the rehearing of the appeal in case of such failure to agree as is mentioned in the said subsection (6). (2) The procedure of a valuation and community charge tribunal shall subject to the Drainage Rates (Appeals) Regulations 1970 be such as the tribunal may determine; and the tribunal– (a) shall sit in public, unless the tribunal otherwise orders on the application of any party to the appeal and upon being satisfied that the interests of that party would be prejudicially affected; and (b) may take evidence on oath and shall have power to administer oaths."

(a) 1976 c.70.

(1) *Provision*	(2) *Words to be replaced*	(3) *Words substituted*
section 79(3) and (5)	"a local valuation court"	"a valuation and community charge tribunal"
section 79(4)	"The court to which an appeal is brought"	"The tribunal which is convened to determine an appeal"

5. The Drainage Rates (Appeals) Regulations 1970**(a)** shall have effect as if they were amended as follows:–

(i) in regulation 2, by the substitution of the definitions set out in column 2 of Table 3 for the definitions mentioned in column 1:

TABLE 3

(1)	(2)
"the court"	" 'the tribunal' means the valuation and community charge tribunal convened under section 79(1) of the Land Drainage Act 1976 to hear and determine the appeal;"
"the chairman"	" 'the chairman' means the member of the tribunal presiding at the hearing;"
"panel area"	" 'tribunal area' means the area for which a valuation and community charge tribunal is established in accordance with regulations under Schedule 11 to the Local Government Finance Act 1988;"
"prescribed panel"	" 'prescribed tribunal' has the meaning assigned to it by regulation 3;"
"relevant panel area"	" 'relevant tribunal area', in relation to a divided hereditament, means a tribunal area in which a part of the hereditament is situated;"

(ii) in regulation 2, by the omission of the definition of "panel" and by the substitution of "tribunal area" for "panel area" in the definition of "undivided hereditament";

(iii) in regulations 3 to 9 and 11 to 16 by the substitution of the words in column 2 of Table 4 for the words in column 1:–

TABLE 4

(1)	(2)
"the panel"	"the valuation and community charge tribunal"
"panel area"	"tribunal area"
"prescribed panel"	"prescribed tribunal"
"relevant panel area"	"relevant tribunal area"
"the court"	"the valuation and community charge tribunal".

(a) S.I. 1970/1152. The Regulations have effect as if made under the Land Drainage Act 1976 by virtue of paragraph 6 of Schedule 6 to that Act.

EXPLANATORY NOTE

(This note is not part of the Regulations)

Regulation 3 of these Regulations provides for the transfer to the tribunals established by the Valuation and Community Charge Tribunals Regulations 1989 (S.I. 1989/439) of the jurisdiction of local valuation courts to hear and determine appeals and applications in connection with–

(a) the valuation of property for rating, under the General Rate Act 1967 ("the 1967 Act");

(b) the amounts of rateable value attributable to such parts of institutions as are used for the care and welfare of the disabled, under the Rating (Disabled Persons) Act 1978;

(c) certificates as to the proportion of a mixed hereditament used for the purposes of a private dwelling, in connection with entitlement to domestic rate relief under section 48 of the 1967 Act; and

(d) valuation for drainage rates under the Land Drainage Act 1976.

The transfer is to take place on 1st May 1989, on which date the local valuation courts are wound up.

Regulation 4 makes transitional provision in relation to appeals and applications instituted or made before that date, and includes provision for determining which tribunal is to deal with each. It also introduces Schedule 1, which makes provision for the transfer of local valuation panel staff to the employment of the tribunals.

Regulation 5 makes provision for savings and repeals, and introduces Schedule 2, which in addition to making provision consequential on the transfer of jurisdiction to the tribunals amends the General Rate Act 1967 so that appeals provided for by or under that Act and the Rating (Disabled Persons) Act 1978 can be dealt with, where the parties so agree, by written representations instead of at a hearing.

STATUTORY INSTRUMENTS

1989 No. 441

RATING AND VALUATION

The Valuation for Rating (Plant and Machinery) Regulations 1989

Made - - - -	*12th March 1989*
Laid before Parliament	*17th March 1989*
Coming into force	*7th April 1989*

The Secretary of State for the Environment as respects England, and the Secretary of State for Wales as respects Wales, in exercise of the powers conferred on them by sections 143(2) and 146(6) of and paragraph 2(8) of Schedule 6 to the Local Government Finance Act 1988(**a**), and of all other powers enabling them in that behalf, hereby make the following Regulations:

1. These Regulations may be cited as the Valuation for Rating (Plant and Machinery) Regulations 1989 and shall come into force on 7th April 1989.

2. In relation to any hereditament other than a hereditament which is valued on the profits basis, in applying the provision of sub-paragraphs (1) to (7) of paragraph 2 of Schedule 6 to the Local Government Finance Act 1988–

(a) all such plant or machinery in or on the hereditament as belongs to any of the classes set out in the Schedule shall be assumed to be part of the hereditament; and

(b) the value of all other plant and machinery in or on the hereditament shall be assumed to have no effect on the rent to be estimated as required by paragraph 2(1).

3. The valuation officer shall, on being so required in writing by the occupier of any hereditament, supply to him particulars in writing showing what machinery and plant, or whether any particular machinery or plant, has been assumed in pursuance of regulation 2(a) to form part of the hereditament.

Nicholas Ridley
9th March 1989 — Secretary of State for the Environment

Peter Walker
12th March 1989 — Secretary of State for Wales

(**a**) 1988 c.41.

SCHEDULE

Regulation 2

CLASSES OF PLANT AND MACHINERY TO BE ASSUMED TO BE PART OF THE HEREDITAMENT

CLASS 1A

Machinery and plant specified in Table 1A (together with any of the appliances and structures accessory to such machinery or plant and specified in the List of Accessories) which is used or intended to be used mainly or exclusively in connection with the generation, storage, primary transformation or main transmission of power in or on the hereditament.

"Transformer" means any plant which changes the pressure or frequency or form of current of electrical power to another pressure or frequency or form of current, except any such plant which forms an integral part of an item of plant or machinery in or on the hereditament for manufacturing operations or trade processes.

"Primary transformation of power" means any transformation of electrical power by means of a transformer at any point in the main transmission of power.

"Main transmission of power" means all transmission of power from the generating plant or point of supply in or on the hereditament up to and including–

(i) in the case of electrical power, the first transformer in any circuit, or where the first transformer precedes any distribution board or there is no transformer the first distribution board;

(ii) in the case of transmission by shafting or wheels, any shaft or wheel driven directly from the prime mover;

(iii) in the case of hydraulic or pneumatic power, the point where the main supply ceases, excluding any branch service piping connected with such main supply;

(iv) in a case where, without otherwise passing beyond the limits of the main transmission of power, power is transmitted to another hereditament, the point at which the power passes from the hereditament.

TABLE 1A

(a) Steam boilers (including their settings) and chimneys, flues and dust or grit catchers used in connection with such boilers; furnaces; mechanical stokers; injectors, jets, burners and nozzles; superheaters; feed water pumps and heaters; economisers; accumulators; deaerators; blow-off tanks; gas retorts and charging apparatus, producers and generators.

(b) Steam engines; steam turbines; gas turbines; internal combustion engines; hot-air engines; barring engines.

(c) Continuous and alternating current dynamos; couplings to engines and turbines; field exciter gear; three-wire or phase balancers.

(d) Storage batteries, with stands and insulators, regulating switches, boosters and connections forming part thereof.

(e) Static transformers; auto transformers; motor generators; motor converters; rotary converters; transverters; rectifiers; phase converters; frequency changers.

(f) Cables and conductors; switchboards, distribution boards, control panels and all switchgear and other apparatus thereon.

(g) Water wheels; water turbines; rams; governor engines; penstocks; spillways; surge tanks; conduits; flumes; sluice gates.

(h) Pumping engines for hydraulic power; hydraulic engines; hydraulic intensifiers; hydraulic accumulators.

(i) Air compressors; compressed air engines.

(j) Windmills.

(k) Shafting, couplings, clutches, worm-gear, pulleys and wheels.

(l) Steam or other motors which are used or intended to be used mainly or exclusively for driving any of the machinery and plant falling within this Class.

CLASS 1B

Machinery and plant specified in Table 1B (together with the appliances and structures accessory to such machinery or plant and specified in paragraph 2 of the List of Accessories) which is used or intended to be used mainly or exclusively in connection with the heating, cooling, ventilating, lighting, draining or supplying of water to the land or buildings of which the hereditament consists, or the protecting of the hereditament from fire: but in the case of machinery or plant which is in or on the hereditament for the purpose of manufacturing operations or trade processes, the fact that it is used in connection with those operations or processes for the purposes of heating, cooling, ventilating, lighting, draining, supplying water or protecting from fire shall not cause it to be treated as falling within the classes of machinery and plant specified in the Schedule.

TABLE 1B

(a) GENERAL

Any of the machinery and plant specified in Table 1A and any steam or other motors which are used or intended to be used mainly or exclusively for driving any of the machinery and plant falling within paragraphs (b) to (h) of this Table.

(b) HEATING

(i) Water heaters.

(ii) Headers and manifolds; steam pressure reducing valves; calorifiers; radiators; heating panels; hot-air furnaces with distributing ducts and gratings.

(iii) Gas pressure regulators; gas burners; gas heaters and radiators and the flues and chimneys used in connection therewith.

(iv) Plug-sockets and other outlets; electric heaters.

(c) COOLING

(i) Refrigerating machines.

(ii) Water screens; water jets.

(iii) Fans and blowers.

(d) VENTILATING

Air intakes, channels, ducts, gratings, louvres and outlets; plant for filtering, washing, drying, warming, cooling, humidifying, deodorising and perfuming, and for the chemical and bacteriological treatment of air; fans, blowers; gas burners, electric heaters, pipes and coils when used for causing or assisting air movement.

(e) LIGHTING

(i) Gas pressure regulators; gas burners.

(ii) Plug-sockets and other outlets; electric lamps.

(f) DRAINING

Pumps and other lifting apparatus; tanks; screens; sewage treatment machinery and plant.

(g) SUPPLYING WATER

Pumps and other water-lifting apparatus; sluice-gates; tanks, filters and other machinery and plant for the storage and treatment of water.

(h) PROTECTION FROM FIRE

Tanks; pumps, hydrants; sprinkler systems; fire alarm systems; lightning conductors.

LIST OF ACCESSORIES

1. Any of the following machinery and plant which is used or intended to be used mainly or exclusively in connection with the handling, preparing or storing of fuel required for the generation or storage of power in or on the hereditament–

Cranes with their grabs or buckets; truck or wagon tipplers; elevating and conveying systems, including power winches, drags, elevators, hoists, conveyors, transporters, travellers, cranes, buckets forming a connected part of any such system, and any weighing machines used in connection therewith; magnetic separators; driers; breakers; pulverisers; bunkers; gas-holders; tanks.

2. Any of the following machinery and plant which is used or intended to be used mainly or exclusively as part of or in connection with or as an accessory to any of the machinery and plant falling within Class 1A or Class 1B–

(i) Foundations, settings, gantries, supports, platforms and stagings for machinery and plant;

(ii) Steam-condensing plant, compressors, exhausters, storage cylinders and vessels, fans, pumps and ejectors; ash-handling apparatus;

(iii) Travellers and cranes;

(iv) Oiling systems; earthing systems; cooling systems;

(v) Pipes, ducts, valves, traps, separators, filters, coolers, screens, purifying and other treatment apparatus, evaporators, tanks, exhaust boxes and silencers, washers, scrubbers, condensers, air heaters and air saturators;

(vi) Shafting supports, belts, ropes and chains;

(vii) Cables, conductors, wires, pipes, tubes, conduits, casings, poles, supports, insulators, joint boxes and end boxes;

(viii) Instruments and apparatus attached to the machinery and plant, including meters, gauges, measuring and recording instruments, automatic controls, temperature indicators and alarms and relays.

CLASS 2

Lifts and elevators mainly or usually used for passengers.

CLASS 3

Railway and tramway lines and tracks.

CLASS 4

The following items, except–

(a) any such item which is not, and is not in the nature of, a building or structure;

(b) any part of any such item which does not form an integral part of such item as a building or structure or as being in the nature of a building or structure;

(c) any such item or part of such item which is moved or rotated by motive power as part of the process of manufacture;

(d) so much of any refractory or other lining forming part of any plant or machinery as is customarily renewed by reason of normal use at intervals of less than fifty weeks;

(e) any item in Table B the total cubic capacity of which (measured externally and excluding foundations, settings, supports and anything which is not an integral part of the item) does not exceed two hundred cubic metres, and which is readily capable of being moved from one site and re-erected in its original state on another without the substantial demolition of the item or of any surrounding structure.

TABLE A

Aerial ropeways, supports for;

Blast Furnaces;

Bridges;

Chimneys;

Coking Ovens;

Cooling Ponds;

Elevators and Hoists;

Fan Drifts;

Floating docks and pontoons, with any bridges or gangways not of a temporary nature used in connection therewith;

Flues;

Flumes and conduits;

Foundations, settings, fixed gantries, supports, platforms and stagings for plant and machinery;

Headgear–

Mine, quarry and pit;

Well.

Masts (including guy ropes) and towers for–

Radar;

Television;

Wireless.

Pits, beds and bays–
- Acid neutralising;
- Casting;
- Cooling;
- Drop;
- Inspection or testing;
- Liming, soaking, tanning or other treatment;
- Settling.

Racks;
Slipways, uprights, cradles and grids for ship construction and repair;
Stages, staithes and platforms for loading, unloading and handling material;
Telescopes, including radio telescopes;
Tipplers;
Transversers and turntables;
Walkways, stairways, handrails and catwalks;
Weighbridges;
Well casings and liners;
Windmills.

TABLE B

Accelerators;
Acid concentrators;
Bins, hoppers and funnels;
Boilers;
Bunkers;
Burners, Bessemer converters, forges, furnaces, kilns, ovens and stoves;
Chambers, vessels and containers for–
- Absorption of gases or fumes;
- Aerographing and spraying;
- Bleaching;
- Chemical reaction;
- Conditioning or treatment;
- Cooling;
- Diffusion of gases;
- Drying;
- Dust or fume collecting;
- Fibre Separation (wool carbonising);
- Fuming;
- Impregnating;
- Mixing;
- Refrigerating;
- Regenerating;
- Sandblasting;
- Shotblasting;
- Sterilising;
- Sulphuric Acid;
- Testing.

Condensers and scrubbers–
- Acid;
- Alkali;
- Gas;
- Oil;
- Tar.

Coolers, chillers and quenchers;
Cupolas;
Economisers, heat exchangers, recuperators, regenerators and superheaters;
Evaporators;

Filters and separators;
Hydraulic accumulators;
Precipitators;
Producers, generators, purifiers, cleansers and holders of gas;
Reactors;
Refuse destructors and incinerators;
Retorts;
Silos;
Stills;
Tanks;
Towers and columns for–
  Absorption of gases or fumes;
  Chemical reaction;
  Cooling;
  Oil refining and condensing;
  Treatment;
  Water.
Vats;
Washeries and dry cleaners for coal;
Wind tunnels.

CLASS 5

A pipe-line, that is to say, a pipe or system of pipes for the conveyance of any thing, not being–

(a) a drain or sewer;

(b) a pipe or system of pipes vested in a public gas supplier, in a board established by the Electricity Act 1947, or in the Central Electricity Generating Board;

(c) a pipe or system of pipes forming part of the equipment of, and wholly situate within, a factory or petroleum storage depot or premises comprised in a mine, quarry or mineral field;

and exclusive of so much of a pipe or system of pipes forming part of the equipment of, and situate partly within and partly outside, a factory or petroleum storage depot or premises comprised in a mine, quarry or mineral field as is situate within, as the case may be, the factory or petroleum storage depot or those premises.

In this paragraph–

(i) "factory" has the same meaning as in the Factories Act 1961(**a**);

(ii) "mine" and "quarry" have the same meanings as in the Mines and Quarries Act 1954(**b**);

(iii) "mineral field" means an area comprising an excavation being a well or bore-hole or a well and bore-hole combined, or a system of such excavations, used for the purpose of pumping or raising brine or oil, and so much of the surface (including buildings, structures and works thereon) surrounding or adjacent to the excavation or system as is occupied, together with the excavation or system, for the purpose of the working of the excavation or system;

(iv) "petroleum storage depot" means premises used primarily for the storage of petroleum or petroleum products (including chemicals derived from petroleum) or of materials used in the manufacture of petroleum products (including chemicals derived from petroleum); and

(v) "public gas supplier" has the same meaning as in Part I of the Gas Act 1986(**c**).

(**a**) 1961 c.34. (**b**) 1954 c.70. (**c**) 1986 c.44.

EXPLANATORY NOTE

(This note is not part of the Regulations)

Paragraph 2 of Schedule 6 to the Local Government Finance Act 1988 provides for the valuation of hereditaments subject, on and after 1st April 1990, to non-domestic rating under Part III of that Act by reference to the rent at which it is estimated that the hereditament might reasonably be expected to let from year to year.

Paragraph 2(8) enables the Secretary of State to provide by Regulations that in applying the provisions of the paragraph to determine the rateable value prescribed assumptions shall be made.

Regulation 2 provides that in valuing hereditaments other than on the profits basis, it is to be assumed that certain classes of plant and machinery in or on the hereditament form part of the hereditament, and that the value of other plant or machinery has no effect on the rent estimated to be payable.

The classes of plant and machinery, which are set out in the Schedule, are the same as those deemed to be part of the hereditament before 1st April 1990 in pursuance of section 21 of the General Rate Act 1967 (c.9) and the Plant and Machinery (Rating) Order 1960 (S.I. 1960/122).

Regulation 3 requires the valuation officer on request to supply the occupier of a hereditament with written particulars of the hereditament assumed in pursuance of regulation 2 to form part of the hereditament.

STATUTORY INSTRUMENTS

1989 No. 442

COMMUNITY CHARGES, ENGLAND AND WALES

The Personal Community Charge (Exemptions) Order 1989

Made - - - -	*12th March 1989*
Laid before Parliament	*17th March 1989*
Coming into force	*7th April 1989*

The Secretary of State for the Environment as respects England, and the Secretary of State for Wales as respects Wales, in exercise of the powers conferred on them by sections 143(1) and 146(6) of, and paragraphs 1(7), 4(4) and 9(4) and (6) of Schedule 1 to, the Local Government Finance Act 1988**(a)**, and of all other powers enabling them in that behalf, hereby make the following Order:

Citation, commencement and interpretation

1.—(1) This Order may be cited as the Personal Community Charge (Exemptions) Order 1989 and shall come into force on 7th April 1989.

(2) In this Order "the Act" means the Local Government Finance Act 1988.

Persons in detention

2.—(1) A person is an exempt individual on a particular day if–

(a) at any time on the day he is imprisoned, detained or in custody under the Army Act 1955**(b)**, the Air Force Act 1955**(c)** or the Naval Discipline Act 1957**(d)**, and

(b) the conditions mentioned in paragraph (2) below are fulfilled with respect to the time where they are applicable.

(2) The conditions are that, where the person is in custody under arrest–

(a) he is not in custody under open arrest; and

(b) the custody forms part of a continuous period exceeding 48 hours during which he is under arrest.

(3) A person is to be treated as in custody under open arrest for the purposes of paragraph (2)(a) if he is so treated for the purposes of Queen's Regulations for the Navy, Army or Air Force.

The severely mentally impaired

3. Paragraph 4(2) of Schedule 1 to the Act is amended by adding after paragraph (c)–

"(d) he is entitled for the day to an invalidity pension under section 15 or 16 of the Social Security Pensions Act 1975**(e)**;

(a) 1988 c.41.
(b) 1955 c.18.
(c) 1955 c.19.
(d) 1957 c.53.
(e) 1975 c.60; section 15 was modified by S.I. 1978/529, regulation 2, restricted by the Social Security Act 1979 (c.18), Schedule 1, paragraph 17, and amended by the Social Security Act 1986 (c.50), Schedule 10, paragraph 70; sections 15 and 16 were amended by the Social Security (Miscellaneous Provisions) Act 1977 (c.5), section 4(4); section 16 was restricted by the Social Security Act 1979 (c.18), Schedule 1, paragraph 18.

(e) he is entitled for the day to an unemployability supplement under section 58 of the Social Security Act 1975**(a)**;

(f) he is entitled for the day to an unemployability allowance under-

(i) article 18(1) of the Personal Injuries (Civilians) Scheme 1983**(b)**, or

(ii) article 18(1) of the Naval, Military and Air Forces etc. (Disablement and Death) Service Pensions Order 1983**(c)** (including that provision as applied, whether with or without modifications, by any other instrument).".

Patients in homes

4.—(1) The definition of hostel set out in paragraph (2) below is prescribed under paragraph 9(4) of Schedule 1 to the Act.

(2) A hostel is–

(a) a bail hostel or probation hostel approved under section 49(1) of the Powers of Criminal Courts Act 1973**(d)**, or

(b) a building or part of a building–

(i) which is solely or mainly used for the provision of residential accommodation in other than separate and self-contained sets of premises, together with personal care, for persons who require such personal care by reason of old age, disablement, past or present alcohol or drug dependence or past or present mental disorder, and

(ii) which is not a residential care home, nursing home or mental nursing home for the purposes of paragraph 9 of Schedule 1 to the Act.

(3) In paragraph (2)(b) "disablement" means a disablement within the meaning of Part I of the Registered Homes Act 1984**(e)**, and "personal care" has the same meaning as in that Part.

(4) The definition of residential care home set out in paragraph (5) below is substituted for that set out in paragraph 9(2) of Schedule 1 to the Act.

(5) A residential care home is–

(a) an establishment in respect of which registration is required under Part I of the Registered Homes Act 1984 or would be so required but for section 1(4) or (5)(j) of that Act;

(b) a building or part of a building in which residential accommodation is provided under section 21 of the National Assistance Act 1948**(f)** or paragraph 2(1)(a) of Schedule 8 to the National Health Service Act 1977**(g)**; or

(c) a building or part of a building in which residential accommodation is provided and which is run by the Abbeyfield Society, including all bodies corporate or unincorporate which are affiliated to that Society.

Nicholas Ridley
9th March 1989 Secretary of State for the Environment

Peter Walker
12th March 1989 Secretary of State for Wales

(a) 1975 c.14; section 58 was restricted by the Social Security Act 1986, Schedule 3, paragraphs 4 and 16.
(b) S.I. 1983/686; article 18 was amended by S.I. 1984/1289, 1985/1313 and 1988/367.
(c) S.I. 1983/883; article 18 was amended by S.I. 1984/1154, 1985/1201 and 1988/248, and is applied by S.R. & O. 1944/500, S.I. 1964/1985, 2007 and 2058, the Royal Warrant of 21 December 1964 (1964 III p.5646; Cmnd 2563), the Order by Her Majesty of 22 December 1964 (1964 III p. 5675; Cmnd 2564), and the Order by Her Majesty of 4 January 1971 (Cmnd 4567).
(d) 1973 c.62; section 49(1) was amended by the Criminal Law Act 1977 (c.45), Schedule 12, paragraph 6, and Schedule 13.
(e) 1984 c.23; *see* section 20(1).
(f) 1948 c.29; section 21 was amended by the Local Government Act 1972 (c.70), Schedule 23, paragraph 2(1), the National Health Service Reorganisation Act 1973 (c.32), Schedule 4, paragraph 44, and Schedule 5, the Housing (Homeless Persons) Act 1977 (c.48), the Schedule, the National Health Service Act 1977 (c.49), Schedule 15, paragraph 5, and the Health Services Act 1980 (c. 53), Schedule 1, paragraph 5.
(g) 1977 c.49.

EXPLANATORY NOTE

(This note is not part of the Order)

Schedule 1 to the Local Government Finance Act 1988 provides for certain exemptions from personal community charges arising under the Act. This Order makes further provision in relation to those exemptions.

Article 2 provides that a person is exempt on a day if at any time on the day he is imprisoned, detained or in custody under the Army Act 1955, the Air Force Act 1955 or the Naval Discipline Act 1957, provided that, in the case of a person in custody under arrest, the arrest subsists for a period exceeding 48 hours and he is not under open arrest.

A person who is severely mentally impaired and who holds a certificate of a registered medical practitioner to that effect is exempt from the personal community charge if one or more of the conditions mentioned in paragraph 4(2) of Schedule 1 to the Act is satisfied. Article 3 widens this exemption by adding to the conditions specified in that paragraph.

Paragraph 9 of Schedule 1 to the Act provides for certain patients in homes to be exempt. Amongst these are individuals having their sole or main residence in a hostel or residential care home. Article 4 defines "hostel" for this purpose, and also substitutes a new definition of residential care home so as to include residential accommodation run by the Abbeyfield Society and affiliated bodies.

STATUTORY INSTRUMENTS

1989 No. 443

COMMUNITY CHARGES, ENGLAND AND WALES

The Personal Community Charge (Students) Regulations 1989

Made - - - -	*12th March 1989*
Laid before Parliament	*17th March 1989*
Coming into force -	*1st October 1989*

The Secretary of State for the Environment as respects the community charges of charging authorities in England, and the Secretary of State for Wales as respects the community charges of charging authorities in Wales, in exercise of the powers conferred on them by section 2(2) of the Welsh Language Act 1967**(a)**, sections 30, 143(1) and (2) and 146(6) of, and paragraphs 1 and 9 of Schedule 2 to, the Local Government Finance Act 1988**(b)**, and of all other powers enabling them in that behalf, hereby make the following Regulations:

Citation and commencement

1. These Regulations may be cited as the Personal Community Charge (Students) Regulations 1989 and shall come into force on 1st October 1989.

Interpretation

2.—(1) In regulations 2 to 5–

"full-time course of education" means (subject to paragraph (3)) a course of education–

(a) which subsists for at least one academic year of the educational establishment concerned or, in the case of an educational establishment which does not have academic years, for at least one calendar year,

(b) which persons undertaking it are normally required by the educational establishment concerned to attend (whether at premises of the establishment or otherwise) for periods of at least 24 weeks in each academic or calendar year (as the case may be) during which it subsists, and

(c) the nature of which is such that a person undertaking it would normally require to undertake periods of study, tuition or work experience which together amount in each such academic or calendar year to an average of at least 21 hours a week as respects the periods of attendance mentioned in paragraph (b) above for the year;

"further education" with respect to an educational establishment in England or Wales has the same meaning as in the Education Act 1944**(c)**, with respect to an educational establishment in Scotland has the same meaning as in the Education (Scotland) Act 1980**(d)**, and with respect to an educational establishment in

(a) 1967 c.66.
(b) 1988 c.41.
(c) 1944 c.31; *see* section 41, substituted by section 120(2) of the Education Reform Act 1988 (c.40).
(d) 1980 c.44; *see* section 1(5), to which relevant amendments were made by The Local Government and Planning (Scotland) Act 1982 (c.43), Schedule 3, paragraph 37(b)(i) and Schedule 4, Part I.

Northern Ireland has the same meaning as in article 5(c) of the Education and Libraries (Northern Ireland) Order 1986**(a)**;

"higher education" has the same meaning as in the Education Reform Act 1988**(b)**; and

"relevant educational establishment" means–

(a) a university (including a constituent college, school or other institution of a university);

(b) an institution in England or Wales providing further or higher education which is (within the meaning of the Education Act 1944**(c)**) maintained or assisted by a local education authority, or which is in receipt of grants made under regulations under section 100 of that Act**(d)**;

(c) a central institution or college of education in Scotland within the meaning of the Education (Scotland) Act 1980**(e)**;

(d) a college of education in Northern Ireland within the meaning of the Education and Libraries (Northern Ireland) Order 1986**(f)**;

(e) an institution within the PCFC funding sector for the purposes of the Education Reform Act 1988**(g)**;

(f) a theological college;

(g) any other institution in England or Wales established solely or mainly for the purpose of providing courses of further or higher education;

(h) any other institution in Scotland or Northern Ireland established solely or mainly for the purpose of providing courses of further education.

(2) In determining whether a course falls within the definition of "full-time course of education" in paragraph (1)–

(a) in applying paragraph (c) of that definition, a person is to be treated as undertaking work experience at any time if, as part of the curriculum of the course–

(i) he is at a place of employment of his and is providing services under his contract of employment, or

(ii) he is at a place where a trade, business, profession or other occupation which is relevant to the subject matter of the course is carried on, and he is there for the purposes of gaining experience of that trade, business, profession or other occupation,

and references in paragraph (3) below to periods of work experience shall be construed accordingly;

(b) where the educational establishment concerned does not have academic years, in applying paragraphs (b) and (c) of that definition, the first calendar year shall be treated as beginning with the day on which the course begins, and subsequent calendar years (if any) as beginning on the anniversary of that day;

(c) in applying those paragraphs to a course which begins part-way through an academic year of the educational establishment concerned, the academic year shall be treated as beginning at the beginning of the academic term in which the course begins, and subsequent academic years (if any) as beginning at the beginning of the equivalent term in those years; and

(d) in applying those paragraphs to a course which subsists (or is treated as subsisting) for other than a number of complete academic or calendar years (as the case may be), any last part year of the course shall be disregarded.

(3) But a course of education is not to be treated as a full-time course of education for the purposes of regulations 3 to 5 if the aggregate for the course as a whole of all the periods of work experience a person undertaking it would normally require to undertake

---

(a) S.I. 1986/594 (N.I.3).
(b) 1988 c.40; *see* section 120(1).
(c) *See* section 114(2).
(d) Section 100 was amended by S.I. 1964/490, article 3(2)(a), the Local Government Act 1958 (c.55), Schedule 8, paragraphs 16(2) and 35 and Schedule 9, Part II, the Education Act 1962 (c.12), section 13 and Schedule 2, and the Education Act 1980 (c.20), Schedule 7.
(e) *See* section 135(1).
(f) *See* article 2(2).
(g) *See* section 120(8).

as mentioned in paragraph (c) of the definition of "full-time course of education" above exceeds the aggregate of all the periods of study or tuition not constituting work experience he would so normally require to undertake (counting for this purpose any period of study, tuition or work experience in a part year which might otherwise fall to be disregarded under paragraph (2)(d)).

(4) A person is to be treated as ceasing to undertake a course of education for the purposes of these Regulations if he has completed it, abandoned it or is no longer permitted by the educational establishment to attend it.

Persons undertaking full-time courses of education

3.—(1) The conditions mentioned in paragraph (2) are prescribed for the purposes of section 30(1) of the Local Government Finance Act 1988 (so that a person is to be treated as undertaking a full-time course of education on a particular day for the purposes of Part I of that Act if, and only if, he fulfils those conditions).

(2) The conditions are that–

(a) on the day the person is enrolled with a relevant educational establishment for the purpose of attending a full-time course of education,

(b) the day falls within the period beginning with the day on which he begins the course and ending with the day on which he ceases to undertake it (which period includes any periods of vacation between academic terms and before he ceases to undertake the course), and

(c) if the relevant educational establishment is in England or Wales, he is issued in respect of the day with a certificate supplied under regulation 4 indicating that the day falls within the period beginning with the day which is stated in the certificate as the day on which the course begins and ending with the day which is stated as the day on which it will (or is expected to) cease.

Certification officers

4.—(1) The individual having responsibility for registering the enrolment of students to courses of education provided by an educational establishment which is a relevant educational establishment in England or Wales shall be the certification officer as regards that establishment.

(2) A certification officer shall supply to a person who is pursuing or about to pursue a full-time course of education at the establishment as regards which he is the certification officer a certificate–

(a) in the case of an establishment in England, in the form set out in Part I of the Schedule, or

(b) in the case of an establishment in Wales, in the form set out in Part II of the Schedule,

stating the name of the establishment and the date on which the course begins and on which it will (or is expected to) cease.

(3) A certificate shall be supplied within 21 days of the day on which the certification officer registers the enrolment of the person to the course of education, of the day on which the date that the course begins is determined or of the day on which these Regulations come into force, whichever is the later; and a fresh certificate shall be issued if the expected date of cessation stated in the certificate proves to be inaccurate within 21 days of the day on which the inaccuracy comes to the knowledge of the certification officer.

(4) The failure to supply a certificate to a person in accordance with this regulation is actionable by the person concerned as a breach of statutory duty.

Information from certification officers

5.—(1) The registration officer for a charging authority may, for the purpose of carrying out his functions under Part I of the Local Government Finance Act 1988, request (by notice given in writing) a certification officer to supply to him such information as is mentioned in paragraph (2).

(2) The information is–

(a) the name of each person who (on the day the request is made) is undertaking a full-time course of education at the educational establishment of the certification officer and has his sole or main residence in the area of the charging authority, and

(b) the address of the sole or main residence of each such person.

(3) Information requested under paragraph (1) shall be supplied by the certification officer if it is in his possession or control and shall be so supplied within 21 days of the day on which the request is made.

(4) For the purposes of this regulation–

(a) a certification officer is an individual who is a certification officer by virtue of regulation 4, and

(b) the educational establishment of a certification officer is the educational establishment as regards which he is the certification officer.

Nursing education

6.—(1) Pursuant to section 30(3) of the Local Government Finance Act 1988, in the opinion of the Secretary of State a course constitutes a full-time course of nursing education if it is a course–

(a) which would (if successfully completed) lead to the person undertaking it being registered on a part of the register maintained under section 10(1) of the Nurses, Midwives and Health Visitors Act 1979**(a)**, or which is undertaken by persons so registered with a view to the recording of an additional qualification on the register in accordance with rules made under section 10(3)(a) of that Act;

(b) which subsists for at least one academic year of the educational establishment providing it or, in the case of an establishment which does not have academic years, for at least one calendar year;

(c) which persons undertaking it are normally required by the educational establishment concerned to attend (whether at premises of the establishment or otherwise) for periods of at least 24 weeks in each academic or calendar year (as the case may be) during which it subsists; and

(d) the nature of which is such that a person undertaking it would normally require to undertake periods of study, tuition or other training (including work experience) which together amount in each such academic or calendar year to an average of at least 21 hours a week as respects the periods of attendance mentioned in sub-paragraph (c) for the year.

(2) Regulation 2(2) shall apply to paragraph (1) above as if references to paragraphs (b) or (c) of the definition of "full-time course of education" were references to sub-paragraphs (c) or (d) respectively of paragraph (1) above.

(3) Notwithstanding this regulation, a person is to be treated as undertaking a full-time course of education for the purposes of Part I of the Local Government Finance Act 1988 only if he is to be so treated by virtue of regulation 3.

Nicholas Ridley
9th March 1989 Secretary of State for the Environment

Peter Walker
12th March 1989 Secretary of State for Wales

(a) 1979 c.36.

Regulation 4(2)

SCHEDULE

FORMS OF CERTIFICATE

PART I: ENGLAND

PERSONAL COMMUNITY CHARGE – STUDENT CERTIFICATE

I, [ ], certify pursuant to regulation 4 of the Personal Community Charge (Students) Regulations 1989 that [ ] is enrolled with [ ] for the purpose of attending a full-time course of education, and that the course begins on [ ] and will cease (or is expected to cease) on [ ].

Dated:

Signed:

PART II: WALES

Y TÂL CYMUNEDOL PERSONOL – TYSTYSGRIF MYFYRIWR

PERSONAL COMMUNITY CHARGE – STUDENT CERTIFICATE

Yr wyf fi, [ ], yn tystio yn unol â rheol 4 o'r Personal Community Charge (Students) Regulations 1989 fod [ ] wedi ei gofrestru/ei chofrestru gyda [ ] er mwyn mynychu cwrs addysg amser-llawn, a bod y cwrs yn dechrau ar [ ] ac y daw i ben (neu y disgwylir iddo ddod i ben) ar [ ].

I, [ ], certify pursuant to regulation 4 of the Personal Community Charge (Students) Regulations 1989 that [ ] is enrolled with [ ] for the purpose of attending a full-time course of education, and that the course begins on [ ] and will cease (or is expected to cease) on [ ].

Dyddiedig/Dated:

Llofnod/Signed:

Nodyn/Note:
Gellir llenwi'r dystygrif hon mewn Cymraeg neu Saesneg neu yn y ddwy.
This certificate may be completed in Welsh or English, or in both languages.

EXPLANATORY NOTE

(This note is not part of the Regulations)

These Regulations make provision, as regards the community charges of charging authorities in England and Wales, with respect to persons undertaking full-time courses of education.

Regulation 2 provides relevant definitions, and regulation 3 prescribes, by reference to those definitions, the conditions which must be fulfilled by a person in order that he may be treated as undertaking a full-time course of education for the purposes of Part I of the Local Government Finance Act 1988.

Regulation 4 provides that the individual having responsibility for registering the enrolment of students to a relevant educational establishment in England or Wales is to be the certification officer for the establishment, and that he is to supply appropriate certificates (in the form prescribed in the Schedule) to people pursuing or about to pursue full-time courses of education at the establishment. Provision is made as respects educational establishments in Wales for the form to be given in Welsh. The possession of such a certificate constitutes one of the conditions prescribed under regulation 3.

Regulation 5 enables a community charge registration officer to request a certification officer to supply him with certain information about those undertaking full-time courses of education at the establishment concerned.

Regulation 6 contains the statement required by section 30(3) of the Act of what courses constitute, in the Secretary of State's opinion, full-time courses of nursing education.

STATUTORY INSTRUMENTS

1989 No. 444 (S.55)

EDUCATION, SCOTLAND

The Further Education (Approved Associations) (Scotland) Grant Regulations 1989

Made - - - -	*10th March 1989*
Laid before Parliament	*20th March 1989*
Coming into force	*10th April 1989*

The Secretary of State, in exercise of the powers conferred on him by sections 73(d), (e) and (g) and 74(1) of the Education (Scotland) Act 1980(**a**), and of all other powers enabling him in that behalf, hereby makes the following Regulations:

Citation and commencement

1. These Regulations may be cited as the Further Education (Approved Associations) (Scotland) Grant Regulations 1989 and shall come into force on 10th April 1989.

Persons to whom grant may be paid

2.—(1) The Secretary of State may pay grant to any organised body of persons, whether corporate or unincorporate, whose objects include the development of further education, if he is satisfied as to its constitution, financial stability, and fitness to receive grant and that it is not conducted for private profit.

(2) Such a body shall be known as an approved association.

Power to make grants

3. Subject to the provisions of these Regulations, the Secretary of State may pay to an approved association–

(a) non-recurrent grants, being grants in aid of expenditure on the acquisition of land and buildings, the erection, enlargement and improvement of buildings, the supply of equipment and furnishings, the provision and laying out of premises, including playing fields and other facilities for social activities and physical training, and generally on works of a permanent character; and

(b) recurrent grants, being grants in aid of expenditure on administration, the maintenance of a further education centre or facilities for social activities or physical training, including the employment of, and the provision of courses of training for, members of staff, the development of further education and for other connected purposes including works of a permanent but minor character.

Determination and payment of grants

4.—(1) Grants under these Regulations shall be of such amount or paid at such rate and in respect of such period as the Secretary of State may determine.

(**a**) 1980 c.44.

(2) Grants under these Regulations may be paid as single payments or by instalments of such amounts and at such times as the Secretary of State may determine.

Conditions applicable to all grants

5. The following conditions shall apply to the payment of all grants under these Regulations:–

(a) the accounts of an approved association shall be audited to the satisfaction of the Secretary of State, and the approved association shall, if the Secretary of State intimates to it that he is not so satisfied, make such arrangements for the audit of its accounts as satisfy him;

(b) an approved association shall make such reports and returns and give such information to the Secretary of State as he may reasonably require;

(c) an approved association shall immediately inform the Secretary of State of any change in the circumstances upon which its application for grant was based and, if in the opinion of the Secretary of State such change warrants an alteration in the amount of, or the withholding of, the grant, he may re-assess, vary, make a deduction from or withhold the grant as he thinks fit;

(d) an approved association shall afford to any of Her Majesty's Inspectors of Schools, or any other person appointed by the Secretary of State, all reasonable facilities which he may require to inform himself as to the progress of the work or delivery of the services in aid of which grant was made;

(e) an approved association shall comply with any requirements imposed by these Regulations.

Requirements relating to grants

6. It shall be a requirement when any grant under these Regulations has been paid that the approved association shall, at the request of the Secretary of State, repay to him so much of any grant as has not been used for the purposes for which it was given.

Requirements relating to non-recurrent grants

7.—(1) The following requirements shall apply when an approved association has received non-recurrent grant under these Regulations in respect of the acquisition of, or expenditure on, any property, heritable or moveable:–

(a) the property shall not be disposed of except in accordance with sub-paragraphs (b) and (c) below;

(b) when any such property is no longer required for the purpose for which it was improved or acquired, the approved association may, with the consent of the Secretary of State, and shall, if the Secretary of State so directs, sell or otherwise dispose of the property;

(c) when any such property is sold or disposed of, the approved association shall pay to the Secretary of State such part of the proceeds of such sale or disposal (less any expenses incurred in the disposal) as he may after consultation with the approved association require.

(2) Where any property which was provided with the aid of non-recurrent grant paid to an approved association under the Further Education (Scotland) Regulations 1959(**a**) is no longer required for the purpose for which it was so provided, the approved association shall, with the consent of the Secretary of State and as suitable opportunity offers, sell or otherwise dispose of the said property, and shall pay to him such part of the proceeds of such sale or disposal (less any expenses incurred in the disposal) as he may after consultation with the approved association require.

Power to withhold grants

8. The Secretary of State may reduce or withhold a grant if any condition imposed by these Regulations in relation to that grant is not fulfilled.

(**a**) S.I. 1959/477; the relevant amending instrument is S.I. 1979/1185.

Michael B. Forsyth
Parliamentary Under Secretary of State,
Scottish Office

St. Andrew's House, Edinburgh
10th March 1989

EXPLANATORY NOTE

(This note is not part of the Regulations)

These Regulations empower the Secretary of State to pay recurrent and non-recurrent grants to organisations whose objects include the development of further education, and prescribe the conditions of eligibility for, and payment of, grants and the requirements to be complied with by such organisations in receipt of grant.

Provisions relating to the payment of grants to such organisations were previously contained in Part II of the Further Education (Scotland) Regulations 1959, which has been revoked by the Grant-aided Colleges (Scotland) Grant Regulations 1989 (S.I. 1989/433).

STATUTORY INSTRUMENTS

1989 No. 445 (S.56)

COURT OF SESSION, SCOTLAND

Act of Sederunt (Rules of the Court of Session Amendment No.2) (Solicitors' Fees) 1989

Made - - - -	*9th March 1989*
Coming into force	*12th April 1989*

The Lords of Council and Session, under and by virtue of the powers conferred on them by section 5 of the Court of Session Act 1988(**a**) and of all other powers enabling them in that behalf, do hereby enact and declare:

Citation and commencement

1.—(1) This Act of Sederunt may be cited as the Act of Sederunt (Rules of the Court of Session Amendment No.2) (Solicitors' Fees) 1989 and shall come into force on 12th April 1989.

(2) This Act of Sederunt shall be inserted in the Books of Sederunt.

Solicitors' fees

2. In rule 347 of the Rules of the Court of Session(**b**) (fees of solicitors) in Chapters I and III, there is substituted the table of fees set out under those Chapters in the Schedule to this Act of Sederunt, and the fees so substituted shall apply to work, in respect of which those fees are chargeable, done on or after the date on which this Act of Sederunt comes into force.

Edinburgh
9th March 1989

Emslie
Lord President, I.P.D.

(**a**) 1988 c.36.
(**b**) S.I. 1965/321; relevant amending instrument is S.I. 1988/684.

Paragraph 2

SCHEDULE

CHAPTER I

TABLE OF DETAILED CHARGES

1. (a) Framing precognitions and other papers (but not including affidavits), not drawn by counsel—per sheet ... £5.00

(b) Framing formal documents such as Inventories, title pages and Accounts of Expenses etc.—per sheet ... £2.00

(c) Framing affidavits—per sheet ... £7.50

Notes

1. The sheet throughout this Table shall consist of 250 words or numbers.

2. Each solicitor shall be entitled to charge for copies of the precognitions for the use of counsel and himself.

3. As between party and party charges for the precognitions and attendances of witnesses present at a proof or trial but not examined nor held as concurring with a witness who has been examined may be allowed provided a motion to this effect is made at the close of the proof or trial and the court grants the same and the witnesses' names are noted.

4. Where a skilled witness prepares his own precognition or report the solicitor shall be allowed half drawing fees for revising and adjusting it.

5. Where the business can properly be performed by a local solicitor the Auditor in taxing an account shall allow such expenses as would have been incurred if it had been done by the nearest local solicitor, including reasonable fees for instructing and corresponding with him, unless the Auditor is satisfied that it was in the interests of the client that the solicitor in charge of the case should attend personally.

6. As between party and party, no allowance shall be made for plans or photographs lodged in process or prepared for use of counsel except such as are either ordered or subsequently sanctioned by the court prepared by mutual arrangement of parties, or lodged and proved at the trial or proof.

2. Copying papers by any means (including facsimile transmission)–

1st copy—per sheet ... £1.00

Additional copies—per sheet ... £0.35

When copied by photostatic or similar process each page shall be charged as one sheet.

3. Revising papers drawn by counsel, Open and Closed Records, etc.—for each five sheets or part thereof ... £2.00

4. Citation of parties, witnesses, havers, instructions to Messengers-at-Arms–

Each party ... £5.00

Each witness or haver ... £5.00

Instructing Messenger-at-Arms including examining execution and settling fee £5.00

5. Time Charges–

(a) Attendances at meetings, preparation for proof, trial, debate and, at court, consultation with counsel, etc.–

Per quarter hour ... £10.00

or such other sum as in the opinion of the Auditor is justified.

(b) Perusal of documents–

Per quarter hour ... £10.00

or such other sum as in the opinion of the Auditor is justified.

(c) Allowance for time of clerk—one half of above.

(d) Attendance at court offices for performance of formal work ... £2.00

with the exception of lodging all first steps of process, when the fees shall be £5.00

Plus for making up and lodging process ... £5.00

Notes

1. Time necessarily occupied in travelling to be regarded as if occupied on business. Reasonable travelling and maintenance expenses to be allowed in addition.

2. In the event of a party in a trial or proof being represented by one counsel only, allowance may be made to the solicitor should the case warrant it for the attendance of a clerk at one-half the rate chargeable for the solicitor's attendance.

6. Correspondence–

Letters including instructions to counsel (whether sent by hand, post, telex or facsimile transmission)—each page of 125 words £5.00

Formal letters £1.00

Telephone calls (except those under next item) £2.00

Telephone calls (lengthy), to be charged at attendance rate.

CHAPTER III

PART I—UNDEFENDED ACTIONS

(other than consistorial actions)

In all undefended cases where no proof is led, the pursuer's solicitor may in his option elect to charge an inclusive fee to cover all work from taking instructions up to and including obtaining extract decree. The option shall be exercised by pursuer's solicitor endorsing a minute to the above effect on the principal summons or petition before decree is taken.

Fee to pursuer's solicitor for all work up to and obtaining extract decree £90.00

Outlays to an amount not exceeding £100 shall also be allowed.

PART II—UNDEFENDED CONSISTORIAL ACTIONS

1. Fee for all work (other than precognitions) up to and including the calling of summons in court £127.00

Note:

Precognitions to be charged as in Part IV paragraph 5.

2. Incidental Procedure–

Fixing diet, enrolling action, preparing for proof, citing witnesses, etc. ... £72.00

3. Amendment–

(a) where summons amended, where re-service is not ordered, and motion is not starred £18.00

(b) where summons amended, where re-service is not ordered and motion is starred £26.50

(c) where summons amended and re-service is ordered £33.50

4. Commissions to take evidence on interrogatories–

(a) Basic fee to cover all work up to and including lodging completed interrogatories, but excluding attendance at execution of Commission... ... ... £32.50

(b) Attendance at execution of Commission (if required)—per quarter hour £10.00

(c) In addition to above, a fee per sheet for completed interrogatories, including all copies, of £5.50

5. Commissions to take evidence on Open Commission–

(a) Basic fee to solicitor applying for Commission but excluding attendance at execution thereof £30.00

(b) Attendance at execution of Commission—per quarter hour... ... ... £10.00

6. Where applicable, charges under Part IV paragraphs 6, 7, 10, 14, 16 and 21.

7. Proof and completion fee—excluding Accounts of Expenses but including instructing counsel for proof, attendance at proof, settling with witnesses, borrowing and returning productions, procuring interlocutor, and obtaining Extract Decree of Divorce £90.00

8. Accounts–

Framing and lodging account and attending taxation £28.50

PART IIA—UNDEFENDED CONSISTORIAL ACTIONS: AFFIDAVIT PROCEDURE

1. In any undefended action of divorce or separation where–

(a) the facts set out in section 1(2)(a) (adultery) or 1(2)(b) (unreasonable behaviour) of the Divorce (Scotland) Act 1976 ("the 1976 Act") are relied upon; and

(b) there are no conclusions relating to any ancillary matters; and

(c) the pursuer seeks to prove those facts by means of affidavits,

the pursuer's solicitor may in respect of the work specified in column 1 of Table A charge, in a case where he is an Edinburgh solicitor acting alone, the inclusive fee specified in respect of that work in column 2 of that Table, and in any other case, the inclusive fee specified in respect of that work in column 3 of that Table.

TABLE A

Column 1 *Work done*	Column 2 *Inclusive fee Edinburgh solicitors only*	Column 3 *Inclusive fee Edinburgh solicitors and solicitors outside Edinburgh*
1. All work to and including calling of the summons	£182.50	£208.50
2. All work from calling to and including swearing affidavits	£130.00	£156.50
3. All work from swearing affidavits to and including sending extract decree	£ 40.00	£ 58.50
4. All work to and including sending extract decree	£352.50	£423.50
Add session fee	of 7½%	of 10%

2. In any undefended action of divorce or separation where—

(a) the facts set out in section 1(2)(c) (desertion), 1(2)(d) (2 years non-cohabitation and consent) and 1(2)(e) (5 years non-cohabitation) of the 1976 Act are relied on; and

(b) there are no conclusions relating to any ancillary matters; and

(c) the pursuer seeks to prove those facts by means of affidavits,

the pursuer's solicitor may in respect of the work specified in column 1 of Table B charge, in a case where he is an Edinburgh solicitor acting alone, the inclusive fee specified in respect of that work in column 2 of that Table, and in any other case, the inclusive fee specified in respect of that work in column 3 of that Table.

TABLE B

Column 1 *Work done*	Column 2 *Inclusive fee Edinburgh solicitors only*	Column 3 *Inclusive fee Edinburgh solicitors and solicitors outside Edinburgh*
1. All work to and including calling of the summons	£150.00	£175.50
2. All work from calling to and including swearing affidavits	£ 72.00	£ 92.00
3. All work from swearing affidavits to and including sending extract decree	£ 40.00	£ 58.50
4. All work to and including sending extract decree	£262.00	£326.00
Add session fee	of 7½%	of 10%

3. If—

(a) the pursuer's solicitor charges an inclusive fee under either paragraph 1 or paragraph 2 of this Part, and

(b) the action to which the charge relates includes a conclusion relating to an ancillary matter, in addition to that fee, he may charge in respect of the work specified in column 1 of Table C the inclusive fee specified in respect of that work in column 2 of that Table, being the same additional inclusive fee whether he is an Edinburgh solicitor acting alone or on the instructions of a solicitor outside Edinburgh.

TABLE C

Column 1 *Work done*	Column 2 *Inclusive fee*
1. All work to and including calling of the summons	£36.50
2. All work from calling to and including swearing affidavits	£42.00
3. All work under items 1 and 2	£78.50

Add session fee of 7½% if Edinburgh solicitor only.
Add session fee of 10% if Edinburgh solicitor and solicitor outside Edinburgh.

4. The Lord Ordinary shall, on pronouncing an interlocutor granting decree of divorce or separation in any action to which paragraph 1 or 2 apply, include in that interlocutor, where appropriate, a finding in respect of expenses.

5. On pronouncing an interlocutor under paragraph 4 making a finding in respect of expenses, the Lord Ordinary shall pronounce a further interlocutor decerning for payment of those expenses as taxed by the person found liable to pay them.

PART III—OUTER HOUSE PETITIONS

Unopposed Petitions

1. Fee for all work, including precognitions and all copyings, up to and obtaining Extract Decree–
   Edinburgh solicitors only £187.00
   Edinburgh solicitors and solicitors outside Edinburgh £260.00
   Outlays including duplicating charges to be allowed in addition.

Opposed Petitions

2. Fee for all work (other than precognitions) up to and including lodging Petition, obtaining and executing warrant for service £127.00
   Outlays including Duplicating Charges to be allowed in addition.
3. Where applicable, charges under Part IV paragraphs 2, 3 and 5 to 21 of this Table.
4. Reports in opposed petitions–
   (a) for each report by Accountant of Court £22.50
   (b) for any other report, as under Part IV section 6.
5. Obtaining Bond of Caution £22.50

PART IV—DEFENDED ACTIONS

1. Instruction Fee–
   (a) To cover all work (apart from precognitions) until lodgement of Open Record £175.00
   (b) Instructing re-service where necessary £19.00
   (c) If Counter-Claim lodged, additional fee for each party £37.00
2. Record Fee–
   (a) To cover all work in connection with adjustment and closing of Record including subsequent work in connection with By Order Adjustment Roll £187.00

	(b) To cover all work as above, so far as applicable, where action settled or disposed of before Record closed	£116.00
	(c) If consultation held before Record closed, additional fees may be allowed as follows:–	
	(i) arranging consultation	£19.00
	(ii) attendance at consultation—per quarter hour	£10.00
	(d) Additional fee to (a) and (b) (to include necessary amendments) to the pursuer and existing defender, to be allowed for each pursuer, defender or third party brought in prior to the Record being closed, each of	£55.00
	(e) If an additional pursuer, defender or third party is brought in after Record closed, an additional fee shall be allowed to the existing pursuer and the existing defender or defenders, each of	£82.50
3.	Procedure Roll or Debate Roll–	
	(a) Preparing for discussion and all work incidental thereto including instruction of counsel	£37.00
	(b) Attendance at court—per quarter hour	£10.00
	(c) Fee for advising and work incidental thereto	£28.00
4.	Adjustment of Issues and Counter-Issues–	
	(a) Fee to pursuer to include all work in connection with and incidental to the lodging of an Issue, and adjustment and approval thereof	£35.50
	(b) If one Counter-Issue, additional fee to pursuer of	£10.00
	(c) Where more than one Counter-Issue, an additional fee to pursuer for each additional Counter-Issue	£5.00
	(d) Fee to defender or third party for all work in connection with lodging of Counter-Issue and adjustment and approval thereof	£35.50
	(e) Fee to defender or third party for considering Issue where no Counter-Issue lodged...	£10.00
	(f) Fee to defender or third party for considering each additional Counter-Issue	£5.00
5.	Precognitions–	
	Taking and drawing precognitions—per sheet	£18.00

Notes

1. In addition each solicitor shall be entitled to charge for copies of the precognition for the use of counsel and himself.

2. Charges for the precognitions and attendances of witnesses present at a proof or trial but not examined nor held as concurring with a witness who has been examined may be allowed, provided a motion to this effect is made at the close of the proof or trial and the court grants the same and the witnesses' names are noted.

3. Where a skilled witness prepares his own precognition or report the solicitor shall be allowed, for revising and adjusting it, half of the taking and drawing fee per sheet.

6.	Reports obtained under order of court excluding Auditor's report–	
	(a) Fee for all work incidental thereto	£40.00
	(b) Additional fee per sheet of report to include all copies required (maximum £25)	£5.50
7.	Specification of Documents–	
	(a) Basic fee to cover instructing counsel, revising and lodging and all incidental procedure to obtain a diligence up to and including obtaining interlocutor	£37.00
	(b) Fee to opponent's solicitor	£18.00
	(c) Fee for attendance at execution of commission, per quarter-hour, of	£10.00
	(d) If alternative procedure adopted, a fee per person upon whom order served, of	£14.50

8. Commission to take evidence–

ON INTERROGATORIES

(a) Basic fee to solicitor applying for commission to cover all work up to and including lodging report of commission with completed interrogatories and cross-interrogatories... ... ... £75.00

(b) Basic fee to opposing solicitor if cross-interrogatories lodged £60.00

(c) Fee to opposing solicitor if no cross-interrogatories lodged £22.50

(d) In addition to above, fee per sheet to each party for completed interrogatories or cross-interrogatories, including all copies, of... ... ... £5.50

9. Commission to take evidence–

OPEN COMMISSIONS

(a) Basic fee to solicitor applying for commission up to and including lodging report of commission, but excluding (c) £82.50

(b) Basic fee to opposing solicitor £37.00

(c) Fee for attendance at execution of commission at the rate per quarter-hour of £10.00

10. Miscellaneous motions where not otherwise covered by this Table–

(a) Where attendance of counsel and/or solicitor not required £10.00

(b) Where attendance of counsel and/or solicitor required, inclusive of instruction of counsel—not exceeding half-hour £28.00

(c) Thereafter attendance fee per additional quarter-hour £10.00

(d) Basic fee to solicitor for instructing counsel for a Minute (other than a Minute ordered by the court), revising and lodging as a separate step in process including any necessary action £27.00

11. Incidental procedure (not chargeble prior to approval of Issue or allowance of proof)–

Fixing diet, obtaining Note on the Line of Evidence, etc., borrowing and returning process, lodging productions, considering opponent's productions, and all other work prior to the consultation on the sufficiency of evidence £105.00

12. Amendment of Record–

(a) Amendment of conclusions only—fee to proposer £28.00

(b) Amendment of conclusions only—fee to opponent £10.00

(c) Amendment of pleadings after Record closed, where no answers to the amendment are lodged—fee to proposer £40.50

(d) In same circumstances—fee to opponent £18.50

(e) Amendment of pleadings after Record closed where answers are lodged—fee for proposer and each party lodging answers £95.00

(f) Fee for adjustment of Minute and Answers, where applicable to be allowed in addition to each party of £52.50

13. Preparation for trial or proof to include fixing consultation on the sufficiency of evidence and attendance thereat, fee-funding precept, citing witnesses, all work checking and writing up process, and preparing for trial or proof–

(a) If action settled before trial or proof, or the same lasts only one day, to include, where applicable, instruction of counsel £254.00

(b) For each day or part of a day after the first, including instruction of counsel £22.50

(c) To cover preparing for adjourned diets and all work incidental as in (a), if diet postponed more than 5 days £46.00

14. Copyings–

Productions, Reports of Commissions, Duplicate Inventory, Jury list, List of Witnesses, Lord Ordinary's Opinion, etc.—as per Chapter I paragraph 2.

When copied by photostatic or similar process each page to be charged as one sheet.

15.	Settlement by Tender—Fees for either party–	
	(a) Basic fee for lodging, or for considering, first Tender	£55.00
	(b) Fee for lodging, or for considering, each further Tender	£37.00
	(c) If Tender accepted, an additional fee to each party	£37.00
16.	Extrajudicial settlement–	
	Fee inclusive of Joint Minute (not based on a Judicial Tender)	£92.00
17.	Proof or trial–	
	Attendance fee—per quarter-hour	£10.00
18.	Accounts—to include framing and lodging account, and attending taxation, uplifting account and noting taxations	£67.00
19.	Ordering and obtaining extract	£15.00
20.	Final procedure–	
	(a) If case goes to trial or proof, to include all work to close of litigation, so far as not otherwise provided for, including in particular settling with witnesses and procuring and booking verdict, or attendance at judgment	£75.00
	(b) If case disposed of before trial or proof	£22.50
21.	Session fee—to cover communications with client and counsel–	
	(a) Where no correspondent—7½% of total fees and copyings allowed on taxation	
	(b) Where correspondent involved—10% of total fees and copyings allowed on taxation	

Note

To be charged only on that part of the account charged under Chapter III.

PART V—INNER HOUSE BUSINESS

1.	Reclaiming Motions—	
	(a) Fee for appellant for all work up to interlocutor sending case to Roll	£55.00
	(b) Fee for respondent	£28.00
	(c) Additional fee for each party for every 50 pages of Appendix	£23.00
2.	Appeals from inferior courts–	
	(a) Fees for appellant	£67.00
	(b) Fee for respondent	£33.00
	(c) Additional fee for each party for every 50 pages of Appendix	£22.50
3.	Summar or Short Roll–	
	(a) Preparing for discussion, instructing counsel, and preparing Appendix	£55.00
	(b) Attendance fee—per quarter-hour	£10.00
4.	Where applicable, charges under Part IV of this Chapter.	
5.	Special Cases and Inner House petitions, according to circumstances of the case.	
6.	Obtaining Bond of Caution	£22.50

EXPLANATORY NOTE

(This note is not part of the Act of Sederunt)

This Act of Sederunt substitutes new Chapters I and III of the Table in rule 347 of the Rules of the Court of Session (fees of solicitors) with minor amendments and increases most of the fees in these Chapters by about 8 per cent.

STATUTORY INSTRUMENTS

1989 No. 446 (S.57)

NATIONAL HEALTH SERVICE, SCOTLAND

The National Health Service (Functions of Health Boards) (Scotland) Order 1989

Made - - - -	*10th March 1989*
Laid before Parliament	*15th March 1989*
Coming into force	*5th April 1989*

The Secretary of State, in exercise of the powers conferred on him by sections 2(1) and 105(6) and (7) of the National Health Service (Scotland) Act 1978(**a**), and of all other powers enabling him in that behalf, hereby makes the following Order:

Citation, commencement and interpretation

1.—(1) This Order may be cited as the National Health Service (Functions of Health Boards) (Scotland) Order 1989 and shall come into force on 5th April 1989.

(2) In this Order–

"the Act" means the National Health Service (Scotland) Act 1978; and

"the principal Order" means the National Health Service (Functions of Health Boards) (Scotland) Order 1983(**b**).

Amendments to Article 3 of the principal Order

2.—(1) Article 3(1) of the principal Order shall be amended as follows:–

(a) sub-paragraph (e) shall be deleted;

(b) in sub-paragraph (f) there shall be deleted the words from "but not including" to the end;

(c) for sub-paragraph (g) there shall be substituted the following:–

"(g) section 57(1) and (2) (Accommodation and services for private patients) but not including the functions of the Secretary of State under section 57(1) to authorise accommodation and services to be made available."(**c**)

(d) sub-paragraph (h) shall be deleted;

(e) after sub-paragraph (k) there shall be inserted the following:–

"(kk) section 98 (Charges in respect of non-residents) but only as regards the function of the Secretary of State to determine and, as the case may be, to calculate charges."(**d**)

(2) Article 3(2) and (3) of the principal Order shall be deleted.

(**a**) 1978 c.29; section 2(1) was amended by the Health and Social Services and Social Security Adjudications Act 1983 (c.41) ("the 1983 Act"), Schedule 7, paragraph 1; section 105(7) was amended by the Health Services Act 1980 (c.53), Schedule 6, paragraph 5(1) and Schedule 7, and the 1983 Act, Schedule 9.

(**b**) S.I. 1983/1027.

(**c**) Section 57(1) and (2) was substituted by the Health and Medicines Act 1988 (c.49), section 7(11).

(**d**) Section 98 was amended by the Health and Medicines Act 1988, section 7(13) and (14).

Amendments to Article 4 of the principal Order

3.—(1) In article 4(1) of the principal Order sub-paragraphs (a) and (c) shall be deleted.

(2) In article 4(2) of the principal Order–

(a) the words "but subject to paragraph (1)(c) of this article," shall be deleted; and

(b) for the words "section 79" there shall be substituted the words "section 79(1)".

Savings

4. Nothing in this Order shall affect the power of the Secretary of State to exercise any function conferred upon him by the provisions of the Act.

Michael B. Forsyth
Parliamentary Under Secretary of State,
Scottish Office

St. Andrew's House, Edinburgh
10th March 1989

EXPLANATORY NOTE

(This note is not part of the Order)

This Order which comes into force on 1st April 1989 amends the National Health Service (Functions of Health Boards) (Scotland) Order 1983 ("the principal Order") consequential to the coming into force of section 7 of the Health and Medicines Act 1988 (c.49) ("the 1988 Act") and of other provisions of that Act which amend the National Health Service (Scotland) Act 1978 ("the 1978 Act").

The provisions of article 3(1)(e) and 3(2) of the principal Order are revoked to reflect the repeal of section 50 of the 1978 Act; the provisions of article 3(1)(f), (g) and (h) are amended, and sub-paragraph (kk) is inserted, to enable Health Boards to exercise the functions of the setting of charges for, respectively, amenity accommodation, accommodation and services for private resident and non-resident patients and overseas visitors; paragraph (3) of article 3 is revoked because section 54 of the 1978 Act, following repeal of sections 50 and 53 of the 1978 Act by the 1988 Act, refers only to the supply of blood, which is a function expressly excluded from being exercised by Health Boards in terms of article 3(1)(d) of the principal Order; the provisions of article 4(1)(a) and 4(1)(c) are revoked to remove the limitation on the exercise by Health Boards of functions under section 36 and 79 of the 1978 Act (powers to provide accommodation and premises and to buy and sell land).

STATUTORY INSTRUMENTS

1989 No. 455

SOCIAL SECURITY

The Social Security Benefits Up-rating Regulations 1989

Made - - - -	*13th March 1989*
Laid before Parliament	*17th March 1989*
Coming into force	*10th April 1989*

The Secretary of State for Social Security, in exercise of the powers conferred by sections 17(1)(a), 49(b), 58(3) and 131 of, and Schedule 20 to, the Social Security Act 1975**(a)** and section 64(2) of the Social Security Act 1986**(b)**, and of all other powers enabling him in that behalf, by this instrument, which contains only provisions in consequence of an order under section 63 of the Act of 1986, makes the following Regulations:

Citation, commencement and interpretation

1.—(1) These Regulations may be cited as the Social Security Benefits Up-rating Regulations 1989 and shall come into force on 10th April 1989.

(2) In these Regulations, unless the context otherwise requires—

"the Act" means the Social Security Act 1975;

"the 1986 Act" means the Social Security Act 1986;

"the up-rating order" means the Social Security Benefits Up-rating Order 1989**(c)**;

and any reference in a regulation to a numbered paragraph is to the paragraph of that regulation bearing that number.

Conditions relating to payment of additional benefit under awards made before the appointed or prescribed day

2.—(1) This regulation applies to a case where—

(a) either—

(i) an award of any benefit under Chapters I to III of Part II of the Act has been made before the day appointed or prescribed for the payment of the benefit in question at a higher rate provided in or by virtue of the up-rating order, or

(ii) an award of any benefit under Part II of the Act has been made before the day appointed or prescribed for the payment of the benefit in question at a lower rate provided in or by virtue of the up-rating order;

(b) the period to which the award relates has not ended before that day; and

(c) the award does not, in accordance with the provisions of section 64(3) of the 1986 Act, provide for the payment of the benefit at a higher or lower rate (as the case may be) as from that day.

(a) 1975 c.14; section 58(3) ceased to have effect on 6th April 1987 except in relation to certain beneficiaries—*see* section 39 of and paragraph 4 of Schedule 3 to the Social Security Act 1986 (c.50), and S.I. 1987/354, art. 2 and Schedule 1. Schedule 20 is cited because of the meanings ascribed to the words "Prescribe" and "Regulations".

(b) 1986 c.50.

(c) S.I. 1989/43.

(2) In a case to which this regulation applies, section 64(2) of the 1986 Act shall have effect subject to the condition that if a question arises as to either—

(a) the weekly rate at which the benefit is payable by virtue of the up-rating order; or

(b) whether the conditions for the receipt of the benefit at the altered rate are satisfied,

the benefit shall, until the question has been determined in accordance with the provisions of the Act, be or continue to be payable at the weekly rate specified in paragraph (3).

(3) The weekly rate referred to in paragraph (2) is the weekly rate specified in the award or the weekly rate at which the benefit would have been paid if the question had not arisen, whichever is the lower.

Persons not ordinarily resident in Great Britain

3. Regulation 5 of the Social Security Benefit (Persons Abroad) Regulations 1975**(a)** (application of disqualification in respect of up-rating of benefit) shall apply to any additional benefit payable by virtue of the up-rating order.

Amendment of the Social Security (Unemployment, Sickness and Invalidity Benefit) Regulations 1983

4. Regulation 3 of the Social Security (Unemployment, Sickness and Invalidity Benefit) Regulations 1983**(b)** (persons deemed to be incapable of work) shall be further amended by the substitution in paragraph (3) for "£27·00" of "£28·50".

Amendment of the Social Security (General Benefit) Regulations 1982

5. Regulation 16 of the Social Security (General Benefit) Regulations 1982**(c)** (earnings level for the purpose of unemployability supplement) shall be further amended by the substitution for "£1404·00" of "£1482·00".

Earnings limit

6. The sums specified in paragraph 2B of Schedule 2 to the Social Security Benefit (Dependency) Regulations 1977**(d)** (prescribed circumstances for increase of invalid care allowance) shall be increased from £90, £11 and £90 to £95, £12 and £95 respectively.

Revocation

7. The Social Security Benefits Up-rating Regulations 1988**(e)** are hereby revoked.

Signed by authority of the Secretary of State for Social Security.

Peter Lloyd
Parliamentary Under-Secretary of State,
Department of Social Security

13th March 1989

(a) S.I. 1975/563; the relevant amending instruments are S.I. 1977/342, 1979/1432 and 1988/436.
(b) S.I. 1983/1598; the relevant amending instruments are S.I. 1987/688 and 1988/436.
(c) S.I. 1982/1408; the relevant amending instrument is S.I. 1988/436. Unemployability Supplement is only payable to those beneficiaries in receipt of it immediately before 6th April 1987—*see* Social Security Act 1986, section 39, Schedule 3, paragraph 4 and S.I. 1987/354, art. 2, Schedule 1.
(d) S.I. 1977/343; the relevant amending instruments are S.I. 1984/1699 and 1985/1618.
(e) S.I. 1988/436.

EXPLANATORY NOTE

(This note is not part of the Regulations)

This instrument contains only provisions in consequence of an order under section 63 of the Social Security Act 1986 (up-rating of benefit). Accordingly, by virtue of paragraph 8 of Schedule 16 to the Social Security Act 1975 and paragraph 12(2) of Schedule 3 to the Social Security Act 1980 (c.30), the Secretary of State has not referred proposals to make the regulations contained in this instrument to the Industrial Injuries Advisory Council or to the Social Security Advisory Committee. Paragraph 8 and paragraph 12(2), mentioned above, were amended by the Social Security Act 1986, section 86 and Schedule 10, paragraphs 90 and 99 respectively.

Regulation 2 provides that in certain cases where a question has arisen about the effect of the up-rating order on a benefit already in payment the altered rates will not apply until the question is determined by an adjudicating authority. Regulation 3 applies the provisions of regulation 5 of the Social Security Benefit (Persons Abroad) Regulations 1975 so as to restrict the application of the increases specified in the order in cases where the beneficiary lives abroad.

Regulation 4 raises from £27·00 to £28·50 the earnings limit which applies to those undertaking work in certain circumstnces while receiving sickness or invalidity benefit.

Regulation 5 raises from £1404·00 to £1482·00 a year the earnings limit which applies to unemployability supplement.

Regulation 6 specifies earnings limits for child dependency increases payable with invalid care allowance.

Regulation 7 contains a revocation consequential upon the coming into force of these Regulations.

STATUTORY INSTRUMENTS

1989 No. 462

HEALTH AND SAFETY

The Health and Safety (Fees) Regulations 1989

Made - - - -	*13th March 1989*
Laid before Parliament	*28th March 1989*
Coming into force	*20th April 1989*

The Secretary of State, in exercise of the powers conferred on him by section 43(2), (4), (5), (6) and (9) and 82(3)(a) of the Health and Safety at Work etc. Act 1974**(a)** ("the 1974 Act") and of all other powers enabling him in that behalf and for the purpose of giving effect without modifications to proposals submitted to him by the Health and Safety Commission under section 11(2)(d) of the 1974 Act, hereby makes the following Regulations:–

Citation, commencement and interpretation

1.—(1) These Regulations may be cited as the Health and Safety (Fees) Regulations 1989 and shall come into force on 20th April 1989.

(2) In these Regulations, unless the context otherwise requires–

"approval" unless otherwise stated includes the amendment of an approval, and "amendment of an approval" includes the issue of a new approval replacing the original incorporating an amendment;

"employment medical adviser" means an employment medical adviser appointed under section 56(1) of the Health and Safety at Work etc. Act 1974;

"the mines and quarries provisions" means such of the relevant statutory provisions as relate exclusively to–

(a) mines and quarries within the meaning of section 180 of the Mines and Quarries Act 1954**(b)**;

(b) tips within the meaning of section 2(1) of the Mines and Quarries (Tips) Act 1969**(c)**,

and includes regulations, rules and orders relating to a particular mine (whether they are continued in force by regulation 7(3) of the Mines and Quarries Acts 1954 to 1971 (Repeals and Modifications) Regulations 1974**(d)** or are health and safety regulations);

"original approval" and "original authority" do not include an amendment of an approval or an amendment of an authority;

"renewal of approval" or "renewal of licence" means respectively the granting of an approval or licence to follow a previous approval or licence without any amendment or gap in time;

"respiratory protective equipment" includes any respirator and any breathing apparatus.

(a) 1974 c.37; section 43 was amended by the Employment Protection Act 1975 (c.71), Schedule 15, paragraph 12.
(b) 1954 c.70.
(c) 1969 c.10.
(d) S.I. 1974/2013.

(3) Unless the context otherwise requires, any reference in these Regulations to–

(a) a numbered regulation or Schedule is a reference to the regulation or Schedule in these Regulations so numbered;

(b) a numbered paragraph is a reference to the paragraph so numbered in the regulation or Schedule in which the reference appears.

Fees payable under the mines and quarries provisions

2.—(1) A fee shall be payable by the applicant to the Health and Safety Executive on each application for an original approval, an amendment of approval or a renewal of approval under any of the mines and quarries provisions.

(2) The fee payable under paragraph (1) for each description of plant, apparatus, substance and in any other case set out in column 1 of Part I of Schedule 1 shall be respectively that specified in the corresponding entry in columns 2, 3 and 4 of that Part.

(3) Where the Executive requires testing to be carried out by its staff to decide whether approval can be granted, a fee shall be payable to the Executive by the applicant on the issue by the Executive of its determination in respect of the application for the approval as described below–

(a) in the case of explosives and detonators, for each test specified in column 1 of Part II of Schedule 1, the fee shall be that specified in the corresponding entry in column 2 of that Part;

(b) in any other case, the fee shall be determined under Part III of Schedule 1.

Fees payable in respect of approval of respiratory protective equipment, blasting helmets and automatic safe loading indicators

3.—(1) A fee shall be payable by the applicant to the Health and Safety Executive on each application for approval–

(a) of respiratory protective equipment–

(i) under the Factories Act 1961**(a)**, or any regulations made or having effect as if made under that Act,

(ii) under the Control of Lead at Work Regulations 1980**(b)**,

(iii) under the Ionising Radiations Regulations 1985**(c)**

(iv) under the Control of Asbestos at Work Regulations 1987**(d)**;

(b) of blasting helmets under the Factories Act 1961, or any regulations made or having effect as if made under that Act; and

(c) of automatic safe load indicators under the Construction (Lifting Operations) Regulations 1961**(e)**, and the Shipbuilding and Ship-Repairing Regulations 1960**(f)**.

(2) The fee payable for approval of each item of each subject matter described in column 1 of Part I of Schedule 2 shall be that specified in the corresponding entry in column 2 of that Part.

(3) Where the Executive requires testing to be carried out by its staff to determine whether approval of any item of equipment specified in column 1 of Part II of Schedule 2 can be granted, a fee shall be payable to the Executive by the applicant on the issue by the Executive of its determination in respect of the application for approval and the fee shall be that specified in the corresponding entry in column 2 of that Part.

Fees payable under the Agriculture (Tractor Cabs) Regulations 1974 and the Poisonous Substances in Agriculture Regulations 1984

4.—(1) A fee shall be payable by the applicant to the Health and Safety Executive on each application for approval of plant and equipment under–

(a) the Agriculture (Tractor Cabs) Regulations 1974**(g)**; and

(b) the Poisonous Substances in Agriculture Regulations 1984**(h)**.

(a) 1961 c.34.
(b) S.I. 1980/1248.
(c) S.I. 1985/1333.
(d) S.I. 1987/2115.
(e) S.I. 1961/1581.
(f) S.I. 1960/1932.
(g) S.I. 1974/2034; relevant amending instruments are S.I. 1976/1247, 1980/1036 and 1981/1414.
(h) S.I. 1984/1114.

(2) The fee payable for the approval of each subject matter described in column 1 of Part I of Schedule 3 shall be that specified in the corresponding entry in column 2 of that Part.

(3) Where the Executive requires testing to be carried out by its staff to determine whether approval of respiratory protective equipment can be granted under the Poisonous Substances in Agricuture Regulations 1984, a fee shall be payable to the Executive by the applicant on the issue by the Executive of its determination in respect of the application for approval, and the fee shall be that specified in column 2 of Part II of Schedule 3.

Fee payable under the Freight Containers (Safety Convention) Regulations 1984

5.—(1) A fee shall be payable by the applicant to the Health and Safety Executive on each application for approval of a scheme or programme for examination of freight containers under the Freight Containers (Safety Convention) Regulations 1984**(a)**.

(2) The fee payable for the approval described in column 1 of Schedule 4 shall be that specified in the corresponding entry in column 2 of that Schedule.

Fees payable for a licence under the Asbestos (Licensing) Regulations 1983

6.—(1) A fee shall be payable by the applicant to the Health and Safety Executive on each application for a licence under the Asbestos (Licensing) Regulations 1983**(b)**.

(2) The fee payable for licence of each subject matter described in column 1 of Schedule 5 shall be that specified in the corresponding entry in column 2 of that Schedule.

Fees payable for examination by an employment medical adviser

7.—(1) A fee shall be payable to the Health and Safety Executive by an employer in respect of a medical examination of each of his employees by an employment medical adviser for the purposes of any provision specified in column 1 of Schedule 6.

(2) The fee payable under paragraph (1) shall be a basic fee for each examination together with additional fees for X-rays and laboratory tests where these are taken or carried out in connection with the examination; and for each provision specified in column 1 of Schedule 6–

(a) the basic fee shall be the amount specified in column 3 of that Schedule for that provision;

(b) the additional fee for X-rays shall be the amount specified in column 4 of that Schedule for that provision and shall cover all X-rays taken in connection with any one examination;

(c) the additional fee for laboratory tests shall be the amount specified in column 5 of that Schedule for that provision and shall cover all such tests carried out in connection with any one examination.

(3) Where an employment medical adviser carries out a medical examination of a self-employed person for the purposes of the Control of Asbestos at Work Regulations 1987, that self-employed person shall pay to the Executive fees ascertained in accordance with paragraph (2).

Fees for medical surveillance by an employment medical adviser under the Control of Lead at Work Regulations 1980

8.—(1) A fee shall be payable to the Health and Safety Executive by an employer in respect of medical surveillance of any of his employees by an employment medical adviser for the purposes of the Control of Lead at Work Regulations 1980**(c)**.

(2) The fee payable for each item described in column 1 of Schedule 7 shall be that specified in the corresponding entry in column 2 of that Schedule.

(a) S.I. 1984/1890.
(b) S.I. 1983/1649.
(c) S.I. 1980/1248.

Fees for approval of dosimetry services and for type approval of radiation generators or apparatus containing radioactive substances under the Ionising Radiations Regulations 1985

9.—(1) A fee shall be payable by the applicant to the Health and Safety Executive on each application for an approval of dosimetry services and for the annual reassessment of an approval of dosimetry services previously granted for the purposes of the Ionising Radiation Regulations 1985**(a)**.

(2) A fee shall be payable by the applicant to the Executive on each application for the type approval of a radiation generator or an apparatus containing a radioactive substance.

(3) The fee payable for approval or type approval in respect of each matter described in column 1 of Schedule 8 shall be that specified in the corresponding entry in column 2 of that Schedule, and the fee for annual reassessment of such approval in respect of each such matter shall be that specified in column 3 of that Schedule.

Fees payable under the Explosives Act 1875 and instruments made thereunder, under the Petroleum (Consolidation) Act 1928 and the Petroleum (Transfer of Licences) Act 1936 and under the Gas Cylinders (Conveyance) Regulations 1931

10.—(1) Where any application in relation to a provision specified in column 1 of Part I of Schedule 9 is made for a purpose specified in column 2 of that Part, the fee specified in the corresponding entry in column 3 of that Part shall be payable by the applicant to the Health and Safety Executive.

(2) The fee or maximum fee payable under each provision specified in column 1 of Part II of Schedule 9 for the purpose described in the corresponding entry in column 2 shall be that specified in the corresponding entry in column 3 of that Part.

(3) A fee shall be payable by the applicant to the Executive on each application being made for each purpose specified in column 1 of Parts III, IV, V and VI of Schedule 9, and the fee for each such purpose shall be that specified in the corresponding entry in column 2 of those Parts.

(4) A fee shall be payable to the Executive where the Executive requires any testing to be carried out in connection with any purpose specified in column 1 of Part VII of Schedule 9, and the fee for testing in connection with each such purpose shall be that specified in the corresponding entry in column 2 of that Part for each hour or part of an hour worked in respect of such testing and such fee shall be payable prior to the granting of the application.

Date from which fees are payable under the Petroleum (Consolidation) Act 1928 and the Petroleum (Transfer of Licences) Act 1936

11. Notwithstanding the provisions of section 4 of the Petroleum (Consolidation) Act 1928**(b)** or section 1(4) of the Petroleum (Transfer of Licences) Act 1936**(c)** the fees for petroleum licences prescribed by these Regulations shall be payable for any licence first having effect or any transfer or renewal of a licence first taking effect on or after the coming into force of these Regulations, irrespective of the date of the application for that licence, transfer or renewal.

Fees for testing in connection with application under the Classification and Labelling of Explosives Regulations 1983

12. A fee shall be payable to the Health and Safety Executive by the applicant if any testing is carried out by or on behalf of the Executive with the agreement of the applicant in connection with any purpose specified in column 1 of Schedule 10, and the fee for testing in connection with each such purpose shall be that specified in the corresponding entry in column 2 of that Schedule for each hour or part of an hour worked in respect of such testing and such fee shall be payable prior to the granting of the application.

(a) S.I. 1985/1333.
(b) 1928 c.32; relevant amending instruments are S.I. 1974/1942 and S.I. 1987/52.
(c) 1936 c.27; relevant amending instruments are S.I. 1974/1942 and S.I. 1987/52.

Fees for explosive licences under Part IX of the Dangerous Substances in Harbour Areas Regulations 1987

13.—(1) A fee shall be payable by the applicant to the Health and Safety Executive on each application for an explosives licence under Part IX of the Dangerous Substances in Harbour Areas Regulations**(a)**.

(2) The fee for each item specified in column 1 of Schedule 11 shall be that specified in the corresponding entry in column 2 of that Schedule.

Calculation of hours worked

14. In calculating the number of hours worked for the purpose of determining the amount of a fee payable under regulation 3(2), 4(3), 10(4), 12 or 13(2) no account shall be taken of any typing, messenger or ancillary work (for which no further charge shall be payable).

Revocations

15. The Health and Safety (Fees) Regulations 1988**(b)** are hereby revoked.

Northern Ireland

16. These Regulations shall not apply to Northern Ireland.

Signed by order of the Secretary of State.

Patrick Nicholls
Parlimentary Under Secretary of State,
Department of Employment

13th March 1989

SCHEDULE 1

Regulation 2

PART I

APPROVAL OF PLANT, APPARATUS OR SUBSTANCE UNDER THE MINES AND QUARRIES PROVISIONS

1 *Subject matter of approval*	2 *Fees for an original approval*	3 *Fee for amendment of approval*	4 *Fee for renewal of approval*
(a) Approval of breathing apparatus	£661	£353	£40
(b) Approval of dust respirators	£60	£60	£40
(c) Approval of explosives	£120	£110	£40
(d) Approval of locomotive or other vehicle	£1,514	£348	£40
(e) Approval of signalling apparatus	£100	£112	£40
(f) Approval in any other case	£192	£104	£40

(a) S.I. 1987/37.
(b) S.I. 1988/712.

PART II

FEES FOR TESTING EXPLOSIVES AND DETONATORS UNDER THE MINES AND QUARRIES PROVISIONS

1 *Test*	2 *Fees for test*
Ballistic pendulum shot	£29
Break test shot	£45
Deflagration shot	£24
Detonator test (per 100 shots)	£269
Gallery shot	£63
Mortar shot	£28
Velocity of detonation test (per 3 shots)	£53

PART III

FEES FOR OTHER TESTING

The fee for any testing not fixed by Part II of this Schedule shall be £48 for each man-hour of work done in the testing, excluding any typing, messenger or other ancilliary work (for which no further charge shall be payable).

Regulation 3

SCHEDULE 2

PART I

APPROVALS OF RESPIRATORY PROTECTIVE EQUIPMENT, BLASTING HELMETS AND AUTOMATIC SAFE LOAD INDICATORS

1 *Subject matter of approval*	2 *Fee*
(a) Approval of respiratory protective equipment	£60
(b) Approval of blasting helmets	£40
(c) Approval of automatic safe load indicators	£32 per hour worked

PART II

FEES FOR TESTING RESPIRATORY PROTECTIVE EQUIPMENT AND BLASTING HELMETS

1 *Item of Equipment*	2 *Fee*
Respiratory protective equipment	£48 per hour worked
Blasting helmets	£48 per hour worked

SCHEDULE 3

Regulation 4

PART I

APPROVALS UNDER THE AGRICULTURE (TRACTOR CABS) REGULATIONS 1974, AND POISONOUS SUBSTANCES IN AGRICULTURE REGULATIONS 1984.

1 *Subject matter of approval*	2 *Fee*
(a) Original approval of tractor cab	£145
(b) Revision of an existing approval of a tractor cab	£72
(c) Approval of respiratory protective equipment	£60

PART II

FEES FOR TESTING RESPIRATORY PROTECTIVE EQUIPMENT UNDER THE POISONOUS SUBSTANCES IN AGRICULTURE REGULATIONS 1984.

1 *Test*	2 *Fee*
Respiratory Protective Equipment	£48 per hour worked

SCHEDULE 4

Regulation 5

APPROVAL UNDER THE FREIGHT CONTAINERS (SAFETY CONVENTION) REGULATIONS 1984

1 *Subject matter of approval*	2 *Fee*
Approval of scheme or programme for examination of freight containers	£25

SCHEDULE 5

Regulation 6

LICENCE UNDER THE ASBESTOS (LICENSING) REGULATIONS 1983

1 *Subject matter of Licence*	2 *Fee*
(a) Licence for work with asbestos insulation or asbestos coating	£415
(b) Renewal of original licence granted under (a) above	£208

Regulation 7

SCHEDULE 6

FEES FOR EXAMINATION BY AN EMPLOYMENT MEDICAL ADVISER

Provision		Reference	Basic Fee	*Additional fees where appropriate*	
				Fee for X-Rays	*Fee for Laboratory tests*
1		2	3	4	5
(a)	The Indiarubber Regulations 1922	S.R. & O. 1922/329 (relevant amending instruments are S.I. 1973/36 and S.I. 1980/1248).	£31	£32	£18.50
(b)	The Chemical Works Regulations 1922	S.R. & O. 1922/731 (relevant amending instruments is S.I. 1973/36).	£31	£32	£18.50
(c)	The Patent Fuel Manufacture (Health & Welfare) Special Regulations 1946	S.R. & O. 1946/258 (relevant amending instrument is S.I. 1973/36).	£31	£32	£18.50
(d)	The Mule Spinning (Health) Special Regulations 1953	S.I. 1953/1545 (relevant amending instrument is S.I. 1973/36).	£31	£32	£18.50
(e)	The Work in Compressed Air Special Regulations 1958	S.I. 1958/61 (relevant amending instrument is S.I. 1973/36).	£31	£32	£18.50
(f)	The Carcinogenic Substances Regulations 1967	S.I. 1967/879 (relevant amending instrument is S.I. 1973/36).	£31	£32	£18.50
(g)	The Ionising Radiations Regulations 1985	S.I. 1985/1333	£42	£32	£18.50
(h)	The Control of Asbestos at Work Regulations 1987	S.I. 1987/2115	£37	£29	£16.50
(i)	Surveillance under sub-paragraph (g) above which is confined to examination of, and making of entries in, records.		£13	–	–

SCHEDULE 7

Regulation 8

FEES FOR MEDICAL SURVEILLANCE BY EMPLOYMENT MEDICAL ADVISER UNDER THE CONTROL OF LEAD AT WORK REGULATIONS 1980

1 *Item*	2 *Fee*
On the first assessment of an employee (including any clinical medical examination and laboratory tests in connection with the assessment)	£41
On each subsequent assessment of an employee–	
(i) for laboratory tests where these are carried out	£32
(ii) for a clinical medical examination where this is carried out	£14

SCHEDULE 8

Regulation 9

FEES FOR APPROVAL OF DOSIMETRY SERVICES AND FOR TYPE APPROVAL OF RADIATION GENERATORS OR APPARATUS CONTAINING RADIOACTIVE SUBSTANCES UNDER THE IONISING RADIATIONS REGULATIONS 1985**(a)**

1 *Description*	2 *Fee for approval or type approval*	3 *Fee for annual reassessment*
Approval of Dosimetry Services granted under Regulation 15 of the Ionising Radiations Regulations 1985		
Group I		
Dose record keeping		
(a) Where the application is solely in respect of Group I functions	£335	£98
(b) Where the application for Group I functions is linked to an application for approval in another group	£143	£98
Group II		
External dosimetry		
(a) Whole body (beta, gamma, thermal neutrons) film	£507 for one sub-group and £168 for each additional sub-group	£364 for one sub-group and £98 for each additional sub-group
(b) Whole body (beta, gamma, thermal neutrons) thermoluminescent dosimeter (TLD)		
(c) Whole body (neutron), other than sub-groups (a) or (b)		
(d) Whole body, other than sub-groups (a), (b) or (c)		
(e) Extremity monitoring		
(f) Accident dosimetry, other than in the previous sub-groups		

(a) S.I. 1985/1333.

1 *Description*	2 *Fee for approval or type approval*	3 *Fee for annual reassessment*
Group III Internal Dosimetry		
(a) Strontium 90 and actinides	£634 for one or more radio-isotopes in this sub-group.	£271 for one or more radio-isotopes in this sub-group.
(b) Any other radionuclide	£492 for up to 5 radionuclides and £345 for each additional group of 5 radionuclides or part thereof.	£175 for up to 5 radionuclides and £137 for each additional group of 5 radionuclides or part thereof.
Type approval of a radiation generator or an apparatus containing a radioactive substance under sub-paragraph (f) or (g) respectively of Schedule 3 to the Ionising Radiations Regulations 1985 (which excepts such type approved radiation generators or apparatus containing radio-active substances from the notification requirements of regulation 5 of those Regulations)	£68	

Regulation 10

SCHEDULE 9

FEES PAYABLE UNDER THE EXPLOSIVES ACT 1875 AND INSRUMENTS MADE THEREUNDER, UNDER THE PETROLEUM (CONSOLIDATION) ACT 1928 AND THE PETROLEUM (TRANSFER OF LICENCES) ACT 1936, AND UNDER THE GAS CYLINDERS (CONVEYANCE) REGULATIONS 1931.

PART I

APPLICATIONS FOR FACTORY LICENCES, MAGAZINE LICENCES AND IMPORTATION LICENCES AND AMENDING LICENCES UNDER SECTIONS 6, 12 AND 40(9) OF THE EXPLOSIVES ACT AND REPLACEMENT OF SUCH LICENCES.

1 *Provision under which a licence is granted*	2 *Purpose of application*	3 *Fee*
Explosives Act 1875 c. 17.		
Section 6 (as applied to explosives other than gunpowder by sections 39 and 40)	Factory licence	£642 plus £32 additional fee for each building or other place in which explosives are to be made or kept.
	Factory amending licence	£248 plus £8 additional fee for each building or other place to be specified in the amending licence and in which explosives are to be made or kept.
	Replacement of one of the above licences if lost	£16

1 *Provision under which a licence is granted*	2 *Purpose of application*	3 *Fee*
Section 12 (as applied to explosives other than gunpowder by sections 39 and 40)	Magazine licence	£502 plus £32 additional fee for each building or other place in which explosives are to be kept.
	Magazine amending licence	£39 plus £8 additional fee for each building or other place to be specified in the amending licence and in which explosives are to be kept.
	Replacement of one of the above licences if lost	£16
Section 40(9)	Licence for importation of explosives	£34
	Licence for importation of a consignment of explosives which are not to be distributed in Great Britain but imported for transhipment only	£34
	Replacement of one of the above licences if lost	£16
	Amendment to an existing licence	£12
Section 40(9) as applied to compressed acetylene by The Compressed Acetylene (Importation) Regulations 1978**(a)**	Licence for importation of compressed acetylene	£34
	Replacement of one of the above licences if lost	£16
	Amendment to an existing licence	£12

(a) S.I. 1978/1723.

PART II

FEE OR MAXIMUM FEE PAYABLE IN RESPECT OF GRANTING AND RENEWAL OF AN EXPLOSIVES STORE LICENCE, THE REGISTRATION OR RENEWAL OF REGISTRATION OF PREMISES USED FOR KEEPING EXPLOSIVES AND THE GRANTING AND TRANSFER OF PETROLEUM-SPIRIT LICENCES.

1 *Provision under which a fee or maximum fee is payable*	2 *Purpose of application*	3 *Fee or Maximum fee*
Section 15 (see note 1)	A store licence	£47
Section 18 (see note 1)	Renewal of a store licence	£47
Section 21 (see note 1)	Registration and renewal of registration of premises for the keeping of explosives with a local authority	£8
Petroleum (Consolidation) Act 1928 c. 32		
Section 4 (see notes 2 and 3)	Licence to keep petroleum spirit of a quantity - not exceeding 2,500 litres	£22 for each year of licence
	exceeding 2,500 litres but not exceeding 50,000 litres	£33 for each year of licence
	exceeding 50,000 litres	£65 for each year of licence
Petroleum (Transfer of Licences) Act 1936 c. 27		
Section 1(4)	Transfer of petroleum spirit licence	£6

Note:

1. Part 1 of the Explosives Act 1875 (which includes sections 15, 18 and 21) is applied to explosives other than gunpowder by sections 39 and 40 of that Act.

2. In the case of a solid substance for which by virtue of an Order in Council made under section 19 of the Petroleum (Consolidation) Act 1928 a licence is required, the fee payable under this Schedule shall be calculated as if one kilogram of the substance were equivalent to one litre.

3. The fee payable for a licence of more or less than one year's duration shall be the fee set out above increased or decreased, as the case may be, proportionately according to the duration of the period for which the licence is granted or renewed.

PART III

APPLICATIONS UNDER PARAGRAPH (1) OF THE PROVISO TO ORDER IN COUNCIL (NO. 30) of 2ND FEBRUARY 1937**(a)** FOR APPROVALS OF PREMISES AND APPARATUS IN WHICH ACETYLENE IS TO BE MANUFACTURED OR KEPT

1 *Purpose of application*	2 *Fee*
Original approval of premises in which acetylene is to be manufactured or kept	£352
Amendment of an approval of premises in which acetylene is to be manufactured or kept	£165
Approval of apparatus in which acetylene is to be manufactured or kept	£19

PART IV

APPLICATIONS FOR COMPARISONS AND APPROVALS IN RESPECT OF CONDITIONS (1), (5) AND (8) IN THE ORDER OF THE SECRETARY OF STATE (NO. 9) OF 23RD JUNE 1919**(b)**

1 *Purpose of application*	2 *Fee*
Comparison of a porous substance with a sample porous substance	£19
Approval of an acetylene cylinder design	£53
Original approval of premises in which acetylene is compressed	£352
Amendment of an approval of premises in which acetylene is compressed	£23

PART V

APPLICATIONS FOR APPROVALS FOR THE PURPOSE OF EXEMPTION ORDERS MADE UNDER REGULATION 4 OF THE GAS CYLINDERS (CONVEYANCE) REGULATIONS 1931**(c)**

1 *Purpose of application*	2 *Fee*
Approval of a gas cylinder manufacturer	£7,698
Approval of the design of a gas cylinder	£53
Approval of a supplier of the material of which a gas cylinder is manufactured	£720
Approval of a gas cylinder inspection body	£1,791
Approval of a user of a gas cylinder manufactured and tested in accordance with the provisions of Home Office Specifications LASS 1 or LASW 1	£360

PART VI

MISCELLANEOUS APPLICATIONS

1 *Purpose of application*	2 *Fee*
Authorisation or classification of an explosive to be manufactured for general sale or to be imported for general sale, with or without a licence	£95
Grant of an original special packing authority under Rule 12 of the Packing of Explosive for Conveyance Rules 1949**(d)**	£181
Amendment to a special packing authority as above	£24
Grant of an ammonium nitrate mixtures licence under article 3 of the Ammonium Nitrate Mixtures Exemption Order 1967**(e)**	£88

(a) S.R.& O. 1937/54; relevant amending instruments are S.R. & O. 1947/805 and S.I. 1974/1885.
(b) S.R & O. 1919/809; amended by S.I. 1974/1885.
(c) S.R.& O. 1931/679; relevant amending instruments are S.I. 1947/1594 and 1974/1942.
(d) S.I. 1949/798 to which there are no relevant amendments.
(e) S.I. 1967/1485.

PART VII

FURTHER FEES PAYABLE IN RESPECT OF CERTAIN TESTING REQUIRED BY THE HEALTH AND SAFETY EXECUTIVE

1 *Purpose of application*	2 *Fee*
Application for a licence to be granted under or in pursuance of section 40(9) of the Explosives Act 1875**(a)** for the importation of explosives which are not at the time of application authorised to be manufactured for general sale or imported for general sale	£44 per hour worked
Approval of apparatus in which acetylene is to be manufactured or kept (Part III above)	£44 per hour worked
Comparison of a porous substance with a sample porous substance (Part IV above)	£44 per hour worked
Authorisation of an explosive to be manufactured for general sale or to be imported for general sale, with or without a licence (Part VI above)	£44 per hour worked

Regulation 12

SCHEDULE 10

FEES FOR TESTING IN CONNECTION WITH APPLICATION UNDER THE CLASSIFICATION AND LABELLING OF EXPLOSIVES REGULATIONS 1983**(b)**

1 *Purpose of application*	2 *Fee*
Classification of an article, substance, combination or unit load	£44 per hour worked

Regulation 13

SCHEDULE 11

FEES FOR WORK IN CONNECTION WITH THE APPLICATIONS UNDER PART IX OF THE DANGEROUS SUBSTANCES IN HARBOUR AREA REGULATIONS 1987**(c)**

1 *Purpose of application*	2 *Fee*
Grant of an explosives licence or alteration of the terms of an existing explosives licence	£195 plus £33 per hour worked

(a) 1875 c.17; section 40(9) was amended by Orders in Council (No. 10) of 27th November 1875 (Rev. VII, p.40) and (No. 10A) of 26th June 1884 (Rev. VIII, p. 41) and S.I. 1974/1885 and 1978/1723.
(b) S.I. 1983/1140.
(c) S.I. 1987/37.

EXPLANATORY NOTE

(This note is not part of the Regulations)

1. These Regulations update and replace the Health and Safety (Fees) Regulations 1988 which they revoke (regulation 15). They fix or determine the fees payable by an applicant to the Health and Safety Executive in respect of an application made for–

(a) an approval under mines and quarries legislation (regulation 2 and Schedule 1);

(b) an approval of certain respiratory protective equipment, blasting helmets, and of automatic safe load indicators (regulation 3 and Schedule 2);

(c) an approval of plant or equipment under the Agriculture (Tractor Cabs) Regulations 1974 and the Poisonous Substances in Agriculture Regulations 1984 (regulation 4 and Schedule 3);

(d) an approval of a scheme or programme under the Freight Containers (Safety Convention) Regulations 1984 (regulation 5 and Schedule 4);

(e) a licence under the Asbestos (Licensing) Regulations 1983 (regulation 6 and Schedule 5);

(f) an approval of dosimetry services and for type approval of radiation generators or apparatus containing radioactive substances under the Ionising Radiations Regulations 1985 (regulation 9 and Schedule 8);

(g) an approval, authorisation or licence etc. under the Explosives Act 1875 and certain instruments thereunder, for a licence under the Petroleum (Consolidation) Act 1928, for the transfer of a licence under the Petroleum (Transfer of Licences) Act 1936, and for the purpose of each of the exemption orders made under the Gas Cylinders (Conveyance) Regulations 1931 (regulation 10 and Schedule 9). The Home Office Specifications referred to in Part V of Schedule 9 are obtainable from the Health and Safety Executive, Technology Division 2, Mechanical Systems Unit, Magdalen House, Stanley Precinct, Bootle, Merseyside L20 3QZ.

(h) the classification of an article, substance, combination, or unit load under the Classification and Labelling of Explosives Regulations 1983 (regulation 12 and Schedule 10).

(i) an explosives licence under Part IX of the Dangerous Substances in Harbour Areas Regulations 1987 (regulation 13 and Schedule 11).

2. The Regulations also fix the fees to be paid in respect of medical examinations and surveillance by an employment medical adviser which are required under certain of the relevant statutory provisions (regulations 7 and 8 and Schedules 6 and 7).

3. The new fees compared with those fixed by or determined under the previous Regulations are as follows:

Provision of these Regulations which fixes or determines the fee	*Previous Fee*			*New Fee*		
Schedule 1 Part I						
	Original approval	Amendment of approval	Renewal of approval	Original approval	Amendment of approval	Renewal of approval
Approval of breathing apparatus	£620	£620	£36	£661	£353	£40
Approval of dust respirators	£60	£60	£36	£60	£60	£40
Approval of explosives	£130	£97	£36	£120	£110	£40
Approval of locomotive or other vehicle	£1,381	£502	£36	£1,514	£348	£40
Approval of signalling apparatus	£122	£89	£36	£100	£112	£40
Approval in any other case under the mines and quarries provisions	£179	£97	£36	£192	£104	£40

Provision of these Regulations which fixes or determines the fee	*Previous Fee*	*New Fee*
Part II		
Ballistic pendulum shot	£20	£29
Break test shot	£40	£45
Deflagration shot	£25	£24
Detonator test (per 100 shots)	£201	£269
Gallery shot	£61	£63
Mortar shot	£16	£28
Velocity of detonation test (per 3 shots)	£45	£53
Part III		
Other testing not fixed in Parts I and II	£48 per hour worked	£48 per hour worked
Schedule 2 Part I		
Approval of respiratory protective equipment	£60	£60
Approval of blasting helmets	£40	£40
Approval of safe load indicators	£32 per hour worked	£32 per hour worked
Part II		
Testing respiratory protective equipment	£48 per hour worked	£48 per hour worked
Testing blasting helmets	£48 per hour worked	£48 per hour worked
Schedule 3 Part I		
Original approval of tractor cab	£126	£145
Revision of existing approval of a tractor cab	£62	£72
Approval of respiratory protective equipment	£60	£60
Part II		
Respiratory Protective Equipment	£48 per hour worked	£48 per hour worked
Schedule 4		
Approval of scheme or programme for examination of freight containers	£75	£25
Schedule 5		
Licence for work with asbestos insulations or asbestos coating	£150	£415
Renewal of original licence	£75	£208

Provision of these Regulations which fixes or determines the fee	*Previous Fee*			*New Fee*		
	Basic	X-Rays	Laboratory tests	Basic	X-Rays	Laboratory tests
Schedule 6						
The Indiarubber Regulations 1922	£25	£30	£17.50	£31	£32	£18.50
The Chemical Works Regulations 1922	£29	£30	£17.50	£31	£32	£18.50
The Patent Fuel Manufacture (Health & Welfare) Special Regulations 1946	£25	£30	£17.50	£31	£32	£18.50
The Mule Spinning (Health) Special Regulations 1953	£25	£30	£17.50	£31	£32	£18.50
The Work in Compressed Air Special Regulations 1958	£27.50	£30	£17.50	£31	£32	£18.50
The Carcinogenic Substances Regulations 1967	£30.50	£30	£17.50	£31	£32	£18.50
The Ionising Radiations Regulations 1985	£39	£30	£17.50	£42	£32	£18.50
Control of Asbestos at Work Regulations 1987	£34.50	£27	£15.50	£37	£29	£16.50
Surveillance under the Ionising Radiations Regulations 1985 which is confined to examination of, and making of entries in, records	£12.50	—	—	£13	—	—
Schedule 7						
On the First Assessment of an employee (including any clinical medical examination and laboratory tests in connection with the assessment).	£38.50			£41		
On each subsequent assessment of an employee–						
(i) for laboratory tests where these are carried out	£30			£32		
(ii) for a clinical medical examination where this is carried out	£13			£14		

Provision of these Regulations which fixes or determines the fee	*Previous Fee*		*New Fee*	
Schedule 8	Approval or type approval	Annual reassessment	Approval or type approval	Annual reassessment
Group I				
Dose record keeping where the application is solely in respect of Group I function	£315	£92	£335	£98
Dose record keeping where the application for Group I functions is linked to an application for approval in another group	£133	£92	£143	£98
Group II				
External dosimetry	£475 for one subgroup and £156 for each additional sub-group	£341 for one subgroup and £92 for each additional sub-group	£507 for one subgroup and £168 for each additional sub-group	£364 for one subgroup and £98 for each additional sub-group
Group III				
Internal dosimetry				
(a) Strontium 90 and actinides	£600 for one or more radio-isotopes in this sub-group	£256 for one or more radio-isotopes in this sub-group	£634 for one or more radio-isotopes in this sub-group	£271 for one or more radio-isotopes in this sub-group
(b) Any other radio-nuclide	£460 for up to 5 radionuclides and £325 for each additional group of 5 radionuclides or part thereof	£165 for up to 5 radionuclides and £129 for each additional group of 5 radionuclides or part thereof	£492 for up to 5 radionuclides and £345 for each additional group of 5 radionuclides or part thereof	£175 for up to 5 radionuclides and £137 for each additional group of 5 radionuclides or part thereof
Type approval of a radiation generator or an apparatus containing a radio-active substance under subparagraph (f) or (g) respectively of Schedule 3 to the Ionising Radiations Regulations 1985	£63		£68	
Schedule 9 Part 1				
Factory licence	£572 plus £28 additional fee for each building or other place in which explosives are to be made or kept		£642 plus £32 additional fee for each building or other place in which explosives are to be made or kept	
Factory amending licence	£165 plus £7 additional fee for each building or other place to be specified in the amending licence and in which explosives are to be made or kept		£248 plus £8 additional fee for each building or other place to be specified in the amending licence and in which explosives are to be made or kept	
Replacement of one of the above licences if lost	£14		£16	

Provision of these Regulations which fixes or determines the fee	*Previous Fee*	*New Fee*
Magazine licence	£455 plus £28 additional fee for each building or other place in which explosives are to be kept	£502 plus £32 additional fee for each building or other place in which explosives are to be kept
Magazine amending licence	£33 plus £7 additional fee for each building or other place to be specified in the amending licence and in which explosives are to be kept	£39 plus £8 additional fee for each building or other place to be specified in the amending licence and in which explosives are to be kept
Replacement of one of the above licences if lost	£14	£16
Licence for importation of explosives	£29	£34
Licence for importation of a consignment of explosives which are not to be distributed in Great Britain but imported for transhipment only	£29	£34
Replacement on one of the above licences if lost	£14	£16
Amendment to an existing licence	£10	£12
Licence for importation of compressed acetylene	£29	£34
Replacement of one of the above licences if lost	£14	£16
Amendment to an existing licence	£10	£12
Part II		
A store licence	£44	£47
Renewal of a store licence	£44	£47
Registration and renewal of registration of premises for the keeping of explosives with a local authority	£7.50	£8
Licence to keep petroleum spirit of a quantity not exceeding 2,500 litres	£21 for each year of licence	£22 for each year of licence
exceeding 2,500 litres but not exceeding 50,000 litres	£31 for each year of licence	£33 for each year of licence
exceeding 50,000 litres	£61 for each year of licence	£65 for each year of licence
Transfer of petroleum spirit licence	£5	£6
Part III		
Original approval of premises in which acetylene is to be manufactured or kept	£322	£352

Provision of these Regulations which fixes or determines the fee	*Previous Fee*	*New Fee*
Amendment of an approval of premises in which acetylene is to be manufactured or kept	£56	£165
Approval of apparatus in which acetylene is to be manufactured or kept	£16	£19
Part IV		
Comparison of a porous substance with a sample porous substance	£16	£19
Approval of an acetylene cylinder design	£48	£53
Original approval of premises in which acetylene is compressed	£322	£352
Amendment of an approval of premises in which acetylene is compressed	£37	£23
Schedule 9 Part V		
Approval of a gas cylinder manufacturer	£7,023	£7,698
Approval of the design of a gas cylinder	£48	£53
Approval of a supplier of the material of which a gas cylinder is manufactured	£616	£720
Approval of a gas cylinder inspection body	£1,538	£1,791
Approval of a user of a gas cylinder manufactured and tested in accordance with the provisions of Home Office Specifications LASS 1 or LASW 1	£308	£360
Part VI		
Authorisation or classification of an explosive to be manufactured for general sale or to be imported for general sale with or without a licence	£83	£95
Grant of an original special packing authority	£70	£181

Provision of these Regulations which fixes or determines the fee	*Previous Fee*	*New Fee*
Amendment to a special packing authority	£20	£24
Grant of an ammonium nitrate mixtures licence under Article 3 of the Ammonium Nitrate Mixtures Exemption Order 1967	£81	£88
Part VII		
Application for a licence to be granted for the importation of explosives which are not at the time of application authorised to be manufactured for general sale or imported for general sale	£44 per hour worked	£44 per hour worked
Approval of apparatus in which acetylene is to be manufactured or kept	£44 per hour worked	£44 per hour worked
Comparison of a porous substance with a sample porous substance	£44 per hour worked	£44 per hour worked
Authorisation of an explosive to be manufactured for general sale or to be imported for general sale with or without a licence	£44 per hour worked	£44 per hour worked
Schedule 10		
Classification of an article, substance, combination or unit load	£44 per hour worked	£44 per hour worked
Schedule 11		
Grant of an explosives licence or alteration of the terms of an existing explosives licence	£170 plus £29 per hour worked	£195 plus £33 per hour worked

4. The Regulations do not apply to Northern Ireland.

STATUTORY INSTRUMENTS

1989 No. 463

ECCLESIASTICAL LAW, ENGLAND

The Grants to the Redundant Churches Fund Order 1989

Made - - - -	*13th March 1989*
Coming into force -	*1st April 1989*

The Secretary of State, in exercise of the powers conferred by section 1(1) and (2) of the Redundant Churches and other Religious Buildings Act 1969**(a)** and now vested in him**(b)**, and of all other powers enabling him in that behalf, with the approval of the Treasury, hereby makes the following Order, in the terms of a draft approved by resolution of the House of Commons:

Citation and commencement

1. This Order may be cited as the Grants to the Redundant Churches Fund Order 1989 and shall come into force on 1st April 1989.

Period for grants to the Redundant Churches Fund

2. The period beginning with 1st April 1989 and expiring on 31st March 1994 is hereby specified for the purposes of section 1(1) of the Redundant Churches and other Religious Buildings Act 1969.

Aggregate Amount of Grants

3. The aggregate amount of the grants that may be paid under section 1(1) of the 1969 Act in the period specified in article 2 of this Order shall not exceed £8,700,000.

Nicholas Ridley
2nd March 1989 One of Her Majesty's Principal Secretaries of State

We approve,

David Lightbown
David MacLean
Two of the Lords Commissioners
13th March 1989 of Her Majesty's Treasury

(a) 1969 c.22.
(b) S.I. 1970/1681.

EXPLANATORY NOTE

(This note is not part of the Order)

The Redundant Churches Fund has as its object the preservation, in the interests of the nation and the Church of England, of churches and parts of churches of historic and archaeological interest or architectural quality, together with their contents, which are vested in the Fund by Part III of the Pastoral Measure 1983 (1983 No. 1).

This Order specifies the period 1st April 1989 to 31st March 1994 for the purposes of section 1 of the Redundant Churches and other Religious Buildings Act 1969, thus enabling the Secretary of State with the approval of the Treasury to make grants to the Redundant Churches Fund during that period of such amounts, payable at such times and subject to such conditions, if any, as he may from time to time determine. This Order also specifies the sum of £8,700,000 as the maximum aggregate amount of the grants that may be paid over that period.

STATUTORY INSTRUMENTS

1989 No. 464

TRANSPORT

The Service Subsidy Agreements (Tendering) (Amendment) Regulations 1989

Made - - - -	*9th March 1989*
Laid before Parliament	*21st March 1989*
Coming into force	*11th April 1989*

The Secretary of State for Transport (as respects England), the Secretary of State for Scotland (as respects Scotland) and the Secretary of State for Wales (as respects Wales), in exercise of the powers conferred by sections 91(1) and 134 of the Transport Act 1985(**a**) and of all other powers enabling them in that behalf, hereby make the following Regulations:

1. These Regulations shall be cited as the Service Subsidy Agreements (Tendering) (Amendment) Regulations 1989 and shall come into force on 11th April 1989.

2. The Service Subsidy Agreements (Tendering) Regulations 1985(**b**) shall be amended in accordance with the following Regulations.

3. In regulation 3(1)(b)–

(a) for "£4,000" in both places where it occurs there shall be substituted "£8,000"; and

(b) for "£20,000" there shall be substituted "£40,000".

Paul Channon
3rd March 1989 — Secretary of State for Transport

Malcolm Rifkind
8th March 1989 — Secretary of State for Scotland

Peter Walker
9th March 1989 — Secretary of State for Wales

(**a**) 1985 c.67.
(**b**) S.I. 1985/1921.

EXPLANATORY NOTE

(This note is not part of the Regulations)

These Regulations amend the Service Subsidy Agreements (Tendering) Regulations 1985 ("the 1985 Regulations") so that:–

(a) the exception from the tendering requirements set out in section 89 of the Transport Act 1985 of service subsidy agreements under which the aggregate amount of the service subsidies payable is "less than £4,000" is amended so that the threshold is "less then £8,000"; and

(b) the exception is excluded in the case of agreements–

(i) whose effect is to provide for the operator to receive under service subsidy agreements an aggregate amount of service subsidies of "more than £40,000" (as opposed to "more than £20,000" in the 1985 Regulations); and

(ii) whose effect is to modify agreements so that the aggregate amount of service subsidies payable becomes "£8,000 or more" (as opposed to "£4,000 or more" in the 1985 Regulations).

1989 No. 465

BANKS AND BANKING

The Banking Act 1987 (Exempt Transactions) (Amendment) Regulations 1989

Made - - - -	*14th March 1989*
Laid before Parliament	*14th March 1989*
Coming into force	*4th April 1989*

The Treasury, in exercise of the powers conferred upon them by section 4(4), (5) and (6) of the Banking Act 1987**(a)** and of all other powers enabling them in that behalf, hereby make the following Regulations:

Citation and commencement

1. These Regulations may be cited as the Banking Act 1987 (Exempt Transactions) (Amendment) Regulations 1989 and shall come into force on 4th April 1989.

Interpretation

2. In these Regulations "the principal Regulations" means the Banking Act 1987 (Exempt Transactions) Regulations 1988**(b)**.

Amendment of principal Regulations

3. The principal Regulations shall be amended as follows:

(a) in regulation 1(2) of the principal Regulations–

(i) by inserting after the definition of "exempt transaction" the following new definition–

" "financial year" has the meaning ascribed to it by section 742 of the Companies Act 1985;";

(ii) by inserting after the definition of "the Official List" the following new definition–

" "Recognised Overseas Exchange" means an exchange, market place or association for the time being included in the list published by the Council for the purposes of rule 535.4a of the Rules of The Stock Exchange (permitted dealings in foreign securities) (or any rule of The Stock Exchange having substantially the same effect)**(c)**;"; and

(iii) by substituting for the definition of "successor to the British Steel Corporation" the following new definition–

" "successor", in relation to a body, means any company in which property, rights and liabilities of the body shall have become vested by virtue of an Act; and";

(b) in regulation 10(2) by deleting the words "to the British Steel Corporation";

(a) 1987 c.22.
(b) S.I. 1988/646.
(c) The list and the Rules may be obtained from the Quotations Department, The Stock Exchange, London EC2N 1HP.

(c) by substituting for regulation 13 of the principal Regulations the following new regulation–

"**13.** The acceptance of a deposit by a person (not being a body listed in Schedule 2 to these Regulations) on terms involving the issue of any sterling commercial paper is an exempt transaction if–

(a) the person accepting the deposit is–

(i) a company whose shares or debt securities have been admitted to the Official List (and are not the subject of a notice issued by the Council cancelling or suspending the listing or suspending dealings) or are dealt in on the Unlisted Securities Market (and are not the subject of a Council notice cancelling or suspending dealings); or

(ii) a company not falling within sub-paragraph (a)(i) above which is incorporated in the United Kingdom or whose shares or debt securities have been admitted to listing on a Recognised Overseas Exchange (and are not the subject of official action taken in accordance with the rules of the Recognised Overseas Exchange cancelling or suspending the listing or suspending dealings), which has complied with the requirements of Schedule 3 to these Regulations; or

(iii) the government of any country or territory, or a public authority, outside the United Kingdom the debt securities of which are admitted to trading on The Stock Exchange or on a Recognised Overseas Exchange (and are not the subject of a notice issued by the Council or official action taken in accordance with the rules of the Recognised Overseas Exchange (as the case may be) cancelling or suspending the admission to trading or suspending dealings); or

(iv) a person who does not fall within sub-paragraphs (a)(i) to (iii) above, if either a company which falls within sub-paragraph (a)(i) or an authorised institution has guaranteed to the holder of the sterling commercial paper the repayment of the principal and the payment of any interest or premium in connection therewith;

(b) in the case of a company falling within sub-paragraph (a)(i) or (ii) above, its net assets or, in the case of a person falling within sub-paragraph (a)(iv) above where the guarantor is not an authorised institution, the guarantor's net assets were shown in its last audited individual or group accounts (as the case may be) to be not less than £25 million (or an amount of equivalent value denominated wholly or partly otherwise than in sterling);

(c) in consideration of the deposit a single debt security is issued, in the form of sterling commercial paper, which has a redemption value of not less than £100,000, the whole or part of which may be transferred only if the aggregate redemption value of sterling commercial paper being transferred is not less than £100,000; and

(d) the sterling commercial paper–

(i) is issued and payable in the United Kingdom,

(ii) bears the rubric

"sterling commercial paper issued in accordance with regulations made under section 4 of the Banking Act 1987",

(iii) states the name of the issuer and that the issuer is not an authorised institution and either states that repayment of the principal and the payment of any interest or premium in connection with the sterling commercial paper have not been guaranteed, or, if they have been guaranteed, states that this is the case, the name of the guarantor and whether or not the guarantor is an authorised institution, and

(iv) if it is issued by a company falling within sub-paragraph (a)(i) or (ii) above, or guaranteed by a company falling within sub-paragraph (a)(i) above, and is not offered by a prospectus to which section 56 or 72 of the Companies Act 1985 or the corresponding Northern Ireland legislation applies, includes a statement made by the company accepting the deposit or the guarantor (as the case may be) that the relevant company has complied with its obligations under the relevant rules and that, since the last publication in compliance with the relevant rules of information about the relevant company, the relevant company, having made all reasonable enquiries, has not become aware of any change in circumstances which could reasonably be regarded as significantly and adversely affecting its ability to meet its obligations in respect of the sterling commercial paper as they fall due. In this paragraph "the relevant rules" means–

(aa) in the case of a company whose shares or debt securities have been admitted to the Official List, the listing rules, or

(bb) in the case of a company whose shares or debt securities are dealt in on the Unlisted Securities Market, the terms and conditions of entry to the Unlisted Securities Market, or

(cc) in the case of a company not falling within sub-paragraph (aa) or (bb) above, Schedule 3 to these Regulations.";

(d) in Schedule 2–

(i) after the entry relating to an Area Board within the meaning of section 1(3) of the Electricity Act 1947 there shall be inserted the following new entry–

"Any successor to such an Area Board.";

(ii) the entries relating to the British Steel Corporation and any successor to the British Steel Corporation shall be deleted;

(iii) after the entry relating to the Central Electricity Generating Board there shall be inserted the following new entry–

"Any successor to the Central Electricity Generating Board.";

(iv) after the entry relating to the Housing Corporation there shall be inserted the following new entry–

"London Regional Transport.";

(v) after the entry relating to the North of Scotland Hydro-Electric Board there shall be inserted the following new entry–

"Any successor to the North of Scotland Hydro-Electric Board.";

(vi) for the entry relating to the Northern Ireland Electricity Service there shall be substituted the words "Northern Ireland Electricity.";

(vii) after the entry relating to the Northern Ireland Transport Holding Company there shall be inserted the following new entry–

"The Post Office."; and

(viii) after the entry relating to the South of Scotland Electricity Board there shall be inserted the following new entry–

"Any successor to the South of Scotland Electricity Board."; and

(e) by the addition after Schedule 2 of the following new Schedule–

"SCHEDULE 3

Regulation 13

REQUIREMENTS TO BE COMPLIED WITH BY CERTAIN ISSUERS OF STERLING COMMERCIAL PAPER

Interpretation

1. In this Schedule–

"the issuer" means a company accepting a relevant deposit;

"the relevant date" means the date on which the information set out in paragraph 2 below was first provided by the issuer to The Stock Exchange in accordance with paragraph 4 below; and

"a relevant deposit" means a deposit accepted on terms involving the issue of any sterling commercial paper.

Information to have been notified to The Stock Exchange

2. Not less than fourteen days prior to the acceptance of its first relevant deposit the issuer shall have provided the following information to The Stock Exchange:

The issuer

(a) the name of the issuer and, if the sterling commercial paper was guaranteed, the name of the guarantor;

(b) the country or territory of incorporation of the issuer and, if applicable, the guarantor;

(c) the address of the registered office of the issuer (if it has one) and, if it has no registered office or if its principal place of business was not at its registered office, the address of its principal place of business;

(d) the date on which the issuer was incorporated and, if it has a limited life, the length of its life;

(e) the legislation under which the issuer is incorporated and the legal form which it has adopted under that legislation;

(f) the place of registration of the issuer, if different to the country or territory of incorporation, and the number with which it is registered;

(g) the names and addresses of the issuer's principal bankers;

(h) details of any legal or arbitration proceedings pending or threatened against the issuer or, if it is a member of a group, any member of the group, which might have, or might have had during the twelve months prior to the relevant date, a significant effect on the financial position of the issuer or the group (as the case may be) or, if there were no such proceedings, a statement to that effect;

(i) the address in the City of London where copies of the documents referred to in paragraph 6 of this Schedule were available for inspection;

(j) if the sterling commercial paper was guaranteed by a company falling within regulation 13(a)(i) of these Regulations, an address in the City of London where information about that company was available for inspection in accordance with the listing rules or the terms and conditions of entry to the Unlisted Securities Market (as the case may be);

(k) a description of the principal activities of the issuer, stating the main categories of products sold or services performed, together with, in a case where two or more activities were carried on which were material in terms of profits or losses, such figures and explanations as were necessary to determine the relative importance of each activity;

(l) details of any patent, licence, new manufacturing process or industrial, commercial or financial contract on which the business or profitability of the issuer or its group depended to a material extent;

(m) if the issuer is a member of a group, a brief description of the group and of the issuer's position within it and, if the issuer is a subsidiary, the name of each holding company of the issuer;

Financial information

(n) the amount of the authorised and issued share capital of the issuer, the amount of any share capital agreed to be issued and the number and classes of the shares of which it was composed with details of their principal characteristics; if any part of the issued share capital was still to be paid up, an indication of the number, or total nominal value, and the type of the securities not then fully paid up, broken down, where applicable, according to the extent to which they had been paid up;

(o) information with respect to the profits and losses, assets and liabilities and financial record and position of the issuer and, if it is a member of a group, of the group, set out as a comparative table for each of the latest five financial years of the issuer for which such information was available, together with copies of individual and (if applicable) group accounts for each of the latest two such financial years, including, in the case of a company incorporated in the United Kingdom, all notes, reports or other information required by the Companies Act 1985 or the Companies (Northern Ireland) Order 1986;

(p) if more than nine months had elapsed since the end of the financial year to which the last published annual accounts related, an interim financial statement covering at least the first six months of the then current financial year and if such an interim financial statement had not been audited, a statement to this effect;

(q) the names, addresses and qualifications of the auditors who have audited the issuer's annual accounts for the preceding two financial years and in the case of a company incorporated outside the United Kingdom a statement as to whether or not those accounts conformed to United Kingdom or generally accepted international accounting standards;

(r) if during the two financial years of the issuer preceding the relevant date the issuer's auditors had refused to sign an auditors' report on the annual accounts of the issuer, or had qualified any such report in any way, a copy of the refusal (if in writing) or of the qualification together with details of any reasons given by the auditors for such action;

(s) details as at the most recent practicable date (which shall have been stated) prior to the relevant date of the following, which, if the issuer is a member of a group, shall also have been provided on a consolidated basis:

(i) the total amount of any loan capital outstanding in any member of the group, and loan capital created but unissued, and term loans, distinguishing between loans guaranteed and unguaranteed, and those secured (whether the security is provided by the issuer or by third parties) and unsecured;

(ii) the total amount of all other borrowings and indebtedness in the nature of borrowing of the issuer or the group (as the case may be), distinguishing between guaranteed and unguaranteed and secured and unsecured borrowings and debts, including bank overdrafts and liabilities under acceptances (other than normal trade bills) or acceptance credits or hire purchase commitments;

(iii) all mortgages and charges of the issuer or the group (as the case may be); and

(iv) the total amount of any contingent liabilities and guarantees of the issuer or the group (as the case may be);

if the issuer or the group (as the case may be) had no such loan capital, borrowings, indebtedness or contingent liabilities, this shall have been stated;

no account should have been taken of liabilities between undertakings within the same group, a statement to that effect having been made if necessary;

Directors

(t) the names, home or business addresses and functions within the issuer or its group (if applicable) of the directors of the issuer and an indication of the principal activities performed by them outside the issuer or the group (as the case may be) where these were significant with respect to the issuer or the group (as the case may be);

Recent developments

(u) general information on the trend of the business of the issuer or its group (if applicable) since the end of the financial year to which the last published annual accounts related, in particular:

(i) the most significant recent trends in production, sales and stocks and the state of the order book; and

(ii) recent trends in costs and selling prices;

Overseas companies

(v) where information was being provided by a company whose shares or debt securities have been admitted to listing on a Recognised Overseas Exchange, the name of the Recognised Overseas Exchange and the type of securities listed;

The sterling commercial paper

(w) the total amount which the issuer intended to raise by the issue of sterling commercial paper and details of the intended application of the proceeds raised;

(x) the name and address of any issuing and paying agent for the sterling commercial paper in the United Kingdom and the name and address of any managing agent, if different;

(y) the period after which entitlement to interest or repayment of capital would lapse, or if there was no period after which such entitlement would lapse, a statement to that effect; and

(z) details of the procedures for the delivery of the sterling commercial paper to holders (including any applicable time limits) and whether temporary documents of title would be issued.

3. Prior to the acceptance by the issuer of a further relevant deposit the issuer shall either have complied with paragraph 2 above as if such further deposit were its first relevant deposit or–

(a) the issuer shall have provided to The Stock Exchange details of all material changes to the information provided under paragraph 2 above (other than the information provided under sub-paragraphs (n) to (s) (financial information)) as soon as practicable after each such change occurred;

(b) if no information was required to be provided under sub-paragraph 2(p) above, but the nine months period referred to in that sub-paragraph has since elapsed, the issuer shall have provided the information specified in that sub-paragraph to The Stock Exchange; and

(c) if more than twelve months has elapsed since the relevant date, the issuer shall have provided to The Stock Exchange an updated version of all the information required by paragraph 2 above at intervals of not more than twelve months.

4. The information set out in paragraphs 2 and 3 above shall have been provided in English and in good faith to the Quotations Department of The Stock Exchange in the form of three copies of a document which, in the case of information provided under paragraphs 2 or 3(c) above, shall have been annotated to indicate where each item set out in paragraph 2 above had been met and (in those cases) shall have been accompanied by a declaration by the directors of the issuer in the following form–

"The Directors of the Company accept responsibility for the information provided. To the best of the knowledge and belief of the Directors (who have taken all reasonable care to ensure that such is the case) the information is in accordance with the facts and does not omit anything likely to affect the import of such information.".

5. The issuer shall have made arrangements with The Stock Exchange for The Stock Exchange to make available to the public all information provided to The Stock Exchange by the issuer under this Schedule and at the date of acceptance of the relevant deposit such arrangements are in force.

Information to be available for public inspection

6. The issuer shall have made available at an address in the City of London copies of the following documents during normal business hours for a period beginning on the relevant date and continuing at least until the acceptance of its first relevant deposit:

(i) the memorandum and articles of association or equivalent documents of the issuer;

(ii) any trust deed or other document constituting debt securites of the issuer;

(iii) any contract directly relating to the issue of the sterling commercial paper and any existing or proposed service contract between a director of the issuer and the issuer or any member of its group;

(iv) any report, letter, valuation, statement, balance sheet or other document any part of which is extracted or referred to in any other document provided to The Stock Exchange under this Schedule; and

(v) the audited accounts of the issuer and, if it is a member of a group, the consolidated audited accounts of the group, for each of the two latest financial years preceding the relevant date for which such accounts are available together with, in the case of a company incorporated in the United Kingdom, all notes, reports or other information required by the Companies Act 1985 or the Companies (Northern Ireland) Order 1986 to be attached thereto;

any reference in this paragraph 6 to a document which is not in English shall be taken to include in addition a reference to a translation of that document which is either certified to be correct by a notary public or which has been made by a person certified by a practising solicitor within the meaning of regulation 8 of these Regulations to be in his opinion competent to make such a translation.

7. Prior to the acceptance by the issuer of a further relevant deposit the issuer shall either have complied with paragraph 6 above as if such further deposit were its first relevant deposit or shall have continued to make available at the address for the time being provided to The Stock Exchange under sub-paragraph 2(i) above up-to-date copies of the documents referred to in that paragraph as soon as practicable after they became available.

Information to have been notified to the Bank of England

8. If the relevant deposit is accepted as part of a programme for the issue of sterling commercial paper, the issuer, before it accepted the first deposit relating to the programme, shall have notified to the Bank of England the total amount to be raised under the programme, the maturity period of the sterling commercial paper to be issued under the programme (if known) and a detailed description of the purposes for which the proceeds of the programme would be used; and if the issuer subsequently extended the programme, shall also have notified details of the increased amount to be raised and any other material changes to the information initially provided.

9. If the issuer has provided information to the Bank of England under paragraph 8 in relation to a relevant deposit, it shall also have reported to the Bank of England within one week after the end of each calendar month following the month in which such information was so provided the amount of sterling commercial paper issued by it outstanding at the end of that calendar month and (in the case of a second or subsequent report) the amounts of sterling commercial paper issued and redeemed by it since the date of the previous report, distinguishing in each case between sterling commercial paper guaranteed by an authorised institution and sterling commercial paper not so guaranteed.".

Kenneth Carlisle
Alan Howarth
Two of the Lords Commissioners
of Her Majesty's Treasury

14th March 1989

EXPLANATORY NOTE

(This note is not part of the Regulations.)

These Regulations amend the Banking Act 1987 (Exempt Transactions) Regulations 1988.

First they make changes to the exemption for sterling commercial paper. The main changes are as follows. The classes of person who can accept deposits under the exemption are widened to include companies whose shares or debt are traded on the Unlisted Securities Market, other unlisted UK companies, overseas companies whose shares or debt are listed on certain overseas stock exchanges and overseas governments and public authorities whose debt is traded on The Stock Exchange or on certain overseas exchanges. Others may also issue sterling commercial paper if the paper is guaranteed by an institution authorised under the Banking Act 1987 or by a company whose shares or debt are listed or traded on the Official List of The Stock Exchange or on the Unlisted Securities Market. The minimum net asset requirement (which does not apply to overseas governments and public authorities) is reduced from £50 million to £25 million. The minimum denomination of sterling commercial paper is reduced from £500,000 to £100,000. Unlisted UK companies (whose shares or debt are not traded on the Unlisted Securities Market) and companies whose shares or debt are listed or traded on overseas stock exchanges are required to disclose certain information set out in a new Schedule 3 to the Regulations.

Secondly they amend the list of public undertakings in Schedule 2, the main changes being the deletion of references to the British Steel Corporation and the insertion of references to London Regional Transport, the Post Office and successors to the electricity boards.

STATUTORY INSTRUMENTS

1989 No. 466

TAXES

The Capital Gains Tax (Annual Exempt Amount) Order 1989

Made - - - - 14th March 1989

The Treasury, in pursuance of section 5(1C) of the Capital Gains Tax Act 1979(**a**), hereby make the following Order:

1. This Order may be cited as the Capital Gains Tax (Annual Exempt Amount) Order 1989.

2. The amount specified, which by virtue of section 5 of the Capital Gains Tax Act 1979 is, unless Parliament otherwise determines, the exempt amount for the year 1989–90, is £5,400.

Kenneth Carlisle
Alan Howarth

14th March 1989 Two of the Lords Commissioners of Her Majesty's Treasury

(**a**) 1979 c.14; section 5(1A), (1B) and (1C) was inserted by section 80(2) of the Finance Act 1982 (c.39).

EXPLANATORY NOTE

(This note is not part of the Order)

This Order specifies £5,400 as the amount which, under section 5 of the Capital Gains Tax Act 1979 ("section 5") (as amended by section 77 of the Finance Act 1980 (c.48) and section 80 of the Finance Act 1982), is the exempt amount for the year 1989–90 unless Parliament otherwise determines. The exempt amount for the year 1988–89 was fixed by section 108 of the Finance Act 1988 (c.39) at £5,000. The amount of £5,400 is the amount for 1988–89 increased by the amount of the percentage increase (6.8%) in the retail prices index for December 1988 over that for December 1987. The amount has been rounded up to the nearest £100 in accordance with section 5(1B).

The "retail prices index" is defined in section 24(8) of the Finance Act 1980 (as extended to the Capital Gains Tax Act 1979 by section 80(4) of the Finance Act 1982) as the "general index of retail prices (for all items) published by the Department of Employment". The retail prices index for December 1987 is 103.3 and for December 1988 110.3 (based on January 1987 as 100). (Table 6.4 on pages S60 and S61 of the February 1989 number of the *Employment Gazette*, the official journal of the Department of Employment.)

The exempt amount has several applications for capital gains tax. Under section 5(1) an individual's gains for a year of assessment are chargeable to tax only to the extent that they exceed the exempt amount. Under paragraphs 4 to 6 of Schedule 1 to the Capital Gains Tax Act 1979 ("paragraphs 4 to 6") (as amended by section 77 of the Finance Act 1980, section 89 of the Finance Act 1981 (c.35), section 80 of the Finance Act 1982 and by Schedule 29, paragraphs 15 and 32 to, the Income and Corporation Taxes Act 1988 (c.1)), section 5(1) also applies, subject to detailed rules, to personal representatives, trustees of settlements for mentally disabled persons or persons in receipt of attendance allowance, and, as to one half of the exempt amount, trustees of other settlements.

Under section 5(5) an individual may, if appropriate, and unless an Inspector otherwise requires, satisfy his obligation to make a return of chargeable gains by stating that his gains do not exceed the exempt amount for the year and that the proceeds of his disposals in the year do not exceed an amount equal to twice the exempt amount. Under paragraphs 4 to 6, section 5(5) also applies to personal representatives and, subject to detailed rules, to trustees.

STATUTORY INSTRUMENTS

1989 No. 467

INCOME TAX

The Income Tax (Indexation) Order 1989

Made - - - - 14th March 1989

The Treasury, in pursuance of sections 1(6) and 257(11) of the Income and Corporation Taxes Act 1988**(a)**, hereby make the following Order:

1. This Order may be cited as the Income Tax (Indexation) Order 1989.

2.—(1) The amounts which, unless Parliament otherwise determines, will be treated by virtue of sections 1(4) and 257(9) of the Income and Corporation Taxes Act 1988**(b)** as specified for the year 1989–90 in sections 1(2) and 257(1), (2), (3), (5) and (6) of that Act are set out in paragraphs (2) and (3).

(2) In section 1(2) of the said Act (basic rate limit)—£20,700.

(3) In section 257 of the said Act (personal reliefs)–

(a) in subsection (1)(a) (married allowance)—£4,375;

(b) in subsections (1)(b) (single allowance) and (6) (wife's earned income relief)—£2,785;

(c) in subsection (2)(a) (married allowance: age 65 to 79)—£5,385;

(d) in subsection (2)(b) (single allowance: age 65 to 79)—£3,400;

(e) in subsection (3)(a) (married allowance: age 80 and over)—£5,565;

(f) in subsection (3)(b) (single allowance: age 80 and over)—£3,540;

(g) in subsection (5) (income limit for age allowance)—£11,400.

Kenneth Carlisle
Alan Howarth

14th March 1989 Two of the Lords Commissioners of Her Majesty's Treasury

(a) 1988 c.1; section 1(2), (3), (4) and (6) was amended by section 24 of the Finance Act 1988 (c.39) and section 257 was amended by section 25(1) of the Finance Act 1988. **(b)** Sections 1(4) and 257(9) were disapplied for the year 1988-89 by sections 24(2) and 25(2) respectively of the Finance Act 1988.

EXPLANATORY NOTE

(This note is not part of the Order)

Sections 1(6) and 257(11) of the Income and Corporation Taxes Act 1988 ("the Act") provide that the Treasury shall by order made by statutory instrument before 6th April 1989 specify the amounts which by virtue of those sections shall, unless Parliament otherwise determines, be treated as specified for the year 1989–90. These are the basic rate limit (section 1 of the Act) and the personal reliefs (section 257 of the Act) respectively. The higher rate bands were abolished by the Finance Act 1988 with effect from 6th April 1988. The amounts of the basic rate limit and the personal reliefs for the year 1988–89 were fixed by sections 24(2) and 25(1) respectively of the Finance Act 1988. Those amounts are increased by this order in accordance with the percentage increase (6.8%) in the retail prices index for December 1988 over that for December 1987. Certain of the amounts have been rounded to the nearest £100 in accordance with sections 1(4) and 257(9)(a) of the Act and, in the case of the other amounts, the increases have been rounded to the nearest £10 in accordance with section 257(9)(b) of the Act.

The "retail prices index" is defined in section 833(2) of the Act as the "general index of retail prices (for all items) published by the Department of Employment". The retail prices index for December 1987 is 103.3 and for December 1988 110.3 (based on January 1987 as 100). (Table 6.4 on pages S60 and S61 of the February 1989 number of the *Employment Gazette,* the official journal of the Department of Employment.)

STATUTORY INSTRUMENTS

1989 No. 468

INHERITANCE TAX

The Inheritance Tax (Indexation) Order 1989

Made - - - - 14th March 1989

The Treasury, in pursuance of section 8(4) of the Inheritance Tax Act 1984(**a**), hereby make the following Order:

1. This Order may be cited as the Inheritance Tax (Indexation) Order 1989.

2. The amounts which, unless Parliament otherwise determines, shall be treated by virtue of section 8 of the Inheritance Tax Act 1984 as specified in the Table in Schedule 1 to that Act(**b**) in relation to chargeable transfers on or after 6th April 1989 are as follows–

TABLE OF RATES OF TAX

Portion of value		*Rate of tax*
Lower Limit	*Upper Limit*	*Per cent.*
£	£	
0	118,000	NIL
118,000	—	40

Kenneth Carlisle
Alan Howarth

14th March 1989 Two of the Lords Commissioners of Her Majesty's Treasury

(**a**) 1984 c.51; section 8 was amended by section 101(3) of, and paragraph 3 of Schedule 19 to, the Finance Act 1986 (c.41) with respect to transfers of value made, and other events occurring, on or after 18th March 1986 subject to Part II of Schedule 19 and by section 136 of, and Part X of Schedule 14 to, the Finance Act 1988 (c.39) in relation to transfers of value made on or after 15th March 1988. Section 8(1) was disapplied in relation to chargeable transfers made in the year beginning 6th April 1987 by section 57(1) of the Finance Act 1987 (c.16) and in relation to chargeable transfers made in the year beginning 15th March 1988 by section 136(2) of the Finance Act 1988. By virtue of section 100(1) and (2) of the Finance Act 1986 on and after 25th July 1986 the Capital Transfer Tax Act 1984 may be cited as the Inheritance Tax Act 1984, and any reference in that Act to capital transfer tax is to have effect as a reference to inheritance tax, except where the reference relates to a liability arising before 25th July 1986. (**b**) The Table in Schedule 1 was substituted by section 136(1) of the Finance Act 1988 with application to any chargeable transfer (within the meaning of the Inheritance Tax Act 1984) made on or after 15th March 1988. Previously, the Table in that Schedule was that substituted by section 57(2) of the Finance Act 1987 with respect to transfers of value made, and other events occurring, on or after 17th March 1987. Prior to that, the Table was substituted by section 101(3) of, and paragraph 36 of Schedule 19 to, the Finance Act 1986 with respect to transfers of value made, and other events occurring, on or after 18th March 1986 subject to Part II of Schedule 19.

EXPLANATORY NOTE

(This note is not part of the Order)

By this Order, made under the provisions of section 8 of the Inheritance Tax Act 1984 (formerly the Capital Transfer Tax Act 1984) a new Table of rate bands and rates is substituted in Schedule 1 to that Act for the Table which was substituted by the Finance Act 1988. The figures in the first and second columns of the new Table are the amounts specified in the Table in Schedule 1 to the Inheritance Tax Act 1984 (as so substituted) increased by the amount of the percentage increase (6.8%) in the retail prices index for December 1988 over that for December 1987. The figures are rounded upward to the nearest £1,000 in accordance with section 8(2). The "retail prices index" is defined in section 8(3) as "the general index of retail prices (for all items) published by the Department of Employment". The retail prices index for December 1987 is 103.3 and for December 1988 is 110.3 (based on January 1987 as 100). (Table 6.4 on pages S60 and S61 of the February 1989 number of the *Employment Gazette*, the official journal of the Department of Employment.)

The new Table will apply in relation to chargeable transfers on or after 6th April 1989 unless Parliament otherwise determines.

STATUTORY INSTRUMENTS

1989 No. 469

INCOME TAX

The Personal Equity Plan Regulations 1989

Made - - - -	*14th March 1989*
Laid before the House of Commons	*14th March 1989*
Coming into force	*6th April 1989*

ARRANGEMENT OF REGULATIONS

The Treasury, in exercise of the powers conferred upon them by section 333 of the Income and Corporation Taxes Act 1988**(a)** and section 149D of the Capital Gains Tax Act 1979**(b)**, hereby make the following Regulations:–

Citation and commencement

1. These Regulations may be cited as the Personal Equity Plan Regulations 1989 and shall come into force on 6th April 1989.

Interpretation

2.—(1) In these Regulations unless the context otherwise requires:–

(a) "the Board" means the Commissioners of Inland Revenue;

"gains" means "chargeable gains" within the meaning of the Capital Gains Tax Act 1979;

"investment trust" has the same meaning as in section 842 of the Taxes Act**(c)**;

"the Management Act" means the Taxes Management Act 1970**(d)**;

"market value" shall be construed in accordance with section 150 of the Capital Gains Tax Act 1979;

"notice" means notice in writing and "notify" shall be construed accordingly;

"ordinary share" means a share which forms part of a company's ordinary share capital (within the meaning of section 832(1) of the Taxes Act);

a "plan investment" is an investment under a plan which is a qualifying investment within the meaning of regulation 6;

a "plan investor" is an individual who subscribes to a plan and who is a qualifying individual within the meaning of regulation 7;

a "plan manager" is a person who fulfils the conditions of these Regulations and is approved by the Board for the purposes of these Regulations as a plan manager;

a "portfolio" is a portfolio of plan investments which are held under a plan;

"recognised stock exchange" has the same meaning as in section 841 of the Taxes Act;

"share" includes stock;

"tax" where neither income tax nor capital gains tax is specified means either of those taxes;

"tax credit" means a credit under section 231 of the Taxes Act;

"year" means a year beginning with 6th April in any year and ending with 5th April in the following year;

"the Taxes Act" means the Income and Corporation Taxes Act 1988;

"the 1986 Regulations" means the Personal Equity Plan Regulations 1986**(e)**.

(b) "authorised unit trust" means a unit trust scheme in the case of which an order under section 78 of the Financial Services Act 1986**(f)** is in force and which is an authorised securities scheme within the meaning of the Authorised Unit Trust Scheme (Investment and Borrowing Powers) Regulations 1988**(g)**;

"unit holder" means a person entitled to a share of the investments subject to the trusts of a unit trust scheme;

"unit trust scheme" has the same meaning as in section 469 of the Taxes Act;

and references to a "unit" include references to a fraction of a unit.

(a) 1988 c.1. **(b)** 1979 c.14; section 149D was inserted by paragraph 26 of Schedule 29 to the Income and Corporation Taxes Act 1988 and amended by section 116 of the Finance Act 1988 (c.39). **(c)** Section 842 was amended by section 117(1) of the Finance Act 1988. **(d)** 1970 c.9. **(e)** S.I. 1986/1948, amended by S.I. 1987/2128, 1988/657 and 1348. **(f)** 1986 c.60. **(g)** S.I. 1988/284.

(2) The Table below indexes other definitions in these Regulations:

Term defined	*Regulation*
Annual claim	20
Interim claim	19
Plan	4(1)
Qualifying individual	7
Qualifying investments	6
Subscription limit	4(4)

Introductory

3. These Regulations provide–

(a) for the setting up of plans by plan managers approved by the Board under which individuals may make certain investments, for the conditions under which they may invest and under which those plans are to operate, for relief from tax in respect of plan investments and generally for the administration of tax in relation to plans, and

(b) for transitional arrangements in respect of plans and plan investors under the 1986 Regulations.

General conditions for plans and subscriptions to plans

4.—(1) A plan is a scheme of investment to which an individual who is a qualifying individual may subscribe and in respect of which (subject to regulation 10) the following conditions must be fulfilled–

(a) a qualifying individual may subscribe to only one plan in any year;

(b) subject to paragraph (2)–

(i) the individual may not subscribe to a plan otherwise than by means of a sum or sums of his cash paid directly to the plan manager; and

(ii) the individual's cash subscription may not exceed the subscription limit in any year.

(2) Where, in pursuance of a public offer, an application is made by a qualifying individual for the allotment to him of shares of a company which are qualifying investments and such shares are allotted to that individual, he may, subject to the conditions prescribed by paragraph (3), subscribe to a plan by transferring or renouncing his rights to any shares so allotted to the plan manager or a nominee for the plan manager.

(3) The conditions prescribed by this paragraph are–

(a) that the shares are transferred, or the rights to the shares are renounced, within 30 days of their allotment to the individual;

(b) that any sum payable on such an application and the individual's cash subscription to the plan do not together exceed the subscription limit in any year.

(4) The subscription limit for the purposes of these Regulations is £4,800.

(5) A plan must be managed in accordance with these Regulations by a plan manager and under terms agreed in writing between the plan manager and the plan investor.

(6) Apart from other requirements of these Regulations the terms agreed to which paragraph (5) refers shall include the following conditions–

(a) that the plan investments shall be in the beneficial ownership of the plan investor;

(b) that the title to the plan investments shall be vested in the plan manager or his nominee or jointly in one of them and the plan investor;

(c) that the share certificate or other document evidencing title to a plan investment shall be held by the plan manager or as he may direct;

(d) that the plan manager shall, if the plan investor so elects, arrange for the plan investor to receive a copy of the annual report and accounts issued by every company or other concern in respect of shares or units (as the case may be) which are his plan investments;

(e) that the plan manager shall be under an obligation (subject to any provisions made by or under any other enactment and if the plan investor so elects) to arrange for the plan investor to be able–

(i) to attend shareholders' or unit holders' meetings,

(ii) to vote, and

(iii) to receive, in addition to the documents referred to in paragraph (d) above, any other information issued to shareholders or unit holders;

(f) that at the request of the plan investor and within such time as shall be agreed an entire plan with all rights and obligations of the parties to it may be transferred to another plan manager;

(g) that the plan manager shall notify the plan investor if by reason of any failure to satisfy the provisions of these Regulations a plan has or will become void.

General investment rules

5.—(1) All transactions whether by way of sale, purchase or otherwise by a plan manager in investments under a plan shall be made at the price which those investments might reasonably be expected to fetch in the open market.

(2) Investments, or rights in respect of investments, may not at any time–

(a) be purchased or made otherwise than out of cash which a plan manager holds (and is entitled under the provisions of these Regulations to hold) under a plan at that time; or

(b) be purchased from–

(i) a plan investor, or

(ii) the spouse of a plan investor,

so as to become plan investments under a plan to which the plan investor subscribes or has subscribed.

(3) A plan investor's cash subscription and any other cash held by a plan manager which he is entitled to hold under a plan shall be held only in sterling and be deposited with a deposit-taker or a building society in circumstances where–

(a) the deposit-taker is liable to account for and pay an amount representing income tax on payments of interest in respect of the deposit calculated by applying the composite rate to the grossed-up amount of the payments in accordance with the provisions of section 479 of the Taxes Act, or

(b) the reduced rate amount payable by the building society under regulation 3 of the Income Tax (Building Societies) Regulations 1986**(a)** includes an amount calculated in accordance with those Regulations by applying the reduced rate there referred to to the grossed-up amount of interest paid or credited in respect of the deposit,

and in either case the deposit is designated for the purposes of these Regulations only.

(4) Subject to paragraph (5), cash by way of dividends, other rights or proceeds in respect of shares, not being shares in an investment trust, which are held as plan investments may be invested only by way of cash deposit or in other such shares.

(5) Cash referred to in paragraph (4) may be invested in an authorised unit trust or in an investment trust provided that immediately after such an investment is made the total market value of plan investments in authorised unit trusts and investment trusts does not exceed one half of the market value of the portfolio.

Qualifying investments

6.—(1) This regulation specifies the kind of investments ("qualifying investments") which may be purchased, made or held under a plan.

(2) Qualifying investments to which paragraph (1) refers are–

(a) ordinary shares, not being shares in an investment trust, issued by a company which is incorporated in the United Kingdom and quoted in the official list of

(a) S.I. 1986/482, amended by S.I. 1987/844, 1988/1011 and 1989/36.

a recognised stock exchange in the United Kingdom or dealt in on the Unlisted Securities Market;

(b) subject to the conditions specified in paragraph (3), investments in–

(i) an authorised unit trust, or

(ii) an investment trust;

(c) cash which the plan manager is entitled to hold for investment under a plan.

(3) The conditions specified in this paragraph are–

(a) that the total amount of the cash subscription to the plan invested in authorised unit trusts and investment trusts in any year does not exceed one half of the subscription limit; and

(b) that on and after 6th April 1990 at least 75 per cent. in value of the investments subject to the trusts of a unit trust scheme which is an authorised unit trust or held by an investment trust are qualifying investments within paragraph (2)(a).

Qualifying individuals who may invest under a plan

7.—(1) This regulation specifies the description of individual who may invest under a plan ("qualifying individual").

(2) A qualifying individual to whom paragraph (1) refers is an individual–

(a) who is 18 years of age or over,

(b) who (subject to regulation 10) has not subscribed to any other plan during the year for which he makes an application under regulation 9, and

(c) (i) who is resident and ordinarily resident in the United Kingdom, or

(ii) who, though non-resident, performs duties which by virtue of section 132(4)(a) of the Taxes Act (Crown employees serving overseas) are treated as being performed in the United Kingdom.

Plan investor ceasing to qualify

8. Notwithstanding any other provision of these Regulations a plan investor who, after subscribing to a plan, at any time ceases to fulfil the conditions of regulation 7(2)(c) may retain the benefits of the plan (including the right to any relief or exemption due under the plan) subsisting at that time but, so long as he fails to fulfil those conditions, shall not be entitled to subscribe further to such a plan.

Conditions for application to subscribe to a plan

9.—(1) An application by an individual to subscribe to a plan must be made to a plan manager in a statement in writing and fulfil the conditions specified in paragraphs (2), (3) and (4).

(2) An application must specify the year for which the applicant is to subscribe to a plan.

(3) An application shall provide for a declaration by the applicant that the applicant–

(a) is 18 years of age or over;

(b) fulfils the conditions of regulation 7(2)(b) and (c);

(c) has made no other application to subscribe to another plan in the year to which paragraph (2) refers;

(d) authorises the plan manager in writing–

(i) to hold the applicant's cash subscription, plan investments, interest, dividends and any other rights or proceeds in respect of those investments and any other cash;

(ii) to make on his behalf any claims to relief from tax in respect of plan investments;

(iii) on the applicant's written request to transfer or pay to him, as the case may be, plan investments, interest, dividends, rights or other proceeds in respect of such investments or any cash.

(4) An application must contain–

(a) the applicant's full name,

(b) his permanent address,

(c) his national insurance number, and

(d) where he knows it, his tax office reference.

(5) A plan manager may not accept as a plan investor any individual if he has reason to believe that–

(a) he is not or might not be a qualifying individual, or

(b) he has given untrue information in his application.

(6) Section 95 of the Management Act shall have effect as if–

(a) the statement and declaration to which paragraphs (1) and (3) refer were a statement or declaration, as the case may be, within the meaning of subsection (1)(b), and

(b) there were substituted for subsection (3) the following words–

"(3) The relevant years of assessment for the purposes of this section are the year of assessment in respect of which any claim to relief from tax, in connection with which the statement or declaration is relevant, is made, the next following, and any preceding year of assessment."

Rights issues—relaxation of provisions of regulations 4 and 7

10.—(1) This regulation prescribes the circumstances in which–

(a) notwithstanding regulations 4(1)(a) and 7(2)(b) an individual may subscribe to more than one plan in any year, and

(b) notwithstanding regulation 4(1)(b) or (2) an individual's cash subscription to a plan in any year may exceed the subscription limit.

(2) The prescribed circumstances are circumstances in which–

(a) on the occasion of a new issue of shares a plan manager is entitled, by virtue of a plan investor's beneficial ownership of shares which are plan investments (in this regulation referred to as "original shares"), to subscribe for shares (in this regulation referred to as "new shares") (being qualifying investments) which are offered to shareholders in proportion to (or as nearly as may be in proportion to) their shareholdings; and

(b) the conditions contained in paragraph (3) are fulfilled.

(3) The conditions to which paragraph (2) refers are–

(a) that the plan investor–

(i) was the beneficial owner of the original shares at the end of the day immediately before that on which the right to subscribe for the new shares was announced; and

(ii) subscribes cash not exceeding the total sum payable to acquire the new shares (in this regulation referred to as "the rights subscription"); and

(b) that the rights subscription shall–

(i) be expended only on a subscription for new shares to which paragraph (2) refers, and

(ii) to the extent that it is not so expended, be transferred to the plan investor together with interest (if any) thereon within 14 days after the date by which the rights subscription is payable by the plan manager under the terms of the offer to subscribe for the new shares.

Plan manager—qualifications and Board's approval

11.—(1) This regulation specifies the circumstances ("qualifying circumstances") in which a person may be approved by the Board as a plan manager.

(2) The qualifying circumstances to which paragraph (1) refers are the following–

(a) the person must make written application to the Board for approval in a form prescribed by the Board;

(b) a plan manager must be an authorised person within the meaning of Chapter III of Part I of the Financial Services Act 1986**(a)** ("the 1986 Act"); and

(a) 1986 c.60.

(c) a plan manager must not be prevented from acting as such by any prohibition by or under rules under section 48 of the 1986 Act, by or under the rules of any recognised self-regulating organisation of which the plan manager is a member, or by or under the rules of any recognised professional body by which the plan manager is certified, or by a prohibition imposed under section 65 of the 1986 Act.

(3) The terms of the Board's approval may include conditions designed to ensure that the provisions of these Regulations are satisfied.

Plan manager—withdrawal by Board of approval

12.—(1) This regulation specifies the circumstances ("the disqualifying circumstances") in which the Board may by notice withdraw their approval of a person as a plan manager in relation to a plan.

(2) The disqualifying circumstances to which paragraph (1) refers are that the Board have reason to believe–

(a) that any provision of these Regulations is not or at any time has not been satisfied in respect of a plan managed by the plan manager; or

(b) that a person to whom they have given approval to act as a plan manager is not qualified so to act.

(3) The notice to which paragraph (1) refers shall specify–

(a) the date from which the Board's approval is withdrawn, and

(b) the disqualifying circumstances.

Plan manager—appeal against withdrawal of Board's approval

13.—(1) A plan manager to whom notice of withdrawal of approval has been given under regulation 12 may appeal against the withdrawal by notice given to the Board within 30 days after the date of the notice of withdrawal.

(2) The appeal shall be to the Special Commissioners.

(3) The like provisions as are contained in Part V of the Management Act (appeals and other proceedings)**(a)** shall apply to an appeal and the Special Commissioners shall on appeal to them confirm the notice unless they are satisfied that the notice ought to be quashed.

Plan manager ceasing to act

14. A person shall give notice to the Board and to the subscriber to the plan which he manages of his intention to cease to act as the plan manager within a reasonable time before he so ceases so that his obligations to the Board under the plan can be conveniently discharged at or about the time he ceases so to act.

Plan manager ceasing to qualify

15. A person shall cease to qualify as a plan manager and shall notify the Board forthwith of that fact where–

(a) the person no longer fulfils the conditions of regulation 11;

(b) in the case of an individual, he becomes bankrupt or, in Scotland, his estate is sequestrated, or makes any arrangement or composition with his creditors generally; or

(c) in the case of a company a resolution has been passed or a petition has been presented to wind it up.

(a) 1970 c.9.

Transfer of plans to other plan managers

16. Where arrangements are made by a plan investor to transfer a plan or plans to another plan manager ("the transferee") the transfer shall have effect and a plan shall not be otherwise affected for the purpose of these Regulations by the occasion of transfer, provided that the plan manager making the transfer ("the transferor") has given notice to the Board of the transfer together with the following information–

(a) (i) the name, address and tax office reference of the transferor;

(ii) the name, address and tax office reference of the transferee;

(iii) the effective date of transfer;

(iv) details of plan investors whose plans are being transferred to the transferee showing names, addresses, national insurance numbers and tax office references;

(v) details of plan investors who are to withdraw plan investments.

(b) A declaration by the transferor that he has fulfilled all his obligations to plan investors, to the Board or otherwise, which are imposed by these Regulations.

Exemption from tax of plan income and gains

17. Subject to these Regulations, except interest in respect of plan investments which is not reinvested but is paid to or at the direction of the plan investor or otherwise applied for his benefit, no tax shall be chargeable on the plan manager or his nominee or the plan investor in respect of interest, dividends or gains in respect of plan investments, losses in respect of plan investments shall be disregarded for the purposes of capital gains tax, and relief in respect of tax shall be given in the manner and to the extent provided by these Regulations.

Tax liabilities and reliefs—plan manager to act on behalf of plan investor

18.—(1) A plan manager may under these Regulations make claims, conduct appeals and agree on behalf of the plan investor liabilities for and reliefs from tax in respect of a plan.

(2) Claims shall be made to the Board in accordance with the provisions of regulations 19 and 20.

(3) Where any relief or exemption from tax previously given in respect of a plan has by virtue of these Regulations become excessive, in computing the relief due on any claim there shall be deducted, so that amounts equal to that excess are set-off or repaid to the Board, as the case may be, notwithstanding that those amounts have been invested–

(a) any amount repaid in respect of a tax credit;

(b) any other amount due to the Board by a plan manager in respect of any tax liability in respect of investments under a plan including (but without prejudice to the making of an assessment under the provisions of that section) any amount falling due in respect of a liability under section 737 of the Taxes Act**(a)**.

(4) Any amount deducted under paragraph (3) shall be treated as an amount of income tax deducted at source and not repayable within the meaning and for the purposes of section 95(2)(a) of the Management Act.

Repayments in respect of tax to plan manager—interim claims

19.—(1) Notwithstanding the provisions of any other enactment, the Board shall not be under an obligation to make any repayment in respect of tax under these Regulations earlier than the end of the month following the month in which the claim for the repayment is received.

(2) A claim for repayment in respect of tax which is not an annual claim ("interim claim") may be made only for a period of a month (or a number of months not exceeding six) beginning on the 6th day of the month and ending on the 5th day of the relevant following month.

(a) 1988 c.1.

(3) No claim for repayment may be made for the month ending 5th October or any subsequent month until the annual return due in respect of a plan for the preceding year has been duly made by the plan manager and received by the Board.

(4) Where, on the occasion of a claim, there is due to the Board an amount in respect of tax that amount shall be recoverable by the Board in the same manner as tax charged by an assessment on the plan manager which has become final and conclusive.

Repayments in respect of tax to plan manager—annual returns and annual claims

20.—(1) An annual claim is a claim for repayment in respect of tax for a year and may not be made at any time more than six years after the end of the year.

(2) A plan manager shall within six months after the end of the year make a return of all income and in addition an annual claim to establish the total of repayments due under a plan for that year.

(3) Where the aggregate of the repayments in respect of interim claims for the year shown by an annual claim exceeds the amount repayable for the year shown on the claim, the plan manager shall repay the amount of the excess to the Board with the claim.

(4) If a plan manager fails to make the return and the annual claim required under this regulation within the time limited, the Board may issue a notice to the plan manager showing the aggregate of payments in respect of the interim claims for the year, and stating that the Board are not satisfied that the amount due to the plan manager for that year exceeds the lower amount stated in the notice.

(5) If a return and an annual claim are not delivered to the Board within 14 days after the issue of such a notice under paragraph (4) the amount of the difference between the aggregate and the lower amount stated in the notice shall immediately be recoverable by the Board in the same manner as tax charged by an assessment on the plan manager which has become final and conclusive.

(6) Where a return and an annual claim have been made and the plan manager subsequently discovers that an error or mistake has been made in the return or claim the plan manager may make a supplementary return or annual claim within the time allowed in paragraph (1).

Plan manager's returns and claims—supplementary provisions

21.—(1) Section 42 of the Management Act**(a)** shall not apply to claims under these Regulations.

(2) No appeal shall lie from the Board's decision on an interim claim.

(3) An appeal shall be to the Special Commissioners from the Board's decision on an annual claim, and the appeal shall be brought by giving notice to the Board within 30 days of receipt of notice of the decision.

(4) No payment or repayment made or other thing done on or in relation to an interim claim or a notice under regulation 20(4) shall prejudice the decision on an annual claim.

(5) The like provisions as are contained in Part V of the Management Act (appeals and other proceedings) shall apply to an appeal under paragraph (3) above, and on an appeal the Special Commissioners may vary the decision appealed against whether or not the variation is to the advantage of the appellant.

(6) All such assessments, payments and repayments shall be made as are necessary to give effect to the Board's decision on an annual claim or to any variation of that decision on appeal.

(7) Returns and claims under these Regulations shall be in such form and contain such particulars as the Board prescribe and shall be signed by the plan manager; and forms prescribed for annual claims may require a report to be given by a person qualified for appointment as auditor of a company.

(a) 1970 c.9.

Assessments for withdrawing relief and recovering tax

22.—(1) Where–

(a) any relief or exemption from tax given in respect of income or gains under a plan is found not to be due or to be excessive, or

(b) where the full amount of tax in respect of the income or gains under a plan has not otherwise been fully accounted for and paid to the Board by or on behalf of the plan investor,

an assessment to tax may be made by the Board in the amount or further amount which in their opinion ought to be charged.

(2) An assessment to which paragraph (1) refers may be made on the plan manager or on the plan investor.

(3) If the assessment is made to recover tax in respect of income (including any amount in respect of a tax credit) under a plan it shall be made under Case VI of Schedule D.

Records to be kept by plan manager

23.—(1) A plan manager shall at all times keep sufficient records in respect of a plan to enable the requirements of these Regulations to be satisfied.

(2) The records shall include a valuation of plan investments at their market value as at 5th April each year.

Information to be given to plan investor by plan manager

24.—(1) Where under the terms of a plan a plan manager has discretion to purchase or sell investments he shall give to the plan investor once in every year a statement in writing of his reasons for–

(a) making a purchase or sale within, and

(b) retaining any investment throughout,

the period.

(2) A plan manager who makes a payment to a plan investor out of or in respect of which tax has been deducted shall, if the investor so requests in writing, furnish the investor with a statement in writing showing the gross amount of the payment, the amount deducted and the amount actually paid.

(3) On the transfer to a plan investor of a plan investment the plan manager shall provide for the investor details in writing of the market value on the date of transfer.

Information to be provided to the Board

25. The Board may by notice require any person who is or who at any time has been a plan manager or plan investor to furnish them, within such time (not being less than 14 days) as may be provided by the notice, such information about any plan or about any plan investment (including copies of or extracts from any books or other records) as they may reasonably require for the purposes of these Regulations.

Inspection of records by officer of the Board

26.—(1) The Board may by notice require any person who is or who at any time has been a plan manager or plan investor, within such time (not being less than 14 days) as may be provided in the notice, to make available for inspection by an officer of the Board authorised for that purpose all documents (including books and other records) in his possession or under his control containing information relating to any plan or to any plan investment.

(2) Where records are maintained by computer the person required to make them available for inspection shall provide the officer making the inspection with all the facilities necessary for obtaining information from them.

Capital gains tax—adaptation of enactments

27.—(1) For the purposes of capital gains tax on the occasion when the title to plan investments is transferred from a plan manager to a plan investor there shall be deemed to be a disposal and reacquisition by him of those investments for a consideration equal to their market value.

(2) For the pooling of plan investments for the purposes of Part III of Schedule 19 to the Finance Act 1985**(a)** Part III shall apply for the purposes of these Regulations with the substitution for paragraph 8(2) of the following words–

"(2) This Part of this Schedule shall apply separately to any securities which are plan investments under a plan within the meaning of the Personal Equity Plan Regulations 1989 and, while applying separately to any such securities, this Part of this Schedule shall have effect as if the plan investor held them in a capacity other than that in which he holds any other securities of the same class whether under another plan or otherwise."

(3) Sections 78 to 81 of the Capital Gains Tax Act 1979**(b)** shall not apply in relation to ordinary shares which are held under a plan if there is by virtue of any allotment for payment as is mentioned in section 77(2) of that Act a reorganisation affecting those shares.

Administration of tax in relation to plans—supplementary

28.—(1) Nothing in these Regulations shall be taken to prejudice any powers conferred or duties imposed by or under any enactment in relation to the making of returns of income or gains, or for the recovery of tax, penalties or interest by means of an assessment or otherwise.

(2) Notwithstanding the provisions of these Regulations a plan manager shall not be released from obligations under these Regulations in relation to a plan except under conditions agreed in writing with and notified to that person by the Board.

(3) Subject to the provisions of these Regulations the like provisions as are contained in the Management Act shall apply to any assessment of tax under these Regulations as if it were an assessment of tax for the year in which, apart from these Regulations, the plan investor would have been liable (by reason of his ownership of the investments) and as if–

(a) the assessment were an assessment specified in sections 55(1) (recovery of tax not postponed) and 86(2) (interest on tax), and

(b) the sum charged by the assessment were tax specified in the Table in section 86(4) (reckonable date for interest).

(4) The like provisions as are contained in section 97(1) of the Management Act shall apply as if–

(a) there were inserted after the words "sections 95 and 96 above" the words "or the Personal Equity Plan Regulations 1989", and

(b) there were inserted after the words "that they were" the words "or have become".

(5) Any form prescribed by the Board for the purposes of these Regulations shall provide for a declaration that all the particulars given in the form are correctly stated to the best of the knowledge and belief of the person concerned.

(6) No obligation as to secrecy imposed by statute or otherwise shall preclude the Board from disclosing to a plan manager or plan investor that any provision of these Regulations has not been satisfied or that relief has been given or claimed in respect of investments under a plan.

Transitional provisions—plans and plan investors under the 1986 Regulations

29.—(1) The 1986 Regulations shall continue to apply to annual plans, notwithstanding the entry into force of these Regulations, during the period from 6th April 1989 until the effective date in relation to any such plan, with the modification that the year which began with 1st January 1989 shall be treated as having ended on the effective date.

(2) With effect from the day following the effective date in relation to an annual plan, the provisions of these Regulations shall apply to it in place of the provisions of the 1986 Regulations.

(3) A plan investor who has subscribed to an annual plan during the year which began with 1st January 1989 may not before the day following the effective date in relation to the plan–

(a) 1985 c.54. **(b)** 1979 c.14.

(a) subscribe further to the plan if that subscription and any previous subscription to the plan for that year would together exceed the limit prescribed by Regulation 4(1)(c) of the 1986 Regulations, or

(b) subscribe to a plan under regulation 4 of these Regulations.

(4) These Regulations apply to any plan to which a qualifying individual who was a plan investor in respect of an annual plan subscribes in the period from the day following the effective date until 5th April 1990 as if that period were a year for the purpose of these Regulations.

(5) In this regulation–

"annual plan" means a plan to which the 1986 Regulations applied immediately before the entry into force of these Regulations; and

"effective date" in relation to an annual plan means the date which is the earlier of–

(a) 31st December 1989, and

(b) the date, being a date after 5th April 1989, which–

(i) the plan investor and the plan manager agree in writing, or

(ii) where the terms of the agreement between them permit, the plan manager determines,

to be the date after which the provisions of these Regulations shall apply to the plan in place of the provisions of the 1986 Regulations.

Kenneth Carlisle
Alan Howarth
14th March 1989 Two of the Lords Commissioners of Her Majesty's Treasury

---

EXPLANATORY NOTE

(This note is not part of the Regulations)

These Regulations consolidate the Personal Equity Plan Regulations 1986 (as amended by the Personal Equity Plan (Amendment) Regulations 1987, the Personal Equity Plan (Amendment) Regulations 1988 and the Personal Equity Plan (Amendment No. 2) Regulations 1988) ("the 1986 Regulations") with amendments and have effect from 6th April 1989. The principal amendments of the scheme under the 1986 Regulations are the abolition of the cash investment limit, together with the requirement that interest on amounts deposited with a building society or a deposit taker be paid gross, and the abolition of the minimum holding period and consequently the concept of the mature portfolio.

These Regulations also amend the scheme under the 1986 Regulations by providing for an increase in the annual amount of the cash subscription, for shares allotted in pursuance of a public offer to be subscribed to a plan, for changing from a calendar year to a tax year basis, for switching plan investments from shares into authorised unit trusts and investment trusts and for a reduction in the amount of information to be supplied by a plan manager to a plan investor. Interest on plan investments is no longer payable gross but continues to qualify for relief from income tax at the higher rate, so long as it is reinvested. Tax credits are payable in respect of dividends from plan investments whether or not they are reinvested. Transitional arrangements are provided in respect of plans and plan investors under the 1986 Regulations.

On and after 6th April 1990, the Regulations provide a new rule that an authorised unit trust or an investment trust in which plan investments are held must itself have at least 75 per cent. in value of its investments in shares of companies incorporated in the United Kingdom which are quoted shares or shares dealt in on the Unlisted Securities Market.

Regulation 1 provides for the title to and commencement of the Regulations.

Regulation 2 provides definitions.

Regulation 3 gives a general introduction.

Regulation 4 sets out general conditions for plans and subscriptions to plans.

Regulation 5 provides general rules for investment in plans.

Regulation 6 specifies permitted kinds of investment.

Regulation 7 specifies the description of individuals who may be plan investors.

Regulation 8 provides for consequences when certain individuals become disqualified.

Regulation 9 provides conditions for individual applications.

Regulation 10 provides for relaxation of the provisions of regulations 4 and 7 in respect of rights issues.

Regulation 11 provides for approval of plan managers by the Board.

Regulation 12 provides for the withdrawal of that approval in certain circumstances.

Regulation 13 provides for an appeal against such a withdrawal.

Regulation 14 requires a person to notify the Board and investors when ceasing to be a plan manager.

Regulation 15 provides circumstances in which a person shall cease to qualify as a plan manager.

Regulation 16 provides for transfers of plans from one to another plan manager.

Regulation 17 sets out the tax exemptions for plan investors.

Regulation 18 provides that the plan manager shall act on behalf of the plan investor in respect of tax reliefs and liabilities under the plan.

Regulations 19, 20 and 21 provide for claims for relief and for returns.

Regulation 22 makes provision for the withdrawal of relief and the recovery of tax.

Regulation 23 provides for the keeping of plan records.

Regulation 24 provides for information and for a certificate of tax deducted to be given by plan managers to investors.

Regulations 25 and 26 empower the Board to obtain information and to inspect records.

Regulation 27 adapts statutory capital gains tax provisions in relation to plans.

Regulation 28 makes supplementary provisions for tax administration in relation to plans.

Regulation 29 contains transitional arrangements for plans and plan investors under the 1986 Regulations.

STATUTORY INSTRUMENTS

1989 No. 470

VALUE ADDED TAX

The Value Added Tax (Fund-Raising Events and Charities) Order 1989

Made - - - - - -	*14th March 1989*
Laid before the House of Commons	*14th March 1989*
Coming into force	*1st April 1989*

The Treasury, in exercise of the powers conferred on them by sections 16(4) and 48(6) of the Value Added Tax Act 1983**(a)** and of all other powers enabling them in that behalf, hereby make the following Order:

1. This Order may be cited as the Value Added Tax (Fund-Raising Events and Charities) Order 1989 and shall come into force on 1st April 1989.

2. Group 16 (charities, etc) of Schedule 5**(b)** to the Value Added Tax Act 1983 shall be varied as follows—

(a) by substituting for item 8 the following—

"**8.** The supply to a charity of a publication in any newspaper, journal, poster, programme, annual, leaflet, brochure, pamphlet, periodical or similar publication of an advertisement which is for the raising of money for, or making known the objects or reasons for the objects of, the charity.";

(b) in note 4(a) by inserting after the word "video" the word ", sterilising".

3. Schedule 6 to the Value Added Tax Act 1983 shall be varied by adding after Group 11 the following—

"GROUP 12—FUND-RAISING EVENTS BY CHARITIES AND OTHER QUALIFYING BODIES

Item No.

1. The supply of goods and services by a charity in connection with a fund-raising event organised for charitable purposes by a charity or jointly by more than one charity.

2. The supply of goods and services by a qualifying body in connection with a fund-raising event organised exclusively for its own benefit.

Notes:

(1) For the purposes of items 1 and 2 "fund-raising event" means a fete, ball, bazaar, gala show, performance or similar event, which is separate from and not forming any part of a series or regular run of like or similar events.

(2) For the purposes of item 2 "qualifying body" means any non-profit making body mentioned in either section 47(3) of this Act or item 1 of Group 9 of Schedule 6 to this Act.".

Kenneth Carlisle
Alan Howarth

14th March 1989 — Two of the Lords Commissioners of Her Majesty's Treasury

(a) 1983 c.55.
(b) Group 16 was varied by S.I. 1983/1717, 1984/766, 1986/530, 1987/437.

EXPLANATORY NOTE

(This note is not part of the Order)

This Order extends the zero-rating provisions of Group 16 (charities, etc) of Schedule 5 to the Value Added Tax Act 1983 and adds a new Group 12 to the exemption Schedule of the same Act.

The zero-rating reliefs available under Group 16 have been extended to cover:—

—advertising published for a charity for educational or fund-raising purposes in a programme, annual, leaflet, brochure, pamphlet, poster or similar publication;

—sterilising equipment supplied to certain non-profit-making bodies for use in medical research, diagnosis or treatment.

The new Group 12 exempts supplies made in connection with one-off fund-raising events by charities and certain other non-profit-making bodies such as political parties and trades unions.

STATUTORY INSTRUMENTS

1989 No. 471

VALUE ADDED TAX

The Value Added Tax (Increase of Registration Limits) Order 1989

Made - - - - - - -	*14th March 1989*
Laid before the House of Commons	*14th March 1989*
Coming into force	
articles 1, 2(a) and (b)	*15th March 1989*
article 2(c)	*1st June 1989*

The Treasury, in exercise of the powers conferred on them by paragraph 12 of Schedule 1 to the Value Added Tax Act 1983**(a)**, hereby make the following Order:

1. This Order may be cited as the Value Added Tax (Increase of Registration Limits) Order 1989 and shall come into force on the following dates:

articles 1, 2(a) and (b) 15th March 1989
article 2(c) 1st June 1989

2. Schedule 1**(b)** to the Value Added Tax Act 1983 (provisions as to liability to be registered) shall be amended as follows:

(a) in paragraph 1(1)(a)(i) for the figure "£7,500" there shall be substituted "£8,000",

(b) in paragraphs 1(1)(a)(ii), 1(1)(b), 1(2) and 4(3) for the figure "£22,100" there shall be substituted "£23,600",

(c) in paragraphs 1(3), 2(1) and 2(2) for the figure "£21,100" there shall be substituted "£22,600".

Kenneth Carlisle
Alan Howarth

14th March 1989 Two of the Lords Commissioners of Her Majesty's Treasury

---

(a) 1983 c.55; Schedule 1 was amended by the Finance Act 1984 (c.43) section 12, the Finance Act 1986 (c.41) section 10, the Finance Act 1987 (c.16) sections 13 and 14 and the Finance Act 1988 (c.39) section 14.
(b) Schedule 1 was varied by S.I. 1984/342, 1985/433, 1986/531, 1987/438, 1988/508.

EXPLANATORY NOTE

(This note is not part of the Order)

This Order increases the VAT registration limit from £22,100 to £23,600 per annum and the single quarterly limit from £7,500 to £8,000 with effect from 15th March 1989.

The Order also increases the limit for cancellation of registration from £21,100 to £22,600 with effect from 1st June 1989.

The later date of implementation of the change in the cancellation limits is to allow time for potential applicants for deregistration to consider their position and to make application to their local VAT Office.

STATUTORY INSTRUMENTS

1989 No. 472

VALUE ADDED TAX

The Value Added Tax (Self-supply of Construction Services) Order 1989

Made - - - - - - -	*14th March 1989*
Laid before the House of Commons	*14th March 1989*
Coming into force - - -	*1st April 1989*

The Treasury, in exercise of the powers conferred on them by sections 3(6) and (8) and 29(2) of the Value Added Tax Act 1983**(a)** and of all other powers enabling them in that behalf, hereby make the following Order:

1. This Order may be cited as the Value Added Tax (Self-supply of Construction Services) Order 1989 and shall come into force on 1st April 1989.

2. In this Order "the Act" means the Value Added Tax Act 1983.

3.—(1) Where a person, in the course or furtherance of a business carried on by him, for the purpose of that business and otherwise than for a consideration, performs any of the following services, that is to say–

(a) the construction of a building; or

(b) the extension or other alteration of, or the construction of an annexe to, any building such that additional floor area of not less than 10 per cent of the floor area of the original building is created; or

(c) the construction of any civil engineering work; or

(d) in connection with any such services as are described in sub-paragraph (a), (b) or (c) above, the carrying out of any demolition work contemporaneously with or preparatory thereto,

then, subject to each of the conditions specified in paragraph (2) below being satisfied, those services shall be treated for the purposes of the Act as both supplied to him for the purpose of that business and supplied by him in the course or furtherance of it.

(2) The conditions mentioned in paragraph (1) above are that–

(a) the value of such services is not less than £100,000; and

(b) such services would, if supplied for a consideration in the course or furtherance of a business carried on by a taxable person, be chargeable to tax at a rate other than nil.

(3) The preceding provisions of this article shall apply in relation to any bodies corporate which are treated for the purposes of section 29 of the Act as members of a group as if those bodies were one person, but anything done which would fall to be treated by virtue of this Order as services supplied to and by that person shall be treated as supplied to and by the representative member.

(a) 1983 c.55.

4.—(1) The value of any supply of services which is to be treated as taking place by virtue of this Order is the open market value of such services.

(2) Where any services of a description specified in article 3(1) above are in the process of being performed on the day this Order comes into force, the value of such services for the purposes of this Order shall be the value of such part of those services as are performed on or after that day.

Kenneth Carlisle
Alan Howarth

14th March 1989 Two of the Lords Commissioners of Her Majesty's Treasury

---

EXPLANATORY NOTE

(This note is not part of the Order)

This Order provides for value added tax to be chargeable where a person performs for himself the construction services specified in the Order which–

(a) are of a value of not less than £100,000, and

(b) would be chargeable to tax at the standard rate if performed for a consideration.

STATUTORY INSTRUMENTS

1989 No. 473 (C. 17)

TAXES

The Finance Act 1988 (Commencement) Order 1989

Made - - - - 13th March 1989

The Lord Chancellor, in exercise of the powers conferred on him by section 134(4) of the Finance Act 1988(**a**), hereby makes the following Order:

1. This Order may be cited as the Finance Act 1988 (Commencement) Order 1989.

2. Sections 134 and 135 of the Finance Act 1988 shall come into force on 3rd April 1989.

13th March 1989

Mackay of Clashfern, C.

EXPLANATORY NOTE

(This note is not part of the Order)

This Order brings into force on 3rd April 1989 sections 134 and 135 of the Finance Act 1988 and the repeals made by Part IX of Schedule 14 to that Act.

Section 134 provides for the introduction of General Commissioners of Income Tax in Northern Ireland to hear appeals and other proceedings as they do elsewhere in the United Kingdom.

The section amends the Taxes Management Act 1970 (c.9) ("the Act") to enable General Commissioners to be appointed for Northern Ireland by the Lord Chancellor and provides for appeals and other proceedings previously heard by the Special Commissioners and county courts in Northern Ireland (and which would have been heard by General Commissioners if they were proceedings in Great Britain) to be heard by those General Commissioners. Transitional arrangements are made in respect of proceedings instituted but not determined before the day appointed by this Order.

Section 135 amends the Act by substituting, for the fixed time limit imposed by the Rules of the Supreme Court (Northern Ireland) 1980 (S.R. (N.I.) 1980 No. 346), a requirement that a case to be stated by Commissioners to the Court of Appeal in Northern Ireland must be settled as soon as is reasonably practicable. It also makes consequential amendments following the introduction of General Commissioners in Northern Ireland.

(**a**) 1988 c.39.

STATUTORY INSTRUMENTS

1989 No. 474

SEA FISHERIES

The North Western and North Wales Sea Fisheries District (Variation) Order 1989

Made - - - -	*13th March 1989*
Coming into force -	*1st April 1989*

The Minister of Agriculture, Fisheries and Food and the Secretary of State, acting jointly, on the application of the local fisheries committee for the North Western and North Wales Sea Fisheries District and after consultation with every council concerned, in exercise of the powers conferred by section 1 of the Sea Fisheries Regulation Act 1966**(a)** and now vested in them**(b)** and of all other powers enabling them in that behalf, hereby make the following Order, a draft of which has lain before Parliament for forty days prior to its being made:–

Title, commencement and interpretation

1.—(1) This Order may be cited as the North Western and North Wales Sea Fisheries District (Variation) Order 1989 and shall come into force on 1st April 1989.

(2) In this Order "the principal Order" means the North Western and North Wales Sea Fisheries District Order 1986**(c)**.

Variation of the principal Order

2.—(1) For article 4 of the principal Order there shall be substituted the following:–

"*Expenses*

4. The expenses of the Committee, other than those which may be required to be incurred under section 17(2) of the Act, shall be chargeable to the constituent Councils, for the financial year ending 31st March 1990 in the respective proportions set out in column 3 of Schedule 1 to this Order opposite the reference to each constituent Council, and for each succeeding financial year in the respective proportions set out in column 4 of that Schedule, and shall be expenses for general county or district purposes.".

(2) For Schedule 1 to the principal Order there shall be substituted the following:–

(a) 1966 c.38, amended by the Local Government Act 1985 (c.51), section 16 and Schedule 8, paragraph 19.
(b) By the Transfer of Functions (Wales) Order 1969 (S.I. 1969/388).
(c) S.I. 1986/1201.

SCHEDULE 1

Articles 3 and 4

CONSTITUTION AND EXPENSES

Column 1	*Column 2*		*Column 3*	*Column 4*
Constituent Councils	*Number of representatives*		*Percentage of expenses payable in 1989/90*	*Percentage of expenses payable after 1989/90*
	Until 30 June 1989	*From 1 July 1989*		
Cheshire County Council	3	2	15.55	8.10
Cumbria County Council	2	2	10.63	9.25
Lancashire County Council	3	3	26.80	20.60
Sefton Metropolitan Borough Council	2	2	7.87	8.75
Wirral Metropolitan Borough Council	2	2	9.25	10.50
Clwyd County Council	2	2	6.82	6.65
Dyfed County Council	2	2	6.33	6.65
Gwynedd County Council	2	3	16.75	29.50 ”

In Witness whereof the Official Seal of the Minister of Agriculture, Fisheries and Food is hereunto affixed on 13th March 1989.

John MacGregor
Minister of Agriculture, Fisheries and Food

13th March 1989

Peter Walker
Secretary of State for Wales

EXPLANATORY NOTE

(This note is not part of the Order)

This Order varies the North Western and North Wales Sea Fisheries District Order 1986 (S.I. 1986/1201) so as to alter the representation of two of the constituent Councils of the local fisheries committee with effect from 1st July 1989 and to reapportion the expenses payable by all the constituent Councils for the financial year ending 31st March 1990 and for succeeding years.

STATUTORY INSTRUMENTS

1989 No. 475

COMMUNITY CHARGES, ENGLAND AND WALES
SOCIAL SECURITY

Community Charges (Information Concerning Social Security) Regulations 1989

Made - - - -	*14th March 1989*
Laid before Parliament	*17th March 1989*
Coming into force	*22nd May 1989*

The Secretary of State for Social Security, in exercise of the powers conferred by sections 143(1) and (2) and 146(6) of, and paragraph 14(1) and (2)(c) of Schedule 2 to, the Local Govenment Finance Act 1988(**a**) and of all other powers enabling him in that behalf, hereby makes the following Regulations:

Citation and commencement

1. These Regulations may be cited as the Community Charges (Information Concerning Social Security) Regulations 1989 and shall come into force on 22nd May 1989.

Interpretation

2. In these Regulations –

"the Act" means the Local Government Finance Act 1988;

"the 1986 Act" means the Social Security Act 1986(**b**);

"appropriate social security office" means an office of the Department of Social Security which is normally open to the public for the receipt of claims for income support and includes an office of the Department of Employment which is normally open to the public for the receipt of claims for unemployment benefit;

"community charge benefits" means benefits to which section 20(1)(d) of the 1986 Act(**c**) refers;

"income support" shall be construed in accordance with Part II of the 1986 Act;

"partner" means –

(a) where a person is a member of a married or unmarried couple(**d**), the other member of that couple; or

(b) where a person is polygamously married to two or more members of his household, any such member to whom he is so married;

"registration officer" means a community charges registration officer within the meaning of section 26 of the Act.

(**a**) 1988 c.41; section 146(6) is cited because of the meaning assigned to the word "prescribed".
(**b**) 1986 c.50.
(**c**) Section 20(1)(d) of the 1986 Act was inserted by the 1988 Act, Schedule 10, paragraph 2(2).
(**d**) *See* the definitions of married and unmarried couple in section 20(11) of the 1986 Act.

Supply of relevant information to registration officers

3.—(1) For the purposes of paragraph 14 of Schedule 2 to the Act (information concerning social security) no duty of confidentiality shall prevent the Secretary of State from disclosing relevant information (within the meaning of that paragraph) to a registration officer for a charging authority.

(2) For the purposes of Sub-paragraph (c) of paragraph 14(2) of Schedule 2 to the Act (meaning of relevant information) there is prescribed information of the description set out in paragraphs (3) and (4).

(3) For the period from the coming into force of these Regulations until 31st March 1990 (both dates inclusive), the information is information as to the name and address of any person, aged 18 or over and any partner aged 18 or over of that person, where that person is in receipt of income support at any time within that period but is not receiving housing benefit under Part II of the 1986 Act.

(4) For the period from 1st April 1990 the information is information as to the name and address of any person, aged 18 or over, and any partner aged 18 or over of that person, where that person is awarded income support but has not at the time of the award, made a claim for community charge benefits at the appropriate Social Security office.

Signed by authority of the Secretary of State for Social Security.

Nicholas Scott
Minister of State,
Department of Social Security

14th March 1989

EXPLANATORY NOTE

(This note is not part of the Regulations)

These Regulations prescribe that,

(a) the Secretary of State may, notwithstanding any duty of confidentiality, supply information concerning persons who have been awarded income support to a community charge registration officer for a charging authority; and

(b) the description of the information which may be supplied where obtained by him under his functions under the Social Security Act 1986.

STATUTORY INSTRUMENTS

1989 No. 476 (S.58)

COMMUNITY CHARGES, SCOTLAND
SOCIAL SECURITY
WATER SUPPLY, SCOTLAND

Community Charges (Information Concerning Social Security) (Scotland) Regulations 1989

Made - - - -	*14th March 1989*
Laid before Parliament	*17th March 1989*
Coming into force	*1st April 1990*

The Secretary of State for Social Security, in exercise of the powers conferred by sections 20B(1) and (2)(c), 26(1) and 31(3) of the Abolition of Domestic Rates Etc (Scotland) Act 1987(**a**) and those sections as read with paragraph 11 of Schedule 5 to that Act(**b**) and with the Community Water Charges (Scotland) Regulations 1988(**c**) made thereunder, and of all other powers enabling him in that behalf, hereby makes the following Regulations:

Citation and commencement

1. These Regulations may be cited as the Community Charges (Information Concerning Social Security) (Scotland) Regulations 1989 and shall come into force on 1st April 1990.

Interpretation

2. In these Regulations–

"the Act" means the Abolition of Domestic Rates Etc (Scotland) Act 1987;

"the 1986 Act" means the Social Security Act 1986(**d**);

"appropriate social security office" means an office of the Department of Social Security which is normally open to the public for the receipt of claims for income support and includes an office of the Department of Employment which is normally open to the public for the receipt of claims for unemployment benefit;

"community charge benefits" means benefits to which section 20(1)(d) of the 1986 Act(**e**) refers;

"income support" shall be construed in accordance with Part II of the 1986 Act;

"partner" means–

(**a**) 1987 c.47; section 20B was inserted by the Local Government Finance Act 1988 (c.41), Schedule 12, paragraph 31; section 26(1) contains a definition of "prescribed" relevant to the exercise of the statutory powers under which these Regulations are made.
(**b**) Paragraph 11 was amended by the Local Government Finance Act 1988, Schedule 12, paragraph 38.
(**c**) S.I. 1988/1538.
(**d**) 1986 c.50, as amended by the Local Government Finance Act 1988 (c.41), Schedule 10.
(**e**) Section 20(1)(d) of the 1986 Act was inserted by the Local Government Finance Act 1988, Schedule 10, paragraph 2(2).

(a) where a person is a member of a married or unmarried couple **(a)**, the other member of that couple; or

(b) where a person is polygamously married to two or more members of his household, any such member to whom he is so married;

"registration officer" means a Community Charges Registration Officer within the meaning of section 12 of the Act;

and any reference to a section of the Act includes a reference to that section as read with paragraph 11 of Schedule 5 to the Act and the Community Water Charges (Scotland) Regulations 1988.

Supply of relevant information to registration officers

3.—(1) For the purposes of section 20B of the Act (information concerning social security) it is prescribed that the Secretary of State may, notwithstanding any duty of confidentiality, supply relevant information (within the meaning of that section) to a registration officer.

(2) For the purposes of paragraph (c) of section 20B(2) of the Act (meaning of relevant information) there is prescribed information of the description set out in paragraph (3).

(3) The information to which paragraph (2) refers is information as to the name, address and date of birth of any person aged 18 or over and any partner aged 18 or over of that person, where that person is awarded income support but has not at the time of the award made a claim at the appropriate social security office–

(a) for community charge benefits, or

(b) where the claim for income support is made prior to 1st April 1990, for housing benefit in the form of a community charge rebate**(b)**.

Signed by authority of the Secretary of State for Social Security.

Nicholas Scott
Minister of State,
Department of Social Security

14th March 1989

EXPLANATORY NOTE

(This note is not part of the Regulations)

These Regulations which are made under section 20B of the Abolition of Domestic Rates Etc (Scotland) Act (as inserted by the Local Government Finance Act 1988, Schedule 12, paragraph 31) prescribe–

(a) that the Secretary of State may supply certain "relevant" information to registration officers; and

(b) the description of that information obtained by him under his functions under the Social Security Act 1986.

They replace the Community Charges (Information Concerning Social Security) (Scotland) Regulations 1988 (S.I. 1988/1889 (S.177)), which have effect for the period from 23rd November 1988 to 31st March 1990.

(a) *See* the definitions of married and unmarried couple in section 20(11) of the 1986 Act.

(b) *See* section 28(1)(aa) of the 1986 Act as modified by the Housing Benefit (Social Security Act 1986 Modifications) (Scotland) Regulations 1988 (S.I. 1988/1483) (s.145).

STATUTORY INSTRUMENTS

1989 No. 477

PENSIONS

The Pensions Increase (Review) Order 1989

Made - - - -	*13th March 1989*
Laid before Parliament	*16th March 1989*
Coming into force	*10th April 1989*

Whereas by virtue of section 23(2)**(a)** of the Social Security Pensions Act 1975**(b)** a direction has been given**(c)** under section 63(2) and section 83(3)(d) of the Social Security Act 1986**(d)** by the Secretary of State for Social Services that the sums mentioned in section 63(1)(b) of the Social Security Act 1986 are to be increased;

Now therefore the Treasury, in exercise of the powers conferred by section 59(1), (2) and (5) of the Social Security Pensions Act 1975**(e)** and now vested in them**(f)**, and all other powers enabling them in that behalf, hereby make the following Order:

Citation and commencement

1. This Order may be cited as the Pensions Increase (Review) Order 1989 and shall come into force on 10th April 1989.

Interpretation

2.—(1) In this Order–

"the 1971 Act" means the Pensions (Increase) Act 1971**(g)**;

"the 1974 Act" means the Pensions (Increase) Act 1974**(h)**;

"the 1975 Act" means the Social Security Pensions Act 1975;

"basic rate" has the meaning given by section 17(1) of the 1971 Act as amended by section 1(3) of the 1974 Act;

"the existing Orders" means the Pensions Increase (Annual Review) Order 1972**(i)**, the Pensions Increase (Annual Review) Order 1973**(j)**, the Pensions Increase (Annual Review) Order 1974**(k)**, the Pensions Increase (Annual Review) Order 1975**(l)**, the Pensions Increase (Annual Review) Order 1976**(m)**, the Pensions

(a) Section 23(2) was amended by Schedule 10, paragraph 91 to the Social Security Act 1986 (c.50).
(b) 1975 c.60.
(c) The direction is contained in S.I. 1989/43.
(d) 1986 c.50; section 1 of the Social Security and Housing Benefits Act 1983 (c.36) made provision for increases to reflect actual, rather than estimated, rises in the general level of prices.
(e) Section 59 was amended and section 59A was added by section 11 of the Social Security Act 1979 (c.18). Section 59 was also amended by Schedule 5, paragraph 33 to the Social Security Act 1985 (c.53). Section 59(1) was further amended by Schedule 10, paragraph 93 to the Social Security Act 1986.
(f) S.I. 1981/1670.
(g) 1971 c.56.
(h) 1974 c.9.
(i) S.I. 1972/1298.
(j) S.I. 1973/1370.
(k) S.I. 1974/1373.
(l) S.I. 1975/1384.
(m) S.I. 1976/1356.

Increase (Annual Review) Order 1977**(a)**, the Pensions Increase (Annual Review) Order 1978**(b)**, the Pensions Increase (Review) Order 1979**(c)**, the Pensions Increase (Review) Order 1980**(d)**, the Pensions Increase (Review) Order 1981**(e)**, the Pensions Increase (Review) Order 1982**(f)**, the Pensions Increase (Review) Order 1983**(g)**, the Pensions Increase (Review) Order 1984**(h)**, the Pensions Increase (Review) Order 1985**(i)**, the Pensions Increase (Review) Order 1986**(j)**, the Pensions Increase (Review) Order 1987**(k)**, and the Pensions Increase (Review) Order 1988**(l)**;

"official pension" has the meaning given by section 5(1) of the 1971 Act;

"pension authority" has the meaning given by section 7(1) of the 1971 Act;

"qualifying condition" means one of the conditions laid down in section 3 of the 1971 Act as amended by section 3(2) and (3) of the 1974 Act;

"widow's pension" means a pension payable in respect of the services of the pensioner's deceased husband.

(2) For the purposes of this Order the time when a pension "begins" is that stated in section 8(2) of the 1971 Act, and the "beginning date" shall be construed accordingly.

(3) Where, for the purposes of this Order, it is necessary to calculate the number of complete months in any period an incomplete month shall be treated as a complete month if it consists of at least 16 days.

Pension increases

3. The annual rate of an official pension may, if a qualifying condition is satisfied or the pension is a widow's pension, be increased by the pension authority in respect of any period beginning on or after 10th April 1989 as follows–

(1) a pension beginning before 11th April 1988 may be increased by 5.9 per cent of the basic rate as increased by the amount of any increase under section 1 of the 1971 Act or the existing Orders;

(2) a pension beginning on or after 11th April 1988 and before 10th April 1989 may be increased by 5.9 per cent multiplied by $\frac{A}{B}$ where

(a) A is the number of complete months in the period between the beginning date of the pension and 10th April 1989, and

(b) B is 12.

Increases in certain lump sums

4. In respect of any lump sum or instalment of a lump sum which became payable before 10th April 1989 but on or after 11th April 1988 there may be paid an increase of 5.9 per cent of the amount of the lump sum or instalment (as increased by the amount under section 1 of the 1971 Act or under the existing Orders) multiplied by $\frac{A}{B}$ where

(a) A is the number of complete months in the period between the beginning date for the lump sum or, if later, 11th April 1988 and the date on which it became payable; and

(b) B is 12.

Reductions in respect of guaranteed minimum pensions

5. The amount by reference to which any increase in the rate of an official pension provided for by this Order is to be calculated shall, in the case of a person–

(a) who is entitled to a guaranteed minimum pension on 10th April 1989, and

(b) whose entitlement to that guaranteed minimum pension arises from an employment from which (either directly or by virtue of the payment of a transfer credit) entitlement to the official pension also arises,

(a) S.I. 1977/1387. **(b)** S.I. 1978/1211. **(c)** S.I. 1979/1047.
(d) S.I. 1980/1302. **(e)** S.I. 1981/1217. **(f)** S.I. 1982/1178.
(g) S.I. 1983/1264. **(h)** S.I. 1984/1307. **(i)** S.I. 1985/1575.
(j) S.I. 1986/1116. **(k)** S.I. 1987/130. **(l)** S.I. 1988/217.

be reduced by an amount equal to the rate of the guaranteed minimum pension unless the Treasury(a) shall, in accordance with the provisions of section 59A of the 1975 Act, otherwise direct.

Alan Howarth
David Maclean
13th March 1989 Two of the Lords Commissioners of Her Majesty's Treasury

---

EXPLANATORY NOTE

(This note is not part of the Order)

Under section 59 of the Social Security Pensions Act 1975 as amended by section 11 of the Social Security Act 1979 and as modified by section 59A of the 1975 Act (introduced by section 11(4) of the 1979 Act) the Treasury (in whom the functions conferred by those provisions are now vested) are required to provide by order for the increase in the rates of public service pensions. The increase is the percentage (or in some circumstances a fraction of the percentage) by which the Secretary of State for Social Services has, by directions given under the provisions of section 23(2) of the Social Security Pensions Act 1975 (as amended by Schedule 10, paragraph 91 of the Social Security Act 1986), increased the sums referred to in section 63(1)(*b*) of the Social Security Act 1986. These are the sums which are the additional components in the rates of long term benefits, namely the additional pension entitlements accruing to employees in respect of earnings after 5th April 1978.

For pensions which began before 11th April 1988 the increase is 5.9 per cent. For pensions which began on or after 11th April 1988 the increases are as follows–

Pensions Beginning	*Percentage Increase*	*Pensions Beginning*	*Percentage Increase*
11th April 1988 to 25th April 1988	5.9%	26th September 1988 to 25th October 1988	2.95%
26th April 1988 to 25th May 1988	5.41%	26th October 1988 to 25th November 1988	2.46%
26th May 1988 to 25th June 1988	4.92%	26th November 1988 to 25th December 1988	1.97%
26th June 1988 to 25th July 1988	4.43%	26th December 1988 to 25th January 1989	1.47%
26th July 1988 to 25th August 1988	3.93%	26th January 1989 to 25th February 1989	0.98%
26th August 1988 to 25th September 1988	3.44%	26th February 1989 to 25th March 1989	0.49%

(a) *See* S.I. 1981/1670, articles 2(1)(*c*) and 3(5).

Deferred lump sums beginning on or before 25th March 1989 and which become payable after 9th April 1989 receive the same percentage increase as pensions which began on the same date. Article 4 of the Order provides for increases on certain deferred lump sums which became payable on or after 11th April 1988 and before 10th April 1989.

The Order also makes provision for the amount by reference to which any increase in the rate of an official pension is to be calculated to be reduced by the amount equal to the rate of the guaranteed minimum pension entitlement deriving from the employment which gives rise to the official pension. This is required by section 59(5) of the Social Security Pensions Act 1975 but by virtue of section 59A of that Act and the Transfer of Functions (Minister for the Civil Service and Treasury) Order 1981 the Treasury is empowered to direct that in respect of specified cases or classes of case either no such reduction be made or the reduction shall be less than the rate of the guaranteed minimum pension.

STATUTORY INSTRUMENTS

1989 No. 478

LOCAL GOVERNMENT, ENGLAND AND WALES

The Local Authorities (Armorial Bearings) Order 1989

Made - - - -	*15th March 1989*
Coming into force	*5th April 1989*

At the Court at Buckingham Palace, the 15th day of March 1989

Present,

The Queen's Most Excellent Majesty in Council

Her Majesty, by virtue and in exercise of the powers conferred on Her by section 247 of the Local Government Act 1972(**a**), is pleased, by and with the advice of Her Privy Council, to order, and it is hereby ordered, as follows:

1. This Order may be cited as the Local Authorities (Armorial Bearings) Order 1989 and shall come into force on 5th April 1989.

2. Subject to article 3 of this Order, the town council of Northam may bear and use the armorial bearings which were immediately before 1st April 1974 borne and used by Northam urban district council.

3. Armorial bearings shall not be borne or used pursuant to article 2 of this Order until they have been exemplified according to the laws of arms and recorded in the College of Arms.

G. I. de Deney
Clerk of the Privy Council

EXPLANATORY NOTE

(This note is not part of the Order)

This Order authorises Northam town council to bear and use the armorial bearings of the former Northam urban district council.

(**a**) 1972 c.70.

STATUTORY INSTRUMENTS

1989 No. 479

CHILDREN AND YOUNG PERSONS

The Child Abduction and Custody (Parties to Conventions) Order 1989

Made - - - - 15th March 1989

At the Court at Buckingham Palace, the 15th day of March 1989

Present,

The Queen's Most Excellent Majesty in Council

Her Majesty, in exercise of the powers conferred on Her by section 2 of the Child Abduction and Custody Act 1985(**a**), is pleased, by and with the advice of Her Privy Council, to order, and it is hereby ordered, as follows:

1.—(1) This Order may be cited as the Child Abduction and Custody (Parties to Conventions) Order 1989.

(2) The Child Abduction and Custody (Parties to Conventions) (Amendment) (No. 3) Order 1988(**b**) is revoked.

2. The Child Abduction and Custody (Parties to Conventions) Order 1986(**c**) is amended by deleting Schedule 1 thereto(**d**) and substituting therefor the following –

(**a**) 1985 c.60. (**b**) S.I. 1988/1839. (**c**) S.I. 1986/1159. (**d**) Schedule 1 to S.I. 1986/1159 was substituted by S.I. 1988/1839.

"SCHEDULE 1

Article 2

CONVENTION ON THE CIVIL ASPECTS OF INTERNATIONAL CHILD ABDUCTION, THE HAGUE, 25th OCTOBER 1980

Contracting States to the Convention	*Territories specified in Declarations under Article 39 or 40 of the Convention*	*Date of Coming into Force as between the United Kingdom and the State or Territory*
Australia	Australian States and mainland Territories	1st January 1987
Austria	—	1st October 1988
Canada	Ontario	1st August 1986
	New Brunswick	1st August 1986
	British Columbia	1st August 1986
	Manitoba	1st August 1986
	Nova Scotia	1st August 1986
	Newfoundland	1st August 1986
	Prince Edward Island	1st August 1986
	Quebec	1st August 1986
	Yukon Territory	1st August 1986
	Saskatchewan	1st November 1986
	Alberta	1st February 1987
	Northwest Territories	1st April 1988
The French Republic	—	1st August 1986
The Hungarian People's Republic	—	1st September 1986
The Grand Duchy of Luxembourg	—	1st January 1987
Norway	—	1st April 1989
The Portuguese Republic	—	1st August 1986
Spain	—	1st September 1987
The Swiss Confederation	—	1st August 1986
The United States of America	—	1st July 1988 "

G. I. de Deney
Clerk of the Privy Council

EXPLANATORY NOTE

(This note is not part of the Order)

This Order amends the Child Abduction and Custody (Parties to Conventions) Order 1986. It adds Norway to the list of the Contracting States to the Convention on the Civil Aspects of International Child Abduction signed at The Hague on 25th October 1980 (Cm.33).

STATUTORY INSTRUMENTS

1989 No. 480

INTERNATIONAL IMMUNITIES AND PRIVILEGES

The CSCE Information Forum (Immunities and Privileges) Order 1989

Made - - - -	*15th March 1989*
Laid before Parliament	*23rd March 1989*
Coming into force	*13th April 1989*

At the Court at Buckingham Palace, the 15th day of March 1989

Present,

The Queen's Most Excellent Majesty in Council

Whereas the Conference on Security and Co-operation in Europe (CSCE) Information Forum is to be held in the United Kingdom from 18th April to 12th May 1989 and is to be attended by representatives of the United Kingdom and of the Governments of other sovereign Powers:

Now, therefore, Her Majesty, by virtue and in exercise of the powers conferred on Her by section 6 of the International Organisations Act 1968**(a)** (hereinafter referred to as the Act) or otherwise in Her Majesty vested, is pleased, by and with the advice of Her Privy Council, to order, and it is hereby ordered, as follows:

1. This Order may be cited as the CSCE Information Forum (Immunities and Privileges) Order 1989 and shall come into force on 13th April 1989.

2.—(1) For the purposes of this Order, there are hereby specified the representatives of the sovereign Powers at the CSCE Information Forum.

(2) Except in so far as in any particular case any privilege or immunity is waived by the Governments of the sovereign Powers whom they represent, the persons specified in the preceding paragraph shall enjoy:–

(a) immunity from suit and legal process in respect of things done or omitted to be done by them in their capacity as representatives;

(b) while exercising their functions and during their journeys to and from the place of meeting, the like inviolability of residence, the like immunity from personal arrest or detention and from seizure of their personal baggage, the like inviolability of all papers and documents, and the like exemption or relief from taxes (other than customs and excise duties or value added tax) as are accorded to the head of a diplomatic mission; and

(c) while exercising their functions and during their journeys to and from the place of meeting, the like exemptions and privileges in respect of their personal baggage as in accordance with Article 36 of the Vienna Convention on Diplomatic Relations, which is set out in Schedule 1 to the Diplomatic Privileges Act 1964**(b)**, are accorded to a diplomatic agent.

(a) 1968 c.48; section 6 was amended by the International Organisations Act 1981 (c.9), section 1(3).
(b) 1964 c.81.

(3) Section 6(3) of the Act and Part IV of Schedule 1 to the Act shall not operate so as to confer any privilege or immunity on the official staff of a representative other than delegates, deputy delegates, advisers, technical experts and secretaries of delegations.

(4) Neither this Article nor section 6(3) of the Act and Part IV of Schedule 1 to the Act shall operate so as to confer any privilege or immunity on any person as the representative of the United Kingdom or as a member of the official staff of such a representative or on any person who is a British citizen, a British Dependent Territories citizen, a British Overseas citizen or a British National (Overseas) or who is permanently resident in the United Kingdom.

G. I. de Deney
Clerk of the Privy Council

EXPLANATORY NOTE

(This note is not part of the Order)

This Order confers privileges and immunities upon the representatives of the sovereign Powers at the Conference on Security and Co-operation in Europe (CSCE) Information Forum, which is to be held in the United Kingdom from 18th April to 12th May 1989, and upon certain members of their official staffs.

STATUTORY INSTRUMENTS

1989 No. 481

FOREIGN COMPENSATION

The Foreign Compensation (Financial Provisions) Order 1989

Made - - - -	*15th March 1989*
Laid before Parliament	*17th March 1989*
Coming into force	*30th March 1989*

At the Court at Buckingham Palace, the 15th day of March 1989

Present,

The Queen's Most Excellent Majesty in Council

Her Majesty, by virtue and in exercise of the powers conferred upon Her in that behalf by section 7(2) of the Foreign Compensation Act 1950**(a)** or otherwise in Her Majesty vested, is pleased, by and with the advice of Her Privy Council, to order, and it is hereby ordered, as follows:

1. This Order may be cited as the Foreign Compensation (Financial Provisions) Order 1989 and shall come into force on 30th March 1989.

2. The Foreign Compensation Commission shall pay into the Consolidated Fund not later than 31st March 1989 out of the compensation funds named in Column 1 of the Schedule to this Order the amounts specified in Column 2 of the Schedule which are hereby determined to be the amounts of the expenses of the Commission during the periods specified in Column 3 of the Schedule attributable to the discharge by the Commission of their functions in relation to the distribution of sums from those compensation funds.

G. I. de Deney
Clerk of the Privy Council

(a) 1950 c.12; the application of section 7(2) was extended by section 3(3) of the Foreign Compensation Act 1962 (c.4).

SCHEDULE

Column 1 *Name of Fund*	*Column 2* *Amount*	*Column 3* *Period*
	£	
The Czechoslovakia Compensation Fund	297,042	1st October 1987 30th September 1988
The Union of Soviet Socialist Republics (Tsarist Assets) Fund	880,673	1st October 1987 30th September 1988
The People's Republic of China Fund	983,506	1st October 1987 30th September 1988

EXPLANATORY NOTE

(This note is not part of the Order)

This Order, which is made under section 7(2) of the Foreign Compensation Act 1950, directs the Foreign Compensation Commission to pay into the Consolidated Fund, out of the funds paid to the Commission for the purpose of being distributed under the said Act, an amount in respect of the Commission's expenses in relation to those funds during the periods specified in the Schedule to the Order.

STATUTORY INSTRUMENTS

1989 No. 482

TERRITORIAL SEA

The Territorial Sea (Limits) Order 1989

Made - - - - 15th March 1989

Coming into force 6th April 1989

At the Court at Buckingham Palace, the 15th day of March 1989

Present,

The Queen's Most Excellent Majesty in Council

Her Majesty, in exercise of the powers conferred upon Her by section 1(2) of the Territorial Sea Act 1987(**a**), is pleased, by and with the advice of Her Privy Council, to order, and it is hereby ordered as follows:

1. This Order may be cited as the Territorial Sea (Limits) Order 1989 and shall come into force on 6th April 1989.

2. The seaward limit of the territorial sea adjacent to the United Kingdom between Point 1 and Point 6 indicated in the Schedule to this Order shall consist of a series of straight lines joining, in the sequence given, Points 1 to 6 indicated in the Schedule to this Order.

3. The seaward limit of the territorial sea adjacent to the United Kingdom shall be the median line where the baselines from which the breadth of the territorial sea adjacent to the United Kingdom is measured are less than 24 nautical miles from the baselines from which the breadth of the territorial sea adjacent to the Isle of Man is measured.

4. In this Order–

(a) "straight line" means a loxodromic line;

(b) all positions given by means of co-ordinates are defined on European Datum (1st Adjustment 1950);

(c) "median line" is a line every point of which is equidistant from the nearest points of the baselines from which the breadth of the territorial sea adjacent to the United Kingdom and the Isle of Man respectively is measured.

5. The Territorial Sea (Limits) Order 1987(**b**) is hereby revoked.

G. I. de Deney
Clerk of the Privy Council

(**a**) 1987 c.49.
(**b**) S.I. 1987/1269.

SCHEDULE

LIST OF POINTS

Point	*Position of Point*	
1	50°49′30″95N	01°15′53″43E
2	50°53′47″00N	01°16′58″00E
3	50°57′00″00N	01°21′25″00E
4	51°02′19″00N	01°32′53″00E
5	51°05′58″00N	01°43′31″00E
6	51°12′00″72N	01°53′20″07E

EXPLANATORY NOTE

(This note is not part of the Order)

This Order provides for the seaward limit of the territorial sea adjacent to the United Kingdom in the Straits of Dover and in the vicinity of the Isle of Man. The limit in the Straits of Dover is constituted by straight lines joining the points indicated in the Schedule and follows the line defined in the Agreement of 2nd November 1988 between the Government of the United Kingdom and the Government of the French Republic (Cm. 557) relating to the Delimitation of the Territorial Sea in the Straits of Dover. The limit in the vicinity of the Isle of Man is the median line.

STATUTORY INSTRUMENTS

1989 No. 483

SOCIAL SECURITY

The Social Security (Isle of Man) Order 1989

Made - - - -	*15th March 1989*
Coming into force	*10th April 1989*

At the Court at Buckingham Palace, the 15th day of March 1989

Present,

The Queen's Most Excellent Majesty in Council

Her Majesty, in pursuance of sections 143 and 166(4) of the Social Security Act 1975(**a**), and of all other powers enabling Her in that behalf, is pleased, by and with the advice of Her Privy Council, to order, and it is hereby ordered, as follows:

Citation, commencement and interpretation

1.—(1) This Order may be cited as the Social Security (Isle of Man) Order 1989 and shall come into force on 10th April 1989.

(2) In this Order–

"the Principal Order" means the Social Security (Isle of Man) Order 1977(**b**);

"the Principal Agreement" means the Agreement set out in Schedule 1 to the Principal Order.

Modification of the Social Security Act 1975 and amendment of Principal Order

2. The Social Security Act 1975 shall be modified and the Principal Order shall be varied so as to give effect to the Principal Agreement as amended by the Agreement which is set out in the Schedule to this Order, so far as the same relate to England, Wales and Scotland.

G. I. de Deney
Clerk of the Privy Council

(**a**) 1975 c.14; subsection (1) of section 143 was amended by section 20(1) of the Social Security (Miscellaneous Provisions) Act 1977 (c.5) and section 65(2) of and Schedule 11 to the Social Security Act 1986 (c.50). Subsection (1A) of section 143 was inserted by section 6(1) of the Social Security Act 1981 (c.33).
(**b**) S.I. 1977/2150.

SCHEDULE

Article 2

AGREEMENT RELATING TO SOCIAL SECURITY BETWEEN THE SECRETARY OF STATE FOR SOCIAL SECURITY AND THE DEPARTMENT OF HEALTH AND SOCIAL SERVICES FOR NORTHERN IRELAND OF THE ONE PART AND THE LIEUTENANT-GOVERNOR OF THE ISLE OF MAN, WITH THE ADVICE AND CONSENT OF THE DEPARTMENT OF HEALTH AND SOCIAL SECURITY OF THE ISLE OF MAN OF THE OTHER PART

1. In this Agreement, "the Principal Agreement" means the Agreement relating to Social Security made in 1977 between the Secretary of State for Social Services and the Department of Health and Social Services for Northern Ireland of the one part and the Lieutenant-Governor of the Isle of Man, with the advice and consent of the Isle of Man Board of Social Security, of the other part.

2. Article 2 of the Principal Agreement shall be amended as follows–

(a) the words "Subject to paragraph (5) of this Article," shall be inserted at the beginning of paragraph (1) before the word "For" which shall itself be replaced by the word "for";

(b) a new paragraph shall be added after paragraph (4) which shall read as follows–

"(5) There shall be excluded from this Agreement all or any of the provisions of the systems of social security established by the Acts relating to mobility allowance except that for the purposes of such of those provisions requiring the completion of periods of presence in the territory of the Act which relates to it–

(i) in relation to a person present and ordinarily resident in the United Kingdom, periods of residence and presence completed in the Isle of Man by that person before he attains the age of 65 shall be treated as if they were periods of presence completed during the corresponding period in the United Kingdom;

(ii) in relation to a person present and ordinarily resident in the Isle of Man, periods of residence and presence completed in the United Kingdom by that person before he attains the age of 65 shall be treated as if they were periods of presence completed during the corresponding period in the Isle of Man.".

Given under the Official Seal of the Secretary of State for Social Security this 2nd day of March 1989.

John Moore
Secretary of State for Social Security

Given under the Official Seal of the Department of Health and Social Services for Northern Ireland this 6th day of March 1989.

F. A. Elliott
Permanent Secretary

Given under the hand of the Lieutenant-Governor of the Isle of Man this 3rd day of March 1989.

Laurence New
Lieutenant-Governor

The consent of the Department of Health and Social Security is hereby given to the Agreement.

J. A. Brown
Minister for Health and Social Security

EXPLANATORY NOTE

(This note is not part of the Order)

This Order gives effect to an Agreement made between the Secretary of State for Social Security and the Department of Health and Social Services for Northern Ireland of the one part and the Lieutenant-Governor of the Isle of Man on the other which has the effect of excluding all provisions relating to mobility allowance from the scope of an earlier reciprocal agreement relating to social security entered into by them and their predecessors except for a provision modifying the Social Security Act 1975 so as to permit periods of presence in the Isle of Man to be treated as if they were periods of presence in the United Kingdom for the purposes of entitlement to that allowance.

STATUTORY INSTRUMENTS

1989 No. 485

CRIMINAL LAW, ENGLAND AND WALES

The Drug Trafficking Offences Act 1986 (United States of America) Order 1989

Made - - - -	*15th March 1989*
Coming into force	*29th March 1989*

At the Court at Buckingham Palace, the 15th day of March 1989

Present,

The Queen's Most Excellent Majesty in Council

Whereas a draft of this Order has been approved by a resolution of each House of Parliament:

Now, therefore, Her Majesty, in exercise of the powers conferred upon Her by section 26 of the Drug Trafficking Offences Act 1986(**a**), is pleased, by and with the advice of Her Privy Council, to order, and it is hereby ordered, as follows:

Title and commencement

1. This Order may be cited as the Drug Trafficking Offences Act 1986 (United States of America) Order 1989 and shall come into force on the fourteenth day following the date of making of this Order.

Interpretation

2. In this Order–

"the Act" means the Drug Trafficking Offences Act 1986;

"a court of the United States of America" means a court of the United States of America or of any of its states or territories.

Designation of and application of the Act to the United States of America

3.—(1) The United States of America is hereby designated for the purposes of sections 26 and 26A of the Act.

(2) The Act shall apply, subject to the modifications set out in Schedule 1 to this Order, in relation to an external confiscation order made by a court of the United States of America and to proceedings which have been or are to be instituted in the United States of America and which may result in an external confiscation order being made there, and, accordingly, in relation to such orders and such proceedings, the Act shall have effect as set out in Schedule 2 to this Order.

Orders made in the United States of America

4. For the purposes of section 26 of the Act, and of the Act as applied under article 3 above, in any proceedings in the High Court a certificate issued by or on behalf of the Attorney General of the United States of America stating either–

(**a**) 1986 c. 32, amended by the Criminal Justice (Scotland) Act 1987 (c. 41), section 70 and Schedule 2 and the Criminal Justice Act 1988 (c. 33), section 103 and Schedule 5.

(a) that an order (however described) made by a court of the United States of America has the purpose of recovering payments or other rewards received in connection with drug trafficking or their value, or

(b) that proceedings have been instituted against a person in the United States of America and have not been concluded there,

shall be admissible as evidence of the facts so stated.

Satisfaction of confiscation order in the United States of America

5.—(1) Where–

(a) a confiscation order has been made under section 1 of the Act; and

(b) a request has been made by the Secretary of State for the assistance of the government of the United States of America in enforcing that order; and

(c) in consequence of that request property is recovered in the United States of America which represents, directly or indirectly, proceeds of drug trafficking which were taken into account under section 2 of the Act by the court which made the confiscation order,

the amount payable under the confiscation order shall be treated as reduced by the value of property so recovered.

(2) For the purposes of paragraph (1) above a certificate issued by or on behalf of the Attorney General of the United States of America stating that property has been recovered there in consequence of a request by the Secretary of State and stating the value of the property so recovered shall be admissible as evidence of the facts so stated.

G.I. de Deney
Clerk of the Privy Council

Article 3(2)

SCHEDULE 1

MODIFICATIONS OF THE DRUG TRAFFICKING OFFENCES ACT 1986

1. For section 1 there shall be substituted the following section:

"**Confiscation orders**

1.—(1) An order made by a court of the United States of America for the purpose of recovering payments or other rewards received in connection with drug trafficking or their value is referred to in this Act as a "confiscation order", and for the purposes of its registration under section 26A of this Act, "external confiscation order" means any such order.

(2) In subsection (1) above the reference to an order includes any order, decree, direction or judgment, however described.

(3) A person against whom a confiscation order has been made or a person against whom proceedings which may result in a confiscation order being made have been, or are to be, instituted in a court of the United States of America, is referred to in this Act as "the defendant".".

2. Sections 2 to 4 shall be omitted.

3. In section 5–

(a) for subsection (1) there shall be substituted the following subsection:

"(1) In this Act "realisable property" means, subject to subsection (2) below–

(a) in relation to a confiscation order made in respect of specified property, the property which is specified in the order; and

(b) in any other case, any property held by the defendant."

(b) subsections (3) to (10) shall be omitted.

4. Section 6 shall be omitted.

5. In section 7–

(a) for subsection (1)(a) there shall be substituted:

"(a) proceedings have been instituted against the defendant in the United States of America,";

(b) for subsection (1)(c) there shall be substituted:

"(c) either a confiscation order has been made in the proceedings or it appears to the High Court that there are reasonable grounds for thinking that a confiscation order may be made in them";

(c) for subsection (2) there shall be substituted the following subsection:

"(2) Those powers are also exercisable where the High Court is satisfied that proceedings are to be instituted against a person in the United States of America and it appears to the court that a confiscation order may be made in them.";

(d) subsection (3) shall be omitted; and

(e) for subsection (4) there shall be substituted the following subsection:

"(4) Where the High Court has made an order under section 8(1) of 9(1) of this Act by virtue of subsection (2) above, it shall discharge the order if the proposed proceedings are not instituted within twenty-eight days.".

6. In section 8–

(a) for subsection (2)(a) and (b) there shall be substituted:

"(a) where an application under subsection (4) below relates to a confiscation order made in respect of specified property, to the property which is specified in that order; and

(b) in any other case–

(i) to all realisable property, whether the property is described in the restraint order or not, and

(ii) to realisable property, being property transferred to the defendant after the making of the restraint order.";

(b) in subsection (4) for the words "the prosecutor" there shall be substituted the words "or on behalf of the government of the United States of America";

(c) for subsection (5)(b) there shall be substituted:

"(b) shall be discharged when the proceedings in relation to which the order was made are concluded.";

(d) in subsection (7)(b) and in subsection (8) for the words "Great Britain" there shall be substituted the words "England and Wales";

(e) in subsection (11), for the words "the prosecutor" there shall be substituted the words "A person applying for a restraint order on behalf of the government of the United States of America".

7. In section 9–

(a) for subsection (1)(a) and (b) there shall be substituted the following:

"(a) where a fixed amount is payable under a confiscation order, of an amount not exceeding the amount so payable, and

(b) in any other case, of an amount equal to the value from time to time of the property charged.";

(b) in subsection (3) for the words "the prosecutor" there shall be substituted the words "or on behalf of the government of the United States of America";

(c) in subsection (4)(a) the words "or by a person to whom the defendant has directly or indirectly made a gift caught by this Act" shall be omitted;

(d) in subsection (7) for the words "for the offence" there shall be substituted the words "against the defendant in the United States of America".

8. In section 10, subsection (6) shall be omitted.

9. After section 10 there shall be inserted the following section:

"10A. Notwithstanding anything in rule 3(2) of Order 115 of the Rules of the Supreme Court 1965(**a**), an application under section 8(4) or 9(3) of this Act shall be supported by an affidavit which shall–

(**a**) S.I. 1965/1776. Order 115 was inserted by R.S.C. (Amendment No. 3) 1986 (S.I. 1986/2289).

(a) state, where applicable, the grounds for believing that a confiscation order may be made in the proceedings instituted or to be instituted in the United States of America;

(b) to the best of the deponent's ability, give particulars of the realisable property in respect of which the order is sought and specify the person or persons holding such property;

(c) where proceedings have not been instituted in the United States of America, indicate when it is intended that they should be instituted there,

and the affidavit may, unless the court otherwise directs, contain statements of information or belief with the sources and grounds thereof.".

10. In section 11–

(a) for subsection (1) of section 11 there shall be substituted the following subsection:

"(1) Where a confiscation order has been registered in the High Court under section 26A of this Act, the High Court may, on an application by or on behalf of the government of the United States of America, exercise the powers conferred by subsections (2) to (6) below."; and

(b) in subsection (6) the words "or, as the case may be, the recipient of a gift caught by this Act" shall be omitted.

11. The following section shall be substituted for section 12:

"Application of proceeds of realisation and other sums.

12.—(1) Subject to subsection (2) below, the following sums in the hands of a receiver appointed under section 8 or 11 of this Act or in pursuance of a charging order, that is–

(a) the proceeds of the enforcement of any charge imposed under section 9 of this Act,

(b) the proceeds of the realisation, other than by the enforcement of such a charge, of any property under section 8 or 11 of this Act, and

(c) any other sums, being property held by the defendant,

shall first be applied in payment of such expenses incurred by a person acting as an insolvency practitioner as are payable under section 17A(2) of this Act and then shall, after such payments (if any) as the High Court may direct have been made out of those sums, be paid to the High Court and applied for the purposes specified in subsections (3) to (5) below and in the order so specified.

(2) Where a fixed amount is payable under the confiscation order and, after that amount has been fully paid, any such sums remain in the hands of such a receiver, the receiver shall distribute those sums–

(a) among such of those who held property which has been realised under this Act, and

(b) in such proportions,

as the High Court may direct after giving a reasonable opportunity for such persons to make representations to the court.

(3) Any sums paid to the High Court under subsection (1) above shall first be applied to pay the receiver's remuneration and expenses.

(4) Next, any amount paid under section 18(2) of this Act shall be reimbursed.

(5) Any sums remaining after all the payments required to be made under the foregoing provisions of this section have been made shall be paid to the Secretary of State and any sums so received by the Secretary of State shall be paid into the Consolidated Fund.".

12. In section 13–

(a) in subsection (2), for the words from "making available" to the end of the subsection there shall be substituted the words "recovering property which is liable to be recovered under a confiscation order registered in the High Court under section 26A of this Act or, as the case may be, with a view to making available for recovery property which may become liable to be recovered under any confiscation order which may be made in the defendant's case.";

(b) subsection (3) shall be omitted;

(c) in subsection (4), the words "or the recipient of any such gift" shall be omitted; and

(d) in subsection (6), the words "or of the recipient of any such gift" shall be omitted.

13. Section 14 shall be omitted.

14. In section 15–

(a) subsection (6) shall be omitted; and

(b) in subsection (7), for the words "the date on which the Insolvency Act 1986 comes into force" there shall be substituted the words "29th December 1986 (the date on which the Insolvency Act 1986 came into force)".

15. In section 16, subsection (6) shall be omitted.

16. In subsection (6) of section 17, for the words "the date on which the Insolvency Act 1986 comes into force" there shall be substituted the words "29th December 1986 (the date on which the Insolvency Act 1986 came into force)".

17. In subsection (2) of section 17A, the words "or (3)(za)" shall be omitted.

18. In subsection (2) of section 18, the letter "B" and the words "by the prosecutor or, in a case where proceedings for a drug trafficking offence are not instituted," shall be omitted.

19. Section 19 and sections 24 to 26 shall be omitted.

20. Sections 27 to 32 shall be omitted.

21. In section 33–

(a) in subsection (1), the words "(2) or", and

(b) subsections (2) and (3)

shall be omitted.

22. Sections 34 to 37 shall be omitted.

23. In section 38–

(a) in subsection (1)–

(i) the definitions of "authorised government department", "drug trafficking offence" and "interest" shall be omitted;

(ii) before the definition of "constable" there shall be inserted the following words:

""a court of the United States of America" means a court of the United States of America or of any of its states or territories;"; and

(iii) after the definition of "drug trafficking" there shall be inserted the following words:

""proceeds of drug trafficking" includes any payments or other rewards received by a person at any time (whether before or after the commencement of the Drug Trafficking Offences Act 1986 (United States of America) Order 1989) in connection with drug trafficking carried on by him or another;";

(b) in subsection (2) for the list of expressions and relevant provisions there shall be substituted the following list:

"Expression	Relevant provision
Charging order	Section 9(2)
Confiscation order	Section 1
Dealing with property	Section 8(7)
Defendant	Section 1
Realisable property	Section 5(1)
Restraint order	Section 8(1)";

(c) subsections (4) and (10) shall be omitted;

(d) in subsection (11), for the words from "are instituted" to the end of the subsection, there shall be substituted the words "the United States when an indictment, information or complaint has been filed against a person in respect of an offence."; and

(e) in subsection (12)(b), for the words from "payment" to the end of the subsection there shall be substituted the words "the recovery of all property liable to be recovered, or the payment of any amount due, or otherwise).".

24. In section 39, subsections (2) and (4) shall be omitted.

25. Section 40 shall be omitted.

SCHEDULE 2

Article 3(2)

THE DRUG TRAFFICKING OFFENCES ACT 1986 AS MODIFIED

Confiscation orders

1.—(1) An order made by a court of the United States of America for the purpose of recovering payments or other rewards received in connection with drug trafficking or their value is referred to in this Act as a "confiscation order", and for the purposes of its registration under section 26A of this Act "external confiscation order" means any such order.

(2) In subsection (1) above the reference to an order includes any order, decree, direction or judgment, however described.

(3) A person against whom a confiscation order has been made or a person against whom proceedings which may result in a confiscation order being made have been, or are to be, instituted in a court of the United States of America, is referred to in this Act as "the defendant".

. . . .

Realisable property

5.—(1) In this Act "realisable property" means, subject to subsection (2) below–

(a) in relation to a confiscation order made in respect of specified property, the property which is specified in the order; and

(b) in any other case, any property held by the defendant.

(2) Property is not realisable property if–

(a) an order under section 43 of the Powers of Criminal Courts Act 1973(**a**) (deprivation orders),

(b) an order under section 27 of the Misuse of Drugs Act 1971(**b**) (forfeiture orders), or

(c) an order under section 223 or 436 of the Criminal Procedure (Scotland) Act 1975(**c**) (forfeiture of property),

is in force in respect of the property.

. . . .

Cases in which restraint orders and charging orders may be made

7.—(1) The powers conferred on the High Court by sections 8(1) and 9(1) of this Act are exercisable where–

(a) proceedings have been instituted against the defendant in the United States of America,

(b) the proceedings have not been concluded, and

(c) either a confiscation order has been made in the proceedings or it appears to the High Court that there are reasonable grounds for believing that a confiscation order may be made in them.

(2) Those powers are also exercisable where the High Court is satisfied that proceedings are to be instituted against a person in the United States of America and it appears to the court that a confiscation order may be made in them.

. . . .

(4) Where the High Court has made an order under section 8(1) or 9(1) of this Act by virtue of subsection (2) above, it shall discharge the order if the proposed proceedings are not instituted within twenty-eight days.

Restraint orders

8.—(1) The High Court may by order (in this Act referred to as a "restraint order") prohibit any person from dealing with any realisable property, subject to such conditions and exceptions as may be specified in the order.

(2) A restraint order may apply–

(a) where an application under subsection (4) below relates to a confiscation order made in respect of specified property, to the property which is specified in that order; and

(b) in any other case–

(i) to all realisable property, whether the property is described in the restraint order or not, and

(ii) to realisable property, being property transferred to the defendant after the making of the restraint order.

(3) This section shall not have effect in relation to any property for the time being subject to a charge under section 9 of this Act.

(4) A restraint order–

(a) may be made only on an application by or on behalf of the government of the United States of America,

---

(**a**) 1973 c. 62.
(**b**) 1971 c. 38.
(**c**) 1975 c. 21.

(b) may be made on an ex parte application to a judge in chambers, and

(c) shall provide for notice to be given to persons affected by the order.

(5) A restraint order–

(a) may be discharged or varied in relation to any property, and

(b) shall be discharged when the proceedings in relation to which the order was made are concluded.

(5A) An application for the discharge or variation of a restraint order may be made by any person affected by it.

(6) Where the High Court has made a restraint order, the court may at any time appoint a receiver–

(a) to take possession of any realisable property, and

(b) in accordance with the court's directions, to manage or otherwise deal with any property in respect of which he is appointed,

subject to such exceptions and conditions as may be specified by the court; and may require any person having possession of property in respect of which a receiver is appointed under this section to give possession of it to the receiver.

(7) For the purposes of this section, dealing with property held by any person includes (without prejudice to the generality of the expression)–

(a) where a debt is owed to that person, making a payment to any person in reduction of the amount of the debt, and

(b) removing the property from England and Wales.

(8) Where the High Court has made a restraint order, a constable may for the purpose of preventing any realisable property being removed from England and Wales, seize the property.

(9) Property seized under subsection (8) above shall be dealt with in accordance with the court's directions.

(10) The Land Charges Act 1972(**a**) and the Land Registration Act 1925(**b**) shall apply–

(a) in relation to restraint orders, as they apply in relation to orders affecting land made by the court for the purposes of enforcing judgments or recognisances; and

(b) in relation to applications for restraint orders, as they apply in relation to other pending land actions.

(11) A person applying for a restraint order on behalf of the government of the United States of America shall be treated for the purposes of section 57 of the Land Registration Act 1925 (inhibitions) as a person interested in relation to any registered land to which a restraint order or an application for such an order relates.

Charging orders in respect of land, securities etc.

9.—(1) The High Court may make a charging order on realisable property for securing the payment to the Crown–

(a) where a fixed amount is payable under a confiscation order, of an amount not exceeding the amount so payable, and

(b) in any other case, of an amount equal to the value from time to time of the property charged.

(2) For the purposes of this Act, a charging order is an order made under this section imposing on any such realisable property as may be specified in the order a charge for securing the payment of money to the Crown.

(3) A charging order–

(a) may be made only on an application by or on behalf of the government of the United States of America;

(b) may be made on an ex parte application to a judge in chambers;

(c) shall provide for notice to be given to persons affected by the order; and

(d) may be made subject to such conditions as the court thinks fit and, without prejudice to the generality of this paragraph, such conditions as it thinks fit as to the time when the charge is to become effective.

(4) Subject to subsection (6) below, a charge may be imposed by a charging order only on–

(a) any interest in realisable property, being an interest held beneficially by the defendant–

(i) in any asset of a kind mentioned in subsection (5) below, or

(ii) under any trust, or

(**a**) 1972 c. 61.
(**b**) 1925 c. 21.

(b) any interest in realisable property held by a person as trustee of a trust if the interest is in such an asset or is an interest under another trust and a charge may by virtue of paragraph (a) above be imposed by a charging order on the whole beneficial interest under the first-mentioned trust.

(5) The assets referred to in subsection (4) above are–

(a) land in England and Wales, or

(b) securities of any of the following kinds–

(i) government stock,

(ii) stock of any body (other than a building society) incorporated within England and Wales,

(iii) stock of any body incorporated outside England and Wales or of any country or territory outside the United Kingdom, being stock registered in a register kept at any place within England and Wales,

(iv) units of any unit trust in respect of which a register of the unit holders is kept at any place within England and Wales.

(6) In any case where a charge is imposed by a charging order on any interest in an asset of a kind mentioned in subsection (5)(b) above, the court may provide for the charge to extend to any interest or dividend payable in respect of the asset.

(7) The court may make an order discharging or varying the charging order and shall make an order discharging the charging order if the proceedings against the defendant in the United States of America are concluded or the amount payment of which is secured by the charge is paid into the High Court.

(8) An application for the discharge or variation of a charging order may be made by any person affected by it.

Charging orders—supplementary provisions

10.—(2) The Land Charges Act 1972 and the Land Registration Act 1925 shall apply in relation to charging orders as they apply in relation to orders or writs issued or made for the purpose of enforcing judgments.

(3) Where a charging order has been registered under section 6 of the Land Charges Act 1972, subsection (4) of that section (effect of non-registration of writs and orders registrable under that section) shall not apply to an order appointing a receiver made in pursuance of the charging order.

(4) Subject to any provisions made under section 11 of this Act or by rules of court, a charge imposed by a charging order shall have the like effect and shall be enforceable in the same courts and in the same manner as an equitable charge by the person holding the beneficial interest or, as the case may be, the trustees by writing under their hand.

(5) Where a charging order has been protected by an entry registered under the Land Charges Act 1972 or the Land Registration Act 1925, an order under section 9(7) of this Act discharging the charging order may direct that the entry be cancelled.

. . . .

(7) In this section and section 9 of this Act, "building society", "dividend", "government stock", "stock" and "unit trust" have the same meanings as in the Charging Orders Act 1979(**a**).

10A. Notwithstanding anything in rule 3(2) of Order 115 of the Rules of the Supreme Court 1965(**b**), an application under section 8(4) or 9(3) of this Act shall be supported by an affidavit which shall–

(a) state, where applicable, the grounds for believing that a confiscation order may be made in the proceedings instituted or to be instituted in the United States of America,

(b) to the best of the deponent's ability, give particulars of the realisable property in respect of which the order is sought and specify the person or persons holding such property,

(c) where proceedings have not been instituted in the United States of America, indicate when it is intended that they should be instituted there,

and the affidavit may, unless the court otherwise directs, contain statements of information or belief with the sources and grounds thereof.

Realisation of property

11.—(1) Where a confiscation order has been registered in the High Court under section 26A of this Act, the High Court may, on an application by or on behalf of the government of the United States of America, exercise the powers conferred by subsections (2) to (6) below.

(2) The court may appoint a receiver in respect of realisable property.

(**a**) 1979 c. 53.

(**b**) S.I. 1965/1776. Order 115 was inserted by R.S.C. (Amendment No. 3) 1986 (S.I. 1986/2289).

(3) The court may empower a receiver appointed under subsection (2) above, under section 8 of this Act or in pursuance of a charging order–

(a) to enforce any charge imposed under section 9 of this Act on realisable property or on interest or dividends payable in respect of such property, and

(b) in relation to any realisable property other than property for the time being subject to a charge under section 9 of this Act, to take possession of the property subject to such conditions or exceptions as may be specified by the court.

(4) The court may order any person having possession of realisable property to give possession of it to any such receiver.

(5) The court may empower any such receiver to realise any realisable property in such manner as the court may direct.

(6) The court may order any person holding an interest in realisable property to make such payment to the receiver in respect of any beneficial interest held by the defendant as the court may direct and the court may, on the payment being made, by order transfer, grant or extinguish any interest in the property.

(7) Subsections (4) to (6) above do not apply to property for the time being subject to a charge under section 9 of this Act.

(8) The court shall not in respect of any property exercise the powers conferred by subsections (3)(a), (5) or (6) above unless a reasonable opportunity has been given for persons holding any interest in the property to make representations to the court.

Application of proceeds of realisation and other sums

12.—(1) Subject to subsection (2) below, the following sums in the hands of a receiver appointed under section 8 or 11 of this Act or in pursuance of a charging order, that is–

(a) the proceeds of the enforcement of any charge imposed under section 9 of this Act,

(b) the proceeds of the realisation, other than by the enforcement of such a charge, of any property under section 8 or 11 of this Act, and

(c) any other sums, being property held by the defendant,

shall first be applied in payment of such expenses incurred by a person acting as an insolvency practitioner as are payable under section 17A(2) of this Act and then shall, after such payments (if any) as the High Court may direct have been made out of those sums, be paid to the High Court and applied for the purposes specified in subsections (3) to (5) below and in the order so specified.

(2) Where a fixed amount is payable under the confiscation order and, after that amount has been fully paid, any such sums remain in the hands of such a receiver, the receiver shall distribute those sums–

(a) among such of those who held property which has been realised under this Act, and

(b) in such proportions,

as the High Court may direct after giving a reasonable opportunity for such persons to make representations to the court.

(3) Any sums paid to the High Court under subsection (1) above shall first be applied to pay the receiver's remuneration and expenses.

(4) Next, any amount paid under section 18(2) of this Act shall be reimbursed.

(5) Any sums remaining after all the payments required to be made under the foregoing provisions of this section have been made shall be paid to the Secretary of State and any sums so received by the Secretary of State shall be paid into the Consolidated Fund.

Exercise of powers by High Court or receiver

13.—(1) The following provisions apply to the powers conferred on the High Court by sections 8 to 12 of this Act, or on a receiver appointed under section 8 to 11 of this Act or in pursuance of a charging order.

(2) Subject to the following provisions of this section, the powers shall be exercised with a view to recovering property which is liable to be recovered under a confiscation order registered in the High Court under section 26A of this Act or, as the case may be, with a view to making available for recovery property which may become liable to be recovered under any confiscation order which may be made in the defendant's case.

. . . .

(4) The powers shall be exercised with a view to allowing any person other than the defendant to retain or recover the value of any property held by him.

(5) An order may be made or other action taken in respect of a debt owed by the Crown.

(6) In exercising those powers, no account shall be taken of any obligations of the defendant which conflict with the obligation to satisfy the confiscation order.

. . . .

Bankruptcy of defendant etc.

15.—(1) Where a person who holds realisable property is adjudged bankrupt–

(a) property for the time being subject to a restraint order made before the order adjudging him bankrupt, and

(b) any proceeds of property realised by virtue of section 8(6) or 11(5) or (6) of this Act for the time being in the hands of a receiver appointed under section 8 or 11 of this Act,

is excluded from the bankrupt's estate for the purposes of Part IX of the Insolvency Act 1986(**a**).

(2) Where a person has been adjudged bankrupt, the powers conferred on the High Court by sections 8 to 12 of this Act or on a receiver so appointed shall not be exercised in relation to–

(a) property for the time being comprised in the bankrupt's estate for the purposes of that Part,

(b) property in respect of which his trustee in bankruptcy may (without leave of court) serve a notice under section 307 or 308 of that Act (after-acquired property and tools, clothes etc exceeding value of reasonable repiacement), and

(c) property which is to be applied for the benefit of creditors of the bankrupt by virtue of a condition imposed under section 280(2)(c) of that Act.

(3) Nothing in that Act shall be taken as restricting, or enabling the restriction of, the exercise of those powers.

(4) Subsection (2) above does not affect the enforcement of a charging order–

(a) made before the order adjudging the person bankrupt, or

(b) on property which was subject to a restraint order when the order adjudging him bankrupt was made.

(5) Where, in the case of a debtor, an interim receiver stands appointed under section 286 of that Act and any property of the debtor is subject to a restraint order–

(a) the powers conferred on the receiver by virtue of that Act do not apply to property for the time being subject to the restraint order.

. . . .

(7) In any case in which a petition in bankruptcy is presented, or a receiving order or adjudication in bankruptcy is made, before 29th December 1986 (the date on which the Insolvency Act 1986 came into force) this section has effect with the following modifications–

(a) for references to the bankrupt's estate for the purposes of Part IX of that Act there are substituted references to the property of the bankrupt for the purposes of the Bankruptcy Act 1914,

(b) for references to the Act of 1986 and sections 280(2)(c), 286, 339 and 423 of that Act there are respectively substituted references to the Act of 1914 and to sections 26(2), 8, 27 and 42 of that Act,

(c) the references in subsection (5) to an interim receiver appointed as there mentioned include, where a receiving order has been made, a reference to the receiver constituted by virtue of section 7 of the Act of 1914, and

(d) subsection (2)(b) is omitted.

Sequestration in Scotland of defendant, etc.

16.—(1) Where the estate of a person who holds realisable property is sequestrated–

(a) property for the time being subject to a restraint order made before the award of sequestration, and

(b) any proceeds of property which was held by him and realised by virtue of section 8(6) or 11(5) or (6) of this Act for the time being in the hands of a receiver appointed under section 8 or 11 of this Act,

is excluded from the debtor's estate for the purposes of the Bankruptcy (Scotland) Act 1985.

(2) Where an award of sequestration has been made, the powers conferred on the High Court by sections 8 to 12 of this Act or on a receiver so appointed shall not be exercised in relation to–

(a) property comprised in the whole estate of the debtor within the meaning of section 31(8) of that Act,

---

(**a**) 1986 c. 45

(b) any income of the debtor which has been ordered, under subsection (2) of section 32 of that Act, to be paid to the permanent trustee or any estate which, under subsection (6) of that section, vests in the permanent trustee,

and it shall not be competent to submit a claim in relation to the confiscation order to the permanent trustee in accordance with section 48 of that Act.

(3) Nothing in that Act shall be taken as restricting, or enabling the restriction of, the exercise of those powers.

(4) Subsection (2) above does not affect the enforcement of a charging order–

(a) made before the award of sequestration, or

(b) on property which was subject to a restraint order when the award of sequestration was made.

(5) Where, during the period before sequestration is awarded, an interim trustee stands appointed under the proviso to section 13(1) of that Act and any property in the debtor's estate is subject to a restraint order, the powers conferred on the trustee by virtue of that Act do not apply to property for the time being subject to the restraint order.

. . . .

(7) In any case in which, notwithstanding the coming into force of the Bankruptcy (Scotland) Act 1985 the Bankruptcy (Scotland) Act 1913 applies to a sequestration, subsection (2) above shall have effect as if for paragraphs (a) and (b) thereof there were substituted the following paragraphs–

"(a) property comprised in the whole property of the debtor which vests in the trustee under section 97 of the Bankruptcy (Scotland) Act 1913,

(b) any income of the bankrupt which has been ordered under subsection (2) of section 98 of that Act, to be paid to the trustee or any estate which, under subsection (1) of that section, vests in the trustee";

and subsection (3) above shall have effect as if for the reference therein to the Act of 1985 there was substituted a reference to the Act of 1913.

Winding up of company holding realisable property

17.—(1) Where realisable property is held by a company and an order for the winding up of the company has been made or a resolution has been passed by the company for the voluntary winding up, the functions of the liquidator (or any provisional liquidator) shall not be exercisable in relation to–

(a) property for the time being subject to a restraint order made before the relevant time, and

(b) any proceeds of property realised by virtue of section 8(6) or 11(5) or (6) of this Act for the time being in the hands of a receiver appointed under section 8 or 11 of this Act.

(2) Where, in the case of a company, such an order has been made or such a resolution has been passed, the powers conferred on the High Court by sections 8 to 12 of this Act or on a receiver so appointed shall not be exercised in relation to any realisable property held by the company in relation to which the functions of the liquidator are exercisable–

(a) so as to inhibit him from exercising those functions for the purpose of distributing any property held by the company to the company's creditors, or

(b) so as to prevent the payment out of any property of expenses (including the remuneration of the liquidator or any provisional liquidator) properly incurred in the winding up in respect of the property.

(3) Nothing in the Insolvency Act 1986 shall be taken as restricting, or enabling the restriction of, the exercise of those powers.

(4) Subsection (2) above does not affect the enforcement of a charging order made before the relevant time or on property which was subject to a restraint order at the relevant time.

(5) In this section–

"company" means any company which may be wound up under the Insolvency Act 1986; and

"the relevant time" means–

(a) where no order for the winding up of the company has been made, the time of the passing of the resolution for voluntary winding up,

(b) where such an order has been made and, before the presentation of the petition for the winding up of the company by the court, such a resolution has been passed by the company, the time of the passing of the resolution, and

(c) in any other case where such an order has been made, the time of the making of the order.

(6) In any case in which a winding up of a company has commenced, or is treated as having commenced, before 29th December 1986 (the date on which the Insolvency Act came into force) this section has effect with the substitution for references to that Act of references to the Companies Act 1985.

Insolvency officers dealing with property subject to restraint order

17A.—(1) Without prejudice to the generality of any enactment contained in the Insolvency Act 1986 or in any other Act, where–

(a) any person acting as an insolvency practitioner seizes or disposes of any property in relation to which his functions are not exercisable because it is for the time being subject to a restraint order; and

(b) at the time of the seizure or disposal he believes, and has reasonable grounds for believing, that he is entitled (whether in pursuance of an order of the court or otherwise) to seize or dispose of that property,

he shall not be liable to any person in respect of any loss or damage resulting from the seizure or disposal except in so far as the loss or damage is caused by his negligence in so acting; and a person so acting shall have a lien on the property, or the proceeds of its sale, for such of his expenses as were incurred in connection with the liquidation, bankruptcy or other proceedings in relation to which the seizure or disposal purported to take place and for so much of his remuneration as may reasonably be assigned for his acting in connection with those proceedings.

(2) Any person who, acting as an insolvency practitioner, incurs expenses–

(a) in respect of such property as is mentioned in paragraph (a) of subsection (1) above and in so doing does not know and has no reasonable grounds to believe that the property is for the time being subject to a restraint order; or

(b) other than in respect of such property as is so mentioned, being expenses which, but for the effect of a restraint order, might have been met by taking possession of and realising the property,

shall be entitled (whether or not he has seized or disposed of that property so as to have a lien under that subsection) to payment of those expenses under section 12(1) of this Act.

(3) In this Act, the expression "acting as an insolvency practitioner" shall be construed in accordance with section 388 (interpretation) of the said Act of 1986 except that for the purposes of such construction the reference in subsection (2)(a) of that section to a permanent or interim trustee in sequestration shall be taken to include a reference to a trustee in sequestration and subsection (5) of that section (which provides that nothing in the section is to apply to anything done by the official receiver) shall be disregarded; and the expression shall also comprehend the official receiver acting as receiver or manager of the property.

Receivers: supplementary provisions

18.—(1) Where a receiver appointed under section 8 or 11 of this Act or in pursuance of a charging order takes any action–

(a) in relation to property which is not realisable property, being action which he would not be entitled to take if it were such property,

(b) believing, and having reasonable grounds for believing, that he is entitled to take that action in relation to that property,

he shall not be liable to any person in respect of any loss or damage resulting from his action except in so far as the loss or damage is caused by his negligence.

(2) Any amount due in respect of the remuneration and expenses of a receiver so appointed shall, if no sum is available to be applied in payment of it under section 12(3) of this Act, be paid by the person on whose application the receiver was appointed.

. . . .

Registration of confiscation order

26A.—(1) On an application made by or on behalf of the Government of a designated country, the High Court may register an external confiscation order made there if–

(a) it is satisfied that at the time of registration the order is in force and not subject to appeal;

(b) it is satisfied, where the person against whom the order is made did not appear in the proceedings, that he received notice of the proceedings in sufficient time to enable him to defend them; and

(c) it is of the opinion that enforcing the order in England and Wales would not be contrary to the interests of justice.

(2) In subsection (1) above "appeal" includes–

(a) any proceedings by way of discharging or setting aside a judgment; and

(b) an application for a new trial or a stay of execution.

(3) The High Court shall cancel the registration of an external confiscation order if it appears to the court that the order has been satisfied by payment of the amount due under it or by the person against whom it was made serving imprisonment in default of payment or by any other means.

Miscellaneous and Supplemental

33.—(1) The Chief Land Registrar (in this section referred to as "the registrar") shall, on an application under subsection (4) below made in relation to a person specified in the application or to property so specified, provide the applicant with any information kept by the registrar under the Land Registration Act 1925 which relates to the person or property so specified.

. . . .

(4) An application may be made by a receiver appointed under section 8 or 11 of this Act and on an application under this subsection there shall be given to the registrar–

(a) a document certified by the proper officer of the court to be a true copy of the order appointing the receiver, and

(b) a certificate that there are reasonable grounds for suspecting that there is information kept by the registrar which is likely to facilitate the exercise of the powers conferred on the receiver in respect of the person or property specified in the application.

(5) The reference in subsection (1) above to the provision of information is a reference to its provision in documentary form.

General interpretation

38.—(1) In this Act–

"a court of the United States of America" means a court of the United States of America or of any of its states or territories;

"constable" includes a person commissioned by the Commissioners of Customs and Excise;

"corresponding law" has the same meaning as in the Misuse of Drugs Act 1971;

"drug trafficking" means doing or being concerned in any of the following, whether in England and Wales or elsewhere–

(a) producing or supplying a controlled drug where the production or supply contravenes section 4(1) of the Misuse of Drugs Act 1971 or a corresponding law;

(b) transporting or storing a controlled drug where possession of the drug contravenes section 5(1) of that Act or a corresponding law;

(c) importing or exporting a controlled drug where the importation or exportation is prohibited by section 3(1) of that Act or a corresponding law;

and includes a person doing the following, whether in England and Wales or elsewhere, that is entering into or being otherwise concerned in an arrangement whereby–

(i) the retention or control by or on behalf of another person of the other person's proceeds of drug trafficking is facilitated, or

(ii) the proceeds of drug trafficking by another person are used to secure that funds are placed at the other person's disposal or are used for the other person's benefit to acquire property by way of investment;

"proceeds of drug trafficking" includes any payments or other rewards received by a person at any time (whether before or after the commencement of the Drug Trafficking Offences Act 1986 (United States of America) Order 1989) in connection with drug trafficking carried on by him or another; and

"property" includes money and all other property, real or personal, heritable or moveable, including things in action and other intangible or incorporeal property.

(2) The expressions listed in the left hand column below are respectively defined or (as the case may be) fall to be construed in accordance with the provisions of this Act listed in the right hand column in relation to those expressions.

Expression	**Relevant provision**
Charging order	Section 9(2)
Confiscation order	Section 1
Dealing with property	Section 8(7)
Defendant	Section 1
Realisable property	Section 5(1)
Restraint order	Section 8(1)

(3) This Act applies to property whether it is situated in England and Wales or elsewhere.

. . . .

(5) References in this Act to anything received in connection with drug trafficking include a reference to anything received both in that connection and in some other connection.

(6) The following provisions shall have effect for the interpretation of this Act.

(7) Property is held by any person if he holds any interest in it.

(8) References to property held by a person include a reference to property vested in his trustee in bankruptcy, permanent or interim trustee within the meaning of the Bankruptcy (Scotland) Act 1985 or liquidator.

(9) References to an interest held by a person beneficially in property include a reference to an interest which would be held by him beneficially if the property were not so vested.

. . . .

(11) Proceedings for an offence are instituted in the United States when an indictment, information or complaint has been filed against a person in respect of an offence.

(12) Proceedings for an offence are concluded–

(a) when (disregarding any power of a court to grant leave to appeal out of time) there is no further possibility of a confiscation order being made in the proceedings;

(b) on the satisfaction of a confiscation order made in the proceedings (whether by the recovery of all property liable to be recovered, or the payment of any amount due, or otherwise).

(13) An order is subject to appeal until (disregarding any power of a court to grant leave to appeal out of time) there is no further possibility of an appeal on which the order could be varied or set aside.

39.—(1) Section 28 of the Bankruptcy Act 1914 (effect of order of discharge) shall have effect as if amounts payable under confiscation orders were debts excepted under subsection (1)(a) of that section.

. . . .

(3) In section 1(2)(a) of the Rehabilitation of Offenders Act 1974 (failure to pay fines etc. not to prevent person becoming rehabilitated) the reference to a fine or other sum adjudged to be paid by or imposed on a conviction does not include a reference to an amount payable under a confiscation order.

. . . .

(5) Section 281(4) of the Insolvency Act 1986 (discharge of bankrupt not to release him from liabilities in respect of fines, etc.) shall have effect as if the reference to a fine included a reference to a confiscation order.

(6) Section 55(2) of the Bankruptcy (Scotland) Act 1985 (discharge of debtor not to release him from liabilities in respect of fines etc.) shall have effect as if the reference to a fine included a reference to a confiscation order.

EXPLANATORY NOTE

(This note is not part of the Order)

This Order makes the provision necessary for the operation in England and Wales of the provisions relating to the restraint and confiscation of proceeds of drug trafficking in the Agreement between the government of the United Kingdom and the government of the United States of America concerning the investigation of drug trafficking offences and the seizure and forfeiture of proceeds and instrumentalities of drug trafficking done at London on 9th February, 1988 (Cm. 340).

The Order provides that where property is liable to be recovered under an order made by a court in the United States of America for the purpose of recovering payments or other rewards received in connection with drug trafficking or their value it can be confiscated in England and Wales under the Drug Trafficking Offences Act 1986. It also provides, in *Article 5*, that the value of any property recovered in the United States of America in response to a request by the government of the United Kingdom for assistance in the enforcement of an order is to be treated as reducing the amount payable in England and Wales under a confiscation order made by the Crown Court.

Article 3 of the Order designates the United States of America for the purposes of enforcement of its confiscation orders, and applies the provisions of the Drug Trafficking Offences Act, with appropriate modifications, to confiscation orders of courts in the United States of America and proceedings which may lead to such an order being made. The modifications to the Act are set out in *Schedule 1* to the Order, and *Schedule 2* sets out in full that Act as so modified. *Article 4* makes provision for proof of the purpose of an order made in a court of the United States of America and of the fact that proceedings have been instituted against a person there.

STATUTORY INSTRUMENTS

1989 No. 486

REPRESENTATION OF THE PEOPLE

REDISTRIBUTION OF SEATS

The European Parliamentary Constituencies (England) (Miscellaneous Changes) Order 1989

Made - - - - 15th March 1989

Coming into force in accordance with article 1(2)

At the Court at Buckingham Palace, the 15th day of March 1989

Present,

The Queen's Most Excellent Majesty in Council

Whereas in pursuance of paragraph 3 of Schedule 2 to the European Parliamentary Constituencies Act 1978(**a**), the Boundary Commission for England have submitted to the Secretary of State a supplementary report dated 5th December 1988 with respect to the areas comprised in certain European Parliamentary constituencies in England and showing the European Parliamentary constituencies into which they recommend, in accordance with the provisions of paragraph 9 of the said Schedule 2, that the areas should be divided;

And whereas the Secretary of State has laid that report before Parliament together with the draft of this Order in Council to give effect to the recommendations contained in the report and each House of Parliament has by resolution approved that draft;

Now, therefore, Her Majesty, in pursuance of paragraph 4B of Schedule 2 to the European Parliamentary Elections Act 1978(**b**), is pleased, by and with the advice of Her Privy Council, to order, and it is hereby ordered, as follows:

1.—(1) This Order may be cited as the European Parliamentary Constituencies (England) (Miscellaneous Changes) Order 1989.

(2) Subject to paragraph 8(1) of Schedule 2 to the European Parliamentary Elections Act 1978(**c**), this Order shall come into force forthwith.

2. For the 34 European Parliamentary constituencies of Bedfordshire South, Bristol, Cambridge and Bedfordshire North, Cheshire East, Cheshire West, Cleveland and Yorkshire North, Cornwall and Plymouth, Derbyshire, Devon, Dorset East and Hampshire West, Durham, Essex North East, Essex South West, Hampshire Central, Hertfordshire, Humberside, Kent East, Kent West, Lancashire Central, Lancashire East, Leicester, Lincolnshire, Midlands Central, Nottingham, Oxford and Buckinghamshire, Sheffield, Shropshire and Stafford, Somerset and Dorset West, Staffordshire East,

(**a**) 1978 c.10; paragraph 3 of Schedule 2 was substituted by section 1(3) of the European Parliamentary Elections Act 1981 (c.8) and amended by paragraph 5(3) of Schedule 3 to the Parliamentary Constituencies Act 1986 (c.56); and the words "European Parliamentary" were substituted for the words "European Assembly" in the provisions concerning the citation of the 1978 and 1981 Acts by section 3(1)(b) and (2)(b) of the European Communities (Amendment) Act 1986 (c.58) on the coming into force of the Single European Act on 1st July 1987.

(**b**) Paragraph 4B was inserted by paragraph 5(4) of Schedule 3 to the Parliamentary Constituencies Act 1986.

(**c**) Paragraph 8(1) was amended by paragraph 5(9) of Schedule 3 to the Parliamentary Constituencies Act 1986.

Suffolk, Wight and Hampshire East, Wiltshire, York and Yorkshire West as constituted by the European Parliamentary Constituencies (England) Order 1984(**a**) (and described by reference to the parliamentary constituencies referred to in that Order), there shall be substituted the 34 European Parliamentary constituencies named on the left-hand side of the Schedule to this Order and comprising the parliamentary constituencies which are set out on the right-hand side and which are constituted–

(a) in the case of the Basildon, Brigg and Cleethorpes, Bristol East, Castle Point, Devizes, Glanford and Scunthorpe, Huntingdon, Kingswood, Newcastle-under-Lyme, Nuneaton, Peterborough, Rugby and Kenilworth, South Dorset, Stafford, Stoke-on-Trent North, Swindon, Wansdyke, Wells, West Dorset, Weston-Super-Mare and Woodspring constituencies, by the Parliamentary Constituencies (England) (Miscellaneous Changes) Order 1985(**b**);

(b) in the case of the Basingstoke, Bridgwater, East Hampshire, Eastleigh, Falmouth and Camborne, Fareham, Havant, Keighley, North East Cambridgeshire, North West Hampshire, Romsey and Waterside, St. Ives, Skipton and Ripon, South East Cambridgeshire, South East Cornwall, South West Cambridgeshire, Taunton, Truro and Winchester constituencies, by the Parliamentary Constituencies (England) (Miscellaneous Changes) Order 1986(**c**);

(c) in the case of the Bishop Auckland, City of Durham, Easington, Gainsborough and Horncastle, Grantham, Halton, Hertford and Stortford, Luton South, Mid Bedfordshire, North Durham, North Luton, Oxford West and Abingdon, Salisbury, Sedgefield, South West Bedfordshire, South West Hertfordshire, Stevenage, Stockton North, Warrington South, Welwyn Hatfield, West Hertfordshire, Wantage and Westbury constituencies, by the Parliamentary Constituencies (England) (Miscellaneous Changes) Order 1987(**d**);

(d) in the case of the Amber Valley, Aylesbury, Bolsover, Boothferry, Bosworth, Braintree, Brentwood and Ongar, Broxtowe, Buckingham, Burnley, Canterbury, Chelmsford, Chesham and Amersham, Chorley, Epping Forest, Erewash, Faversham, Folkestone and Hythe, Fylde, Gillingham, Harlow, Hyndburn, Loughborough, Ludlow, Mid Kent, Newark, North Colchester, North East Derbyshire, North West Leicestershire, Nottingham East, Pendle, Plymouth Devonport, Preston, Ribble Valley, Rushcliffe, Rutland and Melton, Ryedale, Scarborough, Selby, Sherwood, Shrewsbury and Atcham, South Hams, South Ribble, Teignbridge, The Wrekin, West Derbyshire and West Lancashire constituencies, by the Parliamentary Constituencies (England) (Miscellaneous Changes) (No. 3) Order 1987(**e**);

(e) in the case of the constituencies of Ipswich and Suffolk Coastal, by the Parliamentary Constituencies (England) (Miscellaneous Changes) (No. 4) Order 1987(**f**), and

(f) in the case of the remaining constituencies, by the Parliamentary Constituencies (England) Order 1983(**g**).

G. I. de Deney
Clerk to the Privy Council

(**a**) S.I. 1984/544; the citation of this Order has been amended by the provisions referred to in the first footnote to this Order.
(**b**) S.I. 1985/1776. (**c**) S.I. 1986/597. (**d**) S.I. 1987/462.
(**e**) S.I. 1987/2208. (**f**) S.I. 1987/2209. (**g**) S.I. 1983/417.

Article 2

SCHEDULE

NAMES AND AREAS OF ALTERED EUROPEAN PARLIAMENTARY CONSTITUENCIES IN ENGLAND

(1) *Name*	(2) *Contents*
Durham	The parliamentary constituencies of– Bishop Auckland Blaydon City of Durham Darlington Easington North Durham North West Durham Sedgefield
Cleveland and Yorkshire North	The parliamentary constituencies of– Hartlepool Langbaurgh Middlesbrough Redcar Richmond (Yorks) Skipton and Ripon Stockton North Stockton South
York	The parliamentary constituencies of– Boothferry Glanford and Scunthorpe Harrogate Ryedale Scarborough Selby York
Humberside	The parliamentary constituencies of– Beverley Bridlington Brigg and Cleethorpes Great Grimsby Kingston upon Hull East Kingston upon Hull North Kingston upon Hull West
Lancashire Central	The parliamentary constituencies of– Blackpool North Blackpool South Chorley Fylde Preston Ribble Valley South Ribble West Lancashire
Lancashire East	The parliamentary constituencies of– Blackburn Burnley Heywood and Middleton

SCHEDULE *(continued)*

(1) *Name*	(2) *Contents*
	Hyndburn Littleborough and Saddleworth Pendle Rochdale Rossendale and Darwen
Yorkshire West	The parliamentary constituencies of– Batley and Spen Bradford North Bradford South Bradford West Calder Valley Halifax Keighley Shipley
Cheshire West	The parliamentary constituencies of– Birkenhead City of Chester Eddisbury Ellesmere Port and Neston Halton Wallasey Wirral South Wirral West
Cheshire East	The parliamentary constituencies of– Congleton Crewe and Nantwich Macclesfield Staffordshire Moorlands Tatton Warrington North Warrington South
Derbyshire	The parliamentary constituencies of– Amber Valley Ashfield Bolsover Derby North Derby South Erewash High Peak West Derbyshire
Sheffield	The parliamentary constituencies of– Chesterfield North East Derbyshire Sheffield, Attercliffe Sheffield, Brightside Sheffield, Central Sheffield, Hallam Sheffield, Heeley Sheffield, Hillsborough
Nottingham	The parliamentary constituencies of– Broxtowe

SCHEDULE *(continued)*

(1) *Name*	(2) *Contents*
	Gedling Mansfield Nottingham East Nottingham North Nottingham South Rushcliffe Sherwood
Lincolnshire	The parliamentary constituencies of– Bassetlaw East Lindsey Gainsborough and Horncastle Grantham Holland with Boston Lincoln Newark Stamford and Spalding
Shropshire and Stafford	The parliamentary constituencies of– Cannock and Burntwood Ludlow Newcastle-under-Lyme North Shropshire Shrewsbury and Atcham South Staffordshire Stafford The Wrekin
Staffordshire East	The parliamentary constituencies of– Burton Mid Staffordshire North West Leicestershire South Derbyshire South East Staffordshire Stoke-on-Trent Central Stoke-on-Trent North Stoke-on-Trent South
Midlands Central	The parliamentary constituencies of– Coventry North East Coventry North West Coventry South East Coventry South West Meriden Rugby and Kenilworth Solihull Warwick and Leamington
Leicester	The parliamentary constituencies of– Bosworth Leicester East Leicester South Leicester West Loughborough North Warwickshire Nuneaton Rutland and Melton

SCHEDULE *(continued)*

(1) *Name*	(2) *Contents*
Cambridge and Bedfordshire North	The parliamentary constituencies of– Cambridge Huntingdon Mid Bedfordshire North Bedfordshire North East Cambridgeshire Peterborough South West Cambridgeshire
Suffolk	The parliamentary constituencies of– Bury St. Edmunds Central Suffolk Ipswich South East Cambridgeshire South Suffolk Suffolk Coastal Waveney
Oxford and Buckinghamshire	The parliamentary constituencies of– Aylesbury Beaconsfield Buckingham Chesham and Amersham Henley Oxford East Oxford West and Abingdon Wycombe
Bedfordshire South	The parliamentary constituencies of– Luton South Milton Keynes North Hertfordshire North Luton South West Bedfordshire Stevenage West Hertfordshire
Hertfordshire	The parliamentary constituencies of– Broxbourne Hertford and Stortford Hertsmere St. Albans South West Hertfordshire Watford Welwyn Hatfield
Essex South West	The parliamentary constituencies of– Basildon Billericay Brentwood and Ongar Castle Point Chelmsford Epping Forest Harlow Thurrock

SCHEDULE *(continued)*

(1) *Name*	(2) *Contents*
Essex North East	The parliamentary constituencies of– Braintree Harwich North Colchester Rochford Saffron Walden South Colchester and Maldon Southend East Southend West
Bristol	The parliamentary constituencies of– Bath Bristol East Bristol North West Bristol South Bristol West Kingswood Northavon Wansdyke
Wiltshire	The parliamentary constituencies of– Devizes Newbury North Wiltshire Salisbury Swindon Wantage Westbury
Cornwall and Plymouth	The parliamentary constituencies of– Falmouth and Camborne North Cornwall Plymouth, Devonport Plymouth, Drake Plymouth, Sutton St. Ives South East Cornwall Truro
Devon	The parliamentary constituencies of– Exeter Honiton North Devon South Hams Teignbridge Tiverton Torbay Torridge and West Devon
Somerset and Dorset West	The parliamentary constituencies of– Bridgwater Somerton and Frome Taunton Wells West Dorset Weston-Super-Mare

SCHEDULE *(continued)*

(1) *Name*	(2) *Contents*
	Woodspring Yeovil
Dorset East and Hampshire West	The parliamentary constituencies of– Bournemouth East Bournemouth West Christchurch New Forest North Dorset Poole Romsey and Waterside South Dorset
Hampshire Central	The parliamentary constituencies of– Aldershot Basingstoke Eastleigh North West Hampshire Southampton, Itchen Southampton, Test Winchester
Wight and Hampshire East	The parliamentary constituencies of– East Hampshire Fareham Gosport Havant Isle of Wight Portsmouth North Portsmouth South
Kent West	The parliamentary constituencies of– Dartford Gillingham Gravesham Medway Mid Kent Sevenoaks Tonbridge and Malling Tunbridge Wells
Kent East	The parliamentary constituencies of– Ashford Canterbury Dover Faversham Folkestone and Hythe Maidstone North Thanet South Thanet

EXPLANATORY NOTE

(This note is not part of the Order)

This Order gives effect without modification to the recommendations contained in the supplementary report of the Boundary Commission for England dated 5th December 1988. The report contains proposals for changes to the areas comprised in the 34 European Parliamentary constituencies referred to in article 2 of this Order where changes to the boundaries of parliamentary constituencies have resulted in inconsistencies between those boundaries and the boundaries of European Parliamentary constituencies. Article 2 of, and the Schedule to, this Order set out the new constituencies, but by virtue of the provision referred to in article 1(2) these constituencies will only have effect from the next European Parliamentary general election.

STATUTORY INSTRUMENTS

1989 No. 487

REPRESENTATION OF THE PEOPLE

REDISTRIBUTION OF SEATS

The European Parliamentary Constituencies (Wales) (Miscellaneous Changes) Order 1989

Made - - - - 15th March 1989

Coming into force in accordance with article 1(2)

At the Court at Buckingham Palace, the 15th day of March 1989

Present,

The Queen's Most Excellent Majesty in Council

Whereas in pursuance of paragraph 3 of Schedule 2 to the European Parliamentary Elections Act 1978(**a**), the Boundary Commission for Wales have submitted to the Secretary of State a supplementary report dated 22nd July 1988 with respect to the areas comprised in certain European Parliamentary constituencies in Wales and showing the European Parliamentary constituencies into which they recommend, in accordance with the provisions of paragraph 9 of the said Schedule 2, that the areas should be divided:

And whereas the Secretary of State has laid that report before Parliament together with the draft of this Order in Council to give effect to the recommendations contained in the report and each House of Parliament has by resolution approved that draft:

Now, therefore, Her Majesty, in pursuance of paragraph 4B of Schedule 2 to the European Parliamentary Elections Act 1978(**b**), is pleased, by and with the advice of Her Privy Council, to order, and it is hereby ordered, as follows:

1.—(1) This Order may be cited as the European Parliamentary Constituencies (Wales) (Miscellaneous Changes) Order 1989.

(2) Subject to paragraph 8(1) of Schedule 2 to the European Parliamentary Elections Act 1978(**c**), this Order shall come into force fourteen days after it is made.

2. For the three European Parliamentary constituencies of Mid and West Wales, South East Wales and South Wales, as constituted by the European Parliamentary Constituencies (Wales) Order 1984(**d**) (and described by reference to the parliamentary constituencies referred to in that Order), there shall be substituted the three European

(**a**) 1978 c.10; paragraph 3 of Schedule 2 was substituted by section 1(3) of the European Parliamentary Elections Act 1981 (c.8) and amended by paragraph 5(3) of Schedule 3 to the Parliamentary Constituencies Act 1986 (c.56); and the words "European Parliamentary" were substituted for the words "European Assembly" in the provisions concerning the citation of the 1978 and 1981 Acts by section 3(1)(b) and (2)(b) of the European Communities (Amendment) Act 1986 (c.58) on the coming into force of the Single European Act on 1st July 1987.

(**b**) Paragraph 4B was inserted by paragraph 5(4) of Schedule 3 to the Parliamentary Constituencies Act 1986.

(**c**) Paragraph 8(1) was amended by paragraph 5(9) of Schedule 3 to the Parliamentary Constituencies Act 1986.

(**d**) S.I. 1984/545; the citation of this Order has been amended by the provisions referred to in the first footnote to this Order.

Parliamentary constituencies named on the left-hand side of the Schedule to this Order and comprising the parliamentary constituencies which are set out on the right-hand side and which are constituted–

(a) in the case of the Cardiff Central, Cardiff North, Cardiff South and Penarth, Cardiff West, Cynon Valley, Islwyn and Vale of Glamorgan constituencies, by the Parliamentary Constituencies (Wales) Order 1983(**a**), and

(b) in the case of the remaining constituencies by the Parliamentary Constituencies (Wales) (Miscellaneous Changes) Order 1987(**b**).

G. I. de Deney
Clerk of the Privy Council

Article 2

SCHEDULE

NEW CONSTITUENCIES

Mid and West Wales	The parliamentary constituencies of– Brecon and Radnor Carmarthen Ceredigion and Pembroke North Gower Llanelli Neath Pembroke Swansea East Swansea West
South East Wales	The parliamentary constituencies of– Blaenau Gwent Caerphilly Cynon Valley Islwyn Merthyr Tydfil and Rhymney Monmouth Newport East Newport West Rhondda Torfaen
South Wales	The parliamentary constituencies of– Aberavon Bridgend Cardiff Central Cardiff North Cardiff South and Penarth Cardiff West Ogmore Pontypridd Vale of Glamorgan

---

(**a**) S.I. 1983/418.
(**b**) S.I. 1987/2050.

EXPLANATORY NOTE

(This note is not part of the Order)

This Order gives effect without modification to the recommendations contained in the supplementary report of the Boundary Commission for Wales dated 22nd July 1988. The report contains proposals for changes to the areas comprised in the European Parliamentary constituencies of Mid and West Wales, South East Wales and South Wales where changes to the boundaries of parliamentary constituencies have resulted in inconsistencies between those boundaries and the boundaries of European Parliamentary constituencies. Article 2 of, and the Schedule to, this Order, set out the new constituencies, but by virtue of the provision referred to in article 1(2) these constituencies will only have effect from the next European Parliamentary general election.

STATUTORY INSTRUMENTS

1989 No. 488

IMMIGRATION

The Immigration (Jersey) (Variation) Order 1989

Made - - - -	*15th March 1989*
Coming into force	*15th April 1989*

At the Court at Buckingham Palace, the 15th day of March 1989

Present,

The Queen's Most Excellent Majesty in Council

Her Majesty, in pursuance of section 36 of the Immigration Act 1971(**a**) as applied by section 2(3) of the Immigration (Carriers' Liability) Act 1987(**b**), is pleased, by and with the advice of Her Privy Council, to order, and it is hereby ordered, as follows:

1. This Order may be cited as the Immigration (Jersey) (Variation) Order 1989 and shall come into force on 15th April 1989.

2. The Immigration (Jersey) Order 1972(**c**) shall be further varied in accordance with the provisions of the Schedule to this Order.

G. I. deDeney
Clerk of the Privy Council

(**a**) 1971 c.77.
(**b**) 1987 c.24.
(**c**) S.I. 1972/1813, as amended by S.I. 1982/1836, 1984/1690.

SCHEDULE

Article 2

VARIATIONS TO THE IMMIGRATION (JERSEY) ORDER 1972

1. After article 4 there shall be inserted the following article:

"5. The provisions of the Immigration (Carriers' Liability) Act 1987 shall extend to the Bailiwick of Jersey with such exceptions, adaptations and modifications as are specified in the Schedule hereto.".

2.—(1) The Schedule shall be varied in accordance with the following provisions of this paragraph.

(2) In paragraph 1(1) after "that Act" there shall be inserted "or to the Immigration (Carriers' Liability) Act 1987 or any provision thereof".

(3) In paragraph 2(2), after "paragraph 1(4)," there shall be inserted "and in section 1(1) and (5) of the Immigration (Carriers' Liability) Act 1987,".

(4) After paragraph 36 there shall be added the following provisions:

"THE IMMIGRATION (CARRIERS' LIABILITY) ACT 1987

Section 1

37. In section 1–

(a) in subsection (1), for the words from "the sum" to the end there shall be substituted "such sum, not exceeding £1000 or such other sum as may be prescribed, as the Committee may determine";

(b) in subsection (3), for the words from "Secretary of State" to the end there shall be substituted "Committee; and the Subordinate Legislation (Jersey) Law 1960 shall apply to any such order", and

(c) in subsection (5), for "into the Consolidated Fund" there shall be substituted "to the Treasurer of the States and credited to the Annual Income of the States".

Section 2

38. In section 2–

(a) subsection (3) shall be omitted, and

(b) in subsection (4), for "4th March 1987" there shall be substituted "the date of the extension of this Act to the Bailiwick of Jersey".".

EXPLANATORY NOTE

(This note is not part of the Order)

This Order varies the Immigration (Jersey) Order 1972, as amended, so as to extend to the Bailiwick of Jersey the Immigration (Carriers' Liability) Act 1987 with exceptions, adaptations and modifications.

STATUTORY INSTRUMENTS

1989 No. 489

POST OFFICE
TELECOMMUNICATIONS

The Interception of Communications Act 1985 (Isle of Man) Order 1989

Made - - - -	*15th March 1989*
Coming into force	*1st April 1989*

At the Court at Buckingham Palace, the 15th day of March 1989

Present,

The Queen's Most Excellent Majesty in Council

Her Majesty, in pursuance of section 12(4) of the Interception of Communications Act 1985(**a**), is pleased, by and with the advice of Her Privy Council, to order, and it is hereby ordered, as follows:

1. This Order may be cited as the Interception of Communications Act 1985 (Isle of Man) Order 1989 and shall come into force on 1st April 1989.

2. It is hereby directed that sections 11(3) and (5) and 12(1) of the Interception of Communications Act 1985 shall extend to the Isle of Man with the following exceptions, adaptations and modifications, that is to say, in section 11(3) –

(a) for "by the Secretary of State under section 2 of the Interception of Communications Act 1985" there shall be substituted "under section 2 of the Interception of Communications Act 1988 (an Act of Tynwald)", and

(b) for "Commissioner under section 8(3)" there shall be substituted "commissioner under section 9(3)".

G. I. de Deney
Clerk of the Privy Council

(**a**) 1985 c.56.

EXPLANATORY NOTE

(This note is not part of the Order)

This Order extends to the Isle of Man sections 11(3) and (5) and 12(1) of the Interception of Communications Act 1985 with the exceptions, adaptations and modifications specified in the Order.

STATUTORY INSTRUMENTS

1989 No. 491

NORTHERN IRELAND

The Local Elections (Variation of Limits of Candidates' Election Expenses) (Northern Ireland) Order 1989

Made - - - - *15th March 1989*

Coming into force *16th March 1989*

At the Court at Buckingham Palace, the 15th day of March 1989

Present,

The Queen's Most Excellent Majesty in Council

Whereas a draft of this Order has been approved by resolution of each House of Parliament:

Now, therefore, Her Majesty, in pursuance of section 38(1)(a) of the Northern Ireland Constitution Act 1973(**a**), is pleased, by and with the advice of Her Privy Council, to order, and it is hereby ordered, as follows:

1.—(1) This Order may be cited as the Local Elections (Variation of Limits of Candidates' Election Expenses) (Northern Ireland) Order 1989 and shall come into force on the day after the day on which it is made.

(2) This Order extends to Northern Ireland only.

2. The Interpretation Act (Northern Ireland) 1954(**b**) shall apply to article 1 and the following provisions of this Order as it applies to a Measure of the Northern Ireland Assembly.

3. In section 42(1) of the Electoral Law Act (Northern Ireland) 1962 (limit on candidates' election expenses)(**c**), for the words "£135" and "2.8p" there shall be substituted the words "£162" and "3.2p", respectively.

G. I. de Deney
Clerk of the Privy Council

(**a**) 1973 c.36; section 38 was amended by the Northern Ireland Act 1982, Schedule 2, paragraph 6.
(**b**) 1954 c.33 (N.I.).
(**c**) 1962 c.14 (N.I.); section 42(1) was amended (so far as material) by the Local Elections (Northern Ireland) Order 1985 (S.I. 1985/454), article 9.

EXPLANATORY NOTE

(This note is not part of the Order)

This Order increases the maximum amount of a candidate's election expenses at local elections in Northern Ireland. The maximum amount of a candidate's election expenses is made up of a fixed sum (expressed in pounds) plus a sum expressed in pence (and fractions of pence) for each entry in the register of electors.

STATUTORY INSTRUMENTS

1989 No. 493

PATENTS

DESIGNS

The Patents, Designs and Marks Act 1986 (Amendments to the Registered Designs Act 1949 and the Patents Act 1977) (Isle of Man) Order 1989

Made - - - -	*15th March 1989*
Coming into force	*1st April 1989*

At the Court at Buckingham Palace, the 15th day of March 1989

Present,

The Queen's Most Excellent Majesty in Council

Her Majesty, in pursuance of section 4(5) of the Patents, Designs and Marks Act 1986(**a**), is pleased, by and with the advice of Her Privy Council, to order, and it is hereby ordered, as follows:

1. This Order may be cited as the Patents, Designs and Marks Act 1986 (Amendments to the Registered Designs Act 1949 and the Patents Act 1977) (Isle of Man) Order 1989 and shall come into force on 1st April 1989.

2.—(1) Sections 1 and 3(1) of the Patents, Designs and Marks Act 1986 so far as they relate to the Registered Designs Act 1949(**b**) and the Patents Act 1977(**c**) shall extend to the Isle of Man, subject to the modification specified in paragraph (2) below.

(2) Any reference to the said Act of 1949 or the said Act of 1977, or to a provision thereof, shall be construed as a reference to it as it has effect in the Isle of Man.

G. I. de Deney
Clerk of the Privy Council

(**a**) 1986 c.39.
(**b**) 1949 c.88; this Act extends to the Isle of Man subject to the modifications in section 47 of it.
(**c**) 1977 c.37; this Act extends to the Isle of Man subject to the modifications in the Patents Act 1977 (Isle of Man) Order 1978 (S.I. 1978/621).

EXPLANATORY NOTE

(This note is not part of the Order)

This Order extends to the Isle of Man, subject to the modification in article 2(2) of this Order, the amendments to the Registered Designs Act 1949 and the Patents Act 1977 made by section 1 of, and Schedule 1 to, the Patents, Designs and Marks Act 1986 and the repeals of provisions in those Acts of 1949 and 1977 made by section 3(1) of, and Schedule 3 to, the Act of 1986.

1989 No. 494

REPRESENTATION OF THE PEOPLE

REDISTRIBUTION OF SEATS

The European Parliamentary Constituencies (Scotland) (Miscellaneous Changes) Order 1989

Made - - - - 15th March 1989

Coming into force in accordance with article 1(2)

At the Court at Buckingham Palace, the 15th day of March 1989

Present,

The Queen's Most Excellent Majesty in Council

Whereas in pursuance of paragraph 3 of Schedule 2 to the European Parliamentary Elections Act 1978(**a**) the Boundary Commission for Scotland have submitted to the Secretary of State a supplementary report dated 5th January 1989 with respect to the areas comprised in certain European Parliamentary constituencies in Scotland and showing the European Parliamentary constituencies into which they recommend that the areas should be divided, in accordance with the provisions of paragraph 9 of the said Schedule 2:

And whereas the Secretary of State has laid that report before Parliament together with the draft of this Order in Council to give effect to the recommendations contained in the report and each House of Parliament has by resolution approved the said draft:

Now, therefore, Her Majesty, in pursuance of paragraph 4B of Schedule 2 to the European Parliamentary Elections Act 1978(**b**), is pleased, by and with the advice of Her Privy Council, to order, and it is hereby ordered, as follows:–

1.—(1) This Order may be cited as the European Parliamentary Constituencies (Scotland) (Miscellaneous Changes) Order 1989.

(2) Subject to paragraph 8(1) of Schedule 2 to the European Parliamentary Elections Act 1978(**c**), this Order shall come into force on the fourteenth day after the day on which it is made.

2. For the six European Parliamentary constituencies of Mid Scotland and Fife, Lothians, South of Scotland, Strathclyde East, Strathclyde West and Glasgow, as constituted by the European Parliamentary Constituencies (Scotland) Order 1984(**d**) (and described by reference to the parliamentary constituencies referred to in that Order), there shall be substituted the six European Parliamentary constituencies named on the left-hand side of the Schedule

(**a**) 1978 c.10; paragraph 3 of Schedule 2 was substituted by section 1(3) of the European Parliamentary Elections Act 1981 (c.8) and amended by paragraph 5(3) of Schedule 3 to the Parliamentary Constituencies Act 1986 (c.56); the words "European Parliamentary" were substituted for the words "European Assembly" in the provisions concerning the citation of the 1978 and 1981 Acts by section 3(1)(b) and (2)(b) of the European Communities (Amendment) Act 1986 (c.58) on the coming into force of the Single European Act on 1st July 1987.

(**b**) Paragraph 4B was inserted by paragraph 5(4) of Schedule 3 to the Parliamentary Constituencies Act 1986.

(**c**) Paragraph 8(1) was amended by paragraph 5(9) of Schedule 3 to the Parliamentary Constituencies Act 1986.

(**d**) S.I. 1984/548; the citation of this Order has been amended by section 3(1)(b) and (2)(b) of the European Communities (Amendment) Act 1986.

to this Order and comprising the parliamentary constituencies which are set out on the right-hand side and which are constituted–

(a) in the case of the Stirling, Edinburgh South, Ayr, Cunninghame South, Roxburgh and Berwickshire, Hamilton and Dumbarton constituencies, by the Parliamentary Constituencies (Scotland) (Miscellaneous Changes) Order 1987(**a**);

(b) in the case of the Clackmannan, Falkirk East, Central Fife, Dunfermline East, Dunfermline West, North East Fife, Perth and Kinross, Edinburgh East, Midlothian, Carrick, Cumnock and Doon Valley, Clydesdale, Galloway and Upper Nithsdale, East Lothian, East Kilbride, Monklands East, Clydebank and Milngavie, Strathkelvin and Bearsden, Glasgow Cathcart, Glasgow Garscadden and Glasgow Maryhill constituencies, by the Parliamentary Constituencies (Scotland) (Miscellaneous Changes) Order 1988(**b**); and

(c) in the case of the remaining constituencies by the Parliamentary Constituencies (Scotland) Order 1983(**c**).

G.I. de Deney
Clerk of the Privy Council

(**a**) S.I. 1987/469.
(**b**) S.I. 1988/1992.
(**c**) S.I. 1983/422.

Article 2

SCHEDULE

NAMES AND AREAS OF ALTERED EUROPEAN PARLIAMENTARY CONSTITUENCIES IN SCOTLAND

Mid Scotland and Fife	The parliamentary constituencies of– Clackmannan Falkirk East Falkirk West Stirling Central Fife Dunfermline East Dunfermline West Kirkcaldy North East Fife Perth and Kinross
Lothians	The parliamentary constituencies of– Edinburgh Central Edinburgh East Edinburgh Leith Edinburgh Pentlands Edinburgh South Edinburgh West Linlithgow Livingston Midlothian
South of Scotland	The parliamentary constituencies of– Ayr Carrick, Cumnock and Doon Valley Clydesdale Cunninghame South Dumfries Galloway and Upper Nithsdale East Lothian Roxburgh and Berwickshire Tweeddale, Ettrick and Lauderdale
Strathclyde East	The parliamentary constituencies of– Cumbernauld and Kilsyth East Kilbride Glasgow Rutherglen Hamilton Kilmarnock and Loudoun Monklands East Monklands West Motherwell North Motherwell South
Strathclyde West	The parliamentary constituencies of– Clydebank and Milngavie Cunninghame North Dumbarton Eastwood Greenock and Port Glasgow Paisley North Paisley South Renfrew West and Inverclyde Strathkelvin and Bearsden
Glasgow	The parliamentary constituencies of– Glasgow Cathcart Glasgow Central Glasgow Garscadden Glasgow Govan Glasgow Hillhead Glasgow Maryhill Glasgow Pollok Glasgow Provan Glasgow Shettleston Glasgow Springburn

EXPLANATORY NOTE

(This note is not part of the Order)

This Order gives effect without modification to the recommendations contained in the supplementary report of the Boundary Commission for Scotland dated 5th January 1989. The report contains proposals for changes to the areas comprised in the European Parliamentary constituencies of Mid Scotland and Fife, Lothians, South of Scotland, Strathclyde East, Strathclyde West, and Glasgow where changes to the boundaries of parliamentary constituencies have resulted in inconsistencies between those boundaries and the boundaries of European Parliamentary constituencies. Article 2 of, and the Schedule to, this Order set out the altered constituencies.

By virtue of the provision referred to in article 1(2), the altered constituencies will only have effect from the next European Parliamentary general election.

STATUTORY INSTRUMENTS

1989 No. 495

MINISTERS OF THE CROWN

The Transfer of Functions (Transport Tribunal) Order 1989

Made - - - -	*15th March 1989*
Laid before Parliament	*23rd March 1989*
Coming into force	*13th April 1989*

At the Court at Buckingham Palace, the 15th day of March 1989

Present,

The Queen's Most Excellent Majesty in Council

Her Majesty, in pursuance of section 1 of the Ministers of the Crown Act 1975**(a)**, is pleased, by and with the advice of Her Privy Council, to order, and it is hereby ordered, as follows:–

Citation and commencement

1.—(1) This Order may be cited as the Transfer of Functions (Transport Tribunal) Order 1989.

(2) This Order shall come into force on 13th April 1989.

Transfer of functions

2.—(1) The functions of the Secretary of State under paragraphs 5 to 7, 10, 11, 14 and 16 of Schedule 4 to the Transport Act 1985**(b)** (certain powers, proceedings and other matters relating to the Transport Tribunal) are hereby transferred to the Lord Chancellor.

(2) In those paragraphs, for the words "Secretary of State", wherever they occur, there shall be substituted the words "Lord Chancellor".

(3) In paragraph 15 of that Schedule (consultation with Lord Advocate), for the words "this Schedule" there shall be substituted the words "paragraph 2 or 3 above".

Supplementary

3.—(1) Any instrument made before the coming into force of this Order shall have effect, so far as may be necessary for the purpose or in consequence of the transfers effected by this Order, as if references to the Secretary of State were references to the Lord Chancellor.

(2) This Order does not affect the validity of anything done by or in relation to the Secretary of State before the coming into force of this Order; and anything which at the time of the coming into force of this Order is in process of being done by or in

(a) 1975 c.26.
(b) 1985 c.67.

relation to the Secretary of State may, if it relates to a function transferred by this Order, be continued by or in relation to the Lord Chancellor.

(3) Where any rule made or other thing done by the Secretary of State under any such provision of Schedule 4 to the Transport Act 1985 as is mentioned in article 2 above is in force or effective at the coming into force of this Order, that rule or other thing shall have effect, so far as required for continuing its effect after the coming into force of this Order, as if made or done by the Lord Chancellor.

G. I. de Deney
Clerk of the Privy Council

EXPLANATORY NOTE

(This note is not part of the Order)

This Order transfers those functions relating to the Transport Tribunal previously exercised by the Secretary of State for Transport which are specified in article 2(1) to the Lord Chancellor.

STATUTORY INSTRUMENTS

1989 No. 496

MEDICAL PROFESSION

The General Medical Council (Constitution) Amendment Order 1989

Made - - - -	*15th March 1989*
Laid before Parliament	*23rd March 1989*
Coming into force	*13th April 1989*

At the Court at Buckingham Palace, the 15th day of March 1989

Present,

The Queen's Most Excellent Majesty in Council

Her Majesty in exercise of the powers conferred upon Her by section 1(2) of, and paragraphs 1, 2, 3 and 8 of Schedule 1 to, the Medical Act 1983**(a)**, and of all other powers enabling Her in that behalf, is pleased, by and with the advice of Her Privy Council, to order, and it is hereby ordered, as follows:

Citation and commencement

1. This Order may be cited as the General Medical Council (Constitution) Amendment Order 1989 and, subject to article 2(3) below, shall come into force on 13th April 1989.

Amendment of the General Medical Council (Constitution) Order 1979

2. The General Medical Council (Constitution) Order 1979**(b)** shall be amended as follows:–

(1) in article 2(*a*) there shall be substituted for the number "50" the number "54";

(2) in article 2(*b*) there shall be substituted for the number "34" the number "35"; and

(3) with effect from 1st November 1989 in column 1 of the Schedule for "and the Faculty of Community Medicine" there shall be substituted ", the Faculty of Community Medicine and the Faculty of Occupational Medicine.".

G. I. de Deney
Clerk of the Privy Council

(a) 1983 c.54.
(b) S.I. 1979/112, amended by S.I. 1987/457.

EXPLANATORY NOTE

(This note is not part of the Order)

This Order, made under the Medical Act 1983, amends article 2 of, and the Schedule to, the General Medical Council (Constitution) Order 1979 so as to increase the number of elected members of the Council from 50 to 54, and to provide for an additional member to be appointed by the Faculty of Occupational Medicine.

STATUTORY INSTRUMENTS

1989 No. 497

REGISTRATION OF BIRTHS, DEATHS, MARRIAGES, ETC.

ENGLAND AND WALES

The Registration of Births and Deaths (Amendment) Regulations 1989

Made - - - -	*15th March 1989*
Coming into force -	*1st April 1989*

The Registrar General, in exercise of the powers conferred by sections 1(1), 5, 9(5), 10(1), 10A(1), 29(2), 39 and 41 of the Births and Deaths Registration Act 1953**(a)**, by section 20(a) and 21(1) of the Registration Service Act 1953**(b)** and of all other powers enabling her in that behalf, with the approval of the Secretary of State for Health**(c)**, hereby makes the following Regulations–

Citation, commencement and interpretation

1.—(1) These Regulations may be cited as the Registration of Births and Deaths (Amendment) Regulations 1989 and shall come into force on 1st April 1989.

(2) In these Regulations "the principal Regulations" means the Registration of Births and Deaths Regulations 1987**(d)**, and unless the context otherwise requires any reference to a numbered regulation or Schedule is a reference to the regulation or Schedule bearing that number in the principal Regulations.

Substitution of regulation 8

2. For regulation 8 (declaration by mother for registration of birth) there shall be substituted the following regulation–

> "**Declaration by parent for registration of birth**
>
> **8.** Form 2 shall be the prescribed form of the declaration to be made by the mother pursuant to section 10(1)(b)(i) of the Act and by the person stating himself to be the father pursuant to section 10(1)(c)(i) of the Act (entry of father's name in register at request of and on declaration by one parent and statutory declaration of other).".

(a) 1953 c.20; sections 1(1) and 5 were amended by the Children Act 1975 (c.72), Schedule 3, paragraph 13(1); section 5 was also amended by the Registration of Births, Deaths and Marriages (Fees) Order 1968 (S.I. 1968/1242), Schedule 2; section 9(5) was added by the Children Act 1975, section 93(3); sections 10 and 10A were substituted by the Family Law Reform Act 1987 (c.42), sections 24 and 25 respectively; *see* the definitions of "the Minister" and "prescribed" in section 41.

(b) 1953 c.37; *see* the definitions of "the Minister" and "prescribed" in section 21(1).

(c) *See* the Secretary of State for Social Services Order 1968 (S.I. 1968/1699), article 2, which transferred all the functions of the Minister of Health to the Secretary of State; the approval of the Secretary of State is required by virtue of section 39 of the Births and Deaths Registration Act 1953 and by virtue of section 20 of the Registration Service Act 1953.

(d) S.I. 1987/2088; the relevant amending instrument is S.I. 1988/638.

Amendment of regulation 9

3.—(1) In regulation 9(4)(b) (entry of particulars on registration within three months from date of birth)–

(a) for the words "by the mother under section 10(c) of the Act" there shall be substituted the words "under section 10(1)(d) of the Act"; and

(b) for the words "order made under section 4 of the Affiliation Proceedings Act 1957 which was produced to him by the mother" there shall be substituted the words "relevant order which was produced to him".

(2) In regulation 9(8)(b) for "section 10(a)" there shall be substituted "section 10(1)(a)".

Amendment of regulation 10

4. In regulation 10(1) (completion of registration)–

(a) in paragraph (b) for "section 10" there shall be substituted "section 10(1)";

(b) in paragraphs (b)(i) and (b)(ii) for the word "section" there shall be substituted the word "sub-section";

(c) for paragraph (b)(iii) there shall be substituted–

"(iii) if made pursuant to paragraph (c) of that sub-section, the person stating himself to be the father of the child, in which case the registrar shall add after his signature the words "Statutory declaration made by .... on ....", inserting the name and surname of the mother and the date on which the statutory declaration was made by her,

(iv) if made pursuant to paragraph (d) of that sub-section, the person making the request, in which case the registrar shall add after his signature the words "Pursuant to section 10(1)(d) of the Births and Deaths Registration Act 1953".".

Amendment of regulation 13

5. In regulation 13(4)(b)(ii) (declaration and registration under section 9 of the Act)–

(a) for the words "paragraph (b) or (c) of section 10" there shall be substituted the words "paragraph (b), (c) or (d) of section 10(1)",

(b) for "(ii) or (iii)" there shall be substituted "(ii), (iii) or (iv)".

Substitution of regulation 16

6. For regulation 16 (declaration by mother for re-registration of birth) there shall be substituted the following regulation–

"Declaration by parent for re-registration of birth

16. Form 2 shall be the prescribed form of the declaration to be made by the mother pursuant to section 10A(1)(b)(i) of the Act and by the person stating himself to be the father pursuant to section 10A(1)(c)(i) of the Act (entry of father's name in register at request of and on declaration of one parent and statutory declaration of other).".

Amendment of regulation 17

7.—(1) For regulation 17(2)(b)(ii) (re-registration of birth) there shall be substituted the following–

" (ii) in a section 10A(1)(c) case, add the words "Statutory declaration made by .... on ....", inserting the name and surname of the mother and the date on which the statutory declaration was made by her,

(iii) in a section 10A(1)(d) case, add the words "Pursuant to section 10A(1)(d) of the Births and Deaths Registration Act 1953";".

(2) In regulation 17(3)(a)–

(a) in paragraph (ii) after "10A(1)(b)" there shall be inserted "or (c)";

(b) in paragraph (iii) for "10A(1)(c)" there shall be substituted "10A(1)(d)".

(3) In regulation 17(3)(b)–

(a) in paragraph (i)–
(i) after "10A(1)(b)" there shall be inserted "or (c)",
(ii) the words "made by the person acknowledging himself to be the father of the child" shall be omitted;
(b) in paragraph (ii)–
(i) for "10A(1)(c)" there shall be substituted "10A(1)(d)",
(ii) for the words "order made under section 4 of the Affiliation Proceedings Act 1957" there shall be substituted the words "the relevant order".

(4) In regulation 17(4)(b)(ii)–
(a) for "or (c)" there shall be substituted ", (c) or (d)";
(b) for "or (ii)" there shall be substituted ", (ii) or (iii)".

(5) In regulation 17(5)–
(a) in paragraph (b) the words "or (c) case" shall be omitted;
(b) after paragraph (b) there shall be inserted–
"(c) in a section 10A(1)(c) case, the father,
(d) in a section 10A(1)(d) case, the mother or the father,".

Amendment of regulation 43

8. In regulation 43(2) (registration where inquest is not held) for the words "section 21 of the Coroners (Amendment) Act 1926" there shall be substituted the words "section 19 of the Coroners Act 1988"**(a)**.

Amendment of regulation 55

9.—(1) In regulation 55(2)(c) (correction of minor clerical errors after completion)–
(a) after "10(1)(b)(ii)" there shall be inserted "(iii) or (iv)";
(b) after "17(2)(b)(i)" there shall be added ", (ii) or (iii)".

(2) For regulation 55(2)(e) there shall be substituted–
"(e) the omission of–
(i) any of the words (including the name, surname and qualification of the registered medical practitioner) "Certified by ...." required to be entered, in space 8 of a death entry, by Regulation 42(4),
(ii) any of the words (including the name, surname and description of the coroner) "Certified by .... after post-mortem without inquest" required to be entered, in space 8 of a death entry by Regulation 43(2),
(iii) any of the words (including the name, surname and description of the coroner and the date of inquest) "Certificate received from .... Inquest held on ...." required to be entered, in space 7 of a death entry, by Regulation 45(b)(i),
(iv) any of the words (including the name, surname and description of the coroner) "Certificate on inquest adjourned received from ...." required to be entered in space 7 of a death entry, by Regulation 45(b)(ii);".

(3) In regulation 55(2)(g)–
(a) after "10(1)(b)(ii)" there shall be inserted "or (iii)";
(b) after "17(2)(b)(i)" there shall be inserted "or (ii)".

Amendment of regulation 56

10. In regulation 56(3) (correction of other minor clerical errors after completion)–
(a) after paragraph (a)(iii) there shall be inserted–
"(iii*a*) in space 7, in the mother's occupation (if entered),",
(b) in paragraph (b)(iv) for the word "latter" there shall be substituted the word "former".

(a) 1988 c.13.

Amendment of regulation 67

11.—(1) In regulation 67(1) (applications for certificate of birth or death for certain purposes)–

(a) for the words "for the purposes of" there shall be substituted the word "where";

(b) after the words "in paragraph (2)" there shall be inserted the word "applies"**(a)**.

(2) In regulation 67(2) sub-paragraphs (b) and (c) shall be omitted.

Substitution of forms 2 and 6 in Schedule 2

12. For forms 2 and 6 in Schedule 2 there shall be substituted respectively the forms 2 and 6 in the Schedule to these Regulations.

Transitional provisions

13. The provisions of the principal Regulations shall continue to apply as though these Regulations had not been made–

(a) as regards any application made under the Affiliation Proceedings Act 1957**(b)** to which paragraph 1 of Schedule 3 to the Family Law Reform Act 1987 applies,

(b) as regards any request to re-register a birth made under paragraph 12 of Schedule 3 to the Family Law Reform Act 1987, and

(c) where before the coming into force of section 25 of the Family Law Reform Act 1987–

(i) a mother had made a request under section 10A(1)(b) or (c) of the Act to re-register a birth, and

(ii) the Registrar General had authorised that re-registration.

Given under my hand on 13th March 1989

G. T. Banks
Registrar General

Signed by authority of the Secretary of State for Health

R. N. Freeman
Parliamentary Under-Secretary of State,
Department of Health

15th March 1989

(a) Section 10 of the Savings Bank Act 1887 (c.40) is applied by regulation 21 of the Savings Contracts Regulations 1969 (S.I. 1969/1342), regulation 32 of the Savings Certificates Regulations 1972 (S.I. 1972/641), regulation 25 of the Premium Savings Bonds Regulations 1972 (S.I. 1972/765), regulation 52 of the National Savings Stock Register Regulations 1976 (S.I. 1976/2012) and regulation 26 of the Savings Certificates (Yearly Plan) Regulations 1984 (S.I. 1984/779).

(b) 1957 c.55.

Regulation 12

SCHEDULE

FORM 2

DECLARATION/STATEMENT FOR THE REGISTRATION/RE-REGISTRATION OF A BIRTH

Regulations 8, 16
17(3)(a)(ii)

Births and Deaths Registration Act 1953, ss.9(5), 10(1)(b)(i) and (c)(i) and 10A(1)(b)(i) and (c)(i)

CHILD

1. Date and place of birth	
2. Name and surname	3. Sex

FATHER

4. Name and surname
5. Place of birth
6. Occupation

MOTHER

7. Name and surname	
8. Place of birth	
9. (*a*) Maiden surname	(*b*) Surname at marriage if different from maiden surname
10. Usual address (if different from place of child's birth)	

INFORMANT

11. Name and surname (if not the mother or father)	12. Qualification
13. Usual address (if different from that in 10 above)	

For use where the child's parents are not married to each other and one parent produces a statutory declaration of parentage made by the other.

* I, ... DO SOLEMNLY DECLARE that I am the mother of the child the particulars of whose birth are specified above and that the person named in space 4 above is the father of the child; and I request that his name should be recorded as such in the register of births.

OR

* I, ... DO SOLEMNLY DECLARE that I am the father of the child the particulars of whose birth are specified above; and I request that my name should be recorded as such in the register of births.

Signature.. Date ....

Signed and declared by the above-named declarant in the presence

of...
Registrar of Births and Deaths/Superintendent Registrar

.... Sub-district .... District

* Delete as appropriate.

FORM 6

STATEMENT BY PARENT FOR THE RE-REGISTRATION OF A BIRTH

Regulation 17(3)(a)(iii) Births and Deaths Registration Act 1953, s.9(5)

CHILD	
1. Date and place of birth	
2. Name and surname	3. Sex
FATHER	
4. Name and surname	
5. Place of birth	
6. Occupation	
MOTHER	
7. Name and surname	
8. Place of birth	
9. (*a*) Maiden surname	(*b*) Surname at marriage if different from maiden surname
10. Usual address (if different from place of child's birth)	
INFORMANT	
11. Name and surname (if not the mother or father)	12. Qualification
13. Usual address (if different from that in 10 above)	

For use where the child's parents are not married to each other and one of them produces a certified copy of a relevant order.

I, ... DO SOLEMNLY DECLARE that I am the *mother/father of the child the particulars of whose birth are specified above and that *the person named in space 4 above is/ I am the father of the child and *is/am named as such in the certified copy of the relevant order relating to the child and produced by me; and I request that *his/my name should be recorded as such in the register of births.

Signature.. Date ....

Signed and declared by the above-named declarant in the presence

of...
Registrar of Births and Deaths/Superintendent Registrar

.... Sub-district .... District

* Delete as appropriate.

EXPLANATORY NOTE

(This note is not part of the Regulations)

These Regulations make minor amendments to the Registration of Births and Deaths Regulations 1987. The amendments fall into three categories.

The first category of amendments are those consequential on the coming into force of sections 24 and 25 of the Family Law Reform Act 1987. The amendments relate to the registration or re-registration of the births of children whose parents are not married to each other.

The second category of amendments relate to the correction of clerical errors in registers and specifies three further errors a registrar may correct without further authority.

The third category is an amendment to the provision relating to certificates for certain purposes and an amendment to take account of the consolidation of the legislation relating to coroners.

STATUTORY INSTRUMENTS

1989 No. 500

PENSIONS

The Personal and Occupational Pension Schemes (Miscellaneous Amendments) Regulations 1989

Made - - - -	*15th March 1989*
Laid before Parliament	*16th March 1989*
Coming into force -	*6th April 1989*

The Secretary of State for Social Security, in exercise of the powers conferred by section 168(1) of, and Schedule 20 to, the Social Security Act 1975**(a)**, section 52 of, and paragraph 6 of Schedule 2 to, the Social Security Pensions Act 1975**(b)**, and sections 1(9), 17(1) and 84(1) of the Social Security Act 1986**(c)** and all other powers enabling him in that behalf, after considering the report of the Occupational Pensions Board on the proposals submitted to them**(d)**, hereby makes the following Regulations:

Citation and commencement

1. These Regulations may be cited as the Personal and Occupational Pension Schemes (Miscellaneous Amendments) Regulations 1989, and shall come into force on 6th April 1989.

Amendment of the Occupational Pension Schemes (Contracting-out) Regulations 1984

2. In regulations 18(3), 23(5)(b)(ii) and 43(1) of the Occupational Pension Schemes (Contracting-out) Regulations 1984**(e)** for "£16" in each place where it appears there is substituted "£17".

Amendment of the Personal and Occupational Pension Schemes (Modification of Enactments) Regulations 1987

3. After regulation 5 of the Personal and Occupational Pension Schemes (Modification of Enactments) Regulations 1987**(f)** there is inserted–

> **"Modification of the provisions of Part VI of the Social Security Act 1986 in consequence of Part I of that Act**
>
> **6.** Where a member of an appropriate personal pension scheme or a money purchase contracted-out scheme continues in employment after attaining pension-

(a) 1975 c.14. *See* definitions of "prescribe" and "regulations" in Schedule 20. Section 168(1) applies, by virtue of section 66(2) of the Social Security Pensions Act 1975 (c.60), to the exercise of certain powers conferred by that Act.
(b) 1975 c.60. Paragraph 6 of Schedule 2 was amended by the Social Security Act 1980 (c.30), section 3(12).
(c) 1986 (c.50). *See* definitions of "modifications" and "regulations" in section 84(1).
(d) *See* section 61(2) and (3) of the Social Security Pensions Act 1975; section 61(2) was amended by the Social Security Act 1986, Schedule 10, paragraph 94, and there are other amendments not relevant to these Regulations.
(e) S.I. 1984/380; the relevant amending instruments are S.I. 1985/1928, 1987/1114, 1988/475.
(f) S.I. 1987/1116, amended by S.I. 1988/474, 1016.

able age and the commencement of his pension under the scheme is postponed, section 63 of the Social Security Act 1986**(a)** shall have effect as if–

(a) the guaranteed minimum pension to which he is treated as entitled by virtue of section 4(1)(a) of that Act or, as the case may be, by virtue of section 29(2A) of the Social Security Pensions Act 1975**(b)** was subject to increases in accordance with the provisions of section 35(6) of the Social Security Pensions Act 1975**(c)**, and

(b) the amounts of any notional increases referred to in paragraph (a) were subject to annual up-rating in the same way as if they were sums to which section 63(1)(d)(i) of the Social Security Act 1986 applied.".

Amendment of the Personal Pension Schemes (Appropriate Schemes) Regulations 1988

4. Regulation 12 of the Personal Pension Schemes (Appropriate Schemes) Regulations 1988**(d)** is amended as follows–

(a) in paragraph (2) for the words "Subject to paragraph (3)" there is substituted "Subject to paragraphs (2A) and (3)";

(b) in paragraph (2)(a) and (c) for the words "the Secretary of State receives the notice" there is substituted "the notice is completed by the earner";

(c) after paragraph (2) there is inserted–

"(2A) A notice given–

(a) pursuant to paragraph (2)(a) must be received by the Secretary of State not later than 17th May in the following tax year;

(b) pursuant to paragraph (2)(c) must be received by the Secretary of State not later than 17th May 1989.".

Signed by authority of the Secretary of State for Social Security.

Nicholas Scott
Minister of State,
Department of Social Security

15th March 1989

EXPLANATORY NOTE

(This note is not part of the Regulations)

These Regulations make miscellaneous amendments to regulations about personal and occupational pension schemes.

Regulation 2 makes amendments to the Occupational Pension Schemes (Contracting-out) Regulations 1984 by providing for an increase, from £16 to £17, in the amount of a state scheme premium below which it need not be paid.

Regulation 3 makes amendments to the Personal and Occupational Pension Schemes (Modification of Enactments) Regulations 1987 by adding a new regulation 6 which provides for the guaranteed minimum pension to which a member of an appropriate personal pension scheme or a money purchase contracted-out scheme is treated as entitled to be treated as if it were also subject to increments on deferment of pension and for those increments to be subject to annual up-rating.

(a) 1986 c.50; section 63 was amended by the Social Security Act 1988 (c.7), Schedule 5.
(b) 1975 c.60; section 29(2A) was inserted by the Social Security Act 1986 (c.50), section 6 and Schedule 2, paragraph 3.
(c) Section 35(6) was amended by the Social Security (Miscellaneous Provisions) Act 1977 (c.5), section 3(2).
(d) S.I. 1988/137, amended by S.I. 1988/830.

Regulation 4 makes amendments to the Personal Pension Schemes (Appropriate Schemes) Regulations 1988. It extends in certain circumstances the deadline for notifying the Secretary of State of the date from which a scheme is to be the earner's chosen scheme.

The report of the Occupational Pensions Board on the draft of these Regulations which had been referred to them, together with a statement showing that the regulations give effect to the Board's recommendations, is contained in Command Paper No. 653 published by Her Majesty's Stationery Office.

STATUTORY INSTRUMENTS

1989 No. 501 (C.18)

EDUCATION, ENGLAND AND WALES

The Education Reform Act 1988 (Commencement No. 6) Order 1989

Made - - - - 13th March 1989

In exercise of the powers conferred by section 236(6) to (8) of the Education Reform Act 1988**(a)** the Secretary of State for Wales hereby makes the following Order:–

Citation and interpretation

1.—(1) This Order may be cited as the Education Reform Act 1988 (Commencement No. 6) Order 1989.

(2) In this Order:–

"the Act" means the Education Reform Act 1988; and

references to the first, second, third and fourth key stages are references to the periods set out in paragraphs (a) to (d) respectively of section 3(3) of the Act.

Coming into force of certain provisions of the Act

2. The provisions of the Act specified in column 1 of Schedules 1 to 3 to this Order (which relate to the matters mentioned in column 2 thereof) shall, except as otherwise provided in the said column 1, come into force on the date specified in relation to each Schedule in the following table:–

Schedule 1	1st August 1989
Schedule 2	1st August 1990
Schedule 3	1st August 1991

Miscellaneous

3. In Schedule 3 to the Education Reform Act 1988 (Commencement No. 4) Order 1988**(b)**, for the words "69 to 79" (relating to Schedule 12 to the Act) there shall be substituted the words "69 to 76, 78, 79".

(a) 1988 c.40.
(b) S.I. 1988/2271.

SCHEDULE 1

PROVISIONS COMING INTO FORCE ON 1st AUGUST 1989

Provisions of the Act	*Subject matter of the provisions*
Section 10(3) (so far as regards the core subjects in relation to pupils at schools in Wales in the first, second or third key stage who do not have a statement of special educational needs)	Duties with respect to certain requirements

SCHEDULE 2

PROVISIONS COMING INTO FORCE ON 1st AUGUST 1990

Provisions of the Act	*Subject matter of the provisions*
(i) Section 10(3) (so far as regards the core subjects in relation to pupils at schools in Wales in the first, second and third key stage who have a statement of special educational needs)	Duties with respect to certain requirements.
(ii) Section 10(3) (so far as regards the other foundation subjects in relation to pupils at schools in Wales in the first, second or third key stage)	Duties with respect to certain requirements
(iii) Section 10(3) (so far as regards the core subjects in relation to pupils at schools in Wales in the first year of the fourth key stage)	Duties with respect to certain requirements

SCHEDULE 3

PROVISIONS COMING INTO FORCE ON 1st AUGUST 1991

Provisions of the Act	*Subject matter of the provisions*
Section 10(3) (so far as regards the core subjects in relation to pupils at schools in Wales in the second year of the fourth key stage)	Duties with respect to certain requirements

Peter Walker
Secretary of State for Wales

13th March 1989

EXPLANATORY NOTE

(This note is not part of the Order)

Article 2 of this Order, which applies only to pupils at schools in Wales, brings into force on various dates the provisions of section 10(3) of the Education Reform Act 1988 in so far as that subsection applies for the various purposes specified in the Order. Section 10(3) of the 1988 Act imposes duties on local education authorities, governing bodies and head teachers of schools with respect to the teaching of subjects in the National Curriculum.

Section 10(3) is brought into force:–

(a) on 1st August 1989 as regards the core subjects (defined in section 3(1) of the 1988 Act) for pupils in the first three key stages (defined in section 3(3) of the 1988 Act) who do not have a statement of special educational needs under the Education Act 1981 (c.60);

(b) on 1st August 1990 as regards the core subjects for pupils in the first three key stages who do have a statement of special educational needs;

(c) on 1st August 1990 as regards the other foundation subjects (defined in section 3(2) of the 1988 Act) for all pupils in the first three key stages;

(d) on 1st August 1990 as regards the core subjects for pupils in the first year of the fourth key stage; and

(e) on 1st August 1991 as regards the core subjects in relation to pupils in the second year of the fourth key stage.

Article 3 of the Order amends Schedule 3 to the Education Reform Act 1988 (Commencement No.4) Order 1988 (S.I. 1988/2271) by deleting the reference to paragraph 77 of Schedule 12 to the Act. That paragraph, amending paragraph 4 of Schedule 2 to the Sex Discrimination Act 1975 (c.65), which extends Section 27 of the Education Act 1980 (c.20) to enable provision to be made for transitional exemption Orders under the 1975 Act, will accordingly not come into force on 1st April 1989.

NOTE AS TO EARLIER COMMENCEMENT ORDERS

(This note is not part of the Order)

The following provisions of the Act have been brought or will be brought into force on the dates specified in the following table:–

Provision	*Date of Commencement*	*S.I.No.*
Sections 27, 28 and 32 (all partially) and section 30.	1st September 1988	1988/1459
Sections 26, 27(4) to (8) and 31(2) (all partially)	1st September 1989	1988/1459
Sections 26, 27(4) to (8) and 31(1) (all partially)	4th August 1990	1988/1459
Sections 17 to 19, 131 to 134 (including Schedule 8 to the extent not already in force), 136, 220 and paragraphs 83 to 85 of Schedule 12.	1st November 1988	1988/1794
Sections 121 (except for Southampton Institute of Higher Education) to 130 (including Schedule 7), 135, 219(2)(e), 226, 227(2) to (4), 228 and 229 and paragraphs 64 and 80 of Schedule 12.	21st November 1988	1988/1794
Sections 106 to 111, 117 and 118 and Schedule 13 as regards the repeal of section 61 of the Education Act 1944.	1st April 1989	1988/1794
Section 114, 214 to 216, and Schedule 13, as regards the repeal of section 3 of the Education Act 1967 and paragraph 14 of Schedule 3 to the Education Act 1980, and section 237(2) so far as it relates thereto.	30th November 1988	1988/2002
Section 218, paragraph 68 of Schedule 12 and section 237(1) so far as relating to those provisions, and Schedule 13, as regards the repeal of section 27 of the Education Act 1980 and paragraph 5 of Schedule 3 to the Education Act 1981, and section 237(2) so far as it relates thereto.	1st April 1989	1988/2002
Section 152(10) section 219 (to the extent not already in force), paragraph 63 of Schedule 12 and section 237(1) so far as relating to those provisions, and Schedule 13 so far as it relates to the repeal of sections 25 and 29(2) to (4) of the Education Act 1944, section 7 of the Education Act 1946, and the whole of the Education (No. 2) Act 1968 and section 237(2) so far as it relates thereto.	1st January 1989	1988/2271
Section 121 (to the extent not already in force).	1st February 1989	1988/2271
Section 120, paragraphs 54 to 57, 59, 61, 62, 65, 66, 69 to 79*, 86 to 98, 100, 101, 103 to 105 and 107 of Schedule 12 and section 237(1) so far as relating to those provisions. Schedule 13 so far as it relates to the repeal of sections 8(1)(b) (part), 42 to 46, 50 (part), 52(1) (part) 54 (part), 60, 62(2), 69 (part), 84 and 114 (part) of the Education Act 1944; section 8(3) of the Education Act 1946; section 31(1) and (4) of the London Government Act 1963; section 16 (part) of the Industrial Training Act 1964; sections 81(4)(a) (part) and 104(2) (part) of the Local Government Act 1972; sections 24 (part) and 25(6)(c)(ii) (part) of the Sex Discrimination Act 1975; sections 19(6)(c)(ii) (part) and 78(1) (part) of the Race Relations Act 1976; and section 56 (part) of the Education (No. 2) Act 1986; and section 237(2) so far as it relates thereto. * As to paragraph 77, see article 3 of this Order	1st April 1989	1988/2271
Section 7 (except in relation to ILEA schools), paragraph 99 of Schedule 12 and section 237(1) so far as relating to those provisions, and Schedule 13 so far as it relates to the repeal of sections 17(1) (part) and (4), 18(3) (part), (4), (6)(c)(ii) (part) and (8) (part), 19(3) and 20 of the Education (No. 2) Act 1986, and section 237(2) so far as it relates thereto.	1st August 1989	1988/2271

Provision	*Date of Commencement*	*S.I.No.*
Section 152 (to the extent not already in force)	1st April 1990	1988/2271
Section 7 (to the extent not already in force)	1st April 1990	1988/2271
Paragraph 58 of Schedule 12 and section 237(1) so far as it relates thereto and section 12 (except in relation to ILEA county schools).	1st March 1989	1989/164
Section 115.	1st May 1989	1989/164
Sections 5, 10(2) and (3) (the latter subsections partially) and 16.	1st August 1989	1989/164
Section 23(2) (except in relation to ILEA schools).	1st September 1989	1989/164
Sections 12 and 23(2) (to the extent not already in force).	1st April 1990	1989/164
Section 10(3) (partially).	1st August 1990	1989/164
Section 10(3) (partially).	1st August 1991	1989/164

STATUTORY INSTRUMENTS

1989 No. 502

REPRESENTATION OF THE PEOPLE

The European Parliamentary Elections (Northern Ireland) (Amendment) Regulations 1989

Made - - - -	*15th March 1989*
Coming into force	*15th March 1989*

Whereas a draft of these Regulations has been approved by a resolution of each House of Parliament;

Now, therefore, in exercise of the powers conferred upon me by paragraph 2 of Schedule 1 to the European Parliamentary Elections Act 1978(**a**), I hereby make the following Regulations:

1.—(1) These Regulations may be cited as the European Parliamentary Elections (Northern Ireland) (Amendment) Regulations 1989.

(2) These Regulations shall extend to Northern Ireland only.

2. In the right-hand column of Schedule 1 (application with modifications of provisions of the Representation of the People Acts) to the European Parliamentary Elections (Northern Ireland) Regulations 1986(**b**):

(a) in subsection (2) of section 76 (limitation of election expenses) of the Representation of the People Act 1983(**c**), as substituted for the purposes of European Parliamentary elections, for the words "£8,000" and "3.5p" there shall be substituted the words "£10,000" and "4.3p", respectively; and

(b) in the modification of rule 9(1) (deposit) of the rules in Schedule 1 to that Act(**d**), in its application for those purposes, for the words "£750" there shall be substituted the words "£1,000".

Northern Ireland Office
15th March 1989

Tom King
One of Her Majesty's Principal Secretaries of State

(**a**) 1978 c.10; the citation of this Act has been amended by section 3(1)(b) and (2)(b) of the European Communities (Amendment) Act 1986 (c.58) on the coming into force of the Single European Act (Cmnd. 9758) on 1st July 1987.

(**b**) S.I. 1986/2250; the citation of this instrument has been amended by the provisions referred to in the first footnote to these Regulations.

(**c**) 1983 c.2.

(**d**) Rule 9 was amended by section 13(a) of the Representation of the People Act 1985 (c.50).

EXPLANATORY NOTE

(This note is not part of the Regulations)

These Regulations, which apply in Northern Ireland only, amend the European Parliamentary Elections (Northern Ireland) Regulations 1986. They increase the maximum amount of a candidate's election expenses at a European Parliamentary election. The maximum amount of a candidate's election expenses is made up of a fixed sum (expressed in pounds) plus a sum expressed in pence (and fractions of pence) for each entry in the register of electors.

These Regulations also increase from £750 to £1,000 the sum which must be deposited with the returning officer by or on behalf of a candidate at a European Parliamentary election. A person cannot be validly nominated as a candidate at such an election unless this deposit has been made.

STATUTORY INSTRUMENTS

1989 No. 503

RIGHTS OF THE SUBJECT

The Access to Personal Files (Housing) Regulations 1989

Made - - - -	*15th March 1989*
Coming into force	*1st April 1989*

The Secretary of State for the Environment, as respects England, and the Secretary of State for Wales, as respects Wales, in exercise of the powers conferred upon them by section 3(1), (2), (3) and (6) of the Access to Personal Files Act 1987**(a)**, and of all other powers enabling them in that behalf, and after consultation with such authorities and bodies representing authorities as they think appropriate, hereby make the following Regulations, a draft of which has been laid before and approved by a resolution of each House of Parliament:–

Citation, commencement and application

1.—(1) These Regulations may be cited as the Access to Personal Files (Housing) Regulations 1989 and shall come into force on 1st April 1989.

(2) These Regulations apply to England and Wales.

Interpretation

2. In these Regulations:–

"the Act" means the Access to Personal Files Act 1987;

"appropriate health professional" means–

(a) the medical practitioner or dental practitioner who is currently or was most recently responsible for the clinical care of the tenant or the member of his family who is the subject of the relevant information in connection with the matters on which information is sought; or

(b) where there is more than one such practitioner, the practitioner who is the most suitable to advise on the matters on which information is sought; or

(c) where there is no practitioner available falling within sub-paragraph (a) or (b), a health professional who has the necessary experience and qualifications to advise on the matters on which information is sought;

"authority" means a "Housing Act local authority";

"care" includes examination, investigation and diagnosis;

"dental practitioner" and "medical practitioner" mean, respectively, a person registered under the Dentists Act 1984**(b)** and the Medical Act 1983**(c)**;

"health authority" has the same meaning as in section 128(1) of the National Health Service Act 1977**(d)**;

(a) 1987 c.37; paragraph 2(2) of Schedule 1 was amended by paragraph 80 of Schedule 17 to the Housing Act 1988 (c.50).

(b) 1984 c.24.

(c) 1983 c.54.

(d) 1977 c.49; this definition was amended by paragraph 11 of Schedule 3 to the Health and Social Security Act 1984 (c.48).

"health professional" means any person listed in the Schedule to these Regulations;

"inaccurate information" means relevant information which is inaccurate;

"relevant information" means, in relation to any tenant, accessible personal information held by the authority to which the tenant has addressed a requirement under these Regulations;

"tenant" means:–

(a) the tenant of a dwelling whose immediate landlord is an authority;

(b) the former tenant of a dwelling where at any time the immediate landlord was an authority;

(c) an individual who is in the process of applying for, or who has applied for, a tenancy of a dwelling from an authority.

An authority's duties as to access

3.—(1) Subject to the following provisions of these Regulations, where a tenant requires an authority in writing to inform him whether that authority holds relevant information of which he is, or under the Act is treated as, the subject, that authority shall within 40 days of receiving that requirement, or within 40 days of the giving of the consent referred to in regulation 4(1)(a)–

(a) inform the tenant in writing whether the authority holds such information, and

(b) if so, then unless the authority otherwise gives the tenant access to such information within that period and the tenant informs the authority that he does not want a copy of it, comply with regulation 5.

(2) The authority's duties under sub-paragraphs (a) and (b) of paragraph (1) arise only where–

(a) the tenant has paid any fee charged by the authority in accordance with paragraph (4), and

(b) the tenant has supplied information reasonably required to establish his identity (or the identity of any relevant member of his family) and to locate the information sought,

and, where sub-paragraphs (a) and (b) of this paragraph are not satisfied at the time of the written requirement referred to in paragraph (1), the time limit referred to in that paragraph runs from the date on which they are satisfied.

(3) The authority's duties under paragraph (1) apply to any relevant information held by the authority at the date of the written requirement, but the authority may supply information taking account of any correction or erasure made between that time and the time when the information is supplied if that correction or erasure would have been made regardless of the receipt of the requirement.

(4) The authority may charge a fee not exceeding £10 to a tenant making a requirement under paragraph (1) and no separate fee shall be charged for giving access to that information under sub-paragraph (b) of paragraph (1).

Information exempt from access

4.—(1) The authority's duty under regulation 3(1)(b) does not arise where–

(a) subject to paragraph (3), the information sought would itself or with other available information identify another individual (other than a member of the tenant's family) who has not consented to the disclosure, including an individual who has provided that information;

(b) the information sought would–

(i) in the opinion of an appropriate health professional expressed in response to a notification under regulation 6(2), or

(ii) in any case to which regulation 6 does not apply, in the opinion of the authority,

if supplied, be likely to cause serious harm to the physical or mental health of the tenant or of any other person;

(c) the information sought is information held by the authority for the purposes of prevention or detection of crime, or apprehension or prosecution of offenders, and disclosure of it would prejudice those matters;

(d) the information sought is information in respect of which a claim to legal professional privilege could be maintained in legal proceedings;

and where any part of the information falls within one or more of sub-paragraphs (a) to (d) the authority's duty arises in relation to the part that does not.

(2) Where the information sought falls within sub-paragraph (a) of paragraph (1), but is not as described in paragraph (3), the authority shall–

(a) within the period referred to in regulation 3(1), supply so much of the information sought as can be supplied without disclosing the identity of the other individual;

(b) within 14 days of its duties arising under regulation 3(1), inform that other individual in writing that the relevant information contains information which would identify him and ask him whether he consents to that information being disclosed to the tenant.

(3) Information falling within sub-paragraph (a) of paragraph (1) is not exempt from disclosure on the ground that it identifies an individual where the individual identified is–

(a) one who is or was a health professional and who provided the information in his capacity as a health professional having been involved with the care of the person the subject of the information; or

(b) one who acted in the course of his employment by the authority in connection with its functions as a landlord or who for reward provided services on behalf of the authority in performance of the authority's duties as a landlord.

(4) Where the information sought falls within sub-paragraph (b) of paragraph (1), the authority shall supply so much of the information sought as can, in the opinion of the appropriate health professional, or, as the case may be, the authority, be supplied without causing serious harm.

Copies of information

5.—(1) This regulation applies where an authority has informed a tenant in accordance with regulation 3(1)(a) that it holds relevant information, unless the authority has given the tenant access to the relevant information by means other than supplying him with a copy of it and the tenant has informed the authority that he does not want a copy of the relevant information.

(2) Where this regulation applies, the authority shall either–

(a) supply a copy of the relevant information free of charge; or

(b) notify the tenant that its duty under regulation 3(1)(b) does not arise because of the provisions of one or more of sub-paragraphs (a) to (d) in regulation 4(1), specifying the relevant sub-paragraph;

and, where its duty arises as to part only of the information, shall comply with paragraph (a) of this paragraph as to that part and with paragraph (b) as to the remainder.

(3) Where a copy of information is supplied to the tenant in terms which cannot easily be understood without explanation, the information shall be accompanied by a written explanation of those terms.

Information as to an individual's health

6.—(1) This regulation applies where the relevant information held relates to the physical or mental health of an individual and the authority believes it was provided by or on behalf of a health professional.

(2) Where this regulation applies the authority shall, within 14 days of its duties arising under regulation 3(1), inform in writing the body which appears to it to be the relevant health authority, or, if there is no such body, the person who appears to it to be the appropriate health professional that this regulation applies in relation to relevant information and that it or he should give the view of an appropriate health professional as to whether regulation 4(1)(b)(i) applies in whole or part to that information.

(3) The relevant health authority or appropriate health professional shall notify the authority of the view of the appropriate health professional within the 40 day period referred to in regulation 3(1).

(4) In this regulation "relevant health authority" means the health authority which employed, or retained the services of, the health professional whom the authority believes to have supplied the information to the authority in the course of his employment.

Correction and erasure of information

7.—(1) A tenant wishing an authority–

(a) to correct or erase inaccurate information of which he is, or under the Act is treated as, the subject; or

(b) to correct relevant information which consists of an expression of opinion about the tenant or a member of his family which is based on inaccurate information or which implies the existence of facts which are incorrect or misleading;

may by notice in writing require the authority to do so, and that requirement shall be accompanied by–

(i) sufficient information to enable the authority to identify the information and the record in which it is held; and

(ii) a statement of the correct information; and

(iii) any written evidence on which the tenant relies as supporting his view that the information is, or is based on or implies the existence of facts which are, incorrect or misleading.

(2) Unless the authority forms the view described in paragraph (4), it shall on receipt of such a requirement to correct or erase inaccurate information correct or erase the information as required by the tenant's notice, and shall as soon as reasonably practicable send a copy of the revised information to the tenant free of charge.

(3) Unless the authority forms the view described in paragraph (4), it shall on receipt of a requirement to correct an expression of opinion referred to in paragraph (1)(b)–

(a) clearly mark any document on which that expression of opinion appears that the authority accepts that the opinion was based on inaccurate information or, as the case may be, implies the existence of facts which are incorrect or misleading, and

(b) as soon as is reasonably practicable send to the tenant a copy of the document so marked free of charge.

(4) Where the authority forms the view that the relevant information is not inaccurate information, or is not an opinion based on facts which are incorrect or misleading or does not imply the existence of incorrect or misleading facts in the manner described by the tenant, it shall–

(a) place a written note recording the tenant's view with the information which it has decided not to correct or erase, and

(b) send a copy of the note referred to in sub-paragraph (a) to the tenant together with a copy of the information to which it relates, and

(c) send a notice, accompanying the copies referred to in (b), to the tenant stating that the information is not inaccurate information or is not an opinion based on facts which are incorrect or misleading or does not imply the existence of incorrect or misleading facts in the manner described by the tenant, and giving its reasons,

and it shall make no charge for supplying the copies referred to in sub-paragraph (b) or for supplying the notice referred to in sub-paragraph (c).

(5) Where the authority forms the view that part only of the relevant information is, or is an opinion based on facts which are, incorrect or misleading, or implies the existence of incorrect or misleading facts in the manner described in the tenant's notice, it shall comply with paragraph (2) or (3), as appropriate as to that part and with paragraph (4) as to the remainder.

Review

8.—(1) Where the tenant is, or under the Act is treated as, the subject of relevant information held by an authority and where he or a member of his family is aggrieved by any decision of that authority concerning his access to, or correction or erasure of, that information, the tenant may within 28 days of his being notified of the decision require that decision to be reviewed or reconsidered by the authority.

(2) The authority shall make such arrangements for the review of the decision as it thinks appropriate to ensure that the decision is either–

(a) reviewed by members of that authority who took no part in making the decision to be reviewed, or

(b) reconsidered by a meeting of the full authority,

and the tenant may make oral or written representations.

Nicholas Ridley
Secretary of State for
the Environment

13th March 1989

Peter Walker
Secretary of State for
Wales

15th March 1989

SCHEDULE

Regulation 2

HEALTH PROFESSIONALS

Description	*Statutory derivation (where applicable)*
Registered medical practitioner.	Medical Act 1983**(a)**, section 55.
Registered dentist.	Dentists Act 1984**(b)**, section 53(1).
Registered optician.	Opticians Act 1958**(c)**, section 30(1).
Registered pharmaceutical chemist.	Pharmacy Act 1954**(d)**, section 24(1).
Registered nurse, midwife or health visitor.	Nurses, Midwives and Health Visitors Act 1979**(e)**, section 10.
Registered chiropodist, dietitian, occupational therapist, orthoptist or physiotherapist (subject to the Note below).	Professions Supplementary to Medicine Act 1960**(f)**, section 1(2).
Clinical psychologist, child psychotherapist or speech therapist.	
Art therapist or music therapist employed by a health authority.	
Scientist employed by such an authority as a head of department.	

Note: This category shall be construed as not including any person belonging to a profession specified in the first column which, by virtue of an Order under section 10 of the Professions Supplementary to Medicine Act 1960, is for the time being treated as if it were not mentioned in section 1(2) of that Act and as including any person belonging to a profession not specified therein which is for the time being treated by virtue of such an Order as if it were mentioned therein.

(a) 1983 c.54.
(b) 1984 c.24.
(c) 1958 c.32.
(d) 1954 c.61.
(e) 1979 c.36.
(f) 1960 c.66; section 1(2) was amended by S.I. 1966/990 and by 1986/630.

EXPLANATORY NOTE

(This note is not part of the Regulations)

These Regulations provide for a tenant of a Housing Act local authority to have access to certain information relating to him or to a member of his family and held by the authority.

The tenant is required to apply in writing, and to pay any fee (not exceeding £10) demanded (regulation 3). The authority must, within the time specified, tell him whether it holds accessible information. Unless any such information is exempt from disclosure (regulations 4 and 6), the authority must give him access to it and, in the circumstances specified in the Regulations, supply him with copies (regulation 5).

Provision is made for inaccurate information, or expressions of opinion based or apparently based on inaccurate information, to be corrected or erased (regulation 7). Provision is also made for decisions made by the authority concerning access to information or its correction or erasure to be reviewed by members of the authority or reconsidered by a meeting of the full authority (regulation 8).

STATUTORY INSTRUMENTS

1989 No. 504

ANIMALS

ANIMAL HEALTH

The Testing of Poultry Flocks Order 1989

Made - - - -	*15th March 1989*
Coming into force	*16th March 1989*

The Minister of Agriculture, Fisheries and Food, the Secretary of State for Scotland and the Secretary of State for Wales, acting jointly, in exercise of the powers conferred on them by sections 1, 72, 86 and 87(5)(b) of the Animal Health Act 1981**(a)** and of all other powers enabling them in that behalf, hereby make the following Order:

Title and commencement

1. This Order may be cited as the Testing of Poultry Flocks Order 1989 and shall come into force on 16th March 1989.

Interpretation

2. In this Order–

"the Act" means the Animal Health Act 1981;

"appropriate Minister" means, in relation to England, the Minister, and in relation to Scotland or to Wales, the Secretary of State;

"chick box liner" means any material used to line a box or other container in which chicks are transported from a hatchery to any rearing premises;

"inspector" means a person appointed to be an inspector for the purposes of the Act by the Minister or by a local authority and, when used in relation to an officer of the Minister, includes a veterinary inspector;

"laboratory" means any laboratory which has the necessary facilities and personnel for carrying out, and is willing to carry out, tests on samples mentioned in Part I of the Schedule to this Order in accordance with the provisions of Part II of that Schedule;

"the Minister" means the Minister of Agriculture, Fisheries and Food;

"poultry" means domestic fowls of any age;

"poultry flock" means any flock of poultry consisting of–

(a) not less than 25 birds which are kept for the production of eggs for human consumption or breeding (including birds which are being reared to produce eggs for either of those purposes); or

(b) less than 25 birds the eggs of which are sold for human consumption;

"rearing premises" means any premises on which 25 or more birds are being reared at any time for the production of eggs for human consumption or breeding;

"veterinary inspector" means a veterinary inspector appointed by the Minister.

(a) 1981 c.22; as applied by S.I. 1989/285; section 86(1) contains a definition of "the Ministers" relevant to the exercise of the statutory powers under which this Order is made.

Taking of samples from poultry flocks for testing

3. It shall be the duty of the owner or person in charge of a poultry flock to ensure that–

(a) samples are taken in respect of the flock in such manner as is specified in Part I of the Schedule to this Order and at such times as are so specified; and

(b) such samples are submitted, within 24 hours of being taken, to a laboratory for testing for the presence of salmonella in accordance with the bacteriological method set out in Part II of that Schedule.

Testing of samples from poultry flocks and reporting of results of tests

4.—(1) It shall be the duty of the person in charge of a laboratory to which a sample has been submitted under article 3(b) above to ensure that–

(a) the sample is tested for the presence of salmonella in accordance with the bacteriological method set out in Part II of the Schedule to this Order; and

(b) the result of such a test is reported in writing as soon as practicable to the person who submitted the sample.

(2) If a person to whom a report is made under article 4(1)(b) above is not the owner or person in charge of the flock in respect of which the sample was taken, he shall immediately pass that report to the owner or person in charge of that flock.

Keeping of records

5. The owner or person in charge of a poultry flock shall–

(a) make a record of the result of any test carried out in accordance with article 3(b) above as soon as practicable after he has received a report of such result in accordance with article 4 above;

(b) retain such record for a period of 3 years from the date of the test; and

(c) produce such record to an inspector or officer of the appropriate Minister on demand being made by such person at any reasonable time during that period and allow a copy of it or an extract from it to be taken.

Offences

6. Any person who, without lawful authority or excuse, proof of which shall lie on him, contravenes or fails to comply with any provision of this Order commits an offence against the Act.

Local authority to enforce Order

7. The provisions of this Order shall, except where otherwise expressly provided, be executed and enforced by the local authority.

In Witness whereof the Official Seal of the Minister of Agriculture, Fisheries and Food is hereunto affixed on 12th March 1989.

(L.S.)

John MacGregor
Minister of Agriculture, Fisheries and Food

13th March 1989

Sanderson of Bowden
Minister of State, Scottish Office

15th March 1989

Peter Walker
Secretary of State for Wales

SCHEDULE

PART I

Article 3(a)

SAMPLES TO BE TAKEN

1. Except as otherwise provided in paragraph 2 below, the number of samples to be taken shall be as follows:–

Number of birds kept in a house or, on premises on which birds have free access to more than one house, number of birds on such premises	*Number of samples to be taken from that house or from those premises*
1–24	A number equal to the total number of birds there
25–29	20
30–39	25
40–49	30
50–59	35
60–89	40
90–199	50
200–499	55
500 or more	60

2. The samples to be taken shall comprise:–

(a) all chick box liners, up to a maximum of 10, from each consignment of chicks delivered to any rearing premises on any day, such samples to be taken on the day of the arrival of the chicks there;

(b) the carcases of all chicks, up to a maximum of 60, which are dead on arrival at any rearing premises and which die within 4 days of their arrival there;

(c) the carcases of all birds which die or are slaughtered when between 3 and 5 weeks of age, up to a maximum of 60;

(d) cloacal swabs taken (at the rate of one swab from each bird) from birds which have attained 4 weeks of age, such swabs being taken within 1 week of the birds attaining that age;

(e) cloacal swabs taken (at the rate of one swab from each bird) from birds which have attained 14 weeks of age, such swabs being taken within 1 week of the birds attaining that age;

(f) cloacal swabs taken (at the rate of one swab from each bird) within 1 week of the birds attaining 22, 26 and 30 weeks of age and at 8 week intervals thereafter, and

(g) the carcases of five birds (or of any such smaller number that there may be) which have died or been slaughtered when between 26 and 30 weeks of age.

3. The samples shall be identified in such a manner as to enable the laboratory to which they are submitted to know the age of the birds to which they relate.

PART II

Article 3(b) and 4

BACTERIOLOGICAL METHOD

Samples submitted for testing for the presence of salmonella shall be examined in the following prescribed manner on consecutive days and, where a laboratory at which samples have been received for testing on any day is unable to commence such an examination on that day, the samples shall be stored in a refrigerator until required for examination.

Day 1

(a) Chick box liners: a one gram portion shall be taken from each liner and the portions from separate liners shall be bulked to 10 grams and placed into 100 ml Selenite F broth(a).

(b) Cloacal swabs: cloacal swabs shall be bulked in batches of up to 25 and placed in 100 ml of Selenite F broth.

(c) Carcases of birds: the following organs shall be removed from the carcases of birds–

(i) from chicks—samples of the yolk sac, liver and terminal intestines (to include portions of small intestines, large intestine and caecal tonsil),

(ii) from birds of between 3 and 5 weeks of age—samples of liver and terminal intestines (to include portions of small intestines, large intestine and caecal tonsil), and

(iii) from adult egg laying birds—samples of ovary, liver and intestines (to include portions of small intestines, large intestines and caecal tonsil).

Samples of similar organs taken from the carcases of birds submitted shall then be bulked up to a maximum of 10 grams and placed into 100 ml Selenite F broth.

The inoculated Selenite F broth shall then be incubated at 37°C for 18–24 hours.

Day 2

The Selenite F broth shall be plated out on to two plates of Brilliant Green Agar ("BGA")(b) using a 2.5 mm diameter loop. The BGA plates shall be inoculated by a droplet taken from the edge of the surface of the fluid by drawing the loop over the whole of one plate in a zigzag pattern and continuing to the second plate without recharging the loop. The space between the loop streaks shall be 0.5 cm–1.0 cm. The plates shall be incubated at 37°C for 18–24 hours.

Day 3

The plates of BGA shall be examined and a minimum of 3 colonies from the plates showing suspicion of salmonella growth shall be subcultured on to a blood agar plate and a MacConkey agar plate and into biochemical composite media or equivalent. These media shall be incubated at 37°C overnight.

Day 4

The incubated plates and composite media or equivalent shall be examined and the findings recorded, discarding cultures which are obviously not salmonella. Slide serological tests shall be performed using salmonella polyvalent "O" and polyvalent "H" (phase 1 and 2) agglutinating sera on selected suspect colonies collected from the blood agar or MacConkey plates. If reactions occur with one or both sera, the colonies shall be typed by slide serology and a subculture sent to the Lasswade Veterinary Laboratory of the Ministry of Agriculture, Fisheries and Food situated at Penicuik, Midlothian (if the laboratory carrying out the test is in Scotland) or to a Veterinary Investigation Centre of that Ministry (if the laboratory carrying out the test is in England or Wales).

(a) Selenite F broth—Liefson (1936)
(commercially available as Oxoid CH 395 and L121, Lab M44a and 44b or equivalent)
The base shall be reconstituted according to the manufacturer's instructions.

(b) Brilliant Green Agar—Edel and Kampelmacher (1973)
(commercially available as Oxoid CM 329, Lab M34 or equivalent)
The agar shall be reconstituted according to the manufacturer's instructions and poured into 9 cm diameter plates.

References: Liefson E (1936) American Journal of Hygiene 24 423–432
Edel W & Kampelmacher EH (1973) Bulletin of the World Health Organisation 48 167

EXPLANATORY NOTE

(This note is not part of the Order)

This Order requires the owner or person in charge of a poultry flock to ensure that samples are taken in respect of the flock and are submitted to a laboratory for testing for the presence of salmonella (article 3 and Schedule). The Order also requires such an owner or person in charge to keep records of all such tests (article 5).

The Order also requires the person in charge of a laboratory to which any such sample has been submitted for testing to ensure that the test is carried out in the required manner and that the result of the test is reported to the person who submitted the sample and who, if he is not the owner or person in charge of the flock in respect of which the sample was taken, is required to pass the report to the owner or person in charge of the flock (article 4).

"Poultry flock" for the purposes of this Order means any flock of poultry consisting of not less than 25 birds which are kept for the production of eggs for human consumption or breeding (including birds which are being reared to produce eggs for either of those purposes) and any flock of poultry consisting of less than 25 birds the eggs of which are sold for human consumption (article 2).

STATUTORY INSTRUMENTS

1989 No. 505 (S.60)

LEGAL AID AND ADVICE, SCOTLAND

The Civil Legal Aid (Scotland) Amendment Regulations 1989

Made - - - -	*15th March 1989*
Laid before Parliament	*20th March 1989*
Coming into force	*10th April 1989*

The Secretary of State, in exercise of the powers conferred on him by sections 17(5), 37(1) and 42 of the Legal Aid (Scotland) Act 1986(**a**) and of all other powers enabling him in that behalf, and with the concurrence of the Treasury, hereby makes the following Regulations:

1.—(1) These Regulations may be cited as the Civil Legal Aid (Scotland) Amendment Regulations 1989 and shall come into force on 10th April 1989.

(2) In these Regulations, "the principal Regulations" means the Civil Legal Aid (Scotland) Regulations 1987(**b**).

2. In regulation 28(2) of the principal Regulations–

(a) in sub-paragraph (a) the figures of £500 and £250 shall be substituted by the figures £750 and £300, respectively;

(b) in sub-paragraph (b) the figure of £120 shall be substituted by the figure £750.

3. In Schedule 2 to the principal Regulations–

(a) after rule 8 there shall be inserted the following:–

"8A. There shall be a deduction in respect of amounts payable or estimated to be payable in the 12 months following the application by the person concerned in respect of community charge and community water charges as defined in section 26(1), and the rate as defined in section 26(2), of the Abolition of Domestic Rates Etc. (Scotland) Act 1987(**c**)," and

(b) in each of rules 9(2)(b) and (4) after the word "rates" there shall be inserted the following:–

"leviable before 1 April 1989 in Scotland and 1 April 1990 in England and Wales".

(**a**) 1986 c.47.
(**b**) S.I. 1987/381, amended by S.I. 1987/431, 1988/490, 1171 and 1891.
(**c**) 1987 c.47.

James Douglas-Hamilton
St. Andrew's House, Edinburgh Parliamentary Under Secretary of State,
14th March 1989 Scottish Office

We concur,

Alan Howarth
David Maclean
15th March 1989 Two of the Lords Commissioners of Her Majesty's Treasury

---

EXPLANATORY NOTE

(This note is not part of the Regulations)

These Regulations amend the Civil Legal Aid (Scotland) Regulations 1987 by–

(a) increasing the amounts by which an assisted person's resources may change before they are required to have them re-assessed (regulation 2) and

(b) providing that account is taken of payments under the provisions of the Abolition of Domestic Rates Etc. (Scotland) Act 1987 in respect of rates and community charges in computing disposable income of legal aid applicants (regulation 3).

STATUTORY INSTRUMENTS

1989 No. 506 (S.61)

LEGAL AID AND ADVICE, SCOTLAND

The Advice and Assistance (Scotland) Amendment Regulations 1989

Made - - - -	*15th March 1989*
Laid before Parliament	*20th March 1989*
Coming into force	*10th April 1989*

The Secretary of State, in exercise of the powers conferred upon him by sections 37(1) and 42 of the Legal Aid (Scotland) Act 1986(**a**) and of all other powers enabling him in that behalf, and with the concurrence of the Treasury, hereby makes the following Regulations:

1.—(1) These Regulations may be cited as the Advice and Assistance (Scotland) Amendment Regulations 1989 and shall come into force on 10th April 1989.

(2) In these Regulations, "the principal Regulations" means the Advice and Assistance (Scotland) Regulations 1987(**b**).

2. In Rule 7(d) of Schedule 2 to the principal Regulations the figures of £200, £120 and £60 shall be substituted by the figures £335, £200 and £100, respectively.

James Douglas-Hamilton
Parliamentary Under Secretary of State,
Scottish Office

St. Andrew's House, Edinburgh
14th March 1989

We concur,

Alan Howarth
David Maclean
Two of the Lords Commissioners of Her Majesty's Treasury

15th March 1989

(**a**) 1986 c.47.
(**b**) S.I. 1987/382, amended by S.I. 1987/883 and 1356, 1988/489 and 1131.

EXPLANATORY NOTE

(This note is not part of the Regulations)

These Regulations amend the Advice and Assistance (Scotland) Regulations 1987 by increasing the allowances for dependants in the assessment of disposable capital. The allowance for the first dependant is increased from £200 to £335, for the second from £120 to £200 and for every other dependant from £60 to £100.

STATUTORY INSTRUMENTS

1989 No. 507 (S.59)

COMMUNITY CHARGES, SCOTLAND

WATER SUPPLY, SCOTLAND

Community Charges (Deductions from Income Support) (Scotland) Regulations 1989

Made - - - -	*15th March 1989*
Laid before Parliament	*17th March 1989*
Coming into force -	*8th April 1989*

The Secretary of State for Social Security in exercise of powers conferred by section 31(3) of and paragraph 7A of Schedule 2 to the Abolition of Domestic Rates Etc. (Scotland) Act 1987**(a)** and those provisions as read with paragraph 11 of Schedule 5 to that Act**(b)** and with the Community Water Charges (Scotland) Regulations 1988**(c)** made thereunder and of all other powers enabling him in that behalf, after consultation with the Council on Tribunals in accordance with section 10 of the Tribunals and Inquiries Act 1971**(d)**, hereby makes the following Regulations:

Citation, commencement and interpretation

1.—(1) These Regulations may be cited as the Community Charges (Deductions from Income Support) (Scotland) Regulations 1989 and shall come into force on 8th April 1989.

(2) In these Regulations, unless the context otherwise requires–

"the 1975 Act" means the Social Security Act 1975**(e)**;

"adjudication officer" means an officer appointed in accordance with section 97(1) of the 1975 Act;

"appropriate social security office" means an office of the Department of Social Security which is normally open to the public for the receipt of claims for income support and includes an office of the Department of Employment which is normally open to the public for the receipt of claims for unemployment benefit;

"Commissioner" means the Chief or any other Social Security Commissioner appointed in accordance with section 97(3) of the 1975 Act or section 13(5) of the Social Security Act 1980**(f)**, and includes a Tribunal of 3 Commissioners constituted in accordance with section 116 of the 1975 Act;

"couple" means a married or unmarried couple;

"debtor" means a person who is in arrears in respect of community charges and against whom a summary warrant or decree has been obtained;

"5 per cent. of the personal allowance for a single claimant aged not less than 25" and

(a) 1987 c.47; paragraph 7A was inserted by the Local Government Finance Act 1988 (c.41), Schedule 12, paragraph 36(10).
(b) Paragraph 11 was amended by the Local Government Finance Act 1988, Schedule 12, paragraph 38.
(c) S.I. 1988/1538.
(d) 1971 c.62.
(e) 1975 c.14.
(f) 1980 c.30.

"5 per cent. of the personal allowance for a couple where both members are aged not less than 18" means, in each case, where the percentage is not a multiple of 5 pence, the sum obtained by rounding that 5 per cent. to the next higher such multiple;

"income support" means income support within the meaning of the Social Security Act 1986(**a**);

"payments to third parties" means direct payments to third parties in accordance with Schedule 9 to the Social Security (Claims and Payments) Regulations 1987(**b**);

"single debtor" means a debtor who is not a member of a couple; and

"tribunal" means a social security appeal tribunal constituted in accordance with section 97(2) to (2E) of the 1975 Act(**c**).

(3) Any reference in these Regulations to community charges includes a reference to those charges as read with paragraph 11 of Schedule 5 to the Abolition of Domestic Rates Etc. (Scotland) Act 1987 and the Community Water Charges (Scotland) Regulations 1988.

(4) Unless the context otherwise requires, any reference in these Regulations to a numbered regulation or Schedule is a reference to the regulation and Schedule bearing that number in the Regulations and any reference in a regulation or Schedule to a numbered paragraph is a reference to the paragraph of that regulation or Schedule having that number.

Deductions from income support

2.—(1) Without prejudice to their right to pursue any other means of recovering arrears of community charges, a levying authority may apply to the Secretary of State asking him to deduct sums from any amount payable to a debtor by way of income support.

(2) An application from a levying authority shall be in writing and shall contain the following particulars–

(a) the name, address and date of birth of the debtor or where the summary warrant or decree names a couple, the names, address and dates of birth of both of them;

(b) the name and place of the court at which the summary warrant or decree was obtained;

(c) the date when the summary warrant or decree was obtained;

(d) the total amount of the arrears specified in the summary warrant or decree;

(e) the amount which the levying authority wishes to have deducted from income support.

(3) Where it appears to the Secretary of State that an application from a levying authority gives insufficient particulars to enable the debtor to be identified he may require the levying authority to furnish such further particulars as may reasonably be required.

(4) Subject to regulation 4(1), where the Secretary of State receives an application from a levying authority, he shall refer it to an adjudication officer who shall determine, so far as is practicable within 14 days of its submission to him, the following questions–

(a) whether there is sufficient entitlement to income support so as to enable the Secretary of State to make any deduction–

(i) in the case of a single debtor or a debtor who is a member of a couple, at a rate of 5 per cent. of the personal allowance for a single claimant aged not less than 25(**d**); or

(ii) in the case where the decree or summary warrant names a couple and income support is payable in respect of both of them at a rate of 5 per cent. of the personal allowance for a couple where both members are aged not less than 18(**e**),

and if the amount payable by way of income support to the debtor were to be 10

(**a**) 1986 c.50.
(**b**) S.I. 1987/1968, amended by S.I. 1988/522, 1725 and 1989/136.
(**c**) Sub-sections 97(2) to (2E) of the 1975 Act were substituted for sub-section 97(2) by the Health and Social Services and Social Security Ajudications Act 1983 (c.41), Schedule 8, paragraph 2 and sub-section 97(2A) was substituted for sub-sections 97(2A) and (2B) by the Health and Social Security Act 1984 (c.48), section 16(a).
(**d**) *See* Schedule 2 to S.I. 1987/1967, paragraph 1(1)(c).
(**e**) *See* Schedule 2 to S.I. 1987/1967, paragraph 1(3)(c).

pence or more after any such deduction, the adjudication officer shall determine that there is sufficient entitlement;

(b) the priority of any sum to be deducted as against any payments to third parties where there is insufficient entitlement to income support to meet both the deduction in respect of arrears of community charges and those payments to third parties, the following priorities shall apply–

(i) any liability mentioned in paragraph 3 (housing costs) of Schedule 9 to the Social Security (Claims and Payments) Regulations 1987;

(ii) any liability mentioned in paragraph 5 (certain service charges for fuel, and rent) of Schedule 9 to those regulations;

(iii) any liability mentioned in paragraph 6 of Schedule 9 to those regulations;

(iv) any liability for arrears in respect of community charges.

(5) Subject to any right of appeal or review under these regulations, the decision of the adjudication officer shall be final.

Notification of decision

3. The Secretary of State shall notify the debtor in writing of the adjudication officer's decision as soon as practicable after he receives that decision and at the same time he shall notify the debtor of his right of appeal.

Circumstances, time of making and termination of deductions

4.—(1) The Secretary of State shall make deductions from income support in respect of community charges only–

(a) where the debtor is entitled to income support throughout any benefit week; and

(b) in respect of one application (the original application) at a time, and where, at the time he is making deductions under the original application, the Secretary of State receives one or more applications under regulation 2(1), he shall not refer them to the adjudication officer until he has ceased making deductions under the original application when he shall forthwith refer the applications to the adjudication officer in the chronological order in which they were made.

(2) The Secretary of State shall make deductions from income support in respect of arrears of community charges at a time which corresponds to the payment of income support to the debtor**(a)** and he shall cease making deductions when–

(a) a payment to a third party has priority;

(b) there is insufficient entitlement to income support to enable him to make the deduction;

(c) entitlement to income support ceases;

(d) the summary warrant ceases to have effect or the decree is rescinded; or

(e) the debt is discharged.

(3) Payments shall be made to the levying authority at such intervals as the Secretary of State may decide.

Appeal

5.—(1) Where the adjudication officer has decided a question under regulation 2(4), the debtor may appeal to a tribunal.

(2) An appeal lies to a Commissioner from any decision of a tribunal on the grounds that the decision of that tribunal was erroneous in point of law and the persons who may appeal are the debtor and the adjudication officer.

(3) If it appears to the Chief Commissioner or, in the case of his inability to act, to such other of the Commissioners as he may have nominated to act for that purpose, that an appeal falling to be heard by one of the Commissioners involves a question of law of special difficulty, he may direct that the appeal be dealt with, not by that Commissioner alone but by a Tribunal consisting of any 3 of the Commissioners.

(a) *See* Schedule 7 to S.I. 1987/1968.

(4) An appeal on a question of law lies to the Court of Session from any decision of a Commissioner on a question of law with the leave of the Commissioner who gave the decision and the persons who may appeal are–

(a) the debtor;

(b) the adjudication officer; and

(c) the Secretary of State.

Review

6.—(1) Any decision under these Regulations of an adjudication officer, a tribunal or a Commissioner may be reviewed at any time by an adjudication officer if–

(a) the officer is satisfied that the decision was given in ignorance of, or was based on a mistake as to, some material fact; or

(b) there has been a relevant change of circumstances since the decision was given.

(2) Any decision of an adjudication officer may be reviewed at any time by an adjudication officer on the grounds that the decision was erroneous in point of law.

(3) A question may be raised with a view to review under this regulation by means of an application in writing to an adjudication officer, stating the grounds of the application.

(4) On receipt of any such application the adjudication officer shall take it into consideration and, so far as is practicable, dispose of it within 14 days of its receipt.

(5) A decision given on review or a refusal to review a decision under this regulation shall be subject to appeal in the same manner as an original decision and regulation 5(1) and Schedule 2 shall apply with the necessary modifications in relation to a decision given on review as they apply to the original decision on a question.

Correction of accidental errors

7.—(1) Subject to regulation 9, accidental errors in any decision or record of a decision made under regulations 2(4), 5 and 6 and Schedule 2 may at any time be corrected by the person or tribunal by whom the decision was made or a person or tribunal of like status.

(2) A correction made to, or to the record of, a decision shall be deemed to be part of the decision, or of that record, and written notice of it shall be given as soon as practicable to every party to the proceedings.

Setting aside decisions on certain grounds

8.—(1) Subject to regulation 9, on application made by a party to the proceedings, a decision made under regulations 2(4), 5, 6 and Schedule 2 by an adjudication officer, tribunal or a Commissioner may be set aside by the person or tribunal by whom the decision was made, or by a person or tribunal of like status, in a case where it appears just to set that decision aside on the grounds that–

(a) a document relating to the proceedings in which the decision was given was not sent to, or was not received at an appropriate time by a party or their representative or was not received at the appropriate time by the person who gave the decision;

(b) a party to the proceedings in which the decision was given or the party's representative was not present at the hearing relating to the proceedings; or

(c) the interests of justice so require.

(2) An application under this regulation shall be made in accordance with regulation 10 and Schedule 1.

(3) Where an application to set aside is entertained under paragraph (1) every party to the proceedings shall be sent a copy of the application and shall be afforded a reasonable opportunity of making representations on it before the application is determined.

(4) Notice in writing of a determination on an application to set aside a decision shall

be given to every party to the proceedings as soon as may be practicable and the notice shall contain a statement giving the reasons for the determination.

(5) For the purpose of determining under these Regulations an application to set aside, there shall be disregarded any provision in any enactment or instrument to the effect that any notice or other document required or authorised to be given or sent to any person shall be deemed to have been given or sent if it was sent to that person's last known notified address.

Provisions common to regulations 7 and 8

9.—(1) In calculating any time specified in Schedule 1 there shall be disregarded any day falling before the day on which notice was given of a correction of a decision or the record thereof pursuant to regulation 7 or on which notice is given that a determination of a decision shall not be set aside following an application under regulation 8, as the case may be.

(2) There shall be no appeal against a correction made under regulation 7 or a refusal to make such a correction or against a determination under regulation 8.

(3) Nothing in regulation 7 or 8 shall be construed as derogating from any power to correct errors or set aside decisions which is exercisable apart from these regulations.

Manner of making applications or appeals and time limits

10.—(1) Any application or appeal set out in Column (1) of Schedule 1 shall be made or given by sending or delivering it to the appropriate office within the specified time.

(2) In this regulation–

(a) "appropriate office" means the office specified in Column (2) of Schedule 1 opposite the description of the relevant application or appeal listed in Column (1); and

(b) "the specified time" means the time specified in Column (3) of that Schedule opposite the description of the relevant application or appeal so listed.

(3) The time specified by this regulation and Schedule 1 for the making of any application or appeal (except an application to the chairman of a tribunal for leave to appeal to a Commissioner) may be extended for special reasons, even though the time so specified may already have expired, and any application for an extension of time under this paragraph shall be made to and determined by the person to whom the application or appeal is sought to be made or, in the case of a tribunal, its chairman.

(4) An application under paragraph (3) for an extension of time which has been refused may not be renewed.

(5) Any application or appeal set out in Column 1 of Schedule 1 shall be in writing and shall contain:–

(a) the name and address of the appellant or applicant;

(b) the particulars of the grounds on which the appeal or application is to be made or given;

(c) his address for service of documents if it is different to that in (a); and

(d) in the case of an appeal to the Commissioner, subject to paragraph 21(2) of Schedule 2, the notice of appeal shall have annexed to it a copy of the determination granting leave to appeal and a copy of the decision against which leave to appeal has been granted.

(6) Where it appears to an adjudication officer, or chairman of a tribunal, or Commissioner that an application or appeal which is made to him, or the tribunal, gives insufficient particulars to enable the question at issue to be determined, he may require, and in the case of a Commissioner, direct that the person making the application or appeal shall furnish such further particulars as may reasonably be required.

(7) The conduct and procedure in relation to any application or appeal shall be in accordance with Schedule 2.

Manner and time for the service of notices etc.

11.—(1) Any notice or other document required or authorised to be given or sent to any person under these Regulations shall be deemed to have been given or sent if it was sent by post properly addressed and pre-paid to that party at his ordinary or last notified address.

(2) Any notice or other document required or authorised to be given to an appropriate social security office or office of the clerk to the tribunal shall be treated as having been so given or sent on the day that it is received in the appropriate social security office or office of the clerk to the tribunal.

(3) Any notice or document required to be given, sent or submitted to, or served on, a Commissioner–

(a) shall be given, sent or submitted to the office of the Social Security Commissioners;

(b) shall be deemed to have been given, sent or submitted if it was sent by post properly addressed and pre-paid to the office of the Social Security Commissioners.

Signed by authority of the Secretary of State for Social Security.

Nicholas Scott
Minister of State,
Department of Social Security

15th March 1989

SCHEDULE 1

Regulation 10(1)

TIME LIMITS FOR MAKING APPLICATIONS OR APPEALS

(1) *Application or appeal*	(2) *Appropriate Office*	(3) *Specified time*
1. Appeal to a tribunal from an adjudication officer's decision (regulation 5).	An appropriate social security office.	3 months beginning with the date when notice in writing of the decision was given to the appellant.
2. Application to the Chairman for leave to appeal to a Commissioner from the decision of a tribunal (paragraph 16, Schedule 2).	The office of the Clerk to the tribunal	3 months beginning with the date when a copy of the record of the decision was given to the applicant.
3. Application to– (a) an adjudication officer; (b) a tribunal; or (c) a Commissioner, to set aside decision (regulation 8).	(a) An appropriate social security office; (b) The Office of the clerk to the tribunal; (c) The office of the Social Security Commissioners.	(a) and (b) 3 months beginning with the date when notice in writing of the decision was given to the applicant. (c) 30 days from the date on which notice in writing of the decision was given to the applicant by the office of the Social Security Commissioners.
4. Application for leave to appeal to the Commissioner where the chairman has refused leave (paragraph 17 Schedule 2).	The office of the Social Security Commissioners.	42 days beginning with the date when notice in writing of the decision by the chairman to refuse leave was given to the applicant.

(1) *Application or appeal*	(2) *Appropriate Office*	(3) *Specified time*
5. Appeal to the Commissioner (regulation 5).	The office of the Social Security Commissioners.	42 days beginning with the date when notice in writing of the decision was given to the applicant.
6. Leave to appeal to the Court of Session (regulation 5(4)).	The Office of the Social Security Commissioners.	3 months beginning with the date when notice in writing of the decision was given to the applicant.

Regulation 10(7)

SCHEDULE 2

CONDUCT AND PROCEDURE IN RELATION TO APPEALS AND APPLICATIONS

Common provisions in connection with appeals and applications

1.—(1) Subject to the provisions of these Regulations–

(a) the procedure in connection with the consideration of any appeal or any application in relation to questions to which these Regulations relate, shall be such as the adjudication officer, chairman of the tribunal or the Commissioner may determine;

(b) any person who by virtue of these Regulations has the right to be heard at a hearing may be accompanied and represented by another person whether having professional qualifications or not, and for the purposes of any proceedings at any hearing any such representative shall have all the rights and powers to which the person whom he represents is entitled under these Regulations.

(2) Nothing in these Regulations shall prevent a member of the Scottish Committee of the Council on Tribunals in his capacity as such from being present at any oral hearing before a tribunal or a Commissioner, notwithstanding that the hearing is not in public.

2. Reasonable notice (being not less than 10 days beginning on the day on which notice is given and ending on the day before the hearing of the appeal) of the time and place of any oral hearing before the tribunal or the Commissioner shall be given to every party to the proceedings, and if such notice has not been given to a person to whom it should have been given under the provisions of this paragraph the hearing may only proceed with the consent of that person.

3. At any oral hearing any party shall be entitled to be present and be heard.

Postponements and adjournments

4.—(1) Where a person to whom notice of an oral hearing has been given wishes to apply for that hearing to be postponed he shall do so in writing to the chairman of the tribunal or the Commissioner stating his reasons for the application and the chairman or the Commissioner may grant or refuse the application as he sees fit.

(2) An oral hearing may be adjourned at any time on the application of any party to the proceedings or of the motion of the tribunal or the Commissioner.

Striking out of proceedings for want of prosecution

5.—(1) The chairman of a tribunal or the Commissioner may, subject to paragraph (2) on the application of any party to the proceedings or of his own motion, strike out any appeal or application for want of prosecution.

(2) Before making an order under paragraph (1) the chairman of a tribunal or the Commissioner, as the case may be, shall send notice to the person against whom it is proposed that any order should be made giving him a reasonable opportunity to show cause why such an order should not be made.

(3) The chairman of a tribunal or the Commissioner, as the case may be, may, on application by the party concerned, give leave to reinstate any application or appeal which has been struck out in accordance with sub-paragraph (1).

APPLICATION AND APPEALS TO THE TRIBUNAL

Procedure in connection with determinations

6. For the purpose of arriving at its decision a tribunal shall, and for the purpose of discussing any question of procedure may, notwithstanding anything in these Regulations, order all persons not being members of the tribunal other than its clerk to withdraw from the sitting of the tribunal except that–

(a) a member of the Scottish Committee of the Council on Tribunals, the President of Social Security Appeal Tribunals and any full time chairman; and

(b) with the leave of the chairman of the tribunal, if no person having the right to be heard objects, any person mentioned in paragraph 13(1)(b) and (d) (except a person undergoing training as an adjudicating officer)

may remain present at any such sitting.

Oral hearings

7. A tribunal shall hold an oral hearing of every appeal made to them.

8. If a party to the proceedings to whom notice has been given under paragraph 2 should fail to appear at the hearing, the tribunal may, having regard to all the circumstances, including any explanation offered for the absence, proceed with the case notwithstanding his absence.

9. Any oral hearing before a tribunal shall be in public except where the debtor requests a private hearing, or (in any case) the chairman is satisfied that intimate personal or financial circumstances may have to be disclosed, or that considerations of public security are involved, in which case the hearing shall be in private.

10. Any case may with the consent of the debtor or his representative but not otherwise, be proceeded with in the absence of any one member other than the chairman.

11. Where an oral hearing is adjourned and at the hearing after the adjournment the tribunal is differently constituted otherwise than through the operation of paragraph 10 the proceedings at that hearing shall be by way of a complete rehearing of the case.

12.—(1) The decision of the majority of the tribunal shall be the decision of the tribunal but, where the tribunal consists of an even number, the chairman shall have a second or casting vote.

(2) The chairman of a tribunal shall–

(a) record in writing all its decisions; and

(b) include in the record of every decision a statement of the reasons for such decision and of their findings on questions of fact material thereto; and

(c) if a decision is not unanimous, record a statement that one of the members dissented and the reasons given by him for so dissenting.

(3) As soon as may be practicable after a case has been decided by a tribunal, a copy of the record of the decision made in accordance with this paragraph shall be sent to every party to the proceedings who shall also be informed of the conditions governing appeals to a Commissioner.

13.—(1) The following persons shall be entitled to be present at an oral hearing (whether or not it is in private) but shall take no part in the proceedings–

(a) the President of Social Security Appeal Tribunals;

(b) any person undergoing training as a chairman or other member of a tribunal, or as a clerk to a tribunal, or as an adjudication officer;

(c) any person acting on behalf of the President of the Social Security Appeal Tribunals, the Chief Adjudication Officer appointed under section 97(1B)**(a)** of the 1975 Act, or the Secretary of State, in the training or supervision of clerks to tribunals or adjudication officers or officers of the Secretary of State or in the monitoring of standards of adjudication by adjudication officers; and

(d) with the leave of the chairman of the tribunal and with the consent of every party to the proceedings actually present, any other person.

(2) Nothing in sub-paragraph (1) affects the rights of any person mentioned in heads (a) and (b) at any oral hearing where he is sitting as a member of the tribunal or acting as its clerk, and nothing in this paragraph prevents the presence at an oral hearing of any witness.

14. Any person entitled to be heard at an oral hearing may address the tribunal, may give evidence, may call witnesses and may put questions directly to any other person called as a witness.

(a) Sub-sections 97(1) to (1E) of the 1975 Act were substituted for sub-section 97(1) by the Health and Social Services and Social Security Adjudications Act 1983 (c.41), Schedule 8, paragraph 2.

Withdrawal of Appeals

15. Any appeal to the tribunal under these Regulations may be withdrawn by the person who made the appeal–

(a) before the hearing begins by giving written notice of intention to withdraw to the tribunal and with the consent in writing of the adjudication officer who made the decision; or

(b) after the hearing has begun with the leave of the chairman of the tribunal at any time before the determination is made.

Application to a Chairman for leave to appeal from a tribunal to a Commissioner

16.—(1) Subject to the following provisions of this paragraph, an application to the chairman of a tribunal for leave to appeal to a Commissioner from a decision of the tribunal shall be made–

(a) orally at the hearing after the decision is announced by the tribunal; or

(b) as provided by regulation 10 and Schedule 1.

(2) Where an application in writing for leave to appeal is made by an adjudication officer, the clerk to the tribunal shall, as soon as may be practicable, send a copy of the application to every other party to the proceedings.

(3) The decision of the chairman on an application for leave to appeal made under sub-paragraph (1)(a) shall be recorded in the record of the proceedings of the tribunal, and an application under sub-paragraph (1)(b) shall be recorded in writing and a copy shall be sent to each party to the proceedings.

(4) Where in any case it is impracticable, or it would be likely to cause undue delay for an application for leave to appeal against a decision of a tribunal to be determined by the person who was the chairman of that tribunal, that application shall be determined by any other person qualified under section 97(2D) of the 1975 Act to act as a chairman of tribunals.

(5) A person who has made an application to the chairman of a tribunal for leave to appeal to a Commissioner may withdraw his application at any time before it is determined by giving written notice of intention to the chairman.

APPLICATIONS AND APPEAL TO A COMMISSIONER

Applications to a Commissioner for leave to appeal from a tribunal

17. Subject to paragraph 18, an application may be made to a Commissioner for leave to appeal against a decision of a tribunal only where the applicant has been refused leave to appeal by the chairman of a tribunal.

18. Where there has been a failure to apply to the chairman for leave to appeal during the time specified in Schedule 1, an application for leave to appeal may be made to a Commissioner who may, if for special reasons he thinks fit, accept and proceed to consider and determine the application.

Notice of Application

19.—(1) Where the applicant has been refused leave to appeal by the chairman of a tribunal otherwise than by a decision recorded in the record of proceedings of the tribunal, the notice shall also have annexed to it a copy of the decision refusing leave and shall state the date on which the applicant was given notice in writing of the refusal of leave.

(2) Where the applicant has failed–

(a) to apply within the specified time to the chairman of a tribunal for leave to appeal; or

(b) to comply with paragraph 4 of Schedule 1;

the notice of application for leave to appeal shall, in addition to complying with regulation 10(5) state the grounds relied upon for seeking acceptance of the application notwithstanding that the relevant period has expired.

20. Where an application for leave to appeal is made by an adjudication officer the applicant shall, as soon as may be practicable, send the respondent a copy of the notice of application for leave to appeal.

Determination of applications for leave

21.—(1) The office of the Social Security Commissioners shall notify the applicant and the respondent in writing of the determination by a Commissioner of the application.

(2) Subject to a direction by a Commissioner to the contrary, where a Commissioner grants leave to appeal on an application notice of appeal shall be deemed to have been duly given on the date when notice of the determination is given to the applicant and the notice of application shall be deemed to be a notice of appeal duly served under paragraph 5 of Schedule 1.

(3) If on consideration of an application for leave to appeal to him from the decision of a tribunal the Commissioner grants leave he may, with the consent of the applicant and each respondent treat the application as an appeal and determine any question arising on the application as though it were a question arising on an appeal.

Acknowledgement of a notice of appeal and notification to each respondent

22. The office of the Social Security Commissioners shall send–

(a) to the appellant an acknowledgement of the receipt of a notice of appeal; and

(b) to each respondent a copy of the notice of appeal.

Respondent's written observations

23.—(1) A respondent who wishes to submit to a Commissioner written observations on the appeal shall do so within 30 days of being given notice in writing of it.

(2) Any such written observations shall include–

(a) the respondent's name and address for service;

(b) in the case of observations on an appeal, a statement as to whether or not he opposes the appeal;

(c) in any case, the grounds upon which the respondent proposes to rely, and

a copy of any written observations from a respondent shall be sent by the office of the Social Security Commissioners to the other parties.

Written observations in reply

24. Any party may, within 30 days of being sent written observations submitted in accordance with paragraph 24 submit to a Commissioner written observations in reply and a copy of any such observations shall be sent by the office of the Social Security Commissioners to the other parties.

Directions

25.—(1) At any stage of the proceedings, a Commissioner may, either of his own motion or on application setting out the direction which the applicant is seeking, give such directions as he considers necessary or desirable for the efficient and effective despatch of the proceedings.

(2) Without prejudice to paragraphs 23 and 24 or to sub-paragraph (1) above, a Commissioner may direct any party to any proceedings before him to make such written observations as may seem to him necessary to enable the question at issue to be determined.

(3) Unless a Commissioner shall otherwise determine, an application made pursuant to sub-paragraph (2) above shall be copied by the office of the Social Security Commissioners to the other parties.

Requests for oral hearing

26.—(1) Subject to sub-paragraphs (2) and (3) a Commissioner may determine an application for leave to appeal or an appeal without an oral hearing.

(2) Where, in any proceedings before a Commissioner, a request is made by any party for an oral hearing the Commissioner shall grant the request unless, after considering all the circumstances of the case and the reasons put forward in the request for the hearing, he is satisfied that the application or appeal can properly be determined without a hearing, in which event he may proceed to determine the case without a hearing and he shall in writing either before giving his determination or decision, or in it, inform the person making the request that it has been refused.

(3) A Commissioner may of his own motion at any stage, if he is satisfied that an oral hearing is desirable, direct such a hearing.

Oral hearings

27.—(1) If any party to the proceedings to whom notice of an oral hearing has been given under paragraph 2 should fail to appear at the hearing, the Commissioner may, having regard to all the circumstances, including any explanation offered for the absence, proceed with the case notwithstanding his absence, or the Commissioner may give such directions with a view to the determination of the case as he thinks fit.

(2) Any oral hearing shall be in public except where the Commissioner is satisfied that intimate personal or financial circumstances may have to be disclosed or that considerations of public security are involved, in which case the hearing or any part of it shall be in private.

(3) Where a Commissioner holds an oral hearing the following persons shall be entitled to be present and be heard–

(a) the person making the application, appeal or reference;

(b) the debtor;

(c) an adjudication officer; or

(d) any other person with the leave of the Commissioner.

Summoning of witnesses

28.—(1) A Commissioner may summon any person to attend as a witness, at such time and place as may be specified in the summons, at an oral hearing of an application to a Commissioner for leave to appeal, or of an appeal to answer any questions or produce any documents in his custody or under his control which relate to any matter in question in the proceedings.

Provided that no person shall be required to attend in obedience to such a summons unless he has been given at least 7 days notice of the hearing or, if less than 7 days, has informed the Commissioner that he accepts such notice as he has been given.

(2) A Commissioner may upon the application of a person summoned under this paragraph set the summons aside.

Withdrawal of applications for leave to appeal and appeals

29. At any time before it is determined–

(a) an application for leave to appeal may be withdrawn by the applicant by giving written notice to a Commissioner of his intention to do so,

(b) an appeal may be withdrawn by the appellant with leave of the Commissioner, and

a Commissioner may, on application by the party concerned give leave to reinstate any application or appeal which has been withdrawn and on giving leave he may give such directions as he thinks fit.

Irregularities

30. Any irregularity resulting from failure to comply with the requirements of these Regulations before a Commissioner has determined the application or appeal shall not by itself invalidate any proceedings, and the Commissioner, before reaching his decision, may waive the irregularity or take such steps as he thinks fit to remedy the irregularity whether by amendment of any document, or the giving of any notice or directions or otherwise.

Determinations and decisions of a Commissioner

31.—(1) The determination of a Commissioner on an application for leave to appeal shall be in writing and signed by him.

(2) The decision of a Commissioner on an appeal shall be in writing and signed by him and, except in respect of a decision made with the consent of the parties, he shall record reasons.

(3) A copy of the determination or decision and any reasons shall be sent to the parties by the office of the Social Security Commissioners.

(4) Without prejudice to sub-paragraphs (2) and (3), a Commissioner may announce his determination or decision at the conclusion of an oral hearing.

General Powers of a Commissioner

32. A Commissioner may, if he thinks fit–

(a) abridge the time specified in these Regulations for doing any act by him; or

(b) expedite the proceedings in such manner as he thinks fit.

Delegation of functions to nominated officers

33.—(1) All or any of the following functions of a Commissioner may be exercised by a nominated officer authorised by the Secretary of State in accordance with section 114(2C)**(a)** of the 1975 Act–

(a) Section 114(2C) of the Social Security Act 1975 was inserted by section 52 of and Schedule 5, paragraph 16 to the Social Security Act 1986 (c.50).

(a) making a direction under regulation 10(6) and paragraph 25;

(b) making orders for oral hearings under paragraph 26(2) and (3);

(c) summoning witnesses under paragraph 28;

(d) ordering a postponement of oral hearings under paragraph 4(1);

(e) giving leave for withdrawal of any appeal under paragraph 29;

(f) making any order for extension of time under regulation 10 or abridgment of time under paragraph 32;

(g) making an order under sub-paragraph (2) below.

(2) Any party may, within 10 days of being given the decision of a nominated officer, in writing request the Commissioner to consider, and confirm or replace with his own, that decision but such a request shall not stop the proceedings unless so ordered by the Commissioner.

APPLICATION TO A COMMISSIONER FOR LEAVE TO APPEAL TO THE COURT OF SESSION

34.—(1) In a case where the Chief Social Security Commissioner considers that it is impracticable, or would be likely to cause undue delay, for an application for leave to appeal to the Court of Session to be determined by the Commissioner who decided the case, that application shall be determined–

(a) where the decision was a decision of an individual Commissioner, by the Chief Social Security Commissioner or a Commissioner selected by him, and

(b) where the decision was a decision of a Tribunal of 3 Commissioners, by a differently constituted Tribunal of 3 Commissioners selected by the Chief Social Security Commissioner.

(2) If the office of Chief Social Security Commissioner is vacant, or if the Chief Social Security Commissioner is unable to act, paragraph (1) above shall have effect as if the expression "the Chief Social Security Commissioner" referred to such other of the Commissioners as may have been nominated to act for the purpose either by the Chief Social Security Commissioner or, if he has not made such a nomination, by the Lord Chancellor.

35.—(1) For the purposes of making an application for leave to appeal where–

(a) a debtor is unable for the time being to act; and

(b) his estate is not being administered by any tutor, curator or other guardian acting or appointed in terms of law,

the Secretary of State may, upon written application made to him by a person who, if a natural person, is over the age of 18, appoint that person to exercise, on behalf of the person who is unable to act, any right to which that person may be entitled.

(2) Where the Secretary of State has made an appointment under paragraph (1)–

(a) he may at any time revoke it;

(b) the person appointed may resign his office after having given one month's notice in writing to the Secretary of State of his intention to do so;

(c) any such appointment shall terminate when the Secretary of State is notified that a person to whom sub-paragraph (1)(b) applies has been appointed.

36. Paragraph 29 shall apply to a Commissioner in an application for leave to appeal as it applies to the proceedings therein set out.

EXPLANATORY NOTE

(This note is not part of the Regulations)

These Regulations provide for deductions to be made from income support towards discharging a debt in respect of community charges where a levying authority (that is the appropriate local authority) has obtained a summary warrant or decree against a person (the debtor).

The Regulations further provide that where the Secretary of State receives a notice from a levying authority asking him to deduct amounts payable by way of income support, he shall refer the matter to an adjudication officer for the determination of the questions as to whether there is enough income support to make such deduction and in the case where other deductions are being made from income support the priority of the community charges debt in relation to those (regulation 2). Payment to the levying authority is to be at such intervals as the Secretary of State may decide.

Provision is also made for appeals by the debtor from the decision of the adjudication officer to a Social Security Appeal Tribunal and for further appeal from that by the debtor and the adjudication officer to the Social Security Commissioners and from there by the debtor, adjudication officer and Secretary of State to the Court of Session.

Incidental provision is made for setting aside decisions, correction of decisions, withdrawal of applications and time limits for making appeals and applications, service of notices and to enable nominated officers to act instead of a Commissioner in certain procedural matters.

STATUTORY INSTRUMENTS

1989 No. 508

OFFSHORE INSTALLATIONS

The Offshore Installations (Safety Zones) Order 1989

Made - - - -	*8th March 1989*
Coming into force	*31st March 1989*

The Secretary of State, in exercise of the powers conferred on him by section 22(1) and (2) of the Petroleum Act 1987**(a)** (hereinafter referred to as "the Act"), and of all other powers enabling him in that behalf, hereby makes the following Order:

1. This Order may be cited as the Offshore Installations (Safety Zones) Order 1989 and shall come into force on 31st March 1989.

2. A safety zone is hereby established around the installation specified in Column 1 of the Schedule hereto (being an installation stationed in waters to which subsection (7) of section 21 of the Act applies) having a radius of five hundred metres from the point as respects that installation which has the co-ordinates of latitude and longitude according to European Datum (1950) specified in Columns 2 and 3 of the Schedule.

Peter Morrison
8th March 1989 — Minister of State, Department of Energy

(a) 1987 c.12.

Article 2

SCHEDULE

SAFETY ZONE

(1) *Name or other designation of the offshore installation*	(2) *Latitude North*	(3) *Longitude East*
Miller Template 16/8B	58°43′19·00″	01°24′07·00″

EXPLANATORY NOTE

(This note is not part of the Order)

This Order establishes, under section 22 of the Petroleum Act 1987, a safety zone, having a radius of 500 metres from a specified point, around the installation specified in the Schedule to this Order and stationed in waters to which section 21(7) of that Act applies (these include territorial waters and waters in areas designated under section 1(7) of the Continental Shelf Act 1964 (c.29)).

Vessels (which for this purpose include hovercraft, submersible apparatus and installations in transit) are prohibited from entering or remaining in the safety zone except with the consent of the Secretary of State or in accordance with regulations made under section 23(1) of the Act (currently the Offshore Installations (Safety Zones) Regulations 1987 (S.I. 1987/1331)).

STATUTORY INSTRUMENTS

1989 No. 509

NORTHERN IRELAND

The Northern Ireland (Emergency Provisions) Acts 1978 and 1987 (Continuance) Order 1989

Made - - - -	*16th March 1989*
Coming into force	*22nd March 1989*

Whereas a draft of this Order has been approved by resolution of each House of Parliament;

Now, therefore, in exercise of the powers conferred upon me by section 33(3)(a) of the Northern Ireland (Emergency Provisions) Act 1978**(a)** and section 26(4)(a) of the Northern Ireland (Emergency Provisions) Act 1987**(b)**, I hereby make the following Order:

1. This Order may be cited as the Northern Ireland (Emergency Provisions) Acts 1978 and 1987 (Continuance) Order 1989 and shall come into force on 22nd March 1989.

2. In this Order—

(a) "the temporary provisions of the 1978 Act"**(c)** means all the provisions of the Northern Ireland (Emergency Provisions) Act 1978, except sections 5 and 28 to 36, Part III of Schedule 4, Schedules 5 and 6 and, so far as they relate to offences which are scheduled offences by virtue of the said Part III, sections 2, 6 and 7; and

(b) "the temporary provisions of the 1987 Act" means Parts II and III of the Northern Ireland (Emergency Provisions) Act 1987.

3. The temporary provisions of the 1978 Act except section 12, Schedule 1 and section 24, and the temporary provisions of the 1987 Act, shall continue in force for a period of twelve months beginning with 22nd March 1989.

Northern Ireland Office

Tom King

16th March 1989 — One of Her Majesty's Principal Secretaries of State

(a) 1978 c.5. Section 33 is amended by section 13 of the Northern Ireland (Emergency Provisions) Act 1987.
(b) 1987 c.30.
(c) Some of the temporary provisions of the 1978 Act are amended by Part I and section 25 of 1987 c.30.

EXPLANATORY NOTE

(This note is not part of the Order)

Apart from this Order, the temporary provisions of the Northern Ireland (Emergency Provisions) Acts 1978 and 1987 would expire with 21st March 1989. They are currently in force by virtue of the Northern Ireland (Emergency Provisions) Acts 1978 and 1987 (Continuance) Order 1988 (S.I. 1988/426). This Order continues in force the temporary provisions of the 1978 and 1987 Acts for a period of twelve months beginning with 22nd March 1989, except for certain provisions of the 1978 Act. These are section 12 and Schedule 1 (which relate to the detention of terrorists) and section 24 (which makes it an offence to fail to disperse when required to do so by a commissioned officer of HM forces or an officer not below the rank of Chief Inspector of the Royal Ulster Constabulary).

STATUTORY INSTRUMENTS

1989 No. 510

NORTHERN IRELAND

The Northern Ireland (Emergency Provisions) (Amendment) Regulations 1989

Made - - - -	*16th March 1989*
Coming into force	*22nd March 1989*

Whereas a draft of these Regulations has been approved by resolution of each House of Parliament;

Now, therefore, in exercise of the powers conferred upon me by section 27(1) of the Northern Ireland (Emergency Provisions) Act 1978**(a)**, I hereby make the following Regulations:

1. These Regulations may be cited as the Northern Ireland (Emergency Provisions) (Amendment) Regulations 1989 and shall come into force on 22nd March 1989.

2. The Northern Ireland (Emergency Provisions) Regulations 1978**(b)** shall be amended as follows:

(a) for regulation 4 (funerals) there shall be substituted—

"**4.** Where it appears to an officer of the Royal Ulster Constabulary not below the rank of chief inspector that a funeral may—

(a) occasion a breach of the peace or serious public disorder, or

(b) cause undue demands to be made on Her Majesty's forces or the police,

he may, where it appears to him to be necessary for the preservation of public order, give directions requiring persons taking part in the funeral to travel in vehicles."; and

(b) regulation 5 (closing of licensed premises, clubs etc.) shall be deleted.

Northern Ireland Office

Tom King

16th March 1989 One of Her Majesty's Principal Secretaries of State

(a) 1978 c.5.
(b) The Regulations are contained in Schedule 3 to the 1978 Act.

EXPLANATORY NOTE

(This note is not part of the Regulations)

These Regulations amend the Northern Ireland (Emergency Provisions) Regulations 1978 by removing the Secretary of State's power to order the closure of licensed premises, clubs etc. and by confining the power of the Royal Ulster Constabulary in relation to funerals to directions that those taking part in a funeral must travel in vehicles.

STATUTORY INSTRUMENTS

1989 No. 511

REGISTRATION OF BIRTHS, DEATHS, MARRIAGES, ETC.

ENGLAND AND WALES

The Registration of Births and Deaths (Welsh Language) (Amendment) Regulations 1989

Made - - - -	*14th March 1989*
Coming into force	*1st April 1989*

The Registrar General, in exercise of the powers conferred by sections 5, 9(5), 10(1), 10A(1), 39 and 41 of the Births and Deaths Registration Act 1953(**a**), sections 20(a) and 21(1) of the Registration Service Act 1953(**b**), as such powers are extended by section 2(2) of the Welsh Language Act 1967(**c**) and of all other powers enabling her in that behalf, with the approval of the Secretary of State for Wales(**d**), hereby makes the following Regulations –

Citation, commencement and interpretation

1.—(1) These Regulations may be cited as the Registration of Births and Deaths (Welsh Language) (Amendment) Regulations 1989 and shall come into force on 1st April 1989.

(2) In these Regulations "the principal Regulations" means the Registration of Births and Deaths (Welsh Language) Regulations 1987(**e**), and unless the context otherwise requires any reference to a numbered regulation or Schedule is a reference to the regulation or Schedule bearing that number in the principal Regulations.

Substitution of forms 2 and 6 in Schedule 2

2. For forms 2 and 6 in Schedule 2 there shall be substituted respectively the forms 2 and 6 in the Schedule to these Regulations.

Amendment of Schedule 3

3. In Schedule 3 –

(a) in the entry relating to Regulation 10(b)(ii), after "Reg.10(b)(ii)" in column (1) there shall be added "and (iii)";

(b) in the entry relating to Regulation 10(b)(iii) –

(**a**) 1953 c.20; section 5 was amended by the Children Act 1975 (c.72), Schedule 3, paragraph 13(1) and further amended by the Registration of Births, Deaths and Marriages (Fees) Order 1968 (S.I. 1968/1242), Schedule 2; section 9(5) was added by the Children Act 1975(c.72), section 93(3); sections 10 and 10A were substituted by the Family Law Reform Act 1987 (c.42), sections 24 and 25 respectively; *see* the definitions of "the Minister" and "prescribed" in section 41. (**b**) 1953 c.37; *see* the definitions of "the Minister" and "prescribed" in section 21(1). (**c**) 1967 c.66. (**d**) *See* the Secretary of State for Social Services Order 1968 (S.I. 1968/1699), article 2, which transferred all the functions of the Minister of Health to the Secretary of State; the approval of the Secretary of State is required by virtue of section 39 of the Births and Deaths Registration Act 1953 and by virtue of section 20 of the Registration Service Act 1953. (**e**) S.I. 1987/2089; the relevant amending instrument is S.I. 1988/687.

(i) for "(iii)" in column (1), there shall be substituted "(iv)",

(ii) for "10(c)" in columns (2) and (3) there shall be substituted "10(1)(d)";

(c) in the entry relating to Regulation 13(4)(b)(ii), for "10(c)" in columns (2) and (3) there shall be substituted "10(1)(d)";

(d) in the entry relating to Regulation 17(2)(b)(i), after "Reg. 17(2)(b)(i)" in column (1) there shall be added "and (ii)";

(e) in the entry relating to Regulation 17(2)(b)(ii) –

(i) for "(ii)" in column (1) there shall be substituted "(iii)", and

(ii) for "10A(1)(c)" in columns (2) and (3) there shall be substituted "10A(1)(d)";

(f) in the entry relating to Regulation 17(4)(b)(ii), for "10A(1)(c)" in columns (2) and (3) there shall be substituted "10A(1)(d)".

Given under my hand on 13th March 1989

G. T. Banks
Registrar General

I approve,

14th March 1989

Peter Walker
Secretary of State for Wales

SCHEDULE

Regulation 2

FORM 2

DECLARATION/STATEMENT FOR THE REGISTRATION/RE-REGISTRATION OF A BIRTH

Regulation 2(a)

Births and Deaths Registration Act 1953, sections 9(5), 10(1)(b)(i), 10(1)(c)(i) 10A(1)(b)(i) and 10A(1)(c)(i)

<table>
<tr><td colspan="2">1. Date and place of birth   CHILD – Y PLENTYN
....
Dyddiad a lle y ganwyd</td></tr>
<tr><td>2. Name and surname
Enw a chyfenw</td><td>3. Sex
....
Rhyw</td></tr>
<tr><td colspan="2">4. Name and surname   FATHER – TAD
Enw a chyfenw</td></tr>
<tr><td>5. Place of Birth</td><td>Lle y ganwyd</td></tr>
<tr><td>6. Occupation</td><td>Gwaith</td></tr>
<tr><td colspan="2">7. Name and surname   MOTHER – MAM
Enw a chyfenw</td></tr>
<tr><td>8. Place of birth</td><td>Lle y ganwyd</td></tr>
<tr><td>9. (a) Maiden surame
Cyfenw morwynol</td><td>(b) Surname at marriage if different from maiden surname
Cyfenw adeg priodi os yn wahanol i'r cyfenw morwynol</td></tr>
<tr><td>10. Usual address (if different from place of child's birth)</td><td>Cyfeiriad arferol (os yn wahanol i le geni'r plentyn)</td></tr>
<tr><td>INFORMANT – HYSBYSYDD
11. Name and surname (if not the mother or father)
Enw a chyfenw (os nad y tad neu'r fam)</td><td>12. Qualification
....
Cymhwyster</td></tr>
<tr><td>13. Usual address (if different from that in 10 above)</td><td>Cyfeiriad arferol (os yn wahanol i'r hyn sydd yn 10 uchod)</td></tr>
</table>

For use where the child's parents are not married to each other and one parent produces a statutory declaration of parentage made by the other parent.
I'w ddefnyddio lle nad yw rhieni'r plentyn yn briod â'i gilydd a lle mae un rhiant yn cyflwyno datganiad statudol ynghylch y rhieni a wnaed gan y rhiant arall.

I,) ....
Yr wyf i,)

*1. DO SOLEMNLY DECLARE that I am the mother of the child the particulars of whose birth are specified above and that the person named in space 4 above is the father of the child; and I request that his name should be recorded as such in the register of births.

YN CYHOEDDI YMA O DDIFRIF mai myfi yw mam y plentyn y rhoddwyd uchod fanylion am ei enedigaeth, ac mai'r person a enwyd yn 4 uchod yw tad y plentyn; a dymunaf i'w enw gael ei gofnodi felly yn y gofrestr genedigaethau.

or/neu

*2. DO SOLEMNLY DECLARE that I am the father of the child the particulars of whose birth are specified above, and I request that my name should be recorded as such in the register of births.

YN CYHOEDDI YMA O DDIFRIF mai myfi yw tad y plentyn y rhoddwyd uchod fanylion am ei enedigaeth, a dymunaf i'm henw gael ei gofnodi felly yn y gofrestr genedigaethau.

Signature) .... Date) ....
Llofnod) Dyddiad)

Signed and declared by the above-named declarant in the presence of
Wedi ei lofnodi a'i ddatgan gan y person a enwyd uchod fel datganwr ac yng ngŵydd

....
Registrar of Births and Deaths/Superintendent Registrar
Cofrestrydd Genedigaethau a Marwolaethau/Cofrestrydd Arolygol

.... { Sub-district / Is-ddosbarth .... { District / Dosbarth

* Delete as appropriate
Dileër fel y bo'n briodol

FORM 6

STATEMENT BY PARENTS FOR THE RE-REGISTRATION OF A BIRTH

Regulation 2(a)

Births and Deaths Registration Act 1953, sections 9(5) and 10A(1)(d)

1. Date and place of birth .... Dyddiad a lle y ganwyd	CHILD – Y PLENTYN
2. Name and surname Enw a chyfenw	3. Sex .... Rhyw
4. Name and surname Enw a chyfenw	FATHER – TAD
5. Place of birth	Lle y ganwyd
6. Occupation	Gwaith
7. Name and surname Enw a chyfenw	MOTHER – MAM
8. Place of birth	Lle y ganwyd
9. (a) Maiden surname Cyfenw morwynol	(b) Surname at marriage if different from maiden surname Cyfenw adeg priodi os yn wahanol i'r cyfenw morwynol
10. Usual address (if different from place of child's birth)	Cyfeiriad arferol (os yn wahanol i le geni'r plentyn)
INFORMANT – HYSBYSYDD 11. Name and surname (if not the mother or father) Enw a chyfenw (os nad y tad neu'r fam)	12. Qualification .... Cymhwyster
13. Usual address (if different from that in 10 above,	Cyfeiriad arferol (os yn wahanol i'r hyn sydd yn 10 uchod)

For use where the child's parents are not married to each other and one of them produces a copy of a relevant order.
I'w ddefnyddio lle nad yw rhieni'r plentyn yn briod â'i gilydd a lle mae un ohonynt yn cyflwyno copi ardystiedig o orchymyn perthnasol.

I,) ....
Yr wyf i,)

DO SOLEMNLY DECLARE that I am the *mother/father of the child the particulars of whose birth are specified above and that *the person named in space 4 above is/I am the father of the child and *is/am named as such in the certified copy of the relevant order relating to the child and produced by me; and I request that *his/my name should be recorded as such in the register of births.

YN CYHOEDDI YMA O DDIFRIF mai myfi yw *mam/tad y plentyn y rhoddwyd uchod fanylion am ei enedigaeth, ac mai'r *person a enwyd yn 4 uchod/myfi yw tad y plentyn ac a enwir felly yn y copi ardystiedig o'r gorchymyn perthnasol sy'n cyfeirio at y plentyn, ac a gyflwynwyd gennyf i; a dymunaf i'w enw/i'm henw gael ei gofnodi felly yn y gofrestr genedigaethau.

Signature) .... Date) ....
Llofnod) Dyddiad)

Signed and declared by the above-named declarant in the presence of
Wedi ei lofnodi a'i ddatgan gan y person a enwyd uchod fel datganwr ac yng ngŵydd

....
Registrar of Births and Deaths/Superintendent Registrar
Cofrestrydd Genedigaethau a Marwolaethau/Cofrestrydd Arolygol

.... {Sub-District / Is-ddosbarth .... {District / Dosbarth

*Delete as appropriate
Dileër fel y bo'n briodol

EXPLANATORY NOTE

(This note is not part of the Regulations)

These Regulations make minor amendments to the Welsh versions of the forms and forms of words prescribed in connection with the registration and re-registration of births. The amendments are consequential on the coming into force of sections 24 and 25 of the Family Law Reform Act 1987.

STATUTORY INSTRUMENTS

1989 No. 512

HOUSING, ENGLAND AND WALES

The Housing (Preservation of Right to Buy) (Amendment) Regulations 1989

Made - - - -	*16th March 1989*
Laid before Parliament	*21st March 1989*
Coming into force	*5th April 1989*

The Secretary of State for the Environment, as respects England, and the Secretary of State for Wales, as respects Wales, in exercise of the powers conferred on them by section 171C of the Housing Act 1985(**a**) and of all other powers enabling them in that behalf hereby make the following Regulations:

1. These Regulations may be cited as the Housing (Preservation of Right to Buy) (Amendment) Regulations 1989 and shall come into force on 5th April 1989.

2. Section 131 of the Housing Act 1985 (limits on amount of discount) as it applies in the circumstances described in section 171A(1) of that Act (cases in which right to buy is preserved) by virtue of the Housing (Preservation of Right to Buy) Regulations 1989(**b**) is amended by the substitution, in paragraph (c), of the sum of £50,000 for the sum of £35,000, and accordingly a similar substitution is made in paragraph 13 of Part I of Schedule 1 and in Schedule 2 to those Regulations.

Nicholas Ridley
15th March 1989 Secretary of State for the Environment

Peter Walker
16th March 1989 Secretary of State for Wales

(**a**) 1985 c.68; sections 171C and 171A were inserted by section 8 of the Housing and Planning Act 1986 (c.63).
(**b**) S.I. 1989/368.

EXPLANATORY NOTE

(This note is not part of the Regulations.)

These Regulations amend section 131 of the Housing Act 1985 (limits on amount of discount) as applied by the Housing (Preservation of Right to Buy) Regulations 1989 ("the previous Regulations"). These Regulations come into force on 5th April 1989 as do the previous Regulations.

Where the preserved right to buy is exercised by a person in accordance with Part V of the Housing Act 1985 (as modified and adapted by the previous Regulations), the price payable by that person is reduced by an amount of discount calculated in accordance with sections 129 to 131 of and Schedule 4 to that Act (as so modified).

The effect of this amendment is to increase from £35,000 to £50,000 the maximum sum by which the price may be reduced.

STATUTORY INSTRUMENTS

1989 No. 513

HOUSING, ENGLAND AND WALES

The Housing (Right to Buy) (Maximum Discount) Order 1989

Made - - - -	*16th March 1989*
Laid before Parliament	*21st March 1989*
Coming into force	*11th April 1989*

The Secretary of State for the Environment, as respects England, and the Secretary of State for Wales, as respects Wales, in exercise of the powers conferred on them by section 131(2) of the Housing Act 1985(**a**), and of all other powers enabling them in that behalf, hereby make the following Order:

1. This Order may be cited as the Housing (Right to Buy) (Maximum Discount) Order 1989 and comes into force on 11th April 1989.

2. The sum of £50,000 is prescribed as the maximum sum by which the price payable for a dwelling-house on a conveyance or grant under Part V of the Housing Act 1985 may be reduced by discount under section 129(**b**) of that Act.

3. The Housing (Right to Buy) (Maximum Discount) Order 1986(**c**) is revoked.

Nicholas Ridley
15th March 1989 Secretary of State for the Environment

Peter Walker
16th March 1989 Secretary of State for Wales

(**a**) 1985 c.68.
(**b**) Section 129 is amended by section 2 of the Housing and Planning Act 1986 (c.63).
(**c**) S.I. 1986/2193.

EXPLANATORY NOTE

(This note is not part of the Order.)

A person exercising the right to buy a dwelling-house in England or Wales under Part V of the Housing Act 1985 may be entitled, under sections 129 to 131 of and Schedule 4 to the Act, to a discount equal to a certain percentage of the price before discount, which price is calculated in accordance with section 126 of the Act.

The discount may not, however, reduce the price by more than such sum as the Secretary of State may by order prescribe. By this Order, £50,000 is prescribed as the maximum discount, in place of £35,000 prescribed by the Housing (Right to Buy) (Maximum Discount) Order 1986. This Order revokes the 1986 Order.

STATUTORY INSTRUMENTS

1989 No. 517

NATIONAL HEALTH SERVICE, ENGLAND AND WALES

The National Health Service (Travelling Expenses and Remission of Charges) Amendment Regulations 1989

Made - - - -	*20th March 1989*
Laid before Parliament	*20th March 1989*
Coming into force	*10th April 1989*

The Secretary of State for Health, in exercise of powers conferred on him by section 83A of the National Health Service Act 1977**(a)** and of all other powers enabling him in that behalf, hereby makes the following Regulations:

Citation and commencement

1. These Regulations may be cited as the National Health Service (Travelling Expenses and Remission of Charges) Amendment Regulations 1989 and shall come into force on 10th April 1989.

Amendment of Regulations

2.—(1) Part II of Schedule 1 to the National Health Service (Travelling Expenses and Remission of Charges) Regulations 1988**(b)** (calculation of requirements) is amended in accordance with the following paragraphs of this regulation.

(2) In paragraph 4 there are added after the words "column 2" the words "except that where a claimant or his partner is liable to a personal community charge under section 8 of the Abolition of Domestic Rates Etc. (Scotland) Act 1987**(c)** or a collective community charge under section 11 of that Act the provisions of those Regulations shall be applied in accordance with the modifications specified in the corresponding entries in column 2 of the National Health Service (Travelling Expenses and Remission of Charges) (Scotland) Regulations 1988**(d)**".

(3) In Table B, in column (2) for the words "As if in paragraph 1" to "omitted" where they appear in relation to the entry in column (1) "Schedule 3", there are substituted the following words:–

"As if in paragraph 1–

for sub-paragraph (aa) there were substituted–

"(aa) payments of interest and capital under a hire purchase agreement to buy the dwelling occupied as a home;"; and

after sub-paragraph (h) there were added–

"(i) mortgage capital payments;

(j) payments in respect of an endowment policy in connection with the purchase of the dwelling occupied as the home;

(a) 1977 c.49; see section 128(1) for the definitions of "prescribed" and "regulations"; section 83A was inserted by section 14(1) of the Social Security Act 1988 (c.7).
(b) S.I. 1988/551.
(c) 1987 c.47.
(d) S.I. 1988/546, amended by S.I. 1989/393.

(k) payments by way of rent which do not otherwise fall within sub-paragraph (c) or (e) of this paragraph;

(l) 80 per cent of the general rates payable in respect of the dwelling occupied as the home.".

As if paragraphs 5(a), 7 and 8 were omitted.

As if in paragraph 9(1) for the words "paragraph 1(c) to (h)" there were substituted the words "paragraph 1(c) to (h) and (k)".

As if paragraph 10 were omitted.

As if in paragraph 11–

for sub-paragraph (1)(a) and (b) there were substituted–

"(a) in respect of a non-dependant aged 18 or more who is in remunerative work or is a person to whom regulation 3(3) applies (non-dependants), £11.20;

(b) in respect of a non-dependant aged 18 or more to whom (a) does not apply–

(i) except where sub-paragraph (ii) applies, £6.45;

(ii) where the non-dependant is aged under 25 and is in receipt of income support, £3.00.";

in sub-paragraph (2) for the words "the deduction specified in sub-paragraph (1)(b) appropriate in his case" there were substituted "£6.45";

sub-paragraphs (7)(d) and (e) were omitted."

Signed by the authority of the Secretary of State for Health

D. Mellor
Minister of State
Department of Health

20th March 1989

EXPLANATORY NOTE

(This note is not part of the Regulations)

These Regulations amend the National Health Service (Travelling Expenses and Remission of Charges) Regulations 1988 ("the 1988 Regulations") which provide for the remission and repayment of certain charges which would otherwise be payable under the National Health Service Act 1977 and for the payment by the Secretary of State of certain travelling expenses.

Regulation 2 amends paragraph 4 and Table B in Part II of Schedule 1 to the 1988 Regulations. Regulation 2(2) provides for taking into account community charges in Scotland. The amendments to Table B in regulation 2(3) provide for capital and interest payments made under a hire purchase agreement to buy a dwelling to be taken into account in assessing housing costs and increases the deductions to be made in respect of housing costs in respect of non-dependants.

STATUTORY INSTRUMENTS

1989 No. 523

SOCIAL SECURITY

The Social Security Benefit (Dependency) Amendment Regulations 1989

Made - - - -	*16th March 1989*
Laid before Parliament	*21st March 1989*
Coming into force	*11th April 1989*

The Secretary of State for Social Security, in exercise of the powers conferred by sections 44(3)(c), 45(2A)(b), 45A(3) (b), 46(4), 47(1A)(b), 47B(2), 49, 66(1)(d), (3), (4)(b) and (5), and 66A(2) of, and Schedule 20 to, the Social Security Act 1975(**a**) and of all other powers enabling him in that behalf, after agreement by the Social Security Advisory Committee that the proposals to make these Regulations should not be referred to it(**b**), hereby makes the following Regulations:

Citation, commencement and interpretation

1.—(1) These Regulations may be cited as the Social Security Benefit (Dependency) Amendment Regulations 1989 and shall come into force on 11th April 1989.

(2) In these Regulations, "the principal Regulations" means the Social Security Benefit (Dependency) Regulations 1977(**c**).

Amendment of regulation 4A.

2. In regulation 4A(1) of the principal Regulations (circumstances in which a person who is not entitled to child benefit is to be treated as if he was so entitled)(**d**) the word "female" shall be omitted.

(**a**) 1975 c.14; section 44(3)(c) was amended by the Child Benefit Act 1975 (c.61), section 21(1), Schedule 4, paragraph 16(b) and the Social Security Act 1980 (c.30), sections 2 and 21, Schedule 1, paragraph 4(a); section 45(2A)(b) was inserted by the Social Security Act 1985 (c.53), section 13(1) and amended by the Social Security Act 1988 (c.7), Schedule 4, paragraph 7(b); section 45A was inserted by the Health and Social Security Act 1984 (c.48), section 12; subsection (3) was substituted by the Social Security Act 1985 (c.53), section 13(2)(b) and amended by the Social Security Act 1988 (c.7), Schedule 4, paragraph 8(b); section 46(4) was substituted by the Social Security Act 1985 (c.53), section 13(3) and amended by the Social Security Act 1988 (c.7), Schedule 4, paragraph 9; section 47(1A) was inserted by the Social Security Act 1985 (c.53), section 13(4)(b); section 47B was inserted by the Health and Social Security Act 1984 (c.48), section 14(a); section 49 was amended by the Health and Social Security Act 1984 (c.48), Schedule 4, paragraph 3; section 66(1)(d) was amended by the Child Benefit Act 1975 (c.61), section 21(1), Schedule 4, paragraph 23 and the Social Security Act 1980 (c.30), sections 2 and 21, Schedule 1, paragraph 4(a); section 66(3)–(5) was inserted by the Social Security (Miscellaneous Provisions) Act 1977 (c.5), section 22(3), and amended by the Social Security Act 1985 (c.53), section 13(5) and by the Social Security Act 1988 (c.7), Schedule 4, paragraph 13; section 66 ceased to have effect on 6th April 1987 except for beneficiaries entitled to unemployability supplement immediately before that date – *see* the Social Security Act 1986 (c.50), Schedule 3, paragraph 4; section 66A(2) was inserted by the Health and Social Security Act 1984 (c.48), section 14(b); sections 44-47 and 66 of the Social Security Act 1975 are modified by section 10 of the Social Security Act 1988 (c.7); Schedule 20 is cited because of the references to "Prescribe", "Regulations" and "Entitled to child benefit". (**b**) *See* section 10(2)(b) of the Social Security Act 1980 (c.30). (**c**) S.I. 1977/343.

(**d**) Regulations 4A and 4B were inserted by regulation 2 of S.I. 1980/585. Paragraph (3) was inserted in regulation 4B by S.I. 1987/355, regulation 3 and amended by S.I. 1988/554, regulation 3.

Amendment of regulation 4B

3. In regulation 4B(3) of the principal Regulations(**a**) (circumstances in which a person entitled to child benefit is to be treated as if he was not so entitled) after the words "For the purposes of sections" there shall be inserted the words "25(1) (entitlement to a widowed mother's allowance)" and for the words "(child receiving financial support under the Employment and Training Act 1973)" there shall be substituted the words "(child receiving training under the youth training scheme)".

Substitution of reference

4. In regulation 8(7) of the principal Regulations (meaning of "week")(**b**) for the words "regulation 16(6) of the Social Security (Claims and Payments) Regulations 1979" there shall be substituted the words "regulation 22 of and paragraph 5 of Schedule 6 to the Social Security (Claims and Payments) Regulations 1987"(**c**).

Apportionment of payments by way of occupational pension made otherwise than weekly.

5. Immediately before regulation 10 of the principal Regulations (increase of benefit for person having care of child) there shall be inserted the following regulation –

> **"Apportionment of payments by way of occupational pension made otherwise than weekly**
>
> 9A. For the purposes of the provisions mentioned in section 47B(1) and in section 66A(1) of the 1975 Act(**d**), (earnings to include occupational pensions for certain purposes) where payment by way of occupational pensions is for any period made otherwise than weekly, the amount of any such payment for any week in that period shall be determined –
>
> (a) where payment is made for a year, by dividing the total by 52;
>
> (b) where payment is made for three months, by dividing the total by 13;
>
> (c) where payment is made for a month, by multiplying the total by 12 and dividing the result by 52;
>
> (d) where payment is made for two or more months, otherwise than for a year or for three months, by dividing the total by the number of months, multiplying the result by 12 and dividing the result of that multiplication by 52; or
>
> (e) in any other case, by dividing the amount of the payment by the number of days in the period for which it is made and multiplying the result by 7.".

Amendment of regulation 10(2)(e)

6. For sub-paragraph (e) of regulation 10(2) of the principal Regulations (increase of benefit for person having care of child)(**e**) there shall be substituted the following sub-paragraph–

> "(e) either –
>
> (i) has no earnings or has earnings but they do not exceed the standard rate of increase (there being disregarded for this purpose any earnings derived from employment by the beneficiary in caring for a child or children in respect of whom the beneficiary is entitled to child benefit), or
>
> (ii) is employed by the beneficiary in caring for such child or children and is not residing with him;".

(**a**) Regulations 4A and 4B were inserted by regulation 2 of S.I. 1980/585. Paragraph (3) was inserted in regulation 4B by S.I. 1987/355, regulation 3 and amended by S.I. 1988/554, regulation 3. (**b**) Regulation 8 was substituted by S.I. 1985/1190, regulation 3. (**c**) S.I. 1987/1968. (**d**) Sections 47B and 66A were inserted by the Health and Social Security Act 1984 (c.48), section 14. (**e**) Regulation 10(2)(e) was substituted by regulation 4 of S.I. 1988/554.

Revocations

7. Regulation 10(2)(f) of the principal Regulations (increase of benefit for a woman having the care of a child) and regulation 2(8) of the Social Security Benefit (Dependency) Amendment Regulations 1984(**a**) (which inserts new sub-paragraph (f) in regulation 10(2) of the principal Regulations) are hereby revoked.

Signed by authority of the Secretary of State for Social Security.

Nicholas Scott
Minister of State,
Department of Social Security

16th March 1989

(**a**) S.I. 1984/1698.

EXPLANATORY NOTE

(This note is not part of the Regulations)

These Regulations make various amendments to the Social Security Benefit (Dependency) Regulations 1977 ("the principal Regulations").

Regulation 2 amends in regulation 4A of the principal Regulations the description of certain statutory provisions. Regulation 3 adds a reference to widowed mother's allowance to the list of benefits for which a person, entitled to child benefit, is treated in some circumstances as not so entitled for the purposes of determining entitlement to those benefits.

Regulation 4 amends the reference in regulation 8(7) of the principal Regulations. Regulation 5 provides for the apportionment of payments by way of occupational pension made otherwise than weekly.

Regulation 6 amends regulation 10(2)(e) to provide that a dependency increase may be payable to a beneficiary where the dependant is employed in caring for the beneficiary's child but is not residing with him.

Regulation 7 provides for the revocation of regulation 10(2)(f) of the principal Regulations and for a consequential revocation.

STATUTORY INSTRUMENTS

1989 No. 524

FOOD

The Welfare Food Amendment Regulations 1989

Made - - - -	*16th March 1989*
Laid before Parliament	*21st March 1989*
Coming into force	*11th April 1989*

In exercise of the powers conferred by sections 13(3), (4) and (8) of the Social Security Act 1988(**a**) and of all other powers enabling me in that behalf, I hereby make the following Regulations:

Citation, commencement and interpretation

1.—(1) These Regulations may be cited as the Welfare Food Amendment Regulations 1989 and shall come into force on 11th April 1989.

(2) In these Regulations "the principal Regulations" means the Welfare Food Regulations 1988(**b**).

Amendment of regulations 5 and 10 of the principal Regulations

2. In regulation 5(1) of the principal Regulations (purchase of welfare food) and in regulation 10(2) of the principal Regulations (inability to purchase dried milk at a reduced price) for "£2.55" in each place where it occurs, there shall be substituted "£2.70".

Amendment of regulation 6 of the principal Regulations

3. In regulation 6 of the principal Regulations (use of milk, dried milk and vitamins) for "regulation 4." there shall be substituted "regulation 4; or

(d) in the case of milk, the person for whom it was obtained is a child under 30 weeks old being suckled by its mother, in which case the milk may be consumed by the mother.".

Amendment of Schedule 1 to the principal Regulations

4. In Schedule 1 to the principal Regulations, after the entry relating to Cow and Gate Premium there shall be inserted–

"Farley's OsterMilk	Farley Health Products Ltd
Farley's OsterMilk Two	Farley Health Products Ltd".

K. Clarke

16th March 1989 — One of Her Majesty's Principal Secretaries of State

(**a**) 1988 c.7.
(**b**) S.I. 1988/536; there are no relevant amending instruments.

EXPLANATORY NOTE

(This note is not part of the Regulations)

These Regulations amend the Welfare Food Regulations 1988 (the 1988 Regulations).

Regulation 2 increases the price of dried milk to be paid by those entitled to purchase it under regulation 5 of the 1988 Regulations from £2.55 to £2.70. The increase is consequent on the annual up-rating of benefits under section 63 of the Social Security Act 1986 (c.50).

Regulation 3 amends regulation 6 of the 1988 Regulations so as to allow milk obtained for a child under 30 weeks old being suckled by its mother, to be consumed by the mother.

Regulation 4 adds two additional brands of dried milk to the list of dried milks specified for the purposes of the 1988 Regulations.

STATUTORY INSTRUMENTS

1989 No. 525

SOCIAL SECURITY

The Workmen's Compensation (Supplementation) Amendment Scheme 1989

Made - - - -	*15th March 1989*
Laid before Parliament	*22nd March 1989*
Coming into force	*12th April 1989*

The Secretary of State for Social Security, with the consent of the Treasury, in exercise of the powers conferred by sections 2 and 4(2) of the Industrial Injuries and Diseases (Old Cases) Act 1975**(a)** and of all other powers enabling him in that behalf, hereby makes, in consequence of the making of the Social Security Benefits Up-rating Order 1989**(b)**, the following Scheme**(c)**:

Citation, interpretation and commencement

1.—(1) This Scheme may be cited as the Workmen's Compensation (Supplementation) Amendment Scheme 1989 and shall come into force on 12th April 1989.

(2) This Scheme shall be read as one with the Workmen's Compensation (Supplementation) Scheme 1982**(d)** ("the principal Scheme").

(3) In this Scheme, "the operative date" means 12th April 1989.

Amendment of article 5 of the principal Scheme

2. Paragraph (2) of article 5 of the principal Scheme shall be amended by substituting for the date "13th April 1988" the date "12th April 1989".

Substitution of Schedule 1 to the principal Scheme

3. For Schedule 1 to the principal Scheme (table of rates of lesser incapacity allowance for beneficiaries to whom article 5(2) applies and table of loss of earnings and corresponding rate of lesser incapacity allowance) there shall be substituted the Schedule set out in the Schedule to this Scheme.

Transitional provision relating to amount of allowance payable

4.—(1) The provisions of paragraph (2) of this article shall apply to a beneficiary who was, before the operative date, in receipt of a lesser incapacity allowance but in respect of whom the final calculation of earnings required by article 7(2) of the principal Scheme had not been made by that date.

(2) In such a case as is referred to in paragraph (1) above the beneficiary shall be treated as entitled from the operative date to an allowance at the rate to which he would have been entitled had the final calculation been made before the operative date.

(a) 1975 c.16.
(b) S.I. 1989/43, made under section 63 of the Social Security Act 1986 (c.50).
(c) *See* the Industrial Injuries and Diseases (Old Cases) Act 1975 c.16, section 4(1).
(d) S.I. 1982/1489; the relevant amending instruments are S.I. 1982/1490, 1983/1361, 1984/1118, 1985/1446, 1986/1174, 1987/419, 429 and 1988/574.

Transitional provision relating to claims not made before the operative date

5.—(1) The provisions of paragraph (2) of this article shall apply to a person whose claim for lesser incapacity allowance was not made before the operative date and who is awarded such allowance for a period after the operative date at one of the rates shown in the second column of Part II of Schedule 1 to the principal Scheme.

(2) Any lesser incapacity allowance which is found to be payable to such a person as aforesaid in respect of a period before the operative date shall–

(a) in so far as it relates to the period from 13th April 1988 to 11th April 1989 inclusive, be paid at the rate shown in the first column of Part I of Schedule 1 to the principal Scheme which corresponds to the rate awarded to him for the period after the operative date; and

(b) in so far as it relates to a period before 13th April 1988 be paid at the rate or rates then in force which corresponds or correspond to the rate awarded to him for the period after the operative date.

Transitional provision relating to claims made but not determined before the operative date

6.—(1) The provision of paragraph (2) of this article shall apply to a person whose claim for lesser incapacity allowance was made but not determined before the operative date.

(2) Any lesser incapacity allowance which is found to be payable to such a person as aforesaid in respect of a period before the operative date shall be paid at the rate or rates in force for that period which corresponds or correspond with that person's loss of earnings.

Transitional provision relating to review and appeal

7. Where a lesser incapacity allowance has been awarded to a person under the principal Scheme before the operative date and a question arises as to the weekly rate of allowance payable in consequence of this Scheme, the case shall be reviewed by the adjudication officer in the light of amendments made by this Scheme and the allowance shall continue to be payable at the weekly rate specified in the award until the question has been determined in accordance with the provisions of the principal Scheme.

Signed by authority of the Secretary of State for Social Security.

Peter Lloyd
Parliamentary Under-Secretary of State,
Department of Social Security

13th March 1989

We consent,

Alan Howarth
David Maclean
Two of the Lords Commissioners of
Her Majesty's Treasury

15th March 1989

Article 3

SCHEDULE

CONTAINING NEW SCHEDULE 1 TO BE SUBSTITUTED IN PRINCIPAL SCHEME

SCHEDULE 1

PART I

TABLE OF RATES OF LESSER INCAPACITY ALLOWANCE FOR BENEFICIARIES TO WHOM ARTICLE 5(2) APPLIES

Rate of Lesser Incapacity Allowance before 12th April 1989 £	*Rate of Lesser Incapacity Allowance from 12th April 1989* £
2.15	2.30
5.50	5.85
9.40	9.95
13.45	14.25
19.45	20.60
24.75	26.20

PART II

TABLE OF LOSS OF EARNINGS AND CORRESPONDING RATE OF LESSER INCAPACITY ALLOWANCE

Loss of Earnings £	*Rate of Lesser Incapacity Allowance* £
7.20	2.30
15.65	5.85
24.15	9.95
28.55	14.25
34.90	20.60
over 34.90	26.20

EXPLANATORY NOTE

(This note is not part of the Scheme)

This Scheme amends the Workmen's Compensation (Supplementation) Scheme 1982 by making adjustments to the lower rates of lesser incapacity allowance consequential upon the increase in the maximum rate of that allowance made by the Social Security Benefits Up-rating Order 1989. The Scheme also makes transitional provision consequent upon that Order.

STATUTORY INSTRUMENTS

1989 No. 526

TERMS AND CONDITIONS OF EMPLOYMENT

The Employment Protection (Variation of Limits) Order 1989

Made - - - -	*16th March 1989*
Coming into force	*1st April 1989*

Whereas in accordance with section 148 of the Employment Protection (Consolidation) Act 1978**(a)** ("the 1978 Act") the Secretary of State has reviewed the limits referred to in sections 15 and 122(5) of, and the limits imposed by paragraph 8(1) of Schedule 14 to, the 1978 Act**(b)**:

And whereas the Secretary of State having regard to the considerations mentioned in section 148(2) of the 1978 Act has determined that certain of those limits shall be varied as hereinafter provided:

And whereas a draft of the following Order was laid before Parliament in accordance with section 148(3) of the 1978 Act and approved by resolution of each House of Parliament:

Now, therefore, the Secretary of State in exercise of the powers conferred on him by sections 15(5), 122(6), 148, 154(3) and 154(4) of, and paragraph 8(2), (3) and (4) of Schedule 14 to, the 1978 Act**(c)** and of all other powers enabling him in that behalf hereby makes the following Order:–

Citation, commencement and revocation

1.—(1) This Order may be cited as the Employment Protection (Variation of Limits) Order 1989 and shall come into force on 1st April 1989.

(2) Subject to article 3(6) below, the Employment Protection (Variation of Limits) Order 1988**(d)** is revoked.

Variation of limits

2. Subject to article 3 below, each limit specified in columns 1 and 2 of the Table below is varied by the substitution of the new figure in column 3 for the old figure in column 4.

(a) 1978 c.44.
(b) These limits were last varied by S.I. 1988/276.
(c) Paragraph 8(3) was amended by paragraph 30(3) of Schedule 3 to the Employment Act 1982 (c.46).
(d) S.I. 1988/276.

Provision	*Nature of Limit*	*New figure*	*Old figure*
1. Section 15(1) of the 1978 Act.	Limit on amount of guarantee payment payable to an employee in respect of any day.	£11.85	£11.30
2. Section 122(5) of the 1978 Act.	Limit on amount payable to an employee in respect of any debt mentioned in section 122(3) of the 1978 Act where that debt is referable to a period of time.	£172.00	£164.00
3. Paragraph 8(1)(a) of Schedule 14 to the 1978 Act.	Limit on amount of "a week's pay" for the purpose of calculating additional award of compensation where employer fails to comply with order for reinstatement or re-engagement under section 69 of the 1978 Act.	£172.00	£164.00
4. Paragraph 8(1)(b) of Schedule 14 to the 1978 Act.	Limit on amount of "a week's pay" for the purpose of calculating basic award of compensation for unfair dismissal under section 73 of the 1978 Act.	£172.00	£164.00
5. Paragraph 8(1)(c) of Schedule 14 to the 1978 Act.	Limit on amount of "a week's pay" for the purpose of calculating redundancy payment.	£172.00	£164.00

Supplementary and transitional provisions

3.—(1) The variation specified in item 1 of the Table in article 2 above shall have effect as respects any day in respect of which an employee becomes entitled to a guarantee payment after this Order comes into force.

(2) The variation specified in item 2 of the Table in article 2 above shall have effect where the relevant date (as defined in section 122(2) of the 1978 Act**(a)**) falls after this Order comes into force.

(3) The variation specified in item 3 of the Table in article 2 above shall have effect as respects an employer's failure to comply with an order for reinstatement or re-engagement where the date (specified under section 69(2)(c) or, as the case may be, section 69(4)(f) of the 1978 Act) by which the order must be complied with falls after this Order comes into force.

(4) The variation specified in item 3 of the Table in article 2 above shall likewise have effect where the appropriate date (as defined in article (6)(a) below) falls after this Order comes into force.

(5) The variation specified in item 4 of the Table in article 2 above shall have effect where the effective date of termination as defined in section 55(4) or, where applicable, section 55(5) or 55(6) of the 1978 Act**(b)** falls after this Order comes into force.

(6) The variation specified in item 4 of the Table in article 2 above shall likewise have effect where the appropriate date falls after this Order comes into force. "Appropriate date" means:–

(a) in the case of a complaint presented under section 4 of the Employment Act 1980**(c)** (complaint of unreasonable exclusion or expulsion from a trade union) the date of the refusal of the application for, or the expulsion from, membership of a trade union, as the case may be; or

(a) Section 122(2) was amended by section 218(3) of the Insolvency Act 1985 (c.65).
(b) Section 55(5) was amended, and section 55(6) inserted, by paragraph 1 of Schedule 3 to the Employment Act 1982.
(c) 1980 (c.42).

(b) in the case of a complaint presented under section 4 of the Employment Act 1988(a) (complaint of unjustifiable discipline by a trade union) the date of the determination which the individual claims constituted an infringement of his right.

(7) The variation specified in item 5 of the Table in article 2 above shall have effect–

(a) as respects a lay-off or a keeping on short-time where the relevant date (as defined in section 90(2) of the 1978 Act) falls after this Order comes into force; and

(b) as respects a dismissal where the relevant date (as defined in section 90(1) or 90(3) of the 1978 Act) falls after this Order comes into force.

(8) Nothing in this Order affects any limit otherwise than as provided by the foregoing provisions of this article and accordingly the limits operative under the Order mentioned in article 1(2) above continue to apply in cases not falling within those provisions.

Signed by order of the Secretary of State.

Patrick Nicholls
Parliamentary Under Secretary of State,
Department of Employment

16th March 1989

EXPLANATORY NOTE

(This note is not part of the Order)

This Order, which comes into force on 1st April 1989, varies certain of the limits which are required to be reviewed annually by the Secretary of State under section 148 of the Employment Protection (Consolidation) Act 1978. The limit on the amount of guarantee payment payable under section 15(1) of the 1978 Act in respect of any day is increased from £11.30 to £11.85. The limit on the amount for the purpose of calculating the sum payable by the Secretary of State under section 122 of the 1978 Act in respect of a debt due to an employee whose employer becomes insolvent is increased from £164 to £172. The limits on the amount of "a week's pay" for the purposes of calculating redundancy payments and basic and additional awards of compensation for unfair dismissal are increased from £164 to £172.

(a) 1988 c.19.

STATUTORY INSTRUMENTS

1989 No. 527

TERMS AND CONDITIONS OF EMPLOYMENT

The Unfair Dismissal (Increase of Compensation Limit) Order 1989

Made - - - -	*16th March 1989*
Coming into force	*1st April 1989*

Whereas a draft of the following Order was laid before Parliament in accordance with section 75(2) of the Employment Protection (Consolidation) Act 1978(**a**) ("the 1978 Act") and approved by resolution of each House of Parliament:

Now, therefore, the Secretary of State, in exercise of the powers conferred on him by sections 75(2), 154(3) and 154(4) of the 1978 Act and of all other powers enabling him in that behalf, hereby makes the following Order:

Citation, commencement and revocation

1.—(1) This Order may be cited as the Unfair Dismissal (Increase of Compensation Limit) Order 1989 and shall come into force on 1st April 1989.

(2) Subject to article 3(2), the Unfair Dismissal (Increase of Compensation Limit) Order 1986(**b**) ("the 1986 Order") is revoked.

Increase of limits

2. Subject to article 3, the limit of compensation specified in section 75(1) of the 1978 Act is increased to £8,925.

Transitional provisions

3.—(1) The increase specified in article 2 shall have effect where the appropriate date falls on or after 1st April 1989.

(2) Notwithstanding the revocation of the 1986 Order, the limits set by or, as the case may be, preserved by articles 3 and 4 of that Order shall continue to have effect as provided by that Order where the appropriate date falls before 1st April 1989.

(3) In this article, "the appropriate date" means–

(a) in the case of a complaint presented under section 67 of the 1978 Act (complaint of unfair dismissal), the effective date of termination;

(b) in the case of a complaint presented under section 4 of the Employment Act 1980(**c**) (complaint of unreasonable exclusion or expulsion from a trade union), the date of the refusal of the application for, or of the expulsion from, membership, as the case may be; or

---

(**a**) 1978 c.44.
(**b**) S.I. 1986/2284; this Order last increased the limit in section 75(1) of the 1978 Act; previous Orders increasing the limit in that section were S.I. 1978/1778, 1979/1723, 1982/76, 1868 and 1984/2020.
(**c**) 1980 c.42.

(c) in the case of a complaint presented under section 4 of the Employment Act 1988(**a**) (complaint of unjustifiable discipline by a trade union), the date of the determination which the individual claims constituted an infringement of his right;

(d) in the case of a complaint presented under section 63 of the Sex Discrimination Act 1975(**b**) or under section 54 of the Race Relations Act 1976(**c**), the date on which the act complained of was done.

and "effective date of termination" has the same meaning as in section 55(4) of the 1978 Act except in a case in which section 55(5) or (6) of that Act(**d**) would have effect so as to treat a later date as the effective date of termination, in which case that later date shall be the effective date for the purposes of this article.

Signed by order of the Secretary of State.

Patrick Nicholls
Parliamentary Under Secretary of State,
Department of Employment

16th March 1989

EXPLANATORY NOTE

(This note is not part of the Order)

This Order, which comes into force on 1st April 1989, increases from £8,500 to £8,925 the limit on the amount of compensation which can be awarded by an industrial tribunal in claims for unfair dismissal as the compensatory award or as compensation for failure fully to comply with the terms of an order for reinstatement or re-engagement. The increase also affects the maximum amount of compensation that shall be awarded by a tribunal in respect of a complaint under section 4 of the Employment Act 1980 (unreasonable exclusion or expulsion from a trade union) or of a complaint under section 4 of the Employment Act 1988 (unjustifiable discipline by a trade union).

(**a**) 1988 c.19. (**b**) 1975 c.65. (**c**) 1976 c.74.
(**d**) Section 55(5) was amended, and section 55(6) inserted, by section 21(2) of and paragraph 1 of Schedule 3 to the Employment Act 1982 (c.46).

STATUTORY INSTRUMENTS

1989 No. 528

TERMS AND CONDITIONS OF EMPLOYMENT

The Unfair Dismissal (Increase of Limits of Basic and Special Awards) Order 1989

Made - - - -	*16th March 1989*
Coming into force	*1st April 1989*

Whereas a draft of the following Order was laid before Parliament in accordance with sections 73(4B) and 75A(7) of the Employment Protection (Consolidation) Act 1978**(a)** ("the 1978 Act") and approved by resolution of each House of Parliament:

Now, therefore, the Secretary of State, in exercise of the powers conferred on him by sections 73(4B), 75A(7), 154(3) and 154(4) of the 1978 Act and of all other powers enabling him in that behalf, hereby makes the following Order:–

Citation, commencement and revocation

1.—(1) This Order may be cited as the Unfair Dismissal (Increase of Limits of Basic and Special Awards) Order 1989 and shall come into force on 1st April 1989.

(2) Subject to article 3(2), the Unfair Dismissal (Increase of Limits of Basic and Special Awards) Order 1988**(b)** ("the 1988 Order") is revoked.

Increase of limits

2.—(1) Subject to article 3, the minimum award of £2,400 provided for by section 73(4A) of the 1978 Act is increased to £2,520.

(2) Subject to article 3, the sum of £11,950 specified in section 75A(1) of the 1978 Act is increased to £12,550.

(3) Subject to article 3, the sum of £23,850 specified in section 75A(1) of the 1978 Act is increased to £25,040.

(4) Subject to article 3, the sum of £17,900 specified in section 75A(2) of the 1978 Act is increased to £18,795.

Transitional provisions

3.—(1) The increases specified in article 2 shall have effect where the appropriate date falls on or after 1st April 1989.

(2) Notwithstanding the revocation of the 1988 Order, the limits set by or, as the case may be, preserved by articles 3 and 4 of that Order shall continue to have effect as provided by that Order where the appropriate date falls before 1st April 1989.

(a) 1978 c.44; sections 73(4A) and 73(4B) were inserted by section 4(1) of the Employment Act 1982 (c.46), and section 75A was inserted by section 5(3) of the Employment Act 1982.

(b) S.I. 1988/277; this Order last increased the limits in sections 73(4A), 75A(1) and 75A(2) of the 1978 Act; previous Orders increasing the limits in those sections were S.I. 1984/2021, 1985/2033 and 1986/2281.

(3) In this article, "the appropriate date" means–

(a) in the case of a complaint presented under section 67 of the 1978 Act (complaint of unfair dismissal), the effective date of termination;

(b) in the case of a complaint presented under section 4 of the Employment Act 1980**(a)** (complaint of unreasonable exclusion or expulsion from a trade union), the date of the refusal of the application for, or of the expulsion from, membership, as the case may be; or

(c) in the case of a complaint presented under section 4 of the Employment Act 1988**(b)** (complaint of unjustifiable discipline by a trade union), the date of the determination which the individual claims constituted an infringement of his right;

and "effective date of termination" has the same meaning as in section 55(4) of the 1978 Act except in a case in which section 55(5) or (6) of that Act**(c)** would have effect so as to treat a later date as the effective date of termination, in which case that later date shall be the effective date for the purposes of this article.

Signed by order of the Secretary of State.

Patrick Nicholls
Parliamentary Under Secretary of State,
Department of Employment

16th March 1989

EXPLANATORY NOTE

(This note is not part of the Order)

This Order, which comes into force on 1st April 1989, increases from £2,400 to £2,520 the minimum basic award (before appropriate reductions) and increases the limits of £11,950, £23,850 and £17,900 to £12,550, £25,040 and £18,795 respectively, applicable to calculation of the special award. These limits and the minimum basic award are relevant to dismissals which are to be regarded as unfair by virtue of section 58 or 59(a) of the Employment Protection (Consolidation) Act 1978. The increase in the minimum basic award also affects the minimum amount of compensation that shall be awarded by the Employment Appeal Tribunal in respect of a complaint under section 4 of the Employment Act 1988 (unjustifiable discipline by a trade union).

(a) 1980 c.42. **(b)** 1988 c.19.
(c) Section 55(5) was amended, and section 55(6) inserted, by section 21(2) of and paragraph 1 of Schedule 3 to the Employment Act 1982.

STATUTORY INSTRUMENTS

1989 No. 529

PUBLIC HEALTH, ENGLAND AND WALES
PUBLIC HEALTH, SCOTLAND
PUBLIC HEALTH, NORTHERN IRELAND

CONTAMINATION OF FOOD

The Food Protection (Emergency Prohibitions) (Sea Fish) Order 1989

Made - - - -	*20th March 1989*
Laid before Parliament	*20th March 1989*
Coming into force -	*21st March 1989*

Whereas the Minister of Agriculture, Fisheries and Food is of the opinion, in accordance with section 1(1)(a) of the Food and Environment Protection Act 1985**(a)**, that there has been or may have been an escape of substances of such descriptions and in such quantities and such circumstances as are likely to create a hazard to human health through human consumption of food;

And whereas the said Minister is of the opinion, in accordance with section 1(1)(b) of the said Act, that in consequence of the said escape of substances food which is or may be in the future in the area described in the Schedule to the following Order, or which is derived or may be in the future derived from anything in that area, is, or may be, or may become, unsuitable for human consumption;

Now, therefore, the said Minister, in exercise of the powers conferred on him by the said section 1(1) and section 24(3) of the said Act, and of all other powers enabling him in that behalf, hereby makes the following Order:–

Title, commencement and interpretation

1.—(1) This Order may be cited as the Food Protection (Emergency Prohibitions) (Sea Fish) Order 1989 and shall come into force on 21st March 1989.

(2) In this Order–

(a) "the Act" means the Food and Environment Protection Act 1985,

(b) "designated area" means the area described in the Schedule to this Order;

(c) "the relevant time" means one minute past midnight on 21st March 1989.

(a) 1985 c.48.

Designated incident

2. In the opinion of the Minister of Agriculture, Fisheries and Food, food in the area described in the Schedule to this Order is, or may be, or may become unsuitable for human consumption in consequence of the likely escape of toxic substances as a result of the sinking in the English Channel of the m.v. Perintis on or about 13th March 1989.

Designated area

3. The area described in the Schedule to this Order is hereby designated for the purposes of Part I of the Act.

Activity prohibited in the designated area

4. No person shall in the designated area fish for or take any fish.

Restrictions throughout the United Kingdom

5. No person shall, in the United Kingdom or in United Kingdom waters–

(a) use any fish taken out of the designated area after the relevant time in the preparation or processing for supply of food or anything from which food could be derived,

(b) land any fish or other form of aquatic produce which was taken from waters in the designated area after the relevant time,

(c) supply, or have in possession for supply, any fish, or any product derived from fish, from which food could be derived if such fish was taken from the designated area after the relevant time,

(d) feed to any creature a feeding stuff in the preparation or processing of which anything was used in contravention of sub-paragraph (a) of this article,

(e) supply, or have in possession for supply, any food or anything from which food could be derived in the preparation or processing of which anything was used in contravention of sub-paragraph (a) of this article.

In witness whereof the Official Seal of the Minister of Agriculture, Fisheries and Food is hereunto affixed on 20th March 1989.

Trumpington
Parliamentary Secretary, Ministry of Agriculture, Fisheries and Food

SCHEDULE

Article 3

THE DESIGNATED AREA

That area of sea lying within a radius of seven nautical miles of a point in 49°53. 2′ north latitude 2°11′ west longitude which lies within British fishery limits.

EXPLANATORY NOTE

(This note is not part of the Order)

This Order contains emergency prohibitions restricting various activities in order to prevent human consumption of food rendered unsuitable for that purpose in consequence of the likely escape of toxic substances as a result of the sinking in the English Channel of the m.v. Perintis on or about 13th March 1989.

The Order designates an area of sea within British fishery limits affected by the likely escape within which fishing is prohibited (article 3 and the Schedule). Certain other restrictions extend throughout the United Kingdom (article 6).

Under section 21 of the Food and Environment Protection Act 1985 the penalty for contravening an emergency prohibition is–

(a) on summary conviction, a fine of an amount not exceeding the statutory maximum (at present £2,000);

(b) on conviction on indictment, an unlimited fine, or imprisonment for a term of not more than two years or both.

Powers of enforcement in relation to emergency prohibitions are conferred by section 4 of, and Schedule 2 to, the 1985 Act. Obstruction of enforcement officers is an offence under paragraph 10 of that Schedule.

STATUTORY INSTRUMENTS

1989 No. 532

TERMS AND CONDITIONS OF EMPLOYMENT

The Redundancy Payments (Local Government) (Modification) (Amendment) Order 1989

Made - - - -	*21st March 1989*
Coming into force	*1st April 1989*

Whereas a draft of the following Order was laid before Parliament in accordance with section 149(4) of the Employment Protection (Consolidation) Act 1978(**a**) ("the 1978 Act") and approved by resolution of each House of Parliament:

Now, therefore, the Secretary of State in exercise of the powers conferred on him by section 149(1)(b) and section 154(3) and (4) of the 1978 Act and of all other powers enabling him in that behalf hereby makes the following Order:

Citation, commencement and interpretation

1.—(1) This Order may be cited as the Redundancy Payments (Local Government) (Modification) (Amendment) Order 1989 and shall come into force on 1st April 1989.

(2) In this Order the "principal Order" means the Redundancy Payments (Local Government) (Modification) Order 1983(**b**).

Amendments to the principal Order

2. The principal Order shall be amended as follows:–

(a) In article 1(2)(a) after the third reference to "the 1978 Act" add– "or, in relation to any person to whom this Order applies by reason of an amendment contained in the Redundancy Payments (Local Government) (Modification) (Amendment) Order 1989, any event occurring on or after the coming into force of that Order on the happening of which an employee may become entitled to a redundancy payment in accordance with the provisions of the 1978 Act".

(b) In article 4(3) after "paragraph (4)" delete "and (5)" and substitute "(5) and (6)".

(c) After article 4(5) add–

"(6) Where a period of employment of a person to whom this Order applies by reason of an amendment contained in the Redundancy Payments (Local Government) (Modification) (Amendment) Order 1989 falls to be computed in accordance with the provisions of the 1978 Act as modified by this Order, the provisions of this Order shall have effect in relation to any period whether falling wholly or partly before or after the coming into force of that Order".

(d) In Schedule 1 after entry 71 there shall be added–

"**72.** A school maintained under Chapter IV of Part I of the Education Reform Act 1988(**c**) (grant maintained schools).

(**a**) 1978 c.44.
(**b**) S.I. 1983/1160, amended by S.I. 1985/1872, 1988/907.
(**c**) 1988 c.40.

73. The Polytechnics and Colleges Funding Council as established by section 132 of the Education Reform Act 1988.

74. An institution falling within section 218(11) of the Education Reform Act 1988 (institutions within the Polytechnics and Colleges Funding Sector).

75. City Technology Colleges and City Colleges for the Technology of the Arts established with the agreement of the Secretary of State for Education and Science under section 105 of the Education Reform Act 1988.

76. Scottish Consultative Council on the Curriculum.

77. The Broads Authority, established under the Norfolk and Suffolk Broads Act 1988(**a**).

78. Countryside Commission for Scotland."

Signed by order of the Secretary of State.

Patrick Nicholls
Parliamentary Under Secretary of State,
Department of Employment

21st March 1989

EXPLANATORY NOTE

(This note is not part of the Order.)

This Order, which comes into force on 1st April 1989, amends the Redundancy Payments (Local Government) (Modification) Order 1983 as amended by the Redundancy Payments (Local Government) (Modification) (Amendment) Order 1985 and by the Redundancy Payments (Local Government) (Modification) (Amendment) Order 1988. Those Orders modified certain redundancy payments provisions of the Employment Protection (Consolidation) Act 1978 in their application to persons employed in relevant local government service so that their employment in the service is to be treated as if it were continuous for the purposes of those provisions. This Order adds to the list of employers to whose employees the 1983 Order as amended applies.

(**a**) 1988 c.4.

STATUTORY INSTRUMENTS

1989 No. 533

FOOD

COMPOSITION AND LABELLING

The Preservatives in Food Regulations 1989

Made - - - -	*21st March 1989*
Laid before Parliament	*6th April 1989*
Coming into force -	*27th April 1989*

The Minister of Agriculture, Fisheries and Food, the Secretary of State for Health and the Secretary of State for Wales, acting jointly, in exercise of the powers conferred by sections 4, 7, 118 and 119 of the Food Act 1984**(a)** and now vested in them**(b)** and of all other powers enabling them in that behalf, hereby make the following Regulations, after consultation in accordance with section 118(6) of the said Act with such organisations as appear to them to be representative of interests substantially affected by the said Regulations:–

Title and commencement

1. These Regulations may be cited as the Preservatives in Food Regulations 1989, and shall come into force on 27th April 1989.

Interpretation

2.—(1) In these Regulations, unless the context otherwise requires–

"the Act" means the Food Act 1984;

"appropriate designation" means, as respects any permitted preservative or any food, a name or description or a name and description sufficiently specific, in each case, to indicate to an intending purchaser the true nature of the permitted preservative or of the food, as the case may be, to which it is applied;

"biscuits" includes wafers, rusks, crispbreads, oatcakes, matzos and chocolate-coated, chocolate-filled or chocolate-flavoured biscuits;

"bread" has the meaning assigned to it by the Bread and Flour Regulations 1984**(c)**;

"canned food" means any food which–

(a) is in a hermetically sealed container, and

(b) (i) has been sufficiently heat processed to destroy any *Clostridium botulinum* in the food or its container, or

(ii) has a pH of less than 4.5,

and "canned", in relation to any food, shall be construed accordingly;

(a) 1984 c.30; section 132(1) contains a definition of "the Ministers" relevant to the exercise of the statutory powers under which these Regulations are made.

(b) In the case of the Secretary of State for Health, by virtue of S.I. 1988/1843.

(c) S.I. 1984/1304, to which there is an amendment not relevant to these Regulations.

"carbohydrate" means any substance containing carbon, hydrogen and oxygen only in which the hydrogen and oxygen occur in the same proportion as in water;

"cheese" and "soft cheese" have the meanings respectively assigned to them by the Cheese Regulations 1970**(a)**;

"Community" means the European Economic Community;

"Community controlled wine" means wine, grape must, sparkling wine, aerated sparkling wine, liqueur wine, semi-sparkling wine and aerated semi-sparkling wine as respectively defined in Annex 1 to Council Regulation (EEC) No. 822/87**(b)** on the common organisation of the market in wine;

"compounded food" means food containing two or more ingredients;

"concentrated fruit juice" has the meaning assigned to it by the Fruit Juices and Fruit Nectars Regulations 1977**(c)**;

"container" includes any form of packaging of food for sale as a single item, whether by way of wholly or partly enclosing the food or by way of attaching the food to some other article, and in particular includes a wrapper or confining band;

"dock" includes any harbour, moorings, wharf, pier, jetty or other works in or at which food can be shipped or unshipped and any warehouse, transit shed or other premises used in connection therewith for the temporary storage or loading for despatch of food which is unshipped or to be shipped;

"flavouring" includes flavouring essence and flavouring extract and means any product consisting of a flavouring agent and such other substances, if any, the use of which in food is not forbidden and which are reasonably necessary to produce a solid, a solution or an emulsion, but no other ingredient or ingredients;

"flavouring agent" means any sapid or odorous substance capable of imparting and primarily intended to impart a specific and distinctive taste or odour to food, but does not include herbs, spices, onions, garlic, salt, fruit juices, soft drinks, fruit acids, acetic acid, any carbohydrate material, any purine derivative, any preparation of yeast, coffee or chicory or any substances prepared by the hydrolysis of protein-containing materials;

"flavouring syrup" means a solution of carbohydrate sweetening matter containing sufficient flavouring to provide, after dilution with milk or water, a drink with that flavour;

"flour confectionery" means any solid or semi-solid product complete in itself and suitable for consumption without further preparation or processing other than heating, of which the characteristic ingredient, apart from any filling, is ground cereal, whether or not flavoured, coated with or containing any carbohydrate sweetening matter, chocolate or cocoa; and includes shortbread, sponges, pastry, pastry cases, crumpets, muffins, macaroons, ratafias, meringues and petits fours, but does not include pharmaceutical products, bread, biscuits, canned puddings, Christmas puddings or any product containing a filling which has as an ingredient any meat or fish or any animal, vegetable or microbial material processed before or during the preparation of the product to resemble the texture of meat or fish;

"food" means food intended for sale for human consumption and includes drink, chewing gum and other products of a like nature and use, and articles and substances used as ingredients in the preparation of food or drink or of such products, but does not include–

(a) water, live animals or birds,

(b) fodder or feeding stuffs for animals, birds or fish, or

(c) articles or substances used only as drugs;

"food and drugs authority" has the meaning assigned to it by section 71 of the Act;

"freeze drink" means any pre-packed liquid which complies with the requirements in the Soft Drinks Regulations 1964**(d)** as to the composition of any soft drink for consumption without dilution and which is clearly and legibly labelled as intended for freezing before consumption;

(a) S.I. 1970/94; relevant amending instruments are S.I. 1974/1122, 1984/649.
(b) OJ No. L84, 27.3.1987, p. 1.
(c) S.I. 1977/927, to which there are amendments not relevant to these Regulations.
(d) S.I. 1964/760; relevant amending instruments are S.I. 1976/295, 1977/927.

"fruit juice" has the meaning assigned to it by the Fruit Juices and Fruit Nectars Regulations 1977;

"fruit spread" means the product obtained by processing fruit, fruit pulp or purée and carbohydrate sweetening matter, with or without the addition of other substances, to a suitable consistency by the application of heat and which is not a product described in column 2 of Schedule 1 to the Jam and Similar Products Regulations 1981**(a)**;

"hermetically sealed container" means a sealed container which is airtight and impermeable to gases;

"human consumption" includes use in the preparation of food for human consumption;

"ice cream" has the meaning assigned to it by the Ice-Cream Regulations 1967**(b)**;

"the Minister" means the Minister of Agriculture, Fisheries and Food;

"permitted antioxidant" means any antioxidant in so far as its use is permitted by the Antioxidants in Food Regulations 1978**(c)**;

"permitted colouring matter" means any colouring matter in so far as its use is permitted by the Colouring Matter in Food Regulations 1973**(d)**;

"permitted emulsifier" means any emulsifier in so far as its use is permitted by the Emulsifiers and Stabilisers in Food Regulations 1980**(e)**;

"permitted miscellaneous additive" means any miscellaneous additive in so far as its use is permitted by the Miscellaneous Additives in Food Regulations 1980**(f)**;

"permitted preservative" means any preservative specified in columns 1 and 2 of Part I of Schedule 1 or, subject to the provisions of paragraph (2) of this regulation, specified in columns 3 and 4 of that Part of that Schedule which, in either case, satisfies the specific purity criteria in relation to that preservative specified or referred to in Part II of that Schedule, and, so far as is not otherwise provided by any such specific purity criteria, satisfies the general purity criteria specified in Part III of that Schedule, or any mixture of two or more such preservatives;

"permitted solvent" means any solvent in so far as its use is permitted by the Solvents in Food Regulations 1967**(g)**;

"permitted stabiliser" means any stabiliser in so far as its use is permitted by the Emulsifiers and Stabilisers in Food Regulations 1980;

"permitted sweetener" means any sweetener in so far as it use is permitted by the Sweeteners in Food Regulations 1983**(h)**;

"pre-packed" means made up in advance ready for retail sale in or on a container; and on any premises where food of any description is so made up, or is kept or stored for sale after being so made up, any food of that description found made up in or on a container shall be deemed to be pre-packed unless the contrary is proved;

"preparation", in relation to food, includes manufacture and any form of treatment;

"preservative" means any substance which is capable of inhibiting, retarding or arresting the growth of micro-organisms or any deterioration of food due to micro-organisms or of masking the evidence of any such deterioration but does not include–

(a) any permitted antioxidant,

(b) any permitted colouring matter,

(c) any permitted emulsifier,

(d) any permitted miscellaneous additive,

(e) any permitted solvent,

(f) any permitted stabiliser,

(g) any permitted sweetener,

(a) S.I. 1981/1063, to which there are amendments not relevant to these Regulations.
(b) S.I. 1967/1866, to which there are amendments not relevant to these Regulations.
(c) S.I. 1978/105; relevant amending instruments are S.I. 1980/1831, 1983/1211, 1984/1304.
(d) S.I. 1973/1340; relevant amending instruments are S.I. 1975/1488, 1976/2086, 1978/1787, 1987/1987.
(e) S.I. 1980/1833; relevant amending instruments are S.I. 1982/16, 1983/1211, 1810, 1984/1304.
(f) S.I. 1980/1834; relevant amending instruments are S.I. 1982/14, 1983/1211, 1984/1304.
(g) S.I. 1967/1582; relevant amending instruments are S.I. 1967/1939, 1980/1832, 1983/1211, 1984/1304.
(h) S.I. 1983/1211, to which there is an amendment not relevant to these Regulations.

(h) vinegar,

(j) any soluble carbohydrate sweetening matter,

(k) potable spirits or wines,

(l) herbs, spices, hop extract or flavouring agents when used for flavouring purposes,

(m) common salt (sodium chloride),

(n) any substance added to food by the process of curing known as smoking;

"processing", in relation to food, includes curing by smoking and any treatment or process resulting in a substantial change in the natural state of the food but does not include boning, paring, grinding, cutting, cleaning or trimming;

"raw peeled potatoes" includes chips, sliced potatoes, diced potatoes and potatoes which have undergone the culinary process known as "blanching";

"reduced sugar jam", "reduced sugar jelly" and "reduced sugar marmalade" have the meanings assigned to them by regulation 2(2) of the Jam and Similar Products Regulations 1981;

"retail sale" means any sale to a person buying otherwise than for the purpose of re-sale, but does not include a sale to a caterer for the purposes of his catering business, or a sale to a manufacturer for the purpose of his manufacturing business;

"sauce" means a liquid, thickened or unthickened, frozen or otherwise, used as a garnish with food and having a colour and flavour derived essentially from ingredients other than meat, but does not include mustard, gravy sauce or any product having characteristics similar to gravy;

"sausage" does not include any cured meat product which has been acidified or fermented;

"sell" includes offer or expose for sale or have in possession for sale, and "sale" and "sold" shall be construed accordingly;

"smoking" means treating food with smoke or smoke solutions derived from wood or ligneous vegetable matter in the natural state, and excludes smoke or smoke solutions derived from wood or ligneous vegetable matter which has been impregnated, coloured, gummed, painted or otherwise treated in a similar manner;

"soft drink" has the meaning assigned to it by the Soft Drinks Regulations 1964;

"specified food" means any food of a description specified in column 1 of Schedule 2;

"specified sugar product" has the meaning assigned to it by the Specified Sugar Products Regulations 1976**(a)**;

"sterile pack" means a hermetically sealed container which has been sufficiently heat processed to destroy any *Clostridium botulinum* in the container or in any food which is in the container;

"storage", in relation to food, means storage at, in or upon any farm, dock, vehicle, warehouse, fumigation chamber, cold store, transportable container, whether refrigerated or not, or any barge, ship, aircraft or hover vehicle whilst, in each case, at, in or upon any port, harbour, airport or hover-port in England and Wales;

"sweetened" means containing any added soluble carbohydrate sweetening matter or added permitted sweetener and "unsweetened" shall be construed accordingly.

(2) Unless a contrary intention is expressed, any permitted preservative specified in columns 3 and 4 of Part I of Schedule 1 may be used as an alternative to the permitted preservative specified in relation thereto in columns 1 and 2 of that Part of that Schedule, if calculated as that permitted preservative, and any reference in these Regulations to any permitted preservative specified in the said columns 1 and 2 shall be construed accordingly.

(3) Unless a contrary intention is expressed, all proportions mentioned in these Regulations are proportions calculated by weight of the product as sold.

(4) Any reference in these Regulations to a label borne on a container shall be construed as including a reference to any legible marking on the container however effected.

(a) S.I. 1976/509; a relevant amending instrument is S.I. 1982/255.

(5) For the purpose of these Regulations, the supply of food, otherwise than by sale, at, in or from any place where food is supplied in the course of a business shall be deemed to be a sale of that food.

(6) Any reference in these Regulations to a numbered regulation or schedule shall be construed as a reference to the regulation or schedule bearing that number in these Regulations.

Exemptions

3. The provisions of these Regulations shall not apply to food having any preservative in it or on it, or to any preservative which, in each case, is intended at the time of sale or importation, as the case may be, for exportation to any place outside the United Kingdom.

Sale, etc. of food containing preservative

4.—(1) Save as hereinafter provided, no food sold or imported into England and Wales shall have in it or on it any added preservative.

(2) Any specified food may have in it or on it permitted preservative of the description and in the proportion specified in relation thereto in columns 2 and 3 respectively of Schedule 2.

(3) Any specified food in relation to which two or more permitted preservatives are specified in Schedule 2 may have in it or on it an admixture of those preservatives as follows:–

(a) in the case of fruit spread, sambal oelek, concentrated snack meals with a moisture content of not less than 15% and not more than 60%, soup concentrates with a moisture content of not less than 25% and not more than 60% or wine, (including alcoholic cordials) other than Community controlled wine, to the maximum quantity of each such preservative appropriate thereto in accordance with that Schedule;

(b) in the case of beer, fruit or plants (including flowers and seeds), crystallised, glacé or drained (syruped), or candied peel or cut and drained (syruped) peel, or grape juice products (unfermented, intended for sacramental use), if the permitted preservative sulphur dioxide is present, to the maximum quantity of that preservative appropriate to that food in accordance with that Schedule and as regards any other such permitted preservative present, only if, when the quantity of each such preservative is expressed as a percentage of the maximum quantity appropriate to that food in accordance with that Schedule, the sum of those percentages does not exceed one hundred;

(c) in the case of preparations of saccharin, sodium saccharin, or calcium saccharin and water only, if the permitted preservative benzoic acid is present, to the maximum quantity of that preservative appropriate to that food in accordance with that Schedule and as regards any other such permitted preservative present, only if, when the quantity of each such preservative is expressed as a percentage of the maximum quantity appropriate to that food in accordance with that Schedule, the sum of those percentages does not exceed one hundred;

(d) in the case of marinated herring whose pH exceeds 4.5, or marinated mackerel whose pH exceeds 4.5, if the permitted preservative hexamine is present, to the maximum quantity of that preservative appropriate to that food in accordance with that Schedule and as regards any other such permitted preservative present, only if, when the quantity of each such preservative is expressed as a percentage of the maximum quantity appropriate to that food in accordance with that Schedule, the sum of those percentages does not exceed one hundred;

(e) in the case of cheese (other than Cheddar, Cheshire, Grana-padano or Provolone type cheeses or soft cheese) or cured meat (including cured meat products), in accordance with the appropriate provisions of that Schedule;

(f) in the case of prawns and shrimps in brine,–

(i) if the permitted preservative sulphur dioxide is present, to the maximum quantity of that preservative appropriate to that food in accordance with that Schedule;

(ii) if the permitted preservative sorbic acid or benzoic acid is present, to the maximum quantity of that preservative appropriate to that food in accordance with that Schedule;

(iii) if the permitted preservatives sorbic acid and benzoic acid are present, only if, when the quantity of each such preservative is expressed as a percentage of the maximum quantity appropriate to that food in accordance with that Schedule, the sum of those percentages does not exceed one hundred; and

(iv) as regards any other such permitted preservative present, only if, when the quantity of each such preservative is expressed as a percentage of the maximum quantity appropriate to that food in accordance with that Schedule, the sum of those percentages does not exceed one hundred;

(g) in any other case, only if, when the quantity of each such preservative present in that food is expressed as a percentage of the maximum quantity of that preservative appropriate to that food in accordance with that Schedule, the sum of those percentages does not exceed one hundred.

(4) Any specified food and any food intended for use in the preparation of a specified food (but excluding any pre-packed food, any specified sugar product or any fruit juice or concentrated fruit juice specified at item 1 or 2 in column 1 of Schedule 3 to the Fruit Juices and Fruit Nectars Regulations 1977) may, on importation into England and Wales or on a sale other than a retail sale have in it or on it permitted preservative of a description appropriate to the specified food in accordance with Schedules 1 and 2 in any proportion if, as the case may be, the seller gives to the importer on or before importation or to the buyer on or before sale a document which complies with the requirements of paragraphs 4, 5 and 6 of Schedule 3.

(5) Any food may have in it or on it any proportion not exceeding five milligrams per kilogram, formaldehyde derived from any wet strength wrapping containing any resin based on formaldehyde or from any plastic food container or utensil manufactured from any resin of which formaldehyde is a condensing component.

(6) The permitted miscellaneous additive dimethylpolysiloxane may contain formaldehyde in any proportion not exceeding one thousand milligrams per kilogram.

(7) Cheese, clotted cream or any canned food may have in it or on it the permitted preservative nisin.

(8) Any food may have in it or on it the permitted preservative nisin introduced in the preparation of that food by the use of any cheese, clotted cream or canned food containing nisin.

(9) Any food may have in it or on it formaldehyde introduced in the preparation of that food by the use of the permitted miscellaneous additive dimethylpolysiloxane if that formaldehyde is present in the food in no greater proportion, in relation to the quantity of dimethylpolysiloxane used, than the proportion specified in relation to dimethylpolysiloxane in paragraph (6) of this regulation.

(10) Flour may contain the permitted preservative sulphur dioxide or sodium metabisulphite as prescribed by the Bread and Flour Regulations 1984.

(11) Community controlled wine may have in it any of the permitted preservatives sulphur dioxide, potassium bisulphite, potassium metabisulphite, sorbic acid and potassium sorbate or any other preservative to the extent, in each case, authorised by any Community Regulation.

(12) No person shall sell or import into England and Wales any food which does not comply with this regulation.

5. Subject to regulation 7, nothing in the preceding regulation shall prohibit the presence in any compounded food of any permitted preservative introduced in the preparation of that food by the use of one or more specified foods (other than any unfermented grape juice product intended for sacramental use) if that permitted preservative–

(a) may under these Regulations be present in any specified food used in the compounded food, and

(b) is present in the compounded food in no greater proportion, in relation to the quantity of the specified food used, than the proportion specified in relation to that specified food in column 3 of Schedule 2:

Provided that–

(i) if the said specified food or foods may under these Regulations contain the permitted preservative sulphur dioxide, the compounded food may contain that permitted preservative in a quantity not exceeding that introduced by the use of any such specified food or fifty milligrams per kilogram, whichever is the greater;

(ii) if the said specified food or foods may under these Regulations contain any of the permitted preservatives benzoic acid, methyl 4-hydroxybenzoate, ethyl 4-hydroxybenzoate or propyl 4-hydroxybenzoate, the compounded food may contain that permitted preservative in a quantity not exceeding that introduced by the use of any such specified food or one hundred and twenty milligrams per kilogram, whichever is the greater;

(iii) if the compounded food is a specified food other than a cured meat product it may not contain any permitted preservative specified in relation thereto in column 2 of Schedule 2 in any greater proportion than is specified in relation thereto in column 3 of that Schedule;

(iv) if the compounded food is ice-cream or an edible ice made with fruit pieces in stabilised syrup which may under these Regulations contain the permitted preservative sorbic acid, the compounded food may not contain that permitted preservative in a quantity exceeding three hundred milligrams per kilogram.

Sale, advertisement and labelling of preservatives

6.—(1) No person shall sell or import into England and Wales or advertise for sale any preservative (including any preservative with which any other substance has been mixed) for use as an ingredient in the preparation of food unless such preservative is a permitted preservative.

(2) No person shall sell any permitted preservative (including any permitted preservative with which any other substance has been mixed) for use as an ingredient in the preparation of food except in a container bearing a label in accordance with the requirements of paragraphs 1, 2, 3 and 6 of Schedule 3.

Food for babies and young children

7. No person shall sell any food specially prepared for babies or young children or for babies and young children if it has in it or on it any added sodium nitrate or sodium nitrite.

Sampling and analysis of citrus fruit

8.—(1) In relation to the sampling of citrus fruit for the purpose of analysis to establish the presence in or absence from that fruit of biphenyl, 2-hydroxybiphenyl or sodium biphenyl-2-yl oxide and the quantity of any such substance present–

(a) the power of a sampling officer or of an officer of the Minister's department under section 78 or 83 respectively of the Act to procure samples shall be exercised in accordance with Part I of Schedule 4;

(b) the duty of a sampling officer or of an officer of the Minister's department under section 80 or 83 respectively of and paragraph 1 of Part I of Schedule 7 to the Act to seal or fasten up each part of the sample shall be performed in accordance with paragraph 1 of Part II of Schedule 4;

(c) the duty of a sampling officer or of an officer of the Minister's department under section 80 or 83 respectively of and paragraph 9 of Part I of Schedule 7 to the Act to submit one part of the sample for analysis by the public analyst shall be performed in accordance with paragraph 2 of Part II of Schedule 4.

(2) The method to be used in analysing citrus fruit for the purpose of establishing–

(a) the presence in or absence from that fruit of biphenyl, 2-hydroxybiphenyl or sodium bipheny-2-yl oxide shall be as specified in Part I of Schedule 5;

(b) the quantity of biphenyl in that fruit shall be as specified in Part II of Schedule 5;

(c) the quantity of 2-hydroxybiphenyl or sodium biphenyl-2-yl oxide in that fruit shall be as specified in Part III of Schedule 5.

(3) The modified Clevenger-type separator to be used in analysing citrus fruit in accordance with the preceding paragraph and Parts II and III of Schedule 5 for the purpose of establishing the quantity of biphenyl, 2-hydroxybiphenyl or sodium biphenyl-2-yl oxide in that fruit shall conform with the diagram in Schedule 6.

Condemnation of food

9. Where any food is certified by a public analyst as being food which it is an offence against regulation 4 to sell or import into England and Wales, that food may be treated for the purposes of section 9 of the Act (under which food may be seized and destroyed on the order of a justice of the peace) as being unfit for human consumption.

Penalties and enforcement

10.—(1) If any person contravenes or fails to comply with any of the foregoing provisions of these Regulations he shall be guilty of an offence and shall be liable on summary conviction to a fine not exceeding £2,000.

(2) Each food and drugs authority shall enforce and execute such provisions in their area:

Provided that each port health authority shall enforce and execute in their district the provisions of regulations 4 and 6 in so far as they relate to importation.

Defences

11.—(1) In any proceedings for an offence against regulation 4 it shall be a defence for the defendant to prove that the presence in any food of any preservative other than a permitted preservative or the presence of a permitted preservative in any food other than a specified food, as the case may be, is solely due to the use of that preservative in food storage or in the preparation of food for storage–

(a) as an acaricide, fungicide, insecticide or rodenticide, for the protection, in each case, of food whilst in storage, or

(b) as a sprout inhibitor or depressant, otherwise than in the place where food is packed for retail sale.

(2) In any proceedings for an offence against these Regulations in relation to the publication of an advertisement, it shall be a defence for the defendant to prove that, being a person whose business it is to publish or arrange for the publication of advertisements, he received the advertisement for publication in the ordinary course of business.

(3) In any proceedings in respect of the sale or importation before 31st December 1989 of food having in it or on it ethylene oxide contrary to regulation 4, it shall be a defence for the defendant to prove that the presence of that substance in or on that food is solely due to the use for pathogen reduction of that food in accordance with the second column of entry C in the Annex to Directive 79/117/EEC of the Council, prohibiting the placing on the market and use of plant protection products containing certain active substances**(a)**.

Application of various sections of the Act

12. Sections 95(5) and (6) (which relate to prosecutions), 97(1) (2) and (3) (which relate to evidence of analysis), 99 (which relates to the power of a court to require analysis by the Government Chemist), 100 (which relates to a contravention due to some person other than the person charged), 102(2) (which relates to the conditions under which a warranty may be pleaded as a defence) and 103 (which relates to offences in

(a) OJ No. L33, 8.2.1979, p. 36; the relevant amending Directive is 86/355/EEC of the Council—OJ No. L212, 2.8.86, p. 33.

relation to warranties and certificates of analysis) of the Act shall apply for the purposes of these Regulations as if references therein to proceedings, or a prosecution, under or brought under the Act included references to proceedings, or a prosecution as the case may be, taken or brought for an offence under these Regulations and as if the reference in the said section 99 to subsection (6) of section 95 included a reference to that subsection as applied by these Regulations.

Revocations

13. The Regulations specified in the first and second columns of Schedule 7 are hereby revoked to the extent specified in relation thereto in the third column of that Schedule.

In Witness whereof the Official Seal of the Minister of Agriculture, Fisheries and Food is hereunto affixed on 13th March 1989.

John MacGregor
Minister of Agriculture, Fisheries and Food

21st March 1989

Kenneth Clarke
Secretary of State for Health

13th March 1989

Peter Walker
Secretary of State for Wales

SCHEDULE 1

Regulation 2(1) and (2)

PART I

PERMITTED PRESERVATIVES

Column 1 *Permitted preservative specified in Schedule 2*	*Column 2* *Serial Number*	*Column 3* *Alternative form in which the permitted preservative may be used (to be calculated as the permitted preservative shown in column 1)*	*Column 4* *Serial Number*
Sorbic acid	E200	Sodium sorbate	E201
		Potassium sorbate	E202
		Calcium sorbate	E203
Benzoic acid	E210	Sodium benzoate	E211
		Potassium benzoate	E212
		Calcium benzoate	E213
Ethyl 4-hydroxybenzoate	E214	Ethyl 4-hydroxybenzoate, sodium salt	E215
Propyl 4-hydroxybenzoate	E216	Propyl 4-hydroxybenzoate, sodium salt	E217
Methyl 4-hydroxybenzoate	E218	Methyl 4-hydroxybenzoate, sodium salt	E219

SCHEDULE 1: Part I – *continued*

Column 1	*Column 2*	*Column 3*	*Column 4*
Permitted preservative specified in Schedule 2	*Serial Number*	*Alternative form in which the permitted preservative may be used (to be calculated as the permitted preservative shown in column 1)*	*Serial Number*
Sulphur dioxide	E220	Sodium sulphite Sodium hydrogen sulphite Sodium metabisulphite Potassium metabisulphite Calcium sulphite Calcium hydrogen sulphite	E221 E222 E223 E224 E226 E227
Potassium bisulphite	E228		
Biphenyl	E230		
2-Hydroxybiphenyl	E231	Sodium biphenyl-2-yl oxide	E232
2-(Thiazol-4-yl) benzimidazole	E233		
Hexamine	E239		
Sodium nitrite	E250	Potassium nitrite	E249
Sodium nitrate	E251	Potassium nitrate	E252
Propionic acid	E280	Sodium propionate Calcium propionate Potassium propionate	E281 E282 E283
Nisin	234		

PART II

Specific Purity Criteria Applicable to Permitted Preservatives

In the case of:–

E200 Sorbic acid
E201 Sodium sorbate
E202 Potassium sorbate
E203 Calcium sorbate
E210 Benzoic acid
E211 Sodium benzoate
E212 Potassium benzoate
E213 Calcium benzoate
E214 Ethyl 4-hydroxybenzoate
Synonyms: Ethyl *para*-hydroxybenzoate
Ethyl ester of *p*-hydroxybenzoic acid
E215 Ethyl 4-hydroxybenzoate, sodium salt
Synonyms: Sodium ethyl *para*-hydroxybenzoate
Sodium ethyl *p*-hydroxybenzoate
E216 Propyl 4-hyroxybenzoate
Synonyms: Propyl *para*-hydroxybenzoate
n-propyl *p*-hydroxybenzoate
E217 Propyl 4-hydroxybenzoate, sodium salt
Synonyms: Sodium propyl *para*-hydroxybenzoate
Sodium *n*-propyl *p*-hydroxybenzoate
E220 Sulphur dioxide
E221 Sodium sulphite (anhydrous or heptahydrate)
E222 Sodium hydrogen sulphite
Synonym: Acid sodium sulphite
E223 Sodium metabisulphite
E250 Sodium nitrite

E251 Sodium nitrate
E252 Potassium nitrate
E280 Propionic acid
E281 Sodium propionate
E282 Calcium propionate

the appropriate specific purity criteria contained in Directive 65/66/EEC of the Council**(a)**.

In the case of:–

E218 Methyl 4-hydroxybenzoate
Synonyms: Methyl *para*-hyroxybenzoate
Methyl *p*-hydroxybenzoate
E219 Methyl 4-hydroxybenzoate, sodium salt
Synonyms: Sodium methyl *para*-hydroxybenzoate
Sodium derivative of methyl *p*-hydroxybenzoate
E226 Calcium sulphite
E227 Calcium hydrogen sulphite
Synonym: Calcium bisulphite
E233 2-(Thiazol-4-yl) benzimidazole
Synonyms: Thiabendazole
2-(4-thiazolyl) benzimidazole (thiabendazole)
E239 Hexamine
Synonym: Hexamethylenetetramine
E249 Potassium nitrite
E283 Potassium propionate

the appropriate specific purity criteria contained in Directive 65/66/EEC of the Council**(b)**.

In the case of:–

E224 Potassium metabisulphite
E230 Biphenyl
E231 2-Hydroxybiphenyl
Synonym: Orthophenylphenol
E232 Sodium biphenyl-2-yl oxide
Synonym: Sodium orthophenylphenate

the appropriate specific purity criteria contained in Directive 65/66/EEC of the Council**(c)**.

In the case of:–

E228 Potassium bisulphite
Synonym: Potassium acid sulphite

the appropriate specific purity criteria contained in Directive 65/66/EEC of the Council**(d)**.

In the case of:–

Nisin

The criteria in the monograph for nisin contained in the Nutrition Meetings Report Series No. 45A (1969) of the United Nations' Food and Agriculture Organisation at page 53.

PART III

General Purity Criteria Applicable to Permitted Preservatives except where otherwise provided by Specific Purity Criteria

Each preservative shall not contain–

(a) more than 3 milligrams per kilogram of arsenic;
(b) more than 10 milligrams per kilogram of lead;
(c) more than 50 milligrams per kilogram of copper, or 25 milligrams per kilogram of zinc, or 50 milligrams per kilogram of any combination of copper and zinc.

(a) OJ No. 22, 9.2.65, p. 373/65 (OJ/SE 1965–1966, p. 25); relevant amending Directives are 67/428/EEC of the Council—OJ No. 148, 11.7.67, p. 10 (OJ/SE 1967, p. 178); 76/463/EEC of the Council—OJ No. L126, 14.5.76, p. 33.

(b) The relevant amending Directive is 76/463/EEC of the Council—OJ No. L126, 14.5.76, p. 33.

(c) The relevant amending Directive is 67/428/EEC of the Council—OJ No. 148, 11.7.67, p. 10 (OJ/SE 1967, p. 178).

(d) The relevant amending Directive is 86/604/EEC of the Council—OJ No. L352, 13.12.1986, p. 45.

Regulations 2(1) and 4

SCHEDULE 2

ARTICLES OF FOOD WHICH MAY CONTAIN PERMITTED PRESERVATIVE AND THE NATURE AND PROPORTION OF PERMITTED PRESERVATIVE IN EACH CASE

Column 1 *Specified food*	*Column 2* *Permitted Preservative*	*Column 3* *Except where otherwise stated, milligrams per kilogram not exceeding–*
Beer	Sulphur dioxide and either	70
	benzoic acid or	70
	methyl 4-hydroxybenzoate or	70
	ethyl 4-hydroxybenzoate or	70
	propyl 4-hydroxybenzoate	70
Beetroot, cooked and pre-packed	Benzoic acid or	250
	methyl 4-hydroxybenzoate or	250
	ethyl 4-hydroxybenzoate or	250
	propyl 4-hydroxybenzoate	250
Bread	Propionic acid	As prescribed by the Bread and Flour Regulations 1984
Cauliflower, canned	Sulphur dioxide	100
Cheese	Sorbic acid	1,000
Cheese, other than Cheddar, Cheshire, Grana-padano or Provolone type of cheeses or soft cheese	Sodium nitrate and sodium nitrite	50 of which not more than 5 may be sodium nitrite, expressed in both cases as sodium nitrite
Provolone cheese	Hexamine	25 (expressed as formaldehyde)
Chicory and coffee essence	Benzoic acid or	450
	methyl 4-hydroxybenzoate or	450
	ethyl 4-hydroxybenzoate or	450
	propyl 4-hydroxybenzoate	450
Christmas pudding	Propionic acid	1,000
Cider	Sulphur dioxide or	200
	sorbic acid	200
Coconut, desiccated	Sulphur dioxide	50
Colouring matter, except E150 Caramel, if in the form of a solution of a permitted colouring matter	Benzoic acid or	2,000
	methyl 4-hydroxybenzoate or	2,000
	ethyl 4-hydroxybenzoate or	2,000
	propyl 4-hydroxybenzoate or	2,000
	sorbic acid	1,000
The permitted colouring matter, E150 Caramel	Sulphur dioxide	1,000
Crabmeat, canned	Sulphur dioxide	30
Desserts, fruit based milk and cream	Sulphur dioxide or	100
	sorbic acid	300
Dessert sauces, fruit based with total soluble solids content of less than 75%	Sulphur dioxide or	100
	benzoic acid or	250
	methyl 4-hydroxybenzoate or	250
	ethyl 4-hydroxybenzoate or	250
	propyl 4-hydroxybenzoate or	250
	sorbic acid	1,000
The permitted miscellaneous additive, Dimethylpolysiloxane	Sulphur dioxide or	1,000
	benzoic acid or	2,000
	methyl 4-hydroxybenzoate or	2,000
	ethyl 4-hydroxybenzoate or	2,000
	propyl 4-hydroxybenzoate or	2,000
	sorbic acid	1,000
Enzymes:		
Papain, solid	Sulphur dioxide	30,000
Papain, aqueous solutions	Sulphur dioxide or	5,000
	sorbic acid	1,000

SCHEDULE 2 – *continued*

Column 1	*Column 2*	*Column 3*
Specified food	*Permitted Preservative*	*Except where otherwise stated, milligrams per kilogram not exceeding–*
Aqueous solutions of enzyme preparations not otherwise specified, including immobilised enzyme preparations in aqueous media	Sulphur dioxide or	500
	benzoic acid or	3,000
	methyl 4-hydroxybenzoate or	3,000
	ethyl 4-hydroxybenzoate or	3,000
	propyl 4-hydroxybenzoate or	3,000
	sorbic acid	3,000
Fat spreads consisting of an emulsion principally of water in oil with a fat content not exceeding 70%	Sorbic acid	2,000
Figs, dried	Sulphur dioxide or	2,000
	sorbic acid	500
Fillings and toppings for flour confectionery which consist principally of a sweetened oil and water emulsion with a minimum sugar solids content of 50%	Sorbic acid	1,000
Finings when sold by retail:		
Wine finings	Sulphur dioxide	12,500
Beer finings	Sulphur dioxide	50,000
Flavourings	Sulphur dioxide or	350
	benzoic acid or	800
	methyl 4-hydroxybenzoate or	800
	ethyl 4-hydroxybenzoate or	800
	propyl 4-hydroxybenzoate	800
Flavouring syrups	Sulphur dioxide or	350
	benzoic acid or	800
	methyl 4-hydroxybenzoate or	800
	ethyl 4-hydroxybenzoate or	800
	propyl 4-hydroxybenzoate	800
Flour confectionery	Propionic acid or	1,000
	sorbic acid	1,000
Foam headings, liquid	Sulphur dioxide or	5,000
	benzoic acid or	10,000
	methyl 4-hydroxybenzoate or	10,000
	ethyl 4-hydroxybenzoate or	10,000
	propyl 4-hydroxybenzoate	10,000
Freeze drinks	Sulphur dioxide or	70
	benzoic acid or	160
	methyl 4-hydroxybenzoate or	160
	ethyl 4-hydroxybenzoate or	160
	propyl 4-hydroxybenzoate or	160
	sorbic acid	300
Fruit based pie fillings	Sulphur dioxide or	350
	benzoic acid or	800
	methyl 4-hydroxybenzoate or	800
	ethyl 4-hydroxybenzoate or	800
	propyl 4-hydroxybenzoate or	800
	sorbic acid	450
Fruit, dried, other than prunes, or figs	Sulphur dioxide	2,000

SCHEDULE 2 – *continued*

Column 1	*Column 2*	*Column 3*
Specified food	*Permitted Preservative*	*Except where otherwise stated, milligrams per kilogram not exceeding–*
Fruit, fresh:		
Bananas	2-(Thiazol-4-yl) benzimidazole	3
Citrus fruit	Biphenyl or	70
	2-hydroxybiphenyl or	12
	2-(Thiazol-4-yl) benzimidazole	10
Grapes	Sulphur dioxide	15
Fruit, fruit pulp or fruit purée (including tomatoes, tomato pulp, tomato paste and tomato purée) which, in each case, is not fresh or canned	Sulphur dioxide or	350
	benzoic acid or	800
	methyl 4-hydroxybenzoate or	800
	ethyl 4-hydroxybenzoate or	800
	propyl 4-hydroxybenzoate	800
Fruit juices:		
Any fruit juice or concentrated fruit juice mentioned in regulation 11(2) of the Fruit Juices and Fruit Nectars Regulations 1977	Sulphur dioxide	As prescribed by the Fruit Juices and Fruit Nectars Regulations 1977
Any other fruit juice or concentrated fruit juice	Sulphur dioxide or	350
	benzoic acid or	800
	methyl 4-hydroxybenzoate or	800
	ethyl 4-hydroxybenzoate or	800
	propyl 4-hydroxybenzoate	800
Fruit or plants (including flowers and seeds), crystallised, glacé or drained (syruped), or candied peel or cut and drained (syruped) peel	Sulphur dioxide and either	100
	benzoic acid or	1,000
	methyl 4-hydroxybenzoate or	1,000
	ethyl 4-hydroxybenzoate or	1,000
	propyl 4-hydroxybenzoate or	1,000
	sorbic acid	1,000
Fruit pieces in stabilised syrup for use as ingredients of ice-cream or other edible ices	Sorbic acid	1,000
Fruit spread	Sulphur dioxide and	100
	sorbic acid	1,000
Garlic, powdered	Sulphur dioxide	2,000
Gelatin	Sulphur dioxide	1,000
Gelatin capsules	Sorbic acid	3,000
Ginger, dry root	Sulphur dioxide	150
Glucose drinks containing not less than 235 grammes of glucose syrup per litre of the drink	Sulphur dioxide or	350
	benzoic acid or	800
	methyl 4-hydroxybenzoate or	800
	ethyl 4-hydroxybenzoate or	800
	propyl 4-hydroxybenzoate	800
Grape juice products (unfermented, intended for sacramental use)	Sulphur dioxide and either	70
	benzoic acid or	2,000
	methyl 4-hydroxybenzoate or	2,000
	ethyl 4-hydroxybenzoate or	2,000
	propyl 4-hydroxybenzoate	2,000
Grape juice, concentrated, intended for home wine making and labelled as such	Sulphur dioxide	2,000
Hamburgers or similar products	Sulphur dioxide	450

SCHEDULE 2 – *continued*

Column 1 *Specified food*	*Column 2* *Permitted Preservative*	*Column 3* *Except where otherwise stated, milligrams per kilogram not exceeding–*
Herring, marinated,		
—whose pH does not exceed 4.5	Benzoic acid or	1,000
	methyl 4-hydroxybenzoate or	1,000
	ethyl 4-hydroxybenzoate or	1,000
	propyl 4-hydroxybenzoate	1,000
—whose pH exceeds 4.5	Hexamine and either	50
	benzoic acid or	1,000
	methyl 4-hydroxybenzoate or	1,000
	ethyl 4-hydroxybenzoate or	1,000
	propyl 4-hydroxybenzoate	1,000
Hops, dried, sold by retail	Sulphur dioxide	2,000
Horseradish, fresh grated, and horseradish sauce	Sulphur dioxide or	200
	benzoic acid or	250
	methyl 4-hydroxybenzoate or	250
	ethyl 4-hydroxybenzoate or	250
	propyl 4-hydroxybenzoate	250
Jam and other products described in column 2 of Schedule 1 to the Jam and Similar Products Regulations 1981:		
Reduced sugar jam, reduced sugar jelly and reduced sugar marmalade	Sulphur dioxide and benzoic acid or methyl 4-hydroxybenzoate or ethyl 4-hydroxybenzoate or propyl 4-hydroxybenzoate or sorbic acid	As prescribed in the Jam and Similar Products Regulations 1981
Any other product described in column 2 of Schedule 1 to the Jam and Similar Products Regulations 1981	Sulphur dioxide	As prescribed in the Jam and Similar Products Regulations 1981
Mackerel, marinated,		
—whose pH does not exceed 4.5	Benzoic acid or	1,000
	methyl 4-hydroxybenzoate or	1,000
	ethyl 4-hydroxybenzoate or	1,000
	propyl 4-hydroxybenzoate	1,000
—whose pH exceeds 4.5	Hexamine and either	50
	benzoic acid or	1,000
	methyl 4-hydroxybenzoate or	1,000
	ethyl 4-hydroxybenzoate or	1,000
	propyl 4-hydroxybenzoate	1,000
Mallow, chocolate covered	Sorbic acid	1,000 (calculated on the weight of the mallow and chocolate together)
Meat, cured (including cured meat products):		
Cured meat (including cured meat products) packed in a sterile pack, whether or not it has been removed from the pack	Sodium nitrate and sodium nitrite	150, of which not more than 50 may be sodium nitrite, expressed in both cases as sodium nitrite

SCHEDULE 2 – *continued*

Column 1 *Specified food*	*Column 2* *Permitted Preservative*	*Column 3* *Except where otherwise stated, milligrams per kilogram not exceeding–*
Acidified and/or fermented cured meat products (including Salami and similar products) not packed in a sterile pack	Sodium nitrate and sodium nitrite	400, of which not more than 50 may be sodium nitrite, expressed in both cases as sodium nitrite
Uncooked bacon and ham; cooked bacon and ham that is not, and has not been, packed in any hermetically sealed container	Sodium nitrate and sodium nitrite	500, of which not more than 200 may be sodium nitrite, expressed in both cases as sodium nitrite
Any cured meat or cured meat product not specified above	Sodium nitrate and sodium nitrite	250, of which not more than 150 may be sodium nitrite, expressed in both cases as sodium nitrite
Mushrooms, frozen	Sulphur dioxide	50
Nut pastes, sweetened	Sorbic acid	1,000
Olives, pickled	Sulphur dioxide or	100
	benzoic acid or	250
	methyl 4-hydroxybenzoate or	250
	ethyl 4-hydroxybenzoate or	250
	propyl 4-hydroxybenzoate	250
	sorbic acid	500
Peas, garden, canned, containing no added colouring matter	Sulphur dioxide	100
Pectin, liquid	Sulphur dioxide	250
Perry	Sulphur dioxide or	200
	sorbic acid	200
Pickles, other than pickled olives	Sulphur dioxide or	100
	benzoic acid or	250
	methyl 4-hydroxybenzoate or	250
	ethyl 4-hydroxybenzoate or	250
	propyl 4-hydroxybenzoate or	250
	sorbic acid	1,000
Potatoes, raw, peeled	Sulphur dioxide	50
Prawns, shrimps and scampi, other than prawns and shrimps in brine	Sulphur dioxide	200 in the edible part
Prawns and shrimps in brine	Sulphur dioxide and either	200 in the edible part
	sorbic acid or benzoic acid and either	2,000
	ethyl 4-hydroxybenzoate or	300
	propyl 4-hydroxybenzoate or	300
	methyl 4-hydroxybenzoate	300
Preparations of saccharin, sodium saccharin or calcium saccharin and water only	Benzoic acid and either	750
	methyl 4-hydroxybenzoate or	250
	ethyl 4-hydroxybenzoate or	250
	propyl 4-hydroxybenzoate	250
Prunes	Sulphur dioxide or	2,000
	sorbic acid	1,000
Salad cream (including mayonnaise) and salad dressing	Sulphur dioxide or	100
	benzoic acid or	250
	methyl 4-hydroxybenzoate or	250
	ethyl 4-hydroxybenzoate or	250
	propyl 4-hydroxybenzoate or	250
	sorbic acid	1,000

SCHEDULE 2 – *continued*

Column 1	*Column 2*	*Column 3*
Specified food	*Permitted Preservative*	*Except where otherwise stated, milligrams per kilogram not exceeding–*
Sambal oelek	Benzoic acid and	850
	sorbic acid	1,000
Sauces, other than horse-radish sauce	Sulphur dioxide or	100
	benzoic acid or	250
	methyl 4-hydroxybenzoate or	250
	ethyl 4-hydroxybenzoate or	250
	propyl 4-hydroxybenzoate or	250
	sorbic acid	1,000
Sausages or sausage meat	Sulphur dioxide	450
Snack meals, concentrated, with a moisture content of not less than 15% and not more than 60%	Sorbic acid and	1,500
	methyl 4-hydroxybenzoate	175
Soft drinks for consumption after dilution not other-wise specified in this Schedule	Sulphur dioxide or	350
	benzoic acid or	800
	methyl 4-hydroxybenzoate or	800
	ethyl 4-hydroxybenzoate or	800
	propyl 4-hydroxybenzoate or	800
	sorbic acid	1,500
Soft drinks for consumption without dilution not otherwise specified in this Schedule	Sulphur dioxide or	70
	benzoic acid or	160
	methyl 4-hydroxybenzoate or	160
	ethyl 4-hydroxybenzoate or	160
	propyl 4-hydroxybenzoate or	160
	sorbic acid	300
Soup concentrates with a moisture content of not less than 25% and not more than 60%	Sorbic acid and	1,500
	methyl 4-hydroxybenzoate	175
Starches, including modified starches	Sulphur dioxide	100
Sugars:		
Specified sugar products	Sulphur dioxide	As prescribed by the Specified Sugar Products Regulations 1976
Hydrolysed starches (other than specified sugar products)	Sulphur dioxide	400
Other sugars except lactose	Sulphur dioxide	70
Tea extract, liquid	Benzoic acid or	450
	methyl 4-hydroxybenzoate or	450
	ethyl 4-hydroxybenzoate or	450
	propyl 4-hydroxybenzoate	450
Vegetables, dehydrated:		
Brussels sprouts	Sulphur dioxide	2,500
Cabbage	Sulphur dioxide	2,500
Potato	Sulphur dioxide	550
Others	Sulphur dioxide	2,000
Vinegar:		
Cider or wine vinegar	Sulphur dioxide	200
Other	Sulphur dioxide	70
Wine (including alcoholic cordials) other than Community controlled wine	Sulphur dioxide and	450 milligrams per litre
	sorbic acid	200 milligrams per litre

SCHEDULE 2 – *continued*

Column 1	*Column 2*	*Column 3*
Specified food	*Permitted Preservative*	*Except where otherwise stated, milligrams per kilogram not exceeding–*
Yogurt, fruit	Sulphur dioxide or benzoic acid or methyl 4-hydroxybenzoate or ethyl 4-hydroxybenzoate or propyl 4-hydroxybenzoate or sorbic acid	60 120 120 120 120 300

Regulation 4(4) and 6(2)

SCHEDULE 3

LABELLING OF PERMITTED PRESERVATIVES

1.—(1) Each container to which regulation 6(2) applies shall bear a label on which is printed a true statement,–

(a) in respect of each permitted preservative present, of the serial number, if any, as specified in relation thereto in column 2 or 4 of Part I of Schedule 1, and of the common or usual name or an appropriate designation of that permitted preservative;

(b) where any other substance or substances is or are present, of the common or usual name or an appropriate designation of each such substance; and

(c) where two or more of the substances referred to in paragraphs 1(1)(a) and (b) of this Schedule are present, of the proportion of each such substance present, save that the label shall only have printed on it a statement of the proportion of any substance present, other than a permitted preservative, if any regulations, other than these Regulations or any amendment to these Regulations, made under the Act contain a requirement to that effect.

(2) The said statement shall be headed or preceded by the words "for foodstuffs (restricted use)".

2. Any statement required by the preceding paragraph–

(a) shall be clear and legible;

(b) shall be in a conspicuous position on the label which shall be marked on, or securely attached to, the container in such a manner that it will be readily discernible and easily read by an intending purchaser under normal conditions of purchase;

(c) shall not be in any way hidden or obscured or reduced in conspicuousness by any other matter, whether pictorial or not, appearing on the label.

3. The figures and the letters in any statement to which the preceding paragraph applies–

(a) shall be in characters of uniform colour and size (being not less than 1.5 millimetres in height for a label on a container of which the greatest dimension does not exceed 12 centimetres, and not less than 3 millimetres in height for a label on a container of which the greatest dimension exceeds 12 centimetres), but so that the initial letter of any word may be taller than any other letter in the word;

(b) shall appear on a contrasting ground, so however that where there is no ground other than such as is provided by a transparent container and the contents of that container are visible behind the letters, those contents shall be taken to be the ground for the purposes of this paragraph;

(c) shall be within a surrounding line and no other written or pictorial matter shall appear within that line.

4.—(1) There shall be printed on each document to which regulation 4(4) refers a true statement–

(a) of the common or usual name or an appropriate designation of the food to which the document relates;

(b) in respect of each permitted preservative present in the food to which the document relates, of the serial number, if any, as specified in relation thereto in column 2 or 4 of Part I of Schedule 1, and of the common or usual name or an appropriate designation of that permitted preservative; and

(c) of the proportion of each permitted preservative present in the food to which the document relates.

(2) The said statement shall include the words "Not for retail sale".

5. Any statement required by the preceding paragraph shall be clear and legible and the figures and the letters in any such statement–

(a) shall be in characters of uniform colour and size and not less than 3 millimetres in height, but so that the initial letter of any word may be taller than any other letter in the word;

(b) shall appear on a contrasting ground;

(c) shall be within a surrounding line and no other written or pictorial matter shall appear within that line.

6. For the purpose of this Schedule–

(a) the height of any lower case letter shall be taken to be the x-height thereof, disregarding any ascender or descender thereof;

(b) any requirement that figures or letters shall be of uniform height, colour or size, shall be construed as being subject to the saving that any inconsiderable variation in height, colour or size, as the case may be, may be disregarded.

SCHEDULE 4

Regulation 8(1)

SAMPLING OF CITRUS FRUIT TREATED WITH BIPHENYL, 2-HYDROXYBIPHENYL OR SODIUM BIPHENYL-2-YL OXIDE

PART I

Procuring of sample

1. A sample shall be procured using scientific methods which ensure that the sample is representative of the lot to which it relates.

2. A sample shall satisfy at least the following requirements–

(a) in the case of goods packaged in crates, boxes or similar containers–

Numbers of containers in the lot	*Up to 1,000*	*Above 1,000*
Minimum number of containers to be sampled … … … …	3	4
Mass, in kg., of fruit to be treated as sample per container … …	2	2

(b) in the case of goods in bulk–

Mass of batch in kg. … … … … … … … … … … … … …	*Up to 500*	*Above 500*
Mass, in kg., to be treated as sample … … … … … … … …	6	8

3. In this Part of this Schedule, the expression "lot" means a part of a consignment, which part has throughout the same characteristics such as variety of fruit, degree of ripeness and type of packaging.

PART II

Packaging and delivery of sample

1. Each part of the sample shall be placed in an air-tight container which shall be sealed.

2. Each part of the sample to be submitted for analysis shall be delivered so packaged as quickly as possible to the test laboratory.

Regulation 8(2)

SCHEDULE 5

ANALYSIS OF CITRUS FRUIT TREATED WITH BIPHENYL, 2-HYDROXYBIPHENYL OR SODIUM BIPHENYL-2-YL OXIDE

PART I

QUALITATIVE ANALYSIS FOR RESIDUES OF BIPHENYL, 2-HYDROXYBIPHENYL AND SODIUM BIPHENYL-2-YL OXIDE IN CITRUS FRUIT

Purpose and scope

1. The method described below enables the presence of residues of biphenyl, 2-hydroxybiphenyl (orthophenylphenol) or sodium biphenyl-2-yl oxide (sodium orthophenylphenate) in the peel of citrus fruit to be detected. The sensitivity limit of this method, in absolute terms, is approximately 5 μg. for biphenyl and 1 μg. for 2-hydroxybiphenyl or sodium biphenyl-2-yl oxide, which is the equivalent of 5 mg. of biphenyl and 1 mg. of 2-hydroxybiphenyl respectively in the peel of 1 kg. of citrus fruit.

Principle

2. An extract is prepared from the peel using dichloromethane in an acid medium. The extract is concentrated and separated by thin layer chromatography using silica gel. The presence of biphenyl, 2-hydroxybiphenyl or sodium biphenyl-2-yl oxide is shown by fluorescence and colour tests.

Reagents

3. The following reagents shall be used–

(a) cyclohexane (analytical reagent grade);
(b) dicholoromethane (analytical reagent grade);
(c) hydrochloric acid 25 per centum (weight/volume);
(d) silica gel GF 254 (Merck or equivalent);
(e) 0.5 per centum (weight/volume) solution of 2,4,7-trinitrofluorenone (TNF) (Fluka, BDH or equivalent) in acetone;
(f) 0.1 per centum (weight/volume) solution of 2,6-dibromo-*p*-benzoquinone-chlorimine in ethanol (stable for up to one week if kept in the refrigerator);
(g) concentrated solution of ammonia, specific gravity: 0.9;
(h) standard 1 per centum (weight/volume) solution of pure biphenyl in cyclohexane;
(j) standard 1 per centum (weight/volume) solution of pure 2-hydroxybiphenyl in cyclohexane.

Apparatus

4. The following apparatus shall be used–

(a) a mixer;
(b) a 250 ml. flask with ground glass joint and with a reflux condenser;
(c) a reduced pressure evaporator;
(d) micropipettes;
(e) a thin layer chromatographic apparatus with plates measuring 20 × 20 cm.;
(f) an ultra-violet lamp (254 nm.), the intensity of which should be such that a spot of 5 μg. of biphenyl is visible;
(g) equipment for pulversing reagents;
(h) an oven.

Method of Analysis

5. The analysis shall be carried out as follows–

(a) Preparation and extraction. All the fruit in the sample for analysis is cut in half. Half of each piece of fruit is kept for quantitative determination of the residue of any biphenyl or 2-hydroxybiphenyl present. Pieces of peel are taken from the other halves to give a sample of about 80 g. These pieces are chopped, crushed in the mixer and placed in the 250 ml. flask; to this is added 1 ml. of 25 per centum hydrochloric acid and 100 ml. dichloromethane. The mixture is heated under reflux for 10 minutes. After cooling and rinsing of the condenser with about 5 ml. of dichloromethane, the mixture is filtered through a fluted filter. The solution is transferred to the evaporator and some anti-bumping granules are added. The solution is concentrated at reduced pressure at a temperature of 60°C. to a final volume of about 10 ml. If a rotary evaporator is used, the flask should be kept in a fixed position to avoid loss of biphenyl through the formation of a film of the product on the upper wall of the flask.

(b) Chromatography: 30 g. of silica gel and 60 ml. of water are placed in a mixer and mixed for one minute. The mixture is then spread on to 5 chromatographic plates to form a layer approximately 0.25 mm. thick. The plates covered with this layer are subjected to a stream of hot air for 15 minutes and then placed in an oven where they are kept for 30 minutes at a temperature of 110°C.

After cooling, the surface layer of each plate is divided into lanes, 2 cm. wide, by parallel lines penetrating the silica gel down to the surface of the glass plate. 50 μl. of the extract to be analysed are applied to each lane as a narrow band of contiguous spots approximately 1.5 cm. from the lower edge of the plate. At least one lane is kept for the controls consisting of a spot of 1 μl. (that is, 10 μg.) of the standard solutions of biphenyl and 2-hydroxybiphenyl, one standard per lane. The chromatographic plates are developed in a mixture of cyclohexane and dichloromethane (25:95) in tanks previously lined with filter paper.

(c) Detection and identification: The presence of biphenyl and 2-hydroxybiphenyl is shown by the appearance of spots in ultra-violet light (254 nm.). The sodium biphenyl-2-yl oxide will have been converted to 2-hydroxybiphenyl during the extraction in an acid medium, and its presence cannot therefore be distinguished from that of 2-hydroxybiphenyl. The products are identified in the following manner–

(i) biphenyl gives a yellow spot in daylight when sprayed with the TNF solution;

(ii) 2-hydroxybiphenyl gives a blue spot when sprayed with the solution of 2,6-dibromo-*p*-benzoquinonechlorimine, followed by rapid passage through a stream of hot air and exposure to an ammonia-saturated atmosphere.

PART II

QUANTITATIVE ANALYSIS OF THE RESIDUES OF BIPHENYL IN CITRUS FRUIT

Purpose and scope

1. The method described below gives a quantitative analysis of the residues of biphenyl in whole citrus fruit. The accuracy of the method is ±10 per centum for a biphenyl content greater than 10 mg. per kg. of fruit.

Principle

2. After distillation in an acid medium and extraction by cyclohexane, the extract is subjected to thin layer chromatography on silica gel. The chromatogram is developed and the biphenyl is eluted and determined spectrophotometrically at 248 nm.

Reagents

3. The following reagents shall be used–

(a) concentrated sulphuric acid solution;

(b) silicone-based anti-foaming emulsion;

(c) cyclohexane (analytical reagent grade);

(d) hexane (analytical reagent grade);

(e) ethanol (analytical reagent grade);

(f) anhydrous sodium sulphate;

(g) silica gel GF 254 (Merck or equivalent);

(h) standard 1 per centum (weight/volume) solution of pure biphenyl in cyclohexane: dilute with cyclohexane to obtain the following three solutions–
   (i) 0.6 μg/μl;
   (ii) 1 μg/μl;
   (iii) 1.4 μg/μl.

Apparatus

4. The following apparatus shall be used–
(a) a 1 litre mixer;
(b) a 2 litre distillation flask with a modified Clevenger-type separator as shown in the diagram in Schedule 6 and a cooled reflux condenser;
(c) a 10 ml. graduated flask;
(d) 50 μl. micropipettes;
(e) a thin layer chromatographic apparatus with 20 × 20 cm. plates;
(f) an oven;
(g) a centrifuge with 15 ml. conical tubes;
(h) an ultra-violet spectrophotometer.

Method of Analysis

5. The analysis shall be carried out as follows–
(a) Preparation and extraction: All the fruit in the sample for analysis is cut in half. Half of each piece of fruit is kept for qualitative analysis for residues of biphenyl, 2-hydroxybiphenyl or sodium biphenyl-2-yl oxide. The other halves are put all together and shredded in a mill or crushed until a homogeneous mixture is obtained. From this at least two sub-samples of 200 g. are taken for analysis in the following manner. Each sub-sample is placed in a mixer with 100 ml. of water and mixed at slow speed for several seconds. Water is added until the volume of the mixture reaches $\frac{3}{4}$ of the capacity of the mixer, and the mixture is then mixed for 5 minutes at full speed. The resulting purée is transferred to the 2 litre distillation flask. The mixer is rinsed with water and the rinsings added to the contents of the flask. (The total quantity of water to be used in mixing and rinsing is 1 litre.) To the mixture are added 2 ml. sulphuric acid, 1 ml. anti-foaming emulsion and several anti-bumping granules. The separator and reflux condenser are fitted on to the flask. Distilled water is poured into the separator until the water level is well past the lower arm of the lateral return tube, followed by 7 ml. cyclohexane. Distillation is carried out for about 2 hours. The lower aqueous layer in the separator is discarded and the upper layer is collected in the 10 ml. graduated flask. The separator is rinsed with about 1.5 ml. of cyclohexane and the rinsings added to the contents of the flask, which are then brought up to volume with cyclohexane. Finally a little anhydrous sodium sulphate is added and the mixture is shaken.
(b) Chromatography: 30 g. of silica gel and 60 ml. of water are placed in a mixer and mixed for one minute. The mixture is then spread on to 5 chromatographic plates to form a layer approximately 0.25 mm. thick. The plates covered with this layer are subjected to a stream of hot air for 15 minutes and then placed in an oven where they are kept for 30 minutes at a temperature of 110°C. After cooling, the surface layer of each plate is divided into 4 lanes, 4.5 cm. wide, by parallel lines penetrating the silica gel down to the surface of the glass plate. 50 μl. of the extract to be analysed are applied to one lane of each plate as a narrow band of contiguous spots approximately 1.5 cm. from the lower edge of the plate. 50 μl. of the standard solutions (i) (ii) and (iii), corresponding respectively to 30, 50 and 70 μg. levels of biphenyl are applied in the same way to the three remaining lanes, one solution to each lane.

   If a large number of samples are being analysed at one time, standard solutions need not be applied to every plate. Reference may be made to a standard curve provided that this curve has been prepared from the average values obtained from 5 different plates to which the same standard solutions have been applied.
(c) Development of chromatograms and elution: The chromatograms are developed with hexane to a height of 17 cm. in tanks previously lined with filter paper. The plates are air dried. By illuminating the plates with ultra-violet light (254 nm.), the areas of silica gel containing biphenyl are located and marked off in rectangles of equal area.

   The entire layer of silica gel within the areas thus marked off is immediately scraped from the plate with a spatula. The biphenyl is extracted by mixing the silica gel with 10 ml. of ethanol and shaking several times over a period of 10 minutes. The mixture is transferred to the centrifuge tubes and centrifuged for 5 minutes at 2,500 revolutions per minute.

A control sample of silica gel is taken by the same method using an area of the same size. If a series of analyses are made, this control area is taken from an unused lane of a plate and below the solvent front; if a single analysis is made the control sample is taken from an area below one of the positions at which the standard biphenyl is located.

(d) Spectrophotometric determination: The supernatant liquid is decanted into the spectrophotometer cells and the absorption determined at 248 nm. against a control extract from a chromatographic area free from biphenyl.

Calculation of results

6. A standard curve is drawn, plotting the biphenyl values of 30, 50 and 70 μg. against the corresponding absorptions, as determined on the spectrophotometer. This gives a straight line which passes through the origin. This graph allows the biphenyl content of the samples to be read directly in mg. per kg. from the absorption value of their extracts.

PART III

QUANTITATIVE ANALYSIS OF THE RESIDUES OF 2-HYDROXYBIPHENYL AND SODIUM BIPHENYL-2-YL OXIDE IN CITRUS FRUIT

Purpose and scope

1. The method described below enables a quantitative analysis of the residues of 2-hydroxybiphenyl and sodium biphenyl-2-yl oxide in whole citrus fruit to be made. The method gives results which for a 2-hydroxybiphenyl or sodium biphenyl-2-yl oxide content of the order of 12 mg. per kg. are low by an average value of between 10 per centum and 20 per centum.

Principle

2. After distillation in an acid medium and extraction by di-isopentyl ether, the extract is purified and treated with a solution of 4-aminophenazone. A red colour develops, the intensity of which is measured spectrophotometrically at 510 nm.

Reagents

3. The following reagents shall be used–

(a) 70 per centum (weight/weight) orthophosphoric acid;

(b) silicone-based anti-foaming emulsion;

(c) di-isopentyl ether (analytical reagent grade);

(d) purified cyclohexane: shake 3 times with a 4 per cent (weight/volume) solution of sodium hydroxide, wash 3 times with distilled water;

(e) 4 per centum (weight/volume) sodium hydroxide solution;

(f) buffer solution at pH 10.4: into a 2 litre graduated flask put 6.64 g. of boric acid, 8.00 g. of potassium chloride and 93.1 ml. of N sodium hydroxide solution; mix and bring up to calibration mark with distilled water;

(g) reagent I: dissolve 1.0 g. of 4-aminophenazone (4-amino-2, 3-dimethyl-1-phenyl-5-pyrazolone; 4-aminoantipyrin) in 100 ml. of distilled water;

(h) reagent II: dissolve 2.0 g. of potassium ferricyanide in 100 ml. of distilled water. Reagents I and II must be kept in brown glass flasks and are only stable for approximately 14 days;

(j) silica gel;

(k) standard solution: dissolve 10 mg. of pure 2-hydroxybiphenyl in 1 ml. of 0.1 N NaOH; dilute to 100 ml. with a 0.2 M sodium borate solution (1 ml.=100 μg. 2-hydroxybiphenyl). For the standard curve, dilute 1 ml. to 10 ml. with the buffer solution.

Apparatus

4. The following apparatus shall be used–

(a) a shredding or crushing mill;

(b) a mixer;

(c) a 1 litre distillation flask with a modified Clevenger-type separator as shown in the diagram in Schedule 6 and a reflux condenser;

(d) an electrically controlled heating mantle;

(e) a 200 ml. separating funnel;

(f) graduated cylinders of 25 and 100 ml.;

(g) graduated flasks of 25 and 100 ml.;

(h) 1 to 10 ml. pipettes;

(j) 0.5 ml. graduated pipettes;

(k) a spectrophotometer with 4 or 5 cm. cells.

Method of Analysis

5. All the fruit in the sample for analysis is cut in half. Half of each piece of fruit is kept for qualitative analysis for residues of biphenyl, 2-hydroxybiphenyl or sodium biphenyl-2-yl oxide. The other halves are put all together and shredded in a mill or crushed until a homogeneous mixture is obtained. From this at least two sub-samples of 250 g. are taken for analysis in the following manner–

Each sub-sample is placed in a mixer with 500 ml. of water and mixed until a very fine homogeneous mixture is obtained in which the oily cells are no longer perceptible. A sample of 150 to 300 g. of the purée is taken, depending on the presumed 2-hydroxybiphenyl content and placed in the 1 litre distillation flask with a quantity of water sufficient to dilute the mixture to 500 g. in the flask. After the addition of 10 ml. of 70 per centum orthophosphoric acid, several anti-bumping granules and 0.5 ml. of anti-foaming emulsion, the separator and the reflux condenser are fitted on to the flask. 10 ml. of di-isopentyl ether are placed in the separator and the flask is heated gently in the electrically controlled heating mantle until the mixture boils. Emulsion formation is minimised if the mixture is boiled gently for the first 10 to 20 minutes. The rate of heating is then gradually increased until the mixture boils steadily and one drop of water reaches the trapping solvent every 3 to 5 seconds. After distilling for 6 hours, the contents of the separator are poured into the 200 ml. separating funnel, and the separator and the condenser are rinsed with 60 ml. of cyclohexane and then with 60 ml. of water. The rinsings are added to the contents of the separating funnel. The mixture is shaken vigorously and when the phases have separated the aqueous phase is discarded.

To extract the 2-hydroxybiphenyl, the organic phase is shaken vigorously 5 times, each time for 3 minutes, with 10 ml. of 4 per centum sodium hydroxide. The alkaline solutions are combined, adjusted to pH 9–10 with orthophosphoric acid in the presence of phenolophthalein paper, and diluted to 100 ml. with distilled water. A pinch of silica gel is added in order to clarify the solution which will have a slightly cloudy appearance. The solution is then shaken and filtered through a dry, fine-grain filter. Since colouring is developed with the maximum of accuracy and precision using quantities of 2-hydroxybiphenyl of between 10 and 70 μg. an aliquot sample of between 0.5 and 10 ml. of solution is taken with a pipette, taking into account the quantities of 2-hydroxybiphenyl which might be expected to be found. The sample is placed in a 25 ml. graduated flask; to this are added 0.5 ml. of reagent I, 10 ml. of the buffer solution and then 0.5 ml. of reagent II. The mixture is made up to the calibration mark with the buffer solution and shaken vigorously.

After 5 minutes the absorption of the red colouring at 510 nm. is measured spectrophotometrically against a control containing no extract. The colour does not lose intensity within 30 minutes. Evaluation is made by reference to a standard curve drawn from determinations using the standard 2-hydroxybiphenyl solution under the same conditions.

Observations

6. For each analysis it is recommended that the spectrophotometric determination be made with two different volumes of the neutralised alkaline extract.

Untreated citrus fruit give by this method a "blank" reading of up to 0.5 mg. per Kg. for oranges and 0.8 mg. per Kg. for lemons.

SCHEDULE 6

Regulation 8(3)

DIAGRAM OF A MODIFIED CLEVENGER-TYPE SEPARATOR

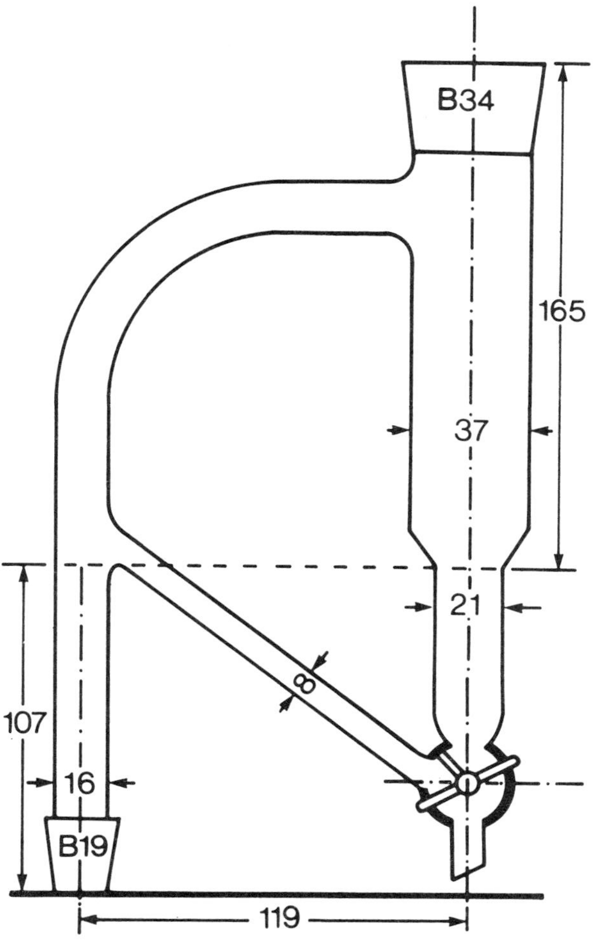

Note: The dimensions in this diagram are given in millimetres.

SCHEDULE 7

Regulation 13

Regulations revoked	*References*	*Extent of revocation*
The Preservatives in Food Regulations 1979	S.I. 1979/752	All the Regulations
The Preservatives in Food (Amendment) Regulations 1980	S.I. 1980/931	All the Regulations
The Jam and Similar Products Regulations 1981	S.I. 1981/1063	Regulation 19 and Schedule 5
The Preservatives in Food (Amendment) Regulations 1982	S.I. 1982/15	All the Regulations
The Fruit Juices and Fruit Nectars (Amendment) Regulations 1982	S.I. 1982/1311	Regulation 9
The Food (Revision of Penalties) Regulations 1982	S.I. 1982/1727	The reference in Schedule 1 to the Preservatives in Food Regulation 1979
The Sweeteners in Food Regulations 1983	S.I. 1983/1211	Schedule 2 paragraph 5
The Bread and Flour Regulations 1984	S.I. 1984/1304	Schedule 6 paragraph 4
The Food (Revision of Penalties) Regulations 1985	S.I. 1985/67	The reference in Part I of the Schedule to the Preservatives in Food Regulation 1979

EXPLANATORY NOTE

(This note is not part of the Regulations)

These Regulations, which apply to England and Wales only, re-enact with amendments the Preservatives in Food Regulations 1979, as amended, and come into force on 27th April 1989. They implement Council Directive 64/54/EEC (OJ No. 12, 27.1.1964, p. 161/64: OJ/SE 1963–1964, p. 99) on the approximation of the laws of Member States concerning the preservatives authorised for use in foodstuffs intended for human consumption, as last amended by Council Directive 85/585/EEC (OJ No. L372, 31.12.85, p. 43), and Council Directive 65/66/EEC (OJ No. 22, 9.2.65, p. 373/65: OJ/SE 1965–1966, p. 25) laying down specific criteria of purity for preservatives authorised for use in foodstuffs intended for human consumption, as last amended by Council Directive 86/604/EEC (OJ No. L352, 13.12.86, p. 45).

The Regulations–

(a) specify permitted preservatives and prescribe purity criteria for those preservatives (regulation 2(1) and (2) and Schedule 1);

(b) prohibit the sale or importation of food having in it or on it any added preservative except specified foods having in them or on them permitted preservatives within prescribed limits or as otherwise prescribed (regulation 4 and Schedule 2 and Schedule 3 paragraphs 4, 5 and 6);

(c) within prescribed limits, permit the presence in compounded food of permitted preservatives introduced in the preparation of that food by the use of one or more foods specified in Schedule 2 (regulation 5);

(d) prohibit the sale, the importation and the advertisement for sale, for use as an ingredient in the preparation of food, of any preservative other than a permitted preservative (regulation 6(1));

(e) prescribe labelling requirements for permitted preservatives when sold as such (regulation 6(2) and Schedule 3 paragraphs 1, 2, 3 and 6);

(f) prohibit the sale of food specially prepared for babies or young children if it has in it or on it any added sodium nitrate or sodium nitrite (regulation 7);

(g) make provision for the sampling and analysis of citrus fruit for the presence of biphenyl, 2-hydroxybiphenyl and sodium bi-phenyl-2-yl oxide (regulation 8 and Schedules 4, 5 and 6).

The principal changes effected by the Regulations are–

(a) the inclusion, in implementation of Directives 85/585 and 86/604, of E228 potassium bisulphite as a permitted preservative with specified purity criteria (regulation 2(1) and Schedule 1); and the confirmation that Community controlled wine may contain this and other preservatives to the extent authorised by any Community Regulation (regulations 2(1) and 4(11));

(b) the substitution for low fat spreads, of fat spreads whose fat content does not exceed 70%, as a specified food permitted to contain sorbic acid (regulation 4(2) and Schedule 2);

(c) the extension of the preservatives permitted in fruit or plants, crystallised, glacé or drained (syruped), or candied peel or cut and drained (syruped) peel to include benzoic acid, hydroxybenzoates or sorbic acid and sulphur dioxide (regulation 4(3)(b) and Schedule 2);

(d) subject to prescribed limits, the authorisation for use in prawns and shrimps in brine of the permitted preservatives, sorbic acid, benzoic acid, ethyl 4-hydroxybenzoate, propyl 4-hydroxybenzoate and methyl 4-hydroxybenzoate as well as sulphur dioxide (regulation 4(3)(f) and Schedule 2);

(e) the provision of a defence to proceedings in respect of sale or importation before 31st December 1989, of food having in it or on it ethylene oxide, where the presence of that substance is due to its use for pathogen reduction in accordance with the provisions of Council Directive 79/117/EEC, as amended by Council Directive 86/355/EEC (regulation 11(3)).

The Nutrition Meetings Report Series No. 45A (1969) of the United Nations' Food and Agriculture Organisation may be inspected at the Ministry of Agriculture, Fisheries and Food, Main Library, 3 Whitehall Place, London SW1A 2HH (telephone 01-270 8419).

1989 No. 534

SOCIAL SECURITY

The Income Support (General) Amendment Regulations 1989

Made - - - -	*22nd March 1989*
Laid before Parliament	*22nd March 1989*
Coming into force -	
regulations 1, 2, 3 and 6 to 9	*10th April 1989*
regulations 4, 5, 10 and 11	*9th October 1989*

The Secretary of State for Social Security in exercise of the powers conferred by sections 20(1) and (12)(k), 21(1A), 22(1), (2), (8) and (9) and 84(1) of the Social Security Act 1986**(a)** and section 166(1) to (3A) of the Social Security Act 1975**(b)** and of all other powers enabling him in that behalf, by this instrument, which is made before the end of a period of 12 months from the commencement of the enactments under which it is made, hereby makes the following Regulations:

Citation, commencement and interpretation

1.—(1) These Regulations may be cited as the Income Support (General) Amendment Regulations 1989 and shall come into force, in relation to a particular claimant, as follows–

(a) regulations 1, 2, 3, 6, 8 and 9 at the beginning of the first benefit week to commence for that claimant on or after 10th April 1989;

(b) regulation 7, on 10th April 1989 immediately after regulation 19 of the Income Support (General) Amendment No. 5 Regulations 1988**(c)** comes into force;

(c) regulations 4, 5, 10 and 11 at the beginning of the first benefit week to commence for that claimant on or after 9th October 1989.

(2) In paragraph (1) the expressions "benefit week' and "claimant" have the same meaning as in the General Regulations and in these Regulations "the General Regulations" means the Income Support (General) Regulations 1987**(d)**.

Amendment of regulation 3 of the General Regulations

2. In regulation 3 of the General Regulations (definition of non-dependant)–

(a) in paragraph (2)(d) for the words "liable to make payments" to the end there shall be substituted the words "liable to make payments to the claimant or the

---

(a) 1986 c.50; section 21(1A) was inserted by the Social Security Act 1988 (c.7), Schedule 4, paragraph 23; and section 84(1) is an interpretation provision and is cited because of the meanings assigned to the words "prescribed" and "regulations".
(b) 1975 c.14, section 166(1) to (3A) is applied to the Social Security Act 1986 by section 83(1) of that Act.
(c) S.I. 1988/2022.
(d) S.I. 1987/1967; amended by S.I. 1988/663, 910, 999, 1228, 1445 and 2022.

claimant's partner or to whom or to whose partner the claimant or the claimant's partner is liable to make payments, in respect of his occupation of the dwelling";

(b) in paragraph (3) the words "in board and lodging accommodation or" shall be omitted;

(c) at the end of paragraph (4) there shall be added the words "but not if each person is separately liable to make payments in respect of his occupation of the dwelling to the landlord".

Amendment of regulation 16 of the General Regulations

3. In regulation 16(3)(c) and (5)(b) of the General Regulations (circumstances in which a person is treated as being or not being a member of the household) for the words "any of sub-paragraphs (a) to (d) of the definition of residential accommodation" there shall be substituted the words "any of sub-paragraphs (a) to (d) (excluding heads (i) to (iii) of sub-paragraph (d)) of the definition of residential accommodation".

Amendment of regulation 71 of the General Regulations

4. In regulation 71(1)(a)(iii) of the General Regulations (applicable amount in urgent cases) for the reference "paragraph 15(2)" there shall be substituted the reference "paragraph 15(2), (2A)".

Amendment of Schedule 2 to the General Regulations

5. In Schedule 2 to the General Regulations (applicable amounts)–

(a) for paragraph 9 there shall be substituted the following paragraphs–

"**Pensioner premium for persons under 75**

9. The condition is that the claimant–

(a) is a single claimant or lone parent aged not less than 60 but less than 75; or

(b) has a partner and is, or his partner is, aged not less than 60 but less than 75.

Pensioner premium for persons 75 and over

9A. The condition is that the claimant–

(a) is a single claimant or lone parent aged not less than 75 but less than 80; or

(b) has a partner and is, or his partner is, aged not less than 75 but less than 80.";

(b) in paragraph 12(1)(c)(i) for the words "solely on account of the maximum age for its payment being reached" there shall be substituted the words "either on account of the maximum age for this payment being reached or the payment of a retirement pension under the Social Security Act";

(c) in paragraph 15–

(i) for sub-paragraph (2) there shall be substituted the following sub-paragraphs–

"(2) Pensioner premium for persons aged under 75–	
(a) where the claimant satisfies the condition in paragraph 9(a);	(2)(a) £11.20;
(b) where the claimant satisfies the condition in paragraph 9(b);	(b) £17.05;
(2A) Pensioner premium for persons aged 75 and over–	
(a) where the claimant satisfies the condition in paragraph 9A(a);	(2A)(a) £13.70;
(b) where the claimant satisfies the condition in paragraph 9A(b);	(b) £20.55;";

(ii) in sub-paragraph (3) for "£13.70" and £19.50" there shall be substituted "£16.20" and "£23.00" respectively(a).

Amendment of paragraph 11 of Schedule 3 to the General Regulations

6. In Schedule 3 to the General Regulations (housing costs)–

(a) in paragraph 4 (circumstances in which a person is or is not to be treated as occupying a dwelling as his home)–

(i) in sub-paragraph (7)(c)(ii) for the reference "paragraph 9," there shall be substituted the reference "paragraph 9, 9A,";

(ii) in sub-paragraph (9)(b)(ii) after the words "(prevention, care and after-care)" there shall be inserted the words "where board is available to the claimant";

(b) in paragraph 11 (non-dependant deductions)–

(i) in sub-paragraph (1) after the words "shall be made in respect of a non-dependant" there shall be inserted the words "or a person who lives in board and lodging accommodation"; and in head (a) of that sub-paragraph after the words "regulation 3(3) applies (non-dependants)" there shall be inserted the words "and in respect of a person who lives in board and lodging accommodation aged 18 or over";

(ii) in sub-paragraph (2) after the words "remunerative work" there shall be inserted the words "and of a person who lives in board and lodging accommodation aged 18 or over in remunerative work"; and after the words "the non-dependant's gross weekly income" there shall be inserted the words "or that of the person in board and lodging accommodation".

Amendment of Schedule 3A to the General Regulations

7. In Schedule 3A to the General Regulations (protected sum)–

(a) in paragraph 1(1)–

(i) for the definition of "eligible housing benefit" there shall be substituted the following definition–

""eligible housing benefit" means–

(a) for the period of 7 consecutive days beginning on 3rd April 1989, the amount of housing benefit to which the claimant or his partner was entitled in that period which relates to the board and lodging accommodation normally occupied as the home by him or, if he has a partner, by him and his partner;

(b) for the period of 7 consecutive days beginning on 10th April 1989 or, in a case to which paragraph 7(7)(b) applies, for the period of 7 consecutive days referred to in that paragraph, the amount of the claimant's or his partner's maximum housing benefit determined in accordance with regulation 61 of the Housing Benefit (General) Regulations 1987**(b)** (maximum housing benefit) which relates to that accommodation;";

(ii) at the end of the definition of "protected sum" there shall be added the words "to a claimant who in the first week is living in board and lodging accommodation or who or whose partner is temporarily absent in that week from that accommodation";

(iii) for the definition of "protected total" there shall be substituted the following definition–

""protected total" means–

(a) the total of the claimant's applicable amount under regulation 20 (applicable amounts for persons in board and lodging accommodation) in the first week or, in a case to which paragraph 7(7) applies, if the protected person or any partner

---

(a) Paragraph 15(3) of Schedule 2 was amended by article 15(5) of, and Schedule 4 to, the Social Security Benefits Up-rating Order 1989 (S.I. 1989/43).

(b) S.I. 1987/1971.

of his is temporarily absent from his accommodation in that week, the amount which would have fallen to be calculated under that regulation for that week as if there had been no temporary absence; and

(b) the amount of any eligible housing benefit for the period of 7 consecutive days beginning 3rd April 1989;";

(iv) after the definition of "second week" there shall be added the following definition–

" "third week" means the benefit week beginning on a day during the period of 7 days commencing on 17th April 1989.";

(b) in paragraph 2–

(i) for the words "Subject to the following provisions" there shall be substituted the words "Subject to sub-paragraph (2) and the following paragraphs";

(ii) in sub-paragraph (b) after the words "the period" there shall be inserted the words "of 7 consecutive days";

(c) at the end of paragraph 2 there shall be added the following sub-paragraphs–

"(2) Where–

(a) in the second week a claimant's income calculated in accordance with Part V or, as the case may be, VI exceeds the aggregate of his applicable amount determined in accordance with the relevant provisions and X; and

(b) the amount of income support to which he is entitled in the first week is more than the amount of housing benefit to which he would, but for this sub-paragraph, have been entitled in the period of 7 consecutive days beginning on 10th April 1989,

the protected sum applicable to the claimant shall, subject to sub-paragraph (3), be an amount equal to X+Y+10 pence.

(3) Where a claimant or his partner is, or both are, entitled in the first, second and third weeks to a relevant social security benefit or to more than one such benefit and consequent upon the Social Security Benefits Up-rating Order 1989**(a)** the claimant or his partner is, or both are, entitled to an increase in any one or more of those benefits in the third week, the protected sum under sub-paragraph (2) shall be increased by an amount equal to the difference between–

(a) the amount of benefit or aggregate amount of those benefits to which the claimant or his partner is, or both are, entitled in the third week; and, if less,

(b) the amount of benefit or aggregate amount of those benefits to which the claimant or his partner is, or both are, entitled in the second week.

(4) In this paragraph–

"X" means the sum which, but for sub-paragraph (2), would be the protected sum applicable under sub-paragraph (1);

"Y" means the amount of the excess to which sub-paragraph (2)(a) refers;

"relevant social security benefit" means–

(a) child benefit;

(b) any benefit under the Social Security Act;

(c) war disablement pension;

(d) war widow's pension;

(e) any payment under a scheme made under the Industrial Injuries and Diseases (Old Cases) Act 1975**(b)**;

(f) any concessionary payment.";

(a) S.I. 1989/43.
(b) 1975 c.16.

(d) in paragraph 3(2) for the words "where he, or any partner of his," to "in respect of" there shall be substituted the words "unless he, or any partner of his, is entitled to housing benefit for the period of 7 consecutive days beginning 10th April 1989 or, where paragraph 7(7)(b) applies, for the period of 7 consecutive days referred to in that paragraph in respect of";

(e) in paragraph 5–

(i) in sub-paragraph (1) for the words "sub-paragraph (2)" there shall be substituted the words "sub-paragraphs (2) and (3)";

(ii) after sub-paragraph (2) there shall be added the following sub-paragraph–

"(3) Where by virtue of the coming into force of regulation 5 of the Income Support (General) Amendment Regulations 1989(**a**) the claimant's applicable amount increases in his benefit week beginning on a day during the period of 7 days commencing on 9th October 1989, no account shall be taken of that increase.";

(f) in paragraph 7, for sub-paragraphs (5) to (7) there shall be substituted the following sub-paragraphs–

"(5) Except where sub-paragraph (7) applies, where a protected sum was applicable to a protected person immediately before he or any partner of his became a patient within the meaning of regulation 21(3) for a period of 14 weeks or less, he shall, subject to sub-paragraph (4)(c), on his or, as the case may be, his partner's ceasing to be a patient, be entitled to a protected sum equal to–

(a) the amount by which his protected total exceeds his applicable amount determined in accordance with the relevant provisions in the first benefit week in which his applicable amount ceases to be determined under paragraph 1 of Schedule 7 and either–

(i) any eligible housing benefit for the period of 7 consecutive days beginning on 10th April 1989; or, if greater,

(ii) in a case where sub-paragraph (7)(b) applied, any eligible housing benefit for the period of 7 consecutive days referred to in that sub-paragraph; or

(b) the amount of the protected sum to which he was entitled in the immediately preceding benefit week,

whichever is the lower.

(6) Paragraph 6(c) shall not apply to a protected person who has ceased to be entitled to income support for a period of not more than 8 weeks–

(a) if immediately before he ceased to be so entitled a protected sum was applicable to him; and

(b) except where sub-paragraph (7) applies, if during that period the protected person becomes re-entitled, or would by virtue of this sub-paragraph be re-entitled, to income support he shall, subject to sub-paragraph (4)(d), be entitled to a protected sum equal to–

(i) the amount by which his protected total exceeds his applicable amount determined in accordance with the relevant provisions in the first benefit week in which he becomes so re-entitled and either any eligible housing beneft for the period of 7 consecutive days beginning 10th April 1989 or, if greater, in a case to which sub-paragraph (7)(b) applied, any eligible housing benefit for the period of 7 consecutive days referred to in that sub-paragraph; or

(ii) the amount of the protected sum to which he was previously entitled,

whichever is the lower.

(7) Where a protected person or any partner of his is temporarily absent

(**a**) S.I. 1989/534.

from his accommodation for a period not exceeding 13 weeks which includes the first or second week (or both)–

(a) in a case where a protected sum was applicable to the protected person immediately before his or, as the case may be, his partner's return to that accommodation and the full charge was made for the accommodation during the temporary absence, on the protected person's or, as the case may be, his partner's return to that accommodation, the protected person shall be entitled to a protected sum equal to–

(i) the amount by which his protected total exceeds his applicable amount determined in accordance with the relevant provisions in the first complete benefit week after his or, as the case may be, his partner's return to that accommodation and any eligible housing benefit for the period of 7 consecutive days beginning 10th April 1989; or

(ii) the amount of the protected sum which was applicable to him in the immediately preceding benefit week,

whichever is the lower;

(b) in a case where–

(i) a protected sum has not at any time been applicable to the protected person; or

(ii) immediately before the protected person's or, as the case may be, his partner's return to that accommodation a protected sum was applicable but a reduced charge was made for the accommodation during the temporary absence,

the protected person on his or, as the case may be, his partner's return to that accommodation shall, subject to sub-paragraph (8), be entitled to a protected sum equal to the amount by which his protected total exceeds his applicable amount determined in accordance with the relevant provisions in the first complete benefit week after his or, as the case may be, his partner's return to that accommodation and the amount of eligible housing benefit for the period of 7 consecutive days beginning on the date determined in accordance with regulation 65 or, as the case may be, 68(2) of the Housing Benefit (General) Regulations 1987 (date on which entitlement is to commence or change of circumstances is to take effect) following that person's return to that accommodation.

(8) Where, in a case to which sub-paragraph (7)(b)(i) applies–

(a) in the first complete benefit week after the protected person's or, as the case may be, his partner's return to his accommodation the protected person's income calculated in accordance with Part V or, as the case may be, VI exceeds the aggregate of his applicable amount determined in accordance with the relevant provisions and X; and

(b) the amount of income support to which he was entitled in the first week is more than the amount of housing benefit to which he would, but for this sub-paragraph, have been entitled in the period of 7 consecutive days beginning on the date determined in accordance with regulation 65 or, as the case may be, 68(2) of the Housing Benefit (General) Regulations 1987 following his or, as the case may be, his partner's return to that accommodation,

the protected sum applicable shall, subject to sub-paragraph (9), be an amount equal to X+Y+10 pence.

(9) Where the protected person or, as the case may be, his partner returns to the accommodation in the second week and he or his partner is, or both are, entitled in the first, second and third weeks to a relevant social security benefit or to more than one such benefit and consequent upon the Social Security Benefits Up-rating Order 1989 he or his partner is, or both are,

entitled to an increase in any one or more of those benefits in the third week, the protected sum under sub-paragraph (8) shall be increased by an amount equal to the difference between–

(a) the amount of benefit or aggregate amount of those benefits to which the protected person or his partner is, or both are, entitled in the third week; and, if less,

(b) the amount of benefit or aggregate amount of those benefits to which the protected person or his partner is, or both are, entitled in the second week.

(10) In sub-paragraph (8)–

"X" means the sum which, but for sub-paragraph (8), would be the protected sum applicable in a case to which sub-paragraph (7)(b)(i) applies;

"Y" means the amount of the excess to which sub-paragraph (8)(a) refers;

"relevant social security benefit" has the same meaning as in paragraph 3(4).".

Amendment of Schedule 4 to the General Regulations

8. In paragraph 11(2) of Schedule 4 to the General Regulations (applicable amounts of persons in residential care homes and nursing homes) for all the words after "specified" there shall be substituted the words "immediately before 10th April 1989 as being within Area 53 in Schedule 6 as then in force".

Amendment of Schedule 7 to the General Regulations

9. In paragraphs 10A, 10B(1) and 16(a) of Schedule 7 to the General Regulations (special cases) for the words "any of sub-paragraphs (a) to (d) of the definition of residential accommodation" there shall be substituted in each of those paragraphs the words "any of sub-paragraphs (a) to (d) (excluding heads (i) to (iii) of sub-paragraph (d)) of the definition of residential accommodation".

Amendment of Schedule 8 to the General Regulations

10. For paragraph 4 of Schedule 8 to the General Regulations (sums to be disregarded in the calculation of earnings) there shall be substituted the following paragraph–

"**4.**—(1) In a case to which this paragraph applies, £15; but notwithstanding regulation 23 (calculation of income and capital of members of claimant's family and of a polygamous marriage), if this paragraph applies to a claimant it shall not apply to his partner except where, and to the extent that, the earnings of the claimant which are to be disregarded under this paragraph are less than £15.

(2) This paragraph applies where the claimant's applicable amount includes, or but for his being an in-patient or in accommodation in a residential care home or nursing home or in residential accommodation would include, an amount by way of a disability premium under Schedule 2 (applicable amounts).

(3) This paragraph applies where–

(a) the claimant is a member of a couple, and–

(i) his applicable amount would include an amount by way of the disability premium under Schedule 2 but for the higher pensioner premium under that Schedule being applicable; or

(ii) had he not been an in-patient or in accommodation in a residential care home or nursing home or in residential accommodation his applicable amount would include the higher pensioner premium under that Schedule and had that been the case he would also satisfy the condition in (i) above; and

(b) he or his partner is under the age of 60 and at least one is engaged in part-time employment.

(4) This paragraph applies where–

(a) the claimant's applicable amount includes, or but for his being an in-patient or in accommodation in a residential care home or nursing home or in residential accommodation would include, an amount by way of the higher pensioner premium under Schedule 2; and

(b) the claimant or, if he is a member of a couple, either he or his partner has attained the age of 60; and

(c) immediately before attaining that age he or, as the case may be, he or his partner was engaged in part-time employment and the claimant was entitled by virtue of sub-paragraph (2) or (3) to a disregard of £15; and

(d) he or, as the case may be, he or his partner has continued in part-time employment.

(5) This paragraph applies where–

(a) the claimant is a member of a couple and–

(i) his applicable amount would include an amount by way of the disability premium under Schedule 2 but for the pensioner premium for persons aged 75 and over under that Schedule being applicable; or

(ii) had he not been an in-patient or in accommodation in a residential care home or nursing home or in residential accommodation his applicable amount would include the pensioner premium for persons aged 75 and over under that Schedule and had that been the case he would also satisfy the condition in (i) above; and

(b) he or his partner has attained the age of 75 but is under the age of 80 and the other is under the age of 60 and at least one member of the couple is engaged in part-time employment.

(6) This paragraph applies where–

(a) the claimant is a member of a couple and he or his partner has attained the age of 75 but is under the age of 80 and the other has attained the age of 60; and

(b) immediately before the younger member attained that age either member was engaged in part-time employment and the claimant was entitled by virtue of sub-paragraph (5) to a disregard of £15; and

(c) either he or his partner has continued in part-time employment.

(7) For the purposes of this paragraph, no account shall be taken of any period not exceeding eight consecutive weeks occurring on or after the date on which the claimant or, if he is a member of a couple, he or his partner attained the age of 60 during which either or both ceased to be engaged in part-time employment or the claimant ceased to be entitled to income support.".

Hostels

11.—(1) The provisions of the General Regulations relating to persons in hostels shall be amended in accordance with Schedule 1 to these Regulations.

(2) In Schedule 1 to these Regulations a reference to a numbered regulation or Schedule is to the regulation in, or Schedule to, the General Regulations bearing that number.

Signed by authority of the Secretary of State for Social Security.

Nicholas Scott

22nd March 1989 Minister of State, Department of Social Security

Regulation 11

SCHEDULE 1

PART I

OMISSION OF REFERENCES TO HOSTEL IN THE GENERAL REGULATIONS AND CONSEQUENTIAL AMENDMENTS

1. In regulation 2(1) (interpretation) in the definition of "residential accommodation" for the reference "regulations 19 and 20 and paragraph 8(c)(i) of Schedule 5" there shall be substituted the reference "regulation 19 and Schedule 3B".

2. In regulation 3 (definition of non-dependant)–
(a) in paragraph (2)(d) the words "subject to paragraph (3)," shall be omitted;
(b) paragraph (3) shall be omitted.

3. In regulation 16(3)(c) and (5)(b) (circumstances in which a person is treated as being or not being a member of the household) for the words "excluding heads (i) to (iii)" there shall be substituted the words "excluding heads (i) and (ii)"**(a)**.

4. Regulation 20 (applicable amounts for persons in hostels) shall be omitted.

5. In regulation 21(3) (special cases) in sub-paragraph (d) of the definition of "residential accommodation"–
(i) in head (d)(i) for the words "where full board is not" there shall be substituted the words "where no board is",
(ii) head (d)(iii) shall be omitted.

6. In regulation 22(1)(b) (reductions in applicable amounts in cases of voluntary unemployment) for the words "regulation 19 or 20" to the end there shall be substituted the words "regulation 19 (applicable amounts for persons in residential care and nursing homes) applies, the amount allowed for personal expenses for him specified in paragraph 13 of Schedule 4.".

7. In regulations 42(4)(a)(ii) (notional income) and 51(3)(a)(ii) (notional capital) the reference "or 20" and the words "or hostels", in each of those regulations shall be omitted.

8. In regulation 71(1)(b) (applicable amounts in urgent cases) the words "a hostel," and–
(i) in head (i) the words "or paragraph 11(b) of Schedule 5 (applicable amounts of persons in board and lodging accommodation or hostels) whichever is appropriate in respect of him";
(ii) in head (ii) the words "or paragraph 11(c) to (f) of Schedule 5, whichever is appropriate,"; and
(iii) in head (iii), the words "or regulation 20 and Schedule 5 whichever is appropriate",
shall be omitted.

9. In regulation 73 (amount of income support payable)–
(a) in paragraph (2) the words "or, as the case may be, 20" and "or board and lodging accommodation or hostels" shall be omitted;
(b) in paragraphs (4) and (5) the words "or, as the case may be, Schedule 5" wherever they occur in those paragraphs shall be omitted;
(c) in paragraph (5), in the definition of "P" the words "or, as the case may be, paragraph 11 of Schedule 5" shall be omitted.

10. In Schedule 3 (housing costs)–
(a) in paragraph 5(b) for the words from "either regulation 19" to "applies" there shall be substituted the words "regulation 19 (applicable amounts for persons in residential care and nursing homes) applies";
(b) in paragraph 11–
(i) in sub-paragraph (1)(a)**(b)** the words "is a person to whom regulation 3(3) applies (non-dependants) and in respect of" shall be omitted;
(ii) in sub-paragraph (7), in head (b), for the words "and he is not a person to whom regulation 3(3) applies (persons in hostels)" and, in heads (c) and (d), for the words

---

(a) Regulation 16(3)(c) and 5(b) is amended by regulation 3 of these Regulations.
(b) Sub-paragraph (1)(a) of paragraph 11 is amended by regulation 6(b)(i) of these Regulations.

"and he is not a person to whom regulation 3(3) applies", there shall be substituted in each of those provisions the words "and is not a person who lives in board and lodging accommodation".

11. In Schedule 3A (protected sums) in paragraph 7(1)(b)(ii) the words from "or a hostel" to "and hostels)" shall be omitted.

12. Schedule 5 shall be omitted.

13. In Schedule 7 (applicable amounts in special cases)–

(a) in paragraphs 10A and 10B(1) in column 1, for the words "excluding heads (i) to (iii)" there shall be substituted the words "excluding heads (i) and (ii)"**(a)**;

(b) in paragraphs 10B(1) and 10C, in column (2), the reference ", 20" in each of those paragraphs shall be omitted;

(c) in paragraph 11, in column (2), for the reference "19 to 21" wherever it occurs there shall be substituted the reference "19 or 21";

(d) in paragraph 12, in column (2), for the reference "18 to 21" wherever it occurs there shall be substituted the reference "18, 19 or 21";

(e) paragraphs 14 and 15 shall be omitted.

(f) in paragraph 16–

(i) in column (1), the reference "or 20" and the words "(persons in hostels)" shall be omitted;

(ii) in column (2), the reference "or paragraph 1(a) of Schedule 5 (applicable amounts of persons in hostels) as the case may be" shall be omitted;

(iii) in sub-paragraph (a), in column (1), for the words "excluding heads (i) to (iii)" there shall be substituted the words "excluding heads (i) and (ii)"**(b)**;

(g) in paragraph 17, in column (2), in sub-paragraphs (b)(ii), (c)(i) and (d)(i) for the reference "regulation 19, 20 or 21" there shall be substituted the reference "regulation 19 or 21";

(h) in paragraph 18 in column (1), the reference "or regulation 20 (persons in hostels)" shall be omitted;

(i) in paragraph 18, in column (2)–

(i) in sub-paragraphs (a)(i) and (ii) the reference "or 20, as the case may be," and the reference "or 20" shall be omitted wherever they occur in each of those sub-paragraphs;

(ii) in sub-paragraph (a)(iii) the reference ", or, as the case may be, paragraph 2 of Schedule 5"; the reference "or paragraph 11 of Schedule 5, as the case may be"; and the reference "or 20" shall be omitted;

(iii) in sub-paragraph (b)(ii), the reference "or, as the case may be, 20"; the reference "or paragraph 2 of Schedule 5"; and the reference "or 20 as the case may be" shall be omitted; and for the reference "either paragraph 13 of Schedule 4 or, as the case may be, paragraph 11 of Schedule 5" there shall be substituted the reference "paragraph 13 of Schedule 4";

(iv) in sub-paragraph (b)(iii) the reference "or, as the case may be, regulation 20"; the reference "or paragraph 2 of Schedule 5, as the case may be"; and the reference "or 20 as the case may be" shall be omitted; and for the reference "either paragraph 13 of Schedule 4 or paragraph 11 of Schedule 5" there shall be substituted the reference "paragraph 13 of Schedule 4";

(v) in sub-paragraph (b)(iv) the reference "or, as the case may be, 20"; the reference "or paragraph 2 of Schedule 5, as the case may be"; and the reference "or 20 as the case may be" shall be omitted; and for the reference "either paragraph 13 of Schedule 4 or paragraph 11 of Schedule 5" there shall be substituted the reference "paragraph 13 of Schedule 4";

(vi) in sub-paragraph (c) the reference "or, as the case may be, regulation 20" shall be omitted.

14. In Schedule 8 (sums to be disregarded in the calculation of earnings)–

(a) in paragraph 5 the words ", hostel," shall be omitted;

(b) in paragraph 15 for the words "residential care home, nursing home, or hostel" there shall be substituted the words "residential care home or nursing home".

(a) Paragraphs 10A and 10B are amended by regulation 9 of these Regulations.
(b) Paragraph 16(a) is amended by regulation 9 of these Regulations.

15. In Schedule 9 (sums to be disregarded in the calculation of income other than earnings) in paragraph 30(d) for the words "actual charge" to the end there shall be substituted the words "actual charge increased, where appropriate, in accordance with paragraph 2 of Schedule 4 exceeds the amount determined in accordance with regulation 19 (residential care and nursing homes).".

16. In paragraph 12 of Schedule 10 (capital to be disregarded) for the reference "Schedules 4 and 5" there shall be substituted the reference "Schedule 4".

PART II

TRANSITIONAL PROVISIONS FOR DETERMINING THE APPLICABLE AMOUNTS OF PERSONS WHO WERE IN HOSTELS PRIOR TO 9TH OCTOBER 1989

17. In regulations 17(1)(g), 18(1)(h) and 71(1)(a)(v) and (d)(iv) (applicable amounts, polygamous marriages and urgent cases) there shall be added at the end of each of those regulations the words "or, as the case may be, 3B".

18. After Schedule 3A (protected sum) there shall be inserted as Schedule 3B the Schedule set out in Schedule 2 to these Regulations.

Regulation 11 and
Schedule 1, paragraph 18

SCHEDULE 2

To be inserted after Schedule 3A to the General Regulations–

"SCHEDULE 3B

Regulations 17(1)(g), 18(1)(h)
and 71(1)(a)(v) and (d)(iv)

PROTECTED SUM

Interpretation

1.—(1) In this Schedule–

"eligible housing benefit" means–

(a) for the period of 7 consecutive days beginning on 2nd October 1989, the amount of housing benefit to which the claimant or his partner was entitled in that period which relates to the hostel normally occupied as the home by him or, if he has a partner, by him and his partner;

(b) for the period of 7 consecutive days beginning on 9th October 1989 or, in a case to which paragraph 6(4)(b) applies, for the period of 7 consecutive days referred to in that paragraph, the amount of the claimant's or his partner's maximum housing benefit determined in accordance with regulation 61 of the Housing Benefit (General) Regulations 1987**(a)** (maximum housing benefit) which relates to that accommodation.

"first week" means the benefit week beginning on a day during the period of 7 days commencing on 2nd October 1989;

"hostel" means any establishment which immediately before the commencement of this Schedule was a hostel within the meaning of regulation 20(2) (applicable amounts for persons in hostels);

"income support" includes any sum payable under Part II of the Income Support (Transitional) Regulations 1987**(b)**;

"March benefit week" means the benefit week beginning on a day during the period of 7 consecutive days beginning 20th March 1989;

"protected sum" means the amount applicable under this Schedule to a claimant who in the first week is living in a hostel or who or whose partner is temporarily absent in that week from that accommodation;

"protected total" means–

(a) the total of the claimant's applicable amount under regulation 20 in the first week or, in a case to which paragraph 6(4) applies, if the claimant or any partner of his is temporarily absent from his accommodation in that week, the amount which would have fallen to be calculated under that regulation for that week as if there had been no temporary absence; and

(a) S.I. 1987/1971.
(b) S.I. 1987/1969.

(b) the amount of any eligible housing benefit for the period of 7 consecutive days beginning 2nd October 1989;

"relevant benefit week" means the benefit week beginning on a day during the period of 7 days commencing on 9th April 1990;

"relevant provisions" means–

(a) regulation 17(1)(a) to (f) (applicable amounts);

(b) regulation 18(1)(a) to (g) (polygamous marriages);

(c) regulation 71(1)(a)(i) to (iv) (urgent cases);

(d) regulation 71(1)(d)(i) to (iii);

(e) in relation to a case to which paragraph 17(b)(ii) or (c)(i) of Schedule 7 (persons from abroad) applies, the regulations specified in that paragraph but as if the reference to regulation 17(1)(g) in that paragraph were omitted; or

(f) in relation to a case to which paragraph 17(d)(i) of that Schedule applies, the regulations specified in that paragraph but as if the reference to regulation 18 were a reference to regulation 18(1)(a) to (g) only;

"second week" means the benefit week beginning on a day during the period of 7 days commencing on 9th October 1989.

(2) For the purposes of this Schedule–

(a) in determining a claimant's applicable amount in his first week, second week or any subsequent benefit week no account shall be taken of any reduction under regulation 22 (reduction in certain cases of unemployment benefit disqualification);

(b) except in so far as it relates to any temporary absence to which paragraph 6(4) refers, where a change of circumstances takes effect in the claimant's second week which, had it taken effect in the first week, would have resulted in a lesser applicable amount in respect of that week, his applicable amount in the first week shall be determined as if the change of circumstances had taken effect in that week.

Protected sum

2.—(1) Subject to the following provisions of this paragraph and the following paragraphs of this Schedule, where the protected total of a claimant is more than–

(a) his applicable amount in the second week determined in accordance with the relevant provisions less the amount of any increase consequent on the coming into force of regulation 5 of the Income Support (General) Amendment Regulations 1989**(a)**; and

(b) any eligible housing benefit for the period of 7 consecutive days beginning 9th October 1989,

the protected sum applicable to the claimant shall be an amount equal to the difference.

(2) Where–

(a) in the second week a claimant's income calculated in accordance with Part V or, as the case may be, VI exceeds the aggregate of his applicable amount determined in accordance with the relevant provisions and X; and

(b) the amount of income support to which he is entitled in the first week is more than the amount of housing benefit to which he would, but for this sub-paragraph, have been entitled in the period of 7 consecutive days beginning on 9th October 1989,

the protected sum applicable to the claimant shall be an amount equal to X+Y+10 pence.

(3) In sub-paragraph (2)–

"X" means the sum which, but for sub-paragraph (2), would be the protected sum applicable under sub-paragraph (1);

"Y" means the amount of the excess to which sub-paragraph (2)(a) refers.

(4) For the period beginning with the claimant's relevant benefit week the protected sum applicable to the claimant shall, subject to sub-paragraph (6) and the following paragraphs of this Schedule, be–

(a) the total of–

(i) the amount of the allowance for personal expenses for the claimant or, if he is a member of a family, for him and for each member of his family in the first week determined, or which, but for any temporary absence, would have been determined, in accordance with paragraph 11 of Schedule 5 as then in force;

(a) S.I. 1989/534.

(ii) the amount of any increase for meals in the first week determined, or which, but for any temporary absence, would have been determined, in accordance with paragraph 2 of that Schedule; and

(iii) the amount or, if he is a member of a family, the aggregate of the amounts determined in accordance with sub-paragraph (5),

less the aggregate of his applicable amount in the second week determined, or which, but for any temporary absence, would have been determined, in accordance with the relevant provisions and, where applicable, the amount of any reduction in the protected sum made by virtue of paragraph 4 in a benefit week occurring before the relevant benefit week; or

(b) the amount of the protected sum which was applicable to him in the immediately preceding benefit week,

whichever is the lower.

(5) For the purposes of sub-paragraph (4)(a), where in the first week the accommodation charge makes or, but for any temporary absence, would have made, provision or no provision for meals, as respects each person an amount shall be determined as follows–

(a) in a case where the provision is for at least three meals a day–

(i) for the claimant, £17.20;

(ii) for a member of his family aged 16 or over, £12.50;

(iii) for a member of his family aged less than 16, £6.25;

(b) except where head (c) applies, in a case where the provision is for less than three meals a day–

(i) for the claimant, £13.85;

(ii) for a member of his family aged 16 or over, £8.30;

(iii) for a member of his family aged less than 16, £4.15;

(c) in a case where the provision is for breakfast only–

(i) for the claimant, £7.05;

(ii) for a member of his family, £1.50;

(d) in a case where there is no provision for meals, for the claimant or, if he is a member of a family, for the claimant and for the members of his family for whom there is no such provision, £5.55;

(6) Where in the relevant benefit week the claimant is in, or only temporarily absent from, residential accommodation, the protected sum applicable to the claimant for the period beginning with that week shall be–

(a) equal to the difference between–

(i) the amount of the allowance for personal expenses for the claimant or, if he is a member of a family, for him and for each member of his family in the first week determined, or which, but for any temporary absence, would have been determined, in accordance with paragraph 11 of Schedule 5 as then in force; and

(ii) the amount of the allowance for personal expenses for the claimant or, if he is a member of a family, for him and for each member of his family in the second week determined, or which, but for any temporary absence would have been determined, under paragraph 13 of Schedule 7 (persons in residential accommodation),

less, where applicable, the amount of any reduction in the protected sum made by virtue of paragraph 4 in a benefit week occurring before the relevant benefit week; or

(b) the amount of the protected sum which was applicable to him in the immediately preceding benefit week,

whichever is the lower.

Persons not entitled to a protected sum

3.—(1) Subject to paragraph 6, a protected sum shall not be applicable to a claimant where he changes or vacates his hostel during the period of 7 consecutive days beginning 9th October 1989.

(2) Except where regulation 8(2)(b) of the Housing Benefit (General) Regulations 1987 (eligible housing costs) applies, a protected sum shall not be applicable to a claimant unless he, or any partner of his, is entitled to housing benefit for the period of 7 consecutive days beginning 9th October 1989 or, where paragraph 6(4)(b) applies, for the period of 7 consecutive days referred to in that paragraph, in respect of the hostel normally occupied as the home by him, or if he has a partner, by him and his partner.

(3) A protected sum shall not be applicable to a claimant where–

(a) he has been or would, but for any temporary absence, have been in the same accommodation in both the March benefit week and the second week, and–

(i) his applicable amount in both those weeks fell or would have fallen, but for any temporary absence, to be determined under paragraph 13(1) of Schedule 7; or

(ii) his applicable amount in the second week fell or would have fallen, but for any temporary absence, to be determined under that paragraph and would also have fallen to be so determined in the March benefit week had his stay in that accommodation been other than temporary; or

(b) his applicable amount in the second week fell or would have fallen, but for any temporary absence, to be determined under that paragraph and would also have fallen to be so determined in the March benefit week had he been in the same accommodation in that week and had his stay in that accommodation been other than temporary.

Reduction of protected sum

4.—(1) Subject to sub-paragraph (2), the protected sum shall be reduced by the amount of any increase, in a benefit week subsequent to the second week, in the claimant's applicable amount determined in accordance with the relevant provisions.

(2) Where regulation 22 (reduction in certain cases of unemployment benefit disqualification) ceases to apply to a claimant and as a result his applicable amount increases no account shall be taken of that increase.

Termination of protected sum

5. Subject to paragraph 6, the protected sum shall cease to be applicable if–

(a) that amount is reduced to nil under paragraph 4; or

(b) the claimant changes or vacates his hostel; or

(c) the claimant ceases to be entitled to income support.

Modifications in cases of temporary absence and loss of entitlement to income support

6.—(1) Paragraph 5(b) shall not apply to a claimant if–

(a) he becomes a patient within the meaning of regulation 21(3) (special cases); or

(b) on his ceasing to be a patient within the meaning of regulation 21(3), he returns to the hostel which he occupied immediately before he became a patient; or

(c) in a case to which sub-paragraph (3) applies, on his becoming re-entitled to income support, he is in the accommodation which he occupied immediately before he ceased to be entitled to income support.

(2) Except where sub-paragraph (4) applies, where a protected sum was applicable to the claimant immediately before he or any partner of his became a patient within the meaning of regulation 21(3) for a period of 14 weeks or less, he shall, subject to sub-paragraph (1)(b), on his or, as the case may be, his partner ceasing to be a patient be entitled to a protected sum equal to–

(a) the amount by which his protected total exceeds his applicable amount determined in accordance with the relevant provisions in the first benefit week in which his applicable amount ceases to be determined under paragraph 1 of Schedule 7 and either–

(i) any eligible housing benefit for the period of 7 consecutive days beginning on 9th October 1989; or, if greater,

(ii) in a case where sub-paragraph (4)(b) applied, any eligible housing benefit for the period of 7 consecutive days referred to in that sub-paragraph; or

(b) the amount of the protected sum to which he was entitled in the immediately preceding benefit week,

whichever is the lower.

(3) Paragraph 5(c) shall not apply to a claimant who has ceased to be entitled to income support for a period of not more than 8 weeks–

(a) if immediately before he ceased to be so entitled a protected sum was applicable to him; and

(b) except where sub-paragraph (4) applies, if during that period he becomes re-entitled, or would by virtue of this sub-paragraph be re-entitled, to income support he shall, subject to sub-paragraph (1)(c), be entitled to a protected sum equal to–

(i) the amount by which his protected total exceeds his applicable amount determined in accordance with the relevant provisions in the first benefit week in which he becomes so re-entitled and either any eligible housing benefit for the period of 7 consecutive days beginning 9th October 1989 or, if greater, in a case to which sub-paragraph (4)(b) applied, any eligible housing benefit for the period of 7 consecutive days referred to in that sub-paragraph; or

(ii) the amount of the protected sum to which he was previously entitled,

whichever is the lower.

(4) Where a claimant or any partner of his is temporarily absent from his accommodation for a period not exceeding 14 weeks which includes the first or second week (or both)–

(a) in a case where a protected sum was applicable to the claimant immediately before his or, as the case may be, his partner's return to that accommodation and the full charge was made for the accommodation during the temporary absence, on the claimant's or, as the case may be, his partner's return to that accommodation, the claimant shall be entitled to a protected sum equal to–

(i) the amount by which his protected total exceeds his applicable amount determined in accordance with the relevant provisions in the first complete benefit week after his, or as the case may be, his partner's return to that accommodation and any eligible housing benefit for the period of 7 consecutive days beginning 9th October 1989; or

(ii) the amount of the protected sum which was applicable to him in the immediately preceding benefit week,

whichever is the lower;

(b) in a case where–

(i) a protected sum has not at any time been applicable to the claimant; or

(ii) immediately before the claimant's or, as the case may be, his partner's return to that accommodation a protected sum was applicable to the claimant but a reduced charge was made for the accommodation during the temporary absence,

the claimant on his or, as the case may be, his partner's return to that accommodation shall, subject to sub-paragraph (5), be entitled to a protected sum equal to the amount by which his protected total exceeds his applicable amount determined in accordance with the relevant provisions in the first complete benefit week after his or, as the case may be, his partner's return to that accommodation and the amount of eligible housing benefit for the period of 7 consecutive days beginning on the date determined in accordance with regulation 65 or, as the case may be, 68(2) of the Housing Benefit (General) Regulations 1987 (date on which entitlement is to commence or change of circumstances is to take effect) following that person's return to that accommodation.

(5) Where, in a case to which sub-paragraph (4)(b)(i) applies–

(a) in the first complete benefit week after the claimant's or, as the case may be, his partner's return to his accommodation the claimant's income calculated in accordance with Part V or, as the case may be, VI exceeds the aggregate of his applicable amount determined in accordance with the relevant provisions and X; and

(b) the amount of income support to which he was entitled in the first week is more than the amount of housing benefit to which he would, but for this sub-paragraph, have been entitled in the period of 7 consecutive days beginning on the date determined in accordance with regulation 65 or, as the case may be, 68(2) of the Housing Benefit (General) Regulations 1987 following his or, as the case may be, his partner's return to that accommodation,

the protected sum applicable to the claimant shall be an amount equal to X+Y+10 pence.

(6) In sub-paragraph (5)–

"X" means the sum which, but for sub-paragraph (5), would be the protected sum applicable in a case to which sub-paragraph (4)(b)(i) applies;

"Y" means the amount of the excess to which sub-paragraph (5)(a) refers.

(7) The foregoing provisions of this paragraph shall not apply to a claimant if he or, if he has a partner, he or his partner, in the first week is temporarily living in a hostel and that accommodation is not the accommodation normally occupied as the home.".

EXPLANATORY NOTE

(This note is not part of the Regulations)

These Regulations further amend the Income Support (General) Regulations 1987 in the following respects–

(a) they introduce an increased pensioner premium for persons aged 75 and over and uprate the amount of the higher pensioner premium with effect from 9th October 1989 (regulations 4 and 5); and provide for an earnings disregard of £15 where but for the new premiums a person would have been entitled to the disability premium (regulation 10);

(b) they make provision for boarders not to be treated as non-dependants if they live in the household of another claimant and for a deduction to be made from a claimant's housing costs in respect of boarders aged 18 or over (regulation 6); make a number of miscellaneous amendments to the provisions for determining a boarder's protected sum and provide for that sum not to be reduced by any increase in his applicable amount consequent on the new premiums (regulation 7);

(c) they make provision for the applicable amount of persons in hostels not to include an amount in respect of accommodation and provide transitional protection for such persons who would otherwise suffer a loss in their benefit income (regulation 10); make an amendment consequential on the omission of board and lodging areas (regulation 8); and make a minor amendment to references to the definition of residential accommodation (regulations 3 and 9).

These Regulations are made before the expiry of 12 months from the commencement of the provisions under which they are made: they are accordingly exempt, by section 61(5) of the Social Security Act 1986, from reference to the Social Security Advisory Committee and have not been so referred.

STATUTORY INSTRUMENTS

1989 No. 535

BETTING, GAMING AND LOTTERIES

The Gaming Clubs (Hours and Charges) (Amendment) Regulations 1989

Made - - - -	*21st March 1989*
Laid before Parliament	*3rd April 1989*
Coming into force	*1st May 1989*

In exercise of the powers conferred on me by sections 14(2) and 51 of the Gaming Act 1968(**a**), and after consultation with the Gaming Board for Great Britain, I hereby make the following Regulations:

1.—(1) These Regulations may be cited as the Gaming Clubs (Hours and Charges) (Amendment) Regulations 1989 and shall come into force on 1st May 1989.

(2) These Regulations do not extend to Scotland.

2. Regulation 5(1) of the Gaming Clubs (Hours and Charges) Regulations 1984(**b**) shall be amended by substituting for the figure "£4.60", in both places where it occurs, the figure "£5".

3. The Gaming Clubs (Hours and Charges) (Amendment) Regulations 1987(**c**) are hereby revoked.

Home Office
21st March 1989

Douglas Hurd
One of Her Majesty's Principal Secretaries of State

EXPLANATORY NOTE

(This note is not part of the Regulations)

These Regulations increase the maximum charges which may be made for admission to gaming on bingo club premises in England and Wales from £4.60 to £5.

(**a**) 1968 c.65.
(**b**) S.I. 1984/248, amended by S.I. 1987/609.
(**c**) S.I. 1987/609.

STATUTORY INSTRUMENTS

1989 No. 536

BETTING, GAMING AND LOTTERIES

The Gaming Act (Variation of Monetary Limits) Order 1989

Made - - - -	*21st March 1989*
Laid before Parliament	*3rd April 1989*
Coming into force	*1st May 1989*

In exercise of the powers conferred on me by sections 20(3) and (8) and 51(4) of the Gaming Act 1968(**a**), I hereby make the following Order:–

1.—(1) This Order may be cited as the Gaming Act (Variation of Monetary Limits) Order 1989 and shall come into force on 1st May 1989.

(2) This Order shall not extend to Scotland.

2. Section 20(3) of the Gaming Act 1968(**b**) (under which the maximum permitted aggregate amount of winnings in respect of games of bingo played in one week simultaneously on different club premises is £3,500) shall have effect with the substitution, for the reference to the sum specified in that subsection, of a reference to the sum of £4,000.

3. Section 20(8) of the Gaming Act 1968(**b**) (under which the maximum amount by which weekly winnings on any particular bingo club premises may exceed the aggregate amount of the stakes hazarded is £1,500) shall have effect with the substitution, for the reference to the sum specified in that subsection, of a reference to the sum of £1,750.

4. The Gaming Act (Variation of Monetary Limits) Order 1987(**c**) is hereby revoked.

Home Office
21st March 1989

Douglas Hurd
One of Her Majesty's Principal Secretaries of State

EXPLANATORY NOTE

(This note is not part of the Order)

This Order increases in England and Wales the monetary limits specified in section 20(3) and (8) of the Gaming Act 1968 and described in articles 2 and 3 of the Order.

(**a**) 1968 c.65; section 20(3) was amended by section 1 of the Gaming (Amendment) Act 1980 (c.8). (**b**) The sums specified in section 20(3) and (8) are as substituted respectively by articles 2 and 3 of the Gaming Act (Variation of Monetary Limits) Order 1987 (S.I. 1987/608). (**c**) S.I. 1987/608.

STATUTORY INSTRUMENTS

1989 No. 537

SEA FISHERIES

CONSERVATION OF SEA FISH

The Cod (Specified Sea Areas) (Prohibition of Fishing) (No. 2) Order 1989

Made - - - -	*22nd March 1989*
Laid before Parliament	*23rd March 1989*
Coming into force	*24th March 1989*

The Minister of Agriculture, Fisheries and Food and the Secretaries of State respectively concerned with the sea fishing industry in Scotland, Wales and Northern Ireland, acting jointly, in exercise of the powers conferred on them by sections 5(1), 15(3) and 20(1) of the Sea Fish (Conservation) Act 1967**(a)**, and of all other powers enabling them in that behalf, hereby make the following Order:

Title, commencement, duration and interpretation

1.—(1) This Order may be cited as the Cod (Specified Sea Areas) (Prohibition of Fishing) (No. 2) Order 1989, shall come into force on 24th March 1989 and shall cease to have effect on 1st July 1989.

(2) In this Order–

"sea area" means a statistical sub-area or division of the International Council for the Exploration of the sea**(b)** or the area known as CECAF Division 34.1.1 (EC Zone) described in the Schedule hereto;

"British fishing boat" means a fishing boat which is registered in the United Kingdom, the Isle of Man or any of the Channel Islands or which, not being so registered, is British-owned.

Prohibition

2. Fishing for cod (*Gadus morhua*)–

(a) within any part of a sea area by any British fishing boat registered in the United Kingdom or the Isle of Man; or

(b) within any part of a sea area which lies inside British fishery limits by any other British fishing boat,

is prohibited.

(a) 1967 c.84; section 5(1) was substituted by section 22(1) of the Fisheries Act 1981 (c.29) and, by virtue of S.I. 1973/238, section 5 applies in relation to British fishing boats registered in the Isle of Man as it applies in relation to British fishing boats registered in the United Kingdom; section 15(3) was substituted by paragraph 38(3) of Schedule 1 to the Sea Fisheries Act 1968 (c.77) and amended by paragraph 16(1) of Schedule 2 to the Fishery Limits Act 1976 (c.86); section 22(2)(a) which contains a definition of "the Ministers" for the purposes of sections 5 and 15(3) was amended by the Fisheries Act 1981, sections 19(2)(d) and 45(b).
(b) Cmnd.2586.

Powers of British sea-fishery officers in relation to fishing boats

3.—(1) For the purpose of the enforcement of this Order a British sea-fishery officer may exercise in relation to any British fishing boat anywhere the powers conferred by paragraphs (2) to (4) of this article.

(2) He may go on board the boat, with or without persons assigned to assist him in his duties, and for that purpose may require the boat to stop and do anything else which will facilitate the boarding of the boat.

(3) He may require the attendance of the master and other persons on board the boat and may make any examination and inquiry which appears to him to be necessary for the purpose mentioned in paragraph (1) of this article and, in particular–

(a) may examine any fish on the boat and the equipment of the boat, including the fishing gear, and require persons on board the boat to do anything which appears to him to be necessary for facilitating the examination;

(b) may require any person on board the boat to produce any document relating to the boat, to its fishing operations or other operations ancillary thereto or to the persons on board which is in his custody or possession and may take copies of any such document;

(c) for the purpose of ascertaining whether the master, owner or charterer of the boat has committed an offence under section 5(1) or (6) of the Sea Fish (Conservation) Act 1967**(a)** as read with this Order, may search the boat for any such document and may require any person on board the boat to do anything which appears to him to be necessary for facilitating the search; and

(d) where the boat is one in relation to which he has reason to suspect that such an offence has been committed, may seize and detain any such document produced to him or found on board for the purpose of enabling the document to be used as evidence in proceedings for the offence;

but nothing in subparagraph (d) above shall permit any document required by law to be carried on board the boat to be seized and detained except while the boat is detained in a port.

(4) Where it appears to a British sea-fishery officer that a contravention of this Order has at any time taken place within British fishery limits, he may–

(a) require the master of the boat in relation to which the offence took place to take, or may himself take, the boat and its crew to the port which appears to him to be the nearest convenient port; and

(b) detain or require the master to detain the boat in the port;

and where such an officer detains or requires the detention of a boat he shall serve on the master a notice in writing stating that the boat will be or is required to be detained until the notice is withdrawn by the service on the master of a further notice in writing signed by a British sea-fishery officer.

Revocation

4. The Cod (Specified Sea Areas) (Prohibition of Fishing) Order 1989**(b)** is hereby revoked.

(a) Sub-section (6) was amended by section 22(2) of the Fisheries Act 1981. By virtue of sub-section (7), where sub-section (6) is not complied with in the case of any fishing boat, the master, the owner and the charterer (if any) are guilty of an offence under that sub-section.
(b) S.I. 1989/142.

In witness whereof the Official Seal of the Minister of Agriculture, Fisheries and Food is hereunto affixed on 19th March 1989.

(L.S.)

John MacGregor
Minister of Agriculture,
Fisheries and Food

22nd March 1989

Sanderson of Bowden
Minister of State, Scottish Office

19th March 1989

Peter Walker
Secretary of State for Wales

20th March 1989

Tom King
Secretary of State for Northern Ireland

Article 1(2)

SCHEDULE

SEA AREAS IN RESPECT OF WHICH PROHIBITION OF FISHING FOR COD APPLIES

ICES Statistical Division VIIb, c (West of Ireland and Porcupine Bank)

The waters bounded by a line beginning at a point on the west coast of Ireland in 54°30′ north latitude; thence due west to 18°00′ west longitude; thence due south to 52°30′ north latitude; thence due east to the coast of Ireland; thence in a northerly direction along the west coast of Ireland to the point of beginning.

ICES Statistical Division VIId (Eastern English Channel)

The waters bounded by a line beginning at a point on the west coast of France in 51°00′ north latitude; thence due west to the coast of England; thence in a westerly direction along the south coast of England to 2°00′ west longitude; thence in a southerly direction to the coast of France at Cape de la Hague; thence in a north-easterly direction along the coast of France to the point of beginning.

ICES Statistical Division VIIe (Western English Channel)

The waters bounded by a line beginning on the south coast of England in 2°00′ west longitude; thence in a southerly and westerly direction along the coast of England to a point on the south-west coast in 50°00′ north latitude; thence due west to 7°00′ west longitude; thence due south to 49°30′ north latitude; thence due east to 5°00′ west longitude; thence due south to 48°00′ north latitude; thence due east to the coast of France; thence in a northerly and north-easterly direction along the coast of France to Cape de la Hague; thence in a northerly direction to the point of beginning.

ICES Statistical Division VIIf (Bristol Channel)

The waters bounded by a line beginning at a point on the south coast of Wales in 5°00′ west longitude; thence due south to 51°00′ north latitude; thence due west to 6°00′ west longitude; thence due south to 50°30′ north latitude; thence due west to 7°00′ west longitude; thence due south to 50°00′ north latitude; thence due east to the coast of England; thence along the south-west coast of England and the south coast of Wales to the point of beginning.

ICES Statistical Division VIIg (South-east of Ireland)

The waters bounded by a line beginning at a point in 9°00′ west longitude on the south coast of Ireland; thence due south to 50°00′ north latitude; thence due east to 7°00′ west longitude; thence due north to 50°30′ north latitude; thence due east to 6°00′ west longitude; thence due north to 51°00′ north latitude; thence due east to 5°00′ west longitude; thence due north to the south coast of Wales; thence in a north-westerly direction along the coast of Wales to a point in 52°00′ north latitude; thence due west to the south-east coast of Ireland; thence in a south-westerly direction along the coast of Ireland to the point of beginning.

ICES Statisical Division VIIh (Little Sole Bank)

The waters bounded by a line beginning at a point in 50°00′ north latitude 7°00′ west longitude; thence due west to 9°00′ west longitude; thence due south to 48°00′ north latitude; thence due east to 5°00′ west longitude; thence due north to 49°30′ north latitude; thence due west to 7°00′ west longitude; thence due north to the point of beginning.

ICES Statistical Division VIIj (Great Sole Bank)

The waters bounded by a line beginning at a point in 52°30′ north latitude on the west coast of Ireland; thence due west to 12°00′ west longitude; thence due south to 48°00′ north latitude; thence due east to 9°00′ west longitude; thence due north to the south coast of Ireland; thence in a Westerly and northerly direction along the coast of Ireland to the point of beginning.

ICES Statistical Division VIIk (West of Great Sole Bank)

The waters bounded by a line beginning at a point in 52°30′ north latitude, 12°00′ west longitude; thence due west to 18°00′ west longitude; thence due south to 48°00′ north latitude; thence due east to 12°00′ west longitude; thence due north to the point of beginning.

ICES Statistical Sub-Area VIII (Bay of Biscay)

The waters bounded by a line beginning at a point on the coast of France in 48°00′ north latitude; thence due west to 18°00′ west longitude; thence due south to 43°00′ north latitude; thence due east to the coast of Spain; thence in a northerly direction along the coasts of Spain and France to the point of beginning.

ICES Statistical Sub-Area IX (Portuguese Waters)

The waters bounded by a line beginning at a point on the coast of Spain in 43°00′ north latitude; thence due west to 10°00′ west longitude; thence due south to 36°00′ north latitude; thence due east to a point on the coast of Spain (Punta Marroqui isthmus) in 5°36′ west longitude; thence in a north-westerly direction along the south-west coast of Spain, the coast of Portugal, and the north-west coast of Spain to the point of beginning.

ICES Statistical Sub-Area X (Azores Grounds)

The waters bounded by a line beginning at a point in 48°00′ north latitude, 18°00′ west longitude; thence due west to 42°00′ west longitude; thence due south to 36°00′ north latitude; thence due west to 18°00′ west longitude; thence due north to the point of beginning.

CECAF Division 34.1.1. (EC Zone)

The waters commonly known as the Moroccan coast bounded by a line drawn from a position on the coast of Spain in 36°00′ north latitude and 5°36′ west longitude (isthmus of Punta Marroqui); thence due west to 13°00′ west longitude; thence due south to 29°00′ north latitude; thence in a southerly and westerly direction to a position in 26°00′ north latitude and 16°00′ west longitude; thence due east to a point on the coast of the continent of Africa in 26°00′ north latitude; thence in a northerly and easterly direction along the coast of the continent of Africa to a point in 5°36′ west longitude; thence due north to the point of commencement.

EXPLANATORY NOTE

(This note is not part of the Order)

This Order prohibits fishing for cod (*Gadus morhua*)–

(a) by any British fishing boat registered in the United Kingdom or the Isle of Man within any part of a sea area specified in the Schedule to the Order, or

(b) by any British fishing boat registered in any of the Channel Islands or by any British-owned fishing boat within any part of such a sea area which lies inside British fishery limits (article 2).

By virtue of section 5(6) of the Sea Fish (Conservation) Act 1967 (as amended by section 22(2) of the Fisheries Act 1981), where, in the course of any fishing operations conducted in any of the above-mentioned sea areas, cod are taken on board a boat to which this Order applies, those fish shall (subject to section 9 of that Act) be returned to the sea forthwith.

British sea-fishery officers are given enforcement powers in relation to boats to which the Order applies (article 3).

The Order revokes the Cod (Specified Sea Areas) (Prohibition of Fishing) Order 1989 which has ceased to have effect (article 4).

The Order ceases to have effect on 1st July 1989.

STATUTORY INSTRUMENTS

1989 No. 538

OVERSEAS DEVELOPMENT AND CO-OPERATION

The African Development Bank (Further Subscription to Capital Stock) Order 1989

Made - - - -	*17th March 1989*
Coming into force	*17th March 1989*

Whereas it is provided in section 4(1) of the Overseas Development and Co-operation Act 1980 ("the Act")(**a**) that if the Government of the United Kingdom becomes bound by arrangements for the making of any further payment to an international development bank beyond the initial subscription or other initial contribution to its capital stock, the Secretary of State may with the approval of the Treasury by Order made by statutory instrument make provision for any of the purposes specified in that subsection;

And whereas a draft of this Order has been laid before the House of Commons in accordance with section 4(3) of the Act and has been approved by a resolution of that House;

Now, therefore, the Secretary of State, in exercise of the powers conferred upon him by section 4 of the Act and with the approval of the Treasury, hereby makes the following Order:

1.—(1) This Order may be cited as the African Development Bank (Further Subscription to Capital Stock) Order 1989 and shall come into force forthwith.

(2) In this Order–

"the Agreement" means the Agreement establishing the African Development Bank dated 4th August 1963, as amended in accordance with Resolution 05–79 adopted by the Board of Governors of the Bank (particulars of which Agreement, as so amended, were laid before Parliament by Command of Her Majesty in July 1981(**b**);

"the Bank" means the African Development Bank established by the Agreement;

"the Resolution" means Resolution B/BG/87/11 concerning the general increase in the capital stock of the Bank adopted by the Board of Governors of the Bank on 11th June 1987.

2. The Secretary of State may, on behalf of the Government of the United Kingdom, out of money provided by Parliament–

(a) make payment of a further subscription to the increased authorised capital stock of the Bank of sums not exceeding in the aggregate the equivalent of Special Drawing Rights 150,400,000 in accordance with arrangements made between the Government and the Bank in accordance with the Agreement and the Resolution; and

(b) make any payments which may become payable in accordance with the said arrangements to maintain the value of the payment mentioned in paragraph (a) above; and

(**a**) 1980 c.63.
(**b**) Cmnd. 8284.

(c) make payment in sterling of sums required to redeem any non-interest-bearing and non-negotiable notes or other obligations which may be issued or created by him and accepted by the Bank in accordance with the said arrangements.

3. Any sums received by the Government of the United Kingdom from the Bank in pursuance of the said arrangements shall be paid into the Consolidated Fund.

Geoffrey Howe
17th March 1989 One of Her Majesty's Principal Secretaries of State

We approve,

David MacLean
David Lightbown
17th March 1989 Two of the Lords Commissioners of Her Majesty's Treasury

---

EXPLANATORY NOTE

(This note is not part of the Order)

This Order provides for the payment to the African Development Bank of a subscription equivalent to 150,400,000 Special Drawing Rights to the increased authorised capital stock of the Bank pursuant to arrangements made with the Bank in accordance with Resolution B/BG/87/11 adopted by the Board of Governors of the Bank on 11th June 1987. The Order also provides for the payment of any sum which may be required to maintain the value of that subscription, and for the redemption of non-interest-bearing and non-negotiable notes issued by the Secretary of State in payment of that subscription. It further provides that certain sums that may be received by the Government of the United Kingdom from the Bank shall be paid into the Consolidated Fund. The provisions of Resolution B/BG/87/11 may be obtained by application to the Overseas Development Administration, Eland House, Stag Place, London SW1E 5DH.

STATUTORY INSTRUMENTS

1989 No. 539

OVERSEAS DEVELOPMENT AND CO-OPERATION

The African Development Fund (Fifth Replenishment) Order 1989

Made - - - -	*20th March 1989*
Coming into force	*20th March 1989*

Whereas it is provided in section 4(1) of the Overseas Development and Co-operation Act 1980 ("the Act")**(a)** that if the Government of the United Kingdom becomes bound by any arrangements for the making of any further payment to an international development bank beyond the initial subscription or other initial contribution to its capital stock, the Secretary of State may with the approval of the Treasury by Order made by statutory instrument make provision for any of the purposes specified in that subsection;

And whereas a draft of this Order has been laid before the House of Commons in accordance with section 4(3) of the Act and has been approved by a resolution of that House;

Now, therefore, the Secretary of State, in exercise of the powers conferred upon him by section 4 of the Act and with the approval of the Treasury, hereby makes the following Order:

1.—(1) This Order may be cited as the African Development Fund (Fifth Replenishment) Order 1989 and shall come into force forthwith.

(2) In this Order–

"the Agreement" means the Agreement establishing the African Development Fund dated 29th November 1972 and ratified by the Government of the United Kingdom on 30th June 1973**(b)**;

"the Fund" means the African Development Fund established by the Agreement;

"the Fifth Replenishment Resolution" means Resolution F/BG/88/01 adopted by the Board of Governors of the Fund on 31st May 1988.

2. The Secretary of State may make payment on behalf of the Government of the United Kingdom out of money provided by Parliament of a further subscription to the Fund of a sum not exceeding £57,883,975 in accordance with arrangements made between the Government and the Fund in accordance with the Fifth Replenishment Resolution.

3. The Secretary of State may out of money provided by Parliament make payment in sterling of sums required to redeem any non-interest-bearing and non-negotiable notes or other obligations which may be issued or created by him and accepted by the Fund in accordance with the Agreement or the said arrangements.

(a) 1980 c.63.
(b) Cmnd. 7551.

4. Any sums received by the Government of the United Kingdom in pursuance of the Agreement or the said arrangements shall be paid into the Consolidated Fund.

Geoffrey Howe
One of Her Majesty's Principal
Secretaries of State

17th March 1989

We approve,

David MacLean
David Lightbown
Two of the Lords Commissioners
of Her Majesty's Treasury

20th March 1989

EXPLANATORY NOTE

(This note is not part of the Order)

This Order provides for the payment to the African Development Fund of a sum not exceeding £57,883,975 as representing the subscription of the Government of the United Kingdom to the Fifth Replenishment of the resources of that Fund, and for the redemption of non-interest-bearing and non-negotiable notes issued by the Secretary of State in respect of the payment. The Order further provides that certain sums which may be received by the Government of the United Kingdom from the Fund shall be paid into the Consolidated Fund. The provisions of Resolution F/BG/88/01 may be obtained by application to the Overseas Development Administration, Eland House, Stag Place, London SW1E 5DH.

STATUTORY INSTRUMENTS

1989 No. 540

PENSIONS

The War Pensions (Miscellaneous Amendments) Order 1989

Made - - - - *20th March 1989*

Coming into force - *1st April 1989*

The Secretary of State for Social Security, in exercise of the powers conferred by section 7(3) of the Pensions (Navy, Army, Air Force and Mercantile Marine) Act 1939**(a)**, and of all other powers enabling him in that behalf, hereby makes the following Order:

Citation and commencement

1. This Order may be cited as the War Pensions (Miscellaneous Amendments) Order 1989, and shall come into force on 1st April 1989.

Public Funds to include reference to community charge

2.—(1) In article 2(9) of the War Pensions (Naval Auxiliary Personnel) Scheme 1964**(b)** (meaning of "public funds") after the words "general or local Act" there shall be inserted the words "moneys provided under the Abolition of Domestic Rates etc. (Scotland) Act 1987**(c)**".

(2) In article 2(26) of the War Pensions (Mercantile Marine) Scheme 1964**(d)** (meaning of "public funds") after the words "general or local Act", there shall be inserted the words "moneys provided under the Abolition of Domestic Rates etc. (Scotland) Act 1987".

(3) In article 1(10) of the War Pensions (Coastguards) Scheme 1944**(e)** (meaning of "public funds"), after the words "general or local Act" there shall be inserted the words "moneys provided under the Abolition of Domestic Rates etc. (Scotland) Act 1987".

Signed by authority of the Secretary of State for Social Security.

Nicholas Scott
Minister of State,
Department of Social Security

20th March 1989

(a) 1939 c.83. The powers conferred by section 7 are now vested in the Secretary of State by the Transfer of Functions (Ministry of Pensions) Order 1953 (S.I. 1953/1198), article 2, the Ministry of Social Security Act 1966 (c.20), section 2, and the Secretary of State for Social Services Order 1968 (S.I. 1968/1699), article 2.
(b) S.I. 1964/1985, to which there are amendments not relevant to this Order.
(c) 1987 c.47.
(d) S.I. 1964/2058, to which there are amendments not relevant to this Order.
(e) S.I. 1944/500, to which there are amendments not relevant to this Order.

EXPLANATORY NOTE

(This note is not part of the Order)

This Order makes amendments to various war pensions schemes consequent upon the abolition in Scotland from 1st April 1989 of domestic rates and their replacement by community charge.

STATUTORY INSTRUMENTS

1989 No. 547

PUBLIC HEALTH, ENGLAND AND WALES
PUBLIC HEALTH, SCOTLAND
PUBLIC HEALTH, NORTHERN IRELAND

The Motor Fuel (Lead Content of Petrol) (Amendment) Regulations 1989

Made - - - -	*22nd March 1989*
Laid before Parliament	*3rd April 1989*
Coming into force	*24th April 1989*

The Secretary of State for Transport, in exercise of the powers conferred by sections 75 and 77(1) of the Control of Pollution Act 1974(**a**), and now vested in him(**b**) and of all other enabling powers, and after consultation with persons appearing to him to represent manufacturers and users of motor vehicles, persons appearing to him to represent the producers and users of fuel for motor vehicles, and persons appearing to him to be conversant with problems of air pollution, in accordance with section 75(2) of that Act, hereby makes the following Regulations:

1. These Regulations may be cited as the Motor Fuel (Lead Content of Petrol) (Amendment) Regulations 1989 and shall come into force on 24th April 1989.

2. The Motor Fuel (Lead Content of Petrol) Regulations 1981(**c**) are hereby further amended in accordance with the following provisions of these Regulations.

3. In regulation 4(2), for sub-paragraph (a) there shall be substituted the following sub-paragraph–

"(a) if the petrol is leaded, it is tested by the method prescribed in the British Standard which is entitled "Method for determination of lead content of gasoline by the iodine monochloride method" and was published on 31st May 1988 under the number BS 5657: 1988 (ISO 3830: 1981);".

4. For regulation 7 (information as to the composition of petrol)(**d**) there shall be substituted the following regulation–

"**7.** Subject to regulation 8, every petrol pump in a petrol filling station which is used or intended to be used to deliver petrol shall be marked by the occupier of the filling station as follows–

(**a**) 1974 c.40.
(**b**) S.I. 1979/571 and 1981/238.
(**c**) S.I. 1981/1523, as amended by S.I. 1985/1728.
(**d**) Regulation 7 of S.I. 1981/1523 was substituted by regulation 5 of S.I. 1985/1728.

(a) in the case of leaded petrol, in accordance with the British Standard which is entitled "Specification for leaded petrol (gasoline) for motor vehicles" and was published on 31st May 1988 under the number BS 4040: 1988; and

(b) in the case of unleaded petrol, in accordance with the British Standard which is entitled "Specification for unleaded petrol (gasoline) for motor vehicles" and was published on 31st May 1988 under the number BS 7070: 1988.".

Signed by authority of the Secretary of State

Peter Bottomley
Parliamentary Under Secretary of State,
Department of Transport

22nd March 1989

EXPLANATORY NOTE

(This note is not part of the Regulations)

These Regulations further amend the Motor Fuel (Lead Content of Petrol) Regulations 1981 in the following ways–

(1) A revised standard test for the lead content of leaded petrol is introduced (regulation 3).

(2) Revised standard specifications for leaded and unleaded petrol are introduced in accordance with Council Directive 85/536/EEC and Community Directive 87/441/EEC on the use of substitute fuel components (oxygenates). The revised standard specification for leaded petrol also limits the benzene content of the fuel to 5% by volume in accordance with Council Directive 85/210/EEC (regulation 4).

Copies of the British Standard specifications mentioned in the Regulations may be obtained from any of the sales outlets operated by the British Standards Institution, or by post from the British Standards Institution at Linford Wood, Milton Keynes MK14 6LE (Telephone number: Milton Keynes (STD 0908) 221166. Copies of the EEC Directives can be obtained from Her Majesty's Stationery Office. Details of the EEC Directives are set out in the table below.

Instrument	*Reference*
Council Directive 85/210/EEC of 20th March 1985	O.J. No. L96, 3.4.85, p.25
Council Directive 85/536/EEC of 5th December 1985	O.J. No. L334, 12.12.85, p.20
Commission Directive 87/441/EEC of 29th July 1987	O.J. No. L238, 21.8.87, p.40

STATUTORY INSTRUMENTS

1989 No. 549

LEGAL AID AND ADVICE, ENGLAND AND WALES

The Civil Legal Aid (Matrimonial Proceedings) Regulations 1989

Made - - - - *23rd March 1989*

Coming into force *1st April 1989*

The Lord Chancellor, in exercise of the powers conferred on him by sections 14(2) and 43 of the Legal Aid Act 1988**(a)**, hereby makes the following Regulations of which a draft has, in accordance with section 36(3)(b) of that Act, been laid before and approved by resolution of each House of Parliament:–

Citation, commencement and revocation

1.—(1) These regulations may be cited as the Civil Legal Aid (Matrimonial Proceedings) Regulations 1989 and shall come into force on 1st April 1989.

(2) The Legal Aid (Matrimonial Proceedings) Regulations 1977**(b)** are hereby revoked.

Proceedings for divorce or judicial separation

2. After paragraph 5 of Part II of Schedule 2 to the Legal Aid Act 1988 there shall be added the following new paragraph:

"**5A.** Proceedings for a decree of divorce or judicial separation unless the cause is defended, or the petition is directed to be heard in open court, or it is not practicable by reason of physical or mental incapacity for the applicant to proceed without representation; except that representation shall be available for the purpose of making or opposing an application–

(a) for an injunction;

(b) for ancillary relief, excluding representation for the purpose only of inserting a prayer for ancillary relief in the petition;

(c) for an order relating to the custody of (or access to) a child, or the education or care or supervision of a child, excluding representation for the purpose only of making such an application where there is no reason to believe that the application will be opposed;

(d) for an order declaring that the court is satisfied as to arrangements for the welfare of the children of the family, excluding representation for the purpose only of making such an application where there is no reason to believe that the application will be opposed; or

(e) for the purpose of making or opposing any other application, or satisfying the court on any other matter which raises a substantial question for determination by the court.".

(a) 1988 c.34.
(b) S.I. 1977/447.

Mackay of Clashfern, C.

Dated 23rd March 1989

EXPLANATORY NOTE

(This note is not part of the Regulations)

These regulations replace the Legal Aid (Matrimonial Proceedings) Regulations 1977 (S.I. 1977/447). Regulation 2 adds a new paragraph to Part II of Schedule 2 to the Legal Aid Act 1988, excluding (with certain exceptions) from the scope of Part IV of the Act, representation in proceedings for divorce or judicial separation.

STATUTORY INSTRUMENTS

1989 No. 550

LEGAL AID AND ADVICE, ENGLAND AND WALES

The Legal Advice and Assistance (Scope) Regulations 1989

Made - - - -	*23rd March 1989*
Coming into force	*1st April 1989*

ARRANGEMENT OF REGULATIONS

The Lord Chancellor, in exercise of the powers conferred on him by sections 8 and 43 of the Legal Aid Act 1988**(a)**, hereby makes the following Regulations of which a draft has, in accordance with section 36(3)(b) of that Act, been laid before and approved by resolution of each House of Parliament:—

PART I

GENERAL

Citation and Commencement

1. These Regulations may be cited as the Legal Advice and Assistance (Scope) Regulations 1989 and shall come into force on 1st April 1989.

(a) 1988 c.34.

Interpretation

2. In these Regulations, unless the context otherwise requires:–

"ABWOR" means assistance by way of representation;

"the Act" means the Legal Aid Act 1988;

"board of visitors" means a board of visitors appointed by the Secretary of State under section 6(2) of the Prison Act 1952**(a)**;

"client" means a person seeking or receiving advice or assistance or on whose behalf advice or assistance is sought;

"conditional sale agreement" has the meaning assigned to it in section 189 of the Consumer Credit Act 1974**(b)**;

"conveyancing services" has the meaning assigned to it in section 11 of the Administration of Justice Act 1985**(c)**;

"mental disorder" has the meaning assigned to it in section 1 of the Mental Health Act 1983**(d)**;

"rental purchase agreement" has the meaning assigned to it in section 88 of the Housing Act 1980**(e)**;

"will" has the meaning assigned to it in section 1 of the Wills Act 1837**(f)**;

PART II

EXCLUSIONS FROM PART III OF THE ACT

Conveyancing Services

3.—(1) Subject to paragraphs (2) and (3), advice and assistance consisting of conveyancing services are excluded from Part III of the Act.

(2) Paragraph (1) does not exclude from Part III of the Act advice or assistance relating to a rental purchase agreement or a conditional sale agreement for the sale of land.

(3) Paragraph (1) does not exclude from Part III of the Act advice or assistance consisting of such conveyancing services as are necessary in order to give effect to an order of the court or, in proceedings under the Matrimonial Causes Act 1973**(g)** or the Matrimonial and Family Proceedings Act 1984**(h)**, the terms of an agreement.

Wills

4.—(1) Except as provided by paragraph (2), advice and assistance in the making of wills are excluded from Part III of the Act.

(2) Advice and assistance in the making of a will are not excluded by paragraph (1) from Part III of the Act where they are given to a client who is–

(a) aged 70 or over; or

(b) blind (or partially sighted), deaf (or hard of hearing), or dumb, or who suffers from mental disorder of any description, or who is substantially and permanently handicapped by illness, injury or congenital deformity; or

(c) a parent or guardian within the meaning of section 87 of the Child Care Act 1980**(i)** of a person to whom any description in (b) applies, where the client wishes to provide in the will for that person; or

---

(a) 1952 c.52; section 6 was amended by the Courts Act 1971 (c.23), Schedule 7 Part II paragraph 4, Schedule 11 Part IV.
(b) 1974 c.39.
(c) 1985 c.61.
(d) 1983 c.20.
(e) 1980 c.51.
(f) 1837 c.26.
(g) 1973 c.18.
(h) 1984 c.42.
(i) 1980 c.5

(d) the mother or father of a minor who is living with the client, where the client is not living with the minor's other parent, and the client wishes to appoint a guardian for that minor under section 4 of the Guardianship of Minors Act 1971**(a)**.

Transition

5. Where advice or assistance has been given before these Regulations come into force, nothing in this Part shall affect further advice or assistance given in relation to the same matter.

PART III

ABWOR

Application of Part III of the Act to ABWOR

6. Part III of the Act does not apply to ABWOR except as provided in this Part.

Proceedings in Magistrates' Courts

7.—(1) Part III of the Act applies to ABWOR given–

(a) to a client for the purposes of the prodeedings in magistrates' courts specified in the Schedule;

(b) at a hearing in any proceedings in a magistrates' court to a party who is not receiving and has not been refused representation in connection with those proceedings, where the court–

(i) is satisifed that the hearing should proceed on the same day;

(ii) is satisfied that that party would not otherwise be represented; and

(iii) requests a solicitor who is within the precincts of the court for purposes other than the provision of ABWOR in accordance with this sub-paragraph, or approves a proposal from such a solicitor, that he provide that party with ABWOR; or

(c) to a person in connection with an application for a warrant of further detention, or for an extension of such a warrant, made in respect of that person to a magistrates' court under section 43 or 44 of the Police and Criminal Evidence Act 1984**(b)**.

(2) Subject to paragraph (3), Part III of the Act also applies, in criminal proceedings in magistrates' courts where the client has not previously received and is not otherwise receiving representation or ABWOR in connection with the same proceedings, to ABWOR given to a client–

(a) in making an application for bail;

(b) at an appearance in court where the client is in custody and wishes the case to be concluded at that appearance, unless the solicitor who is advising him considers that the case should be adjourned in the interests of justice or of the client;

(c) who is before the court as a result of a failure to obey an order of the court, where such failure may lead to his being at risk of imprisonment;

(d) who is not in custody and who in the opinion of the solicitor requires ABWOR.

(3) Paragraph (2) does not apply to committal proceedings, to proceedings in which the client pleads not guilty, nor, unless the solicitor considers the circumstances to be exceptional, to proceedings in connection with a non-imprisonable offence.

(4) Part III also applies to ABWOR given to a defendant in proceedings in a magistrates' court where the defendant is before the court as a result of a failure to pay a fine or other sum which he was ordered on conviction to pay, and such failure may lead to his being at risk of imprisonment.

(a) 1971 c.3.
(b) 1984 c.60.

Proceedings in county courts

8. Part III of the Act applies to ABWOR given by a solicitor at a hearing in any proceedings in a county court to a party who is not receiving and has not been refused representation in connection with those proceedings, where the court–

(i) is satisfied that the hearing should proceed on the same day;

(ii) is satisfied that that party would not otherwise be represented; and

(iii) requests a solicitor who is within the precincts of the court for purposes other than the provision of ABWOR in accordance with this regulation, or approves a proposal from such a solicitor, that he provide that party with ABWOR.

Other Proceedings

9. Part III of the Act applies to ABWOR given–

(a) to a person in proceedings before a Mental Health Review Tribunal under the Mental Health Act 1983 whose case or whose application to the Tribunal is or is to be the subject of the proceedings;

(b) to a prisoner in proceedings before a board of visitors who has been permitted by the board of visitors to be legally represented in those proceedings.

Dated 23rd March 1989

Mackay of Clashfern, C.

SCHEDULE

Regulation 7(1)(a)

PROCEEDINGS IN MAGISTRATES' COURTS IN WHICH ABWOR IS AVAILABLE

1. In this Schedule "proceedings in a magistrates' court" includes giving notice of appeal or applying for a case to be stated within the ordinary time for so doing, and matters preliminary thereto.

2. The proceedings in which Part III of the Act applies to ABWOR under regulation 7(1) (a) are proceedings–

(a) for or in relation to an affiliation order within the meaning of the Affiliation Proceedings Act 1957**(a)**;

(b) for or in relation to an order under Part I of the Domestic Proceedings and Magistrates' Courts Act 1978**(b)**;

(c) under the Guardianship of Minors Act 1971**(c)** and 1973**(d)**;

(d) under section 43 of the National Assistance Act 1948**(e)**, section 22 of the Maintenance Orders Act 1950**(f)**, section 4 of the Maintenance Orders Act 1958**(g)**, section 18 of the Supplementary Benefits Act 1976**(h)**, or section 24 of the Social Security Act 1986**(i)**;

(e) in relation to an application for leave of the court to remove a child from a person's custody under section 27 or 28 of the Adoption Act 1976**(j)** or proceedings in which the making of an order under Part II or section 29 or 55 of the Adoption Act 1976 is opposed by any party to the proceedings;

(f) under Part I of the Maintenance Orders (Reciprocal Enforcement) Act 1972**(k)** relating to a maintenance order made by a court of a country outside the United Kingdom;

(g) under Part II of the Children Act 1975**(l)**;

(a) 1957 c.55.
(b) 1978 c.22.
(c) 1971 c.3.
(d) 1973 c.29.
(e) 1948 c.29; section 43 was amended by the Ministry of Social Security Act 1966 (c.20), Schedule 8, by the Supplementary Benefits Act 1976 (c.71), Schedule 7 paragraph 4, by the Domestic Proceedings and Magistrates' Courts Act 1978 (c.22), Schedule 2 paragraph (6), Schedule 3, by the Justices of the Peace Act 1979 (c. 55), Schedule 2 paragraph 3 and by the Social Security Act 1986 (c.50), Schedule 10 Part II paragraph 33.
(f) 1950 c.37; section 22 was amended by the Domestic Proceedings and Magistrates' Courts Act 1978 (c.22), Schedule 2 paragraph 14.
(g) 1958 c.39; section 4 was amended by the Administration of Justice Act 1970 (c.31), sections 48(2), (3), 54, Schedule 11, by the Administration of Justice Act 1977 (c. 38), Schedule 3 paragraph 3, Schedule 5 Part IV, and by the Matrimonial and Family Proceedings Act 1984 (c. 42), Schedule 1 paragraph 5.
(h) 1976 c.71.
(i) 1986 c.50.
(j) 1976 c.36; sections 27 and 29 were amended by the Health and Social Services and Social Security Adjudications Act 1983 (c.41), Schedule 2 paragraphs 33, 60, Schedule 10 Part I; section 29 was also amended by that Act, Schedule 2 paragraphs 34, 60.
(k) 1972 c.18.
(l) 1975 c.72.

EXPLANATORY NOTE

(This note is not part of the Regulations)

These Regulations replace, with amendments, the provisions in the Legal Advice and Assistance Regulations (No. 2) 1980 (S.I. 1980/1898) which prescribe the scope of advice and assistance (including assistance by way of representation). The other provisions of those Regulations are replaced, with amendments, by the Legal Advice and Assistance Regulations 1989 (S.I. 1989/340).

The main changes are to disapply (with certain exceptions) the provisions of Part III of the Act from advice and assistance consisting of conveyancing services (regulation 3) or in the making of wills (regulation 4).

In accordance with section 8(2) of the Legal Aid Act 1988, the Regulations apply Part III of the Act to assistance by way of representation (as to proceedings in magistrates' courts, regulation 7; as to proceedings in county courts, regulation 8; as to proceedings before Mental Health Review Tribunals and proceedings before boards of prison visitors, regulation 9).

STATUTORY INSTRUMENTS

1989 No. 551

LEGAL AID AND ADVICE, ENGLAND AND WALES

The Legal Aid (Functions) Order 1989

Made - - - -	*23rd March 1989*
Coming into force	*1st April 1989*

The Lord Chancellor, in exercise of the power conferred on him by section 3(4) of the Legal Aid Act 1988**(a)**, hereby makes the following Order, a draft of which has, in accordance with section 36(2)(b) of that Act, been laid before and approved by resolution of each House of Parliament:–

Citation and commencement

1. This Order may be cited as the Legal Aid (Functions) Order 1989 and shall come into force on 1st April 1989.

Functions under Part V of the Legal Aid Act 1988

2. The general function conferred on the Legal Aid Board by section 3(2) of the Legal Aid Act 1988 shall include all such functions mentioned in subsection (4)(b) of that section as are required to be exercised by the Board to enable it–

(a) to determine under the Legal Aid in Criminal and Care Proceedings (General) Regulations 1989**(b)** as respects representation under Part V of that Act:–

(i) an application for review of a refusal by a magistrates' court to grant representation;

(ii) a renewed application for amendment or withdrawal of a grant of representation, or for representation by counsel; and

(iii) an application for prior authority to incur expenditure; and

(b) to promote or assist in the promotion of publicity relating to the functions mentioned in that subsection.

Functions under Part VI of the Legal Aid Act 1988

3. The general function conferred on the Legal Aid Board by section 3(2) of the Legal Aid Act 1988 shall include all such functions mentioned in subsection (4)(c) of that section as are required to be exercised by the Board to enable it to determine under the Legal Aid in Criminal and Care Procedings (General) Regulations 1989 as respects representation under Part VI of that Act:–

(a) a renewed application for amendment or withdrawal of a grant of representation; and

(b) an application for prior authority to incur expenditure.

(a) 1988 c.34.
(b) S.I. 1989/344.

Mackay of Clashfern, C.

Dated 23rd March 1989

EXPLANATORY NOTE

(This note is not part of the Order)

This Order confers on the Legal Aid Board the functions required to enable area committees under the Legal Aid in Criminal and Care Proceedings Regulations 1989 (S.I. 1989/344) to determine the applications mentioned in articles 2 and 3.

In criminal proceedings the relevant applications are applications for review of refusals of representation by magistrates' courts, renewed applications for amendment or withdrawal of representation (or for representation by counsel), and applications for prior authority to incur expenditure.

In care proceedings the relevant applications are renewed applications for amendment or withdrawal of representation, and applications for prior authority to incur expenditure.

Article 2 also confers on the Board the functions required to enable it to promote publicity about Criminal Legal Aid.

STATUTORY INSTRUMENTS

1989 No. 552

SOCIAL SECURITY

The Pneumoconiosis etc. (Workers' Compensation) (Payment of Claims) (Amendment) Regulations 1989

Made - - - -	*22nd March 1989*
Coming into force	*1st April 1989*

The Secretary of State in exercise of the powers conferred on him by sections 1 and 7 of the Pneumoconiosis etc. (Workers' Compensation) Act 1979(**a**) ("the Act") and of all other powers enabling him in that behalf hereby makes the following Regulations, of which a draft has been approved by resolution of each House of Parliament:–

Citation and commencement

1. These Regulations may be cited as the Pneumoconiosis etc. (Workers' Compensation) (Payment of Claims) (Amendment) Regulations 1989 and shall come into force on 1st April 1989.

Interpretation

2. In these Regulations the "principal Regulations" means the Pneumoconiosis etc. (Workers' Compensation) (Payment of Claims) Regulations 1988(**b**).

Amendment of the principal Regulations

3.—(1) The principal Regulations shall be amended in accordance with the following provisions of this regulation.

(2) In regulation 4(6)(a)–

(a) for the word "if" there shall be substituted the words "in cases where";

(b) after the word "dependant" in sub-paragraph (i) there shall be inserted the words "by reason of the deceased's death as a result of the disease".

(3) The following sub-paragraph shall be substituted for sub-paragraph (ii) of regulation 5(1)(a):–

" (ii) where disablement benefit in respect of a disease was not payable to the deceased immediately before he died death benefit is payable to or in respect of the said dependant by reason of the deceased's death as a result of the disease, or"

(4)(a) the Schedule to these Regulations shall be substituted for the Schedule to those Regulations, and

(b) the amount of £1,364 shall be substituted for the amount of £1,263 in regulations 5(1) and 8 of those Regulations, and the amount of £2,822 shall be substituted for the amount of £2,613 in regulation 6(1) of those Regulations,

(**a**) 1979 c.41; sections 1 and 4 of the Act were amended by section 24 of the Social Security Act 1985 (c.53) and section 2 was amended by section 39 of and Schedule 3 to the Social Security Act 1986 (c.50).
(**b**) S.I. 1988/668.

in any case in which a person first satisfies the conditions of entitlement to a payment under the Act on or after the date upon which these Regulations come into force.

Signed by order of the Secretary of State.

Patrick Nicholls
Parliamentary Under Secretary of State,
Department of Employment

22nd March 1989

Regulations 3, 4, 5 and 6

SCHEDULE

TABLE 1

(1) Table 1 is for the determination of payments to disabled persons under regulation 3 (or regulation 6), and for the determination of payments to dependants of deceased sufferers under regulation 4(1).

(2) The relevant period is the period specified in regulation 3(2) or 3(3) or, in the case of a disabled person to whom regulation 6 applies (Payment where pneumoconiosis is accompanied by tuberculosis), the period specified in paragraph (1)(b) of that regulation.

(3) The age to be taken for the purpose of determining the amount payable to a disabled person is his age on the date specified in regulation 3(2) or 3(3) or, in the case of a disabled person to whom regulation 6 applies (Payment where pneumoconiosis is accompanied by tuberculosis) his age on the date specified in paragraph (1) of that regulation. With a view to determining the amount payable to a dependant of a disabled person under regulation 4(1), the age to be taken for the purpose of calculating the sum to be deducted from the amount which would have been payable to the disabled person had he still been alive is the age of the deceased at his last birthday preceding his death.

PART A

PAYMENTS TO DISABLED PERSONS TO WHOM IS PAYABLE DISABLEMENT BENEFIT UNDER SECTION 76 OF THE SOCIAL SECURITY ACT 1975 OR UNDER ANY CORRESPONDING PROVISION OF THE FORMER INDUSTRIAL INJURIES ACTS, OR WOULD BE PAYABLE BUT FOR THE DISABLEMENT AMOUNTING TO LESS THAN THE APPROPRIATE PERCENTAGE.

Age of disabled person	*Percentage assessment for the relevant period*									
	10% or less	11–20%	21–30%	40%	50%	60%	70%	80%	90%	100%
	£	£	£	£	£	£	£	£	£	£
37 and under	15,801	28,216	33,106	34,047	34,988	35,739	36,492	37,244	37,997	38,749
38	15,349	27,087	32,110	33,258	34,234	34,988	35,739	36,492	37,244	37,997
39	14,897	25,958	31,112	32,466	33,483	34,234	34,988	35,739	36,492	37,244
40	14,447	24,829	30,115	31,676	32,730	33,483	34,234	34,988	35,739	36,492
41	13,995	23,701	29,118	30,885	31,978	32,730	33,483	34,234	34,988	35,739
42	13,542	22,572	28,122	30,097	31,225	31,978	32,730	33,483	34,234	34,988
43	12,866	21,255	27,124	29,495	30,699	31,601	32,353	33,106	33,858	34,611
44	12,189	19,938	26,128	28,892	30,172	31,225	31,978	32,730	33,483	34,234
45	11,512	18,622	25,130	28,291	29,645	30,849	31,601	32,353	33,106	33,858
46	10,834	17,305	24,133	27,688	29,118	30,473	31,225	31,978	32,730	33,483
47	10,158	15,989	23,136	27,087	28,592	30,097	30,849	31,601	32,353	33,106
48	9,574	15,461	22,347	25,883	27,688	29,043	29,795	30,548	31,300	32,053
49	8,991	14,936	21,556	24,678	26,786	27,990	28,742	29,495	30,248	31,000
50	8,409	14,408	20,767	23,476	25,883	26,936	27,688	28,441	29,193	29,945
51	7,825	13,882	19,976	22,271	24,980	25,883	26,635	27,387	28,141	28,892
52	7,242	13,355	19,187	21,068	24,077	24,829	25,583	26,334	27,087	27,838
53	6,696	12,415	17,982	20,014	23,174	24,077	24,829	25,583	26,334	27,087
54	6,151	11,474	16,778	18,962	22,271	23,325	24,077	24,829	25,583	26,334
55	5,606	10,533	15,576	17,907	21,368	22,572	23,325	24,077	24,829	25,583
56	5,060	9,594	14,371	16,854	20,467	21,820	22,572	23,325	24,077	24,829
57	4,514	8,653	13,168	15,801	19,563	21,068	21,820	22,572	23,325	24,077
58	4,158	7,864	11,758	14,182	17,605	18,998	19,807	20,598	21,368	22,120
59	3,799	7,072	10,345	12,566	15,649	16,929	17,794	18,622	19,412	20,163
60	3,443	6,282	8,935	10,947	13,695	14,861	15,781	16,648	17,456	18,209
61	3,084	5,492	7,524	9,330	11,738	12,791	13,769	14,672	15,501	16,252
62	2,728	4,702	6,113	7,712	9,782	10,722	11,758	12,698	13,542	14,296
63	2,539	4,251	5,492	6,895	8,701	9,630	10,609	11,512	12,339	13,091
64	2,353	3,799	4,871	6,076	7,619	8,540	9,462	10,327	11,136	11,888
65	2,164	3,349	4,251	5,258	6,536	7,449	8,314	9,142	9,932	10,684
66	1,976	2,898	3,630	4,439	5,456	6,358	7,167	7,957	8,729	9,480
67	1,788	2,444	3,009	3,621	4,374	5,267	6,020	6,772	7,524	8,276
68	1,740	2,369	2,906	3,470	4,223	5,060	5,784	6,564	7,289	8,032
69	1,693	2,294	2,803	3,321	4,073	4,854	5,550	6,358	7,055	7,787
70	1,645	2,219	2,699	3,170	3,922	4,646	5,314	6,151	6,819	7,544
71	1,600	2,144	2,597	3,019	3,771	4,439	5,079	5,945	6,584	7,299
72	1,553	2,069	2,492	2,870	3,621	4,233	4,843	5,737	6,348	7,055
73	1,514	2,033	2,455	2,812	3,565	4,138	4,749	5,587	6,160	6,847
74	1,476	1,993	2,417	2,756	3,510	4,044	4,656	5,436	5,973	6,641
75	1,440	1,957	2,380	2,699	3,451	3,950	4,562	5,286	5,784	6,432
76	1,401	1,918	2,341	2,642	3,395	3,858	4,468	5,136	5,595	6,227
77 and over	1,364	1,881	2,305	2,586	3,338	3,763	4,374	4,986	5,408	6,020

PART B

PAYMENTS TO DISABLED PERSONS TO WHOM IS PAYABLE AN ALLOWANCE UNDER A SCHEME MADE OR HAVING EFFECT AS IF MADE UNDER SECTION 5 OF THE INDUSTRIAL INJURIES AND DISEASES (OLD CASES) ACT 1975 OR UNDER ANY CORRESPONDING PROVISION OF THE FORMER OLD CASES ACTS.

Age of disabled person	*Extent of incapacity for the relevant period*	
	Partial	*Total*
	£	£
37 and under	28,216	38,749
38	27,087	37,997
39	25,958	37,244
40	24,829	36,492
41	23,701	35,739
42	22,572	34,988
43	21,255	34,611
44	19,938	34,234
45	18,622	33,858
46	17,305	33,483
47	15,989	33,106
48	15,461	32,053
49	14,936	31,000
50	14,408	29,945
51	13,882	28,892
52	13,355	27,838
53	12,415	27,087
54	11,474	26,334
55	10,533	25,583
56	9,594	24,829
57	8,653	24,077
58	7,864	22,120
59	7,072	20,163
60	6,282	18,209
61	5,492	16,252
62	4,702	14,296
63	4,251	13,091
64	3,799	11,888
65	3,349	10,684
66	2,898	9,480
67	2,444	8,276
68	2,369	8,032
69	2,294	7,787
70	2,219	7,544
71	2,144	7,299
72	2,069	7,055
73	2,033	6,847
74	1,993	6,641
75	1,957	6,432
76	1,918	6,227
77 and over	1,881	6,020

TABLE 2

(1) Table 2 is for the determination of payments to dependants of deceased sufferers who died as a result of the disease under regulation 4(2) or regulation 4(6).

(2) The relevant period is the period specified in regulation 3(2) or 3(3) or, in the case of a disabled person to whom regulation 6 applies (Payment where pneumoconiosis is accompanied by tuberculosis), the period specified in paragraph (1)(b) of that regulation.

PART A

PAYMENTS TO DEPENDANTS TO WHOM DEATH BENEFIT UNDER SECTION 76 OF THE SOCIAL SECURITY ACT 1975 IS PAYABLE, OR TO DEPENDANTS OF PERSONS TO WHOM DISABLEMENT BENEFIT UNDER THAT SECTION OR UNDER ANY CORRESPONDING PROVISION OF THE FORMER INDUSTRIAL INJURIES ACTS WAS PAYABLE, OR TO DEPENDANTS OF A PERSON TO WHOM DISABLEMENT BENEFIT WOULD HAVE BEEN PAYABLE IMMEDIATELY BEFORE HE DIED BUT FOR THE OCCURRENCE OF ONE OF THE CIRCUMSTANCES LISTED IN REGULATION 5(1)(a)(iii) OR BUT FOR HIS DISABLEMENT AMOUNTING TO LESS THAN THE APPROPRIATE PERCENTAGE, IN CIRCUMSTANCES WHERE THE DISABLED PERSON DIED AS A RESULT OF A DISEASE OTHER THAN DIFFUSE MESOTHELIOMA.

Age of disabled person at his last birthday preceding death	*Percentage assessment for the relevant period*				
	10% or less	11%–20%	21%–30%	40%	50% and over
	£	£	£	£	£
37 and under	7,430	14,485	16,553	17,118	17,589
38	7,204	13,845	15,989	16,553	17,154
39	6,979	13,205	15,424	15,989	16,723
40	6,752	12,566	14,861	15,424	16,289
41	6,527	11,927	14,296	14,861	15,857
42	6,302	11,287	13,731	14,296	15,424
43	5,896	10,458	13,223	13,787	15,011
44	5,492	9,630	12,715	13,280	14,592
45	5,088	8,804	12,208	12,771	14,182
46	4,683	7,975	11,699	12,263	13,769
47	4,279	7,147	11,193	11,758	13,355
48	3,969	6,922	10,817	11,362	12,848
49	3,658	6,696	10,440	10,967	12,339
50	3,349	6,471	10,065	10,571	11,832
51	3,037	6,245	9,688	10,177	11,323
52	2,728	6,020	9,311	9,782	10,817
53	2,586	5,492	8,596	9,236	10,402
54	2,444	4,966	7,880	8,690	9,988
55	2,305	4,439	7,167	8,145	9,574
56	2,164	3,913	6,452	7,600	9,160
57	2,021	3,387	5,737	7,055	8,746
58	1,890	3,009	4,919	6,096	7,600
59	1,758	2,633	4,101	5,136	6,452
60	1,628	2,258	3,282	4,176	5,305
61	1,496	1,881	2,464	3,218	4,158
62	1,364	1,505	1,645	2,258	3,009
63	1,364	1,476	1,590	2,078	2,681
64	1,364	1,448	1,533	1,899	2,353
65	1,364	1,420	1,476	1,721	2,021
66	1,364	1,393	1,420	1,542	1,693
67 and over	1,364	1,364	1,364	1,364	1,364

PART B

PAYMENTS TO DEPENDANTS TO WHOM DEATH BENEFIT UNDER A SCHEME MADE OR HAVING EFFECT AS IF MADE UNDER SECTION 5 OF THE INDUSTRIAL INJURIES AND DISEASES (OLD CASES) ACT 1975 HAS BEEN PAID, OR TO DEPENDANTS OF PERSONS TO WHOM AN ALLOWANCE UNDER SUCH A SCHEME OR UNDER A SCHEME MADE OR HAVING EFFECT AS IF MADE UNDER ANY CORRESPONDING PROVISION OF THE FORMER OLD CASES ACTS WAS PAYABLE, IN CIRCUMSTANCES WHERE THE DISABLED PERSON DIED AS A RESULT OF A DISEASE OTHER THAN DIFFUSE MESOTHELIOMA.

Age of disabled person at his last birthday preceding death	*Extent of incapacity for the relevant period*	
	Partial	*Total*
	£	£
37 and under	14,485	17,589
38	13,845	17,154
39	13,205	16,723
40	12,566	16,289
41	11,927	15,857
42	11,287	15,424
43	10,458	15,011
44	9,630	14,592
45	8,804	14,182
46	7,975	13,769
47	7,147	13,355
48	6,922	12,848
49	6,696	12,339
50	6,471	11,832
51	6,245	11,323
52	6,020	10,817
53	5,492	10,402
54	4,966	9,988
55	4,439	9,574
56	3,913	9,160
57	3,387	8,746
58	3,009	7,600
59	2,633	6,452
60	2,258	5,305
61	1,881	4,158
62	1,505	3,009
63	1,476	2,681
64	1,448	2,353
65	1,420	2,021
66	1,393	1,693
67 and over	1,364	1,364

PART C

PAYMENTS TO DEPENDANTS OF PERSONS WHO DIED AS A RESULT OF DIFFUSE MESOTHELIOMA.

Age of disabled person at his last birthday preceding death	*Payment*
	£
37 and under	17,589
38	17,154
39	16,723
40	16,289
41	15,857
42	15,424
43	15,011
44	14,592
45	14,182
46	13,769
47	13,355
48	12,848
49	12,339
50	11,832
51	11,323
52	10,817
53	10,402
54	9,988
55	9,574
56	9,160
57	8,746
58	7,600
59	6,452
60	5,305
61	4,158
62	3,009
63	2,681
64	2,353
65	2,021
66	1,693
67 and over	1,364

EXPLANATORY NOTE

(This note is not part of the Regulations)

The Pneumoconiosis etc. (Workers' Compensation) (Payment of Claims) Regulations 1988 (the 1988 Regulations) prescribe the amount of payments to be made under the Pneumoconiosis etc. (Workers' Compensation) Act 1979 ("the Act"), as amended by the Social Security Act 1985 and the Social Security Act 1986, to persons disabled by a disease to which the Act applies (namely pneumoconiosis, byssinosis, diffuse mesothelioma, primary carcinoma of the lung (where accompanied by asbestosis or bilateral diffuse pleural thickening) and bilateral diffuse pleural thickening) or to dependants of persons who immediately before they died were disabled by such a disease.

These Regulations amend the 1988 Regulations by increasing the amount of those payments in any case in which a person first becomes entitled to a payment on or after the date when these Regulations come into force. The increase in each case is 8% rounded up or down to the nearest £1 as appropriate. The Regulations also make minor drafting amendments to the 1988 Regulations.

STATUTORY INSTRUMENTS

1989 No. 553

PLANT HEALTH

The Plant Health (Great Britain) (Amendment) Order 1989

Made - - - -	*22nd March 1989*
Laid before Parliament	*5th April 1989*
Coming into force	
Article 2(2)	*1st January 1990*
Remainder	*26th April 1989*

The Minister of Agriculture, Fisheries and Food in relation to England, the Secretary of State for Scotland in relation to Scotland and the Secretary of State for Wales in relation to Wales, in exercise of the powers conferred by sections 1(2)(b), 2, 3(1), (2), (3) and (4) and 4(1) of the Plant Health Act 1967**(a)** and now vested in them**(b)** and of all other powers enabling them in that behalf, hereby make the following Order:

Title, extent, commencement and interpretation

1.—(1) This Order may be cited as the Plant Health (Great Britain) (Amendment) Order 1989, shall apply to Great Britain and except for article 2(2), shall come into force on 26th April 1989.

(2) Article 2(2) of this Order shall come into force on 1st January 1990.

(3) In this Order "the principal Order" means the Plant Health (Great Britain) Order 1987**(c)**.

Amendment of the principal Order

2. The principal Order shall be amended as follows:–

(1) in article 3(1) (interpretation) there shall be inserted, in alphabetical order as appropriate, the following definitions:

" "Beet Rhizomania Disease" means the disease caused by Beet Necrotic Yellow Vein virus;

"Classified basic seed potatoes" means seed potatoes produced in the protected region as defined in article 22 in relation to which a basic seed potatoes certificate has been issued in accordance with the Seed Potatoes Regulations 1984**(d)**;

(a) 1967 c.8; sections 2(1), 3(1) and (2) and 4(1) were amended by the European Communities Act 1972 (c.68), section 4(1) and Schedule 4, paragraph 8; section 3(4) was substituted by section 42 of the Criminal Justice Act 1982 (c.48) and is to be read, as regards England and Wales, with S.I. 1984/447 and section 52(4) of the Criminal Justice Act 1988 (c.33) and, as regards Scotland, with section 289G(13) of the Criminal Procedure (Scotland) Act 1975 (c.21), as inserted by section 66 of the Criminal Justice (Scotland) Act 1987 (c.41), and S.I. 1984/526.
(b) In the case of the Secretary of State for Wales by virtue of S.I. 1978/272.
(c) S.I. 1987/1758.
(d) S.I. 1984/412, amended by S.I. 1987/547, 1988/1759.

"early potatoes" means potatoes–

(a) harvested before 31st July in the year of planting, and

(b) marketed for human consumption immediately after being harvested;

"official label" means a label supplied in accordance with the requirements of the Seed Potatoes Regulations 1984;";

(2) after paragraph (3) of article 22 (restriction on the movement to and planting of potatoes in the protected region) there shall be inserted the following paragraphs–

"(3A) No person shall plant or cause or permit to be planted in the protected region any potatoes other than classified basic seed potatoes or one year's direct progeny of classified basic seed potatoes where that direct progeny has been grown by that person.

(3B) The provisions of paragraph (3A) above shall not apply where the area to be planted is less than 0.1 hectare or is to be used for the production of early potatoes.

(3C) Any person who plants seed potatoes in the protected region other than for the production of seed potatoes shall retain and make available to an authorised officer documentary evidence showing that the seed potatoes planted were classified basic seed potatoes or were one year's direct progeny of classified basic seed potatoes where such progeny has been grown by that person.

(3D) The documentary evidence required by paragraph (3C) of this article shall be in the form of–

(a) an official label together with either an invoice or delivery note; or

(b) a certificate of classification where the potatoes planted are either classified basic seed potatoes, or their direct progeny, and where the seed potatoes, or their direct progeny, were produced by the certificate holder.";

(3) in paragraph (4) of article 22 for the words "paragraph (3)" there shall be substituted the words "paragraphs (3) and (3A)";

(4) in articles 23 (display of notices) and 24 (restriction on entry to infected premises) after the words "Colorado Beetle" there shall be inserted the words "or Beet Rhizomania Disease";

(5) after article 24 there shall be inserted the following article–

"**24A.** The restriction in article 24 shall not apply to a person who enters premises declared infected with Colorado Beetle or Beet Rhizomania Disease for the purpose of saving life or property.";

(6) in paragraph (2) of article 46 for the words "article 4" there shall be substituted the words "article 12";

(7) in article 47 for the words "not exceeding £2,000" there shall be substituted the words "not exceeding level 5 on the standard scale.";

(8) in Part IA of Schedule 1 after Item 18 there shall be inserted the following Items–

"19. *Anomala orientalis* (Waterhouse)—Oriental beetle

20. *Enarmonia prunivora* (Walsh)—Lesser Appleworm

21. *Naccobus aberrans* (Thorne) Thorne & Allen—False Root Knot Nematode

22. *Opogona sacchari* (Bojer)—Sugarcane Borer

23. *Premnotrypes* spp (Non-European)—Andean Potato Weevils

24. *Xiphinema americanum* Cobb *sensu lato* (Non-European populations)—a Dagger Nematode

25. *Thrips palmi* Karny—Palm Thrips.";

(9) in Part IB of Schedule 1 after Item 2 there shall be inserted the following Item–

"3. *Xyella fastidiosa* (Wells *et al.*)—Grapevine Pierce's disease bacterium.";

(10) in Part IC of Schedule 1 after Item 2 there shall be inserted the following Items–

"3. *Gymnosporangium* spp (Non-European)—Fruit Tree/Juniper Rusts.

4. *Sclerotinia fructicola* (Wint.) Rehm (syn *Monilinia fructicola* (Wint.) Honey)—Fruit Brown Rot.

5. *Phoma andina* Turkensteen—Black Potato Blight and Leaf Spot.

6. *Phyllosticta solitaria Ell. and Ev.*—Apple Blotch and Canker.
7. *Septoria lycopersici* var *malaguttii* Ciccarone and Boerema—Annular Potato Leaf Spot.";

(11) in Part IIA of Schedule 1–

(a) after Item 1 there shall be inserted the following Item–

"1A.	*Aphelenchoides besseyi* Christie–Rice White Tip Nematode	Strawberry plants (*Fragaria* L.) other than the fruits and seeds";

(b) in column 3 of Item 3 for the words "Flower bulbs and tubers of potato (*Solanum tuberosum* L.)" there shall be substituted the words "Flower bulbs of the genera *Crocus* L., *Gladiolus* L., *Hyacinthus* L., *Iris* L., *Tigridia* Juss., *Tulipa* L., tubers of potato (*Solanum tuberosum* L.)";

(c) Item 5 (*Caloptilia azaleella*) and Item 6 (*Merodon equestris*) shall be omitted;

(12) in Part IIB of Schedule 1–

(a) Item 5 (*Pseudomonas gladioli*) shall be omitted;

(b) after Item 6 there shall be inserted the following Item–

"6A.	*Pseudomonas syringae p.v. persicae* (Prunier *et al*) Peach Canker	Plants of *Prunus* L. other than fruit and seeds";

(c) after Item 8 there shall be inserted the following Item–

"8A.	*Xanthomonas ampelina* Panagcpoulos—Canker of Grapevine	Plants of vines (*Vitis* L.) other than fruit and seeds";

(13) in Part IIC of Schedule 1–

(a) Item 4 (*Ovulinia azaleae*), Item 9 (*Sclerotinia bulborum*), Item 11 (*Septoria gladioli*) and Item 12 (*Stromatinia gladioli*) shall be omitted;

(b) after Item 8 there shall be inserted the following Item–

"8A.	*Puccinia pitteriana* Hess—Potato Common Rust	Plants of *Solanum* spp.";

(c) after Item 14 there shall be inserted the following Item–

"15.	*Verticillium dahliae* Kleb—Hop Wilt	Plants of Hops (*Humulus Lupulus* L.)";

(14) in Part IID of Schedule 1 in column (2) of Item 8 for the words "Little Cherry pathogen" there shall be substituted the words "Little Cherry disease pathogen";

(15) in Part III of Schedule 1–

(a) in section A the words "5. *Caloptilia azaleella* (Brants) (syn. *Gracilaria azaleella* (Brants)—Azalea Leafminer" and "7. *Merodon equestris* (Fabricius (syn. *Lampetia equestris* Fabricius)—Large Narcissus Fly" shall be omitted;

(b) in section B the words "4. *Pseudomonas gladioli* pv. *gladioli* Severini (syn. *Pseudomonas gladioli* Severini) (syn. *Pseudomonas marginata* (McCulloch Stapp))—Gladiolus Scab and Neck Rot, on gladiolus (*Gladiolus* L.) and freesia (*Freesia* Klatt.)" shall be omitted;

(c) in section C the words "3. *Ovulinia azaleae* Weiss—Rhododendron Petal Blight", "7. *Sclerotinia bulborum* (Wakk.) Rehm—Hyacinth Black Slime" and "8. *Stromatinia gladioli* (Drayt.) Whet.—Gladiolus Dry Rot" shall be omitted;

(d) in section C after the words "5. *Phytophthora fragariae* Hickman—Red Core Disease of Strawberries, in Scotland" there shall be inserted the words "5A. *Puccinia horiana* P. Henn.—Chrysanthemum White Rust";

(16) in Part I of Schedule 2 in Item 3 for the words "other than (1) seeds and (2) plants of the following families" there shall be substituted the words "other than (1) seeds, (2) the genera *Ficus* L. and *Codiaeum* Juss and (3) plants of the following families";

(17) in Part III of Schedule 2–

(a) in column 3 of Item 17 after the word "Austria" there shall be inserted the words "Canary Islands";

(b) after Item 17 there shall be inserted the following Item–

"17A.	Plants of genus *Juniperus* L. other than fruits and seeds.	Countries outside Europe.";

(18) in Schedule 3–

(a) after Item 4 there shall be inserted the following–

"4A.	Plants for planting, other than seeds, originating in countries where *Thrips palmi* Karny is known to occur.	Official statement that:– (a) the place of production has been found free of *Thrips palmi* Karny and (b) that the consignment has undergone appropriate treatment to ensure freedom from *Thysanoptera*.";

(b) after Item 6 there shall be inserted the following Item–

"6A.	Plants of *Chaenomeles* Lindl., *Cydonia* Mill., *Crataegus* L., *Malus* Mill., *Photinia, Prunus* L., *Pyrus* L., and *Rosa* L.	Where the consignment originates in a country outside Europe the plants shall be dormant and free from leaves, flowers and fruit.";

(c) in column 2 of Item 7 after the words "in tissue culture" there shall be inserted the words "and other than plants specified in Item 6A above.";

(d) in Part IIB in column 2 of Item 11 after the words "*Dendrocalamus Nees*" there shall be inserted the words "*Hakonechloa* Mak. ex Honda";

(e) in Part IIC–

(i) in paragraph (a) of column 3 of Item 22 the words "(iii) Lesser Apple Worm (*E. prunivora* (Walsh))" shall be omitted;

(ii) in paragraph (b) of column 3 of Item 22 at the end there shall be inserted the words "and that no symptoms of *S. fructicola* have been observed at the place of production since the beginning of the last complete cycle of vegetation.";

(iii) in paragraph (1)(a) of column 3 of Item 23 after the word "Tortrix" there shall be inserted the word "moth";

(iv) for columns 2 and 3 of Item 24 there shall be substituted the following:–

"Plants of the genera *Cydonia* Mill., *Malus* Mill., *Prunus* L., and *Pyrus* L.	(1) Where the consignment originates in a third country it shall be free from: (a) Western Cherry Fruit Fly (*Rhagoletis indifferens* (Curran)); (b) Apple Curculio (*Tachypterellus quadrigibbus* (Say)); (2) An official statement shall have been made:– (a) either that the plants were grown in a country in which viruses, or virus-like pathogens of a description specified in paragraph (1)(p) of Part ID of Schedule 1 are not known to occur in *Cydonia, Malus, Prunus* or *Pyrus*; or

(b) that the plants were grown at a place of production at which no symptoms of viruses, or virus-like pathogens of a description specified in paragraph (1)(p) of Part ID of Schedule 1 have been observed during at least one official inspection carried out since the beginning of the last complete cycle of vegetation.";

(v) after Item 24 there shall be inserted the following Item–

"24A.	Plants of the genera *Crataegus* L. and *Malus* Mill.	An official statement shall have been made that no symptoms of Apple Blotch and Canker (*Phyllosticta solitaria* (Ell. and Ev.)) have been observed on the plants at the place of production since the beginning of the last complete cycle of vegetation.";

(vi) in paragraph (5)(d) of column 3 of Item 26 for the words beginning with "If the American Leafminer" and ending with "shall have been used." there shall be substituted the words "If the American Leafminer (*Amauromyza maculosa* (Malloch), *Liriomyza huidobrensis* (Blanchard), *L. sativae* Blanchard or *L. trifolii* (Burgess)) has occurred on the place of production within the previous 2 years the second method of treatment shall have been used.";

(vii) paragraph (6) of column 3 of Item 26 shall be omitted;

(viii) after paragraph (1) of Item 27 there shall be inserted the following paragraph–

"(1A) Where the consignment originates in a third country, in addition to being free from the plant pests listed in paragraph (1), the consignment shall be free from Strawberry Weevils (*Anthonomus signatus* (Say) and *Anthonomus bisignifer* (Schenkling)).";

(ix) after paragraph (6) of column 3 of Item 27 there shall be inserted the following paragraph–

"(7) An official statement shall have been made:–

(a) that the plants were grown in a country in which *Aphelenchoides besseyi* Christie is not known to occur; or

(b) where the consignment originates in a country in which *Aphelenchoides besseyi* Christie is known to occur:–

(i) either that no symptoms of *Aphelenchoides besseyi* has been observed on plants at the place of production since the beginning of the last complete cycle of vegetation; or

(ii) that in the case of plants in tissue culture, the plants have been derived from plants which complied with paragraph (7)(b)(i) of this Item or have been officially tested by appropriate nematological methods and have been found free from *Aphelenchoides besseyi*.";

(x) in paragraph (1) of column 3 of Item 30 after the words "(*Verticillium albo—atrum* Reinke and Berth.)" there shall be inserted the words "and of Hop Wilt (*Verticillium dahliae* Kleb.)";

(xi) in paragraph (2) of column 3 of Item 30 the words "that requirement shall also be complied with in respect of Hop Wilt (*Verticillium dahliae* Kleb.) and" shall be omitted;

(f) in Part IV–

(i) in column 2 of Item 56 after the words "pea (*Pisum sativum* L.)" there shall be inserted the words "*Prunus* L.";;

(ii) in column 3 of Item 57 after the words "third country", there shall be inserted the words "it shall be free from Lettuce Mosaic virus and";

(iii) in column 3 of Item 58 after paragraph (3) there shall be inserted the following paragraph–

"(4) Where the consignment originates in a third country, in addition to complying with the requirements specified in paragraphs (1) to (3) of this Item, it shall be free from Verticillium Wilt of Lucerne (*Verticillium albo—atrum* (Reinke and Berth)).";

(g) in Part VB–

(i) in paragraph (3)(c) of column 3 of Item 65 for the words "Apple Fruit Worm (*Enarmonia prunivora* (Walsh))" there shall be substituted the words "Queensland Fruit Fly (*Dacus Tryoni* (Froggatt))";

(ii) after Item 65 there shall be inserted the following Item–

"65A.	Raw fruit from the genus *Prunus* L.	Where the consignment has been landed in Great Britain between 1st March and 30th September (both dates inclusive) and the consignment originates from a country in the Southern Hemisphere an official statement shall have been made:– (a) either that the fruit originates in an area recognised as being free from Fruit Brown Rot (*Sclerotinia fructicola* (Wint.) Rehm) in accordance with the procedure laid down in article 16 of Directive 77/93/EEC; or (b) that the fruits have been subjected to appropriate inspections and treatment procedures prior to harvest or export to ensure freedom from *Sclerotinia fructicola*.";

(h) in Part VC in paragraph (1) of column 3 of Item 72 for the words "(*Rhagoletis menda* Curran)" there shall be substituted the words "(*Rhagoletis mendax* Curran)";

(i) in Part VI in column 2 of Item 74 after the words "Raw vegetables" there shall be inserted the words "with foliage", and at the end the words "with foliage" shall be omitted;

(j) in Part VIIB paragraph (1) of column 3 of Item 78 shall be omitted;

(19) at the end of Schedule 5 there shall be inserted the following instruments–
"Commission Directive 88/271/EEC OJ No. L116, 4.5.88, p.13.
Commission Directive 88/272/EEC OJ No. L116, 4.5.88, p.19.
Commission Directive 88/430/EEC OJ No. L208, 2.8.88, p.36.
Council Directive 88/572/EEC OJ No. L313, 19.11.88, p.39.".

(20) at the end of Schedule 8 there shall be inserted the words "Beet Necrotic Yellow Vein virus, the cause of Beet Rhizomania Disease.".

In Witness whereof the Official seal of the Minister of Agriculture, Fisheries and Food is hereunto affixed on 19th March 1989.

John MacGregor
Minister of Agriculture, Fisheries and Food

22nd March 1989

Saunderson of Bowden
Minister of State,
Scottish Office

20th March 1989

Peter Walker
Secretary of State for Wales

EXPLANATORY NOTE

(This note is not part of the Order)

This Order amends the Plant Health (Great Britain) Order 1987 ("the principal Order") so as to–

(a) impose additional requirements in respect of the planting of potatoes in Scotland, and in parts of the counties of Northumberland and Cumbria (article 2(2));

(b) enable premises to be declared infected with Beet Rhizomania Disease (article 2(1) and (20));

(c) extend to Beet Rhizomania Disease the provisions contained in articles 23 and 24 of the Order which relate to the display of notices on premises declared infected with Colorado Beetle and restriction on entry to such premises (article 2(4));

(d) provide that the restriction on entry to premises declared infected with Colorado Beetle or Beet Rhizomania Disease shall not apply to persons entering such premises for the purpose of saving life or property (article 2(5));

(e) implement, in part, Commission Directives 88/271/EEC, 88/272/EEC, 88/430/EEC and Council Directive 88/572/EEC which amend Council Directive 77/93/EEC, and impose controls or additional controls in relation to certain plant pests, whilst removing or modifying other controls (article 2(8) to (15)(c), (18) and (19).

The Order adds *Puccinia horiana* P. Henn (Chrysanthemum White Rust) to Schedule 1, Part IIIC of the principal Order as being a plant pest normally present in Great Britain which need not be notified (article 2(15)(d)) and adds the Canary Islands to the list of third countries from which the tubers of potatoes other than tubers of potatoes for planting may be imported (article 2(17)). The Order removes the additional conditions concerning the importation of chrysanthemum cut flowers and certain pot plants from the Netherlands (article 2(18)(c)(vii) and article 2(18)(j)).

Article 2(2) of the Order which imposes additional requirements in respect of the planting of potatoes in Scotland, and in parts of Northumberland and Cumbria shall come into force on 1st January 1990 and all the other provisions of the Order shall come into force on 26th April 1989.

STATUTORY INSTRUMENTS

1989 No. 556 (C.19) (S.63)

EVIDENCE

The Civil Evidence (Scotland) Act 1988 (Commencement) Order 1989

Made - - - - 15th March 1989

The Lord Advocate, in exercise of the powers conferred on him by section 11(2) of the Civil Evidence (Scotland) Act 1988(**a**), and of all other powers enabling him in that behalf, hereby makes the following Order:

1. This Order may be cited as the Civil Evidence (Scotland) Act 1988 (Commencement) Order 1989.

2. The provisions of the Civil Evidence (Scotland) Act 1988 shall come into force on 3rd April 1989.

Crown Office, Edinburgh
15th March 1989

Fraser of Carmyllie
Lord Advocate

EXPLANATORY NOTE

(This note is not part of the Order)

This Order brings into force on 3rd April 1989 the provisions of the Civil Evidence (Scotland) Act 1988.

(**a**) 1988 c.32.

STATUTORY INSTRUMENTS

1989 No. 560

LEGAL AID AND ADVICE, ENGLAND AND WALES

The Legal Advice and Assistance (Amendment) Regulations 1989

Made - - - -	*23rd March 1989*
Laid before Parliament	*30th Match 1989*
Coming into force	*1st April 1989*

The Lord Chancellor, in exercise of the powers conferred on him by sections 2, 34 and 43 of the Legal Aid Act 1988**(a)**, having consulted the General Council of the Bar and the Law Society and with the consent of the Treasury, hereby makes the following Regulations:–

Citation and commencement

1. These Regulations may be cited as the Legal Advice and Assistance (Amendment) Regulations 1989 and shall come into force on 1st April 1989.

Basis of assessments

2. For regulation 30 of the Legal Advice and Assistance Regulations 1989**(b)** there shall be substituted the following new regulation:–

"**Basis of assessments**

30.—(1) In any assessment or review of a claim for costs made under these Regulations the amount to be allowed shall, subject to paragraph (2), be assessed in accordance with the provisions of regulation 6 of and Schedule 1, Part I, paragraph 1(a) to the Costs Regulations as if the work done was work to which those provisions applied.

(2) Where the claim is in respect of ABWOR to which regulation 5 applies and which is given in unsocial hours (as defined in regulation 2 of the Legal Advice and Assistance at Police Stations (Remuneration) Regulations 1989**(c)**), by a solicitor designated in accordance with arrangements made by the Board under regulation 6(3), the amount to be allowed under paragraph (1) shall be increased by one third.".

Dated 22nd March 1989

Mackay of Clashfern, C.

We consent

Alan Howarth
Kenneth Carlisle
Two of the Lords Commissioners of Her Majesty's Treasury

Dated 23rd March 1989

(a) 1988 c.34.
(b) S.I. 1989/340.
(c) S.I. 1989/342.

EXPLANATORY NOTE

(This note is not part of the Regulations)

These Regulations amend the provisions of the Legal Advice and Assistance Regulations 1989 (S.I. 1989/340) about remuneration of assistance by way of representation given by duty solicitors in respect of applications for warrants of further detention. Although the intention of regulation 30 of those Regulations was to continue current arrangements, one of its effects would in fact have been to reduce remuneration for the advocacy element of such work. Accordingly, these Regulations restore the current arrangements under which such work is remunerated at a rate one third above the rate for similar work done in normal hours.

STATUTORY INSTRUMENTS

1989 No. 561

TELEGRAPHS

The Wireless Telegraphy (Control of Interference from Fluorescent Lighting Apparatus) (Amendment) Regulations 1989

Made - - - -	*22nd March 1989*
Laid before Parliament	*31st March 1989*
Coming into force	*24th April 1989*

The Secretary of State, in exercise of the powers conferred by section 10 of the Wireless Telegraphy Act 1949(**a**) and now vested in him(**b**), and of all other powers enabling him in that behalf, hereby makes the following Regulations:

1. These Regulations may be cited as the Wireless Telegraphy (Control of Interference from Fluorescent Lighting Apparatus) (Amendment) Regulations 1989 and shall come into force on 24th April 1989.

2. In these Regulations, "the principal Regulations" means the Wireless Telegraphy (Control of Interference from Fluorescent Lighting Apparatus) Regulations 1978(**c**).

3. In regulation 2 of the principal Regulations –

(a) after the definition of "BS5394: 1983" there shall be added the following definition:

"B.S.5394: 1988" means the British Standard Specification for Limits and methods of measurement of radio interference characteristics of fluorescent lamps and luminaires, B.S.5394: 1988, published on 29th July 1988;

(b) for the definition of "the Directive" there shall be substituted the following definition:

"the Directive" means Council Directive No.76/890/EEC(**d**) as amended by Commission Directive No.87/310/EEC(**e**).

4. In regulation 5 of the principal Regulations, after the words "The requirements of Regulation 6 below" there shall be inserted "as originally specified or as subsequently amended".

(a) 1949 c.54; section 10 was amended by section 89, section 109(6) and Part IV of Schedule 7 of or to the Telecommunications Act 1984 (c.12). (**b**) 1969 c.48 (section 3); S.I.1969/1369 (article 3), 1969/1371 (article 2), 1974/691 (article 2). (**c**) S.I. 1978/1268; as amended by S.I.1985/807. (**d**) O.J. No.L336, 4.12.76, p.22.
(**e**) O.J. No.L155, 16.6.87, p.27.

5. For regulation 6 of the principal Regulations there shall be substituted the following regulation:–

6.—(1) Subject to paragraph (3) below, the insertion loss of a luminaire within the meaning of clause 3.5 of BS5394: 1983 or clause 3 of B.S.5394: 1988 as measured by the method prescribed in clause 5 of BS5394: 1983 or clause 5, 6 or 7 of B.S.5394: 1988, as the case may be, shall not be less than the minimum values relevant to that luminaire prescribed in clause 4 of BS5394: 1983 or of B.S.5394: 1988, as the case may be (being values which are related to the frequencies at which the fluorescent lighting apparatus generates electro-magnetic energy).

(2) The relevant procedures, requirements and specifications set out in BS5394: 1983 or B.S.5394: 1988, as the case may be, shall be complied with in the testing of a luminaire and the determination of the minimum values of insertion loss thereof.

(3) On and after 1st January 1990, luminaires which, by virtue of Regulation 4(1), are required to comply with Regulation 6, shall comply only with the relevant procedures, requirements and specifications of B.S.5394: 1988 and, in so far as such luminaires are concerned, the references to BS5394: 1983 in paragraphs (1) and (2) above shall not apply.

Robert Atkins
Parliamentary Under Secretary of State,
Department of Trade and Industry

22nd March 1989

EXPLANATORY NOTES

(This note is not part of the Regulations)

These Regulations amend the Wireless Telegraphy (Control of Interference from Fluorescent Lighting Apparatus) Regulations 1978 (S.I.1978/1268) ("the principal Regulations"), as amended by S.I. 1985/807, which deal with the suppression of radio interference which may be caused by fluorescent lighting apparatus, and luminaires for (or in) such apparatus which are fitted with a starter. Council Directive No.76/890/EEC (as amended by Commission Directive No.82/500/EEC), which formed the basis for the principal Regulations, was adapted to technical progress by Commission Directive No.87/310/EEC. These Regulations apply the standard B.S.5394: 1988 which reflects this adaptation to technical progress.

These Regulations come into force on 24th April 1989. From that date, and until 1st January 1990, apparatus covered by the principal Regulations which is placed on the market must conform either to the existing standard B.S.5394: 1983 or to the new standard B.S.5394: 1988. From 1st January 1990, the new standard alone will apply. For the purposes of regulation 5 of the principal Regulations, which specifies requirements which must be complied with if the apparatus is used within 15 metres of residential accommodation, both those standards and B.S.5394: 1977 which applied under the principal Regulations as originally made will be applicable from 24th April 1989 without time limit.

These Regulations do not extend to the Isle of Man or the Channel Islands since the amendments to section 10 of the Wireless Telegraphy Act 1949 mentioned in footnote (a) above have not yet been extended to those jurisdictions. Accordingly, the principal Regulations, in their unamended form, continue to apply.

Copies of B.S.5394: 1977, B.S.5394: 1983 and B.S.5394: 1988 may be obtained from the British Standards Institution (Sales Department), Linford Wood, Milton Keynes MK14 6LE at a price of £17, £17 and £38, respectively.

STATUTORY INSTRUMENTS

1989 No. 562

TELEGRAPHS

The Wireless Telegraphy (Control of Interference from Household Appliances, Portable Tools etc.) (Amendment) Regulations 1989

Made - - - -	*22nd March 1989*
Laid before Parliament	*31st March 1989*
Coming into force	*24th April 1989*

The Secretary of State, in exercise of the powers conferred by section 10 of the Wireless Telegraphy Act 1949**(a)** and now vested in him**(b)**, and of all other powers enabling him in that behalf, hereby makes the following Regulations:

1. These Regulations may be cited as the Wireless Telegraphy (Control of Interference from Household Appliances, Portable Tools etc.) (Amendment) Regulations 1989 and shall come into force on 24th April 1989.

2. In these Regulations, "the principal Regulations" means the Wireless Telegraphy (Control of Interference from Household Appliances, Portable Tools etc.) Regulations 1978**(c)**.

3. In regulation 2 of the principal Regulations–

(a) after the definition of "B.S. 800: 1983" there shall be added the following definition:

"B.S. 800: 1988" means the British Standard Specification for Limits and methods of measurement of radio interference characteristics of household electrical appliances, portable tools and similar electrical apparatus, B.S. 800: 1988, published on 31st October 1988;

(b) for the definition of "the Directive" there shall be substituted the following definition:

"the Directive" means Council Directive No. 76/889/EEC**(d)** as amended by Commission Directive No. 87/308/EEC**(e)**.

4. In regulation 3 of the principal Regulations, the phrase "(details of which are contained in clause 1.1 of B.S. 800: 1983)" shall be deleted.

5 In regulation 5(1) of the principal Regulations, after the words "The requirements of Regulation 6 below" there shall be inserted "as originally specified or as subsequently amended".

(a) 1949 c.54; section 10 was amended by section 89, section 109(6) and Part IV of Schedule 7 of or to the Telecommunications Act 1984 (c.12).
(b) 1969 c.48 (section 3); S.I. 1969/1369 (article 3), 1969/1371 (article 2), 1974/691 (article 2).
(c) S.I. 1978/1267, as amended by S.I. 1985/808.
(d) O.J. No. L336, 4.12.76, p.1.
(e) O.J. No. L155, 16.6.87, p.24.

6. For regulation 6 of the principal Regulations there shall be substituted the following regulation:–

6.—(1) Subject to paragraph (2) below, the apparatus shall be measured in the manner prescribed by clauses 6 and 7 of B.S. 800: 1983 or of B.S. 800: 1988 and shall comply with the relevant limits of interference prescribed in clause 4 of B.S. 800: 1983 or of B.S. 800: 1988, as the case may be, and, in relation to the testing of the apparatus and the limits of interference thereof, the apparatus shall comply with any other relevant procedures, requirements and specifications set out in B.S. 800: 1983 or B.S. 800: 1988, as the case may be.

(2) On and after 1st January 1990, apparatus which, by virtue of Regulation 4(1), is required to comply with Regulation 6, shall comply only with the relevant procedures, requirements and specifications of B.S. 800: 1988 and, in so far as such apparatus is concerned, the references to B.S. 800: 1983 in paragraph (1) above shall not apply.

Robert Atkins
Parliamentary Under Secretary of State,
Department of Trade and Industry

22nd March 1989

EXPLANATORY NOTE

(This note is not part of the Regulations)

These Regulations amend the Wireless Telegraphy (Control of Interference from Household Appliances, Portable Tools etc.) Regulations 1978 (S.I. 1978/1267) ("the principal Regulations"), as amended by S.I. 1985/808, which relate to the control of radio interference caused by electrical household appliances, portable tools and other equipment causing similar interference. Council Directive No. 76/889/EEC (as amended by Commission Directive No. 82/499/EEC), which formed the basis for the principal Regulations, was adapted to technical progress by Commission Directive No. 87/308/EEC. These Regulations apply the standard B.S. 800: 1988 which reflects this adaptation to technical progress.

These Regulations come into force on 24th April 1989. From that date, and until 1st January 1990, apparatus covered by the principal Regulations which is placed on the market must conform either to the existing standard B.S. 800: 1983 or to the new standard B.S. 800: 1988. From 1st January 1990, the new standard alone will apply. For the purposes of regulation 5 of the principal Regulations, which specifies requirements which must be complied with if apparatus is used by any person, both those standards and B.S. 800: 1977 which applied under the principal Regulations as originally made will be applicable from 24th April 1989 without time limit.

These Regulations do not extend to the Isle of Man or the Channel Islands since the amendments to section 10 of the Wireless Telegraphy Act 1949 mentioned in footnote (a) above have not yet been extended to those jurisdictions. Accordingly, the principal Regulations, in their unamended form, continue to apply.

Copies of B.S. 800: 1977, B.S. 800: 1983 and B.S. 800: 1988 may be obtained from the British Standards Institution (Sales Department), Linford Wood, Milton Keynes MK14 6LE at a price of £28.50, £28.50 and £45, respectively.

STATUTORY INSTRUMENTS

1989 No. 564

POLICE

The Police Federation (Amendment) Regulations 1989

Made - - - -	*23rd March 1989*
Laid before Parliament	*5th April 1989*
Coming into force	*2nd May 1989*

In exercise of the powers conferred on me by section 44 of the Police Act 1964(**a**), and after consultation with the three Central Committees of the Police Federation for England and Wales sitting together as a Joint Committee, I hereby make the following Regulations:

1. These Regulations may be cited as the Police Federation (Amendment) Regulations 1989 and shall come into force on 2nd May 1989.

2. For regulation 20(2) of the Police Federation Regulations 1969(**b**) (hereinafter called "the principal Regulations") there shall be substituted the following paragraphs–

"(2) Federation property and funds held by a central committee shall be vested in three trustees appointed by the committee in question.

(2A) Federation property and funds held by the joint central committee shall be vested in three trustees, of whom each of the central conferences shall have elected one from among the delegates to that conference, appointed by the joint central committee.

(2B) Rules made by the joint central conference may prescribe the term of office of trustees appointed under paragraph (2A) and may provide for the conduct of elections under that paragraph and the filling of casual vacancies among trustees appointed thereunder.".

3. The three persons appointed by the joint central committee to be trustees of the Federation property and funds held by that committee who hold that office immediately before these Regulations come into force shall be deemed to have been so appointed and to hold office under paragraphs (2A) and (2B) of regulation 20 of the principal Regulations.

Home Office
23rd March 1989

Douglas Hurd
One of Her Majesty's Principal Secretaries of State

(**a**) 1964 c.48; section 44 was amended by section 109 of the Police and Criminal Evidence Act 1984 (c.60).
(**b**) S.I. 1969/1787; there are no relevant amendments.

EXPLANATORY NOTE

(This note is not part of the Regulations)

These Regulations amend regulation 20(2) of the Police Federation Regulations 1969 as it relates to Federation property and funds held by the joint central committee of the Police Federation for England and Wales. They make it a requirement to continue the existing practice whereby the three trustees include one representative from each of the federated ranks, elected respectively by the constables', the sergeants' and the inspectors' central conference.

STATUTORY INSTRUMENTS

1989 No. 566

HOUSING, ENGLAND AND WALES
HOUSING, SCOTLAND

The Housing Benefit (General) Amendment No. 2 Regulations 1989

Made - - - -	*28th March 1989*
Laid before Parliament	*30th March 1989*
Coming into force	*1st April 1989*

The Secretary of State for Social Security in exercise of powers conferred by sections 20(1)(c), (8) and (12)(g), 29(3), 51(1)(h) and (q) and 84(1) of the Social Security Act 1986**(a)** and section 166(1) to (3A) of the Social Security Act 1975**(b)** and of all other powers enabling him in that behalf after consultation with organisations appearing to him to be representative of authorities concerned**(c)** and after agreement by the Social Security Advisory Committee that proposals to make these Regulations in so far as they are made under powers in section 51(1) of the Social Security Act 1986 should not be referred to it**(d)**, by this instrument which is otherwise made before the end of a period of 12 months from the commencement of the enactments under which it is made, hereby makes the following Regulations:

Citation, commencement and interpretation

1.—(1) These Regulations may be cited as the Housing Benefit (General) Amendment No. 2 Regulations 1989 and shall come into force on 1st April 1989.

(2) In these Regulations "the General Regulations" means the Housing Benefit (General) Regulations 1987**(e)**.

Amendment of regulation 11 of the General Regulations

2. In regulation 11 of the General Regulations (restrictions on unreasonable rents)–

(a) after paragraph (1) there shall be inserted the following paragraph–

"(1A) Where a rent has been determined by a rent assessment committee in respect of a dwelling under Part I of the Housing Act 1988**(f)** or Part II of the Housing (Scotland) Act 1988**(g)**, the claimant's eligible rent determined

(a) 1986 c.50; section 51(1)(h) was extended by section 121(6) of the Housing Act 1988 (c.50) and section 70(5) of the Housing (Scotland) Act 1988 (c.43); section 84(1) is an interpretation provision and is cited because of the meanings assigned to the words "prescribed" and "regulations".
(b) 1975 c.14; section 166(3A) was inserted by section 62(1) of the Social Security Act 1986 and section 166(1) to (3A) was applied by section 83(1) of that Act.
(c) *See* section 61(7) of the Social Security Act 1986.
(d) *See* section 10(2)(b) of the Social Security Act 1980 (c.30); section 10 was amended by paragraph 98 of Schedule 10 to the Social Security Act 1986.
(e) S.I. 1987/1971, to which there are amendments not relevant to these Regulations.
(f) 1988 c.50.
(g) 1988 c.43.

in accordance with regulation 10 shall not exceed the rent determined by the committee.";

(b) in paragraph (2)–

(i) for the reference "(3) and (4)" there shall be substituted the reference "(3) to (4)";

(ii) at the beginning of sub-paragraphs (a) and (c) there shall be inserted the words "whether by reference to a determination or re-determination made by a rent officer in exercise of a function conferred on him by an order under section 121 of the Housing Act 1988 or, as the case may be, section 70 of the Housing (Scotland) Act 1988, or otherwise";

(c) after paragraph (3) there shall be inserted the following paragraphs–

"(3A) No deduction shall be made under paragraph (2) for a period of 12 months from the date of death of any person to whom paragraph (7) applied or, had a claim been made, would have applied, if the dwelling which the claimant occupies is the same as that occupied by him at that date except where the deduction began before the death occurred.

(3B) For the purposes of paragraph (3A), a claimant shall be treated as occupying the dwelling if paragraph (8) of regulation 5 (circumstances in which a person is to be treated as occupying a dwelling) is satisfied and for that purpose sub-paragraph (b) of that paragraph shall be treated as if it were omitted.".

Amendment of regulation 12 of the General Regulations

3. In regulation 12 of the General Regulations (restrictions on rent increases)–

(a) at the beginning there shall be inserted the words "Subject to paragraph (2),"; and after the words "if it considers" there shall be inserted the words ", whether by reference to a determination or re-determination made by a rent officer in exercise of a function conferred on him by an order under section 121 of the Housing Act 1988 or, as the case may be, section 70 of the Housing (Scotland) Act 1988, or otherwise,";

(b) at the end of that regulation there shall be added the following paragraphs–

"(2) No deduction shall be made under this regulation for a period of 12 months from the date of death of any person to whom paragraph (7) of regulation 11 (restrictions on unreasonable payments) applied or, had a claim been made, would have applied, if the dwelling which the claimant occupies is the same as that occupied by him at that date except where the deduction began before the death occurred.

(3) For the purposes of paragraph (2), a claimant shall be treated as occupying the dwelling if paragraph (8) of regulation 5 (circumstances in which a person is to be treated as occupying a dwelling) is satisfied and for that purpose sub-paragraph (b) of that paragraph shall be treated as if it were omitted.".

Amendment of regulation 82 of the General Regulations

4. In regulation 82 of the General Regulations (procedure on further review) after paragraph (1) there shall be inserted the following paragraph–

"(1A) Notwithstanding paragraph (1) where the appropriate authority has applied for a re-determination by a rent officer in exercise of a function conferred on him by an order under section 121 of the Housing Act 1988 or, as the case may be, section 70 of the Housing (Scotland) Act 1988 the Review Board may, if it considers it appropriate in the circumstances, hold the hearing after the re-determination but as soon as is reasonably practicable thereafter.".

Amendment of regulation 95 of the General Regulations

5. In regulation 95 of the General Regulations (withholding of benefit) after paragraph (6) there shall be added the following paragraph–

"(7) Where a rent officer has notified an authority that he has been denied entry to the dwelling for the purpose of making a determination or re-determination in exercise of a function conferred on him by an order under section 121 of the Housing Act 1988 or, as the case may be, section 70 of the Housing (Scotland) Act 1988, an authority may withhold payment of a rent allowance, if–

(a) in a case where entry has been denied by the claimant, payment would have been made either to the claimant or directly to his landlord; or

(b) in a case where entry has been denied by the landlord, direct payment would have been made to the landlord,

and for so long as the rent officer continues to be denied entry to the dwelling.".

Insertion of Part XIV into the General Regulations

6. After Part XIII of the General Regulations (overpayments) there shall be inserted the following Part–

"PART XIV

MISCELLANEOUS

Evidence and information required by rent officers

106. The appropriate authority shall furnish as soon as is reasonably practicable such information or evidence relating to a claimant and his accommodation obtained by it in exercise of its functions relating to housing benefit as may be required by a rent officer for the purpose of a function conferred on him by an order under section 121 of the Housing Act 1988 or, as the case may be, section 70 of the Housing (Scotland) Act 1988.".

Signed by authority of the Secretary of State for Social Security.

Peter Lloyd
Parliamentary Under-Secretary of State,
Department of Social Security

28th March 1989

EXPLANATORY NOTE

(This note is not part of the Regulations)

These Regulations further amend the Housing Benefit (General) Regulations 1987.

They provide for a claimant's eligible rent not to exceed the rent fixed by a rent assessment committee and for authorities to have regard to determinations made by rent officers in determining eligible rent (regulations 2(a) and (b) and 3(c)); and prohibit an authority from reducing eligible rent for a period of 12 months from the death of a member of the household (regulation 2(c) and 3(b)).

They also provide for payment of a rent allowance to be withheld where a rent officer is denied entry to the dwelling (regulation 5); for an authority to furnish rent officers with information relating to the claimant and his accommodation (regulation 6); and for hearings of a Review Board to be deferred pending a re-determination by a rent officer (regulation 4).

These Regulations, except in so far as they are made under the powers in section 51 of the Social Security Act 1986, are made before the expiry of 12 months from the commencement of the provisions under which they are made; they are accordingly exempt by section 61(5) of that Act from reference to the Social Security Advisory Committee and have not been so referred.

STATUTORY INSTRUMENTS

1989 No. 567

MERCHANT SHIPPING

SAFETY

The Merchant Shipping (Loading and Stability Assessment of Ro/Ro Passenger Ships) (Non-United Kingdom Ships) Regulations 1989

Made - - - -	*28th March 1989*
Coming into force	
regulation 8(2) -	*29th April 1990*

all other regulations: in accordance with regulation 1

Whereas a draft of these Regulations has been laid before Parliament and has been approved by a resolution of each House of Parliament in accordance with section 49(4A) of the Merchant Shipping Act 1979**(a)**;

Now therefore the Secretary of State for Transport, after consulting with the persons referred to in section 22(2) of the Merchant Shipping Act 1979, in exercise of the powers conferred on him by sections 21(1)(c), (3), (5) and (6) and 22(1) of that Act and of all other powers enabling him in that behalf, hereby makes the following Regulations:

Citation and interpretation

1.—(1) These Regulations may be cited as the Merchant Shipping (Loading and Stability Assessment of Ro/Ro Passenger Ships) (Non-United Kingdom Ships) Regulations 1989 and shall come into force on the 7th day after the day on which they are made except for regulation 8(2) which shall come into force on 29th April 1990.

(2) In these Regulations the following expressions have the following meanings respectively:–

"deadweight" has the same meaning as in the Merchant Shipping (Passenger Ship Construction and Survey) Regulations 1984**(b)**;

"deadweight moment" means the total vertical moment about the moulded base line amidships of all the component weights of the total deadweight;

"passenger ship" means a ship carrying more than 12 passengers and propelled by electricity or other mechanical power;

"ro/ro passenger ship" means a passenger ship provided with cargo or vehicle spaces not normally subdivided in any way and extending to either a substantial length or the entire length of the ship in which vehicles or cargo can be loaded or unloaded normally in a horizontal direction;

(a) 1979 c.39; section 21(6) was amended by section 49(3) of the Criminal Justice Act 1982 (c.48) and sections 21 and 49 were amended by section 11 of the Safety at Sea Act 1986 (c.23).
(b) S.I. 1984/1216; relevant amendment is S.I. 1985/661.

"stability information booklet" means the booklet required to be provided in compliance with regulation 9(3) of the Merchant Shipping (Passenger Ship Construction) Regulations 1980**(a)** or regulation 9(3) of the Merchant Shipping (Passenger Ship Construction and Survey) Regulations 1984, as applicable;

"non-United Kingdom passenger ship" means a passenger ship which is not a United Kingdom ship;

"voyage" includes an excursion.

(3) Where a ship is managed by a person other than its owner (whether on behalf of the owner or some other person, or on his own behalf), a reference in these Regulations to the owner shall be construed as including a reference to that person.

(4) A reference in these Regulations to a numbered regulation is a reference to the regulation of that number in these Regulations.

Application

2. These Regulations apply to ro/ro passenger ships other than United Kingdom ships, which are operating as ships of Classes I or II within the meaning of the Merchant Shipping (Passenger Ship Construction and Survey) Regulations 1984, while they are within a port in the United Kingdom.

Information on stability during loading

3.—(1) The owner of every ship shall ensure that the master is provided with information relating to its stability during the process of loading and unloading. The information shall be included in the ship's stability information booklet.

(2) This information shall be so arranged as to enable the master to extract the particular data he requires quickly and easily.

(3) Where any alterations are made or changes occur to the ship so as materially to affect the information supplied to the master in accordance with paragraph (1) of this regulation, amended information shall be provided.

(4) The information provided pursuant to paragraphs (1)–(3) inclusive of this regulation shall be kept on board the ship at all times in the custody of the master.

Stability and freeboard during loading and unloading

4. The master shall use the information provided in accordance with regulation 3 and, when necessary, make calculations or cause calculations to be made in order to ensure that the process of loading and unloading is carried out safely; in particular, he shall ensure that:–

(a) the ship has adequate stability; and

(b) the freeboard at any door giving access to the hull or to an enclosed superstructure is sufficient to prevent the entry of water.

Recording of draught, trim and freeboard prior to departure

5.—(1) On completion of the loading of the ship and before it proceeds on a voyage, the master, or an officer appointed for the purpose by the master shall ascertain:–

(a) the ship's draught at the bow and at the stern;

(b) the trim of the ship by the bow or the stern; and

(c) the vertical distance from the waterline to the appropriate subdivision load line mark on each side of the ship.

(2) The draughts, trim and vertical distances ascertained in accordance with paragraph (1) of this regulation shall be recorded in respect of each voyage in a book retained on board for that purpose..

Calculation of stability prior to departure

6—(1) On completion of the loading of the ship and before the ship proceeds on a voyage the master shall cause the stability of the ship to be calculated and satisfy himself that it is adequate.

(a) S.I. 1980/535; relevant amendment is S.I. 1985/660.

(2) The calculation performed in accordance with paragraph (1) of this regulation shall be made using the actual weights of goods vehicles and other items of cargo required to be determined by regulations made under section 21 of the Merchant Shipping Act 1979. For weights of items not required to be so determined, the declared weights or weights estimated as accurately as possible shall be used.

(3) The calculation in accordance with paragraph (1) of this regulation shall be made using an on-board loading and stability computer, or a reliable shore-based loading and stability computer system, or by such other means as will enable accurate results to be obtained.

(4) The master shall record the result of the calculation in a book specially retained on board for that purpose.

(5) A copy of any print-out of the calculation referred to in paragraph (1), or of any written working of a calculation made in substitution therefor, shall be retained on the ship for at least one calendar month after the calculation was made.

Condition of loading prior to departure to be satisfactory

7. Before the ship proceeds on a voyage the master shall ensure that the condition of loading of the ship, as recorded in accordance with regulations 5(2) and 6(4), satisfies all the relevant requirements prescribed in the stability information booklet.

Draught marks and automatic draught gauge system

8.—(1) Every ship shall have a scale of draughts at the bow and stern on each side of the ship.

(2) Every ship shall be provided with a reliable automatic draught gauge system.

Offences and Penalties

9.—(1) Any contravention of regulation 3(1) and (3) or 8 shall be an offence on the part of the owner and any contravention of regulations 3(4) and 4 to 7 inclusive shall be an offence on the part of the master (except so far as regulation 5(1) imposes a duty on an officer). Any such offence shall be punishable on summary conviction by a fine not exceeding the statutory maximum or on conviction on indictment by imprisonment for a term not exceeding two years, or a fine, or both.

(2) Any contravention of his duty under regulation 5(1) by an officer appointed in accordance with that paragraph shall be an offence on his part punishable on summary conviction by a fine not exceeding level 3 on the standard scale.

Defence

10. It shall be a defence for a person charged with committing an offence under these Regulations to show that he took all reasonable steps to avoid committing the offence.

Detention

11. In any case where a ship does not comply with the requirements of these Regulations, the ship shall be liable to be detained and section 692 of the Merchant Shipping Act 1894**(a)** (which relates to the detention of a ship) shall have effect in relation to the ship, subject to the modification that for the words "this Act" wherever they appear, there shall be substituted "the Merchant Shipping (Loading and Stability Assessment of Ro/Ro Passenger Ships) (Non-United Kingdom Ships) Regulations 1989".

(a) 1894 c.60.

Exemption

12. The Secretary of State may exempt individual ships from the provisions of any of these Regulations, subject to such conditions as he may specify and may, subject to giving reasonable notice, alter or cancel any exemption so granted.

The Lord Brabazon of Tara
Parliamentary Under Secretary of State,
Department of Transport

28th March 1989

EXPLANATORY NOTE

(This note is not part of the Regulations)

These Regulations have the effect of applying to non-United Kingdom ro/ro passenger ships engaged in international voyages from the United Kingdom the principal requirements of the Merchant Shipping (Loading and Stability Assessment of Ro/Ro Passenger Ships) Regulations 1989 (S.I. 1989/100) (which apply only to United Kingdom ships) while they are within a port in the United Kingdom. These Regulations include requirements for the safe loading and unloading of ro/ro passenger ships, the provision of draught marks and the fitting of an automatic draught gauge system.

The Regulations also require records to be made of the ship's draught of water, trim and freeboards and the components of its stability before proceeding on any voyage from a port in the United Kingdom.

STATUTORY INSTRUMENTS

1989 No. 568

MERCHANT SHIPPING

SAFETY

The Merchant Shipping (Weighing of Goods Vehicles and other Cargo) (Application to non-UK Ships) Regulations 1989

Made - - - -	*28th March 1989*
Coming into force	*31st March 1989*

Whereas a draft of these Regulations has been laid before Parliament and has been approved by a resolution of each House of Parliament in accordance with section 49(4A) of the Merchant Shipping Act 1979(**a**).

Now therefore the Secretary of State, after consultation with the persons referred to in section 22(2) of the Merchant Shipping Act 1979, in exercise of the powers conferred on him by section 21(1)(c), (3) to (6) and section 22(1) of that Act, and of all other powers enabling him in that behalf, hereby makes the following Regulations:

1. These Regulations may be cited as the Merchant Shipping (Weighing of Goods Vehicles and other Cargo) (Application to non-UK Ships) Regulations 1989 and shall come into force on 31st March 1989.

2. The Merchant Shipping (Weighing of Goods Vehicles and other Cargo) Regulations 1988(**b**) (which apply only to ro/ro passenger ships which are operating as ships of Class II or II(A) within the meaning of the Merchant Shipping (Passenger Ship Construction and Survey) Regulations 1984(**c**) and are United Kingdom ships) shall apply also to ro/ro passenger ships which are operating as ships of those classes but which are not United Kingdom ships, while they are in a port in the United Kingdom.

The Lord Brabazon of Tara
Parliamentary Under Secretary of State,
Department of Transport

28th March 1989

(**a**) 1979 c.39. Sections 21(1) and (3) and 49 were amended by section 11 of the Safety at Sea Act 1986 (c.23). Section 21(6) was amended by section 49(3) of the Criminal Justice Act 1982 (c.48).
(**b**) S.I. 1988/1275, amended by S.I. 1989/270.
(**c**) S.I. 1984/1216.

EXPLANATORY NOTE

(This note is not part of the Regulations)

These Regulations apply the requirements of the Merchant Shipping (Weighing of Goods Vehicles and other Cargo) Regulations 1988 to non-United Kingdom ro/ro passenger ships of Classes II and II(A) while they are in a port in the United Kingdom. (Those Regulations require the weighing of all road vehicles, except buses, and all non-vehicular items of cargo exceeding, in each case, 7.5 tonnes for all voyages on which passengers are carried.)

STATUTORY INSTRUMENTS

1989 No. 571

SOCIAL SECURITY

The Social Security (Contributions) Amendment (No. 2) Regulations 1989

Made - - - -	*22nd March 1989*
Coming into force	*6th April 1989*

Whereas a draft of the following Regulations was laid before Parliament in accordance with the provisions of section 167(1) of the Social Security Act 1975**(a)** and approved by resolution of each House of Parliament:

Now, therefore, the Secretary of State for Social Security, in conjunction with the Treasury**(b)**, in exercise of powers conferred by sections 129(1) and 166(2) of, and Schedule 20 to, the Social Security Act 1975**(c)** and of all other powers enabling him in that behalf, and after agreement by the Social Security Advisory Committee that proposals to make these Regulations should not be referred to it**(d)**, hereby makes the following Regulations:

Citation and commencement

1. These Regulations may be cited as the Social Security (Contributions) Amendment (No. 2) Regulations 1989 and shall come into force on 6th April 1989.

Amendment to Regulations

2. In regulation 98 of the Social Security (Contributions) Regulations 1979**(e)** (modification of provisions of the Social Security Act 1975 in relation to share fishermen), in paragraph (c) (weekly rate of any Class 2 contributions payable by share fishermen) for "£6.55" there shall be substituted "£5.80".

Signed by authority of the Secretary of State for Social Security.

Nicholas Scott
Minister of State,
Department of Social Security

21st March 1989

Alan Howarth
Kenneth Carlisle
Two of the Lords Commissioners
of Her Majesty's Treasury

22nd March 1989

(a) 1975 c.14; section 167(1) was amended by the Social Security Act 1986 (c. 50), section 62(3).
(b) *See* Social Security Act 1975, section 166(5).
(c) Schedule 20 is cited because of the meaning ascribed to the word "Regulations".
(d) *See* section 61(1)(b) of the Social Security Act 1986 (c.50).
(e) S.I. 1979/591; the relevant amending instrument is S.I. 1986/198.

EXPLANATORY NOTE

(This note is not part of the Regulations)

These Regulations further amend regulation 98 (which relates to share fishermen) of the Social Security (Contributions) Regulations 1979. They amend paragraph (c) in that regulation by reducing the special rate of Class 2 contributions payable by share fishermen from £6.55 to £5.80.

STATUTORY INSTRUMENTS

1989 No. 572

SOCIAL SECURITY

The Social Security (Contributions) Amendment (No. 3) Regulations 1989

Made - - - -	*29th March 1989*
Laid before Parliament	*4th April 1989*
Coming into force	*6th April 1989*

The Secretary of State for Social Security, in exercise of the powers conferred by sections 1(6), 8(1) and 166(3) of, and Schedule 20 to, the Social Security Act 1975**(a)** and of all other powers enabling him in that behalf, after agreement by the Social Security Advisory Committee that proposals to make these Regulations should not be referred to it**(b)**, hereby makes the following Regulations:

Citation, commencement and interpretation

1.—(1) These Regulations may be cited as the Social Security (Contributions) Amendment (No. 3) Regulations 1989 and shall come into force on 6th April 1989.

(2) In these Regulations "the principal Regulations" means the Social Security (Contributions) Regulations 1979**(c)**, and unless the context otherwise requires, any reference in these Regulations to a numbered regulation is a reference to the regulation bearing that number in the principal Regulations.

Amendment of regulation 28

2. Subject to regulation 5 of these Regulations, in sub-paragraph (b) of paragraph (2) of regulation 28**(d)** (precluded Class 3 contributions) for the words "widow's allowance or death grant" there shall be substituted the words "widow's payment".

Amendment of regulation 119

3. For sub-paragraph (e) of paragraph (1) of regulation 119 (conditions as to residence or presence in Great Britain) there shall be substituted the following sub-paragraph:

"(e) as respects entitlement of a person to pay Class 3 contributions in respect of any year, either that–

(i) that person is resident in Great Britain throughout that year; or

(ii) that person has arrived in Great Britain during that year and has been or is liable to pay Class 1 or Class 2 contributions in respect of an earlier period during that year; or

---

(a) 1975 c.14. Section 8(1) was amended by the Education (School-leaving Dates) Act 1976 (c.5), section 2(4), the Health and Social Security Act 1984 (c.48), section 18(1)(a) and S.I. 1988/675, article 4. Schedule 20 is cited because of the meaning it ascribes to the words "Prescribe" and "Regulations".
(b) *See* section 61(1)(b) of the Social Security Act 1986 (c.50).
(c) S.I. 1979/591; the relevant amending instrument is S.I. 1987/2111.
(d) Regulation 28(2)(b) was amended by S.I. 1984/77.

(iii) that person has arrived in Great Britain during that year and was either ordinarily resident in Great Britain throughout the whole of that year or became ordinarily resident during the course of it; or

(iv) that person not being ordinarily resident in Great Britain has arrived in that year or the previous year and has been continuously present in Great Britain for 26 complete contribution weeks, entitlement where the arrival has been in the previous year arising in respect only of the next year.".

Amendment of regulation 121

4.—(1) Regulation 121 (Class 2 and Class 3 contributions for periods abroad) shall be amended in accordance with the following paragraphs of this regulation.

(2) In paragraph (1), for the words "the next succeeding paragraph" there shall be substituted the words "paragraph (2) of this regulation".

(3) After paragraph (1) there shall be inserted the following paragraph–

"(1A) A person who is gainfully employed outside Great Britain and falls within the provisions of sub-paragraph (a) of the last preceding paragraph shall for the purposes of that paragraph be treated as being outside Great Britain for any period during which he is temporarily in Great Britain.".

(4) In paragraph (2), for the words "the last preceding paragraph" there shall be substituted the words "paragraph (1) of this regulation".

Savings

5. For the purposes of determining whether a person is entitled to pay Class 3 contributions under paragraph (2) of regulation 28, sub-paragraph (b) of that paragraph shall continue to have effect in relation to any death occurring before 11th April 1988 as though regulation 2 of these Regulations had not been made.

Signed by authority of the Secretary of State for Social Security.

Nicholas Scott
Minister of State,
Department of Social Security

29th March 1989

EXPLANATORY NOTE

(This note is not part of the Regulations)

These Regulations further amend the Social Security (Contributions) Regulations 1979 ("the principal Regulations").

Regulation 2 amends regulation 28 of the principal Regulations, and is consequential upon the abolition of widow's allowance and death grant. Regulation 5 contains savings provisions.

Regulation 3 amends regulation 119 of the principal Regulations, by providing for entitlement of certain persons arriving in Great Britain from abroad to pay Class 3 contributions.

Regulation 4 amends regulation 121 of the principal Regulations, by extending entitlement to pay Class 2 contributions to those gainfully employed outside Great Britain to cover temporary periods in Great Britain.

STATUTORY INSTRUMENTS

1989 No. 573

COAL INDUSTRY

The Coal Industry (Restructuring Grants) Order 1989

Made - - - -	*23rd March 1989*
Coming into force	*26th March 1989*

The Secretary of State, in exercise of the powers conferred on him by section 3(2)(a), (3), (4)(a) and (6) of the Coal Industry Act 1987(**a**) and with the approval of the Treasury, hereby makes the following Order, a draft of which has been laid before the House of Commons and has been approved by that House in accordance with section 3(10) of that Act:

1. This Order may be cited as the Coal Industry (Restructuring Grants) Order 1989 and shall come into force on the third day after the day on which it is made.

2. In this Order, unless the context otherwise requires–

"the 1989/90 financial year" means the financial year of the British Coal Corporation ending in March 1990;

"the Act" means the Coal Industry Act 1987;

"the Corporation" means the British Coal Corporation or any wholly-owned subsidiary of theirs;

"employees" means employees of the Corporation;

"payments" means periodical or lump sum payments;

"the relevant consolidated profit and loss account" means any consolidated profit and loss account of the British Coal Corporation and their subsidiaries prepared in accordance with a direction given under section 8(1) of the Coal Industry Act 1971(**b**) for the 1989/90 financial year;

and references to payments, contributions or expenditure are references to payments, contributions or expenditure by the Corporation.

3. The 1989/90 financial year shall be a specified financial year for the purposes of section 3(4)(a) of the Act.

4. The kinds of expenditure specified in the Schedule to this Order shall be specified kinds of expenditure for the purposes of section 3(2)(a) of the Act in relation to the 1989/90 financial year.

5. The maximum amount which may be paid under section 3 of the Act by way of grant in respect of the 1989/90 financial year in relation to the kinds of expenditure specified under a Head in the Schedule is that sum which represents 77 per cent. of–

(a) the total amount of the costs of the Corporation which are related to the kinds of expenditure specified under the Head and which fall to be charged to the relevant consolidated profit and loss account; or

(**a**) 1987 c.3; the limit specified in section 3(6) was increased to £500 million by S.I. 1988/456.
(**b**) 1971 c.16.

(b) if a larger amount has been agreed in respect of those costs for the purposes of section 3(2)(b) of the Act, that larger amount.

6. The limit specified in section 3(6) of the Act on the aggregate of grants under section 3(1) thereof is increased from £500 million to £750 million.

Michael Spicer
Parliamentary Under Secretary of State,
Department of Energy

23rd March 1989

We approve,

David Maclean
Kenneth Carlisle
Two of the Lords Commissioners
of Her Majesty's Treasury

23rd March 1989

SCHEDULE

Articles 4 and 5

KINDS OF EXPENDITURE

Head 1: Redundancy and early retirement

(i) Payments in respect of redundant employees made under section 81 of the Employment Protection (Consolidation) Act 1978(**a**).

(ii) Payments made for the purpose of assisting persons who leave the employment of the Corporation by virtue of redundancy or early retirement, being payments made under arrangements established by the Corporation.

(iii) Payments in respect of the loss of superannuation prospects by persons leaving the employment of the Corporation by virtue of redundancy or early retirement.

(iv) Contributions to superannuation funds maintained by virtue of section 37 of the Coal Industry Nationalisation Act 1946(**b**) in respect of any increase in the cost of retirement benefits paid before normal retirement age to persons who leave the employment of the Corporation by virtue of redundancy or early retirement.

Head 2: Changes of work and place of employment

(v) Payments to or for the benefit of employees in connection with their removal or resettlement (with or without their dependants) by virtue of their place of employment being changed.

(vi) Payments to local authorities and housing associations for the provision of housing for employees on account of their place of employment being changed.

(vii) Expenditure on providing travel allowances or transport for employees on account of their place of employment being changed.

(viii) Payments made to supplement temporarily the earnings of employees on account of their place of employment being changed.

(ix) Payments made to compensate employees temporarily for any reduction in their earnings resulting from the nature of their work being changed.

Head 5: Retraining

(x) Expenditure on the provision of retraining for persons who are to leave or have left the employment of the Corporation by virtue of redundancy or incapacity, being retraining provided under arrangements established by the Corporation.

Head 6: New employment

(xi) Payments made under arrangements for the British Coal Corporation to reimburse their wholly-owned subsidiary British Coal Enterprise Limited for losses incurred by it in promoting new employment in coal mining areas or new employment for such persons as are mentioned in paragraph (x) above (whether in such areas or elsewhere).

(**a**) 1978 c.44; section 81(4) was amended by the Employment Act 1982 (c.46), section 20 and Schedule 2, paragraph 6(2).
(**b**) 1946 c.59.

EXPLANATORY NOTE

(This note is not part of the Order)

This Order concerns the making of grants by the Secretary of State to the British Coal Corporation under section 3 of the Coal Industry Act 1987 (grants for workforce redeployment and reduction, etc.).

Article 3 specifies the financial year of the Corporation ending in March 1990 as a year in respect of which such grants may be made.

Article 4 provides for the kinds of expenditure specified in the Schedule to the Order to rank as eligible expenditure of the Corporation and their wholly-owned subsidiaries in relation to the financial year.

Article 5 sets a limit on the amount which may be advanced in relation to the financial year with respect to each head of expenditure specified in the Schedule. The limit is 77 per cent. of the relevant costs appearing in the consolidated profit and loss account or 77 per cent. of such larger amount as may be agreed by the Secretary of State and the Corporation with the approval of the Treasury.

Article 6 increases the limit on the aggregate amount of grants which may be made under section 3 of the 1987 Act from £500 million to £750 million.

STATUTORY INSTRUMENTS

1989 No. 574

AGRICULTURE

The Beef Special Premium (Protection of Payments) Order 1989

Made - - - -	*23rd March 1989*
Laid before Parliament	*31st March 1989*
Coming into force	*3rd April 1989*

The Minister of Agriculture, Fisheries and Food, the Secretary of State for Scotland, (being the Secretary of State concerned with agriculture in Scotland) and the Secretary of State for Wales, acting jointly, in exercise of the powers conferred by sections 5, 9(4) and 35(3) of the Agriculture Act 1957(**a**), as applied in relation to any Community arrangements for or related to the regulation of the market for any agricultural produce by section 6(3) of the European Communities Act 1972(**b**), and now vested in them(**c**), and of all other powers enabling them in that behalf, hereby make the following Order:–

Title, extent and commencement

1. This Order, which may be cited as the Beef Special Premium (Protection of Payments) Order 1989, shall apply in Great Britain and shall come into force on 3rd April 1989.

Interpretation

2.—(1) In this Order, unless the context otherwise requires–

"animal" means an animal of the bovine species;

"approved deadweight centre" means a place for the time being approved by the Board for the making of applications for premium in respect of carcases;

"approved export centre" means a place for the time being approved by the Board for the making of applications for premium in respect of animals to be consigned to another Member State or exported to a third country;

"approved liveweight centre" means a place for the time being approved by the Board for the making of applications for premium in respect of animals;

"authorised officer", in relation to any purpose referred to in this Order, means an officer authorised by the Board to act for that purpose;

"the Board" means the Intervention Board for Agricultural Produce established under section 6 of the European Communities Act 1972;

"the Commission Regulation" means Commission Regulation (EEC) No 714/89(**d**) laying down detailed rules applying to the special premium for beef producers;

(**a**) 1957 c.57.
(**b**) 1972 c.68.
(**c**) In the case of the Secretary of State for Wales, by virtue of S.I. 1978/272.
(**d**) OJ No L 78, 21.3.89, p.38.

"the Meat and Livestock Commission" means the Meat and Livestock Commission established by virtue of section 1(1) of the Agriculture Act 1967(a);

"the Ministers" means the Minister of Agriculture, Fisheries and Food and the Secretaries of State respectively concerned with agriculture in Scotland or Wales;

"premium" means the special premium referred to in Article 4a of Council Regulation (EEC) No 805/68 (b) on the common organisation of the market in beef and veal;

"the prescribed manner" means, in the case of an animal, the manner prescribed in Article 7(3) of the Commission Regulation and, in the case of a carcase, the manner prescribed by the Board;

"slaughter requirements" has the meaning given to it in article 6(1);

(2) Any reference in this Order to the Board other than in this paragraph or in article 8 shall include a reference to the Meat and Livestock Commission when acting for the Board.

(3) Other expressions used in this Order have, in so far as the context admits, the same meanings as in Council Regulation (EEC) No. 468/87 (c) laying down general rules applying to the special premium for beef producers and the Commission Regulation.

(4) In this Order, unless the context otherwise requires, any reference to a numbered article is a reference to the article so numbered in this Order.

Applications for special premium

3.—(1) Subject to paragraph (5) below, a producer on whose holding a male animal was fattened may apply for a premium payment in respect of that animal, or the carcase derived from it, at an approved liveweight centre or an approved deadweight centre respectively, in such form and to such person as the Board may require.

(2) An animal or carcase in respect of which such an application is made shall be examined by a person authorised by the Board for that purpose and shall be marked by him, or under his supervision, in the prescribed manner if he is satisfied–

(a) in the case of an animal, that–

(i) it is a male weighing at least 370 kilograms; and

(ii) it has not been identified or marked in accordance with Article 7 of the Commission Regulation; or

(b) in the case of a carcase, that–

(i) its weight established in accordance with the provisions of Article 5(2) of the Commission Regulation is equal to or exceeds 200 kilograms; and

(ii) it was derived from a male animal which had not been identified or marked in accordance with Article 7 of the Commission Regulation.

(3) Subject to paragraph (5) below, a producer may apply at an approved export centre in such form and to such person as the Board may require for a premium payment in respect of a male animal at least nine months old, to be consigned to another Member State or exported to a third country, which he has kept on his holding for at least two months.

(4) An animal in respect of which such an application is made shall be examined by a person authorised by the Board for that purpose and shall be marked by him in the prescribed manner if he is satisfied that it is a male at least nine months old which has not been identified or marked in accordance with Article 7 of the Commission Regulation.

(5) No application may be made by a producer–

(a) if in any calendar year the total number of animals and carcases in respect of which he has applied for a premium payment (other than applications which have been refused) in that year is equal to or exceeds ninety; or

(b) if pursuant to Article 9(6) of the Commission Regulation he is excluded from the premium scheme.

(a) 1967 c.22.

(b) OJ No L 148, 28.6.68, p.24 (OJ/SE 1968 (I) p.187); Article 4a was inserted by Council Regulation 467/87 (OJ No L 48, 17.2.87, p.1) and amended by Council Regulation 571/89 (OJ No L 61, 4.3.89, p.43).

(c) OJ No L 48, 17.2.87, p.4; amended by Council Regulation 572/89 (OJ No L 63, 7.3.89, p.1).

Records of transactions

4.—(1) A producer who sells an animal in respect of which he has applied for a premium payment, and any person who buys that animal, shall keep a record showing, in respect of that sale or purchase respectively, the particulars specified in the Schedule to this Order and shall retain that record for three years from the end of the calendar year to which it relates.

(2) An invoice or similar account containing the said particulars or some of them, or a copy of such invoice or account, shall with respect to such of the said particulars as are contained therein be a sufficient record for the purposes of this article.

(3) A producer who sells an animal in respect of which he has applied for a premium payment shall retain, in respect of that animal, any account, record, voucher or other document which is relevant to establishing the matters referred to in Article 8(3) of the Commission Regulation for three years from the end of the calendar year to which it relates.

(4) A person who is required by this article to retain an account, record, voucher or other document shall produce it for inspection if so required by an authorised officer.

Production of movement records

5. A person who buys, sells or transports animals and who is required by law to keep or retain a record of their movement shall produce that record for inspection if so required by an authorised officer.

Slaughter requirements

6.—(1) Where an animal is marked at an approved liveweight centre, and the Board have by means of notices prominently displayed at the centre required that animals of a description which includes that animal be slaughtered by a date specified in the notices, or before the end of a period of days so specified beginning with the date on which it was so marked with or without a further requirement that the slaughter shall be at a place or within an area so specified, then–

(a) the owners of the animal at the time of its removal from that centre shall be deemed to have notice of those requirements (which are hereinafter called the slaughter requirements), and

(b) the animal shall be slaughtered in accordance with the slaughter requirements.

(2) Accordingly, references in the following provisions of this article to the date by which an animal must be or should have been slaughtered are references to the date specified under paragraph (1) above or to the last day of the period so specified as the case may require.

(3) No person having notice of the slaughter requirements with respect to an animal shall–

(a) sell the animal on or before the date by which it must be slaughtered without informing the buyer, in writing, of those requirements;

(b) sell the animal after the date by which it should have been slaughtered; or

(c) have the animal in his possession or under his control after the date by which it should have been slaughtered.

(4) Where the slaughter requirements with respect to an animal include a requirement that the animal shall be slaughtered in the United Kingdom, no person having notice of that requirement shall consign that animal to another Member State or export it to a third country.

Removal of ears of carcases

7. An authorised officer at an approved deadweight centre may–

(a) remove or cause to be removed the ears of any carcase marked by him or under his supervision; or

(b) take possession of the ears of any carcase in respect of which or of the animal from which it was derived he reasonably suspects there to have been an offence under section 7 of the Agriculture Act 1957.

Restrictions with respect to marked animals

8. No person shall apply for premium in respect of an animal, or of the carcase derived from an animal, which has been marked in the prescribed manner or permit such an animal to be used for breeding or allow it to have access to any animal with which it may mate.

Powers of entry

9.—(1) For the purposes mentioned in Article 8(1) and (3) of the Commission Regulation an officer of the Board or of one of the Ministers authorised for the purposes of this paragraph may, during a period of three years from the end of the calendar year in which an application for a premium payment was made,–

(a) enter at any reasonable time upon any agricultural land which was, or is alleged by a producer to have been, used for the production of an animal to which that application related;

(b) enter at any reasonable time upon any land which was used for the sale or slaughter of an animal to which that application related;

(c) examine that land and any buildings erected upon it; and

(d) search for, examine, take possession of or copy any account, record, voucher or other document relating to that application.

(2) An officer acting in exercise of the powers conferred by paragraph (1) above shall carry a warrant of his authority so to act, and shall produce it on demand.

Revocation

10. The Beef Premiums (Protection of Payments) Order 1978 **(a)** is hereby revoked.

In witness whereof the Official Seal of the Minister of Agriculture, Fisheries and Food is hereunto affixed on 23rd March 1989.

John MacGregor
Minister of Agriculture, Fisheries and Food

Sanderson of Bowden
23rd March 1989 Minister of State, Scottish Office

Wyn Roberts
23rd March 1989 Minister of State, Welsh Office

(a) S.I. 1978/17.

SCHEDULE

Article 4(1)

PARTICULARS TO BE RECORDED OF PURCHASES AND SALES OF MARKED ANIMALS

1. The date of the transaction.

2. Numbers and descriptions of animals, and the weight of each animal.

3. In the case of a purchase or sale by auction at an auction market, the name and address of the auctioneer, and in any other case the name and address of the other party to the transaction.

4. Where applicable, the dates by which any animals bought or sold are to be slaughtered.

5. Where applicable, the dates of slaughter of unsold animals.

EXPLANATORY NOTE

(This note is not part of the Order)

This Order, which applies in Great Britain, replaces the Beef Premiums (Protection of Payments) Order 1978 which imposed requirements in connection with the payment of beef variable premium which scheme ceased to have effect on 2nd April 1989.

This Order relates to the administration of the beef special premium instituted by Article 4a of Council Regulation 805/68 on the common organisation of the market in beef and veal (inserted by Regulation 467/87 (OJ No L 48, 17.2.87, p.1) and amended by Regulation 571/89 (OJ No L 61, 4.3.89, p.43)) for the application of which general rules are laid down by Council Regulation 468/87 (OJ No L 48, 17.2.87, p.4) as amended by Council Regulation 572/89 (OJ No. L 63, 7.3.89, p.1) and detailed rules by Commission Regulation 714/89 (OJ No L 78, 21.3.89, p.1). The Community scheme governed by these Regulations provides for the payment to a beef producer of a premium in respect of each male beef animal which he has fattened up to a headage limit of 90 animals per producer in any calendar year. In Great Britain the premium will be payable in respect of male animals weighing at least 370 kilograms placed on the market with a view to slaughter at approved livestock markets, male animals at least nine months old intended to be exported from Great Britain and carcases derived from male animals weighing at least 200 kilograms presented at approved abattoirs.

For the purpose of securing that payments are made in proper cases, the Order makes provision–

(a) that applicants who have not yet reached their headage limit and have not been excluded from the scheme may apply for premium–

(i) in the case of animals (other than animals to be exported), at an approved liveweight centre;

(ii) in the case of animals to be exported, at an approved export centre; and

(iii) in the case of carcases, at an approved deadweight centre; and

(b) for the marking of animals or carcases at the appropriate centre by an authorised person if he is satisfied, on examination, that the animals or carcases conform to the scheme's criteria (article 3).

The Order makes further provision for the keeping of records relating to transactions in animals in respect of which premium applications are made and to the establishing of the means of production of applicants and for production of movements records. The Order provides for the imposition by the Intervention Board for Agricultural Produce ("the Board") by means of public notices of a requirement to slaughter animals marked under the scheme within 21 days of the date on which they were marked (articles 4, 5 and 6).

Authorised officers at deadweight centres are authorised to remove ears of carcases when they are marked and to take possession of such ears when an offence under section 7 of the Agriculture Act 1957 is reasonably suspected. There is conferred on authorised officers of the Board a power of entry onto land used for the production, sale or slaughter of animals in respect of which premium has been claimed for the purpose in particular of ascertaining that the headage limit has been respected and that an applicant had sufficient means of production to fatten the animals in respect of which he claimed premium (articles 7 and 9).

Section 7 of the Agriculture Act 1957 creates criminal offences in respect of a contravention of or failure to comply with the Order, wilful obstruction of an authorised officer exercising the powers conferred on him by the Order and the making knowingly or recklessly of a false statement for the purpose of obtaining premium and prescribes maximum penalties for those offences.

STATUTORY INSTRUMENTS

1989 No. 575

AGRICULTURE

The Beef Special Premium (Recovery Powers) Regulations 1989

Made - - - -	*30th March 1989*
Laid before Parliament	*31st March 1989*
Coming into force	*3rd April 1989*

The Minister of Agriculture, Fisheries and Food and the Secretary of State, being Ministers designated(**a**) for the purposes of section 2(2) of the European Communities Act 1972(**b**) in relation to the common agricultural policy of the European Economic Community, acting jointly in exercise of the powers conferred upon them by the said section 2(2) and of all other powers enabling them in that behalf, hereby make the following Regulations:

Title, extent, commencement and interpretation

1.—(1) These Regulations, which may be cited as the Beef Special Premium (Recovery Powers) Regulations 1989, shall apply in Great Britain and shall come into force on 3rd April 1989.

(2) In these Regulations, "The Protection Order" means the Beef Special Premium (Protection of Payments) Order 1989(**c**) and other expressions have, in so far as the context admits, the same meaning as in that Order.

Recovery of premium payments

2. If any person to whom a premium payment has been made–

(a) has made a false statement in connection with that payment; or

(b) has contravened, or failed to comply with, any requirement imposed by or under Council Regulation (EEC) No. 468/87(**d**) laying down general rules applying to the special premium for beef producers or Commission Regulation (EEC) No. 714/89(**e**) laying down detailed rules applying to the special premium for beef producers

the Board may recover from him as a civil debt such of the amount of premium paid to him in the calendar year in which the false statement was made or the contravention or failure to comply occurred as is, in accordance with Article 9 of the Commission Regulation, repayable to the Board together with interest in respect of the period between the date on which any premium was paid and the date on which it was recovered calculated at a rate to be determined by the Minister of Agriculture, Fisheries and Food.

3. If any person has, in contravention of any provision of the Protection Order, in his possession an animal in respect of which a premium payment has been made the Board may recover from him as a civil debt such amount (not exceeding the premium paid in

(**a**) S.I. 1972/1811. (**b**) 1972 c.68. (**c**) S.I. 1989/574.
(**d**) OJ No. L48, 17.2.87, p.4; amended by Council Regulation 572/89 (OJ No. L63, 7.3.89, p.1).
(**e**) OJ No. L78, 21.3.89, p.38.

respect of that animal), together with interest in respect of the period between the date on which that premium was paid and the date on which it was recovered calculated at the rate determined for the purposes of regulation 2 above, as is in accordance with Article 9 of the Commission Regulation due to the Board.

Evidence

4. For the purpose of any proceedings under these Regulations, an animal which is proved to have been marked in the prescribed manner shall be deemed to be an animal in respect of which a premium payment has been made unless the contrary is proved.

Revocation

5. The Beef Premiums (Recovery Powers) Regulations 1978(**a**) are hereby revoked.

In witness whereof the Official Seal of the Minister of Agriculture, Fisheries and Food was hereunto affixed on 23rd March 1989.

John MacGregor
Minister of Agriculture, Fisheries and Food

Sanderson of Bowden
30th March 1989 Minister of State, Scottish Office

EXPLANATORY NOTE

(This note is not part of the Regulations)

These Regulations, which apply in Great Britain, replace the Beef Premiums (Recovery Powers) Regulations 1978 which enabled the Intervention Board for Agricultural Produce ("the Board") to recover a payment of beef variable premium in certain circumstances.

These Regulations, which implement the obligation contained in Article 9(5) of Commission Regulation (EEC) No. 714/89 (OJ No. L78, 21.3.89, p.38) to recover premiums improperly paid together with interest to be fixed by the Member State concerned, enable the Board to recover–

(a) such amount of premium paid to an applicant in a calendar year as is repayable pursuant to that Article together with interest in circumstances where–

(i) he has made a false statement in connection with that payment; or

(ii) he has contravened or failed to comply with any requirement of the Council and Commission Regulations laying down general and detailed rules respectively applying to the special premium for beef producers; and

(b) from a person who, in contravention of that Order, has in his possession an animal in respect of which a premium payment has been made such amount (not exceeding that premium) together with interest as is due to the Board pursuant to that Article.

(**a**) S.I. 1978/18.

STATUTORY INSTRUMENTS

1989 No. 576

AGRICULTURE

The Cereals Co-responsibility Levy (Amendment) Regulations 1989

Made - - - -	*23rd March 1989*
Laid before Parliament	*7th April 1989*
Coming into force	*28th April 1989*

The Minister of Agriculture, Fisheries and Food and the Secretary of State, being Ministers designated(**a**) for the purposes of section 2(2) of the European Communities Act 1972(**b**) in relation to the common agricultural policy of the European Economic Community, acting jointly in exercise of the powers conferred on them by the said section 2(2) and of all other powers enabling them in that behalf, hereby make the following Regulations:–

Title and commencement

1. These Regulations may be cited as the Cereals Co-responsibility Levy (Amendment) Regulations 1989 and shall come into force on 28th April 1989.

Amendment of the Cereals Co-responsibility Levy Regulations 1988

2. The Cereals Co-responsibility Levy Regulations 1988(**c**) are hereby amended in accordance with the following provisions of these Regulations.

3. In regulation 2(1) (interpretation)–

(a) for the definition of "the Commission Regulation" there shall be substituted the following definition–

'"the Commission Regulation" means Commission Regulation (EEC) No. 1432/88 laying down detailed rules for applying the co-responsibility levy in the cereals sector(**d**), as amended by Commission Regulation (EEC) No. 2324/88(**e**) and Commission Regulation (EEC) No. 3858/88(**f**) ;';

(b) for the definition of "trader" there shall be substituted the following definition–

'"trader" means–

(a) any person who purchases from their producer cereals other than cereals placed on the market in the framework of a forward transaction; or

(b) any person who places on the market cereals produced by him–

(i) by way of direct export from the United Kingdom;

(ii) in the form of cereal products; or

(iii) in the framework of a forward transaction.'.

(**a**) S.I. 1972/1811.
(**b**) 1972 c.68.
(**c**) S.I. 1988/1001.
(**d**) OJ No. L131, 27.5.88, p.37.
(**e**) OJ No. L202, 27.7.88, p.39.
(**f**) OJ No. L343, 13.12.88, p.21.

4. In regulation 5(3) (registration of traders) for the words "incapacitated or" there shall be substituted the words "incapacitated by reason of physical or mental illness or becomes".

In witness whereof the Official Seal of the Minister of Agriculture, Fisheries and Food is hereunto affixed on 23rd March 1989.

John MacGregor
Minister of Agriculture, Fisheries and Food

23rd March 1989

Sanderson of Bowden
Minister of State, Scottish Office

EXPLANATORY NOTE

(This note is not part of the Regulations)

These Regulations amend the Cereals Co-responsibility Levy Regulations 1988 ("the principal Regulations") which provide for the administration, collection and enforcement of co-responsibility levy imposed in respect of specified cereals by Article 4 of Council Regulation (EEC) 2727/75 (OJ No. L281, 1.11.1975, p.1), as amended in particular by Council Regulation (EEC) 1097/88 (OJ No. L110, 29.4.88, p.7). These Regulations amend the principal Regulations in consequence of amendments to the detailed rules for the application of the levy laid down by Commission Regulation (EEC) 1432/88 (OJ No. L131, 27.5.88, p.37) set out in Commission Regulation (EEC) 2324/88 (OJ No. L202, 27.7.88, p.39).

Commission Regulation 2324/88 which, inter alia, gives effect to the judgment of the Court of Justice in Case 300/86 handed down on 29th June 1988 provides that–

(a) cereals placed on the market by their producer in the form of processed products are subject to co-responsibility levy; but

(b) cereals delivered but not sold by their producer to a processor with a view to the production of animal feedingstuffs to be used on that producer's farm are not subject to co-responsibility levy.

In implementation of those provisions these Regulations–

(a) amend the definition of "the Commission Regulation" so as to refer to its amendment by Commission Regulations 2324/88 and 3858/88; and

(b) amend the definition of "trader" so as to exclude from its scope persons who process cereals on behalf of their producer and to include therein persons who place on the market cereals produced by them in the form of cereal products (regulation 3).

In addition these Regulations amend regulation 5 of the principal Regulations so as to make clear that the reference therein to persons becoming incapacitated is a reference to persons becoming incapacitated by reason of physical or mental illness (regulation 4).

STATUTORY INSTRUMENTS

1989 No. 577 (S.64)

TOWN AND COUNTRY PLANNING, SCOTLAND

The Town and Country Planning (Determination of Appeals by Appointed Persons) (Prescribed Classes) (Scotland) Amendment Regulations 1989

Made - - - -	*22nd March 1989*
Laid before Parliament	*10th April 1989*
Coming into force	*1st May 1989*

The Secretary of State, in exercise of the powers conferred on him by sections 273 and 275(1) of, and paragraph 1 of Schedule 7 to, the Town and Country Planning (Scotland) Act 1972(**a**) and of all other powers enabling him in that behalf, hereby makes the following Regulations:

Citation and commencement

1. These Regulations may be cited as the Town and Country Planning (Determination of Appeals by Appointed Persons) (Prescribed Classes) (Scotland) Amendment Regulations 1989 and shall come into force on 1st May 1989.

Amendment

2. Schedule 1 to the Town and Country Planning (Determination of Appeals by Appointed Persons) (Prescribed Classes) (Scotland) Regulations 1987(**b**) shall be amended as follows:–

(a) for paragraph (1) there shall be substituted the following paragraph:–

"(1)(a) section 33 of the Act (appeals against planning decisions);

(b) section 33 as applied by section 34 of the Act (appeals in default of planning decisions);

(c) section 33 of the Act (including that section as applied by section 34 of the Act) as applied by section 51 of the Act (appeals against determinations as to whether a use or operation constitutes or involves development);

(d) any of the provisions of the Act referred to in sub-paragraphs (a) to (c) above as applied by–

(i) an order made under section 58 of the Act or under section 58 of the Act and section 2 of the 1984 Act (appeals in relation to consent to felling etc of trees subject to a tree preservation order);

(ii) regulations made under section 61 of the Act (appeals in relation to consent to display of advertisements);

(iii) section 179 of the Local Government (Scotland) Act 1973(**c**) (appeals against decisions by regional planning authorities);

(**a**) 1972 c.52; section 275(1) contains a definition of "prescribed" relevant to the exercise of the statutory powers under which these Regulations are made.
(**b**) S.I. 1987/1531.
(**c**) 1973 c.65; section 179 was substituted by the Local Government and Planning (Scotland) Act 1982 (c.43), section 69(2), Schedule 3, paragraph 24.

(iv) section 1 of the 1984 Act (appeals against planning decisions etc in relation to disposal of Crown land).

(b) for paragraph (3) there shall be substituted the following paragraph:–

"(3)(a) section 85 of the Act (appeals against enforcement notices);

(b) section 85 as applied by–

(i) regulations made under sections 61 and 101 of the Act (appeals in relation to enforcement of advertisement controls);

(ii) section 3 of the 1984 Act (appeals against special enforcement notices relating to development on Crown land);".

James Douglas-Hamilton
Parliamentary Under Secretary of State,
Scottish Office

St. Andrew's House, Edinburgh
22nd March 1989

EXPLANATORY NOTE

(This note is not part of the Regulations)

These Regulations add to the classes of appeal under the Town and Country Planning (Scotland) Act 1972 which are to be determined by a person appointed for the purpose by the Secretary of State instead of being determined by the Secretary of State. They do so by amending the Town and Country Planning (Determination of Appeals by Appointed Persons) (Prescribed Classes) (Scotland) Regulations 1987.

Regulation 2(a) of the amending Regulations re-states those classes of appeal falling under section 33 of the 1972 Act (appeals against planning decisions), including that section as applied by other statutory provisions, which are to be determined by a person appointed by the Secretary of State. The re-statement includes for the first time appeals relating to the control of the display of advertisements. The relevant provision is at sub-paragraph (d)(ii) of the new paragraph (1) of Schedule 1 to the 1987 Regulations as substituted by Regulation 2(a).

Regulation 2(b) of the amending Regulations re-states those classes of appeal falling under section 85 of the Act (appeals against enforcement notices), including that section as applied by other statutory provisions, which are to be determined by a person appointed by the Secretary of State. This re-statement involves a new reference to appeals in relation to enforcement of advertisement controls.

STATUTORY INSTRUMENTS

1989 No. 578 (S.65)

HOUSING, SCOTLAND

The Rent Officers (Additional Functions) (Scotland) Order 1989

Made - - - - 23rd March 1989

Coming into force 1st April 1989

The Secretary of State, in exercise of the powers conferred on him by section 70 of the Housing (Scotland) Act 1988(**a**), and of all other powers enabling him in that behalf, hereby makes the following Order, a draft of which has been laid before and approved by a resolution of each House of Parliament:

Citation and commencement

1. This Order may be cited as the Rent Officers (Additional Functions) (Scotland) Order 1989 and shall come into force on 1st April 1989.

Interpretation

2.—(1) In this Order, unless the context otherwise requires–

"determination" means a determination (including an interim and a further determination) in accordance with Schedule 1 to this Order;

"dwelling" has the same meaning as in the Social Security Act 1986(**b**);

"excluded tenancy" means a tenancy of a category listed in Schedule 2 to this Order;

"local authority" has the same meaning as it has in the Social Security Act 1986 in relation to Scotland;

"occupier" means a person (whether or not identified by name) who is stated, in the application for a determination, to occupy the dwelling;

"rent" has the same meaning as in section 25 of the Housing (Scotland) Act 1988, except that the reference to the house in subsection (3) shall be construed as a reference to the dwelling;

"size criteria" means the standards relating to bedrooms and rooms suitable for living in specified in Schedule 3 to this Order;

"tenancy" includes any other right of occupancy and references to a tenant, a landlord or any other expression appropriate to a tenancy shall be construed accordingly.

(2) In this Order any reference to a notice or application is to a notice or application in writing, and any notice by a rent officer may be sent by post.

Additional Functions

3.—(1) Where, in connection with housing benefit and rent allowance subsidy, a local authority applies to a rent officer for determinations relating to a tenancy of a dwelling, the rent officer shall (subject to article 5) make the determinations and give notice in accordance with Schedule 1 to this Order.

(**a**) 1988 c.43.
(**b**) 1986 c.50.

(2) If a rent officer needs further information in order to make a determination, he shall serve notice on the local authority requesting that information and until he receives it paragraph (1) shall not apply to the making of that determination.

4. If, within the period of 10 weeks beginning with the date on which the local authority was given notice of a determination, the local authority applies (in connection with housing benefit and rent allowance subsidy) to a rent officer for a re-determination, a rent officer (subject to article 5) shall make the re-determination and give notice in accordance with Schedule 4 to this Order and a rent officer whose advice is sought as provided for in that Schedule shall give that advice.

5.—(1) No determination or re-determination shall be made if the application for it is withdrawn or relates to an excluded tenancy.

(2) No determination or re-determination shall be made under paragraph 1 of Schedule 1 (or that paragraph as applied by Schedule 4) if the tenancy is an assured tenancy and–

(a) the rent payable under the tenancy on the date the application for the determination (or, as the case may be, re-determination) was received was an amount determined under section 34 of the Housing (Scotland) Act 1988 or,

(b) the rent so payable on that date was an amount determined under section 25 of that Act and that rent took effect within the period of 12 months ending with the date the application was received.

James Douglas-Hamilton
Parliamentary Under Secretary of State,
Scottish Office

St. Andrew's House, Edinburgh
23rd March 1989

Articles 2(1) and 3(1)

SCHEDULE 1

DETERMINATIONS

Rent Determinations

1.—(1) The rent officer shall determine whether, in his opinion, the rent payable under the tenancy of the dwelling at the time the application for the determination is made is significantly higher than the rent which the landlord might reasonably be expected to obtain under the tenancy at that time, having regard to the level of rent under similar tenancies of similar dwellings in the locality (or as similar as regards tenancy, dwelling and locality as is reasonably practicable), but on the assumption that no person who would have been entitled to housing benefit had sought or is seeking the tenancy.

(2) If the rent officer determines under sub-paragraph (1) that the rent is significantly higher, the rent officer shall also determine the rent which the landlord might reasonably be expected to obtain under the tenancy at the time the application for a determination is made, having regard to the same matter and on the same assumption as in sub-paragraph (1).

Size and Rent Determinations

2.—(1) The rent officer shall determine whether the dwelling exceeds the size criteria for its occupiers.

(2) If the rent officer determines that the dwelling exceeds the size criteria, the rent officer shall also determine the rent which a landlord might reasonably be expected to obtain, at the time the application for the determination is made, for a tenancy which is similar to the tenancy of the dwelling, on the same terms (other than the term relating to the amount of rent), and of a dwelling which is in the same locality as the dwelling, but which–

(a) accords with the size criteria for the occupiers;

(b) is in a reasonable state of repair; and

(c) corresponds in other respects, in the rent officer's opinion, as closely as is reasonably practicable to the dwelling.

(3) When making a determination under paragraph 2(2), the rent officer shall have regard to the same matter and make the same assumption as in paragraph 1(1), except that in judging the similarity of other tenancies and dwellings the comparison shall be with the tenancy of the second dwelling referred to in paragraph 2(2) and the assumption shall be made in relation to that tenancy.

Services Determinations

3.—(1) Where the rent officer makes a determination under paragraph 1(2) or 2(2), he shall also determine whether, in his opinion, any of the rent is fairly attributable to the provision of services which are ineligible to be met by housing benefit and, if so, the amount which in his opinion is so attributable (except where he considers the amount is negligible).

(2) In sub-paragraph (1) "rent" means the rent determined under paragraph 1(2) or 2(2); and "services" means services performed or facilities (including the use of furniture) provided for, or rights made available to, the tenant.

Interim and Further Determinations

4. If notice of a determination under paragraph 1 or 3 is not given to the local authority within the 5 day period mentioned in paragraph 5(a) solely because the rent officer intends to arrange an inspection of the dwelling before making such a determination, the rent officer shall make an interim determination and a further determination.

Notifications

5. The rent officer shall give notice to the local authority of a determination–

(a) except in the case of a further determination, within the period of 5 working days beginning with the date on which the rent officer received the application or, where the rent officer requests further information under article 3(2), with the date on which he received the information, or as soon as practicable after that period.

(b) in the case of a further determination within the period of 20 working days beginning with the date on which notice of the interim determination was given to the local authority, or as soon as practicable after that period.

6.—(1) If the rent officer becomes aware that the tenancy is an excluded tenancy, the rent officer shall give the local authority notice that it is such a tenancy.

(2) If the rent officer is precluded by article 5(2) from making a determination or a re-determination under paragraph 1 (or that paragraph as applied by Schedule 4), the rent officer shall give the local authority notice of the rent determined by the rent assessment committee.

SCHEDULE 2

Article 2(1)

EXCLUDED TENANCIES

1. A tenancy for which a rent officer has made a determination (other than an interim determination) within the 12 months ending on the date the rent officer received the application for a new determination (or a tenancy of the same dwelling on terms which are substantially the same, other than the term relating to the amount of rent, as the terms of that tenancy were at the time of the determination) unless since the earlier application for a determination was made –

(a) the number of occupiers of the dwelling has changed;

(b) there has been a substantial change in the condition of the dwelling (including the making of improvements) or the terms of the tenancy (other than a term relating to rent); or

(c) there has been a rent increase under a term of the tenancy which was in effect when the earlier application for the determination was made (and that determination was not made under paragraph 1(2) or 2(2) of Schedule 1 and any re-determination of that determination under Schedule 4 was not made under either of those sub-paragraphs as applied by Schedule 4), or under a term substantially the same as such a term.

2. An assured tenancy where the landlord is a registered housing association within the meaning of the Housing Associations Act 1985(**a**), unless the local authority states in the application for determinations that the circumstances in regulation 11(2)(a) or (c) of the Housing Benefit (General) Regulations 1987(**b**) exist.

(**a**) 1985 c.69.
(**b**) S.I. 1987/1971; relevant amending instrument is S.I. 1989/416.

3. A tenancy entered into before the relevant date where there is, current on that date, a benefit period (within the meaning of regulation 66 of the Housing Benefit (General) Regulations 1987) relating to a claim for housing benefit in relation to the tenancy–

(a) unless and until a change of circumstances takes effect (within the meaning of regulation 68 of those Regulations) provided it takes effect after 16th April 1989, or

(b) until the benefit period ends (or if it ends before 17th April 1989, the next benefit period ends).

4. A tenancy entered into before 2nd January 1989.

5. A regulated tenancy within the meaning of the Rent (Scotland) Act 1984(**a**).

6. A tenancy to which Part VI of that Act applies.

7. In paragraph 3 "relevant date" means

(a) except where (b) applies 1st April 1989;

(b) in the case of a tenancy where one of the occupiers of the dwelling immediately before 10th April 1989 is in receipt of income support under the Social Security Act 1986 and whose applicable amount immediately before that date is calculated in accordance with regulation 20 or 71(1)(b) of, or paragraph 17 of Schedule 7 to the Income Support (General) Regulations 1987(**b**), 10th April 1989.

Article 2(1)

SCHEDULE 3

SIZE CRITERIA

1. One bedroom shall be allowed for each of the following categories of occupiers (and each occupier shall come within only the first category for which he is eligible)–

(a) a married couple or an unmarried couple (within the meaning of Part II of the Social Security Act 1986),

(b) an adult,

(c) two children of the same sex,

(d) two children who are less than ten years old,

(e) a child.

2. The number of rooms (excluding any allowed as a bedroom under paragraph 1) suitable for living in allowed are–

(a) if there are fewer than four occupiers, one,

(b) if there are more than three and fewer than seven occupiers, two,

(c) in any other case, three.

Article 4

SCHEDULE 4

RE-DETERMINATIONS

1. Schedules 1 to 3 (except paragraph 4 of Schedule 1) shall apply in relation to a re-determination as they apply to a determination, subject to the following:

(a) references in Schedule 1 to the time of an application for a determination shall be references to the time of the application for the original determination; and

(b) for sub-paragraphs (a) and (b) of paragraph 5 of Schedule 1 there shall be substituted "within the period of 20 working days beginning with the date of receipt of the application for a re-determination, or as soon as is reasonably practicable after that period.".

2. The rent officer making the re-determination shall seek and have regard to the advice of one or two other rent officers in relation to the re-determination.

(**a**) 1984 c.58.
(**b**) S.I. 1987/1967; relevant amending instruments are S.I. 1988/663 and 1445.

EXPLANATORY NOTE

(This note is not part of the Order)

This Order confers functions on rent officers in connection with housing benefit and rent allowance subsidy. Article 3 provides that where a local authority applies to a rent officer for determinations relating to a tenancy or other right of occupancy of a dwelling, the rent officer must make the determinations (and give notice to the local authority) in accordance with Schedule 1 to the Order. The determinations relate to the level of rent, the size of the dwelling and rent attributable to the provision of services. Article 4 provides for a rent officer, with the advice of one or two other rent officers, to make a re-determination if a local authority applies for one.

Article 5 prevents determinations and re-determinations being made if the tenancy is one of those described in Schedule 2 to the Order or if the application is withdrawn and certain determinations and re-determinations cannot be made if the tenancy is an assured tenancy and the circumstances are those described in article 5(2).

1989 No. 581 (S.66)

FOOD

COMPOSITION AND LABELLING

The Preservatives in Food (Scotland) Regulations 1989

Made - - - -	*23rd March 1989*
Laid before Parliament	*12th April 1989*
Coming into force	*3rd May 1989*

The Secretary of State, in exercise of the powers conferred on him by sections 4, 7, 26(3), 56 and 56A of the Food and Drugs (Scotland) Act 1956(**a**) and of all other powers enabling him in that behalf, and after consultation in accordance with section 56(6) of the said Act with such organisations as appear to him to be representative of interests substantially affected by these Regulations, hereby makes the following Regulations:

Title and commencement

1. These Regulations may be cited as the Preservatives in Food (Scotland) Regulations 1989, and shall come into force on 3rd May 1989.

Interpretation

2.—(1) In these Regulations, unless the context otherwise requires–

"the Act" means the Food and Drugs (Scotland) Act 1956;

"appropriate designation" means, as respects any permitted preservative or any food, a name or description or a name and description sufficiently specific, in each case, to indicate to an intending purchaser the true nature of the permitted preservative or of the food, as the case may be, to which it is applied;

"biscuits" includes wafers, rusks, crispbreads, oatcakes, matzos and chocolate-coated, chocolate-filled or chocolate-flavoured biscuits;

"bread" has the meaning assigned to it by the Bread and Flour (Scotland) Regulations 1984(**b**);

"canned food" means any food which–

(a) is in a hermetically sealed container, and

(b) (i) has been sufficiently heat processed to destroy any *Clostridium botulinum* in the food or its container, or

(ii) has a pH of less than 4.5,

and "canned", in relation to any food, shall be construed accordingly;

(**a**) 1956 c.30; section 4(1) was amended by the European Communities Act 1972 (c.68), Schedule 4, paragraph 3(1); section 26(3) was amended by the Local Government (Scotland) Act 1973 (c.65), Schedule 27, Part II, paragraph 123(a) and by the Local Government and Planning (Scotland) Act 1982 (c.43), Schedule 4, Part I; section 7 and section 56 were amended by the Weights and Measures Act 1963 (c.31), Schedule 9, Parts I and II; section 56 was also amended by the Criminal Justice Act 1982 (c.48), Schedule 15, paragraph 8 and by the Law Reform (Miscellaneous Provisions) (Scotland) Act 1985 (c.73), section 41 and is to be read with section 289GA(2) of the Criminal Procedure (Scotland) Act 1975 (c.21) (inserted by section 66 of the Criminal Justice (Scotland) Act 1987 (c.41); section 56A was added by the European Communities Act 1972, Schedule 4, paragraph 3(2).

(**b**) S.I. 1984/1518, to which there is an amendment not relevant to these Regulations.

"carbohydrate" means any substance containing carbon, hydrogen and oxygen only in which the hydrogen and oxygen occur in the same proportion as in water;

"cheese" and "soft cheese" have the meanings respectively assigned to them by the Cheese (Scotland) Regulations 1970(**a**);

"Community" means the European Economic Community;

"Community controlled wine" means wine, grape must, sparkling wine, aerated sparkling wine, liqueur wine, semi-sparkling wine and aerated semi-sparkling wine as respectively defined in Annex 1 to Council Regulation (EEC) No. 822/87(**b**) on the common organisation of the market in wine;

"compounded food" means food containing two or more ingredients;

"concentrated fruit juice" has the meaning assigned to it by the Fruit Juices and Fruit Nectars (Scotland) Regulations 1977(**c**);

"container" includes any form of packaging of food for sale as a single item, whether by way of wholly or partly enclosing the food or by way of attaching the food to some other article, and in particular includes a wrapper or confining band;

"dock" includes any harbour, moorings, wharf, pier, jetty or other works in or at which food can be shipped or unshipped and any warehouse, transit shed or other premises used in connection therewith for the temporary storage or loading for despatch of food which is unshipped or to be shipped;

"flavouring" includes flavouring essence and flavouring extract and means any product consisting of a flavouring agent and such other substances, if any, the use of which in food is not forbidden and which are reasonably necessary to produce a solid, a solution or an emulsion, but no other ingredient or ingredients;

"flavouring agent" means any sapid or odorous substance capable of imparting and primarily intended to impart a specific and distinctive taste or odour to food, but does not include herbs, spices, onions, garlic, salt, fruit juices, soft drinks, fruit acids, acetic acid, any carbohydrate material, any purine derivative, any preparation of yeast, coffee or chicory or any substances prepared by the hydrolysis of protein-containing materials;

"flavouring syrup" means a solution of carbohydrate sweetening matter containing sufficient flavouring to provide, after dilution with milk or water, a drink with that flavour;

"flour confectionery" means any solid or semi-solid product complete in itself and suitable for consumption without further preparation or processing other than heating, of which the characteristic ingredient, apart from any filling, is ground cereal, whether or not flavoured, coated with or containing any carbohydrate sweetening matter, chocolate or cocoa; and includes shortbread, sponges, pastry, pastry cases, crumpets, muffins, macaroons, ratafias, meringues and petits fours, but does not include pharmaceutical products, bread, biscuits, canned puddings, Christmas puddings or any product containing a filling which has as an ingredient any meat or fish or any animal, vegetable or microbial material processed before or during the preparation of the product to resemble the texture of meat or fish;

"food" means food intended for sale for human consumption and includes drink, chewing gum and other products of a like nature and use, and articles and substances used as ingredients in the preparation of food or drink or of such products, but does not include–

(a) water, live animals or birds,

(b) fodder or feeding stuffs for animals, birds or fish, or

(c) articles or substances used only as drugs;

"freeze drink" means any pre-packed liquid which complies with the requirements in the Soft Drinks (Scotland) Regulations 1964(**d**) as to the composition of any soft drink for consumption without dilution and which is clearly and legibly labelled as intended for freezing before consumption;

"fruit juice" has the meaning assigned to it by the Fruit Juices and Fruit Nectars (Scotland) Regulations 1977;

"fruit spread" means the product obtained by processing fruit, fruit pulp or purée and carbohydrate sweetening matter, with or without the addition of other substances, to

---

(**a**) S.I. 1970/108; relevant amending instruments are S.I. 1974/1337 and 1984/847.
(**b**) O.J. No. L84, 27.3.1987, p.1.
(**c**) S.I. 1977/1026; relevant amending instruments are S.I. 1977/1883 and 1982/1619.
(**d**) S.I. 1964/767; relevant amending instruments are S.I. 1969/1847, 1970/1619, 1976/442 and 1977/1026.

a suitable consistency by the application of heat and which is not a product as described in column 2 of Schedule 1 to the Jam and Similar Products (Scotland) Regulations 1981(**a**);

"hermetically sealed container" means a sealed container which is airtight and impermeable to gases;

"human consumption" includes use in the preparation of food for human consumption;

"ice cream" has the meaning assigned to it by the Ice-Cream (Scotland) Regulations 1970(**b**);

"permitted antioxidant" means any antioxidant in so far as its use is permitted by the Antioxidants in Food (Scotland) Regulations 1978(**c**);

"permitted colouring matter" means any colouring matter in so far as its use is permitted by the Colouring Matter in Food (Scotland) Regulations 1973(**d**);

"permitted emulsifier" means any emulsifier in so far as its use is permitted by the Emulsifiers and Stabilisers in Food (Scotland) Regulations 1980(**e**);

"permitted miscellaneous additive" means any miscellaneous additive in so far as its use is permitted by the Miscellaneous Additives in Food (Scotland) Regulations 1980(**f**);

"permitted preservative" means any preservative specified in columns 1 and 2 of Part I of Schedule 1 or, subject to the provisions of paragraph (2) of this regulation, specified in columns 3 and 4 of that Part of that Schedule which, in either case, satisfies the specific purity criteria in relation to that preservative specified or referred to in Part II of that Schedule, and, so far as is not otherwise provided by any such specific purity criteria, satisfies the general purity criteria specified in Part III of that Schedule, or any mixture of two or more such preservatives;

"permitted solvent" means any solvent in so far as its use is permitted by the Solvents in Food (Scotland) Regulations 1968(**g**);

"permitted stabiliser" means any stabiliser in so far as its use is permitted by the Emulsifiers and Stabilisers in Food (Scotland) Regulations 1980;

"permitted sweetener" means any sweetener in so far as its use is permitted by the Sweeteners in Food (Scotland) Regulations 1983(**h**);

"pre-packed" means made up in advance ready for retail sale in or on a container; and on any premises where food of any description is so made up, or is kept or stored for sale after being so made up, any food of that description found made up in or on a container shall be deemed to be pre-packed unless the contrary is proved;

"preparation", in relation to food, includes manufacture and any form of treatment;

"preservative" means any substance which is capable of inhibiting, retarding or arresting the growth of micro-organisms or any deterioration of food due to micro-organisms or of masking the evidence of any such deterioration but does not include–

(a) any permitted antioxidant,
(b) any permitted colouring matter,
(c) any permitted emulsifier,
(d) any permitted miscellaneous additive,
(e) any permitted solvent,
(f) any permitted stabiliser,
(g) any permitted sweetener,
(h) vinegar,
(i) any soluble carbohydrate sweetening matter,
(j) potable spirits or wines,
(k) herbs, spices, hop extract or flavouring agents when used for flavouring purposes,
(l) common salt (sodium chloride),
(m) any substance added to food by the process of curing known as smoking;

(**a**) S.I. 1981/1320, to which there are amendments not relevant to these Regulations.
(**b**) S.I. 1970/1285, to which there are amendments not relevant to these Regulations.
(**c**) S.I. 1978/492; relevant amending instrument is S.I. 1980/1886.
(**d**) S.I. 1973/1310; relevant amending instruments are S.I. 1975/1595, 1976/2232, 1979/107 and 1987/1985.
(**e**) S.I. 1980/1888; relevant amending instruments are S.I. 1982/514 and 1983/1815.
(**f**) S.I. 1980/1889; relevant amending instrument is S.I. 1982/515.
(**g**) S.I. 1968/263; relevant amending instrument is S.I. 1980/1887.
(**h**) S.I. 1983/1497, to which there is an amendment not relevant to these Regulations.

"processing", in relation to food, includes curing by smoking and any treatment or process resulting in a substantial change in the natural state of the food but does not include boning, paring, grinding, cutting, cleaning or trimming;

"raw peeled potatoes" includes chips, sliced potatoes, diced potatoes and potatoes which have undergone the culinary process known as "blanching";

"reduced sugar jam", "reduced sugar jelly" and "reduced sugar marmalade" have the meanings assigned to them by regulation 2(2) of the Jam and Similar Products (Scotland) Regulations 1981;

"retail sale" means any sale to a person buying otherwise than for the purpose of re-sale, but does not include a sale to a caterer for the purposes of his catering business, or a sale to a manufacturer for the purpose of his manufacturing business;

"sauce" means a liquid, thickened or unthickened, frozen or otherwise, used as a garnish with food and having a colour and flavour derived essentially from ingredients other than meat, but does not include mustard, gravy sauce or any product having characteristics similar to gravy;

"sausage" does not include any cured meat product which has been acidified or fermented;

"sell" includes offer or expose for sale or have in possession for sale, and "sale" and "sold" shall be construed accordingly;

"smoking" means treating food with smoke or smoke solutions derived from wood or ligneous vegetable matter in the natural state, and excludes smoke or smoke solutions derived from wood or ligneous vegetable matter which has been impregnated, coloured, gummed, painted or otherwise treated in a similar manner;

"soft drink" has the meaning assigned to it by the Soft Drinks (Scotland) Regulations 1964;

"specified food" means any food of a description specified in column 1 of Schedule 2;

"specified sugar product" has the meaning assigned to it by the Specified Sugar Products (Scotland) Regulations 1976(**a**);

"sterile pack" means a hermetically sealed container which has been sufficiently heat processed to destroy any *Clostridium botulinum* in the container or in any food which is in the container;

"storage", in relation to food, means storage at, in or upon any farm, dock, vehicle, warehouse, fumigation chamber, cold store, transportable container, whether refrigerated or not, or any barge, ship, aircraft or hover vehicle whilst, in each case, at, in or upon any port, harbour, airport or hover-port in Scotland;

"sweetened" means containing any added soluble carbohydrate sweetening matter or added permitted sweetener and "unsweetened" shall be construed accordingly.

(2) Unless a contrary intention is expressed, any permitted preservative specified in columns 3 and 4 of Part I of Schedule 1 may be used as an alternative to the permitted preservative specified in relation thereto in columns 1 and 2 of that Part of that Schedule, if calculated as that permitted preservative, and any reference in these Regulations to any permitted preservative specified in the said columns 1 and 2 shall be construed accordingly.

(3) Unless a contrary intention is expressed, all proportions mentioned in these Regulations are proportions calculated by weight of the product as sold.

(4) Any reference in these Regulations to a label borne on a container shall be construed as including a reference to any legible marking on the container however effected.

(5) For the purpose of these Regulations, the supply of food, otherwise than by sale, at, in or from any place where food is supplied in the course of a business shall be deemed to be a sale of that food.

(6) Any reference in these Regulations to a numbered regulation or Schedule shall be construed as a reference to the regulation or Schedule bearing that number in these Regulations.

(**a**) S.I. 1976/946; relevant amending instrument is S.I. 1982/410.

Exemptions

3. The provisions of these Regulations shall not apply to food having any preservative in it or on it, or to any preservative which, in each case, is intended at the time of sale or importation, as the case may be, for exportation to any place outside the United Kingdom.

Sale, etc. of food containing preservative

4.—(1) Save as hereinafter provided, no food sold or imported into Scotland shall have in it or on it any added preservative.

(2) Any specified food may have in it or on it permitted preservative of the description and in the proportion specified in relation thereto in columns 2 and 3 respectively of Schedule 2;

(3) Any specified food in relation to which two or more permitted preservatives are specified in Schedule 2 may have in it or on it an admixture of those preservatives as follows:–

(a) in the case of fruit spread, sambal oelek, concentrated snack meals with a moisture content of not less than 15% and not more than 60%, soup concentrates with a moisture content of not less than 25% and not more than 60% or wine (including alcoholic cordials) other than Community controlled wine, to the maximum quantity of each such preservative appropriate thereto in accordance with that Schedule;

(b) in the case of beer, fruits or plants (including flowers and seeds), crystallised, glacé, drained (syruped) or candied peel or cut and drained (syruped) peel, or grape juice products (unfermented, intended for sacramental use), if the permitted preservative sulphur dioxide is present, to the maximum quantity of that preservative appropriate to that food in accordance with that Schedule and as regards any other such permitted preservative present, only if, when the quantity of each such preservative is expressed as a percentage of the maximum quantity appropriate to that food in accordance with that Schedule, the sum of those percentages does not exceed one hundred;

(c) in the case of preparations of saccharin, sodium saccharin, or calcium saccharin and water only, if the permitted preservative benzoic acid is present, to the maximum quantity of that preservative appropriate to that food in accordance with that Schedule and as regards any other such permitted preservative present, only if, when the quantity of each such preservative is expressed as a percentage of the maximum quantity appropriate to that food in accordance with that Schedule, the sum of those percentages does not exceed one hundred;

(d) in the case of marinated herring whose pH exceeds 4.5, or marinated mackerel whose pH exceeds 4.5, if the permitted preservative hexamine is present, to the maximum quantity of that preservative appropriate to that food in accordance with that Schedule and as regards any other such permitted preservative present, only if, when the quantity of each such preservative is expressed as a percentage of the maximum quantity appropriate to that food in accordance with that Schedule, the sum of those percentages does not exceed one hundred;

(e) in the case of cheese (other than Cheddar, Cheshire, Grana-padano or Provolone type cheeses or soft cheese) or cured meat (including cured meat products), in accordance with the appropriate provisions of that Schedule;

(f) in the case of prawn and shrimps in brine,–

(i) if the permitted preservative sulphur dioxide is present, to the maximum quantity of that preservative appropriate to that food in accordance with that Schedule;

(ii) if the permitted preservative sorbic acid or benzoic acid is present, to the maximum quantity of that preservative appropriate to that food in accordance with that Schedule;

(iii) if the permitted preservatives sorbic acid and benzoic acid are present, only if, when the quantity of each such preservative is expressed as a percentage of the maximum quantity appropriate to that food in accordance with that Schedule, the sum of those percentages does not exceed one hundred; and

(iv) as regards any other such permitted preservative present, only if, when the quantity of each such preservative is expressed as a percentage of the maximum quantity appropriate to that food in accordance with that Schedule, the sum of those percentages does not exceed one hundred;

(g) in any other case, only if, when the quantity of each such preservative present in that food is expressed as a percentage of the maximum quantity of that preservative appropriate to that food in accordance with that Schedule, the sum of those percentages does not exceed one hundred.

(4) Any specified food and any food intended for use in the preparation of a specified food (but excluding any pre-packed food, any specified sugar product or any fruit juice or concentrated fruit juice specified at item 1 or 2 in column 1 of Schedule 3 to the Fruit Juices and Fruit Nectars (Scotland) Regulations 1977) may, on importation into Scotland or on a sale other than a retail sale, have in it or on it permitted preservative of a description appropriate to the specified food in accordance with Schedules 1 and 2 in any proportion if, as the case may be, the seller gives to the importer on or before importation or to the buyer on or before sale a document which complies with the requirements of paragraphs 4, 5 and 6 of Schedule 3.

(5) Any food may have in it or on it any proportion not exceeding five milligrams per kilogram, formaldehyde derived from any wet strength wrapping containing any resin based on formaldehyde or from any plastic food container or utensil manufactured from any resin of which formaldehyde is a condensing component.

(6) The permitted miscellaneous additive dimethylpolysiloxane may contain formaldehyde in any proportion not exceeding one thousand milligrams per kilogram.

(7) Cheese, clotted cream or any canned food may have in it or on it the permitted preservative nisin.

(8) Any food may have in it or on it the permitted preservative nisin introduced in the preparation of that food by the use of any cheese, clotted cream or canned food containing nisin.

(9) Any food may have in it or on it formaldehyde introduced in the preparation of that food by the use of the permitted miscellaneous additive dimethylpolysiloxane if that formaldehyde is present in the food in no greater proportion, in relation to the quantity of dimethylpolysiloxane used, than the proportion specified in relation to dimethylpolysiloxane in paragraph (6) of this regulation.

(10) Flour may contain the permitted preservative sulphur dioxide or sodium metabisulphite as prescribed by the Bread and Flour (Scotland) Regulations 1984.

(11) Community controlled wine may have in it any of the permitted preservatives sulphur dioxide, potassium bisulphite, potassium metabisulphite, sorbic acid and potassium sorbate or any other preservative to the extent, in each case, authorised by any Community Regulation.

(12) No person shall sell or import into Scotland any food which does not comply with this regulation.

5. Subject to regulation 7, nothing in the preceding regulation shall prohibit the presence in any compounded food of any permitted preservative introduced in the preparation of that food by the use of one or more specified foods (other than any unfermented grape juice product intended for sacramental use) if that permitted preservative–

(a) may under these Regulations be present in any specified food used in the compounded food, and

(b) is present in the compounded food in no greater proportion, in relation to the quantity of the specified food used, than the proportion specified in relation to that specified food in column 3 of Schedule 2:

Provided that–

(i) if the said specified food or foods may under these Regulations contain the permitted preservative sulphur dioxide, the compounded food may contain that permitted preservative in a quantity not exceeding that introduced by the use of any such specified food or fifty milligrams per kilogram, whichever is the greater;

(ii) if the said specified food or foods may under these Regulations contain any of the permitted preservatives benzoic acid, methyl 4-hydroxybenzoate, ethyl 4-hydroxybenzoate or propyl 4-hydroxybenzoate, the compounded food may contain that permitted preservative in a quantity not exceeding that introduced by the use of any such specified food or one hundred and twenty milligrams per kilogram, whichever is the greater;

(iii) if the compounded food is a specified food other than a cured meat product it may not contain any permitted preservative specified in relation thereto in column 2 of Schedule 2 in any greater proportion than is specified in relation thereto in column 3 of that Schedule;

(iv) if the compounded food is ice-cream or an edible ice made with fruit pieces in stabilised syrup which may under these Regulations contain the permitted preservative sorbic acid, the compounded food may not contain that permitted preservative in a quantity exceeding three hundred milligrams per kilogram.

Sale, advertisement and labelling of preservatives

6.—(1) No person shall sell or import into Scotland or advertise for sale any preservative (including any preservative with which any other substance has been mixed) for use as an ingredient in the preparation of food unless such preservative is a permitted preservative.

(2) No person shall sell any permitted preservative (including any permitted preservative with which any other substance has been mixed) for use as an ingredient in the preparation of food except in a container bearing a label in accordance with the requirements of paragraphs 1, 2, 3 and 6 of Schedule 3.

Food for babies and young children

7. No person shall sell any food that is specially prepared for babies or young children or for babies and young children if it has in it or on it any added sodium nitrate or sodium nitrite.

Sampling and analysis of citrus fruit

8.—(1) In relation to the sampling of citrus fruit for the purpose of analysis to establish the presence in or absence from that fruit of biphenyl, 2-hydroxybiphenyl or sodium biphenyl-2-yl oxide and the quantity of any such substance present–

(a) the power of a sampling officer or of an officer under section 28 or 32 respectively of the Act to procure samples shall be exercised in accordance with Part I of Schedule 4;

(b) the duty of a sampling officer or of an officer under section 30 or 32 respectively of the Act to seal or fasten up each part of the sample shall be performed in accordance with paragraph 1 of Part II of Schedule 4;

(c) the duty of a sampling officer or of an officer under section 30 or 32 respectively of the Act to submit one part of the sample for analysis by the public analyst shall be performed in accordance with paragraph 2 of Part II of Schedule 4.

(2) The method to be used in analysing citrus fruit for the purpose of establishing–

(a) the presence in or absence from that fruit of biphenyl, 2-hydroxybiphenyl or sodium biphenyl-2-yl oxide shall be as specified in Part I of Schedule 5;

(b) the quantity of biphenyl in that fruit shall be as specified in Part II of Schedule 5;

(c) the quantity of 2-hydroxybiphenyl or sodium biphenyl-2-yl oxide in that fruit shall be as specified in Part III of Schedule 5.

(3) The modified Clevenger-type separator to be used in analysing citrus fruit in accordance with the preceding paragraph and Parts II and III of Schedule 5 for the purpose of establishing the quantity of biphenyl, 2-hydroxybiphenyl or sodium biphenyl-2-yl oxide in that fruit shall conform with the diagram in Schedule 6.

Condemnation of food

9. Where any food is certified by a public analyst as being food which it is an offence against regulation 4 to sell or import into Scotland, that food may be treated for the purposes of section 9 of the Act (under which food may be seized and destroyed on the order of a justice of the peace) as being unfit for human consumption.

Penalties and enforcement

10.—(1) If any person contravenes or fails to comply with any of the foregoing provisions of these Regulations he shall be guilty of an offence and shall be liable–

(a) on summary conviction to a fine not exceeding the statutory maximum, or

(b) on conviction on indictment to a fine or to imprisonment for a term not exceeding one year, or both.

(2) Each district and islands council shall enforce and execute these Regulations in its area.

Defences

11.—(1) In any proceedings for an offence against regulation 4 it shall be a defence for the accused to prove that the presence in any food of any preservative other than a permitted preservative or the presence of a permitted preservative in any food other than a specified food, as the case may be, is solely due to the use of that preservative in food storage or in the preparation of food for storage–

(a) as an acaricide, fungicide, insecticide or rodenticide, for the protection, in each case, of food whilst in storage, or

(b) as a sprout inhibitor or depressant, otherwise than in a place where food is packed for retail sale.

(2) In any proceedings for an offence against these Regulations in relation to the publication of an advertisement, it shall be a defence for the accused to prove that, being a person whose business it is to publish or arrange for the publication of advertisements, he received the advertisement for publication in the ordinary course of business.

(3) In any proceedings in respect of the sale or importation before 31st December 1989 of food having in it or on it ethylene oxide contrary to regulation 4, it shall be a defence for the accused to prove that the presence of that substance in or on that food is solely due to its use for pathogen reduction of that food in accordance with the second column of entry C in the Annex to Directive 79/117/EEC of the Council, prohibiting the placing on the market and use of plant protection products containing certain active substances(**a**).

Application of various sections of the Act

12. Sections 41(2) and (5) (which relate to proceedings), 42(1), (2) and (3) (which relate to evidence of analysis), 44 (which relates to the power of a court to require analysis by the Government Chemist), 45 (which relates to a contravention due to default by some person other than the person charged), 46(2) (which relates to the conditions under which a warranty may be pleaded as a defence) and 47 (which relates to offences in relation to warranties and certificates of analysis) of the Act shall apply for the purposes of these Regulations as if references therein to proceedings, or a prosecution, under or taken or brought under the Act included references to proceedings, or a prosecution as the case may be, taken or brought for an offence under these Regulations and as if the reference in the said section 44 to section 41(5) included a reference to that subsection as applied by these Regulations.

Revocation

13. The Regulations specified in the first column of Schedule 7 are hereby revoked to the extent specified in relation thereto in the third column of that Schedule.

Sanderson of Bowden
Minister of State,
Scottish Office

St. Andrew's House, Edinburgh
23rd March 1989

(**a**) O.J. No. L33, 8.2.1979, p.36; the relevant amending Directive is 86/355/EEC of the Council – O.J. No. L212, 2.8.86, p.33.

Regulation 2(1) and (2)

SCHEDULE 1

PART I

PERMITTED PRESERVATIVES

Column 1 *Permitted preservative specified in Schedule 2*	*Column 2* *Serial Number*	*Column 3* *Alternative form in which the permitted preservative may be used (to be calculated as the permitted preservative shown in column 1)*	*Column 4* *Serial Number*
Sorbic acid	E200	Sodium sorbate Potassium sorbate Calcium sorbate	E201 E202 E203
Benzoic acid	E210	Sodium benzoate Potassium benzoate Calcium benzoate	E211 E212 E213
Ethyl 4-hydroxybenzoate	E214	Ethyl 4-hydroxybenzoate, sodium salt	E215
Propyl 4-hydroxybenzoate	E216	Propyl 4-hydroxybenzoate, sodium salt	E217
Methyl 4-hydroxybenzoate	E218	Methyl 4-hydroxybenzoate, sodium salt	E219
Sulphur dioxide	E220	Sodium sulphite Sodium hydrogen sulphite Sodium metabisulphite Potassium metabisulphite Calcium sulphite Calcium hydrogen sulphite	E221 E222 E223 E224 E226 E227
Potassium bisulphite	E228		
Biphenyl	E230		
2-Hydroxybiphenyl	E231	Sodium biphenyl-2-yl oxide	E232
2-(Thiazol-4-yl) benzimidazole	E233		
Hexamine	E239		
Sodium nitrite	E250	Potassium nitrite	E249
Sodium nitrate	E251	Potassium nitrate	E252
Propionic acid	E280	Sodium propionate Calcium propionate Potassium propionate	E281 E282 E283
Nisin	234		

PART II

SPECIFIC PURITY CRITERIA APPLICABLE TO PERMITTED PRESERVATIVES

In the case of–

E200 Sorbic acid

E201 Sodium sorbate

E202 Potassium sorbate

E203 Calcium sorbate

E210 Benzoic acid

E211 Sodium benzoate

E212 Potassium benzoate

E213 Calcium benzoate

E214 Ethyl 4-hydroxybenzoate
Synonyms: Ethyl *para*-hydroxybenzoate
Ethyl ester of *p*-hydroxybenzoic acid

E215 Ethyl 4-hydroxybenzoate, sodium salt
Synonyms: Sodium ethyl *para*-hydroxybenzoate
Sodium ethyl *p*-hydroxybenzoate

E216 Propyl 4-hydroxybenzoate
Synonyms: Propyl *para*-hydroxybenzoate
n-propyl *p*-hydroxybenzoate

E217 Propyl 4-hydroxybenzoate, sodium salt
Synonyms: Sodium propyl *para*-hydroxybenzoate
Sodium *n*-propyl *p*-hydroxybenzoate

E220 Sulphur dioxide

E221 Sodium sulphite (anhydrous or heptahydrate)

E222 Sodium hydrogen sulphite
Synonyms: Acid sodium sulphite

E223 Sodium metabisulphite

E250 Sodium nitrite

E251 Sodium nitrate

E252 Potassium nitrate

E280 Propionic acid

E281 Sodium propionate

E282 Calcium propionate

the appropriate specific purity criteria contained in Directive 65/66/EEC of the Council(**a**).

In the case of–

E218 Methyl 4-hydroxybenzoate
Synonyms: Methyl *para*-hydroxybenzoate
Methyl *p*-hydroxybenzoate

E219 Methyl 4-hydroxybenzoate, sodium salt
Synonyms: Sodium methyl *para*-hydroxybenzoate
Sodium derivative of methyl *p*-hydroxybenzoate

E226 Calcium sulphite

E227 Calcium hydrogen sulphite
Synonym: Calcium bisulphite

E233 2-(Thiazol-4-yl) benzimidazole
Synonyms: Thiabendazole
2-(4-thiazolyl) benzimidazole (thiabendazole)

E239 Hexamine
Synonym: Hexamethylenetetramine

E249 Potassium nitrite

E283 Potassium propionate

the appropriate specific purity criteria contained in Directive 65/66/EEC of the Council(**b**).

In the case of–

E224 Potassium metabisulphite

E230 Biphenyl

E231 2-Hydroxybiphenyl
Synonym: Orthophenylphenol

(**a**) O.J. No. 22, 9.2.65, p.373/65 (O.J./S.E. 1965-1966, p.25); relevant amending Directives are 67/428/EEC of the Council – O.J. No. 148, 11.7.67, p.10 (O.J./S.E. 1967, p.178); 76/463/EEC of the Council – O.J. No. L126, 14.5.76, p.33.

(**b**) The relevant amending Directive is 76/463/EEC of the Council – O.J. No. L126, 14.5.76, p.33.

E232 Sodium biphenyl-2-yl oxide
Synonym: Sodium orthophenylphenate

the appropriate specific purity criteria contained in Directive 65/66/EEC of the Council(**a**).

In the case of–

E228 Potassium bisulphite
Synonym: Potassium acid sulphite

the appropriate specific purity criteria contained in Directive 65/66/EEC of the Council(**b**).

In the case of–

Nisin

the criteria in the monograph for nisin contained in the Nutrition Meetings Report Series No. 45A (1969) of the United Nations' Food and Agriculture Organisation at page 53.

PART III

GENERAL PURITY CRITERIA APPLICABLE TO PERMITTED PRESERVATIVES EXCEPT WHERE OTHERWISE PROVIDED BY SPECIFIC PURITY CRITERIA

Each preservative shall not contain–

(a) more than 3 milligrams per kilogram of arsenic;

(b) more than 10 milligrams per kilogram of lead;

(c) more than 50 milligrams per kilogram of copper, or 25 milligrams per kilogram of zinc, or 50 milligrams per kilogram of any combination of copper and zinc.

(**a**) The relevant amending Directive is 67/428/EEC of the Council – O.J. No. 148, 11.7.67, p.10 (O.J./S.E. 1967, p.178).

(**b**) The relevant amending Directive is 86/604/EEC of the Council – O.J. No. L352, 13.12.1986, p.45.

SCHEDULE 2

Regulations 2(1) and 4(2)

ARTICLES OF FOOD WHICH MAY CONTAIN PERMITTED PRESERVATIVE AND THE NATURE AND PROPORTION OF PERMITTED PRESERVATIVE IN EACH CASE

Column 1 *Specified food*	*Column 2* *Permitted preservative*	*Column 3* *Except where otherwise stated milligrams per kilogram not exceeding –*
Beer	Sulphur dioxide and either benzoic acid or methyl 4-hydroxybenzoate or ethyl 4-hydroxybenzoate or propyl 4-hydroxybenzoate	70 70 70 70 70
Beetroot, cooked and prepacked	Benzoic acid or methyl 4-hydroxybenzoate or ethyl 4-hydroxybenzoate or propyl 4-hydroxybenzoate	250 250 250 250
Bread	Propionic acid	As prescribed by the Bread and Flour (Scotland) Regulations 1984
Cauliflower, canned	Sulphur dioxide	100
Cheese	Sorbic acid	1,000
Cheese, other than Cheddar, Cheshire, Grana-padano or Provolone type of cheeses or soft cheese	Sodium nitrate and sodium nitrite	50 of which not more than 5 may be sodium nitrite, expressed in both cases as sodium nitrite
Provolone cheese	Hexamine	25 (expressed as formaldehyde)
Chicory and coffee essence	Benzoic acid or methyl 4-hydroxybenzoate or ethyl 4-hydroxybenzoate or propyl 4-hydroxybenzoate	450 450 450 450
Christmas pudding	Propionic acid	1,000
Cider	Sulphur dioxide or sorbic acid	200 200
Coconut, desiccated	Sulphur dioxide	50
Colouring matter, except E150 Caramel, if in the form of a solution of a permitted colouring matter	Benzoic acid or methyl 4-hydroxybenzoate or ethyl 4-hydroxybenzoate or propyl 4-hydroxybenzoate or sorbic acid	2,000 2,000 2,000 2,000 1,000
The permitted colouring matter, E150 Caramel	Sulphur dioxide	1,000
Crabmeat, canned	Sulphur dioxide	30
Desserts, fruit based milk and cream	Sulphur dioxide or sorbic acid	100 300
Dessert sauces, fruit based with a total soluble solids content of less than 75%	Sulphur dioxide or benzoic acid or methyl 4-hydroxybenzoate or ethyl 4-hydroxybenzoate or propyl 4-hydroxybenzoate or sorbic acid	100 250 250 250 250 1,000
The permitted miscellaneous additive, Dimethylpolysiloxane	Sulphur dioxide or benzoic acid or methyl 4-hydroxybenzoate or ethyl 4-hydroxybenzoate or propyl 4-hydroxybenzoate or sorbic acid	1,000 2,000 2,000 2,000 2,000 1,000

Column 1 *Specified food*	*Column 2* *Permitted preservative*	*Column 3* *Except where otherwise stated milligrams per kilogram not exceeding –*
Enzymes:		
Papain, solid	Sulphur dioxide	30,000
Papain, aqueous solutions	Sulphur dioxide or sorbic acid	5,000 1,000
Aqueous solutions of enzyme preparations not otherwise specified, including immobilised enzyme preparations in aqueous media	Sulphur dioxide or benzoic acid or methyl 4-hydroxybenzoate or ethyl 4-hydroxybenzoate or propyl 4-hydroxybenzoate or sorbic acid	500 3,000 3,000 3,000 3,000 3,000
Fat spreads consisting of an emulsion principally of water in oil with a fat content not exceeding 70%	Sorbic acid	2,000
Figs, dried	Sulphur dioxide or sorbic acid	2,000 500
Fillings and toppings for flour confectionery which consist principally of a sweetened oil and water emulsion with a minimum sugar solids content of 50%	Sorbic acid	1,000
Finings when sold by retail:		
Wine finings	Sulphur dioxide	12,500
Beer finings	Sulphur dioxide	50,000
Flavourings	Sulphur dioxide or benzoic acid or methyl 4-hydroxybenzoate or ethyl 4-hydroxybenzoate or propyl 4-hydroxybenzoate	350 800 800 800 800
Flavouring syrups	Sulphur dioxide or benzoic acid or methyl 4-hydroxybenzoate or ethyl 4-hydroxybenzoate or propyl 4-hydroxybenzoate	350 800 800 800 800
Flour confectionery	Propionic acid or sorbic acid	1,000 1,000
Foam headings, liquid	Sulphur dioxide or benzoic acid or methyl 4-hydroxybenzoate or ethyl 4-hydroxybenzoate or propyl 4-hydroxybenzoate	5,000 10,000 10,000 10,000 10,000
Freeze drinks	Sulphur dioxide or benzoic acid or methyl 4-hydroxybenzoate or ethyl 4-hydroxybenzoate or propyl 4-hydroxybenzoate or sorbic acid	70 160 160 160 160 300
Fruit based pie fillings	Sulphur dioxide or benzoic acid or methyl 4-hydroxybenzoate or ethyl 4-hydroxybenzoate or propyl 4-hydroxybenzoate or sorbic acid	350 800 800 800 800 450
Fruit, dried, other than prunes, or figs	Sulphur dioxide	2,000
Fruit, fresh:		
Bananas	2-(Thiazol-4-yl) benzimidazole	3

Column 1 *Specified food*	*Column 2* *Permitted preservative*	*Column 3* *Except where otherwise stated milligrams per kilogram not exceeding –*
Citrus fruit	Biphenyl or 2-hydroxybiphenyl or 2-(Thiazol-4-yl) benzimidazole	70 12 10
Grapes	Sulphur dioxide	15
Fruit, fruit pulp or fruit purée (including tomatoes, tomato pulp, tomato paste and tomato purée) which, in each case, is not fresh or canned	Sulphur dioxide or benzoic acid or methyl 4-hydroxybenzoate or ethyl 4-hydroxybenzoate or propyl 4-hydroxybenzoate	350 800 800 800 800
Fruit juices:		
Any fruit juice or concentrated fruit juice mentioned in regulation 11(2) of the Fruit Juices and Fruit Nectars (Scotland) regulations 1977	Sulphur dioxide	As prescribed by the Fruit Juices and Fruit Nectars (Scotland) Regulations 1977
Any other fruit juice or concentrated fruit juice	Sulphur dioxide or benzoic acid or methyl 4-hydroxybenzoate or ethyl 4-hydroxybenzoate or propyl 4-hydroxybenzoate	350 800 800 800 800
Fruit or plants (including flowers and seeds), crystallised, glacé, drained (syruped) or candied peel or cut and drained (syruped) peel	Sulphur dioxide and either benzoic acid or methyl 4-hydroxybenzoate or ethyl 4-hydroxybenzoate or propyl 4-hydroxybenzoate or sorbic acid	100 1,000 1,000 1,000 1,000 1,000
Fruit pieces in stabilised syrup for use as ingredients of ice-cream or other edible ices	Sorbic acid	1,000
Fruit spread	Sulphur dioxide and sorbic acid	100 1,000
Garlic, powdered	Sulphur dioxide	2,000
Gelatin	Sulphur dioxide	1,000
Gelatin capsules	Sorbic acid	3,000
Ginger, dry root	Sulphur dioxide	150
Glucose drinks containing not less than 235 grammes of glucose syrup per litre of the drink	Sulphur dioxide or benzoic acid or methyl 4-hydroxybenzoate or ethyl 4-hydroxybenzoate or propyl 4-hydroxybenzoate	350 800 800 800 800
Grape juice products (unfermented, intended for sacramental use)	Sulphur dioxide and either benzoic acid or methyl 4-hydroxybenzoate or ethyl 4-hydroxybenzoate or propyl 4-hydroxybenzoate	70 2,000 2,000 2,000 2,000
Grape juice, concentrated, intended for home wine making and labelled as such	Sulphur dioxide	2,000
Hamburgers or similar products	Sulphur dioxide	450
Herring, marinated —whose pH does not exceed 4.5	Benzoic acid or methyl 4-hydroxybenzoate or ethyl 4-hydroxybenzoate or propyl 4-hydroxybenzoate	1,000 1,000 1,000 1,000

Column 1 *Specified food*	*Column 2* *Permitted preservative*	*Column 3* *Except where otherwise stated milligrams per kilogram not exceeding –*
—whose pH exceeds 4.5	Hexamine and either benzoic acid or methyl 4-hydroxybenzoate or ethyl 4-hydroxybenzoate or propyl 4-hydroxybenzoate	50 1,000 1,000 1,000 1,000
Hops, dried, sold by retail	Sulphur dioxide	2,000
Horseradish, fresh grated, and horseradish sauce	Sulphur dioxide or benzoic acid or methyl 4-hydroxybenzoate or ethyl 4-hydroxybenzoate or propyl 4-hydroxybenzoate	200 250 250 250 250
Jam and other products described in column 2 of Schedule 1 to the Jam and Similar Products (Scotland) Regulations 1981:		
Reduced sugar jam, reduced sugar jelly and reduced sugar marmalade	Sulphur dioxide and benzoic acid or methyl 4-hydroxybenzoate or ethyl 4-hydroxybenzoate or propyl 4-hydroxybenzoate or sorbic acid	As prescribed in the Jam and Similar Products (Scotland) Regulations 1981
Any other product described in column 2 of Schedule 1 to the Jam and Similar Products (Scotland) Regulations 1981	Sulphur dioxide	As prescribed in the Jam and Similar Products (Scotland) Regulations 1981
Mackerel, marinated, —whose pH does not exceed 4.5	Benzoic acid or methyl 4-hydroxybenzoate or ethyl 4-hydroxybenzoate or propyl 4-hydroxybenzoate	1,000 1,000 1,000 1,000
—whose pH exceeds 4.5	Hexamine and either benzoic acid or methyl 4-hydroxybenzoate or ethyl 4-hydroxybenzoate or propyl 4-hydroxybenzoate	50 1,000 1,000 1,000 1,000
Mallow, chocolate covered	Sorbic acid	1,000 (calculated on the weight of the mallow and chocolate together)
Meat, cured (including cured meat products):		
Cured meat (including cured meat products) packed in a sterile pack, whether or not it has been removed from the pack	Sodium nitrate and sodium nitrite	150, of which not more than 50 may be sodium nitrite, expressed in both cases as sodium nitrite
Acidified and/or fermented cured meat products (including Salami and similar products) not packed in a sterile pack	Sodium nitrate and sodium nitrite	400, of which not more than 50 may be sodium nitrite, expressed in both cases as sodium nitrite
Uncooked bacon and ham; cooked bacon and ham that is not, and has not been, packed in any hermetically sealed container	Sodium nitrate and sodium nitrite	500, of which not more than 200 may be sodium nitrite, expressed in both cases as sodium nitrite
Any cured meat or cured meat product not specified above	Sodium nitrate and sodium nitrite	250, of which not more than 150 may be sodium nitrite, expressed in both cases as sodium nitrite

Column 1 *Specified food*	*Column 2* *Permitted preservative*	*Column 3* *Except where otherwise stated milligrams per kilogram not exceeding –*
Mushrooms, frozen	Sulphur dioxide	50
Nut pastes, sweetened	Sorbic acid	1,000
Olives, pickled	Sulphur dioxide or benzoic acid or methyl 4-hydroxybenzoate or ethyl 4-hydroxybenzoate or propyl 4-hydroxybenzoate or sorbic acid	100 250 250 250 250 500
Peas, garden, canned, containing no added colouring matter	Sulphur dioxide	100
Pectin, liquid	Sulphur dioxide	250
Perry	Sulphur dioxide or sorbic acid	200 200
Pickles, other than pickled olives	Sulphur dioxide or benzoic acid or methyl 4-hydroxybenzoate or ethyl 4-hydroxybenzoate or propyl 4-hydroxybenzoate or sorbic acid	100 250 250 250 250 1,000
Potatoes, raw, peeled	Sulphur dioxide	50
Prawns, shrimps and scampi, other than prawns and shrimps in brine	Sulphur dioxide	200 in the edible part
Prawns and shrimps in brine	Sulphur dioxide and either sorbic acid or benzoic acid and either ethyl 4-hydroxybenzoate or propyl 4-hydroxybenzoate or methyl 4-hydroxybenzoate	200 in the edible part 2,000 300 300 300
Preparations of saccharin, sodium saccharin or calcium saccharin and water only	Benzoic acid and either methyl 4-hydroxybenzoate or ethyl 4-hydroxybenzoate or propyl 4-hydroxybenzoate	750 250 250 250
Prunes	Sulphur dioxide or sorbic acid	2,000 1,000
Salad cream (including mayonnaise) and salad dressing	Sulphur dioxide or benzoic acid or methyl 4-hydroxybenzoate or ethyl 4-hydroxybenzoate or propyl 4-hydroxybenzoate or sorbic acid	100 250 250 250 250 1,000
Sambal oelek	Benzoic acid and sorbic acid	850 1,000
Sauces, other than horseradish sauce	Sulphur dioxide or benzoic acid or methyl 4-hydroxybenzoate or ethyl 4-hydroxybenzoate or propyl 4-hydroxybenzoate or sorbic acid	100 250 250 250 250 1,000
Sausages or sausage meat	Sulphur dioxide	450
Snack meals, concentrated with a moisture content of not less than 15% and not more than 60%	Sorbic acid and methyl 4-hydroxybenzoate	1,500 175

Column 1 *Specified food*	*Column 2* *Permitted preservative*	*Column 3* *Except where otherwise stated milligrams per kilogram not exceeding –*
Soft drinks for consumption after dilution not otherwise specified in this Schedule	Sulphur dioxide or benzoic acid or methyl 4-hydroxybenzoate or ethyl 4-hydroxybenzoate or propyl 4-hydroxybenzoate or sorbic acid	350 800 800 800 800 1,500
Soft drinks for consumption without dilution not otherwise specified in this Schedule	Sulphur dioxide or benzoic acid or methyl 4-hydroxybenzoate or ethyl 4-hydroxybenzoate or propyl 4-hydroxybenzoate or sorbic acid	70 160 160 160 160 300
Soup concentrates with a moisture content of not less than 25% and not more than 60%	Sorbic acid and methyl 4-hydroxybenzoate	1,500 175
Starches, including modified starches	Sulphur dioxide	100
Sugars:		
Specified sugar products	Sulphur dioxide	As prescribed by the Specified Sugar Products (Scotland) Regulations 1976
Hydrolysed starches (other than specified sugar products)	Sulphur dioxide	400
Other sugars except lactose	Sulphur dioxide	70
Tea extract, liquid	Benzoic acid or methyl 4-hydroxybenzoate or ethyl 4-hydroxybenzoate or propyl 4-hydroxybenzoate	450 450 450 450
Vegetables, dehydrated:		
Brussels sprouts	Sulphur dioxide	2,500
Cabbage	Sulphur dioxide	2,500
Potato	Sulphur dioxide	550
Others	Sulphur dioxide	2,000
Vinegar:		
Cider or wine vinegar	Sulphur dioxide	200
Other	Sulphur dioxide	70
Wine (including alcoholic cordials) other than Community controlled wine	Sulphur dioxide and sorbic acid	450 milligrams per litre 200 milligrams per litre
Yoghurt, fruit	Sulphur dioxide or benzoic acid or methyl 4-hydroxybenzoate or ethyl 4-hydroxybenzoate or propyl 4-hydroxybenzoate or sorbic acid	60 120 120 120 120 300

SCHEDULE 3

Regulations 4(4) and 6(2)

LABELLING OF PERMITTED PRESERVATIVES

1.—(1) Each container to which regulation 6(2) applies shall bear a label on which is printed a true statement–

(a) in respect of each permitted preservative present, of the serial number, if any, as specified in relation thereto in column 2 or 4 of Part I of Schedule 1, and of the common or usual name or an appropriate designation of that permitted preservative;

(b) where any other substance or substances is or are present, of the common or usual name or an appropriate designation of each such substance; and

(c) where two or more of the substances referred to in paragraphs 1(1)(a) and (b) of this Schedule are present, of the proportion of each such substance present, save that the label shall only have printed on it a statement of the proportion of any substance present, other than a permitted preservative, if any regulations, other than these Regulations or any amendment to these Regulations, made under the Act contain a requirement to that effect.

(2) The said statement shall be headed or preceded by the words "for foodstuffs (restricted use)".

2. Any statement required by the preceding paragraph–

(a) shall be clear and legible;

(b) shall be in a conspicuous position on the label which shall be marked on, or securely attached to, the container in such a manner that it will be readily discernible and easily read by an intending purchaser under normal conditions of purchase;

(c) shall not be in any way hidden or obscured or reduced in conspicuousness by any other matter, whether pictorial or not, appearing on the label.

3. The figures and the letters in any statement to which the preceding paragraph applies–

(a) shall be in characters of uniform colour and size (being not less than 1.5 millimetres in height for a label on a container of which the greatest dimension does not exceed 12 centimetres, and not less than 3 millimetres in height for a label on a container of which the greatest dimension exceeds 12 centimetres), but so that the initial letter of any word may be taller than any other letter in the word;

(b) shall appear on a contrasting ground, so however that where there is no ground other than such as is provided by a transparent container and the contents of that container are visible behind the letters, those contents shall be taken to be the ground for the purposes of this paragraph;

(c) shall be within a surrounding line and no other written or pictorial matter shall appear within that line.

4.—(1) There shall be printed on each document to which regulation 4(4) refers a true statement–

(a) of the common or usual name or an appropriate designation of the food to which the document relates;

(b) in respect of each permitted preservative present in the food to which the document relates, of the serial number, if any, as specified in relation thereto in column 2 or 4 of Part I of Schedule 1, and of the common or usual name or an appropriate designation of that permitted preservative; and

(c) of the proportion of each permitted preservative present in the food to which the document relates.

(2) The said statement shall include the words "Not for retail sale".

5. Any statement required by the preceding paragraph shall be clear and legible and the figures and the letters in any such statement–

(a) shall be in characters of uniform colour and size and not less than 3 millimetres in height, but so that the initial letter of any word may be taller than any other letter in the word;

(b) shall appear on a contrasting ground;

(c) shall be within a surrounding line and no other written or pictorial matter shall appear within that line.

6. For the purposes of this Schedule–

(a) the height of any lower case letter shall be taken to be the x-height thereof, disregarding any ascender or descender thereof;

(b) any requirement that figures or letters shall be of uniform height, colour or size shall be construed as being subject to the saving that any inconsiderable variation in height, colour or size, as the case may be, may be disregarded.

SCHEDULE 4

Regulation 8(1)

SAMPLING OF CITRUS FRUIT TREATED WITH BIPHENYL, 2-HYDROXYBIPHENYL OR SODIUM BIPHENYL-2-YL OXIDE

PART I

Procuring of sample

1. A sample shall be procured using scientific methods which ensure that the sample is representative of the lot to which it relates.

2. A sample shall satisfy at least the following requirements–

(a) in the case of goods packaged in crates, boxes or similar containers–

Number of containers in the lot	*Up to 1,000*	*Above 1,000*
Minimum number of containers to be sampled	3	4
Mass, in kg., of fruit to be treated as sample per container	2	2

(b) in the case of goods in bulk–

Number of containers in the lot	*Up to 1,000*	*Above 1,000*
Mass of batch in kg	500	500
Mass, in kg, to be treated as sample	6	8

3. In this Part of this Schedule, the expression "lot" means a part of a consignment, which part has throughout the same characteristics such as variety of fruit, degree of ripeness and type of packaging.

PART II

Packaging and delivery of sample

1. Each part of the sample shall be placed in an air-tight container which shall be sealed.

2. Each part of the sample to be submitted for analysis shall be delivered so packaged as quickly as possible to the test laboratory.

Regulation 8(2)

SCHEDULE 5

ANALYSIS OF CITRUS FRUIT TREATED WITH BIPHENYL, 2-HYDROXYBIPHENYL OR SODIUM BIPHENYL-2-YL OXIDE

PART I

Qualitative analysis for residues of biphenyl, 2-hydroxybiphenyl and sodium biphenyl-2-yl oxide in citrus fruit

Purpose and scope

1. The method described below enables the presence of residues of biphenyl, 2-hydroxybiphenyl (orthophenylphenol) or sodium biphenyl-2-yl oxide (sodium orthophenylphenate) in the peel of citrus fruit to be detected. The sensitivity limit of this method, in absolute terms, is approximately 5 μg for biphenyl and 1 μg for 2-hydroxybiphenyl or sodium biphenyl-2-yl oxide, which is the equivalent of 5 mg of biphenyl and 1 mg of 2-hydroxybiphenyl respectively in the peel of 1 kg of citrus fruit.

Principle

2. An extract is prepared from the peel using dichloromethane in an acid medium. The extract is concentrated and separated by thin layer chromatography using silica gel. The presence of biphenyl, 2-hydroxybiphenyl or sodium biphenyl-2-yl oxide is shown by fluorescence and colour tests.

Reagents

3. The following reagents shall be used–

(a) cyclohexane (analytical reagent grade);

(b) dichloromethane (analytical reagent grade);

(c) hydrochloric acid 25 per centum (weight/volume);

(d) silica gel GF 254 (Merck or equivalent);

(e) 0.5 per centum (weight/volume) solution of 2, 4, 7-trinitrofluorenone (TNF) (Fluka, BDH or equivalent) in acetone;

(f) 0.1 per centum (weight/volume) solution of 2, 6-dibromo-*p*-benzoquinone-chlorimine in ethanol (stable for up to one week if kept in the refrigerator);

(g) concentrated solution of ammonia, specific gravity: 0.9;

(h) standard 1 per centum (weight/volume) solution of pure biphenyl in cyclohexane;

(j) standard 1 per centum (weight/volume) solution of pure 2-hydroxybiphenyl in cyclohexane.

Apparatus

4. The following apparatus shall be used–

(a) a mixer;

(b) a 250 ml flask with ground glass joint and with a reflux condenser;

(c) a reduced pressure evaporator;

(d) micropipettes;

(e) a thin layer chromatographic apparatus with plates measuring 20x20 cm;

(f) an ultra-violet lamp (254 nm), the intensity of which should be such that a spot of 5 mg of biphenyl is visible;

(g) equipment for pulverising reagents;

(h) an oven.

Method of analysis

5. The analysis shall be carried out as follows–

(a) Preparation and extraction: All the fruit in the sample for analysis is cut in half. Half of each piece of fruit is kept for quantitative determination of the residue of any biphenyl or 2-hydroxybiphenyl present. Pieces of peel are taken from the other halves to give a sample of about 80 g. These pieces are chopped, crushed in the mixer and placed in the 250 ml flask; to this is added 1 ml of 25 per centum hydrochloric acid and 100 ml dichloromethane. The mixture is heated under reflux for 10 minutes. After cooling and rinsing of the condenser with about 5 ml of dichloromethane, the mixture is filtered through a fluted filter. The solution is transferred to the evaporator and some anti-bumping granules are added. The solution is concentrated at reduced pressure at a temperature of 60C to a final volume of about 10 ml. If a rotary evaporator is used, the flask should be kept in a fixed position to avoid loss of biphenyl through the formation of a film of the product on the upper wall of the flask.

(b) Chromatography: 30 g of silica gel and 60 ml of water are placed in a mixer and mixed for one minute. The mixture is then spread on to 5 chromatographic plates to form a layer approximately 0.25 mm thick. The plates covered with this layer are subjected to a stream of hot air for 15 minutes and then placed in an oven where they are kept for 30 minutes at a temperature of 110C.

After cooling, the surface layer of each plate is divided into lanes, 2 cm wide, by parallel lines penetrating the silica gel down to the surface of the glass plate. 50 μl of the extract to be analysed are applied to each lane as a narrow band of contiguous spots approximately 1.5 cm from the lower edge of the plate. At least one lane is kept for the controls consisting of a spot of 1 μl (that is, 10 μg) of the standard solutions of biphenyl and 2-hydroxybiphenyl, one standard per lane. The chromatographic plates are developed in a mixture of cyclohexane and dichloromethane (25:95) in tanks previously lined with filter paper.

(c) Detection and identification: The presence of biphenyl and 2-hydroxybiphenyl is shown by the appearance of spots in ultra-violet light (254 nm). The sodium biphenyl-2-yl oxide will have been converted to 2-hydroxybiphenyl during the extraction in an acid medium, and its presence cannot therefore be distinguished from that of 2-hydroxybiphenyl. The products are identified in the following manner–

(i) biphenyl gives a yellow spot in daylight when sprayed with the TNF solution;

(ii) 2-hydroxybiphenyl gives a blue spot when sprayed with the solution of 2,6-dibromo-*p*-benzoquinonechlorimine, followed by rapid passage through a stream of hot air and exposure to an ammonia-saturated atmosphere.

PART II

Quantitative analysis of the residues of biphenyl in citrus fruit

Purpose and scope

1. The method described below gives a quantitative analysis of the residues of biphenyl in whole citrus fruit. The accuracy of the method is ± 10 per centum for a biphenyl content greater than 10 mg per kg of fruit.

Principle

2. After distillation in an acid medium and extraction by cyclohexane, the extract is subject to thin layer chromatography on silica gel. The chromatogram is developed and the biphenyl is eluted and determined spectrophotometrically at 248 nm.

Reagents

3. The following reagents shall be used–

(a) concentrated sulphuric acid solution;

(b) silicone-based anti-foaming emulsion;

(c) cyclohexane (analytical reagent grade);

(d) hexane (analytical reagent grade);

(e) ethanol (analytical reagent grade);

(f) anhydrous sodium sulphate;

(g) silica gel GF 254 (Merck or equivalent);

(h) standard 1 per centum (weight/volume) solution of pure biphenyl in cyclohexane: dilute with cyclohexane to obtain the following three solutions–

(i) 0.6 μg/μl;

(ii) 1 μg/μl;

(iii) 1.4 μg/μl.

Apparatus

4. The following apparatus shall be used–

(a) a 1 litre mixer;

(b) a 2 litre distillation flask with a modified Clevenger-type separator as shown in the diagram in Schedule 6 and a cooled reflux condenser;

(c) a 10 ml graduated flask;

(d) 50 μl micropipettes;

(e) a thin layer chromatographic apparatus with 20x20 cm plates;

(f) an oven;

(g) a centrifuge with 15 ml conical tubes;

(h) an ultra-violet spectrophotometer.

Method of analysis

5. The analysis shall be carried out as follows–

(a) Preparation and extraction: All the fruit in the sample for analysis is cut in half. Half of each piece of fruit is kept for qualitative analysis for residues of biphenyl, 2-hydroxybiphenyl or sodium biphenyl-2-yl oxide. The other halves are put all together and shredded in a mill or crushed until a homogeneous mixture is obtained. From this at least two sub-samples of 200 g are taken for analysis in the following manner. Each sub-sample is placed in a mixer with 100 ml of water and mixed at slow speed for several seconds. Water is added until the volume of the mixture reaches 3/4 of the capacity of the mixer, and the mixture is then mixed for 5 minutes at full speed. The resulting puree is transferred to the 2 litre distillation flask. The mixer is rinsed with water and the rinsings added to the contents of the flask. (The total quantity of water to be used in mixing and rinsing is 1 litre.) To the mixture are added 2 ml sulphuric acid, 1 ml anti-foaming emulsion and several anti-bumping granules. The separator and reflux condenser are fitted on to the flask. Distilled water is poured into the separator until the water level is well past the lower arm of the lateral return tube, followed by 7 ml cyclohexane. Distillation is carried out for about 2 hours. The lower aqueous layer in the separator is discarded and the upper layer is collected in the 10 ml graduated flask. The separator is rinsed with about 1.5 ml of cyclohexane and the rinsings added to the contents of the flask, which are then brought up to volume with cyclohexane. Finally a little anhydrous sodium sulphate is added and the mixture is shaken.

(b) Chromatography: 30 g of silica gel and 60 ml of water are placed in a mixer and mixed for one minute. The mixture is then spread on to 5 chromatographic plates to form a layer approximately 0.25 mm thick. The plates covered with this layer are subjected to a stream of hot air for 15 minutes and then placed in an oven where they are kept for 30 minutes at a temperature of 110C. After cooling, the surface layer of each plate is divided into 4 lanes, 4.5 cm wide, by parallel lines penetrating the silica gel down to the surface of the glass plate. 50 μl of the extract to be analysed are applied to one lane of each plate as a narrow band of contiguous spots approximately 1.5 cm from the lower edge of the plate. 50 μl of the standard solutions (i), (ii) and (iii), corresponding respectively to 30, 50 and 70 μg levels of biphenyl are applied in the same way to the three remaining lanes, one solution to each lane.

If a large number of samples are being analysed at one time, standard solutions need not be applied to every plate. Reference may be made to a standard curve provided that this curve has been prepared from the average values obtained from 5 different plates to which the same standard solutions have been applied.

(c) Development of chromatograms and elution: The chromatograms are developed with hexane to a height of 17 cm in tanks previously lined with filter paper. The plates are air dried. By illuminating the plates with ultra-violet light (254 nm), the areas of silica gel containing biphenyl are located and marked off in rectangles of equal area.

The entire layer of silica gel within the areas thus marked off is immediately scraped from the plate with a spatula. The biphenyl is extracted by mixing the silica gel with 10 ml of ethanol and shaking several times over a period of 10 minutes. The mixture is transferred to the centrifuge tubes and centrifuged for 5 minutes at 2,500 revolutions per minute.

A control sample of silica gel is taken by the same method using an area of the same size. If a series of analyses are made, this control area is taken from an unused lane of a plate and below the solvent front; if a single analysis is made the control sample is taken from an area below one of the positions at which the standard biphenyl is located.

(d) Spectrophotometric determination: The supernatant liquid is decanted into the spectrophotometer cells and the absorption determined at 248 nm against a control extract from a chromatographic area free from biphenyl.

Calculation of results

6. A standard curve is drawn, plotting the biphenyl values of 30, 50 and 70 μg against the corresponding absorptions, as determined on the spectrophotometer. This gives a straight line which passes through the origin. This graph allows the biphenyl content of the samples to be read directly in mg per kg from the absorption value of their extracts.

PART III

Quantitative analysis of the residues of 2-hydroxybiphenyl and sodium biphenyl-2-yl oxide in citrus fruit

Purpose and scope

1. The method described below enables a quantitative analysis of the residues of 2-hydroxybiphenyl and sodium biphenyl-2-yl oxide in whole citrus fruit to be made. The method gives results which for a 2-hydroxybiphenyl or sodium biphenyl-2-yl oxide content of the order of 12 mg per kg are low by an average value of between 10 per centum and 20 per centum.

Principle

2. After distillation in an acid medium and extraction by di-isopentyl ether, the extract is purified and treated with a solution of 4-aminophenazone. A red colour develops, the intensity of which is measured spectrophotometrically at 510 nm.

Reagents

3. The following reagents shall be used–

(a) 70 per centum (weight/weight) orthophosphoric acid;

(b) silicone-based anti-foaming emulsion;

(c) di-isopentyl ether (analytical reagent grade);

(d) purified cyclohexane: shake 3 times with a 4 per cent (weight/volume) solution of sodium hydroxide, wash 3 times with distilled water;

(e) 4 per centum (weight/volume) sodium hydroxide solution;

(f) buffer solution at pH 10.4: into a 2 litre graduated flask put 6.64 g of boric acid, 8.00 g of potassium chloride and 93.1 ml of N sodium hydroxide solution; mix and bring up to calibration mark with distilled water;

(g) reagent I: dissolve 1.0 g of 4-aminophenazone (4-amino-2, 3-dimethyl-1-phenyl-5-pyrazolone; 4-aminoantipyrin) in 100 ml of distilled water;

(h) reagent II: dissolve 2.0 g of potassium ferricyanide in 100 ml of distilled water. Reagents I and II must be kept in brown glass flasks and are only stable for approximately 14 days;

(j) silica gel;

(k) standard solution: dissolve 10 mg of pure 2-hydroxybiphenyl in 1 ml of 0.1 N NaOH; dilute to 100 ml with a 0.2 M sodium borate solution (1 ml = 100 μg 2-hydroxybiphenyl). For the standard curve, dilute 1 ml to 10 ml with the buffer solution.

Apparatus

4. The following apparatus shall be used–

(a) a shredding or crushing mill;

(b) a mixer;

(c) a 1 litre distillation flask with a modified Clevenger-type separator as shown in the diagram in Schedule 6 and a reflux condenser;

(d) an electrically controlled heating mantle;

(e) a 200 ml separating funnel;

(f) graduated cylinders of 25 and 100 ml;

(g) graduated flasks of 25 and 100 ml;

(h) 1 to 10 ml pipettes;

(j) 0.5 ml graduated pipettes;

(k) a spectrophotometer with 4 or 5 cm cells.

Method of Analysis

5. All the fruit in the sample for analysis is cut in half. Half of each piece of fruit is kept for qualitative analysis for residues of biphenyl, 2-hydroxybiphenyl or sodium biphenyl-2-yl oxide. The other halves are put all together and shredded in a mill or crushed until a homogeneous mixture is obtained. From this at least two sub-samples of 250 g are taken for analysis in the following manner.

Each sub-sample is placed in a mixer with 500 ml of water and mixed until a very fine homogeneous mixture is obtained in which the oily cells are no longer perceptible. A sample of 150 to 300 g of the puree is taken, depending on the presumed 2-hydroxybiphenyl content and placed in the 1 litre distillation flask with a quantity of water sufficient to dilute the mixture to 500 g in the flask. After the addition of 10 ml of 70 per centum orthophosphoric acid, several anti-bumping granules and 0.5 ml of anti-foaming emulsion, the separator and the reflux condenser are fitted on to the flask. 10 ml of di-isopentyl ether are placed in the separator and the flask is heated gently in the electrically controlled heating mantle until the mixture boils. Emulsion formation is minimised if the mixture is boiled gently for the first 10 to 20 minutes. The rate of heating is then gradually increased until the mixture boils steadily and one drop of water reaches the trapping solvent every 3 to 5 seconds. After distilling for 6 hours, the contents of the separator are poured into the 200 ml separating funnel, and the separator and the condenser are rinsed with 60 ml of cyclohexane and then with 60 ml of water. The rinsings are added to the contents of the separating funnel. The mixture is shaken vigorously and when the phases have separated the aqueous phase is discarded.

To extract the 2-hydroxybiphenyl, the organic phase is shaken vigorously 5 times, each time for 3 minutes, with 10 ml of 4 per centum sodium hydroxide. The alkaline solutions are combined, adjusted to pH 9-10 with orthophosphoric acid in the presence of phenolphthalein paper, and diluted to 100 ml with distilled water. A pinch of silica gel is added in order to clarify the solution which will have a slightly cloudy appearance. The solution is then shaken and filtered through a dry, fine-grain filter. Since colouring is developed with the maximum of accuracy and precision using quantities of 2-hydroxybiphenyl of between 10 and 70 μg an aliquot sample of between 0.5 and 10 ml of solution is taken with a pipette, taking into account the quantities of 2-hydroxybiphenyl which might be expected to be found. The sample is placed in a 25 ml graduated flask; to this are added 0.5 ml of reagent I, 10 ml of the buffer solution and then 0.5 ml of reagent II. The mixture is made up to the calibration mark with the buffer solution and shaken vigorously.

After 5 minutes the absorption of the red colouring at 510 nm. is measured spectrophotometrically against a control containing no extract. The colour does not lose intensity within 30 minutes. Evaluation is made by reference to a standard curve drawn from determinations using the standard 2-hydroxybiphenyl solution under the same conditions.

Observations

6. For each analysis it is recommended that the spectrophotometric determination be made with two different volumes of the neutralised alkaline extract.

Untreated citrus fruit gives by this method a "blank" reading of up to 0.5 mg per kg for oranges and 0.8 mg per kg for lemons.

SCHEDULE 6

Regulation 8(3)

DIAGRAM OF A MODIFIED CLEVENGER-TYPE SEPARATOR

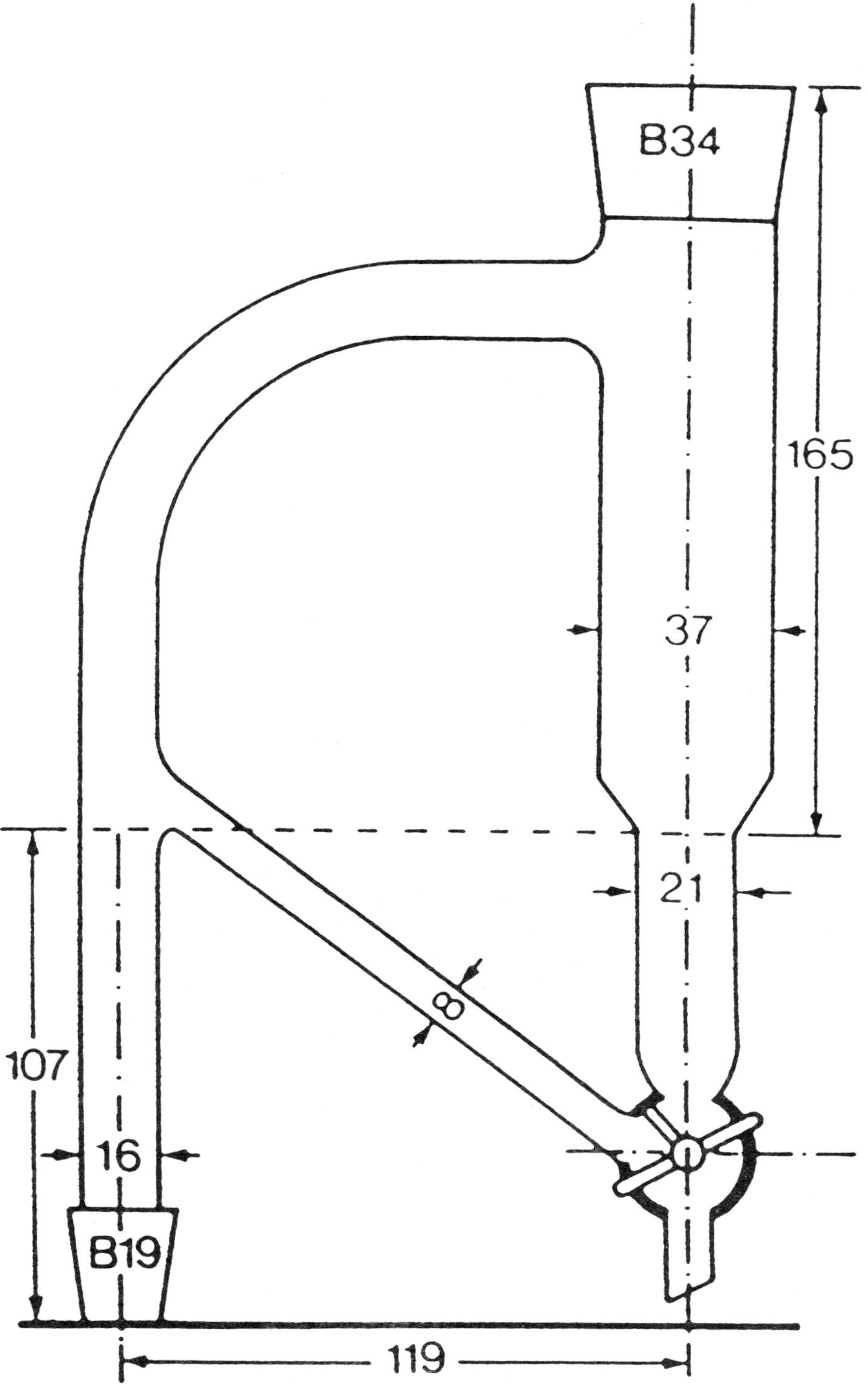

Note: The dimensions in this diagram are given in millimetres.

Regulation 13

SCHEDULE 7

Regulations revoked	*References*	*Extent of revocation*
The Preservatives in Food (Scotland) Regulations 1979	S.I. 1979/1073	All the Regulations
The Preservatives in Food (Scotland) Amendment Regulations 1980	S.I. 1980/1232	All the Regulations
The Jam and Similar Products (Scotland) Regulations 1981	S.I. 1981/1320	Regulation 20 and Schedule 5
The Preservatives in Food (Scotland) Amendment Regulations 1982	S.I. 1982/516	All the Regulations
The Fruit Juices and Fruit Nectars (Scotland) Amendment Regulations 1982	S.I. 1982/1619	Regulation 9
The Food and Drugs (Scotland) Act 1956 (Transfer of Enforcement Functions) Regulations 1983	S.I. 1983/270	The reference in Schedule 2 to the Preservatives in Food (Scotland) Regulations 1989
The Sweeteners in Food (Scotland) Regulations 1983	S.I. 1983/1497	Schedule 2, paragraph 5
The Bread and Flour (Scotland) Regulations 1984	S.I. 1984/1518	Schedule 6, paragraph 4
The Food (Revision of Penalties and Mode of Trial) (Scotland) Regulations 1985	S.I. 1985/1068	The reference in Schedules 1 and 2 to the Preservatives in Food (Scotland) Regulations 1979

EXPLANATORY NOTE

(This note is not part of the Regulations)

These Regulations, which apply to Scotland only, re-enact with amendments the Preservatives in Food (Scotland) Regulations 1979, as amended, and come into force on 3rd May 1989. They implement Council Directive 64/54/EEC (O.J. No. 12, 27.1.1964, p.161/64: O.J./S.E. 1963-1964, p.99) on the approximation of the laws of Member States concerning the preservatives authorised for use in foodstuffs intended for human consumption, as last amended by Council Directive 85/585/EEC (O.J. No. L372, 31.12.85, p.43) and Council Directive 65/66/EEC (O.J. No. 22, 9.2.65, p.373/65: O.J./S.E. 1965-1966, p.25), laying down specific criteria of purity for preservatives authorised for use in foodstuffs intended for human consumption, as last amended by Council Directive 86/604/EEC (O.J. No. L352, 13.12.86, p.45).

The Regulations–

(a) specify permitted preservatives and prescribe purity criteria for those preservatives (regulation 2(1) and (2) and Schedule 1);

(b) prohibit the sale or importation of food having in it or on it any added preservative except specified foods having in them or on them permitted preservatives within prescribed limits or as otherwise prescribed (regulation 4 and Schedule 2 and Schedule 3, paragraphs 4, 5 and 6);

(c) within prescribed limits, permit the presence in compounded food of permitted preservatives introduced in the preparation of that food by the use of one or more foods specified in Schedule 2 (regulation 5);

(d) prohibit the sale, the importation and the advertisement for sale, for use as an ingredient in the preparation of food, of any preservative other than a permitted preservative (regulation 6(1));

(e) prescribe labelling requirements for permitted preservatives when sold as such (regulation 6(2) and Schedule 3, paragraphs 1, 2, 3 and 6);

(f) prohibit the sale of food specially prepared for babies or young children if it has in it or on it any added sodium nitrate or sodium nitrite (regulation 7);

(g) make provision for the sampling and analysis of citrus fruit for the presence of biphenyl, 2-hydroxybiphenyl and sodium bi-phenyl-2-yl oxide (regulation 8 and Schedules 4, 5 and 6).

The principal changes effected by the Regulations are–

(a) the inclusion, in implementation of Directives 85/585/EEC and 86/604/EEC, of E228 potassium-bi-sulphate as a permitted preservative with specified purity criteria (regulation 2(1) and Schedule 1); and the confirmation that Community controlled wine may contain this and other preservatives to the extent authorised by any Community Regulation (regulations 2(1) and 4(11));

(b) the substitution for low fat spreads of fat spreads whose fat content does not exceed 70%, as a specified food permitted to contain sorbic acid (regulation 4(2) and Schedule 2);

(c) the extension of the preservatives permitted in fruit or plants, crystallised, glacé, drained (syruped) or candied peel or cut and drained (syruped) peel to include benzoic acid, hydroxybenzoates or sorbic acid and sulphur dioxide (regulation 4(3)(b) and Schedule 2);

(d) subject to prescribed limits, the authorisation for use in prawns and shrimps in brine of the permitted preservatives, sorbic acid, benzoic acid, ethyl 4-hydroxybenzoate, propyl 4-hydroxybenzoate and methyl 4-hydroxybenzoate as well as sulphur dioxide (regulation 4(3)(f) and Schedule 2);

(e) the provision of a defence to proceedings in respect of sale or importation before 31st December 1989, of food having in it or on it ethylene oxide, where the presence of that substance is due to its use for pathogen reduction in accordance with the provisions of Council Directive 79/117/EEC as amended by Council Directive 86/355/EEC (regulation 11(3)).

The Nutrition Meetings Report Series No. 45A (1969) of the United Nations' Food and Agriculture Organisation may be inspected at the Ministry of Agriculture, Fisheries and Food, Main Library, 3 Whitehall Place, London SW1A 2HH (telephone 01-270-8419).

1989 No. 582 (S.67)

EVIDENCE

The Evidence in Divorce Actions (Scotland) Order 1989

Made - - - -	*23rd March 1989*
Coming into force	*3rd April 1989*

The Lord Advocate, in exercise of the powers conferred on him by section 8(4) of the Civil Evidence (Scotland) Act 1988(**a**), and of all other powers enabling him in that behalf, hereby makes the following Order, a draft of which has been laid before and approved by resolution of each House of Parliament:

1. This Order may be cited as the Evidence in Divorce Actions (Scotland) Order 1989 and shall come into force on 3rd April 1989.

2.—(1) The provisions of this Order shall have effect in relation to the following class of actions, namely actions for divorce in which–

(a) the action is undefended;

(b) the action is brought in reliance on the facts set out in section 1(2)(d) (2 years non-cohabitation and the defender's consent to decree) or in section 1(2)(e) (5 years non-cohabitation) of the Divorce (Scotland) Act 1976(**b**);

(c) no other proceedings are pending in any court which could have the effect of bringing the marriage to an end;

(d) there are no children of the marriage under the age of 16 years;

(e) neither party applies for an order for financial provision on divorce; and

(f) neither party suffers from mental disorder within the meaning of section 1(2) of the Mental Health (Scotland) Act 1984(**c**).

(2) For the purpose of this Order an action shall be treated as undefended when the defender has not entered appearance or, having entered appearance, has not lodged defences or has withdrawn them.

3. Section 8(3) of the Civil Evidence (Scotland) Act 1988 shall not apply in respect of the class of action specified in article 2 above.

Lord Advocate's Chambers
23rd March 1989

Fraser of Carmyllie
Lord Advocate

(**a**) 1988 c.32.
(**b**) 1976 c.39.
(**c**) 1984 c.36.

EXPLANATORY NOTE

(This note is not part of the Order)

This Order provides that the requirement of section 8(3) of the Civil Evidence (Scotland) Act 1988 should not apply to a specified class of divorce action.

Section 8(3) requires that evidence to establish the grounds of action for divorce cases, among others, must consist of or include evidence from a source other than that of a party to the marriage. By means of this Order that requirement is not to apply to actions of divorce brought on the basis of 2 years non-cohabitation and with consent of the defender or of 5 years non-cohabitation where in both cases the action is undefended and certain other criteria are fulfilled. These are actions in which a simplified divorce procedure is available either in the Court of Session under Rule 170E to 170L of the Court of Session Rules (S.I. 1965/321 as amended by S.I. 1982/1679) or in the sheriff court under Ordinary Cause Rules 135 to 143 (the First Schedule to the Sheriff Courts (Scotland) Act 1907 (c. 51) as substituted by S.I. 1983/747 and subsequently amended by S.I. 1984/255, 1986/1230 and 1946).

STATUTORY INSTRUMENTS

1989 No. 583

MEDICINES

The Medicines (Fees Relating to Medicinal Products for Animal Use) Regulations 1989

Made - - - -	*30th March 1989*
Laid before Parliament	*3rd April 1989*
Coming into force	*24th April 1989*

The Secretary of State concerned with health in England, the Secretaries of State respectively concerned with health and with agriculture in Wales and in Scotland, the Minister of Agriculture, Fisheries and Food, the Department of Health and Social Services for Northern Ireland and the Department of Agriculture for Northern Ireland, acting jointly, with the consent of the Treasury, in exercise of the powers conferred by section 1(1) and (2) of the Medicines Act 1971**(a)** and now vested in them**(b)** and of all other powers enabling them in that behalf, after consulting such organisations as appear to them to be representative of interests likely to be substantially affected by these Regulations**(c)**, hereby make the following Regulations:–

PART I

GENERAL

Citation, commencement and scope

1.—(1) These Regulations may be cited as the Medicines (Fees Relating to Medicinal Products for Animal Use) Regulations 1989 and shall come into force on 24th April 1989.

(2) These Regulations apply only to fees payable–

(a) in connection with applications for the grant, variation or renewal of licences or certificates under Part II of the Act relating wholly or partly to medicinal products for animal use; or

(b) in respect of inspections made in connection with applications for the grant, renewal or variation of, or during the currency of any such licence or certificate; or

---

(a) 1971 c.69 as amended by section 21 of the Health and Medicines Act 1988 (c.49); by virtue of section 1(3) of the 1971 Act expressions in that section have the same meaning as in the Medicines Act 1968 (c.67) as amended by the Transfer of Functions (Wales) Order 1969 (S.I. 1969/388). The expression "The Ministers" is defined in section 1(1) of the 1968 Act as so amended.

(b) In the case of the Secretaries of State concerned with health in England and in Wales by virtue of article 2(2) of, and Schedule 1 to, the Transfer of Functions (Wales) Order 1969; in the case of the Secretary of State concerned with agriculture in Wales by virtue of article 2(3) of, and Schedule 1 to, the Transfer of Functions (Wales) (No. 1) Order 1978 (S.I. 1978/272); in the case of the Northern Ireland Departments by virtue of section 40 of, and Schedule 5 to, the Northern Ireland Constitution Act 1973 (c.36) and section 1(3) of, and paragraph 2(1)(b) of Schedule 1 to, the Northern Ireland Act 1974 (c.28).

(c) *See* section 129(6) of the Medicines Act 1968 as extended to include Regulations made under the Medicines Act 1971 by section 1(3)(b) of that latter Act.

(c) in respect of samples submitted for testing in connection with applications for the grant, renewal or variation of, or during the currency of a product licence.

Interpretation

2.—(1) In these Regulations, unless the context requires otherwise—

"the Act" means the Medicines Act 1968**(a)**;

"annual fee" in relation to any product licence means the appropriate amount calculated in accordance with the provisions of Part II of Schedule 4;

"capital fee" means any fee (other than an annual fee) payable under the provisions of these Regulations;

"licence year" means the period beginning with the first day of April and ending with the last day of March of the year next ensuing;

"medicinal product" includes any substance or article specified in any Order made under (a) section 104 or 105(1)(a) of the Act which directs that Part II of the Act shall have effect in relation to such substance or article; or (b) section 130(3A) of the Act which provides that such substance or article shall, or shall not, be treated as a medicinal product.

(2) In these Regulations any reference to a regulation or a Schedule shall be construed as a reference to a regulation contained in these Regulations, or as the case may be, to a Schedule thereto, and any reference in a regulation or a Schedule to a paragraph shall be construed as a reference to a paragraph of the regulation or, as the case may be, Schedule.

PART II

CAPITAL FEES FOR APPLICATIONS FOR LICENCES OR CERTIFICATES AND FOR INSPECTIONS IN CONNECTION THEREWITH

Applications for Licences

3. Subject to regulations 22 and 24, in connection with an application for a product licence, a manufacturer's licence or a wholesale dealer's licence there shall be payable by the applicant–

(a) the fee prescribed in Part II of Schedule 1 in connection with that application;

(b) in respect of any inspection of a description falling within paragraph 1 of Schedule 2 made in connection with that application the fee payable in accordance with paragraphs 2 to 5 of that Schedule; and

(c) if appropriate, the fee prescribed in Part III of Schedule 1 in respect of samples submitted for testing at the request of the Licensing Authority in connection with that application.

Applications for Animal Test Certificates

4. Subject to regulation 24, in connection with an application for an animal test certificate, there shall be payable by the applicant a fee of £2,500.

Applications for certificates for exports of medicinal products

5.—(1) In connection with an application for a certificate issued under section 50 of the Act, there shall be payable by the applicant–

(a) if the applicant requests that the certificate be issued within 24 hours of receipt of the application, a fee of £100; or

(b) in any other case, a fee of £50; and

(a) 1968 c.67.

(c) in either case–
  (i) a fee of £10 for each certified copy of the original certificate requested by the applicant in excess of four, and
  (ii) a fee of £50 for each set of certificates requested by the applicant in addition to one.

(2) In paragraph (1)(c)(ii) "set of certificates" means the original certificate plus up to four certified copies of that certificate.

PART III

FEES FOR APPLICATIONS FOR VARIATIONS OF LICENCES OR CERTIFICATES AND FOR INSPECTIONS IN CONNECTION THEREWITH

Variations of Licences

6. Subject to regulations 8, 9, 22 and 24, in connection with an application under section 30 of the Act for the variation of a provision of a product licence, a manufacturer's licence or a wholesale dealer's licence, there shall be payable by the applicant–

(a) the fee prescribed in Part IV of Schedule 1; and

(b) in respect of any inspection of a description referred to in paragraph 1 of Schedule 2 made in connection with that application, the fee payable in accordance with paragraphs 2 to 5 of that Schedule.

Variations of Animal Test Certificates

7.—(1) Subject to paragraph (2) and regulations 8, 9, 22 and 24, in connection with an application under section 39(4) of the Act for the variation of a provision of an animal test certificate, there shall be payable by the applicant a fee of £200.

(2) Where an application is made for a variation to a provision of the animal test certificate and the variation applied for consists of no more than a change of either or both the name and address of the holder of the certificate, there shall be payable by the applicant a fee of £50.

Applications for Multiple Variations

8. A separate fee shall be payable in respect of each variation of each provision of a licence or certificate applied for in any one application except that no separate fee shall be payable in respect of any variation which is related to or is consequential upon another variation of a provision of the same licence or certificate which is applied for in the same application.

Variations at the Invitation of the Licensing Authority

9. Where an application for a variation is made at the express written invitation of the Licensing Authority, no fee shall be payable under this Part of these Regulations.

PART IV

FEES FOR APPLICATIONS FOR RENEWALS OF LICENCES OR CERTIFICATES AND FOR INSPECTIONS IN CONNECTION THEREWITH

Renewal of Licences

10. Subject to regulations 12, 22 and 24, in connection with an application under section 24(2) of the Act for renewal of a product licence, a manufacturer's licence or a wholesale dealer's licence, there shall be payable by the applicant–

(a) the appropriate fee prescribed in Part V of Schedule 1; and

(b) in respect of any inspection of a description referred to in paragraph 1 of Schedule 2 made in connection with that application a fee payable in accordance with paragraphs 2 to 5 of that Schedule.

Renewal of Certificates

11. Subject to regulations 12 and 24, in connection with an application under section 38(2) of the Act for renewal of an animal test certificate there shall be payable by the applicant a fee of £500.

Renewals in terms which are not identical to the existing licence or certificate

12. Where an applicant applies for renewal of a licence, or as the case may be, an animal test certificate so as to contain provisions which are not identical to that licence or certificate as in force at the date of that application, the fee payable under this Part of these Regulations shall be increased by an amount equal to the fee which would have been payable under Part III of these Regulations had he made a separate application for each variation of that licence or certificate.

PART V

FEES FOR INSPECTIONS MADE DURING THE CURRENCY OF A LICENCE

13.—(1) Subject to paragraph (4) and to regulations 22 and 24, a fee in accordance with paragraphs 2 to 5 of Schedule 2 shall be payable in respect of any inspection of a site made during the currency of a product licence, a manufacturer's licence or a wholesale dealer's licence (except for any inspection in respect of which a fee is otherwise payable under Parts III or IV of these Regulations).

(2) The fee payable under paragraph (1) in respect of an inspection of a site made during the currency of a manufacturer's licence or a wholesale dealer's licence shall be payable by the holder of the manufacturer's licence or, as the case may be, the wholesale dealer's licence.

(3) Where a fee is payable under paragraph 1 in respect of an inspection of a site located outside the United Kingdom, the fee shall be payable in equal proportions by each holder of a product licence in which that site is named as a possible site for manufacture of the medicinal product in respect of which the product licence is granted.

(4) No fee shall be payable in respect of any inspection of a site carried out within 6 months of a previous inspection in order to ascertain whether alterations or improvements to the premises concerned, which were required in writing by the Licensing Authority as the result of that previous inspection, have been implemented.

PART VI

FEES FOR BATCH CONTROL TESTING DURING THE CURRENCY OF A LICENCE

14.—(1) A fee calculated in accordance with paragraph (2) shall be payable in respect of each product licence held, in which, as a condition of that licence there is a requirement that the licence holder shall submit for testing samples of each batch of the medicinal product which he has manufactured.

(2) During any licence year the fees referred to in paragraph (1) shall be—

(a) for the first sample and up to and including three samples, a fee of £600, payable by the licence holder at the time the first sample is submitted for testing;

(b) for four samples and up to and including ten samples, an additional fee of £200, payable by the licence holder at the time the fourth sample is submitted for testing;

(c) for ten samples or more, a further additional fee of £200 payable by the licence holder at the time the tenth sample is submitted for testing.

PART VII

ANNUAL FEES

Product Licences—annual fee

15.—(1) Subject to paragraph (3) and regulation 24 in connection with any application for the grant or renewal of any product licence there shall be payable by the applicant an annual fee in respect of each licence year during any part of which a product licence, granted or renewed in pursuance of the application is in force, or a product licence already held by the applicant, is in force, save that no annual fee shall be payable in respect of the licence year during which the last to expire of such product licences expires if that licence expires on a date earlier than the anniversary of that date on which that licence was granted which falls in that licence year.

(2) The annual fee shall be calculated in accordance with Schedule 4.

(3) The annual fee may be adjusted or refunded in any of the circumstances set out in Schedule 5.

PART VIII

ADMINISTRATION

Payment of fees to Ministers

16. Any sums which under the provisions of these Regulations become payable by way of, or on account of, fees shall be paid to one of the Agriculture Ministers specified in section 1(1)(b) of the Act as appropriate.

Time for payment of capital fees in connection with applications or inspections and refunds of such fees

17.—(1) Subject to paragraphs (2) and (3), all sums payable by way of capital fees under these Regulations in connection with any application shall be payable at the time of the application.

(2) If, following either the determination of an application or an inspection, it becomes apparent that–

(a) a lesser fee was properly payable, the excess shall be refunded to the applicant, or as the case may be, the holder of the licence or certificate concerned; or

(b) a higher fee was properly payable, the balance due shall be payable within 14 days following written notice from the Licensing Authority to the applicant or, as the case may be, the holder of the licence or certificate concerned.

(3) All sums payable by way of fees in respect of inspections made either in connection with an application or during the currency of a licence or certificate or in respect of samples submitted for testing shall become payable within 14 days following written notice from the Licensing Authority.

Time for payment of annual fees

18.—(1) Subject to paragraphs (2) and (3), all annual fees shall be payable on 1st April of the licence year to which they relate:

Provided that the annual fee payable under these Regulations for the licence year beginning 1st April 1989 shall not become payable until 1st September 1989.

(2) Subject to the proviso to paragraph (1), where an applicant first becomes liable to make any payment by way of annual fees of a particular kind during the course of a licence year, such fees shall be payable forthwith.

(3) Where an application is made by an applicant who has not previously held a product licence he shall be liable to pay a sum at the basic rate referred to in Part II of Schedule 4 at the time of the application in respect of the licence year in which the licence is granted.

Late payment of annual fees

19.—(1) Where an annual fee has not been paid by the holder or former holder of the licence by the end of the period of three months from the due date, a further fee, calculated in accordance with the provisions of the following paragraphs, shall be payable.

(2) The further fee referred to in the preceding paragraph shall be an amount equivalent to 1 per cent of the annual fee payable multiplied by the number of complete months contained in the period from the day after the end of the period of three months from the due date until the date when the annual fee is paid, rounded down to the nearest £10. Where the annual fee payable is less than £10, no such fee shall be payable.

(3) Where the holder or former holder of a licence has not furnished evidence of his annual turnover in accordance with the provisions of Part I of Schedule 4 so that the annual fee payable in respect of a licence year cannot be determined before the due date, he may make a payment of an amount on account of the annual fee payable by him (in this regulation referred to as a "payment on account").

(4) Where the holder or former holder of a licence has made a payment on account in the circumstances mentioned in the preceding paragraph the further fee payable by him shall be calculated as if in paragraph (2) above the reference to the annual fee payable were to the difference between the payment on account and the amount of the annual fee as subsequently determined.

(5) In this regulation–

(a) "due date" means the date upon which an annual fee became payable in accordance with the provisions of these Regulations;

(b) references to a period calculated from a day are references to the period inclusive of that day.

Suspension of Licences

20. Where any sum due by way of, or on account of, any fee or any part thereof payable under these Regulations remains unpaid by the holder of a licence or certificate, the Licensing Authority may serve a notice on him requiring payment of the sum unpaid and, if after a period of one month from the date of service of such notice, or such longer period as the Licensing Authority may allow, the said sum remains unpaid, the Licensing Authority may forthwith suspend the licence or certificate until such sum has been paid.

Civil proceedings to recover unpaid fees

21. All unpaid sums due by way of, or on account of, any fees payable under these Regulations shall be recoverable as debts due to the Crown.

Waiver, Reduction or Refund of Fees

22. The Licensing Authority may waive payment of, reduce any fee or part of a fee otherwise payable under these Regulations or refund the whole or part of any fee already so paid in exceptional circumstances or in any of the circumstances specified in Schedule 3.

PART IX

REVOCATION, SAVINGS AND TRANSITIONAL PROVISIONS

Revocation and Savings

23.—(1) Subject to paragraph (2), the Regulations specified in Schedule 6 are hereby revoked in so far as they apply in relation wholly or partly to medicinal products for animal use.

(2) Paragraph (1) shall not affect–

(a) any annual fee or part of such a fee under any of the Regulations specified in Schedule 6;

(b) any notice given or any suspension made under the Regulations specified in Schedule 6 and any such notice or suspension shall have effect as if given or made under these Regulations; and

(c) any proceedings constituted under the Regulations specified in Schedule 6 for the recovery of any fees due as debts due to the Crown.

Transitional provisions

24.—(1) Subject to paragraphs (2) and (3), these Regulations shall not apply to any application made before the date these Regulations come into force.

(2) A fee shall be payable in respect of any inspection made or any sample testing required after the date these Regulations come into force in connection with any application made before that date as if these Regulations applied to that application.

(3) Where an application is made before the date these Regulations come into force to review a licence or certificate which is due to expire on or after 1st October 1989 a fee shall be payable in accordance with Part IV of these Regulations in connection with that application within 14 days following written notice from the Licensing Authority.

Kenneth Clarke
Secretary of State for Health

23rd March 1989

Peter Walker
Secretary of State for Wales

20th March 1989

Sanderson of Bowden
Minister of State, Scottish Office

22nd March 1989

In Witness whereof the Official Seal of the Minister of Agriculture, Fisheries and Food is hereunto affixed on 19th March 1989.

(L.S.)

John MacGregor
Minister of Agriculture, Fisheries and Food

Sealed with the Official Seal of the Department of Health and Social Services for Northern Ireland 30th March 1989.

(L.S.)

Zelma I. Davies
Under Secretary

Sealed with the Official Seal of the Department of Agriculture for Northern Ireland 30th March 1989.

(L.S.)

J. C. Chalmers
Under Secretary

We consent,

Kenneth Carlisle
David Maclean
Two of the Lords Commissioners
of Her Majesty's Treasury

20th March 1989

SCHEDULE 1

Regulations 3(a) and (c), 6(a) and 10(a)

CAPITAL FEES FOR APPLICATIONS, VARIATIONS AND RENEWALS OF LICENCES

PART I

INTERPRETATION

1. In this Schedule–

"active ingredient" means the ingredient of a medicinal product in respect of which efficacy is claimed;

"biological medicinal product" includes an antigen, toxin, antitoxin, serum, antiserum or vaccine;

"complex application" means an application, other than a major application, for a product licence or, as the case may be, for a variation to a product licence where the application–

(a) is subject to the procedure laid down in Article 17 of Council Directive 81/851/EEC**(a)** (notification to five or more Member States);

(b) relates to a medicinal product which is intended to be used in accordance with an indication for use in respect of a different species of animal or as treatment for a new medicinal purpose;

(c) relates to a medicinal product containing a new combination of active ingredients which have not previously been included in that combination in a medicinal product in respect of which a product licence for animal use (other than a product licence of right) has previously been granted in the United Kingdom;

(d) relates to a medicinal product containing a new adjuvant or a new excipient;

(e) relates to a medicinal product which is intended to be administered by a route of administration different from that used in the administration of any medicinal product which contains the same active ingredient as the product in question and in respect of which a product licence for animal use (other than a product licence of right) has previously been granted in the United Kingdom;

(f) relates to a sterile medicinal product the manufacture of which involves a method of sterilisation different from that used in the manufacture of any medicinal product which contains the same active ingredient as the product in question and in respect of which a product licence for animal use (other than a product licence of right) has previously been granted in the United Kingdom;

(g) relates to a medicinal product containing an active ingredient the manufacture of which involves a route of synthesis (or, in the case of a medicinal product not synthetically produced, a method of manufacture) different from that used in the manufacture of the active ingredient of any medicinal product which contains the same active ingredient as the product in question and in respect of which a product licence for animal use (other than a product licence of right) has previously been granted in the United Kingdom;

(h) relates to a biological medicinal product containing an active ingredient, the manufacture of which involves a growth substrate different from that used in the manufacture of the active ingredient of any medicinal product which contains the same active ingredient as the product in question and in respect of which a product licence has previously been granted in the United Kingdom;

(i) relates to a medicinal product which is a controlled release preparation and a product licence for animal use (other than a product licence of right) for such a preparation constituting the same active ingredient as the product in question has not previously been granted in the United Kingdom;

(j) relates to a sterile medicinal product the container of which is directly in contact with the medicinal product and is made from different material from the container of any medicinal product which contains the same active ingredient as the product in question and in respect of which a product licence for animal use (other than a product licence of right) has previously been granted in the United Kingdom;

(k) names as manufacturer of the active ingredient of the medicinal product in question a different manufacturer from the manufacturer of the active ingredient of any medicinal product which contains the same active ingredient as the medicinal product in question and in respect of which a product licence for animal use (other than a product licence of right) has previously been granted in the United Kingdom; or

(a) O.J. No. L317, 28.9.81 p.1.

(l) relates to a biological medicinal product containing an active ingredient derived from a strain of micro-organism different from that used in the manufacture of the active ingredient of any medicinal product which contains the same active ingredient as the product in question and in respect of which a product licence has previously been granted in the United Kingdom;

"major application" means an application for a product licence in respect of a medicinal product containing a new active ingredient;

"new active ingredient" means–

(a) an active ingredient that has not previously been included as an active ingredient in a medicinal product in respect of which a product licence for animal use (other than a product licence of right) has previously been granted in the United Kingdom; or

(b) an active ingredient in a medicinal product derived from genetically engineered micro-organisms, recombinant DNA technology or monoclonal antibodies; or

(c) in the case of a biological medicinal product, a vaccine of a particular micro-organism whether in a live or inactivated form, but this does not include a vaccine of a particular micro-organism which is derived from a strain of micro-organism which is antigenetically similar to that used in the manufacture of the active ingredient of a medicinal product in respect of which a product licence (not being a product licence of right) has previously been granted in the United Kingdom;

"new excipient" means any ingredient of a medicinal product, other than an active ingredient, that has not previously been included in a medicinal product–

(a) which is intended to be administered by the same route of administration as the product in question; and

(b) in respect of which a product licence for animal use (other than a product licence of right) has previously been granted in the United Kingdom

except that, in the case of a medicinal product intended to be administered orally, the expression does not include any ingredient specified in any enactment (including an enactment comprised in subordinate legislation) as an approved ingredient or additive–

(i) in food or food products; or

(ii) in animal feedingstuffs where that product is intended for administration after being incorporated in the feedingstuff;

"simple application" means an application for a product licence when the application–

(a) is made by reference to an application for a particular product ("the existing product") in respect of which a product licence for animal use (other than a product licence of right) has previously been granted;

(b) is made by permission of the licence holder for the existing product;

(c) relates to a product which is in all the following respects the same as the existing product–

(i) it contains the same combination of active ingredients;

(ii) it is intended to be used in accordance with the same indications;

(iii) it is intended to be administered by the same route of administration;

(iv) the manufacturer named in the application is the same as the manufacturer of the existing product;

(v) the method of manufacture is the same;

(vi) in the case of a sterile product the method of sterilisation is the same and the container which is directly in contact with the product is made from the same material;

"standard application" means–

(a) any application in respect of a medicinal product for animal use specified in Annex 1 of Council Directive 70/524/EEC**(a)** or made pursuant to the Medicines (Exportation of Specified Veterinary Products) Order 1971**(b)**, which is not a simple application;

(b) any other application which is not a major, complex or simple application.

PART II

CAPITAL FEES FOR APPLICATIONS FOR LICENCES

Product Licences

1. Subject to paragraph 2, the fee payable under regulation 3(a) in connection with an application for a product licence of a kind described in Column 1 of the following Table shall be the fee specified in the corresponding entry in Column 2 of that Table:

(a) O.J. No. L270, 23.11.70 p. 1, as amended by Council Directive 84/587/EEC, O.J. No. L319, 8.12.84 p. 13.
(b) S.I. 1971/1309.

Column 1 *Kind of application*	Column 2 *Appropriate Fee*
1. Major application	1. £8,000
2. Complex application	2. £4,500
3. Standard application	3. £2,000
4. Simple application	4. £500

2. Where a major or a complex application is made by a person who is already the holder of an animal test certificate, in respect of a medicinal product containing the same active ingredient as the medicinal product in respect of which the product licence is applied for, the fee payable under regulation 3(a) in connection with that application shall be reduced by the amount of the fee paid in connection with the application for that certificate.

3.—(1) Subject to sub-paragraphs (2) and (3), where an application for a product licence consists of an application for more than one such licence each relating to a product containing the same active ingredient or combination of ingredients, the fee payable under regulation 3(a) shall be of an amount equal to the aggregate of the amounts payable under paragraph 1 in respect of a separate application for each such licence.

(2) If the application is a major application, the amount payable shall be the amount payable in respect of a major application under paragraph 1 plus–

(a) in respect of each additional product licence applied for which relates to a medicinal product of a different dosage form, the amount payable in respect of a complex application under paragraph 1; and

(b) in respect of each additional product licence applied for which relates to a medicinal product of the same dosage form but of a different strength of active ingredient or different combination of active ingredients, the amount payable in respect of a standard application under paragraph 1.

(3) If the application is a complex application, the amount payable shall be the amount payable in respect of a complex application under paragraph 1 plus–

(a) in respect of each additional product licence applied for which relates to a medicinal product of a different dosage form, the amount payable in respect of a complex application under paragraph 1; and

(b) in respect of each additional product licence applied for which relates to a medicinal product of the same dosage form but of a different strength of active ingredient or different combination of active ingredients, the amount payable in respect of a standard application under paragraph 1.

Manufacturers' Licences

4.—(1) The fee payable under regulation 3(a) in connection with an application for a manufacturer's licence shall be–

(a) in a case to which sub-paragraph (2) below applies, £50; or

(b) in any other case £1,000; and

(c) in either case, if appropriate, a fee calculated in accordance with Schedule 2 in respect of any inspection made in connection with that application.

(2) This sub-paragraph applies to the case of an application for a manufacturer's licence which is limited solely to the manufacture or assembly of–

(a) medicinal products the sale or supply of which do not require a product licence and to which Article 2(2)(i)(e) of the Medicines (Exemption from Licences) (Special and Transitional Cases) Order 1971**(a)** applies; or

(b) emergency vaccines for use in poultry or other animals.

(3) For the purposes of sub-paragraph (2)(b) "emergency vaccines" means (a) no other suitable licensed vaccines are readily available for such use and (b) the vaccines are manufactured or assembled only from material obtained from the particular animal, flock or herd intended to be vaccinated.

Wholesale Dealers' Licences

5. The fee payable under regulation 3(a) in connection with an application for a wholesale dealer's licence shall be £650.

(a) S.I. 1971/1450; the relevant amending instrument is S.I. 1972/1200.

PART III

CAPITAL FEES FOR SAMPLE TESTING IN CONNECTION WITH APPLICATIONS FOR LICENCES

The fee payable under regulation 3(c) in respect of a sample requested by the Licensing Authority to be submitted for testing in connection with an application for a product licence of a kind described in Column 1 of the following Table shall be the fee specified in the corresponding entry in Column 2 of that Table:

Column 1 *Kind of application*	Column 2 *Appropriate Fee*
1. Major application	1. £4,200
2. Complex application	2. £3,700
3. Standard application	3. £3,700
4. Simple application	4. £2,000

PART IV

FEES FOR APPLICATIONS FOR VARIATIONS OF LICENCES OR CERTIFICATES

Product Licences

1. Subject to paragraph 4, the fee payable under regulation 6(a) in connection with an application for variation of a product licence shall be–

(a) in the case of a complex application £600; and

(b) in any other case £200.

Manufacturers' Licences

2. Subject to paragraph 4, the fee payable under regulation 6(a) in connection with an application for variation of a manufacturer's licence shall be–

(a) in the case of a manufacturer's licence referred to in paragraph 4(2) of Part II of this Schedule, £50;

(b) in any other case, £175.

Wholesale Dealers' Licences

3. Subject to paragraph 4, the fee payable under regulation 6(a) in connection with an application for variation of a wholesale dealer's licence shall be £175.

Other Variations

4. The fee payable under regulation 6(a) in connection with an application for variation of a product licence, a manufacturer's licence or a wholesale dealer's licence shall be £50 where–

(a) the variation applied for consists of no more than a change of either or both the name and the address of the holder of the licence; and

(b) in the case of an application for variation of a manufacturer's licence or a wholesale dealer's licence only, any change of address does not involve a change of the site of manufacture or wholesale dealing.

PART V

FEES FOR APPLICATIONS FOR RENEWALS OF LICENCES

Product Licences

1. The fee payable under regulation 10(a) in connection with an application for renewal of a product licence shall be £250.

Manufacturers' Licences

2. The fee payable under regulation 10(a) in connection with an application for renewal of a manufacturer's licence shall be–

(a) in the case of a manufacturer's licence referred to in paragraph 4(2) of Part II of this Schedule, £50;

(b) in any other case, £500.

Wholesale Dealers' Licences

3. The fee payable under regulation 10(a) in connection with an application for renewal of a wholesale dealer's licence shall be £325.

SCHEDULE 2

Regulations 3(b), 6(b), 10(b) and 13

FEES FOR INSPECTIONS

Interpretation

1.—(1) In this Schedule–

"major inspection" means an inspection at a site at which 60 or more relevant persons are employed;

"minor inspection" means an inspection at a site at which fewer than 10 relevant persons are employed;

"relevant person" means any person directly or indirectly engaged in, or assisting in, the manufacture or assembly of medicinal products and also includes any person connected with such production who is involved in management, quality control, site maintenance, packing, storage or distribution;

"standard inspection" means an inspection at a site at which 10 or more, but fewer than 60, relevant persons are employed.

(2) In calculating the number of relevant persons for the purposes of this Schedule, any person partly engaged or assisting in the manufacture or assembly of medicinal products (whether as a part-time employee or by virtue of being only partly employed in such work) shall be included in the calculation but only as a fraction calculated by reference to the amount of time spent by that person engaged or assisting in the manufacture or assembly of medicinal products or, where such a calculation is inappropriate, by reference to the percentage of his job which relates to the manufacture or assembly of such products and, in either case, by comparison with the average working week of a relevant person engaged in full-time employment at the same site.

Fees

2. Subject to paragraphs 3 to 5, the fee payable in respect of an inspection under these Regulations shall be–

(a) except in the case of an inspection falling within sub-paragraphs (b) to (d) below–
  (i) in respect of a minor inspection, £750;
  (ii) in respect of a standard inspection, £1,500;
  (iii) in respect of a major inspection, £3,000;

(b) where the site inspected is wholly or partly concerned with the manufacture of sterile products or the filling of the containers directly in contact with such products–
  (i) in respect of a minor inspection, £1,250;
  (ii) in respect of a standard inspection, £2,500;
  (iii) in respect of a major inspection, £5,000;

(c) except in the case of an inspection falling within sub-paragraph (b) above or sub-paragraph (d) below, where the site inspected is concerned only with the assembly of medicinal products–
  (i) in respect of a minor inspection, £500;
  (ii) in respect of a standard inspection, £1,000;
  (iii) in respect of a major inspection, £2,000;

(d) where the site inspected is limited solely to the manufacture or assembly of–
   (i) medicinal products, the sale or supply of which do not require a product licence and to which Article 2(2)(i)(e) of the Medicines (Exemption from Licences) (Special and Transitional Cases) Order 1971 applies; or
   (ii) emergency vaccines for use in poultry or other animals;

   £50.

(e) For the purposes of sub-paragraph (d)(ii) "emergency vaccines" means (i) no other suitable licensed vaccines are readily available for such use and (ii) the vaccines are manufactured or assembled only from material obtained from the particular animal, flock or herd intended to be vaccinated.

3.—(1) Subject to paragraph (2), unless the applicant or, as the case may be, the holder of the licence establishes that an inspection is a minor inspection or a standard inspection, the fee payable shall be the appropriate fee specified in paragraph 2 above for a major inspection.

(2) If, following an inspection, it becomes apparent that the inspection fell into a different category from that established by the applicant or the holder of the licence, the fee payable under these Regulations in respect of that inspection shall be the fee payable in respect of an inspection falling within the category into which the inspection should have fallen.

4. In the case of an inspection in connection with the grant, variation or renewal of a wholesale dealer's licence or during the currency of such a licence, the fee payable under these Regulations shall be–

(a) except in a case falling within sub-paragraph (b), £650;

(b) where the site is that of a wholesale dealer whose licence is limited to dealing only in medicinal products falling within a description or class of such products specified in an Order made under section 51(1) of the Act, £250.

5. The fee payable in respect of an inspection at a site outside the United Kingdom shall be increased by an amount equal to the travelling and subsistence costs of the inspector relating to the inspection and any additional costs reasonably incurred by him in respect of that inspection as a result of its being at a site outside the United Kingdom (such as interpreter's fees).

Regulation 22

SCHEDULE 3

WAIVER, REDUCTION OR REFUND OF CAPITAL FEES

1. Where the manufacture, assembly, sale or supply of medicinal products of a particular class or description will be, or is likely to be, interrupted for a period, and in consequence thereof the health of animals will be, or is likely to be, put at risk, the Licensing Authority may decide that any fees otherwise payable under these Regulations–

(a) in connection with an application for the grant (variation or renewal) of a product licence relating to a medicinal product falling within that class or description; or

(b) in respect of any inspection made during the currency of such a licence

shall be waived during that particular period or, if the period will, or is likely to, exceed 3 months, during the first 3 months of that period.

2. The Licensing Authority may waive or reduce the payment of any capital fee payable under these Regulations in circumstances where–

(a) in its opinion the interests of human or animal health require a licence or certificate to be granted or an inspection to be made; and

(b) the medicinal product in respect of which an application for a licence or certificate has been made–
   (i) is not intended for sale; or
   (ii) is intended only for use in the treatment of rare conditions or in the treatment of a minor species of animal or as an emergency vaccine.

For the purposes of sub-paragraph (b)(ii) "emergency vaccine" means (i) no other suitable licensed vaccine is readily available and (ii) the vaccine is manufactured or assembled only from material obtained from the particular animal, flock or herd intended to be vaccinated.

3.—(1) Subject to sub-paragraphs (2) to (5), where the Licensing Authority–

(a) is satisfied that the annual turnover (as calculated in accordance with Part I of Schedule 4) of a medicinal product during any calendar year of the first five years of the currency of the product licence, has not exceeded, or is unlikely to exceed, £30,000; and

(b) is of the opinion that the interests of human or animal health require a product licence to be granted any capital fee otherwise payable under these Regulations in connection with an application for a product licence or an inspection during the currency of that licence or a request to submit samples for testing, may be reduced or, if such a fee has already been paid, be refunded in part in proportion to the difference between the maximum turnover in any calendar year (during the first five years of the currency of the licence) and the sum of £30,000.

(2) Before a licence holder pays any reduced fee or receives any refund pursuant to sub-paragraph (1), he shall furnish evidence to the satisfaction of the Licensing Authority of the amount of annual turnover, in respect of the particular medicinal product, in each calendar year of the first five years of the currency of the licence.

(3) Where a reduced fee is determined in accordance with sub-paragraph (1) at the time of application on the basis of the estimated likely maximum turnover of the medicinal product during the first five years of the currency of the licence, any fee so determined shall be regarded as a provisional payment on account.

(4) Where a provisional payment on account is made in accordance with sub-paragraph (3) and subsequently the turnover in any calendar year in the first five years of the currency of the licence exceeds £30,000, the licence holder shall be liable to pay the balance of the full fee otherwise payable under these Regulations.

(5) Where any provisional payment on account is made in accordance with sub-paragraph (3), the reduced fee shall be recalculated in accordance with the provisions of sub-paragraph (1) at the end of five years from the date of the grant of the licence and any difference between the fee so calculated and the provisional payment on account shall be payable by the applicant or, as the case may be, refunded to the applicant by the Licensing Authority.

4. Where an application for the grant or renewal of a product licence is made at the specific written request of the Licensing Authority any fee otherwise payable under these Regulations in connection with that application shall be waived.

5.—(1) Subject to sub-paragraph (2), where an application for a product licence is withdrawn before determination by the Licensing Authority, the following percentage of the fee otherwise payable (under regulation 3(a)) in connection with that application shall be refunded or, if it has not yet been paid, shall be waived–

(a) if the application has been received but no medical, scientific or pharmaceutical assessment thereof has begun, 90%;

(b) except in a case to which paragraph (c) below applies, medical, scientific or pharmaceutical assessment has begun but not been completed, 50%;

(c) if a request for further information in connection with the application has been made by the Licensing Authority under section 44(1) of the Act, 25%.

(2) If an application for a product licence is withdrawn either after medical, scientific and pharmaceutical assessment has been completed or following consideration of that application by a committee established under section 4 of the Act or by the Medicines Commission, no refund or waiver of the fee payable (under regulation 3(a) of these Regulations) in connection with that application shall be made under this paragraph.

(3) Where the same site is inspected at the same time in connection with applications for the grant, variation, or renewal of both a manufacturer's licence and a wholesale dealer's licence or during the currency of both such licences, the fee otherwise payable under these Regulations in respect of the inspection relating to the wholesale dealer's licence shall be waived.

SCHEDULE 4

Regulation 15

ANNUAL FEES FOR PRODUCT LICENCES

PART I

CALCULATION OF TURNOVER

1. In relation to the calculation of turnover in any calendar year in accordance with the provisions of the succeeding paragraphs of this Part of this Schedule, "manufacturers' prices" shall mean, subject to the provisions of paragraph 2, the prices charged by manufacturers to wholesalers, except where medicinal products are supplied by manufacturers direct to retailers, in which case the prices charged by the licence holder may be reduced by such sum as, in the opinion of the Licensing Authority represents the difference between the prices paid by wholesalers and those normally charged by them to retailers according to the practice prevailing during the licence year in question with regard to such products.

2. Where a licence holder sells or supplies medicinal products which he has neither manufactured nor obtained from the manufacturer, in relation to the calculation of turnover in any calendar year in accordance with the provisions of the succeeding paragraphs of this Part of this Schedule "manufacturers' prices" shall mean the prices paid by, or on behalf of, the licence holder for those medicinal products.

3. For the purpose of calculating annual fees for product licences of a particular kind, "turnover" means the gross value at manufacturers' prices of all medicinal products sold or supplied by the applicant in the United Kingdom during the calendar year which ends 15 months before the end of a licence year. For the purposes of this paragraph medicinal products sold or supplied by the licence holder or applicant shall comprise only those products in respect of which a licence is held or for which application for a licence has been made.

4. (a) For the purpose of satisfying the Licensing Authority for the purposes of Part II of this Schedule, an applicant shall state the amount of the turnover, calculated in accordance with the preceding paragraphs of this Part in respect of the calendar year which ends 15 months before the end of the licence year during which the application is made and in respect of each subsequent calendar year which ends 15 months before the end of any subsequent licence year during any part of which licences are held;

(b) where the licence holder fails to furnish evidence of the amount of annual turnover to the satisfaction of the Licensing Authority the Licensing Authority may require the licence holder to furnish an auditor's certificate containing such evidence. If within one month of the date by which such certificate is required to be furnished, or such longer period as the Licensing Authority may allow, the licence holder has failed to furnish such certificate the sum payable by way of fees for the licence year in question shall be calculated as provided for in paragraph 7 of Part II of this Schedule or shall be such lesser sum as the Licensing Authority shall specify in a notice served on the licence holder.

5. Where an applicant for a licence was not dealing in medicinal products during the calendar year which ends 15 months before the end of the licence year in which the application is made, but has taken over an existing business or concern, whether by purchase or merger or otherwise, the gross value of sales of that business or concern during the calendar year which ends 15 months before the end of the licence year in which the application is made may be treated as the gross value of sales for the purpose of calculating the turnover of that business or concern.

PART II

CALCULATION OF ANNUAL FEES

1. Subject to the provisions of these Regulations annual fees shall be payable at the basic rate of £250 or 0.4% of turnover, whichever is the greater.

2. For the purpose of calculating annual turnover the provisions of Part I of this Schedule shall apply.

3. The amount payable by way of annual fees in accordance with this Schedule shall, when calculated on the basis of turnover, be rounded up to the nearest £10.

4. Where an application is made by an applicant who was not dealing in medicinal products during the calendar year which begins 15 months before the end of the licence year in which the application was made, he shall be liable to pay in respect of the year in which the licence is granted the sum of £250 until such time as the fee calculated in accordance with paragraph (1) is greater than that sum.

5. Where a licence holder has duly paid an annual fee of the appropriate kind at the rate applicable for any licence year, no additional annual fee shall be payable by that person for that year in respect of any application made earlier in that licence year.

6. Where applications are made on more than one occasion in the same licence year for product licences of the same kind, one annual fee only shall be payable which shall be regarded as having been paid in respect of all such applications made in that licence year.

7. Where in any licence year the licence holder does not submit evidence of turnover in relation to the relevant calendar year to the satisfaction of the Licensing Authority the annual fee payable by him in respect of that licence year shall be the sum of £10,000 together with an additional £2,000 for each description of medicinal product in respect of which a licence is held by the licence holder.

8. Where the holder of, or an applicant for a product licence is liable to pay an annual fee and his turnover for the purpose of calculating such a fee exceeds £30 million, one half of such turnover which is the excess of the said amount of £30 million shall be deducted from such turnover for the purpose of calculating the said annual fee.

PART III

LESSER AMOUNTS OF FEES

1. Where the holder of a product licence sells or supplies emergency vaccines for use in poultry or other animals, the annual fee payable shall, instead of the amount otherwise payable under this Schedule, be 0.4% of turnover, calculated in accordance with paragraph 2 of Part I rounded up to the nearest £1, except that the minimum sum payable under this provision shall not be less than £10.

2. For the purposes of paragraph 1, "emergency vaccines" means (a) no other suitable licensed vaccines are readily available for such use and (b) the vaccines are manufactured or assembled only from material obtained from the particular animal, flock or herd intended to be vaccinated.

SCHEDULE 5

Regulation 15(3)

ADJUSTMENT OR REFUND OF ANNUAL FEES

1. Where an annual fee has been paid in accordance with these Regulations and the Licensing Authority is subsequently satisfied as to the gross value of sales in accordance with paragraph 4(a) of Part I of Schedule 4 the difference between the amount so paid and the annual fee so calculated may be refunded by the Licensing Authority.

2. Where, after payment of any annual fee payable in accordance with the provisions of these Regulations, the licence in respect of which such fee has been paid is revoked or expires on a date earlier than the date of expiry stated in the licence, the Licensing Authority may refund to the applicant the whole or any part of the difference between such annual fee as has been paid and the amount of the annual fee payable on the basis of the actual duration of the licence up to the date of such revocation or expiry.

3. In addition to the refunds (if any) payable under the provisions of the preceding paragraph, where the date of revocation or expiry as aforesaid is not an anniversary of the date on which the licence commenced and does not fall within a period of 3 months before any such anniversary, the Licensing Authority may refund to the applicant a sum equivalent to the fee for the appropriate portion of the licence year during which the said licence is not in force.

4. Where, after the payment of the whole or part of the fees in respect of a licence, the application is withdrawn before determination, the Licensing Authority may at the time of such withdrawal refund to the applicant the whole or any part of the fees paid.

5. Any sums payable to an applicant by way of refund of any fees under the provisions of this Schedule may be treated as having been paid on account of any other fee which the applicant is liable to pay (whether by instalments or otherwise) under the provisions of these Regulations.

Regulation 23(1)

SCHEDULE 6

REVOCATIONS

Regulations revoked	*Reference*
The Medicines (Fees) Regulations 1978	S.I. 1978/1121
The Medicines (Fees) Amendment Regulations 1979	S.I. 1979/899
The Medicines (Fees) Amendment Regulations 1980	S.I. 1980/16
The Medicines (Fees) Amendment (No. 2) Regulations 1980	S.I. 1980/1126
The Medicines (Fees) Amendment Regulations 1982	S.I. 1982/1121
The Medicines (Fees) Amendment Regulations 1983	S.I. 1983/1731
The Medicines (Fees) Amendment Regulations 1985	S.I. 1985/1231
The Medicines (Fees) Amendment Regulations 1987	S.I. 1987/1439

EXPLANATORY NOTE

(This note is not part of the Regulations)

These Regulations which replace the Medicines (Fees) Regulations 1978 (as amended) prescribe fees in connection with applications and inspections relating to licences and certificates granted under the Medicines Act 1968 in so far as they apply to medicinal products for animal use only.

The Regulations provide for increased fees to be payable for applications for the grant of product licences, manufacturers' licences, wholesale dealers' licences, animal test certificates and export certificates (Part II).

The Regulations also provide for increased fees to be payable for applications for variations of such licences or certificates (Part III) and for renewal thereof (Part IV). The Regulations provide for increased fees to be payable in respect of inspections of sites carried out in connection with such applications for such licences or certificates and during the currency thereof (Part V).

In addition the Regulations provide for increased annual fees to be payable, calculated on the basis of annual turnover, in connection with applications for the grant or renewal of any product licence (Part VII).

Administrative provisions (Part VIII) deal with time of payment and waiver or refund of fees in specified circumstances.

Part IX of the Regulations deals with revocations, savings and transitional provisions.

The only change of substance is the introduction of a fee to be payable in respect of the testing of samples where batch control sample testing is a condition of the licence (Part VI).

STATUTORY INSTRUMENTS

1989 No. 590

HOUSING, ENGLAND AND WALES

The Rent Officers (Additional Functions) Order 1989

Made - - - -	*28th March 1989*
Coming into force -	*1st April 1989*

The Secretary of State for the Environment, as respects England, and the Secretary of State for Wales, as respects Wales, in exercise of the powers conferred upon them by section 121 of the Housing Act 1988**(a)**, and of all other powers enabling them in that behalf, hereby make the following Order, a draft of which has been laid before and approved by a resolution of each House of Parliament–

Citation and commencement

1. This Order may be cited as the Rent Officers (Additional Functions) Order 1989 and shall come into force on 1st April 1989.

Interpretation

2.—(1) In this Order, unless the context otherwise requires–

"determination" means a determination (including an interim and a further determination) in accordance with Schedule 1 to this Order;

"dwelling" has the same meaning as in the Social Security Act 1986**(b)**;

"excluded tenancy" means a tenancy of a category listed in Schedule 2 to this Order;

"local authority" has the same meaning as it has in the Social Security Act 1986 in relation to England and Wales;

"occupier" means a person (whether or not identified by name) who is stated, in the application for a determination, to occupy the dwelling;

"rent" has the same meaning as in section 14 of the Housing Act 1988, except that the reference to the dwelling-house in subsection (4) shall be construed as a reference to the dwelling;

"size criteria" means the standards relating to bedrooms and rooms suitable for living in specified in Schedule 3 to this Order;

"tenancy" includes "licence" and references to a tenant, a landlord or any other expression appropriate to a tenancy shall be construed accordingly.

(2) In this Order any reference to a notice or application is to a notice or application in writing.

Additional Functions

3.—(1) Where, in connection with housing benefit and rent allowance subsidy, a local

---

(a) 1988 c.50.
(b) 1986 c.50.

authority applies to a rent officer for determinations relating to a tenancy of a dwelling, the rent officer shall (subject to article 5) make the determinations and give notice in accordance with Schedule 1 to this Order.

(2) If a rent officer needs further information in order to make a determination, he shall serve notice on the local authority requesting that information and until he receives it paragraph (1) shall not apply to the making of that determination.

4. If, within the period of 10 weeks beginning with the date on which the local authority was given notice of a determination, the local authority applies (in connection with housing benefit and rent allowance subsidy) to a rent officer for a re-determination, a rent officer shall (subject to article 5) make the re-determination and give notice in accordance with Schedule 4 to this Order and a rent officer whose advice is sought as provided for in that Schedule shall give that advice.

5.—(1) No determination or re-determination shall be made if the application for it is withdrawn or relates to an excluded tenancy.

(2) No determination or re-determination shall be made under paragraph 1 of Schedule 1 (or that paragraph as applied by Schedule 4) if the tenancy is an assured tenancy or an assured agricultural occupancy and–

(a) the rent payable under the tenancy on the date the application for the determination (or, as the case may be, re-determination) was received was an amount determined under section 22 of the Housing Act 1988, or

(b) the rent so payable on that date was an amount determined under section 14 of that Act and that rent took effect within the period of 12 months ending with the date the application was received.

Nicholas Ridley
28th March 1989 Secretary of State for the Environment

Peter Walker
23rd March 1989 Secretary of State for Wales

SCHEDULE 1

DETERMINATIONS

Rent Determinations

1.—(1) The rent officer shall determine whether, in his opinion, the rent payable under the tenancy of the dwelling at the time the application for the determination is made is significantly higher than the rent which the landlord might reasonably be expected to obtain under the tenancy at that time, having regard to the level of rent under similar tenancies of similar dwellings in the locality (or as similar as regards tenancy, dwelling and locality as is reasonably practicable), but on the assumption that no person who would have been entitled to housing benefit had sought or is seeking the tenancy.

(2) If the rent officer determines under sub-paragraph (1) that the rent is significantly higher, the rent officer shall also determine the rent which the landlord might reasonably be expected to obtain under the tenancy at the time the application for a determination is made, having regard to the same matter and on the same assumption as in sub-paragraph (1).

Size and Rent Determinations

2.—(1) The rent officer shall determine whether the dwelling exceeds the size criteria for its occupiers.

(2) If the rent officer determines that the dwelling exceeds the size criteria, the rent officer shall also determine the rent which a landlord might reasonably be expected to obtain, at the time the application for the determination is made, for a tenancy which is similar to the tenancy of the

dwelling, on the same terms (other than the term relating to the amount of rent) and of a dwelling which is in the same locality as the dwelling, but which–

(a) accords with the size criteria for the occupiers;

(b) is in a reasonable state of repair, and

(c) corresponds in other respects, in the rent officer's opinion, as closely as is reasonably practicable to the dwelling.

(3) When making a determination under paragraph 2(2), the rent officer shall have regard to the same matter and make the same assumption as in paragraph 1(1), except that in judging the similarity of other tenancies and dwellings the comparison shall be with the tenancy of the second dwelling referred to in paragraph 2(2) and the assumption shall be made in relation to that tenancy.

Services Determinations

3.—(1) Where the rent officer makes a determination under paragraph 1(2) or 2(2), he shall also determine whether, in his opinion, any of the rent is fairly attributable to the provision of services which are ineligible to be met by housing benefit and, if so, the amount which in his opinion is so attributable (except where he considers the amount is negligible).

(2) In sub-paragraph (1) "rent" means the rent determined under paragraph 1(2) or 2(2); and "services" means services performed or facilities (including the use of furniture) provided for, or rights made available to, the tenant.

Interim and Further Determinations

4. If notice of a determination under paragraph 1 or 3 is not given to the local authority within the 5 day period mentioned in paragraph 5(a) solely because the rent officer intends to arrange an inspection of the dwelling before making such a determination, the rent officer shall make both an interim determination and a further determination.

Notifications

5. The rent officer shall give notice to the local authority of a determination–

(a) except in the case of a further determination, within the period of 5 working days beginning with the date on which the rent officer received the application or, where the rent officer requests further information under article 3(2), with the date on which he received the information, or as soon as practicable after that period,

(b) in the case of a further determination within the period of 20 working days beginning with the date on which notice of the interim determination was given to the local authority, or as soon as practicable after that period.

6.—(1) If the rent officer becomes aware that the tenancy is an excluded tenancy, the rent officer shall give the local authority notice that it is such a tenancy.

(2) If the rent officer is precluded by article 5(2) from making a determination or a re-determination under paragraph 1 (or that paragraph as applied by Schedule 4), the rent officer shall give the local authority notice of the rent determined by the rent assessment committee.

SCHEDULE 2

EXCLUDED TENANCIES

1. A tenancy for which a rent officer has made a determination (other than an interim determination) within the 12 months ending on the date the rent officer received the application for a new determination (or a tenancy of the same dwelling on terms which are substantially the same, other than the term relating to the amount of rent, as the terms of that tenancy were at the time of the determination) unless since the earlier application for a determination was made–

(a) the number of occupiers of the dwelling has changed,

(b) there has been a substantial change in the condition of the dwelling (including the making of improvements) or the terms of the tenancy (other than a term relating to rent), or

(c) there has been a rent increase under a term of the tenancy which was in effect when the earlier application for the determination was made (and that determination was not made under paragraph 1(2) or 2(2) of Schedule 1 and any re-determination of that determination under Schedule 4 was not made under either of those sub-paragraphs as applied by Schedule 4), or under a term substantially the same as such a term.

2. An assured tenancy or an assured agricultural occupancy, where the landlord is a registered housing association within the meaning of the Housing Associations Act 1985**(a)**, the Housing Corporation or Housing for Wales, unless the local authority states in the application for determinations that the circumstances set out in regulation 11(2)(a) or (c) of the Housing Benefit (General) Regulations 1987**(b)** exist.

3.—(1) A tenancy entered into before the relevant date where there is, current on that date, a benefit period (within the meaning of regulation 66 of the Housing Benefit (General) Regulations 1987) relating to a claim for housing benefit in relation to the tenancy–

(a) unless and until a change of circumstances takes effect (within the meaning of regulation 68 of those Regulations), provided it takes effect after 16th April 1989, or

(b) until the benefit period ends (or, if it ends before 17th April 1989, the next benefit period ends).

(2) In sub-paragraph (1) "relevant date" means–

(a) except were (b) applies, 1st April 1989;

(b) in the case of a tenancy where one of the occupiers of the dwelling immediately before 10 April 1989 is in receipt of income support under the Social Security Act 1986 and whose applicable amount immediately before that date is calculated in accordance with regulation 20 or regulation 71(1)(b) of, or paragraph 17 of Schedule 7 to, the Income Support (General) Regulations 1987 **(c)**, 10th April 1989.

4. A tenancy entered into before 15th January 1989.

5. A regulated tenancy within the meaning of the Rent Act 1977**(d)**.

6. A housing association tenancy within the meaning of Part VI of that Act.

7. A protected occupancy or statutory tenancy within the meaning of the Rent (Agriculture) Act 1976**(e)**

8. A tenancy at a low rent within the meaning of Part I of the Landlord and Tenant Act 1954**(f)**.

SCHEDULE 3

SIZE CRITERIA

1. One bedroom shall be allowed for each of the following categories of occupiers (and each occupier shall come within only the first category for which he is eligible)–

(a) a married couple or an unmarried couple (within the meaning of Part II of the Social Security Act 1986),

(b) an adult,

(c) two children of the same sex,

(d) two children who are less than ten years old,

(e) a child.

2. The number of rooms (excluding any allowed as a bedroom under paragraph 1) suitable for living in allowed are–

(a) if there are less than four occupiers, one,

(b) if there are more than three and less than seven occupiers, two,

(c) in any other case, three.

SCHEDULE 4

RE-DETERMINATIONS

1. Schedules 1 to 3 (except paragraph 4 of Schedule 1) shall apply in relation to a re-determination as they apply to a determination, subject to the following–

(a) 1985 c.69.
(b) S.I. 1987/1971; relevant amending instrument is S.I. 1989/566.
(c) S.I. 1987/1967; relevant amending instruments are S.I. 1988/663 and 1445.
(d) 1977 c.42.
(e) 1976 c.80.
(f) 1954 c.56.

(a) references in Schedule 1 to the time of an application for a determination shall be references to the time of the application for the original determination, and

(b) for sub-paragraphs (a) and (b) of paragraph 5 of Schedule 1 there shall be substituted "within the period of 20 working days beginning with the date of receipt of the application for a re-determination, or as soon as is reasonably practicable after that period.".

2. The rent officer making the re-determination shall seek and have regard to the advice of one or two other rent officers in relation to the re-determination.

EXPLANATORY NOTE

(This note is not part of the Order)

This Order confers functions on rent officers in connection with housing benefit and rent allowance subsidy. Article 3 provides that where a local authority applies to a rent officer for determinations relating to a tenancy or a licence of a dwelling, the rent officer must make the determinations (and give notice to the local authority) in accordance with Schedule 1 to the Order. The determinations relate to the level of rent, the size of the dwelling and rent attributable to the provision of services. Article 4 provides for a rent officer, with the advice of one or two other rent officers, to make a re-determination if a local authority applies for one.

Article 5 prevents determinations and re-determinations being made if the tenancy or licence is one of those described in Schedule 2 to the Order or if the application is withdrawn; and certain determinations and re-determinations cannot be made if the tenancy or licence is an assured tenancy or agricultural occupancy and the circumstances are those described in article 5(2).

STATUTORY INSTRUMENTS

1989 No. 591

CONSUMER CREDIT

The Consumer Credit (Cancellation Notices and Copies of Documents) (Amendment) Regulations 1989

Made - - - -	*3rd April 1989*
Laid before Parliament	*10th April 1989*
Coming into force	*3rd May 1989*

The Secretary of State, in exercise of the powers conferred on him by sections 180(3) and 182(2) of the Consumer Credit Act 1974(**a**) and of all other powers enabling him in that behalf, hereby makes the following Regulations:

1. These Regulations may be cited as the Consumer Credit (Cancellation Notices and Copies of Documents) (Amendment) Regulations 1989 and shall come into force on 3rd May 1989.

2. The Consumer Credit (Cancellation Notices and Copies of Documents) Regulations 1983(**b**) are hereby amended in regulation 11 by the addition of the following paragraph–

"(h) in the case of an unexecuted or executed agreement where the prospective regulated agreement or regulated agreement as the case may be is to be or is secured on land, any document referred to in the unexecuted agreement or executed agreement as the case may be in a case where the debtor or hirer has earlier been supplied with a copy of that document in an identical form by virtue of any requirement of the Act."

Francis Maude
Parliamentary Under-Secretary of State,
3rd April 1989 Department of Trade and Industry

EXPLANATORY NOTE

(This note is not part of the Regulations)

These Regulations amend the Consumer Credit (Cancellation Notices and Copies of Documents) Regulations 1983 by providing that further copies of a document referred to in an executed or unexecuted agreement secured or to be secured on land need not be provided in a case where the debtor or hirer has already been supplied with a copy of that document in an identical form.

(**a**) 1974 c.39.
(**b**) S.I. 1983/1557, to which there are amendments not relevant to these Regulations.

STATUTORY INSTRUMENTS

1989 No. 596

CONSUMER CREDIT

The Consumer Credit (Total Charge for Credit and Rebate on Early Settlement) (Amendment) Regulations 1989

Made - - - -	*3rd April 1989*
Laid before Parliament	*14th April 1989*
Coming into force	*30th June 1989*

The Secretary of State, in exercise of his powers under sections 20, 95 and 182(2) of the Consumer Credit 1974(**a**) and of all other powers enabling him in that behalf, hereby makes the following Regulations:

1. These Regulations may be cited as the Consumer Credit (Total Charge for Credit and Rebate on Early Settlement) (Amendment) Regulations 1989 and shall come into force on 30th June 1989.

2. The Consumer Credit (Total Charge for Credit) Regulations 1980(**b**) are hereby amended–

(a) in regulation 1(2), in the definition of "transaction", by inserting after the words "any contract for the provision of security relating to the agreement" the words ", any credit brokerage contract relating to the agreement"; and

(b) in regulation 5(1)(d), by inserting, after the words "any charge", the words "(other than a fee or commission charged by a credit-broker)".

3. The Consumer Credit (Rebate on Early Settlement) Regulations 1983(**c**) are hereby amended in regulation 3(2) by adding after subparagraph (c) the following–

"(d) any fee or commission paid by the debtor or a relative of his under a credit brokerage contract relating to the agreement."

Francis Maude
Parliamentary Under-Secretary of State,
Department of Trade and Industry

3rd April 1989

(**a**) 1974 c.39.
(**b**) S.I. 1980/51, to which there are amendments not relevant to these Regulations.
(**c**) S.I. 1983/1562.

EXPLANATORY NOTE

(This note is not part of the Regulations)

These Regulations amend the Consumer Credit (Total Charge for Credit) Regulations 1980 by requiring the inclusion in the calculation of the total charge for credit fees payable by the debtor under a credit brokerage agreement relating to an actual or prospective consumer credit agreement.

They also amend the Consumer Credit (Rebate on Early Settlement) Regulations 1983 to provide that a broker's fee which is included in the total charge for credit by virtue of the above amendment shall not be taken into account in calculation of any rebate payable by the creditor on early settlement by the debtor.

STATUTORY INSTRUMENTS

1989 No. 597

EDUCATION, ENGLAND AND WALES
EDUCATION, SCOTLAND

The Education (Listed Bodies) (Amendment) Order 1989

Made - - - - - -	*4th April 1989*
Coming into force	*14th April 1989*

In exercise of the powers conferred by section 216(2) of the Education Reform Act 1988(**a**) the Secretary of State for Education and Science hereby makes the following Order:

1. This Order may be cited as the Education (Listed Bodies) (Amendment) Order 1989 and shall come into force on 14th April 1989.

2. To the list of bodies in Part 1 of the Schedule to the Education (Listed Bodies) Order 1988(**b**) there shall be added (at their appropriate places in alphabetical order) the bodies named Harper Adams Agricultural College and the Royal Northern College of Music, being bodies which appear to the Secretary of State to fall within section 216(3) of the Education Reform Act 1988.

Kenneth Baker
4th April 1989 Secretary of State for Education and Science

(**a**) 1988 c.40.
(**b**) S.I. 1988/2034.

EXPLANATORY NOTE

(This note is not part of the Order)

This Order adds Harper Adams Agricultural College and the Royal Northern College of Music to the list of bodies in the Education (Listed Bodies) Order 1988. A body so listed is not a recognised body within section 214(2)(a) or (b) of the Education Reform Act 1988 but either

(a) provides any course which is in preparation for a degree to be granted by such a recognised body and is approved by or on behalf of that body; or

(b) is a constituent college, school or hall or other institution of a university which is such a recognised body.

A recognised body within section 214(2)(a) or (b) of the 1988 Act is one which is authorised by Royal Charter or Act of Parliament to grant degrees or one which is permitted by a body so authorised to act on its behalf in the granting of degrees. Such degrees are "recognised awards" and the provision in section 214(1) of that Act, which makes it an offence to grant, offer to grant or issue any invitation relating to certain unrecognised degrees and awards, does not apply to them.

STATUTORY INSTRUMENTS

1989 No. 598

EDUCATION, ENGLAND AND WALES
EDUCATION, SCOTLAND

The Education (Recognised Awards) (Amendment) Order 1989

Made - - - -	*4th April 1989*
Coming into force	*14th April 1989*

In exercise of the powers conferred by section 214(2)(c) and (3) of the Education Reform Act 1988(**a**) the Secretary of State for Education and Science hereby makes the following Order:

1. This Order may be cited as the Education (Recognised Awards) (Amendment) Order 1989 and shall come into force on 14th April 1989.

2. At the end of the Schedule to the Education (Recognised Awards) Order 1988(**b**) there shall be inserted the following award–

"Degree of Barrister-at-Law	Benchers of the Honorable Society of the Inn of Court of Northern Ireland".

Kenneth Baker
4th April 1989 Secretary of State for Education and Science

EXPLANATORY NOTE

(This note is not part of the Order)

This Order adds the Degree of Barrister-at-Law awarded by the Benchers of the Honorable Society of the Inn of Court of Northern Ireland to the list of awards contained in the Education (Recognised Awards) Order 1988. That Order lists particular awards granted by certain persons which are recognised awards for the purposes of section 214 of the Education Reform Act 1988. Recognised awards are not awards of the kind referred to in section 214(1), which makes it an offence to grant, offer to grant, or issue any invitation relating to certain unrecognised degrees and awards.

(**a**) 1988 c.40.
(**b**) S.I. 1988/2035.

STATUTORY INSTRUMENTS

1989 No. 602 (S.68)

NATIONAL HEALTH SERVICE, SCOTLAND

The National Health Service (General Dental Services) (Scotland) Amendment Regulations 1989

Made - - - -	*4th April 1989*
Laid before Parliament	*7th April 1989*
Coming into force	*1st May 1989*

The Secretary of State, in exercise of powers conferred on him by sections 25(1), (2) and (5), 105 and 108(1) of the National Health Service (Scotland) Act 1978(**a**) and of all other powers enabling him in that behalf, hereby makes the following Regulations:

Citation and commencement

1. These Regulations may be cited as the National Health Service (General Dental Services) (Scotland) Amendment Regulations 1989 and shall come into force on 1st May 1989.

Amendment of Regulations

2. Regulation 36 of the National Health Service (General Dental Services) (Scotland) Regulations 1974(**b**) (amount and time of payments in consequence of suspension) shall be amended as follows:–

(a) in paragraph (1)(a)(i) for "£1,935" there shall be substituted "£2,243";

(b) in paragraph (1)(a)(ii) for "£967" there shall be substituted "£1,121";

(c) in paragraph (1)(b)(i) for "£967" there shall be substituted "£1,121";

(d) in paragraph (1)(b)(ii) for "£1,935" there shall be substituted "£2,243"; and

(e) in paragraph (2) for "£107,103" in both places where it occurs there shall be substituted "£117,689".

Michael B. Forsyth
Parliamentary Under Secretary of State,
Scottish Office

St. Andrew's House, Edinburgh
4th April 1989

(**a**) 1978 c.29; section 25(2) was amended by S.I. 1981/432; section 25(5) was added by section 16(a) of the Health and Social Services and Social Security Adjudications Act 1983 (c.41) ("the 1983 Act"); section 105, which was amended by the Health Services Act 1980 (c.53), Schedule 6, paragraph 5 and Schedule 7, paragraph 24 and by the 1983 Act, Schedule 9, contains provisions relevant to the making of Regulations. Section 108(1) contains definitions of ‹prescribed' and ‹regulations' relevant to the exercise of the statutory powers under which these Regulations are made.

(**b**) S.I. 1974/505; relevant amending instrument is S.I. 1987/1634.

EXPLANATORY NOTE

(This note is not part of the Regulations)

These Regulations amend the National Health Service (General Dental Services) (Scotland) Regulations 1974, which provide for the arrangements under which dentists provide general dental services under the National Health Service in Scotland.

These Regulations increase the amounts of and the amounts used in calculating payments to dentists during periods when their registration under the Dentists Act 1984 (c.24) is suspended by an interim suspension order or by a direction or order of the Health Committee.

STATUTORY INSTRUMENTS

1989 No. 603

TOWN AND COUNTRY PLANNING, ENGLAND AND WALES

The Town and Country Planning General Development (Amendment) Order 1989

Made - - - -	*4th April 1989*
Laid before Parliament	*10th April 1989*
Coming into force -	*1st May 1989*

The Secretary of State for the Environment, as respects England, and the Secretary of State for Wales, as respects Wales, in exercise of the powers conferred on them by sections 24 and 287(3) of the Town and Country Planning Act 1971**(a)** and all other powers enabling them in that behalf, hereby make the following Order–

1. This Order may be cited as the Town and Country Planning General Development (Amendment) Order 1989 and shall come into force on 1st May 1989.

2. The Town and Country Planning General Development Order 1988**(b)** is hereby amended as follows–

(1) For article 1(4) (interpretation) there shall be substituted the following paragraph–

"(4) References to land used for a specified purpose do not include references to land which is being used in contravention of Part III of the Act or in contravention of previous planning control".

(2) In article 1(6) after the words "National Parks and adjoining land" there shall be inserted "and the Broads".

(3) In Schedule 1 Part 1 (National Parks, areas of outstanding natural beauty and conservation areas etc), there shall be inserted at the end–

"(e) the Broads."

(4) In Schedule 1 Part 2 (National Parks and adjoining land etc) in paragraph (a) after the words "In England," there shall be inserted the words "the Broads or".

(5) In Schedule 2 Part 1 (development within the curtilage of a dwellinghouse)–

(a) for paragraphs A.1(b) to (d) in Class A there shall be substituted the following paragraphs–

"(b) the part of the building enlarged, improved or altered would exceed in height the highest part of the roof of the original dwelling;

(a) 1971 c.78; there are amendments to section 24 not relevant to this Order.
(b) S.I. 1988/1813.

(c) the part of the building enlarged, improved or altered would be nearer to any highway which bounds the curtilage of the dwellinghouse than–

(i) the part of the original dwellinghouse nearest to that highway; or

(ii) 20 metres

whichever is the nearest to the highway;

(d) the part of the building enlarged, improved or altered would be within 2 metres of the boundary of the curtilage of the dwellinghouse and would exceed 4 metres in height;";

(b) in paragraph A.3(a)(ii) for the word "is" there shall be substituted the words "would be";

(c) in paragraph B.1(d)(ii) after the words "more than 70" there shall be inserted the word "cubic";

(d) in paragraphs E, E.2 and F after the words "purpose incidental to the enjoyment of the dwellinghouse" there shall be inserted the words "as such".

(6) In Schedule 2 Part 4 (temporary buildings and uses) in paragraph B.2 paragraph (c) (clay pigeon shooting) shall be deleted.

(7) In Schedule 2 Part 6 (agricultural buildings and operations) in paragraph A.2(2) after the words "In the case of article 1(6) land, development consisting of the erection, extension or alteration of a building" there shall be inserted the words "or the formation or alteration of a private way" and after the words "siting, design and external appearance of the building" in paragraph A.2(2)(b) there shall be inserted the words "and the siting and means of construction of the private way".

(8) In Schedule 2 Part 23 (removal of material from mineral-working deposits) for paragraph C.1(b) there shall be substituted the following paragraph–

"(b) the deposit covers a ground area exceeding 2 hectares, unless the deposit contains no mineral or other material which was deposited on the land more than 5 years before the development; or".

(9) In Schedule 5 Part 1 (certificates under section 27 of the Act etc) in Certificate D for the words "at the beginning of the period of 21 days beginning with the date of the application/appeal*" there shall be substituted the words "at the beginning of the period of 21 days ending with the date of the application/appeal*".

(10) In Schedule 5 Part 2 (notice under section 27 of the Act) and Part 3 (notice of appeal under sections 27 and 36 of the Act)–

(a) after the words "(*to be published in a local newspaper or to be served on an owner**" there shall be inserted the words "*or agricultural tenant‡*";

(b) after the words "Any owner*" there shall be inserted the words "/agricultural tenant‡†";

(c) after the definition of "owner" the following definition shall be inserted–

‡"agricultural tenant" means a tenant of an agricultural holding.

3. The Town and Country Planning General Development (Amendment) Order 1988**(a)** is hereby revoked.

Nicholas Ridley
Secretary of State for the Environment

3rd April 1989

Signed by authority of the Secretary of State

Ian Grist
Parliamentary Under-Secretary of State,
Welsh Office

4th April 1989

(a) S.I. 1988/2091.

EXPLANATORY NOTE

(This note is not part of the Order)

This Order makes various minor amendments to the Town and Country Planning General Development Order 1988 (the 1988 Order). It supersedes the Town and Country Planning General Development (Amendment) Order 1988, which is consequently repealed.

This Order introduces into Schedule 1 to the 1988 Order references to the Broads, as defined in section 290 of the Town and Country Planning Act 1971. The definition was inserted by the Norfolk and Suffolk Broads Act 1988 (c.4).

The Order also makes minor changes to the interpretation provisions of the 1988 Order and to the categories of permitted development in Schedule 2 to the 1988 Order, including in particular–

(a) the widening of the circumstances in which minor extensions of residential buildings are permitted (article 2(5));

(b) the extension of permitted development rights for clay pigeon shooting from 14 to 28 days a year, (article 2(6));

(c) changes to the classes relating to agricultural development in Schedule 2, Part 6 to the 1988 Order and mineral tipping (Schedule 2, Part 23 to the 1988 Order) (articles 2(7) and (8)).

Minor changes are also made to the prescribed forms in Schedule 5 to the 1988 Order.

STATUTORY INSTRUMENTS

1989 No. 604

TELEGRAPHS

The Wireless Telegraphy Apparatus (Low Power Devices) (Exemption) Regulations 1989

Made - - - -	*4th April 1989*
Laid before Parliament	*7th April 1989*
Coming into force	*1st May 1989*

The Secretary of State, in exercise of the powers conferred by sections 1 and 3 of the Wireless Telegraphy Act 1949(**a**) ("the 1949 Act") and now vested in him(**b**), the power conferred on him by section 84 of the Telecommunications Act 1984(**c**) ("the 1984 Act"), and of all other powers enabling him in that behalf, hereby makes the following Regulations:–

Citation and Commencement

1. These Regulations may be cited as the Wireless Telegraphy Apparatus (Low Power Devices) (Exemption) Regulations 1989 and shall come into force on 1st May 1989.

Interpretation

2. In these Regulations –

"ERP" means effective radiated power, as defined in the Radio Regulations;

"EIRP" means equivalent isotropically radiated power, as defined in the Radio Regulations;

"field strength" means the magnitude of a component of specified polarisation of the electric or magnetic field, and a reference to the field strength of any signal means the field strength of that signal when measured at a distance of 10 metres;

"the Radio Regulations" means the 1982 edition of the Radio Regulations, as revised in 1985, 1986 and 1988, annexed to the International Telecommunication Convention 1982(**d**) pursuant to Articles 43 and 83 of that Convention; and

"relevant apparatus" means wireless telegraphy apparatus or apparatus designed or adapted for use in connection with wireless telegraphy apparatus.

Exemption

3. Subject to regulation 4, and except as provided for in regulation 5, the establishment, installation and use of any station or apparatus for wireless telegraphy of a description set out in the Schedule hereto (hereinafter referred to as a "relevant low power device") are hereby exempted from the provisions of section 1(1) of the 1949 Act.

(**a**) 1949 c.54. (**b**) Post Office Act 1969 (c.48), section 3; S.I. 1969/1369, article 3, 1969/1371, article 2, and 1974/691, article 2. (**c**) 1984 c.12. (**d**) Cmnd. 9557.

Terms, provisions and limitations

4. The exemption provided for in regulation 3 shall be subject to the terms, provisions and limitations that –

(a) the relevant apparatus comprised in the relevant low power device shall be for the time being approved under section 84 of the 1984 Act; and

(b) the relevant low power device shall not –

(i) infringe any requirements for the time being applied to it by or under any enactment for the purpose of preventing it from causing interference with any wireless telegraphy; or

(ii) cause undue interference with any wireless telegraphy.

Exceptions

5. The exemption provided for in regulation 3 shall not extend to any station or apparatus for wireless telegraphy the establishment, installation or use of which is exempted from the provisions of section 1(1) of the 1949 Act by –

(a) the Wireless Telegraphy (Exemption) Regulations 1980(**a**);

(b) the Wireless Telegraphy (Broadcast Licence Charges and Exemption) Regulations 1984(**b**); or

(c) the Wireless Telegraphy Apparatus (Receivers) (Exemption) Regulations 1989(**c**).

Restrictions on use

6. Where the Secretary of State has reasonable cause to believe that a relevant low power device is causing undue interference with any wireless telegraphy, any person who is in possession or control of that device shall on the demand in that behalf of any person authorised for such purpose by the Secretary of State ("the authorised person") forthwith cause the use of that device to –

(a) cease; or

(b) be restricted in the manner specified by the authorised person.

Robert Atkins
Parliamentary Under Secretary of State,
Department of Trade and Industry

4th April 1989

(**a**) S.I. 1980/1848, regulation 3. These Regulations were amended by S.I. 1987/776. (**b**) S.I. 1984/1053, regulations 3 and 4. There are amendments to S.I. 1984/1053 not relevant to these Regulations. (**c**) S.I. 1989/123, regulation 3.

SCHEDULE

Regulation 3

DESCRIPTIONS OF RELEVANT LOW POWER DEVICES

Emergency alarms

1. Wireless telegraphy apparatus designed or adapted –

(a) for the sole purpose of sending and receiving non-verbal signals in order to summon assistance to those persons who may require it by reason of old age or infirmity; and

(b) so as to be capable of use only –

(i) at a power not exceeding 0.5 mW ERP; and

(ii) on one or more of the frequencies listed below –

27.450 MHz	34.950 MHz
34.925 "	34.975 ".

Field disturbance and Doppler apparatus

2. Wireless telegraphy apparatus –

(a) designed or adapted to produce a radiated field and respond to a variation in that field as a result of any intrusion or movement within that field by other devices, objects or persons in order to detect or monitor the movement of such devices, objects or persons; and

(b) constructed so as to be capable of use only on frequencies, and at a power, or field strength, as the case may be, not exceeding the maximum, specified for each category of apparatus in the table below –

Category	*Description of apparatus*	*Frequencies*	*Maximum power EIRP*	*Maximum field strength*
1	Apparatus designed solely to detect resonant circuits for use on a frequency of 13.56 MHz ± 0.2%	13.56 MHz ± 0.2 %		4500 μV/m
2	Apparatus (other than category 1 above) designed solely to detect resonant circuits	2 – 32 MHz		1000 μV/m
3	Apparatus designed solely for outdoor use	10.577 – 10.597 GHz	1.0 W	
4	Apparatus designed solely for indoor use	10.675 – 10.699 GHz	1.0 W	
5	Apparatus designed solely for use at a fixed location	24.150 – 24.250 GHz	2.0 W	
6	Apparatus designed solely for use in a mobile application	24.250 – 24.350 GHz	2.0 W	
7	Anti-collision devices	31.80 – 33.40 GHz	5.0 W	
8	Any apparatus not within any category above	2.445 – 2.455 GHz	0.1 W	

Induction system apparatus

3. That part of an induction system –

(a) designed or adapted to produce –

(i) a controlled magnetic field; and

(ii) a predetermined recognisable signal when operating within that magnetic field; and

(b) constructed so as to be capable of use only on frequencies, and at an output power, or field strength, as the case may be, not exceeding the maximum for such frequencies for each description of apparatus, specified in the table below –

Frequencies	*Apparatus with terminals for connection to an external loop antenna: Maximum output power*	*Apparatus with ferrite or coil antennas: Maximum field strength*
0 – 185 kHz	10 W	265 μA/m or 100 mV/m
240 – 315 kHz	10 W	17 μA/m or 6.4 mV/m

Narrow band radio microphones

4. Any wireless telegraphy apparatus incorporating a microphone which is –

(a) designed or adapted for transmission on a bandwidth not exceeding 25 kHz; and

(b) constructed so as to be capable of use only –

(i) at an ERP not exceeding 5 mW; and

(ii) on one or more of the frequencies listed below –

174.600 MHz	174.885 MHz
174.675 "	175.020 ".
174.770 "	

Radio hearing aids

5. Any hearing aid operating by means of wireless telegraphy which is constructed so as to be capable of use only –

(a) at an ERP not exceeding 2 mW; and

(b) on one or more of the frequencies listed below –

173.350 MHz	173.695 MHz	174.120 MHz
173.400 "	173.775 "	174.185 "
173.465 "	173.825 "	174.270 "
173.545 "	173.950 "	174.360 "
173.640 "	174.070 "	174.415 "

Telemetry and telecommand apparatus

6. Wireless telegraphy apparatus –

(a) designed or adapted for –

(i) automatically indicating or recording measurements at a distance from the measuring instrument; or

(ii) the transmission of signals to initiate, modify or terminate functions of equipment situated at a distance from such apparatus; and

(b) constructed so as to be capable of use only on frequencies, and at a power not exceeding the maximum for such frequencies, specified in the table below –

Frequencies	*Maximum power ERP*
26.995 MHz, 27.045 MHz, 27.095 MHz, 27.145 MHz or 27.195 MHz	1 mW
173.200 – 173.350 MHz	1 mW
417.90 – 418.10 MHz	250 μW
458.5 – 458.8 MHz	500 mW

Wide band radio microphones

7. Any wireless telegraphy apparatus incorporating a microphone which is –

(a) designed or adapted for transmission on a bandwidth of not less than 25 kHz; and

(b) constructed so as to be capable of use only –

(i) at an ERP not exceeding 2 mW; and

(ii) on one or more of the frequencies listed below –

173.800 MHz	174.800 MHz
174.100 "	175.000 " .
174.500 "	

General purpose devices

8. Any wireless telegraphy apparatus, which is designed or adapted so as to be capable of use only –

(a) within the frequency band 49.82 MHz to 49.98 MHz; and

(b) at an ERP not exceeding 10 mW.

EXPLANATORY NOTE

(This note is not part of the Regulations)

These Regulations provide for the exemption from the provisions of section 1(1) of the Wireless Telegraphy Act 1949 of various low power devices. Accordingly it will not be necessary to hold a licence to install and use apparatus to which these Regulations apply. The descriptions of low power devices which are exempt are set out in the Schedule.

Regulation 4 provides that, for the exemption to apply, certain conditions must be complied with. The low power device must be for the time being approved under section 84 of the Telecommunications Act 1984. Devices exempted from licensing by these Regulations must not cause interference.

The Regulations do not apply to apparatus which is exempt from the licensing requirement under certain other instruments (regulation 5).

Regulation 6 requires that the use of the device must cease, or its operation must be restricted, on the demand of a person authorised in that behalf by the Secretary of State. Failure to comply with such a demand is an offence under section 3 of the Wireless Telegraphy Act.

STATUTORY INSTRUMENTS

1989 No. 607

HOUSING, ENGLAND AND WALES
HOUSING, SCOTLAND

The Housing Benefit (Subsidy) Order 1989

Made - - - -	*4th April 1989*
Laid before Parliament	*10th April 1989*
Coming into force	*1st May 1989*

The Secretary of State for Social Security, with the consent of the Treasury(**a**), in exercise of the powers conferred by section 30(2), (3) and (11) of the Social Security Act 1986(**b**), section 166(1) to (3A) of the Social Security Act 1975(**c**) and of all other powers enabling him in that behalf, after consultation, in accordance with section 61(7) of the Social Security Act 1986, with organisations appearing to him to be representative of the authorities concerned, hereby makes the following Order:

Citation, commencement and interpretation

1.—(1) This Order which may be cited as the Housing Benefit (Subsidy) Order 1989 shall come into force on 1st May 1989.

(2) In this Order, unless the context otherwise requires–

"the Act" means the Social Security Act 1986;

"the Regulations" means the Housing Benefit (General) Regulations 1987(**d**);

"allowance" means a rent allowance;

"authority" means a housing, rating or local authority;

"rebate" means a rent or rate rebate;

"relevant year" means the year ending 31st March 1989;

"scheme" means the housing benefit scheme as defined in section 28 of the Act;

"subsidy" means subsidy under section 30(1) of the Act (rate rebate, rent rebate and rent allowance subsidy);

and other expressions shall have the same meaning as in the Regulations.

(3) In this Order "qualifying expenditure" means the total of rebates and allowances granted by the authority during the relevant year, less–

(a) the deductions specified in article 10; and

(b) where, under subsection (6) of section 28 of the Act (arrangements for housing benefit), the authority has modified any part of the scheme administered by it, any amount by which the total of the rebates or allowances which it granted under the scheme during the relevant year exceeds the total of those which it would have granted if the scheme had not been so modified.

(**a**) *See* section 83(5) of the Social Security Act 1986 (c.50).

(**b**) 1986 c.50; section 30(2) was amended by regulation 3 of S.I. 1988/458. Section 30(11) was added by the Social Security Act 1988 (c.7), Schedule 4, paragraph 20.

(**c**) 1975 c.14; section 166(1) to (3A) is applied by section 83(1) of the Social Security Act 1986.

(**d**) S.I. 1987/1971, amended by S.I. 1988/661, 909, 1444 and 1971.

(4) In this Order, reference to a numbered article or Schedule is to the article in, or Schedule to, this Order bearing that number and, unless the context otherwise requires, reference in an article or a Schedule to a numbered paragraph is to the paragraph bearing that number in that article or that Schedule.

Amount of subsidy

2. The amount of an authority's subsidy for the relevant year–

(a) for the purposes of section 30(2) of the Act (subsidy in respect of rebates or allowances) shall be the amount or total of the amounts calculated in accordance with article 3;

(b) for the purposes of section 30(3) of the Act (subsidy in respect of the costs of administering housing benefit) may include an additional sum in respect of the cost of administering housing benefit calculated in accordance with Schedule 1.

Rebates and allowances

3.—(1) For the purposes of section 30(2) of the Act, an authority's subsidy for the relevant year shall, subject to paragraph (2), be–

(a) in the case of an authority to which articles 4, 5, 6, 7 and 8 do not apply, 97 per cent. of its qualifying expenditure;

(b) in the case of an authority to which at least one of those articles is relevant–

(i) 97 per cent. of so much of its qualifying expenditure as remains after deducting the amount of the rebates or allowances to which each of those articles which is relevant applies; and

(ii) the amount calculated in respect of the rebates or allowances under each such article,

plus, in each case, the addition, where applicable, under article 9.

(2) Where the authority is the Scottish Special Housing Association or a new town corporation in Scotland, its subsidy for the relevant year shall include a further sum being–

(a) in the case of an authority to which sub-paragraph (a) of paragraph (1) applies, 3.5 per cent. of its qualifying expenditure but subject to the relevant maximum specified in column (2) of Schedule 2;

(b) in the case of an authority to which sub-paragraph (b) of paragraph (1) applies, 3.5 per cent. of so much of its qualifying expenditure as remains after the deduction set out in paragraph (1)(b)(i), but subject to the relevant maximum specified in column (2) of Schedule 2.

Backdated payments

4.—(1) Subject to paragraph (2), where–

(a) during the relevant year an authority has, under paragraph (15) of regulation 72 of the Regulations (time and manner in which claims are to be made), treated any claim for a rebate or allowance as made on a day earlier than that on which it is made; and

(b) any part of that authority's qualifying expenditure is attributable to such earlier period,

that authority's subsidy for the relevant year in respect of such part shall be 25 per cent. of the qualifying expenditure so attributable.

(2) This article shall not apply in a case to which article 7 applies.

Treatment of rent increases

5.—(1) Subject to paragraph (3), where any part of an authority's qualifying expenditure is attributable to an increase exceeding 13 per cent. in the average of the eligible rents of the persons to whom it granted allowances, that authority's subsidy for the relevant year in respect of such part shall be 25 per cent. of an amount calculated in accordance with Schedule 3.

(2) In this article "rent" includes all the payments in respect of a dwelling specified in paragraph (1) of regulation 10 of the Regulations (rent), less, except where a person is separately liable for rates or charges for water, sewerage or allied environmental services, the deductions in respect of rates and such charges set out in paragraph (6) of that regulation.

(3) This article shall not apply in a case to which article 7 applies.

Treatment of high rents

6.—(1) Subject to paragraphs (3) and (4), where any part of the qualifying expenditure of an authority within an area listed in column (1) of Schedule 4 is attributable to any allowance granted in respect of a person whose weekly eligible rent exceeds the threshold specified in relation to that authority in column (2) of that Schedule the amount of the authority's subsidy under this article in respect of that allowance shall be calculated in accordance with paragraph (2).

(2) Where paragraph (1) applies–

(a) if the allowance granted is the same as or less than the excess of eligible rent over the threshold, the amount shall be 25 per cent. of the qualifying expenditure attributable to such allowance;

(b) if the allowance granted is greater than the excess of the eligible rent over the threshold, the amount shall be the aggregate of 25 per cent. of the portion of the qualifying expenditure attributable to such allowance which is equal to the excess and 97 per cent. of the balance.

(3) Paragraph (1) shall not apply to an allowance payable by an authority in respect of–

(a) rents which exceed the threshold and which are registered in respect of a dwelling under Part IV, V or VI of the Rent Act 1977(**a**) or Part V, VI or VII of the Rent (Scotland) Act 1984(**b**) or which have been determined by a rent assessment committee in respect of a dwelling under Part I of the Housing Act 1988(**c**) or Part II of the Housing (Scotland) Act 1988(**d**);

(b) rents which exceed the threshold but which have been referred to the rent officer and not registered by him because he is satisfied the rent is at or below the fair rent level and he has in writing so notified the authority; or

(c) rents which exceed the threshold where the relevant tenancy is one to which, before 15th January 1989, the provisions of sections 56 to 58 of the Housing Act 1980 applied(**e**).

(4) This article shall not apply in a case to which article 7 applies.

Treatment of certain residential accommodation

7.—(1) Where any part of an authority's qualifying expenditure is attributable to rebates or allowances granted under the Social Security and Housing Benefits Act 1982(**f**) to persons in respect of accommodation provided under–

(a) sections 21 to 24 and 26 of the National Assistance Act 1948(**g**) (provision of accommodation);

(**a**) 1977 c.42. (**b**) 1984 c.58. (**c**) 1988 c.50.
(**d**) 1988 c.43.
(**e**) 1980 c.51; sections 56 to 58 were partially repealed by section 140 of, and Schedule 18 to, the Housing Act 1988.
(**f**) 1982 c.24.
(**g**) 1948 c.29; section 21 was amended by the Local Government Act 1972 (c.70), Schedule 23, paragraphs 1 and 2 and Schedule 30; the National Health Service Reorganisation Act 1973 (c.32), Schedule 4, paragraph 44 and Schedule 5; the Housing (Homeless Persons) Act 1977 (c.48), Schedule; the National Health Service Act 1977 (c.49), Schedule 15, paragraph 5; the Health Services Act 1980 (c.53), Schedule 1, Part I, paragraph 5. Section 22 was amended by the Social Work (Scotland) Act 1968 (c.49), section 87(4) and Schedule 9, Part I; the Supplementary Benefits Act 1976 (c.71), Schedule 7, paragraph 3; the Housing (Homeless Persons) Act 1977 (c.48), Schedule; the Social Security Act 1980 (c.30), section 20, Schedule 4, paragraph 2(1) and Schedule 5, Part II; the Health and Social Services and Social Security Adjudications Act 1983 (c.41), section 20(1)(a) and the Social Security Act 1986 (c.50), section 86 and Schedule 10, Part II, paragraph 32. Section 24 was amended by the National Assistance (Amendment) Act 1959 (c.30), section 1(1); the National Health Service (Scotland) Act 1972 (c.58), Schedule 6, paragraph 82; the Local Government Act 1972 (c.70), Schedule 23, paragraph 2; the National Health Service Reorganisation Act 1973 (c.32), Schedule 4, paragraph 45 and the Housing (Homeless Persons) Act 1977 (c.48), Schedule. Section 26 was amended by the Health Services and Public Health Act 1968 (c.46), section 44 and Schedule 4 and the Social Work (Scotland) Act 1968 (c.49), Schedule 9, Part I and applied by section 87(3); the Local Government Act 1972 (c.70), Schedule 23, paragraph 2; the Housing (Homeless Persons) Act 1977 (c.48), Schedule and the Health and Social Services and Social Security Adjudications Act 1983 (c.41), section 20(1)(b).

(b) section 21(1) of, and paragraph 1 or 2 of Schedule 8 to, the National Health Service Act 1977(**a**) (prevention, care and after-care); or

(c) section 59 of the Social Work (Scotland) Act 1968(**b**) (provision of residential and other establishments) where board is available to the claimant,

that authority's subsidy for the relevant year in respect of such part shall be 90 per cent. of the qualifying expenditure so attributable.

(2) This article shall not apply in a case to which article 8 applies.

Overpayment of rebates or allowances

8.—(1) Where any part of an authority's qualifying expenditure is attributable to an overpayment of rebates or allowances its subsidy for the year in respect of such part shall be calculated in accordance with paragraph (2).

(2) Subject to paragraph (3), the amount of that subsidy shall be–

(a) in the case of an overpayment caused by an error of the authority making the payment, 15 per cent. of the qualifying expenditure attributable to the overpayment;

(b) in the case of an overpayment caused by an error of a local office of the Department of Social Security, 97 per cent. of so much of the qualifying expenditure attributable to the overpayment as has not been recovered by the authority; or

(c) in the case of any other overpayment, 30 per cent. of the qualifying expenditure attributable to the overpayment.

(3) This article shall not apply in a case to which paragraph (15) of regulation 72 of the Regulations (time and manner in which claims are to be made) applies.

Addition to subsidy

9. Where, following the loss, destruction or non-receipt, or alleged loss, destruction or non-receipt, of original instruments of payment, an authority makes duplicate payments and the original instruments have been or are subsequently encashed, the addition referred to in article 3(1) shall be equal to 30 per cent. of the amount of the duplicate payments.

Deductions to be made in calculating subsidy in respect of rebates or allowances

10. The deductions referred to in article 1(3) are of the following amounts where–

(a) a tenant of an authority, who is in receipt of rent rebate, while continuing to occupy, or when entering into occupation of, a dwelling as his home, either under his existing tenancy agreement or by entering into a new tenancy agreement–

(i) is during, or was at any time prior to, the relevant year able to choose whether or not to be provided with any services, facilities or rights and chooses or chose to be so provided; or

(ii) is during, or was at any time prior to, the relevant year able to choose either to be provided with any services or facilities or, whether or not in return for an award or grant from the authority, to provide such services or facilities for himself; or

(iii) would be able during, or would have been able at any time prior to, the relevant year to exercise the choice set out in sub-paragraph (i) or (ii) of this paragraph if he were not or had not at that time been in receipt of a rent rebate,

the amounts attributable during the relevant year to such services, facilities or rights whether they are or would be expressed as part of the sum fixed as rent, otherwise reserved as rent or expressed as an award or grant from the authority;

(b) during the relevant year a person becomes entitled to a rent-free period which

(**a**) 1977 c.49; paragraphs 1 and 2 of Schedule 8 were amended by section 30, Schedule 10, Part I of the Health and Social Services and Social Security Adjudications Act 1983 (c.41); paragraph 1 was also amended by the Education Reform Act 1988 (c.40), section 237 and Schedule 12, Part I, paragraph 22; paragraph 2 was also amended by section 148, Schedule 4, of the Mental Health Act 1983 (c.20).

(**b**) 1968 c.49.

has not been, or does not fall to be, taken into account in calculating the amount of rent rebate to which he is entitled under the Regulations, the amount of rebate which is or was payable to him in respect of such rent-free period;

(c) during the relevant year an award in the form of a payment of money or monies worth, a credit to the person's rent account or in some other form is made by an authority to one of its tenants in receipt of rent rebate, whether or not the person is immediately entitled to the award, the amount or value of the award, but no such deduction shall be made in respect of an award–

(i) made to a tenant for a reason unrelated to the fact that he is a tenant;

(ii) made under a statutory obligation;

(iii) made under section 137 of the Local Government Act 1972(**a**) (Power of local authorities to incur expenditure for certain purposes not otherwise authorised);

(iv) except where paragraph (a)(ii) applies, made as reasonable compensation for reasonable repairs or redecoration the tenant has, or has caused to be, carried out whether for payment or not and which the authority would otherwise have carried out or have been required to carry out; or

(v) of a reasonable amount made as compensation for loss, damage or inconvenience of a kind which occurs only exceptionally suffered by the tenant by virtue of his occupation of his home;

(d) during the relevant year the weekly amount of rebate or allowance is increased under paragraph (8) of regulation 69 of the Regulations (calculations of weekly amounts), the amount of such increase;

(e) during the relevant year a rebate has been paid in advance and an overpayment has occurred because a change in the circumstances of the recipient has reduced or eliminated entitlement to such rebate, the amount overpaid calculated from the end of the second benefit week after the recipient has disclosed such change of circumstances to the authority;

(f) during the relevant year an overpayment of rebate or allowance has occurred in circumstances to which regulation 91A of the Regulations(**b**) (payment on account of a rent or rate rebate), or regulation 4A of the Housing Benefit (Transitional) Regulations 1987(**c**) (payments on account of housing benefit) applies, the amount of such overpayment;

(g) during the relevant year rebate or allowance has been granted under the Social Security and Housing Benefits Act 1982 in excess of entitlement to a person in respect of accommodation provided under–

(i) sections 21 to 24 and 26 of the National Assistance Act 1948 (provision of accommodation);

(ii) section 21(1) of and paragraph 1 or 2 of Schedule 8 to the National Health Service Act 1977 (prevention, care and after-care); or

(iii) section 59 of the Social Work (Scotland) Act 1968 (provision of residential and other establishments) where board is available to the claimant,

the amount of such overpayment.

Modification of subsidy on payments in excess of entitlement made before 1st April 1988

11.—(1) Notwithstanding any provision made under the Social Security and Housing Benefits Act 1982 in respect of housing benefit paid in excess of entitlement, where an overpayment of benefit to which any such provision applies made before 1st April 1988 under that Act is discovered on or after 1st July 1988, an authority's subsidy in respect of such a payment shall be calculated as set out in paragraph (2).

(2) The amount of that subsidy shall be–

(a) in the case of an overpayment caused by an error of the authority making the payment, 15 per cent. of the overpayment;

(b) in the case of an overpayment caused by an error of a local office of the

(**a**) 1972 c.70; section 137 was amended by the Local Government (Miscellaneous Provisions) Act 1982 (c.30), section 44; the Local Government Finance Act 1982 (c.32), section 34, Schedule 5, paragraph 5; and by the Local Government Act 1986 (c.10), section 3.
(**b**) Regulation 91A was inserted by S.I. 1988/661, regulation 8.
(**c**) S.I. 1987/1972; regulation 4A was inserted by S.I. 1988/458, regulation 2.

Department of Social Security, 97 per cent. of so much of the overpayment as has not been recovered by the authority; or

(c) in the case of any other overpayment, 30 per cent. of the overpayment.

Signed by authority of the Secretary of State for Social Security.

Peter Lloyd
Parliamentary Under-Secretary of State,
Department of Social Security

28th March 1989

We consent,

David Maclean
Kenneth Carlisle
Two of the Lords Commissioners
of Her Majesty's Treasury

4th April 1989

SCHEDULE 1

Article 2

CALCULATION OF SUBSIDY IN RESPECT OF ADMINISTRATION COSTS

1. Subject to paragraphs 3, 4, 5 and 6, the additional sum which may be paid to an authority under section 30(3) of the Act (referred to in this Schedule as "the additional sum") shall be calculated in accordance with the following formula–

$$A \times \left(\frac{0.6B}{C} + \frac{0.4D}{E}\right)$$

Where–

A is the amount available as subsidy in respect of the costs of administering housing benefit being–

(a) in the case of new town corporations in England, Wales or Scotland, the Development Board for Rural Wales, or the Scottish Special Housing Association, £1,861,106; or

(b) in the case of authorities other than those specified in sub-paragraph (a) of this paragraph–

(i) in England, £110,935,584;

(ii) in Wales, £4,879,336; or

(iii) in Scotland, £10,158,941;

B is the estimate of administration costs for the two years immediately preceding the relevant year submitted by that authority before 11th December 1987;

C is the total of such estimates submitted by all authorities in the category specified in sub-paragraph (a), (b)(i), (b)(ii) or (b)(iii), as the case may be, of the definition of A;

D is the figure for that authority's workload, calculated in accordance with paragraph 2;

E is the total of the figures for the workload, of all authorities in the category specified in sub-paragraph (a), (b)(i), (b)(ii) or (b)(iii), as the case may be, of the definition of A.

2. The figure for an authority's workload shall be the aggregate of the amounts obtained by applying the relevant formula to each of the categories of rebates and allowances applicable to that authority listed in column (1) of Table 2 below, that formula being–

(a) in the case of an authority specified in column (1) of Table 1 below, F × G × H;

(b) in the case of any other authority, F × G

Where–

F is the estimate, submitted by that authority before 11th December 1987, of the number of persons in each of the categories listed in column (1) of Table 2 below who are likely to receive rebates or allowances from it during the year immediately preceding the relevant year;

G is the figure specified in relation to that category in whichever of columns (2) to (6) of that Table is appropriate to that authority;

H is the cost adjustment figure specified in column (2) of Table 1 below.

TABLE 1

(1) *Authority*	(2) *Cost Adjustment Figure*
BARKING	1.094
BARNET	1.094
BASILDON	1.033
BASILDON NEW TOWN	1.033
BEXLEY	1.094
BRACKNELL	1.033
BRENT	1.094
BRENTWOOD	1.033
BROMLEY	1.094
BROXBOURNE	1.049
CAMDEN	1.121
CITY OF LONDON	1.204
CHILTERN	1.033
CRAWLEY	1.033
CRAWLEY NEW TOWN	1.033
CROYDON	1.094
DACORUM	1.033
DARTFORD	1.049
EALING	1.094
EAST HERTFORDSHIRE	1.033
ELMBRIDGE	1.049
ENFIELD	1.094
EPPING FOREST	1.049
EPSOM AND EWELL	1.049
GREENWICH	1.121
GUILDFORD	1.033
HACKNEY	1.121
HAMMERSMITH	1.121
HARINGEY	1.094
HARLOW	1.033
HARROW	1.094
HAVERING	1.094
HEMEL HEMPSTEAD NEW TOWN	1.049
HERTSMERE	1.049
HILLINGDON	1.094
HOUNSLOW	1.094
ISLINGTON	1.121
KENSINGTON AND CHELSEA	1.121
KINGSTON UPON THAMES	1.094
LAMBETH	1.121
LEWISHAM	1.121
MERTON	1.094
MOLE VALLEY	1.033
NEWHAM	1.094
REDBRIDGE	1.094
REIGATE AND BANSTEAD	1.049
RICHMOND UPON THAMES	1.094
RUNNYMEDE	1.033
SEVENOAKS	1.033
SLOUGH	1.049
SOUTH BUCKINGHAMSHIRE	1.049
SOUTHWARK	1.121
SPELTHORNE	1.049
ST ALBANS	1.033
SURREY HEATH	1.033
SUTTON	1.094
TANDRIDGE	1.033
THREE RIVERS	1.049
THURROCK	1.033
TOWER HAMLETS	1.121
WALTHAM FOREST	1.094
WANDSWORTH	1.121

(1) Authority	(2) Cost Adjustment Figure
WATFORD	1.049
WAVERLEY	1.033
WELWYN HATFIELD	1.033
WESTMINSTER	1.121
WINDSOR AND MAIDENHEAD	1.033
WOKING	1.033

TABLE 2

(1) *Category of case*	(2) *Non-metropolitan authorities and new town corporations in England*	(3) *Non-metropolitan authorities and new town corporations in Scotland and the Scottish Special Housing Association*	(4) *Non-metropolitan authorities and new town corporations in Wales and the Development Board for Rural Wales*	(5) *Metropolitan authorities*	(6) *London Boroughs*
Cases to which regulation 9(1) of the Housing Benefits Regulations 1985(**a**) *applied*					
(a) Tenants of an authority–					
(i) rent rebate	7.98	8.27	9.55	8.49	8.83
(ii) rate rebate	7.93	8.32	8.99	8.36	9.05
(b) Other tenants–					
(i) rent allowance	43.86	46.23	43.46	38.85	42.55
(ii) rate rebate	39.52	40.76	35.12	36.26	40.81
(c) Persons other than tenants–					
(i) rate rebate	7.31	7.03	8.55	7.12	7.66
Other cases					
(a) Tenants of an authority–					
(i) rent rebate	8.02	6.55	8.94	9.48	9.43
(ii) rate rebate	6.74	5.57	7.58	7.90	8.12
(b) Other tenants–					
(i) rent allowance	33.20	23.65	33.60	36.91	35.67
(ii) rate rebate	31.21	22.60	31.18	33.40	36.72
(c) Persons other than tenants–					
(i) rate rebate	5.33	4.44	5.40	5.53	6.33

3.—(1) If the additional sum, as calculated under paragraph 1–

(a) exceeds 140 per cent. of an amount calculated in accordance with sub-paragraph (2) of this paragraph, the additional sum for that authority for that year shall be 140 per cent. of such amount; or

(b) is less than 90 per cent. of an amount calculated in accordance with sub-paragraph (2) of this paragraph, the additional sum for that authority for that year shall be 90 per cent. of such amount.

(**a**) S.I. 1985/677.

(2) The amount referred to in sub-paragraph (1) shall be–

(a) in the case of a new town corporation in England, Wales or Scotland, the Development Board for Rural Wales, or the Scottish Special Housing Association, 100 per cent.; or

(b) in the case of an authority other than one specified in sub-paragraph (a) of this paragraph–

(i) in England, 60 per cent.;

(ii) in Wales, 70 per cent.; or

(iii) in Scotland, 65 per cent.,

of that authority's estimate of administration costs for the financial year ending 31st March 1988 submitted by that authority before 11th December 1987.

4. Where the total of the additional sums calculated under paragraphs 1 and 3 is less or more than–

(a) for new town corporations in England, Wales or Scotland, the Development Board for Rural Wales or the Scottish Special Housing Association, £1,861,106; or

(b) for authorities other than those specified in sub-paragraph (a) of this paragraph–

(i) in England, £110,935,584;

(ii) in Wales, £4,879,336; or

(iii) in Scotland, £10,158,941,

the amount of the additional sum for an authority to which paragraph 3 does not apply shall be calculated, subject to paragraph 5, in accordance with the following formula–

$$J \times \frac{L}{K}$$

Where–

J is the additional sum calculated under paragraph 1 in respect of the authority;

K is the total of the additional sums calculated under paragraph 1 in respect of all authorities, to which paragraph 3 does not apply, in the category specified in sub-paragraph (a), (b)(i), (b)(ii) or (b)(iii) of this paragraph respectively;

L is the balance of the total amount specified in paragraph 1 available as subsidy in respect of the cost of administering housing benefit for authorities in the category specified in sub-paragraph (a), (b)(i), (b)(ii) or (b)(iii) of this paragraph respectively, after deduction of the additional sums for such authorities to which paragraph 3 applies.

5.—(1) If the additional sum for an authority for the relevant year as calculated under paragraph 4–

(a) exceeds 140 per cent. of the amount for that authority for that year calculated under paragraph 3(2), the additional sum for that authority for that year shall be 140 per cent. of such amount; or

(b) is less than 90 per cent. of the amount for that authority for that year calculated under paragraph 3(2), the additional sum for that authority for that year shall be 90 per cent. of such amount.

6. Until the aggregate of the additional sums calculated under paragraphs 3, 4 and 5 equals the amount available as subsidy in respect of the cost of administering housing benefit for authorities in the category specified in sub-paragraph (a), (b)(i), (b)(ii) or (b)(iii) respectively of paragraph 4, the formula set out in paragraph 4 and paragraph 5 shall, subject to the modifications specified below, continue to apply to calculate the additional sum for those authorities to which neither paragraph 3 nor paragraph 5 has applied; and for that purpose–

(a) J shall apply as if the additional sum were the sum calculated under paragraph 4, or, if by virtue of this paragraph there has been more than one calculation, last calculated under that paragraph in respect of the authority;

(b) K shall apply as if the total of the additional sums were the total of the additional sums calculated under paragraph 4, or, if by virtue of this paragraph there has been more than one calculation, last calculated under that paragraph, in respect of all authorities to which paragraph 5 did not apply in that calculation; and

(c) L shall apply as if the amount to be deducted to determine the balance of the total amount available were the additional sums for authorities to which, in the calculation under paragraphs 4 and 5, or, if there has been more than one calculation under those paragraphs, the last such calculation, paragraph 5 applied.

SCHEDULE 2

Article 3

MAXIMUM AMOUNTS OF SUBSIDY PAYABLE IN RESPECT OF CERTAIN AUTHORITIES IN SCOTLAND

(1) *Authority granting rebates or allowances*	(2) *Maximum amount of subsidy*
	£
Scottish Special Housing Association	1,130,866
Cumbernauld	127,374
East Kilbride	177,474
Glenrothes	110,173
Irvine	65,085
Livingston	144,718

SCHEDULE 3

Article 5

CALCULATION OF SUBSIDY IN RESPECT OF RENT INCREASES

For the purposes of article 5(1) the amount shall be calculated in accordance with the following formula–

$$A - \left(\frac{A \times 113}{B}\right)$$

Where–

A is the amount of the qualifying expenditure attributable to allowances granted by the authority in the relevant year;

B is the average of the eligible rents of those persons in receipt, on 31st May 1989, of an allowance from the authority, expressed as a percentage of the average of the eligible rents of those persons so in receipt on 31st March 1988.

SCHEDULE 4

Article 6

THRESHOLD ABOVE WHICH REDUCED SUBSIDY IS PAYABLE ON RENT ALLOWANCES

(1) *Area*	(2) *Threshold* *(weekly sum)*
	£
Barking	56.58
Barnet	77.32
Bexley	57.32
Brent	62.43
Bromley	71.67
Camden	88.09
City of London	85.97
Croydon	74.41
Ealing	70.55
Enfield	60.69
Greenwich	55.13

(1) *Area*	(2) *Threshold (weekly sum)*
	£
Hackney	59.55
Hammersmith	61.85
Haringey	63.91
Harrow	66.02
Havering	63.53
Hillingdon	66.71
Hounslow	69.75
Islington	64.15
Kensington & Chelsea	76.31
Kingston upon Thames	71.15
Lambeth	62.89
Lewisham	54.41
Merton	72.77
Newham	54.88
Redbridge	55.54
Richmond upon Thames	74.83
Southwark	56.41
Sutton	68.96
Tower Hamlets	58.83
Waltham Forest	48.73
Wandsworth	69.64
Westminster	114.89
Avon	52.34
Bedfordshire	43.00
Berkshire	50.83
Buckinghamshire	48.51
Cambridgeshire	47.33
Cheshire	45.80
Cleveland	41.71
Cornwall	51.95
Cumbria	31.00
Derbyshire	38.42
Devon	51.53
Dorset	45.32
Durham	38.89
East Sussex	53.27
Essex	47.30
Gloucestershire	49.15
Greater Manchester	50.30
Hampshire	47.68
Hereford and Worcester	46.45
Hertfordshire	42.88
Humberside	34.89
Isles of Scilly	51.95
Isle of Wight	43.22
Kent	54.63
Lancashire	60.48
Leicestershire	39.19
Lincolnshire	41.53
Merseyside	41.96
Norfolk	47.38
Northamptonshire	43.69
Northumberland	43.50
Nottinghamshire	40.98
North Yorkshire	43.55
Oxfordshire	54.48
Shropshire	44.65
Somerset	45.42
South Yorkshire	36.84
Staffordshire	39.19
Suffolk	44.65

(1) *Area*	(2) *Threshold (weekly sum)*
	£
Surrey	52.34
Tyne and Wear	39.27
Warwickshire	38.76
West Midlands	39.05
West Sussex	50.98
West Yorkshire	38.93
Wiltshire	49.69
Clwyd	40.70
Dyfed	44.00
Gwent	39.61
Gwynedd	35.24
Mid-Glamorgan	41.63
Powys	38.54
South Glamorgan	48.31
West Glamorgan	39.32
Borders	72.00
Central	72.99
Dumfries & Galloway	60.94
Fife	61.72
Grampian	63.50
Highland	54.50
Lothian	62.08
Orkneys	37.06
Shetlands	37.06
Strathclyde	55.03
Tayside	64.88
Western Isles	54.50

EXPLANATORY NOTE

(This note is not part of the Order)

This Order makes provision for the calculation of housing benefit subsidy payable under section 30(2) and (3) of the Social Security Act 1986 to authorities who grant rebates or allowances under that Act or the Social Security and Housing Benefits Act 1982, in the year ending 31st March 1989.

The Order sets out the manner in which the total figure for an authority's subsidy in respect of rebates and allowances for the year is calculated (articles 2(a) and 3 to 10 and Schedules 2, 3 and 4), and the manner of calculating the additional sum payable to an authority in respect of the cost of administering housing benefit (article 2(b) and Schedule 1).

The Order also makes provision for the modification of the provisions for subsidy in respect of payments of housing benefit in excess of entitlement, made before 1st April 1988 under section 32 of the Social Security and Housing Benefits Act 1982 and discovered after 1st July 1988 (article 11).

STATUTORY INSTRUMENTS

1989 No. 613

NATIONAL HEALTH SERVICE, ENGLAND AND WALES

The National Health Service (General Dental Services) Amendment Regulations 1989

Made - - - -	*6th April 1989*
Laid before Parliament	*10th April 1989*
Coming into force	*1st May 1989*

The Secretary of State for Health, in exercise of powers conferred by sections 35(1) and (4), 36(1) and 126(4) of the National Health Service Act 1977(**a**) and of all other powers enabling him in that behalf, hereby makes the following Regulations:

Citation and commencement

1. These Regulations may be cited as the National Health Service (General Dental Services) Amendment Regulations 1989 and shall come into force on 1st May 1989.

Amendment of Regulations

2. Regulation 26D of the National Health Service (General Dental Services) Regulations 1973(**b**) (amount and time of payments in consequence of suspension) shall be amended as follows:–

(a) in paragraph (1)(a)(i) for "£1935" there shall be substituted "£2,243";
(b) in paragraph (1)(a)(ii) for "£967" there shall be substituted "£1,121";
(c) in paragraph (1)(b)(i) for "£967" there shall be substituted "£1,121";
(d) in paragraph (1)(b)(ii) for "£1935" there shall be substituted "£2,243"; and
(e) in paragraph (2) for "£107,103" in both places where it occurs there shall be substituted "£117,689".

Signed by authority of the Secretary of State for Health

D. Mellor
Minister of State
Department of Health

6th April 1989

(**a**) 1977 c.49; section 35(1) was substituted by the Family Practitioner Committees (Consequential Modifications) Order 1985 (S.I. 1985/39), article 7(9). Section 35(4) was added by section 15(a) of the Health and Social Services and Social Security Adjudications Act 1983 (c.41). For amendments to section 35(3), *see* paragraph 8 of Schedule 5 to the Dentists Act 1984 (c.24). Section 36 was amended by the Health and Social Security Act 1984 (c.48), Schedule 3, paragraph 5. For the definition of "regulations" *see* section 128(1) of the National Health Service Act 1977. (**b**) S.I. 1973/1468; relevant amending instruments are S.I. 1974/53, 1987/736 and 1512.

EXPLANATORY NOTE

(This note is not part of the Regulations)

These Regulations amend the National Health Service (General Dental Services) Regulations 1973, which provide for the arrangements under which dentists provide general dental services under the National Health Service in England and Wales.

These Regulations increase the amounts of, and amounts used in calculating, payments to dentists during periods of suspension of their registration under the Dentists Act 1984 by an interim suspension order or a direction or order of the Health Committee.

STATUTORY INSTRUMENTS

1989 No. 614

NATIONAL HEALTH SERVICE, ENGLAND AND WALES

The National Health Service (Travelling Expenses and Remission of Charges) Amendment (No. 2) Regulations 1989

Made - - - -	*6th April 1989*
Laid before Parliament	*7th April 1989*
Coming into force	*10th April 1989*

The Secretary of State for Health, in exercise of powers conferred by section 83A of the National Health Service Act 1977(**a**) and of all other powers enabling him in that behalf, hereby makes the following Regulations:

Citation and commencement

1. These Regulations may be cited as the National Health Service (Travelling Expenses and Remission of Charges) Amendment (No. 2) Regulations 1989 and shall come into force on 10th April 1989 immediately after the coming into force of the National Health Service (Travelling Expenses and Remission of Charges) Amendment Regulations 1989(**b**).

Amendment of Regulations

2. In column (2) of Table B in Schedule 1 to the National Health Service (Travelling Expenses and Remission of Charges) Regulations 1988(**c**), in the entry relating to paragraph 11 of Schedule 3 to the Income Support (General) Regulations 1987(**d**) –

(a) for "£11.20" there shall be substituted "£12.50";

(b) for "£6.45" in both places where it occurs there shall be substituted "£7.20";

(c) for "£3.00" there shall be substituted "£3.35".

Signed by the authority of the Secretary of State for Health.

D. Mellor
Minister of State,
Department of Health

6th April 1989

(**a**) 1977 c.49; see section 128(1) for the definitions of "prescribed" and "regulations"; section 83A was inserted by section 14(1) of the Social Security Act 1988 (c.7).
(**b**) S.I. 1989/517.
(**c**) S.I. 1988/551, amended by S.I. 1989/517.
(**d**) S.I. 1987/1967; the relevant amending instruments are S.I. 1988/1445 and S.I. 1989/43.

EXPLANATORY NOTE

(This note is not part of the Regulations)

These Regulations effect amendments to the National Health Service (Travelling Expenses and Remission of Charges) Regulations 1988 which provide for the remission and repayment of certain charges which would otherwise be payable under the National Health Service Act 1977 and for payment by the Secretary of State of certain travelling expenses.

They increase the amounts to be deducted, in the calculation of a person's entitlement to remission or repayment, for housing costs in respect of non-dependants. These amendments are consequential upon the uprating of social security benefits on 10th April 1989.

STATUTORY INSTRUMENTS

1989 No. 615

HEALTH AND SAFETY

The Road Traffic (Carriage of Explosives) Regulations 1989

Made - - - -	*5th April 1989*
Laid before Parliament	*11th April 1989*
Coming into force -	
for the purposes of all regulations except regulation 14	*3rd July 1989*
for the purposes of regulation 14	*3rd January 1990*

ARRANGEMENT OF REGULATIONS

Schedule 1—Exceptions.

Schedule 2—Limits on quantities of explosives permitted to be carried.

Schedule 3—Mixed loads.

Schedule 4—Marking of Vehicles.

Part I —Requirements.
Part II—Exceptions.

The Secretary of State, in exercise of the powers conferred on him by sections 15(1), (2), (3)(a) and (c), (4), (5)(b), 80(1) and (4) and 82(3)(a) of, and paragraphs 1(1), 3, 7, 12, 14, 15(1), 16 and 20 of Schedule 3 to, the Health and Safety at Work etc. Act 1974**(a)** ("the 1974 Act") and of all other enabling powers:–

(a) for the purpose of giving effect without modifications to proposals submitted to him by the Health and Safety Commission under section 11(2)(d) of the 1974 Act after the carrying out by the said Commission of consultations in accordance with section 50(3) of that Act; and

(b) it appearing to him that the repeal of paragraph 4 of Schedule 2 to the Emergency Laws (Miscellaneous Provisions) Act 1947**(b)** provided for by section 80(1) of the 1974 Act is expedient, after consulting the Health and Safety Executive being the only body appearing to him to be appropriate to consult in accordance with subsection (4) of that section,

hereby makes the following Regulations:

Citation and commencement

1. These Regulations may be cited as the Road Traffic (Carriage of Explosives) Regulations 1989 and shall come into force on 3rd July 1989, except regulation 14 which shall come into force on 3rd January 1990.

Interpretation

2.—(1) In these Regulations, unless the context otherwise requires–

"the 1983 Regulations" means the Classification and Labelling of Explosives Regulations 1983**(c)**;

"attendant" means a person who accompanies the driver in the vehicle during the journey to help ensure the safety and security of the explosives;

"blasting explosive" means the explosive substance allocated on classification the UN Number 0081, 0082, 0083, 0084, 0241, 0331 or 0332;

"carriage" and related expressions shall be construed in accordance with paragraphs (5) to (7);

"Class 1" has the meaning assigned to it by regulation 2(1) of the 1983 Regulations;

"classified" means classified under the 1983 Regulations, and "classification" and "unclassified" shall be construed accordingly;

"Compatibility Group" and "Compatibility Group letter" have the meanings assigned to them by regulation 2(1) of the 1983 Regulations;

"consignor" means a person who consigns (whether as principal or as agent for another) explosives for carriage by road;

"detonating cord" means the explosive article allocated on classification the UN Number 0065 or 0289;

"detonating fuzes" means the explosive articles allocated on classification the UN Number 0106, 0107, 0257 or 0367;

"detonators" means the explosive articles allocated on classification the UN Number 0029, 0030, 0255, 0267, 0360, 0361, 0455 or 0456;

"Division" and "Division number" have the meanings assigned to them by regulation 2(1) of the 1983 Regulations;

(a) 1974 c.37; sections 15 and 50 were amended by the Employment Protection Act 1975 (c.71), Schedule 15, paragraphs 6 and 16 respectively.
(b) 1947 c.10 (11 and 12 Geo.6).
(c) S.I. 1983/1140.

"explosives" means explosive articles or explosive substances which–

(a) have been assigned on classification to Class 1; or

(b) are unclassified;

"explosive article" means an article containing one or more explosive substances;

"explosive substance" means–

(a) a solid or liquid substance, or

(b) a mixture of solid or liquid substances or both,

which is capable by chemical reaction in itself of producing gas at such a temperature and pressure and at such a speed as could cause damage to surroundings or which is designed to produce an effect by heat, light, sound, gas or smoke or a combination of these as a result of non-detonative self-sustaining exothermic chemical reactions;

"freight container" means a container as defined in regulation 2(1) of the Freight Containers (Safety Convention) Regulations 1984**(a)**;

"gunpowder" means the explosive substance allocated on classification the UN Number 0027;

"military explosive" has the meaning assigned to it by regulation 2(1) of the 1983 Regulations;

"motor vehicle" means a mechanically propelled vehicle intended or adapted for use on roads;

"operator" means in relation to a vehicle–

(a) the person who holds an operator's licence (granted under Part V of the Transport Act 1968**(b)**) for the use of that vehicle for the carriage of goods on a road; except that where by virtue of regulation 32(1) to (3) of the Goods Vehicles (Operators' Licences, Qualifications and Fees) Regulations 1984**(c)** the vehicle is included in a licence held by a holding company and that company is not operating the vehicle at the relevant time, the "operator" shall be the subsidiary company specified in the application made under the said regulation 32(1) or, if more than one subsidiary company is so specified, whichever one is operating the vehicle at the relevant time, and in this sub-paragraph "holding company" and "subsidiary company" have the same meanings as in the said Regulations of 1984;

(b) where no such licence is held, the keeper of the vehicle, and for this purpose, where the vehicle is on hire or lease to another person that other person shall be treated as being the keeper;

"road" means–

(a) as respects England and Wales, a road within the meaning of section 192(1) of the Road Traffic Act 1988**(d)**;

(b) as respects Scotland, a road within the meaning of section 151 of the Roads (Scotland) Act 1984**(e)**;

"semi-trailer" has the same meaning as in column 2 of the Table set out in regulation 3(2) of the Road Vehicles (Construction and Use) Regulations 1986**(f)**;

"smokeless powder" means (except in paragraph 9(c) of Part II of Schedule 4) the explosive substance allocated on classification the UN Number 0160 or 0161;

"trailer" means a vehicle drawn by a motor vehicle but does not include a semi-trailer;

"UN Number" means United Nations Serial Number, that is to say, one of the four digit numbers devised by the United Nations and allocated by the Health and Safety Executive or the Secretary of State to an explosive article or explosive substance as a means of identification;

"vehicle" includes a motor vehicle, trailer and semi-trailer.

(a) S.I. 1984/1890.
(b) 1968 c.73; section 60(1) was modified by S.I. 1980/637.
(c) S.I. 1984/176.
(d) 1988 c.52.
(e) 1984 c.54.
(f) S.I. 1986/1078; the relevant amending instrument is S.I. 1987/676.

(2) Unless the context otherwise requires, any reference in these Regulations to–

(a) a numbered regulation or Schedule is a reference to the regulation or Schedule in these Regulations so numbered;

(b) a numbered paragraph is a reference to the paragraph so numbered in the regulation or Schedule in which that reference appears.

(3) Any reference in these Regulations to an explosive specified in Part I, Part II or Part III of Schedule 1 is a reference to an explosive of the description specified in column 1 of the said Part I, Part II or Part III, as the case may be, allocated on classification the UN Number specified opposite thereto in column 2 of that Part.

(4) Any reference in these Regulations to the quantity of any explosive shall be construed as a reference to the net mass of explosive substance.

(5) Any reference in these Regulations to the carriage of explosives in a vehicle includes a reference to the carriage of explosives on a vehicle or in a freight container attached to a vehicle, and, for the purposes of these Regulations, a motor vehicle and a trailer or semi-trailer attached to it shall be deemed to be one vehicle, and articles or substances or both of them carried in one vehicle shall be deemed to be carried together.

(6) Subject to paragraph (7), a vehicle shall be deemed for the purposes of these Regulations to be used for the carriage of explosives from the commencement of loading the vehicle with the explosives for the purpose of carrying the explosives on a road until all the explosives have been unloaded, whether or not the vehicle is on a road at the material time.

(7) A trailer or semi-trailer containing explosives shall not be deemed for the purposes of these Regulations to be used for the carriage of explosives if it is not attached to a motor vehicle at the material time, and accordingly if the trailer or semi-trailer is loaded with the explosives before it is attached to the motor vehicle the carriage begins when the trailer or semi-trailer is attached to the motor vehicle for the purpose of carrying the explosives on a road and ends when it is detached from the vehicle, or when all the explosives have been unloaded, if earlier.

Application

3.—(1) These Regulations shall apply to or in relation to the carriage of explosives by road.

(2) Regulations 6 to 15 shall not apply to the carriage of explosives in a vehicle being used to carry passengers for hire or reward.

(3) Regulations 4(1), 6 to 10 and 11(2) to 15 shall not apply to carriage by members, acting in the course of their duties, of–

(a) Her Majesty's forces;

(b) visiting forces within the meaning of any of the provisions of Part 1 of the Visiting Forces Act 1952**(a)**;

(c) any headquarters or organisation designated for the purposes of the International Headquarters and Defence Organisations Act 1964**(b)**;

(4) Regulations 4, 6 to 10 and 11(2) to 15 shall not apply to carriage for the purposes of explosive ordnance disposal (other than in connection with dumping at sea) under the direction of a member of Her Majesty's forces, a police officer, or a person authorised by the Secretary of State for Defence.

(5) Regulations 8, 9 and 10 shall not apply where–

(a) the vehicle carrying the explosives has been exempted from excise duty by the Secretary of State under section 7(1) of the Vehicles (Excise) Act 1971**(c)**; or

(b) the vehicle carrying the explosives is one which is only used on roads for delivering goods between private premises and a vehicle in the immediate vicinity of those premises or in passing from one part of such premises to another in the immediate vicinity.

(a) 1952 c.67.
(b) 1964 c.5.
(c) 1971 c.10.

(6) Except for regulations 11 and 13, these Regulations shall not apply where–

(a) the vehicle carrying the explosives is engaged in an international transport operation within the meaning of the Convention concerning International Carriage by Rail (COTIF)**(a)** as revised or re-issued from time to time; and

(b) such carriage conforms in every respect to the provisions of the Uniform Rules concerning the Contract for International Carriage of Goods by Rail (CIM) which forms Appendix B to that Convention and to the regulations (RID) made thereunder.

(7) These Regulations shall not apply to any explosive nuclear device or any component thereof.

Prohibition on the carriage of certain explosives

4.—(1) No person shall carry explosives in Compatibility Group K in a vehicle.

(2) No person shall carry unclassified explosives in a vehicle except–

(a) solely in connection with an application for their classification; and

(b) in accordance with such conditions as are approved in writing for the time being by the Health and Safety Executive or in the case of military explosives, by the Secretary of State for Defence, for the purposes of this regulation.

Carriage of explosives in vehicles used to carry passengers for hire or reward

5.—(1) No person shall carry explosives in a vehicle being used to carry passengers for hire or reward except in accordance with the conditions specified in paragraph (2).

(2) The said conditions are:–

(a) the only explosives carried by that person are any of the explosives specified in Parts I or II of Schedule 1, gunpowder or smokeless powder, or any mixture of them;

(b) the maximum total quantity of explosives carried by that person does not exceed 2 kilograms;

(c) the explosives are kept with that person and are kept properly packed;

(d) all reasonable precautions are taken by that person for the prevention of accidents arising from the explosives.

(3) For the purposes of this regulation, where explosives are being carried by a passenger the driver and operator of the vehicle shall not be treated as carrying them as well.

Suitability of vehicles and freight containers and limits on quantities

6.—(1) The operator of a vehicle used for the carriage of explosives shall ensure that the vehicle and any freight container so used are suitable for the safety and security of the explosives having regard to the type and quantity of explosives being carried.

(2) The operator of a vehicle shall ensure that there is not carried in that vehicle at any one time explosives of the type specified in column 1 of Schedule 2 in excess of the quantity specified for that type of explosive in the corresponding entry in column 2 thereof.

(3) In a case where explosives in different Compatibility Groups or Divisions are being carried together, Schedule 2 shall be applied in accordance with the provisions of paragraphs 1, 2(a) and 3 of Schedule 3.

(4) Nothing in paragraph (2) shall be construed as allowing a greater quantity of explosives to be carried than that for which the vehicle and freight container are suitable as described in paragraph (1).

Mixed loads

7.—(1) The operator of a vehicle used for the carriage of explosives shall ensure that–

(a) Cmnd 8535.

(a) explosives in different Compatibility Groups are not carried together unless–

(i) such carriage is permitted by paragraph 4 of Schedule 3; or

(ii) subject to paragraph (2), effective measures have been taken to ensure that the carriage of such a mixed load is no more dangerous than the carriage of the same quantity of explosives in any one of the Compatibility Groups carried;

(b) explosive substances and explosive articles in the same Compatibility Group are not carried together unless–

(i) such carriage is permitted by paragraph 4 of Schedule 3; or

(ii) subject to paragraph (2), effective measures have been taken to ensure that the carriage of such a mixed load is no more dangerous than the carriage of the same quantity of explosives in the form of explosive substances or explosive articles alone;

(c) unclassified explosives are not carried with classified explosives except those in Compatibility Group S.

(2) Notwithstanding paragraph (1)(a)(ii) and (b)(ii) the operator of a vehicle used for the carriage of explosives shall ensure that–

(a) explosives in Compatibility Groups A, H or L are not carried together or with explosives in any other Compatibility Group;

(b) explosives in Compatibility Group L are not carried with a different type of explosive in the same Compatibility Group.

(3) The operator of a vehicle used for the carriage of explosives shall ensure that the explosives are not carried with any other substance which is dangerous for conveyance (within the meaning of the Classification, Packaging and Labelling of Dangerous Substances Regulations 1984**(a)**, unless all reasonably practicable measures have been taken to prevent the explosives being brought into contact with, or otherwise endangering or being endangered by, any such substance.

Marking of vehicles

8.—(1) The operator and the driver of a vehicle used for the carriage of explosives shall, subject to the exceptions specified in Part II of Schedule 4, ensure that the requirements specified in Part I of that Schedule are complied with.

(2) In a case where explosives in different Divisions are being carried together, Schedule 4 shall be applied in accordance with the provisions of paragraphs 2(b) and 3 of Schedule 3.

Consignment

9.—(1) The operator of a vehicle used for the carriage of explosives shall ensure that he has obtained from the consignor of the explosives or some other person acting on his behalf such information as will enable the operator to comply with his duties under these Regulations.

(2) It shall be the duty of the consignor to ensure that the information referred to in paragraph (1)–

(a) is provided to the operator in writing; and

(b) is accurate and sufficient for the purposes of that paragraph.

(3) The operator of a vehicle used for the carriage of explosives shall not remove any explosives from the consignor's premises unless he is ready immediately to despatch them to the consignee or other person referred to in regulation 13(1)(c).

Information in writing to be available during carriage

10.—(1) The operator of a vehicle used for the carriage of explosives shall ensure that the driver or any attendant thereof has in his possession the following information in writing at the start of the journey:–

(a) S.I. 1984/1244, amended by S.I. 1986/1922 and 1988/766.

(a) in the case of classified explosives, the Division and Compatibility Group of each type of explosive carried;

(b) the net mass (in tonnes or kilograms) of each type of explosive carried, except that the gross mass (in tonnes or kilograms) may be stated instead if the operator does not know and could not reasonably ascertain what the net mass is;

(c) whether, in the case of explosives in Compatibility Group C, D or G, the explosives carried are explosive substances or explosive articles;

(d) the name and address of the consignor, the operator of the vehicle and the consignee;

(e) such other information as will enable the driver and any attendant to know the nature of the dangers to which the explosives carried may give rise and the action to be taken in an emergency.

(2) The driver and attendant shall not carry explosives in the vehicle unless–

(a) the said information in writing referred to in paragraph (1) is kept on the vehicle from the start of the journey and is thereafter readily available at all times while the explosives are being carried; and

(b) the information in writing relating to any explosives which are not being carried at that time is deleted, destroyed, removed from the vehicle, or placed in a securely closed container clearly marked to show that the information does not relate to explosives then being carried.

(3) The driver or attendant shall on request show to any police officer or traffic examiner the information in writing referred to in paragraph (1).

(4) Nothing in paragraph (2)(a) shall prevent the removal from the vehicle of the information in writing for the purposes of showing it, or otherwise communicating the information, to the police, fire brigade, a traffic examiner, or an inspector.

(5) In this regulation "traffic examiner" means a goods vehicle examiner within the meaning of section 68(2) of the Road Traffic Act 1988.

(6) This regulation shall not apply to the carriage of–

(a) any explosives specified in Part I of Schedule 1;

(b) gunpowder or smokeless powder, or a mixture of them, if the total quantity of such explosives does not exceed 5 kilograms;

(c) any explosives specified in Parts II or III of Schedule 1 if–

(i) throughout the carriage the explosives are accompanied by a person who has knowledge of the matters specified in paragraph (1); and

(ii) the quantity of such explosives does not exceed 50 kilograms, except that if other explosives are being carried pursuant to sub-paragraph (b) above in the same vehicle, the total quantity of explosives carried pursuant to that sub-paragraph and this sub-paragraph shall not exceed 50 kilograms.

Duty to ensure safe and secure carriage

11.—(1) The operator of a vehicle used for the carriage of explosives and any person engaged in the carriage, or having custody or control of the explosives during the carriage, shall take such steps as it is reasonable for persons in their positions to take to–

(a) prevent accidents and minimise the harmful effects of any accident which may occur; and

(b) prevent unauthorised access to, or removal of, all or part of the load.

(2) The operator and driver of a vehicle used for the carriage of explosives shall, subject to paragraph (4), ensure that a competent person is constantly in attendance with the vehicle whenever the driver is not present except–

(a) during stops in a safe and secure place (within the meaning of paragraph (3)); or

(b) where the vehicle is on a site where some or all of the explosives are to be used that day and–

(i) the only explosives in the vehicle are blasting explosives not exceeding 50 kilograms in quantity, detonating cord not exceeding 10 kilograms in quantity, detonators not exceeding 100 grams in quantity or 100 in number, or a mixture of them; and

(ii) adequate security precautions are taken.

(3) In paragraph (2)(a) "a safe and secure place" means a safe and secure place–

(a) within a factory or magazine licensed under the Explosives Act 1875**(a)** or lawfully existing under that Act or by virtue of a certificate of exemption granted pursuant to the Explosives Act 1875 (Exemptions) Regulations 1979**(b)**; or

(b) within premises under the control of the Ministry of Defence.

(4) Paragraph (2) shall not apply to the carriage of any explosives specified in Parts I to III of Schedule 1.

(5) The operator and driver of a vehicle used for the carriage of more than 5 tonnes of explosives in Division 1.1 shall ensure that the route followed is the route, or one of the routes, agreed with the chief officers of police of the relevant police districts.

Procedure in the event of accident

12.—(1) The driver of a vehicle used for the carriage of explosives, or if he is not present, the person in attendance having custody or control of the explosives, shall in the event of–

(a) spillage of the explosives such as to constitute a risk to safety;

(b) damage to the explosives or their packaging such as to constitute a risk to safety;

(c) the vehicle overturning; or

(d) a fire or explosion on the vehicle,

ensure that the police, fire brigade and operator of the vehicle are informed by the quickest practicable means.

(2) On being informed of the occurrence of any event referred to in sub-paragraphs (a) to (d) of paragraph (1), the operator of the vehicle shall inform the Health and Safety Executive by the quickest practicable means of the occurrence of that event.

(3) On the occurrence of any event referred to in sub-paragraphs (a) to (d) of paragraph (1), the operator and the driver (or if the driver is not present the person in attendance having custody or control of the explosives) shall ensure that all proper precautions are taken for the security of the explosives and the safety of persons likely to be affected by ignition or initiation of the explosives.

Duration of carriage and delivery

13.—(1) The operator and the driver of a vehicle used for the carriage of explosives shall ensure–

(a) that the carriage is completed within a reasonable length of time having regard to the distance involved;

(b) that any explosives intended to be delivered to a particular place are unloaded from the vehicle as soon as is reasonably practicable after it arrives at that place;

(c) that the explosives are delivered to–

(i) the consignee or his agent, or

(ii) any other person who accepts custody of the explosives for onward despatch, provided that they are delivered to either a safe and secure place (within the meaning of regulation 11(3)) or a designated parking area in an airport, a railway transhipment depot or siding, a harbour, or a harbour area;

and, that if they cannot be so delivered, they are returned to the consignor or his agent; and

(a) 1875 c.17; the relevant amending instrument is S.I. 1974/1885.
(b) S.I. 1979/1378.

(d) that any trailer, semi-trailer or freight container containing explosives is not detached from the vehicle except–

(i) in either a safe and secure place (within the meaning of regulation 11(3)) or a designated parking area in an airport, a railway transhipment depot or siding, a harbour, or a harbour area; or

(ii) in an emergency.

(2) In this regulation–

(a) "harbour" and "harbour area" have the meanings assigned to them by regulation 2(1) of the Dangerous Substances in Harbour Areas Regulations 1987**(a)**;

(b) "designated parking area" means–

(i) in relation to an airport or railway transhipment depot or siding, an area allocated by the occupier as an area for parking vehicles carrying explosives;

(ii) in relation to a harbour or harbour area, a parking area designated for the purposes of regulation 32 of the Dangerous Substances in Harbour Areas Regulations 1987.

Training and instruction of drivers and attendants

14.—(1) The operator of a vehicle used for the carriage of explosives shall ensure that the driver and any attendant have received adequate training and instruction to enable them to understand–

(a) the nature of the dangers to which the explosives carried may give rise and the action to be taken in an emergency;

(b) their duties under these Regulations and under the Health and Safety at Work etc. Act 1974.

(2) The operator shall keep a record of such training and instruction received–

(a) by himself, if he is a driver or attendant; and

(b) by drivers and attendants in his employment, to whom a copy shall be made available.

(3) This regulation shall not apply to the carriage of–

(a) any explosives specified in Part I of Schedule 1;

(b) gunpowder or smokeless powder, or a mixture of them, if the total quantity of such explosives does not exceed 5 kilograms; or

(c) any explosives specified in Part II of Schedule 1, if the quantity of such explosives does not exceed 50 kilograms, except that if other explosives are being carried pursuant to sub-paragraph (b) above in the same vehicle, the total quantity of explosives carried pursuant to that sub-paragraph and this sub-paragraph shall not exceed 50 kilograms.

Minimum age limits for persons engaged in the carriage of explosives

15.—(1) Subject to paragraph (2) no person under the age of 18 years shall–

(a) use any vehicle for the carriage of explosives;

(b) be employed as the driver or attendant of such a vehicle;

(c) be made responsible for the security of the explosives;

(d) be allowed to go on or in such a vehicle except in the presence and under the supervision of a competent person who is at least 18 years of age.

(2) Paragraph (1) shall not apply to the carriage of–

(a) any explosives specified in Part I of Schedule 1; or

(b) any explosives specified in Part II of Schedule 1, if the total quantity of such explosives does not exceed 50 kilograms.

(a) S.I. 1987/37.

Enforcement

16. Notwithstanding regulation 3 of the Health and Safety (Enforcing Authority) Regulations 1977**(a)**, the enforcing authority for these Regulations shall be the Health and Safety Executive.

Certificates of exemption

17.—(1) Subject to paragraph (2), the Health and Safety Executive may, by a certificate in writing, exempt from all or any requirements or prohibitions imposed by these Regulations any particular, or class of, explosive, person or vehicle and any such exemption may be granted subject to conditions and to a limit of time and may be revoked by a certificate in writing at any time.

(2) The Executive shall not grant any such exemption unless, having regard to the circumstances of the case, and in particular to–

(a) the conditions, if any, which it proposes to attach to the exemption; and

(b) any other requirements imposed by or under any enactment which apply to the case,

it is satisfied that neither the health and safety of persons who are likely to be affected by the exemption nor the security of the explosives will be prejudiced.

(3) The Secretary of State for Defence may in the interests of national security exempt by a certificate in writing from all or any requirements or prohibitions imposed by these Regulations any particular, or class of–

(a) military explosive;

(b) person engaged in the carriage of military explosive;

(c) vehicle used for the carriage of military explosive,

and any such exemption may be granted subject to conditions and to a limit of time and may be revoked by a certificate in writing at any time.

Amendment of the Explosives Act 1875

18. In proviso (2) to section 5 of the Explosives Act 1875, except in so far as it applies to Northern Ireland, for the words "with respect to the conveyance of gunpowder" there shall be substituted "and of any health and safety regulations (within the meaning of Part I of the Health and Safety at Work etc. Act 1974) which apply to that conveyance."

Repeals and revocations

19.—(1) Section 97(5) of the Explosives Act 1875 and paragraph 4 of Schedule 2 to the Emergency Laws (Miscellaneous Provisions) Act 1947 are hereby repealed.

(2) The Order of the Secretary of State No 11 dated 20th September 1924**(b)** (except byelaw 3) is hereby revoked to the extent it relates to conveyance by road.

(3) The Conveyance by Road of Military Explosives Regulations 1977**(c)** are hereby revoked.

(4) The Acts, Order and Regulations specified in this regulation are not repealed or revoked in relation to their application in Northern Ireland.

Signed by authority of the Secretary of State

Peter Bottomley
Parliamentary Under Secretary of State,
Department of Transport

5th April 1989

(a) S.I. 1977/746, to which there are amendments not relevant to these Regulations.
(b) S.R. and O. 1924/1129, amended by S.R. and O. 1939/1787, 1943/1252, 1944/139; S.I. 1951/869, 1958/230, 1984/510.
(c) S.I. 1977/888.

Regulations 2(3), 5(2)(a), 10(6), 11(4), 14(3), and 15(2)

SCHEDULE 1

EXCEPTIONS

PART I

1 *Explosives*	2 *UN Number*
ARTICLES, PYROTECHNIC for technical purposes	0432
CARTRIDGES, POWER DEVICE	0323
CARTRIDGES, SIGNAL	0405
CARTRIDGES, SMALL ARMS	0012
CARTRIDGES, SMALL ARMS, BLANK	0014
CASES CARTRIDGE, EMPTY, WITH PRIMER	0055
CUTTERS, CABLE, EXPLOSIVE	0070
FIREWORKS	0337
FLARES, AERIAL	0404
FUSE, SAFETY	0105
IGNITERS	0454
LIGHTERS, FUSE	0131
PRIMERS, CAP TYPE	0044
SIGNAL DEVICES, HAND	0373
SIGNALS, RAILWAY TRACK, EXPLOSIVE	0193

PART II

1 *Explosives*	2 *UN Number*
CARTRIDGES, SMALL ARMS*	0328
CARTRIDGES, SMALL ARMS	0339
CARTRIDGES, SMALL ARMS, BLANK*	0327
CARTRIDGES, SMALL ARMS, BLANK	0338
CASES, CARTRIDGE, EMPTY WITH PRIMER	0379
FIREWORKS*	0333
FIREWORKS*	0334
FIREWORKS*	0335
FIREWORKS	0336
SIGNAL DEVICES, HAND	0191
SIGNALS, DISTRESS, SHIP*	0195

* These explosives are referred to in paragraph 9(c)(i) of Part II of Schedule 4.

PART III

1 *Explosives*	2 *UN Number*
ARTICLES, PYROTECHNIC for technical purposes	0428
ARTICLES, PYROTECHNIC for technical purposes	0429
ARTICLES, PYROTECHNIC for technical purposes	0430
ARTICLES, PYROTECHNIC for technical purposes	0431
CARTRIDGES, OIL WELL	0277
CARTRIDGES, OIL WELL	0278
CARTRIDGES, POWER DEVICE	0275
CARTRIDGES, POWER DEVICE	0276
CARTRIDGES, POWER DEVICE	0381
CARTRIDGES, SIGNAL	0054
CARTRIDGES, SIGNAL	0312
CASES, COMBUSTIBLE EMPTY, WITHOUT PRIMER	0446
CASES, COMBUSTIBLE EMPTY, WITHOUT PRIMER	0447
CORD, IGNITER	0066
DINITROSOBENZENE	0406
FLARES, AERIAL	0093
FLARES AERIAL	0403
FLARES, SURFACE	0092
FLASH POWDER	0094
FLASH POWDER	0305
FUSE, INSTANTANEOUS NON-DETONATING; (QUICKMATCH)	0101
IGNITERS	0121
IGNITERS	0314
IGNITERS	0315
IGNITERS	0325
5-MERCAPTO-TETRAZOLE-1-ACETIC ACID	0448
P0TASSIUM SALTS OF AROMATIC NITRO-DERIVATIVES, explosive	0158
PRIMERS, CAP TYPE	0377
PRIMERS, CAP TYPE	0378
ROCKETS, LINE THROWING	0238
ROCKETS, LINE THROWING	0240
ROCKETS, LINE THROWING	0453
SIGNALS, DISTRESS, ship	0194
SIGNALS, RAILWAY TRACK, EXPLOSIVE	0192
SIGNALS, SMOKE with explosive sound unit	0196
SIGNALS, SMOKE without explosive sound unit	0197
SODIUM DINITRO-o-CRESOLATE, dry or wetted with less than 15% water by mass	0234
SODIUM PICRAMATE, dry or wetted with less than 20% water by mass	0235
TETRAZOLE-1-ACETIC ACID	0407
ZIRCONIUM PICRAMATE dry or wetted with less than 20% water by mass	0236

Regulation 6

SCHEDULE 2

LIMITS ON QUANTITIES OF EXPLOSIVES PERMITTED TO BE CARRIED

1 *Type of explosives*		2 *Maximum Quantity*
Division	Compatibility Group	
1.1	A	500 kilograms
1.1	B, F, G, or L	5 tonnes
1.1	C, D, E or J	16 tonnes
1.2	Any	16 tonnes
1.3	Any	16 tonnes
Unclassified explosives carried solely in connection with an application for their classification		500 kilograms

Regulations 6(3), 7(1)(a)(i), (b)(i), and 8(2)

SCHEDULE 3

MIXED LOADS

Compatibility Groups

1. Where explosives in different Compatibility Groups are carried together, they shall, for the purpose of applying Schedule 2, all be deemed to be in the Group amongst them which comes highest in the following list, that is, Group B (highest), F, G, C, D, E and J (lowest).

Divisions

2. Where explosives in different Divisions are carried together then, subject to paragraph 3–

(a) for the purpose of applying Schedule 2, all the explosives (with the exception of those in Division 1.4) shall be deemed to be in the Division amongst them which comes highest in the following list, that is Division 1.1 (highest), 1.2, 1.3, and 1.5 (lowest);

(b) for the purpose of applying Schedule 4, all the explosives shall be deemed to be in the Division amongst them which comes highest in the following list, that is Division 1.1 (highest), 1.2, 1.3, 1.5 and 1.4 (lowest).

3. Where explosives in Division 1.5 are carried with explosives in Division 1.2 then, for the purpose of applying Schedules 2 and 4, they shall all be deemed to be in Division 1.1.

Permitted mixed loads

4. The following mixed loads are permitted to be carried for the purposes of regulation 7(1)(a)(i) and (b)(i)–

(a) detonating fuzes in Compatibility Group B may be carried with explosive articles in Compatibility Group D, E or F of which the fuzes are components;

(b) explosive substances in Compatibility Group C or D may be carried–

(i) together,

(ii) with explosive articles in Compatibility Group C, D or E, or

(iii) with explosive articles in Division 1.4 in Compatibility Group G,

or any combination of them may be carried;

(c) explosive articles in Compatibility Group C, D or E may be carried–

(i) together,

(ii) with explosive articles in Compatibility Group F, or

(iii) with explosive articles in Compatibility Group G,

or any combination of them may be carried except a combination of the explosives mentioned in paragraphs (ii) and (iii) of this sub-paragraph;

(d) explosive substances or explosive articles in Compatibility Group S may be carried together or with explosive substances or explosive articles in Compatibility Group B, C, D, E, F, G or J, or with a mixture of explosive substances or explosive articles in those Compatibility Groups if such a mixture is permitted to be carried by virtue of sub-paragraphs (a) to (c) above.

SCHEDULE 4

Regulation 8

MARKING OF VEHICLES

PART I

REQUIREMENTS

1. At all times when explosives are carried–

(a) two blank rectangular reflectorised orange-coloured plates conforming to the requirements of paragraphs 2 and 4 shall be affixed, one at the front and the other at the rear of the vehicle,

(b) two placards conforming to the requirements of paragraphs 3 to 8 shall be affixed, one to each side of the vehicle, trailer, semi-trailer or freight container in which the explosives are actually carried.

2. Each plate referred to in paragraph 1(a) shall–

(a) be in the form of the following diagram and comply with the measurements in the diagram, and

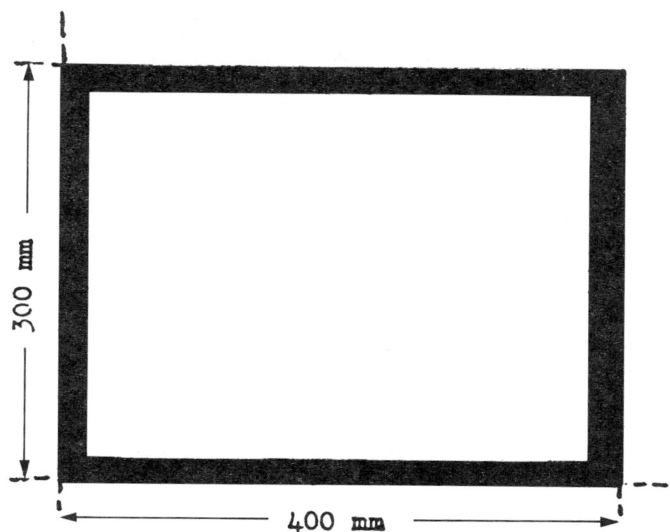

(b) have a black border not more than 15 millimetres wide.

3. Each placard referred to in paragraph 1(b) shall–

(a) be in the form of a square set with its side at an angle of 45° to the vertical, and

(b) have an orange-coloured background with a black border; and any figure, letter or pictograph required by the following provisions of this Schedule shall be in black.

4. Each plate and placard referred to in paragraph 1 shall–

(a) be clearly visible,

(b) so far as is reasonably practicable, be kept clean and free from obstruction at all times when explosives are being carried, and

(c) be completely covered or completely removed when all explosives have been removed from the vehicle, trailer, semi-trailer or freight container on which it was displayed.

5. In the case of explosives in Division 1.1, 1.2 or 1.3 each placard referred to in paragraph 1(b) shall–

(a) be in the form of the following diagram (the Division number "1.2" and the Compatibility Group letter "E" are only examples);

(b) comply with the measurements in the diagram except that larger measurements may be used in which case the measurements shall be increased proportionally;

(c) have a pictograph of a bomb blast filling most of its upper half;

(d) have the Division number and Compatibility Group letter appropriate to the explosives being carried written in its lower half; and

(e) have the class number "1" written in its bottom corner below the Division number and Compatibility Group letter.

6. In the case of explosives in Division 1.4 or 1.5 each placard referred to in paragraph 1(b) shall–

(a) be in the form of the following diagram (the Division number "1.4" and the Compatibility Group letter "E" are only examples);

(b) comply with the measurements in the diagram except that larger measurements may be used in which case the measurements shall be increased proportionally;

(c) have the Division number appropriate to the explosives being carried written on its upper half;

(d) have the Compatibility Group letter appropriate to the explosives being carried written on its lower half; and

(e) have the class number "1" written in its bottom corner below the Compatibility Group letter.

7. In the case of a vehicle carrying explosives of different Compatibility Groups, no Compatibility Group letter shall be written on the placards.

8. In the case of explosives which are carried solely in connection with an application for their classification, each placard referred to in paragraph 1(b) shall–

(a) be in the form of the following diagram; and

(b) comply with the measurements in the diagram, except that larger measurements may be used in which case the measurements shall be increased proportionally.

PART II

EXCEPTIONS

9. Part I of this Schedule shall not apply where–

(a) the explosives carried are substances in Compatibility Group G not exceeding 1 kilogram in quantity;

(b) the explosives carried are in Compatibility Group B or are unclassified explosives not exceeding (in either case) 10 kilograms in quantity;

(c) the explosives carried are–

(i) explosives of a type marked with an asterisk in Part II of Schedule 1; or

(ii) smokeless powder in Division 1.3 (being the explosive substance allocated on classification the UN Number 0161),

and the total quantity of all explosives carried in the vehicle does not exceed 100 kilograms;

(d) the explosives carried are in Division 1.4 and (except in the case of explosives in Compatibility Group S) do not exceed 500 kilograms in quantity;

(e) the explosives carried are other than those specified in the preceding provisions of this paragraph and do not exceed a total quantity of 50 kilograms;

(f) the explosives are being carried for or in connection with the carriage of those explosives by sea, if the vehicle or any freight container on the vehicle is placarded in accordance with the appropriate provisions of the International Maritime Dangerous Goods Code issued by the International Maritime Organisation, as revised or re-issued from time to time; or

(g) the explosives are being carried for or in connection with the carriage of those explosives by air if the explosives are packaged and labelled in accordance with the appropriate provisions of the Technical Instructions for the Safe Transport of Dangerous Goods by Air issued by the International Civil Aviation Organisation.

10. While the vehicle is being loaded or unloaded–

(a) paragraph 1(b) of this Schedule shall not apply,

(b) sub-paragraphs (a) and (b) of paragraph 4 of this Schedule shall not apply to the orange-coloured plate at the rear of the vehicle.

EXPLANATORY NOTE

(This note is not part of the Regulations)

These Regulations impose requirements with respect to the safety and security of explosives carried by road.

The Regulations:–

(a) prohibit the carriage of explosives in Compatibility Group K, and also prohibit the carriage of explosives which have not been classified under the Classification and Labelling of Explosives Regulations 1983 unless they are carried in connection with an application for classification and in accordance with conditions approved by the Health and Safety Executive or (in the case of military explosives) by the Secretary of State for Defence (regulation 4);

(b) prohibit the carriage of explosives in a vehicle used to carry passengers for hire or reward except in accordance with specified conditions including conditions as to the type and quantity of explosives carried (regulation 5);

(c) require vehicles and freight containers to be suitable having regard to the type and quantity of explosives carried, and impose quantity limits for various types of explosives (regulation 6 and Schedule 2);

(d) prohibit the carriage of mixed loads of explosives except in specified circumstances, and require measures to be taken to prevent explosives being brought into contact with dangerous substances or endangering or being endangered by such substances (regulation 7 and Schedule 3);

(e) impose requirements with respect to the marking of vehicles, subject to specified exceptions (regulation 8 and Schedule 4);

(f) prohibit the removal of explosives from the consignor's premises unless the operator is ready immediately to despatch them (regulation 9);

(g) require the consignor to give the operator of the vehicle written information about the load; and require specified information to be kept on the vehicle throughout the journey and shown on request to any police officer or traffic examiner, subject to exceptions for specified types and quantities of explosives (regulations 9 and 10);

(h) require the operator of the vehicle and any person engaged in the carriage or having custody or control of the explosives during the carriage to take such steps as it is reasonable for persons in their positions to take to ensure a safe and secure carriage (regulation 11(1));

(i) require a competent person to be in attendance with the vehicle whenever the driver is not present except in specified circumstances or in respect of certain types of explosives (regulation 11(2) to (4) and Schedule 1);

(j) require the operator and driver to follow a route agreed with the police if more than 5 tonnes of explosives in Division 1.1 are being carried (regulation 11(5));

(k) require the police, fire brigade, operator of the vehicle and Health and Safety Executive to be informed in the event of an accident, and require proper precautions to be taken in such an event (regulation 12);

(l) require the carriage to be completed within a reasonable length of time and require the explosives to be unloaded from the vehicle as soon as is reasonably practicable after it arrives at its destination (regulation 13);

(m) require the explosives to be delivered only to the consignee or his agent, or to a place specified in the Regulations where a person accepts custody of them for onward despatch (regulation 13);

(n) require that a trailer, semi-trailer or freight container containing explosives is not detached from the vehicle except in places specified in the Regulations or in an emergency (regulation 13);

(o) impose requirements with respect to the training of the driver and any attendant of the vehicle, subject to exceptions for specified types and quantities of explosives (regulation 14);

(p) impose a minimum age limit of 18 for persons engaged in the carriage of explosives subject to exceptions for specified types and quantities of explosives (regulation 15).

The requirements mentioned in sub-paragraphs (c) to (p) above do not apply to the carriage of explosives in vehicles used to carry passengers for hire or reward.

Certain requirements of the Regulations do not apply to carriage for the purposes of ordnance disposal, vehicles excepted from excise duty, vehicles only used on roads when passing between private premises in the immediate vicinity, vehicles engaged in specified international journeys, and carriage by HM Forces and visiting forces. The Regulations do not apply to any explosive nuclear device or any component thereof (regulation 3).

The Regulations provide for their enforcement by the Health and Safety Executive (regulation 16) and enable the Executive and (in the case of military explosives) the Secretary of State for Defence to grant certificates of exemption (regulation 17).

The Regulations repeal Section 97(5) of the Explosives Act 1875, repeal paragraph 4 of Schedule 2 to the Emergency Laws (Miscellaneous Provisions) Act 1947, revoke Order of the Secretary of State No. 11 (except byelaw 3) to the extent it relates to conveyance by road, and revoke the Conveyance by Road of Military Explosives Regulations 1977. The Regulations also make a consequential amendment to Section 5 of the 1875 Act (regulations 18 and 19).

Copies of relevant documents may be obtained as follows:–

(a) Regulations concerning the International Carriage of Dangerous Goods by Rail (RID) [ISBN 0 11 550814 7], from Her Majesty's Stationery Office;

(b) the International Maritime Dangerous Goods Code [Volumes I to IV ISBN 92 801 1055 1, Volume V ISBN 92 801 1125 6], from the International Maritime Organisation, 4 Albert Embankment, London SE1 7SR;

(c) the Technical Instructions for the Safe Transport of Dangerous Goods by Air (1989–90 English language edition), from either Freight Merchandising Services, c/o Vidap Freight Services Ltd., Green Lane, Hounslow, Middlesex TW4 6DD or IAL – International Aeradio Plc, Aeradio House, Hayes Road, Southall, Middlesex UB2 5NJ.

STATUTORY INSTRUMENTS

1989 No. 616 (S.69)

NATIONAL HEALTH SERVICE, SCOTLAND

The National Health Service (Travelling Expenses and Remission of Charges) (Scotland) Amendment (No.2) Regulations 1989

Made - - - -	*6th April 1989*
Laid before Parliament	*7th April 1989*
Coming into force	*10th April 1989*

The Secretary of State for Scotland, in exercise of the powers conferred on him by sections 75A, 105 and 108(1) of the National Health Service (Scotland) Act 1978(**a**), and of all other powers enabling him in that behalf, hereby makes the following Regulations:

Citation, commencement and interpretation

1. These Regulations may be cited as the National Health Service (Travelling Expenses and Remission of Charges) (Scotland) Amendment (No.2) Regulations 1989 and shall come into force on 10th April 1989 immediately after the coming into force of the National Health Service (Travelling Expenses and Remission of Charges) (Scotland) Amendment Regulations 1989(**b**).

Amendment of Table B in Part II of Schedule 1 to the principal Regulations

2. In Column 2 of Table B in Part II of Schedule 1 to the National Health Service (Travelling Expenses and Remission of Charges) (Scotland) Regulations 1988(**c**) in the entry relating to paragraph 11 of Schedule 3 to the Income Support (General) Regulations 1987(**d**),

(a) for "£8.20" there shall be substituted "£9.15";

(b) for "£11.20" there shall be substituted "£12.50";

(c) for "£3.45" there shall be substituted "£3.85";

(d) for "£6.45" there shall be substituted "£7.20"; and

(e) for "£3.00" there shall be substituted "£3.35".

(**a**) 1978 c.29; section 75A was inserted by section 14(2) of the Social Security Act 1988 (c.7); section 105, which was amended by the Health Services Act 1980 (c.53), Schedule 6, paragraph 5(1) and Schedule 7 and by the Health and Social Services and Social Security Adjudications Act 1983 (c.41), Schedule 9, paragraph 24, contains provisions relevant to the making of regulations; section 108(1) contains definitions of "prescribed" and "regulations" relevant to the exercise of the statutory powers under which these Regulations are made.

(**b**) S.I. 1989/393.

(**c**) S.I. 1988/546; the relevant amending instrument is S.I. 1989/393.

(**d**) S.I. 1987/1967; the relevant amending instruments are S.I. 1988/1445 and 1989/43.

Michael B. Forsyth
Parliamentary Under Secretary of State,
Scottish Office

St. Andrew's House, Edinburgh
6th April 1989

EXPLANATORY NOTE

(This note is not part of the Regulations)

These Regulations effect amendments to the National Health Service (Travelling Expenses and Remission of Charges) (Scotland) Regulations 1988 which provide for the remission and repayment of certain charges which would otherwise be payable under the National Health Service (Scotland) Act 1978 and for payment by the Secretary of State of certain travelling expenses.

They increase the amounts to be deducted, in the calculation of a person's entitlement to remission or repayment, for housing costs in respect of non-dependants. These amendments are consequential upon the uprating of social security benefits on 10th April 1989.

STATUTORY INSTRUMENTS

1989 No. 619

PUBLIC HEALTH, ENGLAND AND WALES
PUBLIC HEALTH, SCOTLAND
PUBLIC HEALTH, NORTHERN IRELAND

CONTAMINATION OF FOOD

The Food Protection (Emergency Prohibitions) (Sea Fish) (Revocation) Order 1989

Made - - - -	*6th April 1989*
Laid before Parliament	*6th April 1989*
Coming into force	*7th April 1989*

Whereas the Minister of Agriculture, Fisheries and Food was of the opinion, in accordance with section 1(1) of the Food and Environment Protection Act 1985(**a**), that in consequence of the likely escape of toxic substances as a result of the sinking in the English Channel of the m.v. Perintis on or about 13th March 1989, food might have been or might have become unsuitable for human consumption;

And whereas the said Minister was of the opinion that the said toxic substances were in the area designated in the Schedule to the Food Protection (Emergency Prohibitions) (Sea Fish) Order 1989(**b**);

And whereas the said Minister is now of the opinion that the said toxic substances are not in the said area;

Now, therefore, the said Minister, in exercise of the powers conferred on him by the said section 1(1) and section 1(10) of the said Act, and of all other powers enabling him in that behalf, hereby makes the following Order:

Title and commencement

1. This Order may be cited as the Food Protection (Emergency Prohibitions) (Sea Fish) (Revocation) Order 1989 and shall come into force on 7th April 1989.

Revocation

2. The Food Protection (Emergency Prohibitions) (Sea Fish) Order 1989 is hereby revoked.

(**a**) 1985 c.48.
(**b**) S.I. 1989/529.

In witness whereof the Official Seal of the Minister of Agriculture, Fisheries and Food is hereunto affixed on 6th April 1989.

John MacGregor
Minister of Agriculture, Fisheries and Food

EXPLANATORY NOTE

(This note is not part of the Order)

This Order revokes the Food Protection (Emergency Prohibitions) (Sea Fish) Order 1989, which contained emergency prohibitions restricting various activities in order to prevent human consumption of food rendered unsuitable for that purpose in consequence of the likely escape of toxic substances as a result of the sinking in the English Channel of the m.v. Perintis on or about 13th March 1989.

STATUTORY INSTRUMENTS

1989 No. 620

FEES AND CHARGES

The Measuring Instruments (EEC Requirements) (Fees) (Amendment) Regulations 1989

Made - - - -	*5th April 1989*
Laid before Parliament	*7th April 1989*
Coming into force	*30th April 1989*

The Secretary of State for Trade and Industry, with the consent of the Treasury, in exercise of the powers conferred on him by section 56(1) and (2) of the Finance Act 1973(**a**), and of all other powers enabling him in that behalf, hereby makes the following Regulations:

1. These regulations may be cited as the Measuring Instruments (EEC Requirements) (Fees) (Amendment) Regulations 1989 and shall come into force on 30th April 1989.

2. The Measuring Instruments (EEC Requirements) (Fees) Regulations 1988(**b**) are hereby amended as follows–

(a) in regulation 3(2), for "£24.20" there shall be substituted "£26.20", and the words from "except that" to the end shall be omitted;

(b) in paragraph (a) of Schedule 2, for "£41.20" there shall be substituted "£44.60"; and

(c) in paragraph 1(1)(a) of Schedule 3, for "£34.40", "£28.00" and "£10.40" there shall be substituted respectively "£37.20", "£30.20" and "£11.20".

Eric Forth
Parliamentary Under-Secretary of State,
Department of Trade and Industry

30th March 1989

We consent,

Alan Howarth
Kenneth Carlisle
Two of the Lords Commissioners of Her Majesty's Treasury

5th April 1989

(**a**) 1973 c.51.
(**b**) S.I. 1988/1184.

EXPLANATORY NOTE

(This note is not part of the Regulations)

These Regulations increase the fee payable in connection with services provided by the Department of Trade and Industry in respect of EEC initial verification of all classes of alcoholometers and alcohol hydrometers from £24.20 to £26.20, and abolish the fee for batches of 10 or more applications. They also increase the fees for EEC pattern approval as follows: for examiner staff time from £34.40 per hour to £37.20 per hour, for equipment test unit staff time from £28.00 per hour to £30.20 per hour and for use of an environmental testing chamber from £10.40 per hour to £11.20 per hour.

STATUTORY INSTRUMENTS

1989 No. 621

DISTRESS

The Distress for Rates (Amendment) Order 1989

Made - - - -	*5th April 1989*
Coming into force -	*1st May 1989*

The Secretary of State for the Environment, in exercise of the powers conferred by sections 101 and 114(3) of the General Rate Act 1967**(a)** and now vested in him**(b)**, and of all other powers enabling him in that behalf, hereby makes the following Order:

Citation, commencement and interpretation

1.—(1) This Order may be cited as the Distress for Rates (Amendment) Order 1989 and shall come into force on 1st May 1989.

(2) In this Order "the principal Order" means the Distress for Rates Order 1979**(c)**.

Amendments to the principal Order

2.—(1) In item 1 of article 3 of, and in article 4A(1) of, the principal Order–

(a) for "£33" (in all places where references to that amount occur in those provisions) there is substituted "£100";

(b) for "£2.50" in those provisions there is substituted "£12.50"; and

(c) for the words "7½ per cent. on the first £100, 2½ per cent. on the next £400, 1½ per cent. on the next £1,000, 1 per cent. on the next £2,500, ½ per cent. on the next £6,000" in those provisions there are substituted the words "12½ per cent. on the first £100 of the sum due, 4 per cent. on the next £400, 2½ per cent. on the next £1,500, 1 per cent. on the next £8,000".

(2) In item 3 of article 3 of the principal Order, for "£2.50" there is substituted "£4.50", and for "25p" there is substituted "45p".

(3) In item 4 of that article, for the words from "5 per cent." to "for each broker" there are substituted the words "Reasonable fees, charges and expenses of the broker appraising".

(4) In item 5A of that article–

(a) after the words "commission on, sale" there are inserted the words "by auction";

(b) for the words from "15 per cent." to "any additional sum" there are substituted the words "The auctioneer's commission fee and out-of-pocket expenses (but not exceeding in aggregate 15 per cent. of the sum realised), together with reasonable costs and fees incurred in respect of advertising"; and

---

(a) 1967 c.9; section 101(2) was amended by the Local Government, Planning and Land Act 1980 (c.65), section 38.
(b) S.I. 1970/1681.
(c) S.I. 1979/1038, amended by S.I. 1980/2013.

(c) for the words from "Out of pocket" to "the sum realised" there are substituted the words "The auctioneer's commission fee (but not exceeding $7\frac{1}{2}$ per cent. of the sum realised), together with the out-of-pocket expenses of the auctioneer and reasonable costs and fees incurred in respect of advertising".

(5) In item 5B of that article, after the words "proposed sale" there are inserted the words "by auction".

Transitional provision

3. The amendments made by this Order do not have effect in relation to cases where the distress concerned is made (or, as regards the amendments to article 4A(1) of the principal Order, attempted) before 1st May 1989.

Nicholas Ridley
Secretary of State for the Environment

5th April 1989

EXPLANATORY NOTE

(This note is not part of the Order)

This Order amends (and in certain cases increases) the charges recoverable under the Distress for Rates Order 1979 in the levying of distress for rates under the General Rate Act 1967.

STATUTORY INSTRUMENTS

1989 No. 622 (S.70)

BETTING, GAMING AND LOTTERIES

The Gaming Clubs (Hours and Charges) (Scotland) Amendment Regulations 1989

Made - - - -	*3rd April 1989*
Laid before Parliament	*10th April 1989*
Coming into force	*1st May 1989*

The Secretary of State, in exercise of the powers conferred on him by sections 14(2) and (3) and 51 of the Gaming Act 1968(**a**), and of all other powers enabling him in that behalf, and after consultation with the Gaming Board for Great Britain in accordance with section 51(2) of that Act, hereby makes the following Regulations:

1.—(1) These Regulations may be cited as the Gaming Clubs (Hours and Charges) (Scotland) Amendment Regulations 1989, and shall come into force on 1st May 1989.

(2) These Regulations shall extend to Scotland only.

2. In regulation 5(1) of the Gaming Clubs (Hours and Charges) (Scotland) Regulations 1984(**b**) (bingo charges)–

(a) for the sum "£4.60" in both places where it occurs there shall be substituted the sum "£5.00", and

(b) for the sum "£3.45" in both places where it occurs there shall be substituted the sum "£3.75".

3. The Gaming Clubs (Hours and Charges) (Scotland) Amendment Regulations 1987(**c**) are revoked.

James Douglas-Hamilton
Parliamentary Under Secretary of State,
Scottish Office

St. Andrew's House, Edinburgh
3rd April 1989

(**a**) 1968 c.65.
(**b**) S.I. 1984/470, amended by S.I. 1984/1804 and 1987/631.
(**c**) S.I. 1987/631.

EXPLANATORY NOTE

(This note is not part of the Regulations)

These Regulations increase the maximum charges which may be made for admission to gaming on bingo club premises in Scotland.

The maximum charge in respect of a charging period other than the shorter period permitted on a Sunday is increased from £4.60 to £5.00.

The maximum charge in respect of the shorter charging period permitted on a Sunday is increased from £3.45 to £3.75.

STATUTORY INSTRUMENTS

1989 No. 623 (S.71)

BETTING, GAMING AND LOTTERIES

The Gaming Act (Variation of Monetary Limits) (Scotland) Order 1989

Made - - - -	*3rd April 1989*
Laid before Parliament	*10th April 1989*
Coming into force	*1st May 1989*

The Secretary of State, in exercise of the powers conferred on him by sections 20(3) and (8) and 51(4) of the Gaming Act 1968(**a**), and of all other powers enabling him in that behalf, hereby makes the following Order:

1.—(1) This Order may be cited as the Gaming Act (Variation of Monetary Limits) (Scotland) Order 1989 and shall come into force on 1st May 1989.

(2) This Order shall extend to Scotland only.

2. Section 20(3) of the Gaming Act 1968(**b**) (which specifies the maximum permitted aggregate winnings in respect of bingo played in one week simultaneously on different club premises) shall have effect as if for the reference to the sum of £3,500 there were substituted a reference to the sum of £4,000.

3. Section 20(8) of the Gaming Act 1968(**c**) (which specifies the maximum amount by which weekly winnings on any particular bingo club premises may exceed the aggregate amount of the stakes hazarded) shall have effect as if for the reference to the sum of £1,500 there were substituted a reference to the sum of £1,750.

4. The Gaming Act (Variation of Monetary Limits) (Scotland) Order 1987(**d**) is revoked.

James Douglas-Hamilton
Parliamentary Under Secretary of State,
Scottish Office

St. Andrew's House, Edinburgh
3rd April 1989

(**a**) 1968 c.65; section 20(3) was amended by section 1 of the Gaming (Amendment) Act 1980 (c.8).
(**b**) The sum specified by section 20(3) is as substituted by S.I. 1987/630.
(**c**) The sum specified in section 20(8) is as substituted by S.I. 1987/630.
(**d**) S.I. 1987/630.

EXPLANATORY NOTE

(This note is not part of the Order)

This Order, which extends to Scotland only–

(a) increases from £3,500 to £4,000 the maximum aggregate sum permitted to be paid to players as winnings in respect of all "linked" games of bingo (article 2); and

(b) increases from £1,500 to £1,750 the maximum amount by which weekly winnings in bingo clubs may exceed the stakes hazarded (article 3).

STATUTORY INSTRUMENTS

1989 No. 632

SEEDS

The Seed Potatoes (Fees) Regulations 1989

Made - - - -	*6th April 1989*
Laid before Parliament	*10th April 1989*
Coming into force	*1st May 1989*

The Minister of Agriculture, Fisheries and Food in relation to England and the Secretary of State in relation to Wales, in exercise of the powers conferred by section 16(1) and (1A)(e) of the Plant Varieties and Seeds Act 1964(**a**) and now vested in them(**b**), and of all other powers enabling them in that behalf, after consultation in accordance with section 16(1) of the said Act with representatives of such interests as appear to them to be concerned, hereby make the following Regulations:

Title and commencement

1. These Regulations may be cited as the Seed Potatoes (Fees) Regulations 1989 and shall come into force on 1st May 1989.

Revocation of previous regulations

2. The Seed Potatoes (Fees) Regulations 1987(**c**) are hereby revoked.

Fees

3. There shall be paid in advance, in respect of the matters referred to in the first column of the Schedule hereto arising under the Seed Potatoes Regulations 1984(**d**), the fees respectively specified in the second column of the said Schedule opposite the references to those matters.

4. The said fees shall be payable to the Minister of Agriculture, Fisheries and Food (hereinafter referred to as "the Minister").

5. If an application for the classification of a crop of seed potatoes is withdrawn before the arrival of an inspector for the purpose of inspecting the crop for the first time any fee paid in respect of that crop in accordance with regulation 3 of these Regulations, less an amount of £5 in respect of each half-hectare or part thereof of that crop, shall be repaid to the applicant.

6. The Minister may refund in whole or in part fees paid under regulation 3 of these Regulations if, in his opinion, an effective health assessment of a crop or part of a crop is not possible for reasons beyond the control of the grower.

(**a**) 1964 c.14; section 16 was amended by the European Communities Act 1972 (c.68), Schedule 4, paragraph 5(1) and (2).
(**b**) In the case of the Secretary of State by virtue of S.I. 1978/272.
(**c**) S.I. 1987/649.
(**d**) S.I. 1984/412 amended, by S.I. 1987/547, 1988/1759.

In Witness whereof the Official Seal of the Minister of Agriculture, Fisheries and Food is hereunto affixed on 6th April 1989.

John MacGregor
Minister of Agriculture, Fisheries and Food

Peter Walker
Secretary of State for Wales

6th April 1989

Regulation 3

SCHEDULE

Matter	Total fee New fee	Old fee
Crop inspection and provision of seals and labels in respect of crops for which an application has been made for classification as:	£	£ (**a**)
A. Basic Seed Potatoes		
(a) VTSC class per half-hectare or part thereof	44.00	(38.00)
(b) Super Elite class per half-hectare or part thereof	39.50	(34.00)
Minimum fee	79.00	(68.00)
(c) Elite class per half-hectare or part thereof	38.50	(33.00)
Minimum fee	77.00	(66.00)
(d) AA class per half-hectare or part thereof	26.50	(22.50)
Minimum fee	53.00	(45.00)
B. Certified Seed Potatoes (that is to say CC class) per half-hectare or part thereof	26.00	(22.50)
Minimum fee	52.00	(45.00)

(**a**) The figures in parentheses are the fees which were charged under the Seed Potatoes (Fees) Regulations 1987 which are revoked by these Regulations.

EXPLANATORY NOTE

(This note is not part of the Regulations)

These Regulations, which revoke and replace the Seed Potatoes (Fees) Regulations 1987, prescribe the fees payable in respect of certain matters arising under the Seed Potatoes Regulations 1984, as amended.

The fees for crop inspections have been increased by £6 per half-hectare or part thereof inspected for the VTSC class, £5.50 for the Super Elite and Elite classes, £4 for the AA class and £3.50 for the CC class. In addition, the minimum fees payable for crop inspections have been increased by £11 for the Super Elite and Elite classes, £8 for the AA class and £7 for the CC class (regulation 3 and Schedule).

The fee to be retained by the Minister of Agriculture, Fisheries and Food in respect of an application for the classification of a crop of seed potatoes which is withdrawn remains at £5 in respect of each half-hectare or part thereof of that crop (regulation 5).

STATUTORY INSTRUMENTS

1989 No. 633

REPRESENTATION OF THE PEOPLE

The European Parliamentary Elections (Amendment) Regulations 1989

Made - - - -	*10th April 1989*
Coming into force	*10th April 1989*

Whereas a draft of these Regulations has been approved by a resolution of each House of Parliament:

Now, therefore, in exercise of the powers conferred upon me by paragraph 2 of Schedule 1 to the European Parliamentary Elections Act 1978**(a)**, I hereby make the following Regulations:

1.—(1) These Regulations may be cited as the European Parliamentary Elections (Amendment) Regulations 1989.

(2) These Regulations shall not extend to Northern Ireland.

2. In the right-hand column of Schedule 1 (application with modifications of provisions of the Representation of the People Acts) to the European Parliamentary Elections Regulations 1986**(b)**:

(a) in subsection (2) of section 76 (limitation of election expenses) of the Representation of the People Act 1983**(c)**, as substituted for the purposes of European Parliamentary elections, for the words "£8,000" and "3.5p" there shall be substituted the words "£10,000" and "4.3p", respectively; and

(b) in the modification of rule 9(1) (deposit) of the rules in Schedule 1 to that Act**(d)**, in its application for those purposes, for the words "£750" there shall be substituted the words "£1,000".

Home Office
10th April 1989

Douglas Hurd
One of Her Majesty's Principal Secretaries of State

(a) 1978 c.10; the citation of this Act has been amended by section 3(1)(b) and (2)(b) of the European Communities (Amendment) Act 1986 (c.58) on the coming into force of the Single European Act (Cmnd. 9758) on 1st July 1987.

(b) S.I. 1986/2209; the citation of this instrument has been amended by the provisions referred to in the first footnote to these Regulations.

(c) 1983 c.2.

(d) Rule 9 was amended by section 13(a) of the Representation of the People Act 1985 (c.50).

EXPLANATORY NOTE

(This note is not part of the Regulations)

These Regulations, which apply in Great Britain, amend the European Parliamentary Elections Regulations 1986. They increase the maximum amount of a candidate's election expenses at a European Parliamentary election. The maximum amount of a candidate's election expenses is made up of a fixed sum (expressed in pounds) plus a sum expressed in pence (and fractions of pence) for each entry in the register of electors.

These Regulations also increase from £750 to £1,000 the sum which must be deposited with the returning officer by or on behalf of a candidate at a European Parliamentary election. A person cannot be validly nominated as a candidate at such an election unless this deposit has been made.

STATUTORY INSTRUMENTS

1989 No. 634

REPRESENTATION OF THE PEOPLE

The Representation of the People (Variation of Limits of Candidates' Election Expenses) Order 1989

Made - - - -	*10th April 1989*
Coming into force	*11th April 1989*

Whereas a draft of this Order has been approved by resolution of each House of Parliament:

And whereas in my opinion there has been a change in the value of money since 13th May 1987 justifying the variations made by this Order:

Now, therefore, in exercise of the powers conferred upon me by sections 76A(1) and 197(3) of the Representation of the People Act 1983**(a)**, I hereby make the following Order:–

1.—(1) This Order may be cited as the Representation of the People (Variation of Limits of Candidates' Election Expenses) Order 1989 and shall come into force on the day after the day on which it is made.

(2) Articles 4, 5 and 6 of this Order do not extend to Northern Ireland.

(3) In this Order "the Act of 1983" means the Representation of the People Act 1983.

2. The maximum amount of a candidate's election expenses at a parliamentary election in a county constituency shall be varied by substituting, for the words "£3,370" and "3.8p" in section 76(2)(a)(i) of the Act of 1983**(b)**, the words "£3,648" and "4.1p", respectively.

3. The maximum amount of a candidate's election expenses at a parliamentary election in a borough constituency shall be varied by substituting, for the words "£3,370" and "2.9p" in section 76(2)(a)(ii) of the Act of 1983**(b)**, the words "£3,648" and "3.1p", respectively.

4. The maximum amount of a candidate's election expenses at a local government election to which section 76(2)(b)(ii) of the Act of 1983**(b)** applies shall be varied by substituting, for the words "£150" and "3p" in that provision, the words "£162" and "3.2p", respectively.

5. The maximum amount of a candidate's election expenses at a ward election in the City of London shall be varied by substituting for the words "£150" and "3p" in section 197(1) of the Act of 1983**(c)**, the words "£162" and "3.2p", respectively.

(a) 1983 c.2; section 76A was inserted by section 14(4) of the Representation of the People Act 1985 (c.50) and section 197(3) was amended by paragraph 67(b) of Schedule 4 to that Act.
(b) The sums in section 76(2) are as substituted by S.I. 1987/903.
(c) The sums in section 197 are as substituted by S.I. 1987/903.

6. The maximum amount of a candidate's election expenses at an election by liverymen in common hall shall be varied by substituting, for the words "15.8p" in section 197(2) of the Act of 1983**(a)**, the words "17.1p".

7. Articles 2, 3, 5, 6 and 7 of the Representation of the People (Variation of Limits of Candidates' Election Expenses) Order 1987**(b)** shall cease to have effect.

Home Office
10th April 1989

Douglas Hurd
One of Her Majesty's Principal Secretaries of State

EXPLANATORY NOTE

(This note is not part of the Order)

This Order increases the maximum amounts of candidates' election expenses at parliamentary elections in the United Kingdom (articles 2 and 3), local government elections in Great Britain (article 4) and ward elections (article 5) and elections by liverymen in common hall (article 6) in the City of London.

The increases are such as are justified by the change in the value of money since the last occasion on which those maximum amounts were fixed. The last occasion was 13th May 1987 when the Representation of the People (Variation of Limits of Candidates' Election Expenses) Order 1987 was made.

Except in the case of the election by liverymen in common hall, the maximum amount of a candidate's election expenses is made up of a fixed sum (expressed in pounds) plus a sum expressed in pence (and fractions of pence) for, in the case of parliamentary and local government elections, each entry in the register of electors or, in the case of ward elections in the City of London, each elector. The maximum amount of a candidate's election expenses at the election by liverymen in common hall is calculated by allowing an amount in pence (and fractions of pence) for every elector on the common hall register to be used at the election.

(a) The sums in section 197 are as substituted by S.I. 1987/903.
(b) S.I. 1987/903.

STATUTORY INSTRUMENTS

1989 No. 635

HEALTH AND SAFETY

The Electricity at Work Regulations 1989

Made - - - -	*7th April 1989*
Laid before Parliament	*25th April 1989*
Coming into force	*1st April 1990*

ARRANGEMENT OF REGULATIONS

PART I
Introduction

PART II
General

PART III
Regulations Applying to Mines Only

PART IV
Miscellaneous and General

The Secretary of State, in exercise of the powers conferred on him by sections 15(1), (2), (3)(a) and (b), (4)(a), (5)(b), (6)(b), (8) and (9) and 82(3)(a) of, and paragraphs 1(1)(a) and (c), (2) and (3), 6(2), 9, 11, 12, 14, 15(1), 16 and 21(b) of Schedule 3 to, the Health and Safety at Work etc. Act 1974(**a**) ("the 1974 Act"), and of all other powers enabling him in that behalf and for the purpose of giving effect without modifications to proposals submitted to him by the Health and Safety Commission under section 11(2)(d) of the 1974 Act, after the carrying out by the said Commission of consultations in accordance with section 50(3) of that Act, hereby makes the following Regulations:

(**a**) 1974 c.37; sections 15 and 50 were amended by the Employment Protection Act 1975 (c.71), Schedule 15, paragraphs 6 and 16 respectively.

PART I

INTRODUCTION

Citation and commencement

1. These Regulations may be cited as the Electricity at Work Regulations 1989 and shall come into force on 1st April 1990.

Interpretation

2.—(1) In these Regulations, unless the context otherwise requires–

"approved" means approved in writing for the time being by the Health and Safety Executive for the purposes of these Regulations or conforming with a specification approved in writing by the Health and Safety Executive for the purposes of these Regulations;

"circuit conductor" means any conductor in a system which is intended to carry electric current in normal conditions, or to be energised in normal conditions, and includes a combined neutral and earth conductor, but does not include a conductor provided solely to perform a protective function by connection to earth or other reference point;

"conductor" means a conductor of electrical energy;

"danger" means risk of injury;

"electrical equipment" includes anything used, intended to be used or installed for use, to generate, provide, transmit, transform, rectify, convert, conduct, distribute, control, store, measure or use electrical energy;

"firedamp" means any flammable gas or any flammable mixture of gases occurring naturally in a mine;

"injury" means death or personal injury from electric shock, electric burn, electrical explosion or arcing, or from fire or explosion initiated by electrical energy, where any such death or injury is associated with the generation, provision, transmission, transformation, rectification, conversion, conduction, distribution, control, storage, measurement or use of electrical energy;

"safety-lamp mine" means–

(a) any coal mine; or

(b) any other mine in which–

(i) there has occurred below ground an ignition of firedamp; or

(ii) more than 0.25% by volume of firedamp is found on any occasion at any place below ground in the mine;

"system" means an electrical system in which all the electrical equipment is, or may be, electrically connected to a common source of electrical energy, and includes such source and such equipment.

(2) Unless the context otherwise requires, any reference in these Regulations to–

(a) a numbered regulation or Schedule is a reference to the regulation or Schedule in these Regulations so numbered;

(b) a numbered paragraph is a reference to the paragraph so numbered in the regulation or Schedule in which the reference appears.

Persons on whom duties are imposed by these Regulations

3.—(1) Except where otherwise expressly provided in these Regulations, it shall be the duty of every–

(a) employer and self-employed person to comply with the provisions of these Regulations in so far as they relate to matters which are within his control; and

(b) manager of a mine or quarry (within in either case the meaning of section 180 of the Mines and Quarries Act 1954(**a**)) to ensure that all requirements or prohibitions imposed by or under these Regulations are complied with in so far as they relate to the mine or quarry or part of a quarry of which he is the manager and to matters which are within his control.

(**a**) 1954 c.70; section 180 was amended by S.I. 1974/2013.

(2) It shall be the duty of every employee while at work–

(a) to co-operate with his employer so far as is necessary to enable any duty placed on that employer by the provisions of these Regulations to be complied with; and

(b) to comply with the provisions of these Regulations in so far as they relate to matters which are within his control.

PART II

GENERAL

Systems, work activities and protective equipment

4.—(1) All systems shall at all times be of such construction as to prevent, so far as is reasonably practicable, danger.

(2) As may be necessary to prevent danger, all systems shall be maintained so as to prevent, so far as is reasonably practicable, such danger.

(3) Every work activity, including operation, use and maintenance of a system and work near a system, shall be carried out in such a manner as not to give rise, so far as is reasonably practicable, to danger.

(4) Any equipment provided under these Regulations for the purpose of protecting persons at work on or near electrical equipment shall be suitable for the use for which it is provided, be maintained in a condition suitable for that use, and be properly used.

Strength and capability of electrical equipment

5. No electrical equipment shall be put into use where its strength and capability may be exceeded in such a way as may give rise to danger.

Adverse or hazardous environments

6. Electrical equipment which may reasonably foreseeably be exposed to–

(a) mechanical damage;

(b) the effects of the weather, natural hazards, temperature or pressure;

(c) the effects of wet, dirty, dusty or corrosive conditions; or

(d) any flammable or explosive substance, including dusts, vapours or gases,

shall be of such construction or as necessary protected as to prevent, so far as is reasonably practicable, danger arising from such exposure.

Insulation, protection and placing of conductors

7. All conductors in a system which may give rise to danger shall either–

(a) be suitably covered with insulating material and as necessary protected so as to prevent, so far as is reasonably practicable, danger; or

(b) have such precautions taken in respect of them (including, where appropriate, their being suitably placed) as will prevent, so far as is reasonably practicable, danger.

Earthing or other suitable precautions

8. Precautions shall be taken, either by earthing or by other suitable means, to prevent danger arising when any conductor (other than a circuit conductor) which may reasonably foreseeably become charged as a result of either the use of a system, or a fault in a system, becomes so charged; and, for the purposes of ensuring compliance with this regulation, a conductor shall be regarded as earthed when it is connected to the general mass of earth by conductors of sufficient strength and current-carrying capability to discharge electrical energy to earth.

Integrity of referenced conductors

9. If a circuit conductor is connected to earth or to any other reference point, nothing which might reasonably be expected to give rise to danger by breaking the electrical continuity or introducing high impedance shall be placed in that conductor unless suitable precautions are taken to prevent that danger.

Connections

10. Where necessary to prevent danger, every joint and connection in a system shall be mechanically and electrically suitable for use.

Means for protecting from excess of current

11. Efficient means, suitably located, shall be provided for protecting from excess of current every part of a system as may be necessary to prevent danger.

Means for cutting off the supply and for isolation

12.—(1) Subject to paragraph (3), where necessary to prevent danger, suitable means (including, where appropriate, methods of identifying circuits) shall be available for–

(a) cutting off the supply of electrical energy to any electrical equipment; and

(b) the isolation of any electrical equipment.

(2) In paragraph (1), "isolation" means the disconnection and separation of the electrical equipment from every source of electrical energy in such a way that this disconnection and separation is secure.

(3) Paragraph (1) shall not apply to electrical equipment which is itself a source of electrical energy but, in such a case as is necessary, precautions shall be taken to prevent, so far as is reasonably practicable, danger.

Precautions for work on equipment made dead

13. Adequate precautions shall be taken to prevent electrical equipment, which has been made dead in order to prevent danger while work is carried out on or near that equipment, from becoming electrically charged during that work if danger may thereby arise.

Work on or near live conductors

14. No person shall be engaged in any work activity on or so near any live conductor (other than one suitably covered with insulating material so as to prevent danger) that danger may arise unless–

(a) it is unreasonable in all the circumstances for it to be dead; and

(b) it is reasonable in all the circumstances for him to be at work on or near it while it is live; and

(c) suitable precautions (including where necessary the provision of suitable protective equipment) are taken to prevent injury.

Working space, access and lighting

15. For the purposes of enabling injury to be prevented, adequate working space, adequate means of access, and adequate lighting shall be provided at all electrical equipment on which or near which work is being done in circumstances which may give rise to danger.

Persons to be competent to prevent danger and injury

16. No person shall be engaged in any work activity where technical knowledge or experience is necessary to prevent danger or, where appropriate, injury, unless he possesses such knowledge or experience, or is under such degree of supervision as may be appropriate having regard to the nature of the work.

PART III

REGULATIONS APPLYING TO MINES ONLY

Provisions applying to mines only

17.—(1) The provisions of regulations 18 to 28 and Schedule 1 shall apply to mines only; and the provisions of that Schedule shall have effect in particular in relation to the use below ground in a coal mine of any film lighting circuit (as defined by paragraph 1 of that Schedule) at or in close proximity to a coal face.

(2) Expressions to which meanings are assigned by the Mines and Quarries Act 1954 shall, unless the contrary intention appears, have the same meanings in regulations 18 to 27 and Schedule 1.

Introduction of electrical equipment

18. Before electrical equipment (other than equipment approved for the purposes of regulation 20(1)) is first introduced into any underground part of a safety-lamp mine to which the Coal and Other Mines (Surveyors and Plans) Regulations 1956 (**a**) apply, the manager shall submit to an inspector a copy of the ventilation plan required to be kept for that part by regulation 9 of those Regulations, on which the intended locations of that equipment shall be shown, together with a copy of any schematic diagram relating to that part prepared for the purposes of regulation 24(1).

Restriction of equipment in certain zones below ground

19.—(1) At every safety-lamp mine containing any zones below ground in which firedamp whether or not normally present is likely to occur in a quantity sufficient to indicate danger, there shall be prepared a suitable plan identifying such zones.

(2) Electrical equipment shall not be energised in such zones unless it is–

(a) equipment of a kind approved for that purpose;

(b) equipment approved pursuant to regulation 20(1);

(c) equipment the use of which was lawful in such zones immediately before the coming into force of these Regulations;

(d) equipment which has received a certificate of conformity or a certificate of inspection in accordance with Council Directive 82/130/EEC(**b**) on the approximation of the laws of the Member States concerning electrical equipment for use in potentially explosive atmospheres in mines susceptible to firedamp, as adapted to technical progress by Commission Directive 88/35/EEC(**c**) ;

(e) equipment such as is specified in regulation 21(2);

(f) equipment which is not capable of producing incendive electrical sparks in normal use; or

(g) electrically-powered equipment not permanently installed in the mine but required occasionally for monitoring, testing, recording and measurement, and used where the concentration of firedamp is 0.8% by volume or less in accordance with suitable rules drawn up by the manager to ensure that danger will not thereby arise, which rules shall in particular include provision for personal supervision of that equipment by a competent person and testing for firedamp when it is in use;

and any lights which conform with this paragraph shall be permitted lights in any mine such as is specified in paragraph (1).

Cutting off electricity or making safe where firedamp is found either below ground or at the surface

20.—(1) Where any person at a mine detects firedamp in a concentration exceeding 1.25% by volume in the general body of the air either below ground at that mine or at any place on the surface thereat where any exhauster in a firedamp drainage system is installed, firedamp is monitored or its heat content measured, he shall forthwith–

(**a**) S.I. 1956/1760, to which there are amendments not relevant to these Regulations.
(**b**) OJ No. L59, 2.3.82, p.10.
(**c**) OJ No. L64, 10.3.88, p.36.

(a) cut off the supply of electricity to any electrical equipment situated at the place where the said concentration was detected; or

(b) (where this is not possible) take all reasonably practicable steps to make such equipment safe; or

(c) (if the taking of the measures specified in sub-paragraphs (a) and (b) above does not fall within the scope of his normal duties) report the matter to an official of the mine who shall ensure that those measures are taken;

except that the provisions of sub-paragraphs (a) to (c) above shall not apply if the electrical equipment is approved for the purpose of remaining energised in such circumstances or (in the case of a safety-lamp mine) is electrical equipment such as is specified in regulation 21(2).

(2) If the supply of electricity to electrical equipment is cut off or the equipment made safe in accordance with paragraph (1), it shall remain in that condition until the senior official on duty at the mine having determined that it is safe to do so, directs that such precautions are no longer necessary.

(3) If the supply of electricity to electrical equipment is cut off or the equipment made safe in accordance with paragraph (1), details of the time, duration and location shall be recorded.

Approval of certain equipment for use in safety-lamp mines

21.—(1) Subject to paragraph (2), no electric safety-lamp, gas detector, telephone or signalling equipment or other equipment associated therewith or required for the safety of persons shall be taken or used below ground at any safety-lamp mine unless it is equipment which has been approved pursuant to regulation 20(1) or (in the case of electric safety-lamps) is of a type for the time being approved pursuant to section 64(2) of the Mines and Quarries Act 1954.

(2) Nothing in paragraph (1) shall prevent the taking or use below ground at any safety-lamp mine of any electrical equipment which was, before the coming into force of these Regulations, approved pursuant to regulations 20 and 21A of the Coal and Other Mines (Electricity) Regulations 1956(**a**).

Means of cutting off electricity to circuits below ground

22. At every mine at which electrical equipment which may give rise to danger is installed below ground and is supplied from a power source at the surface of the mine, switchgear shall be provided at the surface for cutting off the supply of current to that equipment, and adequate provision shall be made for the operation of that switchgear, including such means of communication as will, so far as is reasonably practicable, enable the switchgear to be operated in case of danger.

Oil-filled equipment

23. Electrical equipment using oil as a means of cooling, insulation or arc suppression shall not be introduced below ground at a mine.

Records and information

24.—(1) Suitable schematic diagrams of all electrical distribution systems intended to be operated at the mine (other than those operating at a voltage not exceeding 250 volts) shall, so far as is reasonably practicable–

(a) be prepared and kept in the office at the mine; and

(b) show the planned settings of any circuit electrical protective devices.

(2) Copies of such portions of the schematic diagrams prepared pursuant to paragraph (1) as are necessary to prevent danger and which show at least those parts of the electrical system which are served by switchgear operating at a voltage in excess of 250 volts shall be displayed at each place where such switchgear is installed.

(a) S.I. 1956/1766; the relevant amending instruments are S.I. 1974/1853 and 1977/1205.

(3) Plans on a suitable scale shall be kept in the office at the mine showing, so far as is reasonably practicable, the position of all permanently installed electrical equipment at the mine supplied at a voltage in excess of 250 volts.

Electric shock notices

25. Where, at any place at a mine, electric arc welding is taking place or electrical energy is being generated, transformed or used at a nominal voltage in excess of 125 volts a.c. or 250 volts d.c., a notice shall be displayed in a form which can be easily read and understood and containing information on the appropriate first-aid treatment for electric shock and details of the emergency action to be taken in the event of electric shock.

Introduction of battery-powered locomotives and vehicles into safety-lamp mines

26. No locomotive or vehicle which uses an electrical storage battery, either partly or wholly, as a power source for traction purposes shall be introduced below ground at a safety-lamp mine unless it is an approved locomotive or vehicle.

Storage, charging and transfer of electrical storage batteries

27. At any mine in which electrical storage batteries are used below ground, those batteries shall, so far as is reasonably practicable, be used, stored, charged and transferred in a safe manner.

Disapplication of section 157 of the Mines and Quarries Act 1954

28. Section 157 of the Mines and Quarries Act 1954(**a**) (which provides a defence in legal proceedings and prosecutions in certain circumstances) shall not apply in relation to any legal proceedings or prosecutions based on an allegation of a contravention of a requirement or prohibition imposed by regulations 18 to 27 or by or under Schedule 1.

PART IV

MISCELLANEOUS AND GENERAL

Defence

29. In any proceedings for an offence consisting of a contravention of regulations 4(4), 5, 8, 9, 10, 11, 12, 13, 14, 15, 16 or 25, it shall be a defence for any person to prove that he took all reasonable steps and exercised all due diligence to avoid the commission of that offence.

Exemption certificates

30.—(1) Subject to paragraph (2), the Health and Safety Executive may, by a certificate in writing, exempt–

(a) any person;
(b) any premises;
(c) any electrical equipment;
(d) any electrical system;
(e) any electrical process;
(f) any activity,

or any class of the above, from any requirement or prohibition imposed by these Regulations and any such exemption may be granted subject to conditions and to a limit of time and may be revoked by a certificate in writing at any time.

(2) The Executive shall not grant any such exemption unless, having regard to the circumstances of the case, and in particular to–

(a) the conditions, if any, which it proposes to attach to the exemption; and

(**a**) 1954 c.70; section 157 was amended by S.I. 1974/2013.

(b) any other requirements imposed by or under any enactment which apply to the case,

it is satisfied that the health and safety of persons who are likely to be affected by the exemption will not be prejudiced in consequence of it.

Extension outside Great Britain

31. These Regulations shall apply to and in relation to premises and activities outside Great Britain to which sections 1 to 59 and 80 to 82 of the Health and Safety at Work etc. Act 1974 apply by virtue of Articles 6 and 7 of the Health and Safety at Work etc. Act 1974 (Application outside Great Britain) Order 1977(**a**) as they apply within Great Britain.

Disapplication of duties

32. The duties imposed by these Regulations shall not extend to–

(a) the master or crew of a sea-going ship or to the employer of such persons, in relation to the normal ship-board activities of a ship's crew under the direction of the master; or

(b) any person, in relation to any aircraft or hovercraft which is moving under its own power.

Revocations and modifications

33.—(1) The instruments specified in column 1 of Part I of Schedule 2 are revoked to the extent specified in the corresponding entry in column 3 of that Part.

(2) The enactments and instruments specified in Part II of Schedule 2 shall be modified to the extent specified in that Part.

(3) In the Mines and Quarries Act 1954, the Mines and Quarries (Tips) Act 1969(**b**) and the Mines Management Act 1971(**c**), and in regulations made under any of those Acts, or in health and safety regulations, any reference to any of those Acts shall be treated as including a reference to these Regulations.

Signed by order of the Secretary of State.

Patrick Nicholls
Parliamentary Under Secretary of State,
Department of Employment

7th April 1989

SCHEDULE 1

Regulation 17

PROVISIONS APPLYING TO MINES ONLY AND HAVING EFFECT IN PARTICULAR IN RELATION TO THE USE BELOW GROUND IN COAL MINES OF FILM LIGHTING CIRCUITS

1. In this Schedule, "film lighting circuit" means any electric circuit at a coal mine, not being permanently installed thereat, and required occasionally to supply mains electricity to electric lights for the purpose of providing illumination for photography or video-recording, and includes the said lights and any other electrical apparatus in that circuit.

2. A film lighting circuit shall not be used unless–

(a) not less than 7 days prior to such use, details of when and where it is to be used have been notified to the Health and Safety Executive; and

(b) within the 24 hours immediately preceding such use–

(i) it has been externally examined; and

(ii) the insulation thereof and the conductance of every conductor of every flexible cable forming part of it have been tested.

(**a**) S.I. 1977/1232. (**b**) 1969 c.10. (**c**) 1971 c.20.

3. The manager shall make, and ensure the carrying out of, arrangements to prevent the accumulation of dust on any surface of any luminaire or apparatus in sufficient quantities to give rise to spontaneous ignition.

4. The manager shall make suitable rules with respect to the use of film lighting circuits, for the purpose of ensuring, so far as is reasonably practicable, that such use will not give rise to danger; and those rules shall in particular require–

(a) continuous testing for firedamp when a film lighting circuit is in use; and

(b) the operation of any such circuit to be personally supervised by a competent person.

5. No person shall fire any shot or round of shots in a place in which, or in the vicinity of which, any part of a film lighting circuit is installed.

Regulation 33

SCHEDULE 2

REVOCATIONS AND MODIFICATIONS

PART I

REVOCATIONS

Column 1 *Regulations and orders revoked*	Column 2 *Reference*	Column 3 *Extent of revocation*
The Electricity Regulations 1908	S.R. & O. 1908/1312	The whole Regulations
The Manufacture of Cinematograph Film Regulations 1928	S.R. & O. 1928/82	Regulation 12
The Cinematograph Film Stripping Regulations 1939	S.R. & O. 1939/571	Regulation 14
The Electricity (Factories Act) Special Regulations 1944	S.R. & O. 1944/739	The whole Regulations
The Factories (Testing of Aircraft Engines and Accessories) Special Regulations 1952	S.I. 1952/1689	In regulation 2(2), the definitions of "Earthed", "Flameproof" and "Intrinsically safe"; regulations 14, 15, 16, 17 and 18
The Coal and Other Mines (General Duties and Conduct) Regulations 1956	S.I. 1956/1761	Regulation 6(2)
The Coal and Other Mines (Safety-Lamps and Lighting) Regulations 1956	S.I. 1956/1765	Regulations 4, 18, 18A and 19
The Coal and Other Mines (Electricity) Order 1956	S.I. 1956/1766	The whole Order
The Miscellaneous Mines (Electricity) Order 1956	S.I. 1956/1779	The whole Order
The Quarries (Electricity) Order 1956	S.I. 1956/1781	The whole Order
The Dragonby Ironstone Mine (Diesel, Diesel-Electric and Storage Battery Vehicles) Special Regulations 1958	S.I. 1958/320	The whole Regulations
The Winn's Ironstone Mine (Diesel, Diesel-Electric and Storage Battery Vehicles) Special Regulations 1958	S.I. 1958/321	The whole Regulations
The Silverwood Mine (Electric Trolley Locomotives) Special Regulations 1958	S.I. 1958/1276	The whole Regulations
The Gasswater A Mine (Storage Battery Locomotives) Special Regulations 1959	S.I. 1959/37	The whole Regulations

Column 1 *Regulations and orders revoked*	Column 2 *Reference*	Column 3 *Extent of revocation*
The Gasswater B Mine (Storage Battery Locomotives) Special Regulations 1959	S.I. 1959/38	The whole Regulations
The Glass Houghton Mine (Shuttle Cars) Special Regulations 1959	S.I. 1959/663	The whole Regulations
The Heights Mine (Storage Battery Locomotives) Special Regulations 1960	S.I. 1960/223	The whole Regulations
The Coal Mines (Firedamp Drainage) Regulations 1960	S.I. 1960/1015	Regulation 12(1)(b)
The Construction (General Provisions) Regulations 1961	S.I. 1961/1580	Regulation 44
The Hopton Mine (Locomotives and Diesel Vehicles) Special Regulations 1961	S.I. 1961/1583	The whole Regulations
The Cocklakes Mine (Locomotives and Diesel Vehicles) Special Regulations 1961	S.I. 1961/1769	The whole Regulations
The Long Meg Mine (Locomotives and Diesel Vehicles) Special Regulations 1961	S.I. 1961/1774	The whole Regulations
The Sandwith Anhydrite Mine (Lighting) Special Regulations 1962	S.I. 1962/192	The whole Regulations
The Thistleton Mine Special Regulations 1962	S.I. 1962/364	Regulations 4, 22 to 42, and 53 to 80
The Force Crag Mine (Storage Battery Locomotives) Special Regulations 1962	S.I. 1962/1501	The whole Regulations
The Potts Ghyll Mine (Storage Battery Locomotives) Special Regulations 1963	S.I. 1963/270	The whole Regulations
The Chislet Mine (Electric Trolley Locomotives) Special Regulations 1963	S.I. 1963/896	The whole Regulations
The Llanharry Mine (Storage Battery Locomotives) Special Regulations 1963	S.I. 1963/906	The whole Regulations
The Easton Mine (Diesel, Diesel-Electric and Storage Battery Vehicles) Special Regulations 1963	S.I. 1963/1074	The whole Regulations
The Guildie Howes Mine (Locomotives and Diesel Vehicles) Special Regulations 1965	S.I. 1965/33	The whole Regulations
The Muirshiel Barytes Mine (Storage Battery Locomotives) Special Regulations 1965	S.I. 1965/120	The whole Regulations
The Dragonby Ironstone Mine (Diesel, Diesel-Electric and Storage Battery Vehicles) (Amendment) Special Regulations 1965	S.I. 1965/1299	The whole Regulations
The Coal and Other Mines (Mechanics and Electricians) Regulations 1965	S.I. 1965/1559	Regulation 11(3)
The Redburn Mine (Storage Battery Locomotives) Special Regulations 1965	S.I. 1965/1698	The whole Regulations
The Settlingstones Mine (Storage Battery Locomotives) Special Regulations 1966	S.I. 1966/351	The whole Regulations
The Coal and Other Mines (Electricity) (Amendment) Regulations 1967	S.I. 1967/1083	The whole Regulations
The Aberllefeni Mine (Storage Battery Locomotives) Special Regulations 1967	S.I. 1967/1395	The whole Regulations
The Braich Goch Mine (Storage Battery Locomotives) Special Regulations 1967	S.I. 1967/1396	The whole Regulations

Column 1 *Regulations and orders revoked*	Column 2 *Reference*	Column 3 *Extent of revocation*
The Preston Manor Mine (Lighting) Special Regulations 1968	S.I. 1968/38	The whole Regulations
The Chudleigh Knighton Tunnel Mine (Lighting) Special Regulations 1968	S.I. 1968/39	The whole Regulations
The West Golds Mine (Lighting) Special Regulations 1968	S.I. 1968/40	The whole Regulations
The Broadway New Pit Tunnel Mine (Lighting) Special Regulations 1968	S.I. 1968/103	The whole Regulations
The Mainbow Mine (Lighting) Special Regulations 1968	S.I. 1968/104	The whole Regulations
The Nangiles and the Janes Mine (Storage Battery Locomotives) Special Regulations 1968	S.I. 1968/868	The whole Regulations
The Camborne Mine (Storage Battery Locomotives) Special Regulations 1969	S.I. 1969/570	The whole Regulations
The Cotgrave Mine (Suspended Monorail Diesel Locomotives) Special Regulations 1969	S.I. 1969/744	The whole Regulations
The Levant Mine (Storage Battery Locomotives) Special Regulations 1969	S.I. 1969/1236	The whole Regulations
The No. 4 Adit Mine (Lighting) Special Regulations 1970	S.I. 1970/1103	The whole Regulations
The Rixey Park Mine (Lighting) Special Regulations 1970	S.I. 1970/1547	The whole Regulations
The Horden Mine (Cable Reel Shuttle Cars) Special Regulations 1971	S.I. 1971/18	The whole Regulations
The Mount Wellington Mine (Storage Battery Locomotives) Special Regulations 1971	S.I. 1971/1270	The whole Regulations
The Cornish Hush Mine (Storage Battery Locomotives) Special Regulations 1972	S.I. 1972/348	The whole Regulations
The Beckermet Mine (Storage Battery Locomotives) Special Regulations 1972	S.I. 1972/396	The whole Regulations
The Burtree Pasture Mine (Storage Battery Locomotives) Special Regulations 1972	S.I. 1972/483	The whole Regulations
The Haile Moor Mine (Storage Battery Locomotives) Special Regulations 1972	S.I. 1972/1235	The whole Regulations
The Carrock Fell Mine (Storage Battery Locomotives) Special Regulations 1972	S.I. 1972/1236	The whole Regulations
The Prince of Wales Mine (Storage Battery Locomotives) Special Regulations 1972	S.I. 1972/1393	The whole Regulations
The Rixey Park Mine (Storage Battery Locomotives) Special Regulations 1973	S.I. 1973/1208	The whole Regulations
The Beaumont Mine (Storage Battery Locomotives) Special Regulations 1974	S.I. 1974/1654	The whole Regulations
The Coal and Other Mines (Electricity) (Second Amendment) Regulations 1974	S.I. 1974/1853	The whole Regulations
The Ledston Luck Mine (Cable Reel Shuttle Cars) Special Regulations 1974	S.I. 1974/1929	The whole Regulations
The Factories Act 1961 etc. (Repeals and Modifications) Regulations 1974	S.I. 1974/1941	Regulation 3(2)(a)
The Hendre Mine (Storage Battery Locomotives) Special Regulations 1974	S.I. 1974/1985	The whole Regulations

Column 1 *Regulations and orders revoked*	Column 2 *Reference*	Column 3 *Extent of revocation*
The Mines and Quarries Acts 1954 to 1971 (Repeals and Modifications) Regulations 1975	S.I. 1975/1102	The entry in Schedule 2 relating to the Coal and Other Mines (Electricity) Regulations 1956
The South Leicester Mine (Electric Lighting) Regulations 1976	S.I. 1976/696	The whole Regulations
The Coal and Other Mines (Electricity) (Third Amendment) Regulations 1977	S.I. 1977/1205	The whole Regulations
The Bolsover Mine (Cable Reel Shuttle Cars) Regulations 1977	S.I. 1977/2035	The whole Regulations
The Ackton Hall Mine (Cable Reel Load-Haul-Dump Vehicles) Regulations 1978	S.I. 1978/1539	The whole Regulations
The Coal and Other Mines (Metrication) Regulations 1978	S.I. 1978/1648	The entries in the Schedule relating to– (a) regulation 18 of the Coal and Other Mines (Safety-Lamps and Lighting) Regulations 1956; and (b) the Coal and Other Mines (Electricity) Regulations 1956
The Coal and Other Mines (Electric Lighting for Filming) Regulations 1979	S.I. 1979/1203	The whole Regulations
The Scraithole Mine (Storage Battery Locomotives) Regulations 1979	S.I. 1979/1658	The whole Regulations
The Lynemouth Mine (Electric Lighting) Regulations 1980	S.I. 1980/1395	The whole Regulations
The Manton Mine (Electric Lighting) Regulations 1980	S.I. 1980/1396	The whole Regulations
The Vane Tempest Mine (Electric Lighting) Regulations 1980	S.I. 1980/1397	The whole Regulations
The Yew Tree Mine (Storage Battery Locomotives) Regulations 1980	S.I. 1980/1405	The whole Regulations
The Coal and Other Mines (Safety-Lamps and Lighting) (Amendment) Regulations 1983	S.I. 1983/710	The whole Regulations
The Miscellaneous Mines (Metrication) Regulations 1983	S.I. 1983/994	In regulation 1(2), the reference to the Miscellaneous Mines (Electricity) Regulations 1956; and in the Schedule the entries relating to those 1956 Regulations
The Quarries (Metrication) Regulations 1983	S.I. 1983/1026	In regulation 1(2), the reference to the Quarries (Electricity) Regulations 1956; and in the Schedule the entries relating to those 1956 Regulations
The Mines (Miscellaneous Amendments) Regulations 1983	S.I. 1983/1130	The whole Regulations

PART II
MODIFICATIONS

1. The Mines and Quarries Act 1954 shall be modified as follows–

(a) in section 64(2) (which relates to safety-lamps) after the word "one" insert "conforming with the provisions of regulation 19(2)(a) to (d) of the Electricity at Work Regulations 1989 or";

(b) in section 182(1) (which defines "permitted lights") the words "or health and safety regulations" shall be substituted for the words "or Regulations 18 and 18A of the Coal and Other Mines (Safety-Lamps and Lighting) Regulations 1956 as substituted and inserted respectively by the Coal and Other Mines (Safety-Lamps and Lighting) (Amendment) Regulations 1983".

2. Regulation 4 of the Coal and Other Mines (Fire and Rescue) Regulations 1956(**a**) (which relates to the provision of dust or sand in relation to electric motors) shall be modified by substituting the words "which is not electrical apparatus that is designed to be moved while working" for the words "which is not portable apparatus for the purposes of the Coal and Other Mines (Electricity) Regulations 1956".

3. The Shipbuilding and Ship-repairing Regulations 1960 (**b**) shall be modified as follows–

(a) in regulation 51(3)(c) (which requires the provision of lamps and torches in confined spaces in vessels) the words "of an appropriate type" shall be substituted for the words "of a safety type approved for the purpose of this Regulation";

(b) in paragraphs (1) and (3) of regulation 59 (which impose restrictions with respect to the application etc. of naked lights, fires, lamps and heated rivets in oil-carrying vessels), the words "a lamp of an appropriate type" shall be substituted for the words "a safety lamp of a type approved for the purpose of this Regulation" where they respectively appear.

4. Section 1(4) of the Mines Management Act 1971 (which relates to exceptions from statutory responsibilities that may be placed on managers' assistants) shall be modified by the substitution of the following paragraphs for paragraph (d)–

"(d) responsibility for making rules under regulation 19(2)(g) of the Electricity at Work Regulations 1989; and

(e) such other responsibilities as may be prescribed.".

EXPLANATORY NOTE

(This note is not part of the Regulations)

These Regulations impose health and safety requirements with respect to electricity at work.

The Regulations impose duties upon employers, self-employed persons, managers of mines and quarries and employees (*regulation 3*). The duties imposed by the Regulations do not, however, extend to the master or crew of a sea-going ship or to their employer in relation to the normal ship-board activities of a ship's crew under the direction of the master (*regulation 32(a)*); nor do those duties extend to any person in relation to any aircraft or hovercraft which is moving under its own power (*regulation 32(b)*).

The Regulations–

(a) impose requirements with regard to the construction and maintenance of electrical systems (*regulation 4(1)* and *(2)*);

(b) impose requirements with regard to the carrying out of work activities (including the operation, use and maintenance of electrical systems and work near electrical systems) (*regulation 4(3)*);

(c) impose requirements with regard to the provision of protective equipment (*regulation 4(4)*);

(**a**) S.I. 1956/1768, to which there are amendments not relevant to these Regulations.
(**b**) S.I. 1960/1932; the relevant amending instrument is S.I. 1983/644.

(d) impose requirements with regard to the putting into use of electrical equipment (*regulation 5*);

(e) impose requirements with regard to the construction and protection of electrical equipment which may reasonably foreseeably be exposed to adverse or hazardous environments (*regulation 6*);

(f) impose requirements with regard to the insulation and protection of, and the taking of precautions in respect of, conductors (*regulation 7*);

(g) impose requirements with regard to the taking of precautions to prevent danger in respect of certain conductors (*regulation 8*);

(h) impose restrictions with regard to the placing of any thing which might give rise to danger in any circuit conductor which is connected to earth or to any other reference point (*regulation 9*);

(i) impose requirements with regard to the mechanical and electrical suitability for use of joints and connections in electrical systems (*regulation 10*);

(j) impose requirements with regard to the protection from excess currents of electrical systems (*regulation 11*);

(k) impose requirements with regard to the availability of suitable means for cutting off the supply of electrical energy to, and the isolation of, electrical equipment which is not itself a source of electrical energy (*regulation 12(1)*) and (where necessary) the taking of such other precautions as will, so far as reasonably practicable, prevent danger in respect of electrical equipment which is itself a source of electrical energy (*regulation 12(3)*);

(l) impose requirements with regard to the taking of such precautions in respect of electrical equipment which has been made dead in order to prevent danger while work is carried on or near it as will prevent that equipment from becoming electrically charged (*regulation 13*);

(m) impose restrictions on persons being engaged in work activities on or near certain live conductors (*regulation 14*);

(n) impose requirements with regard to the provision of adequate working space, adequate lighting and adequate means of access at specified electrical equipment (*regulation 15*);

(o) impose restrictions with regard to who may be engaged in work activities where technical knowledge or experience is necessary to prevent danger or injury (*regulation 16*);

(p) impose requirements with regard to the use of film lighting circuits below ground in coal mines (*regulation 17(1)* and *Schedule 1*);

(q) impose conditions with regard to the introduction of specified electrical equipment into underground parts of specified safety-lamp mines (*regulation 18*);

(r) impose requirements with regard to the preparation of plans identifying zones underground in safety-lamp mines where firedamp is likely to occur in quantities sufficient to indicate danger (*regulation 19(1)*) and specify that only certain electrical equipment may be energised in those zones and deem any lights which may be energised in such zones to be "permitted lights" as defined by section 182(1) of the Mines and Quarries Act 1954 (*regulation 19(2)*). Among the electrical equipment which may be energised in such zones is that which has been certified in accordance with Council Directive 82/130/EEC (OJ No. L59, 2.3.82, p.10) (which relates to the approximation of the laws of the Member States concerning electrical equipment for use in potentially explosive atmospheres in mines susceptible to firedamp), as adapted to technical progress by Commission Directive 88/35/EEC (OJ No. L64, 10.3.88, p.36);

(s) impose requirements with regard to cutting off the supply of electricity to electrical equipment (or making it safe) when firedamp is found in concentrations exceeding 1.25% by volume in the general body of the air either below ground at, or at specified places on the surface of, mines (*regulation 20*);

(t) impose restrictions with regard to the taking or use below ground at safety-lamp mines of electric safety-lamps, gas detectors, telephone and signalling equipment and other equipment associated therewith or required for the safety of persons (*regulation 21*);

(u) impose requirements with regard to the provision and operation of switchgear in respect of electrical equipment which may give rise to danger and which is installed below ground at a mine, but which is supplied from a power source at the surface (*regulation 22*);

(v) impose a prohibition on the introduction below ground at mines of electrical equipment using oil as a means of cooling, insulation or arc suppression (*regulation 23*);

(w) impose requirements with regard to the preparation, keeping and display of schematic diagrams and plans of electrical distribution systems and permanently installed electrical equipment at mines (*regulation 24*);

(x) (in circumstances where, at any place at a mine, electric arc welding is taking place or electrical energy is being generated, transformed or used at a nominal voltage in excess of 125 volts a.c. or 250 volts d.c.) impose requirements with regard to the display of notices giving information on the appropriate first-aid treatment for electric shock and details of what emergency action should be taken in the event of electric shock (*regulation 25*);

(y) impose restrictions with regard to the introduction below ground at safety-lamp mines of locomotives and vehicles which use electrical storage batteries, either partly or wholly, as a power source (*regulation 26*);

(z) impose requirements with regard to the use below ground at mines of electrical storage batteries (*regulation 27*).

The Regulations disapply section 157 of the Mines and Quarries Act 1954 (defence in certain legal proceedings) in relation to any legal proceedings or prosecutions arising out of regulations 18 to 27 and Schedule 1 (*regulation 28*) and provide a defence in the case of a contravention of certain of the Regulations (*regulation 29*). The Regulations provide for the issue of certificates of exemption by the Health and Safety Executive (*regulation 30*). The Regulations also provide that they shall apply outside Great Britain to the extent specified in regulation 31.

The Regulations revoke the instruments specified in Part I of Schedule 2 (*regulation 33(1)*), modify the enactments and instruments specified in Part II of Schedule 2 (*regulation 33(2)*) and provide that any reference to the Mines and Quarries Act 1954, the Mines and Quarries (Tips) Act 1969 or the Mines Management Act 1971 in any of those Acts, in regulations made under any of those Acts, or in health and safety regulations, shall be treated as including a reference to these Regulations (*regulation 33(3)*).

STATUTORY INSTRUMENTS

1989 No. 636

MONOPOLIES AND MERGERS

The Merger Reference (Strong & Fisher, Hillsdown and Pittard Garnar) (Revocation) Order 1989

Made - - - -	*6th April 1989*
Coming into force	*11th April 1989*
Laid before Parliament	*11th April 1989*

The Secretary of State, in exercise of the powers conferred on him by sections 74(1)(a), 75(4) and 134(2) of the Fair Trading Act 1973(**a**), hereby makes the following Order:

1. This Order may be cited as the Merger Reference (Strong & Fisher, Hillsdown and Pittard Garnar) (Revocation) Order 1989 and shall come into force on 11th April 1989.

2. The following Orders are hereby revoked–

(i) the Merger Reference (Strong & Fisher (Holdings) plc and Pittard Garnar plc) Order 1988(**b**);

(ii) the Merger Reference (Hillsdown Holdings plc and Pittard Garnar plc) Order 1988(**c**).

Francis Maude
Parliamentary Under Secretary of State for Corporate Affairs,
6th April 1989 Department of Trade and Industry

EXPLANATORY NOTE

(This note is not part of the Order)

This Order revokes two Orders made to prevent prejudicial action during investigation by the Monopolies and Mergers Commission of proposed mergers between Pittard Garnar plc and (i) Strong & Fisher (Holdings) plc and (ii) Hillsdown Holdings plc respectively. The two earlier Orders prohibited Strong & Fisher and Hillsdown from taking their holdings of Pittard Garnar shares over 15%, exercising 15% or more of voting rights in Pittard Garnar or making agreements with others to secure control of Pittard Garnar. Strong & Fisher and Hillsdown are now released from those prohibitions. The relevant reports of the Monopolies and Mergers Commission are Cm. 663 and Cm. 665, published by Her Majesty's Stationery Office.

(**a**) 1973 c.41.
(**b**) S.I. 1988/2058.
(**c**) S.I. 1988/2178.

STATUTORY INSTRUMENTS

1989 No. 637

TOWN AND COUNTRY PLANNING, ENGLAND AND WALES

The Unitary Development Plans (Tyne and Wear) (Appointed Day) Order 1989

Made - - - -	*10th April 1989*
Laid before Parliament	*17th April 1989*
Coming into force	*8th May 1989*

The Secretary of State for the Environment in exercise of the powers conferred on him by section 4(1) of the Local Government Act 1985(**a**) and of all other powers enabling him in that behalf, hereby makes the following Order:

1. This Order may be cited as the Unitary Development Plans (Tyne and Wear) (Appointed Day) Order 1989 and shall come into force on 8th May 1989.

2. 8th May 1989 is appointed as the day on which Part I of Schedule 1 to the Local Government Act 1985 shall come into force in the areas of the local planning authorities listed in the Schedule hereto.

Nicholas Ridley
Secretary of State for the Environment

10th April 1989

SCHEDULE

Gateshead Metropolitan Borough Council
City of Newcastle upon Tyne
North Tyneside Metropolitan Borough Council
South Tyneside Metropolitan Borough Council

(**a**) 1985 c.51.

EXPLANATORY NOTE

(This note is not part of the Order)

The Local Government Act 1985 abolished the Greater London Council and metropolitan county councils. The Act consequently provides for the replacement in their areas of the existing structure and local development plans under town and country planning legislation by "unitary development plans". This Order brings the provisions of the 1985 Act relating to unitary development plans into force in the county of Tyne and Wear other than the metropolitan district of Sunderland on 8th May 1989.

STATUTORY INSTRUMENTS

1989 No. 638

EUROPEAN COMMUNITIES

The European Economic Interest Grouping Regulations 1989

Made - - - -	*10th April 1989*
Laid before Parliament	*19th April 1989*
Coming into force	*1st July 1989*

The Secretary of State, being a Minister designated**(a)** for the purposes of section 2(2) of the European Communities Act 1972**(b)** in relation to measures relating to European Economic Interest Groupings and their members, in exercise of the powers conferred on him by that section and of all other powers enabling him in that behalf, hereby makes the following Regulations:—

PART I

GENERAL

Citation, commencement and extent

1. These Regulations, which extend to Great Britain, may be cited as the European Economic Interest Grouping Regulations 1989 and shall come into force on 1st July 1989.

Interpretation

2.—(1) In these Regulations—

" the 1985 Act " means the Companies Act 1985**(c)**;

" the contract " means the contract for the formation of an EEIG;

" the EC Regulation " means Council Regulation (EEC) No. 2137/85**(d)** set out in Schedule 1 to these Regulations;

" EEIG " means a European Economic Interest Grouping being a grouping formed in pursuance of article 1 of the EC Regulation;

" officer ", in relation to an EEIG, includes a manager, or any other person provided for in the contract as an organ of the EEIG; and

" the registrar " has the meaning given by regulations 9(1) and 12(1) below;

and other expressions used in these Regulations and defined by section 744 of the 1985 Act or in relation to insolvency and winding up by the Insolvency Act 1986**(e)** have the meanings assigned to them by those provisions as if any reference to a company in any such definition were a reference to an EEIG.

(a) S.I. 1988/785.
(b) 1972 c.68.
(c) 1985 c.6.
(d) OJ No. L199, 31.7.1985, p.1.
(e) 1986 c.45.

(2) A Form referred to in these Regulations by "EEIG" followed by a number means the Form so numbered in Schedule 2 to these Regulations.

(3) In these Regulations, "certified translation" means a translation certified to be a correct translation—

(a) if the translation was made in the United Kingdom, by

(i) a notary public in any part of the United Kingdom;

(ii) a solicitor (if the translation was made in Scotland), a solicitor of the Supreme Court of Judicature of England and Wales (if it was made in England or Wales), or a solicitor of the Supreme Court of Judicature of Northern Ireland (if it was made in Northern Ireland); or

(iii) a person certified by a person mentioned above to be known to him to be competent to translate the document into English; or

(b) if the translation was made outside the United Kingdom, by—

(i) a notary public;

(ii) a person authorised in the place where the translation was made to administer an oath;

(iii) any of the British officials mentioned in section 6 of the Commissioners for Oaths Act 1889**(a)**;

(iv) a person certified by a person mentioned in sub-paragraph (i), (ii) or (iii) of this paragraph to be known to him to be competent to translate the document into English.

PART II

PROVISIONS RELATING TO ARTICLES 1–38 OF THE EC REGULATION

Legal personality (Article 1(3) of the EC Regulation)

3. From the date of registration of an EEIG in Great Britain mentioned in a certificate given under regulation 9(5) below the EEIG shall, subject to regulation 11 below, be a body corporate by the name contained in the contract.

Transfer of official address (Article 14 of the EC Regulation)

4.—(1) Notice of any proposal to transfer the official address of an EEIG registered in Great Britain to any other place shall, where such transfer would result in a change in the law applicable to the contract under article 2 of the EC Regulation, be filed at the registry where the EEIG was registered by delivery of a notice in Form EEIG 4 in pursuance of regulation 13(1) below.

(2) Where the registrar, being the competent authority within the meaning of article 14(4) of the EC Regulation, receives a notice under paragraph (1) above within the period of two months beginning with its publication in the Gazette under regulation 15(1) below and opposes that transfer on the grounds of public interest, that transfer shall not take effect.

Managers (Article 19(2) of the EC Regulation)

5.—(1) A manager of an EEIG registered in Great Britain may be a legal person other than a natural person, on condition that it designates one or more natural persons to represent it and notice of particulars of each such person is sent to the registrar in Form EEIG 3 as though he were a manager.

(2) Any natural person designated under paragraph (1) above shall be subject to the same liabilities as if he himself were a manager.

(a) 1889 c.10; section 6 was amended by the Oaths and Evidence (Overseas Authorities and Countries) Act 1963 (c.27), section 3.

(3) There shall be delivered to the registrar in accordance with the provisions of regulation 13(1) below notice of appointment of any manager and the following particulars with respect to each manager—

(a) (i) his present Christian name and surname;
(ii) any former Christian name or surname;
(iii) his usual residential address;
(iv) his nationality;
(v) his business occupation (if any); and
(vi) the date of his birth; and

(b) in the case of a legal person other than a natural person, its name and registered or principal office.

(4) Section 289(2) of the 1985 Act applies as regards the meaning of "Christian name", "surname" and "former Christian name or surname".

Cessation of membership (Article 28(1) of the EC Regulation)

6. For the purposes of national law on liquidation, winding up, insolvency or cessation of payments, a member of an EEIG registered under these Regulations shall cease to be a member if—

(a) in the case of an individual—
(i) a bankruptcy order has been made against him in England and Wales; or
(ii) sequestration of his estate has been awarded by the court in Scotland under the Bankruptcy (Scotland) Act 1985**(a)**;

(b) in the case of a partnership—
(i) a winding up order has been made against the partnership in England and Wales;
(ii) a bankruptcy order has been made against its members in England and Wales on a bankruptcy petition presented under article 13(1) of the Insolvent Partnerships Order 1986**(b)**; or
(iii) sequestration of the estate of the partnership has been awarded by the court in Scotland under the Bankruptcy (Scotland) Act 1985;

(c) in the case of a company, the company goes into liquidation in Great Britain; or

(d) in the case of any legal person or partnership, it is otherwise wound up or otherwise ceases to exist after the conclusion of winding up or insolvency.

Competent authority (Articles 32(1) and (3) and 38 of the EC Regulation)

7.—(1) The Secretary of State shall be the competent authority for the purposes of making an application to the court under article 32(1) of the EC Regulation (winding up of EEIG in certain circumstances).

(2) The court may, on an application by the Secretary of State, order the winding up of an EEIG which has its official address in Great Britain, if the EEIG acts contrary to the public interest and it is expedient in the public interest that the EEIG should be wound up and the court is of the opinion that it is just and equitable for it to be so.

(3) The court, on an application by the Secretary of State, shall be the competent authority for the purposes of prohibiting under article 38 of the EC Regulation any activity carried on in Great Britain by an EEIG where such an activity is in contravention of the public interest there.

Winding up and conclusion of liquidation (Articles 35 and 36 of the EC Regulation)

8.—(1) Where an EEIG is wound up as an unregistered company under Part V of the Insolvency Act 1986, the provisions of Part V shall apply in relation to the EEIG as if any reference in that Act and the 1985 Act to a director or past director of a company included a reference to a manager of the EEIG and any other person who has or has had control or management of the EEIG's business and with the modification that in section 221(1) after the words "all the provisions" there shall be added the words "of Council Regulation (EEC) No. 2137/85 and".

(2) At the end of the period of three months beginning with the day of receipt by the registrar of a notice of the conclusion of the liquidation of an EEIG, the EEIG shall be dissolved.

(a) 1985 c.66.
(b) S.I. 1986/2142.

PART III

REGISTRATION ETC (ARTICLE 39 OF THE EC REGULATION)

Registration of EEIG whose official address is in Great Britain

9.—(1) The registrar for the purposes of registration of an EEIG in Great Britain where its official address is in Great Britain shall be the registrar within the meaning of the 1985 Act and the contract shall be delivered—

(a) to the registrar or other officer performing under that Act the duty of registration of companies in England and Wales, if the contract states that the official address of the EEIG is to be situated in England and Wales, or that it is to be situated in Wales; and

(b) to the registrar or other officer performing under that Act the duty of registration of companies in Scotland, if the contract states that the official address of the EEIG is to be situated in Scotland.

(2) With the contract there shall be delivered a registration form in Form EEIG 1 containing a statement of the names and the particulars set out in article 5 of the EC Regulation.

(3) The registrar shall not register an EEIG under this regulation unless he is satisfied that all the requirements of these Regulations and of the EC Regulation in respect of registration and of matters precedent and incidental to it have been complied with but he may accept a declaration in Form EEIG 1 as sufficient evidence of compliance.

(4) Subject to paragraph (3) above, the registrar shall retain the contract, and any certified translation, delivered to him under this regulation and register the EEIG.

(5) On the registration of an EEIG the registrar shall give a certificate that the EEIG has been registered stating the date of registration.

(6) The certificate may be signed by the registrar, or authenticated by his official seal.

(7) A certificate of registration given in respect of an EEIG under this regulation is conclusive evidence that the requirements of these Regulations and of the EC Regulation in respect of registration and of matters precedent and incidental to it have been complied with, and that the EEIG is an organisation authorised to be registered, and is duly registered, under these Regulations.

(8) Where an EEIG is to be registered with the contract written in any language other than English, the contract to be delivered under paragraph (1) above may be in the other language provided that it is accompanied by a certified translation into English.

(9) Where an EEIG has published a proposal to transfer its offical address to a place in Great Britain under article 14(1) of the EC Regulation, the registrar responsible for the registration of the EEIG with the new official address shall, where the transfer of the official address has not been opposed under paragraph (4) of that article, register the EEIG with its new official address on receipt of a registration form in Form EEIG 1 containing—

(a) evidence of the publication of the transfer proposal; and

(b) a statement that no competent authority has opposed the transfer under article 14(4) of the EC Regulation.

(10) Any communication or notice may be addressed to an EEIG where its official address is in Great Britain at its official address stated on Form EEIG 1 or in the case of any change in the situation of that address at any new official address stated on Form EEIG 4.

Prohibition on registration of certain names

10.—(1) An EEIG shall not be registered in Great Britain under regulation 9 above by a name which includes any of the following words or expressions, or abbreviations thereof, that is to say, "limited", "unlimited" or "public limited company" or their Welsh equivalents.

(2) In determining for the purposes of section 26(1)(c) of the 1985 Act (as applied by regulation 18 of, and Schedule 4 to, these Regulations) whether one name is the same as another, there are to be disregarded the words "European Economic Interest Grouping" or the initials "EEIG" or their authorised equivalents in official languages of the Economic Community, other than English, the authorised equivalents being set out in Schedule 3 to these Regulations.

Change of name

11.—(1) Regulation 10(2) above applies in determining under section 28(2) of the 1985 Act as applied by regulation 18 of, and Schedule 4 to, these Regulations whether a name is the same as or too like another.

(2) Where an EEIG changes its name the registrar shall (subject to the provisions of section 26 of the 1985 Act which apply by virtue of regulation 18 of, and Schedule 4 to, these Regulations and regulation 10 above) enter the new name on the register in place of the former name, and shall issue a certificate of registration altered to meet the circumstances of the case.

(3) A change of name has effect from the date on which the altered certificate is issued.

Registration of establishment of EEIG whose official address is outside the United Kingdom

12.—(1) The registrar for the purposes of registration under this regulation of an EEIG establishment situated in Great Britain where the EEIG's official address is outside the United Kingdom shall be the registrar within the meaning of the 1985 Act.

(2) For the purposes of registration under paragraph (1) above there shall be delivered, within one month of the establishment becoming so situated at any place in Great Britain, to the registrar at the registration office in England and Wales or Scotland, according to where the establishment is situated, a certified copy of the contract together with—

(a) a certified translation into English of the contract and other documents and particulars to be filed with it under article 10 of the EC Regulation if the contract and other documents and particulars, or any part thereof, are not in English; and

(b) a registration form in Form EEIG 2 containing a statement of the names and particulars set out in articles 5 and 10 of the EC Regulation.

(3) Paragraph (2) above shall not apply where an establishment is already registered in Great Britain under paragraph (1) above.

(4) The registrar shall not register an EEIG establishment under this regulation unless he is satisfied that all the requirements of these Regulations and of the EC Regulation in respect of registration and of matters precedent and incidental to it have been complied with but he may accept a declaration in Form EEIG 2 as sufficient evidence of compliance.

(5) Subject to paragraph (4) above, the registrar shall retain the copy of the contract, and any certified translation, delivered to him under paragraph (2) above and register the EEIG establishment.

(6) Any communication or notice may be addressed to an EEIG where its official address is outside the United Kingdom at any of its establishments in Great Britain.

(7) Regulation 10 above shall apply to an EEIG establishment to be registered under this regulation as it applies to an EEIG to be registered under regulation 9.

(8) If an EEIG fails to comply with any provision of paragraph (2) above, the EEIG, and any officer of it who intentionally authorises or permits the default, is guilty of an offence and liable on summary conviction to a fine not exceeding level 3 on the standard scale and if the failure to comply with any such provision continues after conviction, the EEIG and any such officer shall be guilty of a further offence of failure to comply with that provision and shall be liable to be proceeded against and punished accordingly.

Filing of documents

13.—(1) The documents and particulars referred to in paragraphs (a) to (j) of article 7 of the EC Regulation and required to be filed under that article in Great Britain shall be filed within 15 days (or, in the case of an EEIG whose official address is outside the United Kingdom, 30 days) of the event to which the document in question relates by delivery to the registrar for registration of a notice, together with a certified translation into English of any documents and particulars, or any part thereof, which are not in English—

(a) in the case of paragraph (d) where the official address of the EEIG is in Great Britain, in Form EEIG 3 of the names of the managers and the particulars referred to in regulation 5(3) above, of particulars of whether they may act alone or must act jointly and of the termination of any manager's appointment;

(b) in the case of paragraphs (a), (c) and (e) to (j), and in the case of paragraph (d) where the official address of the EEIG is outside the United Kingdom, in Form EEIG 4 of the documents and particulars referred to in that Form; and

(c) in the case of paragraph (b), in Form EEIG 5 of the setting up or closure of an establishment of an EEIG in Great Britain, except where regulation 12(1) above applies.

(2) The registrar shall retain the documents and particulars and any certified translation delivered to him under this regulation.

(3) If an EEIG fails to comply with any provision of paragraph (1) above, the EEIG, and any officer of it who intentionally authorises or permits the default, is guilty of an offence and liable on summary conviction to a fine not exceeding level 3 on the standard scale and if the failure to comply with any such provision continues after conviction, the EEIG and any such officer shall be guilty of a further offence of failure to comply with that provision and shall be liable to be proceeded against and punished accordingly.

Inspection of documents

14. Any person may—

(a) inspect any document or particulars kept by the registrar under these Regulations or a copy thereof; and

(b) require the registrar to deliver or send by post to him a copy or extract of any such document or particulars or any part thereof.

Publication of documents in the Gazette and Official Journal of the Communities

15.—(1) The registrar shall cause to be published in the Gazette—

(a) the documents and particulars issued or received by him under these Regulations and referred to in article 8(a) and (b) of the EC Regulation; and

(b) in the case of those documents and particulars referred to in article 7(b) to (j) of the EC Regulation a notice (stating in the notice the name of the EEIG, the description of the documents or particulars and the date of receipt).

(2) The registrar shall forward to the Office for Official Publications of the European Communities the information referred to in article 11 of the EC Regulation within one month of the publication of the relevant documents and particulars in the Gazette under paragraph (1) above.

EEIG identification

16.—(1) If an EEIG fails to comply with article 25 of the EC Regulation it is guilty of an offence and liable on summary conviction to a fine not exceeding level 3 on the standard scale.

(2) If an officer of an EEIG or a person on its behalf issues or authorises the issue of any letter, order form or similar document not complying with the requirements of article 25 of the EC Regulation, he is guilty of an offence and liable on summary conviction to a fine not exceeding level 3 on the standard scale.

PART IV

SUPPLEMENTAL PROVISIONS

Application of the Business Names Act 1985

17. The Business Names Act 1985**(a)** shall apply in relation to an EEIG which carries on business in Great Britain as if the EEIG were a company formed and registered under the 1985 Act.

Application of the Companies Act 1985

18. The provisions of the 1985 Act specified in Schedule 4 to these Regulations shall apply to EEIGs, and their establishments, registered or in the process of being registered under these Regulations, as if they were companies formed and registered or in the process of being registered under the 1985 Act and as if in those provisions any reference to the Companies Act included a reference to these Regulations and any reference to a registered office included a reference to an official address, but subject to any limitations mentioned in relation to those provisions in that Schedule and to the omission of any reference to a daily default fine.

Application of Insolvency Act 1986

19.—(1) Part III of the Insolvency Act 1986 shall apply to EEIGs, and their establishments, registered under these Regulations, as if they were companies registered under the 1985 Act.

(2) Section 120 of the Insolvency Act 1986 shall apply to an EEIG, and its establishments, registered under these Regulations in Scotland, as if it were a company registered in Scotland the paid-up or credited as paid-up share capital of which did not exceed £120,000 and as if in that section any reference to the Company's registered office were a reference to the official address of the EEIG.

Application of the Company Directors Disqualification Act 1986

20. Where an EEIG is wound up as an unregistered company under Part V of the Insolvency Act 1986, the provisions of sections 1, 2, 4 to 11, 12(2), 15 to 17, 20 and 22 of, and Schedule 1 to, the Company Directors Disqualification Act 1986**(b)** shall apply in relation to the EEIG as if any reference to a director or past director of a company included a reference to a manager of the EEIG and any other person who has or has had control or management of the EEIG's business and the EEIG were a company as defined by section 22(2)(b) of that Act.

Penalties

21. Nothing in these Regulations shall create any new criminal offence punishable to a greater extent than is permitted under paragraph 1(1)(d) of Schedule 2 to the European Communities Act 1972.

Francis Maude
Parliamentary Under Secretary of State,
Department of Trade and Industry

10th April 1989

(a) 1985 c.7.
(b) 1986 c.46.

SCHEDULE 1

Regulation 2(1)

COUNCIL REGULATION (EEC) No. 2137/85 OF 25TH JULY 1985
on the European Economic Interest Grouping (EEIG)

THE COUNCIL OF THE EUROPEAN COMMUNITIES

Having regard to the Treaty establishing the European Economic Community, and in particular Article 235 thereof,

Having regard to the proposal from the Commission,[1]

Having regard to the opinion of the European Parliament,[2]

Having regard to the opinion of the Economic and Social Committee,[3]

Whereas a harmonious development of economic activities and a continuous and balanced expansion throughout the Community depend on the establishment and smooth functioning of a common market offering conditions analogous to those of a national market; whereas to bring about this single market and to increase its unity a legal framework which facilitates the adaptation of their activities to the economic conditions of the Community should be created for natural persons, companies, firms and other legal bodies in particular; whereas to that end it is necessary that those natural persons, companies, firms and other legal bodies should be able to co-operate effectively across frontiers;

Whereas co-operation of this nature can encounter legal, fiscal or psychological difficulties; whereas the creation of an appropriate Community legal instrument in the form of a European Economic Interest Grouping would contribute to the achievement of the abovementioned objectives and therefore proves necessary;

Whereas the Treaty does not provide the necessary powers for the creation of such a legal instrument;

Whereas a grouping's ability to adapt to economic conditions must be guaranteed by the considerable freedom for its members in their contractual relations and the internal organization of the grouping;

Whereas a grouping differs from a firm or company principally in its purpose, which is only to facilitate or develop the economic activities of its members to enable them to improve their own results, whereas, by reason of that ancillary nature, a grouping's activities must be related to the economic activities of its members but not replace them so that, to that extent, for example, a grouping may not itself, with regard to third parties, practise a profession, the concept of economic activities being interpreted in the widest sense;

Whereas access to grouping form must be made as widely available as possible to natural persons, companies, firms and other legal bodies, in keeping with the aims of this Regulation; whereas this Regulation shall not, however, prejudice the application at national level of legal rules and/or ethical codes concerning the conditions for the pursuit of business and professional activities;

Whereas this Regulation does not itself confer on any person the right to participate in a grouping, even where the conditions it lays down are fulfilled;

Whereas the power provided by this Regulation to prohibit or restrict participation in a grouping on grounds of public interest is without prejudice to the laws of Member States which govern the pursuit of activities and which may provide further prohibitions or restrictions or otherwise control or supervise participation in a grouping by any natural person, company, firm or other legal body or any class of them;

Whereas, to enable a grouping to achieve its purpose, it should be endowed with legal capacity and provision should be made for it to be represented *vis-à-vis* third parties by an organ legally separate from its membership;

Whereas the protection of third parties requires widespread publicity; whereas the members of a grouping have unlimited joint and several liability for the grouping's debts and other liabilities, including those relating to tax or social security, without, however, that principle's affecting the freedom to exclude or restrict the liability of one or more of its members in respect of a particular debt or other liability by means of a specific contract between the grouping and a third party;

[1] OJ No. C.14, 15.2.1974. p. 30 and OJ C.103, 28.4.1978. p.4.

[2] OJ No. C.163, 11.7.1977. p. 17.

[3] OJ No. C.108, 15.5.1975. p. 46.

Whereas matters relating to the status or capacity of natural persons and to the capacity of legal persons are governed by national law;

Whereas the grounds for winding up which are peculiar to the grouping should be specific while referring to national law for its liquidation and the conclusion thereof;

Whereas groupings are subject to national laws relating to insolvency and cessation of payments; whereas such laws may provide other grounds for the winding up of groupings;

Whereas this Regulation provides that the profits or losses resulting from the activities of a grouping shall be taxable only in the hands of its members; whereas it is understood that otherwise national tax laws apply, particularly as regards the apportionment of profits, tax procedures and any obligations imposed by national tax law;

Whereas in matters not covered by this Regulation the laws of the Member States and Community law are applicable, for example with regard to:

(a) social and labour laws,

(b) competition law,

(c) intellectual property law;

Whereas the activities of groupings are subject to the provisions of Member States' laws on the pursuit and supervision of activities; whereas in the event of abuse or circumvention of the laws of a Member State by a grouping or its members that Member State may impose appropriate sanctions;

Whereas the Member States are free to apply or to adopt any laws, regulations or administrative measures which do not conflict with the scope or objectives of this Regulation;

Whereas this Regulation must enter into force immediately in its entirety; whereas the implementation of some provisions must nevertheless be deferred in order to allow the Member States first to set up the necessary machinery for the registration of groupings in their territories and the disclosure of certain matters relating to groupings; whereas, with effect from the date of implementation of this Regulation, groupings set up may operate without territorial restrictions,

HAS ADOPTED THIS REGULATION:

Article 1

1. European Economic Interest Groupings shall be formed upon the terms, in the manner and with the effects laid down in this Regulation.

Accordingly, parties intending to form a grouping must conclude a contract and have the registration provided for in Article 6 carried out.

2. A grouping so formed shall, from the date of its registration as provided for in Article 6, have the capacity, in its own name, to have rights and obligations of all kinds, to make contracts or accomplish other legal acts, and to sue and be sued.

3. The Member States shall determine whether or not groupings registered at their registries, pursuant to Article 6, have legal personality.

Article 2

1. Subject to the provisions of this Regulation, the law applicable, on the one hand, to the contract for the formation of a grouping, except as regards matters relating to the status or capacity of natural persons and to the capacity of legal persons and, on the other hand, to the internal organization of a grouping shall be the internal law of the State in which the official address is situated, as laid down in the contract for the formation of the grouping.

2. Where a State comprises several territorial units, each of which has its own rules of law applicable to the matters referred to in paragraph 1, each territorial unit shall be considered as a State for the purposes of identifying the law applicable under this Article.

Article 3

1. The purpose of a grouping shall be to facilitate or develop the economic activities of its members and to improve or increase the results of those activities; its purpose is not to make profits for itself.

Its activity shall be related to the economic activities of its members and must not be more than ancillary to those activities.

2. Consequently, a grouping may not:

(a) exercise, directly or indirectly, a power of management or supervision over its members' own activities or over the activities of another undertaking, in particular in the fields of personnel, finance and investment;

(b) directly or indirectly, on any basis whatsoever, hold shares of any kind in a member undertaking; the holding of shares in another undertaking shall be possible only in so far as it is necessary for the achievement of the grouping's objects and if it is done on its members' behalf;

(c) employ more than 500 persons;

(d) be used by a company to make a loan to a director of a company, or any person connected with him, when the making of such loans is restricted or controlled under the Member States' laws governing companies. Nor must a grouping be used for the transfer of any property between a company and a director, or any person connected with him, except to the extent allowed by the Member States' laws governing companies. For the purposes of this provision the making of a loan includes entering into any transaction or arrangement of similar effect, and property includes moveable and immoveable property;

(e) be a member of another European Economic Interest Grouping.

ARTICLE 4

1. Only the following may be members of a grouping:

(a) companies or firms within the meaning of the second paragraph of Article 58 of the Treaty and other legal bodies governed by public or private law, which have been formed in accordance with the law of a Member State and which have their registered or statutory office and central administration in the Community; where, under the law of a Member State, a company, firm or other legal body is not obliged to have a registered or statutory office, it shall be sufficient for such a company, firm or other legal body to have its central administration in the Community;

(b) natural persons who carry on any industrial, commercial, craft or agricultural activity or who provide professional or other services in the Community.

2. A grouping must comprise at least:

(a) two companies, firms or other legal bodies, within the meaning of paragraph 1, which have their central administrations in different Member States, or

(b) two natural persons, within the meaning of paragraph 1, who carry on their principal activities in different Member States, or

(c) a company, firm or other legal body within the meaning of paragraph 1 and a natural person, of which the first has its central administration in one Member State and the second carries on his principal activity in another Member State.

3. A Member State may provide that groupings registered at its registries in accordance with Article 6 may have no more than 20 members. For this purpose, that Member State may provide that, in accordance with its laws, each member of a legal body formed under its laws, other than a registered company, shall be treated as a separate member of a grouping.

4. Any Member State may, on grounds of that State's public interest, prohibit or restrict participation in groupings by certain classes of natural persons, companies, firms, or other legal bodies.

ARTICLE 5

A contract for the formation of a grouping shall include at least:

(a) the name of the grouping preceded or followed either by the words 'European Economic Interest Grouping' or by the initials 'EEIG', unless those words or initials already form part of the name;

(b) the official address of the grouping;

(c) the objects for which the grouping is formed;

(d) the name, business name, legal form, permanent address or registered office, and the number and place of registration, if any, of each member of the grouping;

(e) the duration of the grouping, except where this is indefinite.

ARTICLE 6

A grouping shall be registered in the State in which it has its official address, at the registry designated pursuant to Article 39(1).

ARTICLE 7

A contract for the formation of a grouping shall be filed at the registry referred to in Article 6.

The following documents and particulars must also be filed at that registry:

(a) any amendment to the contract for the formation of a grouping, including any change in the composition of a grouping;

(b) notice of the setting up or closure of any establishment of the grouping;

(c) any judicial decision establishing or declaring the nullity of a grouping, in accordance with Article 15;

(d) notice of the appointment of the manager or managers of a grouping, their names and any other identification particulars required by the law of the Member State in which the register is kept, notification that they may act alone or must act jointly, and the termination of any manager's appointment;

(e) notice of a member's assignment of his participation in a grouping or a proportion thereof, in accordance with Article 22(1);

(f) any decision by members ordering or establishing the winding up of a grouping, in accordance with Article 31, or any judicial decision ordering such winding up, in accordance with Articles 31 or 32;

(g) notice of the appointment of the liquidator or liquidators of a grouping, as referred to in Article 35, their names and any other identification particulars required by the law of the Member State in which the register is kept, and the termination of any liquidator's appointment;

(h) notice of the conclusion of a grouping's liquidation, as referred to in Article 35(2);

(i) any proposal to transfer the official address, as referred to in Article 14(1);

(j) any clause exempting a new member from the payment of debts and other liabilities which originated prior to his admission, in accordance with Article 26(2).

Article 8

The following must be published, as laid down in Article 39, in the gazette referred to in paragraph 1 of that Article:

(a) the particulars which must be included in the contract for the formation of a grouping pursuant to Article 5, and any amendments thereto;

(b) the number, date and place of registration as well as notice of the termination of that registration;

(c) the documents and particulars referred to in Article 7(b) to (j).

The particulars referred to in (a) and (b) must be published in full. The documents and particulars referred to in (c) may be published either in full or in extract form or by means of a reference to their filing at the registry, in accordance with the national legislation applicable.

Article 9

1. The documents and particulars which must be published pursuant to this Regulation may be relied on by a grouping as against third parties under the conditions laid down by the national law applicable pursuant to Article 3(5) and (7) of Council Directive 68/151/EEC of 9 March 1968 on co-ordination of safeguards which, for the protection of the interests of members and others, are required by Member States of companies within the meaning of the second paragraph of Article 58 of the Treaty, with a view to making such safeguards equivalent throughout the Community.[1]

2. If activities have been carried on on behalf of a grouping before its registration in accordance with Article 6 and if the grouping does not, after its registration, assume the obligations arising out of such activities, the natural persons, companies, firms or other legal bodies which carried on those activities shall bear unlimited joint and several liability for them.

Article 10

Any grouping establishment situated in a Member State other than that in which the official address is situated shall be registered in that State. For the purpose of such registration, a grouping shall file, at the appropriate registry in that Member State, copies of the documents which must be filed at the registry of the Member State in which the official address is situated, together, if necessary, with a translation which conforms with the practice of the registry where the establishment is registered.

Article 11

Notice that a grouping has been formed or that the liquidation of a grouping has been concluded stating the number, date and place of registration and the date, place and title of publication, shall be given in the *Official Journal of the European Communities* after it has been published in the gazette referred to in Article 39(1).

[1] OJ No. L65, 14.3.1968, p.8.

Article 12

The official address referred to in the contract for the formation of a grouping must be situated in the Community.

The official address must be fixed either:

(a) where the grouping has its central administration, or

(b) where one of the members of the grouping has its central administration or, in the case of a natural person, his prinicipal activity, provided that the grouping carries on an activity there.

Article 13

The official address of a grouping may be transferred within the Community.

When such a transfer does not result in a change in the law applicable pursuant to Article 2, the decision to transfer shall be taken in accordance with the conditions laid down in the contract for the formation of the grouping.

Article 14

1. When the transfer of the official address results in a change in the law applicable pursuant to Article 2, a transfer proposal must be drawn up, filed and published in accordance with the conditions laid down in Articles 7 and 8.

No decision to transfer may be taken for two months after publication of the proposal. Any such decision must be taken by the members of the grouping unanimously. The transfer shall take effect on the date on which the grouping is registered, in accordance with Article 6, at the registry for the new official address. That registration may not be effected until evidence has been produced that the proposal to transfer the official address has been published.

2. The termination of a grouping's registration at the registry for its old official address may not be effected until evidence has been produced that the grouping has been registered at the registry for its new official address.

3. Upon publication of a grouping's new registration the new official address may be relied on as against third parties in accordance with the conditions referred to in Article 9(1); however, as long as the termination of the grouping's registration at the registry for the old official address has not been published, third parties may continue to rely on the old official address unless the grouping proves that such third parties were aware of the new official address.

4. The laws of a Member State may provide that, as regards groupings registered under Article 6 in that Member State, the transfer of an official address which would result in a change of the law applicable shall not take effect if, within the two-month period referred to in paragraph 1, a competent authority in that Member State opposes it. Such opposition may be based only on grounds of public interest. Review by a judicial authority must be possible.

Article 15

1. Where the law applicable to a grouping by virtue of Article 2 provides for the nullity of that grouping, such nullity must be established or declared by judicial decision. However, the court to which the matter is referred must, where it is possible for the affairs of the grouping to be put in order, allow time to permit that to be done.

2. The nullity of a grouping shall entail its liquidation in accordance with the conditions laid down in Article 35.

3. A decision establishing or declaring the nullity of a grouping may be relied on as against third parties in accordance with the conditions laid down in Article 9(1).

Such a decision shall not of itself affect the validity of liabilities, owed by or to a grouping, which originated before it could be relied on as against third parties in accordance with the conditions laid down in the previous subparagraph.

Article 16

1. The organs of a grouping shall be the members acting collectively and the manager or managers.

A contract for the formation of a grouping may provide for other organs; if it does it shall determine their powers.

2. The members of a grouping, acting as a body, may take any decision for the purpose of achieving the objects of the grouping.

Article 17

1. Each member shall have one vote. The contract for the formation of a grouping may, however, give more than one vote to certain members, provided that no one member holds a majority of the votes.

2. A unanimous decision by the members shall be required to:

(a) alter the objects of a grouping;

(b) alter the number of votes allotted to each member;

(c) alter the conditions for the taking of decisions;

(d) extend the duration of a grouping beyond any period fixed in the contract for the formation of the grouping;

(e) alter the contribution by every member or by some members to the grouping's financing;

(f) alter any other obligation of a member, unless otherwise provided by the contract for the formation of the grouping;

(g) make any alteration to the contract for the formation of the grouping not covered by this paragraph, unless otherwise provided by that contract.

3. Except where this Regulation provides that decisions must be taken unanimously, the contract for the formation of a grouping may prescribe the conditions for a quorum and for a majority, in accordance with which the decisions, or some of them, shall be taken. Unless otherwise provided for by the contract, decisions shall be taken unanimously.

4. On the initiative of a manager or at the request of a member, the manager or managers must arrange for the members to be consulted so that the latter can take a decision.

Article 18

Each member shall be entitled to obtain information from the manager or managers concerning the grouping's business and to inspect the grouping's books and business records.

Article 19

1. A grouping shall be managed by one or more natural persons appointed in the contract for the formation of the grouping or by decision of the members.

No person may be a manager of a grouping if:

(a) by virtue of the law applicable to him, or

(b) by virtue of the internal law of the State in which the grouping has its official address, or

(c) following a judicial or administrative decision made or recognized in a Member State

he may not belong to the administrative or management body of a company, may not manage an undertaking or may not act as manager of a European Economic Interest Grouping.

2. A Member State may, in the case of groupings registered at their registries pursuant to Article 6, provide that legal persons may be managers on condition that such legal persons designate one or more natural persons, whose particulars shall be the subject of the filing provisions of Article 7(d) to represent them.

If a Member State exercises this option, it must provide that the representative or representatives shall be liable as if they were themselves managers of the groupings concerned.

The restrictions imposed in paragraph 1 shall also apply to those representatives.

3. The contract for the formation of a grouping or, failing that, a unanimous decision by the members shall determine the conditions for the appointment and removal of the manager or managers and shall lay down their powers.

Article 20

1. Only the manager or, where there are two or more, each of the managers shall represent a grouping in respect of dealings with third parties.

Each of the managers shall bind the grouping as regards third parties when he acts on behalf of the grouping, even where his acts do not fall within the objects of the grouping, unless the grouping proves that the third party knew or could not, under the circumstances, have been unaware that the act fell outside the objects of the grouping; publication of the particulars referred to in Article 5(c) shall not of itself be proof thereof.

No limitation on the powers of the manager or managers, whether deriving from the contract for the formation of the grouping or from a decision by the members, may be relied on as against third parties even if it is published.

2. The contract for the formation of the grouping may provide that the grouping shall be validly bound only by two or more managers acting jointly. Such a clause may be relied on as against third parties in accordance with the conditions referred to in Article 9(1) only if it is published in accordance with Article 8.

ARTICLE 21

1. The profits resulting from a grouping's activities shall be deemed to be the profits of the members and shall be apportioned among them in the proportions laid down in the contract for the formation of the grouping or, in the absence of any such provision, in equal shares.

2. The members of a grouping shall contribute to the payment of the amount by which expenditure exceeds income in the proportions laid down in the contract for the formation of the grouping or, in the absence of any such provision, in equal shares.

ARTICLE 22

1. Any member of a grouping may assign his participation in the grouping, or a proportion thereof, either to another member or to a third party; the assignment shall not take effect without the unanimous authorization of the other members.

2. A member of a grouping may use his participation in the grouping as security only after the other members have given their unanimous authorization, unless otherwise laid down in the contract for the formation of the grouping. The holder of the security may not at any time become a member of the grouping by virtue of that security.

ARTICLE 23

No grouping may invite investment by the public.

ARTICLE 24

1. The members of a grouping shall have unlimited joint and several liability for its debts and other liabilities of whatever nature. National law shall determine the consequences of such liability.

2. Creditors may not proceed against a member for payment in respect of debts and other liabilities, in accordance with the conditions laid down in paragraph 1, before the liquidation of a grouping is concluded, unless they have first requested the grouping to pay and payment has not been made within an appropriate period.

ARTICLE 25

Letters, order forms and similar documents must indicate legibly:

(a) the name of the grouping preceded or followed either by the words 'European Economic Interest Grouping' or by the initials 'EEIG', unless those words or initials already occur in the name;

(b) the location of the registry referred to in Article 6, in which the grouping is registered, together with the number of the grouping's entry at the registry;

(c) the grouping's official address;

(d) where applicable, that the managers must act jointly;

(e) where applicable, that the grouping is in liquidation, pursuant to Article 15, 31, 32 or 36.

Every establishment of a grouping, when registered in accordance with Article 10, must give the above particulars, together with those relating to its own registration, on the documents referred to in the first paragraph of this Article uttered by it.

ARTICLE 26

1. A decision to admit new members shall be taken unanimously by the members of the grouping.

2. Every new member shall be liable, in accordance with the conditions laid down in Article 24, for the grouping's debts and other liabilities, including those arising out of the grouping's activities before his admission.

He may, however, be exempted by a clause in the contract for the formation of the grouping or in the instrument of admission from the payment of debts and other liabilities which originated before his admission. Such a clause may be relied on as against third parties, under the conditions referred to in Article 9(1), only if it is published in accordance with Article 8.

ARTICLE 27

1. A member of a grouping may withdraw in accordance with the conditions laid down in the contract for the formation of a grouping or, in the absence of such conditions, with the unanimous agreement of the other members.

Any member of a grouping may, in addition, withdraw on just and proper grounds.

2. Any member of a grouping may be expelled for the reasons listed in the contract for the formation of the grouping and, in any case, if he seriously fails in his obligations or if he causes or threatens to cause serious disruption in the operation of the grouping.

Such expulsion may occur only by the decision of a court to which joint application has been made by a majority of the other members, unless otherwise provided by the contract for the formation of a grouping.

ARTICLE 28

1. A member of a grouping shall cease to belong to it on death or when he no longer complies with the conditions laid down in Article 4(1).

In addition, a Member State may provide, for the purposes of its liquidation, winding up, insolvency or cessation of payments laws, that a member shall cease to be a member of any grouping at the moment determined by those laws.

2. In the event of the death of a natural person who is a member of a grouping, no person may become a member in his place except under the conditions laid down in the contract for the formation of the grouping or, failing that, with the unanimous agreement of the remaining members.

ARTICLE 29

As soon as a member ceases to belong to a grouping, the manager or managers must inform the other members of that fact; they must also take the steps required as listed in Articles 7 and 8. In addition, any person concerned may take those steps.

ARTICLE 30

Except where the contract for the formation of a grouping provides otherwise and without prejudice to the rights acquired by a person under Articles 22(1) or 28(2), a grouping shall continue to exist for the remaining members after a member has ceased to belong to it, in accordance with the conditions laid down in the contract for the formation of the grouping or determined by unanimous decision of the members in question.

ARTICLE 31

1. A grouping may be wound up by a decision of its members ordering its winding up. Such a decision shall be taken unanimously, unless otherwise laid down in the contract for the formation of the grouping.

2. A grouping must be wound up by a decision of its members:

(a) noting the expiry of the period fixed in the contract for the formation of the grouping or the existence of any other cause for winding up provided for in the contract, or

(b) noting the accomplishment of the grouping's purpose or the impossibility of pursuing it further.

Where, three months after one of the situations referred to in the first subparagraph has occurred, a members' decision establishing the winding up of the grouping has not been taken, any member may petition the court to order winding up.

3. A grouping must also be wound up by a decision of its members or of the remaining member when the conditions laid down in Article 4(2) are no longer fulfilled.

4. After a grouping has been wound up by decision of its members, the manager or managers must take the steps required as listed in Articles 7 and 8. In addition, any person concerned may take those steps.

ARTICLE 32

1. On application by any person concerned or by a competent authority, in the event of the infringement of Articles 3, 12 or 31(3), the court must order a grouping to be wound up, unless its affairs can be and are put in order before the court has delivered a substantive ruling.

2. On application by a member, the court may order a grouping to be wound up on just and proper grounds.

3. A Member State may provide that the court may, on application by a competent authority, order the winding up of a grouping which has its official address in the State to which that authority belongs, wherever the grouping acts in contravention of that State's public interest, if the law of that State provides for such a possibility in respect of registered companies or other legal bodies subject to it.

ARTICLE 33

When a member ceases to belong to a grouping for any reason other than the assignment of his rights in acordance with the conditions laid down in Article 22(1), the value of his rights and obligations shall be determined taking into account the assets and liabilities of the grouping as they stand when he ceases to belong to it.

The value of the rights and obligations of a departing member may not be fixed in advance.

Article 34

Without prejudice to Article 37(1), any member who ceases to belong to a grouping shall remain answerable, in accordance with the conditions laid down in Article 24, for the debts and other liabilities arising out of the grouping's activities before he ceased to be a member.

Article 35

1. The winding up of a grouping shall entail its liquidation.

2. The liquidation of a grouping and the conclusion of its liquidation shall be governed by national law.

3. A grouping shall retain its capacity, within the meaning of Article 1(2), until its liquidation is concluded.

4. The liquidator or liquidators shall take the steps required as listed in Articles 7 and 8.

Article 36

Groupings shall be subject to national laws governing insolvency and cessation of payments. The commencement of proceedings against a grouping on grounds of its insolvency or cessation of payments shall not by itself cause the commencement of such proceedings against its members.

Article 37

1. A period of limitation of five years after the publication, pursuant to Article 8, of notice of a member's ceasing to belong to a grouping shall be substituted for any longer period which may be laid down by the relevant national law for actions against that member in connection with debts and other liabilities arising out of the grouping's activities before he ceased to be a member.

2. A period of limitation of five years after the publication, pursuant to Article 8, of notice of the conclusion of the liquidation of a grouping shall be substituted for any longer period which may be laid down by the relevant national law for actions against a member of the grouping in connection with debts and other liabilities arising out of the grouping's activities.

Article 38

Where a grouping carries on any activity in a Member State in contravention of that State's public interest, a competent authority of that State may prohibit that activity. Review of that competent authority's decision by a judicial authority shall be possible.

Article 39

1. The Member States shall designate the registry or registries responsible for effecting the registration referred to in Articles 6 and 10 and shall lay down the rules governing registration. They shall prescribe the conditions under which the documents referred to in Articles 7 and 10 shall be filed. They shall ensure that the documents and particulars referred to in Article 8 are published in the appropriate official gazette of the Member State in which the grouping has its official address, and may prescribe the manner of publication of the documents and particulars referred to in Article 8(c).

The Member States shall also ensure that anyone may, at the appropriate registry pursuant to Article 6 or, where appropriate, Article 10, inspect the documents referred to in Article 7 and obtain, even by post, full or partial copies thereof.

The Member States may provide for the payment of fees in connection with the operations referred to in the preceding subparagraphs; those fees may not, however, exceed the administrative cost thereof.

2. The member states shall ensure that the information to be published in the *Official Journal of the European Communities* pursuant to Article 11 is forwarded to the Office for Official Publications of the European Communities within one month of its publication in the official gazette referred to in paragraph 1.

3. The Member States shall provide for appropriate penalties in the event of failure to comply with the provisions of Articles 7, 8 and 10 on disclosure and in the event of failure to comply with Article 25.

ARTICLE 40

The profits or losses resulting from the activities of a grouping shall be taxable only in the hands of its members.

ARTICLE 41

1. The Member States shall take the measures required by virtue of Article 39 before 1 July 1989. They shall immediately communicate them to the Commission.

2. For information purposes, the Member States shall inform the Commission of the classes of natural persons, companies, firms and other legal bodies which they prohibit from participating in groupings pursuant to Article 4(4). The Commission shall inform the other Member States.

ARTICLE 42

1. Upon the adoption of this Regulation, a Contact Committee shall be set up under the auspices of the Commission. Its function shall be:

(a) to facilitate, without prejudice to Articles 169 and 170 of the Treaty, application of this Regulation through regular consultation dealing in particular with practical problems arising in connection with its application;

(b) to advise the Commission, if necessary, on additions or amendments to this Regulation.

2. The Contact Committee shall be composed of representatives of the Member States and representatives of the Commission. The chairman shall be a representative of the Commission. The Commission shall provide the secretariat.

3. The Contact Committee shall be convened by its chairman either on his own initiative or at the request of one of its members.

ARTICLE 43

This Regulation shall enter into force on the third day following its publication in the *Official Journal of the European Communities*.

It shall apply from 1 July 1989, with the exception of Articles 39, 41 and 42 which shall apply as from the entry into force of the Regulation.

This Regulation shall be binding in its entirety and directly applicable in all Member States.

Done at Brussels, 25 July 1985.

For the Council
The President
J. POOS

Regulations 2(2), 4(1), 5(1), 9(2), (3), (9) and (10), 12(2) and (4), 13(1) and 18, and Schedule 4, paragraph 14

SCHEDULE 2

FORMS RELATING TO EEIGS

EUROPEAN ECONOMIC INTEREST GROUPING FORM No. 1

Statement of name, official address, members, objects and duration for EEIG whose official address is in Great Britain

Please do not write in this margin

Pursuant to Articles 5, 6, 7 and 39 of Council Regulation (EEC) No. 2137/85 and Regulation 9 of the European Economic Interest Grouping Regulations 1989

Please complete legibly, preferably in black type, or bold block lettering

To the Registrar of Companies
(address overleaf)

For official use

Name of grouping

* insert full name of grouping

*

The official address of the grouping is as stated below

Postcode

ø delete if inappropriate

1. The contract establishing the above named grouping [and that contract not being written in English, a certified translation of it]ø[is][are] delivered for registration.
2. The name(s) (include business name if different) and particulars of the members of the grouping are as follows:

§ Insert "natural person" if an individual, "legal person" if a body corporate or "partnership" as appropriate

† Business address or registered office address as appropriate

Name

Registered Number and Place of Registration (if any)

Legal Form§

Address†

Postcode

Name

Registered Number and Place of Registration (if any)

Legal Form§

Address†

Postcode

Particulars of further members should be given on the prescribed continuation sheet

PLEASE TURN OVER

Presentor's name address telephone number and reference (if any):

For official Use

Post room

Please do not write in this margin

The objects of the grouping are:-

The duration of the grouping (if indefinite this should be noted)

Complete this section only if this form relates to an existing grouping transferring its official address to a place in Great Britain in accordance with Article 14(1) of the EC Regulation.

I attach a copy of ______________________ as evidence of the publication of the transfer proposal and confirm that no competent authority has opposed the transfer under Article 14(4) of the EC Reglation.

Signed ______________________ member/on behalf of a member

I, ______________________ a member/authorised on behalf of a memberø of the above grouping, declare that all the requirements of the above Regulations in respects of the registration of the above grouping and of matters precedent and incidental to it have been complied with. This declaration is made by virtue of the provisions of the Statutory Declarations Act 1835.

ø delete as appropriate

Declared by ______________________

at ______________________

____

____

on ______________________

before me ______________________

A Commissioner for Oaths or Notary Public or Justice of the Peace or Solicitor having the powers conferred on a Commissioner for Oaths

Number of continuation sheets attached ☐

If the official address is in England and Wales or Wales this form together with the contract establishing the grouping, a certified translation if the contract is written other than in English and the appropriate fee must be sent to:-

The Registrar of Companies
Companies House
Crown Way
Cardiff
CF4 3UZ

or, if the official address is in Scotland to:-

The Registrar of Companies
Companies House
100-102 George Street
Edinburgh
EH2 3DJ

EUROPEAN ECONOMIC INTEREST GROUPING FORM No. 2

Statement of name, establishment address in Great Britain and members of an EEIG whose official address is outside the UK

Pursuant to Articles 5 and 10 of Council Regulation (EEC) No. 2137/85 and Regulation 12 of the European Economic Interest Grouping Regulations 1989

Please do not write in this margin

To the Registrar of Companies
(address overleaf)

For official use

Name of grouping

Please complete legibly, preferably in black type, or bold block lettering

Member State in which official address is situated

Establishment address in Great Britain is situated at

Postcode

† delete if inappropriate

1 A certified copy of the contract of the above-named grouping [and, that contract not being written in English, a certified translation of it]†[is][are] delivered for registration

2 The name(s) (include business name if different) and particulars of the members of the grouping are as follows:

§ Insert "natural person" if an individual, "legal person" if a body corporate or "partnership" as appropriate

ø Business address or registered office address as appropriate

Name

Registered Number and Place of Registration (if any)

Legal Form§

Address ø

Postcode

Name

Registered Number and Place of Registration (if any)

Legal Form§

Address ø

Postcode

PLEASE TURN OVER

Presentor's name address, telephone number and reference (if any):

For official Use

Post room

Name	
Registered Number and Place of Registration (if any)	
Legal Form§	
Address ø	
	Postcode

Name	
Registered Number and Place of Registration (if any)	
Legal Form§	
Address ø	
	Postcode

Please do not write in this margin.

Please complete legibly, preferably in black type, or bold block lettering

§ Insert "natural person" if an individual, "legal person" if a body corporate or "partnership" as appropriate

ø Business address or registered office address as appropriate

Particulars of further members should be given on the prescribed continuation sheet.

I, ______________________ a member/authorised on behalf of a member† of the above grouping, declare that all the requirements of the above Regulations in respect of the registration of the above grouping and of matter precedent and incidental to it have been complied with. This declaration is made by virtue of the provisions of the Statutory Declarations Act 1835.

† Delete as appropriate

Declared by ______________________

at ______________________

____

____

on ______________________

before me ______________________

A Commissioner for Oaths or Notary Public or Justice of the Peace or Solicitor having the powers conferred on a Commissioner for Oaths

Number of continuation sheets attached ☐

If the address of the establishment is in England and Wales or Wales this form and the certified copy of the contract must be sent to:-

The Registrar of Companies
Companies House
Crown Way
Cardiff
CF4 3UZ

or, If the address of the establishment is in Scotland to:-

The Registrar of Companies
Companies House
100-102 George Street
Edinburgh
EH2 3DJ

EUROPEAN ECONOMIC INTEREST GROUPING FORM No. 3

Notice of manager's particulars, and of termination of appointment where the official address of the EEIG is in Great Britain

Please do not write in this margin

Pursuant to Article 7(d) of Council Regulation (EEC) No. 2137/85 and Regulations 5 and 13(1)(a) of the European Economic Interest Grouping Regulations 1989

To the Registrar of Companies
(address overleaf)

Grouping number

Please complete legibly, preferably in black type, or bold block lettering

Name of grouping

* insert full name of grouping

*

ø specify the change (including termination of an appointment) and date thereof and if this consists of the appointment of a manager complete the box below.

notifies you of the following details (see **note 1 overleaf**):

ø

Particulars of manager **(note 2 overleaf)**

Name **(note 3)**	Business occupation
Previous name(s)	Nationality
Address **(note 4)**	Date of birth
Postcode	

† delete as appropriate

I consent to act singly/jointly† as manager of the grouping named above

Signature Date

If the grouping has more than one manager does the manager have the power to bind the grouping acting singly? **YES/NO†**

If **NO** please specify the conditions under which managers can bind the grouping:

Signature [Member][Manager]† Date

Presentor's name address, telephone number and reference (if any):

For official Use

Post room

Notes

1. Notice relating to managers of an EEIG with an official address outside Great Britain must be given by form EEIG 4

2. A separate form must be completed in respect of each manager and if that manager is not a natural person it must designate one or more natural persons to represent it (regulation 5(1)). A Form EEIG3 must also be completed in respect of each natural person and be sent to the relevant Registrar.

3. For a natural person, his present christian name(s) and surname must be given, together with any previous Christian name(s) or surname(s).

   "Christian name" includes a forename. In the case of a peer or person usually known by a title different from his surname, "surname" means that title. In the case of a corporation, its corporate name must be given.

   A previous christian name or surname need not be given if:-

   (a) in the case of a married woman, it was a name by which she was known before her marriage; or

   (b) it was changed or ceased to be used at least 20 years ago, or before the person who previously used it reached the age of 18; or

   (c) in the case of a peer or person usually known by a British title different from his surname, it was a name by which he was known before he adopted the title or succeeded to it.

4. Usual residential address must be given. In the case of a corporation, give the registered or principal office.

5. If the official address is in England and Wales or Wales this form must be sent to:-

   The Registrar of Companies
   Companies House
   Crown Way
   Cardiff
   CF4 3UZ

   or,

   if the official address is in Scotland this form must be sent to:—

   The Registrar of Companies
   Companies House
   100-102 George Street
   Edinburgh
   EH2 3DJ

EUROPEAN ECONOMIC INTEREST GROUPING FORM No. 4

Notice of documents and particulars required to be filed

Pursuant to Articles 7 and 10 of Council Regulation (EEC) No. 2137/85 and Regulations 4(1) and 13(1)(b) of the European Economic Interest Grouping Regulations 1989

Please do not write in this margin

To the Registrar of Companies
(address overleaf)

Grouping number

Please complete legibly, preferably in black type, or bold block lettering

Name of grouping

* insert full name of grouping

*
Member State in which official address is situated

gives notice that the following is/are† attached:

Please tick appropriate box(es)

† delete as appropriate

- [ ] 1 an amendment to the grouping's formation contract
- [ ] 2 a document evidencing a judicial decision regarding nullity
- [ ] 3 an assignment of all/part† of a member's participation
- [ ] 4 a members' order/judicial decision† to wind up the grouping
- [ ] 5 Liquidator(s) appointment/termination of appointment†
- [ ] 6 a document evidencing the conclusion of liquidation
- [ ] 7 a proposal to transfer the official address as referred to in Article 14(1) of the EC Regulation
- [ ] 8 an exemption clause relieving a new member from payment of debts and other liabilities which originated before his admission

Except where stated all items apply irrespective of the situation of the official address of the grouping

The following apply only if the grouping has its official address outside the United Kingdom.

- [ ] 9 notice of the appointment of a manager or managers, name(s) and other identification particulars as required by the Member State where the grouping has its official address together with notification as to whether they may act alone or must act jointly
- [ ] 10 notice of termination of a manager's appointment

Note

If any document or particulars are not written in English a certified translation must also be attached

Signed [Member][Manager]† Date

Presentor's name address, telephone number and reference (if any):	For official Use	Post room

Notes

If the official address is in England and Wales or Wales or Form EEIG2 has been delivered to the Registrar of Companies in Cardiff this form must be sent to:-

The Registrar of Companies
Companies House
Crown Way
Cardiff
CF4 3UZ

or, if the official address is in Scotland or Form EEIG2 has been delivered to the Registrar of Companies in Edinburgh this form must be sent to:-

The Registrar of Companies
Companies House
100-102 George Street
Edinburgh
EH2 3DJ

EUROPEAN ECONOMIC INTEREST GROUPING FORM No. 5

Notice of setting up or closure of an establishment of an EEIG

Please do not write in this margin

Pursuant to Articles 7(b) and 10 of Council Regulation (EEC) No. 2137/85 and Regulation 13(1)(c) of the European Economic Interest Grouping Regulations 1989

Please complete legibly, preferably in black type, or bold block lettering

To the Registrar of Companies
(address overleaf)

Grouping number

Name of grouping

* insert full name of grouping

*

Member State in which official address is situated

SECTION A to be completed in all cases

gives notice that it has set up/closed † an establishment at:

Postcode

SECTION B to be completed in appropriate circumstances

If: (a) this notice is in respect of an EEIG whose official address is not in the United Kingdom, <u>and</u>
(b) this form is being used to report the opening or closure of an establishment in Great Britain, <u>and</u>
(c) the EEIG will then have more than one establishment in the United Kingdom,

then it may if it wishes write in this box an address in the United Kingdom at which it would be most convenient to receive correspondence.

Postcode

† delete as appropriate

Signed [Member][Manager]† Date

Presentor's name address, telephone number and reference (if any):

For official Use

Post room

Notes

If the official address is in England and Wales or Wales or Form EEIG2 has been delivered to the Registrar of Companies in Cardiff this form must be sent to:-

The Registrar of Companies
Companies House
Crown Way
Cardiff
CF4 3UZ

or, if the official address is in Scotland or Form EEIG2 has been delivered to the Registrar of Companies in Edinburgh this form must be sent to:—

The Registrar of Companies
Companies House
100-102 George Street
Edinburgh
EH2 3DJ

EUROPEAN ECONOMIC INTEREST GROUPING FORM No. 6

Statement of name, other than registered name, under which an EEIG whose official address is outside Great Britain proposes to carry on business in Great Britain

Please do not write in this margin

Pursuant to Article 39 of Council Regulation (EEC) No. 2137/85 and Section 694(4)(a) of the Companies Act 1985 as applied by Regulation 18 of and Schedule 4 to the European Economic Interest Grouping Regulations 1989

Please complete legibly, preferably in black type, or bold block lettering

To the Registrar of Companies
(address overleaf)

Grouping number

* enter registered name

Name of grouping

*

§ enter name approved by the Secretary of State

The name approved by the Secretary of State, other than its registered name in the Member State where it has its official address, under which the grouping proposes to carry on business in Great Britain is §

† delete as appropriate

Signed [Member][Manager]† Date

Presentor's name address, telephone number and reference (if any):

For official Use

Post room

Notes

If the address of the establishment is in England and Wales or Wales this form must be sent to:-

The Registrar of Companies
Companies House
Crown Way
Cardiff
CF4 3UZ

or, if the address of the establishment is in Scotland to:—

The Registrar of Companies
Companies House
100-102 George Street
Edinburgh
EH2 3DJ

EUROPEAN ECONOMIC INTEREST GROUPING FORM No. 7

Statement of name, other than registered name, under which an EEIG whose official address is outside Great Britain proposes to carry on business in substitution for name previously approved

Please do not write in this margin

Pursuant to Article 39 of Council Regulation (EEC) No. 2137/85 and Section 694(4)(b) of the Companies Act 1985 as applied by Regulation 18 of and Schedule 4 to the European Economic Interest Grouping Regulations 1989

Please complete legibly, preferably in black type, or bold block lettering

To the Registrar of Companies
(address overleaf)

Grouping number

Name of grouping

* insert present name approved by Secretary of State

*

ø enter registered name in the Member State where the grouping has its official address

The name approved by the Secretary of State, other than its registered name, under which ø

§ enter name approved by the Secretary of State

proposes to carry on business in Great Britain is §

This name is in substitution for that currently approved.

† delete as appropriate

Signed [Member][Manager]† Date

Presentor's name address, telephone number and reference (if any):

For official Use

Post room

Notes

If the address of the establishment is in England and Wales or Wales this form must be sent to:-

The Registrar of Companies
Companies House
Crown Way
Cardiff
CF4 3UZ

or, if the address of the establishment is in Scotland to:—

The Registrar of Companies
Companies House
100-102 George Street
Edinburgh
EH2 3DJ

EUROPEAN ECONOMIC INTEREST GROUPING FORMS Nos 1 and 2 (cont)

Statement of members (continuation)

Continuation sheet No ____________
to Form No EEIG [1][2]†

† Delete as appropriate

Name of grouping

*

Name	
Registered Number and Place of Registration (if any)	
Legal Form	
Address	
	Postcode

Name	
Registered Number and Place of Registration (if any)	
Legal Form	
Address	
	Postcode

Name	
Registered Number and Place of Registration (if any)	
Legal Form	
Address	
	Postcode

Regulation 10(2)

SCHEDULE 3

AUTHORISED EQUIVALENTS IN OTHER COMMUNITY OFFICIAL LANGUAGES OF "EUROPEAN ECONOMIC INTEREST GROUPING" AND "EEIG"

DANISH:	Europæiske Økonomiske Firmagruppe (EØFG)
DUTCH:	Europese Economische Samenwerkingsverbanden (EESV)
FRENCH:	Groupement Européen d'intérêt économique (GEIE)
GERMAN:	Europäische Wirtschaftliche Interessenvereinigung (EWIV)
GREEK:	Ευρωπαϊκός όμιλος οικονομικού σκοπού (ΕΟΟΣ) (written phonetically in letters of the Latin alphabet as "Evropaikos omilos economicou skopou (EOOS)")
IRISH:	Grupail Eorpach um Leas Eacnamaioch (GELE)
ITALIAN:	Gruppo Europeo di Interesse Economico (GEIE)
PORTUGUESE:	Agrupamento Europeu de Interesse Econômico (AEIE)
SPANISH:	Agrupación Europea de Interés Económico (AEIE)

Regulation 18

SCHEDULE 4

PROVISIONS OF COMPANIES ACT 1985 APPLYING TO EEIGS AND THEIR ESTABLISHMENTS

1. section 26(1)(c) to (e), (2) and (3).

2. section 28(2) to (5) and (7) so far as it relates to a direction given under subsection (2).

3. section 29(1)(a).

4. Part XII for the purpose of the creation and registration of charges to which it applies.

5. section 432(1) and (2).

6. section 434 so far as it refers to inspectors appointed under section 432 as applied by regulation 18 above and this Schedule.

7. section 436 so far as it refers to inspectors appointed under section 432, and to section 434, as applied by regulation 18 above and this Schedule.

8. sections 437 to 439.

9. section 441 so far as it applies to inspectors appointed under section 432 as applied by regulation 18 above and this Schedule.

10. section 447, as if paragraph (1)(d) referred to any EEIG which is carrying on business in Great Britain or has at any time carried on business there, whether or not any such EEIG is a body corporate.

11. sections 448 to 452.

12. section 458.

13. Part XVIII relating to floating charges and receivers (Scotland).

14. section 694 as if it referred to—

(a) the registered name of an EEIG whose establishment is registered or is in the process of being registered under regulation 12 above with the necessary modifications;

(b) regulation 10 above as applied by regulation 12(7) in addition to section 26;

(c) in subsection (4)(a), a statement in Form EEIG 6; and

(d) in subsection (4)(b), a statement in Form EEIG 7.

15. section 697(2) as if it referred to an EEIG whose establishment is registered or is in the process of being registered under regulation 12 above.

16. section 704(5).

17. section 705(2).

18. sections 706, 707 and 710(1) to (3) and (5) as if they referred to documents and particulars delivered to or furnished by the registrar under these Regulations.

19. section 714(1) as if it referred to EEIGs or their establishments registered under these Regulations or in Northern Ireland.

20. section 718(2) as if it included a reference to an EEIG registered in Great Britain under these Regulations.

21. section 725.

22. section 730 and Schedule 24 so far as they refer to offences under sections applied by regulation 18 above and this Schedule.

23. section 731.

24. sections 732 and 733 so far as they refer to sections 447 to 451 as applied by regulation 18 above and this Schedule.

EXPLANATORY NOTE

(This note is not part of the Regulations)

These Regulations make provisions in respect of European Economic Interest Groupings formed under article 1 of the Council Regulation (EEC) No. 2137/85, which provides a legal framework for groupings of natural persons, companies, firms and other legal entities to enable them to co-operate effectively when carrying on business activities across national frontiers within the European Community. Such groupings, which have their official address in Great Britain, when registered there under these Regulations are bodies corporate and their members have unlimited joint and several liability for the debts and liabilities of such groupings.

The EC Regulation is directly applicable in UK law but these Regulations are necessary for implementation in part of the Community obligations and for other purposes mentioned in section 2(2) of the European Communities Act 1972. In particular certain provisions are left for national law by the EC Regulation. Articles 35 and 36 provide that groupings shall be subject to national laws governing their winding up and the conclusion of their liquidation and insolvency and cessation of payments. Regulation 8 of these Regulations provides for modifications to Part V of the Insolvency Act 1986, where a grouping is wound up as an unregistered company under Part V. Accordingly the Court has power to wind up a grouping in the circumstances set out in articles 31 and 32 or the grouping may be wound up voluntarily in the circumstances set out in article 31; and a grouping is dissolved after 3 months of the receipt by the registrar of a notice of the conclusion of the liquidation, whether or not the grouping has been wound up by the Court.

STATUTORY INSTRUMENTS

1989 No. 639

NATIONAL DEBT

The Premium Savings Bonds (Amendment) Regulations 1989

Made - - - -	*11th April 1989*
Laid before Parliament	*12th April 1989*
Coming into force	*1st July 1989*

The Treasury, in exercise of the powers conferred on them by section 11 of the National Debt Act 1972(**a**) and of all other powers enabling them in that behalf, hereby make the following Regulations:

Citation and commencement

1. These Regulations may be cited as the Premium Savings Bonds (Amendment) Regulations 1989 and shall come into force on 1st July 1989.

Amendment of principal Regulations

2. The Premium Savings Bonds Regulations 1972(**b**) shall be amended by substituting the following regulation for regulation 6 –

"6(1) Except in the case of bonds purchased under regulation 4(3)(a) of these Regulations (bonds purchased on behalf of a person under the age of sixteen years), not less than one hundred bond units shall be purchased in the name of any one person at any time. In the case of bonds purchased under regulation 4(3)(a) of these Regulations, not less than ten bond units shall be purchased in the name of any one person at any time. In either case, bonds shall not be purchased except in multiples of ten bond units.

(2) The foregoing paragraph shall not operate to prevent the purchase of less than one hundred bond units or the purchase of bonds in multiples of less than ten bond units if it appears to the Director of Savings that the purchase was made through an agent of the Director who did not make the purchaser aware of the limits contained in the foregoing paragraph and the Director in his discretion considers it just and reasonable that the purchase be treated as valid.".

Stephen Dorrell
David Maclean
Two of the Lords Commissioners
of Her Majesty's Treasury

11th April 1989

(**a**) 1972 c.65, to which there are amendments not relevant to these Regulations. (**b**) S.I. 1972/765; the relevant amending instrument is S.I. 1985/861.

EXPLANATORY NOTE

(This note is not part of the Regulations)

These Regulations amend the Premium Savings Bonds Regulations 1972. They increase the minimum purchase of bonds, except bonds purchased on behalf of minors under 16, from £10 to £100. The minimum purchase of bonds purchased on behalf of minors under 16 remains at £10. The smallest multiple in which bonds may be purchased is increased from £5 to £10 in both cases. The Director of Savings has discretion to accept purchases of less than £100 or purchases in multiples smaller than £10 in certain circumstances.

STATUTORY INSTRUMENTS

1989 No. 644

AGRICULTURE

The Pig Carcase (Grading) (Amendment) Regulations 1989

Made - - - -	*11th April 1989*
Laid before Parliament	*20th April 1989*
Coming into force	*11th May 1989*

The Minister of Agriculture, Fisheries and Food and the Secretary of State, being Ministers designated (**a**) for the purposes of section 2(2) of the European Communities Act 1972(**b**) in relation to the common agricultural policy of the European Economic Community, acting jointly in exercise of the powers conferred upon them by the said section 2(2) and of all other powers enabling them in that behalf, hereby make the following Regulations:–

Title, extent and commencement

1. These Regulations, which may be cited as the Pig Carcase (Grading) (Amendment) Regulations 1989, shall apply in Great Britain and shall come into force on 11th May 1989.

Amendment of the Pig Carcase (Grading) Regulations 1988

2. The Pig Carcase (Grading) Regulations 1988(**c**) shall be amended:

(a) by substituting for the definition of "the Commission Decision" in regulation 2(1) thereof the following definition:

""the Commission Decision" means Commission Decision No. 88/234/EEC authorising the methods for grading pig carcases in the United Kingdom(**d**), as amended by Commission Decision No. 88/478/EEC(**e**)";

(b) by substituting for paragraph 1(iv) of the Schedule thereto (particulars of the occupier of a slaughterhouse to be notified to the appropriate Minister) the following sub-paragraph:

"(iv) If the council of a London borough the name and address of the council.".

(**a**) S.I. 1972/1811. (**b**) 1972 c.68. (**c**) S.I. 1988/1180. (**d**) OJ No. L105, 26.4.88, p.15. (**e**) OJ No. L234, 24.8.88, p.17.

In Witness whereof the Official Seal of the Minister of Agriculture, Fisheries and Food is hereunto affixed on 11th April 1989.

John MacGregor
Minister of Agriculture, Fisheries and Food

11th April 1989

Sanderson of Bowden
Minister of State, Scottish Office

EXPLANATORY NOTE

(This note is not part of the Regulations)

These Regulations amend the Pig Carcase (Grading) Regulations 1988 in two respects:

(a) by up-dating the definition of the Commission Decision following an amendment to that Decision authorising the methods for grading pig carcases in the United Kingdom (regulation 2(a)); and

(b) by making a minor clarification of the particulars to be notified by an occupier of a slaughterhouse to the appropriate Minister (regulation 2(b)).

STATUTORY INSTRUMENTS

1989 No. 645

HIGHWAYS, ENGLAND AND WALES

The New Street Byelaws (Extension of Operation) (Amendment) Order 1989

Made - - - - 11th April 1989

The Secretary of State for the Environment, as respects England, and the Secretary of State for Wales, as respect Wales, in exercise of the powers conferred by paragraph 11 of Schedule 23 to the Highways Act 1980(**a**) and now vested in them (**b**) and of all other powers enabling them in that behalf hereby make the following Order:

Citation

1. This Order may be cited as the New Street Byelaws (Extension of Operation) (Amendment) Order 1989.

Extension

2. In article 2 of the New Street Byelaws (Extension of Operation) Order 1980(**c**) for "31st March 1989" there shall be substituted, "31st March 1991".

Revocation

3. The Orders specified in column (1) of the Schedule to this Order are hereby revoked.

11th April 1989

Nicholas Ridley
Secretary of State for the Environment

21st March 1989

Peter Walker
Secretary of State for Wales

(**a**) 1980 c.66. (**b**) As respects the Secretary of State for the Environment, S.I. 1970/1681 and as respects the Secretary of State for Wales, S.I. 1965/319. (**c**) S.I. 1980/457.

SCHEDULE

REVOCATIONS

(1)	(2)
Orders revoked	*References*
The New Street Byelaws (Extension of Operation) Order 1962	S.I. 1962/645.
The New Street Byelaws (Extension of Operation) Order 1967	S.I. 1967/512.
The New Street Byelaws (Extension of Operation) Order 1972	S.I. 1972/595.
The New Street Byelaws (Extension of Operation) Order 1974	S.I. 1974/645.
The New Street Byelaws (Extension of Operation) Order 1977	S.I. 1977/502.
The New Street Byelaws (Extension of Operation) Variation Order 1983	S.I. 1983/483.
The New Street Byelaws (Extension of Operation) Variation Order 1986	S.I. 1986/610.

EXPLANATORY NOTE

(This note is not part of the Order)

This Order extends until 31st March 1991 the period during which certain new street byelaws continue in force. The byelaws were made before the commencement of the Highways Act 1959 (c.25) under enactments which were repealed by that Act. Section 312(6) of that Act kept those byelaws in force until 30th April 1962 and subsequent orders (revoked, with the exception of S.I. 1980/457, by this Order) under that section and paragraph 11 of Schedule 23 to the Highways Act 1980 have continued the byelaws in force until 31st March 1989.

STATUTORY INSTRUMENTS

1989 No. 652

NATIONAL DEBT

The National Savings Stock Register (Amendment) Regulations 1989

Made - - - -	*12th April 1989*
Laid before Parliament	*13th April 1989*
Coming into force	*24th April 1989*

The Treasury, in exercise of the powers conferred on them by section 3 of the National Debt Act 1972 **(a)**, and of all other powers enabling them in that behalf, hereby make the following Regulations:

Citation and commencement

1. These Regulations may be cited as the National Savings Stock Register (Amendment) Regulations 1989 and shall come into force on 24th April 1989.

Amendment of principal Regulations

2. The National Savings Stock Register Regulations 1976 **(b)** shall be amended by the insertion of the following regulation after regulation 11:

"The sale of stock to the Bank of England

11A.—(1) Where the Bank of England has given notice that it is prepared to purchase stock of any description, the holder of any such stock may make application to the Director of Savings requesting him to offer the stock for sale through the Commissioners to the Bank of England. If such an application is made the transaction shall be subject to this regulation and regulation 11 shall not apply to it.

(2) An application to the Director of Savings to offer stock for sale to the Bank of England under this regulation shall be made by sending to the Director of Savings an application in writing in the approved form together with any certificate relating to the stock to be offered for sale.

(3) Upon receipt of an application made in accordance with this regulation the Director of Savings shall cause the stock which is the subject of the application to be offered for sale through the Commissioners to the Bank of England.

(4) An application made in accordance with this regulation may not be withdrawn without the consent of the Director of Savings.

(5) Where the Bank of England rejects any offer made to it to sell stock in accordance with this regulation, the Director of Savings shall notify the holder of that stock and shall return the certificate to him as soon as practicable.

(a) 1972 c.65; section 3 was amended by paragraph 19 of Schedule 5 and Schedule 6 to the Trustee Savings Banks Act 1976 (c.4). **(b)** S.I. 1976/2012, to which there are amendments not relevant to these Regulations.

(6) Notwithstanding anything in these Regulations, no commission shall be payable to the Director of Savings on the sale of stock under this regulation.

(7) This regulation shall apply only to stock which is of a description corresponding to stock or securities transferable in the books of the Bank of England.".

David Maclean
Stephen Dorrell
Two of the Lords Commissioners of Her Majesty's Treasury

12th April 1989

EXPLANATORY NOTE

(This note is not part of the Regulations)

These Regulations amend the National Savings Stock Register Regulations 1976 to permit the holders of securities registered on the National Savings Stock Register and which are transferable in the books of the Bank of England, to request the Director of Savings to cause any such securities to be offered for sale to the Bank of England where the Bank of England has given notice that it is prepared to purchase the securities. The Regulations also provide that such sales shall not be subject to any commission charges.

STATUTORY INSTRUMENTS

1989 No. 655

PUBLIC HEALTH, ENGLAND AND WALES
PUBLIC HEALTH, SCOTLAND
PUBLIC HEALTH, NORTHERN IRELAND

CONTAMINATION OF FOOD

The Food Protection (Emergency Prohibitions) Amendment Order 1989

Made - - - -	*12th April 1989*
Laid before Parliament	*14th April 1989*
Coming into force	*17th April 1989*

Whereas the Secretary of State is of the opinion, as mentioned in section 1(1)(a) of the Food and Environment Protection Act 1985(**a**), that there has been or may have been an escape of substances of such descriptions and in such quantities and such circumstances as are likely to create a hazard to human health through human consumption of food;

And whereas he is of the opinion, as mentioned in section 1(1)(b) of the said Act, that in consequence of the said escape of substances food which is, or may be in the future, in the areas described in the Schedule to the Food Protection (Emergency Prohibitions) Order 1989(**b**) or which is, or may be in the future, derived from anything in those areas is, or may be, or may become, unsuitable for human consumption;

Now, therefore, in exercise of the powers conferred on him by sections 1(1) and (2), and 24(1) and (3) of the said Act(**c**), and of all other powers enabling him in that behalf, he hereby makes the following Order:

Title, commencement and interpretation

1. This Order may be cited as the Food Protection (Emergency Prohibitions) Amendment Order 1989 and shall come into force on 17th April 1989.

Partial revocation and amendment

2. The Food Protection (Emergency Prohibitions) Order 1989 is revoked to the extent that it imposes prohibitions on–

(a) the slaughter of any sheep which was moved from any place in accordance with a consent given under section 2(1) of the Food and Environment Protection Act 1985 on or before 8th January 1989 which consent was subject to the condition that the sheep to which it applies should be marked with a blue mark; and

(**a**) 1985 c.48.
(**b**) S.I. 1989/3.
(**c**) Section 24(1) contains a definition of "the Ministers" relevant to the exercise of the statutory powers under which this Order is made.

(b) the supply or having in possession for supply of meat, or food containing meat, derived from any sheep described in paragraph (a) of this article,

and accordingly that Order is amended in accordance with the following provisions of this Order.

3. In article 5, for paragraph (2) there shall be substituted the following paragraph:–

"(2) Paragraph (1) above shall not apply in the case of–

(a) any sheep which was moved from any place in accordance with a consent given under section 2(1) of the said Act which consent did not require that the sheep to which it applies should be marked;

(b) any sheep which was moved from any place in accordance with a consent given under section 2(1) of the said Act which consent was subject to the condition that the sheep to which it applies should be marked with a red mark;

(c) any sheep which was moved from any place in accordance with a consent given on or before 31st July 1988 under section 2(1) of the said Act which consent was subject to the condition that the sheep to which it applies should be marked with an apricot mark;

(d) any sheep which was moved from any place in accordance with a consent given on or before 2nd October 1988 under section 2(1) of the said Act which consent was subject to the condition that the sheep to which it applies should be marked with a green mark;

(e) any sheep which was moved from any place in accordance with a consent given on or before 8th January 1989 under section 2(1) of the said Act which consent was subject to the condition that the sheep to which it applies should be marked with a blue mark;

(f) any sheep which was moved from any place in accordance with a consent given on or after 9th January 1989 under section 2(1) of the said Act which consent was subject to the condition that the sheep to which it applies should be marked with an apricot mark.".

4. In article 6, for paragraph (2) there shall be substituted the following paragraph:–

"(2) Paragraph (1) above shall not apply in the case of–

(a) any sheep which was moved from any place in accordance with a consent given under section 2(1) of the said Act which consent did not require that the sheep to which it applies should be marked;

(b) any sheep which was moved from any place in accordance with a consent given on or before 31st July 1988 under section 2(1) of the said Act which consent was subject to the condition that the sheep to which it applies should be marked with an apricot mark;

(c) any sheep which was moved from any place in accordance with a consent given on or before 2nd October 1988 under section 2(1) of the said Act which consent was subject to the condition that the sheep to which it applies should be marked with a green mark;

(d) any sheep which was moved from any place in accordance with a consent given on or before 8th January 1989 under section 2(1) of the said Act which consent was subject to the condition that the sheep to which it applies should be marked with a blue mark;

(e) any sheep which–

(i) was moved from any place in accordance with a consent given under section 2(1) of the said Act which consent was subject to the condition that the sheep to which it applies should be marked with a red mark, or

(ii) was moved from any place in accordance with a consent given on or after 9th January 1989 under section 2(1) of the said Act which consent was subject to the condition that the sheep to which it applies should be marked with an apricot mark, and which in either case has been examined and marked with an ear-tag by a person authorised in that behalf by one of the Ministers.".

N. E. Sharp
Assistant Secretary,
Scottish Office

St. Andrew's House, Edinburgh
12th April 1989

EXPLANATORY NOTE

(This note is not part of the Order)

The Food Protection (Emergency Prohibitions) Order 1989 contains emergency prohibitions restricting various activities in order to prevent human consumption of food rendered unsuitable for that purpose in consequence of the escape in April 1986 of radioactive substances from a nuclear reactor situated at Chernobyl in the Ukraine, USSR.

This Order excepts from the prohibition on slaughter throughout the United Kingdom any sheep, and from the prohibition on the supply throughout the United Kingdom any meat derived from such sheep, identified by a blue paint mark and which has been moved in accordance with a consent given under section 2(1) of the Food and Environment Protection Act 1985 on or before 8th January 1989.

STATUTORY INSTRUMENTS

1989 No. 656

MEDICAL PROFESSION

The General Medical Council Preliminary Proceedings Committee and Professional Conduct Committee (Procedure) Rules (Amendment) Order of Council 1989

Made - - - -	*13th April 1989*
Laid before Parliament	*17th April 1989*
Coming into force	*10th May 1989*

At the Council Chamber, Whitehall, the 13th day of April 1989

By the Lords of Her Majesty's Most Honourable Privy Council

Whereas in pursuance of paragraphs 1 and 5 of Schedule 4 to the Medical Act 1983**(a)** the General Medical Council, on 3rd November 1988, made the General Medical Council Preliminary Proceedings Committee and Professional Conduct Committee (Procedure) Rules 1988 after consulting with such bodies of persons representing medical practitioners as appeared to the General Medical Council to be requisite, in accordance with paragraph 1(4) of that Schedule**(b)**:

And whereas by the General Medical Council Preliminary Proceedings Committee and Professional Conduct Committee (Procedure) Rules Order of Council 1988**(c)** made on 21st December 1988 the Lords of the Privy Council, in pursuance of sub-paragraph (5) of the said paragraph (1), approved the said Rules as set out in the Appendix to that Order:

And whereas Their Lordships' approval given in the aforesaid Order of 21st December 1988 did not extend to the paragraph (2) of Rule 4 of the Rules duly made by the General Medical Council on 3rd November 1988, after such consultation as aforesaid, and set out in the Appendix to this Order:

Now, therefore, Their Lordships, in further exercise of their powers under the said sub-paragraph (5) of paragraph 1 of Schedule 4 to the said Act, are pleased to approve that paragraph.

This Order shall come into force on 10th May 1989.

G.I. de Deney

Clerk of the Privy Council

(a) 1983 c.54 **(b)** Paragraphs 1(4) and (5) of Schedule 4 apply to rules made under paragraph 5 of that Schedule by virtue of paragraph 5(3). **(c)** S.I. 1988/2255.

APPENDIX

Rule 4(2) of the General Medical Council Preliminary Proceedings Committee and Professional Conduct Committee (Procedure) Rules 1988.

"(2) Subject to paragraph (3), the Council shall appoint the President under this rule."

EXPLANATORY NOTE

(This note is not part of the Order)

The paragraph approved by this Order was inadvertently omitted from the version of the rules submitted by the General Medical Council to the Privy Council for approval and which was approved by the Privy Council by the General Medical Council Preliminary Proceedings Committee and Professional Conduct Committee (Procedure) Rules Order of Council 1988 (S.I. 1988/2255).

STATUTORY INSTRUMENTS

1989 No. 658

PUBLIC HEALTH, ENGLAND AND WALES
PUBLIC HEALTH, SCOTLAND
PUBLIC HEALTH, NORTHERN IRELAND

CONTAMINATION OF FOOD

The Food Protection (Emergency Prohibitions) (England) Amendment No. 2 Order 1989

Made - - - -	*13th April 1989*
Laid before Parliament	*14th April 1989*
Coming into force	*17th April 1989*

Whereas the Minister of Agriculture, Fisheries and Food is of the opinion, in accordance with section 1(1)(a) of the Food and Environment Protection Act 1985**(a)**, that there has been or may have been an escape of substances of such descriptions and in such quantities and such circumstances as are likely to create a hazard to human health through human consumption of food;

And whereas the said Minister is of the opinion, in accordance with section 1(1)(b) of the said Act, that in consequence of the said escape of substances food which is or may be in the future in the area described in Schedule 1 to the Food Protection (Emergency Prohibitions) (England) Order 1987**(b)**, or which is derived or may be in the future derived from anything in that area, is, or may be, or may become, unsuitable for human consumption;

Now, therefore, the said Minister, in exercise of the powers conferred on him by the said section 1(1) and section 24(3) of the said Act, and of all other powers enabling him in that behalf, hereby makes the following Order:–

Title and commencement

1. This Order may be cited as the Food Protection (Emergency Prohibitions) (England) Amendment No. 2 Order 1989 and shall come into force on 17th April 1989.

Partial revocation and amendment

2. The Food Protection (Emergency Prohibitions) (England) Order 1987 is revoked to the extent that it imposes prohibitions on–

(a) the slaughter of a sheep which was moved from any place in accordance with a consent given under section 2(1) of the Food and Environment Protection Act 1985 on or before 8th January 1989 which consent was subject to the condition that the sheep to which it applies should be marked with a blue mark; and

(b) the supply or having in possession for supply of meat, or food containing meat, derived from a sheep described in paragraph (a) of this article,

(a) 1985 c.48.
(b) S.I. 1987/1893, amended by S.I.s 1988/7, 954, 1292, 1679 and 1989/6.

and accordingly that Order is further amended in accordance with the following provisions of this Order.

3. In article 6, for paragraph (2) there shall be substituted the following paragraph–

"(2) Paragraph (1) above shall not apply in the case of–

(a) any sheep which was moved to a market in accordance with a consent given under section 2(1) of the Act which consent did not require that the sheep to which it applies should be marked in a manner specified therein;

(b) any sheep which was moved from any place in accordance with a consent given under the said section 2(1) on or before 8th January 1989 which consent was subject to the condition that the sheep to which it applies should be marked with a blue mark;

(c) any sheep which was moved from any place in accordance with a consent given under the said section 2(1) on or before 31st July 1988 which consent was subject to the condition that the sheep to which it applies should be marked with an apricot mark;

(d) any sheep which was moved from any place in accordance with a consent given under the said section 2(1) on or before 2nd October 1988 which consent was subject to the condition that the sheep to which it applies should be marked with a green mark; or

(e) any sheep which–

(i) was moved from any place in accordance with a consent given under the said section 2(1) which consent was subject to the condition that the sheep to which it applies should be marked with a red mark; or

(ii) was moved from any place in accordance with such a consent given on or after 9th January 1989 which consent was subject to the condition that the sheep to which it applies should be marked with an apricot mark,

and which, in any case, has been examined and marked with an ear-tag by a person authorised in that behalf by one of the Ministers.".

In witness whereof the Official Seal of the Minister of Agriculture, Fisheries and Food is hereunto affixed on 13th April 1989.

John MacGregor
Minister of Agriculture, Fisheries and Food

EXPLANATORY NOTE

(This note is not part of the Order)

The Food Protection (Emergency Prohibitions) (England) Order 1987 contains emergency prohibitions restricting various activities in order to prevent the human consumption of food which has been or which may have been rendered unsuitable for that purpose in consequence of the escape of radioactive substances from a nuclear reactor situated at Chernobyl in the USSR.

This Order excepts from the prohibition on slaughter throughout the United Kingdom any sheep, and from the prohibition on supply throughout the United Kingdom any meat derived from such a sheep, identified by a blue paint mark and which has been moved in accordance with a consent given under section 2(1) of the Food and Environment Protection Act 1985 on or before 8th January 1989.

STATUTORY INSTRUMENTS

1989 No. 659

ANIMALS

ANIMAL HEALTH

The Export of Sheep (Prohibition) (No. 2) Amendment No. 2 Order 1989

Made - - - -	*13th April 1989*
Coming into force	*17th April 1989*

The Minister of Agriculture, Fisheries and Food, in exercise of the powers conferred by sections 11 and 86 of the Animal Health Act 1981(**a**) and of all other powers enabling him in that behalf, hereby makes the following Order:

Title and commencement

1. This Order may be cited as the Export of Sheep (Prohibition) (No. 2) Amendment No. 2 Order 1989 and shall come into force on 17th April 1989.

Amendment of the Export of Sheep (Prohibition) (No. 2) Order 1987

2. The Export of Sheep (Prohibition) (No. 2) Order 1987(**b**) is hereby amended by substituting for article 2(4)(b) the following sub-paragraph–

"(b) any sheep which was marked, as a condition of the granting of a consent under section 2(1) of that Act to its removal from a designated area–

(i) with an apricot mark, in the case of a consent given on or before 31st July 1988; or

(ii) with a green mark, in the case of a consent given on or before 2nd October 1988; or

(iii) with a blue mark, in the case of a consent given on or before 8th January 1989.".

Revocation

3. The Export of Sheep (Prohibition) (No. 2) Amendment Order 1989(**c**) is hereby revoked.

In witness whereof the Official Seal of the Minister of Agriculture, Fisheries and Food is hereunto affixed on 13th April 1989.

John MacGregor
Minister of Agriculture, Fisheries and Food

(**a**) 1981 c.22.
(**b**) S.I. 1987/1808.
(**c**) S.I. 1989/5.

EXPLANATORY NOTE

(This note is not part of the Order)

This Order amends the Export of Sheep (Prohibition) (No. 2) Order 1987, as amended, ("the principal Order") which prohibits, subject to exceptions, the export from Great Britain to a Member State of the European Communities of–

(a) sheep moved from a place in an area designated for the purposes of Part I of the Food and Environment Protection Act 1985 (c.48) in accordance with the terms of a consent under section 2(1) of that Act which required that the sheep to which it applies should be marked in a specified manner; and

(b) sheep which have been moved in contravention of a restriction imposed by an Order made under section 1 of that Act.

The principal Order does not apply to those sheep which have been examined and subsequently marked with an ear-tag by an officer authorised by the Minister of Agriculture, Fisheries and Food, the Secretary of State for Scotland or Wales or the Department of Agriculture for Northern Ireland or to those sheep moved from a place in a designated area in accordance with the terms of a consent given on or before 31st July 1988, 2nd October 1988 or 10th January 1988 which required them to be marked with an apricot, green or a blue mark respectively. This Order extends the exception in the principal Order to any sheep moved from a place in a designated area in accordance with the terms of a consent given on or before 8th January 1989, which required it to be marked with a blue mark.

The Order revokes and replaces the Export of Sheep (Prohibition) (No. 2) Amendment Order 1989 (S.I. 1989/5) (article 3).

STATUTORY INSTRUMENTS

1989 No. 660

PUBLIC HEALTH, ENGLAND AND WALES
PUBLIC HEALTH, SCOTLAND
PUBLIC HEALTH, NORTHERN IRELAND

CONTAMINATION OF FOOD

The Food Protection (Emergency Prohibitions) (Wales) (No. 5) Amendment No. 2 Order 1989

Made - - - -	*13th April 1989*
Laid before Parliament	*14th April 1989*
Coming into force	*17th April 1989*

Whereas the Secretary of State is of the opinion, as mentioned in section 1(1)(a) of the Food and Environment Protection Act 1985**(a)**, that there has been or may have been an escape of substances of such descriptions and in such quantities and such circumstances as are likely to create a hazard to human health through human consumption of food;

And whereas the Secretary of State is of the opinion, as mentioned in section 1(1)(b) of the said Act, that in consequence of the said escape of substances food which is or may be in the future in the areas described in the Schedule to the Food Protection (Emergency Prohibitions) (Wales) (No. 5) Order 1987**(b)**, or which is derived or may be in the future derived from anything in those areas, is, or may be, or may become, unsuitable for human consumption;

Now, therefore, the Secretary of State, in exercise of the powers conferred on him by the said section 1(1) and (2) and section 24(1) and (3) of the said Act, and of all other powers enabling him in that behalf, hereby makes the following Order:–

Title and commencement

1. This Order may be cited as the Food Protection (Emergency Prohibitions) (Wales) (No. 5) Amendment No. 2 Order 1989 and shall come into force on 17th April 1989.

Partial revocation and amendment

2. The Food Protection (Emergency Prohibitions) (Wales) (No. 5) Order 1987 is revoked to the extent that it imposes prohibitions on–

(a) the slaughter of a sheep which was moved from any place in accordance with a consent given under section 2(1) of the Food and Environment Protection Act 1985 on or before 8th January 1989 which consent was subject to the condition that the sheep to which it applies should be marked with a blue mark; and

(b) the supply or having in possession for supply of meat, or food containing meat, derived from a sheep described in paragraph (a) of this article,

(a) 1985 c.48.
(b) S.I. 1987/1894, amended by S.I. 1988/9, 951, 1329, 1680 and 1989/2.

and accordingly that Order is further amended in accordance with the following provisions of this Order.

3. In article 6, for paragraph (2) there shall be substituted the following paragraph–

"(2) Paragraph (1) above shall not apply in the case of–

(a) any sheep which was moved to a market in accordance with a consent given under section 2(1) of the Act which consent did not require that the sheep to which it applies should be marked in a manner specified therein;

(b) any sheep which was moved from any place in accordance with a consent given under the said section 2(1) on or before 31st July 1988 which consent was subject to the condition that the sheep to which it applies should be marked with an apricot mark;

(c) any sheep which was moved from any place in accordance with a consent given under the said section 2(1) on or before 2nd October 1988 which consent was subject to the condition that the sheep to which it applies should be marked with a green mark;

(d) any sheep which was moved from any place in accordance with a consent given under the said section 2(1) on or before 8th January 1989 which consent was subject to the condition that the sheep to which it applies should be marked with a blue mark; or

(e) any sheep which–

(i) was moved from any place in accordance with a consent given under the said section 2(1) which consent was subject to the condition that the sheep to which it applies should be marked with a red mark; or

(ii) is moved from any place in accordance with such a consent given on or after 9th January 1989 which consent is subject to the condition that the sheep to which it applies should be marked with an apricot mark,

and which, in any case, has been examined and marked with an ear-tag by a person authorised in that behalf by one of the Ministers.".

13th April 1989

Peter Walker
Secretary of State for Wales

EXPLANATORY NOTE

(This note is not part of the Order)

The Food Protection (Emergency Prohibitions) (Wales) (No. 5) Order 1987, as amended by S.I. 1988/9, 951, 1329, 1680 and 1989/2 contains emergency prohibitions restricting various activities in order to prevent human consumption of food which has been or which may have been rendered unsuitable for that purpose in consequence of the escape of radioactive substances from a nuclear reactor situated at Chernobyl in the USSR.

The Order excepts from the prohibition on slaughter throughout the United Kingdom any sheep, and from the prohibition on supply throughout the United Kingdom any meat derived from such a sheep, identified by a blue paint mark and which has been moved in accordance with a Ministerial consent given under section 2(1) of the Food and Environment Protection Act 1985 on or before 8th January 1989.

STATUTORY INSTRUMENTS

1989 No. 661

ANIMALS

ANIMAL HEALTH

The Processed Animal Protein Order 1989

Made - - - -	*13th April 1989*
Coming into force	
Article 5	*13th June 1989*
Remainder	*14th April 1989*

The Minister of Agriculture, Fisheries and Food, the Secretary of State for Scotland and the Secretary of State for Wales, acting jointly, in exercise of the powers conferred on them by sections 1, 72, 86(1) and 87(2) and (5)(a) of the Animal Health Act 1981**(a)** and of all other powers enabling them in that behalf, hereby make the following Order:

Title and commencement

1.—(1) This Order may be cited as the Processed Animal Protein Order 1989 and, except for article 5, shall come into force on 14th April 1989.

(2) Article 5 of this Order shall come into force on 13th June 1989.

Extension of definitions of "animals" and "poultry"

2. For the purposes of the Act in its application to this Order–

(a) the definition of "animals" in section 87(1) of the Act is hereby extended so as to comprise–

(i) any kind of mammal except man, and

(ii) any kind of four-footed beast which is not a mammal; and

(b) the definition of "poultry" in section 87(4) of the Act is hereby extended so as to comprise quails.

Interpretation

3.—(1) In this Order, unless the context otherwise requires–

"the Act" means the Animal Health Act 1981;

"animal" means any kind of mammal except man, and any kind of four-footed beast which is not a mammal;

"animal protein" means any material which may be used for feeding to livestock or poultry which contains the whole or any part of any dead animal or bird, or of any fish, reptile, crustacean or other cold-blooded creature or any product derived from them and includes blood, hatchery waste, eggs, egg shells, hair, horns, hides, hoofs, feathers and manure, any material which contains human effluent and any protein obtained from any of these materials by heat, sedimentation, precipitation, ensiling or any other system of treatment or procedure but does not include milk or milk products, shells other than egg shells, fat or dicalcium bone phosphate;

(a) 1981 c.22 as applied by S.I. 1989/285; section 86(1) contains a definition of "the Ministers" relevant to the exercise of the statutory powers under which this Order is made.

"the appropriate Minister" means, in relation to England, the Minister, and in relation to Scotland or to Wales, the Secretary of State;

"authorised laboratory" means a laboratory authorised by the Minister in writing;

"authorised officer" means a veterinary inspector or an officer authorised by the appropriate Minister;

"day" means the period of twenty-four hours which begins with one midnight and ends with the next;

"fat" means any vegetable or mineral oil or any other oleaginous product obtained by a rendering or a refining process;

"laboratory" means any laboratory which has the necessary facilities and personnel for carrying out tests on samples mentioned in paragraph (1) or (2) of Part I of Schedule 1 to this Order in accordance with either of the methods set out in Part II of that Schedule;

"livestock" means cattle, sheep, pigs, goats, horses (including asses and mules), deer, and rabbits which are kept for commercial purposes;

"the Minister" and "the Ministry" mean respectively the Minister and the Ministry of Agriculture, Fisheries and Food;

"poultry" means live birds of the following species, that is to say, domestic fowls, turkeys, geese, ducks, guinea-fowls, pigeons, pheasants, partridges and quails;

"processed", in relation to animal protein, means animal protein which has been subjected to heat, sedimentation, precipitation, ensiling, milling, grinding, or any other system of treatment or procedure so as to render it suitable for use (whether with or without further treatment or procedure) as a feeding stuff or as an ingredient in a feeding stuff for livestock or poultry; and cognate expressions shall be construed accordingly;

"the Register" means the Register kept by the Minister under article 5 of this Order;

"Registered person" means the person whose name is entered in the Register;

"veterinary inspector" means a veterinary inspector appointed by the Minister.

(2) Until the coming into force of article 5 to this Order, any reference in this Order to a Registered person shall be a reference to the owner or person in charge of the premises the address of which will be required to be entered in the Register in accordance with article 5 when that article comes into force.

(3) After 13th August 1989 any reference in this Order to a laboratory shall be a reference to an authorised laboratory.

Scope

4. The provisions of this Order shall not apply to waste food defined in, and required to be processed under, the provisions of the Diseases of Animals (Waste Food) Order 1973**(a)**.

Registration of animal protein processors

5.—(1) No person shall, in the course of a business carried on by him, process any animal protein unless his name and the address of the premises used by him for the purpose of processing any animal protein are entered in the Register.

(2) The Minister shall not enter the name of a person in the Register unless all the particulars specified in Schedule 2 to this Order are notified to him in writing.

(3) The Registered person shall notify the Minister in writing of any change in the particulars previously notified to the Minister, such notification to be made within 14 days of any such change.

Taking of samples for testing

6.—(1) It shall be the duty of a Registered person to ensure that–

(a) on each day on which any supplies of processed animal protein are consigned from the premises in respect of which his name is entered in the Register, a

(a) S.I. 1973/1936, amended by S.I. 1987/232.

sample is taken in the manner described in paragraph (2) of Part I of Schedule 1 to this Order from the processed animal protein which forms those supplies, and

(b) the sample is submitted forthwith to a laboratory for testing (at his expense) in accordance with either of the methods set out in Part II of Schedule 1 to this Order.

(2) Where processed animal protein produced on any premises is incorporated in a feeding stuff for livestock or poultry kept on those premises, it shall be the duty of the Registered person to ensure that–

(a) on each day immediately before any supplies of any such processed animal protein are incorporated in such feeding stuff, a sample is taken in the manner mentioned in paragraph (1)(a) above from those supplies, and

(b) the sample is submitted for testing (at his expense) in accordance with the provisions of paragraph (1)(b) above.

(3) After a sample has been tested in accordance with paragraph (1)(b) or (2)(b) above by a laboratory it shall be destroyed by that laboratory.

Duty to prevent movement of contaminated processed animal protein and incorporation of such animal protein in a feeding stuff

7. It shall be the duty of a Registered person who knows that a test carried out on a sample taken from the processed animal protein produced on premises in respect of which his name is entered on the Register has resulted in the isolation of salmonella from that sample, to ensure that during the period of one month from the date on which he becomes aware of such result–

(a) no processed animal protein produced on those premises is removed from any premises occupied by him or under his control; and

(b) no such processed animal protein which remains under his control is incorporated in a feeding stuff for livestock or poultry,

unless–

(i) such processed animal protein is not taken from the same storage facility as that used to store the processed animal protein from which the sample was taken, or

(ii) such processed animal protein is treated in such manner as to ensure freedom from salmonella and a test carried out by a laboratory in accordance with either of the methods set out in Part II of Schedule 1 to this Order on a sample taken from the processed animal protein so treated does not result in the isolation of salmonella from that sample, or

(iii) under the authority of a licence issued by an authorised officer and in accordance with the conditions, if any, of that licence.

Powers of authorised officers

8.—(1) An authorised officer may at any reasonable time and on production of his authority on demand–

(a) enter any premises which he has reasonable grounds for supposing are being used for the purpose of processing animal protein;

(b) take a sample in the manner described in paragraph (1) or (2) of Part I of Schedule 1 to this Order from such premises of any material or substance which he has reasonable grounds for supposing to be processed animal protein;

(c) at the request of the Registered person or person in charge of the premises, take and give to him a like sample to that taken under sub-paragraph (b) above–

(2) An authorised officer entering any premises by virtue of paragraph (1) above–

(a) shall, if required by the Registered person or person in charge of the premises, state his reasons for entering, and

(b) may take with him such other persons and such equipment as appear to him to be reasonably necessary for the proper performance of his functions under this Order.

(3) The Registered person or person in charge of premises referred to in paragraph (1) above shall give all reasonable assistance to an authorised officer and any person accompanying him so as to enable the power conferred by this article to be properly exercised.

Testing of samples taken by authorised officers

9.—(1) On taking a sample as referred to in article 8(1)(b) above the authorised officer shall submit it to a laboratory for testing in accordance with either of the methods set out in Part II Schedule 1 to this Order.

(2) The result of the test carried out under paragraph (1) above shall be notified in writing by an authorised officer to the Registered person or person in charge of the premises with all practicable speed.

(3) After a sample has been tested in accordance with paragraph (1) above by a laboratory it shall be destroyed by that laboratory.

Tampering with samples

10.—(1) No person shall treat or otherwise tamper with a sample of processed animal protein taken under this Order.

(2) For the purposes of this article a person shall be deemed to have treated a sample if he does anything in relation to it with intent to affect the result of the test required to be carried out under this Order.

Keeping of records

11. A Registered person shall–

(a) make a record of the result of any test carried out in accordance with article 6(1)(b) or (2)(b) above as soon as practicable after he has received a report of such result;

(b) retain such record for a period of 12 months from the date of the test; and

(c) produce such record to an authorised officer on demand being made by him at any reasonable time during that period and allow him to take a copy of it or an extract from it.

Information to be given

12. Where as a result of a test carried out in accordance with the provisions of this Order salmonella is isolated from a sample of processed animal protein, a Registered person shall, with a view to enabling an authorised officer to trace the processed animal protein from which the sample was taken, give to the authorised officer any information that he has concerning any consignments of or from that processed animal protein, such information to be given on demand being made by the authorised officer at any reasonable time.

Offences

13. Any person who, without lawful authority or excuse, proof of which shall lie on him–

(a) contravenes any provision of this Order or any provision of a licence issued under it; or

(b) fails to comply with any such provision or with a condition of such licence; or

(c) knowingly causes or permits any such contravention or non-compliance,

commits an offence against the Act.

Local authority to enforce Order

14. The provisions of this Order shall, except where otherwise expressly provided, be executed and enforced by the local authority.

Revocation

15. The Diseases of Animals (Protein Processing) Order 1981**(a)** and the Diseases of Animals (Protein Processing) (Amendment) Order 1989**(b)** are revoked.

In Witness whereof the Official Seal of the Minister of Agriculture, Fisheries and Food is hereunto affixed on 13th April 1989.

John MacGregor
Minister of Agriculture, Fisheries and Food

Sanderson of Bowden
Minister of State,
Scottish Office

12th April 1989

Peter Walker
Secretary of State for Wales

13th April 1989

Articles 3, 6, 7, 8 and 9

SCHEDULE 1

PART I

Manner of sampling processed animal protein

A sample of processed animal protein to be submitted to a laboratory for testing in accordance with the methods set out in Part II of this Schedule shall be obtained by the methods described in paragraph (1) or (2) of this Part of this Schedule.

(1) Sample portion shall be the total load or throughput—either bulk or bags	Number of incremental samples of approximately equal proportions which shall be extracted evenly throughout the sampled portion	Number of aggregate samples which shall be obtained by pooling a relevant number of incremental samples	
A. Loose animal protein			Aggregate sample shall be placed into separate sterile receptacle and each shall be thoroughly mixed by stirring or shaking
1 tonne	7	1	
1.1–2.5 tonnes	7	2	
2.6–10 tonnes	$\sqrt{20 \times \text{size of sampled portion}}$	2	
10.1–40 tonnes	$\sqrt{20 \times \text{size of sampled portion}}$	3	
over 40 tonnes	$\sqrt{20 \times \text{size of sampled portion}}$ (maximum—40 incremental samples)	4	
B. Bagged animal protein			
1–16 bags	4	1	
17–200 bags	$\sqrt{\text{no of bags in sampled portion}}$	2	
201–800 bags	$\sqrt{\text{no of bags in sampled portion}}$	3	
over 800 bags	$\sqrt{\text{no of bags in sampled portion}}$ (maximum—40 incremental samples)	4	

(a) S.I. 1981/676.
(b) S.I. 1989/139.

The final sample shall be obtained by the extraction of an approximately equal amount of the sampled portion from each aggregate sample so as to provide a single final sample of approximately 500 grams. This final sample shall be transferred into a suitable sterile wide-mouthed, screw top polypropylene container sealed and marked to indicate the name and address of the premises and the date of sampling.

(2) Sample portion shall be the total quantity of supplies consigned from the premises or incorporated in a feeding stuff on the day in question	Number of incremental samples of approximately equal proportions which shall be extracted evenly throughout the sampled portion	Number of aggregate samples which shall be obtained by pooling a relevant number of incremental samples	
Loose or bagged animal protein			
1–5 consignments	1 per consignment	1	Aggregate sample shall be placed into separate sterile receptacle and each shall be thoroughly mixed by stirring or shaking
6–10 consignments	1 per consignment	2	
11–15 consignments	1 per consignment	3	
Over 15 consignments	1 per consignment	4	

(For the purpose of this paragraph "consignment" means the total quantity of processed animal protein loaded onto a single vehicle or trailer for movement to other premises or for movement to a place for incorporation in a feeding stuff).

The final sample shall be obtained by the extraction of an approximately equal amount of the sampled portion from each aggregate sample so as to provide a single final sample of approximately 500 grams. This final sample shall be transferred into a suitable sterile wide-mouthed, screw top polypropylene container sealed and marked to indicate the name and address of the premises and the date of sampling.

PART II

a. Bacteriological method for the isolation of salmonella from animal protein

Samples of processed animal protein submitted for testing shall be examined on the first working day which allows the following method to be completed. Samples not examined on the day of receipt shall be stored in a refrigerator until required. Examination shall be carried out in duplicate using two 25 gram portions of each sample submitted for testing.

Day 1

The sample shall be removed from refrigeration and left at room temperature for at least four hours. Thereafter, 25 grams shall be added aseptically to a jar containing 225 ml BPW(a) and incubated overnight at 37°C for 18 hours.

Day 2

0.1 ml from the jar of incubated BPW shall be inoculated into 10 ml RV(b) broth and incubated at 42.5 ± 0.5°C for 24 hours.

Day 3

(i) The RV broth shall be plated out on to two plates of BGA(c) using a 2.5 mm diameter loop. The BGA plates shall be inoculated with a droplet taken from the edge of the surface of the fluid by drawing the loop over the whole of one plate in a zig zag pattern and continuing to the second plate without recharging the loop. The space between the loop streaks shall be 0.5 cm–1.0 cm. The plates shall be incubated at 37°C overnight.

(ii) The residual RV broth shall be reincubated at 42.5 ± 0.5°C for a further 24 hours.

Day 4

(i) The plates of BGA shall be examined and a minimum of 3 colonies from the plates showing suspicion of salmonella growth shall be subcultured onto a blood agar plate and a MacConkey agar plate and into biochemical composite media or equivalent. These media shall be incubated at 37°C overnight.

(ii) The reincubated RV broth shall be plated out as described in (i) of Day 3.

Day 5

(i) The incubated composite media or equivalent shall be examined and the findings recorded, discarding cultures which are obviously not salmonella. Slide serological tests shall be performed using salmonella polyvalent "O" and polyvalent "H" (phase 1 and 2) agglutinating sera on selected suspect colonies collected from the blood agar or MacConkey plates. If reactions occur with one or both sera, the colonies shall be typed by slide serology and a subculture sent (in Scotland) to the Veterinary Laboratory, Lasswade, Midlothian and (in England and Wales) to a Veterinary Investigation Centre of the Ministry for further typing.

(ii) The plates referred to in (ii) of Day 4 shall be examined and further action taken as in (i) of Day 4 and (i) of Day 5.

(a) Buffered Peptone Water—Edel and Kampelmacher (1973)
(Commercially available as Oxoid CM 509, Lab M46 or equivalent).

(b) Rappaports Vassiliadis (RV) Broth—Vassiliadis et al (1976)
(Commercially available as Oxoid CM 669 or equivalent).

(c) Brilliant Green Agar (Modified)—Edel and Kampelmacher (1969)
(Commercially available as Oxoid CM 329, Lab M34 or equivalent).

The agar shall be reconstituted according to the manufacturer's instructions and poured on to 9 cm diameter culture plates.

References:

Edel W. & Kampelmacher E. H. (1969) Bulletin of the World Health Organisation 41 297-306.

Edel W. & Kampelmacher E. H. (1973) Bulletin of the World Health Organisation 48 167-174.

Vassiliadis, P., Pateraki, E., Papaiconomou, N., Papadakis, J. A., and Trichopoulos, D. (1976) Annales de Microbiologie (Institut Pasteur) 127B 195-200.

b. Electrical conductance method for the detection and isolation of salmonella from animal protein

Samples of processed animal protein submitted for testing shall be examined on the first working day which allows the following method to be completed. Samples not examined on the day of receipt shall be stored in a refrigerator until required. Examination shall be carried out in duplicate using two 25 gram portions of each sample submitted for testing.

Day 1

The sample shall be received or removed from refrigeration and left at room temperature for at least 4 hours. Thereafter 25 grams shall be added aseptically to a jar containing 225 ml BPW/L/G(a) and incubated at 37°C for 18 hours.

Day 2

Volumes of the incubated BPW/L/G inoculated with the samples under test shall be transferred to SC/T/D(b) and LD/G(c) media in electrical conductance cells or wells. For cells or wells containing >5 ml medium 0.2 ml shall be transferred and for cells or wells containing <5 ml medium 0.1 ml shall be transferred.

Cells or wells shall be connected to appropriate electrical conductance measuring equipment set to monitor and record changes in electrical conductance at 6 minute intervals over a 24 hour period. The temperature of cells and wells shall be controlled at 37°C.

Day 3

At the end of the 24 hour period, the information recorded by the conductance measuring equipment shall be analysed and interpreted using criteria defined by the manufacturers of the equipment.

Where a well or cell is identified as being positive for salmonella, the result shall be confirmed by subculturing the contents of the well or cell on to two plates BGA(d) using a 2.5 mm diameter loop. The BGA plates shall be inoculated with a droplet taken from the edge of the surface of the fluid by drawing the loop over the whole of one plate in a zig zag pattern and continuing to the second plate without recharging the loop. The space between the loop streaks shall be 0.5 cm–1.0 cm. The plates shall be incubated at 37°C overnight.

Day 4

The plates of BGA shall be examined and a minimum of 3 colonies from the plates showing suspicion of salmonella growth shall be subcultured on to a blood agar plate and a MacConkey agar plate and into biochemical composite media or equivalent. These media shall be incubated at 37°C overnight.

Day 5

The incubated composite media or equivalent shall be examined and the findings recorded, discarding cultures which are obviously not salmonella. Slide seriological tests shall be performed using salmonella polyvalent "O" and polyvalent "H" (phase 1 and 2) agglutinating sera on selected suspect colonies collected from the blood agar or MacConkey plates. If reactions occur with one or both sera, the colonies shall be typed by slide serology and a subculture sent (in Scotland) to the Lasswade Veterinary Laboratory situated at Penicuik, Midlothian, and (in England and Wales) to a Veterinary Investigation Centre of the Ministry for further typing.

(a) Buffered Peptone Water/Lysine/Glucose (BPW/L/G)—Ogden (1988)
(b) Selenite Cystine TMAO Dulcitol (SC/T/D)—Eastern and Gibson (1985)
(c) Lysine Decarboxylase Glucose (LD/G)—Ogden (1988)
(d) Brilliant Green Agar (Modified) (BGA)—Edel and Kampelmacher (1969)

References:

Ogden I. D. (1988) International Journal of Food Microbiology 7 287-297.
Easter M. C. and Gibson D. M. (1985) Journal of Hygiene 94 245-262.
Edel W. & Kampelmacher E. H. (1969) Bulletin of the World Health Organisation 41 297-306.
Edel W. & Kampelmacher E. H. (1973) Bulletin of the World Health Organisation 48 167-174.

SCHEDULE 2

Article 5(2)

Particulars to be notified to the Minister for the purposes of article 5

(i) The business name, if any.
(ii) The address of the person who carries on the business.
(iii) The address and telephone number of the business.
(iv) The address of each premises at which animal protein is processed in the course of the business.
(v) The description of raw material processed.
(vi) The source of raw material processed.
(vii) The description of the processed animal protein produced.
(viii) Whether processed animal protein is intended for incorporation in animal feeding stuffs.

Note:

In the case of a person who intends to commence business after the coming into force of article 5(2), the above particulars shall be modified so as to require that person to notify the Minister of his intentions in connection with the proposed business.

EXPLANATORY NOTE

(This note is not part of the Order)

This Order re-enacts the Diseases of Animals (Protein Processing) Order 1981 ("the 1981 Order") with amendments. It continues to enable authorised officers to take for testing at a laboratory samples of processed animal protein from premises where it is produced (article 8).

The Order makes the following changes of substance by–

1. requiring the registration of animal protein processors (article 5);
2. imposing a duty on the Registered person to ensure the taking of samples from processed animal protein and its submission to a laboratory for testing for salmonella (article 6);
3. imposing a duty on the Registered person to ensure (where he knows that a test on a sample has proved positive) that for a period of one month no processed animal protein produced on premises in respect of which his name is entered in the Register is (without further treatment and testing) removed from premises occupied by him or under his control and is not incorporated in a feeding stuff for livestock or poultry, unless the processed animal protein to be removed is taken from a separate storage facility or under the authority of a licence (article 7);
4. prohibiting any tampering with samples (article 10); and
5. requiring Registered persons to keep records of the results of tests on samples (article 11) and to give information to enable the tracing of contaminated feeding stuffs (article 12).

The provisions requiring the registration of animal protein processors shall come into force on 13th June 1989. Until that date the duties of a Registered person under the Order shall be the duties of the owner or person in charge of the premises which are used in the course of a business for processing animal protein (articles 1(2) and 3(2)).

Until 13th August 1989 samples taken under the Order are required to be tested at laboratories which have the necessary facilities and personnel for carrying out the tests in accordance with the Order and after that date the samples are required to be tested at laboratories authorised in writing by the Minister of Agriculture, Fisheries and Food for this purpose.

STATUTORY INSTRUMENTS

1989 No. 662

MERCHANT SHIPPING

The Merchant Shipping (Merchant Navy Reserve) Regulations 1989

Made - - - -	*11th April 1989*
Laid before Parliament	*21st April 1989*
Coming into force	*12th May 1989*

The Secretary of State for Transport in exercise of the powers conferred on him by section 28(4) of the Merchant Shipping Act 1988**(a)** and of all other powers enabling him in that behalf hereby makes the following Regulations:

Citation and commencement

1. These Regulations may be cited as the Merchant Shipping (Merchant Navy Reserve) Regulations 1989 and shall come into force on 12th May 1989.

Call-out

2. The Secretary of State may call-out members of the Merchant Navy Reserve if appropriate in the light of the state of international tension and the need to prepare for the defence of the realm. Such call-out may apply to all members of the Merchant Navy Reserve, or to individual members or classes of members.

Notification

3. Each member of the Merchant Navy Reserve shall be served notice of any call-out by such means as the Secretary of State thinks fit. Such notice shall specify a place to which the member must report, if different from his allocated reporting station, and a time by which he must report. In addition the Secretary of State may generally notify members of a call-out by television or radio broadcasts, or notices in newspapers with national circulations.

Reporting

4. Members of the Merchant Navy Reserve personally notified of a call-out shall report to their allocated reporting station or other place of which they are notified, as the case may be, within the time specified: provided that any member who is unable to do so within that specified time shall report as soon as possible to the nearest office of the Merchant Navy Establishment Administration or to the nearest Department of Transport Marine Office.

Service

5.—(1) Service by a member in the Merchant Navy Reserve shall commence when he reports for duty, wherever that takes place, in response to a call-out by the Secretary of State.

(a) 1988 c.12.

(2) Where a member has commenced service in accordance with paragraph (1), he shall serve on any vessel, or at any place of duty, to which he is assigned without absence.

(3) Service in the Merchant Navy Reserve shall continue until a member is notified by the Secretary of State that his call-out is ended, or until the Secretary of State makes a general notification (in the manner specified in regulation 3) that call-out for all or specified members or classes of members is finished, whichever is the sooner (so far as appropriate to him).

Offences

6.—(1) Contravention of the requirement to report for duty in regulation 4 or of the requirement to serve in regulation 5(2) shall be an offence punishable on summary conviction by a fine not exceeding the third level on the standard scale.

(2) It shall be a defence to a charge of contravention of the requirement in regulation 5(2) to serve without absence that the member can show that he had been granted leave of absence.

Signed by authority of the Secretary of State

Michael Portillo
11th April 1989 Minister of State, Department of Transport

EXPLANATORY NOTE

(This note is not part of the Regulations)

These Regulations make arrangements for the operation of the Merchant Navy Reserve which the Secretary of State is empowered to establish under section 28 of the Merchant Shipping Act 1988. They set out terms by which the Merchant Navy Reserve can be called-out for service and how members of the Reserve will be notified of a call-out. The Regulations also provide for the reporting of members of the Reserve for service, and define the commencement and ending of that service. Requirements are made of Reservists to report for service when they are personally notified of a call-out and to serve without absence, unless leave has been granted, on any vessel, or at any place of duty, to which they are assigned. Contravention of these requirements constitutes an offence.

STATUTORY INSTRUMENTS

1989 No. 666 (S.72)

EDUCATION, SCOTLAND

The Teachers' Superannuation (Scotland) Amendment Regulations 1989

Made - - - -	*11th April 1989*
Laid before Parliament	*28th April 1989*
Coming into force	*1st June 1989*

The Secretary of State, in exercise of the powers conferred on him by sections 9 and 12 of the Superannuation Act 1972(**a**) and of all other powers enabling him in that behalf, after consulting with representatives of local education authorities and of teachers and with such representatives of other persons likely to be affected by these Regulations as appear to him to be appropriate, in accordance with section 9(5) of that Act, and with the consent of the Treasury(**b**), hereby makes the following Regulations:

Citation and commencement

1.—(1) These Regulations may be cited as the Teachers' Superannuation (Scotland) Amendment Regulations 1989 and may be cited together with the Teachers' Superannuation (Scotland) Regulations 1977 to 1988 as the Teachers' Superannuation (Scotland) Regulations 1977 to 1989.

(2) These Regulations shall come into force on 1st June 1989 and shall have effect from 6th April 1988 except for regulations 3(a), 7, 24 and 25 which shall have effect from 1st June 1989.

Interpretation

2. In these Regulations, a reference to "the principal Regulations" is a reference to the Teachers' Superannuation (Scotland) Regulations 1977(**c**).

Definitions

3. In regulation 3 of the principal Regulations–

(a) after the definition of "Act of 1939" there shall be inserted the following definition:–

""the 1965 family benefit regulations" means the Teachers (Superannuation) (Family Benefits) (Scotland) Regulations 1965(**d**);";

(b) after the definition of "agreed" there shall be inserted the following definition:–

""appropriate personal pension scheme" means a personal pension scheme for which there is in force a certificate issued in accordance with section 2 of the Social Security Act 1986(**e**);";

(c) after the definition of "disqualifying income" there shall be inserted the following definition:–

(**a**) 1972 c.11.
(**b**) The function was transferred to the Treasury by S.I. 1981/1670.
(**c**) S.I. 1977/1360, amended by S.I. 1977/1808, 1978/1507, 1980/344, 1983/639 and 1431, 1984/2028 and 1988/1618.
(**d**) S.I. 1965/680.
(**e**) 1986 c.50.

““earnings factors” has the same meaning as in section 13 of the Social Security Act 1975(**a**);”;

(d) after the definition of “employer” there shall be inserted the following definition:–

““excluded employment” has the meaning given by regulation 4A(2);”;

(e) after the definition of “Pensions Act” there shall be inserted the following definition:–

““personal pension scheme” has the same meaning as in section 84(1) of the Social Security Act 1986;”; and

(f) after the definition of “Salaries Memorandum” there shall be inserted the following definition:–

““Self-employed pension arrangement” means a personal pension scheme within the meaning of Chapter IV of Part XIV of the Income and Corporation Taxes Act 1988(**b**) which is approved by the Inland Revenue under that Chapter; but which is neither a personal pension scheme within the meaning of the Social Security Act 1986 nor a contract or a scheme approved under Chapter III of Part XIV of the Income and Corporation Taxes Act 1988;”;

(g) for the definition of “widower” there shall be substituted:-

““widower” means the husband of a deceased woman teacher;”.

Voluntary Membership

4.—(1) In regulation 4(2) of the principal Regulations, after sub-paragraph (d) there shall be inserted the words “except at any time when his employment is excluded employment by reason of regulation 4A”.

(2) After regulation 4 of the principal Regulations there shall be inserted the following Regulations:–

“**Voluntary Membership**

4A.—(1) Notwithstanding the provisions of regulation 4(2), a teacher who–

(a) is employed in reckonable service, or

(b) is not so employed but expects to enter an employment in which he would be so employed,

may at any time, by giving written notice to the Secretary of State, make an election under this Regulation.

(2) As from the date from which the election has effect, the employment referred to in paragraph (1) and any subsequent periods of employment which would otherwise be reckonable service shall, subject to regulation 4B below, not be reckonable service, and employment where this paragraph applies is in these Regulations referred to as “excluded employment”.

(3) An election under this regulation shall have effect–

(a) where paragraph (1)(a) applies, from the first day of the pay period after that in which the notice was recieved by the Sectretary of State;

(b) where paragraph (1)(b) applies, if the notice is received by the Secretary of State within the first pay period of commencing employment, from the date on which the teacher became so employed.

(4) For the purposes of this regulation and regulation 4B–

“pay period” means the period of employment at the end of which a teacher receives payment of salary from his employer.

Resumption of Membership

4B.—(1) Subject to paragraphs (4) and (5), a teacher who has made an election under regulation 4A, who has since been in excluded employment and who–

(a) is in excluded employment, or

(**a**) 1975 c.14; section 13 was amended by the Social Security Pensions Act 1975 (c.60), Schedule 4, Part I, paragraph 38, by the Social Security Act 1979 (c.18), Schedule 3, paragraph 5, by the Social Security Act 1980 (c.30), section 5, by the Social Security (No. 2) Act 1980 (c.39), Schedule, by the Social Security Act 1985 (c.53), Schedule 5, paragraph 6, and by the Social Security Act 1986 (c.50), Schedule 8, paragraph 2 and Schedule 11.

(**b**) 1988 c.1.

(b) is not in, but expects to enter, employment which is excluded employment by virtue of his having previously made an election under regulation 4A,

may, at any time, by giving written notice to the Secretary of State, make an election under this regulation.

(2) As from the date on which the election has effect, subject to regulation 4A, any excluded employment on or after that date shall become employment in reckonable service.

(3) An election under this regulation shall have effect–

(a) where paragraph (1)(a) applies, from the first day of the pay period after that in which the notice was received by the Secretary of State; and

(b) where paragraph (1)(b) applies, if the notice is received by the Secretary of State within the first pay period of commencing that employment, from the date on which he became so employed.

(4) If after making an election under this regulation a teacher makes a further election under regulation 4A above, he may make a further election under this regulation only if, since he made the further election under regulation 4A, there has been a period of not less than 5 years during which he was not in any excluded employment.

(5) For the purposes of this regulation the Secretary of State may in a particular case–

(a) accept an election where the period specified in paragraph (4) is less than 5 years; or

(b) refuse to accept an election where the teacher is on sick leave."

Part-time service

5. In regulation 5 of the principal Regulations–

(a) in paragraph (1), there shall be inserted at the beginning the words "Subject to paragraph (6)";

(b) in paragraph (2), there shall be inserted at the beginning the words "Subject to regulation 4A"; and

(c) after paragraph (5) there shall be added the following paragraph:–

"(6) Paragraph (1) shall not apply to a teacher who has made an election under regulation 4A.".

Service not reckonable

6. Regulation 6(3)(b) of the principal Regulations is revoked.

Contributions for pre-April 1972 family pensions

7. For regulations 30 to 38 of the principal Regulations there shall be substituted the following regulation:–

"Additional contributions for family benefits

30.—(1) Parts I and III of Schedule 4 have effect for enabling men and unmarried women to pay additional contributions ("family benefit contributions") in order to secure, or to increase, family benefits in respect of reckonable service before 1st April 1972.

(2) Parts II and III of Schedule 4 have effect for enabling married women to pay family benefit contributions in respect of reckonable service before 6th April 1988.".

Return of contributions on cessation of employment

8. In regulation 39 of the principal Regulations–

(a) there shall be inserted at the beginning of paragraph (1) the words "Subject to paragraph (2)";

(b) there shall be substituted for sub-paragraph (a) of paragraph (1) the following:–

"(a) (i) he is not entitled to any benefit; or

(ii) subject to paragraph (3), he is not qualified by virtue of service under regulation 46;";

(c) after paragraph (1) there shall be added the following proviso:–

"Provided that the sum payable to a teacher whose application for a refund of contributions under this regulation was received by the Secretary of State before 6th April 1988 shall be reduced in respect of tax chargeable only by the sum by which it would have been reduced if the payment had been made by the Secretary of State on 5th April 1988."; and

(d) for paragraphs (2) and (3) there shall be substituted the following paragraphs:–

"(2) For the purposes of paragraph (1), the making of an election under regulation 4A shall be treated as ceasing to be employed in reckonable service.

(3) This regulation shall not apply where a transfer value has been paid to the Secretary of State by the trustees or managers of a personal pension scheme in respect of a teacher notwithstanding that he has less than 2 years' service.".

Calculation for the purposes of regulations 39 and 41

9. In regulation 42 of the principal Regulations, paragraphs (10) and (11) are revoked.

Return of member's contributions

10. At the end of regulation 43(1) of the principal Regulations there shall be added the following proviso:–

"Provided that the sum payable to a member whose application for a refund of contributions under this regulation was received by the Secretary of State before 6th April 1988 shall be reduced in respect of tax chargeable only by the sum by which it would have been reduced if the payment had been made by the Secretary of State on 5th April 1988.".

Guaranteed Minimum Pension

11. In regulation 45A of the principal Regulations–

(a) for paragraphs (2) and (3) there shall be substituted the following:–

"(2) The words and expressions used in this regulation shall have the same meaning as in the Pensions Act(**a**).

(3) If a teacher has a guaranteed minimum in accordance with section 35 of the Pensions Act(**b**) in relation to the pension provided for him under these Regulations–

(a) he shall be entitled to receive from state pension age an annual pension payable at a rate equivalent to a weekly rate of not less than the guaranteed minimum;

(b) if the member is a man and dies at any time leaving a widow, in relation to the weekly rate of the pension provided for her under this scheme, she shall be entitled, during any such period as is mentioned in section 36(6) of the Pensions Act, to a long term pension which shall not be less than half that member's guaranteed minimum;

(c) if the member is a woman and dies on or after 6th April 1989 leaving a widower, in relation to the weekly rate of the pension provided for him under this scheme, he shall be entitled to a long term pension which shall not be less than half of that part of the member's guaranteed minimum which is attributable to earnings factors for the tax year 1988/89 and subsequent tax years.

(4) The guaranteed minimum pensions referred to in paragraph (3) shall, insofar as they are attributable to earnings factors in the tax years from (and including) 1988/89, be increased in accordance with the requirements of section 37A of the Pensions Act(**c**) and to the extent of any orders made thereunder.

(5) If the commencement of any member's guaranteed minimum pension is postponed for any period, his guaranteed minimum shall be increased to the extent,

---

(**a**) The Social Security Pensions Act 1975 (c.60).

(**b**) Section 35 was amended by the Social Security (Miscellaneous Provisions) Act 1977 (c.5), section 3(2), by the Social Security Act 1979 (c.18), Schedule 3, paragraphs 13 and 18, by the Social Security Act 1985 (c.53), Schedule 3, paragraph 2, and by the Social Security Act 1986 (c.50), section 9(1) and (2) and Schedule 8, paragraph 8.

(**c**) Section 37A was inserted by the Social Security Act 1986 (c.50), section 9(7).

if any, specified in section 35(6), (6A) and (6B) of the Pensions Act, as amended from time to time.".

Entitlement to retiring allowances on grounds of age or redundancy

12. In regulation 46 of the principal Regulations–

(a) in paragraph (1), for sub-paragraphs (a) to (f), there shall be substituted the following:–

"(a) was on 6th April 1988 employed in reckonable service and has been employed in such service, whether before or after that date, for at least 2 years; or

(b) has been employed in reckonable service after 5th April 1988 for at least 2 years; or

(c) served in reckonable service before 6th April 1988 and has been employed in reckonable service or partly in reckonable service and partly in employment of a description specified in Schedule 5, for at least 5 years; or

(d) not being such a person as aforesaid, has been employed in reckonable service during a period in respect of which he has a guaranteed minimum pension being a period in respect of which contributions equivalent premium cannot be paid."; and

(b) in paragraph (3), for the words "5 years" in both places where they occur, there shall be substituted the words "2 years".

Reckonable service for entitlement and for benefit

13. In regulation 49(2) of the principal Regulations, sub-paragraphs (cc) and (ccc) are revoked.

Enhancement of reckonable service

14. In regulation 51 of the principal Regulations–

(a) in paragraph (1), there shall be inserted, before the words "If while he is employed", the words "Subject to paragraph (1A),";

(b) in paragraph (1)(a), there shall be inserted, after the words "if he has completed", the words "5 years but"; and

(c) after paragraph (1) there shall be inserted the following:–

"**(1A)** In relation to a teacher employed in part-time service, paragraph (1) shall apply if–

(a) the period over which the part-time service was recorded as reckonable service, in accordance with regulation 5(4)(a), extends to at least 5 years, and

(b) for the purposes of calculating the retiring allowance under regulation 47 the reference in paragraph (1) to years completed shall be construed as a reference to the reckonable service calculated in accordance with regulation 5(4)(b).".

Death gratuities

15. In regulation 57(2)(b) of the principal Regulations, for the words "5 years", there shall be substituted the words "2 years".

Abatement of annual pension

16. In regulation 60(1) of the principal Regulations, the following paragraph shall be added after paragraph (a):–

"(aa) excluded employment by virtue of an election made under regulation 4A.".

Short-term pensions

17. In regulation 63(2)(b) of the principal Regulations, for "5", there shall be substituted "2".

Long-term pensions

18. In regulation 64 of the principal Regulations–

(a) in paragraph (1), there shall be inserted at the beginning the words "Subject to paragraph (1B)," and for "5" there shall be substituted "2";

(b) in paragraph (1A), for the words "46(1)(e)", there shall be substituted the words "46(1)(d)";

(c) there shall be inserted after paragraph (1A) the following:–

"**(1B)** In respect of a teacher such as is mentioned in paragraph (1), who dies while employed in reckonable service, or to whom retiring allowances were paid on grounds of incapacity by virtue of regulation 47, and whose service counting for benefit is less than 5 years, in calculating any long-term pension Note 2 to Table 2 shall be disregarded.";

(d) in paragraph (4), for the words "widow or", there shall be substituted "widow, widower,"; and

(e) for paragraph (8) there shall be substituted the following:–

"Notwithstanding the provisions of this regulation and Schedules 8 and 9, in the case of a widow of a teacher who was employed in reckonable service after 5th April 1978, or in the case of a widower of a teacher last employed after 5th April 1988, where the marriage took place after the day on which the teacher was last employed in reckonable service, the reckonable service counting for benefit shall in respect of a widow or widower be the reckonable service after 5th April 1978 and 5th April 1988 respectively.".

Widowers' long term pension

19. After regulation 64 of the principal Regulations there shall be inserted the following:–

"**Widowers' long-term pension**

64A.—(1) Subject to regulation 64B, on the death of a teacher who was employed in reckonable service for at least 2 years, there shall be paid to her widower a pension calculated in accordance with paragraph (3).

(2) In respect of a teacher referred to in paragraph (1) who dies while employed in reckonable service or while in receipt of an incapacity pension by virtue of regulation 47 and who has at least 5 years' reckonable service, the reckonable service in paragraph (3) shall be enhanced by such number of years as bears to any period which (disregarding any past added years which she elects to purchase) was or could have been added to her reckonable service by virtue of regulation 51 the same as the number of years of her reckonable service after 5th April 1988 bears to her total reckonable service.

(3) Subject to paragraph (2) the pension payable to a widower shall be calculated by multiplying 1/160th of the teacher's pensionable salary by the number of years of her reckonable service after 5th April 1988 together with any period for which family benefit contributions have been paid in accordance with an election made under Parts I or II of Schedule 4, any period of reckonable service credited by virtue of the receipt of, after 5th April 1988, a transfer value under regulation 73 and any past added years the teacher elected to purchase after 5th April 1988 under Part III.

64B. Where a married woman teacher has before 6th April 1988 nominated under previous provisions a person, other than a spouse, to receive a pension under this Part, and she is entitled to a guaranteed minimum pension in relation to benefits under these Regulations, the long term pension payable to her widower following her death, if the nomination has not been revoked, shall be the aggregate of the following amounts:–

(a) a pension equal to one half of that part of the teacher's guaranteed minimum which is attributable to earnings for the tax year 1988/89 and subsequent tax years; and

(b) a pension calculated in the manner prescribed in regulation 64A(3) for any period for which family benefit contributions have been paid in accordance with an election made under Parts I or II of Schedule 4.".

Nomination of beneficiaries

20. Regulation 65 of the principal Regulations shall be substituted by the following:–

"**Nomination of beneficiaries**

65.—(1) Subject to paragraph (2), an unmarried person ("the appointer") may at any time while employed in reckonable service, by giving written notice to the Secretary of State, nominate an eligible person who is wholly or mainly financially dependent on the appointer and who is not a child to receive a pension under regulations 63 and 64.

(2) No person may be nominated while a previous nomination under this regulation has effect.

(3) The eligible persons are–

(a) a parent of the appointer,

(b) an unmarried brother or sister of the appointer, and

(c) a widowed step-parent of the appointer.

(4) A nomination under this regulation may be revoked by giving written notice to the Secretary of State, and if not previously revoked ceases to have effect–

(a) on the death or marriage (or, as the case may be, remarriage) of the person nominated, and

(b) on the marriage of the appointer.

(5) The references in paragraphs (2) and (4) to a nomination under this regulation include references to a nomination made before 6th April 1988 for the purposes of this Part or of previous provisions relating to family benefits.".

Special pension for widow

21. In regulation 66(b) of the principal Regulations, for the words "5/160ths", there shall be substituted the words "1/80th".

Payment of transfer values

22. In regulation 72 of the principal Regulations–

(a) in paragraph (1), for the words "(hereafter referred to as his "old employment"),", there shall be substituted the words "or is a person who entered excluded employment by virtue of an election made under regulation 4A,";

(b) in paragraph (1)(a), for the words "his old employment terminated", there shall be substituted the words "he ceased to be employed in reckonable service or entered excluded employment";

(c) in paragraph (1)(b)(ii), for the words "leaving his old employment", there shall be substituted the words "ceasing to be employed in reckonable service" and for the words "6 months", there shall be substituted the words "12 months";

(d) at the end of paragraph (1)(b)(ii), for the semi-colon, there shall be substituted the word "or" and the following head shall be added:–

"(iii) who after ceasing to be employed in reckonable service or entering excluded employment participates in a personal pension scheme or a self-employed pension arrangement and has within 12 months of beginning to so participate made an application such as is mentioned in sub-paragraph (d) for payment of a transfer value;";

(e) in paragraph (1)(c), for the words "old employment" where they first occur, there shall be substituted the words "reckonable service" and, where they next both occur, the words "in his old employment" shall be deleted;

(f) in paragraph (1)(d)(ii), for the words "his old employment terminated", there shall be substituted the words "he ceased to be employed in reckonable service or entered excluded employment"; and

(g) after paragraph (5) there shall be inserted the following:–

"(6) When the payment of a transfer value is made, the teacher's accrued rights, within the meaning given in Schedule 10, to which it relates, shall cease to be treated as such for all purposes of these Regulations.".

Receipt of transfer values

23. In regulation 73 of the principal Regulations–

(a) in paragraph (1), after "superannuation scheme", there shall be inserted the words ", a personal pension scheme or a self-employed pension arrangement";

(b) in paragraph (1)(a), after the words "superannuation scheme", there shall be inserted the words ", personal pension scheme or self-employed pension arrangement"; and

(c) in paragraph (1)(b), after the words "superannuation scheme", there shall be inserted the words "personal pension scheme or self-employed pension arrangement".

Purchase of Past Added Years – current provisions

24.—(1) Part I of Schedule 2A to the principal Regulations is amended–

(a) in paragraph 2(1), by deleting the words "not less than 5 in number";

(b) in paragraph 3(2), by inserting after the words "Table 1" the words "or, as the case may be, Table 1A"; and

(c) by inserting after Table 1 the following:–

"TABLE 1A

Period of contribution in years	1	2	3	4
Teachers' age	Percentage contribution in respect of each year purchased			
20	32.96	15.97	10.35	7.59
21	31.79	15.32	9.88	7.20
22	30.66	14.71	9.45	6.84
23	29.59	14.15	9.05	6.52
24	28.57	13.62	8.69	6.24
25	27.61	13.14	8.36	5.99
26	26.63	12.71	8.10	5.81
27	25.74	12.31	7.86	5.64
28	24.93	11.95	7.64	5.50
29	24.20	11.63	7.45	5.37
30	23.55	11.34	7.28	5.26
31	23.04	11.12	7.15	5.17
32	22.59	10.91	7.03	5.10
33	22.18	10.73	6.93	5.03
34	21.83	10.58	6.85	4.98
35	21.52	10.45	6.78	4.94
36	21.31	10.37	6.73	4.92
37	21.14	10.30	6.70	4.90
38	20.99	10.25	6.67	4.89
39	20.87	10.21	6.66	4.89
40	20.78	10.18	6.65	4.89
41	20.75	10.18	6.65	4.90
42	20.74	10.18	6.67	4.91
43	20.74	10.20	6.68	4.93
44	20.76	10.22	6.70	4.95
45	20.81	10.25	6.73	4.97
46	20.87	10.29	6.76	5.00
47	20.94	10.33	6.80	5.03
48	21.04	10.39	6.84	5.06
49	21.16	10.45	6.89	5.10
50	21.29	10.52	6.94	5.15
51	21.44	10.61	7.00	5.20
52	21.61	10.70	7.07	5.25
53	21.80	10.80	7.15	5.32
54	22.01	10.92	7.23	5.39
55	22.23	11.04	7.32	5.46
56	22.59	11.24	7.47	5.58
57	23.00	11.48	7.64	5.73
58	23.47	11.74	7.84	5.89
59	23.99	12.04	8.07	6.08
60	24.57	12.38	8.31	6.28
61	24.05	12.12	8.14	6.15
62	23.53	11.85	7.96	6.02
63	23.01	11.59	7.79	5.88
64	20.28	10.14	6.76	5.07
65	21.97	11.07	7.43	5.62
66	21.44	10.78	7.23	
67	20.91	10.49		
68	20.39			

".

(2) Part III of Schedule 2A to the principal Regulations is amended–

(a) in paragraph 2(1)(a)(ii), by substituting for the words "less than 5 nor" the words "less than one year nor";

(b) in paragraph 2(1)(b), by inserting after the words "a period of" the words "not less than one year nor more than";

(c) in paragraph 3, by deleting the words "or 5";

(d) in paragaph 4(1), by deleting the words from "In the case" to "election";

(e) in paragraph 4(2), by deleting the words "In such case" and by substituting for the words "the following Table 4" the words "the appropriate Table";

(f) by inserting after paragraph 4(2) the following:–

"(2A) The appropriate Table–

(a) in the case of a teacher who has not attained the age of 55 on 1st October next following his giving notice of his election, is Table 4 or, as the case may be, Table 4A below, and

(b) in any other case, is Table 5 below.";

(g) by deleting paragraph 5; and

(h) by inserting after Table 4 the following:–

"TABLE 4A

Range within which relevant rate of interest falls %	Contribution period in years			
	1	2	3	4
5.00– 5.49	0.0859	0.0441	0.0302	0.0233
5.50– 5.99	0.0861	0.0444	0.0305	0.0235
6.00– 6.49	0.0863	0.0446	0.0307	0.0238
6.50– 6.99	0.0865	0.0448	0.0309	0.0240
7.00– 7.49	0.0868	0.0450	0.0311	0.0242
7.50– 7.99	0.0870	0.0452	0.0314	0.0244
8.00– 8.49	0.0872	0.0455	0.0316	0.0247
8.50– 8.99	0.0874	0.0457	0.0318	0.0249
9.00– 9.49	0.0877	0.0459	0.0320	0.0251
9.50– 9.99	0.0879	0.0461	0.0323	0.0254
10.00–10.49	0.0881	0.0463	0.0325	0.0256
10.50–10.99	0.0883	0.0466	0.0327	0.0258
11.00–11.49	0.0886	0.0468	0.0329	0.0260
11.50–11.99	0.0888	0.0470	0.0332	0.0263
12.00–12.49	0.0890	0.0472	0.0334	0.0265
12.50–12.99	0.0892	0.0475	0.0336	0.0268
13.00–13.49	0.0894	0.0477	0.0338	0.0270
13.50–13.99	0.0897	0.0479	0.0341	0.0272
14.00–14.49	0.0899	0.0481	0.0343	0.0275
14.50–14.99	0.0901	0.0484	0.0345	0.0277
15.00–15.49	0.0903	0.0486	0.0348	0.0279
15.50–15.99	0.0906	0.0488	0.0350	0.0282
16.00–16.49	0.0908	0.0490	0.0352	0.0284
16.50–16.99	0.0910	0.0493	0.0355	0.0287
17.00–17.49	0.0912	0.0495	0.0357	0.0289
17.50–17.99	0.0914	0.0497	0.0359	0.0292
18.00–18.49	0.0917	0.0499	0.0362	0.0294
18.50–18.99	0.0919	0.0502	0.0364	0.0296
19.00–19.49	0.0921	0.0504	0.0366	0.0299
19.50–19.99	0.0923	0.0506	0.0369	0.0301

TABLE 5

Range within which relevant rate of interest falls %	Contribution period in years				
	1	2	3	4	5
5.00– 5.49	0.0860	0.0443	0.0304	0.0235	0.0194
5.50– 5.99	0.0863	0.0445	0.0306	0.0237	0.0196
6.00– 6.49	0.0865	0.0448	0.0309	0.0239	0.0198
6.50– 6.99	0.0867	0.0450	0.0311	0.0242	0.0200
7.00– 7.49	0.0869	0.0452	0.0313	0.0244	0.0203
7.50– 7.99	0.0872	0.0454	0.0315	0.0246	0.0205
8.00– 8.49	0.0874	0.0456	0.0318	0.0249	0.0207
8.50– 8.99	0.0876	0.0459	0.0320	0.0251	0.0210
9.00– 9.49	0.0878	0.0461	0.0322	0.0253	0.0212
9.50– 9.99	0.0881	0.0463	0.0324	0.0256	0.0214
10.00–10.49	0.0883	0.0465	0.0327	0.0258	0.0217
10.50–10.99	0.0885	0.0468	0.0329	0.0260	0.0219
11.00–11.49	0.0887	0.0470	0.0331	0.0263	0.0222
11.50–11.99	0.0890	0.0472	0.0334	0.0265	0.0224
12.00–12.49	0.0892	0.0474	0.0336	0.0267	0.0226
12.50–12.99	0.0894	0.0476	0.0338	0.0270	0.0229
13.00–13.49	0.0896	0.0479	0.0340	0.0272	0.0231
13.50–13.99	0.0898	0.0481	0.0343	0.0274	0.0234
14.00–14.49	0.0901	0.0483	0.0345	0.0277	0.0236
14.50–14.99	0.0903	0.0485	0.0347	0.0279	0.0239
15.00–15.49	0.0905	0.0488	0.0350	0.0282	0.0241
15.50–15.99	0.0907	0.0490	0.0352	0.0284	0.0244
16.00–16.49	0.0910	0.0492	0.0354	0.0287	0.0246
16.50–16.99	0.0912	0.0494	0.0357	0.0289	0.0249
17.00–17.49	0.0914	0.0497	0.0359	0.0291	0.0251
17.50–17.99	0.0916	0.0499	0.0361	0.0294	0.0255
18.00–18.49	0.0919	0.0501	0.0364	0.0296	0.0257
18.50–18.99	0.0921	0.0504	0.0366	0.0299	0.0260
19.00–19.49	0.0923	0.0506	0.0369	0.0301	0.0262
19.50–19.99	0.0925	0.0508	0.0371	0.0304	0.0265"

Family benefit contributions

25. For Schedule 4 to the principal Regulations there shall be substituted the Schedule set out in the Schedule to these Regulations.

Schedule 7 (Short-term pensions)

26. In Schedule 7 to the principal Regulations–

(a) in Table 1, for the words "Widow or widower or other adult nominated beneficiary", where they appear against categories 1, 2 and 3, there shall be substituted the words "Widow, widower or adult nominated beneficiary";

(b) note 1 shall be substituted by the following:–

"An adult nominated beneficiary includes a widower of a teacher who was nominated before 6th April 1988.";

(c) in note 3 the word "other" shall be deleted; and

(d) for note 4 there shall be substituted the following:–

"**4.** Subject to note 5, in relation to a widower of a teacher who was in reckonable service on or after 6th April 1988, in the heading of Tables 1 and 2 for the words "service counting for benefit under Schedule 9" there shall be substituted the words "reckonable service" and in the heading of Table 3 for the words "5 or more years' reckonable service counting for benefit under Schedule 9" there shall be substituted the words "2 or more years' reckonable service".

5. In relation to a teacher to whom regulation 64(1A) applies, the words "5 or more years' service counting for benefit under Schedule 9" in the heading of Table 2 and the words "with 5 or more years' service counting for benefit under Schedule 9" in the heading of Table 3, as varied by note 4, shall be omitted.".

Schedule 8 (Amount of adults' long-term pension)

27. In Schedule 8 to the principal Regulations–

(a) in the headings of columns 1 and 2 in Table 2, there shall be added, after the word "widow" the word ", widower"; and

(b) for Note 3 to Table 2 there shall be substituted the following:–

"**3.** Where the pension received by a widow, widower or adult nominated beneficiary ceases for any reason, any child's pension payable under column (1) shall become payable under column (2) as from the date of cessation.".

Schedule 9 (Service counting for benefit)

28. In paragraph 2(i) of Schedule 9 to the principal Regulations, there shall be inserted, after the words "by virtue of regulation 47,", the words "and whose reckonable service amounted to at least 5 years,".

Schedule 10 (Transfer values)

29. In Schedule 10 to the principal Regulations–

(a) for paragraph 3 there shall be substituted the following paragraphs:–

"**3.** Where a person requests that a transfer value be paid to–

(a) (i) a superannuation scheme which is not contracted out within the meaning of section 32 of the Pensions Act(**a**); or

(ii) a personal pension scheme which is not an appropriate personal pension scheme; or

(iii) a self-employed pension arrangement; and

(b) the trustees or managers of the superannuation scheme, personal pension scheme or self-employed pension arrangement are able or willing to have transferred to it only the liabilities for a member's accrued rights other than his or her and their respective spouses' rights to guaranteed minimum pensions; and

(c) the member does not require the Secretary of State to use that portion of the transfer value that represents guaranteed minimum pension in one of the ways specified in regulation 72(1),

the member's transfer value shall be reduced by the amount of a state scheme premium sufficient for the Secretary of State for Social Services to meet his liability in respect of the member's and his or her spouse's guaranteed minimum pensions.

3A.(a) Subject to sub-paragraph (b), in respect of a person who is in excluded employment by virtue of an election under regulation 4A, the transfer value calculated in accordance with this Part shall be the aggregate of the following:

(i) in relation to the person's retiring allowance, that part of his accrued rights which bears the same proportion to his total accrued rights as his reckonable service after 5th April 1988 bears to his total reckonable service; and

(ii) in relation to his spouse's pension, that part of his accrued rights applicable to service after 5th April 1988;

(b) Sub-paragraph (a) shall not apply to a person whose reckonable service before 6th April 1988 amounts to less than 2 years.

(c) Where–

(**a**) Section 32 was amended by the Social Security and Housing Benefits Act 1982 (c.24), Schedule 4, paragraph 20 and by the Social Security Act 1986 (c.50), Schedule 2, paragraph 5, Schedule 10, paragraph 16 and Schedule 11.

(i) a transfer value limited in accordance with sub-paragraph (a) has been paid in respect of a person; and

(ii) that person has subsequently ceased to be employed in excluded employment other than by virtue of an election under regulation 4B before attaining the age of 60 years, or, where regulation 72(2) applies, the age of 59 years,

a right to a transfer value in respect of any part of his accrued rights to which, but for the operation of sub-paragraph (a), he would have been entitled on ceasing to be employed in reckonable service, shall accrue to the person on the date on which he ceased to be employed in excluded employment and shall be valued accordingly.

(d) In relation to any person to whom sub-paragraph (c) applies–

(i) regulation 72(1)(d)(ii) shall have effect as if for the words "he ceased to be employed in reckonable service or entered excluded employment" there were substituted the words "he terminated excluded employment"; and

(ii) the definition of "material date" in paragraph 4(c) shall have effect as if for the words "ceased to be employed in reckonable service or entered excluded employment" there were substituted the words "terminated excluded employment".

(e) For the purposes of this paragraph, where a person ceases to be employed in excluded employment other than by virtue of an election under regulation 4B but that person enters again into excluded employment or enters reckonable service, then, if there is between those two employments–

(i) an interval not exceeding one month; or

(ii) an interval of any length if the second of the employments results from the exercise of a right to return to work under section 45(1) of the Employment Protection (Consolidation) Act 1978(**a**) (right to return to work following pregnancy or confinement),

they shall be treated as a single employment.";

(f) in the definition of "material date" in paragraph 4(c), after the words "employed in reckonable service", there shall be inserted the words "or entered excluded employment"."

Teachers' superannuation account

30. In the form of account in Part I of Schedule 11 to the principal Regulations, after Head BI(iv), there shall be inserted the following:–

"v. Widowers' pension ....", and

items "v", "vi" and "vii" shall be renumbered "vi", "vii" and "viii" respectively.

Transitional provisions

31. The amendments made by regulations 12, 14 and 15 shall apply only where the person ceased to hold the employment concerned, or (in relation to regulations 17 to 19) where the death concerned occurred, on or after 5th April 1988.

Right to opt out

32. No provision of these Regulations shall apply to any person to whom at any time before 1st June 1989 any benefit including a return of contributions was or may become payable if–

(a) he is placed by that provision in a worse position than he would have been in if it had not applied in relation to that benefit; and

(b) that provision relates to a benefit paid or payable in respect of a person who–

(i) ceased before 1st June 1989 to be in reckonable service; or

(ii) died before that date while employed in reckonable service; and

(**a**) 1978 c.44.

(c) the person first mentioned in this regulation elects by giving notice in writing to the Secretary of State within 6 months after 1st June 1989, that the provision shall not apply to him.

Michael B. Forsyth
Parliamentary Under Secretary of State,
Scottish Office

St. Andrew's House, Edinburgh
4th April 1989

We consent,

David Lightbown
David Maclean
Two of the Lords Commissioners of Her Majesty's Treasury

11th April 1989

Regulation 25

SCHEDULE

SCHEDULE SUBSTITUTED FOR SCHEDULE 4 TO THE PRINCIPAL REGULATIONS

"SCHEDULE 4

Regulation 30

FAMILY BENEFIT CONTRIBUTIONS

PART I

MEN AND UNMARRIED WOMEN

1.—(1) In this Part–

"the Fund" means the Teachers' Family Benefits Fund established by regulation 37 of the 1965 family benefit regulations and continued by regulation 13 of the 1971 family benefit regulations;

"member" means a man who–

(a) has been employed in reckonable service at any time after 31st March 1972;

(b) immediately before 1st April 1972 had service counting for benefit within the meaning of regulation 37 of the 1971 family benefit regulations; and

(c) has not received a repayment of contributions paid by him under the 1965 family benefit regulations or the 1971 family benefit regulations; and

"non-member" means a man other than a member, who

(a) has been employed in reckonable service at any time after 31st March 1972; and

(b) is entitled to count a period that ended before 1st April 1972 as reckonable service.

(2) A member's normal contributions are the contributions paid by him under regulation 6 of the 1965 family benefit regulations or regulation 25 of the 1971 family benefit regulations, and his normal service is the period in respect of which he paid them.

(3) A member's additional contributions are any contributions paid by him under regulation 9 of the 1965 family benefit regulations or under regulation 26 or 27 of the 1971 family benefit regulations, and the additional period is the period in respect of which he elected to pay them.

(4) A member's deemed normal service is two-thirds of any service before 1st April 1972 in respect of which the full amount of normal contributions was held in the Fund immediately before that date.

(5) A member's deemed additional service is $\frac{A \times B}{C}$, where–

A is the factor ascertained from Table 1 below,

B is the amount of the additional contributions held in the Fund immediately before 1st April 1972, and

C is the annual rate of his salary at that time.

TABLE 1

Age at last birthday before 1st April 1972	*Factor*	*Age at last birthday before 1st April 1972*	*Factor*
18	21.4	40	50.3
19	23.9	41	50.2
20	26.2	42	50.0
21	28.4	43	49.8
22	30.6	44	49.6
23	32.6		
24	34.5	45	49.4
		46	49.3
25	36.3	47	49.2
26	38.0	48	49.1
27	39.6	49	49.0
28	41.1		
29	42.6	50	49.0
		51	49.0
30	43.9	52	49.0
31	45.2	53	48.9
32	46.4	54	48.9
33	47.4		
34	48.4	55	48.8
		56	48.8
35	49.2	57	48.7
36	49.8	58	48.7
37	50.0	59	48.6
38	50.2		
39	50.3	60 and over	48.6

(6) A member's credited service is 165.6% of the total of his deemed normal service and any deemed additional service.

(7) References in this Part to "Method I", "Method II" and "Method III" are references to the Methods so designated in the 1965 family benefit regulations.

2.—(1) Subject to sub-paragraph (3) and paragraph 4, a member who elected to pay additional contributions by Method I or Method II may elect to pay family benefit contributions in respect of all or part of a period not exceeding in length the difference between his credited service and the total of the additional period and his normal service.

(2) Subject to sub-paragraph (3) and paragraph 4, a member who elected to pay additional contributions by Method III may by an election under this paragraph–

(a) revoke the earlier election, or

(b) revoke the earlier election and elect to pay family benefit contributions in respect of the additional period, or part of it, or

(c) vary the earlier election so as to relate to part only of the additional period and elect to pay family benefit contributions in respect of the remaining part.

(3) The period in respect of which a member elects to pay family benefit contributions as mentioned in sub-paragraph (1) or (2) is not to exceed $A - (B + \frac{5 \times (C - B)}{6})$, where–

A is the length of reckonable service attributable to any period that ended before 1st April 1972,

B is the total length of his normal service and the additional period, and

C is the length of his credited service.

(4) A member may elect to pay family benefit contributions in respect of all or part of any period in respect of which he could have elected, but did not elect, to pay additional contributions.

3. Subject to paragraph 4, a non-member or an unmarried woman may elect to pay family benefit contributions in respect of the whole or a part of any reckonable service attributable to a period that ended before 1st April 1972.

4.—(1) A man who has become entitled to payment of allowances may not make an election under paragraph 2 or 3.

(2) An election under paragraph 2 or 3 must–

(a) be made by giving written notice to the Secretary of State within the period specified in sub-paragraphs (3) to (5),

(b) specify the period in respect of which it is made, and

(c) specify the rate at which family benefit contributions are to be paid, which must comply with paragraph 13(2) and (3),

and has effect from the date on which the notice is received by the Secretary of State, and, except as provided in paragraph 13(4), is irrevocable.

(3) Subject to sub-paragraph (4), a man may only make an election under paragraph 2 or 3 within 6 months after–

(a) his marriage while in employment in reckonable service, or

(b) his returning to employment in reckonable service after becoming married while not in such employment, or

(c) where he is a person who was not continuously employed in reckonable service for a period of 6 months during either of the periods mentioned in sub-paragraph 4(a) or (b) and ceases to be employed within 6 months of his returning to such employment, his returning again to such employment.

(d) his nomination of a beneficiary under regulation 65,

whichever occurs first.

(4) An election under paragraph 2 or 3 may be made by

(a) a member who was not continuously in employment in reckonable service for 6 months or more after 31st October 1974 and before 31st July 1977, or

(b) a non-member who was not continuously in such employment for 6 months or more after 8th January 1974 and before 1st August 1977,

only within 6 months after returning to reckonable service.

(5) A woman may only make an election under paragraph 3 within 6 months after nominating a beneficiary.

5.—(1) Where a person has made an election under paragraph 2(2) or (4) or paragraph 3 the period during which, subject to paragraph 13(7) to (10), the family benefit contributions are to be paid ("the payment period") is to be ascertained from, or where the period in respect of which the election was made is not an exact number of years by extrapolation from, Table 2 below.

TABLE 2

Age on date from which contributions are payable	*Period in years for which contributions are to be paid in respect of each year of election period*								
	Rate of contributions								
	1%	2%	3%	4%	5%	6%	7%	8%	9%
32 or under	3.15	1.58	1.05	.79	.63	.525	.45	.395	.35
33–37	3.20	1.60	1.07	.80	.64	.535	.46	.40	.355
38–42	3.30	1.65	1.10	.82	.66	.55	.47	.41	.365
43–47	3.35	1.68	1.12	.84	.67	.56	.48	.42	.37
48 and over	3.40	1.70	1.13	.85	.68	.565	.485	.425	.375

(2) Where a man has made an election under paragraph 2(1) the payment period is, subject to paragraph 13(7) to (10), 5/6ths of the period ascertained in accordance with sub-paragraph (1).

6.—(1) This paragraph applies where a member who elected to pay additional contributions by thod III has not revoked that election, and he–

(a) dies in employment in reckonable service leaving a widow or having nominated a beneficiary under regulation 65, or

(b) becomes qualified for allowances while married or after nominating a beneficiary.

(2) Where this paragraph applies there is to be deducted from the appropriate terminal sum an amount of $\frac{A \times B}{100} \times \frac{5 \times C}{6}$, where–

A is the member's average salary,

B is the factor ascertained from Table 3 below, and

C is the period calculated in accordance with sub-paragraph (3).

TABLE 3

Age	*Factor*
39 or under	3.8
40 to 49	3.7
50	3.6
51	3.6
52	3.6
53	3.6
54	3.5
55	3.5
56	3.5
57	3.4
58	3.4
59	3.3
60	3.3
61	3.2
62	3.1
63	3.1
64 and over	3.0

(3) The period is (D + E) – (F + G + H), where–

D is the additional period in respect of which he elected to pay contributions by Method III, together with any additional period for which he elected to pay contributions by Method I or II,

E is his normal service,

F is his credited service,

G is any period or periods for which he has elected to pay family benefit contributions under paragraph 2, and

H is any additional period in respect of which he elected to pay contributions by Method I or II, less his credited service in respect of deemed additional service attributable to contributions so paid, and less any period for which he has elected under paragraph 2(1) to pay family benefit contributions.

7.—(1) Subject to sub-paragraphs (2) and (3), a member or non-member who–

(a) is not employed in reckonable service and has become entitled to payment of allowances, and

(b) would otherwise have been able to make an election under paragraph 2 or 3,

may make a corresponding election under this paragraph.

(2) An election under this paragraph–

(a) must be made by giving written notice to the Secretary of State within 6 months after the date on which the man became entitled to payment of allowances,

(b) must specify the period in respect of which it is made, and

(c) is irrevocable.

(3) The family benefit contributions payable as a result of an election under this paragraph consist of a lump sum of $\frac{A}{100} \times (B \times C)$, where–

A is the annual rate at which his salary was last payable,

B is the length, expressed in years and any fraction of a year, of the period in respect of which the election was made, and

C is the factor ascertained from Table 4 below,

but where the election made corresponds to one that could have been made under paragraph 2(1), B is reduced by 1/6th.

TABLE 4

Age on date of election	*Factor*
32 or under	3.15
33–37	3.20
38–42	3.30
43–47	3.35
48 and over	3.40

8.—(1) This paragraph applies where–

(a) a member or non-member dies before becoming entitled to payment of allowances, and

(b) he has not made an election under paragraph 2 or 3, but could still have done so if he had not died, and

(c) he leaves a widow.

(2) Where this paragraph applies the widow may, subject to sub-paragraph (3), elect to pay family benefit contributions in respect of a period comprising all or part of so much of the deceased's reckonable service as would otherwise not count in the calculation of family benefits.

(3) An election under this paragraph–

(a) must be made by giving written notice to the Secretary of State within 3 months after the death,

(b) must specify the period in respect of which it is made, and

(c) must result in a total of not less than 2 years' reckonable service counting in the calculation of family benefits, and

(d) ceases to have effect if the family benefit contributions are not paid within 3 months after its date.

(4) The family benefit contributions payable as a result of an election under this paragraph consist of a lump sum which is the actuarial equivalent of the contributions that would have been payable by the deceased if–

(a) he had made an election under paragraph 2, or as the case may be paragraph 3, in respect of the same period, and

(b) notice of that election had been given on the day before his death and had specified as the rate at which family benefit contributions were to be paid the maximum allowed by paragraph 13(2) and (3).

PART II

MARRIED WOMEN

9.—(1) Subject to sub-paragraph (3) and paragraph 10, a woman in relation to whom the election conditions are satisfied may elect to pay family benefit contributions in respect of the whole or a part of any reckonable service attributable to a period–

(a) that ended before 1st April 1972, or

(b) for which contributions have been paid under regulations 21 to 28 (past and current added years)

or attributable to the receipt, before 6 April 1988, of a transfer value.

(2) Subject to sub-paragraph (3) and paragraph 10, a woman in relation to whom the election conditions are satisfied may elect to pay family benefit contributions in respect of the whole or a part of any reckonable service attributable to a period that–

(a) began after 31st March 1972 and ended before 6th April 1988, and

(b) would otherwise not count in calculating any pension becoming payable to her widower.

(3) Where an election is made in respect of a part only of any service, the part must consist of one or more whole years.

(4) The election conditions are that she is married, and either–

(a) is employed in reckonable service, or

(b) ceased after 5th April 1988 and before 1st January 1990 to be so employed and immediately became entitled to payment of retiring allowances.

10.—(1) An election under paragraph 9(1) or (2)–

(a) must be made by giving written notice to the Secretary of State within the period specified in sub-paragraphs (2) to (4),

(b) must specify the period in respect of which it is made,

(c) must state whether the contributions are to be paid by Method A (periodical payments) or by Method B (lump sum),

(d) if the contributions are to be paid by Method A, must specify the rate at which they are to be paid, which must comply with paragraph 13(2) and (3),

(e) has effect from the date on which the notice is received by the Secretary of State, and

(f) except as provided in paragraph 13(4), is irrevocable.

(2) The period within which an election may be made is one of 6 months beginning on the relevant date.

(3) Where paragraph 9(4)(b) applies, the relevant date is 1st July 1989; in any other case, subject to sub-paragraph (4), the relevant date is the first date after 30th June 1989 on which the election conditions are satisfied.

(4) If, during the period of 6 months beginning on that first date, the election conditions cease to be satisfied, the relevant date becomes the first date on which they are again satisfied.

(5) A woman who could make an election under paragraph 9(2) may only make one under paragraph 9(1) if, and at the same time as, she elects under paragraph 9(2) to pay family benefit contributions in respect of the whole of the reckonable service there mentioned.

(6) Where elections are made both under paragraph 9(1) and under paragraph 9(2) they must specify the same method of payment.

(7) Payment may not in any case be made by Method A if–

(a) the payment period would be less than one year, or

(b) the woman's employment in reckonable service is part-time; or

(c) she is not employed in reckonable service.

11.—(1) Subject to sub-paragraph (2), where payment is to be made by Method A the payment period is to be ascertained from, or where the period in respect of which the election was made is not an exact number of years by extrapolation from, Table 5 below.

TABLE 5

Period in years for which contributions are to be paid in respect of each year of period specified in election

Rate of contributions	*Election under paragraph 9(1)*	*Election under paragraph 9(2)*
1%	1.45	0.42
2%	0.69	0.20
3%	0.46	0.14
4%	0.33	0.10
5%	0.27	0.08
6%	0.22	0.07
7%	0.18	0.06
8%	0.16	0.05
9%	0.14	0.04

(2) If the period ascertained in accordance with sub-paragraph (1) ("the Table period") does not end with the last day of a month, the payment period ends with the last day of the month in which the Table period ends.

(3) Where payment is to be made by Method B the lump sum payable, which must be payable within 3 months after its amount is notified by the Secretary of State, is–

(a) for each year of service in respect of which an election was made under paragraph 9(1), 1.25%, and

(b) for each year of service in respect of which an election was made under paragraph 9(2), 0.4%,

of the appropriate amount, and pro rata for any period of less than a year.

(4) The appropriate amount is–

(a) where the woman was employed in reckonable service when the election took effect, the annual rate of her salary at that time, and

(b) in any other case, her pensionable salary.

12.—(1) The widower of a woman who–

(a) died during the period beginning on 6th April 1988 and ending with 31st December 1989 without having made an election under paragraph 9, and

(b) either was employed in reckonable service when she died or had ceased during that period to be so employed,

may make a corresponding election under this paragraph.

(2) A married woman who–

(a) ceased to be employed in reckonable service during the period mentioned in sub-paragraph (1), and

(b) on ceasing to be so employed did not immediately become entitled to payment of retiring allowances,

may make a corresponding election under this paragraph if the conditions in sub-paragraph (3) are satisfied.

(3) The conditions are that–

(a) she did not again become employed in reckonable service, and

(b) she has become entitled to payment of retiring allowances.

(4) Where a woman to whom sub-paragraphs (2) and (3) would otherwise have applied dies before becoming entitled to payment of allowances, her widower may make a corresponding election under this paragraph.

(5) An election under this paragraph–

(a) must be made by giving written notice to the Secretary of State within the appropriate period,

(b) must specify the period in respect of which it is made, and

(c) is to be treated as an election to make payment by Method B.

(6) The appropriate period is–

(a) where sub-paragraph (1) applies, the period beginning on 1st July 1989 and ending with 31st December 1989,

(b) where sub-paragraphs (2) and (3) apply, 6 months from the date on which she became entitled to payment of retiring allowances, and

(c) where sub-paragraph (4) applies, 3 months from the date of her death.

PART III

COMMON PROVISIONS

13.—(1) This paragraph applies where–

(a) an election is made under paragraph 2 or 3, or

(b) an election is made under paragraph 9 to pay family benefit contributions by Method A.

(2) The rate at which family benefit contributions are to be paid, and any higher rate substituted by an election under sub-paragraph (4), must be an integral percentage, not in any case exceeding 9, of the person's salary.

(3) If he is paying additional contributions for past added years, or towards the provision of a pension otherwise than under these Regulations, sub-paragraph (2) has effect with the substitution for "9" of the number obtained by deducting from 9 the percentage rate of those contributions.

(4) The election may at any time be varied by an election to pay the family benefit contributions at a specified higher rate.

(5) An election under sub-paragraph (4) must be made by giving written notice to the Secretary of State, and has effect from the first day of the month following that in which the notice is received by him.

(6) The payment period begins on the first day of the month following that in which it is notified to the person by the Secretary of State.

(7) If after the start of the payment period there is an interval of more than 30 days during which the person is not employed in reckonable service or paying additional contributions for current added years–

(a) the interval is not part of the payment period, but

(b) the end of the payment period is postponed by the length of the interval.

(8) If after the start of the payment period the person becomes employed part-time in reckonable service, the length of the payment period is increased by so much of the period of part-time employment as does not count as reckonable service.

(9) If the original election is varied by one made under sub-paragraph (4) ("the further election"), the length of the payment period is reduced to $A - (\frac{B}{C} \times D)$, where–

A is what the length of the payment period would have been if the increased rate had been specified in the original election,

B is the rate specified in the original election,

C is the increased rate, and

D is the period from the start of the payment period to the effective date of the further election.

(10) The contributions–

(a) are payable from the start of the payment period,

(b) continue to be payable while the person is employed in reckonable service or paying additional contributions for current added years, and

(c) cease to be payable if he dies or becomes entitled to retiring allowances before the end of the payment period.

14.—(1) This paragraph–

(a) applies where family benefit contributions to which paragraph 13 applies cease to be payable before the end of the payment period, and

(b) has effect subject to paragraph 15.

(2) Where the person paying the contributions dies before attaining the age of 60, or (whether or not he later re-enters employment in reckonable service) becomes entitled to payment of retiring allowances by virtue of regulation 47–

(a) contributions are to be treated as having been paid in respect of the whole of the period in respect of which the election was made, but

(b) if part of the payment period falls after his 60th birthday, the actuarial equivalent of the contributions that would have been payable during that part is to be deducted from the appropriate terminal sum.

(3) Where the person dies, or becomes entitled to payment of retiring allowances, after attaining the age of 60–

(a) contributions are to be treated as having been paid in respect of the whole of the period in respect of which the election was made, but

(b) there is to be deducted from the appropriate terminal sum an amount of $(A \times \frac{B}{100}) \times C$, where–

A is the annual rate at which his salary was last payable,

B is the rate at which the contributions were last payable, and

C is the multiplier ascertained from, or if the remainder of the payment period is not an exact number of years by extrapolation from, Table 6 below.

TABLE 6

Years in remainder of payment period	*Multiplier*
1	0.990
2	1.961
3	2.913
4	3.846
5	4.760
6	5.657
7	6.536
8	7.398
9	8.244
10	9.072
11	9.884
12	10.681
13	11.461
14	12.227
15	12.977
16	13.713
17	14.434
18	15.141
19	15.835
20	16.514

(4) Where the person becomes entitled to payment of allowances by virtue of regulation 46(2)(c)–

(a) he may, by giving written notice to the Secretary of State within 3 months after the end of his employment in reckonable service, elect to pay a lump sum which is the actuarial equivalent of the contributions that would have been payable during the remainder of the payment period,

(b) if he does so elect, on payment of the lump sum contributions are to be treated as having been paid in respect of the whole of the period in respect of which the original election was made, and

(c) if he does not so elect, contributions are to be treated as having been paid in respect of $D \times \frac{E}{F}$,

where–

D is the period in respect of which the original election was made,

E is the period during which contributions were paid, and

F is the payment period.

15. Where–

(a) a deduction has fallen to be made under paragraph 14(2) or (3) or an election has been made under paragraph 14(4), and

(b) there is then a retrospective increase in the person's salary, and

(c) the consequent recalculation of the amount of the deduction or lump sum and of the appropriate terminal sum results in a greater increase in the amount of the deduction or lump sum than in the terminal sum,

the person, or as the case may be his widow or widower or a beneficiary nominated under regulation 65, may notify the Secretary of State in writing that the amount of the deduction made is not to be increased."

EXPLANATORY NOTE

(This note is not part of the Regulations)

These Regulations further amend the Teachers' Superannuation (Scotland) Regulations 1977.

There are added a number of definitions of expressions used in later provisions concerning mainly amendments to the transfer value provisions (regulation 3).

Inserted in the 1977 Regulations are new regulations 4A and 4B. Regulation 4A reconciles the 1977 Regulations with section 10 of the Social Security Act 1986 (which makes void, inter alia, any rule to the effect that an earner must be a member of a particular occupational pension scheme), by conferring a right on a teacher to elect to cease to be, or not to become, subject to the 1977 Regulations as an employee in reckonable service. Regulation 4B allows any person who has made such an election to elect to become subject again to the 1977 Regulations (regulation 4).

Regulation 5 of the 1977 Regulations is amended as a consequence of regulation 4 of these Regulations to enable part-time teachers currently superannuable by virtue of an election they have made to elect to cease to be subject to the 1977 Regulations (regulation 5).

Regulation 6(3)(b) of the 1977 Regulations is revoked. This regulation permitted late entrants (age 55 and over) who entered teaching for the first time to elect not to be superannuable. This separate provision is no longer required as any teacher can so elect under new regulation 4A (regulation 6).

Regulations 30 to 38 and Schedule 4 to the 1977 Regulations are replaced by a new regulation and Schedule encompassing in one place extended and existing provisions relating to additional contributions which may be paid by teachers to increase reckonable service counting for family benefits. The effect of the new provisions is that married women are enabled to pay additional contributions in respect of service before 6th April 1988 which would not otherwise count towards widowers' benefits (regulations 7 and 25).

Regulation 39 of the 1977 Regulations is amended as follows:–

1. The general conditions for entitlement to a refund of contributions are amended consequentially upon amendments to regulation 12, ie refunds are available only where a person has less than 2 years' service.
2. Entitlement to a refund of contributions is extended to teachers who elect to cease to be subject to the 1977 Regulations.
3. By precluding a refund of contributions to a teacher with less than 2 years' service if part of that service was credited by virtue of a transfer value received from a personal pension scheme.
4. By providing that the increased rate of tax deductible from refunds of contributions, effective from 6th April 1988, will not be applied in respect of refunds paid after this date but for which application was lodged before this date.

The scope of regulation 45A of the 1977 Regulations, which provides entitlement to a guaranteed minimum pension for teachers and for teachers' widows, is extended to include teachers' widowers and, in addition, provides that all such pensions shall be increased in accordance with the requirements of section 37A of the Social Security Act 1975 (regulation 11).

Regulation 46 of the 1977 Regulations is amended by reducing from 5 years to 2 years, and from 10 years to 5 years, the periods of service giving rise, in differing circumstances, to an entitlement to benefits (immediate or deferred, according to age) on ceasing to be employed in reckonable service (regulation 12).

Regulation 51 of the 1977 Regulations is amended to clarify (a) that benefits payable early by reason of incapacity will be enhanced only if 5 or more years' service have been completed, and (b) how these provisions apply in relation to part-time teachers (regulation 14).

The period of service required for payment of a death gratuity is also reduced from 5 years to 2 years (regulation 15).

Provision is made for the abatement provisions to apply in the case of a retired teacher who, on being re-employed, does not become subject to the 1977 Regulations by virtue of an election made under new Regulation 4A (regulation 16).

Apart from the minor consequential amendments, regulation 64 of the 1977 Regulations is amended to clarify that, corresponding to the amendment introduced by regulation 14, the service counting for a spouse's pension will not be enhanced if the teacher's service amounts to less than 2 years and alters the provisions governing post-retirement marriages following the introduction of widowers' benefits (regulation 18).

Provision is made for the payment of pensions to widowers in respect of service accrued by a teacher after 5th April 1988. Such a pension is, however, limited to one half of the teacher's guaranteed minimum pension if there is in existence a nomination made by the teacher in respect of a person other than her spouse (regulation 19).

Regulation 65 of the 1977 Regulations is amended to take account of the introduction of automatic widowers' benefits so that from 6th April 1988 married women teachers can no longer make a nomination. In addition, the categories of persons who may be nominated are amended to prevent a child, however related to any teacher, from being nominated (regulation 20).

Regulation 72 of the 1977 Regulations is amended to extend to those teachers who elect to opt out of the Scheme a right to a transfer value. Further amendments allow transfer values to be paid to personal and self employed pension schemes and ensure that, following payment of a transfer value, the 1977 Regulations cease to apply to the accrued rights to which it relates (regulation 22).

Regulation 73 of the 1977 Regulations is amended to reflect that transfer values may be received from institutions managing personal pension schemes or self employed pension arrangements (regulation 23).

Following changes to legislation governing tax relief on pension contributions, the minimum contribution period for the purchase of past added years can be reduced from 5 years to one year for certain methods of payment. Schedule 2A to the 1977 Regulations is accordingly amended and new tables are supplied.

Schedule 7 to the 1977 Regulations is amended to take account of the introduction of widowers' benefits and the reduction in the period giving rise to entitlement of benefits. The reduction in the period giving rise to entitlement to benefits, however, has not been carried through to Tables 1 and 2, thus improving entitlement to short-term pensions (regulation 26).

Schedule 8 to the 1977 Regulations is amended to take account of the introduction of widowers' benefits and to make one improvement in relation to children's pensions when a widow's, widower's or adult nominated beneficiary's pension ceases for any reason (regulation 27).

Schedule 10 to the 1977 Regulations is extended to take account of personal pension schemes and self employed pension schemes which cannot accept that part of a transfer value which represents guaranteed minimum pension liability and, to provide for this, reduction of a transfer value where a teacher opts out of the Scheme (regulation 29).

Regulation 31 provides that certain provisions of these Regulations apply only where cessation of employment or death occurred after 6th April 1988.

These Regulations, apart from regulations 3(a), 7, 24 and 25, have retrospective effect as authorised by section 12 of the Superannuation Act 1972.

Regulation 32 permits a person to opt out if placed in a worse position by any of these Regulations.

The remaining regulations are consequential.

STATUTORY INSTRUMENTS

1989 No. 669

CIVIL AVIATION

The Air Navigation (General) (Third Amendment) Regulations 1989

Made - - - -	*13th April 1989*
Coming into force	*1st June 1989*

The Secretary of State for Transport, in exercise of his powers under article 29(1) of the Air Navigation Order 1985 (**a**) and of all other powers enabling him in that behalf, hereby makes the following Regulations:

1. These Regulations may be cited as the Air Navigation (General) (Third Amendment) Regulations 1989 and shall come into force on 1st June 1989.

2. The Air Navigation (General) Regulations 1981 (**b**) shall be amended as follows–

(1) For regulation 7(7)(a), there shall be substituted the following–

"(7)(a) (i) In the case of a turbine-jet powered aeroplane, the landing distance required does not exceed at the aerodrome at which it is intended to land or at any alternate aerodrome, as the case may be, the landing distance available on–

(aa) the most suitable runway for a landing in still air conditions; and

(bb) the runway that may be required for landing because of the forecast wind conditions.

(ii) In the case of an aeroplane powered by turbine propeller or piston engines, the landing distances required, respectively specified as being appropriate to aerodromes of destination and alternate aerodromes, do not exceed at the aerodrome at which it is intended to land or at any alternate aerodrome, as the case may be, the landing distance available on–

(aa) the most suitable runway for a landing in still air conditions; and

(bb) the runway that may be required for landing because of the forecast wind conditions:

Provided that if an alternate aerodrome is designated in the flight plan, the specified landing distance required may be that appropriate to an alternate aerodrome when assessing the ability of the aeroplane to satisfy this condition at the aerodrome of destination.".

Signed by authority of the Secretary of State

Peter Bottomley
Parliamentary Under Secretary of State,
Department of Transport

13th April 1989

(**a**) S.I. 1985/1643, to which there are amendments not relevant to these Regulations.
(**b**) S.I. 1981/57; the relevant amending instrument is S.I. 1987/2078.

EXPLANATORY NOTE

(This note is not part of the Regulations)

These Regulations amend the Air Navigation (General) Regulations 1981. The Regulations eliminate the distinction between destination and alternate aerodromes for calculating the landing distances required by turbine-jet powered aeroplanes.

STATUTORY INSTRUMENTS

1989 No. 670

TOWN AND COUNTRY PLANNING, ENGLAND AND WALES

The Town and Country Planning (Control of Advertisements) Regulations 1989

Made - - - -	*13th April 1989*
Laid before Parliament	*26th April 1989*
Coming into force -	*22nd May 1989*

ARRANGEMENT OF REGULATIONS

PART IV

Areas of Special Control

PART V

Miscellaneous

SCHEDULES

The Secretary of State for the Environment, as respects England, and the Secretary of State for Wales, as respects Wales, in exercise of the powers conferred upon them by sections 63**(a)**, 109(1) and (2)**(b)**, 176 and 287(1) of the Town and Country Planning Act 1971**(c)** and all other powers enabling them in that behalf, hereby make the following Regulations:–

(a) Section 63 has been amended by section 45 of the Housing and Planning Act 1986 (c.63).
(b) Section 109(2) has been amended by section 46 of the Criminal Justice Act 1982 (c.48) and Schedule 11, paragraph 13 of the Housing and Planning Act 1986.
(c) 1971 c.78.

PART I

GENERAL

Citation and Commencement

1. These Regulations may be cited as the Town and Country Planning (Control of Advertisements) Regulations 1989 and shall come into force on 22nd May 1989.

Interpretation

2.—(1) In these Regulations–

"the Act" means the Town and Country Planning Act 1971;

"advertisement" does not include anything employed wholly as a memorial or as a railway signal;

"area of outstanding natural beauty" means an area designated as such by an order made under section 87 of the National Parks and Access to the Countryside Act 1949**(a)**;

"area of special control" means an area designated by an order under regulation 18;

"balloon" means a tethered balloon or similar object;

"deemed consent" has the meaning given by regulation 5;

"discontinuance notice" means a notice served under regulation 8;

"express consent" has the meaning given by regulation 5;

"illuminated advertisement" means an advertisement which is designed or adapted to be illuminated by artificial lighting, directly or by reflection, and which is so illuminated;

"National Park" has the meaning given by section 5 of the National Parks and Access to the Countryside Act 1949;

"site" means any land or building, other than any advertisement, on which an advertisement is displayed;

"standard conditions" means the conditions specified in Schedule 1 to these Regulations;

"statutory undertaker" includes, in addition to any person mentioned in section 290(1) of the Act, the Civil Aviation Authority, any relevant airport operator within the meaning of section 57 of the Airports Act 1986**(b)**, the British Airports Authority, the British Coal Corporation, any public gas supplier within the meaning of Part I of the Gas Act 1986**(c)** and any telecommunications code system operator; and statutory undertaking shall be interpreted accordingly;

"telecommunications code system operator" means a person who has been granted a licence under section 7 of the Telecommunications Act 1984**(d)** which applies the telecommunications code to him in pursuance of section 10 of that Act;

"vehicle" includes a vessel on any inland waterway.

(2) In these Regulations, "local planning authority" means–

(a) for land in the area of an urban development corporation, which is the local planning authority for the purposes of sections 63 and 109 of the Act, and except in regulation 18, that corporation;

(b) for land in a National Park outside the metropolitan counties, the county planning authority for the area; and

(c) in any other case, the district planning authority for the area.

(3) Any reference in these Regulations to the person displaying an advertisement includes–

(a) 1949 c.97.
(b) 1986 c.31.
(c) 1986 c.44.
(d) 1984 c.12.

(a) the owner and occupier of the land on which the advertisement is displayed;
(b) any person to whose goods, trade, business or other concerns publicity is given by the advertisement; and
(c) the person who undertakes or maintains the display of an advertisement.

(4) Except in Schedule 2, Class A, any reference in these Regulations to the land, the building, the site or premises on which the advertisement is displayed includes, in the case of an advertisement which is displayed on, or which consists of, a balloon, a reference to the land, the building, the site or other premises to which the balloon is attached and to all land, buildings or other premises normally occupied therewith.

Application

3.—(1) These Regulations apply to the display on any site in England or Wales of any advertisement.

(2) Parts II and III of these Regulations do not apply to an advertisement within any description set out in Schedule 2, which complies with–
(i) any conditions and limitations there specified; and
(ii) the standard conditions, except that paragraph 4 of Schedule 1 does not apply in the case of any Class G advertisement.

Powers to be exercised in the interests of amenity and public safety

4.—(1) A local planning authority shall exercise their powers under these Regulations only in the interests of amenity and public safety, taking account of any material factors and in particular–
(a) in the case of amenity, of the general characteristics of the locality, including the presence of any feature of historic, architectural, cultural or similar interest, disregarding, if they think fit, any advertisements being displayed there;
(b) in the case of public safety–
(i) the safety of any person who may use any road, railway, waterway (including coastal waters), docks, harbour or airfield;
(ii) whether any display of advertisements is likely to obscure, or hinder the ready interpretation of, any road traffic sign, railway signal, or aid to navigation by water or air.

(2) In determining an application for consent for the display of advertisements, or considering whether to make an order revoking or modifying a consent, the local planning authority may have regard to any material change in circumstances likely to occur within the period for which the consent is required or granted.

(3) Unless it appears to a local planning authority to be required in the interests of amenity or public safety, an express consent for the display of advertisements shall not contain any limitation or restriction relating to the subject matter, content or design of what is to be displayed.

(4) A consent for the display of advertisements shall take effect as consent for the use of the site for the purposes of the display, whether by the erection of structures or otherwise, and for the benefit of any person interested in the site.

Requirement for consent

5. Except as provided by regulation 3(2) and regulation 19(1)(a), no advertisement may be displayed without consent granted by the local planning authority or by the Secretary of State on an application in that behalf (referred to in these Regulations as "express consent"), or granted by regulation 6 below (referred to in these Regulations as "deemed consent").

PART II

DEEMED CONSENT

Deemed consent for the display of advertisements

6.—(1) Subject to regulations 7 and 8 below, deemed consent is hereby granted for the display of an advertisement falling within any class specified in Part I of Schedule 3, subject–

(a) to any conditions and limitations specified in that Part in relation to that class; and

(b) to the standard conditions.

(2) Part II of Schedule 3 applies for the interpretation of that Schedule.

Directions restricting deemed consent

7.—(1) If the Secretary of State is satisfied, upon a proposal made to him by the local planning authority, that the display of advertisements of any class or description specified in Schedule 3, other than Class 11B, 12 or 13, should not be undertaken in any particular area or in any particular case without express consent, he may direct that the consent granted by regulation 6 for that class or description shall not apply in that area or in that case, for a specified period or indefinitely.

(2) Before making any such direction, the Secretary of State shall–

(a) where the proposal relates to a particular area, publish, or cause to be published, in at least one newspaper circulating in the locality, and on the same or a subsequent date in the London Gazette, a notice that such a proposal has been made, naming a place or places in the locality where a map or maps defining the area concerned may be inspected at all reasonable hours; and

(b) where the proposal relates to a particular case, serve, or cause to be served, on the owner and occupier of the land affected and on any other person who, to his knowledge, proposes to display on such land an advertisement of the class or description concerned, a notice that a proposal has been made, specifying the land and the class or description of advertisement in question.

(3) Any notice under paragraph (2) above shall state that any objection to the making of a direction may be made to the Secretary of State in writing within such period (not being less than 21 days from the date when the notice is given) as may be specified.

(4) The Secretary of State shall not make a direction under this regulation until after the expiry of the specified period.

(5) In determining whether to make a direction, the Secretary of State–

(a) shall take into account any objections made in accordance with paragraph (3) above;

(b) may modify the proposal of the local planning authority if–

(i) he has notified, in writing, that authority and any person who has made an objection or representation to him of his intention and the reasons for it and has given them a reasonable opportunity to respond; and

(ii) the intended modification does not extend the area of land specified in the proposal.

(6) Where the Secretary of State makes a direction, he shall send it to the local planning authority, with a statement in writing of his reasons for making it, and shall send a copy of that statement to any person who has made an objection in accordance with paragraph (3) above.

(7) Notice of the making of any direction for a particular area shall be published by the local planning authority in at least one newspaper circulating in the locality and, unless the Secretary of State otherwise directs, on the same or a subsequent date in the London Gazette, and such a notice shall–

(a) contain a full statement of the effect of the direction;

(b) name a place or places in the locality where a copy of the direction and of a map defining the area concerned may be seen at all reasonable hours; and

(c) specify a date when the direction shall come into force, at least 14 and not more than 28 days after the first publication of the notice.

(8) Notice of the making of any direction for a particular case shall be served by the local planning authority on the owner and on any occupier of the land to which the direction relates, and on any other person who, to the knowledge of the authority, proposes to display on such land an advertisement of the class or description affected.

(9) A direction for an area shall come into force on the date specified in the notice given under paragraph (7) above; and a direction for a particular case shall come into force on the date on which notice is served on the occupier or, if there is no occupier, on the owner of the land affected.

Discontinuance of deemed consent

8.—(1) The local planning authority may serve a notice requiring the discontinuance of the display of an advertisement, or the use of a site for the display of an advertisement, for which deemed consent is granted under regulation 6–

(a) if they are satisfied it is necessary to do so to remedy a substantial injury to the amenity of the locality or a danger to members of the public; and

(b) in the case of any advertisement within Class 12 in Schedule 3, if the advertisement is not also within Class F or G in Schedule 2.

(2) A discontinuance notice–

(a) shall be served on the advertiser and on the owner and occupier of the site on which the advertisement is displayed;

(b) may, if the local planning authority think fit, also be served on any other person displaying the advertisement;

(c) shall specify the advertisement or the site to which it relates;

(d) shall specify a period within which the display or the use of the site (as the case may be) is to be discontinued; and

(e) shall contain a full statement of the reasons for taking discontinuance action.

(3) Subject to paragraphs (4) and (5) below, a discontinuance notice shall take effect at the end of the period (being at least 8 weeks after the date on which it is served) specified in the notice.

(4) If an appeal is made to the Secretary of State under regulation 15, the notice shall be of no effect pending the final determination or withdrawal of the appeal.

(5) The local planning authority, by a notice served on the advertiser, may withdraw a discontinuance notice at any time before it takes effect or may, where no appeal to the Secretary of State is pending, from time to time vary a discontinuance notice by extending the period specified for the taking effect of the notice.

(6) The local planning authority shall, on serving on the advertiser a notice of withdrawal or variation under paragraph (5) above, send a copy to every other person served with the discontinuance notice.

PART III

EXPRESS CONSENT

Applications for express consent

9.—(1) An application for express consent shall be made–

(a) where it relates to land in a National Park outside a metropolitan county, to the district planning authority; and

(b) in any other case, to the local planning authority.

(2) In a case to which paragraph (1)(a) above applies–

(a) the district planning authority shall transmit the application to the county planning authority; and

(b) the application shall be treated as if made on the day on which it is received by the county planning authority.

(3) Such an application shall be made on a form–

(a) provided by the local planning authority; and

(b) containing the particulars required by the form, accompanied by such plans as the authority may require and by 2 copies of the form and plans.

(4) The local planning authority may, if they think fit, accept an application in writing which does not comply with any of the provisions of paragraph (3).

Secretary of State's directions

10. The Secretary of State may give directions to a local planning authority, either generally or in relation to a particular case or class of case, specifying the kinds of particulars, plans or information to be contained in an application for express consent.

Receipt of applications

11. On receipt of an application for express consent, the local planning authority–

(a) shall send an acknowledgement in writing to the applicant;

(b) may direct the applicant in writing to provide one of their officers with such evidence as may be reasonably called for to verify any particulars or information given to them.

Duty to consult

12.—(1) Before granting an express consent, a local planning authority shall consult–

(a) any neighbouring local planning authority, any part of whose area appears likely to be affected;

(b) where they consider that a grant of consent may affect the safety of persons using any trunk road (as defined in section 329 of the Highways Act 1980**(a)**) in England, the Secretary of State for Transport;

(c) where they consider that a grant of consent may affect the safety of persons using any railway, waterway (including any coastal waters), dock, harbour or aerodrome (civil or military), the person responsible for the operation thereof, and, in the case of coastal waters, the Corporation of Trinity House.

(2) The local planning authority shall give anyone whom they are required to consult at least 14 days' notice that the relevant application is to be considered and shall take into account any representations made by any such person.

Power to deal with applications

13.—(1) Subject to regulation 19 below, where an application for express consent is made to the local planning authority, they may–

(a) refuse consent; or

(b) grant consent, in whole or in part, subject to the standard conditions and to such additional conditions as they think fit, subject to paragraphs (3) to (6) below.

(2) An express consent may be–

(a) for the display of a particular advertisement or advertisements with or without illumination, as the applicant specifies;

(a) 1980 c.66.

(b) for the use of a particular site for the display of advertisements in a specified manner, whether by reference to the number, siting, size or illumination of the advertisements, or the structures intended for such display, or the design or appearance of any such structure, or otherwise; or

(c) for the retention of any display of advertisements or the continuation of the use of a site begun before the date of the application.

(3) The conditions imposed under paragraph (1)(b) above may in particular include conditions–

(a) regulating the display of advertisements to which the consent relates;

(b) regulating the use for the display of advertisements of the site to which the application relates or any adjacent land under the control of the applicant, or requiring the carrying out of works on any such land;

(c) requiring the removal of any advertisement or the discontinuance of any use of land authorised by the consent, at the end of a specified period, and the carrying out of any works then required for the reinstatement of the land.

(4) The local planning authority shall not, under paragraph (1)(b) above, impose any conditions in relation to the display of an advertisement within any class specified in Schedule 3, more restrictive than those imposed by that Schedule in relation to that class.

(5) Subject to paragraph (4) above, an express consent shall be subject to the condition that it expires at the end of–

(a) a period of 5 years from the date of the consent, or

(b) such longer or shorter period as the local planning authority may specify in granting the consent.

(6) A local planning authority may specify a period under paragraph (5)(b) above as a period running in the alternative, from the date of commencement of the display or a specified date not later than 6 months after the consent is granted, whichever is the earlier.

(7) An application for the renewal of an express consent may not be made at a date earlier than 6 months before the expiry of that consent.

Notification of decision

14.—(1) The grant or refusal of an express consent by a local planning authority shall be notified in writing to the applicant within a period of 8 weeks from the date of the receipt of the application or such longer period as the applicant may, before that date, agree in writing.

(2) The authority shall state in writing their reasons for–

(a) any refusal of consent in whole or in part;

(b) any decision to attach any condition under regulation 13(1)(b) to a consent, except a condition specified in Schedule 3 in a case to which regulation 13(4) applies; and

(c) any condition imposing a shorter period than that specified in regulation 13(5)(a), except where the application specified that shorter period.

Appeals to the Secretary of State

15.—(1) Sections 36 and 37 of the Act shall apply, in relation to applications for express consent under these Regulations, subject to the modifications set out in Part I of Schedule 4.

(2) The provisions of sections 36 and 37, as modified under paragraph (1) above, are set out in Part II of Schedule 4.

(3) Where a discontinuance notice is served under regulation 8, section 36 of the Act shall apply with the modifications specified in Part III of Schedule 4.

Revocation or modification of express consent

16.—(1) If a local planning authority are satisfied that it is expedient, they may by order revoke or modify an express consent, subject to paragraphs (2) to (6) below.

(2) An order under paragraph (1) above shall not take effect without the approval of the Secretary of State, which may be granted with or without modifications.

(3) When an authority submit an order made under this regulation to the Secretary of State for approval, they shall serve notice on the person who applied for the express consent, the owner and the occupier of the land affected and any other person who, in their opinion, will be affected by the order, specifying a period of at least 28 days from the service of the notice, within which an objection may be made, as provided in paragraph (4) below.

(4) If, within the period specified in the notice, an objection to the order is received by the Secretary of State from any person on whom notice is served, the Secretary of State shall, before approving the order, give to that person and to the local planning authority an opportunity of appearing before and being heard by a person appointed by him.

(5) The power to make an order under this regulation may be exercised–

(a) in a case which involves the carrying out of building or other operations, at any time before those operations have been completed;

(b) in any other case, at any time before the display of advertisements is begun.

(6) In a case to which paragraph (5)(a) above applies, the revocation or modification of consent shall not affect such operations as have already been carried out.

Compensation for revocation or modification

17.—(1) Where–

(a) an order under regulation 16 takes effect; and

(b) a claim is made in accordance with paragraph (2) below,

a local planning authority shall pay compensation to any person suffering loss or damage in the circumstances and to the extent specified in paragraph (3) below.

(2) A claim for compensation shall be made in writing and served on the local planning authority, by delivery at the offices of the authority or by post to their offices, within 6 months of the approval of the order to which it relates.

(3) Compensation is payable if, and to the extent that, any person has–

(a) incurred expenditure in carrying out abortive work, including the preparation of plans or similar material;

(b) otherwise sustained loss or damage directly attributable to the order, other than loss or damage consisting of any depreciation in value of any interest in land,

but excluding any work done, or loss or damage arising out of anything done or not done before the grant of consent.

PART IV

AREAS OF SPECIAL CONTROL

Area of Special Control Orders

18.—(1) Every local planning authority shall from time to time consider whether any part or additional part of their area should be designated as an area of special control.

(2) An area of special control shall be designated by an area of special control order made by the local planning authority and approved by the Secretary of State, in accordance with the provisions of Schedule 5.

(3) An area of special control order may be revoked or modified by a subsequent order

made by the authority and approved by the Secretary of State, in accordance with the provisions of Schedule 5.

(4) Where an area of special control order is in force, the local planning authority shall consider at least once in every 5 years whether it should be revoked or modified.

(5) Before making an order under this regulation, a local planning authority shall consult–

(a) where it appears to them that the order will be likely to affect any part of the area of a neighbouring local planning authority, that authority;

(b) where the order will relate to any land within a National Park, any district planning authority within whose area any of that land is situated.

(6) A local planning authority shall not exercise their power under this regulation in the interests of public safety within the meaning of regulation 4(1).

Control in areas of special control

19.—(1) No advertisements may be displayed in an area of special control unless they come within–

(a) Classes B to J in Schedule 2;

(b) Classes 1 to 3 and 5 to 14 in Schedule 3; or

(c) paragraphs (2) to (5) below.

(2) Advertisements of the following descriptions may be displayed in an area of special control with express consent, subject to paragraph (3) below–

(a) hoardings or similar structures to be used only for the display of notices relating to local events, activities or entertainments;

(b) any advertisement for the purpose of announcement or direction in relation to buildings or other land in the locality, reasonably required having regard to the nature and situation of such buildings or other land;

(c) any advertisement required in the interests of public safety;

(d) any advertisement which could be displayed under paragraph (1) above but for some non-compliance with a condition or limitation as respects size, height from the ground, number or illumination imposed by Schedule 3.

(3) Express consent may not be given for the purposes of paragraph (2) above for an illuminated advertisement, other than one illuminated for the purpose of indicating that medical or similar services or supplies are available at the premises on which the advertisement is displayed.

(4) On the coming into force of an area of special control order–

(a) any advertisement within paragraph (2)(d) above for which express consent has been granted may continue to be displayed after the expiry of that consent, by virtue of Class 14 in Schedule 3, subject to the power of the local planning authority to serve a discontinuance notice under regulation 8;

(b) any other advertisement for which express consent has been given may continue to be displayed for 6 months from the date on which the order comes into force or for the remainder of the term of the consent, whichever is the longer; and

(c) any other advertisement displayed in accordance with these Regulations may continue to be displayed for 8 months from the date on which the order comes into force.

(5) Where paragraph (4)(b) or (c) above applies, the relevant advertisement shall be removed forthwith, at the end of the relevant period, unless a further consent is granted for its continued display in accordance with this regulation.

(6) Nothing in the foregoing provisions of this regulation shall–

(a) affect a notice served under regulation 8 at any time;

(b) override any condition attached to a consent, whereby the advertisement is required to be removed;

(c) restrict the powers of a local planning authority, or of the Secretary of State, in regard to any contravention of these Regulations;

(d) restrict the power of the local planning authority, or of the Secretary of State, to consent to the display, in an area of special control, of an advertisement of a class in respect of which a direction under regulation 7 is in force.

PART V

MISCELLANEOUS

Compensation under section 176 of the Act

20.—(1) The time limit prescribed for the purpose of making a claim for compensation under section 176 of the Act is a period of 6 months from the completion of works carried out–

(a) to remove an advertisement displayed on 1st August 1948; or

(b) to discontinue the use for the display of advertisements of a site used since that date.

(2) Any such claim shall contain such information as the local planning authority consider is required to enable them properly to determine the claim.

Register of applications

21.—(1) Every local planning authority shall keep a register containing particulars of–

(a) any application made to them for express consent for the display of an advertisement, including the name and address of the applicant, the date of the application and the type of advertisement concerned;

(b) any direction given under these Regulations relating to the application;

(c) the date and effect of any decision of the local planning authority on the application;

(d) the date and effect of any decision of the Secretary of State on an appeal.

(2) The register shall include an index to enable a person to trace any entry therein.

(3) Any part of the register which relates to land within a particular part of the area of a local planning authority may be kept at a place within or convenient to that part of their area.

(4) Subject to paragraph (3) above, the register shall be kept at the office of the local planning authority.

(5) Every entry in the register consisting of particulars of an application shall be made within 14 days of the receipt of that application.

(6) The register shall be open to public inspection at all reasonable hours.

Powers of the Secretary of State

22.—(1) The Secretary of State may give a direction to a local planning authority, or to such authorities generally, requiring them to provide him with information required for the purpose of any of his functions under these Regulations.

(2) Subject to regulation 23 below, if it appears to the Secretary of State, after consultation with the local planning authority, that–

(a) a discontinuance notice should be served under regulation 8; or

(b) an area of special control order or a revocation order under regulation 18 should be made,

he may himself serve such a notice or make such an order.

(3) Where the Secretary of State proposes to exercise his power under paragraph (2) above, the provisions of regulations 8, 15 and 18 shall apply, with such modifications as may be necessary, as they apply to the action of a local planning authority.

Secretary of State's discontinuance notice

23.—(1) If the Secretary of State is satisfied that it is necessary to remedy a substantial injury to the amenity of the locality or a danger to members of the public, he may serve a discontinuance notice under regulation 8 above in relation to an advertisement within Class 1B in Schedule 3.

(2) Paragraphs (2), (5) and (6) of regulation 8 shall apply to a discontinuance notice to which paragraph (1) above applies as if references to the local planning authority were references to the Secretary of State.

(3) Regulation 15(3) above shall apply to a discontinuance notice to which paragraph (1) above applies, with such modifications as may be necessary.

Extension of time limits

24. The Secretary of State may, in any particular case, extend the time within which anything is required to be done under these Regulations or within which any objection, representation or claim for compensation may be made.

Directions

25. Any power conferred by these Regulations to give a direction includes power to cancel or vary the direction by a subsequent direction.

Contravention of Regulations

26. A person displaying an advertisement in contravention of these Regulations shall be liable on summary conviction of an offence under section 109(2) of the Act to a fine of an amount not exceeding level 3 on the standard scale and, in the case of a continuing offence, £40 for each day during which the offence continues after conviction.

Statutory Instruments revoked

27. The Town and Country Planning (Control of Advertisements) Regulations 1984**(a)**, the Town and Country Planning (Control of Advertisements) (Amendment) Regulations 1987**(b)** and the Town and Country Planning (Control of Advertisements) (Amendment No. 2) Regulations 1987**(c)** are hereby revoked.

Nicholas Ridley
13th April 1989 Secretary of State for the Environment

Peter Walker
13th April 1989 Secretary of State for Wales

Regulation 2(1)

SCHEDULE 1

STANDARD CONDITIONS

1. Any advertisements displayed, and any site used for the display of advertisements, shall be maintained in a clean and tidy condition to the reasonable satisfaction of the local planning authority.

2. Any structure or hoarding erected or used principally for the purpose of displaying advertisements shall be maintained in a safe condition.

(a) S.I. 1984/421.
(b) S.I. 1987/804.
(c) S.I. 1987/2227.

3. Where an advertisement is required under these Regulations to be removed, the removal shall be carried out to the reasonable satisfaction of the local planning authority.

4. No advertisement is to be displayed without the permission of the owner of the site or any other person with an interest in the site entitled to grant permission.

5. No advertisement shall be sited or displayed so as to obscure, or hinder the ready interpretation of, any road traffic sign, railway signal or aid to navigation by water or air, or so as otherwise to render hazardous the use of any highway, railway, waterway (including any coastal waters) or aerodrome (civil or military).

SCHEDULE 2

Regulation 3

CLASSES OF ADVERTISEMENTS TO WHICH PARTS II AND III OF THESE REGULATIONS DO NOT APPLY

Description of advertisement	*Conditions, limitations and interpretation*
CLASS A	
The display of an advertisement on or consisting of a balloon not more than 60 metres above ground level.	1. The site of the advertisement is not within an area of outstanding natural beauty, a conservation area, a National Park, the Broads or an area of special control. 2. Not more than one such advertisement may be displayed at any time. 3. The site may not be used for the display of advertisements on more than 10 days in total in any calendar year. 4. For the purposes of Class A, "the site" means– (a) in a case where the advertisement is being displayed by a person (other than the occupier of the land) who is using, or proposing to use, the land to which the balloon is attached for a particular activity (other than the display of advertisements) for a temporary period, the whole of the land used, or to be used, for that activity; or (b) in any other case, the land to which the balloon is attached and all land normally occupied together therewith.
CLASS B	
An advertisement displayed on enclosed land.	1. The advertisement is not readily visible from outside or from any place to which the public have a right of access. 2. For the purposes of Class B, "enclosed land" includes any railway station (and its yards) or bus station, together with its forecourt, whether enclosed or not; but does not include any public park, public garden or other land held for the use or enjoyment of the public, or (save as herein specified) any enclosed railway land normally used for the carriage of passengers or goods by rail.

SCHEDULE 2 – *continued*

Description of advertisement	*Conditions, limitations and interpretation*
CLASS C	
An advertisement displayed on or in a vehicle.	1. The vehicle is not– (a) normally employed except as a moving vehicle; or (b) used principally for the display of advertisements.
CLASS D	
An advertisement incorporated in the fabric of a building.	1. The building or any external face of it is not used principally for the display of advertisements. 2. For the purposes of Class D– (a) an advertisement fixed to, or painted on, a building is not to be regarded as incorporated in its fabric; (b) a hoarding or similar structure is to be regarded as a building used principally for the display of advertisements.
CLASS E	
An advertisement displayed on an article for sale or on the container in, or from which, an article is sold.	1. The advertisement refers only to the article for sale. 2. The advertisement may not be illuminated. 3. It may not exceed 0.1 square metre in area. 4. For the purposes of Class E, "article" includes a gas or liquid.
CLASS F	
An advertisement relating specifically to a pending Parliamentary, European Assembly or local government election.	1. The advertisement shall be removed within 14 days after the close of the poll in the election to which it relates.
CLASS G	
An advertisement required to be displayed by Standing Orders of either House of Parliament or by any enactment or any condition imposed by any enactment on the exercise of any power or function.	1. If the advertisement would, if it were not within this Class, fall within any Class in Schedule 3, any conditions imposed on that Class as to size, height or number of advertisements displayed shall apply to it. 2. In a case to which paragraph 1 does not apply, the size, height, and number of advertisements displayed shall not exceed what is necessary to achieve the purpose for which the advertisement is required. 3. The advertisement may not be displayed after the expiry of the period during which it is required or authorised to be displayed, or, if there is no such period, the expiry of a reasonable time after its purpose has been satisfied.

SCHEDULE 2–*continued*

Description of advertisement	*Conditions, limitations and interpretation*
CLASS H	
A traffic sign.	1. The sign is one approved under the Traffic Signs Regulations and General Directions 1981**(a)**, or any directions made under those Regulations, or one for whose display the authorisation of the Secretary of State has been given under section 64 of the Road Traffic Regulation Act 1984**(b)**.
CLASS I	
The national flag of any country.	1. Each flag is to be displayed on a single vertical flagstaff. 2. Neither the flag nor the flagstaff may display any advertisement or subject matter additional to the design of the flag.
CLASS J	
An advertisement displayed inside a building.	1. The advertisement may not be illuminated. 2. The building in which the advertisement is displayed is not used principally for the display of advertisements. 3. No part of the advertisement may be within 1 metre of any external door, window or other opening, through which it is visible from outside.

SCHEDULE 3

Regulation 6

CLASSES OF ADVERTISEMENTS WHICH MAY BE DISPLAYED WITH DEEMED CONSENT

PART I

SPECIFIED CLASSES AND CONDITIONS

Class 1 **Functional advertisements of local authorities, statutory undertakers and public transport undertakers**

Description **1A.** An advertisement displayed wholly for the purpose of announcement or direction in relation to any of the functions of a local authority or to the operation of a statutory undertaking or a public transport undertaking, which–

(a) is reasonably required to be displayed for the safe or efficient performance of those functions, or operation of that undertaking, and

(b) cannot be displayed by virtue of any other specified class.

Conditions and Limitations **1A.**—(1) Illumination is not permitted unless reasonably required for the purpose of the advertisement.

Description **1B.** An advertisement displayed by a local planning authority on land in their area.

Conditions and Limitations **1B.**—(1) In an area of special control, no advertisement may be displayed for which the authority could not have granted express consent.

(a) S.I. 1981/859.
(b) 1984 c.27.

Class 2	**Miscellaneous advertisements relating to the premises on which they are displayed**
Description	**2A.** An advertisement displayed for the purpose of identification, direction or warning, with respect to the land or building on which it is displayed.
Conditions and Limitations	**2A.**—(1) No such advertisement is to exceed 0.3 square metre in area. (2) Illumination is not permitted. (3) No character or symbol on the advertisement may be more than 0.75 metre in height, or 0.3 metre in an area of special control. (4) No part of the advertisement may be more than 4.6 metres above ground level, or 3.6 metres in an area of special control.
Description	**2B.** An advertisement relating to any person, partnership or company separately carrying on a profession, business or trade at the premises where it is displayed.
Conditions and Limitations	**2B.**—(1) No advertisement is to exceed 0.3 square metre in area. (2) No character or symbol on the advertisement may be more than 0.75 metre in height, or 0.3 metre in an area of special control. (3) No part of the advertisement may be more than 4.6 metres above ground level, or 3.6 metres in an area of special control. (4) Not more than one such advertisement is permitted for each person, partnership or company or, in the case of premises with entrances on different road frontages, one such advertisement at each of two such entrances. (5) Illumination is not permitted unless the advertisement states that medical or similar services or supplies are available on the premises and the illumination is in a manner reasonably required for that purpose.
Description	**2C.** An advertisement relating to any institution of a religious, educational, cultural, recreational or medical or similar character, or to any hotel, inn or public house, block of flats, club, boarding house or hostel, at the premises where it is displayed.
Conditions and Limitations	**2C.**—(1) Not more than one such advertisement is permitted in respect of each premises or, in the case of premises with entrances on different road frontages, one such advertisement at each of two such entrances. (2) No such advertisement may exceed 1.2 square metres in area. (3) No character or symbol on the advertisement may be more than 0.75 metre in height, or 0.3 metre in an area of special control. (4) No part of the advertisement may be more than 4.6 metres above ground level, or 3.6 metres in an area of special control. (5) Illumination is not permitted unless the advertisement states that medical or similar services or supplies are available at the premises and the illumination is in a manner reasonably required for that purpose.
Class 3	**Miscellaneous temporary advertisements**
Description	**3A.** An advertisement relating to the sale or letting, for residential, agricultural, industrial or commercial use or for development for such use, of the land or premises on which it is displayed.
Conditions and Limitations	**3A.**—(1) (a) Not more than one such advertisement, consisting of a single board or two joined boards, is permitted. (b) Where more than one such advertisement is displayed, the first to be displayed shall be taken to be the one permitted. (2) No advertisement may be displayed indicating that land or premises have been sold or let, other than by the addition to an existing advertisement of a statement that a sale or letting has been agreed, or that the land or premises have been sold or let, subject to contract. (3) Any Class 3A advertisement shall be removed within 14 days after the sale is completed or a tenancy is granted.

(4) No such advertisement may exceed in area–

(a) where the advertisement relates to residential use or development, 0.5 square metre or, in the case of two joined boards together, 0.6 square metre in aggregate;

(b) where the advertisement relates to any other use or development, 2 square metres or, in the case of two joined boards, 2.3 square metres.

(5) Where the advertisement is displayed on a building, the maximum projection permitted from the face of the building is 1 metre.

(6) Illumination is not permitted.

(7) No character or symbol on the advertisement may be more than 0.75 metre in height, or 0.3 metre in an area of special control.

(8) No part of the advertisement may be higher above ground level than 4.6 metres, or 3.6 metres in an area of special control or, in the case of a sale or letting of part only of a building, the lowest level of that part of the building on which display is reasonably practicable.

Description

3B. An advertisement announcing the sale of goods or livestock, and displayed on the land where the goods or livestock are situated or where the sale is held, not being land which is normally used, whether at regular intervals or otherwise, for the purpose of holding such sales.

Conditions and Limitations

3B.—(1) (a) Not more than one such advertisement may be displayed at any one time on the land concerned.

(b) Where more than one such advertisement is displayed, the first to be displayed shall be taken to be the one permitted.

(2) No such advertisement may be displayed earlier than 28 days before the day (or first day) on which the sale is due to take place.

(3) Any such advertisement shall be removed within 14 days after the sale is completed.

(4) No such advertisement may exceed 1.2 square metres in area.

(5) Illumination is not permitted.

(6) No character or symbol on the advertisement may be more than 0.75 metre in height, or 0.3 metre in an area of special control.

(7) No part of the advertisement may be more than 4.6 metres above ground level, or 3.6 metres in an area of special control.

Description

3C. An advertisement relating to the carrying out of building or similar work on the land on which it is displayed, not being land which is normally used, whether at regular intervals or otherwise, for the purposes of carrying out such work.

Conditions and Limitations

3C.—(1) (a) Not more than one such advertisement shall be displayed at any time, on each road frontage of the land, in respect of each separate development project, except in the case mentioned in paragraph (4) below.

(b) Where more than one such advertisement is displayed, the first to be displayed shall be taken to be the one permitted.

(2) No such advertisement may be displayed except while the relevant works are being carried out.

(3) No such advertisement may exceed in aggregate–

(a) in the case of an advertisement referring to one person–

(i) if the display is more than 10 metres from a highway, 3 square metres in area; or

(ii) in any other case, 2 square metres;

(b) in the case of an advertisement referring to more than one person–

(i) if the display is more than 10 metres from a highway, 3 square metres plus 0.6 square metre for each additional person, or

(ii) in any other case, 2 square metres plus 0.4 square metre for each additional person,

together with 0.2 of the area permitted under sub-paragraph (a) or (b) above for the name, if any, of the development project.

(4) Where any such advertisement does not refer to any person carrying out such work, that person may display a separate advertisement with a maximum area of 0.5 square metre, which does so refer, on each frontage of the land for a maximum period of 3 months.

(5) Illumination is not permitted.

(6) No character or symbol on the advertisement may be more than 0.75 metre in height, or 0.3 metre in an area of special control.

(7) No part of the advertisement may be more than 4.6 metres above ground level, or 3.6 metres in an area of special control.

Description

3D. An advertisement–

(i) announcing any local event of a religious, educational, cultural, political, social or recreational character,

(ii) relating to any temporary matter in connection with an event or local activity of such a character,

not being an event or activity promoted or carried on for commercial purposes.

Conditions and Limitations

3D.—(1) No such advertisement may exceed 0.6 square metre in area.

(2) No such advertisement may be displayed earlier than 28 days before the day (or first day) on which the event is due to take place.

(3) Any such advertisement shall be removed within 14 days after the end of the event.

(4) Illumination is not permitted.

(5) No character or symbol on the advertisement may be more than 0.75 metre in height, or 0.3 metre in an area of special control.

(6) No part of the advertisement may be more than 4.6 metres above ground level, or 3.6 metres in an area of special control.

Description

3E. An advertisement relating to any demonstration of agricultural methods or processes, on the land on which it is displayed.

Conditions and Limitations

3E.—(1) No such advertisement may be displayed for more than 6 months in any period of 12 months.

(2) The maximum area of display permitted in respect of each demonstration is 1.2 square metres.

(3) No single advertisement within such a display may exceed 0.4 square metre in area.

(4) No such advertisement may be displayed earlier than 28 days before the day (or first day) on which the demonstration is due to take place and shall be removed within 14 days after the end of the demonstration.

(5) Illumination is not permitted.

(6) No character or symbol on the advertisement may be more than 0.75 metre in height, or 0.3 metre in an area of special control.

(7) No part of the advertisement may be more than 4.6 metres above ground level, or 3.6 metres in an area of special control.

Description

3F. An advertisement relating to the visit of a travelling circus, fair or similar travelling entertainment to any specified place in the district.

Conditions and Limitations

3F.—(1) No such advertisement may exceed 0.6 square metre in area.

(2) No such advertisement may be displayed earlier than 14 days before the first performance or opening of the entertainment at the place specified.

(3) Any such advertisement shall be removed within 7 days after the last performance or closing of the specified entertainment.

(4) At least 14 days before the advertisement is first displayed, the local planning authority are to be notified in writing of the first date on which, and of the site at which, it is to be displayed.

(5) Illumination is not permitted.

(6) No part of the advertisement may be more than 3.6 metres above ground level.

Class 4 **Illuminated advertisements on business premises**

Description

4A. An illuminated advertisement displayed on the frontage of premises within a retail park, which overlook or face on to a communal car park wholly bounded by the retail park, where the advertisement refers wholly to the business carried on, and the name and qualifications of the person carrying on a business from the premises.

Conditions and Limitations

4A.—(1) Subject to paragraph (11) below, no such advertisement is permitted within a conservation area, an area of outstanding natural beauty, a National Park, an area of special control or the Broads.

(2) In the case of a shop, no such advertisement may be displayed except on a wall containing a shop window.

(3) Not more than one such advertisement parallel to a wall and one projecting at right angles from such a wall is permitted, and in the case of any projecting advertisement–

(a) no surface may be greater than 1 square metre in area;

(b) the advertisement may not project more than 1 metre from the wall; and

(c) it may not be more than 1.5 metres high.

(4) Each character of the advertisement but no part of the background is to be illuminated from within.

(5) No such advertisement may include any intermittent light source, moving feature, exposed cold cathode tubing, animation or reflective material.

(6) The luminance of any such advertisement may not exceed the limits specified in paragraph 3 of Part II of this Schedule.

(7) In the case of any advertisement consisting of a built-up box containing the light source, the distance between–

(a) the face of the advertisement and any wall parallel to which it is displayed, at the point where it is affixed, or

(b) the two faces of an advertisement projecting from a wall,

may not exceed 0.25 metre.

(8) The lowest part of any such advertisement must be at least 2.5 metres above ground level.

(9) No character or symbol on the advertisement may be more than 0.75 metre in height.

(10) No part of the advertisement may be higher above ground level than 4.6 metres or the bottom level of any first floor window in the wall on which the advertisement is displayed, whichever is the lower.

(11) Any such advertisement displayed on the date of designation of the relevant area, for the purposes of paragraph (1) above, may continue to be displayed for a period of 5 years from that date.

Description

4B. An illuminated advertisement, other than one falling within Class 4A, displayed on business premises wholly with reference to the business carried on and the name and qualifications of the person carrying on a business from those premises.

Conditions and Limitations

4B.—(1) Subject to paragraph (12) below, no such advertisement is permitted within a conservation area, an area of outstanding natural beauty, a National Park, an area of special control or the Broads.

(2) In the case of a shop, no such advertisement may be displayed except on a wall containing a shop window.

(3) Not more than one such advertisement parallel to a wall and one projecting at right angles from such a wall is permitted, and in the case of any projecting advertisement–

(a) no surface may be greater than 0.75 square metre in area;

(b) the advertisement may not project more than 1 metre from the wall or two thirds of the width of any footway or pavement below, whichever is the less;

(c) it may not be more than 1 metre high; and

(d) it may not project over any carriageway.

(4) Each character of the advertisement but no part of the background is to be illuminated from within.

(5) No such advertisement may include any intermittent light source, moving feature, exposed cold cathode tubing, animation or reflective material.

(6) The luminance of any such advertisement may not exceed the limits specified in paragraph 3 of Part II of this Schedule.

(7) In the case of any such advertisement consisting of a built-up box containing the light source, the distance between–

(a) the face of the advertisement and any wall parallel to which it is displayed, at the point where it is affixed, or

(b) the 2 faces of an advertisement projecting from a wall,

may not exceed 0.25 metre.

(8) The lowest part of any such advertisement shall be at least 2.5 metres above ground level.

(9) No surface of any advertisement may exceed one sixth of the frontage on which it is displayed, measured up to a height of 4.6 metres from ground level or 0.2 of the frontage measured to the top of the advertisement, whichever is the less.

(10) No character or symbol on the advertisement may be more than 0.75 metre in height.

(11) No part of the advertisement may be higher above ground level than 4.6 metres or the bottom level of any first floor window in the wall on which the advertisement is displayed, whichever is the lower.

(12) Any such advertisement displayed on the date of designation of the relevant area, for the purposes of paragraph (1) above, may continue to be displayed for a period of 5 years from that date.

Class 5 **Advertisements (other than illuminated advertisements) on business premises**

Description

5. Any advertisement which does not fall within Class 4A or 4B displayed on business premises wholly with reference to the business carried on, the goods sold or services provided, and the name and qualifications of the person carrying on the business, or supplying the goods or services, on those premises.

Conditions and Limitations

5.—(1) In the case of a shop, no such advertisement may be displayed, except on a wall containing a shop window.

(2) In an area of special control, the space occupied by any such advertisement may not exceed 0.1 of the overall area of the face of the building on which it is displayed, up to a height of 3.6 metres from ground level; and the area occupied by any such advertisement shall, notwithstanding that it is displayed in some other manner, be calculated as if the whole advertisement were displayed flat against the face of the building.

(3) Illumination is not permitted.

(4) No character or symbol on the advertisement may be more than 0.75 metre in height, or 0.3 metre in an area of special control.

(5) No part of the advertisement may be higher above ground level than whichever is the lower of–

(a) 4.6 metres, or 3.6 metres in an area of special control; or

(b) the bottom level of any first floor window in the wall on which the advertisement is displayed.

Class 6 **An advertisement on a forecourt of business premises**

Description

6. An advertisement displayed on any forecourt of business premises, wholly with reference to all or any of the matters specified in Class 5.

Conditions and Limitations

6.—(1) Advertisements displayed on any such forecourt or, in the case of a building with a forecourt on two or more frontages on each of those frontages, shall not exceed in aggregate 4.5 square metres in area.

(2) Illumination is not permitted.

(3) No character or symbol on the advertisement may be more than 0.75 metre in height, or 0.3 metre in an area of special control.

(4) No part of the advertisement may be more than 4.6 metres above ground level, or 3.6 metres in an area of special control.

Class 7 **Flag advertisements**

Description

7. An advertisement in the form of a flag attached to a single flagstaff projecting vertically from the roof of a building.

Conditions and Limitations

7.—(1) No such advertisement is permitted other than one–

(a) bearing the name or device of any person occupying the building; or

(b) referring to a specific event (other than the offering of named goods for sale) of limited duration, which is taking place in the building, for the duration of that event.

(2) No character or symbol on the flag may be more than 0.75 metre in height, or 0.3 metre in an area of special control.

Class 8 **Advertisements on hoardings**

Description

8. An advertisement on a hoarding which encloses, either wholly or in part, land on which building operations are taking place or are about to take place, if those operations are in accordance with a grant of planning permission (other than outline permission) for development primarily for use for commercial, industrial or business purposes.

Conditions and Limitations

8.—(1) Subject to paragraph (7) below, no such advertisement shall be displayed in a conservation area, an area of special control, a National Park, an area of outstanding natural beauty or the Broads.

(2) No such advertisement may be displayed earlier than one month before the commencement of the building operations.

(3) Any such advertisement shall be at least 1.5 metres high and 1 metre long and not more than 3.1 metres high and 6.1 metres long.

(4) At least 14 days before the advertisement is first displayed, the local planning authority shall be notified in writing by the person displaying it of the date on which it will first be displayed and shall be sent a copy of the relevant planning permission.

(5) No such advertisement shall be displayed for more than 2 years.

(6) Illumination is permitted in a manner and to the extent reasonably required to achieve the purpose of the advertisement.

(7) Any such advertisement displayed on the date of designation of the relevant area, for the purposes of paragraph (1) above, may continue to be displayed for a period of 1 year from that date or 2 years from the date of commencement of the display, whichever is the later.

Class 9 **Advertisements on highway structures**

Description

9. An advertisement displayed on a part of an object or structure designed to accommodate four-sheet panel displays, the use of which for the display of such advertisements is authorised under section 115E(1)(a) of the Highways Act 1980**(a)**.

Conditions and Limitations

9.—(1) No such advertisement may exceed 1.6 square metres in area.

(2) Illumination is not permitted.

(3) No character or symbol on the advertisement may be more than 0.75 metre in height, or 0.3 metre in an area of special control.

(4) No part of the advertisement may be more than 4.6 metres above ground level, or 3.6 metres in an area of special control.

(a) 1980 c.66; section 115E was inserted by the Local Government (Miscellaneous Provisions) Act 1982 (c.30), Schedule 5, Part I.

Class 10 **Advertisements for neighbourhood watch and similar schemes**

Description

10. An advertisement displayed on or near highway land (but not in the window of a building), to give notice that a neighbourhood watch scheme or a similar scheme established jointly by the police authority and a local committee or other body of persons is in operation in the area.

Conditions and Limitations

10.—(1) No such advertisement may exceed 0.2 square metre in area.

(2) No such advertisement may be displayed on highway land without the consent of the highway authority.

(3) The local planning authority shall, at least 14 days before the advertisement is first displayed, be given particulars in writing of the place at which it is to be displayed and a certificate–

(a) that the scheme has been properly established;

(b) that the police authority have agreed to the display of the advertisement; and

(c) where relevant, that the consent of the highway authority has been given.

(4) Any such advertisement shall be removed within 14 days after–

(a) the relevant scheme ceases to operate;

(b) the relevant scheme ceases to be approved by the police authority; or

(c) the highway authority withdraw their consent to its display.

(5) Illumination is not permitted.

(6) No character or symbol on the advertisement may be more than 0.75 metre in height, or 0.3 metre in an area of special control.

(7) No part of the advertisement may be more than 3.6 metres above ground level.

Class 11 **Directional advertisements**

Description

11A. An advertisement on a single flat surface directing potential buyers and others to a site where residential development is taking place.

Conditions and Limitations

11A.—(1) No such advertisement may exceed 0.15 square metre in area.

(2) No part of the advertisement may be of a reflective material.

(3) The design of the advertisement may not be similar to that of a traffic sign.

(4) The advertisement is to be displayed on land adjacent to highway land, in a manner which makes it reasonably visible to an approaching driver, but not within 50 metres of a traffic sign intended to be observed by persons approaching from the same direction, or within 25 metres of a Class 11B advertisement.

(5) No advertisement may be more than two miles from the main entrance of the site.

(6) The local planning authority shall, at least 14 days before the advertisement is first displayed, be notified in writing of the place at which, and the first date on which, it will be displayed.

(7) No such advertisement may be displayed after the development of the site is completed or, in any event, for more than 2 years.

(8) Illumination is not permitted.

(9) Any character or symbol on the advertisement shall be at least 0.04 metre high.

(10) No character or symbol on the advertisement may be more than 0.25 metre high.

(11) No part of the advertisement may be more than 4.6 metres above ground level, or 3.6 metres in an area of special control.

Description

11B. In the Ashford, Dover and Shepway experimental area, an advertisement displayed to direct visitors to the locality of a tourist attraction or a tourist facility.

Conditions and Limitations

11B.—(1) Any such advertisement is to consist of white characters or symbols on a brown background.

(2) No such advertisement may exceed 0.5 square metre in area.

(3) No part of any such advertisement may be of a reflective material or illuminated.

(4) Any such advertisement is to be displayed on land adjacent to a highway (but not on highway land), by which the specified tourist attraction or facility may be approached.

(5) Except for one advertisement which may be displayed at or immediately opposite the main entrance to the attraction or facility, any such advertisement is to be single-sided and displayed so as to be reasonably visible to a driver of a vehicle approaching it and may not be displayed–

(a) within 50 metres of an existing traffic sign, if it faces in the same direction as that traffic sign;

(b) within 25 metres of an existing directional advertisement for any tourist attraction or facility;

(c) if there is already an existing directional advertisement for the specified tourist attraction or facility, on the same approach route to that attraction or facility; and

(d) outside a radius of 2 miles from the main entrance to that attraction or facility.

(6) The advertiser shall, not later than 21 days before the date on which it is first displayed–

(a) notify the local planning authority in writing of the date on which the advertisement will be displayed, the precise location of the advertisement, and the tourist attraction or facility specified; and

(b) provide the local planning authority, by means of a scale drawing, or a plan, or a coloured photograph, with a description from which the advertisement may be readily identified.

(7) Any character or symbol on the advertisement shall be at least 0.04 metre high.

(8) No character or symbol on the advertisement may be more than 0.25 metre high.

(9) No part of the advertisement may be more than 4.6 metres above ground level, or 3.6 metres in an area of special control.

Class 12 **Advertisements inside buildings**

Description

12. An advertisement displayed inside a building which does not fall within Class J in Schedule 2.

Class 13 **Sites used for the display of advertisements on 1st April 1974**

Description

13. An advertisement displayed on a site which was used for the display of advertisements without express consent on 1st April 1974 and has been so used continually since that date.

Conditions and Limitations

13.—(1) No substantial increase in the extent, or substantial alteration in the manner, of the use of the site for the display of advertisements on 1st April 1974 is permitted.

(2) If any building or structure on which such an advertisement is displayed is required by any enactment to be removed, no erection of any building or structure to continue the display is permitted.

Class 14	**Advertisements displayed after expiry of express consent**
Description	**14.** An advertisement displayed with express consent, after the expiry of that consent, unless– (a) a condition to the contrary was imposed on the consent, or (b) a renewal of consent was applied for and refused.
Conditions and Limitations	**14.**—(1) Any condition imposed on the relevant express consent is to continue to apply to any such advertisement. (2) No advertisement may be displayed under this class except on a site which has been continually used for the purpose since the expiry of the express consent.

PART II

INTERPRETATION

1.—(1) In Part I of this Schedule–

(1) "business premises" means any building or part of a building normally used for the purpose of any professional, commercial or industrial undertaking, or for providing services to members of the public or of any association, and includes a public restaurant, licensed premises and a place of public entertainment, but not–

(a) a building used as an institution of a religious, educational, cultural, recreational, or medical or similar character;

(b) a building designed for use as one or more separate dwellings, unless it was normally used, immediately before 1st September 1949, for any such purpose or has been adapted for use for any such purpose by the construction of a shop front or the making of a material alteration of a similar kind to its external appearance;

(c) any forecourt or other land forming part of the curtilage of a building;

(d) any fence, wall or similar screen or structure, unless it forms part of the fabric of a building;

"existing directional advertisement" does not include any advertisement displayed without express or deemed consent;

"forecourt" includes any fence, wall or similar screen or structure enclosing a forecourt and not forming part of the fabric of a building constituting business premises;

"ground level", in relation to the display of advertisements on any building, means the ground-floor level of that building;

"joined boards" means boards joined at an angle, so that only one surface of each is usable for advertising;

"public transport undertaking" means an undertaking engaged in the carriage of passengers in a manner similar to that of a statutory undertaking;

"retail park" means a group of 3 or more retail stores, at least one of which has a minimum internal floor area of 1,000 square metres and which–

(a) are set apart from existing shopping centres but within an existing or proposed urban area;

(b) sell primarily goods other than food;

(c) share one or more communal car parks.

"traffic sign" means a sign falling within Class H of Schedule 2 to these Regulations.

(2) Where a maximum area is specified, in relation to any class in this Schedule, in the case of a double-sided board, the area of one side only shall be taken into account.

2. For the purposes of assessing the effect on amenity and public safety of advertisements falling within the description in Class 11B, an area comprising the borough of Ashford, and the districts of Dover and Shepway is defined as the Ashford Dover and Shepway experimental area for a period of 2 years beginning on 1st July 1987.

3.—(1) The permitted limits of luminance for advertisements falling within Class 4A or 4B are, subject to sub-paragraph (2), for an illuminated area measuring not more than–

(a) 0.5 square metre, 1,000 candela,

(b) 2 square metres, 800 candela,

(c) 10 square metres, 600 candela,

and for any greater area, 400 candela.

(2) For the purposes of calculating the relevant area for the permitted limits–

(a) each advertisement, or in the case of a double-sided projecting advertisement, each side of the advertisement is to be taken separately;

(b) no unilluminated part of the advertisement is to be taken into account.

SCHEDULE 4

Regulation 15

APPEALS TO THE SECRETARY OF STATE

PART I

MODIFICATIONS OF THE ACT (APPLICATIONS FOR EXPRESS CONSENT)

1. In section 36 of the Act–

(a) in subsection (1), for the words from "for planning permission" to "permission, consent, agreement or approval," substitute "for express consent under the Town and Country Planning (Control of Advertisements) Regulations 1989 and";

(b) for subsection (2), substitute the following subsections:–

"(2) Notice of appeal shall be given in writing to the Secretary of State within 8 weeks from the date of receipt of notification of the local planning authority's decision, or such longer period as the Secretary of State may at any time allow, and the notice shall be accompanied by a copy of each of the following documents:–

(a) the application made to the local planning authority;

(b) all relevant plans and particulars submitted to them;

(c) the notice of decision; and

(d) all other relevant correspondence with the authority.

(2A) Where an appeal is brought under this section, the Secretary of State may require the applicant or the local planning authority to submit to him, within such period as he may specify, a statement in writing in respect of such matters relating to the application as he may specify, and if, after considering the grounds of appeal and any such statement, the Secretary of State is satisfied that he has sufficient information to enable him to determine the appeal he may, with the agreement in writing of both the applicant and the local planning authority, determine the appeal without complying with subsection (4) of this section.";

(c) after subsection (3), insert–

"(3A) The Secretary of State may, in granting an express consent, specify that the term thereof shall run for such longer or shorter period than five years as he considers expedient, having regard to regulation 4 of the Regulations and to any period specified in the application for consent.";

(d) subsection (5) shall be omitted;

(e) at the end of subsection (6), add the words "and shall otherwise have effect as if it were a decision of the local planning authority";

(f) in subsection (7), for the words from "in respect of an application for planning permission" to "planning permission for that development", substitute the words "in respect of an application for express consent under the Regulations, the Secretary of State forms the opinion that, having regard to the Regulations and to any direction given under them, consent".

2. In section 37–

(a) for the words from the beginning to "order" in the first place where it appears, substitute "Where any such application as is mentioned in section 36(1) of this Act (as applied and modified by the Town and Country Planning (Control of Advertisements) Regulations 1989) is made to a local planning authority then, unless within the period of 8 weeks from the date when the application was received by the local planning authority";

(b) for the words from "either" to "section 35 of this Act" substitute "give notice to the applicant of their decision on the application";

(c) for the words "permission or approval", substitute "consent";

(d) after the words "of this Act" insert "(as so modified)"; and

(e) for the words "at the end of the period prescribed by the development order" substitute "at the end of the period referred to above".

PART II

SECTIONS 36 AND 37 OF THE ACT AS MODIFIED (APPLICATIONS FOR EXPRESS CONSENT)

"36.—(1) Where an application is made to a local planning authority for express consent under the Town and Country Planning (Control of Advertisements) Regulations 1989 and is refused by that authority or granted by them subject to conditions, the applicant, if he is aggrieved by their decision, may by notice under this section appeal to the Secretary of State.

(2) Notice of appeal shall be given in writing to the Secretary of State within 8 weeks from the date of receipt of notification of the local planning authority's decision, or such longer period as the Secretary of State may at any time allow, and the notice shall be accompanied by a copy of each of the following documents:–

(a) the application made to the local planning authority;

(b) all relevant plans and particulars submitted to them;

(c) the notice of decision; and

(d) all other relevant correspondence with the authority.

(2A) Where an appeal is brought under this section, the Secretary of State may require the applicant or the local planning authority to submit to him, within such period as he may specify, a statement in writing in respect of such matters relating to the application as he may specify; and if, after considering the grounds of appeal and any such statement, the Secretary of State is satisfied that he has sufficient information to enable him to determine the appeal he may, with the agreement in writing of both the applicant and the local planning authority, determine the appeal without complying with subsection (4) of this section.

(3) Where an appeal is brought under this section from a decision of a local planning authority, the Secretary of State, subject to the following provisions of this section, may allow or dismiss the appeal, or may reverse or vary part of the decision of the local planning authority, whether the appeal relates to that part thereof or not, and may deal with the application as if it had been made to him in the first instance.

(3A) The Secretary of State may, in granting an express consent, specify that the term thereof shall run for such longer or shorter period than five years as he considers expedient having regard to regulation 4 of the Regulations and any period specified in the application for consent.

(4) Before determining an appeal under this section, other than an appeal referred to a Planning Inquiry Commission under section 48 of this Act, the Secretary of State shall, if either the applicant or the local planning authority so desire, afford to each of them an opportunity of appearing before, and being heard by, a person appointed by the Secretary of State for the purpose.

(6) The decision of the Secretary of State on any appeal under this section shall be final and shall otherwise have effect as if it were a decision of the local planning authority.

(7) If, before or during the determination of an appeal under this section in respect of an application for express consent under the Regulations, the Secretary of State forms the opinion that, having regard to the Regulations and to any direction given under them, consent could not have been granted by the local planning authority or could not have been granted by them otherwise than subject to the conditions imposed by them, he may decline to determine the appeal or to proceed with the determination of it.

(8) Schedule 9 to this Act applies to appeals under this section, including appeals under this section as applied by or under any provision of this Act.

37. Where any such application as is mentioned in section 36(1) of this Act (as applied and modified by the Town and Country Planning (Control of Advertisements) Regulations 1989) is made to a local planning authority then, unless within the period of 8 weeks from the date when the application was received by the local planning authority, or within such extended period as may at any time be agreed upon in writing between the applicant and the local planning authority, the local planning authority give notice to the applicant of their decision on the application, the provisions of section 36 of this Act (as so modified) shall apply in relation to the application as if the consent to which it relates had been refused by the local planning authority, and as if notification of their decision had been received by the applicant at the end of the period referred to above, or at the end of the said extended period, as the case may be".

PART III

MODIFICATIONS OF THE ACT (DISCONTINUANCE NOTICES)

1. In section 36 for subsections (1) and (2) substitute–

"(1) Where a discontinuance notice has been served on any person by a local planning authority under regulation 8 of the Town and Country Planning (Control of Advertisements)

Regulations 1989 that person may, if he is aggrieved by the notice, appeal by notice under this section to the Secretary of State.

(2) Notice of appeal shall be given in writing to the Secretary of State at any time before the date on which the discontinuance notice is due to take effect under regulation 8(3) taking account, where appropriate, of any extension of time under regulation 8(5) of the 1989 Regulations, or such longer period as the Secretary of State may allow, and the notice shall be accompanied by a copy of each of the following documents:–

(a) the discontinuance notice;

(b) any notice of variation thereof; and

(c) any relevant correspondence with the authority.

(2A) Where an appeal is brought under this section, as applied by regulation 15(3) of the 1989 Regulations, the Secretary of State may require the appellant or the local planning authority to submit to him, within such period as he may specify, a statement in writing in respect of such matters relating to the discontinuance notice as he may specify and if, after considering the grounds of appeal and any such statement, the Secretary of State is satisfied that he has sufficient information to enable him to determine the appeal, he may, with the agreement in writing of both the appellant and the local planning authority, determine the appeal without complying with subsection (4) of this section.".

2. In subsection (3)–

(i) omit the words "from a decision of a local planning authority";

(ii) for the words, "any part of the decision," substitute "any part of the discontinuance notice"; and

(iii) for the words "may deal with the application as if it had been made to him in the first instance.", substitute "may deal with the matter as if an application for express consent had been made and refused for the reasons stated for the taking of discontinuance action.".

3. For subsection (5), substitute–

"(5) On the determination of an appeal under this section, as applied by regulation 15(3) of the 1989 Regulations, the Secretary of State shall give such directions as may be necessary for giving effect to his determination, including, where appropriate, directions for quashing the discontinuance notice or for varying its terms in favour of the appellant.".

4. Subsection (7) shall be omitted.

SCHEDULE 5

Regulation 18

AREA OF SPECIAL CONTROL ORDERS

PART I

PROCEDURE FOR AREA OF SPECIAL CONTROL ORDERS

1. A local planning authority who propose–

(a) to designate an area of special control; or

(b) to modify an area of special control order,

shall make an area of special control order designating the area or indicating the modifications by reference to an annexed map.

2. If an area of special control order contains any descriptive matter relating to the area or the modifications in question, that descriptive matter shall prevail, in the case of any discrepancy with the map, unless the order provides to the contrary.

3. As soon as may be after the making of an area of special control order, the authority shall submit it to the Secretary of State for approval, together with–

(a) two certified copies of the order;

(b) a full statement of their reasons for making it;

(c) in the case of an order modifying an existing order, unless the boundaries of the existing area of special control are indicated on the map annexed to the order, a plan showing both these boundaries and the proposed modifications; and

(d) any additional certified copy of any of the material in subparagraphs (a) to (c) above, which the Secretary of State requires.

4. The authority shall forthwith publish in the London Gazette, and in two successive weeks in at least one newspaper circulating in the locality, a notice in prescribed Form 1.

5. If any objection is made to an order, in the manner and within the time provided for in the prescribed form, the Secretary of State–

(a) may offer all interested parties an opportunity to make representations to him in writing about any such operation, before such date as he may specify;

(b) may, and at the request of any interested party shall, either provide for a local inquiry to be held or afford to the parties an opportunity of a hearing before a person appointed by him.

6. After considering any representations or objections duly made and not withdrawn and, where applicable, the report of any person holding an inquiry or hearing, the Secretary of State may, subject to paragraph 7 below, approve the order with or without modifications.

7. If the Secretary of State proposes to make a modification for the inclusion of additional land in an order, he shall–

(a) publish notice of his intention to do so;

(b) afford an opportunity for the making of objections to, or representations about, the proposed modification; and

(c) if he considers it expedient, provide for a further inquiry or hearing to be held.

8. As soon as may be after the order has been approved, the local planning authority shall publish in the London Gazette, and in two successive weeks in at least one newspaper circulating in the locality, a notice of its approval in prescribed Form 2.

9. An area of special control order shall come into force on the date on which the notice of its approval is published in the London Gazette.

10. Where a local planning authority propose to make an order revoking an area of special control order, a map showing the existing area shall be annexed to the order, and the procedure prescribed in paragraphs 2 to 9 of this Schedule in relation to an order modifying an existing order shall be followed, subject to the modification that the prescribed forms of notice under paragraphs 4 and 8 respectively are prescribed Forms 3 and 4.

11. Any reference in this Part of this Schedule to a prescribed form is to the form bearing that number in Part II of this Schedule or a form substantially to the like effect.

PART II

FORMS OF NOTICE

FORM 1

Notice of an area of special control order

TOWN AND COUNTRY PLANNING ACT 1971

Town and Country Planning (Control of Advertisements) Regulations 1989

1. We, the (*insert name of Council*) give notice that we have submitted an area of special control order, made under regulation 18 of the Town and Country Planning (Control of Advertisements) Regulations 1989, to the Secretary of State *for the Environment/for Wales for approval under Schedule 5 to the Regulations.

2. *The order designates the area of land described in the Schedule hereto and shown on the map accompanying the order.

Or

*The order modifies the (*insert name of relevant order*) by *adding/removing the area of land described in the Schedule hereto and shown on the map accompanying the order.

3. A copy of the order and of the statement of the reasons for making it have been deposited at and will be available for inspection free of charge between the hours of

4. The order is about to be considered by the Secretary of State. Any objection to it must be made in writing, stating the grounds of objection, and sent to the *Department of the Environment/Welsh Office at
before (*insert a date at least 28 days from the date of 1st publication of the local advertisement*).

Signed ....
On behalf of ....
Date ....

*Delete whichever is inappropriate

SCHEDULE

(insert description of land)

FORM 2

Notice of approval of an area of special control order

TOWN AND COUNTRY PLANNING ACT 1971

Town and Country Planning (Control of Advertisements) Regulations 1989

1. We, the (*insert name of Council*) give notice that the Secretary of State *for the Environment/for Wales has approved *with modifications the (*insert name of order*) for the purposes of Schedule 5 to the Town and Country Planning (Control of Advertisements) Regulations 1989.

2. The order *designates as an area of special control the land described in the Schedule hereto/modifies the (*insert name of relevant order*) by adding/removing the land described in the Schedule hereto.

3. The order comes into force on (*insert date of publication in London Gazette*).

4. A copy of the order as approved has been deposited at
and will be available for inspection free of charge between the hours of

IMPORTANT

Regulation 19 of the 1989 Regulations contains important provisions about–

The advertisements permitted in an area of special control.
The circumstances in which existing advertisements must be removed after this order comes into force.

Signed ....
On behalf of ....
Date ....

*Delete inappropriate words

SCHEDULE

(insert description of land)

FORM 3

Notice of revocation of an area of special control order

TOWN AND COUNTRY PLANNING ACT 1971

Town and Country Planning (Control of Advertisements) Regulations 1989

1. We, the (*insert name of Council*) give notice that we have submitted an order revoking the (*insert name of relevant order*) made under regulation 18 of the Town and Country Planning (Control of Advertisement) Regulations 1989 to the Secretary of State *for the Environment/for Wales for approval under Schedule 5 to the Regulations.

2. A copy of the revocation order and of the statement of the reasons for making it have been deposited at
and will be available for inspection free of charge between the hours of

3. The revocation order is about to be considered by the Secretary of State. Any objection to it must be made in writing, stating the grounds of objection, and sent to the *Department of the Environment/Welsh Office at
before (*insert a date at least 28 days after the first publication of the local advertisement*).

Signed ....
On behalf of ....
Date ....

*Delete whichever is inappropriate

FORM 4

Notice of approval of an order revoking an area of special control order

TOWN AND COUNTRY PLANNING ACT 1971

Town and Country Planning (Control of Advertisements) Regulations 1989

1. We, the (*insert name of Council*) give notice that the Secretary of State *for the Environment/for Wales has approved an order revoking the (*insert name of order revoked*) for the purposes of Schedule 5 to the Town and Country Planning (Control of Advertisements) Regulations 1989.

2. The revocation order comes into force on (*insert date of publication in London Gazette*).

3. A copy of the revocation order as approved has been deposited at
and will be available for inspection free of charge between the hours of

Signed ....
On behalf of ....
Date ....
*Delete whichever is inapplicable

EXPLANATORY NOTE

(This note is not part of the Regulations)

These Regulations consolidate with amendments the Town and Country Planning (Control of Advertisements) Regulations 1984 and subsequent amending instruments.

The main provisions of the Regulations, which apply in England and Wales, concern the control by local planning authorities of the display of outdoor advertisements. Specified classes of advertisements are excluded from the Regulations and others may be displayed with deemed consent, subject to conditions and limitations and the power of local planning authorities to serve discontinuance notices (Part II). Applications to the local planning authority for express consent and the granting of consent subject to conditions are provided for, as are appeals to the Secretary of State where consent is refused or granted conditionally, and the revocation or modification of express consent (Part III). Part IV deals with the designation of areas of special control and Parts I and V with general and miscellaneous provisions.

The main changes made by the Regulations are–

(a) modification of the powers of the Secretary of State in directing that, in a specified case or class of case, advertisements should not be displayed without express consent (regulation 7);

(b) revision of the criteria on which a local planning authority may serve a discontinuance notice withdrawing deemed consent under Schedule 3 (regulation 8);

(c) clarification of the powers of a local planning authority to grant consent for part only of an application, with or without conditions (regulation 13);

(d) the introduction of two new classes of illuminated advertisement with deemed consent (Classes 4A and 4B in Schedule 3);

(e) other minor modifications to the Classes of advertisement with deemed consent (regulation 6 and Schedule 3);

(f) introduction of a power for an objection to an area of special control order to be dealt with by written representations, instead of a hearing, if the parties agree (Schedule 5, paragraph 5).

STATUTORY INSTRUMENTS

1989 No. 672

HEALTH AND SAFETY

The Health and Safety at Work etc. Act 1974 (Application outside Great Britain) (Variation) Order 1989

Made - - - -	*18th April 1989*
Laid before Parliament	*26th April 1989*
Coming into force	*22nd May 1989*

At the Court at Windsor Castle the 18th day of April 1989

Present,

The Queen's Most Excellent Majesty in Council

Her Majesty, in exercise of the powers conferred by section 84(3) and (4) of the Health and Safety at Work etc. Act 1974**(a)**, is pleased to order, by and with the advice of her Privy Council, and it is hereby ordered, as follows:–

Citation and commencement

1. This Order may be cited as the Health and Safety at Work etc. Act 1974 (Application outside Great Britain) (Variation) Order 1989 and shall come into force on 22nd May 1989.

Offshore Installations

2. For article 4(2) (definition of "offshore installation") of the Health and Safety at Work etc. Act 1974 (Application outside Great Britain) Order 1977**(b)** ("the 1977 Order") there shall be substituted the following provision–

"(2) In this Article–

"offshore installation" means an offshore installation within the meaning of section 1 of the Mineral Workings (Offshore Installations) Act 1971**(c)** which is within territorial waters or a designated area."

Pipelines

3. In article 5(2) of the 1977 Order (definition of "pipeline")

(a) after sub-paragraph (a) in the definition of "pipeline", there shall be inserted the following sub-paragraph–

(a) 1974 c.37.
(b) S.I. 1977/1232.
(c) 1971 c.61; section 1 was substituted by the Oil and Gas (Enterprise) Act 1982 (c.23), section 24.

"(aa) any apparatus for treating or cooling any thing which is to flow through, or through part of, the pipe or system;" and

(b) in sub-paragraph (ii) the words "and is capable of being manned" shall be omitted.

G. I. de Deney
Clerk of the Privy Council

EXPLANATORY NOTE

(This note is not part of the Order)

The Order varies the Health and Safety at Work etc. Act 1974 (Application outside Great Britain) Order 1977 by adopting the definition of "offshore installation" contained in the Mineral Workings (Offshore Installations) Act 1971 as amended by the Oil and Gas (Enterprise) Act 1982 (article 2). The principal effect is to apply the Health and Safety at Work etc. Act 1974 to gas storage and accommodation installations and installations in transit. The definition of "pipeline" is extended to bring it more closely into line with the definition in the Petroleum and Submarine Pipe-lines Act 1975 (c.74), as amended by the Oil and Gas (Enterprise) Act 1982 (article 3).

STATUTORY INSTRUMENTS

1989 No. 673

TRUSTS

The Recognition of Trusts Act 1987 (Overseas Territories) Order 1989

Made - - - -	*18th April 1989*
Laid before Parliament	*26th April 1989*
Coming into force	*1st June 1989*

At the Court at Windsor Castle, the 18th day of April 1989

Present,

The Queen's Most Excellent Majesty in Council

Her Majesty, by and with the advice of Her Privy Council, and by virtue of the authority conferred upon Her by sections 2(2) and 2(3) of the Recognition of Trusts Act 1987**(a)** and of all other powers enabling Her in that behalf, is pleased to direct, and it is hereby directed, as follows:

1. This Order may be cited as the Recognition of Trusts Act 1987 (Overseas Territories) Order 1989 and shall come into force on 1st June 1989.

2.—(1) The Recognition of Trusts Act 1987 and the Schedule thereto, modified as in Schedule 1 hereto, shall form part of the law of the Territories specified in Schedule 2 hereto.

(2) For the purpose of construing the said Act as part of the law of any Territory to which it extends "the Territory" means that Territory.

G. I. de Deney
Clerk of the Privy Council

(a) 1987 c.14.

SCHEDULE 1 TO THE ORDER

Article 2(1)

THE RECOGNITION OF TRUSTS ACT 1987 AND THE SCHEDULE THERETO AS MODIFIED AND EXTENDED TO THE TERRITORIES SPECIFIED IN SCHEDULE 2 TO THE ORDER

1.—(1) The provisions of the Convention set out in the Schedule to this Act shall have the force of law in the Territory.

(2) Those provisions shall, so far as applicable, have effect not only in relation to the trusts described in Articles 2 and 3 of the Convention but also in relation to any other trusts of property arising under the law of the Territory or by virtue of a judicial decision whether in the Territory or elsewhere.

(3) In accordance with Articles 15 and 16 such provisions of the law as are there mentioned shall, to the extent there specified, apply to the exclusion of the other provisions of the Convention.

(4) In Article 17 the reference to a State includes a reference to any country or territory (whether or not a party to the Convention) which has its own system of law.

(5) Article 22 shall not be construed as affecting the law to be applied in relation to anything done or omitted before the coming into force of this Act.

3.—(1) This Act may be cited as the Recognition of Trusts Act 1987.

(3) This Act binds the Crown.

SCHEDULE TO THE ACT

Section 1

CONVENTION ON THE LAW APPLICABLE TO TRUSTS AND ON THEIR RECOGNITION

CHAPTER I – SCOPE

ARTICLE 1

This Convention specifies the law applicable to trusts and governs their recognition.

ARTICLE 2

For the purposes of this Convention, the term "trust" refers to the legal relationship created – inter vivos or on death – by a person, the settlor, when assets have been placed under the control of a trustee for the benefit of a beneficiary or for a specified purpose.

A trust has the following characteristics —

(a) the assets constitute a separate fund and are not a part of the trustee's own estate;

(b) title to the trust assets stands in the name of the trustee or in the name of another person on behalf of the trustee;

(c) the trustee has the power and the duty, in respect of which he is accountable, to manage, employ or dispose of the assets in accordance with the terms of the trust and the special duties imposed upon him by law.

The reservation by the settlor of certain rights and powers, and the fact that the trustee may himself have rights as a beneficiary, are not necessarily inconsistent with the existence of a trust.

ARTICLE 3

The Convention applies only to trusts created voluntarily and evidenced in writing.

ARTICLE 4

The Convention does not apply to preliminary issues relating to the validity of wills or of other acts by virtue of which assets are transferred to the trustee.

ARTICLE 5

The Convention does not apply to the extent that the law specified by Chapter II does not provide for trusts or the category of trusts involved.

CHAPTER II – APPLICABLE LAW

ARTICLE 6

A trust shall be governed by the law chosen by the settlor. The choice must be express or be implied in the terms of the instrument creating or the writing evidencing the trust, interpreted, if necessary, in the light of the circumstances of the case.

Where the law chosen under the previous paragraph does not provide for trusts or the category of trust involved, the choice shall not be effective and the law specified in Article 7 shall apply.

ARTICLE 7

Where no applicable law has been chosen, a trust shall be governed by the law with which it is most closely connected.

In ascertaining the law with which a trust is most closely connected reference shall be made in particular to —

(a) the place of administration of the trust designated by the settlor;
(b) the situs of the assets of the trust;
(c) the place of residence or business of the trustee;
(d) the objects of the trust and the places where they are to be fulfilled.

ARTICLE 8

The law specified by Article 6 or 7 shall govern the validity of the trust, its construction, its effects and the administration of the trust.

In particular that law shall govern —

(a) the appointment, resignation and removal of trustees, the capacity to act as a trustee, and the devolution of the office of trustee;
(b) the rights and duties of trustees among themselves;
(c) the right of trustees to delegate in whole or in part the discharge of their duties or the exercise of their powers;
(d) the power of trustees to administer or to dispose of trust assets, to create security interests in the trust assets, or to acquire new assets;
(e) the powers of investment of trustees;
(f) restrictions upon the duration of the trust, and upon the power to accumulate the income of the trust;
(g) the relationships between the trustees and the beneficiaries including the personal liability of the trustees to the beneficiaries;
(h) the variation or termination of the trust;
(i) the distribution of the trust assets;
(j) the duty of trustees to account for their administration.

ARTICLE 9

In applying this Chapter a severable aspect of the trust, particularly matters of administration, may be governed by a different law.

ARTICLE 10

The law applicable to the validity of the trust shall determine whether that law or the law governing a severable aspect of the trust may be replaced by another law.

CHAPTER III – RECOGNITION

ARTICLE 11

A trust created in accordance with the law specified by the preceding Chapter shall be recognised as a trust.

Such recognition shall imply, as a minimum, that the trust property constitutes a separate fund, that the trustee may sue and be sued in his capacity as trustee, and that he may appear or act in this capacity before a notary or any person acting in an official capacity.

In so far as the law applicable to the trust requires or provides, such recognition shall imply in particular —

(a) that personal creditors of the trustee shall have no recourse against the trust assets;
(b) that the trust assets shall not form part of the trustee's estate upon his insolvency or bankruptcy;
(c) that the trust assets shall not form part of the matrimonial property of the trustee or his spouse nor part of the trustee's estate upon his death;
(d) that the trust assets may be recovered when the trustee, in breach of trust, has mingled trust assets with his own property or has alienated trust assets. However, the rights and obligations of any third party holder of the assets shall remain subject to the law determined by the choice of law rules of the forum.

ARTICLE 12

Where the trustee desires to register assets, movable or immovable, or documents of title to them, he shall be entitled, in so far as this is not prohibited by or inconsistent with the law of the State where registration is sought, to do so in his capacity as trustee or in such other way that the existence of the trust is disclosed.

ARTICLE 14

The Convention shall not prevent the application of rules of law more favourable to the recognition of trusts.

CHAPTER IV – GENERAL CLAUSES

ARTICLE 15

The Convention does not prevent the application of provisions of the law designated by the conflicts rules of the forum, in so far as those provisions cannot be derogated from by voluntary act, relating in particular to the following matters —

(a) the protection of minors and incapable parties;
(b) the personal and proprietary effects of marriage;
(c) succession rights, testate and intestate, especially the indefeasible shares of spouses and relatives;
(d) the transfer of title to property and security interests in property;
(e) the protection of creditors in matters of insolvency;
(f) the protection, in other respects, of third parties acting in good faith.

If recognition of a trust is prevented by application of the preceding paragraph, the court shall try to give effect to the objects of the trust by other means.

ARTICLE 16

The Convention does not prevent the application of those provisions of the law of the forum which must be applied even to international situations, irrespective of rules of conflict of laws.

ARTICLE 17

In the Convention the word 'law' means the rules of law in force in a State other than its rules of conflict of laws.

ARTICLE 18

The provisions of the Convention may be disregarded when their application would be manifestly incompatible with public policy.

ARTICLE 22

The Convention applies to trusts regardless of the date on which they were created.

Article 2(1)

SCHEDULE 2 TO THE ORDER

Bermuda
British Antarctic Territory
Falkland Islands
St Helena and Dependencies
South Georgia and the South Sandwich Islands
Sovereign Base Areas of Akrotiri and Dhekelia
Virgin Islands

EXPLANATORY NOTE

(This note is not part of the Order)

This Order directs that the Recognition of Trusts Act 1987 and the Schedule thereto, subject to modifications, shall form part of the law of the Territories specified in Schedule 2 hereto.

STATUTORY INSTRUMENTS

1989 No. 674

CRIMINAL LAW, ENGLAND AND WALES

The Criminal Justice Act 1987 (Guernsey) Order 1989

Made - - - -	*18th April 1989*
Coming into force	*18th May 1989*

At the Court at Windsor Castle, the 18th day of April 1989

Present,

The Queen's Most Excellent Majesty in Council

Her Majesty, in pursuance of section 17(6) of the Criminal Justice Act 1987**(a)**, is pleased, by and with the advice of Her Privy Council, to order, and it is hereby ordered, as follows:

1.—(1) This Order may be cited as the Criminal Justice Act 1987 (Guernsey) Order 1989 and shall come into force on 18th May 1989.

(2) Without prejudice to its earlier revocation and subject to article 3 below this Order shall cease to have effect on the expiration of two years beginning with the date of its coming into force.

2. Section 2 of the Criminal Justice Act 1987**(b)** shall extend to the Bailiwick of Guernsey subject to the modifications specified in the Schedule to this Order.

3. In any case in which a request under section 2(1) of the Criminal Justice Act 1987, as modified in its extension to the Bailiwick of Guernsey by paragraph 2 of the Schedule to this Order, is made before the date on which this Order ceases to have effect by virtue of article 1(2) above, the powers of the Attorney General shall continue to be exercisable under that section as so modified as if this Order had not ceased to have effect.

G. I. de Deney
Clerk of the Privy Council

(a) 1987 c.38.
(b) Section 2 was amended by section 143 of, and paragraph 113 of Schedule 15 to, the Criminal Justice Act 1988 (c.33).

Article 2

SCHEDULE

MODIFICATIONS TO SECTION 2 OF THE CRIMINAL JUSTICE ACT 1987 AS EXTENDED TO THE BAILIWICK OF GUERNSEY

1. Any reference to section 2 of the Criminal Justice Act 1987 or any provision thereof shall be construed, unless the contrary intention appears, as a reference to it as it has effect in the Bailiwick of Guernsey; and any reference to section 1 of that Act shall be construed as a reference to it as it has effect in England and Wales and Northern Ireland.

2. In subsection (1)–

(a) for "Director" there shall be substituted "Attorney General", and

(b) for the words from "only" to "the request" there shall be substituted "only on a request made by the Director of the Serious Fraud Office for the purposes of an investigation under section 1 of this Act, or on a request made by the Lord Advocate for the purposes of an investigation under legislation corresponding to that section and having effect in Scotland".

3. In subsection (2)–

(a) for "Director" there shall be substituted "Attorney General", and

(b) after "specified place" there shall be inserted "in the Bailiwick of Guernsey".

4. In subsection (3)–

(a) for "Director" in each place where it occurs there shall be substituted "Attorney General", and

(b) after "such place" there shall be inserted "in the Bailiwick of Guernsey".

5. In subsection (4)–

(a) for "on information on oath laid by a member of the Serious Fraud Office, a justice of the peace" there shall be substituted "on an application by the Attorney General, the Bailiff", and

(b) for "the information" there shall be substituted "the application".

6. In subsection (5)–

(a) for "constable" there shall be substituted "police officer", and

(b) for "information" there shall be substituted "application".

7. For subsection (6) there shall be substituted the following subsection–

"(6) A police officer executing a warrant issued under subsection (4) above may be accompanied by any person or persons expressly authorised for that purpose by the Attorney General.".

8. For subsection (7) there shall be substituted the following subsection–

"(7) Without prejudice to his power to enter into agreements apart from this subsection, the Attorney General may enter into a written agreement for the supply of information to or by him subject, in either case, to an obligation not to disclose the information concerned otherwise than for a specified purpose.".

9. In subsection (9), for "High Court" there shall be substituted "Royal Court".

10. In subsection (10), for paragraph (b) there shall be substituted the following paragraph:–

"(b) the Attorney General has authorised the making of the requirement.".

11. For subsection (11) there shall be substituted the following subsection–

"(11) The Attorney General may authorise any Advocate to exercise on his behalf all or any of the powers conferred by this section, but no such authority shall be granted except for the purpose of investigating the affairs, or any aspect of the affairs, of a person specified in the authority.".

12. In subsection (15), for "not exceeding the statutory maximum" there shall be substituted "on level 5 of the standard scale".

13. In subsection (16)(a), after "Serious Fraud Office" there shall be inserted "or an officer nominated by the Lord Advocate".

14. In subsection (17), for paragraphs (a) and (b) there shall be substituted "on conviction, be liable to imprisonment for a term not exceeding 7 years or to a fine or to both".

15. For subsection (19), there shall be substituted the following subsection–

"(19) In this section, the expression–

"police officer" means an officer of the salaried police force of the Island of Guernsey;

"Serious Fraud Office" means the Serious Fraud Office constituted under section 1 of this Act.".

16. After subsection (19) there shall be inserted the following subsection–

"(20) In the application of subsection (4) above–

(a) to Alderney, the reference to "the Bailiff" shall include a reference to the President of the Court of Alderney or a jurat of that Court, and

(b) to Sark, the reference to "the Bailiff" shall include a reference to the Seneschal of Sark;

and in its application to Alderney and Sark the reference to "the Attorney General" shall include a reference to a police officer acting on the authority of the Attorney General.".

EXPLANATORY NOTE

(This note is not part of the Order)

This Order extends to the Bailiwick of Guernsey section 2 of the Criminal Justice Act 1987 subject to the modifications specified in the Schedule to the Order.

STATUTORY INSTRUMENTS

1989 No. 675

CRIMINAL LAW, ENGLAND AND WALES

The Criminal Justice Act 1987 (Jersey) Order 1989

Made - - - -	*18th April 1989*
Coming into force	*18th May 1989*

At the Court at Windsor Castle, the 18th day of April 1989

Present,

The Queen's Most Excellent Majesty in Council

Her Majesty, in pursuance of section 17(6) of the Criminal Justice Act 1987(**a**), is pleased, by and with the advice of Her Privy Council, to order, and it is hereby ordered, as follows:

1.—(1) This Order may be cited as the Criminal Justice Act 1987 (Jersey) Order 1989 and shall come into force on 18th May 1989.

(2) Without prejudice to its earlier revocation and subject to article 3 below this Order shall cease to have effect on the expiration of two years beginning with the date of its coming into force.

2. Section 2 of the Criminal Justice Act 1987(**b**) shall extend to the Bailiwick of Jersey subject to the modifications specified in the Schedule to this Order.

3. In any case in which a request under section 2(1) of the Criminal Justice Act 1987, as modified in its extension to the Bailiwick of Jersey by paragraph 2 of the Schedule to this Order, is made before the date on which this Order ceases to have effect by virtue of article 1(2) above, the powers of the Attorney General shall continue to be exercisable under that section as so modified as if this Order had not ceased to have effect.

G. I. de Deney
Clerk of the Privy Council

(**a**) 1987 c.38.
(**b**) Section 2 was amended by section 143 of, and paragraph 113 of Schedule 15 to, the Criminal Justice Act 1988 (c.33).

SCHEDULE

Article 2

MODIFICATIONS TO SECTION 2 OF THE CRIMINAL JUSTICE ACT 1987 AS EXTENDED TO THE BAILIWICK OF JERSEY

1. Any reference to section 2 of the Criminal Justice Act 1987 or any provision thereof shall be construed, unless the contrary intention appears, as a reference to it as it has effect in the Bailiwick of Jersey; and any reference to section 1 of that Act shall be construed as a reference to it as it has effect in England and Wales and Northern Ireland.

2. In subsection (1)–

(a) for "Director" there shall be substituted "Attorney General", and

(b) for the words from "only" to "the request" there shall be substituted "only on a request made by the Director of the Serious Fraud Office for the purposes of an investigation under section 1 of this Act, or on a request made by the Lord Advocate for the purposes of an investigation under legislation corresponding to that section and having effect in Scotland".

3. In subsection (2)–

(a) for "Director" there shall be substituted "Attorney General", and

(b) after "specified place" there shall be inserted "in the Bailiwick of Jersey".

4. In subsection (3)–

(a) for "Director" in each place where it occurs there shall be substituted "Attorney General", and

(b) after "such place" there shall be inserted "in the Bailiwick of Jersey".

5. In subsection (4)–

(a) for "on information on oath laid by a member of the Serious Fraud Office, a justice of the peace" there shall be substituted "on an application by the Attorney General, the Bailiff", and

(b) for "the information" there shall be substituted "the application".

6. In subsection (5)–

(a) for "constable" there shall be substituted "police officer", and

(b) for "information" there shall be substituted "application".

7. For subsection (6) there shall be substituted the following subsection–

"(6) A police officer executing a warrant issued under subsection (4) above may be accompanied by any person or persons expressly authorised for that purpose by the Attorney General.".

8. For subsection (7) there shall be substituted the following subsection–

"(7) Without prejudice to his power to enter into agreements apart from this subsection, the Attorney General may enter into a written agreement for the supply of information to or by him subject, in either case, to an obligation not to disclose the information concerned otherwise than for a specified purpose.".

9. In subsection (9), for "High Court" there shall be substituted "Royal Court".

10. In subsection (10), for paragraph (b) there shall be substituted the following paragraph–

"(b) the Attorney General has authorised the making of the requirement.".

11. For subsection (11) there shall be substituted the following subsection–

"(11) The Attorney General may authorise any Crown Advocate to exercise on his behalf all or any of the powers conferred by this section, but no such authority shall be granted except for the purpose of investigating the affairs, or any aspect of the affairs, of a person specified in the authority.".

12. In subsection (13), for the words from "summary conviction" to the end there shall be substituted "conviction to imprisonment for a term not exceeding six months or to a fine or to both".

13. In subsection (15), for paragraphs (a) and (b) there shall be substituted "on conviction, be liable to imprisonment for a term not exceeding two years or to a fine or to both".

14. In subsection (16)(a), after "Serious Fraud Office" there shall be inserted "or an officer nominated by the Lord Advocate".

15. In subsection (17), for paragraphs (a) and (b) there shall be substituted "on conviction, be liable to imprisonment for a term not exceeding 7 years or to a fine or to both".

16. For subsection (19), there shall be substituted the following subsection–

"(19) In this section, the expression–

"police officer" means a member of the Honorary Police or a member of the States of Jersey Police Force;

"Serious Fraud Office" means the Serious Fraud Office constituted under section 1 of this Act.".

EXPLANATORY NOTE

(This note is not part of the Order)

This Order extends to the Bailiwick of Jersey section 2 of the Criminal Justice Act 1987 subject to the modifications specified in the Schedule to the Order.

STATUTORY INSTRUMENTS

1989 No. 676

IMMIGRATION

The Immigration (Guernsey) (Variation) Order 1989

Made - - - -	*18th April 1989*
Coming into force	*18th May 1989*

At the Court at Windsor Castle, the 18th day of April 1989

Present,

The Queen's Most Excellent Majesty in Council

Her Majesty, in pursuance of section 36 of the Immigration Act 1971(**a**) as applied by section 2(3) of the Immigration (Carriers' Liability) Act 1987(**b**), is pleased, by and with the advice of Her Privy Council, to order, and it is hereby ordered, as follows:

1. This Order may be cited as the Immigration (Guernsey) (Variation) Order 1989 and shall come into force on 18th May 1989.

2. The Immigration (Guernsey) Order 1972(**c**) shall be further varied in accordance with the provisions of the Schedule to this Order.

G.I. de Deney
Clerk of the Privy Council

SCHEDULE

Article 2

VARIATIONS TO THE IMMIGRATION (GUERNSEY) ORDER 1972

1. After article 4 there shall be inserted the following article:

"**5.** The provisions of the Immigration (Carriers' Liability) Act 1987 shall extend to the Bailiwick of Guernsey with such exceptions, adaptations and modifications as are specified in the Schedule hereto.".

2.—(1) The Schedule shall be varied in accordance with the following provisions of this paragraph.

(**a**) 1971 c.77. (**b**) 1987 c.24. (**c**) S.I. 1972/1719, as amended by S.I. 1982/1834, 1983/1897.

(2) In paragraph 1(1), after "that Act" there shall be inserted "or to the Immigration (Carriers' Liability) Act 1987 or any provision thereof".

(3) In paragraph 2, there shall be added at the end the following provision:

"(3) In section 1(1) of the Immigration (Carriers' Liability) Act 1987, for the reference to the Secretary of State there shall be substituted a reference to the States.".

(4) After paragraph 35 there shall be added the following provisions:

"THE IMMIGRATION (CARRIERS' LIABILITY) ACT 1987

Section 1

36. In section 1–

(a) in subsection (3), for the words from "an order" to the end there shall be substituted "Ordinance of the States", and

(b) subsection (5) shall be omitted.

Section 2

37. In section 2–

(a) subsection (3) shall be omitted, and

(b) in subsection (4), for "4th March 1987" there shall be substituted "the date of the extension of this Act to the Bailiwick of Guernsey".".

EXPLANATORY NOTE

(This note is not part of the Order)

This Order varies the Immigration (Guernsey) Order 1972, as amended, so as to extend to the Bailiwick of Guernsey the Immigration (Carriers' Liability) Act 1987 with exceptions, adaptations and modifications.

STATUTORY INSTRUMENTS

1989 No. 678

NORTHERN IRELAND

The Matrimonial and Family Proceedings (Northern Ireland Consequential Amendment) Order 1989

Made - - - - 18th April 1989

Coming into force in accordance with Article 1(2)

At the Court at Windsor Castle, the 18th day of April 1989

Present,

The Queen's Most Excellent Majesty in Council

Whereas a draft of this Order has been approved by a resolution of each House of Parliament:

Now, therefore, Her Majesty, in exercise of the powers conferred by section 38(2) of the Northern Ireland Constitution Act 1973**(a)** as extended by paragraph 1(7) of Schedule 1 to the Northern Ireland Act 1974**(b)**, and of all other powers enabling Her in that behalf, is pleased, by and with the advice of Her Privy Council, to order, and it is hereby ordered as follows:–

Title, commencement and extent

1.—(1) This Order may be cited as the Matrimonial and Family Proceedings (Northern Ireland Consequential Amendment) Order 1989.

(2) This Order shall come into force on the day appointed under article 1(3) of the Matrimonial and Family Proceedings (Northern Ireland) Order 1989**(c)** for the coming into operation of Part IV of that Order.

(3) This Order extends to the whole of the United Kingdom.

Amendment of Maintenance Orders Act 1950

2. In section 16(2)(c) of the Maintenance Orders Act 1950**(d)** after sub-paragraph (viii)**(e)** there shall be inserted the following sub-paragraph–

"(ix) Article 18 or 21 of the Matrimonial and Family Proceedings (Northern Ireland) Order 1989;".

G. I. de Deney
Clerk of the Privy Council

(a) 1973 c.36; section 38 was amended by paragraph 6 of Schedule 2 to the Northern Ireland Act 1982 (c.38).
(b) 1974 c.28.
(c) S.I. 1989/677 (NI4).
(d) 1950 c.37.
(e) Inserted by paragraph 39 of Schedule 10 to the Social Security Act 1986 (c.50).

EXPLANATORY NOTE

(This note is not part of the Order)

This Order makes an amendment to the Maintenance Orders Act 1950 which is consequential on the Matrimonial and Family Proceedings (Northern Ireland) Order 1989. The Order brings orders under articles 18 and 21 of the Matrimonial and Family Proceedings (Northern Ireland) Order 1989 within the definition of maintenance order for the purposes of Part II of the Maintenance Orders Act 1950, thereby rendering such orders enforceable in other parts of the United Kingdom in accordance with that Part.

STATUTORY INSTRUMENTS

1989 No. 679

MERCHANT SHIPPING

The Merchant Shipping Act 1988 (Isle of Man) Order 1989

Made - - - -	*18th April 1989*
Laid before Parliament	*26th April 1989*
Coming into force	*18th May 1989*

At the Court at Windsor Castle, the 18th day of April 1989

Present,

The Queen's Most Excellent Majesty in Council

Her Majesty, in pursuance of section 738 of the Merchant Shipping Act 1894**(a)** and section 56 of the Merchant Shipping Act 1988**(b)**, is pleased, by and with the advice of Her Privy Council, to order, and it is hereby ordered, as follows:

1. This Order may be cited as the Merchant Shipping Act 1988 (Isle of Man) Order 1989 and shall come into force on 18th May 1989.

2. The provisions of the Merchant Shipping Act 1988 specified in Part I of the Schedule to this Order shall extend to the Isle of Man with the modifications specified in Part II of that Schedule.

3. Notwithstanding the extension of paragraph 2(b) of Schedule 1 to the Merchant Shipping Act 1988 (which amends section 7 of the Merchant Shipping Act 1894 by the omission of subsection (2) thereof) the power of exemption given to the Secretary of State by that subsection shall continue to have effect in relation to any class of ship in respect of which it was exercised immediately before the date of that extension.

G. I. de Deney
Clerk of the Privy Council

(a) 1894 c.60. **(b)** 1988 c.12.

Article 2

SCHEDULE

PART I

PROVISIONS OF THE MERCHANT SHIPPING ACT 1988 EXTENDED TO THE ISLE OF MAN

Sections 1 to 5, 7 to 10, 51, 53, 54, 57 and 58.
Schedule 1.

PART II

MODIFICATIONS IN THE EXTENSION OF PROVISIONS OF THE MERCHANT SHIPPING ACT 1988 TO THE ISLE OF MAN

1.—(1) Subject to sub-paragraph (2), any reference to an enactment shall, unless the contrary intention appears, be construed as a reference to that enactment as it has effect in the Isle of Man.

(2) Any reference to Part II, or to any provision thereof, of the Merchant Shipping Act 1988 shall be construed as a reference to any provision contained in, or made under, an Act of Tynwald which has the equivalent effect to that Part or, as the case may be, provision.

(3) Any reference to the Secretary of State shall be construed as a reference to the Department of Highways, Ports and Properties.

(4) For the words "United Kingdom" wherever they occur, except in the expression "Her Majesty's Government in the United Kingdom" and unless the contrary intention appears from the following provisions of this Schedule, there shall be substituted "Isle of Man".

2. In section 2, subsection (2) shall be omitted.

3. In section 4(1), for "sections 6 and 7 below" there shall be substituted "section 7 below and section 1 of the Merchant Shipping (Registration) Act 1984 (an Act of Tynwald) and any provision of an Act of Tynwald amending or replacing that section".

4. In section 7(3) –

(a) for paragraph (a) there shall be substituted the follow paragraph –

"(a) that, having regard to –

(i) the matters mentioned in subsection (1)(a) of section 1 of the Merchant Shipping (Registration) Act 1984 (an Act of Tynwald) and any provision of an Act of Tynwald amending or replacing that section, or

(ii) any order made under subsection (1)(b) of that section, or

(iii) the condition of the ship so far as relevant to any risk of pollution,

it would be inappropriate for a registered ship to continue to be registered, or",

and

(b) in paragraph (b), after "Merchant Shipping Acts" there shall be inserted "or any Act of Tynwald relating to merchant shipping or pollution of the sea from ships".

5. In section 8(1)(a), the words "6(1) or" shall be omitted.

6. In section 10(1), the words from "which include" to the end shall be omitted.

7. In section 53, for subsection (1) there shall be substituted the following subsection:

"(1) Regulations under Part I of this Act shall be laid before Tynwald.".

8.—(1) In section 54(1), "or II" shall be omitted.

(2) In section 54(2) –

(a) "or II",

(b) "or registered fishing vessel", and

(c) in paragraph (b), "or in the case of a fishing vessel",

shall be omitted.

(3) In section 54(3), for "the appropriate register" there shall be substituted "the register in which the ship is registered under Part I of the 1894 Act".

(4) In section 54(4) –

(a) the definitions of "the appropriate register" and "registered fishing vessel" shall be omitted, and

(b) in the definition of "registered owner", the words from "or Part II" to the end shall be omitted.

9.—(1) In section 57(2) –

(a) the definition of "modifications" shall be omitted, and

(b) in the definition of "relevant overseas territory" for "Isle of Man" there shall be substituted "United Kingdom".

(2) For subsections (3) to (5) there shall be substituted the following subsection –

"(3) Sections 51 and 52 of the Merchant Shipping Act 1906(**a**) are hereby repealed.".

10. In section 58, subsections (2) to (5) shall be omitted.

11.—(1) Without prejudice to paragraph 1 above, Schedule 1 shall have effect with the following modifications.

(2) Any reference to the omission of a provision shall be construed as a reference to the repeal thereof.

(3) In paragraph 2(a) –

(a) for "Commissioners of Customs and Excise" there shall be substituted "Department of Highways, Ports and Properties", and

(b) for "Commissioners" there shall be substituted "Department".

(4) In paragraph 12(c), in the provisions which are inserted thereby, subsections (5)(b) and (6)(b) shall be omitted.

(5) In paragraph 13, in section 22 which is substituted thereby, in subsection (1) for "Registrar-General of Shipping and Seamen" there shall be substituted "Registrar of British Ships in the Isle of Man".

(6) In paragraph 14 –

(a) paragraphs (a) and (c) shall be omitted, and

(b) for "United Kingdom" there shall be substituted "British Islands".

(7) In paragraph 19, in the subsection substituted thereby, for paragraphs (a) and (b) there shall be substituted "Her Majesty's High Court of Justice of the Isle of Man".

(8) In paragraph 20, for the provisions substituted thereby there shall be substituted "Her Majesty's High Court of Justice of the Isle of Man".

(9) In paragraph 28, for "United Kingdom" there shall be substituted "British Islands".

(10) In paragraph 30, in subsection (5) of section 53A inserted thereby, for "Isle of Man" there shall be substituted "United Kingdom".

(11) For paragraph 36 there shall be substituted the following paragraph –

"36. In section 62 (application of fees), for the words from "if taken in any part" to the end there shall be substituted "form part of the General Revenue of the Isle of Man".

(12) In paragraph 38(c), in the provisions substituted thereby –

(a) in subsection (3), paragraph (b) and the words ", and in Scotland sufficient evidence," shall be omitted;

(b) in subsection (5), the words ", and (in Scotland) of subsection (4)," shall be omitted, and

(c) in subsection (6), for the words from "such fee" to the end there shall be substituted "such reasonable fee as may be determined by the Department of Highways, Ports and Properties".

(13) In paragraph 42, in section 70 substituted thereby, the words "any part of" in paragraph (a) shall be omitted.

(14) In paragraph 47(2), for paragraph (b) there shall be substituted the following paragraph –

"(b) for the words from "the High Court" to "dominions" substitute "Her Majesty's High Court of Justice of the Isle of Man";".

(**a**) 1906 c.48.

(15) After paragraph 47 there shall be inserted the following paragraph –

"47A. For section 83 substitute –

"Fees for measurement 83. Such fees as the Department of Highways, Ports and Properties determine shall be paid in respect of the measurement of a ship's tonnage."."

(16) In paragraph 48, after sub-paragraph (b) there shall be inserted the following sub-paragraph –

"(bb) for "Board of Trade" substitute "Department of Highways, Ports and Properties"; and".

(17) After paragraph 49 there shall be inserted the following paragraph –

"49A. In section 86 (surveyors and regulations for measurement of ships) for "Board of Trade" there shall be substituted "Department of Highways, Ports and Properties".".

(18) For paragraph 51 there shall be substituted the following paragraph –

"51. In section 91(**a**) –

(a) omit paragraphs (d), (i) and (j);

(b) for "Governor in Council" and "Isle of Man Harbour Board" wherever occurring substitute "Department of Highways, Ports and Properties", and

(c) in paragraph (f) for "Isle of Man Finance Board" substitute "Department of Highways, Ports and Properties".".

EXPLANATORY NOTE

(This note is not part of the Order)

This Order extends the provisions of the Merchant Shipping Act 1988 specified in Part I of the Schedule to the Isle of Man subject to the modifications specified in Part II of that Schedule (article 2).

Article 3 of the Order makes supplementary provision for the Isle of Man similar to that made for the United Kingdom by article 3 of the Merchant Shipping Act 1988 (Commencement No. 3) Order 1989 (S.I. 1989/353).

(**a**) Section 91 was amended by the Isle of Man (Transfer of Functions) Order 1980 (S.I. 1980/399).

STATUTORY INSTRUMENTS

1989 No. 681

PARLIAMENT

The Lord Chancellor's Salary Order 1989

Made - - - - *18th April 1989*

Coming into force - *18th April 1989*

At the Court at Windsor Castle, the 18th day of April 1989

Present,

The Queen's Most Excellent Majesty in Council

Whereas a draft of this Order has been approved by resolution of each House of Parliament:

Now, therefore, Her Majesty, in pursuance of section 1(4) of the Ministerial and other Salaries Act 1975**(a)** and of all other powers enabling Her in that behalf, is pleased, by and with the advice of Her Privy Council, to order, and it is hereby ordered, as follows:–

Citation, commencement and revocation

1.—(1) This Order may be cited as the Lord Chancellor's Salary Order 1989.

(2) This Order shall come into force on the day on which it is made.

(3) The Lord Chancellor's Salary Order 1988**(b)** is hereby revoked.

Increase of Lord Chancellor's salary

2. For the amount specified in subsection (2) of section 1 of the Ministerial and other Salaries Act 1975**(a)** as the aggregate annual amount of the salary payable to the Lord Chancellor under that subsection and the salary payable to him as Speaker of the House of Lords there shall be substituted £91,500.

G. I. de Deney
Clerk of the Privy Council

(a) 1975 c.27.
(b) S.I. 1988/1088.

EXPLANATORY NOTE

(This note is not part of the Order)

This Order increases the total salary payable to the Lord Chancellor under the Ministerial and other Salaries Act 1975 and as Speaker of the House of Lords. The Order provides for the Lord Chancellor to receive a £2,000 lead over the Lord Chief Justice.

STATUTORY INSTRUMENTS

1989 No. 682

HEALTH AND SAFETY

The Health and Safety Information for Employees Regulations 1989

Made - - - -	*18th April 1989*
Laid before Parliament	*26th April 1989*
Coming into force -	*18th October 1989*

ARRANGEMENT OF REGULATIONS

The Secretary of State, in exercise of the powers conferred on him by sections 15(1), (2), (3)(a), (4)(a), (5)(b) and (6)(b) of, and paragraph 15(1) of Schedule 3 to, the Health and Safety at Work etc. Act 1974**(a)** ("the 1974 Act") and of all other powers enabling him in that behalf and for the purpose of giving effect without modifications to proposals submitted to him by the Health and Safety Commission under section 11(2)(d) of the 1974 Act after the carrying out by the said Commission of consultations in accordance with section 50(3) of that Act, hereby makes the following Regulations:

Citation and commencement

1. These Regulations may be cited as the Health and Safety Information for Employees Regulations 1989 and shall come into force on 18th October 1989.

(a) 1974 c.37; sections 15 and 50 were amended by the Employment Protection Act 1975 (c.71), Schedule 15, paragraphs 6 and 16 respectively.

Interpretation and application

2.—(1) In these Regulations, unless the context otherwise requires–

"the 1974" Act means the Health and Safety at Work etc. Act 1974;

"the approved poster" and "the approved leaflet" have the meanings assigned by regulation 3;

"employment medical advisory service" means the employment medical advisory service referred to in section 55 of the 1974 Act;

"ship" has the meaning assigned to it by section 742 of the Merchant Shipping Act 1894**(a)**.

(2) Any reference in these Regulations to the enforcing authority for premises is a reference to the enforcing authority which has responsibility for the enforcement of section 2 of the 1974 Act in relation to the main activity carried on in those premises.

(3) Any reference in these Regulations to–

(a) a numbered regulation is a reference to the regulation so numbered in these Regulations;

(b) a numbered paragraph is a reference to the paragraph so numbered in the regulation in which the reference appears.

(4) These Regulations shall have effect for the purpose of providing information to employees relating to health, safety and welfare but they shall not apply in relation to the master and crew of a sea going ship.

Meaning of and revisions to the approved poster and leaflet

3.—(1) In these Regulations "the approved poster" or "the approved leaflet" means, respectively, a poster or leaflet in the form approved and published for the purposes of these Regulations by the Health and Safety Executive, as revised from time to time in accordance with paragraph (2).

(2) The Health and Safety Executive may approve a revision (in whole or in part) to the form of poster or leaflet; and where it does so it shall publish the revised form of poster or leaflet and issue a notice in writing specifying the date the revision was approved.

(3) Such a revision shall not take effect until nine months after the date of its approval, but during that time the employer may use the approved poster or the approved leaflet incorporating that revision for the purposes of regulation 4(1).

Provision of poster or leaflet

4.—(1) An employer shall, in relation to each of his employees–

(a) ensure that the approved poster is kept displayed in a readable condition–

(i) at a place which is reasonably accessible to the employee while he is at work, and

(ii) in such a position in that place as to be easily seen and read by that employee; or

(b) give to the employee the approved leaflet.

(2) An employer shall be treated as having complied with paragraph (1)(b) from the date these Regulations come into force or the date the employee commences employment with him (if later) if he gives to the employee the approved leaflet as soon as is reasonably practicable after that date.

(3) Where the form of poster or leaflet is revised pursuant to regulation 3(2), then on or before the date the revision takes effect–

(a) an employer relying on compliance with paragraph (1)(a) shall ensure that the approved poster displayed is the one as revised;

(b) an employer relying on compliance with paragraph (1)(b) shall either give to the employees concerned fresh approved leaflets (as so revised) or bring the revision to their notice in writing.

(a) 1894 c.60.

Provision of further information

5.—(1) An employer relying on compliance with regulation 4(1)(a) shall, subject to paragraph (2), ensure that the following information is clearly and indelibly written on the poster in the appropriate space–

(a) the name of the enforcing authority for the premises where the poster is displayed and the address of the office of that authority for the area in which those premises are situated; and

(b) the address of the office of the employment medical advisory service for the area in which those premises are situated.

(2) Where there is a change in any of the matters referred to in paragraph (1) it shall be sufficient compliance with that paragraph for the corresponding amendment to the poster to be made within six months from the date thereof.

(3) An employer who gives to his employee a leaflet pursuant to regulation 4(1)(b) shall give with the leaflet a written notice containing–

(a) the name of the enforcing authority for the premises where the employee works, and the address of the office of that authority for the area in which those premises are situated; and

(b) the address of the office of the employment medical advisory service for the area in which those premises are situated.

(4) Where the employee works in more than one location he shall, for the purposes of paragraph (3), be treated as working at the premises from which his work is administered, and if his work is administered from two or more premises, the employer may choose any one of them for the purpose of complying with that paragraph.

(5) Where an employer relies on compliance with regulation 4(1)(b) and there is a change in any of the matters referred to in paragraph (3) the employer shall within six months of the date thereof give to the employee a written notice specifying the change.

Exemption certificates

6.—(1) Subject to paragraph (2) the Health and Safety Executive may, by a certificate in writing, exempt any person or class of persons from all or any of the requirements imposed by these Regulations and any such exemption may be granted subject to conditions and to a limit of time and may be revoked in writing at any time.

(2) The Executive shall not grant any such exemption unless, having regard to the circumstances of the case, and in particular to–

(a) the conditions if any, which it proposes to attach to the exemption; and

(b) any other requirements imposed by or under any enactment which apply to the case;

it is satisfied that the health, safety and welfare of persons who are likely to be affected by the exemption will not be prejudiced in consequence of it.

Defence

7. In any proceedings for an offence for a contravention of these Regulations it shall be a defence for the accused to prove that he took all reasonable precautions and exercised all due diligence to avoid the commission of that offence.

Repeals, revocations and modifications

8.—(1) The enactments specified in column 1 of Part I of the Schedule to these Regulations are hereby repealed to the extent specified in the corresponding entries in column 2 thereof.

(2) The instruments specified in column 1 of Part II of the Schedule to these Regulations are hereby revoked to the extent specified in the corresponding entries in column 3 thereof.

(3) The instrument specified in column 1 of Part III of the Schedule to these Regulations is hereby modified to the extent specified in the corresponding entry in column 3 thereof.

Signed by order of the Secretary of State.

Patrick Nicholls
Parliamentary Under Secretary of State,
Department of Employment

18th April 1989

Regulation 8

THE SCHEDULE

REPEALS, REVOCATIONS AND MODIFICATIONS

PART I

REPEALS

Column 1 *Enactments*	Column 2 *Repeals*
Factories Act 1961**(a)**	In section 125(2)(j) the words "the abstract of this Act and". In section 127(2)(j), the words "the abstract of this Act and". In section 127(5), the words "the prescribed abstract of this Act and of" and the words "of the abstract of this Act and". In section 138(1), paragraphs (a), (b) and (c). In section 153(1), paragraph (b).
Employment Medical Advisory Service Act 1972**(b)**	Schedule 2, in so far as it relates to the amendment of section 138(1) of the Factories Act 1961.

PART II

REVOCATIONS

Column 1 *Title of instrument*	Column 2 *Reference*	Column 3 *Extent of revocation*
The Information for Employees Regulations 1965.	S.I. 1965/307 amended by S.I. 1982/827.	The whole Regulations.
The Abstract of Factories Act Order 1973.	S.I. 1973/7 amended by S.I. 1983/978.	The whole Order.
The Offices, Shops and Railway Premises Act 1963 etc. (Metrication) Regulations 1982.	S.I. 1982/827.	The Schedule in so far as it relates to the amendment of the Information for Employees Regulations 1965.
The Factories Act 1961 etc. (Metrication) Regulations 1983.	S.I. 1983/978.	Regulation 5 and Schedule 3.

(a) 1961 c.34.
(b) 1972 c.28.

PART III

MODIFICATIONS

Column 1 *Title of instrument*	Column 2 *Reference*	Column 3 *Extent of modification*
The Construction (General Provisions) Regulations 1961.	S.I. 1961/1580 to which there are amendments not relevant to these Regulations.	For regulation 5(2) substitute– "The name of every person so appointed shall be entered by the contractor or employer appointing him on the copy or abstract of these Regulations required to be posted up in accordance with sections 139 and 127 of the Factories Act 1961."

EXPLANATORY NOTE

(This note is not part of the Regulations)

These Regulations require information relating to health, safety and welfare to be furnished to employees by means of posters or leaflets in the form approved and published for the purposes of the Regulations by the Health and Safety Executive (regulations 3 and 4). A copy of the form of poster or leaflet so approved may be obtained from Her Majesty's Stationery Office.

The Regulations also require the name and address of the enforcing authority and the address of the employment medical advisory service to be written in the appropriate space on the poster (regulation 5(1)); and where the leaflet is given the same information should be specified in a written notice accompanying it (regulation 5(3)).

The Regulations provide for the issue of certificates of exemption by the Health and Safety Executive (regulation 6), provide for a defence for contravention of the regulations (regulation 7) and repeal, revoke and modify various enactments and instruments relating to the provision of information to employees (regulation 8). The Regulations do not apply in relation to the master and crew of a sea going ship (regulation 2(4)).

1989 No. 683

LOCAL GOVERNMENT, ENGLAND AND WALES

The Local Government (Allowances) (Amendment) Regulations 1989

Made - - - -	*14th April 1989*
Laid before Parliament	*24th April 1989*
Coming into force -	*15th May 1989*

The Secretary of State for the Environment as respects England, and the Secretary of State for Wales as respects Wales, in exercise of the powers conferred upon them by sections 173, 177A and 270(1) of the Local Government Act 1972**(a)**, and of all other powers enabling them in that behalf, hereby make the following Regulations:

1. These Regulations may be cited as the Local Government (Allowances) (Amendment) Regulations 1989 and shall come into force on 15th May 1989.

2. In these Regulations "the principal Regulations" means the Local Government (Allowances) Regulations 1986**(b)**.

3.—(1) For regulations 3 and 4 of the principal Regulations there shall be substituted:–

"**3.**—(1) The prescribed amount of attendance allowance shall be £19.50 for any period of 24 hours beginning at 3 am.

(2) The prescribed amount of finanical loss allowance shall be:

(a) £16.15 for any period not exceeding 4 hours;

(b) £32.35 for any period exceeding 4 hours but not exceeding 24 hours;

(c) for a period exceeding 24 hours, £32.35 for each period of 24 hours plus the amount specified above which is appropriate to the remainder of the period.

4.—(1) The rate which a special responsibility allowance shall not exceed in any financial year beginning with the financial year ending on 31st March 1990 is:–

(a) in the case of a principal council belonging to the description of councils in paragraph 8(e) of Schedule 1 hereto, £560; and

(b) in any other case, one third of the total amount which that principal council may pay in that year by way of such allowances or £5,580, whichever is the less.

(a) 1972 c.70. *See* the definition of "prescribed" in section 270(1). Section 177A was inserted by, and section 173 was amended by, section 24 of the Local Government, Planning and Land Act 1980 (c.65). Section 177A was amended by paragraph 20 of Schedule 14 to the Local Government Act 1985 (c.51).

(b) S.I. 1986/724, amended by S.I. 1987/1483, 1988/358.

(2) The total amount payable by a principal council by way of special responsibility allowances in any financial year beginning with the financial year ending on 31st March 1990 shall not exceed the figure specified in Schedule 1 to these Regulations in respect of that council or the description of councils to which it belongs.".

(2) For Schedule 1 to the principal Regulations there shall be substituted the Schedule set out in the Schedule to these Regulations.

14th April 1989

Nicholas Ridley
Secretary of State for the Environment

14th April 1989

Peter Walker
Secretary of State for Wales

SCHEDULE

Regulation 4

SCHEDULE SUBSTITUTED IN THE PRINCIPAL REGULATIONS

"SCHEDULE 1

(TOTAL AMOUNT AVAILABLE FOR PAYMENT UNDER SECTION 177A OF THE ACT)

1 *(Name or Class of Authority)*	2 *(Amount)*
1. The Inner London Education Authority	22,290
2. The London Fire and Civil Defence Authority	11,135
3. An outer London borough	12,555
4. An inner London borough	6,965
5. A joint authority (other than the London Fire and Civil Defence Authority), the population of whose area is estimated on 1st April in the relevant financial year to exceed 2 million	5,565
6. A joint authority (other than the London Fire and Civil Defence Authority), the population of whose area is estimated on 1st April in the relevant financial year to not exceed 2 million	4,880
7. A county council or a metropolitan district council, the population of whose area is estimated on 1st April in the relevant financial year–	
(a) to exceed 1 million	20,915
(b) to exceed 500,000 but not to exceed 1 million	19,520
(c) to exceed 250,000 but not to exceed 500,000	13,940
(d) not to exceed 250,000	12,555
8. A non-metropolitan district council, the population of whose area is estimated on 1st April in the relevant financial year–	
(a) to exceed 400,000	6,965
(b) to exceed 200,000 but not to exceed 400,000	5,580
(c) to exceed 150,000 but not to exceed 200,000	4,185
(d) to exceed 100,000 but not to exceed 150,000	2,790
(e) not to exceed 100,000	1,390"

EXPLANATORY NOTE

(This note is not part of the Regulations)

These Regulations further amend the Local Government (Allowances) Regulations 1986 as amended by the Local Government (Allowances) (Amendment) Regulations 1987 and the Local Government (Allowances) (Amendment) Regulations 1988. They increase the amounts of attendance allowance, financial loss allowance, and special responsibility allowance payable under the Local Government Act 1972 to members of local authorities and certain other bodies for the performance of approved duties.

The maximum amount of attendance allowance payable to members of local authorities who are councillors is increased from £18.25 to £19.50. The maximum amount of financial loss allowance payable to members of local authorities and other bodies who are not entitled to attendance allowance, and to councillors who opt to receive it instead of attendance allowance, is increased from £29.70 to £32.35 for each 24 hour period and from £14.85 to £16.15 for a period of less than 4 hours.

The total amounts which a principal council may pay in any financial year by way of special responsibility allowances under the Act, and the maximum rate, are increased by 7% over those specified for the financial year ending 31st March 1989.

STATUTORY INSTRUMENTS

1989 No. 684

FEES AND CHARGES

The Medicines (Fixing of Fees Relating to Medicinal Products for Human Use) Order 1989

Made - - - - 17th April 1989

Coming into force - 18th April 1989

Whereas a draft of this Order has been approved by a resolution of the House of Commons in pursuance of section 102(5) of the Finance (No. 2) Act 1987**(a)**:

Now, therefore, the Secretaries of State for Health, for Wales, for Scotland and for Northern Ireland and the Minister of Agriculture, Fisheries and Food, being the Ministers of the Crown determined by the Treasury to be the appropriate authority in relation to the power to fix fees under section 1(1) of the Medicines Act 1971**(b)** acting jointly in exercise of the powers conferred by section 102 of the Finance (No. 2) Act 1987, hereby make the following Order:–

Citation, commencement and interpretation

1.—(1) This Order may be cited as the Medicines (Fixing of Fees Relating to Medicinal Products for Human Use) Order 1989 and shall come into force on the day after the day on which it is made.

(2) In this Order–

"the 1968 Act" means the Medicines Act 1968**(c)**;

"the 1971 Act" means the Medicines Act 1971**(d)**;

"the 1987 Act" means the Finance (No. 2) Act 1987;

"medicinal product" includes any substance or article specified in any order made under section 104 or 105(1)(a) of the 1968 Act which directs that Part II of that Act shall have effect in relation to such substance or article;

and other expressions have the same meaning as in the 1968 Act.

Functions the costs of which are to be taken into account in fixing fees under the 1971 Act

2. In relation to the power of the Ministers under section 1(1) of the 1971 Act to make regulations providing for the payment of such fees as are prescribed by the regulations with regard to the matters specified in that subsection, the functions specified for the purpose of section 102(3) of the 1987 Act are, as respects matters relating to medicinal products for human use, those functions set out in Schedule 1 to this Order.

(a) 1987 c.51.
(b) *See* section 102(2)(b) of the Finance (No. 2) Act 1987.
(c) 1968 c.67.
(d) 1971 c.69, as amended by section 21 of the Health and Medicines Act 1988 (c.49).

Matters to be taken into account in determining the costs of functions specified in Schedule 1 hereto

3. In relation to each of the functions specified by article 2 of, and Schedule 1 to, this Order for the purposes of section 102(3) of the 1987 Act, the matters specified for the purposes of section 102(4) of that Act are those set out in Schedule 2 to this Order.

Signed by authority of the Secretary of State for Health

D. Mellor
Minister of State,
Department of Health

13th April 1989

Peter Walker
Secretary of State for Wales

12th April 1989

Malcolm Rifkind
Secretary of State for Scotland

12th April 1989

Tom King
Secretary of State for Northern Ireland

17th April 1989

In Witness whereof the Official Seal of the Minister of Agriculture, Fisheries and Food is hereto affixed on 13th April 1989.

John MacGregor
Minister of Agriculture, Fisheries and Food

Article 2

SCHEDULE 1

FUNCTIONS THE COSTS OF WHICH ARE TO BE TAKEN INTO ACCOUNT IN FIXING FEES UNDER THE 1971 ACT

1. Functions of the Ministers under Parts I, II, III, V, VI and, subject to paragraph 11 below, VIII of the 1968 Act and under the 1971 Act.

2. Functions of the Licensing Authority under Part II of the 1968 Act.

3. Functions (except those under Part VII of the 1968 Act) of the Medicines Commission established under section 2 of the 1968 Act.

4. Functions of the following Committees established under section 4 of the 1968 Act: the Committee on Safety of Medicines, the Committee on Review of Medicines and the Committee on Dental and Surgical Materials.

5. Functions of the Ministers or the Licensing Authority in relation to anything done by the European Communities or any of their institutions with respect to the control of medicinal products.

6. Functions of the Ministers or the Licensing Authority in relation to anything done by the World Health Organisation with respect to the control of medicinal products.

7. Without prejudice to paragraphs 5 and 6, functions of the Ministers or the Licensing Authority arising under any international instrument relating to the control of medicinal products.

8. Functions of persons appointed under the 1968 Act.

9. Functions of the Medicines Testing Laboratory of the Royal Pharmaceutical Society of Great Britain under arrangements made with Ministers in respect of work relating to enforcement of the 1968 Act.

10. Without prejudice to the generality of the foregoing paragraphs, the following functions of the Ministers:–

(a) review of the functioning of the laws relating to the control of medicinal products (including whether or not a product or class of articles or substances should be made subject to such control) and development of proposals for legislation relating thereto;

(b) maintenance of relations with persons and organisations both within the United Kingdom and abroad in respect of matters relating to the control of medicinal products;

(c) subject to paragraph 11 below, enforcement of the 1968 Act and regulations and orders made under it, including investigation and prosecution of offences thereunder;

(d) the conduct of civil proceedings for the recovery of debt arising in relation to any of the functions otherwise specified in this Schedule.

11. Paragraphs 1 and 10(c) above do not apply to the function of Ministers under the 1968 Act to enforce that Act and regulations and orders made under it in so far as that function consists of the enforcement of provisions relating to the retail sale, or supply in circumstances corresponding to retail sale, of medicinal products.

SCHEDULE 2

Article 3

MATTERS TO BE TAKEN INTO ACCOUNT IN DETERMINING THE COST OF FUNCTIONS SPECIFIED IN SCHEDULE 1

1. All costs (including capital costs) incurred by the Ministers, the Licensing Authority, the Medicines Commission, the Committees established under section 4 of the 1968 Act specified in paragraph 4 of Schedule 1 above, appointed persons referred to in paragraph 8 of Schedule 1 above, and the Royal Pharmaceutical Society of Great Britain which are directly attributable to the functions specified in Schedule 1 above.

2. That proportion of the costs (including capital costs), not falling within paragraph 1 above, incurred by or on behalf of any of the persons or organisations specified in paragraph 1 above in relation to staff, equipment, premises, facilities and matters connected therewith (whether directly or indirectly), being the proportion which falls to be attributed to any of the functions specified in Schedule 1 above.

3.—(1) In so far as the capital cost of any capital asset employed wholly by any of the persons or organisations referred to in paragraph 1 above in relation to any of the functions specified in Schedule 1 to this Order has not been taken into account under that paragraph, an allowance, calculated in accordance with sub-paragraph (3) below for depreciation of that asset.

(2) In so far as the capital cost of any capital asset employed partly by any of the persons or organisations referred to in paragraph 1 above in relation to any of the functions specified in Schedule 1 to this Order has not been taken into account under paragraph 2 above, an allowance, calculated in accordance with sub-paragraph (3) below for depreciation of that asset.

(3) The allowance for depreciation of a capital asset referred to in sub-paragraphs (1) and (2) above shall be calculated at a rate which takes into account the anticipated useful future life of the asset in question and the current replacement cost of that asset.

4. A return on the resources employed in carrying out any of the functions specified in Schedule 1 above.

5. The allocation of a sum in respect of matters which would otherwise be covered by insurance, the allocation of a sum in respect of superannuation payments and provision for bad debts in relation to any of the functions specified in Schedule 1 above.

6. The recovery of any past deficits in relation to any of the functions specified in Schedule 1 above.

7. The allocation over a period of years of an initial or exceptional cost in relation to any of the functions specified in Schedule 1 above.

8. In respect of any function of any of the persons or organisations specified in paragraph 1 above consisting of the payment or remittance of any sum or amount, both the sum or amount in question and the cost incurred in effecting the payment or remittance.

EXPLANATORY NOTE

(This note is not part of the Order)

This Order specifies functions and matters which are to be taken into account in the determination of the fees prescribed under the Medicines Act 1971 in respect of applications for, variations or renewals of, or inspections related to, licences, certificates or directions for medicinal products under Part II of the Medicines Act 1968.

STATUTORY INSTRUMENTS

1989 No. 685 (S.73)

LANDLORD AND TENANT, SCOTLAND

The Assured Tenancies (Rent Information) (Scotland) Order 1989

Made - - - -	*14th April 1989*
Laid before Parliament	*26th April 1989*
Coming into force	*17th May 1989*

The Secretary of State, in exercise of the powers conferred on him by section 49 of the Housing (Scotland) Act 1988(**a**) and of all other powers enabling him in that behalf, hereby makes the following Order:

1. This Order may be cited as the Assured Tenancies (Rent Information) (Scotland) Order 1989 and shall come into force on 17th May 1989.

2. The information with respect to rents under assured tenancies to be kept by the rent assessment panel (whether it is kept in documentary form or otherwise) shall be kept in such manner–

(a) that the entry in respect of each tenancy shows, or

(b) if kept otherwise than in documentary form that each entry when displayed or printed shows,

the information specified in the Schedule to this Order.

3. The rent assessment panel shall keep the specified information available for public inspection without charge during usual office hours at the office of the panel.

4. A person requiring a copy of any specified information certified under the hand of an authorised officer of the rent assessment panel shall be entitled to obtain it on payment of a fee of £1.50 for the specified information relating to each entry.

James Douglas-Hamilton
Parliamentary Under Secretary of State,
Scottish Office

St. Andrew's House, Edinburgh
14th April 1989

(**a**) 1988 c.43.

Article 2

SCHEDULE

Information with respect to rents under assured tenancies to be kept by rent assessment panel:

1. Address and description of subjects of let.

2. Details of any accommodation which is shared including whether it is shared with the landlord or somebody else.

3. Names and addresses of landlord and tenant.

4. Duration of tenancy if short assured tenancy.

5. Rent applying before application is made.

6. Details of any furniture and services provided by the landlord and the amount of the rent which is attributable to the use of furniture or for services.

7. Kind of application, for example, whether (a) proposing new terms and rent, (b) proposing new rent or (c) determination of rent for short assured tenancy.

8. Date and details of determination including revised rent and whether or not linked with change in the terms of the tenancy.

9. Reasons for a refusal to make a determination of the kind mentioned in 7(c) above.

10. Any other factor taken into consideration by the rent assessment committee in making a determination.

EXPLANATORY NOTE

(This note is not part of the Order)

This Order specifies the information on rents of assured tenancies which is to be made publicly available by the rent assessment panel, the manner in which it is to be made available and the fee to be charged for the supply of a certified copy of such information.

STATUTORY INSTRUMENTS

1989 No. 687

SEA FISHERIES

MARKETING

The Sea Fish (Marketing Standards) (Amendment) Regulations 1989

Made - - - -	*18th April 1989*
Laid before Parliament	*27th April 1989*
Coming into force	*18th May 1989*

The Minister of Agriculture, Fisheries and Food and the Secretary of State, being Ministers designated**(a)** for the purposes of section 2(2) of the European Communities Act 1972**(b)** in relation to the common agricultural policy of the European Economic Community, acting jointly, in exercise of the powers conferred on them by the said section 2(2) and of all other powers enabing them in that behalf, hereby make the following Regulations:—

Title, commencement and interpretation

1.—(1) These Regulations may be cited as the Sea Fish (Marketing Standards) (Amendment) Regulations 1989 and shall come into force on 18th May 1989.

(2) In these Regulations "the principal Regulations" means the Sea Fish (Marketing Standards) Regulations 1986**(c)**.

Amendment of the principal Regulations

2. The principal Regulations are hereby amended as follows—

(a) by substituting in regulation 2 thereof (interpretation) for the definitions of Regulations 103/76 and 104/76 the following definitions—

'"Regulation 103/76" means Council Regulation (EEC) No. 103/76 laying down common marketing standards for certain fresh or chilled fish**(d)** as amended by Council Regulation (EEC) No. 3396/85**(e)**, Commission Regulations (EEC) Nos. 3856/87**(f)** and 3940/87**(g)** and Council Regulation (EEC) No. 33/89**(h)** and read with Commission Regulation (EEC) No. 3703/85 laying down detailed rules for applying the common marketing standards for certain fresh or chilled fish**(i)**;

(a) By S.I. 1972/1811.
(b) 1972 c.68; section 2 is subject to Schedule 2 to that Act and is to be read, as regards England and Wales, with sections 37, 40 and 46 of the Criminal Justice Act 1982 (c.48) and S.I. 1984/447, as regards Scotland, with sections 289F and 289G of the Criminal Procedure (Scotland) Act 1975 (c.21), as inserted by section 54 of the Criminal Justice Act 1982 and amended by section 66 of the Criminal Justice (Scotland) Act 1987 (c.41), and with S.I. 1984/526, and, as regards Northern Ireland, with S.I. 1984/703 (N.I. 3) and S.R. (N.I.) 1984 No. 253.
(c) S.I. 1986/1272, to which there are amendments not relevant to these Regulations.
(d) OJ No. L20, 28.1.76, p.29.
(e) OJ No. L322, 3.12.85, p.1.
(f) OJ No. L363, 23.12.87, p.25.
(g) OJ No. L373, 31.12.87, p.6.
(h) OJ No. L5, 7.1.89, p.18.
(i) OJ No. L351, 28.12.85, p.63.

"Regulation 104/76" means Council Regulation (EEC) No. 104/76 laying down common marketing standards for shrimps (*Crangon crangon*), edible crabs (*Cancer pagurus*) and Norway lobsters (*Nephrops norvegicus*)**(a)**, as amended by Council Regulations (EEC) Nos. 3575/83**(b)** and 3118/85**(c)** and Commission Regulations (EEC) Nos. 3940/87 and 4213/88**(d)** and read with Commission Regulation (EEC) No. 1048/86 defining the coastal areas of the United Kingdom to which a minimum marketing size for crabs shall apply**(e)**;';

(b) by substituting in column 1 of the Schedule thereto (specified Community provisions)—

(i) for the words 'Article 11(1) of Regulation 103/76' the words 'Article 10(1) of Regulation 103/76';

(ii) for the words 'Article 11(2) of Regulation 103/76' the words 'Article 10(2) of Regulation 103/76'.

In witness whereof the Official Seal of the Minister of Agriculture, Fisheries and Food is hereunto affixed on 17th April 1989.

Trumpington
Parliamentary Secretary — Ministry of Agriculture, Fisheries and Food

Sanderson of Bowden
18th April 1989 — Minister of State, Scottish Office

EXPLANATORY NOTE

(This note is not part of the Regulations)

These Regulations amend the Sea Fish (Marketing Standards) Regulations 1986 ("the principal Regulations"), which make provision for the enforcement of certain of the enforceable Community restrictions and obligations concerning common marketing standards and related rules as to marketing for certain species of sea fish, including shellfish, which are contained in Council Regulations (EEC) Nos. 103/76 and 104/76 ("the Council Regulations").

In consequence of amendments made to the Council Regulations by Commission Regulations (EEC) Nos. 3856/87, 3940/87 and 4213/88 and Council Regulation (EEC) No. 33/89, these Regulations amend the definitions of the Council Regulations in regulation 2 of the principal Regulations (interpretation) so as to provide for the inclusion of those amendments in those definitions. They also make a consequential amendment to the Schedule to the principal Regulations (regulation 2).

(a) OJ No. L20, 28.1.76, p.35.
(b) OJ No. L356, 20.12.83, p.6.
(c) OJ No. L297, 9.11.85, p.3.
(d) OJ No. L370, 31.12.88, p.33.
(e) OJ No. L96, 11.4.86, p.14.

STATUTORY INSTRUMENTS

1989 No. 689

MERCHANT SHIPPING

PILOTAGE

The Pilotage Authorities (1988 Returns) Order 1988

Made - - - -	*26th September 1988*
Coming into force	*30th September 1988*

The Secretary of State for Transport in exercise of the powers conferred by section 19 of the Pilotage Act 1983(**a**) ("the 1983 Act") and of all other powers enabling him in that behalf, hereby makes the following Order:–

1. This Order may be cited as the Pilotage Authorities (1988 Returns) Order 1988 and shall come into force on 30th September 1988.

2. The 1988 returns to be delivered by a pilotage authority to the Secretary of State pursuant to section 19(1) of the 1983 Act shall give the particulars with respect to pilotage in their district indicated in Form "A" in the Schedule to the Pilotage Authorities (Returns) Order 1978(**b**) ("the 1978 Order") and shall be delivered in that form or in a form substantially to the same effect, but any reference in that Form to the year (except in relation to item 6) or to the year ended 31st December shall be taken as a reference to the period from 1st January 1988 until 30th September 1988 (inclusive), any other reference in the Form to 31st December shall be taken as a reference to 30th September 1988, and the reference to the year in item 6 shall be taken as a reference to the year ended 30th June 1988.

3. The 1988 statement of accounts to be furnished by a pilotage authority to the Secretary of State pursuant to section 19(2) of the 1983 Act shall be in the form set out as Form "B" in the Schedule to the 1978 Order or a form substantially to the same effect, but the reference to the year ended 31st December shall be taken as a reference to the period from 1st January 1988 until 30th September 1988 (inclusive).

Signed by authority
of the Secretary of State
26th September 1988

J. W. S. Dempster
An Under Secretary in the
Department of Transport

(**a**) 1983 c.21.

(**b**) S.I. 1978/852.

EXPLANATORY NOTE

(This note is not part of the Order)

This Order prescribes the particulars and form of returns and statements of accounts to be given by pilotage authorities for the period of their operation immediately preceding their abolition on 1st October 1988.

STATUTORY INSTRUMENTS

1989 No. 693

BETTING, GAMING AND LOTTERIES

The Gaming (Bingo) Act (Fees) (Amendment) Order 1989

Made - - - -	*20th April 1989*
Laid before Parliament	*27th April 1989*
Coming into force	*29th May 1989*

In exercise of the powers conferred on me by paragraph 5(1) of the Schedule to the Gaming (Bingo) Act 1985**(a)**, I hereby make the following Order:

1. This Order may be cited as the Gaming (Bingo) Act (Fees) (Amendment) Order 1989 and shall come into force on 29th May 1989.

2. In article 2(b) of the Gaming (Bingo) Act (Fees) Order 1986**(b)** for "£30,000" there shall be substituted "£70,000".

Home Office
20th April 1989

Douglas Hurd
One of Her Majesty's Principal Secretaries of State

EXPLANATORY NOTE

(This note is not part of the Order)

This Order amends article 2(b) of the Gaming (Bingo) Act (Fees) Order 1986 so as to increase from £30,000 to £70,000 the fee payable to the Gaming Board for Great Britain for the continuing in force, for a period of three years, of a certificate issued by the Board to an organiser of games of multiple bingo under the Schedule to the Gaming (Bingo) Act 1985.

(a) 1985 c.35. **(b)** S.I. 1986/833.

STATUTORY INSTRUMENTS

1989 No. 694

POLICE

The National Police Records (Recordable Offences) (Amendment) Regulations 1989

Made - - - -	*20th April 1989*
Laid before Parliament	*27th April 1989*
Coming into force	*1st June 1989*

In exercise of the powers conferred on me by section 27(4) of the Police and Criminal Evidence Act 1984**(a)**, I hereby make the following Regulations:

1. These Regulations may be cited as the National Police Records (Recordable Offences) (Amendment) Regulations 1989 and shall come into force on 1st June 1989.

2. In regulation 2(1) of the National Police Records (Recordable Offences) Regulations 1985**(b)** there shall be substituted for the words following "telecommunications system);" the following provisions:

"(c) section 29 of the Road Traffic Act 1972 (penalisation of tampering with vehicles);

(d) section 1 of the Malicious Communications Act 1988 (offence of sending letters etc. with intent to cause distress or anxiety); and

(e) section 139(1) of the Criminal Justice Act 1988 (offence of having article with blade or point in public place).".

Home Office
20th April 1989

Douglas Hurd
One of Her Majesty's Principal Secretaries of State

(a) 1984 c.60.
(b) S.I. 1985/1941; there are no amending Regulations.

EXPLANATORY NOTE

(This note is not part of the Regulations)

These Regulations amend the National Police Records (Recordable Offences) Regulations 1985, which make provision for recording in national police records convictions for offences punishable with imprisonment and for specified offences which are not so punishable.

The Regulations add to the offences specified in the 1985 Regulations offences under section 1 of the Malicious Communications Act 1988 (c.27), for which the maximum penalty is a fine not exceeding level 4 on the standard scale, and section 139(1) of the Criminal Justice Act 1988 (c.33), for which the maximum penalty is a fine not exceeding level 3.

The Regulations come into force on 1st June 1989.

STATUTORY INSTRUMENTS

1989 No. 701

ELECTRICITY

The Meters (Certification) (Fees) Regulations 1989

Made - - - -	*15th April 1989*
Laid before Parliament	*27th April 1989*
Coming into force	*1st June 1989*

The Secretary of State, in exercise of the powers conferred on him by section 50A(4) of the Schedule to the Electric Lighting (Clauses) Act 1899(**a**) as incorporated with the Electricity Act 1947(**b**), hereby makes the following Regulations:

Citation and commencement

1. These Regulations may be cited as the Meters (Certification) (Fees) Regulations 1989 and shall come into force on 1st June 1989.

Meter certification fees

2.—(1) The fee to be paid to the Secretary of State by the holder of an authorisation under section 50A(2) of the 1899 Schedule towards administrative expenses incurred by him by virtue of section 50A of the 1899 Schedule shall be increased from 15 pence to 16 pence for each meter certified.

(2) For the purposes of this Regulation–

"the 1899 Schedule" means the Schedule to the Electric Lighting (Clauses) Act 1899 as incorporated with the Electricity Act 1947; and

"meter certified" means a meter certified under section 50 of the 1899 Schedule.

3. The Meters (Certification) (Fees) Regulations 1988(**c**) are hereby revoked.

Michael Spicer
Parliamentary Under Secretary of State,
Department of Energy

15th April 1989

(**a**) 1899 c.19; section 50A was inserted by the Energy Act 1983 (c.25), Schedule 1, paragraph 6.
(**b**) 1947 c.54; section 57(2) incorporates the Schedule to the Electric Lighting (Clauses) Act 1899 with adaptations and modifications.
(**c**) S.I. 1988/457.

EXPLANATORY NOTE

(This note is not part of the Regulations)

These Regulations supersede the Meters (Certification) (Fees) Regulations 1988 which apply to persons who manufacture or repair meters and who are authorised by the Secretary of State for Energy under section 50A(2) of the Schedule to the Electric Lighting (Clauses) Act 1899 to certify, in accordance with section 50 of that Schedule, meters manufactured or repaired by them.

The Regulations increase the amount of the fee payable by the holders of such authorisations to the Secretary of State towards administrative expenses incurred by him by virtue of section 50A of the Schedule from 15 pence to 16 pence for each meter certified.

1989 No. 702 (S.74)

POLICE

The Police Cadets (Scotland) Amendment Regulations 1989

Made - - - -	*16th April 1989*
Laid before Parliament	*28th April 1989*
Coming into force	*19th May 1989*

The Secretary of State, in exercise of the powers conferred on him by section 27 of the Police (Scotland) Act 1967(**a**), and of all other powers enabling him in that behalf, and after taking into consideration the recommendations made by the Police Negotiating Board for the United Kingdom and furnishing the said Board with a draft of the Regulations in accordance with section 2(1) of the Police Negotiating Board Act 1980(**b**), hereby makes the following Regulations:

Citation

1. These Regulations may be cited as the Police Cadets (Scotland) Amendment Regulations 1989.

Commencement

2. These Regulations shall come into force on 19th May 1989 and shall have effect for the purposes of regulation 4 as from 1st September 1988.

Interpretation

3. In these Regulations any reference to "the principal Regulations" is a reference to the Police Cadets (Scotland) Regulations 1968(**c**).

Amendment of the principal Regulations

4. For the Table in Schedule 1 to the principal Regulations (which contains scales of pay) there is substituted the following Table:

"TABLE

Age	*Annual Pay*
Under 17 years	£3,384
17 years	£3,588
18 years or over	£3,996

".

5. In Schedule 2 to the principal Regulations (which relates to charges for board and lodging), for the sum "£444" there is substituted the sum "£471".

(**a**) 1967 c.77; section 27 was amended by the Police and Criminal Evidence Act 1984 (c.60), section 111(2).
(**b**) 1980 c.10.
(**c**) S.I. 1968/208; the relevant amending instrument is S.I. 1987/1878.

St. Andrew's House, Edinburgh
16th April 1989

James Douglas-Hamilton
Parliamentary Under Secretary of State,
Scottish Office

EXPLANATORY NOTE

(This note is not part of the Regulations)

These Regulations further amend the Police Cadets (Scotland) Regulations 1968.

Regulation 4 increases the pay of police cadets with retrospective effect from 1st September 1988. Retrospection is authorised by section 27(2) of the Police (Scotland) Act 1967.

Regulation 5 increases the charges payable by cadets for board and lodging provided by police authorities from £444 per annum to £471 per annum with effect from 19th May 1989.

STATUTORY INSTRUMENTS

1989 No. 711

PENSIONS

The Pensions Increase (Approved Schemes) (National Health Service) Amendment Regulations 1989

Made - - - -	*21st April 1989*
Laid before Parliament	*24th April 1989*
Coming into force	*15th May 1989*

The Secretary of State for Health, in exercise of the powers conferred by sections 13(2), (4) and (5) of the Pensions (Increase) Act 1971**(a)** and of all other powers enabling him in that behalf, with the approval of the Treasury**(b)**, hereby makes the following Regulations:

Citation and commencement

1. These Regulations may be cited as the Pensions Increase (Approved Schemes) (National Health Service) Amendment Regulations 1989, and shall come into force on 15th May 1989.

Amendment of Regulations

2.—(1) The Pensions Increase (Approved Schemes) (National Health Service) Regulations 1976**(c)** shall be amended in accordance with the provisions of this regulation.

(2) In regulation 2(1) (interpretation)–

(a) for the definition of "reckonable service" there shall be substituted the following definition–

" 'reckonable service' has the meaning assigned to it by the civil service regulations, in relation to a person to whom regulation 4C applies; by the local government regulations, in relation to a person to whom regulation 4D applies; and by the schedule to these regulations, in relation to any other person;";

(b) for the words " 'regulation 75(1) optant' means a person to whom the provisions of regulation 75(1) of the 1961 regulations" there shall be substituted the words " 'regulation 79(1) optant' means a person to whom the provisions of regulation 79(1) of the 1980 regulations";

(c) in the definition of "superannuation scheme" for "75(1)" there shall be substituted "79(1)";

(d) in the definition of "superannuable under the Regulations" for the words "43, 45 and 75 of the 1961 regulations" there shall be substituted the words "44, 48 and 79 of the 1980 regulations";

(e) in the definition of "the previous regulations" for the words "25th July 1961" there shall be substituted the words "6th March 1980" and after the words

(a) 1971 c.56.
(b) *See* the Transfer of Functions (Minister for the Civil Service and Treasury) Order 1981 (S.I. 1981/1670), article 2.
(c) S.I. 1976/1451.

"National Health Service Act 1946" there shall be inserted "or section 10 of the Superannuation Act 1972**(a)**";

(f) in the definition of "the Regulations" for the words "the 1961 regulations" there shall be substituted the words "the 1980 regulations";

(g) for the definition of "the 1961 regulations" there shall be substituted the following definition–

" 'the 1980 regulations' means the National Health Service (Superannuation) Regulations 1980"**(b)**;

(h) after the definition of "the retirement regulations" there shall be inserted the following definitions–

" 'the civil service regulations' means the Pensions Increase (Federated Superannuation Scheme for Nurses and Hospital Officers) (Civil Service) Regulations 1972**(c)**;

'the local government regulations' means the Pensions Increase (Approved Schemes) (Local Government) Regulations 1972**(d)**;".

(3) In regulation 3 (application), for the words "described in regulation 4 hereof" there shall be substituted the words "to whom any of regulations 4 to 4D of these regulations applies".

(4) For the heading to regulation 4 there shall be substituted the heading "Persons remaining in or leaving reckonable service with an employing authority who are entitled to benefits under a superannuation scheme".

(5) In regulation 4(1), for the words "These regulations" there shall be substituted the words "This regulation".

(6) In regulation 4(1)(b), for the words "75(1) optant" there shall be substituted the words "79(1) optant".

(7) In regulation 4(1)(c)(ii), for the words "disabled by physical or mental infirmity" there shall be substituted the words "permanently incapacitated by physical or mental infirmity from engaging in any regular full-time employment".

(8) In regulation 4(2), for the words "75(1) optant" there shall be substituted the words "79(1) optant" and for the words "these regulations insofar as they apply" there shall be substituted the words "this regulation insofar as it applies".

(9) After regulation 4 there shall be inserted the following regulations–

"**Persons becoming superannuable under the Regulations on relinquishing options or on re-employment**

4A. This regulation shall apply to any person who–

(a) either–

(i) has ceased to be employed by an employing authority, and immediately before doing so was in that employment subject to a superannuation scheme, or

(ii) has ceased to be subject to a superannuation scheme while remaining in the employment of an employing authority;

and

(b) within 12 months, or such longer period as the Secretary of State may allow, of that cessation has become superannuable under the Regulations; and

(c) does not satisfy the requirements of regulation 4(1)(a)(ii) of these regulations but would satisfy them if the length of time during which he has been superannuable under the Regulations were added both to the length of time which he has spent in reckonable service and to his age at the time of the ceasing mentioned in paragraph (a) of this regulation.

(a) 1972 c.11.
(b) S.I. 1980/362, amended by S.I. 1981/1205, 1982/288, 1765, 1985/39, 1987/2218.
(c) S.I. 1972/395, amended by S.I. 1973/1068, 1984/1751.
(d) S.I. 1972/931, amended by S.I. 1975/503.

Persons entering other employment on leaving reckonable service with an employing authority

4B. This regulation shall apply to any person who–

(a) has ceased to be employed by an employing authority and immediately before doing so was in that employment subject to a superannuation scheme; and

(b) within 12 months, or such longer period as the Secretary of State may allow, of that cessation has entered other employment which is either–

(i) employment related to the provision of health or allied services, or

(ii) employment in the civil service of the State, local government, education, the police or the fire service;

and

(c) is not a person–

(i) to whom the civil service regulations apply, or

(ii) to whom those regulations would apply if regulation 3(2) of those regulations were disregarded, or

(iii) to whom the local government regulations apply;

and

(d) has within 6 months, or such longer period as the Secretary of State may allow, of the coming into operation of this regulation, applied for, and been granted, the Secretary of State's approval, for the purposes of this regulation, of the employment referred to in paragraph (b) of this regulation; and

(e) does not satisfy the requirements of regulation 4(1)(a)(ii) of these regulations but would satisfy them if the length of time during which he has been employed in the employment which is approved by the Secretary of State under paragraph (d) of this regulation were added both to the length of time which he has spent in reckonable service and to his age at the time of the ceasing mentioned in paragraph (a) of this regulation.

Special provision for persons becoming superannuable under the Regulations after employment in the civil service

4C. This regulation shall apply to any person who–

(a) either–

(i) has ceased to be employed in the civil service of the State, and immediately before doing so was in that employment subject to a superannuation scheme, or

(ii) has ceased to be subject to a superannuation scheme while remaining in employment in the civil service of the State;

and

(b) within 12 months, or such longer period as the Secretary of State may allow, of that cessation has become superannuable under the Regulations; and

(c) does not qualify for a payment under the civil service regulations for any one or more of the following reasons (but for no other reason), namely–

(i) that when he ceased to be in employment in the civil service of the State he had not completed the requisite period of reckonable service,

(ii) that when he ceased to be in that employment he had not attained the requisite age, or

(iii) that he ceased to be in that employment before 12th April 1972,

but would qualify for a payment under those regulations if the length of time during which he has been superannuable under the Regulations were added both to the length of time which he has spent in reckonable service and to his age at the time of the ceasing mentioned in paragraph (a) of this regulation and the application of the civil service regulations were not restricted to persons retiring from the civil service of the State on or after 12th April 1972.

Special provision for persons becoming superannuable under the Regulations after employment by a local authority

4D. This regulation shall apply to any person who–

(a) either–

(i) has ceased to be employed by a local authority and immediately before doing so was in that employment subject to a superannuation scheme, or

(ii) has ceased to be subject to a superannuation scheme while remaining in the employment of a local authority;

and

(b) within 12 months, or such longer period as the Secretary of State may allow, of that cessation has become superannuable under the Regulations; and

(c) does not qualify for a payment under the local government regulations for either or both of the following reasons (but for no other reason), namely–

(i) that when he ceased to be in that employment he had not completed the requisite period of reckonable service, or

(ii) that when he ceased to be in that employment he had not attained the requisite age,

but would qualify for a payment under those regulations if the length of time during which he has been superannuable under the Regulations were added both to the length of time which he has spent in reckonable service and to his age at the time of the ceasing mentioned in paragraph (a) of this regulation."

(10) Regulations 5(1) and (7) (notional pension and lump sum) shall be amended by the substitution, for the words "these regulations apply", of the words "any of regulations 4 to 4D of these regulations applies".

(11) Regulation 6 (payments of benefits equivalent to statutory pension increases) shall be redesignated paragraph (1) of regulation 6, and for the words from "The Secretary of State shall," to "these regulations apply" there shall be substituted the words "Subject to paragraph (2) of this regulation, the Secretary of State shall, in respect of the appropriate period as specified in paragraph (3) of this regulation, pay to a person to whom any of regulations 4 to 4D of these regulations applies".

(12) After paragraph (1) of regulation 6 there shall be added the following paragraphs–

"(2) The Secretary of State shall not pay the amounts referred to in paragraph (1) of this regulation to any person to whom any of regulations 4A to 4D of these regulations applies unless the person first makes a claim in writing to the Secretary of State.

(3) The appropriate period referred to in paragraph (1) of this regulation is–

(a) in relation to a person to whom regulation 4 of these regulations applies–

(i) any period beginning on or after 1st March 1975 if he is a regulation 79(1) optant, and

(ii) any period beginning on or after 1st December 1974 if he is not;

and

(b) in relation to a person to whom any of regulations 4A to 4D of these regulations applies, any period beginning on or after 15th May 1989."

(13) In paragraph 1(a) of the schedule (meaning of reckonable service) for the words "75(1) optant" there shall be substituted the words "79(1) optant" and in paragraph 4 of the schedule for the words "22 of the 1961 regulations" there shall be substituted the words "24 of the 1980 regulations".

Signed by authority of the Secretary of State for Health.

D. Mellor
Minister of State,
Department of Health

19th April 1989

We approve

David Lightbown
Nigel Lawson
Lords Commissioners of Her Majesty's Treasury

21st April 1989

EXPLANATORY NOTE

(This note is not part of the Regulations)

These Regulations amend the Pensions Increase (Approved Schemes) (National Health Service) Regulations 1976 ("the 1976 Regulations"). Those Regulations provide for payments to certain persons who, having elected to secure their superannuation benefits through schemes which operate by way of insurance policies to produce lump sums or annuities, or both, on retirement (persons who so elect being known as "optants"), have retired from employment in the National Health Service, and would have been eligible for increases under the Pensions (Increase) Act 1971 had they been pensionable under the National Health Service superannuation scheme.

The main provisions of these Regulations bring within the scope of the 1976 Regulations certain persons who were hitherto not covered, namely persons who have ceased to be optants and within 12 months (or a longer period if allowed by the Secretary of State) of so ceasing have either become members of the National Health Service superannuation scheme or entered employment which is related to the provision of health or allied services and approved for the purpose of these Regulations by the Secretary of State. Provision is also made for persons who made similar arrangements in relation to their superannuation benefits whilst employed in the civil service or local government but subsequently became superannuable under the National Health Service superannuation scheme. Persons in these various categories may have ceased to be optants at any time but are entitled to payments by virtue of these Regulations only from the operative date of these Regulations.

In addition these Regulations make an amendment to the wording in the 1976 Regulations which relates to those persons who qualify for payments partly by reason of disablement.

STATUTORY INSTRUMENTS

1989 No. 712

COMMUNITY CHARGES, ENGLAND AND WALES

The Community Charges (Administration and Enforcement) (Amendment) Regulations 1989

Made - - - -	*24th April 1989*
Laid before Parliament	*28th April 1989*
Coming into force	*19th May 1989*

The Secretary of State for the Environment as respects England, and the Secretary of State for Wales as respects Wales, in exercise of the powers conferred on them by paragraph 27 of Schedule 4 to the Local Government Finance Act 1988(**a**), and of all other powers enabling them in that behalf, hereby make the following Regulations:

1. These Regulations may be cited as the Community Charges (Administration and Enforcement) (Amendment) Regulations 1989 and shall come into force on 19th May 1989.

2. For regulation 51(1)(b) of the Community Charges (Administration and Enforcement) Regulations 1989(**b**) there is substituted–

"(b) in supplying information in purported compliance with that regulation he makes a statement which he knows to be false in a material particular or recklessly makes a statement which is false in a material particular.".

20th April 1989

Nicholas Ridley
Secretary of State for the Environment

24th April 1989

Peter Walker
Secretary of State for Wales

(**a**) 1988 c.41.
(**b**) S.I. 1989/438.

EXPLANATORY NOTE

(This note is not part of the Regulations)

These Regulations correct an error in the Community Charges (Administration and Enforcement) Regulations 1989. They substitute a new regulation 51(1)(b) in those Regulations so that that provision accords with paragraph 27(1)(b) of Schedule 4 to the Local Government Finance Act 1988. The result is that a person commits an offence by making a statement which is false in a material particular in purported compliance with a request under regulation 31(2)(b) of those Regulations only if he does so knowingly or recklessly.

STATUTORY INSTRUMENTS

1989 No. 713

ROAD TRAFFIC

The Motorcycles (Sound Level Measurement Certificates) (Amendment) Regulations 1989

Made - - - -	*24th April 1989*
Laid before Parliament	*3rd May 1989*
Coming into force	*24th May 1989*

The Secretary of State for Transport, being a Minister designated**(a)** for the purposes of section 2(2) of the European Communities Act 1972**(b)** in relation to the type, description, construction or equipment of vehicles, and of components of vehicles, and in particular any vehicle type approval scheme, in exercise of the powers conferred on him by the said section 2(2), and of all other enabling powers, hereby makes the following Regulations:

1. These Regulations may be cited as the Motorcycles (Sound Level Measurement Certificates) (Amendment) Regulations 1989 and shall come into force on 24th May 1989.

2. The Motorcycles (Sound Level Measurement Certificates) Regulations 1980**(c)** are hereby amended in accordance with the following provisions of these Regulations.

3. In paragraph (2) of regulation 4, after sub-paragraph (a) there shall be inserted–

"(aa) the vehicle is one of a type which complies with the harmonised requirements specified in the Council Directive, and".

Signed by authority of the Secretary of State

Peter Bottomley
Parliamentary Under Secretary of State,
Department of Transport

24th April 1989

(a) S.I. 1972/1811.
(b) 1972 c.68.
(c) S.I. 1980/765, as amended by S.I. 1988/1640.

EXPLANATORY NOTE

(This note is not part of the Regulations)

These Regulations further amend the Motorcycles (Sound Level Measurement Certificates) Regulations 1980, by inserting a new sub-paragraph in regulation 4(2), to make it clear that certificates are only to be issued when the relevant standards of Council Directive 78/1015/EEC as amended by Council Directive 87/56/EEC are met.

Copies of the EEC Directives can be obtained from Her Majesty's Stationery Office. The details of the Directives are set out below.

Instrument	*Reference*
Council Directive 78/1015/EEC of 23rd November 1978	OJ No. L349, 13.12.78, p.21.
Council Directive 87/56/EEC of 18th December 1986	OJ No. L24, 27.1.87, p.24.

STATUTORY INSTRUMENTS

1989 No. 719 (C.20)

EDUCATION, ENGLAND AND WALES

The Education Reform Act 1988 (Commencement No. 7) Order 1989

Made - - - - 26th April 1989

In exercise of the powers conferred by section 236(6) to (8) of the Education Reform Act 1988**(a)** the Secretary of State for Education and Science hereby makes the following Order:

Citation and interpretation

1.—(1) This Order may be cited as the Education Reform Act 1988 (Commencement No. 7) Order 1989.

(2) In this Order–

"the Act" means the Education Reform Act 1988.

Coming into force of certain provisions of the Act

2. The provisions of the Act specified in column 1 of the Schedule to this Order (which relate to the matters mentioned in column 2 thereof) shall, except as otherwise provided in the said column 1, come into force on 1st May 1989.

SCHEDULE

PROVISIONS COMING INTO FORCE ON 1st MAY 1989

Provisions of the Act	*Subject matter of the provisions*
Section 210	Grants for the education of travellers and displaced persons.
Section 211	Grants in respect of special provision for immigrants.
Section 237(2) and Schedule 13, so far as they relate to the repeals set out in the Appendix to this Schedule	Repeals.

(a) 1988 c.40.

APPENDIX TO SCHEDULE

Chapter	*Short title*	*Extent of repeal*
9 & 10 Geo. 6. c.50.	The Education Act 1946	In section 1(1), the words "(hereinafter referred to as 'the principal Act')".
1978 c.44.	The Employment Protection (Consolidation) Act 1978	In section 29(1)(e), the word "or" at the end.
1980 c.20.	The Education Act 1980	In section 35(5), the words "section 27(1)(a), (2), or (3) or". In Schedule 1, paragraph 25.
1980 c.65.	The Local Government, Planning and Land Act 1980	In Schedule 10, Part I.
1985 c.51.	The Local Government Act 1985	Section 22.
1986 c.61.	The Education (No. 2) Act 1986	Section 29. In section 47(5)(a)(ii), the word "or". In Schedule 4, paragraph 4.
1987 c.44.	The Local Government Act 1987.	Section 2.

Kenneth Baker
26th April 1989 Secretary of State for Education and Science

EXPLANATORY NOTE

(This note is not part of the Order)

This Order brings into force on 1st May 1989 section 210 of the Act, which empowers the Secretary of State to make Regulations providing for the payment of grants to local education authorities in respect of the provision of education for travellers and displaced persons. It also brings into force on that date section 211, which extends section 11 of the Local Government Act 1966 (c.42) (grants in respect of special provision for immigrants) by enabling the Secretary of State to pay such grants in respect of grant-maintained schools, city technology colleges and city colleges for the technology of the arts, and institutions within the PCFC funding sector.

Also brought into force on 1st May 1989 are various consequential repeals.

NOTE AS TO EARLIER COMMENCEMENT ORDERS

(This note is not part of the Order)

The following provisions of the Act have been brought or will be brought into force on the dates specified in the following table:–

Provision	*Date of Commencement*	*S.I. No.*
Sections 27, 28 and 32 (all partially) and section 30.	1st September 1988	1988/1459
Sections 26, 27(4) to (8) and 31(2) (all partially)	1st September 1989	1988/1459
Sections 26, 27(4) to (8) and 31(1) (all partially)	4th August 1990	1988/1459
Sections 17 to 19, 131 to 134 (including Schedule 8 to the extent not already in force). 136, 220 and paragraphs 83 to 85 of Schedule 12.	1st November 1988	1988/1794
Sections 121 (except for Southampton Institute of Higher Education) to 130 (including Schedule 7). 135, 219(2)(e), 226, 227(2) to (4), 228 and 229 and paragraphs 64 and 80 of Schedule 12.	21st November 1988	1988/1794
Sections 106 to 111, 117 and 118 and Schedule 13 as regards the repeal of section 61 of the Education Act 1944.	1st April 1989	1988/1794
Section 114, 214 to 216, and Schedule 13, as regards the repeal of section 3 of the Education Act 1967 and paragraph 14 of Schedule 3 to the Education Act 1980, and section 237(2) so far as it relates thereto.	30th November 1988	1988/2002
Section 218, paragraph 68 of Schedule 12 and section 237(1) so far as relating to those provisions, and Schedule 13, as regards the repeal of section 27 of the Education Act 1980 and paragraph 5 of Schedule 3 to the Education Act 1981, and section 237(2) so far as it relates thereto.	1st April 1989	1988/2002
Section 152(10) section 219 (to the extent not already in force), paragraph 63 of Schedule 12 and section 237(1) so far as relating to those provisions, and Schedule 13 so far as it relates to the repeal of sections 25 and 29(2) to (4) of the Education Act 1944, section 7 of the Education Act 1946, and the whole of the Education (No. 2) Act 1968 and section 237(2) so far as it relates thereto.	1st January 1989	1988/2271
Section 121 (to the extent not already in force).	1st February 1989	1988/2271
Section 120, paragraphs 54 to 57, 59, 61, 62, 65, 66, 69 to 76, 78, 79*, 86 to 98, 100, 101, 103 to 105 and 107 of Schedule 12 and section 237(1) so far as relating to those provisions. Schedule 13 so far as it relates to the repeal of sections 8(1)(b) (part), 42 to 46, 50 (part), 52(1) (part) 54 (part), 60, 62(2), 69 (part), 84 and 114 (part) of the Education Act 1944; section 8(3) of the Education Act 1946; section 31(1) and (4) of the London Government Act 1963; section 16 (part) of the Industrial Training Act 1964; section 81(4)(a) (part) and 104(2) (part) of the Local Government Act 1972; sections 24 (part) and 25(6)(c)(ii) (part) of the Sex Discrimination Act 1975; sections 19(6)(c)(ii) (part) and 78(1) (part) of the Race Relations Act 1976; and section 56 (part) of the Education (No. 2) Act 1986; and section 237(2) so far as it relates thereto. * As to paragraph 77, see article 3 of the Education Reform Act 1988 (Commencement No. 6) Order 1989 (S.I. 1989/501).	1st April 1989	1988/2271
Section 7 (except in relation to ILEA schools), paragraph 99 of Schedule 12 and section 237(1) so far as relating to those provisions, and Schedule 13 so far as it relates to the repeal of sections 17(1) (part) and (4), 18(3) (part), (4), (6)(c)(ii) (part) and (8) (part), 19(3) and 20 of the Education (No. 2) Act 1986, and section 237(2) so far as it relates thereto.	1st August 1989	1988/2271

Provision	*Date of Commencement*	*S.I. No.*
Section 152 (to the extent not already in force).	1st April 1990	1988/2271
Section 7 (to the extent not already in force).	1st April 1990	1988/2271
Paragraph 58 of Schedule 12 and section 237(1) so far as it relates thereto and section 12 (except in relation to ILEA county schools).	1st March 1989	1989/164
Section 115.	1st May 1989	1989/164
Section 5, 10(2) and (3) (the latter subsection partially) and 16.	1st August 1989	1989/164
Section 23(2) (except in relation to ILEA schools).	1st September 1989	1989/164
Section 12 and 23(2) (to the extent not already in force).	1st April 1990	1989/164
Section 10(3) (partially).	1st August 1990	1989/164
Section 10(3) (partially).	1st August 1991	1989/164
Section 10(3) (partially).	1st August 1989	1989/501
Section 10(3) (partially).	1st August 1990	1989/501
Section 10(3) (partially).	1st August 1991	1989/501

STATUTORY INSTRUMENTS

1989 No. 720 (S.75)

LEGAL AID AND ADVICE, SCOTLAND

The Civil Legal Aid (Financial Conditions) (Scotland) Regulations 1989

Made - - - - 19th April 1989

Coming into force 20th April 1989

The Secretary of State, in exercise of the powers conferred on him by section 36(2)(b) of the Legal Aid (Scotland) Act 1986(**a**), and of all other powers enabling him in that behalf, hereby makes the following Regulations, a draft of which has been laid before, and approved by a resolution of, each House of Parliament:

1.—(1) These Regulations may be cited as the Civil Legal Aid (Financial Conditions) (Scotland) Regulations 1989 and shall come into force on 20th April 1989.

(2) In these Regulations "the Act" means the Legal Aid (Scotland) Act 1986.

2. For the yearly sum of £5,765 specified in section 15(1) of the Act(**b**), there is hereby substituted the yearly sum of £6,035.

3. For the sum of £5,000 specified in section 15(2)(a) of the Act, there is hereby substituted the sum of £6,000.

4. For the yearly sum of £2,400 specified in section 17(2)(a) of the Act, there is hereby substituted the yearly sum of £2,515.

5. The Civil Legal Aid (Financial Conditions) (Scotland) Regulations 1988(**c**) are hereby revoked.

James Douglas-Hamilton
Parliamentary Under Secretary of State,
Scottish Office

St. Andrew's House, Edinburgh
19th April 1989

(**a**) 1986 c.47; section 36(2)(b) was amended by the Legal Aid Act 1988 (c. 34), Schedule 4, paragraph 6.
(**b**) The existing figures referred to in regulations 2 to 4 were inserted in sections 15 and 17 of the Act by virtue of S.I. 1988/686.
(**c**) S.I. 1988/686.

EXPLANATORY NOTE

(This note is not part of the Regulations)

These Regulations increase certain of the financial limits of eligibility for civil legal aid under the Legal Aid (Scotland) Act 1986.

The income limits are increased to make legal aid available to persons with disposable incomes of not more than £6,035 a year (instead of £5,765) and available without payment of a contribution to those with disposable incomes of less than £2,515 a year (instead of £2,400).

The lower limit of disposable capital below which no contribution in respect of capital may be required remains at £3,000, while the upper limit of disposable capital, above which legal aid may be refused if it appears that applicants could afford to proceed without it, is increased from £5,000 to £6,000.

STATUTORY INSTRUMENTS

1989 No. 721 (S.76)

LEGAL AID AND ADVICE, SCOTLAND

The Advice and Assistance (Financial Conditions) (Scotland) Regulations 1989

Made - - - -	*19th April 1989*
Coming into force	*20th April 1989*

The Secretary of State, in exercise of the powers conferred on him by sections 11(2), 36(2)(b) and 37(1) of the Legal Aid (Scotland) Act 1986(**a**), and of all other powers enabling him in that behalf, hereby makes the following Regulations, a draft of which has been laid before, and approved by a resolution of, each House of Parliament:

1.—(1) These Regulations may be cited as the Advice and Assistance (Financial Conditions) (Scotland) Regulations 1989 and shall come into force on 20th April 1989.

(2) In these Regulations, "the Act" means the Legal Aid (Scotland) Act 1986.

2. For the weekly sum of £122 specified in section 8(a) of the Act(**b**), there is hereby substituted the weekly sum of £128.

3. For the capital sum of £850 specified in section 8 of the Act, there is hereby substituted the capital sum of £890.

4. For the weekly sum of £58 specified in section 11(2)(a) of the Act, there is hereby substituted the weekly sum of £61.

5. The maximum amount of fees or outlays which a client shall be liable to pay under section 11(2) of the Act(**c**), where his disposable income falls within a range specified in the first column of the following table, shall be the amount specified in relation to that range in the second column:–

	Disposable income range	*Maximum contribution*
1	Exceeding £61 but not exceeding £69 a week	£5
2	Exceeding £69 but not exceeding £75 a week	£12
3	Exceeding £75 but not exceeding £81 a week	£19
4	Exceeding £81 but not exceeding £87 a week	£25
5	Exceeding £87 but not exceeding £93 a week	£32
6	Exceeding £93 but not exceeding £98 a week	£37
7	Exceeding £98 but not exceeding £103 a week	£42

(**a**) 1986 c.47; section 36(2)(b) was amended by the Legal Aid Act 1988 (c. 34), Schedule 4, paragraph 6.
(**b**) The existing figures referred to in regulations 2 to 4 were inserted in sections 8 and 11 of the Act by virtue of S.I. 1988/685.
(**c**) The existing maximum amounts are specified in S.I. 1988/685.

	Disposable income range	*Maximum contribution*
8	Exceeding £103 but not exceeding £108 a week	£48
9	Exceeding £108 but not exceeding £113 a week	£53
10	Exceeding £113 but not exceeding £118 a week	£59
11	Exceeding £118 but not exceeding £123 a week	£64
12	Exceeding £123 but not exceeding £128 a week	£70

6. The Advice and Assistance (Financial Conditions) (Scotland) Regulations 1988(**a**) are hereby revoked.

James Douglas-Hamilton
Parliamentary Under Secretary of State,
Scottish Office

St Andrew's House, Edinburgh
19th April 1989

EXPLANATORY NOTE

(This note is not part of the Regulations)

These Regulations increase the disposable income limit for eligibility for advice and assistance under the Legal Aid (Scotland) Act 1986 from £122 a week to £128 a week, the disposable capital limit from £850 to £890 and the weekly disposable income above which a person is required to pay a contribution from £58 to £61. They also prescribe the scale of contributions to be paid where the weekly disposable income exceeds £61 but does not exceed £128.

(**a**) S.I. 1988/685.

STATUTORY INSTRUMENTS

1989 No. 728

CONSUMER PROTECTION

The Low Voltage Electrical Equipment (Safety) Regulations 1989

Made - - - -	*26th April 1989*
Laid before Parliament	*10th May 1989*
Coming into force	*1st June 1989*

Whereas the Secretary of State has, in accordance with section 11(5) of the Consumer Protection Act 1987**(a)**, consulted such organisations as appear to him to be representative of interests substantially affected by these Regulations, such other persons as he considers appropriate and the Health and Safety Commission:

And whereas the Secretary of State is a Minister designated **(b)** for the purposes of section 2 of the European Communities Act 1972**(c)** in relation to measures for safety and consumer protection as respects electrical equipment and any provisions concerning the composition, labelling, marketing, classification or description of electrical equipment:

Now, therefore, the Secretary of State in exercise of powers conferred on him by section 11 of the said Act of 1987, by section 2 of the said Act of 1972 and by the Consumer Protection Act 1987 (Commencement No. 1) Order 1987**(d)** and of all other powers enabling him in that behalf hereby makes the following Regulations:–

Citation and commencement

1. These Regulations may be cited as the Low Voltage Electrical Equipment (Safety) Regulations 1989 and shall come into force on 1st June 1989.

Revocations, disapplications and defence

2.—(1) The Electric Blankets (Safety) Regulations 1971**(e)**, the Electric Blankets (Safety) Regulations (Northern Ireland) 1972**(f)**, the Electrical Equipment (Safety) Regulations 1975**(g)**, the Electrical Equipment (Safety) (Amendment) Regulations 1976**(h)** and the Electrical Equipment (Safety) Regulations (Northern Ireland) 1977**(i)** are hereby revoked.

(a) 1987 c.43.
(b) S.I. 1972/1811.
(c) 1972 c.68.
(d) S.I. 1987/1680.
(e) S.I. 1971/1961.
(f) S.R. & O. (N.I.) 1972 No. 69.
(g) S.I. 1975/1366.
(h) S.I. 1976/1208.
(i) S.R. (N.I.) 1977 No. 137.

(2) The Heating Appliances (Fireguards) Regulations 1973**(a)** and the Heating Appliances (Fireguards) Regulations (Northern Ireland) 1975**(b)** shall cease to have effect in so far as they relate to electrical equipment.

(3) In any proceedings against a person for an offence under any of the relevant statutory provisions (as defined in section 53(1) of the Health and Safety at Work etc. Act 1974**(c)** or article 2(2) of the Health and Safety at Work (Northern Ireland) Order 1978**(d)**) which impose requirements with respect to any matter it shall be a defence for that person to show that the requirements of these Regulations were satisfied in relation to that matter.

(4) Where an improvement notice or a prohibition notice has been served on any person pursuant to section 21 or, as the case may be, section 22 of the Health and Safety at Work etc. Act 1974**(e)** (or pursuant to article 23 or, as the case may be, article 24 of the Health and Safety at Work (Northern Ireland) Order 1978**(f)**), if the person upon whom the notice was served appeals to an industrial tribunal pursuant to section 24 of the said Act (or article 26 of the said Order) and shows that the notice relates to any matter in respect of which the requirements of these Regulations are satisfied, the tribunal shall cancel the notice.

Interpretation

3.—(1) In these Regulations–

"the 1987 Act" means the Consumer Protection Act 1987**(g)**;

"CENELEC Harmonisation Documents HD 21" means those documents relating to polyvinyl chloride insulated cables which contain technical specifications relating to the construction and testing of flexible cables and cords, that is, harmonisation documents numbered HD 21.1 S2, HD 21.2 S2, HD 21.5 S2 all published on 1st July 1984 and Amendment 1 to harmonisation document HD 21.5 S2 published on 1st January 1988, subject to any amendments made to any document in the series and approved by the Secretary of State;

"CENELEC Harmonisation Documents HD 22" means those documents relating to rubber insulated cables which contain technical specifications relating to the construction and testing of flexible cables and cords, that is, harmonisation documents numbered HD 22.1 S2, HD 22.2 S2, HD 22.3 S2 and HD 22.4 S2 all published on 1st July 1984, subject to any amendments made to any document in the series and approved by the Secretary of State;

"Community certification body" means a body which has been notified under article 11 of the low voltage Directive as a body which may establish the marks and certificates in accordance with article 10 of that Directive;

"electrical equipment" means, unless the context otherwise requires, any electrical equipment to which these Regulations apply by virtue of regulation 4 below;

"harmonised standard" means a standard harmonised in accordance with article 5 of the low voltage Directive;

"international safety provision" means a safety provision of a standard which has been published by the International Commission on the Rules for the Approval of Electrical Equipment or the International Electrotechnical Commission and which has been published in the Official Journal of the Communities pursuant to article 6 of the low voltage Directive;

"the low voltage Directive" means Council Directive No. 73/23/EEC**(h)** on the harmonisation of the laws of member States relating to electrical equipment designed for use within certain voltage limits;

"national safety provision" means a safety provision which has the force of law in a member State of the European Economic Community or which is contained in a standard published and not withdrawn by a national standards body, not being a

(a) S.I. 1973/2106.
(b) S.R. (N.I.) 1975 No. 310.
(c) 1974 c.37.
(d) S.I. 1978/1039 (N.I.9).
(e) S.I. 1974 c.37.
(f) S.I. 1978/1039 (N.I.9); relevant amending instruments are S.I. 1984/1159 (N.I.9) and S.I. 1987/2049 (N.I.20).
(g) 1987 c.43.
(h) OJ No. L77, 26.3.73, p.29.

safety provision which is to the same effect as a safety provision of a harmonised standard or as an international safety provision;

"national standards body" means a body which has been notified under article 11 of the low voltage Directive for the purposes of article 5 of that Directive;

"safe" has the same meaning as in section 19(1) of the 1987 Act, except that, for the purpose of these Regulations, the references in that subsection to "risk" shall be construed as including references to any risk of–

(a) death or injury to domestic animals; and

(b) damage to property;

and as excluding any risk arising from the improper installation or maintenance of the electrical equipment in question or from the use of the equipment in applications for which it is not made;

"safety provision" means a provision made for the purpose of ensuring that the equipment in question is safe;

"supply" (except in reference to the electricity supply) includes offering to supply, agreeing to supply, exposing for supply and possessing for supply, and cognate expressions shall be construed accordingly.

(2) For the purposes of regulation 7(2) below a national safety provision is applicable to equipment in a particular member State of the European Economic Community if–

(a) the provision has the force of law in that member State or the national standards body publishing it has its principal office there, and

(b) the equipment was not manufactured in any other member State of the European Economic Community.

(3) Any reference in these Regulations to an electric shock is a reference to an electric shock of such severity as to be liable to cause death or personal injury.

Application

4.—(1) Subject to paragraphs (2) and (3) below, these Regulations apply to any electrical equipment (including any electrical apparatus or device) designed or adapted for use with voltage (in the case of alternating current) of not less than 50 volts nor more than 1,000 volts or (in the case of direct current) of not less than 75 volts nor more than 1,500 volts.

(2) These Regulations do not apply to the electrical equipment set out in Schedule 1 to these Regulations.

(3) These Regulations do not apply to any electrical equipment supplied for export to a place which is not within any member State of the European Economic Community.

Requirement for electrical equipment to be safe etc.

5.—(1) Electrical equipment shall be–

(a) safe; and

(b) constructed in accordance with principles generally accepted within the member States of the European Economic Community as constituting good engineering practice in relation to safety matters.

(2) Subject to regulations 6 and 7 below, in determining whether electrical equipment satisfies the requirements of paragraph (1) above due regard shall be had to the principal elements of the safety objectives for electrical equipment in Annex I to the low voltage Directive as set out in Schedule 2 to these Regulations.

(3) In determining whether electrical equipment satisifies the requirements of paragraph (1) above, no regard shall be had to any liability of the equipment to cause radio-electrical interference.

Harmonised standards

6. Subject to regulation 8 below, electrical equipment which satisfies the safety provisions of harmonised standards shall be taken to satisfy the requirements of regulation 5(1) above.

Conformity with other standards and requirements

7.—(1) Subject to regulation 8 below, where there are no relevant harmonised standards, electrical equipment which satisfies international safety provisions shall be taken to satisfy the requirements of regulation 5(1) above.

(2) Subject to regulation 8 below, where there are no relevant harmonised standards and no relevant international safety provisions, electrical equipment which–

(a) has been manufactured in accordance with the national safety provisions applicable to that equipment in a member State and the compliance of the equipment with such provisions results in the equipment being at the time when the equipment is supplied in the United Kingdom at least as safe as it would be if it satisfied the requirements of regulation 5(1) above; or

(b) satisfies the safety provisions contained in standards published by national standards bodies which are approved in accordance with the provisions of the Approval of Safety Standards Regulations 1987**(a)** and which are appropriate to that equipment,

shall be taken to satisfy the requirements of regulation 5(1) above.

(3) Electrical equipment to which the requirements of the relevant statutory provisions (as defined in section 53(1) of the Health and Safety at Work etc. Act 1974)**(b)** or article 2(2) of the Health and Safety at Work (Northern Ireland) Order 1978**(c)**) apply shall be taken to satisfy the requirements of regulation 5(1) above if the requirements of those provisions are satisfied in relation to that equipment.

Conditions which all electrical equipment (except that mentioned in regulation 7(3)) must satisfy in order to satisfy regulation 5(1).

8. Electrical equipment, other than the equipment referred to in regulation 7(3) above, shall be taken to satisfy the requirements of regulation 5(1) above only if the conditions set out below are satisfied in relation to that equipment–

(a) the equipment is designed and constructed to ensure that it is safe when connected to the electricity supply system and provides an equivalent level of protection against electric shock as equipment which relies on a combination of insulation and the protective earthing conductor contained within that system;

(b) flexible cables and cords intended for the connection of equipment to the electricity supply system comply with CENELEC Harmonisation Documents HD 21 or HD 22 or an equivalent standard of safety; and

(c) where it is necessary for the safe use of any equipment to which these regulations apply that the user should be aware of any particular characteristic of the equipment, the necessary information is given in markings on the equipment itself or, where this is not practicable, in a notice accompanying the equipment. It is not sufficient compliance with this condition to give the information only in a language other than English.

Reports on safety etc. of electrical equipment

9. Where any electrical equipment may not be taken by virtue of regulations 6 or 7 above to satisfy the requirements of regulation 5(1) above and the question of whether or not it satisfies those requirements has arisen (whether in any proceedings or otherwise) any report prepared by a body notified in accordance with the procedure set out in article 11 of the low voltage Directive for the purposes of article 8 of that Directive may be relied upon for the purpose of establishing that the equipment does in fact satisfy those requirements and due regard shall be had to any such report by any person or court by whom that question falls to be determined.

Marks as to conformity

10. Where electrical equipment bears a mark distinctive of a Community certification body or is accompanied by a certificate issued by such a body or, where such a certificate has not been issued or is not available, by a written declaration of conformity made by

(a) S.I. 1987/1911.
(b) 1974 c.37.
(c) S.I. 1978/1039 (N.I.9).

the manufacturer of the equipment, and the mark indicates, or the certificate or declaration is to the effect, that the equipment satisfies–

(a) the safety provisions of harmonised standards;

(b) international safety provisions; or

(c) sub-paragraph (a) or (b) or regulation 7(2) above,

then the equipment shall, unless the contrary be proved, be taken to satisfy those safety provisions, international safety provisions or the relevant sub-paragraph, as the case may be.

Prohibition on supply

11. No person shall supply–

(a) any electrical equipment in respect of which the requirements of regulation 5(1) above are not satisfied; or

(b) any goods which are designed to be used as component parts of any type of electrical equipment to which these Regulations apply by virtue of regulation 4 above and which would, if so used, cause equipment of that type to contravene those requirements.

Duties of enforcement authorities

12. Every authority and council on whom a duty is imposed by virtue of section 27 of the 1987 Act–

(a) shall have regard, in performing that duty in so far as it relates to any provision of these Regulations, to matters specified in any direction issued by the Secretary of State with respect to that provision; and

(b) shall give immediate notice to the Secretary of State of any suspension notice served by it or any application made by it for an order for forfeiture of any goods to which these Regulations apply or any other thing done in respect of any such goods for the purposes of or in connection with sections 14 to 17 of that Act.

Commencement of Proceedings

13. In England, Wales and Northern Ireland a magistrates' court may try an information (in the case of England and Wales) or a complaint (in the case of Northern Ireland) in respect of an offence comitted under section 12 of the 1987 Act in relation to a contravention of these Regulations if (in the case of England and Wales) the information is laid or (in the case of Northern Ireland) the complaint is made within twelve months from the time when the offence is committed, and in Scotland summary proceedings for such an offence may be begun at any time within twelve months from the time when the offence is committed.

Regulations to be treated as safety regulations within the meaning of the 1987 Act.

14.—(1) Subject to paragraph (2) below, these Regulations shall be treated for all purposes as if they were safety regulations within the meaning of section 45(1) of the 1987 Act.

(2) Where a contravention of regulation 11 above arises from the supply of electrical equipment which fails to satisfy the requirements of regulation 5(1) above or of goods which would cause the relevant equipment to contravene those requirements because there is in each case a risk of death or injury to domestic animals or damage to property, or both, but no risk of the death of a person or of personal injury, the person who contravenes regulation 11 shall be guilty of an offence punishable on summary conviction with imprisonment for not more than three months or with a fine not exceeding level five on the standard scale.

Eric Forth
Parliamentary Under-Secretary of State,
Department of Trade and Industry

26th April 1989

Regulation 4(2)

SCHEDULE 1

ELECTRICAL EQUIPMENT EXCLUDED FROM THESE REGULATIONS

Equipment for use in an explosive atmosphere
Equipment for radiology and medical purposes

Parts for goods lifts and passenger lifts

Electricity supply meters
Plugs, socket outlets and adaptors for domestic use
Fence controllers

Specialised electrical equipment for use on ships, aircraft or railways, which complies with the safety provisions drawn up by international bodies in which the member States participate

Regulation 5(2)

SCHEDULE 2

PRINCIPAL ELEMENTS OF THE SAFETY OBJECTIVES FOR ELECTRICAL EQUIPMENT DESIGNED FOR USE WITHIN CERTAIN VOLTAGE LIMITS

1. General conditions

(a) The essential characteristics, the recognition and observance of which will ensure that electrical equipment will be used safely and in applications for which it was made, shall be marked on the equipment, or, if this is not possible, on an accompanying notice.

(b) The manufacturer's or brand name or trade mark should be clearly printed on the electrical equipment or, where that is not possible, on the packaging.

(c) The electrical equipment, together with its component parts should be made in such a way as to ensure that it can be safely and properly assembled and connected.

(d) The electrical equipment should be so designed and manufactured as to ensure that protection against the hazards set out in points 2 and 3 of this Schedule is assured providing that the equipment is used in applications for which it was made and is adequately maintained.

2. Protection against hazards arising from the electrical equipment

Measures of a technical nature should be prescribed in accordance with point 1, in order to ensure:

(a) that persons and domestic animals are adequately protected against danger of physical injury or other harm which might be caused by electrical contact direct or indirect;

(b) that temperatures, arcs or radiation which would cause a danger, are not produced;

(c) that persons, domestic animals and property are adequately protected against non-electrical dangers caused by the electrical equipment which are revealed by experience;

(d) that the insulation must be suitable for foreseeable conditions.

3. Protection against hazards which may be caused by external influences on the electrical equipment.

Technical measures are to be laid down in accordance with point 1, in order to ensure:

(a) that the electrical equipment meets the expected mechanical requirements in such a way that persons, domestic animals and property are not endangered;

(b) that the electrical equipment shall be resistant to non-mechanical influences in expected environmental conditions, in such a way that persons, domestic animals and property are not endangered;

(c) that in foreseeable conditions of overload the electrical equipment shall not endanger persons, domestic animals and property.

EXPLANATORY NOTE

(This note is not part of the Regulations)

These Regulations implement Council Directive No. 73/23/EEC (OJ No. L77, 26.3.73, p.29) on the harmonisation of the laws of member States relating to electrical equipment designed for use within certain voltage limits. They revoke the Electric Blankets (Safety) Regulations 1971, the Electric Blankets (Safety) Regulations (Northern Ireland) 1972, the Electrical Equipment (Safety) Regulations 1975, the Electrical Equipment (Safety) (Amendment) Regulations 1976 and the Electrical Equipment (Safety) Regulations (Northern Ireland) 1977 and provide that the Heating Appliances (Fireguards) Regulations 1973 and the Heating Appliances (Fireguards) Regulations (Northern Ireland) 1975 no longer apply to electrical equipment to which these Regulations apply, that is, any electrical equipment designed or adapted for use with voltage (in the case of alternating current) of between 50 and 1,000 volts or (in the case of direct current) of between 75 and 1,500 volts, except equipment mentioned in Schedule 1 to the Regulations or supplied for export to a place outside the European Economic Community.

The Regulations require electrical equipment to be safe and constructed in accordance with engineering practice generally accepted as good in the EEC (regulation 5(1)). "Safe" has the same meaning as in section 19(1) of the Consumer Protection Act 1987 except that the risk of death or injury to domestic animals or of damage to property is treated as being included in the risks there mentioned and a risk arising from the improper installation or maintenance of the equipment or from its use for unintended purposes is treated as being excluded (regulation 3(1)).

The Regulations require due account to be taken of the principal elements of the safety objectives for electrical equipment in Schedule 2 to the Regulations when deciding whether regulation 5(1) is satisfied (regulation 5(2)).

The following electrical equipment is to be taken (subject to regulation 8) to satisfy article 5(1):–

equipment which satisfies the safety provisions of standards harmonised in accordance with article 5 of the Directive (regulation 6);

if there are no relevant harmonised standards, equipment which satisfies international safety provisions, that is, the safety provisions of standards published by the International Commission on the Rules for the Approval of Electrical Equipment or the International Electrotechnical Commission and published in the Official Journal of the Communities (regulation 7(1));

if there are no harmonised standards and no international safety provisions–

equipment manufactured in accordance with national safety provisions of a member State, where compliance has the result that when it is supplied in the United Kingdom it is at least as safe as if it complied with regulation 5(1) (regulation 7(2)(a));

equipment which satisfies the safety provisions in standards published by national standards bodies which have been approved under the Approval of Safety Standards Regulations 1987 (regulation 7(2)(b)).

Equipment to which the relevant statutory provisions of the Health and Safety at Work etc. Act 1974 or of the Health and Safety at Work (Northern Ireland) Order 1978 and which complies with those provisions is to be taken as complying with regulation 5(1) (regulation 7(3)).

Regulation 8 (which lays down conditions which are designed to ensure that the equipment can be safely used in the United Kingdom) applies to all electrical equipment except that to which regulation 7(3) applies.

Regulation 9 provides that for the purpose of showing that electrical equipment complies with regulation 5(1) a report of a body notified under the Directive procedure may be relied upon and requires any person or court called upon to decide whether regulation 5(1) is satisfied to take due account of any such report.

Regulation 10 provides that electrical equipment is to be taken, unless the contrary is proved, as complying with the safety provisions of harmonised standards, international safety provisions or regulation 7(2)(a) or (b) where it bears the mark of a body notified under article 11 of the Directive or is accompanied by a certificate issued by such a body or, in the absence of such a certificate, by the manufacturer's written declaration indicating (in each case) such compliance.

Regulation 11 prohibits the supply of electrical equipment which does not satisfy regulation 5(1) and of goods designed to be used as parts of electrical equipment which would, if used in that way, result in the equipment not complying with that regulation. Contravention of regulation 11 is a criminal offence by virtue of section 12 of the 1987 Act.

Regulation 13 enables summary proceedings to be instituted for an offence under the Regulations within twelve months of the commission of the offence.

Regulation 14 provides that where a contravention of regulation 11 arises from the supply of goods which involve a risk of injury to animals or damage to property (or both), but no risk to human beings, the person who contravenes the regulation is to be guilty of an offence punishable on summary conviction with a maximum of three months' imprisonment or a fine not exceeding level 5 on the standard scale. In other cases the penalty for a contravention of regulation 12 is a maximum of six months' imprisonment or a fine not exceeding level 5 on the standard scale, or both, by virtue of section 12(5) of the 1987 Act.

Copies of the CENELEC Harmonisation Documents, harmonised standards and international safety provisions referred to in the Regulations may be obtained from the Marketing Department, BSI, Linford Wood, Milton Keynes, MK14 6LE.

STATUTORY INSTRUMENTS

1989 No. 730

BUILDING SOCIETIES

The Building Societies (Money Transmission Services) Order 1989

Made - - - -	*25th April 1989*
Coming into force	*1st July 1989*

The Treasury, in exercise of the powers conferred on them by section 19 of the Building Societies Act 1986(**a**), and of all other powers enabling them in that behalf, hereby make the following Order, a draft of which has been laid before and approved by resolution of each House of Parliament:

Title and commencement

1. This Order may be cited as the Building Societies (Money Transmission Services) Order 1989 and shall come into force on 1st July 1989.

Interpretation

2. In this Order–

"the Act" means the Building Societies Act 1986;

"the 1987 Order" means the Building Societies (Limited Credit Facilities) Order 1987(**b**); and

"society" means a building society.

Money transmission service debts and accounts

3.—(1) The forms of property which, by virtue of this Order, a society is to have power, subject to the provisions of this Order, to acquire, hold and dispose of as class 3 assets are money transmission service debts.

(2) For the purposes of this Order–

(a) "money transmission service debt" means the sum in which a person is indebted to a society on a money transmission service account (whether that sum represents principal, interest or other sums payable on the money transmission service account and whether it is immediately payable or not),

(b) "money transmission service account holder" means that person, and

(c) "money transmission service account" means an account which is provided by a society to a person to facilitate the provision of money transmission services by the society to that person and on which that person may, temporarily or occasionally, in the course of and as an incident of receiving money transmission services from the society, become indebted to the society.

(**a**) 1986 c.53. Schedule 8 was amended by the Banking Act 1987 (c.22), Schedule 6, paragraph 26(8), and varied by S.I. 1988/1141.
(**b**) S.I. 1987/1975.

Societies to which power is available

4. The power conferred by this Order is not available to a society which does not for the time being have a qualifying asset holding, but the cessation of its availability does not require the disposal of any property.

Limit on power

5. A society may acquire, hold and dispose of a money transmission service debt only where it is owed by a person other than an individual.

Class 3 asset limits

6. The aggregate of money transmission service debts owing to a society shall count in accordance with section 20 (commercial asset structure requirements) of the Act towards the limits applicable to class 3 assets under that section, and in calculating that aggregate–

(a) where the society has the power conferred by section 34(1) of and item 1 of Part I of Schedule 8 to the Act (power to provide banking services) and the power conferred by this Order, any current overdraft which could be permitted under either of those powers shall be treated as a money transmission service debt;

(b) where a money transmission service account holder holds other accounts with the society, the value of any shares or deposits in those other accounts shall not be taken into account;

(c) where the society has money transmission service accounts upon which there is no current indebtedness to the society, the balance of such accounts shall not be taken into account.

Amendment of the 1987 Order

7. For article 7 of the 1987 Order there shall be substituted the following article–

"Class 3 asset limits

7. The aggregate of facility debts owing to a society shall count in accordance with section 20 (commercial asset structure requirements) of the Act towards the limits applicable to class 3 assets under that section, and in calculating that aggregate–

(a) where the society has the power conferred by section 16 of the Act and the power conferred by this Order, and the society has made arrangements which could be made under either of those powers, the society shall, in respect of each such arrangement, record the power under which it is to be treated as having been made;

(b) where the society has the power conferred by section 34(1) of and item 1 of Part I of Schedule 8 to the Act (power to provide banking services) and the power conferred by this Order, any current overdraft which could be permitted under either of those powers shall be treated as a facility debt;

(c) where a facility account holder holds other accounts with the society, the value of any shares or deposits in those other accounts shall not be taken into account; and

(d) where the society has facility accounts in respect of which there are no current facility debts, the balance of such accounts shall not be taken into account.".

David Lightbown
David Maclean

25th April 1989

Two of the Lords Commissioners
of Her Majesty's Treasury

EXPLANATORY NOTE

(This note is not part of the Order)

This Order empowers building societies with commercial assets of at least £100 million to operate accounts on which a person other than an individual can overdraw, temporarily or occasionally, in the course of receiving money transmission services. Any such indebtedness will count as a class 3 asset. Class 3 assets may not currently exceed more than 5 per cent of a society's total commercial assets.

The Order also amends article 7 of the Building Societies (Limited Credit Facilities) Order 1987 so that the aggregation of facility debts for the purposes of calculating the limits applicable to class 3 assets is made in the same manner as the aggregation of money transmission service debts under article 6 of this Order.

1989 No. 731

FIRE SERVICES

SUPERANNUATION

The Firemen's Pension Scheme (Amendment) Order 1989

Made - - - -	*26th April 1989*
Laid before Parliament	*10th May 1989*
Coming into force -	*15th June 1989*

In exercise of the powers conferred upon me by section 26 of the Fire Services Act 1947**(a)** I hereby, with the approval of the Treasury**(b)** and after consultation with the Central Fire Brigades Advisory Council and the Scottish Central Fire Brigades Advisory Council, make the following Order:

1.—(1) This Order may be cited as the Firemen's Pension Scheme (Amendment) Order 1989.

(2) This Order shall come into force on 15th June 1989 and shall have effect as from 16th March 1988.

2.—(1) The Firemen's Pension Scheme 1973, set out in Appendix 2 to the Firemen's Pension Scheme Order 1973**(c)** shall be amended in accordance with the following provisions of this article.

(2) In Part I of Schedule 3–

(a) in paragraph 1(2), for "12.5%" there shall be substituted "18.75%", and

(b) in paragraph 1(3), for "4 or more" there shall be substituted "3 or more".

Home Office
20th April 1989

Douglas Hurd
One of Her Majesty's Principal Secretaries of State

We approve,

Kenneth Carlisle
David Lightbown

26th April 1989 — Two of the Lords Commissioners of Her Majesty's Treasury

---

(a) 1947 c.41. Section 26 was amended and extended by section 42 of the Reserve and Auxiliary Forces (Protection of Civil Interests) Act 1951 (c.65) and sections 12 and 16 of the Superannuation Act 1972 (c.11).
(b) Formerly the Minister for the Civil Service: *see* S.I. 1981/1670.
(c) S.I. 1973/966. The relevant amending instruments are S.I. 1978/1228, 1980/1615, 1983/1409, 1987/1302.

EXPLANATORY NOTE

(This note is not part of the Order)

This Order, which comes into force on 15th June 1989, amends the Firemen's Pension Scheme Order 1973 with effect from 16th March 1988 (retrospection is authorised by sections 12 and 16 of the Superannuation Act 1972).

Article 2 amends Schedule 3 of the Scheme set out in Appendix 2 to the Order of 1973 by increasing from 12.5% to 18.75% the maximum rate at which a child's ordinary allowance is payable in respect of the death of a regular fireman. The total amount payable by way of children's ordinary allowances in respect of the death remains 37.5% of the deceased's pension or notional pension (or, where appropriate, of the alternative amount specified in the Schedule); consequently, where 3 or more such allowances are payable, the rate is reduced to provide an equal share of that total amount (the number was previously 4 or more).

STATUTORY INSTRUMENTS

1989 No. 732

FIRE SERVICES

SUPERANNUATION

The Firemen's Pension Scheme (Amendment) (No. 2) Order 1989

Made - - - -	*26th April 1989*
Laid before Parliament	*10th May 1989*
Coming into force	*1st June 1989*

In exercise of the powers conferred upon me by section 26 of the Fire Services Act 1947**(a)**, I hereby, with the approval of the Treasury**(b)** and after consultation with the Central Fire Brigades Advisory Council and the Scottish Central Fire Brigades Advisory Council, make the following Order:

1. This Order may be cited as the Firemen's Pension Scheme (Amendment) (No. 2) Order 1989 and shall come into force on 1st June 1989.

2.—(1) The Scheme set out in Appendix 2 to the Firemen's Pension Scheme Order 1973**(c)** shall be amended in accordance with the following provisions of this article.

(2) In article 55(1) (*pensionable pay*), at the end there shall be added the following provision–

"Provided that, in the case of a person by whom pension contributions become payable under article 56 on or after 1st June 1989, no account shall be taken, for the purposes of determining his pensionable pay, of any amount by which that pay exceeds an amount equivalent to an annual rate of £60,000.

In this paragraph a reference to contributions becoming payable is a reference to their becoming payable either for the first time or following any period in respect of which they were not payable.".

Home Office
21st April 1989

Douglas Hurd
One of Her Majesty's Principal Secretaries of State

We approve,

Kenneth Carlisle
David Lightbown

26th April 1989

Two of the Lords Commissioners of Her Majesty's Treasury

(a) 1947 c.41. Section 26 was amended and extended by section 42 of the Reserve and Auxiliary Forces (Protection of Civil Interests) Act 1951 (c.65) and sections 12 and 16 of the Superannuation Act 1972 (c.11).
(b) Formerly the Minister for the Civil Service: *see* S.I. 1981/1670.
(c) S.I. 1973/966, to which there are amendments not relevant to this Order.

EXPLANATORY NOTE

(This note is not part of the Order)

This Order amends the Firemen's Pension Scheme Order 1973 by limiting the amount of pay which may be counted for the purposes of determining the pensionable pay of a regular fireman to £60,000.

STATUTORY INSTRUMENTS

1989 No. 733

POLICE

The Police Pensions (Amendment) Regulations 1989

Made - - - -	*26th April 1989*
Laid before Parliament	*10th May 1989*
Coming into force	*1st June 1989*

In exercise of the powers conferred upon me by section 1 of the Police Pensions Act 1976**(a)**, and after consultation with the Police Negotiating Board for the United Kingdom, I hereby with the consent of the Treasury**(b)** make the following Regulations:

1. These Regulations may be cited as the Police Pensions (Amendment) Regulations 1989 and shall come into force on 1st June 1989.

2.—(1) The Police Pensions Regulations 1987**(c)** shall be amended in accordance with the following provisions of this regulation.

(2) In regulation G1(1) (*pensionable pay*), at the end there shall be added the following provision–

"Provided that, in the case of a person by whom pension contributions become payable under regulation G2 on or after 1st June 1989, no account shall be taken, for the purposes of determining his pensionable pay, of any amount by which that rate exceeds an annual rate of £60,000.

In this paragraph a reference to contributions becoming payable is a reference to their becoming payable either for the first time or following any period in respect of which they were not payable.".

Home Office
21st April 1989

Douglas Hurd
One of Her Majesty's Principal Secretaries of State

We consent,

Kenneth Carlisle
David Lightbown
26th April 1989
Two of the Lords Commissioners of Her Majesty's Treasury

(a) 1976 c.35, as amended by section 2(3) of the Police Negotiating Board Act 1980 (c.10).
(b) Formerly the Minister for the Civil Service: *see* S.I. 1981/1670.
(c) S.I. 1987/257, to which there are amendments not relevant to these Regulations.

EXPLANATORY NOTE

(This note is not part of the Regulations)

These Regulations amend the Police Pensions Regulations 1987 by limiting the rate of pay which may be counted for the purposes of determining the pensionable pay of a member of a police force to £60,000.

Selected Local Statutory Instrument

STATUTORY INSTRUMENTS

1989 No. 86

HARBOURS, DOCKS, PIERS AND FERRIES

The Mostyn Docks (Pilotage) Harbour Revision Order 1989

Made - - - - 19th January 1989

Coming into force 20th January 1989

ARRANGEMENT OF ARTICLES

The Secretary of State for Transport in exercise of the powers conferred by section 14 of the Harbours Act 1964(**a**) and now vested in him(**b**) and of all other powers enabling him in that behalf, and on the application of Mostyn Docks Limited in accordance with section 7(5) of the Pilotage Act 1987(**c**), hereby makes the following Order:–

Citation and commencement

1. This Order may be cited as the Mostyn Docks (Pilotage) Harbour Revision Order 1989 and shall come into force on 20th January 1989.

Interpretation

2. In this Order–

"the Company" means Mostyn Docks Limited;

"the harbour" has the same meaning as in the Mostyn Docks Harbour Empowerment Order 1988(**d**);

Extension of limits of jurisdiction for purposes of pilotage

3.—(1) The limits within which the Company shall have jurisdiction for the purposes of pilotage under Part I of the Pilotage Act 1987 shall include (in addition to the harbour)–

(**a**) 1964 c. 40; section 14 and Schedule 3 were amended by the Transport Act 1981 (c. 56), section 18 and Schedule 6, paragraphs 2 to 4.
(**b**) S.I. 1981/238.
(**c**) 1987 c. 21.
(**d**) S.I. 1988/1677.

the waters of the River Dee from immediately below the Old Dee bridge at Chester to the imaginary straight lines mentioned in paragraph (2) below.

(2) The lines referred to in paragraph (1) above are–

(a) a line from a point at latitude 53° 21′.35N, longitude 3° 19′.20W, to a point at latitude 53° 22′.00N, longitude 3° 18′.20W; and

(b) a line from that point to a point at latitude 53° 23′.15N, longitude 3° 11′.83W.

J.W.S. Dempster
An Under Secretary
in the Department of Transport

Signed by authority of the Secretary of State
19th January 1989

EXPLANATORY NOTE

(This note is not part of the Order)

By virtue of section 7(5) of the Pilotage Act 1987 a direction given by a harbour authority for the purpose of making pilotage compulsory for ships navigating in a specified area shall not apply to any area which is outside the authority's harbour unless the limits of jurisdiction of the authority for pilotage purposes have been extended to cover that area.

This Order accordingly extends the limits of jurisdiction of Mostyn Docks Limited for pilotage purposes under Part I of the Pilotage Act 1987 so as to include certain areas outside the harbour of Mostyn in respect of which the Company considers that pilotage should be compulsory.

The applicant for this Order is Mostyn Docks Limited.

APPENDIX

Selected Instruments not registered as Statutory Instruments

ORDERS IN COUNCIL

LETTERS PATENT

ROYAL INSTRUCTIONS

ROYAL PROCLAMATIONS ETC.

BY THE QUEEN

A PROCLAMATION

DETERMINING THE SPECIFICATIONS AND DESIGN FOR, AND GIVING CURRENCY TO GOLD COINS IN OUR COLONY OF GIBRALTAR

ELIZABETH R.

We, in exercise of the powers conferred by section 11 of the Coinage Act 1870, section 2(3) of the Decimal Currency Act 1967, and of all other powers enabling Us in that behalf, do hereby, by and with the advice of Our Privy Council, proclaim, direct and ordain as follows:—

1. This Proclamation shall be published in the Official Gazette of Gibraltar and shall come into force there on the date of such publication.

2.—(1) New gold coins of the denomination of five pounds, two pounds, one sovereign, half sovereign and quarter sovereign, shall be made.

(2) In the making of the said coins the fineness, diameter, weight and other specifications shall be as set out in the Schedule to this Our Proclamation.

(3) In the making of the said coins a remedy (that is a variation from the minimum weight) shall be allowed as set out in the said Schedule to this Our Proclamation.

3. The design of the said coins shall be as follows:

(a) All coins shall bear on the obverse impression Our effigy with the inscription "ELIZABETH II" to the left and the inscription "GIBRALTAR . 1989" to the right.

(b) The reverse impression shall bear the design of a lion standing holding the key of Gibraltar in its front left paw and a female allegorical figure holding the orb and sceptre with the inscription "MONETAE REGIAE GIBRALTARICA" above and the inscriptions "MCMLXXXIX" and "SESQUICENTENARIUM" below, with a surrounding border.

(c) All coins shall have a milled rim which continues around the edge.

4. The said coins shall be current and legal tender within Our Colony of Gibraltar.

5. For the purposes of this Our Proclamation there shall be substituted for references to "the Mint" in the Coinage Act 1870 as it applies to Gibraltar, references to "the Pobjoy Mint Ltd.".

Given at Our Court at Windsor Castle, this eighteenth day of April in the year of our Lord One thousand nine hundred and eighty-nine and in the thirty-eighth year of Our Reign.

GOD SAVE THE QUEEN

Modifications to Legislation

For List of Abbreviations used in this table, see p.ix in Section 1.

Year and Number (or date)	*Act or Instrument*	*How affected*
1817	Distress (Costs) Act (c. 93)	**excl**, 1989/438
1827	Distress (Costs) Act (c. 17)	**restr**, 1989/438
1875	Explosives Act (c. 17)	s. 5, proviso (2) **am** (not NI), 1989/615 15, 18, 21 **am**, 1989/462 97(5) **r** (not NI), 1989/615
	Intestates Widows and Children (S) Act (c. 41)	s. 3 **am**, Schs. A, B **am**, 1989/289
1876	Small Testate Estates (S) Act (c. 24)	s. 3 **am**, Sch. A **am**, 1989/289
1894	Arbitration (S) Act (c. 13)	**excl**, 1989/380
	Merchant Shipping Act (c. 60)	s. 460(1) **applied** subject to **mods**, 1989/102 692 **applied** subject to **mods**, 1989/100, 102, 567
1906	Alkali, etc Works Regulation Act (c. 14)	s. 9(3)(4)**r**, 9(7) **r** (with saving), 1989/318
1907	Sheriff Cts (S) Act (c. 51)	First Sch, rule 72A **inserted**, 1989/436
1922		
329	Indiarubber Regs	**am**, 1989/462
731	Chemical Works Regs.	**am**, 1989/462
1335	Maintenance Orders (Facilities for Enforcement) Rules	**am**, 1989/384
1924		
1129	Conveyance of explosives by road, etc—O (No.11)	**r** in pt (not NI), 1989/615
1925	Land Registration Act (c. 21)	**ext**, s. 49(1)(g) **am**, 1989/438
1093	Land Registration Rules	**am**, 1989/801
1928	Petroleum (Consolidation) Act (c. 32)	s. 4 **am/excl**, 1989/462
82	Manufacture of Cinematograph Film Regs	**am**, 1989/635
1933		
878	Alkali, etc Works Regulation O (S)	**r** (with saving), 1989/318
1936	Petroleum (Transfer of Licences) Act (c. 27)	s. 1(4) **am/excl**, 1989/462
1939	HC Members' Fund Act (c. 49)	**am**, 1989/365
571	Cinematograph Film Stripping Regs	**am**, 1989/635
1944	Education Act (c. 31)	s. 29(1) **applied (mods)**, Sch. 5 **applied (mods)**, 1989/46
500	War Pensions (Coastguards) Scheme	**am**, 1989/540
739	Electricity (Factories Act) Special Regs ..	**r**, 1989/635
1946		
258	Patent Fuel Manufacture (Health & Welfare) Special Regs	**am**, 1989/462

Year and Number (or date)	*Act or Instrument*	*How affected*
1947	Emergency Laws (Misc Provns) Act (c. 10)	Sch 2, para 4 **r** (not NI), 1989/615
1949	Wireless Telegraphy Act (c. 54)	s. 1(1) **excl**, 1989/604
1950	Arbitration Act (c. 27)	**excl**, 1989/380 s. 31 **applied**, 1989/439
	Maintenance Orders Act (c. 37)	s. 16(2)(c)(ix) **inserted**, 1989/678
1952		
1689	Factories (Testing of Aircraft Engines and Accessories) special Regs	**am**, 1989/635
1953		
1545	Mule Spinning (Health Special Regs)	**am**, 1989/462
1954	Mines and Quarries Act (c. 70)	**ext**, s. 64(2) **am**, 157 **excl**, 182(1) **am**, 1989/635
698	Horses (Landing from NI and the Republic of Ireland) O	**r**, 1989/23
1956	Food and Drugs (S) Act (c. 30)	s. 41(2) **ext**, (5) **ext**, (1)–(3) **ext**, 44–48 **ext**, 1989/581
1797	Misc Mines (Electricity) O	**r**, 1989/635
1781	Quarries (Electricity) O	**r**, 1989/635
1957		
2208	Alkali, etc Works (Registration) O	**r** (with saving), 1989/318
1958	Agriculture Marketing Act (c. 47)	s. 47(2) **excl**, 1989/380
61	Work in Compressed Air Special Regs	**am**, 1989/462
320	Dragon by Ironstone Mine (Diesel, Diesel-Electric and Storage Battery Vehicles) Special Regs	**r**, 1989/635
321	Winn's Ironstone Mine (Diesel, Diesel-Electric and Storage Battery Vehicles) Special Regs	**r**, 1989/635
1276	Silverwood Mine (Electric Trolley Locomotives) Special Regs	**r**, 1989/635
1959		
3	Magistrates' Cts (Maintenance Orders Act 1958) Rules 1959	**am**, 1989/384
477	Further Education (S) Regs	**am**, 1989/433
663	Glass Houghton Mine (Shuttle Cars) Special Regs	**r**, 1989/635
1960		
1015	Coal Mines (Firedamp Drainage) Regs	**am**, 1989/635
1932	Shipbuilding and Ship-repairing Regs	**am**, 1989/635
1961	Factories Act (c. 34)	s. 125(2)(j) **am**, 127(2)(j)(5) **am**, 138(1)(a)–(c) **r**, 153(1)(b) **r**, 1989/682
1580	Construction (Gen Provns) Regs	**am**, 1989/635, 682
1582	Hopton Mine (Locomotives and Diesel Vehicles) Special Regs	**r**, 1989/635
1769	Cocklakes Mines (Locomotives and Diesel Vehicles) Special Regs	**r**, 1989/635
1774	Long Meg Mine (Locomotives and Diesel Vehicles) Special Regs	**r**, 1989/635

Year and Number (or date)	Act or Instrument	How affected
1962		
192	Sandwith Anhydrite Mine (Lighting) Special Regs	**r**, 1989/635
364	Thistleton Mine Special Regs	**am**, 1989/635
645	New Street Byelaws (Ext of Operation) O ..	**r**, 1989/645
1501	Force Crag Mine (Storage Battery Locomotives) Special Regs	**r**, 1989/635
1963		
270	Potts Ghyll Mine (Storage Battery Locomotives) Special Regs	**r**, 1989/635
896	Chislet Mine Electric Trolley Locomotives) Special Regs	**r**, 1989/635
906	Llanharry Mine (Storage Battery Locomotives) Special Regs	**r**, 1989/635
1074	Easton Mine (Diesel, Diesel-Electric and Storage Battery Vehicles) Special Regs	**r**, 1989/635
1964		
388	Prison Rules	**am**, 1989/330
1985	War Pensions (Naval Auxiliary Personnel) Scheme	**am**, 1989/540
2058	War Pensions (Mercantile Marine) Scheme	**am**, 1989/540
1965	National Insurance Act (c. 51)	s. 36(1) **am**, 1989/43
33	Guildie Howes Mine (Locomotives and Diesel Vehicles) Special Regs	**r**, 1989/635
120	Muirshiel Barytes Mine (Storage Battery Locomotives) Special Regs	**r**, 1989/635
307	Information for Employees Regs	**r**, 1989/682
321	AS (Rules of Ct consolidation and amendment)	**am**, 1989/435, 445
534	Water Resources (Licences) Regs	**am**, 1989/336
1299	Dragonby Ironstone Mine (Diesel, Diesel-Electric and Storage Battery Vehicles (Amdt) Special Regs	**r**, 1989/635
1559	Coal and Other Mines (Mechanics and Electricians) Regs	**am**, 1989/635
1698	Redburn Mine (Storage Battery Locomotives) Special Regs	**r**, 1989/635
1776	Rules of the Supreme Ct	**am**, 1989/177, 386
1995	Industrial and Provident Societies Regs	**am**, 1989/357
1966		
351	Settlingstones Mine (Storage Battery Locomotives) Special Regs	**r**, 1989/635
1967	General Rate Act (c. 9)	s. 70(5), 72(1), 73(1)(2)(b), 74(2)(3), 75(b) **am**, 76(1)(2) **replaced**, 76(3)–(5), 77, 78(1)(3), 83(5)(b)(6)–(9) **am**, 88(1)–(4) **r** (1–5–89), (5)–(6) **replaced**, 89–92 **r** (1–5–89), 93(1) **am**, 94 **r** (1–5–89) 108(1)(c) **am**, 1989/440
512	New Street Byelaws (Ext of Operation) ..	**r**, 1989/645
636	Local Valuation Panels (Jurisdiction) Regs ..	**am** (with saving), 1989/440
637	Mixed Hereditament (Certificate) Regs ..	**am**, 1989/440
879	Carcinogenic Substances Regs	**am**, 1989/462

Year and Number (or date)	Act or Instrument	How affected
1967—*contd*		
1083	Coal and Other Mines (Electricity) (Amdt) Regs	**r**, 1989/635
1310	Industrial and Provident Societies Regs	**am**, 1989/357
1395	Aberllefeni Mine (Storage Battery Locomotives) Special Regs	**r**, 1989/635
1396	Braich Goch Mine (Storage Battery Locomotives) Special Regs	**r**, 1989/635
1968	International Organisations Act (c. 48)	s. 6(3) **excl**, Sch 1, Pt 1V **excl**, 1989/480
	Gaming Act (c. 65)	s. 20(3)(8) **am** (E and W) 1989/536 **am** (S) 1989/623 48(3)(a)–(g)(4)(a)(b) **am** (E and W), 1989/294 **am** (S) 1989/362
38	Preston Manor Mine (Lighting) Special Regs	**r**, 1989/635
39	Chudleigh Knighton Tunnel Mine (Lighting) Special Regs	**r**, 1989/635
40	West Golds Mine (Lighting) Special Regs	**r**, 1989/635
103	Broadway New Pit Tunnel Mine (Lighting) Special Regs	**r**, 1989/635
104	Mainbow Mine (Lighting) Special Regs	**r**, 1989/635
182	Bermuda Constitution O	**am**, 1989/151
208	Police Cadets (S) Regs	**am**, 1989/702
868	Nangiles and the Janes Mine (Storage Battery Locomotives) Special Regs	**r**, 1989/635
1231	Legal Aid in Criminal Proceedings (Gen) Regs	**r**, 1989/344
1969	Mines and Quarries (Tips) Act (c. 10)	**ext**, 1989/635
177	Cts-Martial Appeal Legal Aid (Gen) Regs	**r**, 1989/344
570	Camborne Mine (Storage Battery Locomotives) Special Regs	**r**, 1989/635
744	Cotgrave Mine (Suspended Monorail Diesel Locomotives) Special Regs	**r**, 1989/635
1236	Levant Mine (Storage Battery Locomotives) Special Regs	**r**, 1989/635
1787	Police Federation Regs	**am**, 1989/564
1970	Taxes Management Act (c. 9)	**applied** with **mods**, 1989/469 s. 33(1), 34(1), 37(1), 40(1)(2) **applied (mods)**, 1989/421 42 **excl**, 1989/469 43(1) **applied (mods)**, 1989/421 Pt V **applied** 1989/469 95 **applied** with **mods**, 95(2)(a) **mod**, 97(1) **applied** with **mods**, 1989/469 113(1B)(3) **applied**, 114(2) **applied**, 1989/421
	Income and Corporation Taxes Act (c. 10)	s. 168(1) **applied (mod)**, 1989/421
	Merchant Shipping Act (c. 36)	s. 21 **r**, 22(1) **am**, 76(3) **am**, 1989/102
294	Merchant Shipping (Certificates of Competency as A.B.) Regs	**am**, 1989/323
616	Elections (Welsh Forms) O	**r**, 1989/429
1103	No.4 Adit Mine (Lighting) Special Regs	**r**, 1989/635

Year and Number (or date)	*Act or Instrument*	*How affected*
1970—*contd*		
1152	Drainage Rates (Appeals) Regs	**am**, 1989/440
1547	Rixey Park Mine (Lighting) Special Regs	**r**, 1989/635
1980	Legal Aid in Criminal Proceedings (Gen) (Amdt) Regs	**r**, 1989/344
1971	Mines Management Act (c. 20)	**ext**, s. 1(4)(d) **substituted** (4)(e) **inserted**, 1989/635
1971	Finance Act (c. 68)	s. 23(2)(4) **applied (mods)**, 1989/421
	Town and Country Planning Act (c. 78)	s. 36, 37 **applied** with **mods**, 1989/670
18	Horden Mine (Cable Reel Shuttle Cars) Special Regs	**r**, 1989/635
1270	Mount Wellington Mine (Storage Battery Locomotives) Special Regs	**r**, 1989/635
1961	Electric Blankets (Safety) Regs	**r**, 1989/728
1991	Magistrates' Cts (Blood Tests) Rules	**am**, 1989/384
1972	Employment Medical Advisory Service Act (c. 28)	Sch 2 **am**, 1989/682
	Land Charges Act (c. 61)	**ext**, 1989/438
	Local Govt Act (c. 70)	s. 85 **applied** Sch 12, Pt V1 (exc para 45) **applied**, 1989/304
348	Cornish Hush Mine (Storage Battery Locomotives) Special Regs	**r**, 1989/635
396	Beckermet Mine (Storage Battery Locomotives) Special Regs	**r**, 1989/635
483	Burtree Pasture Mine (Storage Battery Locomotives) Special Regs	**r**, 1989/635
595	New Street Byelaws (Ext of Operation) O	**r**, 1989/645
764	Nat Savings Bank Regs	**am**, 1989/25
765	Premium Savings Bonds Regs	**am**, 1989/639
1235	Haile Moor Mine (Storage Battery Locomotives) Special Regs	**r**, 1989/635
1236	Carrock Fell Mine (Storage Battery Locomotives) Special Regs	**r**, 1989/635
1393	Prince of Wales Mine (Storage Battery Locomotives) Special Regs	**r**, 1989/635
1719	Immigration (Guernsey) O	**am**, 1989/676
1813	Immigration (Jersey) O	**am**, 1989/488
1871	Merchant Shipping (Provns and Water) Regs	**r**, 1989/102
1872	Merchant Shipping (Provns and Water) (Fishing Vessels) Regs	**r**, 1989/102
1973	Fair Trading Act (c. 41)	**mod**— Sch 3, Pt 11 para 10(1) **am**, 10(1A) **inserted**, 1989/122
	Finance Act (c. 51)	Sch 16A **applied** (with **mods**), 1989/421
	Land Compensation (S) Act (c. 56)	s. 28 **replaced**, 30(4) **r**, 1989/47
966	Fireman's Pension Scheme O	**am**, 1989/731, 732
1165	Town and Country Planning (Use Classes) (S) O	**r**, 1989/147

Year and Number (or date)	Act or Instrument	How affected
1973—*contd*		
1208	Rixey Park Mine (Storage Battery Locomotives) Special Regs	**r**, 1989/635
1468	NHS (Gen Dental Services) Regs	**am**, 1989/394, 613
1936	Diseases of Animals (Waste Food) O	**excl**, 1989/661
2106	Heating Appliances (Fireguards) Regs	**am**, 1989/728
1974	Local Govt Act (c. 7)	s. 21(3) **am**, 1989/440
284	NHS (Charges for Appliances) Regs	**am**, 1989/394
505	NHS (Gen Dental Services) (S) Regs	**am**, 1989/363, 602
645	New Street Byelaws (Ext of Operation) O	**r**, 1989/645
706	Magistrates' Cts (Guardianship of Minors) Rules	**am**, 1989/384
1654	Beaumont Mine (Storage Battery Locomotives) Special Regs	**r**, 1989/635
1740	Pensions Increase (Local Authies' etc Pensions) Regs	**am**, 1989/417
1853	Coal and Other Mines (Electricity) (Second Amdt) Regs	**am**, 1989/635
1910	NHS (Charges for Appliances) (S) Regs	**am**, 1989/363
1929	Ledston Luck Mine (Cable Reel Shuttle Cars) Special Regs	**r**, 1989/635
1941	Factories Act 1961 etc (Repeals and Mods) Regs	**am**, 1989/635
1985	Hendre Mine (Storage Battery Locomotives) Special Regs	**r**, 1989/635
1975	Social Security Act (c. 14)	**mod**, 1989/483 s. 4(6B) (6E) **am**, 7(1)(5), 8(1), 9(2), 10(1) **am**, 1989/26 30(1)(1)(a)(b) **am**, 41(2B) **am**, 1989/43 134(4) defn of "appropriate national health service allocation" **am**, 1989/26 Sch 4 Pts I, III–V **am**, 1989/43
	Industrial Injuries and Diseases (Old Cases) Act (c. 16)	s. 2(6)(c) **am**, 7(2)(b) **am**, 1989/43
	Ministerial and Other Salaries Act (c. 27)	s.1(2) **am**, 1989/681
	Social Security Pensions Act (c. 60)	s. 6(1)(a) **am**, Sch 1 **am**, 1989/43
205	Friendly Societies Regs	**am**, 1989/356
299	Land Tribunal Rules	**am**, 1989/440
536	Trade Unions and Employers' Assocns (Amalgamations, etc) Regs	**am**, 1989/205
686	Local Authies (Allowances) (S) Regs	**am**, 1989/301
733	Merchant Shipping (Provns and Water) (Fishing and Other Vessels) (Amdt) Regs	**r**, 1989/102
1030	Zoonoses O	**r**, 1989/285
1102	Mines and Quarries Acts 1954–1971 (Repeals and Mods) Regs	**am**, 1989/635
1366	Electrical Equipment (Safety) Regs	**r**, 1989/728
1976	Adoption Act (c. 36)	s. 57(7) **r**, 1989/166
	Land Drainage Act (c. 70)	s. 78(5)(a)(b) **replaced**, 78(6) **am**, 79(1)(2) **replaced**, 79(3)(4)(5) **am**, 79(8) **r**, 1989/440
476	AS (Summary Cause Rules, Sheriff Ct)	**am**, 1989/436
696	South Leicester Mine (Electric Lighting) Regs	**r**, 1989/635

Year and Number (or date)	*Act or Instrument*	*How affected*
1976—*contd*		
790	Legal Aid in Criminal Proceedings (Gen) (Amdt) Regs	**r**, 1989/344
1208	Electrical Equipment (Safety) (Amdt) Regs ..	**r**, 1989/728
1267	Child Benefit and Social Security (Fixing and Adjustment of Rates) Regs	**am**, 1989/43
1451	Pensions Increase (Approved Schemes) (NHS) Regs	**am**, 1989/711
1987	Teachers' Supn Regs	**mod**, 1989/378
2007	Fire Precautions Act 1971 (Mods) Regs ..	**r**, 1989/79
2008	Fire Precautions (Application for Certificate) Regs	**r**, 1989/77
1009	Fire Precautions (Factories, Offices, Shops and Railway Premises) O	**r**, 1989/76
2010	Fire Precautions (Non-Certificated Factory, Office, Shop and Railway Premises) Regs ..	**r**, 1989/78
2012	Nat Savings Stock Register Regs	**am**, 1989/652
1977		
343	Social Security Benefit (Dependency) Regs ..	**am**, 1989/455, 523
447	Legal Aid (Matrimonial Proceedings) Regs ..	**r**, 1989/549
502	New Street Byelaws (Ext of Operation) O ..	**r**, 1989/645
888	Conveyance by Road of Military Explosives Regs	**r** (not NI), 1989/615
1205	Coal and Other Mines (Electricity) (Third Amdt) Regs	**r**, 1989/635
1360	Teachers' Supn (S) Regs	**am**, 1989/666
2035	Botsover Mine (Cable Reel Shuttle Cars) Regns	**r**, 1989/635
2150	Social Security (Is of Man) O	**mod**, 1989/483
1978	NI (Emergency Provns) Act (c. 5)	temp provns (exc s. 12, Sch 1, s. 24) **cont** until 21-3-90, 1989/509 Sch 3: reg 4 **replaced**, 5 **r**, 1989/510
	Adoption (S) Act (c. 28)	s. 51(8) **r**, 1989/194
1978	Rating (Disabled Persons) Act (c. 40)	s. 2(5B) **am**, (5C) **replaced**, Sch 1, para 11(2) **am**, 11(3) **replaced**, 1989/440
	Finance Act (c. 42)	s. 30(1) **applied (mod)**, 1989/421
	Protection (Consolidation) Act (c. 44)	15(1) **am**, 1989/526 73(4A) **am**, 1989/528 75(1) **am**, 1989/527 75A(1)(2) **am**, 1989/528 122(5) **am**, Sch 14, para 8(1)(a)–(c) **am**, 1989/526
17	Beef Premiums (Protection of Payments) O	**r**, 1989/574
18	Beef Premiums (Recovery Powers) Regs	**r**, 1989/575
32	Diseases of Animals (Approved Disinfectants) O	**am**, 1989/144
36	Merchant Shipping (Provn and Water) Regs	**r**, 1989/102
322	Babies' Dummies (Safety) Regs (NI)	**r**, 1989/141
323	Home Loss Payments (S) O	**r**, 1989/47
393	Social Security (Graduated Retirement Benefit) (No. 2) Regs	**am**, 1989/43
738	Price Marking (Food) O	**am**, 1989/218

Year and Number (or date)	Act or Instrument	How affected
1978—*contd*		
795	Merchant Shipping (Crew Accommodation) Regs	**am**, 1989/184
836	Babies' Dummies (Safety) Regs	**r**, 1989/141
1121	Medicines (Fees) Regs	**am**, 1989/418, 583
1267	Wireless Telegraphy (Control of Interference from Household Appliances, Portable Tools etc) Regs	**am**, 1989/562
1268	Wireless Telegraphy (Control of Interference from fluorescent Lighting Apparatus) Regs	**am**, 1989/561
1344	Trade Unions and Employers' Assocns (Amalgamations, etc) (Amdt) Regs	**am**, 1989/205
1539	Ackton Hall Mine (Cable Reel Load-Haul-Dump Vehicles) Regs	**r**, 1989/635
1648	Coal and Other Mines (Metrication) Regs	**am**, 1989/635
1727	Fire Services (Appointments and Promotion) (S) Regs	**am**, 1989/49
1979	Capital Gains Tax Act (c. 14)	s. 78–81 **excl**, 1989/469
112	Gen Medical Council (Constitution) O	**am**, 1989/496
368	European Parliamentary Elections (Welsh Forms) O	**r**, 1989/428
554	Customs Duties (Standard Exchange Relief) Regs	**r**, 1989/116
555	Outward Processing Relief Regs	**r**, 1989/116
591	Social Security (Contributions) Regs	**am**, 1989/345, 571, 572
705	NHS (Dental and Optical Charges) (S) Regs ..	**am**, 1989/363
752	Preservatives in Food Regs	**r**, 1989/533
899	Medicines (Fees) Amdt Regs	**am**, 1989/418, 583
937	Industrial and Provident Societies (Credit Unions) Regs	**am**, 1989/358
1038	Distress for Rates O	**am**, 1989/621
1073	Preservatives in Food (S) Regs	**r**, 1989/581
1185	Further Education (S) Amdt Regs	**am**, 1989/433
1203	Coal and other Mines (Electric Lighting for Filming) Regs	**r**, 1989/635
1658	Scraithole Mine (Storage Battery Locomotives) Regs	**r**, 1989/635
1980	Magistrates' Cts Act (c. 43)	s. 55(2) **rest**, 1989/438 77(1) **applied**, 78 **applied**, 1989/217 125(3) **applied**, 127(1) **excl**, 1989/438
16	Medicines (Fees) Amdt Regs	**am**, 1989/418, 583
51	Consumer Credit (Total Charge for Credit) Regs	**am**, 1989/596
457	New Street Byelaws (Ext of Operation) O	**am**, 1989/645
661	Legal Aid in Criminal Proceedings (Gen) (Amdt) Regs	**r**, 1989/344
765	Motorcycles (Sound Level Measurement Certificates) Regs	**am**, 1989/713
931	Preservatives in Food (Amdt) Regs	**r**, 1989/533
986	NHS (Gen Dental Services) Amdt Regs ..	**am**, 1989/394
1126	Medicines (Fees) Amdt (No.2) Regs	**am**, 1989/418, 583
1220	NHS (Gen Dental Services) (S) Amdt Regs ..	**am**, 1989/363
1232	Preservatives in Food (S) Amdt Regs	**r**, 1989/581
1395	Lynemouth Mine (Electric Lighting) Regs	**r**, 1989/635
1396	Manton Mine (Electric Lighting) Regs	**r**, 1989/635
1397	Vane Tempest Mine (Electric Lighting) Regs	**r**, 1989/635

Year and Number (or date)	*Act or Instrument*	*How affected*
1980—*contd*		
1405	Yew Tree Mine (Storage Battery Locomotives) Regs	**r**, 1989/635
1503	NHS (Charges for Drugs and Appliances) Regs	**r**, 1989/419
1630	Legal Aid (Assessment of Resources) Regs	**r**, 1989/338
1651	Legal Aid in Criminal Proceedings (Gen) (Amdt No.2) Regs	**r** 1989/344
1674	NHS (Charges for Drugs and Appliances) (S) Regs	**r**, 1989/326
1894	Legal Aid (Gen) Regs	**r**, 1989/339
1898	Legal Advice and Assistance Regs (No.2)	**r**, 1989/340
1981	HC Members' Fund and Parliamentary Pensions Act (c. 7)	s. 2(1)(b) **substituted**, 1989/365
	Judicial Pensions Act (c. 20)	s. 21(1)(c)(ii) **am**, 1989/187
	Animal Health Act (c. 22)	s. 87(1) defn of ''animals'' **ext**, 87(4) defn of ''poultry'' **ext**, various provns **applied**, 1989/285
57	Air Navigation (Gen) Regs	**am**, 1989/669
173	Legal Aid (Gen) (Amdt) Regs	**r**, 1989/339
257	Public Service Vehicles (Conditions of Fitness Equipment, Use and Certification) Regs ..	**am**, 1989/322
354	Merchant Shipping (Light Dues) Regs	**r** (1-6-89), 1989/305
533	Magistrates' Cts (Forms) Rules	**am**, 1989/384
552	Magistrates' Cts Rules	**am**, 1989/300, 384, 438
630	Education (School Information) Regs	**am**, 1989/398
676	Diseases of Animals (Protein Processing) O	**r**, 1989/661
830	Town and Country Planning (Gen Devpt) (S) O	**am**, 1989/148
1063	Jam and Similar Products Regs	**am**, 1989/533
1086	Education (Schools and Further Education) Regs	**am**, 1989/351
1221	Central Institutions (S) Amdt Regs	**am**, 1989/433
1320	Jam and Similar Products (S) Regs	**am**, 1989/581
1523	Motor Fuel (Lead Content of Petrol) Regs	**am**, 1989/547
1687	Country Ct Rules	**am**, 1989/236, 381
1694	Motor Vehicles (Tests) Regs	**am**, 1989/321
1714	NHS (Charges for Drugs and Appliances) Amdt Regs	**am**, 1989/419
1717	NHS (Charges for Drugs and Appliances) (S) Amdt (No.2) Regs	**am**, 1989/326
1982	Social Security and Housing Benefits Act (c. 24)	s.7(1)(a)(b) **am**, 1989/43
15	Preservatives in Food (Amdt) Regs	**r**, 1989/533
168	Sea Fish Industry Authy (Levy) Regs 1982 Confirmatory O	**r**, 1989/425
218	Poisons Rules	**am**, 1989/112
234	Warble Fly (E and W) O	**am**, 1989/244
287	NHS Functions (Directions to Authies and Admin Arrangements)	**r**, 1989/51
315	Authies for London Post-Graduate Teaching Hospital Regs	**am**, 1989/238
516	Preservatives in Food (S) Amdt Regs	**r**, 1989/581
793	Outward Processing Relief (Amdt) Regs	**am**, 1989/116
827	Offices, Shops and Railway Premises Act 1963 etc (Metrication) Regs	**am**, 1989/682
863	NHS (Charges to Overseas Visitors) (No.2) Regs	**r**, 1989/306
898	NHS (Charges to Overseas Visitors) (S) Regs	**r**, 1989/364

Year and Number (or date)	Act or Instrument	How affected
1982—*contd*		
1009	Local Govt (Compensation for Premature Retirement) Regs	**am**, 1989/372
1109	Crown Ct rules	**am**, 1989/299
1121	Medicines (Fees) Amdt Regs	**r** in pt, 1989/418, 583
1311	Fruit Juices and Fruit Nectars (Amdt) Regs	**am**, 1989/533
1408	Social Security (Gen Benefit) Regs	**am**, 1989/455
1489	Workmen's Compensation (Supplementation) Scheme	**am**, 1989/525
1577	NHS (Charges to Overseas Visitors) (Amdt) Regs	**r**, 1989/306
1592	Legal Advice and Assistance (Amdt) Regs	**r**, 1989/340
1619	Fruit Juices and Fruit Nectars (S) Amdt Regs	**am**, 1989/581
1727	Food (Revision of Penalties) Regs	**am**, 1989/533
1743	NHS (Charges to Overseas Visitors) (S) Amdt Regs	**r**, 1989/364
1752	Merchant Shipping (Section 52 Inquiries) Rules	**am**, 1989/84
1983	Representation of the People Act (c. 2) ..	s. 76(2)(a)(i)(ii) **am**, (2)(b)(ii) **am** (GB) 197(1)(2) **am** (City of London), 1989/634
	VAT Act (c.55)	Sch 1, para 1(1)(a)(i)(ii) **am**, (1)(b)(2)(3) **am**, 2(1)(2) **am**, 4(3) **am**, 1989/471 5, Group 16, item 8 **replaced**, note 4 (a) **am**, 1989/470 6, Group 6, item 1 **am**, note (1) **am**, note (3A) **inserted**, 1989/267 Group 12 **added**, 1989/470
270	Food and Drugs (S) Act 1956 (Transfer of Enforcement Functions) Regs	**am**, 1989/581
302	NHS (Charges to Overseas Visitors) Amdt Regs	**r**, 1989/306
306	NHS (Charges for Drugs and Appliances) Amdt Regs	**r**, 1989/419
334	NHS (Charges for Drugs and Appliances) (S) Amdt Regs	**r**, 1989/326
362	NHS (Charges to Overseas Visitors) (S) Amdt Regs	**r**, 1989/364
423	Legal Aid (Assessment of Resources) (Amdt) Regs	**r**, 1989/338
424	Legal Aid (Gen) (Amdt) Regs	**r**, 1989/339
470	Legal Advice and Assistance (Amdt) (No.2) Regs	**r**, 1989/340
483	New Street Byelaws (Ext of Operation) Variation O	**r**, 1989/645
667	Nurses, Midwives and Health Visitors (Parts of the Register) O	**am**, 1989/104
686	Personal Injuries (Civilians) Scheme	**am**, 1989/415
710	Coal and Other Mines (Safety-Lamps and Lighting) (Amdt) Regs	**r**, 1989/635
713	Civil Cts O	**am**, 1989/106, 107

Year and Number (or date)	Act or Instrument	How affected
1983—*contd*		
873	Nurses, Midwives and Health Visitors Rules Approval O	**am**, 1989/109
883	Naval, Military and Air Forces etc (Disablement and Death) Service Pensions O	**am**, 1989/156
943	Health and Safety (Emissions into the Atmosphere) Regs	**am**, 1989/319
978	Factories Act 1961 etc (Metrication) Regs	**am**, 1989/682
994	Misc Mines (Metrication) Regs	**am**, 1989/635
1026	Quarries (Metrication) Regs	**am**, 1989/635
1027	NHS (Functions of Health Bds) (S) O	**am**, 1989/446
1130	Mines (Misc Amdts) Regs	**r**, 1989/635
1142	Legal Advice and Assistance (Amdt) (No.3) Regs	**r**, 1989/340
1160	Redundancy Payments (Local Govt) (Modification) O	**am**, 1989/532
1165	NHS (Charges for Drugs and Appliances) Amdt (No.2) Regs	**r**, 1989/419
1172	NHS (Charges for Drugs and Appliances) (S) (No.2) Amdt Regs	**r**, 1989/326
1211	Sweetners in Food Regs	**am**, 1989/533
1483	Legal Aid (Gen) (Amdt No.2) Regs	**r**, 1989/339
1497	Sweetners in Food (S) Regs	**am**, 1989/581
1557	Consumer Credit (Cancellation Notices and Copies of Documents) Regs	**am**, 1989/591
1562	Consumer Credit (Rebate on Early Settlement) Regs	**am**, 1989/596
1598	Social Security, (Unemployment, Sickness and Invalidty Benefit) Regs	**am**, 1989/455
1619	Town and Country Planning (Use Classes) (S) Amdt O	**r**, 1989/147
1674	Town and County Planning (Fees for Applications and Deemed Applications) Regs	**r** (with saving), 1989/193
1731	Medicines (Fees) Amdt Regs	**r** in pt 1989/418, 583
1784	Legal Advice and Assistance (Financial Conditions) (No.2) Regs	**r**, 1989/340
1785	Legal Advice and Assistance (Prosp Cost) (No.2) Regs	**r**, 1989/340
1863	Legal Aid in Criminal Proceedings (Gen) (Amdt) Regs	**r**, 1989/344
1935	Legal Advice and Assistance (Amdt) (No.5) Regs	**r**, 1989/340
1963	Legal Advice and Assistance (Amdt) (No.6) Regs	**r**, 1989/340
1984	Food Act (c. 30)	s.95(5)(6)**ext**, 97(1)–(3), 99, 100, 102(2), 103 **applied** with **mods**, 1989/533
	Inheritance Tax Act (c. 51)	Sch 1, Table **replaced**, 1989/468
241	Legal Advice and Assistance (Amdt) Regs	**r**, 1989/340
248	Gaming Clubs (Hours and Charges) Regs	**am** (E and W), 1989/535
252	High Ct of Justiciary Fees O	**am**, 1989/258
256	Ct of Session etc Fees O	**am**, 1989/260
292	NHS (Charges for Drugs and Appliances) (S) Amdt Regs	**r**, 1989/326
295	NHS (Charges to Overseas Visitors) (S) Amdt Regs	**r**, 1989/364

Year and Number (or date)	*Act or Instrument*	*How affected*
1984—*contd*		
298	NHS (Charges for Drugs and Appliances) Amdt Regs	**am**, 1989/419
300	NHS (Charges to Overseas Visitors) Amdt Regs	**r**, 1989/306
380	Occupational Pension Schemes (Contracting-out) Regs	**am**, 1989/500
421	Town and Country Planning (Control of Advertisements) Regs	**r**, 1989/690
470	Gaming Clubs (Hours and Charges) (S) Regs	**am**, 1989/622
519	Legal Aid (S) (Fees in Civil Proceedings) Regs	**am**, 1989/389
520	Legal Aid (S) (Fees in Criminal Proceedings) Regs	**am**, 1989/390
544	European Assembly Constituencies (E) O	**am**, 1989/486
545	European Assembly Constituencies (W) O	**am**, 1989/487
548	European Assembly Constituencies (S) O	**am**, 1989/494
611	Magistrates' Cts (Adoption) Rules	**am**, 1989/384
637	Legal Advice and Assistance (Amdt) (No.2) Regs	**r**, 1989/340
647	Probation Rules	**am**, 1989/265
1053	Wireless Telegraphy (Broadcast Licence Charges and Exemption) Regs	**am**, 1989/96, 325
1173	Housing (Right to Buy) (Prescribed Persons) O	**am**, 1989/174
1304	Bread and Flour Regs	**am**, 1989/533
1404	Motor Vehicles (Type Approval and Approval Marks) (Fees) Regs	**r**, 1989/350
1518	Bread and Flour (S) Regs	**am**, 1989/581
1577	NHS Functions (Directions to Authies and Admin Arrangements) Amdt Regs	**r**, 1989/51
1698	Social Security Benefit (Dependency) Amdt Regs	**am**, 1989/523
1716	Legal Aid in Criminal Procedings (Gen) (Amdt) Regs	**r**, 1989/344
1848	Confirmation to Small Estates (S) O	**r**, 1989/289
1985	Companies Act (c. 6)	**mod/am**, s. 26(1)(c)–(e)(2)(3), 28(2)–(5)(7), 29(1)(a) **ext** with **mods**, 289(2) **applied**, Pt XII **ext** with **mods**, s. 432(1)(2), 434, 436–439, 441, 447–452, 458 **ext** with **mods**, Pt XVIII **ext** with **mods**, s. 694, 697(2), 704(5), 705(2), 706, 707, 710(1)–(3)(5), 714(1), 718(2), 725, 730–733 **ext** with **mods**, Sch 24 **ext** with mod 1989/638
	Business Names Act (c. 7)	**ext**, 1989/638
	Finance Act (c. 54)	Sch 19, Pt 111 **applied** with **mod** 1989/469
	Interception of Communications Act (c.56)	s. 11(3)(5), 12(1) **ext** to Is of Man with **exceptions, adaptations** and **mods**, 1989/489

Year and Number (or date)	Act or Instrument	How affected
1985—*contd*		
	Transport Act (c. 67)	Sch 4, paras 5–7, 10, 11, 14–16 **am**, 1989/495
	Housing Act (c. 68)	Pt V **mod**, 1989/368 s. 131 **mod**, 1989/512
67	Food (Revision of Penalties) Regs	**am**, 1989/533
160	Civil Aviation (Route Charges for Navigation Services) (Amdt) Regs	**r**, 1989/303
292	Home Loss Payments (S) O	**r**, 1989/47
326	NHS (Charges for Drugs and Appliances) Amdt Regs	**r**, 1989/419
353	NHS (Charges for Drugs and Appliances (S) Amdt Regs	**r**, 1989/326
371	NHS (Charges to Overseas Visitors) Amdt Regs	**r**, 1989/306
373	Public Trustee (Fees) O	**am**, 1989/437
383	NHS (Charges to Overseas Visitors) (S) Amdt Regs	**r**, 1989/364
827	Sheriff Ct Fees O (Registers) Regs	**am**, 1989/259
1029	Agriculture Improvement Scheme	**am**, 1989/128
1068	Food (Revision of Penalties and Mode of Trial) (S) Regs	**am**, 1989/581
1163	Napier College of Commerce and Technology (No.2) Regs	**am**, 1989/433
1164	Glasgow College of Technology (No.2) Regs	**am**, 1989/433
1181	Teachers (Compensation for Redundancy and Premature Retirement) Regs	**r**, 1989/298
1182	Town and Country Planning (Fees for Applications and Deemed Applications) (Amdt) Regs	**r** (with saving), 1989/193
1231	Medicines (Fees) Amdt Regs	**r** in Pt, 1989/418, 583
1266	Agriculture Improvement Regs	**am**, 1989/219
1333	Ionising Radiations Regs	**am**, 1989/462
1411	Statutory Sick Pay (Additional Compensation of Employers and Consequential Amdts) Regs	**am**, 1989/286
1491	Legal Advice and Assistance (Amdt) Regs	**r**, 1989/340
1632	Legal Aid in Criminal Proceedings (Gen) (Amdt) Regs	**r**, 1989/344
1656	Motor Vehicles (Type Approval and Approval Marks) (Fees) (Amdt) Regs	**r**, 1989/350
1671	NHS (Charges for Drugs and Appliances) Amdt (No.2) Regs	**r**, 1989/419
1695	Magistrates' Cts (Custodianship Orders) Rules	**am**, 1989/383
1714	Rules of the Air and Air Traffic Control Regs	**am**, 1989/30
840	Legal Advice and Assistance (Prospective Cost) Regs	**r**, 1989/340
1879	Legal Advice and Assistance (Amdt) (No.2) Regs	**r**, 1989/340
1916	Civil Aviation (Route Charges for Navigation Services) (Second Amdt) Regs	**r**, 1989/303
1921	Service Subsidy Agreements (Tendering) Regs	**am**, 1989/464
1941	Nat Police Records (Recordable Offences) Regs	**am**, 1989/694

Year and Number (or date)	*Act or Instrument*	*How affected*
1986	Drug Trafficking Offences Act (c.32)	**applied** subject to **mods**, s. 1 **substituted**, 2–4 **r**, 5(1) **substituted**, 5(3)–(10), 6 **r**, 7(1)(a)(c)(2) **substituted**, (3) **r**, 7(4), 8(2)(a)(b) **substituted**, 8(4) **am**, (5)(b) **substituted**, (7)(b)(8)(11) **am**, 9(1)(a)(b) **substituted**, (3)(4)(a)(7) **am**, 10(6) **r**, 10A **inserted**, 11(1) **substituted**, (6) **am**, 12 **substituted** 13(2) **am**, (3) **r**, (4)(6) **am**, 14, 15(6) **r**, 15(7) **am**, 16(6) **r**, 17(6) **am**, 17A(2), 18(2) **am**, 19, 24–32 **r**, 33(1) **am**, 33(2)(3), 34–37 **r**, 38(1), defns of "authorized government department", "drug trafficking offence", "interest" **r**, defns of "a court of the United States of America", "proceeds of drug trafficking" **inserted**, 38(2) **am**, (4)(10) **r**, (11)(12)(b) **am**, 39(2)(4), 40 **r**, 1989/485
	Patents, Designs and Marks Act (c. 39)	s. 1, 3(1) **ext** to Is of Man subject to **mod**, 1989/493
	Insolvency Act (c. 45)	Pt 111 **ext**, s. 120 **ext** with **mods (S)** 1989/638 122(1)(f) **mod**, 1989/438 Pt V **mod**, s. 221(1) **mod**, 1989/638 267 **mod**, 1989/438
	Company Directors Disqualification Act (c. 46)	ss. 1, 2, 4–11, 12(2), 15–17, 20 22 and Sch 1 **ext** with **mods**, 1989/638
	Legal Aid (S) Act (c. 47)	s. 8(a), 8 **am**, 11(2)(a) **am**, 1989/721 15(1)(2)(a) **am**, 17(2)(a) **am**, 1989/720

Year and Number (or date)	Act or Instrument	How affected
1986—*contd*		
	Social Security Act (c. 50)	s. 23(5)(b) **am**, 1989/43
	Financial Services Act (c. 60)	s. 76(1) **excl**, 1989/28 142 **applied**, 1989/29
24	Local Govt Supn Regs	**am**, 1989/371, 372
272	Legal Aid (Gen) (Amdt) Regs	**r**, 1989/339
274	Legal Aid in Criminal Proceedings (Gen) (Amdt) Regs	**r**, 1989/344
275	Legal Advice and Assistance (Amdt) Regs	**r**, 1989/340
276	Legal Aid (Assessment of Resources) (Amdt) Regs	**r**, 1989/338
403	Civil Aviation (Navigation Services Changes) Regs	**am**, 1989/349
416	Misuse of Drugs (Licence Fees) Regs	**am**, 1989/245
459	NHS (Charges to Overseas Visitors) Amdt Regs	**r**, 1989/306
470	Dairy Produce Quotas Regs	**r**, 1989/380
482	Income Tax (Building Societies) Regs	**am**, 1989/36
610	New Street Byelaws (Ext of Operation) Variation O	**r**, 1989/645
724	Local Govt (Allowances) Regs	**am**, 1989/683, 693
924	NHS (Charges to Overseas Visitors) (S) Amdt (No.2) Regs	**r**, 1989/364
950	NHS (Charges to Overseas Visitors) Amdt (No.2) Regs	**r**, 1989/306
965	NHS (Gen Ophthalmic Services) (S) Regs	**am**, 1989/387
966	NHS (Payments for Optical Appliances) (S) Regs	**r**, 1989/392
975	NHS (Gen Ophthalmic Service) Regs	**am**, 1989/395
976	NHS (Payments for Optical Appliances) Regs	**r**, 1989/396
1136	NHS (Payments for Optical Appliances) Amdt Regs	**r**, 1989/396
1159	Child Abduction and Custody (Parties to Conventions) O	**am**, 1989/479
1186	Legal Aid (Gen) (Amdt) (No.2) Regs	**r**, 1989/339
1192	NHS (Payments for Optical Appliances) (S) Amdt Regs	**r**, 1989/392
1201	Northern Western and North Wales Sea Fisheries District O	**am**, 1989/474
1272	Sea Fish (Marketing Standards) Regs	**am**, 1989/687
1620	Saithe (Channel, Western Waters and Bay of Biscay) (Prohibition of Fishing) (Revn) O	**r**, 1989/142
1878	Building Societies (Designated Capital Resources) O	**r**, 1989/208
1925	Insolvency Rules	**am**, 1989/397
1936	Sole (Irish Sea and Sole Bank) (Prohibition of Fishing) O	**r**, 1989/142
1951	Road Traffic (Carriage of Dangerous Substances in Packages Etc) Regs	**am**, 1989/105
1960	Statutory Maternity Pay (Gen) Regs	**am**, 1989/43
2060	Sole (Specified Sea Areas) (Prohibition of Fishing) O	**r**, 1989/142
2090	Sea Fishing (Enforcement of Community Conservation Measures) O	**am**, 1989/426
2092	Local Govt Reorganisation (Preservation of Right to Buy) O	**excl**, 1989/368
2120	Civil Aviation (Route Charges for Navigation Services) (Third Amdt) Regs	**r**, 1989/303
2122	Herring (Firth of Clyde) (Prohibition of Fishing) O	**r**, 1989/142

Year and Number (or date)	Act or Instrument	How affected
1986—*contd*		
2135	Legal Aid (Gen) (Amdt) (No.3) Regs	**r**, 1989/339
2193	Housing (Right to Buy) (Maximum Discount) O	**r**, 1989/513
2194	Housing (Right to Buy) (Prescribed Forms) Regs	**am**, 1989/239
2209	European Assembly Elections Regs	**am**, 1989/633
2250	European Parliamentary Elections (NI) Regs	**am**, 1989/502
2284	Unfair Dismissal (Increase of Compensation Limit) O	**r**, 1989/527
1987	Recognition of Trusts Act (c.14)	**mod** and **ext** to various Overseas Territories, 1989/673
	Banking Act (c.22)	Sch 2 **am**, 1989/125
	NI (Emergency Provns) Act (c.30)	temp provns **cont** until 21-3-90, 1989/509
	Criminal Justice Act (c.38)	s. 2 **ext** to Bailiwick of Guernsey subject to **mods** (until 17-5-91), 1989/674 **ext** to Bailiwick of Jersey subject to **mods** (until 17-5-89), 1989/675
	Abolition of Domestic Rates Etc (S) Act (c.47)	Sch 1A, para 4(2) **am**, 1989/63
91	Statutory Maternity Pay (Compensation of Employers) Regs	**am**, 1989/286
101	Town and Country Planning (Fees) for Applications and Deemed Applications) (Amdt) Regs	**r**, (with saving), 1989/193
188	Seeds (Nat Lists of Varieties)(Fees) Regs	**am**, 1989/275
189	Plant Breeder's Right (Fees) Regs	**am**, 1989/276
212	Milk and Dairies and Milk (Special Designation) (Charges) Regs	**am**, 1989/376
245	NHS Functions (Amdt of Directions to Authies) Regs	**am**, 1989/51
257	Police Pensions Regs	**am**, 1989/733
309	Colleges of Education (S) Regs	**am**, 1989/433
315	Motor Vehicles (Type Approval and Approval Marks) (Fees) (Amdt) Regs	**r**, 1989/350
367	NHS (Charges for Drugs and Appliances) (S) Amdt Regs	**r**, 1989/326
368	NHS (Charges for Drugs and Appliances) Amdt Regs	**r**, 1989/419
371	NHS (Charges to Overseas Visitors) Amdt Regs	**r**, 1989/306
381	Civil Legal Aid (S) Regs	**am**, 1989/505
382	Advice and Assistance (S) Regs	**am**, 1989/506
387	NHS (Charges to Overseas Visitors) (S) Amdt Regs	**r**, 1989/364
396	Legal Advice and Assistance (Financial Conditions) (No.2) Regs	**r**, 1989/340
402	Control of Pollution (Landed Ships' Waste) Regs	**am**, 1989/65
422	Legal Aid in Criminal Procedings (Gen) (Amdt) Regs	**r**, 1989/344
443	Legal Advice and Representation (Duty Solicitor) (Remuneration) Regs	**r**, 1989/341
481	Social Fund Maternity and Funeral Expenses (Gen) Regs	**am**, 1989/379
608	Gaming Act (Variation of Monetary Limits) O	**r** (E and W) 1989/536

Year and Number (or date)	Act or Instrument	How affected
1987—*contd*		
609	Gaming Clubs (Hours and Charges) (Amdt) Regs	**r** (E and W) 1989/535
630	Gaming Act (Variation of Monetary Limits) (S) O	**r** 1989/623
631	Gaming Clubs (Hours and Charges) (S) Amdt Regs	**r**, 1989/622
649	Seed Potatoes (Fees) Regs	**r**, 1989/632
746	Merchant Shipping (Light Dues) (Amdt No.2) Regs	**r**, 1989/305
804	Town and Country Planning (Control of Advertisements) (Amdt) Regs	**r**, 1989/670
903	Representation of the People (Variation of Limits of Candidates' Election Expenses) O	**am**, 1989/634
1116	Personal and Occupational Pension Schemes (Incentive Payments) Regs	**am**, 1989/500
1227	Plaice and Saithe (Specified Sea Areas) (Prohibition of Fishing) O	**r**, 1989/142
1264	Consular Fees O	**r**, 1989/152
1269	Territorial Sea (Limits) O	**r**, 1989/482
1378	Motor Vehicles (Driving Licences) Regs	**am**, 1989/373
1439	Medicines (Fees) Amdt Regs	**r** in pt, 1989/418, 583
1531	Town and Country Planning (Determination of Appeals by Appointed Persons) (Prescribed Classes) (S) Regs	**am**, 1989/577
1556	Motor Vehicles (Type Approval and Approval marks) (Fees) (Amdt) (No.2) Regs	**r**, 1989/350
1758	Plant Health (GB) O	**am**, 1989/553
1808	Export of Sheep (Prohibition) (No.2) O	**am**, 1989/5, 659
1850	Local Govt Supn (S) Regs	**am**, 1989/422
1893	Food Protection (Emergency Prohibitions) (England) O	**am**, 1989/6, 658
1894	Food Protection (Emergency Prohibitions) (W) (No.5) O	**am**, 1989/2, 660
1900	Saithe (Specified Sea Areas) (Prohibition of Fishing) (Revn) O	**r**, 1989/142
1967	Income Support (Gen) Regs	**am**, 1989/43, 534
1968	Social Security (Claims and Payments) Regs	**am**, 1989/136
1971	Housing Benefit (Gen) Regs	**am**, 1989/43, 416, 566
1973	Family Credit (Gen) Regs	**am**, 1989/43
1975	Building Societies (Limited Credit Facilities) O	**am**, 1989/730
2011	Plaice (Specified Sea Areas) (Prohibition of Fishing) O	**r**, 1989/142
2083	Civil Aviation (Route Charges for Navigation Services) (Fourth Amdt) Regs	**r**, 1989/303
2088	Registration of Births and Deaths Regs	**am**, 1989/497
2089	Registration of Births and Deaths (Welsh Language) Regs	**am**, 1989/511
2115	Control of Asbestos at Work Regs	**am**, 1989/462
2192	Cod (Specified Sea Areas) (Prohibition of Fishing) O	**r**, 1989/142
2227	Town and Country Planning (Control of Advertisements) (Amdt No.2) Regs	**r**, 1989/670
2279	Rate Support Grant (S) (No.3) O	**am**, 1989/68

Year and Number (or date)	Act or Instrument	How affected
1988	Income and Corporation Taxes Act (c. 1)	s. 1(2) **am**, 1989/467 76(7) **mod**, 1989/2 257(1)(a)(b) **am**, (2)(a)(b) **am**, (3)(a)(b)(5)(6) **am**, 1989/467
	Merchant Shipping Act (c. 12)	s. 1–5 **ext** to Is of Man with **mods**, 7–10 **ext** with **mods** to Is of Man 46, 48, 50 **ext** subject to **mods** to Bermuda, 51 **ext** to Is of Man with **mods**, 1989/679 53, 54, 57, 58 **ext** to Is of Man with **mods**, 1989/679 Sch. 1 **ext** to Is of Man with **mods** (saving re ext of para 2(b)), 1989/679
	Civil Evidence (S) Act (c. 32)	s. 8(3) **excl**, 1989/582
	Legal Aid Act (c. 34)	s. 3(2) **ext**, 1989/551 Pt 111 **restr/applied**, 1989/550 s. 10(1) **excl**, 11(2)(b) **excl**, 1989/340 16(6) **applied**, 17(1) **applied**, 1989/339 Sch 2, Pt 11, para 5A **added**, 1989/549
	Education Reform Act (c. 40)	11 **applied (mods)/restr**, 13 **applied (mods)**, 23(1) **applied (mods)/restr**, 1989/46 130 **applied**, 1989/282
	Local Govt Finance Act (c. 41)	s. 11(4) **ext**, 23(2)(e) **excl**, 1989/438 117(1) **excl**, 1989/440 Sch 1, para 4(2)(d)–(f) **inserted**, 9(2) defn of "residential care home" **replaced**, 1989/442 Sch 2, para 21 **inserted**, 1989/438 4, para 1(1)(ee) **inserted**, V1A **inserted**, 1989/438 11, para 9, 10, **mod/applied**, 1989/439 13, Pt 1 **excl**, 1989/440
8	NHS (Charges to Overseas Visitors) Amdt Regs	**r**, 1989/306
11	Food Protection (Emergency Prohibitions) O	**r**, 1989/3
13	NHS (Charges to Overseas Visitors) (S) Amdt Regs	**r**, 1989/364
110	Act of Adj (Consolidation)	**am**, 1989/48
136	Third County Fishing (Enforcement) O	**r**, 1989/217
137	Personal Pension Schemes (Appropriate Schemes) Regs	**am**, 1989/500
223	Supn (Children's Pensions) (Earnings Limit)	**r**, 1989/187
224	Diseases of Animals (Approved Disinfectants) (Amdt) O	**r**, 1989/144
234	Nat Assistance (Charges for Accommodation) Regs	**r**, 1989/307
270	Home Purchase Assistance (Price-Limits) O	**r**, 1989/137
276	Employment Protection (Variation of Limits) O	**r**, 1989/526

Year and Number (or date)	Act or Instrument	How affected
1988—*contd*		
277	Unfair Dismissal (Licence of Limits of Basic and Special Awards) O	**r**, 1989/528
310	Certification Officer (Amdt of Fees) Regs	**am**, 1989/205
330	Merchant Shipping (Light Dues) (Amdt) Regs	**r**, 1989/305
331	Nat Assistance (Charges for Accommodation) (S) Regs	**r**, 1989/432
334	Gaming Act (Variation of Fees) (No.2) O	**r** (E and W), 1989/294
335	Lotteries (Gaming Board Fees) O	**r**, 1989/295
352	Insurance (Fees) Regs	**r**, 1989/293
359	Local Govt Reorganisation (Capital Money) (Greater London) O	**r** (with savings), 1989/255
365	NHS (Charges for Drugs and Appliances) (S) Amdt Regs	**r**, 1989/326
372	Local Authies (Allowances) (S) Amdt Regs	**r**, 1989/301
373	Gaming Act (Variation of Fees) (S) (No.2) O	**r**, 1989/362
376	Wireless Telegraphy (Broadcast Licence Charges and Exemption) (Amdt) Regs	**r**, 1989/325
395	Registered Housing Assocns (Accounting Requirements) O	**am**, 1989/327
423	Legal Aid in Criminal Proceedings (Costs) Regs	**r** (with saving), 1989/343
427	NHS (Charges for Drugs and Appliances) Amdt Regs	**r**, 1989/419
428	NHS (Payments for Optical Appliances) Amdt Regs	**r**, 1989/396
436	Social Security Benefits Up-rating Regs	**r**, 1989/455
437	Education (Grants for Training of Teachers and Community Education Workers) (S) Regs	**r**, 1989/185
446	Legal Advice and Assistance at Police Stations (Remuneration) Regs	**r**, 1989/342
447	Legal Advice and Representation (Duty Solicitor) (Remuneration) (Amdt) Regs	**r**, 1989/341
448	Building Societies (Gen Charges and Fees) Regs	**r**, 1989/355
449	Friendly Societies (Fees) Regs	**r**, 1989/356
450	Industrial and Provident Societies (Amdt of Fees) Regs	**r**, 1989/357
451	Industrial and Provident Societies (Credit Unions) (Amdt of Fees) Regs	**r**, 1989/358
453	Industrial Assurance (Fees) Regs	**r**, 1989/328
457	Meters (Certification) (Fees) Regs	**r**, 1989/701
459	Legal Advice and Assistance (Financial Conditions) (No.2) Regs	**r**, 1989/340
460	Legal Aid (Gen) Amdt Regs	**r**, 1989/339
461	Legal Advice and Assistance (Amdt) Regs	**r**, 1989/340
462	NHS (Charges to Overseas Visitors) (S) Amdt (No.2) Regs	**r**, 1989/364
463	NHS (Payments for Optical Appliances) (S) Amdt Regs	**r**, 1989/392
464	NHS (Dental Charges) (S) Regs	**r**, 1989/363
467	Legal Aid (Assessment of Resources) (Amdt) Regs	**r**, 1989/338
468	Legal Aid in Criminal Proceedings (Gen) (Amdt) Regs	**r**, 1989/344
472	NHS (Charges to Overseas Visitors) Amdt (No.2) Regs	**r**, 1989/306
473	NHS (Dental Charges) Regs	**am**, 1989/394
534	Dairy Produce Quotas (Amdt) Regs	**r**, 1989/580
536	Welfare Food Regs	**am**, 1989/524

Year and Number (or date)	*Act or Instrument*	*How affected*
1988—*contd*		
545	NHS (Payments for Optical Appliances) (S) Amdt (No.2) Regs	**r**, 1989/392
546	NHS (Travelling Expenses and Remission of Charges) (S) Regs	**am**, 1989/393, 616
551	NHS (Travelling Expenses and Remission of Charges) (S) Regs	**am**, 1989/394, 517, 614
552	NHS (Payments for Optical Appliances) (Amdt) (No.2) Regs	**r**, 1989/396
632	Personal Community Charge (Students) (S) Regs	**r**, 1989/32
646	Banking Act 1987 (Exempt Transactions) Regs	**am**, 1989/465
664	Social Security (Payments on account, Overpayments and Recovery) Regs	**am**, 1989/136
666	Legal Advice and Assistance (Financial Conditions) Regs	**r**, 1989/340
667	Legal Aid (Financial Conditions) Regs ..	**r**, 1989/338
668	Pneumoconiosis etc (Workers' Compensation) (Payments of Claims) Reg	**am**, 1989/552
681	AS (Fees of Solicitors in the Sheriff Ct)	**r**, 1989/434
685	Advice and Assistance (Financial Conditions) (S) Regs	**r**, 1989/721
686	Civil Legal Aid (Financial Conditions) (S) Regs	**r**, 1989/720
712	Health and Safety (Fees) Regs	**r**, 1989/462
798	High Ct of Justiciary Fees Amdt O	**r**, 1989/258
799	Ct of Session etc Fees Amdt O	**r**, 1989/260
851	Welfare of Poultry (Transport) O	**am**, 1989/52
864	NHS Functions (Directions to Authies and Admin Arrangements) Amdt Regs	**r**, 1989/51
866	NHS (Gen Medical and Pharmaceutical Services and Charges for Drugs) Amdt Regs	**am**, 1989/419
913	Magistrates' Cts (Children and Young Persons) Rules	**r**, 1989/384
925	Consular Fees (Amdt) O	**r**, 1989/152
1001	Cereals Co-responsibility Levy Regs	**am**, 1989/576
1073	NHS (Gen Medical and Pharmaceutical Services and Charges for Drugs) (S) Amdt Regs	**am**, 1989/326
1088	Lord Chancellor's Salary O	**am**, 1989/681
1180	Pig Carcase (Grading)	**am**, 1989/644
1184	Measuring Instrt (EEC Requirements) (Fees) Regs	**am**, 1989/620
1196	Building Societies (Designation of Qualifying Bodies) O	**am**, 1989/215
1264	Sole (Specified Sea Areas) (Prohibition of Fishing) O	**r**, 1989/142
1275	Merchant Shipping (Weighing of Goods Vehicles and Other Cargo) Regs	**am**, 1989/270
1286	Rate Support Grant (S) O	**am**, 1989/68
1305	Gen. Optical Council (Contact Lens (Qualifications etc) Rules) O of C	**am**, 1989/375
1328	Matrimonial Causes (Costs) Rules	**am**, 1989/385
1422	Young Offender Institution Rules	**am**, 1989/331
1425	NHS (Payments for Optical Appliances) (S) Amdt (No.3) Regs	**r**, 1989/392
1435	NHS (Payments for Optical Appliances) Amdt (No.3) Regs	**r**, 1989/396
1453	Diseases of Animals (Approved Disinfectants) (Amdt) (No.2) O	**r**, 1989/144

Year and Number (or date)	Act or Instrument	How affected
1988—*contd*		
1468	Local Govt Act 1988 (Defined Activities) (Competition) (W) Regs	**am**, 1989/138
1478	Goods Vehicles (Plating and Testing) Regs	**am**, 1989/320
1485	Merchant Shipping (Fees) Regs	**r**, 1989/323
1541	Personal Community Charge (Exemption for the Severely Mentally Impaired) (S) Regs	**r**, 1989/63
1652	Teachers' Supn (Consolidation) Regs	**am**, 1989/378
1678	Export of Sheep (Prohibition) (No.2) Amdt No.3 O	**r**, 1989/5
1725	Social Security (Common Provns) Misc Amdt Regs	**am**, 1989/136
1761	Cod (Specified Sea Areas) (Prohibition of Fishing) (Variation) O	**r**, 1989/142
1813	Town and Country Planning Gen Devpt O	**am**, 1989/603
1839	Child Abduction and Custody (Parties to Conventions) (Amdt) (No.3) O	**r**, 1989/479
1890	Housing Benefit (Community Charge Rebates) (S) Regs	**am**, 1989/43, 361
1929	Merchant Shipping (Fees) (Amdt) Regs	**r**, 1989/323
1935	NHS (Payments for Optical Appliances) Amdt (No.4) Regs	**r**, 1989/396
1938	Legal Aid (Gen) (Amdt) (No.2) Regs	**r**, 1989/339
1950	NHS (Payments for Optical Appliances) (S) Amdt (No.4) Regs	**r**, 1989/392
1986	Consular Fees (Amdt) (No.2) O	**r**, 1989/152
2034	Education (Listed Bodies) O	**am**, 1989/597
2035	Education (Recognised Awards) O	**am**, 1989/598
2058	Merger Reference (Strong & Fisher (Holdings) plc and Pittard Ganar plc) O	**r**, 1989/636
2071	Cod (Specified Sea Areas) (Prohibition of Fishing) (Revn) O	**r**, 1989/142
2091	Town and Country Planning Gen Devpt (Amdt) O	**r**, 1989/603
2117	Trade Union Ballots and Elections (Independent Scrutineer Qualifications) O	**am**, 1989/31
2130	Civil Aviation (Route Charges for Navigation Services) (Fifth Amdt) Regs	**r**, 1989/303
2178	Merger Reference (Hillsdown Holdings plc and Pittard Garnar plc) O	**r**, 1989/636
2197	Plaice (Specified Sea Areas) (Prohibition of Fishing) O	**r**, 1989/142
2203	Assured Tenancies and Agricultural Occupancies (Forms) Regs	**am**, 1989/146
2255	Gen Medical Council Preliminary Proceedings Ctee and Professional Conduct Ctee (Procedure) Rules	**am**, 1989/656
2271	Education Reform Act 1988 (Commencement No.4) O	**am**, 1989/501
2300	Sea Fishing (Enforcement of Community Conservation Measures) (Amdt) (No.2) O	**r**, 1989/426
2302	Legal Aid in Criminal Proceedings (Costs) (Amdt) Regs	**r** (with saving), 1989/343
2303	Legal Aid in Criminal Proceedings (Gen) (Amdt) (No.2) Regs	**r**, 1989/344
1989		
3	Food Protection (Emergency Prohibitions) O	**r** in pt, 1989/655
5	Export of Sheep (Prohibition) (No.2) Amdt O	**r**, 1989/659
16	Dairy Produce Quotas (Amdt) Regs	**r**, 1989/380

Year and Number (or date)	Act or Instrument	How affected
1989—*contd*		
139	Diseases of Animals (Protein Processing) (Amdt) O	**r**, 1989/661
142	Cod (Specified Sea Areas) (Prohibition of Fishing) O	**r**, 1989/537
340	Legal Advice and Assistance Regs	**am**, 1989/560
438	Community Charges (Administration and Enforcement) Regs	**am**, 1989/712
529	Food Protection (Emergency Prohibitions) (Sea Fish) O	**r**, 1989/619

Index to Part I

An instrument that has been classified as local is distinguished by an entry **(L)** after its title.